Morocco

Mediterranean Coast & the Rif
p218

Atlantic Coast
p153

Fez, Meknès & the Middle Atlas
p284

Marrakesh & Central Morocco
p46

Southern Morocco & Western Sahara
p352

Jessica Lee, Brett Atkinson, Paul Clammer, Virginia Maxwell, Lorna Parkes and Regis St Louis

Contents

NEJJARINE FOUNTAIN, FEZ P286

JULIAN LOVE/LONELY PLANET ©

MOROCCAN CUISINE P470

BARTOSZ LUCZAK/SHUTTERSTOCK ©

Contents

SPICES & HERBS IN A MARRAKESH MARKET P47

Welcome to Morocco

Morocco is a gateway to Africa, and a country of dizzying diversity. Here you'll find epic mountain ranges, ancient cities, sweeping deserts – and warm hospitality.

Mountains & Desert

From Saharan dunes to the peaks of the High Atlas, Morocco could have been tailor-made for travellers. Lyrical landscapes carpet this slice of North Africa like the richly coloured and patterned rugs you'll lust after in local cooperatives. The mountains – not just the famous High Atlas but also the Rif and suntanned ranges leading to Saharan oases – offer simple, breathtaking pleasures: night skies glistening in the thin air, and views over a fluffy cloudbank from the Tizi n'Test pass. On lower ground, there are rugged coastlines, waterfalls and caves in forested hills, and the mighty desert.

Ancient Medinas

Morocco's cities are some of the most exciting on the continent. Join the centuries-old trail of nomads and traders to their ancient hearts, from the winding medina maze of Fez to the carnivalesque street-theatre of the Djemaa el-Fna in Marrakesh. In the rocky deserts medinas are protected by kasbahs, on the coast by thick sea walls. But it's not just a heritage trip, as Morocco's cities are forward-facing too, with glitzy new urban design in Casablanca, Rabat and Tangier looking to the future as well as paying homage to their roots.

Moroccan Activities

Enjoying Morocco starts with nothing more strenuous than its national pastime – people-watching in a street cafe with a coffee or a mint tea. Use the opportunity to plan your next moves – hiking up North Africa's highest peak, learning to roll couscous, camel trekking in the desert, shopping in the souqs or getting lost in the medina. Between the activities, you can sleep in boutique riads, relax on panoramic terraces and grand squares, and mop up delicately flavoured tajines – before sweating it all out in a restorative hammam.

Traditional Life

Morocco is a storied country, that has over the centuries woven its ties to Sub-Saharan Africa, Europe and the wider Middle East into whole cloth. Its mixed Arab and Berber population forms a strong national identity, but an increasingly youthful one, taking the best of its traditions and weaving the pattern anew – from the countryside to the city, from the call to prayer from the mosque to the beat of local hip hop. Morocco has a hundred faces and sounds, all ready to welcome the traveller looking for spice and adventure.

Why I Love Morocco

By Paul Clammer, Writer

In the 20-something years that I've been visiting Morocco – from a student backpacker through leading tour groups and writing travel guides to having my own front door key to a medina house – it's always the first mint tea that grounds me in the place. The ceremonial pouring and re-pouring from silver teapots. The tall glasses stuffed with viridescent leaves that scald to the touch. The impossible sweetness that would be cloying anywhere else in the world. Back then, mint tea was the taste of somewhere new. Now, it's the reassurance that I'm back in a country I love. For me, there's nothing more Moroccan.

For more about our writers, see p512

Above: Erg Chebbi (p148)

Morocco

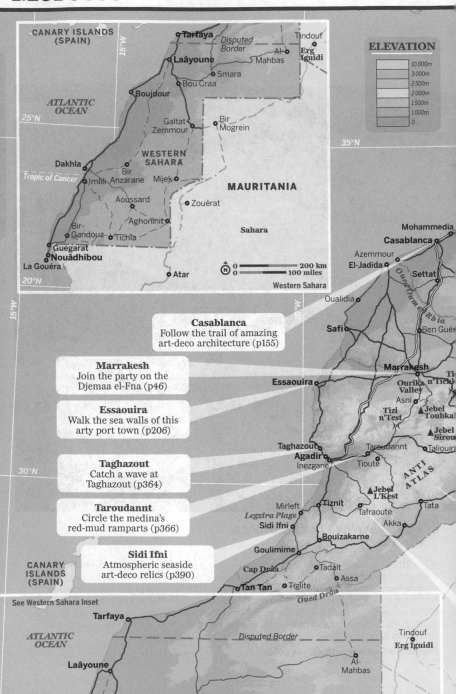

ELEVATION

	10 000m
	3 000m
	2 500m
	2 000m
	1 500m
	1 000m
	0

Casablanca
Follow the trail of amazing
art-deco architecture (p155)

Marrakesh
Join the party on the
Djemaa el-Fna (p46)

Essaouira
Walk the sea walls of this
arty port town (p206)

Taghazout
Catch a wave at
Taghazout (p364)

Taroudannt
Circle the medina's
red-mud ramparts (p366)

Sidi Ifni
Atmospheric seaside
art-deco relics (p390)

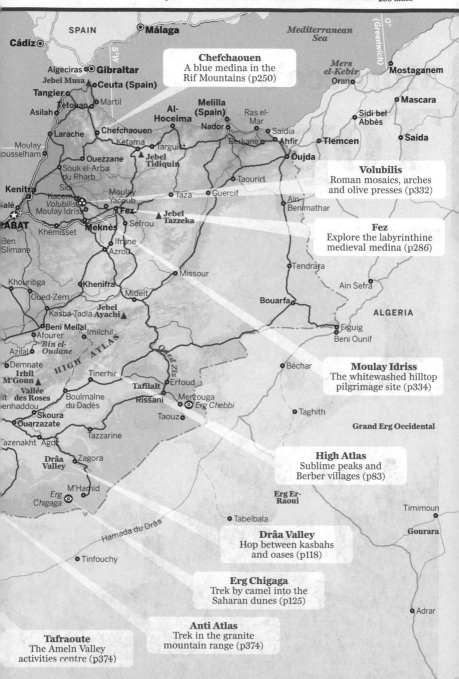

N 0   0   400 km
                     200 miles

Chefchaouen
A blue medina in the
Rif Mountains (p250)

Volubilis
Roman mosaics, arches
and olive presses (p332)

Fez
Explore the labyrinthine
medieval medina (p286)

Moulay Idriss
The whitewashed hilltop
pilgrimage site (p334)

High Atlas
Sublime peaks and
Berber villages (p83)

Drâa Valley
Hop between kasbahs
and oases (p118)

Erg Chigaga
Trek by camel into the
Saharan dunes (p125)

Anti Atlas
Trek in the granite
mountain range (p374)

Tafraoute
The Ameln Valley
activities centre (p374)

SPAIN · Málaga · Mediterranean Sea · Mers el-Kebir · Mostaganem · Oran · Cádiz · Algeciras · Gibraltar · Jebel Musa · Ceuta (Spain) · Tangier · Asilah · Tétouan · Martil · Al-Hoceima · Melilla (Spain) · Ras el-Mar · Mascara · Sidi bel Abbès · Saida · Larache · Chefchaouen · Ketama · Targuist · Nador · Berkane · Saïdia · Ahfir · Tlemcen · Moulay Bousselham · Souk el-Arba du Rharb · Ouezzane · Jebel Tidiquin · Taza · Guercif · Aïn Benimathar · Oujda · Taourirt · Kenitra · Salé · Sidi Kacem · Volubilis · Moulay Yacoub · Moulay Idriss · Fez · Meknès · Sefrou · Jebel Tazzeka · RABAT · Khémisset · Ifrane · Azrou · Tendràra · Aïn Sefra · Ben Slimane · Missour · Bouarfa · ALGERIA · Khouribga · Khenifra · Midelt · Oued-Zem · Kasba-Tadla · Jebel Ayachi · Figuig · Beni Ounif · Beni Mellal · Afourer · Imilchil · Azilal · Bin el-Oudane · Demnate · Irhil M'Goun · HIGH ATLAS · Tinerhir · Oued Ziz · Béchar · Taghith · Grand Erg Occidental · Vallée des Roses · Aït Benhaddou · Boulmalne du Dadès · Tafilalt · Erfoud · Merzouga · Erg Chebbi · Skoura · Rissani · Ouarzazate · Tazzarine · Taouz · Tazenakht · Agdz · Drâa Valley · Zagora · Erg Er-Raoui · Timimoun · Gourara · Erg Chigaga · M'Hamid · Tabelbala · Hamada du Drâa · Tinfouchy · Adrar

Morocco's
Top 17

Djemaa el-Fna Street Theatre

1 Circuses can't compare to the madcap, Unesco-acclaimed *halqa* (street theatre) in Marrakesh's main square (p50). By day, 'La Place' draws crowds with astrologers, snake-charmers, acrobats and dentists with jars of pulled teeth. Around sunset, 100 restaurant stalls kick off the world's most raucous grilling competition. 'I teach Jamie Oliver everything he knows!' brags a chef. 'We're number one...literally!' jokes the cook at stall number one. After dinner, Djemaa music jam sessions get under way – audience participation is always encouraged, and spare change ensures encores. Gnaoua musicians

Fez Medina

2 The Fez medina (p287) is the maze to end all mazes. The only way to experience it is to plunge in head first, and don't be afraid of getting lost – follow the flow of people to take you back to the main thoroughfare, or pay a small boy to show you the way. It's an adventure into a medieval world of hidden squares, enormous studded doors and colourful souqs. Remember to look up and see intricate plasterwork, magnificent carved cedarwood and curly Arabic calligraphy, while at your feet are jewel-like mosaics. View to the Medina from Medersa Bou Inania

TIM GERARD BARKER/GETTY IMAGES ©

SABINO PARENTE/500PX ©

The High Atlas

3 Zaouiat Ahansal (p88) is the Chamonix of the eastern Atlas. Hemmed in by the cracked and fissured summit of Aroudane (3359m), the valley is characterised by kilometres of cliffs, soaring buttresses and dramatic slot canyons. With the arrival of a paved road in 2013, this natural canvas is just beginning to attract attention. Rafters and kayakers whip between 8ft-wide limestone walls; while for climbers and trekkers the extreme topography and huge routes offer ridiculous views and a thrilling sense of wilderness.

Chefchaouen Medina

4 Steep and cobbled, the Chefchaouen medina (p251) tumbles down the mountainside in a shower of red roofs, wrought-iron balconies and geraniums. The blue-washed lanes enchant, making the town a photographer's dream-come-true. With a grand red-hued kasbah lording it over the cafe-packed main square, you could be content for hours just people-watching over a mint tea. But if you're feeling more active, amble down the riverside walk or stroll to the Spanish mosque on the hill.

Life in the Palmeraies

5 Thick with palms and networked by communal wells and *khettara* (irrigation channels) the palm groves of Figuig (p143), Ziz Valley, Tinejdad, Tinerhir and Skoura are the historical lifeblood of the Moroccan south. Even today they continue to play a vital role in oasis life, with plots beneath the shaded canopy providing a surprising bounty of barley, tomatoes, mint, pomegranates, apricots, figs and almonds sustaining generation after generation. Skoura palmeraie (p128)

Drâa Valley Kasbah Trail

6 Roads now allow safe, speedy passage through the final stretches of ancient caravan routes from Mali to Marrakesh, but beyond the rocky gorges glimpsed through car windows lies the Drâa Valley (p118) of desert-traders' dreams. The palms and cool mud-brick castles of Tamegroute, Zagora, Timidarte and Agdz must once have seemed like mirages after two months in the Sahara. Fortifications that housed gold-laden caravans are now open to overnight guests, who wake to this realisation: speed is overrated. Agdz (p118)

Tafraoute

7 The Anti Atlas' main town, Tafraoute (p374) has a jumble of pink houses and market streets with extraordinary surroundings. The Ameln Valley is dotted with *palmeraies* and Berber villages, and the looming mountains stage a twice-daily, ochre-and-amber light show. With a relatively undeveloped tourist industry, despite the region's many charms, it's a wonderful base for activities including mountain biking and seeking out prehistoric rock carvings. As if the granite cliffs and oases weren't scenic enough, a Belgian artist applied his paint brush to some local boulders – with surreal results.

PATRICE SCHWARZ/500PX ©

Surfing

8 You can surf all along Morocco's Atlantic coast, but the best place to catch waves is Taghazout (p364; pictured above left). It's clear what floats the village's board as soon as you arrive: the usual cafes and *téléboutiques* are joined by surf shops, where locals and incomers wax boards and wax lyrical about the nearby beaches. On the same stretch of coast between Agadir and Essaouira, Tamraght and Sidi Kaouki are also set up for surfing; further south, Mirleft is Morocco's newest surf destination, with an annual longboard championship.

Anti Atlas Trekking

9 A sunburned granite range leading to the Sahara, the Anti Atlas (p374) remains unexplored compared with the High Atlas. The star attraction for trekkers is the quartz massif Jebel L'Kest, the 'amethyst mountain', accessed via the lush Ameln Valley. More farming villages and crumbling kasbahs are found around Jebel Aklim, another of the excellent trekking possibilities in this area of blue skies and Berber shepherds. The landscape has enough variety, from palm-filled gorges to brooding, volcanic Jebel Siroua, to justify multiple treks.

Sidi Ifni

10 Shhh! Don't tell your travelling friends, but this formerly Spanish seaside town (p390), a camel ride from the Sahara, is every bit as dilapidated, breezy and magical as well-trodden Essaouira. You can walk out along the sweep of Legzira Plage, or just explore the blue-and-white backstreets of one of southern Morocco's most alluring hang-outs. The best time to appreciate the art-deco relics – more reminiscent of Cuba than Casa – is sunset, when the Atlantic winds bend the palms and fill the air with a cooling sea mist.

Essaouira

11 Freshened by the endless Atlantic breeze, the old sea walls and gleaming white medina of Essaouira (p206) help make one of Morocco's most charming and laid-back destinations. There are swish riads, the freshest seafood unloaded from the small port, and a vibe that seamlessly blends an old visual arts tradition with the active sea sports that the coast here is increasingly known for. As any resident will tell you, Jimi Hendrix was a fan – and you soon will be too.

Fès Festival of World Sacred Music

12 With intimate concerts in mosaic-studded riads, harmonics at the Batha Museum, Sufi Nights in a Pasha's garden and grand performances in the magnificent Bab al Makina, this festival (p299) still charms and impresses after 20 years. A love of music that engenders harmony between civilisations and religions is the cornerstone here, and you'll experience sacred music from every corner of the world: from Mongolian fiddles or Sufi *qawwali* to Irish laments. Qawwals from the Faiz Ali Faiz ensemble

11

12

Moulay Idriss

13 Named for Morocco's most revered saint, this little town (p334) contains his mausoleum and is one of the most important pilgrimage spots in the country. It straddles two hills and, whichever side of town you're on, the views across the green roofs and out to the rolling countryside beyond are arrestingly pretty, especially in the evening light. At the very top is Morocco's only cylindrical minaret, which is well worth the climb, while spread at its feet are olive groves that produce a fragrantly tasty oil.

Volubilis

14 Berber king Juba II, whose wife was the daughter of Antony and Cleopatra, was installed at Volubilis (p331) by the Romans. The town became a thriving farming community producing olive oil, wheat and wine for the Roman army. Stand on the basilica steps today, look out over the same fertile fields and survey his kingdom. This World Heritage site has few rules about where you can walk, little signage and lots of storks nesting on columntops. It has some dazzling mosaics and a brand-new museum.

VIXIT/SHUTTERSTOCK ©

JOHN COPLAND/SHUTTERSTOCK ©

Taroudannt

15 With views of both the High Atlas and the Anti Atlas, this Souss Valley trading centre (p366) is known as Little Marrakesh, offering a medina and souqs without the big-city hustlers. Day trippers from Agadir will certainly find it charming. The town's red-mud ramparts are unique, changing colour according to the time of day. Circle the 7.5km perimeter by foot, bike or horse-drawn calèche, then return to the medina through one of the gates. After the sunset glow fades from the walls, the town is a relaxing, everyday place with some good restaurants.

Camel Trekking in the Sahara

16 When you pictured dashing into the sunset on your trusty steed, you probably didn't imagine there'd be quite so much lurching involved. Don't worry: no one is exactly graceful clambering onto a saddled hump. But even if your dromedary leaves you knock-kneed, you'll instinctively find your way to the summit of the dunes at nightfall. Stars have never seemed clearer, and with good reason: at Erg Chigaga (p125), you're not only off the grid, but several days' camel trek from the nearest streetlights.

Meknès

17 Morocco has four old imperial cities. Rabat is the go-ahead capital, Marrakesh has the tourist bling, Fez its epic medina and Meknès... well, Meknès (p320) is unfairly overlooked by far too many visitors. It has a wealth of grand architecture, from the incredible grain stores of Heri es-Souani to the imposing gate of Bab Mansour and the Mausoleum of Moulay Ismail (currently under restoration). Place el-Hedim is a mini Djemaa el Fna but without the tourist focus, and it's only a hop and skip away to the Roman ruins at Volubilis. Zellij on the Bab el Mansour (p323)

Need to Know

For more information, see Survival Guide (p461)

Currency
Dirham (Dh)

Languages
Moroccan Arabic (Dari-ja), Berber (Amazigh), French

Visas
Visas are not generally required for stays of up to 90 days.

Money
ATMS are widely available. Credit cards are accepted in most midrange hotels and above, and at top-end restaurants.

Mobile Phones
GSM phones work on roaming. For unlocked phones, local mobile SIM cards are a cheaper option.

Time
GMT/UTC

When to Go

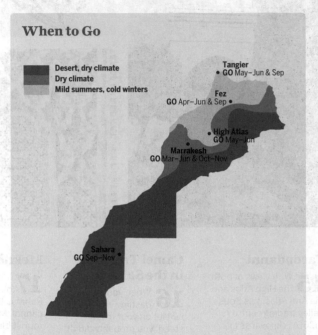

Desert, dry climate
Dry climate
Mild summers, cold winters

Tangier
GO May–Jun & Sep

Fez
GO Apr–Jun & Sep

High Atlas
GO May–Jun

Marrakesh
GO Mar–Jun & Oct–Nov

Sahara
GO Sep–Nov

High Season
(Nov–Mar)

➜ Spring and autumn are the most popular times to visit.

➜ Accommodation prices are highest.

➜ Marrakesh and the south are popular at Christmas and New Year, but the north of the country can be chilly and wet.

Shoulder
(Apr & Oct)

➜ Spring sandstorms in the Sahara and persistent rain in the north; popular elsewhere.

➜ Accommodation prices and demand jump around Easter.

Low Season
(May–Sep)

➜ Discounts in accommodation and souqs.

➜ Domestic tourism keeps prices high on the coast, where this is shoulder season

➜ 2017–20 Ramadan will commence between the end of April and late May. Eid al-Adha will fall around August.

Useful Websites

The View from Fez (http://riadzany.blogspot.com) News and opinions.

Visit Morocco (www.visitmorocco.com) Moroccan National Tourist Office website.

Maroc Mama (http://maroc-mama.com) Morocco-themed food and travel blog.

Al-Bab (www.al-bab.com/maroc) Handy links.

Morocco World News (www.moroccoworldnews.com) Moroccan news portal.

Lonely Planet (www.lonelyplanet.com/morocco) Destination information, hotel bookings, traveller forum and more.

Important Numbers

Always dial the local four-digit area code even if you are dialling from the same town or code area.

Ambulance	🕿15
Fire	🕿15
Police (city)	🕿19
Gendarmerie (police outside cities)	🕿177

Exchange Rates

Australia	A$1	Dh7.36
Canada	C$1	Dh7.18
Europe	€1	Dh10.94
Japan	Y100	Dh9.57
Mauritania	UM100	Dh2.71
New Zealand	NZ$1	Dh7.07
UK	UK$1	Dh12.16
USA	US$1	Dh9.70

For current exchange rates, see www.xe.com.

Daily Costs

Budget: Less than Dh500

➡ Basic double (shared bathroom): from Dh50

➡ Soup or sandwich: Dh4–30

➡ Four-hour local bus trip: Dh60

Midrange: Dh500–1400

➡ Admission to sights: Dh10–50

➡ Hotel room: Dh400–800

➡ Dinner main: Dh70–150

Top end: More than Dh1400

➡ Hire a car: Dh300

➡ Day tour: Dh300

➡ Double in a city riad: from Dh1000

Opening Hours

Morocco keeps the Western working week, but some businesses may close early/completely on the Muslim prayer day or Friday. Exact opening hours may vary.

Banks 8.30am to 6.30pm Monday to Friday

Bars 4pm till late

Government offices 8.30am to 6.30pm Monday to Friday

Post offices 8.30am to 4.30pm Monday to Friday

Restaurants noon to 3pm and 7pm to 10pm (cafes generally open earlier and close later)

Shops 9am to 12.30pm and 2.30pm to 8pm Monday to Saturday (often closed longer at noon for prayer)

Work hours may be severely truncated during Ramadan.

Arriving in Morocco

Mohammed V International Airport (Casablanca) Trains run to Casa Voyageurs station (Dh43, 35 minutes) hourly from 6am to 10pm, and again at 11.45pm; taxis to central Casablanca cost Dh300 to Dh350 (45 minutes).

Tanger Med ferry terminal Shuttle buses run hourly to central Tangier (Dh25, 45 minutes).

Menara Airport (Marrakesh) Buses to central Marrakesh (Dh30) run every 20 minutes; taxis to central Marrakesh cost Dh70/100 petit taxi/grand taxi (50% more at night); private hotel transfer to the city costs around Dh200.

Fes–Saïss Airport (Fez) Taxis to central Fez/medina cost Dh200.

Getting Around

Transport in Morocco is reasonably priced, and mostly quick and efficient.

Train Reasonably priced, with good coverage and frequent departures between the major cities, but no lines in the south or along the Mediterranean coast.

Car Useful for travelling at your own pace, or for visiting regions with minimal public transport. Cars can be hired in every town or city. Drive on the right, but beware erratic Moroccan drivers.

Bus Cheaper and slower than trains, ranging from modern coaches to rickety local affairs. Useful for destinations not serviced by trains.

Taxi Mercedes 'grands taxis' run set routes between nearby towns and cities. Cheap but cramped.

For much more on **getting around**, see p481

If You Like...

Medinas

If you pause for a moment in the medina, stepping out of the stream of shoppers, you can watch Morocco's very essence flash by. These ancient, crowded quarters – with winding lanes, dead ends, riad hotels, piles of spices, traders, tea drinkers, and a sensory assault around every corner – offer a strong dose of Morocco's famous Maghrebi mystique.

Fez The world's largest living Islamic medieval city, with goods still carried by donkey and mule. (p287)

Marrakesh Exuberant Marrakshis course between souqs, palaces and the Djemaa el-Fna within the medina's ramparts. (p50)

Tangier Hop off the ferry for a fitting introduction to North Africa in this compact medina. (p221)

Chefchaouen Medinas aren't always like diving from the top board; smaller examples include this blue-washed treat. (p251)

Craft & Culture

Whether you want to catch some Gnaoua (bluesy music developed by freed slaves), see the Maghreb's hottest contemporary art or transform your mantel with quality craftwork, Morocco will inundate you with options.

Taroudannt Pick up Chleuh silver jewellery, influenced by Saharan tribes and Jewish silversmiths, in the souqs. (p371)

Fès Festival of World Sacred Music In June, Morocco's premier music festival features international names and intimate concerts by *tariqas* (Sufi orders). (p299)

Marrakesh Shop beyond the souqs, alongside collectors in the hip art galleries of Guèliz. (p78)

Carpets Towns such as Ouarzazate (p117) and Tafraoute (p376) are low-pressure spots to bag a tasselled souvenir.

Tangier The American Legation Museum is devoted to Paul Bowles, William Burroughs and the Beat writers. (p221)

Off the Beaten Track

Morocco's small towns and picturesque villages are ideal for unwinding and meeting the locals over mint tea.

Afella-Ighir The road to these oasis villages is little visited; in Tiwadou, stay in an *auberge* (inn) with a local museum. (p382)

Agdz Enjoy the Drâa Valley from the palm groves and mudbrick kasbahs of Agdz. (p118)

Imilchil The Middle Atlas village is famous for its marriage *moussem* (festival), but the journey there is stunning year-round. (p138)

Tarfaya Clean up in a tented pool hall near a shipwrecked ferry, and watch the Saharawi world go by. (p398)

Around Essaouira Leave the crowds in the medina and follow the surf trail south to Sidi Kaouki (p217) and Taghazout (p364).

Bhalil A friendly hillside village dating back to the 4th century, unusual for its troglodyte cave dwellings. (p315)

Food Adventures

Morocco offers culinary adventures from couscous rolling to eating camel tajine.

Fez Take a street-food tour, roll your own couscous and visit the communal bread ovens. (p297)

M'hamid Learn Saharawi recipes or the secrets of elaborate traditional couscous at M'Hamid's Saharan retreats. (p126)

Marrakesh Buy your ingredients at the souq, and feast on the results in a riad kitchen. (p65)

Top: A woman in Berber costume
Bottom: Entrance to Rissani

Seafood Buy your dinner fresh off the boat in the ports of Al Hoceima (p265) and Essaouira (p213).

Taliouine Tour saffron and argan producers and learn how to make a saffron-tinted tajine. (p372)

Demnate Try local almonds, olive oil and wildflower honey in this Berber foodie hub near Marrakesh. (p83)

Architecture

Morocco's buildings, whether being reinvented as a boutique medina retreat or crumbling into a hillside, reflect the country's long history as a cultural melting pot.

Ali ben Youssef Medersa Inside this splendid 14th-century theological seminary in Marrakesh are five-colour *zellij* (tilework) walls and stucco archways. (p51)

Art deco The Atlantic Coast has wonderful art-deco architecture, in Casablanca (p157) and Sidi Ifni (p390).

Kairaouine Mosque & University One of Africa's largest mosques and the world's oldest university, founded in Fez 1200 years ago. (p289)

Rabat Morocco's capital looks to its past with its Almohad Tour de Hassan minaret, and to the future with the Zaha Hadid designed Grand Theatre of Rabat. (p172)

Rissani Tour a *zawiya* (shrine), a ruined Saharan trading post, and multiple desert *ksour* (castle). (p146)

Berber Culture

Morocco's proud indigenous people are a memorable part of many travellers' journeys here. Their Amazigh colour and character are a big part of special spots such as Marrakesh and the Atlas.

Regional costumes From Riffian hats to colourful dresses, women display their local cultural roots. (p51)

Demnate Immersion in indigenous culture awaits, with fine olive oil and a Berber Romeo and Juliet. (p83)

Imilchil Berbers look for marriage material at the annual moussem in the Middle Atlas village. (p138)

Maison Tiskiwin Understand how the Berbers fit into the rest of North Africa in Marrakesh's museum of trans-Saharan culture. (p56)

Al-Hoceima The seaside town is the unofficial capital of Morocco's northern Berbers. (p263)

Beaches

Its coastline stretching from the Mediterranean to the Sahara, Morocco packs in beaches for every taste between its coves, cliffs, boardwalks and ports. Some are fit for family fun, others wait and will development to happen, and many are untrodden, apart from the odd surfer and migratory bird.

Marabout's Beach Lined with savage rocks, this is the most dramatic of Mirleft's Atlantic beaches. (p388)

Agadir Agadir's long, curving (and clean) beach has families scrambling for buckets and spades. (p356)

Yellich This Mediterranean village has a fine beach with an island you can walk out to. (p268)

Tangier Head for Plage Robinson, at the northwestern extremity of Africa's Atlantic Coast. (p236)

Deserts

Morocco's Saharan expanses are some of Africa's safest and most evocative places to experience the great desert. Not only can you see curvy dunes and harsher *hammada* (stony desert), you can also meet blue-robed Berbers and try the nomadic lifestyle.

Erg Chebbi This classic Saharan sandscape can be explored by camel, 4WD or sandboard. (p148)

Figuig It's worth trekking east to Morocco's oasis par excellence, with *palmeraies*, *ksour* and Algerian views. (p143)

Erg Chigaga Enlist a 'Blue Man' in M'Hamid, to explore these mountainous sand dunes. (p125)

Drâa Valley Timbuktu-bound caravans once passed through this valley; now you can explore its oases by camel. (p118)

Mountains

With Berber villages nestling beneath snowy peaks, the High Atlas is one of the world's most awe-inspiring mountain ranges. Whether you want to climb, trek, experience rural life or just escape the rat race far below, Morocco's other mountains are also worth exploring.

Jebel Toubkal Trek to the top of North Africa for thin air and views across the High Atlas. (p103)

Ameln Valley Stay in a traditional village house among *palmeraies* and the gold-pink Anti Atlas. (p378)

Middle Atlas The mellower northern Atlas range is ideal for day hikes through hills and forests. (p340)

Jebel el-Kelaâ This Rif mountain is walkable in a day from the blue-washed town of Chefchaouen. (p250)

Eastern Atlas Barren, Martian-red mountains overlook the Ziz Gorges and the wedding-festival village of Imilchil (p142)

Month by Month

TOP EVENTS
....

Fès Festival of World Sacred Music, June

Festival of Popular Arts, July

Marriage Moussem, September

Marathon des Sables, March

Riffian Trekking, April

January

Moroccan winter: the north is wet and snow makes many mountains impassable for trekkers and even motorists. Marrakesh and the south receive the most tourists, especially around New Year.

🏃 Marrakesh Marathon

The year-round Djemaa el-Fna carnival acquires a sporty dimension with this annual road race, when 5000 marathoners cross the finish line on the grand square. The route follows the city ramparts and alleys of palms, orange and olive trees. (p66)

February

Winter continues: the weather is generally poor, although drier, balmier spots, such as Marrakesh and Agadir, are bearable. Apart from overlanders and city-breakers, few visitors are spotted.

🎎 Moussem of Sidi ben Aïssa

One of Morocco's largest *moussems* (festivals) takes place at the Sufi saint's mausoleum, outside Meknès medina walls. Public displays of glass-eating, snake bites and ritual body piercing are no longer allowed, but *fantasias* (musket-firing cavalry charges), fairs and the usual singing and dancing are.

🎎 Marrakech Biennale

Held on even-numbered years, the Marrakech Biennale is the city's foray into both high and popular artistic culture, with every thing from public art displays to chin-scratching conceptual installations. (p67)

March

The country wakes up with the beginning of spring, when the mountains thaw and wildflowers and almond and cherry trees blossom. Winds begin to disturb the desert and Souss Valley, continuing through April.

🎎 Almond Blossom Festival

A very pretty festival held in the Anti Atlas in spring, when the Tafraoute area is awash with blossoms. Traditionally about celebrating the harvest in Morocco's almond capital, the festival is now also about local folklore, with singing, dancing, theatre and storytelling. (p374)

🎎 Marathon des Sables

Starting and finishing in Morocco's movie town, Ouarzazate, the Saharan ultramarathon is as epic as films made in 'Ouallywood'. The gruelling six-day challenge, held in March or April, crosses 243km of desert. Water is provided. (p114)

April

Spring continues: the country is lush and green and temperatures are now reliably hot nationwide. Tourist numbers are high, particularly around Easter, when prices jump.

✯ Festival of Sufi Culture

This Fez festival hosts events including films and lectures, and concerts with Sufi musicians from around the world. The setting is the Andalucian-style garden of the Batha Museum, which is housed in a 19th-century summer palace. (p299)

✯ Jazzablanca

Casablanca's popular jazz festival has been taking over the city for more than a decade now, and is currently held in April. Expect the best local and international names to hit the stage. (p161)

🏃 Riffian Trekking

Between the wet northern winter and fierce summer, spring is perfect for trekking trails in the Rif Mountains. The best scenery is found in Talassemtane National Park, including the God's Bridge rock formation and, closer to the Mediterranean, the Al-Hoceima National Park.

May

Prices drop in hotels and souqs as the tourist season ends, although the heaviest summer heat is yet to come; the average daily temperature in Marrakesh is about 28°C. Ideal for mountain trekking.

✯ Festival Mawazine

This popular and free music festival in Rabat grows every year, and attracts big names from the Arabic, African and Western spheres. Expect anything from Elton John to Afrobeat and Lebanese divas. (p177)

✯ Rural Festivals

During the Festival du Desert Er-Rachidia hosts performers from across the Sahara, including local Gnaoua band Les Pigeons du Sable. Down the Dadès Valley, garlands come out for Kelaâ M'Gouna's festival to celebrate the rose harvest. (p142)

June

Summer is hotting up, although High Atlas peaks are still snowy. Northern Morocco and the coast are good places to be. During the Fès Festival of World Sacred Music there is major demand for local accommodation.

✯ Cherry Festival

Sleepy Sefrou awakes for Morocco's longest-running town festival, held in mid-June. Folk music, artists' displays, parades, *fantasias* and sports events celebrate the cherry harvest – culminating in the picturesque crowning of the Cherry Queen. (p314)

✯ Fès Festival of World Sacred Music

Fez's successful world-music festival has hosted everyone from Youssou N'Dour to Bjork. Equally impressive are the concerts by Moroccan *tariqas* (Sufi orders); fringe events include exhibitions, films and talks. May be held in May depending on Ramadan dates. (p299)

✯ Gnaoua & World Music Festival

A passionate celebration held in Essaouira in late June, with concerts featuring international, national and local performers, and art exhibitions. A great chance to hear some bluesy Gnaoua, developed here by freed slaves. (p211)

July

Snow melts from the mountains, the High Atlas is scorching and Ramadan adds intensity to the temperatures, hovering around 30°C. The beaches are breezy, but busy with domestic and European tourists in the north.

✯ Asilah Festival

Asilah confirms its arty leanings with this cultural jamboree, which attracts some 200,000 spectators to three weeks of public art demonstrations, workshops, concerts and exhibitions. A concurrent three-day horse festival features a *fantasia*. (p195)

✯ Festival of Popular Arts

This street-theatre festival is a typically colourful Marrakshi event, highlighting the best of Moroccan traditional and popular culture. Djemaa el-Fna is even more anarchic than usual during the opening-night parade, featuring 500-plus performers. (p67)

August

This month is a scorcher with an average of 40°C in Marrakesh, and it can easily exceed that in the interior. Head to southern Atlantic beaches to avoid the crowds.

Moussems

During Morocco's largest *moussem*, picturesque whitewashed Moulay Idriss fills with *fantasias*, markets and music. Five pilgrimages to this *moussem* are said to equal one to Mecca. *Moussems* also take place in Setti Fatma, southeast of Marrakesh, and Ouarzazate. (p335)

September

With autumn, Morocco is once again prime territory for foreign travellers. Beaches empty of local holidaymakers and even the desert is pleasant with the scent of dates and gentle breezes. Eid al-Adha interrupts transport and business in August/September.

Marriage Moussem

At this famous three-day festival in the Middle Atlas village of Imilchil, local Berbers search for a partner. Everyone looks their best, sporting woollen cloaks, white *jellabas* (flowing garments) and elaborate jewellery.

Religous Moussems

Hamdouchi Moussem is a dance-off between religious fraternities outside Demnate's two *zawiyas* (shrines); Fez' Moussem of Moulay Idriss sees a musical, rosewater-showered procession through the medina; thousands of pilgrims head east to the *moussem* at Sidi Yahia Ben Younes, which includes a *fantasia*. (p299)

TANJAzz

Attracting an ever-growing roster of international as well as local musicians, Tangier's annual jazz festival is a great way to take in the cosmopolitan side of Morocco's music scene. (p226)

October

Another popular month to visit, although, rain is beginning to set in north of the Middle Atlas.

Nuits Sonores Tanger

Tangier shows as the city that always moves with times, with its new cutting-edge electronic music festival. (p226)

Rallye Toulouse Saint-Louis

In late September/early October, this event in Tarfaya remembers the colonial French airmail service that stopped here, and its most famous pilot, the writer Antoine de Saint-Exupéry. Planes pass through en route from Toulouse in France to Saint Louis in Senegal. (p398)

November

A busy time in Marrakesh and further south, with more people heading to the desert or trekking nearby. Birdwatchers stake out wetlands and Mauritania-bound overlanders roll through.

Harvests

Around the Immouzzer des Ida Outanane waterfalls in the High Atlas foothills, villagers climb into the trees to shake olives from the branches. In Taliouine, a festival celebrates the saffron harvest, and you can see locals picking the flowers.

December

The country is busy at the end of the month with Christmas holidaymakers. Snow closes High Atlas passes, but the white blanket is good news for skiers.

Marrakesh International Film Festival

The Marrakesh event lives up to its name, with stars from Hollywood to Bollywood jetting in to walk the red carpet. The week culminates in wildly eclectic awards shows – with honours going to everything from art-house dramas to Bollywood spectaculars. (p67)

Itineraries

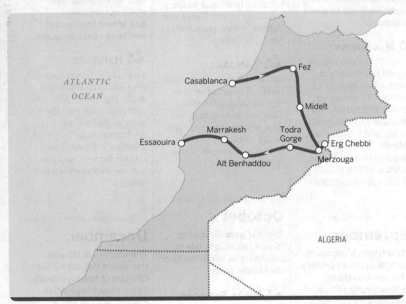

ATLANTIC
OCEAN

Fez

Casablanca

Midelt

Marrakesh

Todra
Gorge

Essaouira

Erg Chebbi

Aït Benhaddou

Merzouga

ALGERIA

Essential Morocco

Morocco is a big country, but in two weeks you can still comfortably cover a lot of ground and explore the best of what it has to offer, from imperial cities to mountains and desert.

Touch down in **Casablanca**, the commercial capital, and start with a tour of the stupendous Hassan II Mosque. Head by train to venerable **Fez**, with its ancient yet thriving medina.

Next, cross the Middle Atlas via **Midelt** for your first startling taste of Moroccan kasbah architecture, and the abandoned mining town of Aouli, dropped into the crevasse of a pretty gorge. Continue all the way to **Merzouga**, Morocco's gateway to the Sahara. Saddle up your camel and sleep under the stars amid the perfectly sculpted **Erg Chebbi**.

Shadowing the High Atlas as you head west brings you to the **Todra Gorge** for a day's hiking amid the canyons and *palmeraies* (palm groves). From here, head past Ouarzazate to **Aït Benhaddou**, with its fairy-tale-like 11th-century kasbah.

En route to the Atlantic, check into a riad in **Marrakesh**, and spend as many sunsets as possible on the theatrical Djemaa el-Fna, then don't stop until you reach artsy seaside medina and fishing port **Essaouira**.

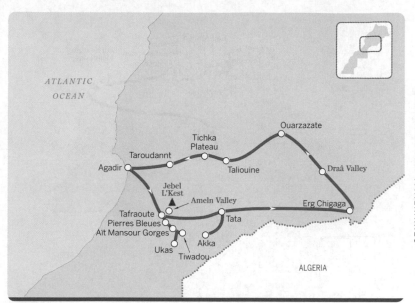

 Circling the South

This itinerary takes you deep into the south for wild mountain and desert landscapes, far from clicking cameras, and with plenty of activities to stimulate the mind and body.

Agadir is a handy entry point, but adventurers will want to leave quickly. Head to tiny but vibey **Tafraoute**, surrounded by beautiful Anti Atlas scenery such as the **Ameln Valley**, with its lush *palmeraies* and pink-hued houses. Spend a few days trekking through the valley and up **Jebel L'Kest**, bike past rock formations and engravings to the surreal **Pierres Bleues**, known as the Painted Rocks, and continue south through the **Aït Mansour Gorges**. At the far end of the gorges, where the beautiful scenery belies the ancient slave routes that passed this way, stay in the Afella-Ighir oasis. Use **Tiwadou** as a base for more trekking or discovering the rock carvings at **Ukas**.

By now you'll have developed a taste for Morocco's secluded southern corners. Once back in Tafraoute, wind east through the Anti Atlas and descend to the equally silent and epic Sahara. The last stop before Jebel Bani and a whole lot of *hammada* (stony desert), **Tata** makes a convenient base for exploring the oases, kasbahs, *agadirs* (fortified granaries) and magnificent rock engravings in spots such as **Akka**. A dusty journey to the east, the yellow-gold dunes of **Erg Chigaga** are more remote and less visited than Merzouga. In nearby M'Hamid, find yourself a camel to lead you north into the kasbah-littered **Drâa Valley**.

At the top of valley, head back towards the mountains. Commandeer a bike (mountain or motor), horse, mule or dromedary in film favourite **Ouarzazate**, where the stony desert landscape has been a celluloid stand-in for Tibet, Rome, Somalia and Egypt. Return to the coast via **Taliouine**, where you can buy the world's most expensive spice in Africa's saffron capital. Pause here, or in **Taroudannt**, for a trekking reprise in a mountainous area such as the **Tichka Plateau**. With its red walls and backdrop of snowcapped peaks, Taroudannt has hassle-free echoes of Marrakesh. Its souqs and squares are pleasant places to relax, and it's handy for Agadir's Al-Massira Airport.

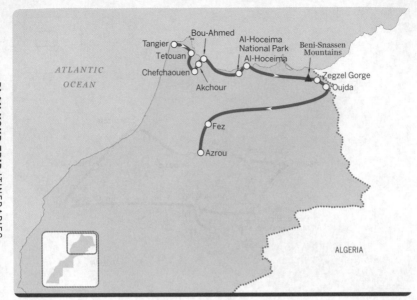

3 WEEKS The Med & the Mountains

In the north the Mediterranean littoral and the Rif Mountains have seen huge investment from the government. Domestic tourism has boomed as a result, but travellers are yet to discover the region in numbers.

Start in **Tangier**, ideally arriving by ferry across the Strait of Gibraltar to feel the thrill of crossing from Europe to Africa. In the mid-20th century, characters from gunrunners to beatnik literati mixed in this legendary port city. After a few days taking in the history, nightlife and restaurants, skip inland to **Tetouan**, the old capital of Spanish Morocco, with its charming blend of Arab medina and Andalucian architecture. The Spanish left a lighter imprint on nearby **Chefchaouen**, nestled in the Rif Mountains with its gorgeous blue-painted medina. It's tempting to spend a string of sunsets listening to the minarets chorus each other's call to prayer, but this is also a good trekking spot. You can head deep into the mountains on a five-day trek via riverside **Akchour** to **Bou-Ahmed**, a fishing village in the Oued Bouchia valley.

Continue east along the coast to the proud, modern seaside resort of **Al-Hoceima**, gateway to the dry canyons and limestone cliffs of the **Al-Hoceima National Park**. Walk to the park along the coast, or book a memorable tour including hiking or mountain biking and a homestay with a Berber family. En route to the Algerian border, there's more fine scenery in the **Beni-Snassen Mountains**, which you can enjoy in a swimming pool with mountain views, or a 300-year-old rural lodge. With its gorges, caves, mesa and Barbary sheep, this verdant area is far removed from classic images of Morocco. In the **Zegzel Gorge**, pluck a cumquat and see why the Romans remarked on this small citrus fruit.

From here, head to **Oujda** to refresh yourself with some city comforts, before taking the train to that grandest of imperial cities, **Fez**. Dive into the medina and relax in a riad, but if you find yourself missing the countryside, you can make an easy day (or several-day) trip into the cedar-clad Middle Atlas around the Berber market town of **Azrou**.

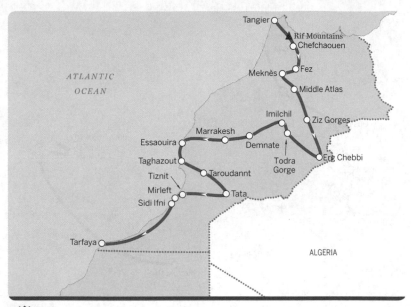

 6 WEEKS **Highlights & Hidden Gems**

Given six weeks you can really dive deep into Morocco: explore its big-ticket destinations while still having plenty of time to discover its more hidden corners – getting off the beaten track or just taking more time to soak the country in.

Climb off a ferry in famously decadent **Tangier**, with its Europe-facing medina, and head into the **Rif Mountains**. European influence continues in **Chefchaouen**, with its bright blue, Andalucian-tiled medina. Further south, the imperial cities of **Fez** and **Meknès** are more quintessentially Moroccan in their ancient medinas. After a few days of labyrinthine lanes and dye pits, you'll be ready for more mountains. Wind through the **Middle Atlas** and on through the Martian landscape of the **Ziz Gorges**. It's now just a few dusty hours to **Erg Chebbi**, the achingly beautiful expanse of rolling dunes, which you can explore on a camel or sandboard.

Brush off the Sahara and return to the High Atlas at **Todra Gorge**. Hike between the enclosing rock walls, then jump in a market-bound truck through tiny villages and deeper into the mountains. **Imilchil**, surrounded by red rock and turquoise lakes, is the site of a wedding *moussem* (festival) in September. Descend through the High Atlas and turn southwest, pausing to refuel in Berber foodie and cultural hub **Demnate**. The next stop is **Marrakesh**, with its famous riad hotels, medina shopping and Djemaa el-Fna. Hit the wild west coast at hippie-turned-boutique hang-out **Essaouira**, then head south to vibrant **Taghazout**, Morocco's premier surf spot. Then take the N10 to **Taroudannt**, the Souss Valley's prettiest market town with its mud-walled medina and kasbah.

Travel barren mountains and empty roads to **Tata**, a Saharan gateway where blue-robed guides can show you the desert. The road back to the Atlantic passes oases, *palmeraies*, kasbahs, *agadirs* and rock carvings. Near the coast, detour north to the **Tiznit** jewellery souq, particularly if it's a Thursday (market day).

Arcing west and south, you come to **Mirleft**, with its pink-and-blue arches, and **Sidi Ifni**, a jumble of wind-whipped art-deco relics surrounded by coastal walks. End your journey on the edge of the Western Sahara in sandy, gloriously isolated **Tarfaya**.

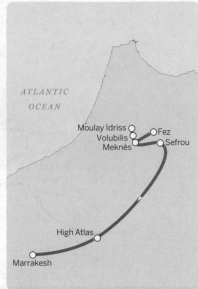

 Atlantic Adventure
3 WEEKS

Morocco's Atlantic seaboard takes you from the clamour of the north to the quieter coastline of the south. It's a landscape where cities give way to dramatic sea cliffs, long sandy beaches and picturesque fishing ports. Take the ferry from Spain to **Tangier**, at once a quintessentially Moroccan mosaic and a decadent outpost of Europe. Catch the train south, first to chilled-out **Asilah**, with its whitewashed charms, and then to **Rabat**, with its colonial architecture and palm-lined boulevards. Follow Casablanca's suburbanites taking the spectacular ocean road to **Oualidia**, the St Tropez lookalike with a perfect crescent lagoon. Further south, the hippies once gravitated to **Essaouira**, and its white-walled ramparts, bohemian beat and renovated riads still make travellers linger. When you've eaten your fill at the outdoor fish grills, follow Jimi Hendrix and today's surfers to the peaceful beaches at **Diabat** and **Sidi Kaouki**. Past more surf spots, **Agadir** is a modern family-friendly seaside resort, but the beaches and boutique accommodation of **Mirleft** may be more appealing for other travellers, along with the Spanish art-deco treasures of **Sidi Ifni**.

Empire & Atlas
10 DAYS

This short route gives a fast-paced introduction into the best that Morocco has to offer – its ancient storied cities and medinas, and the mighty Atlas mountains that ripple in waves down the length of the country. This itinerary begins in two cities once ruled by enlightened dynasties. Throw back a shot of Maghrebi exoticism in **Fez**, where modern Morocco and its rich past crowd for space in the extraordinary medina. Next, catch your breath in nearby **Meknès**, bypassed by many travellers despite its echoes of Sultan Moulay Ismail's glory days. A detour north takes you to **Volubilis**, Morocco's best-preserved ancient city, and testament to the Roman Empire's astonishing breadth. Nearby **Moulay Idriss**, with the mausoleum of the founder of Morocco's first imperial dynasty, is another wonderful antidote to urban clamour. Head south into the Middle Atlas, stopping at the Berber town **Sefrou**, with its charming medina. From here, take the cross-country route via Beni Mellal, skirting the edge of the **High Atlas** to the icon of contemporary Morocco: **Marrakesh**. The city's souqs, street performers and imperial architecture form an intoxicating mix.

Plan Your Trip
Morocco Outdoors

Morocco's diverse terrain means there are many outdoor activities on offer besides trekking. Birdwatching enthusiasts, cyclists, climbers and horse riders will all find options to challenge and excite. Another bonus: whether you're skiing, surfing or camel trekking, between activities you can enjoy the Moroccan culture and hospitality.

Birdwatching

Morocco is a birdwatcher's paradise. A startling array of species inhabits the country's diverse ecosystems and environments, especially the coastal wetlands.

Around 460 species have been recorded in the country, many of them migrants passing through in spring and autumn, when Morocco becomes a way station between Sub-Saharan Africa and breeding grounds in Scandinavia, Greenland and northern Russia. Other birds fly to Morocco to avoid the harsh northern European winters. The lagoon at Merja Zerga National Park (p188), near Moulay Bousselham, is the best site in the country for migratory birds.

A pleasant time for birdwatching is March through May, when the weather is comfortable and a wide variety of species is usually present. The winter is also a particularly active time in the wetlands and lagoons.

Guides & Tours

In addition to local birdwatching guides, the following UK-based companies offer Moroccan tours:

Birdfinders (www.birdfinders.co.uk)

Naturetrek (www.naturetrek.co.uk)

Wild Insights (www.wildinsights.co.uk)

Top Activity Spots

Mountains

Hoist yourself up here for rock climbing, from bouldering to mountaineering; downhill skiing and ski trekking; wildlife spotting, including apes, sheep and leopards, all of the Barbary variety; trekking; mountain biking; and white-water rafting.

Desert

Hotfoot it to the Sahara to take part in camel treks, moonlight dune hikes and sandboarding, and to watch wildlife – including desert warblers and the bat-eared fennec fox – and sleep in a Berber tent.

Coast

Hit the beach for surfing, windsurfing, kitesurfing, kayaking and canoeing; and for marine mammals and birdlife such as the endangered bald ibis.

Camel Treks

Exploring the Sahara by camel – whether on an overnight excursion or a longer desert safari – is one of Morocco's signature activities and most rewarding wilderness experiences.

Morocco's most evocative stretches of Saharan sand are Erg Chebbi, near Merzouga, and Erg Chigaga, near M'Hamid and Zagora, and past the more accessible Tinfou Dunes.

Only consider doing a camel trek in autumn (September and October) or winter (November to early March). Outside these months, you'll experiences gruelling extremes of heat, plus sandstorms in spring.

Prices start at around Dh300 per person per day, but vary depending on the number of people, the length of the trek and your negotiating skills.

The agency will organise the bivouac (temporary camp), which may be a permanent camp for shorter trips, and may offer Berber music and *mechoui* (whole roast).

Organising a Camel Trek

Travellers with lots of time can organise a guide and provisions in situ. This benefits the local community and counters the trend towards young guides leaving home to look for work in the more popular tourist centres.

M'Hamid is probably the most hassle-free of the main desert gateways, although the choice is wider at Zagora and Merzouga. Try to get recommendations from other travellers.

It's quicker and easier, involving less negotiations and waiting, to organise a trip in advance – either through an international tour operator or a company based in Ouarzazate or Marrakesh.

Horse Riding

Southern Morocco is popular for horse riding, from beaches such as Diabat to hills, mountains, valleys, gorges and the desert.

Specialist travel companies offer guided horse-riding tours:

Club Farah (www.clubfarah.com) Based near Mèknes.

Unicorn Trails (www.unicorntrails.com)

Mountain Biking

Ordinary cycling is possible in Morocco, but mountain biking opens up the options considerably.

For the very fit, the vast networks of *pistes* (dirt tracks) and footpaths in the High Atlas offer the most rewarding biking. The Anti Atlas, the Jebel Saghro plateau and the Drâa Valley also offer excellent trails.

Travel agencies, hotels and shops hire out mountain bikes, for example in Tafraoute, but the quality isn't really high enough for an extended trip. Adventure-tour companies cater to serious cyclists.

The following operators offer mountain-bike tours in Morocco:

Biking Morocco (www.mountain-bike-morocco.com)

Freeride Morocco (www.freeridemorocco.com)

Saddle Skedaddle (www.skedaddle.co.uk)

Rock Climbing

There is a growing climbing scene in Morocco, with some sublime routes. Anyone contemplating climbing should have plenty of experience and be prepared to bring all their own equipment.

The Anti Atlas and High Atlas offer everything from bouldering to very demanding mountaineering routes that shouldn't be attempted unless you have a great deal of experience.

The Dadès and Todra Gorges are prime climbing territory.

Des Clark's guidebook *Mountaineering in the Moroccan High Atlas* (2011), subtitled 'walks, climbs and scrambles over 3000m', is destined to become a classic. It covers some 50 routes and 30 peaks in handy pocket-sized, plastic-covered form, with plenty of maps, photos and practical information. Another excellent guide is *Morocco Rock* (www.moroccorock), which is particularly good on the Anti Atlas. The authors run an active Facebook community.

The Royal Moroccan Ski & Mountaineering Federation (www.frmsm.ma) has lists of climbing routes. A good local climbing tour operator is **Climb Morocco** (http://climbmorocco.com).

Skiing

Skiing is viable from November to April, although Morocco's ski stations are somewhat ramshackle. For more information, including local ski clubs, contact the Royal Moroccan Ski & Mountaineering Federation (www.frmsm.ma).

Downhill Skiing

Popular resort Oukaïmeden, about 70km south of Marrakesh, has North Africa's highest ski lift, and equipment for hire. There are other spots dotted around the Middle Atlas, most notably Mischliffen, near Fez, although some seasons the snow is thin on the ground. There's ad hoc equipment hire, but no ski-lift.

Ski Trekking

Ski randonnée is increasingly popular, especially from late December to February, when the Aït Bougomez Valley has prime routes.

Surfing, Windsurfing & Kitesurfing

With thousands of kilometres of coastline, the Moroccan Atlantic is a fine, if underrated, destination for surfing, windsurfing and kitesurfing. Lessons, equipment hire and surf holidays are available.

Northern & Central Morocco

North of Rabat, Mehdiya Plage has strong currents, but reliable year-round breaks.

Moving south, Plage des Nations and Temara Plage, both within 20km of Rabat, are also good for surfing. Sidi Bouzid and the beaches around El-Jadida also attract surfers.

Oualidia is known for surfing, windsurfing and kitesurfing. En route to Safi, the Lalla Fatna area has some of Morocco's best breaks: one of the world's longest tubular right-handers has drawn some of the biggest names in surfing.

Southern Morocco

Essaouira has been singled out by some surfers, although the 'Windy City of Africa' is a better windsurfing and kitesurfing destination year-round. Nearby Sidi Kaouki is an upcoming destination for all three sports.

Near Agadir, the Taghazout area has some of Morocco's best surfing beaches and numerous businesses catering to surfers.

Other destinations to consider in southern Morocco are Agadir, Aglou Plage, Mirleft and Sidi Ifni.

White-Water Rafting & Kayaking

Although white-water rafting and kayaking are underdeveloped in Morocco, the rivers in the High Atlas near Bin el-Ouidane have stunning scenery. **Water By Nature** (www.waterbynature.com) is a specialist rafting operator running tours in Morocco.

Plan Your Trip

Trekking in Morocco

Morocco is blessed with some of the world's most beautiful mountains, and is a year-round trekking destination. In summer, head to Jebel Toubkal (North Africa's highest peak). In winter, when snow closes the High Atlas, there's Jebel Saghro to explore, while the Rif Mountains are ideal for the seasons in between.

Trekking Regions

High Atlas

Tackle North Africa's highest peak, Jebel Toubkal, and meet the Berbers on the longer Toubkal Circuit.

Escape the crowds and be inspired by the remote M'Goun Massif's spectacular valleys and beautiful villages.

Jebel Saghro

Head southeast to some of Morocco's most rugged and stunning scenery, perfect for winter walking.

The Rif

Take a gentler path through little-visited cedar forests in the Talassemtane National Park, near Chefchaouen.

Anti Atlas

Visit a few of the Ameln Valley's 26 villages, en route to an ascent of the 'amethyst mountain', Jebel L'Kest.

Enjoy serious trekking and stark beauty among the remote villages and tremendous gorges beneath volcanic Jebel Siroua.

Getting Started

Where to Trek

Toubkal Summit & Circuit

An ascent of Jebel Toubkal, North Africa's highest peak (4167m), is Morocco's most iconic trek. The two-day hike starts at Imlil near Marrakesh; those wanting more can hire mules to make a Toubkal Circuit trek of up to 10 days.

M'Goun Traverse

Despite the sometime fearsome reputation of the M'Goun Massif, this four-day trek is suitable for most levels of fitness. The landscape is both varied and spectacular, from dry gorges to lush valleys, but be prepared to get your feet wet hopping or wading across shallow rivers.

Rif Mountains

Morocco's lowest mountain range is ideal for springtime trekking, when the Rif's oak forests are in their greenest leaf and the slopes carpeted with wildflowers. Trek through the Talassemtane National Park, past Berber villages to arrive at the audacious natural rock formation of God's Bridge.

Trekking Areas

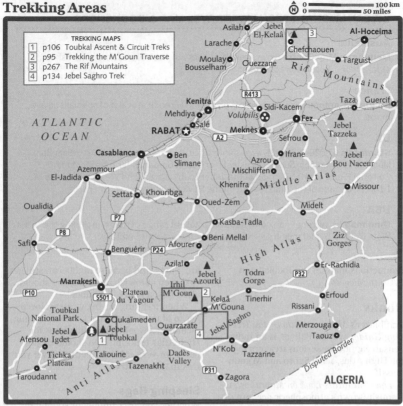

TREKKING MAPS
1 p106 Toubkal Ascent & Circuit Treks
2 p95 Trekking the M'Goun Traverse
3 p267 The Rif Mountains
4 p134 Jebel Saghro Trek

Jebel Sarhro

This trek of five to six days threads a path between the High Atlas and the Dadès Valley. The traverse of Jebel Saghro is arid but starkly beautiful, and is a prime winter trek when other mountain trails are closed due to snow.

Anti Atlas

The Anti Atlas is where Morocco's ripple of mountains finally peter out into the Sahara. In these much-overlooked mountains hardcore trekkers can take a week to tackle the volcanic peak of Jebel Siroua, or hike for five days through the villages of the Ameln Valley to Jebel L'Kest.

Maps

Morocco is covered by a 1:100,000 and also a 1:50,000 topographical map series.

Some of the 1:50,000 series are unavailable to the public; travellers exploring wide areas are advised to stick to the 1:100,000 series.

Although marked in Cyrillic script, 1:100,000 maps of Morocco made by the Soviet military are as topographically accurate as any available.

The best place in Morocco to buy maps is **Direction de la Cartographie** (☏0660 10 26 83; www.ancfcc.gov.ma; cnr Aves My Youssef & My Hassan I) in Rabat, which lists the maps it sells online.

Maps and photocopies are also available at other bookshops around Morocco, as well as at stalls around the Djemaa el-Fna (p50) in Marrakesh and, as a last resort, on the approaches to the Atlas trekking routes.

Websites, including Amazon (www. amazon.com), sell maps such as West Col

Productions maps of the Toubkal and M'Goun Massifs.

Books

Trailblazer's *Moroccan Atlas – the Trekking Guide,* by Alan Palmer, is an indispensable guide for serious trekkers to the High Atlas, Jebel Sahro and M'goun Massif.

The Mountains Look on Marrakech is Hamish Brown's atmospheric account of a 96-day trek across the mountains.

If you can find it in Morocco, the old booklet *Morocco: Mountain and Desert Tourism* (2005), published by Office National Marocain du Tourisme (ONMT), is still a good introduction to trekking in Morocco, though some contact details in its listings sections are now out of date. You should be able to pick it up in ONMT offices overseas and in Marrakesh and other major cities, or at Imlil's bureau des guides.

Clothing & Equipment

All year round you will need to pack strong, well-broken-in walking boots. You will also need a waterproof and windproof outer layer. It's amazing how quickly the weather can change, so you'll also need a sunhat, sunglasses and high-factor sunscreen.

In summer (June to August) light, baggy cotton trousers and long-sleeved shirts are musts, and because nights can still get cold even at lowish altitudes, you should also bring a fleece or jumper.

When trekking during winter (November to March) always pack warm clothing, including a woollen hat and gloves for High Atlas trekking. You should be prepared for very cold weather wherever you trek in the country.

Sleeping Bags
Whether you are camping or staying in houses, a four-season sleeping bag is essential for the High Atlas and Jebel Saghro from September to early April, when temperatures as low as –10°C are not unknown.

In lower ranges, even in high summer, a bag comfortable at 0°C is recommended. A thick sleeping mat or thin foam mattress is a good idea since the ground is extremely rocky. Guides can usually supply these.

Stoves
Many *gîtes* (hostels) have cooking facilities, but you may want to bring a stove if you are camping. Multifuel stoves that burn anything from aviation fuel to diesel are ideal.

Methylated spirits is hard to get hold of, but kerosene is available. Pierce-type butane gas canisters are also available, but not recommended for environmental reasons. Your guide will be able to offer advice.

Tents

The key decision, when planning a route, is whether or not to sleep in a tent. A good tent opens up endless trekking possibilities and will get you away from the crowds.

You can hire tents from tour operators and guides, and at trailheads.

If you would rather not carry a tent, in most regions you can stay in the villages.

Other Equipment

Bring a basic medical kit as well as water-purification tablets or iodine drops or a mechanical purifier. All water should be treated unless you take it directly from the source.

To go above 3000m between November and May, as well as having experience in winter mountaineering, you will need essentials including crampons, ice axes and snow shovels. Again, this equipment is available for hire.

If you are combining trekking with visits to urban areas, consider storing extra luggage before your trek rather than lugging around unwanted gear. Most hotels will let you leave luggage, sometimes for a small fee. Train stations in larger cities have secure left-luggage facilities.

Guides

However much trekking and map-reading experience you have, we strongly recommend that you hire a qualified guide – if for no other reason than to be your translator (how is your Tashelhit?), chaperone *faux guides* (unofficial guides) – they won't come near you if you are with a guide, deal-getter and vocal guidebook.

A good guide will also enhance your cultural experience. They will know local people, which will undoubtedly result in invitations for tea and food, and richer experiences of Berber life.

If something goes wrong, a local guide will be the quickest route to getting help. Every year foreigners die in the Moroccan mountains. Whatever the cause – a freak storm, an unlucky slip, a rock slide – the presence of a guide would invariably have increased their chances of survival. So however confident you feel, we recommend that you never walk into the mountains unguided.

Choosing a Guide

A flash-looking, English-speaking *faux guide* from Marrakesh is no substitute for a gnarled, old, local mountain guide who knows the area like the back of his hand.

Official guides carry photo-identity cards. Guides should be authorised by the Fédération Royale Marocaine de Ski et Montagne or l'Association Nationale des Guides et Accompagnateurs en Montagne du Maroc. They should be credited as *guides de montagne* (mountain guides), which requires study for at least six months at the Centre de Formation aux Métiers de Montagne, a school for mountain guides at Tabant in the Aït Bougomez valley.

Accompagnateurs (escorts) will have had only one week's training, and will not be insured to lead mountain trips; *guides de tourisme* (tourist guides) are not qualified to lead treks.

Official mountain guides, who can always show an identity card as proof of their status, have been trained in mountain craft, including first aid. In times of uncertain weather or in an emergency, they will be infinitely more efficient than a cheaper guide lacking proper training. If a guide is reluctant to show a photo card, it probably means they either don't have one or it has expired (they should be renewed every three years).

Some *guides de montagne* have additional training in rock climbing, canyoning and mountaineering. All guides speak French, and some also speak English, Spanish or German. Several young Moroccan female guides, who have succeeded in breaking into the previously all-male world of mountain guiding, are in high demand.

Hiring a Guide

There are more than 400 accredited mountain guides in Morocco, and many can be found through the *bureaux des guides* in Imlil, Setti Fatma, Chefchaouen, and Maroc Profond in Tabant (Aït Bougomez Valley).

At the time of writing, the minimum rate for official guides was Dh350 per day (per group, not per person). This rate can vary according to season and location. The rates do not include food and accommodation expenses.

Guides generally get free accommodation in *refuges* and *gîtes,* but you may be asked to cover their meals. If you walk a linear route, you'll also be expected to pay for their return journey.

Negotiate all fees before departure and count on giving at least a 10% tip at the end, unless you have been unhappy with the service.

If your guide is organising your trip (rather than a tour operator), be sure to go through all aspects of the trek ahead of time. Discuss where each day will start and end; whether tents will be shared (most guides have a tent and/or sleeping bag); how many mules will be hired; who will be cooking (if there are enough of you, the guide may insist on hiring a cook, usually for about Dh100 a day); food preferences; water provision; and the division of food and equipment among the group.

Mules

Mules (and the odd donkey) are widely used in Morocco for transporting goods through the mountains, and you can easily hire one to carry your gear.

If you are relying on heavy local supplies, or are in a large group, hiring a mule makes especially good sense. As a rough guide, mules can carry up to 120kg – or up to four sets of gear. If the route is very steep or demanding, the muleteer may insist upon carrying less. He will have the wellbeing of his meal ticket in mind, although Moroccans are generally unsentimental about their pack animals.

Some trekking routes are not suitable for mules, although detours (for the mule) are often possible. If high passes are covered in snow, porters may have to be used instead of mules (one porter can carry up to 18kg).

There is usually a standard charge for a mule and muleteer of about Dh100 per day. As with guides, if you trek a linear route, you'll also be expected to pay for the muleteer's return journey.

On the Trek

Accommodation

If you would rather not carry a tent, you can often stay in *refuges* and in villages at either *gîtes d'étape* (basic homestays or hostels) or *chez l'habitant* (in someone's home). Especially in remote areas, village rooms may not even have a mattress on the floor, although in places such as Imlil they often come with the luxury of a bed.

The bulk of trekking accommodation options in the High and Middle Atlas are *gîtes.* In the Rif and Anti Atlas, *gîtes* are uncommon, and accommodation is more often in local homes or in tents.

Gîtes d'Étape

Gîtes provide basic accommodation, often offering little more than a foam mattress in an empty room, or on a roof terrace or balcony. They have basic bathrooms and toilets, although the better ones have hot showers. Given notice, the proprietor can rustle up a tajine.

At the time of writing, the standard rate was Dh50 per person per night, although prices can vary according to season and location. Meals are extra (usually Dh30 to Dh50 per person), as are hot showers (usually Dh10 to Dh15 per shower).

The more upscale, privately owned *gîtes* typically charge up to Dh200 per person for half-board, while rooms at one luxury kasbah in Imlil cost up to Dh280.

Refuges

CAF operates *refuges* in Imlil, Oukaïmeden, Tazaghart, Tacheddirt and on Toubkal. Officially, bookings should be made in advance through the Oukaïmeden *refuge.* However, in practice you can usually find out if space is available at the other *refuges* in the Toubkal region by asking in Oukaïmeden or Imlil. *Refuges* are often packed in July and August.

CAF members and HI members get the cheapest price for a bed. Members of affiliated and recognised alpine organisations (eg the UK's Alpine Club) and children aged under 16 years are also eligible for discounts.

Food

The choice of dry rations is limited in rural Morocco. You cannot be sure of finding much beyond powdered milk, a range of dried fruit and sachets of soup, biscuits, some tinned fish and dates. Supermarkets in larger towns and cities are a much better option, and if you take a mule, you will be able to plan a more varied diet.

Bread, eggs, vegetables and some basic supplies (eg tea and tinned tuna) may be available in some mountain villages, but you cannot count on it. Meals can also be arranged in some villages (Dh30 to Dh50 per person is standard), especially at *gîtes* and *refuges,* although they usually need to be ordered in advance. Again, do not rely on local suppliers as your only source of food unless you have made previous arrangements.

Change money in the nearest major town and ensure that you have plenty of small notes. If you do get stuck, euro notes may be accepted.

Transport

Many trailheads are off the beaten path as far as public transport goes. You might need to factor in the cost of hiring a grand taxi to get you to where you can start walking.

Responsible Trekking

Morocco is being developed as a walking destination, but many regions are still remote – and susceptible to the cultural and environmental impact of tourism. Many travellers return home warmed and heartened by Berber hospitality, but as visitor numbers increase so too does the pressure on locals. In response, travellers should adopt an appropriate code of behaviour.

Cross-Cultural Considerations

Dress

The way you dress is important, especially among remote mountain people, who remain conservative. In villages, wear buttoned shirts or T-shirts and not sleeveless vests, which villagers use as underwear. Above all, trousers should be worn rather than shorts. This applies equally to men and women.

The importance of dress in the villages cannot be overemphasised (as many a frustrated and embarrassed trekking tour leader will affirm). However much you might disagree with this conservatism, respecting local traditions will bring great rewards, not least by way of contact, hospitality and assistance.

Hospitality

Invitations for tea and offers of food are common in the mountains. By taking a guide, who may have friends in many villages, you'll open yourself up to even more offers of genuine hospitality.

While these offers are unconditional, it is worth bearing in mind that the mountain economy is one of basic subsistence farming. No one has large supplies, and in outlying villages there may be no surplus

---

TREKKING GUIDEBOOKS

➡ *Great Atlas Traverse* by Michael Peyron. The two-volume work by the Morocco-based British writer is the definitive text for the great traverse. Less useful for the casual trekker.

➡ *The Atlas Mountains: A Walking and Trekking Guide* by Karl Smith. Published by the walking specialist Cicerone, this has route descriptions and information on subjects such as ski-touring, although it gets mixed reviews.

➡ *Mountaineering in the Moroccan High Atlas* by Des Clark. Also published by Cicerone, this guide – subtitled 'walks, climbs and scrambles over 3000m' – is destined to become a classic. It covers some 50 routes and 30 peaks in handy pocket-sized, plastic-covered form, with plenty of maps, photos and practical information.

➡ *Trekking in the Moroccan Atlas* by Richard Knight. Has 43 maps and information ranging from green hiking tips to language advice, although it also has both fans and detractors. Likely to be the most useful book for inexperienced trekkers, but also the bulkiest.

WORDS TO TREK BY

Even just a few words in a foreign language can make a big difference to your experience. The following words may be helpful on these treks. '(A)' indicates Arabic, '(B)' indicates Berber; other useful Arabic and Berber words can be found in the Glossary (p500).

adfel (B) – snow

adrar (B) – mountain (plural *idraren*)

afella (B) – summit

agdal (B) – pasture (also *aougdal*)

aghbalu (B) – water spring

ain (A) – water spring

aman (B) – water

anzar (B) – rain

argaz (B) – man

asserdoun (B) – mule

assif (B) – watercourse, river

azaghar (B) – plane, plateau (also *izwghar*)

azib (B) – seasonal shelter for shepherds

brhel (A) – mule

châba (B) – ravine

iferd (B) – lake

ifri (B) – cave

jebel (A) – mountain or hill

kerkour (B) – cairn

taddart (B) – house

talat (B) – dried-up ravine or watercourse

tamada (B) – lake

tigm (B) – house

tizi (B) – mountain pass

food. Offering your hosts some Chinese gunpowder tea and some sugar (preferably in cones) is a very welcome gesture. Dried fruits are also appreciated, as is a taste of any imported food you may have.

For this reason, it is important to be generous when buying provisions for yourself and guides.

Medicine

In remote areas, people along the way will often ask for medicine, from disinfectant and bandages to painkillers or cream for dry skin (which many children have). Always make sure the guide explains what to do with what you offer – how often to take it and so on.

Environmental Considerations

Rubbish

Carry out all your rubbish; never bury it or burn it (Western-style packaging never burns well) or allow your guide to hurl it over a cliff.

Don't rely on bought water in plastic bottles, as disposal of these bottles is creating a major problem in Morocco. Instead purify locally sourced water.

Human Waste Disposal

It's important to avoid contamination of water sources. Where there is a toilet, use it; where there is none, bury your waste. Dig a small hole 15cm (6in) deep and at least 60m from any watercourse – an important point to remember, given how many trekking routes follow rivers and streams. Consider carrying a lightweight trowel: in the arid Atlas Mountains, digging without one can be difficult. In snow, dig down to the soil; otherwise, your waste will be exposed when the snow melts.

Use toilet paper sparingly, burn it when possible or bury it with the waste. Cover the waste with soil and a rock.

Washing

Don't use detergents or toothpaste in or near watercourses, even if they are biodegradable. For personal washing use biodegradable soap and wash at least 50m away from any watercourse. Disperse the waste water widely to allow the soil to filter it fully before it makes its way back to the watercourse. Use a scourer, sand or snow to wash cooking utensils rather than detergent. Again, make sure you're at least 50m from any watercourse.

Camping

Vegetation at high altitude is highly sensitive. When camping, minimise your impact on the environment by not removing or disturbing the vegetation around your campsite. Sufficient fodder (barley) for all baggage mules and donkeys should be brought in.

Low-Impact Cooking

Don't depend on open fires for cooking: cutting wood for fires has caused widespread deforestation in Morocco. Ideally, cook on a lightweight multifuel or kerosene stove and avoid those powered by disposable butane gas canisters. If you do make a fire, ensure it is fully extinguished after use.

Erosion

Hillsides and mountain slopes, especially at high altitudes, are prone to erosion. Stick to existing tracks and avoid short cuts that bypass a switchback. If you blaze a new trail straight down a slope, it will turn into a watercourse with the next heavy rainfall, eventually causing soil loss and deep scarring.

Plan Your Trip
Travel with Children

Morocco has plenty to capture a child's imagination. The souqs of Marrakesh and Fez are an endlessly fascinating sensory explosion, and nights around a campfire or camel rides on the beach are equally memorable – but factor in some time by the hotel pool at the end of a hot day.

Best Regions for Kids

Marrakesh

All generations can retire to pool, park, horse-drawn calèche or camel back. The Djemaa el-Fna is Morocco's carnival capital.

Atlantic Coast

The Atlantic Coast offers plenty of beaches and water and wind sports. Agadir's long, sandy beach is popular; mix it with somewhere more colourful such as Essaouira, with its fun-to-explore ramparts and medina.

Drâa Valley

Tour Ouarzazate's film studios and kasbah, then head down the valley for dunes and dromedary rides.

Rabat

With souqs, ruins and gardens, this is a relatively mellow slice of urban Morocco. Attractions include the beach, amusement park and pony rides.

Middle Atlas

For mountain scenery, waterfalls, forest walks and less hair-raising passes than the High Atlas. Easily visited from spots such as Azrou and Fez.

Morocco for Kids

Morocco is ideal for parents who once travelled to intrepid destinations, and don't necessarily fancy a Western poolside now they have knee-high travelling companions. Compared with Asia, Morocco is easily accessed from Europe and North America; Marrakesh is less than four hours from London. And when you touch down, you'll find that children open numerous doors, getting you closer to the heart of this family-oriented country.

Meeting the Locals

Moroccans love children so much that you may even want to bring a backpack to carry smaller kids, in case they grow tired of the kissing, hugging, gifts and general adulation. Locals have grown up in large families, so children help break the ice and encourage contact with Moroccans, who are generally very friendly, helpful and protective towards families.

As you travel the countryside, women may pick up their own child and wave from their doorway. Such moments emphasise your children's great benefit: having yet to acquire any stereotypes about Africa and the Middle East, their enduring impression of Morocco is likely to be its people's warmth and friendliness.

Of course, this certainly doesn't mean parents receive special treatment from the salesmen in the country's souqs. However, even the grizzliest shopkeepers generally welcome Western women and children, as it gives their store the image of having a broad, family-friendly appeal. Letting your kids run amok in carpet shops can also be an excellent bargaining technique!

Adapting to Morocco

Morocco is a foreign environment and children will probably take a day or so to adapt, but it has plenty of familiar and fun aspects that kids can relate to. In the countryside, simple things like beehives and plants endlessly fascinate children. Dedicated play facilities in parks and public gardens are very rare.

Taking Your Time

A key to successful family travel in Morocco is to factor in lots of time to acclimatise at the beginning, and to just relax and muck about at the end. Trying to cram everything in, as you might if you were by yourself, will lead to tired, cranky kids. Distances are deceptive due to factors such as bad roads, and you need to build in contingency plans in case children become ill. However, having to slow your pace to that of your kids – for example, having to stay put in the hottest hours between noon and 4pm – is another way children draw you closer to the Moroccan landscape, people and pace of life.

Eating Out

Tajines contain many familiar elements, such as potatoes and carrots. Although you may want to encourage your child to try Moroccan food, you may struggle if they don't like potatoes or bread; in which case Western foods, such as pasta, pizza and fries, are available. High chairs are not always available in restaurants, although staff are almost universally accommodating with children.

Be careful about choosing restaurants; steer clear of salads and stick to piping-hot tajines, couscous, omelettes and soups such as *harira* (lentil soup). Markets sell delicious fruit and veggies, but be sure to wash or peel them. Local fried doughnuts are a sweet sticky treat.

To avoid stomach upsets, stick to purified or bottled water. Milk is widely available – UHT, pasteurised and powdered – but baked beans are not, and you should bring any special foods you require.

Children's Highlights

Animal Encounters

Mountain walk, High Atlas Travelling by road to a High Atlas trailhead such as Imlil, then taking a day walk in the mountains with a guide and mule. (p101)

Camel ride, Essaouira Camel or horse rides along the beaches around Essaouira or in the Sahara, with accessible dunes in the Drâa Valley and Merzouga. (p206)

Calèche ride, Marrakesh Calèche (horse-drawn carriage) rides around the ramparts of places such as Marrakesh, Meknès and Taroudannt. (p82)

Splashing Around

Water sports, Essaouira Wind and water sports around Essaouira (p209), or the beach at Agadir (p356) for young children.

Oualidia lagoon Safe, calm waters and a wide, sandy beach. (p202)

Parque Marítimo del Mediterráneo Ceuta's creative maritime park, its pools surrounded by restaurants and cafes. (p240)

Jnan Sbil, Fez These shady gardens (p293) have plenty of fountains for cooling down amid leafy surrounds.

Fun & Games

Marrakesh Explore Jardin Majorelle (p60) and its collection of desert plants at Djemaa el-Fna, (p50), children enjoy amusements such as the 'fishing for a bottle' game.

Ouarzazate The Atlas Film Corporation Studios (p114) features sets and props from famous films made in the area.

Fez Cooking classes at Café Clock (p307) Good for children of most ages – from making spice mixes to kneading dough and taking bread to the communal oven. Kefta tajine is a good knife-free meal to prepare. There's also a Cafe Clock in Marrakech which is popular with families.

Planning

If you look hard enough, you can buy just about anything you need for young children in Morocco. Before leaving home, think about what you can take with you to Morocco's various environments; wet-weather gear is vital in the mountains in case the weather turns bad.

Lonely Planet's *Travel with Children* has more information and tips.

Accommodation

Some hotels are more family-friendly than others, so check your children will be well catered for before booking.

Like the airlines, many hotels will not charge children under two years of age. For those between two and 12 years sharing a room with their parents, it's often 50% off the adult rate. If you want reasonable toilet and bathroom facilities, you'll need to stay in midrange hotels.

Transport

Northern Morocco has a great rail infrastructure and travel by train may be the easiest, most enjoyable option: children can stretch their legs and fold-out tables are useful for drawing and games. Travellers with children can buy discount cards for rail travel.

Grands taxis and buses can be a real squeeze with young children, who count not as passengers in their own right but as wriggling luggage, and have to sit on your lap. The safety record of buses and shared taxis is poor, and many roads are potholed.

Hiring a vehicle – a taxi in Marrakesh or a 4WD to the mountains – is well worth the extra expense. You might bring a child seat, but note that many taxis don't have seatbelts to help attach them. Hire-car companies normally don't have them; child seats generally cost more in Morocco than in Europe.

Health & Hygiene

Hand sanitiser (alcohol gel) is essential, as children tend to touch everything. Disposable nappies are readily available. All travellers with children should know how to treat minor ailments and when to seek medical treatment.

Make sure the children are up to date with routine vaccinations, and discuss possible travel vaccines well before departure, as some are not suitable for children aged less than a year.

Upset stomachs are always a risk for children when travelling, so take particular care with diet. If your child is vomiting or experiencing diarrhoea, lost fluid and salts must be replaced. It may be helpful to take rehydration powders for reconstituting with sterile water; ask your doctor. Be aware that at roadside stops and cheaper hotels, squat-style toilets are more common than Western-style toilets.

In Morocco's often-searing heat, sunburn, heat exhaustion and dehydration should all be guarded against, even on cloudy days. Bring high-factor sunscreen with you, and avoid travelling in the interior or during midsummer, when temperatures rise to 40°C plus.

Encourage children to avoid dogs and other mammals because of the risk of rabies and other diseases – although there isn't likely to be a risk on camel rides in the desert, or with donkeys and mules working in places like Fez medina.

Regions at a Glance

Marrakesh & Central Morocco

Architecture
Desert
Trekking

Marble & Mudbrick Marvels

The skinny lanes of Marrakesh's medina lead to lavish palaces, tombs and religious monuments decked out in marble, tilework and honeycombed *muqarnas* (ornamented vaulting). While red-earth kasbahs and *ksour* (fortified strongholds) stand guard over High Atlas valleys and the old desert caravan routes.

Sahara Exploits

The days of the great caravans to Timbuktu are done, but you can still saddle up your camel and trek into the great sand sea of the Sahara, and sleep under the stars in a traditional Berber encampment.

High Atlas Trails

The High Atlas mountains are a destination tailor-made for trekking. Hike for an afternoon or a week, or take the option to tackle Mt Toubkal, North Africa's highest peak.

p48

Atlantic Coast

Beaches
Architecture
Outdoor Activities

Seaside Breaks

This stretch encompasses the aptly named Paradise Beach, a bus-ride from Asilah, and Sidi Kaouki, a top surfing and windsurfing spot. In between, Temara Plage and Haouzia beach are near Rabat and Casablanca, laid-back Oualidia has a sand-fringed lagoon, while the beach at Moulay-Bousselham is a gorgeous stretch of golden sand.

Mauresque & Medinas

Gems include Essaouira, a fortified seaside town with wave-lashed ramparts. Hispano-Moorish Larache recalls its two spells under Spanish rule and murals decorate nearby Asilah's medina. Mauresque beauties and the world's third-largest mosque are found in Casablanca, and Rabat is home to a superb kasbah.

Birdwatching

Beaches and coastal wetlands offer excellent birdwatching, particularly around Moulay Bousselham: Merja Zerga (Blue Lagoon) attracts thousands of birds. Lac de Sidi Bourhaba is one of the last places to see large numbers of marbled ducks.

p153

Mediterranean Coast & the Rif

Coast
Nature
Mountains

Beaches

From beaches near Tangier – such as bracing Plage Robinson – the Mediterranean coast ripples east. Top beaches include Oued Laou, Cala Iris, Al-Hoceima and Saïdia, all unruffled in comparison with Europe's Mediterranean beaches.

National Parks

Two stunning national parks offer the best of the region's coastline and mountains. Talassemtane National Park encompasses green mountains, tiny villages, an eco-museum and the God's Bridge rock formation. The Al-Hoceima National Park's great mesas, dry canyons and thuya forests lead to limestone sea cliffs.

Riffian Trekking

Trekking through the Rif Mountains in Talassemtane National Park is superb, and the park is largely undiscovered compared with High Atlas routes. From Chefchaouen, multiday trails lead through forests of cedar, cork oak and fir.

p218

Fez, Meknès & the Middle Atlas

Souqs
History
Food

Handicraft Shopping

Fez medina includes the Henna Souq, the recently restored Dyers' Souq and the Carpenter's Souq, with thrones built for weddings. Meknès has souqs devoted to textiles, jewellery, carpets and embroidery, and Middle Atlas souqs are piled with local produce and the occasional Berber carpet.

Minarets & Mosaics

Fez medina is the world's largest living medieval Islamic city, and the Fès Festival of World Sacred Music showcases Sufi music. Elsewhere, memories of Meknès' past glories remain; Volubilis was a Roman outpost; Moulay Idriss is dedicated to its 8th-century namesake; and an 11th-century minaret overlooks oasis town Figuig.

Street Eats

The Fassi cuisine of Fez is the envy of Morocco, while the Middle Atlas is Morocco's bread basket: seek out homegrown delights such as Sefrou cherries, the olive oils of Moulay Idriss and Meknés wines.

p284

Southern Morocco & Western Sahara

Off the Beaten Track
Oases
Activities

Coastal Hideaways

En route to the Sahara, remote seaside escapes offer empty beaches and dilapidated charm. Mirleft is a favourite hang-out with its cafes and boutique accommodation; art-deco Sidi Ifni is as perfectly faded as a sepia photo; and Tarfaya's colonial Spanish relics peel between the eddying sands.

Palmeraies

Beneath ochre cliffs, palms worthy of *Lawrence of Arabia* nestle in the Aït Mansour Gorges and Ameln Valley. Palms also line the winding road through Paradise Valley, and refresh Saharan travellers around Tata and Tighmert.

Sand & Surf

Taghazout is Morocco's premier surf spot; the sun-and-sand fun continues year-round in Agadir; and Mirleft and Sidi Ifni offer wind and water sports. Inland, the Anti Atlas is a trekking and mountain-biking playground, and Tata is an emerging destination for desert excursions.

p352

On the Road

Mediterranean Coast & the Rif
p218

Atlantic Coast
p153

Fez, Meknès & the Middle Atlas
p284

Marrakesh & Central Morocco
p46

Southern Morocco & Western Sahara
p352

Marrakesh & Central Morocco

مراكش ووسط المغرب

Why Go?

Marrakesh is most people's first taste of Morocco and what an introduction it is. Somewhere between the donkey-cart swerving souq action, the tilework and marble monument overload, and the hundredth time you find yourself lost amid the medina's doodling alleyways, this great city of the Maghreb will work its magic on you. But when you've finally found your way out of the old city, Marrakesh is a jumping-off point to some of Morocco's most stunning landscapes, set against the soaring peaks of the Atlas mountains.

Hike along craggy clifftops to tiny Berber villages in the High Atlas, or amid orchards and wind-whittled rock formations inside the lush Dadès Gorge. Then explore the palm-studded Drâa Valley and its slumping mudbrick kasbahs and *ksour* on your way east to the Sahara. Sitting atop a sculpted sand dune at sunrise is the perfect orange-hued curtain call to this extraordinary region.

Best Places to Eat

➜ Amal Center (p74)

➜ Al Fassia (p75)

➜ Douyria (p116)

➜ Chez Pierre (p137)

➜ Dar Anika (p74)

Best Places to Sleep

➜ Riad Azoulay (p70)

➜ L'Ma Lodge (p130)

➜ Tizouit (p85)

➜ Maison Merzouga (p148)

➜ Riad Bledna (p71)

➜ Riad Dar Sofian (p123)

When to Go
Marrakesh

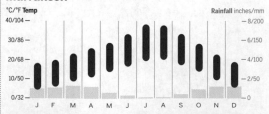

Mar–Apr Mountains thaw, wildflowers bloom. Though skip Easter holidays in

Marrakesh when prices jump.
May–Jun Pull on your hiking boots and hit the High Atlas trails.

Oct–Nov Dune escapades beckon. Prime desert time with gentle breezes and dates galore.

MARRAKESH

مراكش

POP 1,323,005

Prepare for your senses to be slapped. Marrakesh's medina, wrapped within powder-pink *pisé* (rammed earth) ramparts, is a show-stopping muddle of crowded souqs where sheep carcasses swing from hooks next door to twinkling lamps, and squiggling ochre-dusted lanes lead to nowhere. The main artery into this labyrinthine web is the vast square of Djemaa el-Fna, where it's carnival night every night and musicians, acrobats, and slapstick acting troupes tap into the old city's frenetic pulse.

Raised, razed, and then raised again; almost 1000 years after its founding, Morocco's Red City continues to evolve. Today its caravanserai culture and craft heritage lay alongside a contemporary arts scene that brings festivals and design initiatives to its door. Chi-chi boutiques sit next to bazaar-stalls within the souqs, and the traders of old have long since been swapped for groups of tourists goggling at palace and mansion frippery where the one percenters of past centuries once lived.

Rapid growth though, has brought its attendant problems. Congestion, pollution and creeping urbanisation have become environmental issues while the recent economic downturn has exposed the fragility of tourism-driven economy. But this is a city that refuses to sit still and it's that abundant energy that will help steer Marrakesh forward.

More than anywhere else in Morocco, this is where tradition and modernity merge. Marrakesh will dazzle, frazzle and enchant. Put on your tassle-toed *babouches* (leather slippers) and dive right in.

History

The Berber Sanhaja tribe founded the Almoravid dynasty in the 11th century and swept through the south of Morocco, demolishing opponents as they rode north. They pitched their campsite on a desolate swath of land that would become Marrakesh.

Almoravid Berber leader Youssef ben Tachfine and his savvy wife Zeinab recognised its strategic potential, and built ramparts around the encampment in AD 1062. The Almoravids established the city's *khettara* (underground irrigation system) and signature pink mudbrick architecture.

At the age of almost 80, Youssef ben Tachfine launched successful campaigns securing Almoravid control of Andalucia. Marrakesh, once just a patch of dirt, became the operational centre of an empire that stretched right up to Barcelona's city limits.

Almohad warriors stormed the city in 1147 and left only the plumbing and the Koubba Ba'adiyn intact. Almohad ruler Yacoub al-Mansour remodelled Marrakesh with a fortified kasbah, glorious gardens, *qissaria* (covered markets), a rebuilt Koutoubia and a triumphal gate (Bab Agnaou). But the Almohads lost their showpiece to the Merenids in 1269, who turned royal attention to Meknès and Fez.

After centuries of playing second fiddle under Merenid rule, Marrakesh regained it's crown in the 16th century, when the Saadians established their dynasty in the city. Marrakesh thrived as the crux of lucrative sugar-trade routes, and a trading centre for Christians and a protected *mellah* (Jewish quarter) were established in 1558. Ahmed al-Mansour ed-Dahbi (the Victorious and Golden) paved the Badi Palace with gold and took opulence to the grave in the gilded Saadian Tombs.

The Saadian dynasty crumbled in the 17th century, paving the way for the Alawites to seize the reins. Alawite leader Moulay Ismail preferred Meknès to Marrakesh, and moved his headquarters there – though not before looting the Badi Palace. Stripped of its role as the imperial base, Marrakesh entered its Wild West period with big guns vying for control. Those who prevailed built extravagant riads, though much of the population lived hand to mouth in crowded *fondouqs* (rooming houses).

After 1912, when Morocco was handed to the French protectorate, Thami el-Glaoui was installed as pasha of Marrakesh. While he went to work terrorising southern Morocco, French and Spanish colonists were busy building themselves a *ville nouvelle* (new town) outside of Marrakesh's city walls.

After independence in 1956, Marrakesh was left without a clear role and resumed its fallback career as a caravanserai – becoming the nation's breakaway success. Roving hippies built the city's mystique in the 1960s and '70s, and visits by the Rolling Stones, Beatles and Led Zeppelin gave the city star power. In the 1990s private medina mansions were converted into B&Bs, as low-cost airlines delivered weekenders to brass-studded riad doors.

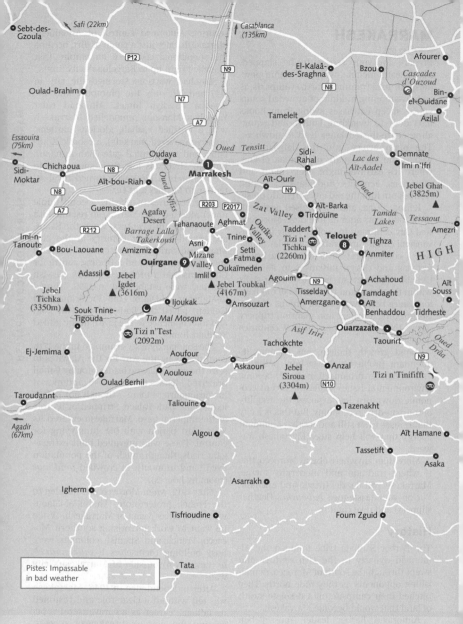

Marrakesh & Central Morocco Highlights

1 Marrakesh (p50)
Succumbing to the Djemaa's all-out chaos then throwing away the map to meander medina lanes.

2 Aït Bougomez Valley

(p90) Walking through Morocco's stunning Shangri-la.

3 Dadès Gorge (p135)
Descending into this valley of timewarp villages and crumbling kasbahs, framed by wacky, weathered rock.

4 Erg Chigaga (p125)
Absorbing stark Saharan beauty and star-filled nights amid rolling dunes.

5 Ahansal Valley (p88)
Fuelling your adventure-itch by

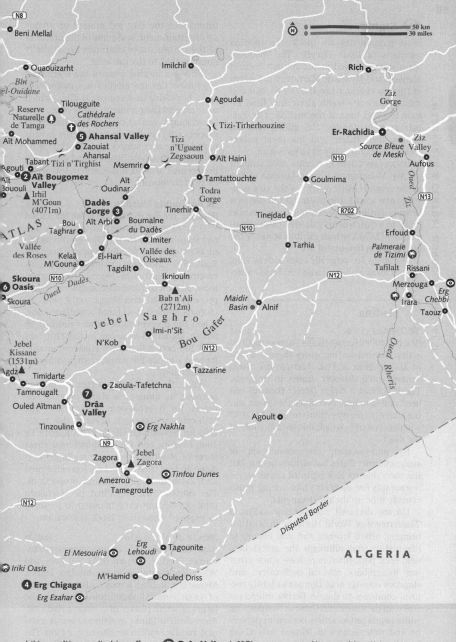

hiking, rafting or climbing off
the beaten trail.

◉ Sights

Most monuments are inside the medina ramparts (a 19km circuit). The medina's main souqs, as well as the Ali ben Youssef Medersa and Musée de Marrakech are north of Djemaa el-Fna, while the Dar Si Said and Bahia Palace are south along Rue Riad Zitoun el-Jedid toward the *mellah*. The kasbah area, containing the gilded Saadian Tombs, Badi Palace and the royal palace (closed to visitors), is just to the south.

It's an easy 20- to 25-minute stroll straight up Ave Mohammed V from Djemaa el-Fna to the central Guéliz district of the ville nouvelle (new town). The main sight in the new town is Jardin Majorelle, but Guéliz is also home to a clutch of art galleries, most significantly MACMA, which exhibits some of the big names in Orientalist art.

The souqs are generally open 9am to 7pm, though many stalls are closed on Friday afternoon.

◉ Medina

★ Djemaa el-Fna
SQUARE

(Map p56; off Pl de Foucald) FREE Think of it as live-action channel-surfing: everywhere you look in the Djemaa el-Fna, Marrakesh's main square, you'll discover drama in progress. The hoopla and *halqa* (street theatre) has been non-stop here ever since this plaza was the site of public executions around AD 1050 – hence its name, which means 'assembly of the dead'.

By mid-morning the soundtrack of snake-charmer flutes has already begun, but the show doesn't kick off until sunset when restaurants fire up their grills, cueing musicians to tune up their instruments.

Unesco declared the Djemaa el-Fna a 'Masterpiece of World Heritage' in 2001 for bringing urban legends and oral history to life nightly and although the storytellers who once performed here have since given way to acrobats, musical performers, and slapstick comedy acts, Djemaa's nightly carnival continues to dazzle. Berber musicians strike up the music and Gnaoua troupes sing while henna tattoo artists beckon to passers by and water-sellers in fringed hats clang brass cups together, hoping to drive people to drink. This is a show you don't want to miss and it's a bargain too. Applause and a few dirhams ensure an encore.

The square's many eclectic exhibitions are not without a darker side though; you are very likely to see monkeys, kept in cages throughout the day, led around on chains for entertainment, and some of the practices of the plaza's snake charmers are ethically questionable, to say the least.

While wandering around the Djemaa at any time of day stay alert to cars, motorbikes and horse-drawn-carriage traffic, which whiz around the perimeter of the plaza. Also be on guard against pickpockets and rogue gropers who are known to work the crowds particularly after sunset. To nab prime seats on makeshift stools (women and elders get preference) around musician circles, arrive early in the evening.

★ Koutoubia Mosque
MOSQUE

(Map p53; cnr Rue el-Koutoubia & Ave Mohammed V; ⊘ closed to non-Muslims) Five times a day, one voice rises above the Djemaa din as the muezzin calls the faithful to prayer from the Koutoubia Mosque minaret. Excavations confirm a Marrakshi legend: the original mosque, built by Almoravid architects, wasn't properly aligned with Mecca, so the pious Almohads levelled it to build a realigned one. When the present mosque was finished by Sultan Yacoub el-Mansour in the 12th century, 100 booksellers were clustered around its base – hence the name, from *kutubiyyin* (booksellers).

While the Koutoubia serves a spiritual purpose, its minaret is also a point of reference for international architecture. The 12th-century 70m-high tower is the prototype for Seville's La Giralda and Rabat's Le Tour Hassan, and it's a monumental cheat sheet of Moorish ornament: scalloped keystone arches, jagged *merlons* (crenellations) and mathematically pleasing proportions. The minaret was sheathed in Marrakshi pink plaster, but experts opted to preserve its exposed stone in its 1990s restoration.

Musée de Mouassine
MUSEUM

(Map p56; ☑ 0524 38 57 21; www.museedemouassine.com; 5 Derb el Hammam; Dh30; ⊘ 9.30am-7pm) While house-hunting in the medina, Patrick Menac'h stumbled across a historic treasure of great cultural significance. Beneath the layers of white plaster of a modest riad's 1st-floor *douiria* (guest apartment) was a jewel of domestic Saadian architecture, c 1560. The riad's ground-floor rooms hold a small collection of Berber artefacts, but the painstakingly restored interior of the upstairs salons, with their intricate cornice friezes and painted woodwork, are the true star of this charming museum.

> **DON'T MISS**
>
> ## MEDINA PRIVATE MUSEUMS
>
> Within the looping *derbs* (alleyways) of the medina you'll find a clutch of newly opened private museums, which allow a window on Marrakshi culture and history. Here are three of our favourites:
>
> **Le Jardin Secret** (☎0524 39 00 40; www.lejardinsecretmarrakech.com; 121 Rue Mouassine; adult/child Dh50/free, tower Dh30/20; ☺10.30am-7pm) Take a souq time-out to enjoy a traditional medina garden revived for the 21st century. This historic riad was once owned by powerful *caid* (local chief) U-Bihi, who was poisoned by Mohammed IV. The palatial grounds comprise both an exotic and traditional Islamic garden fed by a restored original *khettara* (underground irrigation system), a pavilion with exhibits on the riad's history (including a fascinating documentary on the restoration process), a cafe, and a tower with views across the medina.
>
> **Heritage Museum** (Musée du Patrimoine; www.heritagemuseummarrakech.com; 25 Zinkat Rahba; Dh30; ☺9am-5pm) The Alouani Bibi family have thrown open the doors of this old riad to display their eclectic and fascinating collection of Moroccan artefacts. From Berber costumes and jewellery to Roman amphorae, the exhibits (all labelled in English and French) cover the arc of Moroccan history and culture. The rooftop cafe is a tranquil spot to hang out in amid the souq hustle.
>
> **Musée Boucharouite** (☎0524 38 38 87; Derb El Cadi; adult/child Dh40/free; ☺9.30am-6pm Mon-Sat, closed Aug) Berber *boucharouites* (rag rugs made from recycled cloth) may be a poor cousin to the famous jewel-toned Moroccan carpets, but this beautifully collated gallery housed in an 18th-century riad displays the artistry of this lesser-known craft. The museum is the work of avid collector Patrick de Maillard and, in addition to *boucharouites*, the rooms are scattered with a lovely jumble of Moroccan popular art, from agricultural implements to painted doors. The terrace upstairs serves refreshments.

The other major projects of this period, when the Saadians were busy transforming Marrakesh into their Imperial capital, are all grand in scale – the mosques at Mouassine, Bab Doukkala, Ben-Youssef and Sidi Bel-Abbes. But this bijou 1st-floor *douiria* was created by a *chorfa* (noble) family after the Saadians relocated the Mouassine Jews to the *mellah* and gave the city a new dynamic.

The *douiria,* in its restored form, is thus an important example of domestic architecture in this era and a commentary on the courtly art of hospitality. Imagine the mindset of travel-weary guests as they entered the main salon with its symphony of colour: flowers and birds in saffron, verdigris and apricot climb the walls in a vertical garden, while bedrooms are trimmed with sculpted Kufic script framed by azure blue and finished with a fine Pompeian red skirting. You may assume the vivid colours on show are the work of the 24-man restoration team, but the decor is, amazingly, original – their vibrancy preserved beneath layers of plaster for centuries. In the side salon you can view a fascinating short video of some of the restoration methods.

The staff here are passionate about the *douiria* and its restoration process and are more than happy to guide you through the rooms offering insight and explanations.

Souq des Teinturiers SOUQ
(Map p56, Souq des Teinturiers; ☺irregular hours) The dyers' souq is one of Marrakesh's most colourful market sights. Here you'll find skeins of coloured wool draped from the rafters and a rainbow of colour pigment pots outside the stalls.

★**Ali ben Youssef Medersa** ISLAMIC SITE
(Map p56; ☎0524 44 18 93; Pl ben Youssef; Dh20; ☺9am-7pm, to 6pm winter) 'You who enter my door, may your highest hopes be exceeded' reads the inscription over the entryway to the Ali ben Youssef Medersa, and after almost six centuries, the blessing still charms visitors. Sight lines are lifted in the entry with carved Atlas cedar cupolas and *mashrabiyya* (wooden-lattice screen) balconies, while the courtyard is a mind-boggling profusion of Hispano-Moresque ornament: five-colour *zellij* walls, stucco archways, cedar windows, and a marble *mihrab* (niche in a mosque indicating the direction of Mecca).

Marrakesh

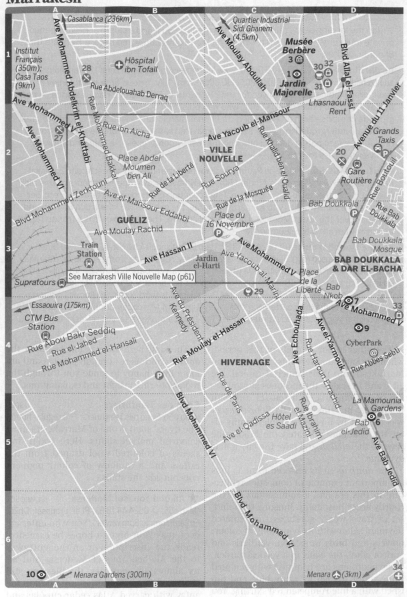

Casablanca (236km)

Quartier Industrial Sidi Ghanem (4.5km)

Ave Mohammed Abdelkrim el-Khattabi

Ave Moulay Abdullah

Musée Berbère

3

30 32

1

31

Jardin Majorelle

Blvd Allal el-Fassi

Institut Français (350m); Casa Taos (9km)

Hôpital ibn Tofaïl

28

Rue Abdelouahab Derraq

Ave Mohammed VI

27

Rue Mohammed Bakka

Rue ibn Aicha

Ave Yacoub el-Mansour

VILLE NOUVELLE

Lhasnaoui Rent

Avenue du 11 Janvier

Grands Taxis

Place Abdel Moumen ben Ali

Rue de la Liberté

Rue Sourya

Rue Khalid ben el-Oualid

20

Gare Routière

Rue Boutouil

Blvd Mohammed Zerktouni

Ave el-Mansour Eddahbi

Rue de la Mosquée

Bab Doukkala

Rue Bab Doukkala

GUÉLIZ

Ave Moulay Rachid

Place du 16 Novembre

Bab Doukkala Mosque

Train Station

Ave Hassan II

Jardin el-Harti

Ave Yacoub el-Marini

Ave Mohammed V

BAB DOUKKALA & DAR EL-BACHA

See Marrakesh Ville Nouvelle Map (p61)

Place de la Liberté

Bab Nkob

Bab Mohammed V

7

33

Supratours

29

Essaouira (175km)

CTM Bus Station

Rue Abou Bakr Seddiq

Rue el-Jahed

Rue Mohammed el-Hansali

Ave du Président Kennedy

Rue Moulay el-Hassan

HIVERNAGE

Ave Echouhada

Ave el-Yarmouk

Rue Haroun Errachid

9

CyberPark

Rue Abbes Sebti

Rue de Paris

Blvd Mohammed VI

Ave el-Qadissa

Hôtel es Saadi

Rue Ibrahim el Mazini

Rue el-Jedid

La Mamounia Gardens

Bab el-Jedid

6

Ave Bab Jedid

Blvd Mohammed VI

10

Menara Gardens (300m)

Menara (3km)

34

Founded in the 14th century under the Merenids, but fully kitted-out with its exuberantly ornate decoration in 1565 in the Saadian era, this Quranic learning centre was once the largest in North Africa, and remains among the most splendid.

The *medersa* (theological college) is affiliated with nearby **Ali ben Youssef Mosque** (Map p56; ☉closed to non-Muslims), and once 900 students in the 132 dorms arranged around the courtyard studied religious and legal texts here. Despite upgrades with its

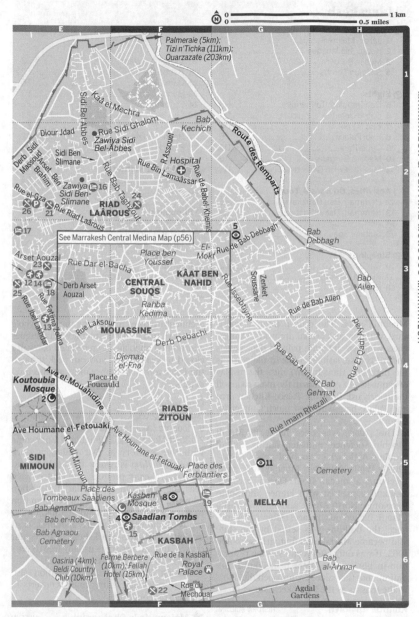

Palmeraie (5km);
Tizi n'Tichka (111km);
Ouarzazate (203km)

See Marrakesh Central Medina Map (p56)

19th-century renovation, the Ali ben Youssef Medersa gradually lost students to its collegiate rival, the Medersa Bou Inania in Fez, but even today – long after the students finally left – this old seminary still exudes magnificent, studious calm.

★ **Musée de Marrakech**   MUSEUM
(Map p56; ☑ 0524 44 18 93; www.museedemar rakech.ma; Pl ben Youssef; adult/child Dh50/free; ☺ 9am-7pm, to 6pm Oct-Mar) The Musée de Marrakech exhibits a collection of Moroccan art forms within the decadent salons of the

Marrakesh

Mnebhi Palace. The central internal courtyard, with its riot of cedar archways, stained-glass windows, intricate painted door panels and, of course, lashings of *zellij* tile work, is the highlight, though don't miss the display of exquisite Fez ceramics in the main room off the courtyard. Both the Palace Kitchen area and Palace hammam host much simpler interiors.

The palace was once home to Mehdi Mnebhi, defence minister during Sultan Moulay Abdelaziz's troubled reign (1894–1908). While Minister Mnebhi was away receiving a medal from Queen Victoria, England conspired with France and Spain to colonise North Africa, and autocrat Pasha Glaoui filched his palace. After independence, the building was seized by the state and became Marrakesh's first girls' school in 1965. It was only after a painstaking restoration in 1997, by the Omar Benjelloun Foundation, that the palace swung open the doors to the masses as the Marrakech Museum.

Koubba Ba'adiyn   HISTORIC BUILDING
(Map p56; Pl ben Youssef) The Almohads destroyed almost everything their Almoravid predecessors built in Marrakesh, but overlooked this small, graceful 12th-century *koubba* (shrine) – probably used for ablutions – across from Ali ben Youssef Mosque (p52). This relic reveals what Hispano-Morish architecture owes to the Almoravids: keyhole arches, ribbed vaulting, interlaced arabesques and domed cupolas on crenellated bases. It's closed to visitors, but you can peek through the fence to get a glimpse of its architectural details.

Dar Bellarj   GALLERY
(Map p56; ☑0524 44 45 55; www.darbellarj.org; 9-7 Toualate Zaouiate Lahdar; ⊙9.30am-12.30pm & 2-5.30pm Mon-Sat) **FREE** Flights of fancy come with the territory at Dar Bellarj, a stork hospital (*bellarj* is Arabic for stork) turned into Marrakesh's premier arts centre. Each year the nonprofit Dar Bellarj Foundation adopts a program theme, ranging from film to women's textiles and storytelling. Calligraphy demonstrations, art openings, craft exhibits and arts workshops are regular draws, and admission is usually free (there's a charge for some events).

During Ramadan, the foundation also hosts a series of evening music concerts in the central courtyard.

★ **Maison de la Photographie**   MUSEUM
(Map p56; ☑0524385721; www.maisondelaphotographie.ma; 46 Souq el-Fassi; adult/child Dh40/free; ⊙9.30am-7pm) When Parisian Patrick Menac'h and Marrakshi Hamid Mergani realised they were both collecting vintage Moroccan photography, they decided to open a photography museum to show their collections

in context. Together they 'repatriated' 4500 photos, 2000 glass negatives and 80 documents dating from 1870 to 1950; select works on view here fill three floors, organised by region and theme, and include a rare, full-colour 1957 documentary shot in Morocco. Most works are editioned prints from original negatives, and are for sale.

Afterwards, head up to the rooftop terrace for a coffee or pot of tea. If you're heading to Ourika Valley, be sure to check out their second venture, the Ecomusée Berbere (p98).

Bab Debbagh Tanneries   AREA
(Map p53; Rue de Bab Debbagh; ⊘ Sat-Thu) The acrid smell assaulting your nose announces your arrival in Marrakesh's tannery area. You'll find tanneries scattered on either side of Rue de Bab Debbagh – generally with touts stationed at the gates, offering tours for a tip. The best time to come is in the morning when you'll usually be able to see tanners at work, transforming leather hides into a rainbow of hues. It's hard, dirty work and dangerous too, now that natural dyes have been eschewed for chemical colours.

In exchange for a tip, you'll usually also be offered to see a view of the tanneries from above, from one of the houses near the Bab Debbagh gate. The views are definitely worth it, but be aware that many of the 'houses' are actually leatherware shops and touts can be pushy. Don't feel pressured into having to buy something if you don't want to.

Zawiya Sidi Bel-Abbes   SHRINE
(Map p53; Rue Sidi Ghalom; ⊘ closed to non-Muslims) This *zawiya* – shrine to a *marabout* (saint) is Marrakesh's most important and has been finely restored. The current building dates from the Saadian era and honours the renowned holy man Sidi Bel-Abbes – who died and was buried here in 1205. Non-Muslims can't enter the hallowed confines, but can walk through the arched arcade (note the intricate stucco-work on both gates) and into the courtyard to view its minaret, fountain and the elaborately decorated entrance way of the shrine itself.

★ **Dar Si Said**   MUSEUM
(Map p56; ☑ 0524 38 95 64; Derb Si Said; adult/child Dh10/3; ⊘ 9am-4.45pm Wed-Mon) A monument to Moroccan *mâalems* (master artisans), the residence of Bou Ahmed's brother Si Said is home to the **Museum of Moroccan Arts**. On display is a collection of granary doors, Tuareg leather bags, ceramics, embroidery, carpets, weaponry, and Berber jewellery within its salons. The highlight of a visit here is the spectacular painted and domed wedding-reception chamber flanked by flower-painted musicians' balconies; it's credited to artisans from Fez.

LOCAL KNOWLEDGE

CARAVANSERAI HERITAGE

From loaded-down camel caravans coming in from the desert to the carpet shops and souvenir stalls of today, Marrakesh is first and foremost a magnificent caravanserai city. Since medieval times, *fondouqs* (rooming houses) provided ground-floor stables and workshops downstairs, and rented rooms for desert traders and travelling merchants upstairs. As trading communities became more stable and affluent though, the need for *fondouqs* declined.

Today only 140 remain in the medina, many of them now converted into artisan complexes, and although you'll find them in various states of disrepair, many retain fragments of fine woodcarving and even stucco work. The best to poke your head into and admire their shop-worn glory are found on Rue Dar el-Bacha and Rue Mouassine. Our two favourites are:

Fondouq el-Amir (Rue Dar el-Bacha) This well-preserved *fondouq* would have once been the staging post for medieval merchants, here to do business in the city, but today the courtyard chambers are filled with small artisan shops. It's particularly noteworthy for the red-ochre geometric decoration of diamonds, hexagons and stars that border its internal stone arches.

Fondouq Kharbouch (Rue Dar el-Bacha) The inner courtyard of this *fondouq* may now be home to a ramshackle collection of workshops, with power lines strung precariously between windows, but the spacious grace and pleasing proportions of this old merchant inn haven't been lost. The upper balconies still cling to threads of wooden ceilings now supported by plain white plaster pillars.

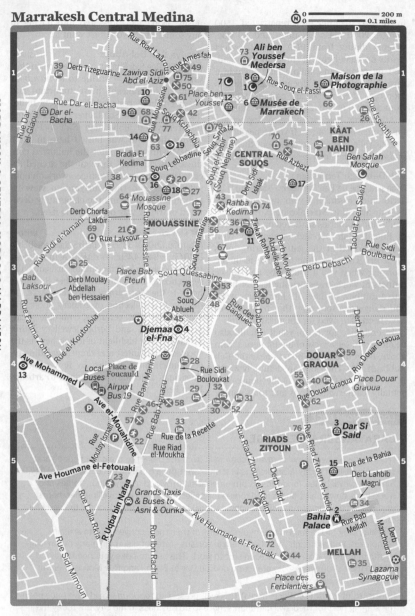

Maison Tiskiwin   MUSEUM
(Map p56; ☎ 0524 38 91 92; www.tiskiwin.com; 8
Rue de la Bahia; adult/child Dh20/10; ☉ 9.30am-
12.30pm & 2.30-6pm) Travel to Timbuktu and
back again via Dutch anthropologist Bert
Flint's art collection, displayed at Maison
Tiskiwin. Each room represents a caravan
stop along the Sahara-to-Marrakesh route,
presenting indigenous crafts from Tuareg
camel saddles to High Atlas carpets. The accompanying text is often more eccentric than
explanatory (eg 'By modifying his pristine
nakedness Man seeks to reveal his image of
himself'), but Tiskiwin's well-travelled arte-

Marrakesh Central Medina

facts offer tantalising glimpses of Marrakesh's trading-post past.

★ **Bahia Palace** PALACE
(Map p56; ☑ 0524 38 95 64; Rue Riad Zitoun el-Jedid; adult/child Dh10/3; ⊙9am-4.30pm) Imagine what you could build with Morocco's top artisans at your service for 14 years, and here you have it.

The salons of both the **petit riad** and **grand riad** host intricate marquetry and *zouak* (painted wood) ceilings while the vast **grand courtyard**, trimmed in jaunty blue and yellow, leads to the **Room of Honour**, with a spectacular cedar ceiling.

The **harem** offers up yet more dazzling interiors with original woven-silk panels, stained glass windows and rose-bouquet painted ceilings.

The floor-to-ceiling decoration here was begun by Grand Vizier Si Moussa in the 1860s and embellished from 1894 to 1900

Marrakesh Medina

A HALF-DAY TOUR OF THE MEDINA

To discover the medina's hidden treasures begin this leisurely stroll at **❶ Dar Si Said**, the home of tastemaker Si Said, a model of restrained 19th-century elegance. Then head north up Rue Riad Zitoun el-Jedid and emerge into the **❷ Djemaa el-Fna**, from where you can see the iconic **❸ Koutoubia minaret**. You'll need to dodge scooters and snake charmers as you cross the plaza to Pl Bab Fteuh in the northwest corner. On your right is the Bab Fteuh Funduq where jewellery and trays are hammered out in crammed studios.

Follow Rue el-Mouassine north past the Mouassine mosque and duck down a small *derb* (alley) beside the monumental **❹ Mouassine Fountain** to marvel at the 16th-century splendour of the **❺ Musée de Mouassine**, with its finely restored Saadian era douiria (guest apartment) and interesting cultural exhibits in the downstairs salons. Emerge dazzled into the sun and continue north.

At the next arched junction with Rue Dar el-Bacha you'll spot grand courtyard **❻ funduqs** (medieval merchant inns). Some date back to the 16th century and most are populated by artisan workshops. Lunch a few steps further north in the tranquil shaded courtyard of **❼ Le Jardin**.

Refuelled, turn right out of Le Jardin and right again after the small arch onto Rue Amesfah, which takes you past more *funduqs* and the Ben Youssef Mosque, before you see signs for the **❽ Ali ben Youssef Medersa**. Once the most splendid Quranic school in North Africa, it's decorated with Hispano-Moresque wonders wrought in high-lustre *zellij* (mosaic) and intricate stucco. Finish the tour amid vintage photographs of the medina and a spectacular sunset view from the rooftop of **❾ Maison de la Photographie**.

Funduqs
These medieval caravanserai once provided lodging and stabling for desert traders visiting the souqs. Of the 140 remaining in the medina, many have now been converted into artisan workshops.

Mouassine Fountain
Built in the mid-16th century by Abdallah el Ghalib, the Mouassine Fountain is one of 80 original medina fountains. Its installation was a pious act, providing water for people and animals.

LONELY PLANET/GETTY IMAGES ©

MAURIZIO DE MATTEI/SHUTTERSTOCK ©

Koutoubia Minaret
This 12th-century, 70m-high tower is the architectural prototype for Seville's La Giralda, and it's a monumental cheat sheet of Moorish ornamentation: scalloped keystone arches, jagged *merlons* and mathematically pleasing proportions.

e Jardin

his popular medina hang-out is a true urban
asis. The lush green colour scheme echoes the
oothing canopy of palms and banana trees that
hade the 17th-century riad courtyard, which
omes complete with trilling songbirds.

Maison de la Photographie

This riad gallery displays fascinating works from
1870 to 1960, including a 1907 Djemaa el-Fna
vista, a 1920 photo of Ali ben Youssef Medersa
with students, and a rare 1957 documentary
shot in Morocco.

SAIKO3P/SHUTTERSTOCK ©

Ali ben Youssef Medersa

In its heyday, 900
students lived in
the medersa's
132 dorms – and
shared one bath-
room. Upstairs,
a 3-sq-metre
room shows how
students lived,
with a sleeping
mat, writing
implements and
Quran bookstand.

BVVALET/SHUTTERSTOCK ©

Musée de Mouassine

The central room of the restored *douiria* (guest
apartment) here is covered with stucco in brightly
coloured *testir*, geometric tracery radiating from a
central star called 'the cobwebs of the Prophet'.

Djemaa el-Fna

PT Barnum was
bluffing when he
called his circus
'the greatest show
on earth'; that title
has belonged to
the Djemaa el-Fna
ever since this
plaza was used for
public executions
in about 1050.

Dar Si Said

Si Said's artisans outdid themselves in the
upstairs wedding chamber, covering the walls,
musicians' balconies and ceiling with a truly
joyous profusion of floral ornament.

by slave-turned-vizier Abu 'Bou' Ahmed. In 1908 the palace's beguiling charms attracted warlord Pasha Glaoui, who claimed it as a suitable venue to entertain French guests. They, in turn, were so impressed that they booted out their host in 1911, installing the protectorate's resident-general in his place.

Though today only a portion of the palace's eight hectares and 150 rooms is open to the public, there's still plenty of ornamental frippery on show. While admiring the tranquil grand courtyard with its floor laid in white Carrara marble, remember this is where people waited in the sun for hours to beg for Bou Ahmed's mercy. Bou Ahmed's four wives and 24 concubines all lived in the lavish interiors of the harem's small salons.

Badi Palace
HISTORIC SITE

(Map p53; Pl des Ferblantiers; adult/child Dh10/3, Koutoubia minbar extra Dh10; ⊙9am-5pm) As 16th-century sultan Ahmed al-Mansour was paving the Badi Palace with gold, turquoise and crystal, his court jester wisecracked, 'It'll make a beautiful ruin.' That jester was no fool: 75 years later the place was looted and today only remnants remain. El-Badi's vast courtyard, with its four sunken gardens and reflecting pools, give a hint of the palace's former majesty and the views from the pisé ramparts, where storks nest, are magnificent.

The building just west of the Khaysuran Pavilion holds the 12th-century Koutoubia minbar (prayer pulpit); a masterwork by Cordoban artisans.

The entire Badi Palace complex was closed to the public for a long-overdue and ambitious restoration project. Be aware that the complex, or parts of the complex, may not be fully open when you visit.

To reach the entrance, head through Pl des Ferblantiers and turn right along the ramparts.

Lazama Synagogue
SYNAGOGUE

(Map p56; Derb Manchoura; Dh10; ⊙9am-5pm Sun-Thu, 9am-1pm Fri, closed on Jewish holidays) In the *mellah* (Jewish quarter), the Lazama Synagogue is still used by Marrakesh's dwindling Jewish community. A nondescript door leads into a pretty blue-and-white courtyard with the synagogue on the right-hand side. Inside the austere worship area, note the *zellij* tilework's Star of David motif. The courtyard's surrounding ground-floor rooms have exhibits of Moroccan Jewish life.

Miaâra Jewish Cemetery
CEMETERY

(Map p53; Rue el-Miaâra; entry by donation Dh10; ⊙Sun-Thu 9am-5pm, Fri 8am-1pm, closed Jewish holidays) In this sprawling walled cemetery, the exceptionally helpful gatekeeper admits visitors who wish to pay their respects to whitewashed tombs topped with rocks for remembrance.

Your donation towards the cemetery's upkeep gets you a map of the *mellah*, so it's well worth visiting the Miaâra first before diving into the Jewish quarter's back streets.

★ Saadian Tombs
HISTORIC SITE

(Map p53; Rue de la Kasbah; adult/child Dh10/3; ⊙9am-4.45pm) Anyone who says you can't take it with you hasn't seen the Saadian Tombs, near the Kasbah Mosque. Saadian Sultan Ahmed al-Mansour ed-Dahbi spared no expense on his tomb, importing Italian Carrara marble and gilding honeycomb *muqarnas* (decorative plasterwork) with pure gold to make the **Chamber of the 12 Pillars** a suitably glorious mausoleum.

Al-Mansour played favourites even in death, keeping alpha-male princes handy in the **Chamber of the Three Niches**, and relegating to garden plots some 170 chancellors and wives – though some trusted Jewish advisors earned pride of place, literally closer to the king's heart than his wives or sons. All tombs are overshadowed by his mother's in the courtyard, carved with poetic, weathered blessings and vigilantly guarded by stray cats.

Al-Mansour died in splendour in 1603, but a few decades later Alawite Sultan Moulay Ismail walled up the Saadian Tombs to keep his predecessors out of sight and mind. Accessible only through a small passage in the Kasbah Mosque, the tombs were neglected by all except the storks, until aerial photography exposed them in 1917.

⊙ Ville Nouvelle

★ Jardin Majorelle
GARDENS

(Map p52; ☑0524 31 30 47; www.jardinmajorelle. com; cnr Aves Yacoub el-Mansour & Moulay Abdullah; adult/child Dh70/free; ⊙8am-6pm, to 5.30pm Oct-Apr) Other guests bring flowers, but Yves Saint Laurent gifted the Jardin Majorelle to Marrakesh, the city that adopted him in 1964. Saint Laurent and his partner Pierre Bergé bought the electric-blue villa and its garden to preserve the vision of its original owner, landscape painter Jacques Majorelle, and keep it open to the public. The garden began cultivating in 1924 and thanks to Marrakshi

Marrakesh Ville Nouvelle

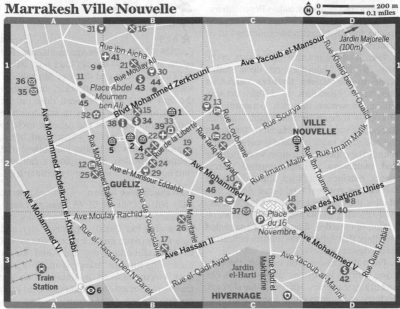

Marrakesh Ville Nouvelle

ethnobotanist Abderrazak Benchaâbane, the psychedelic desert mirage of 300 plant species from five continents continues to be preserved.

Even if you're not that into plants, come here to visit Majorelle's art deco studio, home to the **Musée Berbère** (adult/child Dh30/free; ◷8am-6pm, to 5.30pm Oct-Apr), which showcases the rich panorama of Morocco's indigenous inhabitants through displays of some 600 artefacts. By far one of the country's most beautifully curated museums, the collection includes wood, leather and metalwork, textiles, musical instruments, religious trappings, and a display of the various regional traditional dress. Best of all is the mirrored, midnight-black octagonal chamber displaying a sumptuous collection of chiselled, filigreed and enamelled jewellery that reflect into infinity beneath a starry desert sky.

From the museum you exit into the boutique with its handsome coffee-table books and pricey souvenirs: Majorelle blue slippers, perfume and pillows embroidered with YSL.

Another museum, dedicated to Yves Saint Laurent, is due to open within the gardens in late 2017.

MACMA
GALLERY
(Map p61; Musee d'Art et de Culture de Marrakech; ☎0524 44 83 26; 61 Passage Ghandouri, Rue de Yougoslavie; adult/student Dh40/20; ◷10am-7pm Mon-Sat) It may be small but the big guns of Orientalist painting are all on display at this suave gallery, opened in early 2016. The impressive collection of 19th- and 20th-century European artists who fell for Morocco's landscapes and peoples include Henri Le Riche, Edy Legrand, Roger Marcel Limouse and, of course, Jacques Majorelle – he of garden fame (p60).

Menara Gardens
GARDENS
(Map p52; Ave de la Menara, Hivernage; garden free, picnic pavilion Dh20; ◷9am-5pm) Local lore tells of a sultan who seduced guests over dinner, then lovingly chucked them in the Menara's reflecting pools to drown. Nowadays dunking seems the furthest thing from the minds of couples canoodling amid these royal olive groves, or families picnicking in the stately 19th-century pavilion. The vast olive groves themselves hold little interest, but on clear days come for dromedary rides and photo ops of the pavilion and reflecting pool against the Atlas Mountain backdrop.

🏃 Activities

Cycling

★AXS
CYCLING
(☎0524 40 02 07; www.argansports.com; Rue Fatima al Fihria; half-day city tours from Dh350; ♿) Get on a bike and discover Marrakesh's sights on a classic city ride, or munch through street stalls between rides on the tasting tour. Those up for more adventure can mountain bike in the Atlas or cycle to Essaouira. High-quality Giant road bikes, mountain bikes (including kid's bikes) and helmets provided. Solo explorers can also rent bikes here for single and multiday trips.

Marrakech Bike Action
CYCLING
(Map p61; ☎0661 24 01 45; www.marrakechbikeaction.com; 1st fl, 212 Ave Mohammed V; city or palmeraie tour Dh250) Organises city and *palmeraie* (palm grove) tour circuits as well as mountain-biking day trips and longer excursions into the Atlas region. They also have electric-assisted mountain bikes for travellers worried about their ability to keep up with the rest of the group.

Horse Riding

Les Cavaliers de L'Atlas
HORSE RIDING
(☎0611 81 68 06; www.lescavaliersdelatlas.com; Rte de Casablanca; half/full day €50/90) Run by passionate horsewoman Sophie Chauvat, this is a professional stable with a mix of Arab, Anglo-Arab and Berber horses and Welsh and Shetland ponies. Options range from half-day rides through the *palmeraie* to multiday horse treks in the Atlas.

All equipment is provided, including riding caps, half-chaps and body protectors for children.

The centre is located five-minutes north of Marrakesh, just off the Rte de Casablanca (N9) and is clearly signposted on the road. For those that want to make their holiday all about riding, their guesthouse **Dar Guerris** (double/suites including breakfast €90/150) is onsite.

Public Hammams

For an authentic Moroccan spa experience, head to your local neighbourhood hammam. Entry costs about Dh10 with optional massage Dh50 to Dh100. All public hammams are single sex (or have separate hours for women and men). It's best to ask for public hammam recommendations from locals as a few don't accept non-Muslims.

BYO hammam kit: towel, flip-flops, plastic mat and a change of underwear (you'll be ex-

MARRAKESH FOR CHILDREN

The mutual admiration between kids and Marrakesh is obvious. Kids will gaze in wonderment at fairytale souq scenes, herbalists trading concoctions straight out of *Harry Potter*, cupboard-sized shops chock-a-block with spangled Cinderella-style slippers, and the chaotic, thrumming spectacle of Djemaa el-Fna lit up at night.

The key to a successful trip is child-friendly accommodation. Fair warning: riad plunge pools and steep stairs aren't exactly childproof, and sound reverberates through riad courtyards. Most riad owners and staff, however, dote on babies and will provide cots and high chairs, and prepare special meals on request.

Entertainment That Costs Nothing

Marrakesh museums are a poor substitute for the live theatre of the souqs and the Djemaa el-Fna (p50).

➡ Early mornings are quieter in the souqs, meaning less hassle and a better view of craftspeople at work.

➡ Early evenings (6pm to 8pm) are best for Djemaa dance troupes and musicians, and offer chance encounters with Moroccan families also doing the rounds.

Discover Marrakshi Culture

Let the kids dig a bit deeper into Marrakshi culture.

➡ They'll be souq-ready with Cafe Clock's (p72) 'Kech Download, a 90-minute crash course in Moroccan culture and common phrases.

➡ For family-friendly activities such as a task-filled medina hunt and henna-art workshops, try Creative Interactions (p66).

Alternative Sightseeing

Calèche rides When kids' legs and parents' backs start to give out, do what Moroccan parents do: hire a horse carriage in the Djemaa el-Fna and take a grand tour.

Dromedary rides Head out to the *palmeraie* (palm grove) where dromedaries await in the parking lot of the Café le Palmier d'Or. About Dh50 to Dh70 should cover a 15- to 30-minute guided ride (bargaining required).

Horse riding For professional lessons and horse treks in the *palmeraie* and Atlas Mountains, try the stables at Les Cavaliers de L'Atlas (p62).

Biking Explore Marrakesh or the Atlas Mountains beyond, on a family-friendly bike tour with AXS (p62).

When The City Gets Too Much...

Beldi Country Club (p65) A 15-hectare country retreat designed with families in mind; includes a kid's pool and child-focused activities ranging from bread baking to horse riding.

Terres d'Amanar (☑ 0524 43 81 03; www.terresdamanar.com; Douar Akli, Tahanaoute; activities from Dh100; ⊕) Adrenaline-packed activities to balance out all that souq strolling. This outdoor centre, 36km south of Marrakesh, offers zip lines, a forest adventure course, mountain biking and horse riding.

Oasiria (☑ 0524 38 04 38; www.oasiria.com; Rte d'Amizmiz, Km4; adult/child Dh210/130; ⊙10am-6pm; ⊕) Beat the heat with nine pools, a kamikaze slide and a pirate lagoon.

Need To Know

Admission The majority of museums have reduced rates for under-12s.

Challenges Strollers are impractical in the medina, baby-changing facilities are scarce – and restaurants make few dietary concessions.

Practical shopping Nappies, infant formula and other necessities can be found at Carrefour (p78) in Guéliz.

MARRAKESH MODERN ART SCENE

While the tourist market still trades in harem girls, men with muskets and other Orientalist clichés, these galleries offer original talent.

Musée Farid Belkahia (☎0524 32 89 59; off Rte de Fez; adult/child Dh50/30; ⊙10am-7pm) Farid Belkahia (1934–2014) was one of the most well-known figures in 20th-century Moroccan art. This museum, housed in the artist's old villa, exhibits a selection of his work, including some of the multimedia pieces that he was known for.

To get here, follow the signs from Musée de la Palmeraie.

Galerie Rê (☎0524 43 22 58; www.galeriere.com; Résidence Al Andalous III, cnr Rues de la Mosquée & Ibn Toumert; ⊙10am-1pm & 3-8pm Mon-Sat) Head across Ave Mohammed V and down Rue ibn Toumert to check out next-generation art stars at Galerie Ré. Keep an eye out for Amina Benbouchta's hieroglyphically minimalist paintings, Mauoal Bouchaïb's petroglyph-inspired etchings, editions of poetry illustrated by gallery artists, and gallery opening soirees (always packed, always fabulous).

David Bloch Gallery (☎0524 45 75 95; www.davidblochgallery.com; 8 bis Rue des Vieux Marrakchis; ⊙10.30am-1.30pm & 3.30-7.30pm Tue-Sat, 3.30-7.30pm Mon) Artists from both sides of the Mediterranean strike fine lines between traditional calligraphy and urban graffiti in a series of temporary exhibitions. Catch the work of up-and-coming abstract artists.

Galerie Noir sur Blanc (☎0524 42 24 16; www.galerienoirsurblanc.com; 1st fl, 48 Rue de Yougoslavie; ⊙3-7pm Mon, 10am-1pm & 3-7pm Tue-Sat) The Galerie Noir sur Blanc showcases major Moroccan talent complemented by temporary exhibits focused on local artists.

Gallery 127 (☎0524 43 26 67; www.galerienathalielocatelli.com; 2nd fl, 127 Ave Mohammed V; ⊙2-7pm Tue-Sat) Like any worthwhile Chelsea gallery, this one is up a dim, once-grand staircase, in an industrial-chic chamber with the obligatory exposed brick-and-concrete wall. It exhibits a range of new and vintage works by international photographers (mostly Mediterranean) with shows varying from straightforward travel photography to more interpretive works.

Musée de la Palmeraie (☎0661 09 53 52; off Rte de Fez; adult/child Dh40/free; ⊙9am-6pm) Set in a collection of adobe houses, the Musée de la Palmeraie displays a collection of Moroccan modern art that includes calligraphy, photography, painting and sculpture. Some of the art is so-so, but outside, the museum's immaculate Andalusian and cacti gardens are a tranquil escape from the city.

pected to wear yours). You can also bring your own black soap and hammam mitt (buy them from the many stalls around town).

Hammam Mouassine HAMMAM
(Map p56; Derb el-Hammam; hammam & gommage Dh100; ⊙5am-midnight) A proper public hammam that also caters for travellers looking for an authentic experi ence. In business since 1562, Hammam Mouassine has charming and professional staff who will wash and then scrub you down *(gommage)* with Morocco's famed rhassoul clay until you're squeaky clean. As with other public hammams, you could also DIY it here and pay just the entrance fee Dh10.

Men enter the hammam the marked archway on the east side of the Mouassine fountain. The women's entrance is through the signposted alleyway on the west side.

Hammam Dar el-Bacha HAMMAM
(Map p53; 20 Rue Fatima Zohra; Dh10; ⊙men 7am-1pm, women 1-9pm) The city's largest traditional hammam, with star-shaped vents in the vast domed ceiling. It's the public hammam of choice for women, who get prime afternoon and evening hours here.

Hammam Bab Doukkala HAMMAM
(Map p53; Rue Bab Doukkala; Dh10; ⊙women noon-7pm, men from 8pm) A historic hammam in the southeast corner of Bab Doukkala Mosque, dating from the 17th century. It has heated *tadelakt* (polished plaster) floors in good repair and a mellow atmosphere during men's hours.

Private Hammams
Heritage Spa HAMMAM
(Map p53; ☎0524 38 43 33; www.heritagespamarrakech.com; 40 Derb Arset Aouzal; hammam &

gommage from Dh290; ⊘10am-8pm) Forget any illusions of authentically local hammams and bliss out in this private spa-hammam with a deep-cleansing sea-salt exfoliation (Dh300) or a detoxing black-soap and bitter-orange scrub (Dh290). Afterwards, stressed travellers can soothe jet-lagged skin with a pampering massage using essential oils (from Dh450).

Le Bain Bleu   HAMMAM
(Map p56; ☑0524 38 38 04; www.lebainbleu. com; 32 Derb Chorfa Lakbir; hammam & gommage Dh200, with massage from Dh600; ⊘10am-11pm) Top-notch pampering awaits. Follow signs for Dar Cherifa off Rue el-Mouassine onto Derb Chorfa Lakbir, where this riad spa-hammam features secluded patios, sleek subterranean steam rooms and professional treatments to soothe the souq-weary. Couples hammam packages, plus facials, manicures and pedicures available.

Sultana Spa   HAMMAM
(Map p56; ☑0524 38 80 08; www.lasultanamarrakech.com; Rue de la Kasbah; hammam & gommage Dh400) An opulent, all-marble spa near the Saadian Tombs offering services from a basic hammam experience to pampering massages (Dh600 to Dh1400), signature cinnamon body scrubs and facial treatments using argan and prickly-pear oils.

Swimming
★Beldi Country Club   SWIMMING
(Map p53; ☑0524 38 39 50; www.beldicountryclub. com; Rte de Barrage 'Cherifa', Km6; adult/child pool day-pass Dh200/100, incl lunch Dh370/250; ☑) Located just 6km south of the city centre, the Beldi feels a million miles away from the dust and chaos of the medina. Lie back and smell the 15,000 roses at Dominique Leymarie's eco-chic paradise with its pools, spa, hammam, tennis courts and plenty of family-friendly activities on offer.

Riad Bledna   SWIMMING
(☑0661 18 20 90; www.riadbledna.com; off Rte de Ouarzazate, Km19, 31°35'46.8"N 7°52'28.5"W; per person, incl lunch & transfer €25) This 1.5-hectare organic garden retreat is in a quiet Marrakesh suburb east of the city centre. Day rates offer superb value, covering use of the oxygen-filtered pool, tasty homemade lunches and transfers to and from Djemaa el-Fna.

Ferme Berbère   SWIMMING
(Map p53; ☑0661 92 09 41; www.fermeberbere.com; Rte d'Ourika, Km9; lunch with pool access Dh165,

lunch, pool & hammam package Dh450; ☑) We can think of a better way to spend a lazy afternoon than lolling on a sun-lounger at this rustic adobe-walled retreat. A great escape from the medina hustle, with good getaway deals for families: lunch for two adults and two children, pool access, family hammam, and donkey rides for the kids cost Dh750. You'll find it 9km south on Rte d'Ourika.

🎓 Courses
Cafe Clock (p72) is a one-stop shop for a fascinating range of courses from oud lessons to calligraphy to language classes.

Many riads in the medina organise cooking sessions with their chef. The Amal Center (p74) also offers highly recommended cooking courses.

★Ateliers d'Ailleurs   ART
(☑0672 81 20 46; www.ateliersdailleurs.com; workshops €35-69) Engaging a select network of professional craftsmen with robust businesses in pottery, tadelakt, woodwork, zellij tiling, embroidery and much more, these ateliers (studios) offer a unique insight into traditional-craft techniques. During the two-to five-hour workshops, you work alongside craftsmen utilising traditional materials, with enough time to practice several techniques and to realise your own objects.

Souk Cuisine   COOKING
(Map p56; ☑0673 80 49 55; www.soukcuisine.com; Zniquat Rahba, 5 Derb Tahtah; class incl meal & wine €50) Learn to cook as the dadas (chefs) do: shop in the souq for ingredients with English-speaking Dutch hostess Gemma van de Burgt, work alongside two Moroccan dadas, then enjoy the four-course lunch you helped cook. Courses run for two to 12 participants; vegetarian courses possible.

Bled Al Fassia   COOKING
(☑0661 43 34 26; www.bledalfassia.com; Rte de Ouarzazate, Km9; per person Dh600) Learn the secrets of the chefs behind Al Fassia restaurant (p75) in this spotless luxury villa kitchen on the outskirts of Marrakesh. Rates include transfers from central Marrakesh. Minimum of two participants.

Study Arabic in Marrakech   LANGUAGE
(☑0672 86 90 36; www.studyarabicmarrakech.com; off Rte de Casablanca; private/group lessons per hr Dh100/70; ⊘9am-1pm & 3-7pm Mon-Fri) Has both short-term programs for travellers wanting to pick up some Darija (Moroccan Arabic) and

long-term courses in both Darija and modern standard Arabic. Private classes available.

Creative Interactions LANGUAGE

(Map p61; ☑0524 42 16 87; www.creative-interactions.com; Apt 47, Immeuble El Khalil Bldg, Ave des Nations Unies; 1½hr private/group €40/35, 3hr €65/60) Moroccan Arabic classes designed for short-term travellers. These fun and friendly workshops allow even travellers on a very short stay a chance to learn the basics they'll most need on their visit. A fantastic idea for those who want to dive a little further into Marrakesh culture. Three-hour sessions include a cooking demonstration and lunch.

Also runs four-week intensive Arabic courses.

Centre for Language and Culture LANGUAGE

(Map p61; ☑0524 44 76 91; www.clcmorocco.org; off Rue Sourya, Guéliz) American and Moroccan teachers with years of experience offer summer language courses with homestay hookups. Lessons are immersive and the school applies the Communicative Language Learning (CLL) technique in its Arabic language classes, the only school in Morocco to do so.

☞ Tours

Guided tours of the medina will help you cover specific landmarks in an hour or two. Just don't expect sweet souq deals: guides get commissions on whatever you buy. Hotels, riads and travel agencies can arrange guides, or you can book official guides directly via the tourist office for Dh250/400 for a half/full day.

★ Tawada Trekking TREKKING

(☑0618 24 44 31; www.tawadatrekking.com; Hay Ezzaitoun) Trekking tours into the Atlas Mountains, rafting trips and cultural immersion experiences are the speciality of this small, professional company run by Hafida H'doubane, one of the first Moroccan women to be licensed as a mountain guide. They can also organise 4WD trips into the Atlas region and desert beyond.

Morocco Adventure & Rafting RAFTING

(Map p65; ☑0661 77 52 51; www.rafting.ma; Rue Beni Marine; half-day rafting trip €95) This local company has been leading rafting expeditions (February to May) in the Atlas for over 12 years, with a team of local and international guides all with a minimum of five years' guiding experience. Excursions range from a half-day whitewater rafting trip to Ourika to a three-day or week-long rafting excursion in the Ahansel Valley.

In addition, it organises city tours of Marrakesh as well as desert trips and excursions into the Atlas. Every April it runs a seasonal kayak school for beginners at Bin el-Ouidane, and kayak clinics for the more experienced. Groups are limited to 12 to 16 people.

Inside Morocco Travel TOURS

(Map p61; ☑0524 43 00 20; www.insidemoroccotravel.com; 4th fl, 29 Rue de Yougoslavie; ☺8.30am-4.30pm) Get to know Morocco on bespoke adventures designed by multilingual Mohamed Nour and his team. Specialises in trekking trips into the High Atlas and combined 4WD excursions exploring the desert and mountains. Their day trip visiting the Agafay Desert, Lalla Takerkoust and hiking around Imlil (from €60 per person) is worthwhile if you're short of time.

Mountain Voyage TOURS

(Map p61; ☑0524 42 19 96; www.mountain-voyage.com; 2nd fl, Immeuble El Batoul, 5 Ave Mohammed V; ☺9am-12.30pm & 3.30-7pm Mon-Sat) This British-owned, Marrakesh-based company provides licensed, English-speaking guides for tailor-made Marrakesh tours, sustainable tourism excursions in the Middle Atlas, and High Atlas excursions with stays at its own property, the Kasbah du Toubkal.

Marrakech Food Tours FOOD, DRINK

(www.marrakechfoodtours.com; US$65; ☺1pm & 6pm Sat-Thu) Munch your way through the medina: weave through the souqs tucking into *tanjia* (slow-cooked stew), sampling Marrakshi street food and slurping down avocado milkshakes. Hosts Youssef and Amanda take groups (up to six participants) on a whirlwind tour of Marrakshi flavours. Bring your appetite.

Desir du Maroc TOURS

(☑0661 16 35 85; www.desirdumaroc.com) Marrakshi Abdelhay Sadouk has 30 years' experience introducing visitors to Moroccan culture, leading history and culture tours around Marrakesh's lesser-known sites and further afield to the coast, desert and mountains.

⁕ Festivals & Events

Marrakesh Marathon SPORTS

(www.marathon-marrakech.com; half-/full-marathon fee €50/70; ☺Jan) Run like there's a carpet salesman after you from the Djemaa to the *palmeraie* and back for this yearly marathon.

Marrakech Biennale

ART

(www.marrakechbiennale.org; ☉ Feb-May) Promoting debate and dialogue through artistic exchange, this major trilingual (Arabic, French and English) festival invites local and international artists to create literary, artistic, architectural and digital works throughout the city. Held every other year (even years).

Marrakech Festival
of Popular Arts
PERFORMING ARTS

(☉ Jul) The only thing hotter than Marrakesh in July is this free-form folk fest. Berber musicians, dancers and street performers from around the country pour into Marrakesh to thrill the masses.

Oasis Festival
MUSIC

(www.oasisfest.com; ☉ Sep) Oasis brings together Morocco's best electronica talent with DJs from Europe for a music festival with a distinctly Moroccan twist. In the afternoon there's swimming, a souq, yoga and henna art; once dusk sets in the DJs hit the decks. In 2016 the festival was held at the Source hotel, 10km from the city, with shuttle transport available from the centre.

Advance booking essential. Tickets available on the website.

MadJazz
MUSIC

(www.madjazz-festival.com; ☉ May) Marrakech invents new sounds nightly with Gnaoua castanets, jazz riffs and Jimi Hendrix guitar licks.

Marrakech International
Film Festival
FILM

(www.festivalmarrakech.info/en; ☉ Dec) Stars from Hollywood to Bollywood strut the Berber red carpet at this week-long festival, culminating in wildly unpredictable awards shows. There are also movie screenings at Djemaa el-Fna.

🛏 Sleeping

Marrakesh has it all: you can sleep anywhere from the funkiest fleapit to palaces straight out of some Orientalist Hollywood fantasy. Take your pick: authentic riads hidden in the heart of the medina; budget-friendly inns right off the Djemaa; ville nouvelle hotels, ranging from budget to business class; or *palmeraie* villas, with pools amid swaying palms.

Booking ahead is crucial for medina riads due to limited rooms.

Room rates in Marrakesh are the highest in Morocco. Many budget hotels keep the same rates all year round but with negotia-

THE UBIQUITOUS OURIKA VALLEY DAY TRIP

Every travel agency in town touts day trips to the Ourika Valley. Be aware that although the trip does offer a quick taste of the Moroccan countryside, it isn't for everyone. Expect a long drive, few actual stops and crowds at Setti Fatma. The typical trip stops first at a lookout (with an optional, very quick camel ride), a shopping stop at an argan oil workshop, and then onwards to Setti Fatma for what is usually a very crowded hike up to the cascades (with local guides pulling less-able hikers up the rocks), and then lunch.

ble prices for longer stays or quiet periods. Some riads only raise their prices over the winter and Easter holiday period while others have various different pricing scales for low and high seasons.

🛏 Medina

★ Le Gallia
HOTEL €

(Map p56; ☎ 0524 44 59 13; www.hotellegallia.com; 30 Rue de la Recette; s/d/tr incl breakfast Dh350/550/850; ❄ ☎) Madcap Djemaa el-Fna is around the corner, but Le Gallia maintains the calm and grace of another era with comfortable, neat-as-a-pin rooms, all with aircon, heating and reliable hot water, arranged around a courtyard trimmed with colourful *beldi* tiles and shaded by orange trees. Run by the French Galland family since 1929, it's often packed with repeat visitors.

Note that prices are often cheaper than their official room rates.

★ Equity Point Hostel
HOSTEL €

(Map p56; Riad Amazigh; ☎ 0524 44 07 93; www.equity-point.com; 80 Derb el-Hammam, Mouassine; 8-/6-/4-bed dm incl breakfast €13/16/20; ❄ ☎❄) Courtyard pool – yep. *Zellij*-tastic *bhous* (nooks), brass lanterns and carved cedar door trimmings – yep. Usual riad price-tag – nope. Equity Point converted this labyrinthine old mansion into a wallet-friendly backpacker's boutique with a bar, a restaurant, oodles of cushioned lounging areas, and on-point dorms (both mixed and female-only), which come with lockers, air-con and en suite.

Hotel du Trésor
RIAD €

(☎ 0524 37 51 13; www.hotel-du-tresor.com; 77 Derb Sidi Bouloukat; incl breakfast s €37-42, d €50-90;

✻ 🛈 ⊠) This exceedingly good-value riad brims with whimsy and rock-and-roll style from the mod Panton chairs beside the plunge pool to the snug rooms chock-a-block with eclectic razzle dazzle. Behind painted doors are walls of vintage mirrors reclaimed from the Mamounia, crystal chandeliers over a red-velvet-padded bed, and in the terrace Blue Suite, a soaking tub and gold-mosaic fireplace.

Jnane Mogador   RIAD €

(Map p56; 🖉 0524 42 63 24; www.jnanemogador.com; 116 Derb Sidi Bouloukat; s/d/tr Dh360/480/580; ✻ @ 🛈) A 19th-century riad with small rooms cheerfully decorated with plenty of traditional flourishes and a prime location just off Rue Riad Zitoun el-Kedim. There's an in-house hammam, tea salon, double-decker roof terraces and laid-back hospitality from owner Mohammed. Quiet, airy upper-floor rooms are the pick of the bunch. Breakfast is an extra Dh40.

Riad Elkarti   RIAD €

(Map p56; 🖉 0610 31 32 18; www.facebook.com/riadelkarti/; 8 Derb Tahta; d €25-35; ✻ 🛈) Marrakech riad-chic without the price-tag? Step up Riad Elkarti. Owned by young Marrakshi designer Ahmed Abidine, it features five bijou rooms in warm-toned *tadelakt,* set around a white courtyard trimmed in Majorelle blue. This is a friendly, laid-back place to stay with an arty slant and a lot more style than you'd expect for the room rates.

Young & Happy Hostel   HOSTEL €

(Map p53; 🖉 0524 38 33 88; www.youngandhappymarrakech.com; 113 Rue de Berrima; 2-6-8-bed dm incl breakfast Dh105/95/85; ⊜ ✻ 🛈) If you can get past the cringe-worthy name, this cosy hostel is a brilliant deal. Neat and tidy dorms come with cheerfully painted bunks and lockers, shared bathrooms are modern and clean, and staff go out of their way to help.

Hôtel Sherazade   INN €

(Map p56; 🖉 0524 42 93 05; www.hotelsherazade.com; 3 Derb Djemaa; s Dh220-550, d Dh270-550, ste Dh690, without bathroom s/d Dh180/230; ✻ 🛈) Conversation comes easily at this inn run by a Moroccan-German family, with 23 rooms (18 with air-con), sunny terraces and a mellow-yellow courtyard with a trickling fountain. Terrace rooms are bargains, but you'll want earplugs to sleep through the muezzin's call and the breakfast rush (Dh50 extra). Light sleepers should ask for rooms in the ivy-covered rear courtyard.

Hôtel Cecil   HOTEL €

(Map p56; 🖉 0524 44 22 03; www.djemaaelfnahotelcecil.org; Rue Sidi Bouloukat; s/d/tr incl breakfast Dh286/340/440, d/tr without bathroom Dh240/340; ✻ 🛈) Cecil's twin courtyards framed by fat pink pillars and comfy sofas offer digs minutes from Djemaa el-Fna. Rooms with bathroom have more pizazz, thanks to brightly painted furniture and the addition of air-con. For those sharing bathrooms there are toilets and showers on each floor while breakfast is on the roof terrace beneath a Berber tent.

Hotel Essaouira   HOTEL €

(Map p56; 🖉 0524 44 38 05; 3 Derb Sidi Bouloukat; s/d without bathroom Dh70/100, r with bathroom Dh380-480) No frills, just the cheapest hotel in the medina with 28 rooms still holding on to scraps of lovely tile detail, decently clean

---

THE RIAD EXPERIENCE

Paris has its cathedrals, New York its skyscrapers, but riads are what set Marrakesh apart. These spectacular mudbrick courtyard mansions are oases of calm in the bustling medina: push through the brass-studded ancient door and you'll find yourself listening to songbirds, ice clinking in drinks and your own thoughts – suddenly, Marrakesh's balance of extremes makes perfect sense.

Over the past decade, hundreds of these historic family homes have been sold and reinvented as guesthouses, mainly by Europeans. The best are not just marvels of the Marrakshi tradition of craftsmanship – which guesthouses helped revive – but unforgettable experiences of Marrakshi hospitality, complete with insights into the local culture and shifting social mores, home-cooked meals and prime opportunities for relaxation and cultural immersion. Staying in a riad isn't just about sleeping in posh digs; it's about gaining an understanding of Marrakesh behind those studded doors.

Hip Marrakech (www.hipmarrakech.com) Riad accommodation specialist with a good range of options.

Marrakech Riads (www.marrakech-riads.com) A selection of nine medina riads.

Marrakech Medina (www.marrakech-medina.com) Local riad booking agency.

shared bathrooms and a roof terrace with breakfast (Dh20) views of the Koutoubia.

★ **Riad Le J** RIAD €€
(Map p56; ☑ 0524 39 17 87; www.riadlej.com; 67 Derb el-Hammam; r incl breakfast €75-105; ❋ 🛜) What do you get if you cross Italian furniture designers with Marrakshi craftsmanship? An achingly cool hideaway where art deco Mamounia mirrors meet silk kaftans hung as art, and *zouak* (painted wood) ceilings merge with retro lamps. There are just four spicy rooms on offer – Mint, Saffron, Pepper and Cinnamon – and the welcome is as genuine and personal as the interiors are beautiful.

Tchaikana RIAD €€
(Map p56; ☑ 0524 38 51 50; www.tchaikana.com; 25 Derb el Ferrane, Azbest; incl breakfast r €90-100, ste €150; ❋ 🛜) The skinny, winding *derb* (alleyway) that leads here belies what lies inside the front door. With a Tuareg tent-post bed in one room and African artefacts artfully scattered throughout, Tchaikana is Marrakesh's luxurious pad for travellers with a nomadic spirit. Plot souq forays over lavish breakfasts hosted by English-speaking Belgian owner Jean-Francois, and return at happy hour to plan Sahara eco-adventures.

Riad Tizwa RIAD €€
(Map p56; www.riadtizwa.com; 26 Derb Gueraba, Dar el-Bacha; r incl breakfast €75-140; ❋ 🛜) The Bee brothers bring their signature style to Marrakech with this intimate hideaway, sister to their property in Fez. Pops of colour add a modern freshness to the six quirky rooms, that still have original stucco and antique tile decorative features. Beds are so comfortable you may not want to get up.

Dar Attajmil RIAD €€
(Map p56; ☑ 0524 42 69 66; www.darattajmil.com; 23 Rue Laksour; r incl breakfast €90-110; ❋ @ 🛜) Lucrezia and her attentive staff offer a warm welcome and an even warmer rooftop hammam at this relaxed and elegant riad of blush-pink *tadelakt* walls, cosy lounging salons and banana-tree shaded courtyard. Just four rooms – home to softly sumptuous furnishings and wood ceilings – guarantee a personal touch. There are also Moroccan-Italian dinners, a babysitting service, cooking classes and Essaouira escapes.

Dar Zaman RIAD €€
(Map p52; ☑ 0524 37 66 12; www.darzaman.com; 29 Derb Bouelilou, Sidi Ben Slimane; r incl breakfast €95-105; ❋ 🛜) What Dar Zaman may lack in size it makes up for in heart, with extraordi-nary personal attention from Peter, Hassan, Karima and Yassine. Other guests obviously think the same, as dinner dates quickly transform into social events offering opportunities to trade tips on overnight excursions and hammams – certainly, no one seems keen to retire to their snug, stylish rooms.

Riad UP RIAD €€
(Map p56; ☑ 0665 36 79 36; www.riadup.com; Derb Boutouil 41, Kennaria; d €65-80, ste €90; ❂ ❋ 🛜 🞉) Mallorcan chic meets medina living. Elsa Bauza oversaw every aspect of her riad's renovation retaining its handsome central courtyard, installing a plunge pool in the patio and a sleek *tadelakt* fireplace in the salon, while stripping rooms down to their elegant essentials to create tranquil, minimalist spaces that deserve a spread in *Architectural Digest*.

Riad Helen RIAD €€
(Map p53; ☑ 0524 37 86 11; www.riadhelen.com; 138 Derb Arset Aouzal; r incl breakfast €65-75; ❋ 🛜) This quaint *dar* (small house), down funky Derb Arset Aouzal and its alley-wall mural art, is home to Maxime and Mario and offers five of the best-value riad rooms in town. There's a breezy style here, using lashings of white-trim with sea-green shuttered windows and French doors, while good-sized 1st-floor rooms are dressed in soft pastels and flooded with light.

Marhbabikoum RIAD €€
(Map p56; ☑ 0524 37 52 04; www.marhbabikoum. com; 43 Derb Lahbib Magni; s/d/q incl breakfast €55/90/115; ❂ ❋ 🛜) The name means 'welcome', and you'll feel it as soon as you step through the door. Khalil and Véronique run a mellow, family-style riad, so you're automatically invited for tea, chats, card games and Moroccan jam sessions already in progress. If you can tear yourself away, rooms – like the atmosphere – are homey and colourful.

★ **Riad L'Orangeraie** RIAD €€€
(Map p57; ☑ 0661 23 87 89; www.riadorangeraie. com; 61 Rue Sidi el-Yamani; incl breakfast r €140-150, ste €180; ❋ 🛜 🞉) Substance as well as style. From Moroccan sweets and fresh flowers in your room to top-notch, personal service provided by owner Cyril and manager Ismail, Riad L'Orangeraie gets all the finer details right. Amply proportioned rooms come with bathrooms of perfectly buffed *tadelakt* walls and massaging showers (the best in town), while the courtyard rimmed by cosy sitting alcoves leads out to a generous pool.

With five employees looking after seven rooms, excellent breakfasts, soothing hammam treatments, a babysitting service and full concierge services to help you make the most out of your stay, this really is the ultimate five-star boutique experience.

★ Riad Azoulay
RIAD €€€

(Map p56; ☑ 0524 38 37 29; www.riad-azoulay. com; 3 Derb Jamaa Kebir; incl breakfast d €100-130, ste from €170; ✆ ❄ 🛜 🏊) The restoration of this 300-year-old mansion, once home to the wealthy Azoulay family, who served as advisors to the royal family, was a labour of love for owner Sandro. The result is a haven of casual luxury where original cedar ceilings and plasterwork decor sit comfortably alongside modern art, painted-wood antique furniture and sumptuously coloured kilims.

Service is sublime, meals mix Moroccan and Italian influences to create a fresh menu of Mediterranean flavours, the private hammam dishes up pampering treats, and the plunge pool in the central courtyard provides the perfect antidote after a long day treading the medina streets.

Riad Al Massara
RIAD €€€

(Map p53; ☑ 0524 38 32 06; www.riadalmassarah. com; 26 Derb Jedid; d incl breakfast Dh1150-1950; ❄ 🛜 🏊) 🍃 The ultimate feel-good getaway: British-French owners Michel and Michael redesigned this ancient riad to maximise comfort and sunlight, and minimise electrical and water waste, putting the well-being of guests and the planet first. Each guest room is distinct, with original art, handmade textiles, and *tadelakt* fireplaces. The riad's local engagement and energy-saving efforts have earned it a Travelife gold award. Children under 12 years are not accepted.

Dar Housnia
RIAD €€€

(Map p56; ☑ 0524 37 66 97; www.dar-housnia. com; 2 Derb Lalla Azzouna, Kâat Benahid; r incl breakfast €135-165, 4-person douiria €340; 🛜 🏊) Tradition and modernity blend seamlessly in Eveline Donnez's quietly stylish *dar,* where a thoughtful approach to luxury puts the well-being of guests ahead of glitzy frippery. Winding staircases lead to a hammam, a sun-lounger-speckled roof terrace and a secret courtyard with a generous plunge pool. The spacious rooms, meanwhile, feature art on the walls and buffed *tadelakt* bathrooms.

For friends, or family travelling together, the riad's self-contained *douiria* (guest apartment) with it's own lounging salon and terrace, is a suitably suave choice.

🛏 Ville Nouvelle

Hôtel Toulousain
GUESTHOUSE €

(Map p61; ☑ 0524 43 00 33; www.hoteltoulousain. ma; 44 Rue Tariq ibn Ziyad; incl breakfast new s/d Dh300/400, old Dh250/300, without bathroom Dh150/220; 🅿 🛜) An easygoing hotel arranged around a shady courtyard and run by a kind Moroccan-American family in a prime Guéliz location. There's a variety of rooms (which come in a highly confusing number of configurations); the pick of the bunch is the new 'traditional-style' with their beige *tadelakt* walls and stained-glass detailing. Older rooms are decked out in classic blue *beldi* tiles.

Be aware, upstairs rooms here swelter in midsummer. Mobile fans (and heaters in winter) can be provided, but you need to ask.

Hôtel du Pacha
HOTEL €

(Map p61; ☑ 0524 43 13 27; www.hotelpacha.net; 33 Rue de la Liberté; s/d Dh330/420; ❄ 🛜) Novels beg to be set in this faded colonial hotel, with tall French windows to catch breezes and neighbourhood gossip. Ground-floor rooms come with marble sinks and dark woodwork, while those upstairs are snug, but brightened by stripy red bed linens and drapes. The shadowy stuccoed entry, hidden courtyard and salon club chairs add *noir*-novel intrigue.

Blue Sea Le Printemps
HOTEL €€

(Map p61; ☑ 0524 43 29 92; www.blueseahotels. com; 19 Ave el-Mansour Eddahbi; d Dh600, ste from Dh1500, all incl breakfast; 🅿 ✆ ❄ 🛜 🏊) This 140-room hotel, run by the Spanish Blue Sea Hotels Group, is a great alternative to Marrakesh's bland mega-hotels. It's a winner for families and travellers seeking full facilities. Check the website for offers; rooms are often half-price.

🛏 Palmeraie & Outskirts

When the medina seems a bit much, villas in the *palmeraie* and on the outskirts of the city allow you to chill out. Once your blood pressure dips and you begin to miss the madness of Marrakesh, it's only a 15- to 20-minute drive back to the heart of the action. A taxi into town is the easiest way, but is rather costly (Dh150 to DH250) since you often have to pay for the driver's round-trip to fetch you.

⭐ Riad Bledna
GUESTHOUSE €€

(☑0661 18 20 90; www.riadbledna.com; off Rte de Ouarzazate, Km19, N 31°35'46.8, W 7°52'28.5; d incl breakfast €70; 🅿🍴) 🏵 Welcome to the garden villa of the Moroccan-British Nour family, who pamper visitors as if they are favourite house guests. With five rooms of spice-toned *tadelakt* walls and traditional *tataoui* ceilings, a filtered pool and delicious home cooking (with produce from their organic four-acre garden) this is a peaceful and thoroughly homey cocoon to retreat to after the medina hustle.

Your hosts can arrange airport pickups, medina transfers, babysitting, desert trips, mountain eco-excursions and hands-on Moroccan crafts workshops.

You'll find it 19km east of Marrakesh, signposted off the Rte de Ouarzazate. From the turn-off it's a further 2.5km to the house.

Jnane Tamsna
RESORT €€€

(☑0524 32 94 23; www.jnane.com; Douar Abiad, Palmeraie; d incl breakfast €195-395; ✴🛜🍴) 🏵 Sustainability meets style at Meryanne Loum-Martin's oasis. Paths thread through landscaped gardens (planted by her ethnobotanist husband, Gary Martin) leading to swimming pools, tennis courts and large rooms scattered with antiques, art and Moroccan textiles. A home-away-from-home for discerning jet-setter families, expect organic cuisine, Marrakesh jaunts and lazy days lapping up the secluded beauty of the nine-acre palm-fringed property.

You'll find it 15 minutes northwest of Marrakesh in Douar Abiad, off the Circuit de la Palmeraie. Transfers from the medina can be arranged.

For those who can't stay, Jnane Tamsna offers lunch with pool access for Dh400 per person.

Casa Taos
GUESTHOUSE €€€

(Map p52; ☑0661 20 04 14; www.casataos.net; Rte de Targa, Km8; r incl breakfast €175-235; 🅿✴🛜🍴) Hicham and family ladle out lashings of hospitality at this colourful, quirky villa with rooms kitted out in an eclectic fusion melding modern and traditional Moroccan design with art deco. Wipe off the medina dust and loll by the large pool under swaying palm trees. At mealtimes, feast on innovative Mediterranean menus made from this foodie family's organic garden produce.

With advance booking, non-guests can savour Casa Taos' genial ambience as well as lunch and pool formulas for Dh350.

Al Fassia Aguedal
BOUTIQUE HOTEL €€€

(☑0524 38 38 39; www.alfassia.com; 9 bis Rte de l'Ourika, Km2, Zone Aguedal; incl breakfast d Dh1500-1800, ste Dh2250; ✴🛜🍴) Want relaxed ambience but a location that's closer to the medina than the luxury pads of the *palmeraie?* This boutique hotel offers spacious, light-filled rooms decked out with traditional flourishes yet with all mod-cons provided – a spa, pool, restaurant and peaceful garden abloom with flowers. Same owners as the long-running restaurant Al Fassia (p75) in Guéliz.

✖ Eating

Marrakesh's culinary scene has improved considerably with a flurry of new restaurants opening in both the medina and ville nouvelle. That said, as traditionally Marrakshis don't eat out often, most medina restaurants are aimed squarely at the tourist market and meals can be hit-and-miss. In middle-class Guéliz, there's more of a local dining vibe with both Moroccan and international restaurants.

✖ Medina

Hadj Mustapha
MOROCCAN €

(Map p56; Souq Ablueh, east side; tanjia with bread & olives Dh70; ☺noon-8pm) Several stalls at Souq Ablueh offer up paper-sealed crockpots of *tanjia*, but Hadj Mustapha's is the most renowned for sampling this famed 'bachelor's stew', with basic but clean seating inside a well-scuffed stall. Use bread as your utensil to scoop up *tanjia;* sprinkle with cumin and salt; and chase with olives.

Djemaa El-Fna Food Stalls
MOROCCAN €

(Map p56; mains Dh30-50; ☺sunset-1am) Grilled meat and tajines as far as the eye can see! Plus Moroccan specialities of snail soup, sheep's brains and skewered hearts for the more adventurous gourmet. Eating amid the mayhem of the Djemaa food stalls at least once in your trip is not to be missed. Always go for the busiest stalls as they'll have the freshest meat.

Marrakech Henna Art Cafe
CAFE €

(Map p56; ☑0524 38 14 10; www.marrakech-hennaartcafe.com; 35 Derb Siquya; mains Dh40; ☺10am-9pm; 🛜🏵) This charming cafe and art space is a cosy retreat dishing up a mixed menu of North African (the Berber omelette and turkey *brochettes* with caramelised pumpkin are winners) and healthy-leaning sandwiches. True to its name there are local art exhibits, a collection of Berber artefacts, wall murals and the opportunity to get your own piece of henna body art.

Roti d'Or
INTERNATIONAL €

(Map p56; Kennaria Dabbachi; mains Dh25-40; ⊙10.30am-9pm) Blink and you'd miss it, but Roti d'Or is not a place to miss if you're looking for a good-value non-Moroccan meal in the medina. Enchiladas, a Tex-Mex burger and felafel sandwiches feature on the menu, all served with a tangy rice salad and chips.

Café des Épices
CAFE €

(Map p56; ✐0254 39 17 70; Pl Rahba Kedima; sandwich & salads Dh45-60; ⊙8am-9pm; 🕾) A traveller's institution parked in prime position on Rahba Kedima. Watch the henna artists and basket sellers tout for business from your shady stool while munching on sandwiches or sipping a fresh beetroot, apple and ginger juice. We like the Paris Marrakech burger stuffed with cheese and aubergine.

Henna Cafe
CAFE, MOROCCAN €

(Map p53; www.hennacafemarrakech.com; 93 Arset Aouzal; mains Dh40, tattoos from Dh50; ⊙11am-8pm; 🕾🍴) 🍃 Tea, coffee, salad, henna tattoo, Darija class...they're all on the menu at this funky cafe, where a local *nquasha* (henna artist) draws intricate designs on hands and feet and you can munch on felafel platters and *khleer* (cured lamb) sandwiches on the rooftop terrace. All profits go to local residents in need.

Babouche Café
MOROCCAN €

(Map p53; ✐0675 36 94 68; Rue el-Giza; mains Dh25-55; ⊙11.30am-11.30pm Mon-Sat; 🕾) First, the bad news: it's in a hilariously bad location right next to a car park. Now the good: this scrubbed up hole-in-the-wall cafe with its shady patio of maroon walls framed by palms (rubbing up against aforementioned car park) may just dish up some of the tastiest tajines in the medina. The *harira* (lentil soup; Dh15), in particular, is delicious.

Fox Art Food
CAFE €

(Map p56; Riad Zitoun el-Kedim; mains Dh35-50; ⊙11am-10pm) Overseen by the fox-headed mannequin out front, this funky, fun cafe is run by a group of local artists as a means to support their work. Pull up a stool (made from old crates and recycled denim) and order lunch from the small menu that trips from sandwiches, salads, burgers and tajines.

Latitude 31
MEDITERRANEAN €€

(Map p53; ✐0524 38 49 34; www.latitude31marrakech.com; 186 Rue el Giza; mains Dh130-210; ⊙6-11pm; 🕾) It's difficult to tweak heavily traditional cuisines without raising eyebrows but Latitude 31 pretty much pulls it off. Not all of it completely gels, but the complimentary pumpkin crème brûlée starter is luscious and their take on *mrouzia* (lamb tajine cooked with honey, raisins and almonds) is a sweet-sticky-savoury delight. Service is stellar.

Souk Kafé
MOROCCAN €€

(Map p56; ✐0662 61 02 29; 11 Derb Sidi Abdelaziz; mains Dh90-120; ⊙9am-9pm; 🌢🕾) Pull up a hand-hewn stool under terrace parasols and stay a while: this is authentic local food worth savouring. The Moroccan *mezze* of six cooked vegetable dishes qualifies as lunch for two, and the vegetarian Berber couscous is surprisingly hearty – but wait until you get a whiff of the aromatic Marrakshi *tanjia*, with its slow-cooked, perfectly falling apart beef.

Cafe Clock
CAFE €€

(Map p53; ✐0524 37 83 67; www.cafeclock.com; 224 Derb Chtouka; mains Dh60-95; ⊙10am-10pm; 🕾🍴) Little sister to the Fez original, Cafe Clock is housed in an old school with sunset views over the Kasbah. The signature camel burger, inventive sandwiches and salads are reason enough to drop in, but the cross-cultural vibe will keep you returning. Every Monday and Thursday they host traditional *hikayat* (storytelling) performances and there's live Gnaoua and Amazigh music on Sundays.

Naranj
LEBANESE €€

(Map p56; ✐0524 38 68 05; www.naranj.ma; 84 Rue Riad Zitoun el-Jedid; mains Dh69-119; ⊙11am-11pm; 🌢) If you know your felafel from your fattoush (salad of toasted bread, tomatoes, onion and mint) make a beeline here. Inside it's a glam mix of funky *khamsa* (traditional amulet) mirrors, low-hanging copper lamps and stripy textiles that wouldn't be out of place in a hipster Beirut cafe. Which is the point, because the menu is of bang-on classic Lebanese favourites, with a couple of modern twists.

Kui-Zin
INTERNATIONAL €€

(Map p56; ✐0524 39 09 84; www.kui-zin.com; 12 Rue Amesfah; mains Dh50-90; ⊙11am-10pm Tue-Sun; 🕾🍴) As you're munching on complimentary olives and fresh-baked bread, choose from a menu that spins from couscous and tajines to vegetable lasagne (actually a delicious, cheesy carrot and courgette pie) and chicken curry. Chef Kenza takes real pride in the preparation, while Hassan serves everything with a heartfelt smile. Come for dinner and get live music thrown in, too.

LOCAL EATS

Mechoui Alley (Souq Ablueh, east side; mechoui Dh50-70; ⊙11am-2pm) Just before noon, the vendors at this row of stalls start carving up steaming sides of *mechoui* (slow-roasted lamb). Point to the best-looking cut of meat, and ask for a *nuss* (half) or *rubb* (quarter) kilo. The cook will hack off falling-from-the-bone lamb and hand it to you with fresh-baked bread, cumin, salt and olives.

Snack al-Bahriya (75 Ave Moulay Rachid, cnr Rue Mauritanie; seafood with chips Dh30-80; ⊙10am-midnight) Fish and chips the Marrakesh way. The entire stretch of Rue Mauritanie is packed with sidewalk stalls and restaurants serving up seafood, but Snack al-Bahriya is our favourite for dishing up fresh fish and perfectly tender fried calamari with generous chunks of lemon, plus salt, cumin and hot sauce.

Plats Haj Boujemaa (65 Rue Mohammed Bakkal; mains Dh25-45; ⊙noon-10pm Tue-Sun) *Brochettes* (kebabs), tajines, pizza, pasta, steak. This unpretentious place covers all the bases, though what it's known for is its perfectly grilled meat. Join the locals who crowd in here on their lunch break for a cheap, tasty meal with friendly service.

Oscar Progrès (20 Rue Bani Marine; mains Dh35-45; ⊙noon-11pm) This brightly lit local canteen serves up huge plates of couscous and sizzling *brochettes* (kebabs) to hungry office workers who take a pew at long communal tables. Despite the dining-hall atmosphere, the food is a good standard and the service efficient and pleasant.

El Bahja (☑0524 44 13 51; 24 Rue Bani Marine; mains Dh35-45; ⊙noon-11pm) Serving up filling portions of *kefta* (meatballs) and Moroccan staples to a steady stream of hungry local workers and travellers, El Bahja is a stalwart of the Djemaa el-Fna scene. The food here isn't going to knock your socks off, but it's always dependable, good value and fresh.

I Limoni   ITALIAN €€
(Map p53; ☑0524 38 30 30; 40 Rue Bab Taghzout; mains Dh80-180; ⊙noon-11pm; ☑) We're kinda partial to any restaurant that has a collection of kitsch snow-globes on display, but I Limoni serves up a fine line of pasta as well. Park yourself up in the lemon-tree-shaded courtyard, order a glass of wine (from Dh50) and tuck into comforting dishes such as ricotta ravioli with parmesan, lemon zest and mint.

Le Jardin   MOROCCAN €€
(Map p56; ☑0524 37 82 95; www.lejardin.ma; 32 Derb Sidi Abdelaziz; mains Dh80-140; ☎☑) Entrepreneur Kamal Laftimi transformed this 17th-century riad in the medina's core into a tranquil oasis where you can lunch beneath a canopy of banana trees, serenaded by songbirds, as tiny tortoises inch across the floor tiles. The menu can be hit and miss, but shines with its big-portioned *brochettes* and whole grilled sardines.

Un Déjeuner à Marrakech   MEDITERRANEAN €€
(Map p56; ☑0524 37 83 87; 2-4 Rue Riad Zitoun el-Jedid, cnr Douar Graoua; mains Dh85-135; ⊙11am-10pm; ✳☎☑) Popular with the lunching crowd, Un Déjeuner dishes up a Mediterranean menu that jumps from Tangier shrimp to steak, mozzarella salad and pumpkin balls. The cactus-lined roof terrace is the place to be on a blue-skied, breezy Moroccan spring day.

Nomad   MEDITERRANEAN €€
(Map p56; ☑0524 38 16 09; www.nomadmarrakech.com; 1 Derb Arjan; mains Dh90-120; ⊙11am-11pm; ☎☑) Nomad's rooftop terrace is one of the medina's buzziest eating venues. The small menu adds contemporary tweaks to North African staples such as a spice-packed Tunisian lamb *brik* (pastry), while keeping the punters happy by also serving up a flavoursome burger. Desserts such as apple and beetroot clafoutis and hibiscus panna cotta add an interesting end-of-dinner twist.

Beats Burger   BURGERS €€
(Map p56; ☑0524 39 12 13; www.beatsburger.com; 35 Souq Jeld Kemakine; mains Dh55-115; ⊙11am-9pm; ☎☑) No, we didn't expect to find a gourmet burger joint sitting amid the souqs either. Sign of the times indeed. If you're tajined-out for the day, hit this place for burgers with a difference – stuffed with hash browns, *harissa* mayonnaise and duck breast – or keep your health halo glowing with a vegan bagel.

Naima   MOROCCAN €€
(Map p56; Derb Sidi Ishak; meals Dh100; ⊙11am-10pm) If you want to eat couscous prepared

DON'T MISS

DJEMAA EL-FNA DINNER THEATRE

Arrive around 4pm to watch chefs set up shop right in the heart of the action in the Djemaa el-Fna. Djemaa stalls have a better turnover of ingredients than most fancy restaurants, where you can't typically check the meat and cooking oil before you sit down to dinner. Despite alarmist warnings, your stomach should be fine if you clean your hands before eating, use your bread instead of rinsed utensils and stick to your own bottled water.

Pull up a bench and enjoy the show: the action continues in 'La Place' until after midnight. Berber bands sing songs near dentists' booths displaying jars of teeth, not far from a performance involving clowns and worryingly amateur boxers. Some of the Djemaa's evening entertainments haven't changed much in a millennium, including astrologers, potion-sellers and cross-dressing belly dancers.

by a proper Marrakshi mamma then Naima is the place to be. Squeeze into the tiny dining room, order either tajine or couscous (there's no menu) and settle back with a mint tea as the women get cooking. Bring your appetite – this is family-style Moroccan food and the portions are huge.

★**Dar Anika** MOROCCAN €€€
(Map p56; 📞0524 39 17 51; www.riaddaranika.com; 112 Riad Zitoun el-Kedim; mains Dh150-200; ⊙11.30am-2.30pm & 6.30-11pm) The small terrace, framed by palms and trailing bougainvillea, is all about romantic candlelit dining. The main courses offer a tastebud tour of Moroccan dishes often missing from medina menus. For a sweet-savoury kick order the chicken *seffa medfouna* (chicken topped with raisin, almond and cinnamon spiked vermicelli) or go full-hog and pre-order (four hours in advance) the camel *tanjia*.

★**PepeNero** ITALIAN, MOROCCAN €€€
(Map p56; 📞0524 38 90 67; www.pepenero-marrakech.com; 17 Derb Cherkaoui; mains Dh120-220, 3-course lunch menu Dh190; ⊙12.30-2.30pm & 7.30-11pm Tue-Sun; 🛜🍽) Housed in part of Riad al Moussika, Thami el Glaoui's one-time pleasure palace, this Italian-Moroccan

restaurant is one of the finest in the medina, with its fresh house-made pasta stealing the show. Request a table beside the courtyard pool, rimmed by citrus trees, to make the most of the occasion. Reservations required.

Le Tobsil MOROCCAN €€€
(Map p56; 📞0524 44 40 52; 22 Derb Abdellah ben Hessaien; 5-course menu incl wine Dh640; ⊙7.30-11pm Wed-Mon) In this intimate riad near Bab Laksour, 50 guests (max) indulge in button-popping, five-course Moroccan menus with aperitifs and wine pairings, as Gnaoua musicians strum quietly in the courtyard. Don't let the belly dancers distract you from your 11 salads, *pastilla* (rich savoury pie), tajines (yes, that's plural) and couscous, capped with mint tea, fruit and Moroccan pastries. Booking required.

La Maison Arabe MOROCCAN €€€
(Map p53; 📞0524 38 70 10; www.lamaisonarabe.com; 1 Derb Assehbe; mains Dh150-200; ⊙7.30pm-midnight; 🛜🍽) La Maison Arabe was serving Moroccan fine dining decades before other riads, and *viva la difference!* The focus here is on the food and service, with excellent classical Andalucian musicians providing subtle background music for traditional tajine and couscous feasts. Make an evening of it and drop into the piano bar for an aperitif before your meal.

✗ Ville Nouvelle

★**Amal Center** MOROCCAN €
(Map p61; 📞0524 44 68 96; amalnonprofit.org; cnr Rues Allal ben Ahmad & Ibn Sina; mains Dh50-60; ⊙noon-4pm) 🍴 Do good while eating delicious food – double bonus. The Amal Center supports and trains disadvantaged Moroccan women in restaurant skills and you get to feast on their flavours. So many Marrakesh restaurants reflect poorly on local cuisine, but here you get the real home-cooking deal. On our last visit we had the best fish tajine we've ever tasted in Morocco.

The menu changes daily but there's always at least three options of starters, mains and dessert; on Fridays couscous is always the star of the show. Prices are locally focused so the restaurant's clientele is a happy mix of local families, expats and in-the-know tourists. Even better, if the spicy zing of your tajine has got your tastebuds craving more, they're now running cooking classes.

Catanzaro ITALIAN €€
(Map p61; ☑0524 43 37 31; 42 Rue Tariq ibn Ziyad; mains Dh50-120; ☺noon-2.30pm & 7.15-11pm Mon-Sat; ❋) This is the best pizza in Morocco. It may even be the best pizza this side of the Med. We realise that's an awfully big call and maybe the very reasonably priced wine here (from Dh160 per bottle) went to our head, but Catanzaro's thin-crust, wood-fired creations (particularly the Neapolitan with capers, local olives and Atlantic anchovies) are a show-stealer.

Loft INTERNATIONAL €€
(Map p61; ☑0524 43 42 16; 18 Rue de la Liberté; mains Dh130-190; ☺noon-midnight; ❋☎) Carnivores unite. From Atlas mountain snails to lamb shank and a divine calf's liver (doused in a luscious garlicky sauce), Loft is a meat-lover's paradise. Framed by huge wall mirrors, the small space buzzes from lunch till late, but exceptionally on-the-ball staff keep service fast and friendly even when it's packed.

Mamma Mia ITALIAN €€
(Map p61; ☑0524 43 44 54; www.restaurant-mammamia.com; 18 Rue de la Liberté; mains Dh50-170; ☺10am-10pm; ❋✐) Full hat-tip to this family-friendly trattoria for its smoke-free section. Take a tajine break and join the punters chowing down on good-value pizzas, generous bowls of pasta or main dishes of veal escalope and steak. Beer and wine are available and there's a full bar out the back (in the smoking section).

Chez Mado SEAFOOD €€
(Map p61; ☑0524 42 14 94; 22 Rue Moulay Ali; mains Dh90-220; ☺noon-3pm & 7-11.30pm Tue-Sun; ❋) With the fragrance of Oualidia's salty shallows still fresh on them, Chez Mado's oysters are the prettiest and plumpest in Marrakesh. Shellfish and seafood are delivered daily here, where under chef Alex Chaussetier's direction they are transformed into the lightest lunches: elegant sole meunière, grilled prawns and mayonnaise, John Dory with chorizo and a seafood platter to blow your mind.

Café 16 CAFE €€
(Map p61; ☑0524 33 96 70; 18 Pl du 16 Novembre; desserts Dh70, sandwiches & salads Dh120-140; ☺9am-midnight) The blonde-wood decor and prices may seem European, but the welcome is Marrakshi – and so are intriguing ice-cream flavours like bergamot orange tea and *kaab el-gazelle* (almond cookie). Great for a coffee or beer in the early evening, or perhaps some gold-leafed chocolate-coffee cream cake or raspberry-mousse cake for dessert.

★**Al Fassia** MOROCCAN €€€
(Map p61; ☑0524 43 40 60; www.alfassia.com; 55 Blvd Mohammed Zerktouni; mains Dh110-175; ☺noon-2.30pm & 7.30-11pm Wed-Mon) In business since 1987, this stalwart of the Marrakesh dining scene is still one of the best. Meals begin with a bang with free 12-dish *mezze* (salads) while Moroccan mains of chicken tajine or caramelised pumpkin and lamb tajine with almonds and eggs – served by an all-female waiter crew – show how the classics should be done. Reservations essential.

Azar MIDDLE EASTERN €€€
(Map p61; ☑0524 43 09 20; www.azarmarrakech.com; Rue de Yougoslavie; mains Dh95-250; ☺7pm-midnight; ❋✐) Imagine a Beirut lounge teleported to Marrakesh via Mars: with space-captain chairs and star-patterned stucco walls, the decor is out of this world – and the Lebnese-inspired fare isn't far behind. The *mezze* is where this place really shines with pleasing *batata harra* (spicy baked potatoes) and *chankliche* (cheese). Shared mixed *mezze* platters (from Dh190) will keep vegetarians happy, and bills in this stratosphere.

SUGAR RUSH: MARRAKESH'S SWEET TREATS

Pâtisserie Amandine (☑0524 44 96 12; www.amandinemarrakech.com; 177 Rue Mohamed El Beqal; sweets & desserts from Dh10; ☺7am-9pm; ❋) Outstanding viennoiserie and multicoloured macarons.

Pâtisserie al-Jawda (☑0524 43 38 97; 11 Rue de la Liberté; ☺8am-7.30pm) Sweet and savoury delicacies featuring figs, orange-flower water and desert honey.

Pâtisserie des Princes (☑0524 44 30 33; 32 Rue Bab Agnaou; ☺9am-9pm; ❋) The city's most famous patisserie, with enough *pain au chocolat* and *mille-feuille* to keep Djemaa el-Fna dentists in business.

Panna Gelato (☑0524 43 65 65; www.pannagelatoitaliano.it; cnr Rue du Capitaine Arrigui & Ave Mohammed V; cone Dh20; ☺7.30am-10pm; ❋) A master *gelato* artisan from Italy, proprietary recipes and top ingredients make Panna the best place for ice cream in Morocco.

♟ Drinking & Nightlife

Dar Cherifa
CAFE

(Map p56; ☑ 0524 42 64 63; 8 Derb Chorfa Lakbir; ⊙ noon-7pm; 🛜) Ring the doorbell to be admitted into this serene late-15th-century Saadian riad. Tea, juice and saffron coffee are served on ultra-comfy yellow sofas in a courtyard framed by soaring blush-pink pillars topped with intricate cedar lintels. Surrounding salons are home to art exhibitions and you'll get great views from the terrace upstairs.

Meals can be underwhelming, which is a shame as the ambience can't be beaten.

Kechmara
BAR

(Map p61; ☑ 0524 42 25 32; www.kechmara.com; 3 Rue de La Liberté; ⊙ 11.30am-1am Mon-Sat; 🛜) Want to hang out with the Marrakshi cool kids? Pull up a Saarinen tulip chair at Kechmara after sunset and watch as the bar packs out with a hip, young crowd. The menu (with great burgers) makes this a nice spot for lunch, but it's after dark when the music starts pumping that Kechmara really comes into its own.

68 Bar à Vin
BAR

(Map p61; ☑ 0524 44 97 42; 68 Rue de la Liberté; ⊙ 7pm-2am) A hip and ultra-lively little wine bar that packs in a nice mixed crowd of Moroccans and foreign residents. There are both European and Moroccan wines on offer as well as beer. Staff are on the ball and friendly. When it gets too smoky later in the evening, escape to the patio bench seating out the front.

Pointbar
BAR

(Map p61; 3 Rue Abou Hayane Taouhidi; ⊙ 6pm-late) A lot of Marrakesh bars can get a bit smoky, which is why Pointbar with its outdoor front courtyard (which has a retractable roof for colder nights) is, literally, a breath of fresh air. Sit yourself down on a comfy sofa or square pouf, order from the tapas set menu (Dh210) and have a few beers.

Grand Café de la Poste
CAFE

(Map p61; ☑ 0524 43 30 38; cnr Blvd el-Mansour Eddahbi & Rue Imam Malik; ⊙ 8am-1am; 🛜) Restored to its flapper-era glory, this landmark bistro oozes colonial decadence in spades. Prices run high for dinner so skip the food and instead lap up the old-world ambience of dark wood and potted palms with a coffee, Darjeeling tea or wine in hand.

Café du Livre
CAFE

(Map p61; ☑ 0524 43 21 49; www.cafedulivre.com; 44 Rue Tariq ibn Ziyad; ⊙ 10am-11pm Mon-Sat; 🛜) This cafe-bar is a chilled-out spot with draft beer, cushy seating, walls of books to browse and quiz nights. Come for happy hour (6pm to 8pm Tuesday to Saturday) for some of the cheapest beer in town (Dh20 to Dh40) when the after-work crowd descends and it takes on a lively pub atmosphere.

Riad Yima
TEAHOUSE

(Map p56; ☑ 0524 39 19 87; www.riadyima.com; 52 Derb Aarjane, Rahba Kedima; ⊙ 9am-6pm Mon-Sat; 🛜) Acclaimed Marrakshi artist and photographer Hassan Hajjaj created this kitsch-crammed tearoom and gallery. Here, all your preconceived notions of Moroccan restaurants and riads, with their Arabian Nights fantasy of candlelit lanterns, arches and belly dancers, are revamped with a tongue-in-cheek sense of humour, accompanied by a traditional glass of mint tea, of course.

Kosybar
BAR

(Map p56; ☑ 0524 38 03 24; http://kozibar.tripod.com; 47 Pl des Ferblantiers; ⊙ noon-1am; 🛜) The Marrakesh-meets-Kyoto interiors are full of plush, private nooks, but keep heading upstairs to low-slung canvas sofas on the rooftop terrace where storks give cocktail-sippers the once-over from nearby nests. Skip the cardboard-esque sushi and stick with the bar snacks.

Café Arabe
BAR

(Map p56; ☑ 0524 42 97 28; www.cafearabe.com; 184 Rue Mouassine; ⊙ 10am-midnight; 🛜) Gloat over souq purchases with cocktails on the roof or alongside the Zen *zellij* courtyard fountain. Prices here are reasonable for such a stylish place, and you can order half bottles of decent Moroccan wines, such as the peppery red Siroua S. The food is bland but the company isn't – artists and designers flock here.

Kaowa
CAFE

(Map p52; ☑ 0524 33 00 72; 34 Rue Yves Saint Laurent; ⊙ 8am-8pm; 🛜) Breezy Kaowa brings a touch of California cool to the Majorelle gardens. The decked terrace attracts a see-and-be-seen crowd who sip detox smoothies and lunch on huge slices of quiche and leafy salads (Dh75 to Dh90).

Bô & Zin
LOUNGE

(☑ 0524 38 80 12; www.bo-zin.com; Rte de Ourika, Km3.5, Zone Aguedal; ⊘ 8pm-late) If you want to hang out with Marrakesh's beautiful people, this is the place to be. This rather chic place, with its garden area under billowing white sails, is both a lounge-style bar and Thai-Moroccan restaurant (mains Dh175 to Dh260) in the early evening, and laid-back club later at night once the DJs hit the decks.

L'auberge Espagnole
BAR

(Map p61; Rue Moulay Ali; ⊘ 5pm-1am) L'auberge Espagnole may not be able to decide if it's a restaurant, tapas bar or sports bar, but heck, who cares? This friendly hang-out, with walls covered in sporting paraphernalia and big-screen TVs does a good line in Spanish tapas as well as imported and local beers.

555 Famous Club
CLUB

(☑ 0678 64 39 40; www.beachclub555.com; Hotel Ushuaia Clubbing, Blvd Mohammed VI, Agdal; entry Dh300; ⊘ 11pm-5am) Most clubbers' venue of choice, 555 has a fun, non-sleazy vibe with tight security on the door, and pumps out house, trance, Europop and RnB until the wee hours. After 1am the scene here can get packed with a good mix of locals and foreign visitors. Women often have free entry until 2am.

Djelabar
CLUB

(Map p52; ☑ 0524 42 12 42; 2 Rue Abou Hanifa, Hivernage; ⊘ 7pm-3am) Lounge-club-restaurant with a cabaret show on the weekends (cue the belly dancers) and plenty of over-the-top kitsch style. The converted stucco-tastic 1940s wedding hall features an eye-popping zellij-backed bar and wall portraits sporting fez-wearing icons from Marilyn Monroe to Michael Jackson. Skip the food and come for a late-night drink.

☆ Entertainment

Djemaa el-Fna is Marrakesh's biggest entertainment venue with its nightly melee of busking street performers and music.

For a good selection of French and sometimes Moroccan films, check out the program at the **Institut Français** (☑ 0524 44 69 30; www.if-maroc.org/marrakech; 60 Rte de Targa, Guéliz; ⊘ 9am-12.30pm & 3-7pm Mon-Sat), where films are usually in French or subtitled in French. Guéliz's **Le Colisée** (☑ 0524 44 88 93; Blvd Mohammed Zerktouni; orchestra/balcony Dh25/35) cinema sometimes shows

films in the original language with subtitles in French.

🛍 Shopping

🛍 Medina

Think of the medina's souqs as a shopping mall, but laid out according to a labyrinthine medieval-era plan. Whether you want to spice up your pantry with North African flavours or buy a carpet to add Moroccan-wow to your house, this magpie's nest of treasures is manna for shop-til-you-drop fanatics.

The main market streets are Souq Semmarine and Souq el-Kebir. If you see something you really like there, fine – but understand prices will be higher. Smaller souqs and souqs dedicated to artisan workshops such as Souq Haddadine (Blacksmith's Souq), where you can buy direct from the producer, generally have the best deals.

Anamil
ARTS & CRAFTS

(Map p56; 48 Derb Sidi Ishak; ⊘ 9.30am-6pm) Step inside this little treasure trove and you're bound to fall in love with at least one beautiful thing. The extremely well collated collection of high-quality ceramics, textiles, soft leather handbags and lamps is full of gorgeous gifts that are a little bit different, and a tad more quirky, than you'll see elsewhere in the souqs.

Al Kawtar
ARTS & CRAFTS

(Map p56; ☑ 0524 38 56 95; www.alkawtar.org; 3 Derb Zaouia Laftihia, Rue Mouassine; ⊘ 9.30am-2pm & 3-6.30pm) 🗡 This nonprofit female collective not only trains women with disabilities in embroidery craft but also sells fine homewares, with a sharp eye for converting traditional needlework into snazzily modern pieces. Pick up a beautiful tablecloth or some gorgeous bed linen here; you know your money's going to a good cause.

Al Nour
ARTS & CRAFTS

(Map p56; ☑ 0524 39 03 23; www.alnour-textiles. com; Rue Laksour 57; ⊘ 9am-2pm & 3-7pm Sat-Wed) 🗡 A smart cooperative that's run by local women with disabilities and where you can find household linens minutely embroidered along the edges. You can also get fabulous hand-stitched Marrakesh-mod tunics, dresses and shirts for men, women and kids, and there's no extra charge for alterations. Purchases pay for salaries, training programs and a childcare centre.

Souq Ableuh FOOD
(Map p56; Souq Ableuh) Swerve off Djemaa el-Fna to this tiny souq dedicated to olives. Green olives, black olives, purple olives, and olives marinated in spicy harissa paste – it's basically olive heaven.

Souq Haddadine ARTS & CRAFTS
(Map p56) The blacksmith's souq is full of busy workshops where the sound of the metalworkers' hammers provides a staccato background beat. If you've been tempted by some of those lovely Moroccan lamps for sale throughout the souqs, buying direct here will probably get you the best price.

Souk Cherifa DESIGN
(Map p56; Souq Kchachbia; ⊙10am-7pm) Short-circuit souq fatigue and head straight for this converted *fondouq* where younger local designers congregate on the upper floor. Pick up funky cushion covers at **Sisi Morocco**, colourful kaftans and clutches made from carpets at **Khmissa**, contemporary embroidered linens from **La Maison Bahira** (www.maisonbahira.com; ⊙10.30am-7pm), and top quality argan oil, *amlou* (argan-nut butter) and beauty products at **Arganino** (⊙10am-7pm).

Creations Pneumatiques ARTS & CRAFTS
(Map p56; 110 Rue Riad Zitoun el-Kedim; ⊙10am-7pm) 🖉 To buy crafts directly from Marrakesh's recycling artisans, head over to Riad Zitoun el-Kedim and check out lanterns, bowls and belts cleverly fashioned from tin cans and tyres. There are several to choose from, but this place (look for the framed Bob Marley poster) has a good selection of Michelin mirrors, inner-tube jewellery boxes, and man-bags with street cred.

Assouss Cooperative d'Argane BEAUTY, FOOD
(Map p56; ☑0524 38 01 25; 94 Rue Mouassine; ⊙9am-1pm & 3-7pm Sat-Thu, 9am-noon Fri) 🖉 This is the Marrakesh retail outlet of a women's argan cooperative outside Essaouira. The all-women staff will ply you with free samples of *amlou* (argan-nut butter) and proudly explain how their ultra-emollient cosmetic oil and gourmet dipping oils are made. You'll find it near Mouassine Fountain.

Fondouq Namas CARPETS
(Map p56; Derb Sidi Ishak; ⊙10am-7.30pm) Several carpet dealers have their shops here with piles and piles of beautiful Berber kilims and *hanbels* (pileless woven carpets) in a range of prices. There are plenty of Berber blankets and other tribal trappings for those looking to take home something smaller as well. Get your glass of mint tea in hand and start carpet-hunting.

Naturom COSMETICS
(Map p56; ☑0673 46 02 09; 213 Rue Riad Zitoun el-Jedid; ⊙9.30am-8pm Sat-Thu, to noon Fri) There are lots of things to like about Naturom, not least its 100% organic certification and the use of pure essences and essential oils (argan, avocado, wheat germ), which ensure that all of the beauty products are completely hypo-allergenic. And with its own medicinal and herbal garden, it has full traceability of all raw materials.

Dar Chrifa Lamrania ART
(Map p56; ☑0663 47 33 23; 11 Zaouit Lahdar; ⊙10.30am-7pm) There are plenty of little art studios dotted around the medina, but this particular one displays some of the more interesting and original paintings by local artists. To find it, head past the Medersa Ali ben Youssef and turn left. It's tucked under the next arch.

Ensemble Artisanal ARTS & CRAFTS
(Map p52; Ave Mohammed V; ⊙9.30am-12.30pm & 3-7pm Mon-Sat) To get a jump-start on the souqs, come to this government-sponsored showcase to glimpse expert artisans at work and see the range of crafts and prices Marrakesh has to offer. The set prices are higher than in the souqs, but it's hassle-free shopping and the producer gets paid directly.

Max & Jan FASHION & ACCESSORIES
(Map p56; ☑0524 37 55 70; www.maxandjan.ma; 14 Rue Amesfah; ⊙10am-7pm) Quirky jewellery sits alongside vintage kaftans, slouchy active-wear and re-imagined salwar pants inside this funky boutique that puts the wacky and inspired into Moroccan fashion.

🛍 Ville Nouvelle

Stock up on essentials at either **Aswak Assalam** (Ave du 11 Janvier; ⊙9am-10pm), the nearest decent-sized supermarket to the medina, or the big **Carrefour** (Eden Centre, Ave Mohammed V; ⊙9am-11pm), which is in central Guéliz and has an alcohol section and many items (including international brands) hard to find elsewhere.

33 Rue Majorelle FASHION, ACCESSORIES
(Map p52; ☑0524 31 41 95; www.33ruemajorelle.com; 33 Rue Yves Saint Laurent; ⊙9.30am-7pm) Over 60 designers, mostly from Morocco, are represented here and co-owner Yehia

Abdelnour dedicates much of his time to sourcing local *maâlems* (master craftsmen) who make the majority of what's on view. Recent finds include super-cool clutches made in vintage upholstery from the Harakat sisters, silk harem pants from couturier Maroc'n Roll and plaited, pop-art charm bracelets from Zinab Chahine.

Sidi Ghanem　　　　　　　　　　DESIGN
(Map p52; www.sidighanem.net; Rte de Safi; ⊙9am-6pm Mon-Fri, 9am-noon Sat) The industrial district of Sidi Ghanem is where the big names in modern Moroccan design have their workshops and showrooms, from ceramics and textiles to furniture and fashion. The quarter is 4km outside of the centre. A round-trip taxi ride from the medina (at a negotiated set rate) will probably cost between Dh150-250.

Darart Librairie　　　　　　　　BOOKS
(Map p52; ☑0524 31 45 93; 79 Rue Yves Saint Laurent; ⊙9am-6pm) This bookshop sells glossy coffee-table books about Morocco, with a small selection of English and French titles. There's also a tiny shelf of Morocco travel guidebooks, good city and country maps, and a decent clutch of Moroccan cookery books.

Atika　　　　　　　　　　　　　SHOES
(Map p61; ☑0524 43 95 76; 34 Rue de la Liberté; ⊙8.30am-12.30pm & 3.30-8pm Mon-Sat) With more colours than a candy store, Atika loafers are a Marrakesh must-have. Some customers have been known to buy their favourite shoe in 10 different colours, and at Dh650 to Dh700 a pair, a quarter of the price of designer-brand lookalikes, who can blame them?

ℹ Information

DANGERS & ANNOYANCES
Hustlers and touts are part and parcel of the medina experience. Marrakesh's *Brigades Touristiques* (Tourist Police) have, in recent years, managed to stymie the worst of the city's hustler problem, but not completely eliminate it. Keep your wits about you and be prepared for a fair amount of hassle.

If you're lost in the medina, ask a shopkeeper for directions. Often bored youths will point you in the wrong way on purpose.

EMERGENCY
Brigade Touristique (Map p56; ☑0524 38 46 01; Rue Ouadi el-Makhazine)
Central Police Station (Map p56; ☑190; Rue Ibn Hanbal, Guéliz; ⊙24hr)

INTERNET ACCESS
Most hotels, riads and many cafes and restaurants offer free wi-fi.

There is still a scattering of cybercafes within the medina, mostly near the Djemaa el-Fna. Look out for signs reading 'c@fe'. Most charge Dh8 to Dh12 per hour and open between 10am and 10pm.

Cyber Café in CyberPark (www.arsatmoula yabdeslam.ma; Ave Mohammed V; per hr Dh10; ⊙9am-6pm) 15 terminals with fast connections amid the oleander trees.

MONEY
ATMs are found around Djemaa el-Fna in the medina and along Ave Mohammed V in the ville nouvelle.

On Sundays, ATMs on Rue Bab Agnaou (near Djemaa el-Fna) and in Rahba Kedima often run out of funds. Try ATMs on Rue Fatima Zohra, near Bab Ksour, or in the ville nouvelle.

The medina souqs are still very much a cash society. Only larger shops will accept credit and debit cards.

Many midrange and top-end accommodations accept payment in euros.

BCMI Bank (Map p56; Ave Mohammed V; ⊙8am-6pm Mon-Fri)
Société Générale (Map p56; Ave Mohammed V; ⊙8am-6pm Mon-Fri)
Voyages Schwartz (Map p61; ☑0524 43 74 69; 22 Rue Moulay Ali; ⊙8.30am-noon & 2.30-6.30pm Mon-Fri, 8.30am-noon Sat) Represents American Express.

MEDICAL SERVICES
A list of pharmacies operating night hours (known as *Pharmacie de Garde*) is posted on or beside the door of all chemists. For public holidays, the list will include pharmacies that are open during the day. For an online list and location map, refer to www.syndicat-pharmaciens-marrakech.com.

Pharmacie Centrale (Map p61; ☑0524 43 01 58; 166 Blvd Mohammed V; ⊙9am-7pm) The go-to place for excellent advice, personal care and a reliable stock of medication.
Pharmacie de l'Unité (Map p61; ☑0524 43 59 82; Ave des Nations Unies; ⊙8.30am-11pm)
Clinique Internationale (☑0524 36 95 95; www.clinique-internationale-marrakech.com; Bab Ighli, off Av Guemassa) This central private hospital is recommended by Marrakesh's foreign residents. It's located east of the Menara Gardens, just off the road to the airport.
Polyclinique du Sud (Map p61; ☑0524 44 79 99; 2 Rue de Yougoslavie; ⊙24hr) Well-regarded private hospital.

POST & TELEPHONE
Public card phones are widely available, especially near Rue de Bab Agnaou in the medina and

Ave Mohammed V in Guéliz. Cards can be bought from news vendors and *téléboutiques*.

DHL (Map p61; ☏ 0524 43 76 48; www.dhl-ma.com; 113 Ave Abdelkrim el-Khattabi; ⊗8.30am-12.30pm & 2.30-6.30pm Mon-Fri, 8.30am-12.30pm Sat) International courier service; insurance subject to surcharge.

FedEx (Map p61; ☏ 0524 31 40 64; 113 Ave Abdelkrim el-Khattabi; ⊗8.15am-12.15pm & 2.30-6.30pm Mon-Fri, 8.15am-12.30pm Sat) International courier service.

Main Post Office (Map p61; ☏ 0524 43 19 63; Place du 16 Novembre; ⊗8am-4pm Mon-Fri, 8.30am-noon Sat) Poste restante is at window 3 and the parcel office is around the corner on Ave Hassan II. The section for stamps and foreign exchange stays open until 8pm Monday to Friday and to 6pm on Saturday.

Post Office (Map p56; Rue de Bab Agnaou; ⊗8am-noon & 3-6pm Mon-Fri) A convenient branch in the medina.

TOURIST INFORMATION

Office National Marocain du Tourisme (Map p61; ONMT; ☏ 0524 43 61 79; Pl Abdel Moumen ben Ali, Guéliz; ⊗8.30am-noon & 2.30-8pm Mon-Thu, 8.30-11.30am & 3-6.30pm Fri) offers pamphlets but little in the way of actual information.

Most hotels and riads can provide free maps of the city.

USEFUL WEBSITES

Lonely Planet (www.lonelyplanet.com/morocco/marrakesh) Destination information, hotel bookings, traveller forum and more.

Marrakech Pocket (www.marrakechpocket.com) Marrakesh's monthly French-language listings guide. Also stocked in most hotels and bars.

Vivre Marrakech (www.vivre-marrakech.com) Events, new openings and listings (all in French). The website's free quarterly guide (in French and English) is available in many hotels and some businesses.

❶ Getting There & Away

AIR

Small, modern **Marrakech Menara Airport** (RAK; ☏ 0524 44 79 10; www.marrakech.airport-authority.com; ⊗information desk 8am-6pm; 🛈) is located 6km southwest of town. Due to the growing number of international and charter flights serving Marrakesh, the airport is expanding and a second terminal is currently being built.

In the arrivals hall you'll find currency exchange, ATMs, an information desk and phone providers where you can equip yourself with a Moroccan SIM card. The currency exchange office stays open until the last flight for the night has arrived.

Royal Air Maroc (Map p61; RAM; ☏ 0524 43 62 05, call centre 0890 00 08 00; www.royalair-maroc.com; 197 Ave Mohammed V; ⊗8.30am-12.20pm & 2.30-7pm) Has several flights daily to and from Casablanca (one-way from about Dh800, 55 minutes), where you can pick up domestic and international connections.

BUS

The **CTM bus station** (Map p52; ☏ 0524 43 44 02; www.ctm.ma; Rue Abou Bakr Seddiq; ⊗6am-10pm) is located southwest of the train station (about 15 minutes on foot). There's not much at the station in the way of facilities, beyond a smoky 24-hour cafe with stuttering wi-fi.

A taxi from the station to Djemaa el-Fna shouldn't cost more than Dh30 (drivers will often quote Dh50).

Supratours (Map p52; ☏ 0524 43 55 25; www.oncf.ma; Ave Hassan II) is located west of the train station, in the old station building. The station has a cafe and a room where you can check baggage (Dh10 per day, open 6am to 10pm). Bus services connect to train departure and arrival times.

The parking lot in front of the Supratours office is the arrival and departure point for most international buses, including **CTM** buses to/from Paris (adult/child Dh2730/2060, 48 hours, Tues and Fri).

Taxis wait in the Supratours parking lot.

The **Gare Routière** (Map p52; Bus Station; ☏ 0524 43 39 33; Bab Doukkala) is where non-CTM and Supratours buses arrive and depart from, just outside the city walls at Bab Doukkala, a 25-minute walk or Dh5- to- Dh10 taxi ride from Djemaa el-Fna. The large main building is lined with booths covering local and long-distance destinations; get tickets for early-morning departures the day before as some booths aren't open first thing.

CAR

If you're coming into town with your own wheels, try to arrive during daylight. Driving through the busy, chaotic traffic at night is stressful for first-time visitors. At all times be alert for scooters, horse carriages, donkeys, pedestrians, and other drivers who rarely obey road rules.

Local car-rental companies often offer more competitive deals than international operators, with quoted rates starting at around Dh350 per day with air-con and unlimited mileage. For 4WD rentals, count on Dh950 to Dh1300 per day with minimal insurance; the top end of the range reflects the largest vehicles, which can carry up to seven people. You should be able to negotiate a 10% to 20% discount in the low season (late October to mid-December and mid-January to the end of February).

A car with a driver starts at an additional Dh150 per day within Marrakesh and Dh200 per day for excursions outside Marrakesh.

International agencies Avis, Hertz, Europcar and Budget all have desks at the airport.

KAT (Map p61; ☑ 0524 43 01 75; www. katcar-marrakech.com; 68 Blvd Mohammed Zerktouni; basic/with air-con per day €24/32; ⊙ 8am-9pm) Friendly, English-speaking agency.

La Plaza Car (Map p61; ☑ 0524 42 18 01; www. laplazacar.com; Immeuble 141, 23 Rue Mohammed el-Beqal; per day from €25; ⊙ 8.30am-noon & 2.30-6.30pm Mon-Sat)

Lhasnaoui Rent (Map p52; ☑ 0524 31 24 15; www.lhasnaouirent.com; cnr Blvd Allal el-Fassi & Ave Yacoub el-Mansour, 15 Immeuble el-Omairi; per day from €25; ⊙ 9am-5pm Mon-Sat)

TAXI

Grands taxis (Rue Uqba bin Nafaa) and minibuses to destinations in the High Atlas, including Asni (Dh30), Ouirgane (Dh40) and Setti Fatma (Dh40), depart from Rue Uqba bin Nafaa, alongside the medina wall, a short walk from Djemaa el-Fna.

Grands taxis (off Ave du 11 Janvier) serving destinations further afield, including those bound for Agadir (Dh150), Azilal (Dh75), Beni Mellal (Dh110), Demnate (Dh70), Essaouira (Dh90), Ouarzazate (Dh120) and Taroudannt (Dh110), gather on a parking lot just outside Bab Doukkala. Prices can fluctuate by Dh10 to Dh20 depending on demand.

TRAIN

Marrakesh's **train station** (Map p52; ☑ 0524 44 77 68; www.oncf.ma; cnr Ave Hassan II & Blvd Mohammed VI) is big, organised and convenient, with ATMs, cafes and fast-food outlets.

Taxis wait just outside. To Djemaa el-Fna it's no more than Dh20 on the meter (Dh30 at night) but drivers are notorious for not putting the meter on. Dh50 is the usual quoted price.

ℹ Getting Around

Compact and flat, Marrakesh was made for walking. The medina's skinny maze of souqs and alleys

CTM Bus Services From Marrakesh

DESTINATION	PRICE (DH)	DURATION (HR)	FREQUENCY (DAILY)
Agadir	120/150 regular/premium	3½-4	17
Casablanca	90/130 regular/premium	3½	15
Er-Rachidia	180	10	1
Essaouira	80	3½	2
Fez	185-190	8-9	6
Laâyoune	350	14-15½	7
Ouarzazate	90	4½	5
Tan Tan	225	9	8
Tiznit	140-150	5½	8
Zagora	155	7½	2

Supratours Bus Services From Marrakesh

DESTINATION	PRICE (DH)	DURATION (HR)	FREQUENCY (DAILY)
Agadir	110/150 regular/comfort plus	4	11
Dakhla	490	23	2
Essaouira	80/110 regular/comfort plus	3½	6
Laâyoune	350	15	6
Ouarzazate	80	4½	3
Tan Tan	205	10	7
Zagora	140	7¾	1

> ### ⓘ FIRST TIME ARRIVING IN MARRAKESH
>
> If it's your first time in Marrakesh, and particularly if you're staying in a medina riad or out in the *palmeraie*, it makes sense to pay extra and organise a private airport transfer to your accommodation. Most riads charge around Dh150 to Dh170 for the service which, if you're heading into the medina, includes being met at the taxi drop-off point (usually Djemaa el-Fna) and being walked to the door.

can only be explored on foot and central Guéliz is only a 20- to 25-minute stroll from Djemaa el-Fna.

TO/FROM THE AIRPORT

Airport bus 19 (one way/return Dh30/50; ⊘ 6.15am-9.30pm) runs a circular route, every 30 minutes, between the airport and central Marrakesh. From the airport, it stops at Pl de Foucauld (a one-minute walk to Djemaa el-Fna), then runs along Ave Mohammed V via Bab Nkob (alight for Bab Doukkala) to Guéliz (passing Pl du 16 Novembre and the train station) before heading back to the airport.

A petit taxi to central Marrakesh from the airport (6km) should be no more than Dh70, but you will most likely have extreme difficulty convincing the driver of this. Late at night, with no other options available, drivers will typically quote between Dh120 and Dh150.

BUS

Local buses are run by **Alsa** (www.alsa.ma; fares Dh4). There's a semi-helpful route map on Alsa's website. Buses heading for the ville nouvelle stop at Pl de Foucauld in front of Djemaa el-Fna. Services start around 6am and finish between 9.30pm and 10pm with buses on most routes running every 15 to 20 minutes.

Key bus lines include the following:

Bus 1 Kasbah–Guéliz–Bab Doukkala (via Djemaa el-Fna and Ave Mohammed V)

Bus 8 & 10 Djemaa el-Fna–train station

Bus 11 Bab Doukkala–Djemaa el-Fna–Menara Gardens

Bus 12 Jardin Majorelle–Bab Doukkala–Hivernage

Bus 16 Djemaa el-Fna–Bab Doukkala–Guéliz–northwest suburbs

CALÈCHES

These green horse-drawn carriages congregate at Pl de Foucauld next to the Djemaa el-Fna. They're a pleasant way to get around, if you avoid the rush hours (8am, noon and 5.30pm to 7.30pm). State-fixed rates of Dh120 per hour apply (rates are posted inside the carriage). Expect a tour of the ramparts to take 1½ hours.

Animal welfare charity SPANA (www.spana. org) works with Marrakesh's calèche drivers, monitoring horse welfare and maintaining water troughs along popular carriage routes.

CAR & MOTORCYCLE

If your accommodation is in the medina, there are guarded car parks on Rue Fatima Zohra (near Djemaa el-Fna), Rue Riad Zitoun el-Jedid (near Bahia Palace) and Rue Abbes Sebti (behind the Koutoubia Mosque). In Guéliz there's a secure underground car park on Av Mohammed V, opposite the post office. Expect to pay Dh20/40 during the day/24 hours.

In Guéliz some roads have parking meters (Dh2 per hour). If you find street parking without a meter, a guardian will expect a Dh10 tip for keeping an eye on your car; look for the guy in the blue coat and pay your tip afterwards.

If you're feeling brave and/or foolhardy, you might join the fray on a scooter or motorcycle. Rentals are available from **Marrakech Roues** (Map p56; ☑ 0663 06 18 92; www.marrakech-roues.com; Imm Roux, 3 Rue Bani Marine; per hr/half-day/full-day Dh50/80/160; ⊘ 9am-1pm & 2-8.30pm Mon & Tue, 9.30am-7.30pm Wed, Thu, Sat & Sun, 9am-12.30 & 2.30-9pm Fri).

TAXI

Metered rates for the city's beige petits taxis around town are between Dh8 and Dh20 with a Dh10 surcharge at night. Many drivers will insist their meter is 'broken' and will quote higher prices, particularly taxis waiting at stands that get a lot of tourist business (the airport, train station, Djemaa el-Fna and Jardin Majorelle are notorious for this). You can usually get a metered rate – or at least, a better quoted price – by flagging a taxi down from the street.

If your party numbers more than three, you must take a grand taxi, which requires negotiation.

AROUND MARRAKESH

Ouirgane

When Marrakesh is baking 60km to the northeast, and tourists and day-trippers are swamping Ourika, Marrakshis sneak off to mellow Ouirgane for High Atlas breezes, peaceful hikes through unspoilt villages and romantic country retreats. For those crossing the Tizi n'Test to or from

Taroudannt, Ouirgane makes an excellent stopover en route to Marrakesh.

🛏 Sleeping

★ Ouirgane Ecolodge   GUESTHOUSE €€
(☑ 0668 76 01 65; www.ouirgane-ecolodge.com; r Dh400-800; ✱🐾🛜🏊) 🥾 For a peaceful escape from the Marrakesh bustle, it's hard to fault this environmentally minded retreat. Rooms boast a warm Berber design, and the lounge is a fine place for a meal or to curl up fireside with a good book. You can also use the hammam (€5), lounge by the pool, hire mountain bikes or take scenic walks in the surrounding countryside.

There are only four rooms, so reserve well ahead.

★ L'Oliveraie
de Marigha   BOUTIQUE HOTEL €€€
(☑ 0524 48 42 81; www.oliveraie-de-marigha. com; Km 59 R203, Douar Marigha; d/ste Dh900/1300; 🅿✱🛜🏊) Weekend escapees come all the way from Casa to lunch on wood-fired pizza in this olive grove and float in the pool admiring High Atlas views. Chic bungalows in subtle earth tones sit amid the trees and are equipped with walnut furniture, double-glazed French doors and shiny, marble bathrooms. Children are made welcome with a separate pool, mini-golf and other amusements (ping-pong, petanque).

Domaine Malika   GUESTHOUSE €€€
(☑ 0524 48 59 21; www.domainemalika.com; Rte d'Amizmiz, Douar Marigha; d from Dh1390, ste Dh1800-2100; 🅿✱🛜🏊) The perfect antidote to inward-facing medina riads, this modern villa with only seven rooms is all about the great outdoors. Floor-to-ceiling patio doors overlook a pool shaded by drooping pepper trees, while 1st-floor rooms enjoy views of High Atlas peaks from double aspect windows and private terraces. The decor, likewise, is modern with a slight vintage vibe and a zesty colour palette. Service and food are impeccable. It's about 6km north of Ouirgane.

THE HIGH ATLAS
Welcome to North Africa's highest mountain range, known by local Berbers as 'Idraren Draren' (Mountains of Mountains), and a trekker's paradise from spring through to autumn. The High Atlas runs diagonally across Morocco for almost 1000km, encircling Marrakesh to the south and east from the Atlantic Coast just north of Agadir to Khenifra in the northeast. Its saw-toothed Jurassic peaks act as a weather barrier between the mild, Mediterranean climate to the north and the encroaching Sahara to the south.

In its highest reaches, snow falls regularly from September to May, allowing for winter sports in Oukaïmeden, while year-round rivers flow northwards towards Marrakesh creating a network of fertile valleys – the Zat, Ourika, Mizane and Ouirgane. Happiest of all are the secluded valleys of the central High Atlas, which include Zaouiat Ahansal, Aït Bougomez, Aït Bououli and Aït Blel.

In the High Atlas the main language is the Berber dialect of Tashelhit, with some pockets of Tamazight.

Central High Atlas
The road less travelled lies to the east of Marrakesh in the central High Atlas, accessible through the regional hub of Demnate. Here a chalky mass of muscular mountains, weatherworn canyons and sculpted gorges (which provide the best climbing in the country) hide fertile valleys, many inaccessible to vehicles until a few years ago. Several peaks in the area exceed 4000m including Irhil M'Goun, which at 4071m is the highest point.

Demnate   دمنات
POP 24,000
The once-grand Glaoui kasbah and mud-brick ramparts have been left to crumble, yet Demnate's fascinating interfaith heritage has survived. At the heart of town is a *mellah* (Jewish quarter), with an entry about 150m on the right after the town's main gate. It's a lively town to explore, though most visitors are only passing through en route to the picturesque gorge of Imi n'Ifri to the east.

The 100-year-old olive groves dotting hillsides around Demnate produce Morocco's best olive oil, with trace mineral salts, a golden colour and subtle woodsy flavours that compare favourably to Tuscan oils. Almonds are another renowned local product, and the flowering of the local orchards makes March a lovely time to visit.

WORTH A TRIP

GREAT ESCAPES: THE AGAFAY DESERT

If you don't have time to traverse mountain passes, you can take an overnight trip to the Agafay Desert: a rough, dry, moon-like expanse 40km southwest of Marrakesh down the Rte d'Amizmiz. This is a favourite playground for weekending Marrakshis who come for horse-riding, dune-gazing and canoeing on Lalla Takerkoust, a man-made reservoir. In spring wheat and wildflowers predominate; in summer and autumn it really does look like the desert.

Desert retreats are the name of the game here. They're all set up for relaxing, unwinding and making the most of the harshly beautiful surrounding countryside.

Unless you have your own wheels, getting to and around the Agafay Desert area is near on impossible. All the resorts in the area can arrange pick-up and drop-off transfers to and from Marrakesh.

Here are four of our favourites:

La Pause (☑0661 30 64 94; www.lapause-marrakech.com; Douar Lmih Laroussiéne, N 31°26.57, W 008°10.31; d per person incl full board in safari tent/lodge €135/200; ☒) Skip off the grid to this desert getaway where you can experience the stark, visceral beauty of Morocco's countryside. This is a chill-out zone for grown-ups, where electricity and smartphone checking is out, hammock swinging and nomad-tent dining is in, and you bed down in rustic-chic bungalows complete with candles, *tataoui* (woven reed) ceilings and Berber carpets.

Scarabeo (☑0662 80 08 23; www.scarabeo-camp.com; d/ste/f incl half-board Dh2055/2755/3080; ⊘closed mid-Jun–mid-Sep) Tuareg nomads never saw camping like this. Scarabeo's white nomad-style tents, complete with carpets and comfy beds, sit amid the barren Agafay desert with panoramic views stretching to the Atlas Mountains. During the day spend your time trekking, riding camels, or exploring by 4WD; at night simply look up for unforgettable stargazing.

Jnane Tihihit (☑0524 38 73 52; www.riad-t.com/jnane-tihihit; Douar Makhfamane; d incl breakfast from Dh940; ℙ☒) Relax as nature intended, on an organic farmstead with solar-heated, whitewashed pisé bungalows amid pomegranate trees. Foodies can tend saffron gardens and learn to make couscous (meals around Dh175), while kids can go riding or head out to the lake-front beach or lounge by the chemical-free pool. It's located about 45km southwest of Marrakesh off the P2009.

Terre des Étoiles (☑0524 44 73 75; www.terredesetoiles.co.uk; N 31°27.50, W 08°11.65; per person incl half-board Dh700-950) Get away from it all at this peaceful spot amid the lunar terrain with fine views of the distant Atlas. Lodging is in one of 10 spacious luxury tents, complete with comfy mattresses, quality furnishings and en suite. You can help out in the garden, head out on an excursion (walking, camel rides, mountain biking) or simply enjoy a life unplugged, beneath star-filled skies by night. It's located about 34km southwest of Marrakesh, off the R212.

🎉 Festivals & Events

Hamdouchi Moussem RELIGIOUS
(⊘Sep) Demnate has two *zawiyas* (Islamic religious shrines), making the annual Hamdouchi Moussem in September twice as raucous. Pilgrims visiting each *zawiya* dance to a different rhythm in an all-day music festival in the town centre before going their separate ways in three-hour parades to the *zawiyas*. Sometimes the *moussem* (festival) peaks in blood purification, with dancers cutting themselves on the scalp in dramatic acts of ritual cleansing.

Jewish Moussem RELIGIOUS
(⊘Jul) Hundreds of Jewish families from Morocco, France, Israel, Canada and the US arrive each July for the Jewish *moussem*, a weeklong mystical event said to offer miracle cures.

🛏 Sleeping & Eating

★Kasbah Timdaf GUESTHOUSE €€€
(☑0523 50 71 78; www.kasbah-timdaf.com; N 31°46.50, W 007°01.13; s/d Dh715/880; ℙ🛜) ✐
A cosy eco-castle 15 minutes from Demnate on the road to Azilal, with artful rooms warmed by vintage wood-burning stoves

and snazzy *tadelakt* (smooth, lustrous lime plaster) bathrooms. It may seem palatial, but this stone and mudbrick kasbah is a working farm surrounded by almond and olive groves, providing inspired Mediterranean-Berber meals (Dh110 to Dh190) on a vine-draped terrace with expansive views.

Owners Jacqueline and Yannick can organise cycling, trekking and fishing trips around Demnate. Transfers to Marrakesh and Ouzoud are available.

Restaurant-Café Itranes   MOROCCAN €
(quarter/whole chicken with chips or bread Dh25/75; ⏱ noon-11pm) Some 300m after the city gate on the left, this sidewalk restaurant serves a mean rotisserie chicken.

Café-Restaurant Al Jazeera   BERBER €€
(🖉 0524 45 82 39; 3-course menu from Dh130; ⏱ 8am-8pm) You have to call ahead to eat here, but it's worth the effort. The meal begins with savoury seasonal salads that are a prelude to Demnate's signature fine-grain couscous, decadently dressed with local olive oil and toasted local almonds. Afterwards, enjoy a refreshing dip in the courtyard pool (open in summer) and an excellent espresso in the garden. It's just near the *gare routière* (central bus station).

You can also come just for a swim (Dh20).

🛍 Shopping

If you don't happen to be in town on Sunday, when the souq is on, you can shop for local ceramics at the potteries northeast of town in the village of Bouglou; turn right at the mosque and head 4km off-road.

Sunday Souq   MARKET
The weekly Sunday souq, 10 minutes south of town by foot, is an opportunity to taste-test local olives, olive oils and almonds and browse Demnate's local woodwork and yellow-glazed pottery painted in henna.

Miel d'Atlas   FOOD
Honey that's considered rare elsewhere abounds in the hills around Demnate. You'll notice a Miel d'Atlas sign with a bee on it at the *hanout* (grocer) on your right on the main road east out of town towards Imi n'Ifri: approach the counter and ask the grocer to let you sample local honey.

The mountain herb and wildflower honey is a standout with its peppery, thyme flavour, while the *zriga* (a local blue wildflower) honey tastes fruity, almost like guava.

ⓘ Getting There & Away

Grands taxis to Marrakesh (Dh60) and Azilal (Dh37.50) leave from the main gate in Demnate.

Buses leave for Marrakesh (Dh40, two hours) from 6am to 9pm and to Azilal (Dh30, one hour) from 7am to noon from the bus station (take the road to the right before the town gate and turn left at the roundabout). To reach nearby Imi n'Ifri, you'll need to take a taxi (Dh40 for the whole taxi).

Imi-n'Ifri

Just 6km east of Demnate along the R307 is Imi n'Ifri ('Grotto's Mouth' in Berber), a natural travertine bridge that formed over a gorge 1.8 million years ago. The two sides of the bridge are said to represent two local lovers whose families kept them apart, so this Romeo and Juliet held hands and turned to stone. You can walk down into the gorge and through this toothy maw by yourself – the paths are clearly marked by the bridge and post office and comprise 300 steps down – but you might want to pay a small tip (Dh20) to a local guide to help you over some tricky boulders and explain local lore.

On the southern side of the gorge is a spring with water rich in natural mineral salts, where brides come for pre-wedding rites; in summer you may hear women singing and playing drums and tambourines at Berber bachelorette parties. On the other side of the gorge is a freshwater spring said to cure acne, which explains the number of teens hanging out here. Pass under the bridge, and suddenly you're in a *Lord of the Rings* setting, with flocks of crows swooping down from dramatic stalactites overhead.

🛏 Sleeping & Eating

A few enterprising locals offer tea and snacks at plastic tables right inside the gorge. Otherwise, most visitors take their meals at their guesthouses or in Demnate.

Gite Kasbah Imi n'Ifri   GUESTHOUSE €
(🖉 0662 10 51 68; thamitrek1@hotmail.com; r per person Dh150, with demi-pension Dh220) A good budget option just a few minutes' stroll from the top of the gorge, this family-run spot has basic rooms with shared bathrooms. The best catch a bit of breeze and have mountain views. Full-day guided hikes (Dh300) are available.

★ Tizouit   GUESTHOUSE €€
(🖉 0658 34 61 48; www.tizouit.ma; Aït Oumghar; r Dh600-660, tr Dh850; P 🛜 ☃) ⟋ Stepped into the hillside overlooking Demnate and

shaded by flourishing gardens filled with banana, pomegranate and olive trees, Tizouit is a labour of love and it shows. Henri and Nadja have created an idyllic escape in this superb ecolodge with its eight individual cottage rooms (each with its own private terrace), natural biological pond, and luxurious native planting scheme.

A relaxed, Euro-ethnic vibe – combining raffia rugs, Moroccan antiques and textiles and squashy European sofas – characterises the living areas and rooms where patio doors open onto sun-kissed views of Demnate's ancient olive groves. Activities are naturally laid-back: long, leisurely walks along ancient irrigation channels to Imi n'Ifri's grotto (Tizouit's four-legged assistant, Charlie, may come with you), or treks in dinosaur footprints at Aït Blel.

ℹ️ Getting There & Away

If you're staying at a guesthouse near Imi n'Ifri, you'll be able to walk to the gorge. Buses and grands taxis stop at Demnate, where you'll need to take an onward taxi to Imi n'Ifri (around Dh40).

Cascades d'Ouzoud

Northeast of Demnate, just 167km from Marrakesh and a world away from the city heat, are the **Cascades d'Ouzoud**, one of the most popular day trips from Marrakesh for tourists and Moroccans alike. The Oued Ouzoud drops 110m into the canyon of Oued el-Abid in three-tiered waterfalls, and the view only gets better as you descend into the cool of the canyon, past the late-afternoon rainbow mists to the pools at its base. The falls are most dramatic from March to June when there's more water, but young Moroccans often camp here in summer on terraces facing the falls.

To reach the falls, walk past the signs for Riad Cascades d'Ouzoud towards the precipice, where converging paths wind down towards the falls.

⊙ Sights & Activities

Locals might lead you into the gorge for a few dirham, but you can follow well-trodden paths to viewing points and down into the gorge. Along the way, Barbary apes clamour for attention – though a signpost advises not to feed them.

At the bottom, you can hike further along the riverbed to more peaceful pools where you can swim, or cross the river to another path

for extended hikes. To see the picturesque Berber village of **Tanaghmelt**, follow the path by the lower pools past a farmhouse and up the slopes for about 1.5km. For longer treks, follow the course of the river to the **Gramaa Nakrouine caves** (two hours) and the **Gorges of Oued el-Abid** (another two hours).

🛏️ Sleeping & Eating

You'll find a growing number of inexpensive guesthouses on the path leading down to the falls. There are also many Moroccans that camp here, but with the amount of garbage left behind, these sites aren't recommended.

Most cafes flanking the falls offer meals comprising of salad, tagine, chicken and chips for Dh60 to Dh80.

★**Camping Zebra** CAMPGROUND, GUESTHOUSE €
(📞 0666 32 85 76; www.campingzebra.com; N 32°00.351, W 006°42.177; 2-person pitch with/without electricity Dh105/85; r with/without bathroom Dh400/250; 🅿️ 🛜 😺) After four years overlanding in their B&W-striped 4WD, Renata and Paul landed in Ouzoud and decided to create their own dream campground. The result is this welcoming mixed site with tent pitches, four garden rooms and a mini kasbah with four en suites.

The decor is as cheerful as your hosts, with brightly painted rooms and a communal *khaima* (tent) decked out in multicoloured Moroccan textiles where you can order meals. If you want to arrange activities, Renata and Paul can put you in touch with guides from Ouzoud. Get in touch before setting out. Note that Camping Zebra was listed for sale when we last passed through.

Hotel Chellal Ouzoud GUESTHOUSE €
(📞 0523 42 91 80; www.hotelchellalouzoud.com; s/d Dh250/350; 🛜) A simple guesthouse with colourful, reasonably priced rooms on the path heading down to the falls (about 400m walk from the top). It's a friendly spot, with some English spoken and a small patio for guests.

Riad Cascades d'Ouzoud GUESTHOUSE €€
(📞 0662 14 38 04; www.ouzoud.com; r Dh450-810; ❄️🛜) This stylish mudbrick guesthouse located just 30m from the top of the cascades offers the best accommodation in Ouzoud, along with a range of activities in the surrounding area. Solar-heated show-

OFF THE BEATEN TRACK

ROAD-TRIPPING DEMNATE TO AÏT BOUGOMEZ

Follow the road that forks to the left at Imi n'Ifri into the breathtaking Aït Blel Valley, which connects to Aït Bougomez Valley via Aït Bououli Valley. In spring, Aït Blel is like an animated Impressionist painting, with the breeze rippling golden wheat fields dotted with red poppies.

The road here is fairly new, so the entire valley seems untouched. Mountains are striped gold, orange and purple, with green crops sprouting from stone-walled terraces. Follow the road 6km from Imi n'Ifri to the village of **Iouaridene** and you're in prehistoric territory. In a fenced area, just off the left side of the road, you'll find what geologists claim are **dinosaur footprints** dating from the mid-Jurassic period, about 170 million years ago (if the gate is locked, ask at the nearby house for a key). Quadruped and carnivorous dinosaurs once roamed this area, and local kids do a mean impersonation of a T-rex.

From Aït Blel the only way is up, east over the **Tizi-n-Oubadou pass** (2173m) towards Aït Bououli, Aït Bougomez and beyond. It's a spectacular drive through mountain oak forests set against striking, vertically striped sedimentary rock formations formed during the Triassic period some 230 million years ago. You'll need a 4WD and dry weather (thunderstorms and flash floods often wipe out bridges) between April and November.

The road sometimes narrows to one lane, but it's paved or graded the entire way. The cliff-edge villages and centuries-old way of life you'll encounter make it worth the additional two hours it takes to reach Aït Bougomez, instead of going the faster route via Aït Mohammed. Gas up before you go: the biggest town is Khemis Aït Blel, with a Tuesday souq and stalls selling sundries and occasionally petrol.

Near the Tizi-n-Oubadou pass, **Gîte Tizi-n-Oubadou** (☑ 0661 44 36 02; www.gitetizinoubadou. com; s/d Dh170/270) offers wraparound views over meticulously trimmed terraces with carob and almond groves. Its five rooms are quite simple but well maintained. If you call as you leave Demnate in the morning, it may be able to provide lunch (Dh60 to Dh90).

ers, ceilings painted with Berber talismans, and family-style welcomes from local staff make you feel part of the scenery. Six rooms also have fireplaces (a welcome feature in winter).

⊙ Getting There & Away

From Marrakesh, it's easiest to get transport direct to Azilal, from where grands taxis run when full to Ouzoud (Dh30/150 per person/taxi). Head back to Azilal before 4pm, when taxis become scarce and drive hard bargains. To avoid backtracking, you can also jump off at the Ouzoud turn-off, 22km west of Azilal and grab a taxi from here (around Dh12).

Azilal أزيلال

POP 29,000

This regional centre is mainly of interest to travellers as a handy transport hub between Demnate, the Cascades d'Ouzoud and the Zaouiat Ahansal and Aït Bougomez Valleys. This is also the last place you'll be able to stock up on cash in the area; it's a good idea to get petrol here too. There's a Thursday souq.

⊙ Sights

Complexe Artisanal MARKET
(⊙9am–4pm Mon-Sat) Right across from the town hall, this market is a fine place to explore the Atlas craft traditions.

🛏 Sleeping & Eating

Hotel Ouzoud GUESTHOUSE €
(☑0523 45 91 53, 0678 90 68 56; Ave Hassan II; s/d without bathroom Dh70/120) A good-value option in the centre of town, with simple but pleasantly set rooms and a small lounge. The best chambers have elaborate ceilings and appealing views. In the works is a new upstairs room with air-con, bathroom and TV (singles/doubles Dh120/200). There's a casual eatery downstairs.

Ajabli GUESTHOUSE €
(☑0523 45 84 04; Hay Oued Edahab Rue 22; s/tw Dh60/120; ☎) Rooms are spotless and freshly painted at this newish spot one block up from the main street. Couples are out of luck as it's mostly twin beds here, and shared bathrooms for all.

Ibnou Ziad Restaurant
MOROCCAN €

(Ave Hassan II; meals Dh40-60; ⊘11am-8pm) A good pit stop for a lunch of rotisserie chicken and chips, though football fans might be delayed by matches shown on TV here. It's on the main street, across from a small square.

ⓘ Information

You'll find a number of banks along Ave Hassan II, including Attijariwafa next to the police station.

Assotech (2nd fl, Ave Hassan II; per hr Dh5; ⊘9am-12.30pm & 2.30-10pm Mon-Thu & Sat, 2.30-10pm Fri) One of the last internet outposts before heading into Aït Bougomez is above the Ben Alal Pharmacy on the main drag.

ⓘ Getting There & Away

Three daily buses run from Azilal to Marrakesh (Dh60, 3½ hours) and Demnate (Dh20, 1½ hours). There's also a 6pm bus to Agadir (Dh150) via Marrakesh. Buses and taxis currently depart from a station behind the main mosque, but plans are afoot to open a new bus station on Ave Hassan II, about 2km west of the centre (and closer to Ouzoud).

Plenty of grands taxis run from Marrakesh to Azilal (Dh90) and, less frequently, from Azilal to Demnate (Dh35). In the afternoon, when full, local minibuses depart from Azilal to Zaouiat Ahansal (Dh50, around three hours) and Tabant (Dh40, three hours), the main town in Aït Bougomez.

Zaouiat Ahansal

Fantastically remote and fiercely independent, Zaouiat Ahansal was founded in the 13th century by travelling Islamic scholar Sidi Said Ahansal, who, according to local legend, was instructed to establish a religious school wherever his cat leapt off his mule. Happily for Sidi Ahansal that location sits astride a prominent crossroads between the Central High Atlas and the plains of Marrakesh and is blessed with fresh water and abundant grazing frequented by the powerful Aït Abdi and Aït Atta nomads.

As a result, the region prospered materially and intellectually. Libraries, religious schools, saints' houses and highly decorative *ighirmin* (collective granaries) testify to this wealthy cultural heritage. Even today a significant number of pilgrims continue to visit the region during the Islamic month of *shawaal,* bearing gifts of clothing and food for Saint Sidi Said Ahansal and his descendants.

Activities

Arriving in Zaouiat Ahansal, cross the bridge towards the mudbrick *douar* (village) atop a steep hill; this structure once housed the entire 300-person community. You can stay here or in the nearby villages of Amezrai or Agoudim (tell the bus driver which village you're getting off at). The village of Taghia is a further three-hour trek upstream and is located at the base of a stunning limestone

---

WORTH A TRIP

KAYAKING AT BIN EL-OUIDANE

From Azilal it's possible to take a detour to the huge dam of Bin el-Ouidane. The dam provides the majority of the electricity in the region, but more importantly it's the location for the increasingly popular 10-day kayak school of **Morocco Adventure & Rafting** (p66). Held once a year between April and May, the school spends two days on the lake running through the basics (no previous experience required) before launching off into the Ahansal river gorge. What follows are seven spectacular days of running rapids through 8ft-wide gorges, river camping and turtle-spotting before returning in a loop to the lake.

Aside from being awesome fun, it's a wonderful way to visit the dramatic Cathédrale des Rochers and Ahansal Valley, and affords a dramatically different perspective of the sheer rock gorges from the valley floor. Groups are limited to 12 people and are accompanied by two guides, a safety kayaker and a photographer. Sleeping bags are also available for hire if you don't want to carry your own. Exclusive trips can also be organised for a minimum of six people.

A shorter, three-day rafting excursion down the Ahansal is also possible, as is canyoning, although a good level of fitness is required for the latter.

cirque. You'll need to hire a mule to reach it (Dh120 including muleteer).

With the tarmac road from Azilal arriving in 2013, Zaouiat Ahansal is only now making a name for itself among serious climbers and adventurous trekkers. To explore the region's dramatic scenery and sights, it's advisable to hire a local, licensed mountain guide (Dh300 to Dh400 per day). Note, though, that these guides are only certified in trekking, hiking and multiday camping excursions – they are not climbing guides.

Tagoujimt n'Tsouiannt · TREKKING

At 853m high, Tagoujimt n'Tsouiannt is the highest, scalable cliff face, accessible also by trek via the aptly named Tire-Bouchon (Corkscrew) Pass, as hikers must 'corkscrew' themselves through a tight and winding series of stone and wood stacks to reach the top.

Other worthwhile local treks include a circumnavigation of Oujdad, the muscular rock formation that defines the valley, and a short walk upstream to 'The Source', an impressive waterfall that marks the start of the Ahansal River.

Kristoffer Erickson · CLIMBING

(day climbs €375) Part-time resident, the North Face athlete and international climbing guide Kristoffer Erickson can be hired to help you scale the region's technical rock face. In the winter months, Erickson also guides single or multiday backcountry ski tours in the surrounding peaks. You can contact him through Atlas Cultural Adventures (p90).

Historic Walking Tours · WALKING

(www.atlasculturalfoundation.org; half-day tour Dh350) Zaouiat Ahansal is blessed with an abundance of historical and natural sites: old saint's houses, places of pilgrimage and hand-tended community gardens. For a more in-depth tour, an Atlas Cultural Foundation (p90) staff member can be hired for half-day and multiday tours of the region and their community projects.

🛏 Sleeping

Advance reservations are recommended for the months of March through to June, and for September and October.

Kasbah Amezray · GUESTHOUSE €

(☑ 0666 53 10 02; www.kasbah-amezray.com; Amezrai; dm/r per person incl half-board Dh150/250;) A fine option in Amezrai, this 12-room *gîte* (hostel) has cosy rooms (five with en suite) with exposed stone walls and wood-

beam ceilings. It's set in front of a photogenic granary, which you can visit. It's a good place to arrange treks, rockclimbing and 4WD trips. Transfers to Marrakesh are available.

Gîte Ahmed El Hansali · GÎTE D'ÉTAPE €

(☑ 0678 53 88 82; amahdar.ahmed@gmail.com; Agoudim; dm incl half-board Dh150) Bunk at Sidi Ahmed Amahdar's *gîte* for hot showers, clean shared bathrooms and a clamorous welcome from the folks who manage the place. It's set below a restored granary (ask Mohammed to give you a tour inside) about 500m after crossing the bridge. Lunch is an extra Dh50.

Gîte Tawajdat · GÎTE D'ÉTAPE €

(☑ 0523 45 92 90; gitesaid@yahoo.fr; Taghia; dm incl full board Dh120) Trekking groups head up to this basic guesthouse at the home of guide Said Massaoudi and his son Mohammad. It consists of mattresses on wooden pallets accompanied by simple but tasty meals. Lunch is an extra Dh50. It's a three-hour walk from Zaouiat Ahansal to get here.

★ Dar Ahansal · GUESTHOUSE €€

(☑ 0678 96 25 84; www.darahansal.net; Amezrai; s/d incl half-board Dh380/560, child incl half-board Dh145, camping/caravan per person Dh50/80;) As you round the final corner to Amezrai, the impressive rock-hewn *dar* (small house) of mountain guide Youssef Oulcadi rises organically out of the tough mountain landscape, its terraces built around Aleppo pines and landscaped with blushing roses and oleanders. Inside, rooms are beautifully finished

VOLUNTEERING IN ZAOUIAT AHANSAL

The **Atlas Cultural Foundation** (ACF; www.atlasculturalfoundation.org) is a registered US non-profit organisation with the mission of helping under-served Moroccans, especially women and children, improve their quality of life through locally determined development projects focusing on cultural preservation, community and environmental health, and education. In partnership with the local Moroccan Association Amezray SMNID, they are responsible for the restoration of three historic saints' houses and the extraordinary communal granaries, which now form some of the major sights in the valley.

Another core component of ACF's work is its programs run through **Atlas Cultural Adventures** (ACA; http://atlasculturaladventures.com). Participants assist in ACF's ongoing community development projects, work side by side with locals, and experience rural Moroccan village life. Programs are focused on community leader capacity building, historic preservation, design and construction of small community projects, public health workshops and sustainable farming. Programs are open to students or independent travellers and are from three days to five weeks in length.

with terracotta floors, *zellij* bathrooms and raffia-framed beds.

The large, cosy dining room and vast terrace overlooks Amezrai's pisé granary (restored by the Atlas Cultural Foundation), as do the camping facilities, which are provided with their own shared shower unit, traditional hammam and washing facilities.

ℹ Information

Youssef Oulcadi, a licensed Moroccan mountain guide and native of the region, can hook you up with guides through his guesthouse **Dar Ahansal** (p89). Alternatively, visit www.rando-maroc.net.

Climbers and trekkers are advised to bring a medical kit as the small clinic in Agoudim has poor facilities. In the case of emergencies, there is a government ambulance that runs between Agoudim and the Azilal hospital.

ℹ Getting There & Away

Zaouiat Ahansal is 84km southeast of Azilal. From Azilal through Aït Mohammed follow the old route for Aït Bougomez for 25km. When you reach the junction below the snowy sail of Azourki, take the left-hand road heading northeast across the Tizi n'Tselli-n-Imanain (2763m) to the market town of Assemsouk. Beyond Assemsouk the road climbs again to Tizi n'Illissi (2606m) and then snakes down the Illissi valley to Zaouiat Ahansal.

Minivans ply the route between Zaouiat Ahansal and Azilal (Dh50, 3½ to four hours, two daily), leaving Zaouiat Ahansal in the morning and returning from Azilal in the afternoon. Grands taxis only originate in Azilal and cost about Dh50 per person.

Cathédrale des Rochers & Reserve Naturelle de Tamga

Continuing north off-road along the main road from Zaouiat Ahansal leads to La Cathédrale des Rochers, the 'rock cathedral', and the Reserve Naturelle de Tamga, a vast national reserve with eight separate parks. Birdwatchers will have a field day (or several) observing 107 species of birds, including rare and endangered species. A botanical garden, 3km from the sign marking the park's entry, highlights the park's diverse flora, including medicinal herbs said to cure rheumatism.

🛏 Sleeping

There are several simple guesthouses here, and a new one was in the works when we last passed through.

Gîte le Cathédrale   GÎTE D'ETAPE €
(📞 0523 44 20 23, 0661 87 64 01; dm/campsite Dh100/30, dm incl half-board Dh200) Overnight stays, camping and meals (Dh50) are available at the simple Gîte le Cathédrale, 2km after the sign for the *cathédrale*. The six basic rooms here share bathrooms.

ℹ Getting There & Away

You'll need your own vehicle to visit the area. The road can be treacherous, and unsuitable for 2WD vehicles after heavy rains. Get the latest info at Zaouiat Ahansal or Ouaouizarht (if coming from the north) before setting out.

Aït Bougomez Valley

Though some roads are still accessible only by mule or 4WD, paved roads have given unprecedented entry to Morocco's 'happy valley' with its mudbrick towers, reddish *ighremt* (stone-reinforced houses) and rich, cultivated terraces. Scattered throughout the valley, 25 *douars* blend mimetically with their spectacular backdrops. Cliff sides are dotted with tiny plots of wheat and barley inside stone-walled terraces. High in the hills, you'll spot villagers collecting wild mountain plants to make herbal remedies and natural dyes, and in the broad alluvial valley are acres of lovingly tended fruit orchards.

The Y-shaped valley centres around the *zawiya* of Sidi Moussa, which sits on a cone-shaped hill at the centre with the villages of Imelgas and Ikhf-n-Ighir to the northeast, Tabant to the east and Tikniouine and Agouti to the southwest. Tabant, with its weekly Sunday souq, school and official mountain-guide training centre, is the heart of the valley and the main transport hub.

Sights & Activities

Although there are plenty of mountainous hikes in the region – with summit-baggers heading straight for **Irhil M'Goun** (4068m) – ambling between villages along the valley floor is enormously rewarding. Along the way, drop in at some of the valley's 40 local associations and cooperatives and find out more about how these mountain communities are evolving their own unique brand of sustainable tourism and providing much needed education to future generations. One such example is the nonprofit École Vivante

(www.ecolevivante.com), a free primary school that is part of a global educational youth project.

At the very upper (northeastern) end of the valley, at Ifrane, a track heads east to Zaouiat Oulmzi. From here you can trek down to the seasonal **Lac Izoughar**, a favoured watering hole for the nomadic Aït Atta tribe.

Exiting the northern end of the valley 5km northeast of Ifrane towards Azilal, you'll crest the dramatic Tizi n''Tirghist pass (2626m). Around this area are petroglyphs some geologists estimate are 4000 years old; ask a local guide to point out the enigmatic symbols, which local lore links to ancient rain-making ceremonies.

★ Sidi Moussa   MONUMENT

For a spectacular sunset, take the road west out of Tabant, and you'll find the trailhead leading up to this Unesco-heritage site, *a zawiya* of local *marabout* Sidi Moussa. You can park near the École Vivante, from which it's a straightforward 25-minute uphill hike (head toward the radio tower and follow the zigzagging path to the top); you won't need a guide.

The round structure served as a collective granary and has been restored through a community effort, with fitted-stone walls and weather-beaten wooden doors making a worthy photo backdrop. When it's open, locals charge Dh10 admission, which includes tea.

LOCAL KNOWLEDGE

ARTISANS ONLINE

Inhabitants of the Aït Bougomez Valley are a surprisingly resourceful bunch, testament of which is the launch of **Anou** (www.theanou.com), a new artisan-managed online platform that enables illiterate artisans to sell their work independently.

Unlike Etsy or eBay, the resource isn't open to anyone, but rather is limited to locally recognised artisans peer-verified by Anou's leadership team, the benchmark being the quality of the products produced and the motivation of the artisans to expand and develop their product line.

Anou then assists artisans in creating a profile page with a biography of each member, photographs of their studio and tools, and GPS coordinates of their workshops. Each piece created is subsequently approved by Anou's administration team before being posted to the site, ensuring that every product you see is exactly the item that will be shipped to you. When products sell, artisans pop the purchased item in the post and, *voilà*, in two to three weeks your new handcrafted carpet, bag or sculpture will arrive on your doorstep.

It's a great resource for travellers, as Anou's primary buyers are, so far, conscientious tourists keen to ensure that they are buying direct from artisans. At the time of writing there were 200 artisans on the site and 35 cooperatives and associations now extending well beyond Aït Bougomez across the whole country.

★ Cooperative
Tikniouine
NOTABLE BUILDING

(☑ 0678 52 08 80; Tikniouine; ⊙ 9am-4pm Mon-Thu & Sat) ⦿ Some 5km east along the main road from Agouti is the village of Tikniouine, a key stop for gourmet treats and cultural immersion. The cooperative was formed in 2005 by plucky young women who secured EU funding to start cultivating organic walnuts, collecting mountain wildflower honey, and making their own mild, aged cow's-milk cheese, which tastes like a cross between gouda and emmental.

At the cooperative's centre, which now employs 17 women full time, you can sample and purchase the products. It is signposted off the main road 50m down a rutted track.

Souq
MARKET

(Tabant; ⊙ 8am-2pm Sun) The valley's main market takes place on Sunday and offers a great insight into valley life. Traders and shoppers start arriving in Tabant on Saturday evening, 'parking' their donkeys at the top of town. Expect an unedited experience of busy butchers stalls and veg vendors, alongside traders selling everything from used clothes to teapots and tajines and even the kitchen sink (literally).

Association Ighrem
Atelier du Sculpture
CULTURAL CENTRE

(☑ 0673 75 31 63; www.theanou.com; ⊙ 8am-6pm Mon-Sat) At this centre in Agouti visitors can watch artisans carve free-form spoons and bowls from fragrant walnut, juniper and boxwood salvaged from fallen trees. With proceeds from sales, the association is reforesting the valley with fast-growing boxwood and planting vetiver to harvest for basket-weaving.

Nearby (on the right), the same association also sells tapestries, bags and jewellery – a great opportunity to buy finely crafted goods straight from the source.

🛏 Sleeping & Eating

The valley is dotted with a network of *gîtes d'etape* (hostels or homestays). Many of them are located within a 30-minute walk west of Tabant in the villages of Imelgas and Ikhf-n-Ighir. Closer to the M'Goun trailhead is Agouti, which is the favoured base for trekkers. Most establishments offer half-board lodging.

Basic cafes and restaurants can be found in Tabant.

Flilou
GÎTE D'ÉTAPE €

(☑ 0524 34 37 98; tamsilt@menara.ma; Agouti; dm/s/d incl half-board Dh160/240/480, d with shared bathroom incl half-board Dh320; 🅿) The first *gîte* on your left as you enter the village offers clean dorms, doubles with hand-painted beds, savoury meals and clean, updated bathrooms. Climb the steep staircase to the roof terrace, where Berber tents beckon and mirrored wedding blankets reflect sunsets. The mattresses are stiff, but the welcome is warm.

Gîte Tawada
GUESTHOUSE €

(☑ 0654 57 49 12; www.terre-d-ame-randonnees-maroc.com; Imelghas; d Dh150, s/d with shared bathrooms Dh60/100) On the main road in Imelghas village, Mohamed Imharkan and his family offer a warm welcome with six simple but well-maintained rooms (three with en suite). This is a great base for outdoor activities and Mohamed is an excellent guide for trekking; you can also hire bikes (Dh150 per day). Meals are available (dinner Dh55, breakfast Dh12).

Gîte Timit-La
Maison Imazighne
HOMESTAY €

(☑ 0673 26 04 38; gite.timit@hotmail.fr; Timit; dm/d incl breakfast Dh80/220) This historic Berber home is a breath of fresh mountain air, with family-friendly dorms and brightly painted doubles. Your host family lives in the rear courtyard, and can arrange birdwatching excursions, treks and botanical hikes. Meals are served family-style on cushions in the living room, under a painted ceiling.

Gîte La Montagne Au Pluriel
GUESTHOUSE €

(☑ 0661 88 24 34; www.lamontagneaupluriel.com; Agouti; s/d/tr/q Dh100/160/225/280, half-board per person Dh100) Offers small but cosy rooms with low ceilings, most with shared bathrooms, at unbeatable prices. The Benali family lays out the welcome mat and has a wealth of information on exploring the area. There's a huge terrace with jaw-dropping views – ask to take your meals here! It's located on the main road through the village.

Gîte Intimou
GÎTE D'ÉTAPE €

(☑ 0670 71 47 12; Ikhf-n-Ighir; per person incl half-board Dh280) Intimou has five sunny doubles and triples and one large dorm room. All of them share gleaming black-and-white-tiled washing facilities, which include two showers and two toilets. You'll find it on the hillside on your left as you head north, opposite the sign for the Association Ikhf-n-Ighir.

★ **Touda Ecolodge** GUESTHOUSE €€
(☑ 0662 14 42 85; www.touda.fr; Zaouiat Oulmzi; per person incl half-board Dh380-490) 🖉 Quite literally off-the-beaten track, Touda is located down a rutted *piste* (track) in the village of Zaouiat Oulmzi, 5km east of Ifrane and the Tizi n'Tirghist pass and 4km west of the seasonal Lac D'Izoughar. Here you'll be overwhelmed by magnanimous Berber hospitality, plentiful home-cooked meals, impromptu fireside music sessions and stunning treks in the foothills of Jebel Azourki (3677m).

Children (aged four to 12) pay half price.

Dar Si Hamou RIAD €€
(☑ 0667 64 48 62; www.nuancesmarocaines.com; Tabant; s/d Dh130/260, r per person incl half-board Dh250-300) Set around a pretty garden courtyard with undisturbed views over emerald-green fields to snowcapped M'Goun beyond, Dar Si Hamou is Tabant's first stylin' guesthouse. Pristine white linens on cosy duvets offset minimal Berber-chic decor of saffron stencils, ochre-and-red-striped woollen cushions and painted chests, while hungry trekkers keep warm around the free-standing fireplace in the salon.

Ecolodge Dar Itrane INN €€€
(☑ 0610 08 69 30; www.origins-lodge.com; Imelghas; r per person incl half-board Dh380-500) 🖉 Located in Imelghas village, an easy 30-minute walk west of Tabant, is this rural-hip ecolodge. Eighteen whitewashed guest rooms are kitted out with handmade Berber-style furnishings, plus en suite in *tadelakt* with solar-powered hot showers. Pack lunches, guide and donkey are all available, as are a whole host of excursions and activities.

❶ Getting There & Away

Access to Aït Bougomez is from Azilal south along the R301. At Aït Mohammed the road forks southeast (accessing the valley from the north over Tizi n'Tirghist and off-*piste* through ancient juniper and oak forests to Aghbalou) and southwest, from where a paved road leads all the way to Agouti.

Minibuses occasionally run from Azilal to Tabant (Dh40, three hours) in the morning when full, from near the mosque. You might share a grand taxi (Dh50 per person) or ride in trucks headed to Azilal on Thursday for its market.

Aït Bououli Valley

Heading southwest from Aït Mohammed you'll pass through hills marking geologic time in red-, purple- and white-striped mineral deposits. Five kilometres before you reach Agouti, adventurers equipped with a 4WD and steely nerves can detour south through a steep red-clay gorge to the Aït Bououli Valley, which until a few years ago was inaccessible even by mule for months at a time.

◉ Sights

Sebt Aït Bououli VILLAGE
In the remote outpost of Sebt Aït Bououli, 14km off the main road, trekkers stock up on food for their M'Goun traverse at the Saturday souq. Some 2.5km beyond Sebt Aït Bououli, you'll have to squint to make out a picturesque trio of villages built right into a two-toned purple and ochre bluff. On green terraces are gambolling lambs that are the valley's claim to fame: Bououli means 'Those who keep sheep'.

🛍 Shopping

★ **Cooperative Feminin de Tissage Aït Bououli** ARTS & CRAFTS
(☑ 0671 41 91 06; ⊘ 8am-5pm) Immediately below Aït Bououli's trio of mimetic villages is a stone-walled community association with a sign pointing visitors toward the Aït Bououli women's carpet-weaving cooperative. This 40-member cooperative takes every aspect of carpet-making into its own hands, tending and shearing sheep; carding and spinning fluffy lambswool into yarn; and collecting plants to dye yarn fascinating tertiary hues.

The members also take turns minding the shop, so you'll be buying carpets from the woman who made it, her sister or her neighbour. If you find the door closed, just call Fatima, the dynamic director, and she'll come down from the village to open the small storeroom.

Trekking the M'Goun Traverse

While crowds flock to Jebel Toubkal, nature lovers head to the M'Goun Massif, where pristine, prehistoric landscapes and some of Morocco's highest peaks make for rewarding challenges for trekkers. Nevertheless, this walk will suit all grades of trekkers, including families.

If you're going in spring, dress warmly and be prepared to get your boots wet: walking river gorges is one of the great pleasures of M'Goun. The M'Goun Traverse follows one river up to its mountain source, crosses the mountain range, and then follows another river down into its valley.

ⓘ BEFORE YOU GO: M'GOUN TRAVERSE TREKKING CHECKLIST

Maps & Books The 1:100,000 survey sheets *Azilal, Zawyat Ahannsal, Qalat M'Gouna* and *Skoura* cover all of the major trekking areas. West Col Productions' 1:100,000 *Mgoun Massif* is occasionally available in Morocco, otherwise try Stanfords (www.stanfords. co.uk) or Omnimap (www.omnimap.com); although devoid of contours, this map is a good trail reference. The German-produced *Kultur Trekking im Zentralen Hohen Atlas* shows the trek from Aït Bougomez to Kelaâ M'Gouna, and usefully marks and grades *gîtes* (maps) throughout the range.

Guide Since Morocco's main mountain-guide school is in Tabant, there are many licensed local guides with M'Goun expertise. Guides with High Atlas training from the Imlil, Marrakesh and Dadès also have the know-how to lead M'Goun trips.

Food Basic food supplies are available in Tabant and sometimes in Abachkou.

Water Purifying locally sourced water is the most responsible option.

Fuel For gas canisters, a supermarket in Marrakesh is the best bet. Petrol, diesel and kerosene can be bought in Azilal.

Gear When walking in spring or after heavy rain, a stick or trekking pole will help you vault over streams. When water is high, you may want plastic or waterproof sandals to wade through rocky riverbeds.

Tent There is no *gîte* in Rougoult, but there is excellent camping beside the river. Your guide should be able to arrange tents. If you don't have a tent and don't want to sleep under the stars, you'll need to spend the night in Sebt Aït Bououli, making the second-day walk longer.

Mule Guides can sort out local muleteers and mules.

ARRIVAL DAY

To stretch your legs and camp overnight, you could stroll down the valley to Agerssif to a riverside camping spot near the bridge. Alternatively, there's accommodation around Tabant and right near the trailhead in Agouti.

DAY 1: AGOUTI TO ROUGOULT

DURATION SIX TO SEVEN HOURS / DISTANCE 17KM / ASCENT & DESCENT 326M

After a leisurely 1½-hour walk south along the road from Agouti, a *piste* road forks to the left. Continue on this road, or take a steeper, shorter path that zigzags down into the valley, rejoining the tarmac road at the village of **Agerssif** (1469m), which you should reach less than three hours from Agouti. Agerssif sits at the confluence of the Lakhdar and Bougomez Rivers, and there's a good resting and camping spot by the bridge.

The Lakhdar Valley narrows as the road climbs its southern side. A half-hour upstream is the picturesque village of **Taghoulit** (1519m), surrounded by juniper trees, and with a simple *gîte* (per person Dh60). The road scales the gorge, then enters the broad, fertile upper valley, until it reaches **Sebt Aït Bououli**; you'll find **Gîte Hassan Benkoum** (per person Dh110) here, but we advise continuing to Rougoult for a head start on day

two. Several valleys meet at Sebt Aït Bououli, and looking up past the village of Abachkou you'll notice **Jebel Rat** (3781m).

A graded *piste* road heads left to the south, through a valley of wheat and barley fields. The village of **Tazouggart**, on the opposite side of the valley, marks a more-than-halfway

THE TREK AT A GLANCE

Duration Four days

Distance 57km

Standard Medium

Start Agouti

Finish Aït Alla

Highest point Tizi n'Rougoult (2860m)

Accommodation Camping and *gîtes*

Public transport Yes

Summary This walk traverses the northeastern slopes of the M'Goun Massif and then drops down into the Tessaout river valley; it will suit most trekkers, even younger ones. There's one long day of walking, but this varied trek crosses stunning mountain landscapes, and travels through river gorges and remote valleys.

M'Goun Traverse Trek

M'Goun Traverse Trek

Jebel Tamadout

Jebel Asselda (2984m)
Jebel Aklim (3432m)
Taouigalt
Tighouzzirine
Taghra
1989m
Irhil M'Goun (4068m)
Jebel Tajouga (3391m)
Jebel Tazoult n'Ouguerd (3481m)
Jebel Wagraraz (3272m)
Amezri (2250m)
Tizi n'Oulawn (2767m)
Tasgaiwalt (2521m)
Imi-n-Ikkis
Tighremt n'Aït Ahmed (2230m)
Ihil Timoughrine
Tizi n'Aït Imi (2905m)
Tizi n'Tanout (3074m)
3266m
3519m
Ifrhin Tgoudnameme
Tizi Asdremt n'Aït Bou Ouilli (3066m)
3996m
3993m
Tizi n'Oumsond (2969m)
Tizi n'Oumassin (3640m)
Jebel n'Nig Oumassine (3883m)
Tabant
Talsnant
Tabant
Arous
START
Agouti
Irni n'Talat
Agerssif (1469m)
Taghoulit
Jebel Tadaghast (2891m)
Jebel Tafenfent (2513m)
Jebel Tifdaniwine (3449m)
Irhil n'Tkkis (3207m)
Sebt Ait Bououli (1858m)
Rougoult (1850m)
Abachkou
Tarbat n'Aït Moussa
Tazzougart
Tazzagalt
Tignousti (3819m)
Tizi n'Tighist (2999m)
Tizi n'Iblouzene
Tizi n'Wani (3017m)
Jebel Rat (3778m)
Aghouild n'Ichbbakne
2809m
2864m
Ichbbakene
Imi-n-Ikkis
Fakhour
Aït Ali n'Ito (1833m)
Ifoujou
END
Aït Alla
Jebel Waguerset (2882m)
Jebel Timilit (2862m)
Tissili
Jebel Aguendra (3060m)
Tizi n'Wawat
Imi n'Larba
Jebel Amerziaz (2522m)
Jebel Azegza (2653m)
Tala n'Izri
Tarbat n'Tirsal
Jebel Alimanne (2586m)
Tagassalt
Taghzout
Assif n'Arous
Assif n'Arous
Assif Arouss
Assif Ikraatten
Assif n'Tizit
Idrmanan
Ifri n'Aït Kherfalla
Jebel Tarkeddid
Tizi n'Taziyt
Assif Aït Toumert
Assif Aït Mallul
Oued l'Essaouid
Assif n'Zaouyat

10 km
5 miles
N

point between Sebt Aït Bououli and **Rougoult** (1850m). In Rougoult you'll find a Tifra River campsite and homestays (per person Dh50) – ask around to see who has space.

DAY 2: ROUGOULT TO AMEZRI

DURATION SIX TO SEVEN HOURS / DISTANCE 14KM / DESCENT 600M / ASCENT 970M

For two hours, the morning walk follows the Tifra along a stony path criss-crossing the river. As the well-trodden mule path climbs, the landscape becomes more barren, occasionally leading above rocky gorges – but the path always follows the course of the river south.

The source of the Tifra River is no more than a trickle at the best of times, as you'll discover just below the pass of **Tizi n'Rougoult** (2860m). From the broad saddle beneath the pass, a path leads left (east) to a ridge that climbs to over 3500m. The well-worn Rougoult pass is straight ahead, and the summit of **Irhil M'Goun** (4068m) – only 100m lower than Jebel Toubkal – due east. In the near distance across the **Tessaout River**, exposed mountain slopes reveal great gashes of rust, green and grey rock.

From the Rougoult pass, the mule path is clearly marked, winding gradually downhill for two hours before reaching the village of **Tasgaïwalt** (2521m). Curious village children may keep you company on the easy 40-minute walk along the track, keeping the river to your left, to the village of **Amezri** (2250m). The **Gîte d'Étape Agnid Mohamed** (per person Dh110) has several large sleeping rooms, some of which overlook the valley, with a rudimentary shower and toilets. There's convenient camping (Dh25) too.

DAY 3: AMEZRI TO AÏT ALI N'ITO

DURATION SIX HOURS / DISTANCE 18KM / DESCENT 427M / ASCENT 150M

Your path follows the Tessaout River, shelving gently from 2250m to 1833m. The valley is flanked by impressive cliffs, particularly the sheer Ichbbakene escarpment, which rises 600m above the river.

The river has few fish, but it does irrigate exceptionally lovely terraces cultivated by Aafan Berbers. In spring, the area is covered with wildflowers and blooming fruit and nut trees. Here the Tessaout flows west, fed by streams of melted mountain snow.

Where the path crosses the river, you can often hop across on stones. In spring, you may have to wade, as at the village of **Imi-n-Ikkis**, 5km from Amezri. The village has a shop (no sign) that sometimes stocks water, soft drinks, tinned food and plastic shoes to ford rivers.

Downstream 1½ hours, the path passes beneath the larger village of **Ichbbakene**, backed by a sheer escarpment. The path becomes a *piste,* and keeping the river on your left for another 2½ hours, it squeezes between the stone and mud houses of **Aït Hamza**. Another hour leads to the village of **Aït Ali n'Ito**, where you'll find great views at the **Gîte d'Étape Assounfou** (☑ 0668 96 82 63; Aït Ali n'Ito; per person incl half-board Dh220), plus electricity, hot showers (Dh10) and even a hammam.

DAY 4: AÏT ALI N'ITO TO AÏT ALLA

DURATION 2½ TO THREE HOURS / DISTANCE 8KM / DESCENT 150M

A dirt road leads alongside the river with gentle climbs to the lovely village of **Fakhour**, where houses scale the hillside. Fakhour is noted for its *agadir* (fortified granary), which can be visited (Dh10 to Dh20 tip for the guardian is customary).

Less than an hour beyond Fakhour, the village of **Ifoulou** sits on a bend of the river and road, drawing villagers from miles around for its Monday souq. From here, a tarmac road leads to the main Demnate–Skoura road by the bridge over the Tessaout River, below the village of **Aït Alla**. This small, peaceful mountain village makes a fine place to unwind after the long days of trekking. From here you can also catch onward transport to Demnate or Ouarzazate.

Western High Atlas

South of Marrakesh, Morocco's highest peak, Jebel Toubkal (4167m), sits at the centre of Toubkal National Park. Since these peaks are just 2½ hours from Marrakesh, Jebel Toubkal is the most frequently visited High Atlas region and has long been a key route south. It is most easily accessible via the Ourika and Mizane Valleys. The heavily touristed Ourika Valley deposits you at the trekking base of Setti Fatma, while the Mizane Valley leads you to the more atmospheric village of Imlil. The ski resort of Oukaïmeden sits between the two.

Zat Valley

When Marrakesh is sweating it out 50km to the northwest, breezes are rippling through barley and swaying poplar trees along this charmed river valley.

To reach Zat Valley from Marrakesh, take the N9 towards Ouarzazate until it crosses the Oued Zat at Aït Ourir, then turn off south and head towards the transport town of **Tighdouine** at the near end of the valley. Tighdouine offers tasty roadside tajines before you enter Zat's land of make-believe: gardens built right into cliff faces, stone houses with bright-blue doors, white-framed windows with families leaning out to say hello. This is all best appreciated on foot or mule.

Three- to five-day walking tours are organised by Inside Morocco Tours (p66). They wend their way up the rich valley (most of Marrakesh's potatoes, turnips, olives, figs and tomatoes come from here) to the village of **Talatassat**, where you can visit the local potteries before continuing on up to the red sandstone **Yaggour Plateau**, the location of an important concentration of prehistoric rock engravings. Nearby **Tizi N'Rhellis** leads to the neighbouring Ourika Valley.

Ourika Valley

Temperatures are cooler in the shadow of snowcapped High Atlas peaks, and this blooming valley a little over 50km south of Marrakesh is the city's escape hatch from the soaring summer heat. The valley is especially mood-altering from February to April, when almond and cherry orchards bloom manically and wildflowers run riot.

Sadly Ourika's beauty and easy accessibility have lead to significant development, which now threatens to mar its mountain-valley vibe. At Oulmes, makeshift cafes and BBQ joints line the riverside strung together by flimsy rope bridges that allow day-trippers to cross the river, while at the end of the valley sits the summer resort and well-worn trekking base of Setti Fatma.

For High Atlas scenery with fewer tourist coaches and moped-mounted salesmen, you may prefer the Mizane or Zat Valleys.

Getting There & Away

Grands taxis and minibuses to Setti Fatma leave frequently from Rue Uqba bin Nafaa, near Bab er-Rob, in Marrakesh (Dh40) and you may also find less-frequent minibuses to Ourika Valley destinations (Dh20 to Dh30). Most grands taxis will drop you anywhere along the Route d'Ourika, but return taxis and minibuses are easiest to find in Setti Fatma, Tnine and Aghbalou. Transport returns when full.

AGHMAT أغمات
POP 2600
Drivers speeding past Aghmat (aka Rhmat, Ghmat or Jemaa Rhmat), 31km from Marrakesh, are missing a key turning point in Moroccan history. This town was an Idrissid dynastic capital from AD 828 to 1058, and an important stop for the camel caravans from Sub-Saharan Africa through Sijilmassa.

When the Almoravids conquered the city in 1058, one of Aghmat's leading citizens was killed in the fray, leaving his brilliant, wealthy widow Zeinab en-Nafzawiyyat free to marry Almoravid leader Abu Bakr. When Abu Bakr was recalled to the Sahara to settle disputes, he divorced Zeinab so that she could remarry his cousin, Yusuf bin Tachfin. With Zeinab's financing and counsel, Yusuf bin Tachfin proved unstoppable, founding a new capitol at Marrakesh and expanding the Almoravid empire to the doorstep of Barcelona.

Once Almoravids moved to Marrakesh, Aghmat became a place of exile for political dissidents, including Andalusian poet-king Al-Mutamid ibn Abbad.

Sights

Visitors can glimpse Aghmat's former glories just behind the town's main marketplace, where Aghmat's Friday souq is held.

Mausoleum HISTORIC SITE
Al-Mutamid's tomb is marked with an Almoravid-style domed mausoleum. It's signed right off the main road after the commune building, inside a garden enclosure 200m along on the left. The dissident's tomb was the site of a 1950 protest against French occupation that was violently suppressed by Pasha Glaoui – an inciting incident in Morocco's independence movement.

LOCAL KNOWLEDGE

LOCAL SOUQ DAYS

In the valleys surrounding Jebel Toubkal, towns have market days featuring local crafts, fresh produce and donkeys on the following days:

Monday Tnine
Tuesday Tahanaoute, Aït-Ourir
Wednesday Tighdouine
Thursday El-Khemis Ouirgane
Friday Aghmat
Saturday Asni
Sunday Setti Fatma

☆☆ Festivals & Events

Awaln'art CULTURAL

(www.awalnart.com; ⊙Apr) Aghmat's big event happens in April when it hosts a colourful outdoor festival of theatre, dance and cabaret.

TNINE

POP 4500

Beyond the turn-off for Aghmat and 33km from Marrakesh along Rte d'Ourika is the town of Tnine (aka Tnin l'Ourika), a worthwhile detour for a visit to its lush saffron and botanical gardens. Tnine is also home to one of the Ourika Valley's finest cultural museums, a good starting point for delving into its Berber heritage. You may run into donkey traffic here when the Monday souq takes place.

⊙ Sights

★Ecomusée Berbere MUSEUM

(✆ Khalid 0610 25 67 34, Salah 0607 59 85 85; www.museeberbere.com; Douar Tafza, Km 37, Rte de l'Ourika, Tafza; adult/child Dh2/free; ⊙9.30am-7pm) ✐ Four kilometres after Tnine a discreet sign points up a dirt path into the Berber village of Tafza: here the three-storey mudbrick *ksar* that once housed the local *caïd* (chief) is now a museum. Enthusiastic guided visits (in English, French or Spanish) cover every detail of household life, from symbols carved in door frames to silver dowry jewellery.

Call ahead to reserve meals on the terrace (Dh70), to arrange visits to Tafza pottery workshops, or for half-day excursions that take in community gardens, pottery workshops and village life.

Safranerie GARDENS

(✆ 0522 48 44 76; www.safran-ourika.com; Km 34 Rte de l'Ourika, Tnine; garden tours adult/child under 16 yr Dh20/free; ⊙7am-5.30pm) Almost anything thrives in Ourika's rich soil, including saffron (*Crocus sativus*), organically grown here from bulbs that are cultivated near Talouine. Saffron is a high-maintenance plant, with flowers harvested before dawn for maximum potency. Guided tours are given by staff who reiterate key points on explanatory placards.

Jardin Bio-Aromatique d'Ourika GARDENS

(Nectarôme; ✆ 0524 48 21 49; www.jardin-bioaromatique-ourika.com; Km 34 Rte de l'Ourika, Tnine; garden visits adult/child Dh20/10, with guide Dh70; ⊙9am-7pm Sep-Jul) Just after the bridge in Tnine, signs off the main road point down a dirt track towards the organic botanical gardens of a Franco-Moroccan natural bath-product company that combines Berber herbal remedies with modern aromatherapy. The garden certainly smells great, and a foot-bath and foot massage with organic essential oils (Dh250) is just the thing after a trek.

🛏 Sleeping

Kasbah Jad Auberge GUESTHOUSE €€

(✆ 0524 48 29 53; jadauberge@gmail.com; d/tr/ste Dh350/495/600; ☎) This appealing place has much to recommend it, starting with attractively furnished rooms, all of which offer memorable views over the valley. Take the spiral staircase to the roof for more great views and a choice spot for meals on request. There's also an indoor pool (open year-round) and a hammam. Good mountain bikes are available for hire (Dh200 per day).

Kasbah Bab Ourika ECOLODGE €€€

(✆ 0668 74 95 47; www.kasbahbabourika.com; Tnine Ourika; d Dh1650-2860, ste Dh3300-7260; P☎🖥) ✐ Occupying an outstanding location in the Ourika Valley, this rammed-earth kasbah puts Richard Branson's bombastic Kasbah Tamadot in the shade. Understated luxuries include uninterrupted views of snowy Atlas peaks, top-quality meals anytime anywhere, superbly finished interiors and sleep-inducing orthopedic mattresses. You can relax beneath olive trees while admiring the view, take a dip in the gorgeous pool or unwind in the hammam.

ⓘ Information

From December to March, flash floods can make hiking dangerous and render parts of Ourika Valley inaccessible – in 1995, winter floods nearly wiped out the village of Oulmes.

Centre d'Informations Touristique Ourika (✆ 0668 46 55 45; ⊙8.30am-7pm Mon-Sat, to 1pm Sun) Just outside Tnine, this local NGO-operated information office sells a sheet map (Dh20) of valley vista points and provides updates on trekking conditions.

AGHBALOU

POP 8400

A red stone mosque and minaret are the signature landmarks of Aghbalou, the Ourika Valley's largest village, located some 47km southwest of Marrakesh. Most buses make a stop here, and from here to Oulmes the river is lined with cafes and restaurants.

🛏 Sleeping & Eating

Cafes dot the riverbanks serving kebabs and salad (Dh50) or tajines big enough for two (Dh60), with carpets spread out under shady trees in good weather.

Auberge le Maquis
HOTEL €€
(📞 0524 48 45 31; www.le-maquis.com; Km 45 Rte de l'Ourika; s/d incl breakfast Dh395/630; 🛜🏊) A warm welcome awaits at this 11-room, family-style getaway and launching pad/finish line for bikers and trekkers. The local management makes meals (mains Dh60 to Dh90) feel like dinners among friends, and there's a play yard where kids can cut loose. Don't miss the fossil and mineral collection (from Jean-Pierre's desert forays) in the restaurant.

The auberge also arranges plenty of treks and excursions, including to the Yaggour plateau petroglyphs (from where you can descend to the Zat Valley) and mule treks for little ones.

Ourika Garden
HOTEL €€
(📞 0670 72 16 06, 0524 48 44 41; www.ourik-agarden.com; Km 49.5 Rte de l'Ourika; r Dh630-840; ✳🛜🏊) A gardener's dream, with flagstone paths through aromatic herbs leading over footbridges to a stone-walled lodge. Guest rooms have fireplaces, seating nooks, hewn-wood furnishings, and en suite with variable hot water (shower early). Breakfasts on the terrace feature High Atlas views, local honey and olive oil, and there's wi-fi by the patio bar.

SETTI FATMA
ستي فاطمة

POP 23,400

A little village that's seen a whole lot of tourist action in the past decade, Setti Fatma is a scenic stop for lunch by the river and for hikes to seven waterfalls. The village is neatly nestled in a canyon beneath the High Atlas mountains at the southern end of the Ourika Valley road, 24km south of the Oukaïmeden turn-off at Aghbalou.

Prime times to visit are in early March when the cherry and almond trees are in bloom, or in August for the four-day *moussem*, with its fair and market at the *koubba* of Setti Fatma. During the summer, the place is clogged with visitors from Marrakesh, so consider heading, instead, to the splendidly untrammelled neighbouring valleys of Zat and Ouirgane.

🏃 Activities

Served by frequent buses and grands taxis, Setti Fatma is the most accessible High Atlas trekking base, although trailheads for many of the more impressive hikes lie on the other side of Tizi n'Tacheddirt pass (3230m) in Imlil. One popular hike has been to traverse the pass via the villages of Tadrart, Timichi, Tacheddirt and Ouaneskra, but now a paved road covers two-thirds of the route forcing trekkers to make a steeper two-day ascent to avoid walking along the road.

Other possible treks from Setti Fatma head east to Tourcht, north to Imi-n-Taddert, to Anammer and Tiz n'Oucheg in the Aït Oucheg Valley, and from the Yaggour Plateau into the Zat Valley, the latter being the most impressive trek on offer.

Waterfall hikes range from 30-minute walks to arduous stream hikes; ignore the faux guides and follow the paths, or find a licensed guide to lead the way on foot or mule.

The **bureau des guides** (📞 0524 42 61 13; ⊙ 9am-5pm) can hook you up with guides.

🛏 Sleeping & Eating

From Oulmes to Setti Fatima, both sides of the river are lined with cafe-restaurants offering tajines priced to move. There's also a couple of reasonable choices in Setti Fatima proper.

★ Eau Bord du l'Eau
GUESTHOUSE €
(📞 0661 22 97 55; www.obordelo.com; d Dh270-400, ste Dh485-550; 🛜) This jaunty little guesthouse is tucked down a steep pebble staircase about 1km (on the left) before reaching Setti Fatma. As a result, it's wonderfully secluded, with just the sound of the rushing river to disturb dreams of summit ascents. With Martine and Poulou's easygoing hosting and shared conversations around central fireplaces, you'll feel right at home.

Hôtel Asgaour
GUESTHOUSE €
(📞 0524 48 52 94; r with/without bathroom Dh200/150; 🛜) Basic but clean rooms with lumpy pillows and hot showers upstairs, plus a restaurant downstairs serving well-caramelised tajines (around Dh50).

Café-Restaurant Azrrabzou
MOROCCAN €
(set meals Dh60; ⊙ 11am-8pm) Set meals of salad, tajine or kebab and bottled water are on offer at this place over a plank bridge in a patch of almond trees (opposite the taxi stand, on the opposite side of the river).

ℹ Information

Bureau des Guides (p99) Located just past the Hôtel Asgaour.

Pharmacy Asgaour (⊙ 10am-8pm) A good selection of first aid, medicine and women's products.

LOCAL KNOWLEDGE

BERBER BOTANY IN THE HIGH ATLAS

Despite icy winters and scalding summers, the High Atlas Mountains are extremely fertile. Overgrazing, agriculture and wood collection for fuel has impacted the High Atlas; much of its indigenous vegetation has disappeared. But through painstaking reforestation and resourceful mountainside terrace farming using *targa* (channel) irrigation, the hills are alive with a diversity of flora.

Here's what you'll spot on High Atlas walks:

Valleys lower than 2400m Riots of flowers erupt in spring, when valley almond, cherry and apricot orchards bloom. In summer, you'll enjoy the shade of carob, quince, pomegranate, apple and fig trees. Resourceful farmers manage to eke multiple crops from terrace plots: barley October through to May, and potatoes, carrots, turnips, onions, lentils and beans from spring through to autumn. Walnuts are a major crop in higher villages, with harvest in late September.

Subalpine zone (2400m to 3200m) Thickets of gnarled Spanish juniper *(Juniperus thurifer)* are blasted into extraordinary shapes by the wind, and exposed roots cling like fingers to the rock. Aleppo pine is being planted to prevent erosion, and replace fragrant Atlas cedar used for woodworking.

High elevations higher than 3200m The easiest to spot are 'hedgehog plants', spiny, domed bushes that briefly burst into flower in spring. Even when you don't spot plants on the trail, you'll get a whiff of lavender, rosemary and wild thyme underfoot, perfuming your boots as you walk.

Oukaïmeden اوكيمدن

This sleepy mountain village, perched at 2650m in the High Atlas, offers a peaceful escape from the hustle of Marrakesh 75km to the north. It's a fine year-round destination with hiking amid wildflower-strewn valleys in springtime and downhill skiing in winter. Aside from its beckoning outdoor adventures, however, there isn't much to Oukaïmeden.

🏃 Activities

In snow season, skiers will find seven ski runs from nursery to black, six tows and the highest ski lift in Africa (3243m). Gear, passes and lessons are available in town at prices that will delight skiers used to European and American rates. Peak season has historically been late January to March, but in recent years snow has been scarce by March. When snow is low on the slopes, skiers can cross-country ski.

Club Alpin Français (CAF) can point you towards trekking trailheads.

🛏 Sleeping

CAF Refuge HOSTEL €
(🕿 0524 31 90 36; dm CAF members/nonmembers Dh90/140; 🛜) Offers heated dormitories, bar-restaurant, well-equipped kitchen, library and wi-fi, but you'll need your own sleeping bag. Bathrooms are on the 1st floor, but the nicest bunk beds are in pine-ceilinged rooms upstairs. Group pick-ups can be arranged from Marrakesh (by grand taxi Dh400 or by minibus or 4WD for nine to 12 passengers Dh700 to Dh900).

Hôtel Chez Juju HOTEL €€€
(🕿 0524 31 90 05; www.hotelchezjuju.com; d incl half-board Dh1100-2600; 🛜) Reliable restaurant with a bar, plus simple alpine-style rooms with en suites. Nicer renovated doubles have mountain views, pine panelling, cotton quilts and flowered drapes; grimmer rooms are in back and best avoided. The hotel also serves up some of the best meals in the village (though there isn't much competition).

ℹ Information

Club Alpin Français (CAF; 🕿 0524 31 90 36; www.ffcam.fr)

ℹ Getting There & Away

If you're not travelling by rental car, your best bet is to arrange transport through **CAF** (p100). Otherwise, you can charter a grand taxi from Marrakesh's Bab er-Rob (Dh400 to Dh600).

Toubkal National Park

For pure mountain air that cuts through the heat and leaves you giddy, don't miss the highest mountain in North Africa: snowcapped

Jebel Toubkal (4167m), situated in the heart of the Toubkal National Park. Mountain trails criss-crossing Jebel Toubkal start from Imlil, which is located at the end of the Mizane Valley. On the way to Imlil, you could make a pit stop 47km south of Marrakesh at Asni for roadside tajines and the Saturday souq.

ⓘ Getting There & Away

Frequent local buses (Dh20, 1½ hours) and grands taxis (Dh20, one hour) leave south of Bab er-Rob in Marrakesh for Asni. Local minibuses and occasional taxis travel the final 17km between Asni and Imlil (Dh12, one hour). Expect a car journey from Marrakesh to Imlil to take at least 2½ hours.

Imlil   إمليل

POP 5100

A favourite hitching post for mountain trekkers, Imlil is just a five-hour hike from the base of Jebel Toubkal, and in spring you won't want to miss waking up in these flowering High Atlas foothills.

🏃 Activities

Imlil is the main trekking base for Jebel Toubkal and the whole town caters to trekkers and their needs. Ascents to the summit leave daily from here, although the traffic in high season may rub the edge off that lone-mountain-ranger fantasy. To escape the well-worn path consider trekking southwest over Tizi n'Mzik (2489m) to the wonderful **Cascades d'Irhoulidene** near Azib Tamsoult and either ascending the Toubkal summit from the west (covered on Days 6 and 7 of the Toubkal Circuit trek), or heading east down the unspoilt **Azzaden Valley**.

If you arrive without having made arrangements, head to the bureau des guides (p102) and let them know your requirements and they'll hook you up with a guide for a fixed-price rate (Dh300/400 per half/full day). Guides speak a range of languages, including French, English, German and Spanish.

If you are really short on time, you can easily walk to the village of Aroumd (p102) and back in a few hours; follow the mule track along the western edge of the Mizane river.

Mountain Travel Morocco   TREKKING
(MTM; ☑ 0524 48 57 84; www.mountain-travel-morocco.com; Imlil; ⊙ 9am-6pm Mon-Sat) Established by four of Imlil's most experienced trekking guides, MTM is Imlil's first fully registered, private guiding outfit offering treks to suit all levels. Guides are also trained in first aid and are experienced in dealing with altitude sickness. To ensure you can undertake the trek you want when you want, book in advance.

**Bike Adventures
in Morocco**   MOUNTAIN BIKING
(☑ 0666 23 82 00; www.bikeadventuresinmorocco.com; Imlil) Run by mountain guide and biking expert Lahcen Jellah, this well-equipped outfit offers a range of itineraries criss-crossing the Atlas. Routes range from an easy four-day Toubkal circuit to an epic 10-day Atlas traverse from Imlil to M'Goun.

🛏 Sleeping

★**Authentic Toubkal**   GUESTHOUSE €
(☑ 0672 84 51 71; www.authentictoubkallodge.com; Arghen Village) 🍃 Run by the youthful Lahcen and his family, this delightful village stay aims to introduce guests to Berber culture, with lessons on mint tea preparation, bread baking and opportunities to interact with village residents. Expect delicious communal meals and ample amusement (you too can dress in Berber finery). It's about a 20-minute uphill walk from town. Call in advance for someone to meet you.

★**Riad Atlas Toubkal**   GUESTHOUSE €
(☑ 0524 48 57 82; www.riadatlastoubkal.com; Imlil; d/tr/ste Dh300/400/600; 🅿⚘🛜) This appealing guesthouse has eight cosy rooms with large picture windows that catch mountain breezes and boast views as fine as those at the pricey kasbah; three rooms also have balconies. Piles of board games and books keep idle hours filled. Guest showers for sweaty trekkers, panoramic views from the restaurant and parking (Dh20) complete the service.

Imlil Lodge   GUESTHOUSE €
(☑ 0671 15 76 36; www.toubkalguide.com; Tamatert; d Dh250-400, f Dh600; ⚘🛜) Run by Jamal Imrehane, one of the founders of Mountain Travel Morocco, this friendly stone-faced guesthouse looks out over Imlil and the Mizane Valley from Tamatert. Arranged around an internal courtyard, riad-style rooms come with fancy stucco ceilings, brass lanterns and stripey Asni blankets. Several rooms have balconies and one also has a fireplace.

Dar Adrar   RIAD €
(☑ 0668 76 01 65; www.daradrar.com; Achayn; s/d/tr incl breakfast from Dh250/300/400; 🛜) Sitting in a shaded grove in the village of Achayn, a steep 10-minute walk uphill from the Atlas Trek Shop in Imlil, Dar Adrar has

simple, comfortable rooms, a flower-filled yard and an in-house hammam (Dh50). The owner, mountain guide Mohamed Aztat, is a cofounder of Mountain Travel Morocco (p101) and also owns the trek shop in Imlil.

Dar Ouassaggou
RIAD €

(☑ 0667 49 13 52; www.guesthouseouassaggou.com; Douar Aït Soukka; d incl breakfast Dh330-490; 🖹 🛜) A walnut orchard shades the valley path east of Imlil to this eight-room guesthouse, where visitors are received like long-lost relatives by Houssein, an English-speaking mountain guide. Cosy, comfortable bedrooms have en suites, one with a *tadelakt* tub. The sunny terrace is ideal after a morning trek, and you can also arrange dinner (Dh100 per person).

Imlil Refuge
HOSTEL €

(☑ 0661 87 37 71; http://imlilrefuge.com; dm incl breakfast Dh90) Imlil Refuge offers the cheapest lodging in town with 10 simple but clean rooms that share bathrooms. There's a sitting room with fireplace, a roof terrace and a shared kitchen. It's a fine bunkhouse for trekkers before or after making the big ascent.

★ Douar Samra
RIAD €€

(☑ 0524 48 40 34; www.douar-samra.net; Tamartert; per person incl half-board Dh485-715; 🛜) At the eastern end of the valley in Tamartert, a trail zigzags among low-slung houses made of pisé; the triple-decker one is Douar Samra. Take the hewn stone steps to candlelit, wood-beamed guest rooms – one of which occupies a treehouse. Donkeys deliver luggage, but there's wi-fi in the organic garden and aperitifs with terrace sunsets.

Kasbah Imlil
GUESTHOUSE €€

(www.kasbah-imlil.com; r €20-45; 🖹🛜) Kasbah Imlil has four handsomely furnished rooms, nicely kitted out with tapestries and warm, earthy hues; two have balconies. You can unwind in the lounge amid Berber rugs and finely crafted lanterns.

Riad Dar Imlil
GUESTHOUSE €€€

(☑ 0524 48 49 17; www.darimlil.com; d Dh800-1500; 🖹🛜) Marrakesh style heads for the mountains at this 20-room stone guesthouse. Bedrooms are comfortable and climate-controlled with hewn wood furnishings, wrought-iron windows and modern en suite with complimentary *babouches* and warm woollen jellabas (garments). Cheaper rooms facing the courtyard are quieter but darker; there's dining on the terrace or by the salon fireplace.

Kasbah du Toubkal
HERITAGE HOTEL €€€

(☑ 0524 48 56 11; www.kasbahdutoubkal.com; dm incl breakfast €40, d €130-250, ste €340-440, villa €820; 🛜) ✈ This converted historic kasbah, at 1800m, lords it over Imlil with grand views over the mountainous landscape. The 11 bedrooms range from quaintly cute to kasbah cool, and 'Berber salons' allow families and groups to bunk communally. Traditional hammam, mountain guides, board games and tasty meals (prix-fixe dinner €20) are on offer.

Minimum two nights in high season. A 5% community tariff has helped build several boarding schools and supply two ambulances.

✖ Eating

Cafe Atlas Toubkal
CAFE €

(mains Dh40-150; ⊙8am-midnight; 🛜) This well-placed eatery in Imlil has a bit of everything: pizzas, brochettes, cakes and the town's best coffees. Head up to the roof deck for superb views over the landscape.

Patisserie La Maison des Association
PASTRIES €

(snacks from Dh4; ⊙10am-7pm) Follow your nose to this tiny pastry shop hidden behind the main street for melt-in-your-mouth, almond-flavoured biscuits and honey sweets baked daily by Berber village girls. Supported by the Kasbah Toubkal, this local association helps villagers learn and perfect new skills.

❶ Information

Bureau Des Guides (☑ 0524 48 56 26; www.bureaudesguidesimlil.com; ⊙8am-7pm; 🛜) This information bureau is open daily during the season. If you arrive without having made arrangements, head here and let them know your requirements and they'll hook you up with a guide for a fixed-price rate (Dh300/400 per half/full day). Guides speak a range of languages, including French, English, German and Spanish.

Trekking maps (Dh80) and free wi-fi are available, and you can leave luggage here (Dh20).

Aroumd

For Berber hospitality above the trekker fray, head 3km up to the hilltop village of Aroumd (also called Armed). You could take the drivable *piste* from Imlil, but the walking path passes a burbling stream, stone houses and shady orchards.

🛏 Sleeping

Les Roches Armed/Chez Lahcen   RIAD €

(📞0667 64 49 15; rochesarmed@yahoo.fr; dm/d per person incl half-board Dh100/200) Atop Aroumd, guests enjoy 360-degree mountain views, admire courtyard gardens, and chat by the living-room fireplace before retreating to private rooms with *tataoui* (woven palm) ceilings or clean dorms. Five shared bathrooms come with hot showers. Hearty High Atlas cooking is served on Berber crockery.

Gîte Le Toubkal Armed   GUESTHOUSE €

(Chez Hadj Omar; 📞0670 41 26 75; r per person without bathroom Dh60, incl half-board Dh200) This well-kept place has simple but comfortably set dorms, with three to six beds in each. The best feature is the tree-lined courtyard patio, which makes a fine place to unwind after a day of hiking.

Dar Warawte/Chez Omar Jellah   RIAD €

(📞0670 41 46 23; toubkal_trek@yahoo.co.uk; per person with/without bathroom Dh300/100) Ideal for families trekking together, this unfussy guesthouse is a fully equipped apartment downstairs from the family home of English-speaking guide Omar Jellah. Through arched doorways is a salon, stucco-edged bedrooms and an enviable kitchen. There's also an upstairs room with en suite.

Jebel Toubkal Ascent

North Africa's tallest peak, **Jebel Toubkal** (4167m) doesn't require climbing experience. In summer, anyone in good physical condition can reach the summit. In early October runners of the **Toubkal Marathon** (www.toubkaltrail.com; ☉Oct) scamper 42km up and down Jebel Toubkal. For extreme ultramarathoners, the organisers tacked a 106km High Atlas trail onto the marathon, calling it the **Toubkal Trail**.

Although the 3313m ascent from Imlil isn't technically difficult, challenges include Toubkal's fast-changing climate, steep slopes of volcanic scree, and altitude sickness. Hikers should factor in sufficient time to ascend slowly and steadily; for a more leisurely ascent, camp en route at Sidi Chamharouch. An ascent of Toubkal can be combined with satellite peaks, and very fit trekkers ascend **Ouanoukrim** (4088m) as well.

THE TREK AT A GLANCE

Duration Two days

Distance 22km

Standard Medium to hard

Start/Finish Imlil village

Highest Point Jebel Toubkal (4167m)

Accommodation Camping and mountain *refuges*

Public Transport Yes

Summary The most popular walk in the High Atlas, with magnificent views. The route is straightforward, but the trek up the scree slope is hard, and trekkers can be struck with altitude sickness. The trek is best in summer and autumn, but check conditions before departure – there can be snow even in June.

ⓘ BEFORE YOU GO: TOUBKAL SUMMIT CHECKLIST

Maps The same maps are recommended as for the Toubkal Circuit.

Water Purifying locally sourced water is a more responsible alternative than bottled water, but don't count on finding available water sources between June and October.

Guide Although the route is marked, a **guide** (p102) is recommended for the ascent, especially for inexperienced mountaineers and in variable conditions from October to June.

Food Meals and snacks are available at Toubkal Refuge and Refuge Mouflon, but you can also find lunch supplies in Imlil and a wide selection of portable snacks in Marrakesh supermarkets.

Mule For this two-day trek with limited gear requirements, most experienced trekkers won't require a mule. If you would prefer one, guides can organise mules and muleteers for you.

Gear Bring a sleeping bag. You won't need a tent, unless you'd rather camp than stay at *refuges* – just ask your guide to arrange tents in advance.

DAY 1: IMLIL TO TOUBKAL REFUGE

DURATION FIVE TO SIX HOURS / DISTANCE 10KM / ASCENT 1467M

Ideally leave **Imlil** early morning – it's uphill all the way, with little shade past Aroumd. Follow the dirt track leading to **Aroumd** (Armed) past the **Kasbah du Toubkal**. Beyond the kasbah, the path zigzags steeply upwards to rejoin the road at Aroumd, where towering slopes begin to close around you.

Past Aroumd, cross the stony valley floor and follow the well-defined mule trail uphill towards a very large rock above the eastern side of the Assif Reraya, which leads to the hamlet and *marabout* of **Sidi Chamharouch** (2310m). Beyond the *marabout*, to the left of the track, are cascades, pools and a prime picnic spot in the shady overhang of the rocks.

After crossing the river by the bridge at Sidi Chamharouch, the rocky path veers away from the river for 2km and zigzags above the valley floor. It then levels off, before rejoining the course of the river. The **Toubkal Refuge** is visible for an hour before you reach it, immediately below the western flank of Jebel Toubkal.

DAY 2: THE ASCENT

DURATION NINE HOURS / DISTANCE 12KM / ASCENT & DESCENT 960M

Set off as early as possible to avoid climbing in the sun – there is no shade, only rocks – and be sure to dress warmly and pack extra water and snacks. If you've trekked here directly from Imlil, you may not be acclimatised, so walk at a steady, slow pace to avoid altitude sickness. If you experience severe headache or vomiting, descend immediately. However tempting, do not lie down to sleep on the slope.

Two *cwms* (valleys formed by glacial activity) run down the western flank of Toubkal, divided by the west-northwest ridge, which leads down from the summit. The southern cwm is the more usual route, and starts immediately below the *refuge* to the left, where you cross the river and head eastwards to the scree slope.

Start to climb the well-defined path to the left of the slope, cross the field of boulders, then follow the path that zigzags up to **Tizi n'Toubkal** (3940m), straight ahead on the skyline. From there the path turns left (northeast) and follows the ridge to the summit (4167m). Allow up to four hours to reach the top, depending on your fitness and weather conditions.

Stick to the same route coming down, bearing left when the *refuge* comes into view.

The descent to the *refuge* should only take 2½ hours, after which you can return to Armoud or Imlil. If you are planning on spending a second night at the *refuge,* you could come down the longer route via the Ihibi sud (south) circuit. It's a straightforward four-hour walk down to the *refuge* for well-earned congratulations and celebratory chocolate.

Toubkal Circuit

Beyond the majestic peaks and fabulous views of Jebel Toubkal, this circuit offers fascinating glimpses into Berber life in remote High Atlas villages. You will need camping gear for this route, though with short detours you could use basic village accommodation and mountain *refuges*.

Since this trek is fairly strenuous, you might want an extra rest day. The ascent of Jebel Toubkal takes place on the sixth day, allowing five days of acclimatisation to altitude. Most of the route is above 2000m, with several passes over 3000m.

Late April to late June is ideal: alpine flowers bloom April to May, and by June daytime temperatures are pleasantly warm. Temperatures often drop below freezing November to May, and snow covers higher peaks and passes. Only lower-valley walking is possible during this season, unless you're prepared to bring ropes and crampons.

Midsummer guarantees long daylight hours and snow-free passes (though not

---

THE TREK AT A GLANCE

Duration Seven to 10 days

Distance 60.2km

Standard Medium to hard

Start/Finish Imlil village

Highest Point Jebel Toubkal (4167m)

Accommodation Camping, village *gîtes* and mountain *refuges*

Public Transport Yes

Summary Easily accessible from Marrakesh, this circuit passes around (and up) Jebel Toubkal passes through landscapes ranging from lush, cultivated valleys and Berber villages to forbidding peaks and bleak passes. This is a demanding trek, with long, gruelling climbs over rocky terrain. A guide is highly recommended, fitness essential.

ℹ BEFORE YOU GO: TOUBKAL CIRCUIT CHECKLIST

Maps The 1:50,000 sheet map *Jebel Toubkal* covers the whole Toubkal Circuit and is sometimes available through the **bureau des guides** (p102) in Imlil. The four-sheet, 1:100,000 topographical *Toubkal Massif Walking Map* also covers the circuit, produced by the Division de la Cartographie (Moroccan Survey) and obtainable from their office in Rabat, in London at Stanfords (www.stanfords.co.uk) or in Marrakesh on the Djemaa el-Fna at Hotel Ali (Dh150). Government-produced 1:100,000 *Cartes des Randonnées dans le Massif du Toubkal* marks trekking routes but includes less topographical detail.

Guide Engage licensed guides at Imlil's *bureau des guides*. Allow at least a day to hire a guide and make trekking arrangements – though if you have specific needs or are travelling in high season, it may take more time.

Mule Mountain guides can organise mules and muleteers for you. Trekkers should be aware that mules have problems crossing Tizi n'Ouanoums, west of Lac d'Ifni, and from November to May, some areas may be impassable. If mules have to take lengthy detours, you may need to carry one day's kit and food. Talk this through with your guide and muleteer.

Food Basic food supplies are available in Imlil, and trail mixes, packaged soups and other light, portable food is stocked by Marrakesh supermarkets.

Water Purifying locally sourced water is a responsible alternative to bottled water, but don't count on finding available water sources – bring your own supply.

Gear A stick or trekking pole is useful. Petrol, diesel and kerosene can be bought in Marrakesh or Asni.

Tent Your guide can arrange tents. The circuit may require some camping, but you could add detours to seek out lodging, or possibly do without tents in summer.

always a snow-free Toubkal), but in the lower valleys temperatures can be extremely hot and water nonexistent. July and August are the busiest months in the High Atlas, but trekking is best done early morning and later in the afternoon.

Flash flooding can occur in summer after thunderstorms – something to bear in mind when deciding where to camp. Rivers have maximum flow in autumn (November) and late spring (April or May).

DAY 1: IMLIL TO TACHEDDIRT
DURATION 3½ TO 4½ HOURS / DISTANCE 9.5KM / ASCENT 560M

Much of the first day's relatively gentle route follows the road linking **Imlil** (1740m) to the village of **Ouaneskra**, 2km west of Tacheddirt (2300m). The road climbs gently eastwards zigzagging up to **Aït Souka**.

After an hour, just past a stream known as Talat n'Aït Souka, you can either take the road north directly to the pass at **Tizi n'Tamatert** (2279m), or follow a fairly well defined but rocky path east, skirting **Tamatert** village. The rocky path continues eastwards for 15 minutes, passing through a small pine grove and crossing the road, before climbing steeply northeast to reach Tizi n'Tamatert. The walk up takes 30 to 45 minutes.

At the pass is **Bivi Thé**, a weather-beaten shack selling pricey soft drinks. To the northeast are great views of **Tizi n'Eddi** (2960m), the pass leading to Oukaïmeden, and **Tizi n'Tacheddirt** (3230m).

The path and tarmac meet at Tizi n'Tamatert, where it's an easy 45-minute walk to Ouaneskra. Along this stretch you'll be treated to views across the valley to neat Berber houses and lush terraces in Talate n'Chaoute, Tamguist and Ouaneskra.

Shortly before Ouaneskra, the path divides. The mule track to the right traverses the southern side of the valley to an ideal camping place near the track, close to the **Irhzer n'Likemt** stream and the starting place for the next day's climb.

The longer route via **Ouaneskra** and **Tacheddirt** takes the northern side of the valley after crossing Tizi n'Tamatert. There are three *gîtes* in Ouaneskra and a pleasant little restaurant – but tomorrow's walk is long, so it's best to have lunch and carry on. The village of **Tacheddirt** is 2km further along the tarmac road. In Tacheddirt, 50 people can sleep at **Tigmi Tacheddirt** (✆0662 10 51 69; www.highatlaslodges.com; per person incl half-board Dh200). From Tacheddirt,

Toubkal Ascent & Circuit Treks

the hiking track loops south, up to the campsite near Irhzer n'Likemt.

DAY 2: TACHEDDIRT TO AZIB LIKEMT

DURATION FIVE TO SIX HOURS / DISTANCE 9KM / ASCENT 1200M / DESCENT 900M

Leave Tacheddirt early to make the two- to three-hour walk up to **Tizi Likemt** (3550m), winding around the head of the valley on a more gentle ascent instead of heading straight down and across the **Assif n'Imenane** and up past the campsite. Though the walk is mostly shaded by mountain shadows in the morning, it's a hard climb, especially a very steep scree slope towards the top.

Close to the campsite, a well-defined rocky path heads up the centre of the gully on the east side of the riverbed (though it crosses over twice). It climbs for about 50

minutes before bearing left (southeast) up to the col (pass). Atop Tizi Likemt are views of verdant valleys and jagged peaks, including Oukaïmeden and Jebel Toubkal on clear days.

The rocky path leading down the other side (southeast) passes a semipermanent water source on the left after 30 minutes, and irrigated pastures above **Azib Likemt** after another hour. An *azib* is a summer settlement, and Azib Likemt (2650m) is occupied from May through October by local people growing crops on irrigated terraces.

You may be offered shelter or a place to pitch your tent in Azib Likemt. Otherwise, walk through terraces down to the **Assif Tifni**, cross the river, turn right and walk upstream to a group of large boulders, where you'll find a flat campsite close to the river.

DAY 3: AZIB LIKEMT TO AMSOUZERT

DURATION SIX TO 6½ HOURS / DISTANCE 15.2KM / ASCENT 470M / DESCENT 1380M

This direct route south to Amsouzert is less demanding, but offers some good ridge walking. From **Azib Likemt**, the well-worn trail leads behind the campsite south, up the mountainside and into the tremendous gorge formed by **Assif n'Tinzer**. Above the river's eastern bank, the trail snakes above the **Tombe Asmine waterfall** before descending close to the river. Follow the river for about two hours past stunning cliffs and through wide pastures, until an obvious track leads up the valley to **Tizi n'Ououraïne** (3120m; also known as Tizi n'Ouaraï) and brilliant views of the eastern face of Toubkal, **Dôme d'Ifni** (3876m) and the rest of the jagged Toubkal massif.

Continue over the col, where the trail traverses the head of the valley to a spur and trail crossroads. Heading southwest, a trail leads down the ridge to **Tagadirt** (after 50m there's a fantastic viewpoint south to **Jebel Siroua**), but turn left (southeast) and follow the mule track south. Traverse the head of another valley and along the side of a spur to reach the ridge after 90 minutes; **Lac d'Ifni** is visible to the west. After a further 15 minutes, just before two pointed outcrops, the path forks. Turn right and continue descending slowly southwards to a large cairn. Descend southwest, then west down to the end of the spur to **Amsouzert** (1797m) in 30 minutes.

Amsouzert is a prosperous village spread on both sides of the river. If you're planning a rest day, this is an excellent place to take it. Next to the school is an outdoor tearoom shaded by an enormous walnut tree where you may able to **camp** (Amsouzert; per tent Dh30). Otherwise, you can stay at **Gîte Himmi Omar** (dm Dh60).

In Amsouzert there are small shops, a couple of cafes west of the river and early morning transport to the N10 highway connecting Marrakesh and Ouarzazate. About 3km south of Amsouzert is another village called Imlil (not to be confused with the Imlil trailhead on the northern side of the range), which hosts a wildly popular **Wednesday souq**.

DAY 4: AMSOUZERT TO AZIB IMI N'OUASSIF

DURATION 5½ TO 6 HOURS / DISTANCE 10.5KM / ASCENT 1100M

Between November and June, mules will not make it much beyond Lac d'Ifni, the largest lake in the High Atlas, which means you'll have to carry your kit to **Azib Imi n'Ouassif** over **Tizi n'Ouanoums** (3600m) to Toubkal Refuge.

From **Amsouzert** follow the level, well-used 4WD track that continues northwest towards Lac d'Ifni above the north side of the river. The path takes you through the villages of **Ibrouane**, **Takatert** and **Tisgouane** before reaching **Aït Igrane**, where there are a couple of cafes and **Gîte Belaïde** (Aït Igrane; dm Dh60). There is also a shady **campsite** (Dh40) on a flat, stony site just beyond the Café Toubkal, with a cold shower and toilet.

Follow the 4WD track along the riverbed northwest out of Aït Igrane, picking up the narrow rocky mule path where the 4WD track crosses the river then turns sharp left. The mule path leads around the north side of **Lac d'Ifni** (2295m), across sharp, rocky, barren, inhospitable terrain. The climb is steep at first, but it descends to the northeastern corner of Lac d'Ifni, an inviting expanse of green water (safe for swimming). The walk to the lake should take three hours. Before you reach the shore, you will pass a **shack** marked 'café'. There's no coffee here, but if it's attended, you may be able to buy water, soft drinks and, with any luck, a tajine.

On the small beach on the northern shore are shady (if occasionally fly-filled) **stone shelters**. If it's rainy, camping nearer the next pass is treacherous, and you're better off finding a campsite above the lake.

Every October, villagers from the surrounding area gather at Lac d'Ifni for a three-day *moussem* in honour of a local *marabout*, whose tomb, **Sidi n'Ifni**, sits high above the southeastern corner of the lake. A track leads from the northeast shore up to the tomb.

From the northwestern side of the lake, the track crosses the wide, dry part of Lac d'Ifni before the long trudge towards **Tizi n'Ouanoums** (3600m). The path climbs through a rocky gorge, keeping to the south side of the river. About 3.5km from the lake, you'll reach **Azib Imi n'Ouassif** (2841m), situated at a crossing of dramatic gorges. Beyond this point the path climbs steeply to Tizi n'Ouanoums, with winds near the summit and small, frigid waterfalls. You'll find flat, rocky areas for pitching tents and shelters in surrounding cliffs long used by local shepherds.

DAY 5: AZIB IMI N'OUASSIF TO TOUBKAL REFUGE

DURATION FOUR HOURS / DISTANCE 4KM / ASCENT 759M / DESCENT 393M

The path to Tizi n'Ouanoums is immediately northwest of the campsite. It's a steep, demanding climb, but the views are spectacular from the top over **Assif n'Moursaïne**, hemmed in by jagged ridges of **Adrar bou Ouzzal** and **Ouimeksane**. The path crosses the river several times after leaving the camp, reaching a stone shelter and water source after an hour and the col another hour further. Even in midsummer it's cold and blustery at the top.

Coming down the other side, there's treacherous loose rock and snow until July. From here you can see Jebel Toubkal and, to the west, the path to **Tizi n'Melloul** (3875m). After the descent, the track levels out and heads due north to Toubkal Refuge (3207m), about two hours from Tizi n'Ouanoums.

CAF's **Toubkal Refuge** ([icon]0661 69 54 63; www.refugedutoubkal.com; dm CAF members/nonmembers from Dh75/145), sometimes labelled Neltner on maps, suffers from overcrowding, damp, and a lack of facilities. The newer **Refuge Mouflon** ([icon]0663 76 37 13; www.refugelesmouflons.com; dm Dh150, r per person incl half-board Dh340) provides more facilities, a better-stocked shop and good meals (Dh90) in the chilly lounge. You can camp downstream from the *refuge* or 20 minutes south of the *refuge* on flat pasture (Dh20).

Assuming you reach the *refuge* before lunch, there are trekking options to occupy the afternoon – including the three- or four-hour descent directly north back to the starting point, Imlil, if you don't want to climb Jebel Toubkal. You could ascend the second-highest mountain in the region, **Jebel Ouanoukrim** (4088m, five to six hours return). The best option is to rest all afternoon to prepare for the climb up Jebel Toubkal the following morning.

DAY 6: TOUBKAL REFUGE TO AZIB TAMSOULT

DURATION FIVE HOURS / DISTANCE 8KM / ASCENT 493M / DESCENT 1300M

From the **Toubkal Refuge** pick up the mule track that heads northwest then gently climbs north across the slope for about 15 minutes. You will come to a fork near a small rounded wall, used as a sheepfold. Turn left, westwards, up the zigzagging mule path, which will bring you to **Tizi n'Aguelzim** (3560m) after two hours. It's a slower trail but less treacherous than the southern route

at Tizi n'Taddert, which is often abruptly closed due to dangerous conditions.

Panoramic views await at Tizi n'Aguelzim pass: east to the Toubkal summit, northeast to the Imlil valley, northwest to Azzadene and west to the Tazaghart plateau. From here, the track twists in some 92 hairpin bends downhill for almost an hour. At the bottom, it crosses a stream. Twenty minutes further on, at a fork, take the left-hand track, and take another left 15 minutes later. Here the track leads uphill for 10 minutes to cosy **CAF Tazaghart Refuge** ([icon]0667 85 27 54, Oukaïmeden 0524 31 90 36; dm CAF members/nonmembers Dh70/145), which sits beside a stunning waterfall. There are mattresses for 22 people, gaslights and a basic kitchen.

You'll probably find the place closed unless you've made a reservation, and the *gardien* (attendant) is based in Tizi Oussem. Phone ahead, or else try passing a message to him via muleteers or shepherds, who may run all the way to Tizi Oussem to fetch him. Campers can pitch tents beside the *refuge*, or on flat ground above the falls.

Tizi n'Melloul (3875m), southeast of Tazaghart *refuge*, offers a harder route to and from the Toubkal Refuge, but provides access to **Afella** (4045m) southeast of the pass and to the jagged ridge leading north to Biginousseun.

The route down to **Azib Tamsoult** (2400m) passes the impressive **Cascades d'Irhoulidene**, where vegetation and tree coverage increases. A five-minute walk from the falls brings you to a pleasant wooded area for camping. To reach the village, walk north for 10 to 15 minutes.

DAY 7: AZIB TAMSOULT TO IMLIL

DURATION FOUR TO FIVE HOURS / DISTANCE 7KM / ASCENT 89M / DESCENT 749M

If you have made good time and you have the legs, you could continue down to Imlil at the end of day six. From the vegetable patches of **Azib Tamsoult**, with the **Assif n'Ouarzane** down to the left, a mule track traversing the forested valley is visible to the north. Head towards it past the village and over the stream, and stay on it, avoiding left forks into the valley.

Climbing slightly and heading steadily northeast, towards the juniper forest with Tizi Oussem due west, you arrive at **Tizi n'Mzik** (2489m), where a sheep shed might serve as shelter. Imlil is a 90-minute descent along a well-worn mule track; there's a spring to the right of the trail after 40 minutes. Comfortable beds and hot tajines await in Imlil.

Tizi n'Test

Blasted through the mountains by the French in the late 1920s, the awe-inspiring road over the Tizi n'Test pass (2092m) was the first modern route linking Marrakesh with the Souss plain. Vital for the control of trade, its hair-raising hairpin bends offer one of the most exhilarating panoramic drives in the country. As if the single-lane road weren't enough of an adventure, the weather is subject to sudden changes. Heavy clouds and mist often cut visibility to near zero and you may find your way blocked by snow in winter.

Heading south from Marrakesh, you'll notice Tin Mal village on the right of the road. The village's Almohad-era mosque (suggested tip Dh10-20) was built in 1156 in honour of the dynasty's strict spiritual leader, Mohammed ibn Tumart, and it a remains an architectural wonder. The mosque is no longer used for prayers, so the guardian will usher you through its massive doors into the serene prayer hall with its intricately carved cedar ceilings.

Beyond Tin Mal, as you approach the pass, you may suddenly break through fog into clear blue sky, and catch breathtaking airplane-window views over cloudbanks. On the south side of the pass, the van ominously embedded into the hillside is your cue for a pit stop at Cafe Dar Issouga (0670 10 65 21; tagine Dh60-100). The balcony offers stunning valley views of green terraces and cypress forests cascading down the hillside all the way to Taroudannt.

THE SOUTHERN OASES

Break through the granite curtain of the High Atlas over the Tizi n'Tichka pass (2260m) and you'll find yourself descending from forested slopes into the flat, stony landscape of Morocco's pre-Sahara. Cypress, juniper and apple blossom quickly give way to thorny acacias and palm trees that flash in sudden bursts of green against a backdrop of mudbrick kasbahs and secretive *ksours*. Snaking through the great *hammada* (stony desert) down to the sandy fringes of the Sahara proper are the southern oases – the Drâa, Dadès and Ziz – long green river valleys thick with date

palms that once served the caravan routes to Timbuktu, Niger and Sudan.

The hub of the region is the administrative centre of Ouarzazate, from where you can embark on excursions south through the Drâa to M'Hamid and the impressive Erg Chigaga dunefield, or east via Skoura along the Dadès Valley to Merzourga and the smaller dunefield of Erg Chebbi.

Tizi n'Tichka

Higher than Tizi n'Test to the west but an easier drive along the N9, the Tizi n'Tichka connects Marrakesh with the southern oases. It was built to bypass the old caravan route to the Drâa, which meandered through the Ounilla Valley and was controlled throughout the 19th century by the powerful Glaoui clan.

If you have a date with the desert, you can make it over Tizi n'Tichka from Marrakesh within three hours. As you pass Aït Ourir, the road ascends and takes a turn for the scenic amid oak trees and walnut groves. Past the village of Taddert, the road gets steeper and the landscape is stripped of colour, except for hardy wildflowers and kids along the road selling geodes dyed shocking red. In winter, check with the Gendarmerie of the Col du Tichka (0524 89 06 15) that the pass is open.

Once over the pass, you can choose one of two routes to Ouarzazate: the quicker journey is to continue along the N9, while the more scenic route takes you via the splendid Glaoui Kasbah (p110) in Telouet and the lush green Ounilla Valley all the way to Aït Benhaddou (p111). You'll find the turn-off to Telouet on the southern side of the road some 20km after the pass. While the road is pockmarked and bumpy, it is possible to navigate all 36km to Aït Benhaddou with a 2WD. The worst section of road is the 11km stretch between Telouet and Anmiter.

If you're not in a rush, it's worth staying in one of the superb guesthouses in the area. I Rocha (p110) and Dar Isselday (p109) both make fine bases to explore this region, and are located about 40km south of the Tizi n'Tichka pass.

🛏 Sleeping

Dar Isselday GUESTHOUSE €
(0666 17 48 81; www.dar-isselday.com; Douar Tisselday; s/d Dh330/440) Najat's traditional lunches prepared with love are served on Dar Isselday's panoramic terrace beneath the shade of a pink peppercorn tree. Inside, six

comfortable rooms sport *tadelakt* bathrooms, and brothers Kamal and Lahcen are on hand to lead interesting walks through the family orchards and to nearby quartz mines. You'll find the house just down the hill from I Rocha on the N9 Marrakesh–Ouarzazate road.

★ **I Rocha** GUESTHOUSE €€
(☑ 0667 73 70 02; www.irocha.com; Douar Tisselday; d/ste incl breakfast Dh690/900; 🛜 ☒) This cliffside stone guesthouse, on the N9 Marrakesh–Ouarzazate road, lifts travel-worn spirits above the green river valley. Ten sunny, cream-coloured rooms have easy-going Berber charm, with wood-beamed ceilings, plush local carpets, and *beldi*-tiled bathrooms. Owners Ahmed and Katherine make terrific French-Moroccan dishes with herbs fresh from the terrace garden (meals around Dh150 per person).

Telouet تيلويت

Telouet occupied a privileged position as the birthplace of French collaborator and autocrat Pasha Glaoui, until he was ousted in 1953 by the Moroccan independence movement. Legend has it that when the imposing doors of Telouet's Glaoui kasbah were thrown open at last, locals who had mysteriously disappeared from their villages years before stum-

bled dazed onto Telouet streets, after years locked in the pasha's basement.

Telouet also once had a thriving Jewish community, entrusted by the Glaoui with managing the all-important salt trade. Salt mines are still active in the area, and prized pink salt found along the nearby Oued Mellah (Salt River) was once accepted as currency. Near the Glaoui Kasbah is what remains of an ancient slave village. But Morocco's government remains ambivalent about the Glaoui clan's home town, and with little outside investment and a highway bypassing the town entirely, Telouet seems arrested in time half a century ago.

◉ Sights & Activities

★ **Glaoui Kasbah** HISTORIC SITE
(admission Dh20; ⊙ 8am-6pm) The once-glorious stronghold has been left to crumble, and the best indication of Telouet's former position as the centre of a trans-Saharan trading empire are the 2nd-floor reception rooms. No less than 300 artisans worked on salons faceted with stucco, *zellij* and painted cedar ceilings that make Marrakesh's royal Bahia Palace seem like a freshman artisan effort.

**Baraka Community
Partnerships** VOLUNTEERING
(www.barakacommunity.com) 🖌 In cooperation with the Tighza Village Association, UK NGO Baraka Community Partnerships offer volunteer vacations in the remote, rural village of Tighza, 16km east of Telouet. Current long-term projects involve the replacement of irrigation channels and larger groups can assist with tree planting.

🛏 Sleeping & Eating

Dar Aissa GÎTE D'ÉTAPE €
(☑ 0670 22 22 47; daraissa@hotmail.fr; Telouet; per person incl breakfast/half-board Dh120/200; @) In downtown Telouet, this simple but welcoming family-run guesthouse offers unfussy rooms in hues of pink and yellow with shared bathrooms set around a modest geranium-filled courtyard. There are sheep and chickens in the yard outside, and Almodhik can advise on treks and other outings in the area.

★ **Riad Kasbah Oliver** GUESTHOUSE €€
(☑ 0677 84 04 87; www.homestaysmorocco.net; Tighza; per person adult/child 6-12yr Dh300/100) 🖌 Owned by Tighza native Mohamed El Qasemy and his British wife, Carolyn, Riad Kasbah Oliver is a labour of love. Built by hand in stone and earth by local village craftsmen, the result

---

WORTH A TRIP

THE OUNILLA VALLEY

Travellers equipped with a sturdy 2WD or 4WD, mountain bikes or good walking shoes can follow the ancient desert caravan routes from Telouet to Aït Benhaddou through the splendid **Ounilla Valley**. Although the first 12km is bumpy and slow going, the remaining 25km to Tamdaght is on good graded *piste*. The fascinating route follows the course of the Oued Mellah passing through **Anmiter** (whose red-tower kasbah gives a glimpse of what Aït Benhaddou may have looked like in its original state), Assaka, Tizgui and other picturesque villages dotting the **Gorge Assaka**. Exiting the Ounilla Valley to the south, you'll spot **limestone threshing terraces** notched into an east-facing hillside. In harvest season, you'll see villagers threshing grain on these stone platforms, just as they've done for centuries.

is simple, sustainable accommodation. Doors were fashioned in Telouet and furniture up-cycled, and hot showers are solar-powered.

Walking tours, salt-mine visits, souk trips and tea with local villagers are just some of the activities that can be arranged. You'll find the turn-off to Tighza 11km east of Telouet, from where it is a 5km drive on rough *piste* to the village.

Le Lion d'Or Atlas
MOROCCAN €

(☑ 0524 88 85 07; meals Dh120) Take a seat on the terrace overlooking the valley and order a tajine with Telouet's speciality figs. You'll find the restaurant on your left 500m from the kasbah. Five simple guest rooms (around Dh250) are also available.

❶ Getting There & Away

From the N9 Marrakesh–Ouarzazate Rd, the turn-off to Telouet is signed 20km beyond the pass. There's a daily bus from Bab Gehmat in Marrakesh (Dh50), which returns to Marrakesh at 7am. Grands taxis are around Dh120 per seat, but you might get stuck paying for all six seats (Dh700). There are no buses from Ouarzazate, only taxis, which charge around Dh60 per seat (or Dh360 for the whole vehicle).

Aït Benhaddou   آيت بن حدو
POP 4200

With the help of some Hollywood touch-ups, this Unesco-protected red mudbrick *ksar* 32km from Ouarzazate seems frozen in time, still resembling its days in the 11th century as an Almoravid caravanserai. Movie buffs may recognise it from *Lawrence of Arabia, Jesus of Nazareth* (for which much of Aït Benhaddou was rebuilt), *Jewel of the Nile* (note the Egyptian towers) and *Gladiator*. A less retouched kasbah can be found 6km north along the tarmac from Aït Benhaddou: the Tamdaght kasbah, a crumbling Glaoui fortification topped by storks' nests.

If you're heading to the desert, Aït Benhaddou is a worthy detour for a tasty lunch and a stroll through the narrow lanes. From the Hôtel la Kasbah, head down past the souvenir stalls to the *ksar* across the parched Oued Ounilla. But where are all the people? The few remaining residents make a few dirham selling souvenirs, carpets and other wares through former homes. One family also operates a small one-room 'museum' (Dh10), with a dusty collection of old door latches, swords, baskets and satchels (plus a vintage record player). Wind your way through winding lanes up to a ruined *aga-dir* with magnificent views of the surrounding *palmeraie* and unforgiving *hammada*.

🛏 Sleeping

Kasbah du Jardin
HOTEL €

(☑ 0524 88 80 19; www.kasbahdujardin.com; camp-site Dh50-70, d Dh250-400; ❋ 🤖 ≋) Near the western entrance to town, the friendly Kasbah du Jardin has decent, nicely equipped rooms set around a sparkling pool – book an upstairs one for better views. You can also pitch a tent here, but there's not much shade.

Etoile Filante d'Or
GUESTHOUSE €€

(☑ 0524 890322; www.etoilefilantedor.com; d incl breakfast from €35; ❋ 🤖) Moonlit desert nights on the Etoile's roof terrace lure guests out of 17 spacious rooms for movie-script-inspiring *ksar* views. Guest rooms feature traditional touches such as *tataoui* ceilings and Berber blankets. The guesthouse also has an inviting restaurant where you can enjoy Moroccan and European fare (three-course dinner Dh100), and a full bar. Nadia, welcoming host, can arrange camel rides, mountain biking and other excursions.

Dar L'Haja
GUESTHOUSE €€

(☑ 0652 03 38 25; www.elhaja-aitbenhaddou.com; s/d Dh350/600) Fuel those Lawrence of Arabia fantasies by overnighting inside the *ksar*. Set along the steps leading through the old fortified village, this guesthouse offers amazing views from the terrace, and the comfortably furnished rooms are nicely maintained.

★ Kasbah Ellouze
HERITAGE HOTEL €€€

(☑ 0524 89 04 59; www.kasbahellouze.com; Tamdaght; s/d/ste incl half-board Dh750/945/1365; ❋ 🤖 ≋) Located 6km north of Aït Benhaddou in the village of Tamdaght, this pisé guesthouse blends in with the adjacent kasbah and makes for a fantastic retreat. The best rooms have orchard views (*luz* means almonds), especially stylish doubles by the heated pool.

Guests gather in the kitchen to learn to make local bread, for aperitifs and wi-fi in the jazz salon, and for watercolour-painting excursions into the Ounilla and Drâa Valleys.

✖ Eating

Chez Brahim
MOROCCAN €€

(☑ 0671 81 63 12; meals Dh100; ⏰ 10am-9pm; 🤖) Sure, there are other tajines in town, but only Brahim's improve international relations: the chef-owner has a letter from Hilary Rodham Clinton thanking him for a

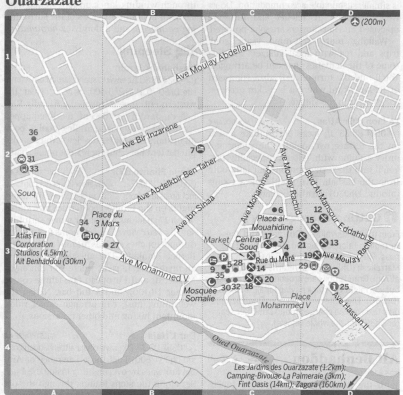

meal in her First Lady days. The set menu includes salads, tajine and dessert in a pisé-walled salon with *ksar* views.

The same family also offers 10 pleasantly set rooms (doubles around Dh300) with fine views.

Auberge Cafe-Restaurant Bilal MOROCCAN €
(📞 0668 24 83 70; mains Dh30-60; ⏰ 10am-9pm; 🛜) For lunch or tea with a magnificent view, pull up a patio chair and gaze at Aït Benhaddou across the way. À la carte options include omelettes, couscous and kebabs.

❶ Getting There & Away

To get here from Ouarzazate take the main road towards Marrakesh to the signposted turn-off (22km); Aït Benhaddou is another 9km down a bitumen road. Cycling from Ouarzazate takes three hours.

Grands taxis run from outside Ouarzazate bus station when full (Dh20 per person) and from the turn-off (around Dh5 per person or Dh30 for the whole vehicle). Minibuses run from Tamdaght to Ouarzazate in the morning when full.

Ouarzazate   ورزازات

POP 62,000

Strategically located Ouarzazate (war-zazat) has gotten by largely on its wits instead of its looks. For centuries, people from the Atlas, Drâa and Dadès Valleys converged to do business at Ouarzazate's sprawling Taourirt Kasbah, and a modern garrison town was established here in the 1920s to oversee France's colonial interests. The movie business gradually took off in Ouarzazate after the French protectorate left in the 1950s, and 'Ouallywood' movie studios have built quite a resume providing convincingly exotic backdrops for movies supposedly set in Tibet, ancient Rome, Somalia and Egypt.

Since King Mohammed VI started visiting here and fixing up the roads, Ouarzazate has been developing quickly with vast

new residential areas marked out to the south of town along with new condo-hotel complexes, a spacious pedestrian plaza and well-stocked supermarkets. With scores of agencies offering bikes, motorbikes and camels, this is an ideal launching pad for mountains, desert and gorges.

◎ Sights

Ouarzazate is more of a staging post in most travel itineraries. If you're here for a day or two, it's worth hiring a taxi and taking a day trip to the nearby **Fint Oasis** or the **Barrage El Mansour Eddahbi**, a popular fishing and birding spot.

From November to March, be prepared for the icy winds that can come whipping down from the High Atlas.

★**Taourirt Kasbah**   MEDINA
(Map p 113;Ave Mohammed V; Dh20; ⊗8am-6.30pm) Unlike other Glaoui kasbahs, Taourirt escaped ruin by moonlighting as a Hollywood backdrop (*Sheltering Sky, Gladiator, Prince of Persia*) and attracting the attention of Unesco, which has carefully restored small sections of the inner sanctum. Follow the maze of stairwells to the top floor, where you'll find a prayer room

through keyhole archways, traces of stucco and an original *tataoui* ceiling.

Afterwards, wander through the village inside the kasbah walls, and you might also find deals on local crafts in backstreet shops.

Atlas Film Corporation Studios
NOTABLE BUILDING

(☑ 0524 88 22 12, 0524 88 22 23; www.studiosat-las.com; adult/child Dh50/35; ☉ 8.15am-5.15pm Oct-Feb, to 6.45pm Mar-Sep) The first 'Ouallywood' studio, established by Mohammed Belghimi in 1983, displays sets and props from movies filmed here, including *Jewel of the Nile, Kingdom of Heaven* and *Kundun*. Guided tours run every 20 to 40 minutes and take you through some of the stages, sets and workshops incorporated in the 150 hectare site. And who knows, you may even get discovered by a talent scout.

Buy tickets at Hotel Oscars next door. The studio is 5km west of town on the Marrakesh road and easily accessible on the green Lux bus (1 or 2, Dh3) that run along Ave Mohammed V.

Musée de Cinema
MUSEUM

(Map p113; ☑ 0524 89 03 46; Ave Mohammed V; adult/student Dh30/15; ☉ 8am-6pm) This small, dusty cinema museum is housed in a former studio and exhibits a collection of old sets, props and cinematic equipment. Located opposite the Taourirt Kasbah, it is a convenient alternative if you can't get to the larger studios out of town.

🚩 Tours

Desert Majesty
TOURS

(Map p 112; ☑ 0524 89 07 65; www.desertmajesty.com; 18 Pl al-Mouahidine; ☉ 9am-12.30pm & 2-8pm Mon-Sat) A highly recommended local agency offering trips to the High Atlas and the desert. Airport pick-ups, multilingual guides originating in Erfoud, Merzouga, M'Hamid and Taouz, and reassuringly safe drivers are offered at competitive prices. Booking queries are handled by Felicity, who is fluent in English, German, French and Darija.

Désert et Montagne
TOURS

(☑ 0524 85 49 49; www.desert-montagne.ma; Dar Daïf, Douar Talmasla) Morocco's first female mountain guide and her company organise trips to meet Berber families in the mountains, walking and 4WD trips in the desert and High Atlas, and longer trips following caravan routes. The agency operates out of Dar Daïf in Douar Talmasla. To reach it, continue south on the N9 and cross the Oued

Ouarzazate, after which it is signposted to the left.

Photo Emotion
TOURS

(☑ 0642 98 89 47; www.rosafrei.com; 1-day workshops per person from Dh3200, 12-day tours €4360; ☉ 10am-4pm Mon-Fri) Swiss photographer and Ouarzazate resident Rosa Frei offers custom-made photography workshops and tours between September and May. Workshops focus on technique, composition, visual awareness and lighting, while tours range down the Drâa and Dadès Valleys to desert and kasbah retreats.

Also possible are shorter trips to the film studios, Fint Oasis and the El Mansour Eddahabi dam. Workshops are in English or German.

Ouarzazate Unlimited
TOURS

(Mapp112; ☑ 0524890641,0661439777; www.ouarzazate-unlimited.com; 6 Rue du Maré) Delivers well-organised camel treks, 4WD desert tours and multi-city itineraries. Select accommodation includes midrange to top-end riads, kasbahs and camps.

Wilderness Wheels
ADVENTURE

(Map p 112; ☑ 0524 88 81 28; www.wildernesswheels.com; 61 Hay al-Qods; 3-day/2-night excursions from €1150) Professionally guided motorbike tours are organised by this British-run company. Prices include overnight stays, complete riding gear and a support car for up to 20 bikes. Sell-out tours include the classic five-day Desert Tour.

Maroc Experience
TOURS

(Map p112; ☑ 0524 88 33 63; www.marocexperiencetours.com; Pl al-Mouahidine; ☉ 9.15am-1pm & 3-7pm Mon-Fri, to 1pm Sat) Italian-owned agency that offers a wide range of tours as well as plane tickets and other travel essentials.

✨ Festivals & Events

The *moussem* of Sidi Daoud is held in Ouarzazate each August.

Marathon des Sables
SPORTS

(www.marathondessables.co.uk; ☉ Mar-Apr) This gruelling six-day, 250km desert ultramarathon changes course each year, and is revealed when runners converge in Ouarzazate.

🛏 Sleeping

Camping-Bivouac La Palmeraie
CAMPGROUND €

(☑ 0676 66 60 64; www.camping-ouarzazate.com; Douar Tajda, N 30°54.151, W 06°53.515; campsite for 2 people incl car/caravan Dh70/75, Berber tent/d incl breakfast Dh250/300, electricity Dh20; P 🛜) Sleep in one of five cosy Berber tents or pitch your own beneath palms and fruit trees in the Ouarzazate *palmeraie*. There's also room for 15 camping cars, and meals are served in the shocking pink salon with its gauzy, tent-like roof. Canoeing excursions and half-day trips to the Fint Oasis are also possible.

Hotel Amlal
HOTEL **€**

(Map p112; 📋 0524 88 40 30; www.amlalhotel. com; 24-25 Rue du Maré; r Dh250, tr/q 300/400; P ✳ 🛜) With its zigzagging tilework and cool terrazzo floors, Hotel Amlal is a decent budget option. Twenty-eight air-con rooms feature simple wood and wrought-iron furnishings, narrow beds and snug, tiled bathrooms. Although the place is showing its age, the location is excellent, with good dining options a short stroll from the hotel.

★ Auberge La Terrasse des Délices
GUESTHOUSE **€€**

(📋 0668 51 56 40; www.terrassedesdelices.com; Oasis de Flint; s/d/tr/q Dh300/450/675/800; ✳ 🈺) It's well worth making the trip out to the Fint Oasis, 13km south of Ouarzazate, for a stay at this idyllic guesthouse. Rachid Azeouane, who hails from the nearby community (his grandfather was the village chief), offers a warm welcome, pleasant rooms set around an interior courtyard and a picturesque terrace in a good spot for gazing out across the oasis and the star-filled skies above.

Rachid can arrange excursions (walks, birdwatching, 4WD trips), and you can come for lunch (sizzling fig tajines are outstanding) and a dip in the pool if you can't stay the night.

★ Dar Bergui
GUESTHOUSE **€€**

(Map p112; 📋 0524 88 77 27; www.darbergui. com; Sidi Hussain Ben Nacer; s/d incl breakfast Dh500/660; ✳ 🛜 🈺) Located with walking distance of the Place al-Mouahidine, this sleek pisé villa with crenellated turrets is the home of Jean-Michel and Martine. The six villa bedrooms arranged around the courtyard swimming pool are simply and tastefully furnished and offer good value for money, especially considering the bountiful breakfast of pancakes, homemade yoghurt, fruit and cake.

Le Petit Riad
GUESTHOUSE **€€**

(Map p113; 📋 0524 88 59 50; http://petitriad. com; Ave Moulay Abdellah, Hay el Wahda; r incl breakfast Dh750; ✳ 🛜 🈺) For those craving light after the shady seclusion of Drâa Valley kasbahs, book a room at the family home of mountain guide Fatima Agoujil. The modern villa has seven large rooms with large picture windows overlooking the flowering gardens and the Atlas mountains. The decor is flamboyant (family artworks, plush quilts, dozens of scatter cushions) and the home-cooked meals are deliciously authentic.

Hotel Azoul
HOTEL **€€**

(Map p112; 📋 0524 88 30 15; www.hotelazoul.com; Av Mohamed V; s/d/ste Dh340/450/650; ✳ 🛜) This good-value place has attractive rooms painted in neutral tones, with silky striped bed covers, carved dark-wood furniture and decent lighting (plus extras like electric

---

DON'T MISS

LA KASBAH DES SABLES

Putting Ouarzazate's film credentials to good use, there is little about **La Kasbah des Sables** (📋 0524 88 54 28; www.lakasbahdessables.com; 195 Hay Aït Kdif; meals Dh200-340; 🕐 noon-2pm & 7-11pm; P) that won't leave you slack-jawed. The 5km journey west of Ouarzazate to the old neighbourhood of Al Kdif is a suitable adventure to whet your appetite for the Arabian Nights spectacle within.

Housed behind the walls of an old Glaoui Kasbah, this 900-sq-metre restaurant is the creation of Brigitte Babolat, who conceived an extraordinary medley of art-filled lounges and nooks arranged around patios hung with grand cut-brass chandeliers dangling like oversized Christmas baubles. The centerpiece is an enormous shallow pool backed by a wall of jewel-coloured lights and surrounded by romantic, candlelit tables where diners are served a mix of Moroccan and French dishes such as barbot and saffron or chicken with Atlas morels. Afterwards, recline in cushion-lined cubbyholes filled with objets d'art crafted in Ouarzazate and Marrakesh. In the morning you'll have to shake yourself and wonder if you didn't dream the whole experience.

> **ℹ STOCK UP BEFORE YOU HIT THE DESERT**
>
> **Supermarché** (Ave Mohammed V; ⏰8am-10pm) Carries all the desert essentials: water, toothpaste, lip balm, packaged soups, cookies, vodka and argan anti-cellulite lotion.
>
> **Supermarket** (Ave Moulay Rachid; ⏰8am-midnight) This large supermarket has imported European foods. Fresh breads are in front on the left.

kettles, mini-fridges and flat-screen TVs). Rooms at the front are brighter with small balconies, but also noisier. It's located on the busy main road, about 13 minutes' walk west of Ouarzazate's centre.

Dar Kamar   GUESTHOUSE €€€
(Map p113; ☑0524 88 87 33; www.darkamar.com; 45 Kasbah Taourirt; s Dh765-1020, d Dh900-1200, ste Dh1360-1900, all incl breakfast; ❄🐾) Once a stern 17th-century Glaoui courthouse, this cosy pisé guesthouse has a sense of humour: upturned tajines serve as sinks and sewing-machine tables are repurposed as desks. Local iron-workers went wild decorating the en suites, though showers are poorly ventilated – a fine excuse to use the in-house hammam and massage room.

✗ Eating

Habous   MOROCCAN €
(Map p112; Pl al-Mouahidine; mains Dh30-70; ⏰restaurant noon-1am, cafe 7am-1am) Overlooking the lively square at the epicentre of Ouarzazate, Habous is the most popular place in town. It has a patisserie, cafe and restaurant, with plenty of outdoor seating for taking in life on the square. The restaurant side (third building on the right) serves up salads, brochettes, sandwiches, pastas and pizzas, plus steaks and *gratin* dishes at reasonable prices.

Chez Nabil   MOROCCAN €
(Map p112; ☑0524 88 45 45; Ave Moulay Rachid; mains Dh45-75; ⏰10am-10pm) With its red-and-white-checked tablecloths and fast, friendly service, Chez Nabil is a local favourite. Choose between quick and easy burgers, chicken skewers and merguez sausages and trad favourites such as liver tajine and couscous.

Aux Delices   PASTRIES €
(Map p112; ☑0524 88 28 29; Ave Moulay Rachid; pastries from Dh5; ⏰6am-midnight) Legendary

for its *chnek* (custard cinnamon-raisin twirl), this patisserie rivals the best in Marrakesh.

Restaurant 3 Thés   MOROCCAN €
(Map p112; ☑0524 88 63 63; Ave Moulay Rachid; mains Dh25-55; ⏰8am-10pm) The wrought-iron sidewalk seating and cosy interiors say Paris cafe, but the menu says cheeseburgers and tasty vegetarian or meaty tajines with figs, prunes or almonds.

★ Douyria   MOROCCAN €€
(Map p113; ☑0524 88 42 62; www.restaurant-ouarzazate.net; 72 Ave Mohammed V; mains Dh60-110; ⏰11am-3pm & 7-11pm; ✎) One of the best eateries in town, Douyria wows dinners with its rooftop terrace, candlelit tables and cushion-lined nooks perfect for taking in the atmospheric surrounds with a cocktail. You can feast on richly flavoured couscous and tajine, including unusual options like roasted goat basted in argan oil or camel with figs; alternatively, stick to well-marinated beef skewers with wild thyme.

Chez Dimitri   FUSION €€
(Map p112; Ave Mohammed V; mains Dh70-120; ⏰noon-3pm & 7-10pm) This historic spot has been around since 1928, when Chez Dimitri played a pivotal role as petrol station, transport hub, restaurant and even dance hall in the fledgling city of Ouarzazate. You can contemplate the past – old sepia prints line the walls – while dining on warm goat's cheese salad, lasagna, lamp chops and the house speciality of moussaka.

Jardin des Arômes   MOROCCAN €€
(Map p112; ☑0524 88 88 02; 69 Ave Mohammed V; mains Dh100-150; ⏰10am-2.30pm & 7-10pm Tue-Sun) Step off busy Ave Mohammed V and climb the steps up to this peaceful *jardin* (garden), with white leather chairs, thick curtains and a tent-like interior overlooking the greenery. Start off with the Lebanese mezzes (taboulet, baba ghanouj, hummus) before moving onto a hearty tajine or a plate of roasted lamb with raisins and almonds.

Accord Majeur   FRENCH, ITALIAN €€€
(Map p112; ☑0524 88 24 73; www.restaurant-accord-majeur.com; Rue Al-Mansour Ad-Dahbi; meals Dh200-275; ⏰11am-10pm Mon-Sat) After a week of desert dining, you may find yourself sleepwalking into this French bistro opposite the Berbère Palace. Here, in cosy nooks lit by a mellow, yellow glow from dozens of brass wall lamps, Aurélie and Charlie serve an impressive menu of foie gras, smoked salmon,

beef carpaccio, duck confit and even home-made liquorice-and-mint ice cream.

If there are any film stars in town, they'll probably be dining here too.

Le Relais Saint Exupéry   FUSION €€€
(☑0524 88 77 79; www.relais-ouarzazate.com; 13 Blvd Moulay Abdellah; mains Dh90-160; ☺11.30am-2.30pm & 6-10pm) The Relais serves creative dishes featuring local ingredients such as Talouine saffron and Saharan salt. Try flaky *pastilla* of fish, or dromedary meat in a Mali-inspired sauce of garlic, cumin, ginger and paprika. It may seem odd to find adventurous gastronomy near the Ouarzazate airport, but this airport was an inspiration to *Little Prince* author and pilot Antoine de Saint-Exupéry.

🛍 Shopping

Horizon Artisanat   ARTS & CRAFTS
(Map p113; ☑0524 88 69 38; 181 Ave An-nasr; ☺9am-7pm) Henna-painted pottery, hand-painted tea glasses, and silver filigree rings are sold at reasonable fixed prices, supporting Horizon's programs to provide vocational training for adults with disabilities and integrate disabled children and adults into the community. The association supports some 2500 people, including 53 permanent staff members.

Complexe Artisanal   ARTS & CRAFTS
(Map p113; Ave Mohammed V; ☺9am 12.30pm & 1.30-6pm Mon-Sat) Opposite the kasbah, this sprawling collection of state-run showrooms features elaborately woven tapestries, local stone carvings, inlaid daggers, metal lanterns and embroidered linens.

Coopérative de Tissage   ARTS & CRAFTS
(Map p113; Weaving Cooperative; ☑0662 61 05 83; Ave Mohammed V; ☺9am-6pm Mon-Sat) Inside the Complexe Artisanal, glimpse women artisans at work (Monday to Friday) on *han-bels* and embroidered straw mats, and take one home at posted fixed prices (Dh550 to Dh1100 per sq metre).

ⓘ Information

EMERGENCY
Police (Map p112; ☑19; Ave Mohammed V)

INTERNET ACCESS
You'll still find a few internet cafes (one hour for around Dh10) around town, including one at the northern end of Ave Mohammed V. Most hotels and guesthouses also offer free wi-fi.

MEDICAL SERVICES
Pharmacies line Ave Mohammed V and post a list of night pharmacies in their windows after hours.

Hôpital Bougafer (Map p112; ☑0524 88 24 44; Ave Mohammed V) Public hospital east of the tourist office.

MONEY
Banks with ATMs line the northern end of Ave Mohammed V.

POST & TELEPHONE
Main Post Office (Map p112; Ave Mohammed V; ☺8.30am-4.30pm Mon-Fri) Postal services and a direct-dial international phone.

TOURIST INFORMATION
Délégation Régionale du Tourisme (Map p112; ONMT; ☑0524 88 24 85; Ave Mohammed V; ☺8.30am-4.30pm) Stocks a few brochures and offers limited advice. Hotels will be able to provide more information.

ⓘ Getting There & Away

AIR
Two kilometres north of town is the **Ouarzazate airport** (Map p112; ☑0522 43 58 58; www.onda.ma). **Royal Air Maroc** (☑0524 88 51 02; www.royalairmaroc.com; 1 Ave Mohammed V) has daily flights direct to Casablanca. Flights arriving in Ouarzazate from Casa tend to land inconveniently just before midnight when night fares apply to taxi services.

During the annual Haj pilgrimage and popular events such as the Marathon des Sables there are extra flights.

BUS
Supratours operates buses from Marrakesh (Dh80, 4½ hours, three daily) and one daily service to Zagora (Dh50, three hours), Er-Rachidia (Dh90, 5½ hours) and Merzouga (Dh140, eight hours). **Supratours Al Hizam** (Map p112; ☑0524 89 07 96; Ave Moulay Abdellah; ☺7.30am-11pm) sells tickets, and the bus stops outside.

CTM (Map p112; ☑0524 88 24 27; Ave Mohammed V; ☺7am-10pm) buses also serve Marrakesh (Dh85, five to seven daily), Agadir (Dh140, 7½ hours, one daily), Er-Rachidia (Dh85, 5½ hours, one daily) and Zagora (Dh60, three hours, two to three daily). During local holidays and busy periods, book your tickets at least a day in advance. The CTM bus station is conveniently located bang in the centre of town, near the post office.

The main, local **bus station** (Gare Routière; Mahta) is 1km northwest of the town centre off Ave Moulay Abdellah. Several buses a day leave from here to Marrakesh (Dh70, four to five hours), Boumalne du Dadès (Dh35), Taroudannt (Dh80, five hours), Tazenakht (Dh25, three hours), Foum Zguid (Dh40, four hours), Tata (Dh80, five hours) and M'Hamid (Dh75, seven hours) via Zagora (Dh45, four hours).

CAR

For desert detours you might want to rent a car (from Dh350 per day); car hire with a driver runs Dh900 (car) to Dh1250 (4WD). There are dozens of agencies in town and international outfits such as **Avis** (Map p112; ✒ 0524 88 80 00; www. avis.com; cnr Ave Mohammed V & Pl du 3 Mars), **Hertz** (Map p112; ✒ 0524 88 20 84; www.hertz. com; 33 Ave Mohammed V), **Budget** (Map p112; ✒ 0524 88 42 02; www.budget.com; 28 Ave Mohammed V; ⊙ 8.30am-noon & 2.30-7pm Mon-Sat) and **National** (Map p112; ✒ 0524 88 20 35; www.nationalcar.com; Place du 3 Mars) all have booths at the airport, although they are more expensive than local operators. Other operators: **Desert Evasion** (Map p112; ✒ 0524 88 86 82; www.desert-evasion.net; Imm El Ghifari, Ave Mohammed V) Payment due upon receipt of keys. Has 4WDs.

ESON Maroc (Map p112; ✒ 0666 89 08 99; www.eson-maroc.com; Ave Mohammed VI) Reliable and much cheaper than the international agencies; also has 4WDs.

TAXI

Grands taxis leave from outside the main bus station to Agdz (Dh40), Boumalne du Dadès (Dh65), Marrakesh (Dh80 to Dh110), Skoura (Dh25 to Dh30), Tinerhir (Dh80) and Zagora (Dh40 to Dh60).

❶ Getting Around

Petits taxis run up and down Ave Mohammed V for flat rates of Dh5 per person (based on three people sharing). There is no bus into town from the airport; taxis to/from town cost between Dh50 and Dh80 depending on the time of day.

DRÂA VALLEY وادي درعة

From Ouarzazate the N9 plunges southeast into the Drâa Valley, formed by a narrow ribbon of water from the High Atlas that occasionally emerges triumphantly in lush oases, particularly between Agdz and Zagora, a stretch of about 95km. The drive from Agdz to Zagora takes three to four hours, though the more scenic Circuits Touristiques route follows the *piste* through the oasis. Beyond that, a road takes you 96km further south to M'Hamid, a town 40km short of the Algerian border that marks the end of the road and the start of the desert proper.

If you don't want to retrace your steps back to Ouarzazate along the N9, it's possible to continue west of M'Hamid through the desert to Foum Zguid, from where you can pick up the N10 north via Tazenakht. For those with more time, it's possible to complete an enormous circuit east on the N12 from Tansikht (29km southeast of Agdz) to the Erg Chebbi dune field near Merzouga and return to Ouarzazate via the Todra and Dades Gorges.

Agdz اكدز
POP 9400

Travellers who zoom from Ouarzazate to Zagora are missing out on Agdz (ag-*daz*), a classic caravanserai oasis with a still-pristine *palmeraie*, ancient mudbrick kasbahs and a secret desert prison. As you approach the town, you'll see tajine-shaped Jebel Kissane on the horizon, and spot mountain bikers heading off from Agdz to 1660m Tizi n'Tinififft, some 20km away. The mountains glisten with what looks like snow, but that's a mirage: it's sunlight bouncing off deposits of reflective mica. Agdz crafts traditions include carving, pottery and basket-weaving, and you might spot a few prime examples outside shops downtown or at the Thursday souq (Oct and Nov).

⊙ Sights

None of Agdz's key attractions are apparent from the main road. The historic centre is east of the N9, about 1.5km along a dusty *piste,* so has been largely bypassed by mass-tourism development schemes. For that very reason, an unusual number of authentic mudbrick kasbahs have been preserved. Overnight visitors might also take a morning stroll through the vast Agdz *palmeraie,* just to the north of the village.

Caïd's Kasbah MEDINA
(Dh30) The 170-year-old kasbah that once belonged to the *caïd* of Agdz is now owned by his descendants. Stop at the reception of Casbah Caïd Ali (p119) next door for admission to the mudbrick structure, and explore a maze of rooms spread over three storeys. The play of light and shade in the ancient kasbah could keep photographers entertained for hours, but best of all are the rooftop views over the neighbouring oasis.

LOCAL KNOWLEDGE

THE IDEAL DATE

For prime date selection, head to **Tinzouline**, about 56km south of Agdz, during the September to November date season. You're getting close when you spot vendors with dates overflowing from palm-frond baskets along the Zagora road. You may run into traffic for the Monday souq, where you'll be elbow to elbow with local grandmothers vying for the best local-speciality boufeggou dates. This is a date to remember: nicely caramelised outside by the desert sun, and tender and savoury-sweet inside.

If you're not visiting the valley in autumn, you still have a standing dessert date in **Timidarte**, where local dates become Slow Food sensations at **Timarine Tijara** (p121), 18km south of Agdz. Head past historic mudbrick kasbahs, through the garden of a traditional family home, and into a spotless white-tiled kitchen with a single industrial cauldron bubbling merrily away and a dozen jars of Timarine Tijara's signature date jam and *tahalout* (date syrup). 'Try drizzling some on warm goat cheese – it brings out the nutty, fruity flavours in our dates', advises owner and date gourmet innovator Abderrahim Ouagarane.

Glaoui Kasbah   MEDINA

(customary tip Dh20) Long-time residents of Agdz report their shock at discovering that the walled Glaoui kasbah in Agdz was used as a secret desert detention centre. Hassan II's purges to suppress political dissidents led to the establishment of such secret detention centres, details of which emerged post-2004 through Morocco's Equity and Reconciliation Commission. It's located on the southern side of the *piste* near Rose du Sable guesthouse and marked 307 on the gate.

If you see the next-door neighbour who keeps an eye on the place, you can ask him to let you in the door to look around.

🛏 Sleeping & Eating

Cafes ring Pl Marché Vert in downtown Agdz.

Dar Jnane   GUESTHOUSE €

(☎0673 18 13 14; www.darjnane-location-sud-maroc.com; r per person Dh350; ❄) Run by a kindly French-Moroccan couple, Dar Jnane has three handsomely furnished bedrooms set amid peaceful gardens roughly 1km (well-signed) off the highway. Meals are available (dinner Dh 60 to Dh90), you can hire mountain bikes, and Lahcen and Dominique can advise on scenic walks in the area.

Casbah Caïd Ali   HERITAGE HOTEL €

(☎0524 84 36 40, 0698 90 65 50; Rue Hassan II; d/tr/q incl breakfast Dh240/350/400, mattress on roof Dh50, campsite for 2 people around Dh60; ❄❄❄) Descendants of the local *caïd* welcome guests to their partially restored kasbah. Courtyard guest rooms are basic, though the colourfully painted ceilings add character. Camping is good beneath the

palms, and you can also sleep outdoors on the terrace beneath star-filled skies.

In early April, the kasbah hosts an international music festival on the grounds – well worth attending if you're passing through.

Dar Amazir   GUESTHOUSE €€

(☎0524 84 37 93; www.daramazir.com; d/ste from Dh600/900; ❄❄❄) A delightful hideaway in Agdz, the Dar Amazir is a rather compact property, with an enticing swimming pool at the centre, and eight lovely rooms set with Malian masks, Berber tapestries on the walls, carved wooden doors and smooth *tadelakt* bathrooms. The friendly host rolls out the welcome mat with mint tea upon arrival, and makes guests feel right at home.

Kasbah Azul   GUESTHOUSE €€€

(☎0524 84 39 31; www.kasbahazul.com; Agdz; d incl breakfast Dh935-1265, ste Dh1430-2100; P❄❄❄) Hiding in a garden at the eastern end of the historic centre like an arty recluse, this seven-room kasbah has beautifully furnished rooms with tadelakt en suites in contrasting hues: acid green and plum, terracotta and powder blue. The owner contributed her own collaged lamps and paintings to this artist's retreat, which also has a keyhole pool and copious breakfasts.

ℹ Getting There & Away

Buses from Ouarzazate (Dh30 to Dh40, one hour) and Zagora (Dh40, two hours) stop in the Grand Place; the CTM office is in the northeast corner of the square. You can also pick up grands taxis here for Ouarzazate (Dh30 to Dh40), Zagora (Dh40) and N'Kob (Dh30). The back country road N12 to Rissani meets the N9 29km east of Agdz.

CIRCUITS TOURISTIQUES

Those with 4WD shouldn't miss the slower, scenic *piste* that runs from Tamnougalt to just north of Zagora, parallel to highway N9. The dirt road winds along the northern side of the valley through palm oases, villages, patchwork fields and river vistas all the way to Zagora. For shorter 4WD excursions along the scenic northern side of the Drâa, follow signposts for 'circuits touristiques' off N9 (near the Afriquia petrol station) just before Ouled Aïtman that lead past **Kasbah Said Arabi** and the **Tinzouline kasbah**. At Tansikht, about 29km before Zagora, look out for the old watchtower guarding the *palmeraie,* signposted 'Oasis Du Drâa.'

Tamnougalt

Perched on a hill 6km from Agdz is a star attraction of the Drâa Valley: a 16th-century fortified village that's among the oldest mudbrick *ksour* still standing.

◉ Sights & Activities

★ Kasbah des Caïds   CASTLE
(Musée du Tamnougalt; Dh20, optional guide Dh50) The maze of rooms at Tamnougalt *ksar* leads through a sizeable *mellah,* dips underground with strategically placed skylights and candle nooks, and emerges into sunny courtyard stables lined with horseshoe arches. See if you can distinguish between the Arab, Andalusian and Berber Jewish motifs that blend so seamlessly here – or at least recognise scenes shot here from Oscar-winning movies *Babel* and *The English Patient.* Purchase tickets at Chez Yacob (p120).

Abdel Jalil   OUTDOORS
(☏0673 61 84 00) Multilingual guide Abdel Jalil has an office just outside the Kasbah des Caïds and offers guided visits of the kasbah (Dh50) as well as longer excursions through the village and *palmeraie* (Dh100). He can also help arrange overnight stays with families living inside the *ksar* and many other activities.

⌂ Sleeping

Chez Yacob   HERITAGE HOTEL €€
(☏0524 84 33 94; www.lavalleedudraa.com; r per person incl half-board Dh300; ❊) Next door to

Tamnougalt's ancient *mellah* are eight snug rooms with en suites ringing a soaring courtyard and capped by a scenic terrace overlooking the *palmeraie*. Set menus (Dh90) are bountiful enough to count as lunch and dinner. It's 2km from Rte de Zagora down an unpaved lane.

★ Bab el Oued   GUESTHOUSE €€€
(☏0660 18 84 84; www.babelouedmaroc.com; d Dh825-935, tr Dh1320, ste Dh935-1815; ℗❊❊)
🍃 Shaded by date palms in a walled organic garden, these ecofriendly bungalows 6km south of Agdz beam with local pride, thanks to wooden doors carved in town, carpets from nearby Tazenakht, palm-beamed ceilings, and glossy *tadelakt* bathrooms. By keeping the pool small and the toilets lowflow, the French- and English-speaking owners conserve enough water to grow 60 types of plants, including herbs and vegetables for Moroccan-Mediterranean meals.

Nonguests can call ahead for delicious organic lunches (Dh176), and nap in hammocks by goldfish ponds afterwards.

❶ Getting There & Away

Turn left off the main road 4km past Agdz, then 2km east up a *piste*. There's no reliable public transport here.

Timidarte

If you want to (all together now) rock the kasbahs, turn west off N9 to check out prime specimens in Timidarte village. The finest example dates from the 17th century, recently converted by Timidarte's tourism association into an authentic kasbah guesthouse, Kasbah Timidarte.

⌂ Sleeping

Kasbah Timidarte   HERITAGE HOTEL €
(☏0668 68 00 47; www.kasbahtimidarte.com; s/d incl half-board Dh300/460, with shared bathroom Dh260/320) Live much like kasbah inhabitants have for centuries. Seven mudbrick rooms are arranged around a central light well, with palm-frond mats and mattresses on floors. Instead of TV, there's socialising under the stars on the roof terrace, next to a Berber bread oven. It's 1km east of Rte de Zagora, 15km south of Agdz.

Some improvements have been made since the 17th century – there's electric light for reading, and several rooms have en suites. Timidarte's tourism association members have taken to the task of cooking for guests with gusto, and home-style Berber meals are a point of pride.

🛍 Shopping

Timarine Tijara FOOD
(☑ 0661 91 32 25; ☺ by appointment) Timidarte is becoming a magnet for foodies with this artisan producer of date jam and syrup – call ahead for tastings and bargain purchases (Dh15 to Dh40).

Zagora زاكورة

POP 36,000

The original, iconic 'Tombouctou, 52 jours' (Timbuktu, 52 days) sign, featuring a nomad with a smirking camel, may have been swept away in an inexplicable government beautification scheme, but Zagora's fame as a desert outpost remains indelible. The Saadians launched their expedition to conquer Timbuktu here in 1591, and desert caravans passing through gave this isolated spot cosmopolitan character. These days Zagora remains a trading post and meeting place, hosting a regional souq on Wednesday and Sunday and putting on a variety of lively festivals.

👁 Sights

★**Musée des Arts et Traditions de la Valleé du Drâa** MUSEUM
(☑ 0667 69 06 02; Kasbah de Tissergat; Dh25; ☺ 8.30am-7pm) Eight kilometres north of town, below a spectacular view point over the *palmeraie,* follow 'Musée' signs to a triple-storey mudbrick home that houses this fascinating desert-culture museum. In the tea salon, you'll find key equipment for desert entertaining c 1930: a vintage ham radio, a gramophone, and tea glasses believed to shatter on contact with poison.

Artifacts are tagged with insightful explanations of their origins and purpose in French and English – very helpful for explaining otherwise mysterious tattooing implements, the intriguing birthing room and markedly different wedding garments from five local tribes. The people behind the museum also run a recommended guesthouse next door.

Amezrou AREA
Zagora's desert-crossroads culture can be glimpsed in the adjacent village (south of downtown Zagora, across the Oued Drâa), where artisans in the historic *mellah* work good-luck charms from African, Berber,

Zagora

❷ Activities, Courses & Tours
1 Caravane Desert et Montagne A2
2 Caravane du Sud B3
3 Caravane Hamada Drâa.....................A2

🛏 Sleeping
4 Auberge Restaurant Chez Ali A2
5 Camping Oasis Palmier......................B2
6 Hotel la Fibule du Draa......................B3
7 La Petite Kasbah................................B3
8 Riad Dar Sofian B2
9 Riad Soleil du Monde.........................B3
10 Villa Zagora.......................................B3

❸ Drinking & Nightlife
11 African Bar B3

❶ Information
12 Banque Populaire...............................A2
13 BMCE..A1
14 Pharmacy Zagora A2

❶ Transport
15 Bus Station.......................................A1
16 CTM Bus Station...............................A2
    Grands Taxis ....(see 15)
17 Supratours...A2

Jewish and Muslim traditions into their designs. In the 1930s, Amezrou had some 400 Jewish households, but almost all had left town by the 1960s.

Ask an elderly resident to point you towards the tiny synagogue. The family opposite will let you into the prayer room (Dh20 tip customary).

Jebel Zagora MOUNTAIN
This spectacular mountain rises over the Oued Drâa – worth climbing for the views, provided you have stamina, water and sunblock and set off in the early morning. The round trip to Jebel Zagora takes about three hours on foot, or 45 minutes by car along the *piste* to the right beyond Camping de la Montagne. Halfway up are the faint ruins of an 11th-century Almoravid fortress, but the military installation at the summit is off-limits.

🏃 Activities

Nearly every tourist in Zagora is heading for the Sahara and many plan their trips here. That said, the desert gateway of M'Hamid is still a three-hour drive further south with the undulating dunes of Erg Chigaga an additional (and expensive) 56km off-road southwest from M'Hamid. When planning trips with local operators make sure you know where your trip is headed. The closest dunes to Zagora are Erg Nakhla (12km northeast of town), Tinfou (25km south beside the N9), El Messouira and Erg Lihoudi (both approximately 90km south near M'Hamid).

For dromedary rides all-inclusive prices range from Dh350 to Dh600, depending on the campsite and the size of the group.

☞ Tours

Wild Morocco TOURS
(☑ 0655 77 81 73; www.wildmorocco.com) This Berber-British partnership run by M'Hamid native Yahya and corporate-escapee Emily distinguishes itself by its professionalism and passion. Abandoning the nomadic life after the damming of the Drâa made it unfeasible, Yahya put his immense knowledge of the desert, its customs, flora and fauna, to service in these well-planned itineraries.

Adventurers can join three- to six-day desert treks following nomadic migration routes, musicians find guitars conjured from neighbours for impromptu desert jam sessions, and budding anthropologists break bread with Drâa Valley families or join Harratin inhabitants in M'Hamid's old *ksar* for tea and local gossip. Larger excursions combining Altas mountain trekking, the gorges and desert tours are also possible, as are desert trips to Erg Chebbi.

Caravane Desert et Montagne OUTDOORS
(Map p121; ☑ 0611 15 37 66; www.caravanedesertetmontagne.com; 112 Blvd Mohammed V) Partners with local nomads to create adventures off the beaten camel track for individuals and small groups.

Caravane du Sud OUTDOORS
(Map p121; ☑ 0524 84 75 69; www.caravanedusud.com; Amezrou; ⊗ 8am-7pm) Three- to 14-day camel treks, 4WD circuits and a three-day round-trip to Erg Chigaga (Dh1900). It also offers cheaper departures from M'Hamid. You'll find it on the roundabout in Amezrou.

Caravane Hamada Drâa OUTDOORS
(Map p121; ☑ 0661 32 81 06; www.hamadadraa.com; Blvd Mohammed V) Treks to nomadic camps by licensed English-speaking guides and native nomad Youssef M'Hidi.

✴ Festivals & Events

Moussem of Sufi
Moulay Abdelkader Jilali RELIGIOUS
This *moussem,* which takes place at the same time as Moulid an-Nabi, is the Drâa's biggest shindig. Members of the Sufi Jilala brotherhood make a pilgrimage to Zagora to pay their respects, and you may hear their hypnotic music of praise and celebration with the *bendir* (hand-held drum).

🛏 Sleeping

★ Auberge Restaurant Chez Ali INN €
(Map p121; ☑ 0524 84 62 58; http://chezali.net; Ave de l'Atlas Zaouiate El Baraka; d incl breakfast without bathroom Dh70-90, with bathroom Dh200-300; ▣✳🖥🏊) The peacocks stalking the pool can't be bothered, but otherwise the welcome here is enthusiastic. Sky-lit upstairs rooms have simple pine furnishings, bathrooms and air-con, and 'traditional' rooms have mattresses on carpets and shared bathrooms. Enjoy fantastic Berber meals (Dh100) and overnight trips run by English-speaking guides Mohamed and Yusuf.

La Petite Kasbah GUESTHOUSE €
(Map p121; ☑ 0524 84 80 43; www.hotelzagora.com; Amezrou; r per person incl breakfast/half-board Dh175/275; ▣🖥) 🍃 Expect a warm welcome and a fresh glass of mint tea when you arrive at La Petite Kasbah. Originally the family home of Brahim Badri, the mini kasbah

MARRAKESH & CENTRAL MOROCCO ZAGORA

now has five rooms around a flower-filled courtyard, a cushion-strewn tea salon and a terrace overlooking the Amezrou *palmeraie*.

Camping Oasis Palmier
CAMPGROUND €

(Map p121; ☑ 0613 98 52 31; pixameharee@hotmail.com; Rte de Nakhla; camping per person Dh20, per Berber tent Dh15-30, per car Dh15, campervans Dh30; P 🛜) Located just north of Amezrou, this campsite has a mixture of palm-shaded pitches and Berber tents. It also has a cafe, free wi-fi, hot showers (Dh10) and electric hook-ups (Dh20), and it'll even deliver fresh bread to your door.

Kasbah Ziwana
GUESTHOUSE €€

(☑ 0667 69 06 02; www.kasbah-ziwana-zagora.com; s/d incl half-board Dh300/600; 🌟) Next to the Musée des Arts in Tissergat, 8km north of Zagora, the Kasbah Ziwana is made of native materials, and has attractively furnished rooms. Relax in the peaceful inner courtyard or on the roof terrace, and get loads of local insight from the kindhearted host Mustapha, a desert guide with many years of experience.

Riad Soleil du Monde
GUESTHOUSE €€

(Map p121; ☑ 0661 68 71 31; almalamzrou@yahoo.fr; d Dh330-540; P 🛜 🏊) Tucked down a narrow dirt road near Amezrou, this four-room guesthouse has beautifully set rooms, with striking coloured glass light fixtures, pisé walls and decorative moulding. The pool, fringed by towering date palms and pomegranate trees, makes a fine retreat on hot days. The warm welcome and idyllic location in the *palmeraie* adds to the appeal.

Villa Zagora
GUESTHOUSE €€

(Map p121; ☑ 0524 84 60 93; www.mavillaausahara.com; Rte de Nakhla, Amezrou; d incl breakfast Dh540-740, ste Dh740-950, Berber tent per person Dh190; 🌟 🛜 🏊) Light, breezy and naturally charming, this converted country home makes desert living look easy. French doors reveal plush Moroccan carpets, soaring ceilings, and an eclectic art collection, including Zagora-inspired abstracts. Staff fuss over you like Moroccan relations you never knew you had, and decadent meals (around Dh160) feature oasis-fresh ingredients.

Riad de Rêve
GUESTHOUSE €€

(☑ 0677 19 13 37; www.facebook.com/riaddereve; 353 Hay Moulay Rachid; s/d/ste incl half-board Dh370/560/1100; 🌟 🛜) Escape the typical tourist accommodation and spend a night at Abdesalem's intimate riad home, where he'll whip up tasty traditional dishes and a variety of home-baked breads. With a nomadic back-

ground and years of experience working in Switzerland, your host is a master of hospitality and a knowledgeable guide to local history and folklore and the surrounding desert.

★ Riad Dar Sofian
GUESTHOUSE €€€

(Map p121; ☑ 0524 84 73 19; www.riaddarsofian.com; Rte de Nakhla, Amezrou; s/d/tr incl breakfast Dh680/880/1100, tents Dh220; P 🌟 🛜 🏊) Setting new standards in Zagora, Dar Sofian is a stunning desert oasis. The fabulous pisé edifice was constructed by a team from Skoura, while Fassi craftsmen executed the acres of tilework inside. The decor is a successful take on contemporary Moroccan with a mix of modern beds and bathrooms, antique furnishings and traditional detailing.

🍴 Eating & Drinking

Hotels provide set meals (Dh100 to Dh150) to guests and nonguests by prior reservation. Auberge Restaurant Chez Ali (p122) is a standout for quality and freshness, and you can join off-duty desert guides at **La Rose des Sables** (☑ 0524 84 72 74; Ave Allal Ben Abdallah; meals Dh40-60). Cafes and *laterie* (juice shops) cluster around the intersection of Boulevard Mohammed V and Ave Allal Ben Abdallah and serve a good selection of staples like roast chicken, tajine and pizza for Dh20 to Dh35.

Picnic ingredients can be found at the supermarket at the northern end of town (no alcohol) and a bakery on Mohammed V.

For a stiff drink, head to the garden bar at **La F** (☑ 0524 84 73 18; Amezrou; s/d/tr incl breakfast from Dh400/540/700; P 🛜)**ibule du Draa** (☑ 0524 84 73 18; Amezrou; s/d/tr incl breakfast from Dh400/540/700; P 🛜 🏊) or the **African Bar** (☑ 0524 84 83 88; www.riadlamane.com; Amezrou) at Riad Lamane.

ℹ️ Information

Most hotels offer wi-fi and there are several internet cafes along Blvd Mohammed V and Ave Allal Ben Abdallah (Dh10 per hour).

Banque Populaire (Map p121; Blvd Mohammed V) Stock up on cash at one of the last ATMs you'll find before you hit the Sahara.

BMCE (Map p121; Blvd Mohammed V) ATM.

Pharmacy Zagora (Map p121; ☑ 0524 84 71 95; Blvd Mohammed V; ⊙ 8.30am-1pm & 3-8pm Mon-Fri, 8.30am-1pm Sat)

ℹ️ Getting There & Away

AIR

Zagora has a small airport, southwest of town off the N12, that has two weekly flights (Monday and Wednesday) from Casablanca with Royal Air Maroc (www.royalairmaroc.com).

BUS

The **CTM bus station** (Map p121; ☑ 0524 84 73 27; Blvd Mohammed V) is at the southwestern end of Mohammed V, while the local **bus station** is beside the mosque, where grands taxis also depart. **Supratours** (Map p121; ☑ 0524 84 76 88; Blvd Mohammed V), near the Banque Populaire, offers a daily 6am bus to Marrakesh (Dh135, 7½ hours) and Ouarzazate (Dh50, 2¾ hours). There is also a daily CTM bus to M'Hamid (Dh35, 2¾ hours) and three daily CTM buses to Ouarzazate (Dh55, three hours), two of which continue to Marrakesh (Dh135, 8½ hours).

Other companies, which are based at the local bus station, have at least one run a day to Marrakesh (Dh120) and Ouarzazate (Dh55, three hours). There are buses to Rissani (Dh100, six hours) via N'Kob (Dh20, two hours) and Tazzarine (Dh35, 2½ hours) three times a week. A bus passes through Zagora to M'Hamid (Dh35, three hours) in the morning. More frequent minibuses run to M'Hamid (Dh30) throughout the day when full.

TAXI

Grands taxis (Map p121; Blvd Mohammed V) can be found in the centre of town beside the the morning. Destinations include Tamegroute (Dh10, 20 minutes), Agdz (Dh35, 1½ hours), Ouarzazate (Dh80, three hours), M'Hamid (Dh35, 1½ hours) and N'Kob (Dh50 to Dh60, 1½ hours).

Tamegroute تامكروت

Stressed out? You've come to the right place: Tamegroute's Zawiya Nassiriyya is said to cure anxiety and high blood pressure, thanks to the post-mortem calming influence of Sidi Mohammed ben Nassir – founder of the influential and learned Nassiri brotherhood, who were famed for their ability in settling

---

QUICK GETAWAY: TINFOU DUNES

M'Hamid's grand **Erg Chigaga** (p125) or the great inland sea of dunes in **Merzouga** (p148) can make this small patch of two to three dunes seem like a child's sandbox by comparison. Around 8km south of Tamegroute, you'll spot them marooned by the road on your left. On busy days it can feel like a playground here, but it's still fun to climb and run down the big dunes.

Drâa Valley disputes in the 17th century. The *zawiya* is still a place of pilgrimage for the sick and a working Quranic school. Bibliophiles should plan desert trips around visits to the *zawiya's* library of ancient illuminated texts or try to coincide with the annual *moussem* (12 to 22 November).

Besides miracle cures, Tamegroute is known for its labyrinth of *ksour*, which you can explore with a local guide or by yourself to test your internal compass. Tamegroute also has a Saturday souq.

◉ Sights

★**Cooperative des Potiers**   GALLERY
(⊙8am-6pm Mon-Fri) Oxidised copper yields the distinctive 'Tamegroute green' glaze used on the local pottery, which originated when the Nassiri brotherhood invited craftsmen from Fez to settle in the village. Two families remain, turning out iridescent rustic bowls, stamped tiles and elegant platters. Heading south, you'll find it on your left as you leave the village.

Zawiya Nassiriyya   ISLAMIC SITE
(suggested donation Dh20; ⊙morning & late afternoon Sat-Thu) Although non-Muslims can't visit Sidi ben Nassir's green-roofed mausoleum, anyone can visit the library inside the adjacent *medersa* for Quranic scholars. Among the 4000 books on these glassed-in shelves are ancient medical, mathematics, algebra and law texts, in addition to splendid 13th-century Qurans written on gazelle hide. You'll find it through an arch in the northwest corner of the main square.

🛏 Sleeping & Eating

**Auberge-Restaurant-
Camping-Jnane Dar Diafa**   GUESTHOUSE €
(☑ 066134 8149; www.jnanedar.ch; s/d Dh300/380, without bathroom from Dh180/220, all incl breakfast) In this breezy garden-gazebo restaurant, enjoy leisurely lunches made with vegetables grown on the premises. Scuffed but winsome pisé-walled guest rooms overlook the garden, some featuring air-con, mosquito nets over beds, and star-patterned walls.

Tamegroute to M'Hamid

From Tamgroute the road south narrows to a single lane highway (being widened at the time of research) and takes you through a dauntingly bleak landscape of sun-scorched rubble, until the road ascends up and over

Tizi Beni Selmane pass. Midway, the village of **Tagounite** has petrol and several cafes. It's also a jumping-off point for the **El Mesouira** and **Erg Lihoudi** dunes, which lie southwest of Tagounite.

🛏 Sleeping

⭐ **La Dune Blanche** CAMPGROUND €€
(📞0667 96 64 64; www.bivouac-ladune blanche-zagora.com; N 29°56'05.53, W 005°41'28.13; per person incl half-/full board Dh370/450) La Dune Blanche offers a great alternative to staying in M'Hamid and gets you into the desert fast. Surrounded by dunes, 22km south of Tagounite, accommodation is in beautiful pisé cottages dressed with fabric inside to mimic the feel of a tent.

Each 'tent' has a different colour and is furnished with comfortable beds dressed in natural woollen blankets, carpets and cut-metal lanterns, which cast swirling patterns on the walls. From here, any number of excursions are possible. Given the location, it is necessary to book in advance. Salah will meet you at the gas station at Tagounite with a 4WD to take you the remainder of the way.

M'Hamid محاميد

POP 3000

Once it was a lonesome oasis, but these days M'Hamid is a wallflower no more. Border tensions between Algeria (which lies just 40km south) and Morocco and the Polisario had isolated this caravan stop until the 1990s, when accords allowed M'Hamid to start hosting visitors again. From here, it doesn't take long to reach the dunes – some nuzzle right up against guesthouses on the western side of town – but to be enveloped by large dunes, you'll have to head out across the *reg* (hard-packed rocky desert) by dromedary or 4WD.

◉ Sights

M'Hamid encompasses two towns and five different ethnic groups: the Harratine, Berber, Chorfa, Beni M'Hamid and the fabled nomadic 'Blue Men'. M'Hamid Jdid, the prematurely aged 'new' town, has a mosque, roadside cafe-restaurants, small budget hotels and a Monday **souq** (⊙6am-noon Mon). There's a frontier-town feel here, with tough guys in *shesh* (turban) and sunglasses hanging around dusty cafes, swapping stories.

The old **kasbah** sits in the *palmeraie*, 3km away across the Oued Drâa. Another worthwhile stop is the **Ksar Ouled Driss**, 5km before M'Hamid, which includes a small **ethnographic museum** (Dh20; ⊙hours vary) displaying traditional household objects in a lovely mudbrick courtyard.

⭐ **Erg Chigaga** DUNES
The star attraction is the misnamed Erg Chigaga, not a single dune *(erg)* but an awesome stretch of golden sand sea some 56km southwest of M'Hamid. It is the largest sand sea in Morocco, snaking along the horizon for 40km and bordered to the north and south by mountain ridges. The best way to reach them is in classic movie style: by camel, which takes five days or a week (from Dh500 to Dh600 per day) round-trip.

To reach the area in just a few hours, a 4WD costs from Dh1000 to Dh1300 per day with insurance, plus another Dh350 to Dh500 for the camp.

This sea of golden crescents, which peak at 300m, hides small, semipermanent camps in its troughs. As a result the desert experience here is quiet and enveloping, offering spectacular night skies illuminated by the enormous arc of the Milky Way.

Erg Ezahar DUNES
This tall 'screaming' dune set amid a sea of smaller dunes wails eerily when the wind kicks up. Located 65km southwest of M'Hamid, it takes three days to reach it by camel, passing an old *marabout* and the flat plain of Bousnaïna where artefacts from a long disappeared village are sometimes turned up. There are no fixed camps here.

El Mesouiria DUNES
Located just 8km northwest of M'Hamid, El Mesouiria is another possibility for an easy overnight camel trek. Dunes range between 60m and 80m in height and are characterised by their white sand and a smattering of tamarisk trees.

Erg Esmar DUNES
Located close to Erg Ezahar, this collection of smaller dunes, rising to just 80m, are well off the main radar with no permanent camps. With its mixture of red and white dunes, it's particularly photogenic at sunset.

Erg Lehoudi DUNES
(Dunes of the Jews) The most easily accessible dunes to M'Hamid are the 100m-high Erg Lihoudi, located 8km northeast of M'Hamid. Characterised by their white river sand, due to their proximity to the Drâa,

ℹ️ BOOKING ERG CHIGAGA EXCURSIONS: TOP TIPS

Book ahead Given the considerable logistics of desert travel (and the fact that top guides are often booked in advance through Marrakesh agencies), it's always best to book ahead. It also gives you time to nail down the details of your camp and itinerary.

First time? Keep it short As any Sufi mystic will attest, being alone with your thoughts in the desert can be an illuminating, uplifting experience – but those not accustomed to such profound isolation may get bored quickly.

Camel riding or camel trekking Be aware that not all camels are for riding. In fact, most dromedaries are used for transporting luggage and food. If you want to ride your camel, you need to specify that at the outset and it may cost more if additional animals are needed.

Before you commit to a longer trip, get names The guide (and the guide's language ability) can make or break your experience. Ask for the name of the guide with whom you'll be travelling, do an internet search for reviews, and solicit feedback.

they are frequented by a higher number of day-trippers and some of the semipermanent camps are in need of attention.

🏃 Activities

Many overnight camel treks from M'Hamid head to Erg Lehoudi (p125) or the smaller dunes of El Mesouiria (p125), 8km from M'Hamid. You can arrive there by *piste,* off the main road 18km before M'Hamid, but a guide is advisable. The highlight is a camel trek to Erg Chigaga (p125). Other nearby desert destinations include Erg Ezahar (p125) and the **Iriki oasis** mirage. And if you get the hang of camel-riding, you might consider an epic 12-day camel trip to **Foum Zguid**.

👉 Tours

Treks on foot, by camel or 4WD to Erg Chigaga can be arranged in Marrakesh, Zagora or M'Hamid. Sales ploys come with the territory, so don't be reeled in by *faux guide* scare tactics. Prices are fairly standard at around Dh350 per person per day for an overnight camel treks and from Dh500 to Dh600 per day for a camel trek to Erg Chigaga. Also bear in mind that many desert tour operators only accept payment in cash.

Most hotels can also arrange excursions and overnight camps in the desert.

★ Sahara Services OUTDOORS
(📞 0661 77 67 66; www.saharaservices.info; per person from €75) Far and away the most professional outfit operating in M'Hamid, Sahara Services offers memorable, all-inclusive desert trips via camel and 4WD, including overnights to an encampment of handsome-

ly set Berber tents in Erg Chigaga. You'll dine well here, enjoy fireside music and watch the night sky light up with stars before falling asleep on a comfy bed surrounded by a sea of silence.

Bivouac Sous Les Étoiles OUTDOORS
(📞 0644 77 74 05; www.bivouacsouslesetoiles.org) Expert and friendly 4WD excursions and camel treks led by the personable Hassan and a team of M'Hamid locals. Operates several desert camps costing between Dh900 and Dh1600 per person.

🛏️ Sleeping

Auberge Kasbah Dar Sahara GUESTHOUSE €
(📞 0667 85 33 17; http://darsaharatour.com; s/d/q Dh150/200/400; 🅿️ 🛜) A big draw for budget travellers, this small, very welcoming place has rustic rooms with shared facilities and relaxing common areas and outdoor space where you can unwind and contemplate the peace of the desert. To get there, head all the way through town and look for the sign leading up to the left.

Auberge la Palmeraie INN €
(📞 0668 72 98 51; www.aubergelapalmeraie.com; per person incl half-board Dh200) Located across the Oued Drâa in the shade of the palm grove is the Laghrissi brothers' budget-friendly camp. It provides simple accommodation, mixing traditional goat-hair Berber tents and modest pisé rooms with mattress beds on flat-weave carpets. Showers and toilets are basic, with the latter being of the squat variety. The brothers are both experienced guides and offer well-priced excursions.

Turn left at the mosque as you enter M'Hamid and you'll find it just past Hamada du Drâa.

Dar Sidi Bounou   GUESTHOUSE €€

(☑ 0677 29 13 10; www.darsidibounou.com; s/d incl half-board Dh460/810, Berber tent per person incl half-board Dh350; **P** 🛜) A desert dream: dunes in the backyard, sand hammams, Saharawi music jam sessions and *mechoui* (whole roast lamb) feasts on starry terraces. Retreat to Berber tents and mudbrick huts that sleep six to eight, sleep on the roof, or curl up between crisp cotton sheets in the main house.

Instead of the usual sandy pool, Dar Sidi Bounou offers desert immersion experiences such as landscape-painting, cooking or belly-dancing classes. It's 4km beyond Ouled Driss.

Le Drom'Blanc   INN €€

(☑ 0524 84 68 52; www.ledromblanc.com; N 29°49.054, W 005°40.681; s/d Dh180/400/550, bivouac/bungalow per person Dh180/210, all incl breakfast; **P** ❄ 🛜) Well off the beaten track down a seemingly endless bumpy *piste*, Le Drom'Blanc is an excellent place for families and groups. Guest rooms are available in the air-conditioned riad or in small cottages dotted around the garden. Your hostess, Maguy, is an excellent cook, and if you book ahead, she'll prepare her famous spice-infused lamb baked in a traditional clay oven in the garden.

Erg Chigaga Luxury
Desert Camp   CAMPGROUND €€€

(☑ 0656 56 33 85; www.desertcampmorocco.com; per person all-inclusive camp Dh2500) Set in the shadow of Erg Chigaga's highest dune is Morocco's most luxurious tented camp. Co-owned by M'Hamid native, Mohammed Boulfrifi (aka Bobo) and British ex-pat Nick Garsten, the 13 sumptuous caidal tents (25 sq metres each) are furnished with wall-to-wall carpets, handcrafted beds, snug duvets, percale cotton sheets and solar-powered lighting.

Camel rides, guided walks, chill-out zones furnished with hammocks, board games and magical evenings filled with Gnawa ballads played with goatskin drums – the experience here is second to none. For those seeking more privacy, the camp also operates two private camps (each with only two tents) and offers the option of wild camping on treks of three days or more.

West of Erg Chigaga

Exiting Erg Chigaga by 4WD, head north to Ouarzazate or Marrakesh via Foum Zguid. En route through the *sahel* and *reg,* you'll pass the **Iriki 'oasis'** under an imposing plateau on your right. From here, you'll spot thirsty birds and gazelles drinking from a vast lake. But look again: 'Lake Iriki' is actually a salt pan shimmering in the heat haze, with deceptive silhouettes of poisonous calitropis bushes.

Travel another 30km or so and you'll hit the N12 tarmac road. From here the road heads south to Tata and north to **Foum Zguid**. Foum Zguid is a strategic military base, so you may be asked to show your passport here. Downtown is a crossroads with all the necessities: water, petrol, a public phone, restaurants and coffee. As you head north out of town, past the guardhouse, a road east leads to the town's two hotels. The road north is rough, ruined by trucks serving the nearby titanium mines, but the scenery is spectacularly barren.

Eighty-five kilometres north of Foum Zguid is **Tazenakht**, a handy stop for a quick bite, coffee, petrol and, yes, carpets. The distinctive local carpets (a mix of flat-weave and thick pile) with their extraordinary zigzagging patterns and bold colour schemes of red, orange and blue, are hung all around town. You can skip the middlemen and browse fixed-price pieces inside the government-run **Agence de L'Artisanat** (☉ 8am-7pm), within a walled compound on your right as you enter the town from the south.

More carpets await discovery 26km north in the village of **Anzal** at **Jemaite Tifawin Carpet Cooperative** (Association of Light; ☑ 0642 59 29 80; Anzal; ☉ carpet showroom 9am-noon & 2-6pm Mon-Thu, studio open house 9am-5pm Sun). If you telephone a week in advance, they will happily organise a studio visit and show you how to create natural dyes and spin raw wool into yarn. Approaching from the south, turn left at the sign for Khouzama in the centre of Anzal.

🛏 Sleeping & Eating

You'll find Foum Zguid's two hotels signposted east at the police checkpoint at the northern entrance to the town.

Maison d'Hôtes Hiba   GUESTHOUSE €

(☑ 0528 21 64 87; www.maisondhoteshiba.com; N° 30°07.549, W°006°52.411, Foum Zguid; per person from Dh250; ❄ 🛏) A rock-studded guesthouse and restaurant serving restorative meals of tajine, salad and fruit on the scenic terrace or in the air-conditioned salon. Comfy grotto-style rooms have en suites making this a welcome overnight stop after roughing it in the desert.

Bab Rimal
HOTEL €€

(☑ 0528 21 62 78; www.maroc-desert.com/hotel; N 30°07.722, W 006°52.062, Foum Zguid; s/d incl half-board from Dh500/740; ꇛ꘎ꗛꗸ) A complex of faux-pisé cottages centred around a large, flower-fringed pool. Standard rooms come with platform beds, *zellij* floor tiles and Tazenakht carpets. More luxurious suites are housed in mini villas with double-aspect windows and their own garden terraces. It's a popular lunch stop for tour groups, who relish a few hours in the pool on the long drive south or north.

Bab Sahara
MOROCCAN €

(☑ 0524 84 10 70; Tazenakht; mains Dh50-90; ⊙8am-11pm; ꘎ꗸ) This Peace Corps–certified hotel on Tazenakht's main drag is a popular pit stop for pizza, brochettes and bubbling tajines. It also does a mean *nous-nous* (half-half) coffee that would almost past muster in an Italian bar.

❶ Getting There & Away

Sitting at the crossroads between Ouarzazate and Agadir, Tazenakht is something of a transport hub, although without your own 4WD transport onward travel to Foum Zguid and Erg Chigaga is impossible from here. If you're driving yourself, fuel up in Tazenakht as the two gas stations further south don't have a reliable supply of petrol. And for those contemplating the westward drive east along the R108, don't attempt it in a 2WD vehicle as the road is particularly bad.

DADÈS VALLEY & THE GORGES
وادي دادس والمضايق

Nomad crossings, rose valleys and two-tone kasbahs: even on paper, the Dadès Valley stretches the imagination. From the daunting High Atlas to the north to the rugged Jebel Saghro range south, the valley is dotted with oases and mudbrick palaces that give the region its fairy-tale nickname – Valley of a Thousand Kasbahs. Some of the best views are only glimpsed when travelling on foot, along hidden livestock tracks between the Dadès and Todra Gorges and nomad routes across the Saghro.

Paved roads from Tinerhir to Imilchil and the intersection of the N8 between Beni Mellal and Khenifra, and from Er-Rachidia north up the N13 to Meknès, allow travellers to connect easily with Middle Atlas itineraries.

Skoura
سكورة
POP 2900

By the time caravans laden with gold and spice reached Skoura, the camels must have been gasping. After a two-month journey across the Sahara, blue-robed Tuareg desert traders offloaded cargo from caravans in Skoura, where Middle Atlas mountaineers packed it onto mules headed to Fez. Ouarzazate is now the region's commercial centre 39km west, but Skoura's historic mudbrick castles remain, and desert traders throng Monday and Thursday souqs brimming with intensely flavourful desert produce. When market days are finished and palm-tree shadows stretch across the road, no one seems in a hurry to leave.

◉ Sights

Navigating the mazelike network of dirt tracks in Skoura's vast *palmeraie* is challenging, so invest in a guide (Dh50 per hour). Most hotels offer their own excursions.

★ Palmeraie
PLANTATION

Skoura's defining features remain its mudbrick kasbahs and vast Unesco-protected *palmeraie*, earning the moniker 'Oasis of 1000 Palms.' Under this green canopy, a 5-mile patchwork of carefully tended garden plots are watered by an ingenious, centuries-old *khettara* system of locks, levers and canals. More than 100 bird species flourish here. Stay overnight in a pisé guesthouse and explore the *palmeraie* on foot or bicycle.

Kasbah Amridil
MEDINA

(☑ 0524 85 23 87; with/without guide Dh60/10; ⊙8am-7pm) Morocco's most coveted kasbah is this 17th-century wonder, which appears on Morocco's 50-dirham note. Signposted just a few hundred metres from the main road, this living museum shows traditional kasbah life over the centuries, with hand-carved door locks, an olive-oil press, still-functioning bread ovens, and stalls where animals were once kept.

Confusingly, there are now two separate entrances, each claiming to be the 'authentic' kasbah. In truth, the original kasbah is on the right; the building on the left was a later addition, and is actually a riad with a garden in the middle (a design not native to the area at all, but imported from Marrakesh).

Skoura Cultural Centre CULTURAL CENTRE
(☎0524 85 23 92; ⏰8.30am-noon & 3.30-5pm) An enterprising NGO, showcases local ingenuity at its crafts centre on the eastern edge of town. Here Skoura residents sell items made with palm fronds, sustainably harvested without harming the trees. For travellers who've admired Morocco's majestic *palmeraie,* these sun hats, bread baskets, mats and glass-lined lanterns make meaningful mementos – and purchases support the centre's palm preservation efforts. It's 300m on the left after the Skoura crossroads to Toundout.

👉 Tours

Toufiq Mousaoui OUTDOORS
(☎0611 72 30 05; tmousaoui0@gmail.com) One of the top guides working in Skoura, Toufiq is young and energetic, and has a wealth of knowledge about the history and culture of the region. You can arrange a wide range of outings with him, including walking or biking tours through the *palmeraie,* lunch with a local family, donkey treks (good for kids), traditional bread baking and other activities.

Nomad Attitude OUTDOORS
(☎0524 85 22 81; www.nomadattitude.com) Run by the owners of L'Ma Lodge (p130), this top-notch outfit offers a wide range of excursions both near and far. You can arrange 4WD trips, multiday treks, desert bivouacs and more.

🛏 Sleeping & Eating

Given this is a small oasis, there are no real restaurants, so hotels offer full board, or half-board with some light lunch options. If you're just passing through, you may be able to book lunch (depending on numbers), but you'll need to reserve ahead.

Kasbah Aït Abou HERITAGE HOTEL €
(☎0524 85 22 34; Palmeraie de Skoura; per person incl half-board Dh250, campsites per person Dh60; P) Sleep like a dignitary in this 1825 kasbah built by the local *caïd,* with a 25m mudbrick tower that's an engineering marvel. Ground-floor rooms are big, plain and naturally cool, with wonky en suites; alternatively, opt for one of the newer rooms set around the vegetable garden. Thanks to a unique partnership with the UCPA youth club, Mohammed can also arrange for horse rides through the *palmeraie.*

Follow the red arrows from the main road.

Sawadi GUESTHOUSE €€
(☎0671 57 01 54; www.sawadi.ma; Douar Tajanate; s/d incl breakfast €60/70, ste €85-120; P❋❅🅟🅦) 🍃 An oasis within an oasis, 9 acres of walled organic gardens make a bucolic setting for pisé bungalows and are used to prepare sumptuous evening meals (around €16). Unwind after visits to local artisans or kasbah architecture tours with a steamy hammam, or chilled white wine by the pool.

Sawadi is also a working farm, with cattle, sheep, rabbits and honey bees. For farm-to-table dining, Sawadi is unrivalled. Follow white triangle markers from the road into the northern end of the oasis.

Skoura Lodge GUESTHOUSE €€
(☎0668 94 35 24; www.skouralodge.com; d €50-60; 🅦) Located just outside of Skoura, this traditional lodge offers rooms set in round African-style bungalows, complete with bamboo

---

EVERY PALM TREE DESERVES A HAND

Walking the Skoura Oasis, feet naturally fall into rhythm with the bossa-nova sway of stately palms. But they're not here for looks: palms have work to do in the oasis, providing dates, shade and fronds to be woven into roofing material, floor coverings and fencing.

Palms are plentiful in this 'Oasis of 1000 Palms', but not one of them can be taken for granted. One concern is Bayoud disease, a fungus that passes from palm to palm. Unesco is taking steps to protect palm oases from Aït Benhaddou to Figuig, declaring the oases a biosphere reserve, and the Moroccan government is planting palms believed to be resistant to Bayoud.

But Skoura's majestic palms face another danger. According to the director of the palm-preservation initiative at Skoura Cultural Centre (p129) the biggest threat isn't Bayoud but rather poverty. During desperate times, when crops fail, some people illegally sell palms to support their families. To address this problem, the centre recently opened an oasis arts showcase. Here Skoura residents sell items made with palm fronds, sustainably harvested without harming the trees.

ceilings, Berber carpets, colourfully woven blankets and handsome bathrooms in *tadelakt*. There are fine views of the Altas Mountains and over the *palmeraie*. Coming from Ouarzazate, it's located about 5km southwest of the centre, signed to the left off the N10.

★ **L'Ma Lodge** GUESTHOUSE €€€
(www.lmalodge.com; r/ste €90/130; ☎0666 64 79 08; ✳🐾🛜🏊) ✎ This gorgeously designed lodge features seven spacious, light-filled rooms, each with antiques, elegant wood furnishings and artwork (from Morocco, West Africa and beyond). There's a garden, where organic fruits feature in the homemade breakfast jams, and you can relax in hammocks, swim in the heated pool, play a few rounds of petanque or arrange a massage. There's also a kids' play area.

The restaurant serves excellent, creative veg-friendly dishes, and the affable hosts have a wealth of information on making the most of the area. To get there, look for the marked turn-off on the N10, just east of Skoura, then follow the signs. Reserve well ahead.

★ **Jardins de Skoura** GUESTHOUSE €€€
(☑0524 85 23 24; www.lesjardinsdeskoura.com; Palmeraie de Skoura; s/d/ste incl breakfast from €75/80/130; ☺closed during Ramadan; ✳🛜🏊) ✎ Low-key, high-romance Skoura style: this garden guesthouse offers intimate rooms with nooks carved from pisé walls, custom-designed rugs and attractive artworks. Lunch on light salads and fresh-baked pizza amid the magical blooming garden, then take a nap beside the small pool beneath your courtesy palm-woven sunhat.

You might struggle to tear yourself away for donkey rides in the *palmeraie,* aperitifs on the roof top and French-Moroccan dinners, but they're worth it. Follow orange triangle markers from the main road.

Dar Lorkam GUESTHOUSE €€€
(☑0524 85 22 40; www.dar-lorkam.com; N 31°05.57, W 06°35.03; d/ste incl half-board from Dh800/1000; ☺closed Jan & Jul; ℗✳🛜🏊) With a garden full of roses and views of Jebel M'Goun from the vine-draped terraces, there's hardly any reason to venture beyond the snug confines of Dar Larkom. Seven cosy rooms with understated decorative details sit beneath shady olive trees overlooking a small, child-friendly pool.

Mornings slip by with walks in the *palmeraie* and visits to the souq, while evenings are best spent in the royal purple hammam. Follow green triangle markers from the main road.

Kasbah Aït ben Moro HERITAGE HOTEL €€€
(☑0524 85 21 16; www.kasbahaitbenmoro.com; r incl breakfast Dh700-1000; ℗✳🛜🏊) An 18th-century kasbah given a stylish makeover that remains true to its desert roots with original palm-beam ceilings, moody low-lit passageways, and water-conserving cactus gardens. The three tower rooms are the sweetest deals, with shared bathrooms and oasis views; ask for the one with a fireplace. It's located on the N10, 2km west of Skoura.

ℹ️ Getting There & Away

There are regular but infrequent buses from Ouarzazate (Dh13, 45 minutes) and Tinerhir (Dh40, two hours) to the centre of Skoura, which lies just off the N10 at the eastern end of the oasis. Grands taxis from Ouarzazate (Dh15) and Kelaâ M'Gouna (Dh22) stop just after the crossroads.

Kelaâ M'Gouna قلعة مغونة

Although it takes its name from the nearby M'Goun mountain, the small town of Kelaâ M'Gouna is famous for roses and daggers. Some 50km from Skoura, pink roses start peeking through dense roadside hedgerows, and you can't miss the bottles of local rosewater for sale in town. During the May rose harvest you'll see rose garlands everywhere, especially during the town's signature rose festival (first weekend of May). At the Wednesday souq, you can load up on dried edible roses.

There's an ATM, pharmacies and internet cafes at Kelaâ's downtown crossroads.

🏃 Activities

To stop and smell the roses on a nature walk, call the **bureau des guides** (☑0662 13 21 92, 0661 79 61 01) or book official guides through local hotels (around Dh350 per day).

🛏️ Sleeping

Kasbah Iswan GUESTHOUSE €€
(☑0524 89 17 71; www.kasbah-iswan.com; Tazroute; per person incl half-board Dh375) Spend a few days at comfortable Kasbah Iswan and you'll start to feel as at home as the storks that nest on the turrets. Nights are dark and peaceful, filled with friendly conversation and delicious plates of couscous and fried sardines, while days can be spent reading in the flower-filled courtyard or wandering through rose gardens

along the M'Goun River. It's 7km north of Kelaâ M'Gouna, in the village of Tazroute.

Kasbah Itran
HERITAGE HOTEL €€

(☑ 0524 83 71 03; www.kasbahitran.com; d incl half-board with shared bathroom Dh400, with bathroom Dh550-600; 🛜) At this striking clifftop perch, you'll find a maze of terraces, fireplaces and simple rooms with all the essentials. The roof deck offers stunning views over the lush valley and the mountains beyond. Most rooms come with en suite (three with air-con), stiff beds and M'Goun River views. It's 2km northwest of Kelaâ M'Gouna; minivans from town run past en route to the village of Torbis (Dh8).

Trekking excursions are also available.

🛍 Shopping

Unité de Distillation de Rose
GIFTS & SOUVENIRS

(☑ 0661 34 81 77; ⊗ 8am-5.30pm) Coming from Skoura, this rosewater distillery is located on your right 500m before you reach town. Rose buds sold here are purchased directly from farmers in the valley. The adjoining showroom offers a full range of perfume, creams and bath products, including uncoloured, untreated rosewater used locally as aftershave.

ℹ Getting There & Away

Buses run between Ouarzazate and Tinerhir via Kelaâ, but are often full. You can catch buses and grands taxis from the centre of Kelaâ, where they pull up beside the road. Taxis serve Ouarzazate (Dh35, 1½ hours), Skoura (Dh20, 45 minutes), Boumalne du Dadès (Dh10, 40 minutes) and Tinerhir (Dh35, 1½ hours).

Boumalne Du Dadès
بومالن دادس

POP 11,200

Twenty-four kilometres northeast of Kelaâ M'Gouna you reach a fork: the main road continues over the river to the hillside town of Boumalne du Dadès while the left-hand road leads into stunning Dadès Gorge. The town itself doesn't have much to offer, aside from being a base to explore the nearby gorge. It's worth stopping here however during the lively Wednesday and Sunday souqs.

🏃 Activities

Vallée des Oiseaux
BIRDWATCHING

(Valley of the Birds) A few kilometres to the east of town, where the *piste* leads south into the seemingly lifeless *hammada* to the village of Tagdilt, you'll find a surprisingly rich variety of bird life in the aptly named Vallée des Oiseaux. Horned lark, wheat-ears, sand grouse, buzzards and eagle owls are just some of the species you may spot here, along with a healthy reptile population and small herds of Edmi gazelle and Addax antelope.

Bureau des Guides
TREKKING, CYCLING

(☑ 0667 59 32 92; hamou57@voila.fr; Ave Mohammed V) Hamou Aït Lhou is a knowledgeable local guide who takes trips to the Vallée des Oiseaux and further afield to Jebel Saghro. The office is located on the main road in Boumalne, about 500m south of the junction for the Dadès Valley.

🛌 Sleeping & Eating

Kasbah Jeanne Ecolodge
GUESTHOUSE €€

(☑ 0667 41 56 97; s/d/tw/tr €45/55/65/70; 🛜) 🍃 This riad-style guesthouse with a garden out back receives high marks for its spacious traditional rooms – complete with pisé walls, poplar wood ceilings and juniper wood doors – and the kind-hearted welcome of the owner, who has loads of tips on exploring the region. Dinner costs Dh125 extra. To get there, follow signs leading north off Ave Mohammed V.

Hôtel Almanader
HOTEL €€

(☑ 0524 83 01 72; www.hotelmanader.com; Ave Mohammed V; s/d incl half-board Dh300/450; ❄🛜) High above the river valley, Almanader makes a splash with colourful murals and 12 tidy, quirky rooms with candy-coloured stucco ceilings; four have air-conditioning. Easygoing staff are quick with hellos, espresso and home-style Berber cooking (mains Dh60 to Dh70).

Xaluca Dadés
HOTEL €€€

(☑ 0535 57 84 50; www.xaluca.com; s/d/ste from Dh740/900/1460; 🅿❄@🛜🌊) A Sub-Saharan makeover transformed this 1970s convention centre into a destination hotel. The 106 guest rooms have balconies with Tuareg chairs, plush beds with thick duvets and mud-cloth bedspreads. Expect all the mod cons, plus hammam (Dh100), a bar, billiards, a panoramic terrace swimming pool, a Jacuzzi, and noisy gym. It's signposted at the top of the hill on Ave Mohammed V, and is just north of the centre of Boumalne du Dadès.

Restaurant Oussikis
MOROCCAN €

(Place de Souk; mains Dh40-100) Inside the souq plaza on your left, you'll spot chef Fadil Faska in his spotless open kitchen transforming fresh, local ingredients into savoury tajines, flaky *pastilla,* or quick, satisfying salads and roast chicken.

Hôtel-Restaurant Adrar　　MOROCCAN €
(📞 0524 83 07 65; Ave Mohammed V; mains Dh40-80; ❄) This clean place, handy to the bus station, serves popular, filling meals of salads and brochettes or the local speciality, *gallia* (game hen) tajine.

ℹ Information

On Ave Mohammed V there's a **Banque Populaire** (Ave Mohammed V), four pharmacies and internet access.

ℹ Getting There & Away

BUS

Supratours offers a daily service to Ouarzazate (Dh40, two hours), Tinerhir (Dh30, 1¼ hours), Marrakesh (Dh115, six hours) and Merzouga (Dh90, six hours). The ticket office is near Banque Populaire and buses stop near the covered market.

Cheaper private buses also leave daily to Ouarzazate (Dh30), Tinerhir (Dh10) and Marrakesh (Dh100), and multiple times daily to Er-Rachidia (Dh40).

TAXI & MINIBUS

You may have to wait a while for a grand taxi or minibus to fill up, but they do go to Ouarzazate (Dh40), Tinerhir (Dh20) and Aït Oudinar (inside the Dadès Gorge; Dh12).

Trekking Jebel Saghro

Few tourists venture into the starkly beautiful Jebel Saghro (aka Jebel Sarhro or Djebel Sahro) as most of the flat-topped mesas, volcanic pinnacles and deep gorges dotted with palm groves are only accessible on foot. This arid, isolated territory is home turf to the seminomadic Aït Atta, legendary warriors famous for their 1933 stand against the French here, on **Jebel Bou Gafer**.

Jebel Saghro is accessed from three trekking hubs: Kelaâ M'Gouna and Boumalne du Dadès on the north side of the range, and the southern village of N'Kob. The most scenic routes head through the heart of the range, between Igli and Bab n'Ali.

This circuit has one big advantage over the classic Saghro north–south traverse: it begins and ends on the north side of the mountains, so you can easily resume journeys to Dadès gorges, Merzouga and the dunes.

THE TREK AT A GLANCE

Duration Five to six days

Distance 56km

Standard Medium

Start Tagdilt

Finish Kelaâ M'Gouna

Highest Point Tizi n'Ouarg (approximately 2300m)

Accommodation Camping and *gîtes/* homestay

Public Transport Yes

Summary A great alternative to the classic Saghro traverse, showcasing the staggering and varied beauty of the range. Given demanding climbs and long days of walking, you might add another night to the route.

When To Go

While many High Atlas trails are impassable between November and February, Saghro is a prime winter trekking destination. Winter temperatures can dip below freezing, and snow may fall as low as 1400m – but even when it does snow, it is usually possible to trek. In autumn and spring, night-time temperatures rarely fall below zero. When summer temperatures get scorching hot (above 40°C), water sources disappear, and even scorpions hunker under rocks for shade.

ℹ Getting There & Away

Minibuses run from Boumalne du Dadès to Ikniouln (Dh28), at the northern edge of the range, departing around noon and returning to Boumalne early the next morning. There may be extra buses on Wednesday, when Ikniouln has its weekly souq.

Day 1: Tagdilt To The Assif Ouarg Valley

DURATION FOUR HOURS / DISTANCE 17KM / ASCENT 200M

Tagdilt is an uninspiring village but a useful trailhead, with three *gîtes* and a daily *camionette* (pick-up truck) from Boumalne. For 2½ hours, you could follow the *piste* used by vans crossing the mountain to N'Kob, or veer onto the track that occasionally strays to the side, rejoining the *piste* further up the slope.

At **Imi n'Ouarg**, the third village above Tagdilt, the path leaves the road (which continues to mines at Tiouit). The path turns right (southwest) beside the village school, marked by a Moroccan flag.

The path follows the right-hand side of the winding Assif Ouarg valley, beneath the summit of **Jebel Kouaouch** (2592m). After an hour (about 3km), there's a farm above terraced fields where you can arrange a **homestay** (☑0661 08 23 21; per person Dh60-70). The host's sons can be hired as muleteers and hot meals may be available.

Day 2: Assif Ouarg Valley To Igli

DURATION SIX TO SEVEN HOURS / DISTANCE 19KM / ASCENT 620M / DESCENT 860M

The most memorable walk on this trek is also the most difficult, starting with a 35-minute climb towards the head of the valley. The path leads left (south) and **Jebel Kouaouch** is the highest of a row of peaks straight ahead. The path zigzags over a stream, up towards Kouaouch and a lone juniper tree – a good place for a breather. Depending on your fitness and the weather, it could take another hour to reach the pass. As you climb, there are good views back towards Tagdilt, and once over the ridge, the High Atlas and Jebel Saghro come into view.

The path drops steeply down ahead, but our track veers right (southwest) across the valley's shoulder and over another ridge, with views south to the palms and kasbahs of N'Kob. Igli is due south over a series of slopes, with the famous **Tête de Chameau** (Camel's Head) cliffs appearing as you walk down towards the settlement. Three low buildings form a **gîte** (per person Dh60) with a toilet

and wood-fired hot showers (Dh10). There's no electricity or sleeping mats here, but the friendly *gardien* runs a shop selling trekkers' necessities, including mule shoes, and if you bring flour, he'll have it baked into bread.

For breathtaking mountain sunsets, you've come to the right place. You might add a round trip to **Bab n'Ali**, one of the most spectacular rock formations in the Saghro, returning to Igli for another night or continuing to the **Irhazzoun n'Imlas gîte** (per person Dh60).

Day 3: Igli To Tajalajt

DURATION SEVEN TO 7½ HOURS / DISTANCE 24KM / ASCENT 350M / DESCENT 400M

Looming on the right-hand side as you walk is the peak of **Jebel Amlal**, sacred to the Aït Atta and the site of August pilgrimages. The morning's walk is gentler than the previous day's, leading through wide, rocky valleys. After 1½ hours, beneath the village of **Taouginte**, the path curves around an **Aït Atta cemetery**, where graves are marked with piles of stone. The path then leads below the **Needles of Saghro**, a long, dramatic cliff that slopes down after another 1½ hours to the Amguis River. Several valleys meet at a beautiful camping spot, amid palms and oleander. Half an hour southwards down the valley is **Irhazzoun n'Imlas**, a village above well-tended fields with a riverside lunch spot.

At Irhazzoun n'Imlas the path joins a *piste* that runs left to N'Kob and right towards the Dadès. Take the right track (northwest) towards a sheer cliff on the left, with the rocky path leading beneath it and up to a broadening valley. The *piste* loops around the north

---

ⓘ BEFORE YOU GO: JEBEL SAGHRO CHECKLIST

Maps The 1:100,000 *Boumalne* and *Tazzarine* maps cover the region, but a more detailed trekking map with history and information on the back is 1:100,000 *Randonnée culturelle dans le Djebel Sarhro*, by Mohamed Aït Hamza and Herbert Popp, published in Germany, written in French and available in Morocco, including at hotels in Boumalne and N'Kob.

Guide Several foreign tour operators run good-value trips here, but many of them sub-contract to local guides. You can find a licensed local guide directly through a *bureau des guides* in any of the three Saghro trekking centres: Kelaâ M'Gouna (p130), Boumalne (p131) and N'Kob (p152). Expect to pay Dh350 a day for a guide and Dh150 for a mule.

Water Dehydration is common any time of the year, so pack extra water.

Food Stock up in Ouarzazate or Boumalne de Dadès. The three Saghro departure towns all have tea, tinned fish, biscuits and bread, and you may find eggs, dates, almonds, bread and tinned sardines in some villages.

Mule Given the amount of water you must carry, mules are a worthwhile investment. Your guide can organise mules and muleteers.

Gear Bring a sleeping bag. You won't need a tent, unless you'd rather camp than stay at *refuges*.

Jebel Saghro Trek

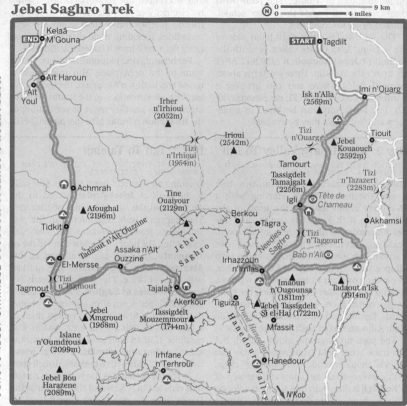

side of **Jebel Tassigdelt Si el-Haj** (1722m) and then south again towards **Tiguiza**, where there is a basic **gîte** (☎ 0671 72 80 06; per person Dh60). Before Tiguiza, another *piste* leads right (west) to **Akerkour village**, into a narrowing valley dotted with palms, and up an incline to **Tajalajt**, where you can arrange a **homestay** (per person Dh60) and maybe obtain basic meals.

Day 4: Tajalajt To Achmrah

DURATION EIGHT TO 8½ HOURS / DISTANCE 26KM / ASCENT 200M / DESCENT 300M

Take the valley *piste* from Tajalajt, above splendid terraced palm and almond groves. Less than 1½ hours brings you to **Assaka n'Aït Ouzzine** (1584m), its ruined kasbah teetering above the beautiful valley. Next, the *piste* leads out of the valley into a rocky, windy steppe.

After 1½ hours from Assaka spent wedged between 2000m ridges, you'll arrive at **Tagmout** (also called Amgroud after one of the mountains overlooking the village) and a well-kept **gîte** (per person Dh60) with electricity, mattresses, blankets and possibly lunch (around Dh30).

From Tagmout the *piste* leads northwest to Kelaâ M'Gouna and south to N'Kob, with transport headed to N'Kob's **Sunday souq**. The trek heads due north, climbing over an hour to **Tizi n'Tagmout** (1754m) for stunning views to the M'Goun Massif. Another hour leads to **El-Mersse**, where shade and a year-round spring facilitate camping.

The track continues due north, mostly in gentle descent, but with occasional climbs. Less than 1½ hours after El-Mersse, there's a riverside camp site under shade trees at **Tidkit** and it may be possible to sleep *chez l'habitant* here or in **Achmrah**, another hour down the track. However, the Berbers on this side of Jebel Saghro are seminomadic and may be absent April to May. If the houses are empty, the animal shelters will be too – a less glamorous but practical place to sleep.

Day 5: Achmrah To Kelaâ M'Gouna

DURATION FOUR HOURS / DISTANCE 14KM / ASCENT 150M / DESCENT 450M

The best parts of this morning walk are the beginning and end. The track north of Achmrah makes a short climb, suddenly revealing M'Goun and Siroua vistas. Less than half an hour later, it crosses a *piste* that leads to an anthracite mine and should not be followed. Instead continue north, occasionally northwest, on a well-worn track that leads down a gully towards the Dadès Valley. As you get closer, you will see the villages of Aït Youl on your left, Aït Haroun on the right, and a valley studded with old kasbahs. Head for Aït Haroun, where there is a bridge over the Dadès River. The Boumalne–Kelaâ M'Gouna road is nearby, but long after you return to the modern world, Saghro's seminomadic spirit stays with you.

Dadès Gorge وادي دادس

As the local saying goes, the wind has a son who lives in Boumalne, which is why he rips down this valley to visit him in winter. Sitting in the rain shadow of the Central Atlas, the Dadès Gorge presents a dramatic landscape: ancient rust-red and mauve mountains stripped back to zigzagging layers of strata and knobbly rock formations reminiscent of Utah. A rush of springtime water puddles in the valley where irrigation channels siphon it off to fields of wheat and orchards of fig, almond and olive trees. A series of crumbling kasbahs and *ksour* line the valley in the Berber villages of Aït Youl, Aït Arbi, Aït Oudinar, Aït Ouffi and Aït Toukhsine.

◉ Sights

Nomads still live in the surrounding mountains with their herds (you can see some of their troglodyte caves from the Berbere de la Montagne campground) and use the valley as a seasonal livestock between their High Atlas summer pastures and their winter home in Jebel Saghro. In spring and autumn, if you're lucky, you'll see them on the move with laden camels and mules.

The R704 road is sealed all the way to **Msemrir**, 63km north of Boumalne de Dadès, but you'll need a 4WD beyond that –

especially for the *piste* that leads southeast into Todra Gorge. If you're up for a challenge, you could travel north from Msemrir over the High Atlas to Imilchil. Lots of transport heads up the valley on Saturday for the Msemrir market. There's also a market in Aït Oudinar on Sunday.

The most dramatic gorge scenery commences 26km up the gorge where the road crosses the river and starts to climb through an extraordinary series of hairpin bends (see www.dangerousroads.org). When the road flattens out again, you might take that as your cue to turn around: you've covered the best gorge scenery you can see without a 4WD or good hiking shoes.

Tamlalt Valley   VALLEY

Eighteen kilometres from Boumalne brings you to extraordinary red rock formations that look like wax, melting right into the green carpet of the *palmeraie* below Aït Arbi. They're known locally as *Les Doigts de Singes* ('Monkey's Fingers') given their bizarre windworn shapes. A little further on is the more colourfully named 'Valley of Human Bodies', where famished travellers are said to have died of hunger and been turned to stone.

Aït Youl   MEDINA

Those art-deco tourism posters you'll see all over Morocco showing a red-and-white kasbah in a rocky oasis aren't exaggerating: just 6.5km into the gorge the old Glaoui kasbah of Aït Youl is set against a lush backdrop of almond and fig trees. A couple of kilometres past Aït Youl, the road crosses an *oued;* this river valley offers a sneaky back way to Kelaâ M'Gouna on foot.

Gorge de Miguirne   GORGE

(Sidi Boubar Gorge) Cresting over a small pass, 14km from Boumalne, is the hidden Gorge de Miguirne, which joins the Dadès Gorge from the south. It offers a pleasant half-day hike amid its springs and rock pools. Ask at your guesthouse for a guide.

Association
Gorge du Dadès   ARTS & CRAFTS

(☑ 0677 90 96 70, 0666 39 69 49; Km 24, Aït Oudinar; ⊗ 2-5pm Mon-Sat) Tufted carpets are made at this weaving cooperative, but soft kilim blankets made with undyed, extra-fluffy lambswool are signature pieces. The women are introducing nonchemical dyes made from local walnuts shells (brown), onion skins (yellow) and poppies (black). Items are sold at fixed prices and the weaver is paid directly.

From the roadside sign, follow arrows to the western bank to find the converted stable currently housing the cooperative.

Activities

There's a good trekking trail heading northwest, beginning just across the river, 28km from Boumalne du Dadès. The energetic could cover the distance from Dadès and Todra Gorges on foot (a two- to three-day walk). Most hotels in the gorge and Boumalne du Dadès can arrange hiking guides (around Dh300 per day), 4WD trips to the Todra Gorge (Dh1500 per day) and bicycle hire (around Dh100).

Bureau des Guides　　　　　TREKKING
(0671 31 09 23; Km 3) Monyr Hammdu runs this small outfit some 3km north of Boumalne, and leads a wide range of treks from one-day outings (around €50) to weeklong excursions. He speaks English, German, French and Dutch.

Sleeping

Most accommodation in the gorge is within 28km of Boumalne du Dadès, and the kilometre markings refer to the distance from Boumalne. Most will let you sleep in the sa-

---

OFF THE BEATEN TRACK

GORGE YOURSELF: DADÈS TO TODRA

The 42km *piste* drive from Dadès Gorge to Tamtattouchte in the Todra Gorge is a tough five-hour journey through twisting hills and the boulder-strewn valley of Tizgui n'Ouadda. The crossing is prone to flash floods, so seek up-to-date advice on the state of the *piste* before setting off. The route starts with a bone-rattling ascent at Tilmi, 15km north of Msemrir, and then crests the 2639m-high **Tizi n'Uguent Zegsaoun** before descending through a long valley to emerge just north of Tamtattouchte.

The trip should only be attempted by 4WD during the summer months (May to September), and a local guide is recommended. In May, many nomadic Berbers with homes in Aït Haini head to this valley to pitch tents and graze large herds of sheep. If you stop, you may be invited into tents to sip tea and swap stories.

---

lon or on the terrace (even in summer you may need a sleeping bag) for around Dh30, or camp by the river for around the same price.

Chez L'Habitant Amazigh　　GUESTHOUSE **€**
(☎0670 71 45 51; zaid.azul@hotmail.fr; Km 20, Aït Arbi; d Dh200-300, s/d incl half-board Dh300/500; 🛜) Spend a night at the Tair family home and you'll get a warm introduction to Berber life, with nightly discussions of history and culture, followed by family music jams (from 8pm to 9pm). Cheerfully decorated pink pisé rooms and exuberantly furnished salons can't compete with first-class terrace views over the river and valley rock formations.

It's also a good place to arrange treks to visit nomad camps, abandoned kasbahs and intriguing rock formations.

Le Berbère de la Montagne　　CAMPGROUND, GUESTHOUSE **€**
(☎0524 83 02 28; www.berbere-montagne.com; Km 34; per person incl half-board Dh250-300, campsite for 2 Dh80; 🅿🌐🛜🐕) With tent pitches overlooking the river, and the hotel within a few metres of the narrowest point of the gorge, this friendly place offers peaceful accommodation far from the madding crowds. It's also perfectly located for hikes into the Petit Gorge and up into the hills to visit nomad encampments and secret caves hung with stalactites.

The 10 pleasant rooms come with *tataoui* ceilings, terracotta tiled floors and pine beds heaped with warm blankets. Laundry facilities/electricity are an additional Dh50/20, and guides Dh200 per day.

Auberge des Gorges du Dadès　　INN **€**
(☎0524 83 02 21; www.aubergeaitoudinar.com; Km 25, Aït Oudinar; camping per person/tent/car Dh10/20/20, s/d per person incl half-board Dh260/200; 🅿🌐) Bubbly with personality and overlooking the river, the Auberge has 30 rooms that cover the waterfront with Moroccan motifs: pisé Amazigh designs in one wing, ornate stucco and eye-catching tiles in another. Some have balconies and all have basic en suites and tiled floors. Guided hikes and 4WD trips are available.

Chez Bassou　　HOTEL **€**
(☎0523 44 24 02; www.chezbassou.com; Imilchil; s/d incl breakfast from Dh250/300; 🛜) This 20-room guesthouse has a fine location in the mountains. Rooms are small but clean and comfortable, with adequate blankets for

cold Atlas nights. Meals are available at the good on-site restaurant.

Hotel Izlane HOTEL €
(✆ 0661 22 48 82; www.hotelizlane.com; Imilchil; s/d incl half-board from Dh250/400) Offers clean, fairly priced rooms and decent meals. Staff are helpful and you can also arrange excursions.

Chez Pierre INN €€
(✆ 0524 83 02 67; www.chezpierre.org; Km 27, Aït Ouffi; s/d/tr/q incl breakfast Dh475/620/800/900; 🛜🏊) Eight light-filled rooms and one apartment are notched right into the gorge wall, with tasteful, minimalist decor, flowering terraces and poolside sun decks. A rosy gorge sunset is the prelude to spectacular five-course dinners (Dh230) featuring inventive appetisers, delicately cooked duck in red wine *jus* and impeccable tarte Tatin served beside the snug wood-burning stove.

Brothers Ismael and Lahcen Sibiri run the inn with great pride and passion and also offer guided day trips in English, French and Spanish. There are also several apartments accommodating six to eight people.

Maison 4 Saisons GUESTHOUSE €€
(✆ 0524 83 17 55; www.chambresdhotesdades.com; Km 24, Aït Oudinar; s/d incl half-board Dh330/500) Book early for one of the four 'seasonal' rooms at Youssef Azrarag's welcoming guesthouse, where Berber hospitality, vintage French furniture and bright local decor blend seamlessly. All the rooms overlook the lovely patio garden where numerous varieties of mountain mint and verveine perfume the air.

⭐**Kasbah de Mimi** GUESTHOUSE €€€
(✆ 0671 52 38 55; http://kasbah-mimi.webliberte. net; Km 12, Aït Ibrine; per person incl half-board €50; ❄🛜🏊) Save yourself the trouble of cultivating friends with fabulous country houses, and book a weekend at one of four rooms at Kasbah de Mimi. At this painstakingly restored cliffside getaway, everything is in excellent taste: Berber *baraka* painted on living-room walls, pâté hors d'ouevres, water-conserving rose gardens tumbling to the valley floor, and a grand piano in the fully stocked library.

The 500m cliffhanger of a driveway is harrowing, but village kids will cheer your arrival.

🍴 Eating

The best dining in the valley is at Chez Pierre (p137). Other than that there are a few casual eateries along the valley. To snap that iconic image of the road snaking up the valley, stop for coffee or a snack at

Hotel Restaurant Timzzillite (mains Dh40-80; ⊙10am-8pm).

Le Jardin de Source MOROCCAN €
(✆ 0670 01 90 30; Km 11, Aït Ibrirne; mains Dh40-100; ⊙11am-9pm; 🛜) Quick lunches at this garden restaurant near the mouth of the gorge include flavourful vegetarian options, omelettes and marinated turkey kebabs. Several good-value rooms (Dh250 per person, including half-board) are also available.

ℹ️ Getting There & Away

Grands taxis and minibuses run up the gorge from Boumalne to the cluster of hotels in Aït Oudinar and Aït Ouffi (Dh10) and to Msemrir (Dh30, 1½ to two hours). To return, flag down a passing vehicle. You can also hire a taxi for a half-day trip (Dh250) into the gorge. Minibuses run up to Msemrir often; the last one back to Boumalne leaves around 4pm.

Tinerhir تنغير
POP 36,000
Charm falls a distant third to dust and hustle in Tinerhir (aka Tinghir), a busy mining-town transit hub recently benefitting from a rash of expansion and construction thanks to an administrative upgrade to independent provincial capital. If you need a break after the 51km drive from Boumalne du Dadès, head to the eastern edge of town, where a palm oasis unfolds like a green umbrella. Under the canopy, you'll discover crumbling kasbahs, the abandoned 19th-century Medersa Ikelane (look for the whitewashed mudbrick cupola) and, to the north of town, the ruins of Ksar Asfalou, where Muslim and Jewish students once studied under the same roof. An enormous souq is held 2.5km west of the centre on Monday, and there's a Saturday livestock souq in town.

Oasis guides are available at Hôtel Tomboctou (p138).

🛏️ Sleeping

Kasbah Petit Nomade HERITAGE HOTEL €
(✆ 0668 49 58 38; http://kasbah-petitnomade. com; N 31°31.683, W 005°33.386, Douar Ichmarine; s/d incl half-board Dh400/660; 🅿❄🛜) 🌿 North of town, Lahcen and Mouna's restored kasbah is a find amid Tinerhir's bleak hotel scene. Three simple rooms decked out in bold reds and mauve sit around an internal courtyard while terrace tables look out over a dense thicket of *palmeraie*. The food here is made with

flair and features a bounty of fresh produce sourced from local farms.

Tours of the *palmeraie* and nearby villages provide fascinating insights, and hiking, climbing or horse riding excursions in the gorge can easily be arranged. You'll find it signed off the highway some 2km north of Tinerhir, at the start of the gorge in the village of Ichmarine.

Hôtel de l'Avenir
HOTEL €

(☑ 0672 52 13 89; 27 Rue Zaid Ouhmed; r from Dh160) Cheap, clean rooms, hot showers and a nice roof terrace on the main market square. Ask for a room away from the square or bring earplugs.

Hôtel Tomboctou
HERITAGE HOTEL €€

(☑ 0524 83 51 91; www.hoteltomboctou.com; 126 Ave Bir Anzarane; s/d/tr incl breakfast Dh475/550/730; ✳✳) Quirky, cosy rooms with en suites in a renovated kasbah built in 1944 for the local *caïd*. Traditional kasbah windows are porthole-sized, but sunshine surrounds the courtyard pool and bar. There's also a good on-site restaurant (menu Dh130). Oasis walking tours and bicycle trips are organised here.

✕ Eating

Grill restaurants line Ave Mohammed V and Ave Hassan II, including **Café des Amis** (Ave Hassan II; mains Dh40-80; ⊙10am-8pm) and **Café Central** (Ave Hassan II; mains Dh30-50; ⊙11am-7pm).

Chez Michelle Supermarket
SUPERMARKET €

(☑ 0524 83 46 68; Ave Mohammed V; ⊙9am-9pm Sat-Thu) Excellent range of trekking provisions and snacks, and the only place that sells alcohol.

ℹ Information

Banks with ATMs flank Ave Mohammed V, including BMCE and Crédit du Maroc. There's a Banque Populaire opposite Pl Principale.

ℹ Getting There & Away

BUS

Buses leave from Pl Principale, off Ave Mohammed V. Supratours stops in Tinerhir en route to Boumalne du Dadès (Dh30, 75 minutes), Ouarzazate (Dh60, three hours), Marrakesh (Dh130, 7½ hours) and, heading in the other direction, Er-Rachidia (Dh40, three hours), Erfoud (Dh60, 3½ hours) and Merzouga (Dh85, 4½ hours). You'll find the ticket office to the right of the bus lot in front of the mosque.

On other lines, there's frequent service from Tinerhir to Marrakesh (Dh130) via Ouarzazate (Dh40), and to Erfoud (Dh40), Meknès (Dh110) and Boumalne du Dadès (Dh20).

TAXI & MINIVAN

Grands taxis to Ouarzazate (Dh60), Alnif (Dh25) and Er-Rachidia (Dh45 to Dh70) leave from Pl Principale, where you'll also find minivans or pick-up trucks into Todra Gorge (Dh10) and beyond to Tamtattouchte (Dh18) and Imilchil (Dh40). Grands taxis to Tamtattouchte (Dh18), Aït Haini (Dh20) and Imilchil (Dh40) leave from between 9am and 1pm.

Todra Gorge   ممضيق تودغا

Being stuck between a rock and a hard place is a sublime experience in the Todra Gorge, where a 300m-deep fault splits the orange limestone into a deep ravine at some points

---

IMILCHIL: MOROCCO'S MEET MARKET

Just another striking Middle Atlas Berber village most of the year, Imilchil is flooded with visitors during its three-day **marriage moussem** (Imilchil; ⊙ Sep) in September. At this huge festival, local Berbers scope the scene for marriage material. Women strut their stuff in striped woollen cloaks and elaborate jewellery, and boys preen in flowing white jellabas (garments).

The festival usually runs Friday to Sunday in the third or fourth week of September; dates are posted at tourist offices throughout the country. Organised tours to the event are available from cities throughout Morocco, and newly paved roads from Rich and Aït Haini to Imilchil have brought busloads of tourists to see romance blossom. With hustlers, faux guides and souvenir stalls eyeing the tourists, onlookers are beginning to outnumber the young lovers – but there's no denying the voyeuristic fascination of the event.

During the festival, the area is covered in tented accommodation. Otherwise, there is basic hotel accommodation at **Chez Bassou** (p136) and **Hotel Izlane** (p137).

just wide enough for a crystal-clear river and single-file trekkers to squeeze through. The road from Tinerhir passes green *palmeraies* and Berber villages until, 15km along, high walls of pink and grey rock close in around the road. The approach is thrilling, as though the doors of heaven were about to close before you.

The best time to visit is in the morning, when the sunshine briefly illuminates the gorge in a golden moment of welcome. Souvenir vendors and tour buses clog the centre in afternoons, until it suddenly turns dark and bitterly cold. Through the gorge and 18km up the road is the Berber village of Tamtattouchte, with Imilchil some 95km beyond.

🏃 Activities

Besides day hikes in and around the gorge, Todra's vertical rock faces offer sublime rock-climbing routes (French grade 5 to 8), some of them bolted. Many of the routes are over 25m long, although there is some spectacular multipitch climbing where routes run over 300m. **Pillar du Couchant**, near the entrance to the gorge, offers classic long climbs, while the **Petite Gorge** is better for novice climbers, with good short routes. Few of the routes are mapped, although many hotels keep logbooks detailing current information on local routes. Otherwise, internationally certified guides and reliable equipment can be hired from Aventures Verticales (p139).

From the centre of the gorge, you can walk back to Tinerhir through *palmeraies* in three or four hours. With a 4WD or a couple of days walking, you can cover the rough *piste* west of Todra to Dadès Gorge. There are no banks in the gorge and limited connectivity and phone coverage, so carry enough cash.

Aventures Verticales   CLIMBING
(📞 0524 89 57 27; www.escalade-au-maroc.com; Km 14, Tizgui; 1hr/half-/full day per person in a group of 3 Dh40/100/150) Todra has a professional climbing outfit with internationally certified guides offering climbing, alpinism and trekking excursions for all levels. The small shop in Tizgui also stocks top gear for hire and sale, including Rock Pillar climbing shoes, Petzl helmets, Beal ropes and powder sacs, plus tents and sleeping bags.

The Moroccan-Portuguese venture hopes to develop a serious climbing scene in the gorge, including establishing a school for climbing guides and developing a series of *via ferrata* routes (permanent, bolted routes linked by a safety cable modelled on

Todra Gorge

those in the Italian Alps), which will facilitate more DIY climbing.

Auberge Cavaliers   HORSE RIDING
(📞 0618 53 07 90; Km 14, Aït Baha Tizgui; per hr/day Dh160/550) At this small guesthouse, you can sign up for treks and horse riding. Advance booking is recommended for overnight horse treks with guide and food.

🛏 Sleeping & Eating

Most visitors take their meals at their guesthouses. If you're not packing a picnic, the best lunch spots are at Camping le Soleil (p140) and the restaurants in the small village of Aït Baha Tizgui.

Hotel Valentine   GUESTHOUSE €
(📞 0524 89 52 25; www.hotel-valentine.net; Km 14, Aït Baha; s/d Dh200/300, incl half-board Dh250/400; ❄🐾) In the village of Aït Baha Tizgui, about 800m before the gorge, Hotel Valentine rolls out the welcome mat with thoughtful service and remarkably budget-friendly rooms. Accommodations are on the small side, and only two of the eight rooms have views, but you can head up to the roof terrace for a splendid panorama over the village, *palmeraie* and chiselled mountains beyond.

LOCAL KNOWLEDGE

DIY TODRA LOOP HIKE

For a vigorous morning hike, try a three-hour loop from north of the gorge to Tizgui, south of the gorge. A 30-minute walk beyond the main gorge is the **Petite Gorge**, where you'll find a trailhead near Auberge le Festival. Take the track leading uphill to the left (southwest) – regular donkey and mule traffic keep this path well defined. Head to the pass, and from there, ascend southeast to the next pass. This would be a good place to stray from the main route to look over the rim of the gorge, but be careful, as the winds are powerful up here. From the second pass, descend to the Berber village of **Tizgui**, where you can stroll through the *palmeraies* back to the gorge.

Auberge Amazigh
GUESTHOUSE €

(☑ 0610 12 75 55; www.amazigh-tamtattouchte.jimdo.com; KM 34; campsites per person Dh50, r per person Dh150-180; P ᗑ) Located 17km past the gorge in the village of Tamtattouchte, Auberge Amazigh has just four small cosy rooms, each with traditional pisé walls carved with Berber motifs and sporting helpful mosquito nets and colourful tapestries. There's also an appealing roof terrace.

Maison la Fleur
GUESTHOUSE €

(☑ 0670 40 43 69; www.maison-lafleur.com; Km 14, Aït Baha Tizgui; dm/d per person incl half-board Dh150/200; P @ ᗑ) Run by a Japanese expat named Noriko, this surprising spot on the main road in Aït Baha Tizgui has six simple rooms (including a five-bed dorm) painted in muted colours, plus a great open terrace. It's an easy 700m walk to the gorge, and probably the only spot in the Atlas mountains where you'll find miso soup on the menu.

Camping le Soleil
CAMPGROUND €

(☑ 0524 89 51 11; Km 8; campsites per person/tent/car/campervan Dh24/23/23/28, d Dh300, d incl half-board Dh440-500; P ᗑᗑᗑ) The first place you reach on the approach to the gorge has pleasantly furnished, motel-style rooms that open onto a wraparound balcony as well as partially shaded campsites. The enticing pool and good restaurant add to the appeal, though sometimes tour buses crowd in at lunchtime. Excursions available.

★ Auberge Le Festival
INN €€

(☑ 0661 26 72 51; www.auberge-lefestival.com; Km 22; tower/cave r per person incl half-board Dh350/500; P ᗑ) ✐ Get back to nature in romantically lit cave rooms dug right into the hillside and finished in moulded *tadelakt*, or rock-walled, solar-powered tower rooms surveying the Petit Gorge. After self-guided treks and climbs (Dh300 per hour) arranged by the multilingual owner, relax on the panoramic terrace or help harvest vegetables in the organic garden for dinner.

★ Palmeraie Guesthouse
GUESTHOUSE €€

(☑ 0524 89 52 09; www.palmeraieguesthouse.com; Km 7; s/d incl half-board Dh300/500, with shared bathroom Dh200/350; ᗑᗑ) Just inside the palmery, this delightful guesthouse has a series of pretty terraces draped with flowering vines and attractive rooms set with Berber carpets, vintage travel posters and touches of artwork. Rachid and Doreen give a warm welcome, and this is a great base for exploring the palmery (ask to take Jack the donkey for a stroll).

You can also take longer promenades to the gorge (a scenic 7km walk). When coming from Tinerhir, park right next to the sign and take the steps down to the guesthouse.

Kasbah Amazir
GUESTHOUSE €€

(☑ 0524 89 51 09; http://kasbahamazir.com; Km 10; s/d/tr Dh350/450/500, incl half-board Dh450/600/800; P ᗑᗑᗑ) This reliable place hits all the right notes, with bright rooms (some with small balconies), a riverside location and friendly service. Some rooms are bigger than others and have better views, so look at a few before committing.

Dar Ayour
GUESTHOUSE €€

(☑ 0524 89 52 71; www.darayour.com; Km 13; s/d incl half-board Dh350/700; P ᗑᗑ) Riads have arrived in Todra at this warm, artsy five-storey guesthouse that's all Middle Atlas rugs, winking mirrorwork pillows, and colourful Berber-inspired abstract paintings. Fall asleep to the sounds of the river rushing past. All 10 rooms have en suites and fine views over the valley; four have balconies. There's also a roof terrace with a 360-degree panorama.

ⓘ Getting There & Away

The now paved road from Aït Haini north to Imilchil and the intersection of the N8 Beni Mellal–Fez road is accessible to normal vehicles. Grands taxis run up the gorge from Tinerhir to Imilchil (Dh40, 2½ hours), and there's usually one transit minivan heading up the gorge every day, with more on Wednesday for Aït Haini's Thursday market and on Friday for Imilchil's Saturday market. Hotels can usually advise on when the next public transport is scheduled.

Tinejdad

POP 7600

Back when caravans arrived loaded with gold, five Berber and Saharan tribes crossed paths at this hitching post (Tinejdad means 'nomad' in Tamazight), quenching their thirsts at the Sources de Lalla Mimouna natural springs, sleeping peacefully in well-fortified *ksour* in the Ferkla oasis and conducting business at 1000-year-old Ksar Asir, a medieval commercial centre that housed an Almoravid mosque and a sizeable Jewish community. Water, shelter, business and *baraka* (blessings): what more could a nomad need?

⊙ Sights

Tinejdad's crossroads culture remains remarkably intact just off the N10. The **Lalla Mimouna springs** are signposted on the left (north) 3km before town, and the green line of the **Ferkla oasis** begins on the southwest edge of town, where you'll spot towering **Ksar Asir**.

To see what treasures you can find from desert traders, hit the Sunday and Wednesday **souqs** on the western side of town.

★ **Musée de Oasis**　　　　MUSEUM
(www.elkhorbat.com/en.museum.htm;　　N 31°29.693, W 005°05.206; Dh20; ⊙9am-7pm) Inside restored Ksar el-Khorbat is this award-winning museum that traces tribal migrations through 22 rooms of carefully curated artefacts of seminomadic life: saddles worn shiny; contracts inscribed on wooden tablets in Arabic and Hebrew; Tinejdad jars for water and preserved butter; heavy silver jewellery; and to protect it all from would-be thieves, inlaid muskets and handcuffs.

Interesting multilingual explanations in French, English and Spanish illuminate tribal and family affiliations and explain the vexing architectural differences between a *ksour* and a *kasbah*. Useful indeed when you wander around the labyrinthine alley of the *ksar* in which the museum is housed and which is still home to some 80 families.

★ **Musée Sources Lalla Mimoun**　MUSEUM
(☑0535 78 67 98; Dh50; ⊙8am-sunset; ℗) This partly outdoor private museum encompasses the fizzing, magnesium-rich springs of Lalla Mimouna and is the passion project of Tinejdad native Zaïd Abbou. Artefacts collected over 30 years – including agricultural implements, textiles, pottery, construction tools, calligraphy tablets and painted prayer books – offer an insight into desert life and are housed in an unfolding series of spaces that encompass an internal garden dotted with words of wisdom from *The Little Prince*.

If Zaïd is on-site, he will happily show you around, which is undoubtedly the highlight of any visit. He will show you how some of the ancient time-measuring devices using water and a bowl worked, demonstrate early primitive locks and keys, and share a bit of the magic and mystery of this place.

🛏 Sleeping

Gîte-Restaurant el-Khorbat　CASTLE €€
(☑0535 88 03 55; www.elkhorbat.com; Ksar el-Khorbat; s/d/tr incl breakfast Dh475/530/625; ❄🛜🏊) 𝒫 Seasonal meals of garden-grown pumpkin soup and beef tajines with dates (Dh80 to Dh100) are served in the walled garden of the *ksar*, a regular stop for 19th-century Aït Merghad nomads. The *ksar* is still inhabited, and you too can spend the night in this living museum.

Ten rooms are big enough to house a small, seminomadic tribe of your own, with en suites, air-con and Tinejdad clay pots as lampshades. Excellent maps of the *palmeraie* enable self-guided wanders.

🛍 Shopping

Galerie d'Art Chez Zaid　ARTS & CRAFTS
(☑0524 83 51 13; ⊙9am-6pm) Snoop around this converted home of a local calligrapher (who also runs the Musée Sources Lall Mimoun) and you might find Tinejdad-made crockery in the courtyard, sand-worn bracelets in the salon, and wonderful, well-patched nickel silver teapots in the kitchen. There's also a restaurant here. Located in downtown Tinejdad, 200m after the Shell station on the right.

ℹ Information

There's an Attijariwafa ATM on the left-hand side of the street across from the Tinejdad commune.

ℹ Getting There & Away

Grands taxis run from the main market in the centre of town to Goulmima (Dh25, 45 minutes), Er-Rachidia (Dh50, 1½ hours) and Tinerhir (Dh20, one hour).

Goulmima كلميمة

POP 17,000

Located midway between Tinejdad and Er-Rachidia, Goulmima was once an ancient hub of Berber culture, but is now little more than a stop-over on journeys east to the desert (ATMs and internet cafes line the main street). In fact, most travellers skip this featureless stretch of the N10 altogether and head direct to Erfoud along the more scenic R702 from Tinejdad.

If you are stopping over here, the main attraction is the labyrinthine **Ksar Aït Goulmima**, a walled village on the southeast end of Goulmima's oasis that's home to several hundred people. A guide can lead you through the *palmeraie* and *ksar* to the 500-year-old mosque and historic *mellah*. To get there, head through downtown and turn right at the Er-Rachidia roundabout; the *ksar* is signed straight on. A pre-Islamic necropolis can be found northeast of town (signposted from N10), and there are also three souqs each week on Tuesday, Thursday and Saturday.

Grands taxis run when full to Er-Rachidia (Dh30) and Tinerhir (Dh15) via Tinejdad.

ZIZ VALLEY & THE TAFILALT

وادي زيز وتافيلالت

Snaking down through the dramatic Ziz Gorges from Rich, the Oued Ziz brings to life the last southern valley of the Ziz and the Tafilalt oases before puttering out in the rose gold dunes of Merzouga. Starting just south of the Middle Atlas town of Rich and about 30km north of Er-Rachidia, the tremendous Ziz Gorges provide a rocky passage south through the Tunnel du Légionnaire (built by the French in 1928). To the south, the valley widens, presenting a spectacular sight: a dense canopy of palms wedged between ancient striated cliffs, which date to the Jurassic period. It's worth taking some time here to explore the rich, untouristed *palmeraie*.

The provincial capital is in Er-Rachidia, a convenient pit stop for those travelling north along the N13 to Midelt and Meknès.

Er-Rachidia الرشيدية

POP 96,000

Established as a military garrison for the French Foreign Legion, the provincial capital of Er-Rachidia is still home to a sizeable military population stationed here to keep an eye on the nearby border with Algeria. Much like Ouarzazate, it is an expanding modern town staking out ever larger residential suburbs thanks to a significant injection of development funds. For those travelling north along the N13 to Midelt and Meknès, it makes a convenient stop.

Garrison towns aren't generally known for their hospitality or culture, but Er-Rachidia is trying to change that – every May, its enormous theatre hosts performers from throughout the Sahara at the **Festival du Desert** (www.festivaldudesert.ma; ⊙May) Market days are Sunday, Tuesday and Thursday.

🛏 Sleeping & Eating

Despite its regional importance, Er-Rachidia has a limited number of decent hotels, so you may want to push on for camping options at Meski and along the road south to Aufous.

Hôtel Errachidia HOTEL €
(☑0535 57 04 53; 31 Rue Ibn Battuta; s/d/tr incl breakfast Dh250/300/350; ❋🤶) Don't be fooled by the setting behind the bus station: inside are 21 simple but clean rooms with en suites and half with air-con. There's also a cafe downstairs.

Hotel le Riad HOTEL €€€
(☑0535 79 10 06; www.hotelleriad.com; Rte de Goulmima; s/d incl breakfast from Dh600/700; 🅿❋@ 🤶❋) Er-Rachidia's best business-class hotel has 27 sprawling guest suites with marble bathtubs, a huge pool, a spa and conference facilities. It's rather expensive for what it is, especially the Dh100 breakfast. You'll find it on your right along the N10 as you drive into town from Goulmima.

Zerda ZMP Restaurant CAFE €
(Ave Moulay Ali Cherif; mains around Dh30; ⊙9am-10pm) On the main road through town, a short stroll from the bus station, this buzzing open-sided eatery is one of the best spots in town for a quick, inexpensive meal of sandwiches, grilled meats and, the speciality, rotisserie chicken.

Restaurant Imilchil MOROCCAN €
(☑0661 60 92 64; Ave Moulay Ali Cherif; mains around Dh35; ⊙7am-11pm) Pop by for a good tajine served on a big terrace or to watch the sports on TV. There's a scruffy garden in back. It's on the main road, a 10-minute walk from the bus station.

FIGUIG

In the days of cross-border tourism, Figuig (fig-eeg) was popular with travellers. Few people make it here now, which is a shame because it is one of Morocco's best oasis towns: seven traditional desert villages amid 200,000 date palms fed by artesian wells. Once a historic way station for pilgrims travelling to Mecca, Figuig now sleeps, only waking for the autumn date harvest.

Figuig has an upper and lower town. The main road, Blvd Hassan II, runs through the upper (new) town, where there are ATMs, a post office and pleasant municipal gardens.

Sights

Where the road passes the Figuig Hotel, it drops downhill towards the lower town – the basin of palms and *ksour* (fortified mudbrick strongholds) that make up the old part of Figuig. This ridge provides a handy landmark as well as views over the *palmeraie* (palm grove) and into Algeria: the best views are from Azrou, where the path leads towards Ksar Zenaga, or from the terrace of the Figuig Hotel.

The seven *ksour* that make up the town each control an area of *palmeraie* and its all-important supply of water.

The crumbling state of many *ksour* lets you see their clever construction: palm-tree trunks plastered with pisé, and ceilings made of palm fronds. It's cool and dark and often eerily quiet. It's easy to get lost; village children will happily guide you for a few dirham.

Ksar Zenaga The largest and most rewarding of the town's seven *ksour* is Ksar Zenaga, south below the ridge splitting the oasis. Take the paths following irrigation channels past palm trees and gardens, then suddenly you're among a warren of covered passages. As you tunnel between the houses, look out for some marvellous, ancient wooden doors; and watch out – you may find yourself in someone's backyard.

Ksar el-Oudahir Close to the upper part of town, to the west of the main road, Ksar el-Oudahir is home to a lovely octagonal minaret built in the 11th century. It's known as the *sawmann al-hajaria* (tower of stone), and its design is quite unlike anything you'll see anywhere else in Morocco, instead echoing the minarets of Mauritania and the Sahel.

Sleeping

Auberge Oasis (☑ 0536 89 92 20; www.auberge-oasis.com; Rue Jamaa, Ksar Zenaga; s/d Dh100/170, incl full board Dh300/600; @) A family home built of adobe in a *ksar*, this auberge is the best way to taste traditional Figuigi life. Rooms are traditionally decorated and have en suites. The home-cooked meals are excellent, and you can relax in the rooftop Berber tent.

Getting There & Away

Always check transport options the day before travelling as schedules and availability of services can change. There are several buses a day to Oujda (around Dh100, six hours), including a daily CTM bus (Dh100, 5½ hours). All stop at Bouarfa, where you can change for connections to Er-Rachidia.

The border with Algeria is closed, but in the unlikely event of it reopening, it's 3km from Figuig to Moroccan customs, and a further 4km to the Algerian town of Béni Ounif.

❶ Information

Banque Populaire and Attajariwafa ATM are on Ave Mohamed V, as is the post office.

❶ Getting There & Away

AIR

Er-Rachidia's Moulay Ali Cherif airport is located about 4km northeast of the city centre. Royal Air Maroc (www.royalairmaroc.com) flies three times a week to/from Casablanca.

BUS

Buses operate out of the central **bus station** (Rue M'Daghra). **CTM** (☑ 0535 57 20 24) has one service daily to Marrakesh (Dh165, 10½ hours) and Meknès (Dh120, six hours) and an overnight service to Fez (Dh130, 7½ hours).

Private buses run to Ouarzazate (Dh75, six hours, three daily), Marrakesh (Dh150, 11 hours, three daily), Fez (Dh95 to Dh110, five daily) and Rissani (Dh25, two hours, nine daily) via Erfoud (Dh20).

TAXI

Grands taxis depart three blocks northeast of the main bus station. Destinations include Erfoud (Dh30, one hour), Meknès (Dh120, five hours), Fez (Dh130, five hours), Tinerhir (Dh60, 1½ hours), Rissani (Dh30, 1½ hours), and Merzouga via Rissani (Dh35, 1½ hours).

Around Er-Rachidia

Driving south to Erfoud you pass the origins of the Oued Ziz at Meski, 17km south of Er-Rachidia. From here the road crests a desert plateau to a striking viewpoint over the Ziz *palmeraie* before descending to the town of Aufous, 40km south of Er-Rachidia and midway to Erfoud. Formidable *ksour* line the route, peeking above the palm tops, and Aufous has some stunning pisé buildings and an impressive kasbah ruin as well as useful services such as petrol, coffee and phones.

◉ Sights

Source Bleue de Meski   SPRING
The origins of the Oued Ziz can be found in Meski, where warm, natural springs bubble to the surface beneath the picturesque ruins of the **Ksar Meski**. The French Foreign Legion extended the main pool and added steps forming a pleasant swimming pool much used by weekending locals. Beside it is a well-shaded campsite, and if you walk downstream and cross over the river, you can hike up to the deserted *ksar* for fabulous sunset views. The spring is signposted about 1km west of the main road.

Cooperative Al Ouaha   CULTURAL CENTRE
(⊙9am-noon Tue, Thu & Sat) ⚑ Seven kinds of date are grown in the Aufous oasis, and you can sample them all here. In the October and November season, the women of this cooperative in Aufous will walk you through a date tasting (Dh20), and in the off-season on Tuesday, Thursday and Sunday, they'll offer you tastes (Dh20) of nutty *tahalout* (date syrup) and natural energy bars made with dates. The cooperative is signed on the main road past the village mosque on the left, next to the village commune.

🛏 Sleeping

★ **Maison Zouala**   GUESTHOUSE €
(☑0672 14 46 33; www.zouala.com; per person incl half-board Dh250-300; 🛜) An icon of rural tourism, this welcoming family-run guesthouse has traditional rooms set with pisé walls, Berber tapestries and pottery-like lamps, and it's a great base for exploring the *palmeraie*. Hamid has a masters degree in history and a wealth of information on the Ziz Valley, its people and culture, and can connect you with village life (including visits to the school and a women's cooperative).

If you don't stay here, you can still stop in for lunch – but you'll need to call ahead. You can also arrange excursions, from walks, bike rides and mule rides through the oasis, to multiday trips to other villages, overnighting with locals on the way (overnight trips start around Dh400 per person per day including food and accommodation).

It's located about 47km north of Erfoud. When traveling north, look for a signed turn-off (leading to the left) on the N13.

Camping Tissirt   CAMPGROUND €
(☑0662 14 13 78; http://campingtissirtziz.free.fr; N 31°78.535, W 004°23.118; per person/car/tent/caravan Dh15/15/15/30, bungalows Dh130, incl half-board per person Dh150; 🛜) At the edge of the *palmeraie*, 12km north of Aufous, is this friendly, palm-shaded camp with three simple pisé bungalows (shared bathrooms) and meals of local *kalia* (spiced beef or chicken; Dh60 to Dh70), best finished with dates cooked in olive oil (Dh40). Showers (Dh10) and electricity (Dh25) are extra. Bicycles are also available for hire.

Maison Vallée de Ziz   GUESTHOUSE €€
(☑0661 83 51 51, 0535 88 21 76; N 31°45.835, W 004°12.220; per person incl half-board Dh350; ❋🛜♨) Ignore the rather featureless facade of this small roadside hotel and walk through to the poolside terrace for gorgeous valley views above the swaying palms and pomegranate trees. Steps down into the *palmeraie* allow for frequent morning and evening walks, after which you can collapse in enormous king-sized beds beneath cut-steel lanterns and oil paintings inspired by desert dreams.

It's also a great place to stop for lunch (Dh80) and a refreshing swim. Mohammed and Said are desert guides, so excursions further afield are easily arranged.

❶ Getting There & Away

Public buses travel from Er-Rachidia to a terminal above the Source Bleue spring (Dh4, 7am to 9pm). Any bus or grand taxi to Erfoud or Aufous can drop you at the turn-off. When leaving, flag down a grand taxi from the main road.

Erfoud

ارفود

POP 24,000

Erfoud makes a pleasant pit stop on the journey heading south to Merzouga from Fez or Meknès, with wood-fired *madfouna* (Berber calzone), fossils dating back hundreds of millions of years and the photogenic ancient Ksar M'Aadid, 5km north of town. The souq at the southern end of Erfoud sells local dates and fresh produce, and in October the town has an increasingly popular date festival, with dancing and music.

◉ Sights

Erfoud lies in the heart of Morocco's fossil beds, and the Paleozoic strata south of the highway between Erfoud and Alnif are a prime hunting ground for diggers. Kilometers of shallow trenches have been hand-dug by Berber miners in their search for trilobite fossils. Few of them are found in perfect condition so diggers take broken trilobites to 'prep' labs, like Brahim Tahiri's facility, where they are restored.

Trilobite replicas can be made from plaster, plastic or auto-body putty, and can be hard to distinguish from real fossils.

Museum of Fossils & Minerals MUSEUM
(☑ 0535 57 68 74; www.tahirimuseum.com; Rte de Rissani; ☺ 8am-7pm) FREE The best place for an introduction to Morocco's fossils is at Brahim Tahiri's Museum of Fossils & Minerals, the only private fossil museum in Morocco, where scientifically important specimens are exhibited beside their lesser cousins for sale in the boutique. Brahim's efforts at raising awareness of Morocco's rich geological heritage have even been recognised internationally with the naming of his very own trilobite, *Asteropyge tahiri*. You'll find the museum around 5km along the Rissani road – easily spotted by the lifesize replicas of dinosaur skeletons out front.

⌂ Sleeping & Eating

Hotel Cannes HOTEL €€
(☑ 0535 57 86 95; www.hotelrestaurantcannes.com; 85 Ave Hassan II; s/d/tr Dh160/210/270; ❀ 🕾) Cheap, clean, central rooms sporting what appear to be swirling, finger-painted walls done in faded pastel colours. Breakfast is an additional Dh25, and the cafe does decent meals. It's within walking distance of the market, CTM and Supratours ticket offices on Ave Mohammed V and the bus stop at Place des FAR.

Kasbah Xaluca Maadid RESORT €€€
(☑ 0535 57 84 50; www.xaluca.com; d/ste from Dh900/1800; 🅿❀🕾❄) A flashy pool-party scene straight out of music videos, only with more kids. Junior suites come with fossilised marble bedsteads and mineral lamps; suites are frilly, with chintz dust ruffles on four-poster beds. Desert travellers appreciate the spa, but kids head for the pool and minigolf course. It's 5km before Erfoud on the right.

★ **Pizzeria-Restaurant des Dunes** BERBER, PIZZA €
(☑ 0535 57 67 93; www.restaurantdesdunes.com; Ave Moulay Ismail; mains Dh50-70; ☺ 9am-10pm; 🕾) Authentic wood-fired pizza includes a house special with heart of palm, olives and oregano. For something a bit different, order the stellar *madfouna* (Berber calzone), a dough pocket stuffed with minced onions and herb-spiked chicken, beef or vegetables, then baked until puffy and golden. There's a pleasant back terrace, where you can dine when the weather cooperates.

Hotel-Restaurant Benhama CAFE €
(☑ 0661 82 64 57; Ave Moulay Ismail; sandwiches Dh20-25; ☺ 8am-9pm) Serves up a mix of the usual tajines, brochettes and couscous, plus pizza. Meals are served at spiffy sidewalk tables on the main road or inside the pleasant, air-conditioned lobby-restaurant.

❶ Information

Banks, internet cafes, the post office and a supermarket are all located along Ave Moulay Ismail.

❶ Getting There & Away

BUS

CTM (☑ 0535 57 68 86; Ave Mohammed V) runs overnight bus service to Meknès (Dh140, 7½ hours) and Fez (Dh150, 8½ hours) via Er-Rachidia (Dh30, 1¼ hours), as well as an early-morning service to Rissani (Dh20, 25 minutes).

Supratours and other buses depart from Pl des FAR for Tinerhir (Dh70, 3½ hours, daily), Ouarzazate (Dh120, 6½ hours, three daily), Marrakesh (Dh190, 11 hours), Meknès (Dh130, eight hours) and Fez (Dh140, nine hours, three daily).

TAXI

Grands taxis and taxi minivans depart Pl des FAR and opposite the post office for Merzouga (Dh35, one hour), Rissani (Dh10, 20 minutes), Er-Rachidia (Dh30, one hour) and Tinerhir (Dh65, five hours).

Rissani الريصاني

POP 21,200

Rissani is where the Oued Ziz quietly ebbs away, but between the 14th and 18th centuries it was the location of the famed desert capital, Sijilmassa, where fortunes in gold and slaves were traded via caravans crossing the *sahel*. Rissani was so strategic that the Filali (ancestors of the ruling Alawite dynasty) staged their epic battle here to supplant the Saadians. Today, Rissani is a dusty shadow of its former self. Barely a quarter of the population live in the 17th-century *ksar* while the modern town constitutes a single street and one square. Still, echoes of the past can still be heard in the epic haggling over birds, sheep and desert jewellery at Sunday, Tuesday and Thursday souqs.

⊙ Sights & Activities

The ruins of Sijilmassa and the Landmark Loop are both signed off the N13 to the west of the town centre. More mudbrick *ksour* flank the road to Merzouga, including **Dar el-Beidha** and **Ksar Haroun**; look for signposts on your left leaving town.

Sijilmassa   HISTORIC SITE

Just before you reach Rissani are the ruins of Sijilmassa, the capital of the first virtually independent Islamic principality in the south. Its foundation is lost in myth, but by the end of the 8th century it was a staging post for trans-Saharan trade. Caravans of up to 20,000 camels departed Sijilmassa for the remote desert salt mines of Taodeni and Tagahaza (in modern-day Mali), then continued to Niger and Ghana, where a pound of Saharan salt was traded for an ounce of African gold.

By the 12th century, Sudanese gold refined in Sijilmassa had made it to Europe, where it was minted into European coins. The identical quality between European and Moroccan coins attests to the importance of trade between these regions. But as Berbers say, where there's gold, there's trouble. Internal feuding led to the collapse of the city in the 14th century, and although it was rebuilt by Alawite Sultan Moulay Ismail in the 18th century, it was finally destroyed by Aït Atta nomadic warriors in 1818. Sijilmassa has remained a ruin ever since, with only two decorated gateways and other partially standing structures.

Ksar El Fida   CASTLE

(suggested donation Dh10; ⊙8am-7pm) This enormous, restored Alawite kasbah (1854–72)

served as the palace for the local *caïd* right up until 1965, after which it housed a museum of archaeology. Now only the son of the former owner remains and is happy to give you a short guided tour in French and Arabic.

Circuit Touristique   ARCHITECTURAL TOUR

Dune-bound visitors may be tempted to zoom through Rissani, but photographers, history buffs and architecture aficionados could spend a few days exploring decrepit *ksour* and artfully crumbling kasbahs on this 21km 'Landmark Loop'. It's best tackled in a clockwise direction from the regal ruins of **Ksar Abbar** – a favourite palace in exile for sidelined members of the Alawite dynasty – past half a dozen crumbling *ksour* to the still-inhabited **Ksar Tinheras** situated on a rise offering spectacular views over the Tafilalt.

Also of note en route are **Zawiya Moulay Ali Ash-Sherif** (⊙8am-6pm) FREE, the shrine built to honour the Alawite dynasty's founder, and the royal **Ksar Oulad Abdelhalim**, a glorious 19th-century ruin with huge ramparts.

The circuit is signed 1.5km west of Rissani along the N13.

🛏 Sleeping

With the dunes barely 35km further south, few people choose to spend the night in Rissani, instead visiting on a day trip either from Erfoud or Merzouga.

Hôtel Sijilmassa   HOTEL €

(☑0535 57 50 42; hotel-sijilmassa@menara.ma; Pl al-Massira al-Khadra; s/d with air-con Dh180/230, without air-con Dh120/180; ❋🐧) Located near the bus and grand taxi station (good for late or early arrivals), Hôtel Sijilmassa has clean, air-conditioned rooms with cramped en suites, plus a downstairs restaurant featuring a hearty *kalia*. Excursions are available here.

❶ Information

There's a post and phone office at the northern end of the medina, and two banks with ATMs on Place al Massira.

❶ Getting There & Away

BUS

CTM (Pl al-Massira) has an office in the centre of town. It runs one bus a day at 8pm to Meknès/Fez (Dh150/160, eight to nine hours) via Erfoud (Dh20, 30 minutes) and Er-Rachidia (Dh35, 1¾ hours).

Rissani & Merzouga

Rissani & Merzouga

⊙ Sights
1 Ksar El Fida	B1
2 Sijilmassa	A1

🛏 Sleeping
3 Auberge Camping Sahara	D1
4 Chez Julia	D3
5 Chez Youssef	D3
6 Hôtel Sijilmassa	A1
7 Kasbah Kanz Erremal	D1
8 Kasbah Mohayut	D1
9 Maison Merzouga	D1
10 Riad Ali	D4

ℹ Information
11 Al Barid Bank	D3

ℹ Transport
12 CTM	A1
Grands Taxis	(see 4)
Grands Taxis	(see 6)
13 Local Bus Station	A1
Supratours	(see 4)

Supratours runs an evening service to Meknès (Dh140) and Fez (Dh140) via Er-Rachidia (Dh40), a morning service to Marrakesh (Dh190, 12 hours) and an early morning and evening service to Merzouga (Dh30, 30 minutes).

Local buses leave from the **central bus station**, 400m north of the square on the road to Erfoud. There are services to Fez (Dh140, 13 hours) via Meknès (Dh110, nine hours) and to Marrakesh (Dh190, 10 hours). Buses run occasionally to Tinerhir (Dh40, six hours); check at the station for departures. There are six buses a day to Er-Rachidia (Dh30, two hours) via Erfoud.

TAXI

Grands taxis run frequently from opposite Hôtel Sijilmassa to Erfoud (Dh10), Er-Rachidia (Dh30), Tinerhir (Dh75), Merzouga (Dh20) and occasionally Taouz (Dh30).

Merzouga

When a wealthy family refused hospitality to a poor woman and her son, God was offended, and buried them under the mounds of sand called Erg Chebbi. So goes the legend of the dunes rising majestically above the twin villages of Merzouga and Hassi Labied, which for many travellers fulfill Morocco's promise as a dream desert destination. But Erg Chebbi's beauty coupled with Merzouga's accessibility has its price. Paved roads across the Middle Atlas from Midelt and east from Ouarzazate mean that desert tourism is booming. In high season, coaches and convoys of 4WDs churn up huge dust clouds as they race across the *hammada* in time for sunset camel rides, and purists lament the encroachment of hotels flanking the western fringes of the dunes – although there's no denying the spectacular dune views from rooms and terraces.

◉ Sights & Activities

The classic Merzouga excursion is to head into the desert and overnight in safari tents. Plan on sunset camel rides, fireside music jams and star-filled nights, followed by an early morning walk to the tallest nearby dune to watch the sunrise. To best experience the desert's ethereal beauty, plan carefully and come out of season. The end of November, and January and February are the quietest times and some of the best weatherwise.

Most hotels offer excursions into the dunes, ranging from Dh150 to Dh300 for two-hour sunrise or sunset camel treks. Overnight trips (Dh350 to Dh700 per person) usually include a bed in a Berber tent, dinner and breakfast; 4WD outings (up to Dh1200 per day) for a vehicle taking up to five passengers are more expensive. Invasive quads (dune buggies), which level dunes and disturb residents and wildlife, are not recommended.

If you show up in town unaccompanied by a guide or a dromedary, you can anticipate repeated offers of both. Try to keep it in perspective: getting by in the desert is notoriously tough. If you feel pressured, step away from the interaction.

★ Erg Chebbi
DUNES

Shape-shifting over 28km from north to south and reaching heights of 160m, Erg Chebbi may be modest compared with the great sand seas of Algeria, Libya and Namibia, but it is extraordinarily scenic. The rose gold dunes rise dramatically above a pancake-flat, black hammada and glow stunning shades of orange, pink and purple as the afternoon sun descends.

Lac Tamezguida
BIRDWATCHING

(Lac de Merzouga, Dayet Sriji) At the southern end of Erg Chebbi, between November and May, you'll find the seasonal lake of Tamezguida. This is perhaps the best area in Morocco for spotting many desert birds, including Egyptian nightjars, desert warblers, fulvous babblers and blue-cheeked bee-eaters. Sometimes, in good years, the lake even attracts flocks of flamingos and other waterbirds.

🍴 Sleeping & Eating

Merzouga has an excellent range of accommodation from humble, family-run guesthouse to lavish kasbah-style hotels. Many hotels are reached by *pistes* that run 1km or more east off the N13 tarmac road. Since they're strung out over 5km between the village of Hassi Labied to the north and Merzouga to the south, book in advance and find out the exact location of your hotel. At some places you can sleep on a terrace mattress or in a Berber tent for Dh30 to Dh60 per person. Bring warm clothing for overnight trips in desert bivouacs as it can get very cold.

There aren't many options when it comes to restaurants; most visitors take their meals at their lodging.

🛏 Hassi Labied

Auberge Camping Sahara   INN, CAMPING €
(📱 0535 57 70 39; www.auberge-sahara-merzouga. com; N 31°08.100, W 004°01.122; d per person incl half-board Dh200-400, terrace camping per person/caravan Dh50/70; 🅿 ❄ 🛜 ♿) Twenty basic, spotless rooms with en suites in a friendly Tuareg-run place with a pool, backing right onto the dunes at the southernmost end of the village. Four rooms feature dune views and three rooms air-con.

★ Maison Merzouga
GUESTHOUSE €€
(📱 0661 25 46 58 0535 57 72 99; www.merzouga-guesthouse.com; N 31°07.869, W 004°01.034; s/d incl half-board from Dh500/700, ste incl half-board Dh1000-2000; ❄ 🛜 ♿) Guests receive a heart-

felt welcome at this family-run guesthouse that focuses on Berber hospitality and not just desert-themed decor. Woven carpets, *tadelakt* walls, stone fireplaces and peaceful terraces with desert views add to the appeal. This is a fine spot to lounge poolside, arrange trips or set off to explore the *palmeraie*.

Kasbah Kanz Erremal
HOTEL €€

(☑ 0535 57 84 82; www.kanzerremal.com; N 31°07.765, W 004°00.769; d/tr/q incl breakfast Dh480/720/950; P ❋ 🐶 🌊) Eschewing the rustic vibe of many other Merzouga hotels, Kanz Erremal favours understated stylish decor. Cushioned banquets line the airy, central courtyard while rooms with desert views are swathed in cool, white linens and gauzy curtains. Best of all is the wide terrace that overlooks the sand and a sleek infinity pool with dreamy dune views.

Kasbah Mohayut
INN €€

(☑ 0666 03 91 85; www.hotelmohayut.com; s/d/ste incl half-board from Dh490/620/840; P 🐶 🌊) Find your niche in 18 sculpted-*tadelakt* guest rooms, in the shade by a small pool or on the roof overlooking the sanddunes. Canopied beds, Berber rugs and *tataoui* ceilings add charm, though the suites are the real draw – each with a rooftop terrace, well placed for taking in the desert views.

🛏 Merzouga

Chez Julia
GUESTHOUSE €

(☑ 0535 57 31 82; www.chez-julia.com; d with/without air-con from Dh300/180; ❋ 🐶) Pure charm in the heart of Merzouga, behind the mosque: seven simply furnished rooms (with three shared bathrooms) in sun-washed colours (rose, lemon, blue) with straw-textured pisé

walls, antique mantelpieces and white-tiled shared bathrooms, plus a furnished family apartment (Dh400 to Dh800). Ask about birdwatching tours, Saharan music concerts, fossil-hunting and overnights in the desert.

Riad Ali
GUESTHOUSE €€

(☑ 0670 62 41 36; www.hotelriadali.com; N 31°05.799, W 004°00.302; s/d incl breakfast Dh400/600; P ❋ 🐶 🌊) A mod kasbah provides instant relief from the desert heat with 11 guest rooms in Majorelle blue and lemon arranged around a shimmering courtyard pool. Overnight dromedary trips are led by an experienced, local official tour leader inclusive of standard, high-end or luxury bivouac accommodation (Dh450 to Dh1300 per person), the latter two boasting en suite showers and toilets.

It's conveniently located 600m from the centre of Merzouga where the bus terminates.

Chez Youssef
GUESTHOUSE €€

(☑ 0666 36 71 74; www.chezyoussef.com; Merzouga Village; d/tr incl breakfast Dh330/440, s/d/tr incl half-board Dh275/510/710; ❋ 🐶) Youssef's simple pisé home offers four rooms arranged around a tiny courtyard shaded by a single palm. The oasis-inspired decor is sparing, but beds are firm, linens are spotlessly clean and food home-cooked. Your host offers good-value camel treks and overnights in a peaceful camp far from the crowds (Dh450 per person).

★ Ali & Sara's Desert Palace
CAMPGROUND €€€

(☑ 0668 95 01 44; thedesertpalace@hotmail.com; per person incl full board Dh975; 🐶) 🛇 Make friends with Romeo, George and Casanova – no they aren't local lads trying it on, but your trusty dromedaries – as you head out from

---

ℹ CAMEL QUERIES

With over 70 camps in the Erg Chebbi dunes, picking your place is key. Before you agree to a dromedary trek, ask the guide the following questions.

How big is your camp, and how many people are headed there tonight? Overnight treks often congregate in the same spot, so if you have a romantic notion of being alone in the dunes under the stars, find an outfit with a separate camp.

How far is it to the camp site? Not everyone is cut out for dromedary-riding – it makes some seasick, and others chafe. For long treks, bring motion-sickness pills and cornstarch or talcum powder.

Does the trek guide speak English, or another language I know? This is important in the unlikely case of emergency in the desert, and to avoid awkward hand-gesture explanations when you need to use the bathroom.

Are the camels well rested? Don't take it personally. Cranky, overtired camels are notorious for sudden shifts, dead stops and throat-rattling spitting.

Merzouga for a trip of a lifetime. Husband-and-wife team, Ali and Sara, have spent four years crafting a personalised experience that gets rave reviews.

Coming from a nomadic family of 11 brothers, Ali's knowledge of the desert is second to none, while Sara's know-how makes for a luxurious and organised camp, first-class cooking and beautifully decorated tents. To keep things small, intimate and hassle-free the camp, 8km east of Merzouga, accommodates only 12 people and rates are fully inclusive, including non-alcoholic drinks. Reserve in advance.

ℹ Information

Al Barid Bank (⊘8am-4.15pm Mon-Fri) Next to the post office at the entrance to Merzouga, this handy bank has the only ATM in town.

Post Office At the entrance to Merzouga.

ℹ Getting There & Away

The N13 runs from Rissani to Merzouga, and the *piste* from Erfoud will probably be sealed in the next few years. That said, most hotels are some distance from the road on *pistes* marked with signs. If you're driving a standard rental car, don't head off-road as you'll likely get stuck in the sand. Minibuses will pick up or drop off in Hassi Labied – your hotel can make arrangements. Minivans run from Merzouga between 7.30am and 9.30am in high season.

Supratours has a daily 8am service from Merzouga to Marrakesh (Dh220, 12½ hours) and a 7pm bus to Fez (Dh170, 10½ hours). The bus stop is on Merzouga's main street, just off the highway leading north to Rissani.

Grands taxis leave from Merzouga centre heading north to Rissani (Dh15). Transport is harder to come by for Taouz to the south; you might have to hire out all six places (Dh100).

Taouz   تاوز

Come to Taouz to spot mineral formations and possibly dinosaur bones where the desert swallows the road. Between Merzouga and Taouz is the village of Khamlia, whose inhabitants are believed to be descended from escaped slaves. This frontier town is home to notable Gnawa musicians, including *Les Pigeons du Sable* (Sand Pigeons). Their music is available online, and they occasionally perform locally and at Er-Rachidia's Festival du Desert. Ask at their house (marked by a banner) for details.

A house beyond Taouz village, **Casa Taouz**, offers tea and occasional food. If you have a

4WD, several places to stay in the desert are signposted from the road with GPS locations.

RISSANI TO ZAGORA

Rather than retracing the N10 back to Marrakesh via Tinerhir and Ouarzazate, adventurous desert travellers opt for the N12, which traces the southern foothils of Jebel Saghro via Alnif, Tazzarine and N'Kob. The road sees little traffic and few tourists and provides an interesting link through prime fossil-hunting territory to the Drâa Valley, where it emerges at Tansikht 63km north of Zagora and 98km south of Ouarzazate. Kasbah-studded N'Kob is the most atmospheric place to stay and provides a good base for Jebel Saghro treks and exploration.

ℹ Getting There & Away

Local buses ply the road between Rissani and Zagora (six hours), via Alnif, Tazzarine and N'Kob. More reliable, though, are grands taxis between Rissani and Alnif (Dh30), Alnif and Tazzarine (Dh30), Alnif and Tinerhir (Dh30) and Tazzarine and Ouarzazate (Dh75).

CTM runs a 6.30am bus from Tazzarine to Marrakesh (Dh135, 7½ hours) via N'Kob (Dh20, 30 minutes) and Ouarzazate (Dh60, three hours).

Alnif   النيف

Much of Morocco's Anti-Atlas Mountains are built of Paleozoic rocks, dating back to between 245 and 570 million years. When these rocks were deposited, a shallow sea covered the region. Trilobites scuttled along the seafloor, and huge schools of *Orthoceras,* squid-like nautiloids with cone-shaped shells, swam above. When they died, their shells were preserved in the limy mud of the Maidir basin located between Erfoud and Alnif, awaiting resurrection as the polished curios, coffee tables and ornamental sinks that now cram Alnif's roadside shops.

Today more than 50,000 Moroccans earn their livelihoods in the fossil and mineral specimen mining and export business. It's hard, labour-intensive work where men work the fossil-rich seams and old mining spoil heaps by with chisels, picks and hoes. Prices depend on rarity, condition and the quality of the workmanship in the preparation, and can range from tens of dirhams to tens of thousands of dirhams for museum-quality specimens.

🏃 Activities

Ihmadi Trilobites Centre · TREKKING
(📞0666 22 15 93; www.alnifearth.com; ⊘9am-5pm) Mohand Ihmadi, the geologist owner, leads short trips to local fossil sites (Dh200 for the afternoon). Ihmadi has a wealth of information on the geological history of the region, and was in the process of creating a new museum nearby (slated to open in 2017). Stop in the shop to get the latest info.

🛏 Sleeping & Eating

Kasbah Meteorites · HERITAGE HOTEL €€
(📞0661 70 26 30; www.kasbahmeteorites.com; per person incl half-board Dh300; ❀🐾🛜🏊) This pleasant pit stop 13km west of Alnif has plain but comfortable air-conditioned rooms and an oversized pool. It's popular with tour groups.

La Gazelle du Sud · MOROCCAN €
(📞0670 23 39 42; mains Dh40-75; ⊘8am-7pm; 🛜) A popular lunch stop, serving large meals of tajine, brochettes or omelettes. It's the calmer of the two hotel-eateries facing each other at the town's main intersection. Simple rooms (doubles from Dh100) are available.

Hotel Restaurant Bougafer · CAFE €
(📞0535 78 38 09; Alnif; meals Dh30-60; ⊘8am-10pm) Bougafer has limited options (tajine or rotisserie chicken and chips), but that hasn't affected its enormous lunchtime popularity.

Tazzarine · تازارين

The small desert town and oasis of Tazzarine is located in the heart of the Aït Atta tribal area, midway between Alnif and N'Kob. Despite many years of drought, the palm groves and henna fields are still a pretty sight. Although there is little to stop for in the small straggling town, a few kilometres southwest you'll find the prehistoric site of Aït Ouazik with its wonderful petroglyphs clearly depicting images of elephants, giraffe, buffalo and antelope. They date from about 5000 BC when the area had a savannah-like character. Also south of Tazzarine is the small, but picturesque dunefield of Foum Tizza, an area of sandy *sahel* contrasting with blue-black rocks. The dunes are rarely visited and offer travellers a chance to appreciate the *désert profond* on a small scale.

🛏 Sleeping

Camping Serdrar · CAMPGROUND €
(📞0667 23 80 22; www.camp-serdrar.com; N 30°43.318, W 005°28.547; Berber tent per person

OFF THE BEATEN TRACK

BEYOND THE END OF THE ROAD: OUZINA

Instead of turning back at Taouz, you could take the *piste* by 4WD about one hour (30km) southwest towards the 2km stretch of dunes at **Ouzina**, a seldom-visited desert destination known only to Sahara savants. Here you'll find **Kasbah Ouzina** (📞0668 98 65 00; www.kasbahouzina.com; s/d incl half-board from Dh500/800), a small, tidy auberge with mercifully sand-free beds. At Ouzina the *piste* turns west toward the Drâa Valley, heading 45km to **Mharje village**, where you can turn north onto a well-graded *piste* to **Alnif**, where it intersects with the tarmac road to Zagora. Otherwise, you could follow a bumpy *piste* from Taouz west towards the Drâa Valley south of Zagora. Either way, the Taouz–Zagora journey takes at least seven hours, equipped with plenty of water, petrol, food, a spare tyre, a mobile phone and a Sahara-savvy guide.

incl half-board Dh200, tent/camper van incl shower Dh60/60, electricity Dh20) For those on a budget Camping Serdrar is a family-run palm farm set in a wonderful location 11km south of Tazzarine and 6km off the main road in the shadow of Jebel Rhart. Sleep in Berber tents or camp beneath the palms. Youssef can guide you to the fossil fields.

Camp Nomades · CAMPGROUND €€€
(📞0524 43 48 08; www.camps-nomades.com; Tazzarine; per person incl full board Dh1135-1900; ⊘closed May-Sep) Marrakesh-based travel specialist Maroc Sur Mesure offer a luxurious camping experience at Camp Nomades. The price includes full board and all activities (including desert walks, mule treks, village visits and cooking demonstrations).

N'Kob · نقوب

One of Morocco's best-kept secrets is the Berber oasis of N'Kob, where 45 mudbrick *ksour* make you stop and stare. The town has a dusty, bustling thoroughfare (which is also the main road leading in and out of town), where you can still find traditional craftsmen at work. On the main square at the eastern edge of town, you might also spot a member of the local Aït Atta warrior tribe striding into the N'Kob post office

LOCAL KNOWLEDGE

LOCAL SHOPPING

Opposite the post office is **Aït Atta Chassures**, a cobbler banging out traditional walking sandals with leather, rope and used tyre treads – more comfortable than they sound and quite stylish (Dh80 to DH130). Wander 500m down the side street with signs for Kasbah Baha Baha and through a doorway bedecked with dented pots to find N'Kob's teapot mender, whose services are in demand during the **Sunday souq**.

wearing a scimitar. The name N'Kob comes from a cave in the area that once served as a lodging of sorts for Aït Atta nomads. Beyond town lies the deep green palms of the oasis and the looming mountains of Jebel Saghro.

 Activities

For trekkers, N'Kob provides a gateway for treks across Jebel Saghro (three days) and is particularly well located for shorter treks to the spectacular rock pinnacles of Bab n'Ali. Also possible is a spectacular off-road drive up over Tizi n'Tazazert (2283m) and through the swirling rock formations of the Taggourt Plateau before dropping down to Ikniouln and the Dades Valley.

The **bureau des guides** (☑ 0667 48 75 09) on the main road can arrange local hikes to explore N'Kob's kasbahs, rock formations and palm oasis.

🛏 Sleeping & Eating

Aside from a few basic eateries along the main road, dining options are limited in N'Kob. Most travellers eat where they're lodging.

N'Kob's main budget option, **Auberge-Camping Ouadjou** (☑ 0524 83 93 14; r incl half-board from Dh250; P ☀), was closed for renovations when we were last in town, so give them a call before you arrive to check if they're open.

Kasbah Baha Baha HERITAGE HOTEL €€
(☑ 0524 83 97 63; www.kasbahabaha.com; N'Kob; s/d/tr from Dh380/500/690, without bathroom Dh250/370/500; P ❄ 🛜 ☀) A gorgeously restored kasbah with a vast Berber botany garden, wood-fired bread oven, gourmet poolside meals (breakfast/dinner from Dh40/120), on-site ethnographic museum (Dh10) and striking oasis views. Rooms come in three styles from simple

accommodations with shared bathrooms (nice rooms but a long walk to the facilities) to pretty duplexes with rooftop decks. All are attractively designed with traditional materials.

Kasbah Ennakhile HERITAGE HOTEL €€
(☑ 0524 839 719; www.kasbah-nkob.com; N'Kob; s/d incl half-board Dh400/560; ❄ 🛜 ☀) Guests give high marks to this friendly, reasonably priced kasbah with essential creature comforts. Rooms have stone floors, pisé walls and traditional details (though the shower which flows from a ceramic Tamegroute pitcher adds a bit of whimsy). The terrace and adjoining pool offer unobstructed views over the *palmeraie* and the thicket of kasbah towers in the village. It's on the road leading east out of town, about 800m past the main square.

Ksar Jenna GUESTHOUSE €€
(☑ 0524 83 97 90; www.ksarjenna.com; d incl breakfast Dh420-460; ❄ 🛜 ☀) Holding its own with Marrakesh riads, Ksar Jenna offers light-filled rooms in pastel blue, lemon yellow and the palest mauve decorated artfully with carved furniture, Tazenakht carpets and designer-fabulous *zellij* and *tadelakt* bathrooms. Dinner is served under the painted dining-room ceiling, breakfasts amid flowering garden, and aperitifs or espresso in the patio bar (it's a Moroccan-Italian venture). It's 2km west of N'Kob.

Kasbah Imdoukal HERITAGE HOTEL €€
(☑ 0524 83 97 98; http://kasbahimdoukal.com; N'Kob; d/tr/ste Dh700/900/1000, d without air-con Dh500; ❄ 🛜 ☀) Berber pride meets minimalist chic: chip-carved beds, Amazigh friezes atop *tadelakt* walls, oasis mule treks followed by poolside lounging, and dinners of *madfouna* (Dh120 to Dh190) by the restaurant fireplace with the occasional concert. Most rooms have air-con.

★**Kasbah Hôtel Aït Omar** HOTEL €€€
(☑ 0524 83 99 81; www.kasbahhotel-aitomar.com; s/d incl breakfast €50/90, d without bathroom €30-40; P ❄ 🛜 ☀) Rebuilt to pisé perfection, Aït Omar's crenellated rooftop and descending terraces offer unparalleled views over N'Kob's forest of kasbahs. Zigzagging staircases reveal private patios with potted citrus trees, a domed, marble hammam and 11 individually decorated rooms linked by turquoise accents in *zellij* tiles, luxe sofa fabrics and mosaic mirrors. In a separate building, the Petite Kasbah offers simpler rooms with shared bathrooms.

Atlantic Coast

شاطئ الاطلنطي

Best Places to Eat

➡ La Table by Madada (p214)

➡ Beachside Shellfish (p205)

➡ Pâtisserie Bennis Habous (p164)

➡ Restaurant Brasserie La Bavaroise (p164)

Best Places to Sleep

➡ Villa Bea (p189)

➡ Jack's Apartments & Suites (p211)

➡ La Sultana (p202)

➡ Riad Meftaha (p178)

➡ L'Alcazar (p178)

Why Go?

This windswept coast is home to Morocco's cultured capital, Rabat, and its economic hub, Casablanca. The refined Mauresque architecture and liberal attitudes on display in both cities are a far cry from the medieval medinas and conservative lifestyles of inland cities such as Fez and Marrakesh.

There's more to see than these big cities, though. Vast swathes of golden sand, small fishing villages, historic ports built by the Portuguese and fortified towns with vibrant medinas are scattered along the ocean's edge. Outside the towns, farmland rolls gently down to the sea and wetland reserves showcase rich migratory birdlife in autumn and spring.

The region is bookended by Asilah and Essaouira, famed for their medinas and surrounding beaches. There's art to view, delicious seafood to eat and an extraordinarily rich history, from the Phoenicians to the protectorates, that is begging to be explored. Don't miss it.

When to Go

Casablanca

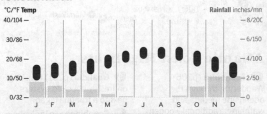

Mar–May Observe huge flocks of migrating birds on lagoons along the coast.

Jun Join world-music devotees at Essaouira's world-famous Gnaoua festival.

Sep Hit the beaches after the Moroccan tourists leave, while the weather's still good.

SPAIN

ATLANTIC
OCEAN

Tangier
Tangier-Boukhalef Airport
Had Gharbia
Asilah • Dchar
• Ghanem
Souq Tnine de
Sidi el-Yamani
Larache • Lixus
Ksar el-
Moulay Kebir
Bousselham ⑤
• Merdja
Merja Zerga Bargha
National Park
Lac de Sidi ⓐ¹ • Souk el-Arba
Boughaba du Rhurb
Sidi-
Kacem
Plage des Nations • **Kenitra**
Salé *Rabat-Salé*
Rabat ② *Airport*
Temara Plage Aïn el-
Mohammedia • Aouda ⓝ⁶ **Meknès**
Sidi- ⓐ²
Casablanca ④ Yahya Khemisset
Ben • ⓟ²²
Slimane Merchouch *Azrou*
Sidi **Rommani** *(25km)*
Mohammed V Bettache
International • Oued-Zem
Azemmour *Airport* Ez-Zhiliga
El Jadida Aïn-Leuh
Sidi Bouzid • ⓐ⁷ Oued
Moulay Abdallah *Mellah*
Settat Khouribga
ⓝ¹ Boulâouane Oued-Zem
Oualidia ③ S-Smaïl ⓝ⁹ Boujad Khenifra
Cap Beddouza S-Bennour
Lalla Fatna Khemis • Skhour Mechra Kasba-Tadla
Rehamna Benâbbou El Borouj • El-Ksiba
Safi Youssoufia Fkih-Ban-
Bouguedra • Salah Beni-Mellal
Souira • Benguérir
Kedima ⓝ⁷ Bin-el-Ouidane
ⓡ²⁰⁴ ⓐ⁷
Sidi-Bou-Othmane Azilal
Oued Tensift **HIGH ATLAS**
Essaouira Demnate
Diabat • *Essaouira*
Île de *Mogador Airport* ⓡ²⁰⁷ Chichaoua ⓝ⁸
Mogador ① *Sidi Kaouki (15km)* **Marrakesh**
Ménara
Airport

Atlantic Coast Highlights

① **Essaouira** (p206)
Wandering through the
oceanside medina and
watching traditional wooden
boats being constructed in the
bustling port.

② **Rabat** (p172) Exploring
the historic walled medina and
evocative kasbah.

③ **Oualidia** (p201) Feasting
on freshly shucked oysters
next to a tranquil lagoon.

④ **Casablanca** (p155)
Admiring this cosmopolitan
city's treasure trove of
Mauresque, art nouveau and
art deco architecture.

⑤ **Merja Zerga National
Park** (p188) Spotting rare
migrating birds from a boat on
the marshy wetlands.

Casablanca (Dar el-Baïda)

الدار البيضاء

POP 3.34 MILLION

Though not as atmospheric as other Moroccan cities, Casablanca is the best representation of the modern nation. This is where money is being made, where young Moroccans come to seek their fortunes and where business and the creative industries prosper.

The number of construction projects currently under way here is simply extraordinary – major redevelopments include those at Pl Mohammed V and the Parc de la Ligue Arabe, and new public buildings include the Grand Théâtre de Casablanca.

The city's handsome Mauresque buildings, which meld French-colonial design and traditional Moroccan style, are best admired in the downtown area. Visitors who spend time there, in the Quartier Habous and in the beachside suburb of Ain Diab, are sure to get into the local swing of things and realise that this old pirate lair is looking towards the future, embracing the European-flavoured urban sophistication that has underpinned life here for the past century.

History

The Phoenicians established a small trading post in the now-upmarket suburb of Anfa in the 6th century BC. In the 7th century AD, Anfa became a regional capital under the Barghawata, a confederation of Berber tribes. The Almohads destroyed it in 1188, and 70 years later, the Merenids took over.

In the early 15th century the port became a safe haven for pirates and racketeers. Anfa pirates became such a serious threat later in the century that the Portuguese sent 50 ships and 10,000 men to subdue them, leaving Anfa in a state of ruins. However, the local tribes continued to terrorise the trade routes, provoking a second attack by the Portuguese in 1515. Sixty years later the Portuguese arrived to stay, erecting fortifications and renaming the port Casa Branca (White House).

The Portuguese abandoned the colony in 1755 after a devastating earthquake severely damaged the walls of Casa Branca. Sultan Sidi Mohammed ben Abdullah subsequently resettled and fortified the town, but it never regained its former importance. By 1830 there were only 600 or so inhabitants.

By the mid-1800s Europe was booming and turned to Morocco for increased supplies of grain and wool. The fertile plains around Casablanca were soon supplying European markets, and agents and traders flocked back to the city. Spanish merchants renamed the city Casablanca and by the beginning of the 20th century the French had secured permission to build an artificial harbour.

Increased trade brought prosperity to the region, but the activities and influence of the Europeans also caused resentment. Violence erupted in 1907 when Europeans desecrated a Muslim cemetery. The procolonialist French jumped at the chance to send troops to quell the dispute; a French warship and a company of marines soon arrived and bombarded the town. By 1912 it was part of the new French protectorate.

◉ Sights

Casablanca is Morocco's commercial hub and locals are more interested in business than in tourism. Tourists are few and far between and there are remarkably few traditional tourist attractions. Other than the grand Hassan II Mosque, the city's main attraction lies in its neighbourhoods: the wonderful Mauresque architecture of the downtown area, the pretty Quartier Habous and the upmarket beachfront suburbs of Anfa and Ain Diab.

◉ Downtown Casa

It is often said that Casablanca has no sights apart from the Hassan II Mosque, but the French-built city centre is packed with grand colonial-era buildings, some of which are being restored. The best way to take it all in is by strolling through the area around the Marché Central (p164).

Abderrahman Slaoui Foundation Museum MUSEUM
(Map p159; ☑ 0522 20 62 17; www.musee-as.ma; 12 Rue du Parc; adult/student/child under 12yr Dh30/10/free; ☉10am-6pm Tue-Sat; 🚇 Place Mohammed V) An attractively presented house museum with a notable collection of Moroccan decorative arts, this privately established and operated institution occupies the former home of businessman Abderrahman Slaoui. The museum showcases his wonderful collection of Orientalist travel posters produced from the 1890s to the 1950s, as well as ceramics, inlaid furniture (including pieces designed by Marrakesh-based Louis Majorelle), ornate Berber jewellery encrusted with semi-precious stones and a stunning collection of ornate and richly

CASABLANCA IN...

One Day

Start your day by visiting the city's major landmark and tourist drawcard, the **Hassan II Mosque** (p165). Next, head to **Sqala** (p164), in the ramparts, or **Restaurant du Port de Pêche** (p164), in the port compound, for lunch, before wandering through the **Old Medina** (p156) and taking an architecture-focused stroll around the downtown area. In the evening, pay homage to a cinema classic by dining at **Rick's Café** (p164) or head to the beachside suburb of Ain Diab to sample traditional Moroccan dishes at **Basmane** (p166) or mod Med creations at ultrachic **Le Cabestan** (p166).

Two Days

With another day to enjoy the city, start in the Quartier Habous, where you can pick up some souvenirs at the souq and buy a selection of Moroccan pastries at **Pâtisserie Bennis Habous** (p164) – enjoy these with a good coffee at **Cafe Imperial** (p168). In the afternoon, pop into the **Abderrahman Slaoui Foundation Museum** (p155) to admire its collection of Moroccan decorative arts, check out an exhibition at the **Villa des Arts de Casablanca** (p157) and then finish the day by enjoying an excellent French dinner at old-fashioned favourite **Restaurant Brasserie La Bavaroise** (p164) followed by a drink and a dance at **La Bodéga** (p164).

coloured glass jewellery boxes and perfume flasks.

Old Medina
AREA

(Map p159; ⌂ Place Nations Unies) Though lacking the medieval magic that characterises many Moroccan medinas, Casablanca's compact 19th-century example is still worth a wander. You're unlikely to find treasures in its humdrum shops (hardware stores, pharmacies and shops selling cheap clothing and shoes predominate), but the crooked lanes, occasional tree-shaded square and well-frequented local cafes contribute to a generally pleasant atmosphere and make it a popular route for those walking between downtown Casablanca and the Hassan II Mosque.

The most heavily used entrances are through Bab Marrakech on Ave Tahar El Alaoui or through the gate next to the rebuilt clock tower at the northeast corner of Pl des Nations Unies. The narrow lanes near these gates are where most shops are found; the rest of the medina remains largely residential.

On the north side of the medina, facing the port, you'll see the last remains of Casablanca's 18th-century fortifications. Known as the **sqala**, the bastion offers panoramic views over the sea.

Clock Tower
LANDMARK

(Map p162) Marking the busiest entrance to the old medina, this 20m-tall clock tower is one of the most recognisable landmarks in downtown Casablanca. The current tower is a 1993 reproduction of the original 1911 structure, which fell into disrepair and was dismantled around 1950.

Church of St John the Evangelist
CHURCH

(Map p162; www.stjohnscasablanca.org; Rue des Anglais; ⌂ Place Nations Unies) The oldest church building still in use in Casablanca, this Anglican house of worship was built in 1906 on land owned by the British Crown. There are services at 9.30am (contemporary) and 11.30am (traditional) each Sunday. The **cemetery** on the site predates the church, having been built in 1864. The pulpit was donated by General George Patton, the WWII general who led Allied troops ashore at Safi in November 1942 as part of Operation Torch.

Place Mohammed V
SQUARE

(Map p162; Ave Hassan II; ⌂ Place Mohammed V) Surrounded by public buildings resplendent with Mauresque details, this central plaza was being redeveloped at the time of research. When reopened it will feature paving, a large fountain and palm trees. Overlooking it will be the the newly constructed Grand Théâtre de Casablanca designed by Moroccan-born French citizen and Pritzker Prize–winning architect Christian de Portzamparc. Both the plaza and the opera house are due to be unveiled in late 2017.

Villa des Arts de Casablanca GALLERY

(Map p159; ☎ 0522 29 50 87; www.fondationona. ma; 30 Blvd Brahim Roudani; ⊙ during exhibitions 9.30am-7pm Tue-Sat; ☒ Avenue Hassan II) **FREE** Located in an elegant 1934 art deco villa dating from 1934, this gallery, near Parc de la Ligue Arabe, is operated by the nonprofit Fondation ONA. It stages exhibitions of contemporary Moroccan and international art.

Parc de la Ligue Arabe PARK

(Map p159; Ave Hassan II; ☒ Place Mohammed V, Avenue Hassan II) This large green space was being redeveloped at the time of research and was due to reopen in March 2017. The rehabilitated park will feature promenades lined with palm trees, water features, a stadium, a skate park and an underground car park. The **Cathédrale du Sacré Coeur**, (Blvd Rachidi; ☒ Place Mohammed V) in its northwest corner, will be retained.

Church of Notre-Dame de Lourdes CHURCH

(Map p159; cnr Ave Mers Sultan & Blvd Mohammed Zerktouni; ☒ Avenue Hassan II) A striking example of European modernism, this 1956 Catholic church is notable for its elongated concrete entrance and its striking stained-glass windows, which were designed by noted French artist Gabriel Loire. It overlooks the Rond-point de l'Europe (aka Mers Sultan Roundabout).

◉ Maarif

Moroccan Jewish Museum MUSEUM

(Map p158; ☎ 0522 99 49 40; www.casajewishmuseum.com; 81 Rue Chasseur Jules Gros, Quartier Oasis; Dh50; ⊙ 10am-5pm Mon-Fri, 11am-3pm Sun; ☒ Gare de l'Oasis) The only Jewish museum in the Arab-speaking world, this institution is set in an attractive garden villa that once functioned as a Jewish orphanage. It traces the 2000-year history of Jews in Morocco, focusing on Casablanca's Jewish community (most of the country's Jews live here). The thoughtfully curated and well-labelled collection includes ornate clothing, traditional tools and ritual objects. Photographs usually feature in the temporary exhibition space, and there's a reconstructed 1930s synagogue from Larache in an adjoining room.

The museum is 1km from the Gare de l'Oasis tram stop. From the tram stop, walk down Route de l'Oasis past the train station and then turn right into Rue Abu Dhabi. Rue Chasseur Jules Gros is the sixth street to the left. A taxi from the city centre will cost Dh40, but note that most taxi drivers are unaware of the museum's existence so will need to be given directions. Also note that it is sensible to call ahead to check that the museum is open as it sometimes closes when the security situation is unsettled. Students are given free entry on Wednesdays.

◉ Quartier Habous (Nouvelle Medina)

The Quartier Habous, or Nouvelle (New) Medina, is Morocco lite – an idealised version of a traditional medina with clean streets, attractive Mauresque buildings and arcades, neat rows of shop stalls and even a small park. Built by the French in the 1930s, it was a unique experiment: a medina built to Western standards to accommodate the first rural exodus in the 1920s. Though undeniably ersatz, it blends Moroccan architecture with French ideals very successfully and its souq offers excellent opportunities to source souvenirs.

The **Royal Palace** (closed to the public) is to the north of the district, while to the south is the old **Mahakma du Pasha** (Blvd Victor Hugo) **FREE**, which has more than 60 rooms decorated with sculpted wooden ceilings, stuccowork, wrought-iron railings and earthenware floors. This is not always open to visitors.

THE CHANGING FACE OF CASABLANCA

The first French resident-general, Louis Hubert Gonzalve Lyautey, hired French architect Henri Prost to redesign Casablanca in the early 20th century as the economic centre of the new protectorate and, indeed, as the jewel of the French colonies. His wide boulevards and modern urban planning still survive, as does a rich and unique heritage of Mauresque architecture, melding French-colonial design and traditional Moroccan style. However, Lyautey underestimated the success of his own plans and the city grew far beyond his elaborate schemes. By the end of WWII, Casablanca had a population of 700,000 and was surrounded by heaving shanty towns. These have only recently been demolished – often controversially – and their residents rehoused on the outer urban edge of the city.

ATLANTIC COAST CASABLANCA (DAR EL-BAÏDA)

Casablanca

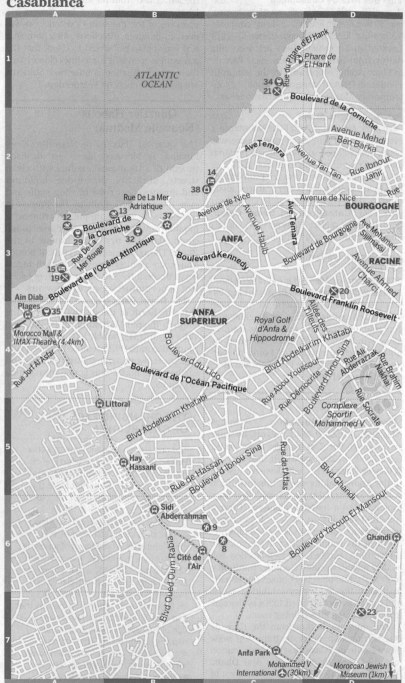

ATLANTIC
OCEAN

Phare de
El Hank

Rue du Phare d'El Hank

34
21

Boulevard de la Corniche

Avenue Mehdi
Ben Barka

Ave Temara

Avenue Tan Tan

Rue Ibnour
Jahir

14
38

Rue De La Mer
Adriatique

Avenue de Nice

Avenue de Nice

Rue

BOURGOGNE

12
29

13

Boulevard de
la Corniche

37

Ave Temara

Avenue Habib

ANFA

Boulevard de Bourgogne

Ave Mohamed
Sijilmassi

RACINE

Rue De La
Mer Rouge

32

Boulevard Kennedy

Avenue Ahmed
Charci

15
19

Boulevard de l'Océan Atlantique

Boulevard Franklin Roosevelt

20

Ain Diab
Plages

35

AIN DIAB

ANFA
SUPERIEUR

Royal Golf
d'Anfa &
Hippodrome

Allée des
Tilleuls

Blvd Abdelkarim Khatabi

Boulevard Ibnou Sina

Rue Ali
Abderrazzak

Rue Brahim
Nakhai

Morocco Mall &
IMAX Theatre (4.4km)

Rue Jorf Al Asfar

Boulevard du Lido

Boulevard de l'Océan Pacifique

Rue Abou Youssouf

Rue Démocrite

Complexe
Sportif
Mohammed V

Rue Socrate

Littoral

Blvd Abdelkarim Khatabi

Hay
Hassani

Rue de Hassan

Boulevard Ibnou Sina

Rue de l'Atlas

Blvd Ghandi

Sidi
Abderrahman

9

8

Cité de
l'Air

Boulevard Yacoub El Mansour

Ghandi

Blvd Oued Oum Rabia

23

Anfa Park

Mohammed V
International (30km)

Moroccan Jewish
Museum (1km)

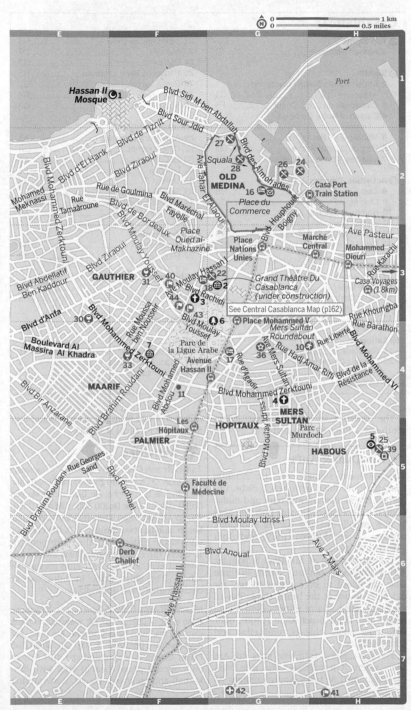

Casablanca

The Quartier is located about 2.5km southeast of Place Mohammed V.

◎ Aïn Diab & Anfa

These affluent suburbs on the Atlantic beachfront are lined with beach clubs, up-market hotels, restaurants, bars and clubs. Long the city's entertainment hub, the area is now equally popular for its shopping, courtesy of the Morocco (p169) and Anfa Place (p169) malls.

The sandy beach at Aïn Diab is popular with young locals but isn't clean, so those who can afford to do so tend to pay for day entry to one of the beach clubs. Two of the better ones, Miami Fitness Club & Spa (p160) and Tahiti Beach Club (p160), offer swimming pools, chaises, umbrellas and other facilities.

The Casablanca tramway goes to Aïn Diab, where it terminates. The ride from Pl Mohammed V takes approximately 35 minutes. A taxi from the centre should cost around Dh35 (Dh70 at night).

🏃 Activities

Tahiti Beach Club   SWIMMING
(Map p158; ☑ 0522 79 80 25; www.tahitibeachclub. ma; Blvd de la Corniche, Aïn Diab; adult Mon-Fri Dh150-200, Sat & Sun Dh200-300, child daily Dh50-100; ⓟ Aïn Diab Plage) The city's most popular beach club has two venues, with the cheaper one on the eastern side the more popular. It offers three restaurants, two swimming pools, a gym, a spa, a kids club and a surf school. The entry price includes use of chaise-lounges and umbrellas.

Miami Fitness Club & Spa   SWIMMING
(Map p158; ☑ 0522 20 67 24; www.miamifitness clubcasa.ma; Blvd de la Corniche, Aïn Diab; per day adult/child Dh80/50; ☺ May-Sep; ⓟ Aïn Diab Plage) As well as a gym and spa, this fitness club offers a *plage* (beach) area with basketball and volleyball courts, a swimming

pool and a restaurant. Cabana/chaise/umbrella hire cost Dh200/25/25.

Club Alpin Français   TREKKING
(Map p158; CAF; ☎ 0522 99 01 41; http://cafmaroc2011.ffcam.fr; 50 Blvd Sidi Abderrahmane, Quartier Beausejour; 🚇 Cité de l'Air) Organises canyoning, trekking, spelunking (caving), kayaking and mountain climbing activities, operates mountain *refuges* (huts) and has an informative French-language website.

Hammam Ziani   HAMMAM
(Map p159; ☎ 0522 31 96 95; 59 Rue Abou Rakrak, Quartier Alsace; Dh50; ⏱ 7am-10pm; 🚇 Avenue Hassan II) Offering the traditional steam room and *gommage* (scrub) for Dh80, this modern spa and hammam also offers massage for Dh100.

Institut Français   LANGUAGE
(Map p159; ☎ 0522 77 98 70; http://if-maroc.org; 121-123 Blvd Mohammed Zerktouni; ⏱ 8.30am-6.30pm Mon-Sat, 10am-2pm Sun; 🚇 Avenue Hassan II) Presents cultural events and offers semester-long French-language courses.

🎉 Festivals & Events

Anfa Festival   MUSIC
(⏱ Jul) Free outdoor music and performance festival staged on the beach in Ain Diab. Includes dance, theatre and music in a variety of genres, with an emphasis on Moroccan *chaabi*.

Jazzablanca   MUSIC
(http://jazzablanca.com; ⏱ Apr) Weeklong jazz festival at the Hippodrome de Casa-Anfa featuring local and international acts.

L'Boulevard Festival of Casablanca   CULTURAL
(www.boulevard.ma; Aux Anciens Abattoirs de Casablanca, Quartier Hay Mohammadi; ⏱ Oct) This five-day music and arts festival in the city's historic abattoirs building features free concerts, circus arts and a handicrafts souq.

🛏 Sleeping

Occupancy rates and prices are higher in Casablanca than elsewhere in Morocco, so it's always a good idea to book your accommodation in advance to secure a room at the best available price.

Budget hotels here are almost uniformly poor value – check for cleanliness before booking in – and good midrange options are few and far between. There are plenty of topend options, predominantly catering to business travellers.

Hotel Guynemer   HOTEL €
(Map p162; ☎ 0522 27 57 64; hotelguynemer@yahoo.com; 2 Rue Mohammed Belloul; s/d incl breakfast Dh350/450, ste s/d incl breakfast Dh450/650; ❄ 🖥; 🚇 Place Mohammed V) Friendly and well-priced, the Guynemer has recently undergone a major renovation but the owners have ensured that many of the building's original features have been retained (most date from the 1930s). Regular rooms are comfortable but slightly cramped (especially the bathrooms); suite rooms are well-sized. All have double-glazed windows, satellite TV and good beds. Parking costs Dh10 per 24 hours.

Hotel Central   HOTEL €
(Map p178; ☎ 022 26 25 25; www.hotelcentralcasa.com; 20 Pl Ahmed El Bidaoui, Old Medina; s/d/tr incl breakfast Dh340/400/500; @) In a somewhat isolated location on the edge of the old medina, this hybrid hotel-hostel occupies a handsome but worn colonial-era building and has helpful staff. To find it, look for the big information sign and multicoloured stairs opposite the port. Be warned that the area isn't particularly safe at night.

There's a pleasant roof terrace with a view across to the Hassan II Mosque. The best rooms are those on the top floor with balcony; others can be dark. Wi-fi is spotty.

Hôtel Astrid   HOTEL €
(Map p162; ☎ 0522 27 78 03; hotelastrid@hotmail.com; 12 Rue 6 Novembre; s/d Dh330/440; 🖥;

CASABLANCA FOR CHILDREN

Casablanca is a huge, dirty and noisy city, so many families travelling with young children choose to retreat from the chaos of the city centre and hang out at the beach or in their hotel. The **Four Seasons Hotel** (p163) and **Hotel Bellerive** (p163) are both on the beach in **Ain Diab** and have a swimming pool, as does the the **Hyatt Regency** (p163) downtown. Alternatively, the beach clubs in Ain Diab have pools, playgrounds and attached terrace cafes specialising in ice cream.

Continuing west from Ain Diab, the upmarket suburb of **Anfa** is home to the enormous **Morocco Mall** (p169), which has a giant aquarium and an **IMAX Theatre** (p169) in addition to shops and a food court. It's a good choice for teens.

Sidebar: ATLANTIC COAST CASABLANCA (DAR EL-BAÏDA)

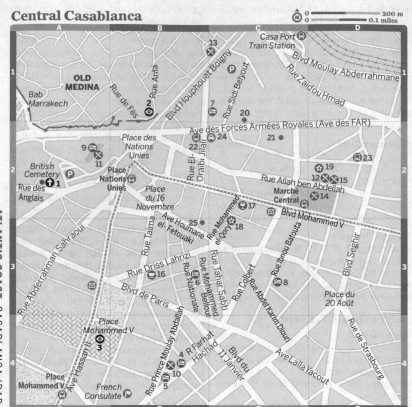

Central Casablanca

Central Casablanca

🏠 Place Mohammed V) Though in dire need of an overhaul (fittings are extremely worn), this dated budget option is worth considering as it is relatively clean, offers good wi-fi and has helpful staff. Credit card payments are not accepted.

Hotel du Palais HOTEL €
(Map p162; ☑ 0522 27 61 91; 68 Rue Farhat Hachad; s/d without bathroom Dh150/230, d/tr with bathroom Dh200/280; 📶; 🏠 Place Mohammed V) The dowdy du Palais offers worn, relatively clean and noisy rooms with decent beds. A warmish shower costs Dh10.

Hôtel Maamoura HOTEL €€
(Map 162; ☑ 0522 45 29 67; www.hotelmaamoura. com; 59 Rue Ibnou Batouta; s/d/tr incl breakfast Dh450/600/700; 🅿️ ❄️ 🛜; 🏠 Marché Central) Popular with small tour companies and regular visitors to the city, this well-priced hotel offers clean and spacious rooms, a good breakfast and helpful staff. Wi-fi can be patchy.

Hôtel les Saisons HOTEL €€
(Map p162; ☑ 0522 49 09 01; www.hotellessaisonsmaroc.ma; 19 Rue el-Oraïbi Jilali; s/d/ste incl breakfast Dh950/1150/1450; ❄️ 🛜; 🏠 Place Nations Unies) This small and efficiently run modern hotel near Casa Port train station offers clean and comfortable rooms, a decent breakfast and an in-house restaurant serving alcohol.

Hotel Bellerive HOTEL €€
(Map p158; ☑ 0522797504; www.hotelbellerive-casablanca.com; 38 Blvd de la Corniche, Ain Diab; s/d/tr/q incl breakfast Dh620/820/1120/1420; 🅿️ ❄️ 🛜 🏊; 🏠 Ain Diab) A beachfront terrace, pool and garden compensate for the dated and slightly grubby rooms at this French-speaking family-run hotel on the Corniche. Many rooms have ocean views, but they also overlook the terrace bar, which is open to the public and can be noisy.

⭐ **Hôtel Le 135** HOTEL €€€
(Map p159; ☑ 0522 27 91 12; www.le135hotel.com; 135 Ave Hassan II; s/d/tr Dh1400/1800/1900; 🅿️ ❄️ 🛜; 🏠 Avenue Hassan II) Good upper-mid-range accommodation choices are few and far between in Casablanca, so the 2016 opening of this 10-room hotel opposite the Parc de la Ligue Arabe was greeted with acclaim by regular visitors to the city. Huge, light-filled rooms are exceptionally well appointed (top-quality bed, satellite TV, bathtub and

shower). Breakfast costs Dh100 per person and parking Dh35 per night.

Four Seasons Hotel Casablanca HOTEL €€€
(Map p158; ☑ 0529073700; www.fourseasons.com/casablanca/; Blvd de la Corniche, Anfa; r Dh3250-4850, ste Dh5250-80,050; 🅿️ ❄️ ❄️ 🛜 🏊 🐕) Located on the beach in Anfa and opened in late 2015, this Foster and Partners–designed hotel has style and swank in spades. Rooms are huge and lavishly appointed, in-house restaurants have seating overlooking the ocean (but no alcohol) and service is exemplary. When not lazing by the heated outdoor pool, guests are often found in the luxury spa.

Breakfast costs Dh350 and the hotel's popular buffet afternoon tea (Friday to Sunday, 4pm to 7pm) costs Dh200.

Le Doge BOUTIQUE HOTEL €€€
(Map p159; ☑ 0522 46 78 00; www.hotelledoge. com; 9 Rue Docteur Veyre; r Dh1640-1840, ste Dh2440-2640; 🅿️ ❄️ 🛜 🏊; 🏠 Place Mohammed V) Casablanca's only boutique hotel occupies a lovingly restored art deco villa in a quiet street near Pl Mohammed V. Its 16 rooms are individually decorated and very comfortable, with quality toiletries. The lounge-library with open fire is a drawcard in winter and the luxe spa is popular at all times. Our only caveat? We found the breakfast (Dh180) very disappointing.

Hyatt Regency Casablanca HOTEL €€€
(Map p162; ☑ 0522 43 12 34; https://casablanca. regency.hyatt.com; Pl des Nations Unies; r Dh2200-2600, ste Dh3900-27,000; 🅿️ ❄️ ❄️ 🍴 🛜 🏊; 🏠 Place Nations Unies) Its central location means that this efficiently operated hotel is a popular meeting place for Casablancais, who enjoy lunch in Café M, a coffee or drink in the foyer, or a meal at swish Moroccan restaurant Dar Beida (p165). Rooms are spacious, comfortable and extremely well equipped; facilities include a fitness centre and an outdoor pool. Service is both friendly and efficient.

🍴 Eating

Fresh fish and seafood are the local speciality. Rue Chaouia, located opposite the Marché Central, is the best place for a quick eat, with a line of rotisseries, stalls and restaurants serving roast chicken, brochettes and sandwiches (Dh20 to Dh30). It's open until about 2am.

✗ Downtown Casa & Maarif

★ Pâtisserie Bennis Habous
BAKERY €

(Map p159; ☑ 0522 30 30 25; 2 Rue Fkih el-Gabbas, Quartier Habous; pastries Dh5; ⊙ 8am-9pm) Secreted in a lane in the Souq Habous, this famous patisserie deserves a dedicated visit. Make your choice of traditional Maghribi pastries such as *cornes de gazelle* (gazelle horns; pastries filled with a paste of almond and orange water) or *akda aux amandes* (almond macaroons), then head to nearby Cafe Imperial to order a coffee and scoff your bounty.

Marché Central
MARKET €

(Map p162; meals from Dh40; ⊙ 9am-6pm; ☐ Marché Central) The Marché Central is a great place to go for lunch – busy tables from a dozen simple eateries are crammed with diners feasting on huge platters of fish, grilled vegetables, bread, salads and seafood soup. Cheap, filling and perfect for people-watching.

★ Restaurant du Port de Pêche
SEAFOOD €€

(Map p159; ☑ 0522 31 85 61; Le Port de Pêche; mains Dh90-135; ⊙ noon-2.30pm & 7-10.30pm) Packed to the gills at lunch and dinner, this tried and trusted restaurant on the upstairs floor of a building in the middle of Casablanca's port serves the city's freshest and best seafood. Fish can be enjoyed fried or grilled, plain or meunière, and there are oysters and other shellfish on offer. Note that smokers on nearby tables are inevitable.

★ Rick's Café
MEDITERRANEAN €€

(Map p159; ☑ 0522 27 42 07; www.rickscafe.ma; 248 Blvd Sour Jdid, Old Medina; mains Dh100-180; ⊙ noon-3pm & 6.30pm-1am) It may be as clichéd as they come, but this tribute bar and restaurant is both endearing and enjoyable. Run by a former American diplomat, it has loads of atmosphere and serves good Moroccan and international food. American crooners dominate the soundtrack when pianist Issam takes a break, and Sunday's jazz sessions, which start at 9.30pm, are everpopular.

La Bodéga
TAPAS €€

(Map p162; ☑ 0522 54 18 42; www.restopro.ma/bodega/; 129 Rue Allah ben Abdellah; tapas Dh45-70, mains Dh80-160; ⊙ noon-3pm Mon-Sat, 7pm-2am daily; 🛜; ☐ Marché Central) Local partygoers of all ages love this hybrid tapas bar-restaurant where meaty dishes are served accompanied by a soundtrack of loud – and often live – music (everything from salsa to Arabic pop). Ri-oja (Spanish wine) flows freely and the dance floor is packed after 10pm on weekends. At other times there may be football on the big screen or even flamenco performances.

Sqala
MOROCCAN €€

(Map p159; ☑ 0522 26 09 60; www.sqala.ma; Blvd des Almohades; set breakfast Dh90, mains Dh75-170; ⊙ noon-3pm & 7-11pm Mon, 8am-11pm Wed-Sun) Nestled in the ochre walls of the *sqala,* an 18th-century fortified bastion on the edge of the old medina, this pretty garden restaurant is a tranquil escape from the downtown bustle. Particularly popular for breakfast, it also serves *briouates* (bite-sized flaky-pastry triangles), tajines, *pastillas* (savoury pies) and brochettes. No alcohol is served, but there's a good selection of fresh juices (Dh22).

La Taverne du Dauphin
FRENCH €€

(Map p162; ☑ 0522 22 12 00; www.taverne-du-dauphin.com; 115 Blvd Houphouët Boigny; mains Dh80-130; ⊙ noon-11pm Mon-Sat; ☐ Place Nations Unies) A Casablanca institution, this staunchly traditional restaurant near Casa Port has been serving up *fruits de mer* (seafood) since it opened in 1958 and is particularly busy at lunchtimes. Service is friendly, there are dedicated smoking and nonsmoking sections and the set menu of three courses plus coffee for Dh120 is a major bargain.

Marny
CAFE €€

(Map p158; ☑ 0522 25 48 10; http://marnymaroc.com/; 45 Cour des Sports, Ferme Bretonne; set breakfast Dh20-65, pastas Dh85-115, burgers Dh85-95; ⊙ 7am-9pm; ☐ Beauséjour) A popular expat haunt, this cafe and bakery located in front of the Cour des Sports rugby club and close to the French Club has a modern airy interior and a pleasant front garden. Bread, pastries and gateaux are the house specialities and are heartily recommended. No alcohol.

★ Restaurant Brasserie La Bavaroise
FRENCH €€€

(☑ 0522 31 17 60; www.bavaroise.ma; 133 Rue Allah ben Abdellah; mains Dh160-230; ⊙ noon-10.30pm Mon-Fri, 7-10.30pm Sat; ❋; ☐ Marché Central) Located in a dishevelled street behind the Marché Centrale, La Bavaroise has been serving an ultraloyal local clientele since 1968 and shows no sign of losing its popularity. The speciality is grass-fed beef from the Atlas served in the form of steak with pommes frites, green salad and French-style sauces. Other highlights include oysters from Dakhla and decadent desserts.

DON'T MISS

HASSAN II MOSQUE

Built by the late King Hassan II to commemorate his 60th birthday, this enormous **mosque** (Blvd Sidi Mohammed ben Abdallah; guided tours adult/student/child 4-12yr Dh120/60/30; ⊙ tours 9am, 10am, 11am, 3pm & 4pm Sat-Fri, plus noon Sat-Thu) was partially funded by public subscription. Set on an outcrop jutting over the ocean and with a 210m-tall minaret that serves as the city's major landmark, it is a showcase of the very best Moroccan artisanship: hand-carved stone and wood, intricate marble flooring and inlay, gilded cedar ceilings and exquisite *zellij* (colourful ceramic tiling) abound. Multilanguage guided tours of the interior are conducted outside prayer times for modestly clad visitors.

The mosque is commonly thought to be the world's third-largest mosque after those in Mecca and Medina, and can accommodate 25,000 worshippers. The mosque complex was designed by French architect Michel Pinseau, took six years to build and was completed in 1993. Its dramatic location overhanging the ocean waves echoes verse from the Quran, which states that God's throne was built upon the water. Believers pray on a centrally heated floor, and can see the Atlantic breaking over the rocks underneath the glass floor in the basement and feel the sunlight through the retractable roof.

The size and elaborate decoration of the prayer hall is simply spectacular. A team of over 6000 master craftspeople was assembled to work on the mosque, delicately carving intricate patterns and designs in cedar from the Middle Atlas and pink granite from Agadir. The gates were made from brass and titanium, and the ablution fountains in the basement, which are shaped like huge lotus flowers, were carved from local marble.

To see the interior visitors must be 'decently and respectfully dressed' (knees and upper arms need to be covered); women do not require a headscarf. Hour-long tours are conducted in French, English, German and Spanish, and take in the prayer hall, subterranean ablutions rooms and never-used hammam.

Le Rouget de L'isle
FRENCH €€€
(Map p159; ☑ 0522 29 47 40; 16 Rue Rouget de l'Isle; mains Dh170-270; ⊙ noon-3pm Mon-Fri, 7.30-11pm Mon-Sat; 🚇 Place Mohammed V) Occupying a charming 1930s villa in a leafy street near the Slaoui Museum, this upmarket restaurant is known for its wonderful garden redolent with night-blooming jasmine. It's a romantic spot for dinner in warm weather – in the cooler months the modern French dishes are enjoyed in the art-adorned dining salon.

Al-Mounia
MOROCCAN €€€
(Map p162; ☑ 0522 22 26 69; 95 Rue Prince Moulay Abdallah; mains Dh120-180; ⊙ noon-3pm & 7-10.30pm Mon-Sat; 🚇 Place Mohammed V) You'll sit in a salon decorated with *zellij* or under an old pepper tree in an attractive courtyard when dining at this long-standing Casablancan favourite. The menu features traditional Moroccan favourites (couscous, tajines, brochettes, *pastilla*). Sadly, service can be a tad unfriendly.

Ostréa
SEAFOOD €€€
(Map p159; ☑ 0522 44 13 90; Le Port de Pêche; mains Dh120-240; ⊙ noon-11.30pm) The Casablanca branch of the famous Oualidia oyster farm and restaurant is located within the port complex. Be sure to start with oysters (au naturel or au gratin) and follow with fresh shellfish or fish.

Dar Beida
MOROCCAN €€€
(Map p162; ☑ 0522 43 12 34; https://casablanca.regency.hyatt.com; Hyatt Regency Casablanca, Pl des Nations Unies; mains Dh190-270; ⊙ 7pm-2am; ❄️🚇; 🚇 Place des Nations Unies) Attentive service and luxurious surrounds are the hallmarks of this reliable restaurant in the Hyatt Regency (p163). You'll dine on a low couch and look your best under the mood lighting – it's a great place for a romantic tête-à-tête, especially as there is live oud (lute) music most nights. Traditional dishes dominate the menu and there's an excellent wine list.

Aïn Diab & Anfa

Frédéric Cassel Haute Patisserie
CAFE €€
(Map p158; ☑ 0522 94 93 82; 8 Blvd Moulay Rachid, Anfa; pastries from Dh12; ⊙ 8am-10pm) This French cafe and patisserie in upmarket Anfa has indoor and outdoor seating, serves good pastries and cakes, and is an popular choice for breakfast.

Basmane
MOROCCAN €€€

(Map p158; ☎0522 79 70 70; www.basmane-restaurant.com; cnr Blvds Océan Atlantique & de la Corniche, Ain Diab; mains Dh165-320; ⊙noon-1am; ❄; ☐ Ain Diab) The moneyed residents of nearby Anfa comprise most of the clientele at this classy restaurant in the Hôtel Club Val d'Anfa, lured by the expertly prepared traditional Moroccan dishes it serves. It's best visited at night, when mood lighting illuminates the *zellij*-covered walls. Service is friendly and there's live music and belly dancers most nights.

Le Cabestan
MEDITERRANEAN €€€

(Map p158; ☎0522 39 11 90; www.le-cabestan.com; 90 Blvd de la Corniche; mains Dh140-290; ⊙noon-2am) The limousines parked outside this ultrafashionable restaurant-bar-club perched on a clifftop beneath the Phare d'El Hank (El Hank Lighthouse) signal the fact that it is the most fashionable venue in the city. The mod Med menu is dominated by fish, and quality is high. Book ahead to request a table on the terrace or next to a panoramic window.

🍷 Drinking & Nightlife

There are plenty of dive bars in the centre of town, but these lack charm and are off-limits for all females except prostitutes. In general, the bars in the larger hotels – especially the Hyatt Regency (p163) or Sofitel Tour Blanche – or trendy restaurants such as Le Cabestan (p166) are better choices.

The beachfront suburb of Ain Diab is the main place for late-night drinking and dancing. However, hanging out with Casablanca's beautiful people for a night on the town doesn't come cheap. Expect to pay at least Dh150 to get into any club and as much again for a drink. Heavy-set bouncers guard the doors and practise tough crowd control – if you don't look the part, you won't get in. Many of these clubs cater for well-heeled Gulf Arabs (a Saudi prince has a palace on the Corniche), and Egyptian or Lebanese performers are popular.

Sky 28
BAR

(Map p159; ☎0522 97 80 00; www.kenzi-hotels.com; 28th fl, Kenzi Tower Hotel, Twin Centre, Blvd Zerktouni, Maarif; ⊙3pm-2am) Well-made expensive cocktails, live music sets and DJs with a fondness for rhythm and blues are the hallmarks of this ritzy restaurant, bar and club on top of the Kenzi Tower Hotel. The sensational view extends across the city towards the Hassan II Mosque and the food menu

🏃 City Walk
Central Casablanca's Mauresque Architecture

START CATHÉDRALE DU SACRÉ COEUR, BLVD RACHIDI
END PL DU 16 NOVEMBRE
LENGTH 3KM, ONE HOUR

Central Casablanca has a rich architectural heritage dominated by a style of architecture commonly known as Mauresque (Moorish). Developed in the 1920s and '30s, this blend of French-colonial design and traditional Moroccan style was heavily influenced by the art deco and art nouveau movements – with ornate wrought-iron balconies, rounded exterior corners and decorative facades and friezes. These were incorporated alongside traditional Moroccan features such as arches, cupolas, columns, *mashrabiyyas* (wooden-lattice screens), *muqarnas* (decorative plaster vaulting) and coloured *zellij* (tilework).

Sadly, most of the city's Mauresque buildings are in an awful state of disrepair. Others have been demolished in recent years to make way for huge development projects This tour identifies some of the most notable examples in the downtown precinct, along with a few art deco and art nouveau gems.

Start on the northwest edge of the Parc de la Ligue Arabe at the unusual white ❶ **Cathédrale du Sacré Coeur** (p157), an extraordinary architectural meld of the art deco, Mauresque and neo-Gothic styles, with twin towers that resemble minarets and decorative aperture-style windows. Walk around the building to see the cathedral's buttresses and spires in all their glory, peek inside to admire the massive stained glass window and then continue southeast along Blvd Rachidi to ❷ **Place Mohammed V** (p156), which was being redeveloped at the time of research. This is surrounded by impressive administrative buildings, with the 1930s ❸ **wilaya** (old police headquarters, now governor's office) dominating the south side. Though topped by a modernist clock tower, the upper-storey detailing has pronounced Gothic and Islamic echoes, making it a true architectural oddity.

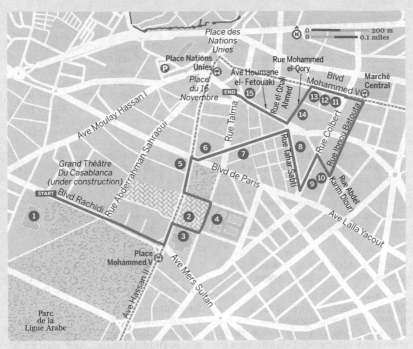

The nearby ④ **Tribunal de Premiere Instance** (*palais de justice* or law courts) dates from 1925. Its entrance was inspired by the Persian *iwan*, a vaulted hall that opens into the central court of the *medersa* (theological college) of a mosque.

On the northern side of the square is Casablanca's ⑤ **main post office** (p170), built between 1918 and 1920, fronted by arches and stone columns and decorated with richly coloured art nouveau–style mosaics. The carved stucco on the facade of the nearby ⑥ **Banque al-Maghrib** on Blvd de Paris, and the ornate main door with its *mashrabiyya*-style detailing, reference traditional Moroccan architecture, although the building's form is decidedly modern.

Next walk east on Rue Driss Lahrizi, where impressive facades line both sides of the street. The most striking of these is ⑦ **La Princière Salon de Thé**, with its huge stone crown on the roofline.

Turn right into Rue Tahar Sabti, which is lined with colonial buildings that are now apartments, hotels and offices. The most impressive of these is the art deco ⑧ **Hotel Amouday** at No 51, with its distinctive ocean-liner-style design. Further on are two striking art deco bars and the empire-style BMCE building.

Take a V-turn left into Rue Colbert and look for ⑨ **Hôtel Transatlantique**, dating from 1922. The filigree-like detailing surrounding the main entrance is quite striking. Then turn right into Rue Abdul Karim Diouri to find ⑩ **Hotel Volubilis** with its recessed balcony, burnished-gold detailing and art nouveau signage.

Go left up Rue Ibnou Batouta and continue to the corner of Blvd Mohammed V. Turn left and look out for an array of wonderful facades along the street's south side. The ⑪ **Central Market Post Office** (p170), with its delicate motifs, and ⑫ **Le Matin/Maroc Soir**, with its classic style, are two of the most impressive.

At the end of this block, on the corner of Rue Mohammed el-Qory, is ⑬ **Petit Poucet** (p168), a bar-cafe once frequented by Antoine de Saint-Exupéry, Édith Piaf and Albert Camus. Turn left here into Rue Mohammed el-Qory to find the ⑭ **Cinéma Rialto** (p169), a hardly changed art deco gem where Michael Curtiz' 1942 film *Casablanca* is still occasionally screened. Continue south to the junction with Ave Houmane el-Fetouaki and turn right to reach ⑮ **Pl du 16 Novembre**, home to plenty of art deco buildings.

For more information on Casablanca's 20th-century architectural heritage see www.casamemoire.org or the Casablanca Histoire et Architecture Facebook page.

CASABLANCA: THE FILM

Memorable performances, a haunting signature song and a sensational script by Julius J Epstein, Philip G Epstein and Howard Koch make the 1942 film *Casablanca* one of Hollywood's greatest achievements. Inspired by Murray Burnett and Joan Allison's unproduced stage play *Everybody Comes to Rick's,* producer Hal B Wallis and director Michael Curtiz put together a stellar cast and crew and shot the film in just over two months at the Warner Bros studio in Burbank, California. No scenes were filmed in Casablanca itself, but the city and its cosmopolitan wartime population were wonderfully evoked, and images of Rick's Café Américain, street cafes and the souq gave many cinema-goers their first-ever visual introduction to the Maghreb.

Watching the film today, it's both fascinating and sobering to consider how its story of refugees and lost souls stranded in a foreign place mirrors the contemporary geopolitical situation and the plight of refugees from Syria and other war-torn countries.

It has become almost obligatory for travellers visiting modern-day Casablanca to pop into Rick's Café (p164) on the edge of the old medina and be serenaded by pianist Issam. When quizzed, Issam says that he can't imagine how many times he has played 'As Time Goes By', but admits that he still enjoys doing so. Here's looking at him.

includes sushi (Dh160 for 12 pieces), Dakhla oysters (Dh150 for six) and burgers (Dh160).

Café Alba
CAFE

(Map p162; ☑ 0522 22 71 54; 59-61 Rue Driss Lahrizi; ◷ 6.30am-9.30pm; 🚇 Marché Central) A hint of colonial elegance and a female-friendly atmosphere differentiate Café Alba from the vast majority of cafes around town. The premium seating is in the front arcade, and the set breakfast deals offer the best value.

Cafe Imperial
CAFE

(Map p159; Quartier Habous; ◷ 8am-10pm) Greatly benefiting from its location on a corner opposite the park behind the Mahkama du Pacha and around the corner from famous Pâtisserie Bennis Habous (p164), this pleasant cafe has a sunny front terrace and serves decent coffee and mint tea.

Le Chester
BAR

(Map p159; ☑ 0522 94 12 82; www.lechester. ma; Rue Abu Faraj el Asbahani, Racine Maarif; ◷ 6pm-1am) Popular with well-heeled local 30-somethings, this bar just off Blvd d'Anfa offers burgers, Caesar salads and other international favourites. Beer is the tipple of choice and the DJ spins funk, pop and rhythm and blues on Tuesdays, Thursdays and Fridays from 7pm.

Le Trica
BAR

(Map p159; ☑ 0522 22 07 06; 5 Rue el-Moutanabi, Quartier Gauthier; ◷ 6.30pm-1am) This American-themed bar-lounge is set over two levels but still gets jam-packed on Friday and Saturday nights, when the DJ spins techno.

It's also a popular place to watch big football matches on the big screen or grab a drink after work (happy hour 6.30pm to 9pm).

Social Club at Le Cabestan
CLUB, BAR

(Map p158; ☑ 0522 39 11 90; www.le-cabestan. com; 90 Blvd de la Corniche; ◷ bar noon-2am, Social Club midnight-5am Sat) Le Cabestan is party central on Saturday nights, when local and international DJs choreograph moves on the downstairs dance floor and the city's young and beautiful work hard to see and be seen. You'll need to dress to impress to get past the door staff. On other nights, the upstairs bar with its panoramic view sees lots of cocktail action.

Petit Poucet
BAR

(Map p162; cnr Blvd Mohammed V & Rue Mohammed el-Qory) A die-hard relic of the 1920s, this bar and cafe was where Saint-Exupéry, the French author and aviator, used to spend time between mail flights across the Sahara. Today, it's a seedy and less-than-inviting place for regulars to get sloshed.

Maison B
CLUB

(Map p158; ☑ 0698 99 94 42; 5 Rue de la Mer Adriatique, Ain Diab; ◷ 7pm-4am) As glam as Casa's club scene gets, this place near the Megarama cinema complex (p169) has a restaurant serving Mediterranean and Asian food and is particularly popular in the warmer months, when its terrace area is invariably packed on weekends. International DJs are regular fixtures, and there are also occasional live acts. Check the Facebook feed for event details.

Armstrong Legend CLUB
(Map p158; ☑ 0522 79 77 58; 41 Blvd de la Corniche)
This small place is one of the few clubs in town
where you can dance to live music; bands concentrate on '80s and '90s rock covers.

VIP Club CLUB
(Map p158; Rue des Dunes) On a hill next to the
Ain Diab tram terminus, this long-established
and expensive venue has a more inclusive vibe
than many clubs in the city. There's a large
dance floor.

☆ Entertainment

**Les Anciens Abattoirs
de Casablanca** PERFORMING ARTS
(☑ 0654 80 05 39; Rue Jaafar Barmaki, Quartier
Hay Mohammadi; ☐ Grand Ceinture) The old
city abattoirs, an art deco complex built in
1922, was transformed into a cultural centre
dubbed the Culture Factory in 2008. Located near Casa Voyageurs railway station, the
centre hosts exhibitions and performances,
plays, concerts and workshops. Check its
Facebook page for program details.

**Complexe Culturel
Sidi Belyout** THEATRE
(Map p162; ☑ 0522 31 67 58; 28 Rue Léon L'Africain;
☐ Marché Central) This 200-seat theatre hosts
plays (usually in Arabic) and the occasional
music recital or dance performance.

☆ Cinemas

Most English-language films are dubbed in
French, unless it specifically mentions 'version originale'.

Megarama CINEMA
(Map p158; ☑ 0522 79 88 88; http://casablanca.
megarama.ma/; Blvd de la Corniche, Ain Diab; tickets Dh45-65; ☐ Ain Diab) The plushest cinema
in town, this huge complex in Ain Diab has
four comfortable theatres that are usually
packed.

Imax Theatre CINEMA
(Map p158; ☑ 0801 00 12 30; www.moroccomall.
ma; Morocco Mall, cnr Blvds de la Corniche & de
l'Océan, Sidi Abderahman; tickets Dh65; ☉ 10am-
9pm Sun-Thu, to 10pm Fri & Sat) Located at glitzy
Morocco Mall, this cinema concentrates on
Hollywood blockbusters.

Cinéma Rialto CINEMA
(Map p162; ☑ 0522 26 26 32; Rue Mohammed
el-Qory; ☐ Marché Central) A classic sin-
gle-screen cinema dating from the 1930s.
Concerts are also staged here.

Cinéma Lynx CINEMA
(Map p159; ☑ 0522 22 02 29; 150 Ave Mers Sultan;
☐ Avenue Hassan II) Spacious and comfortable,
with a good sound system.

🔒 Shopping

Although not an artisan centre, Casablanca
has a good choice of traditional crafts from
around Morocco. The best place to shop for
these is in the Quartier Habous, south of the
centre. There are also crafts shops of varying
(usually low) quality along Blvd Houphouët
Boigny on the edge of the old medina. These
aim to attract the tourist dirham.

Souq Habous MARKET
(Map p159; Quartier Habous) Shopping isn't a
highlight in Casablanca, but those wanting
to snaffle a few souvenirs should head to
the attractive but pricey souq in the streets
east of the central roundabout in the Quartier Habous. Shops sell babouches (leather
slippers), jellabas (robes), soaps, spices and
ceramics. Be prepared to haggle.

Morocco Mall MALL
(Map p158; www.moroccomall.net; Blvd de la
Corniche, Anfa; ☉ 10am-9pm Sun-Thu, to 10pm
Fri & Sat) Morocco's fanciest shopping destination, this large mall in Ain Diab has
stores galore, from recognised international
brands to a dedicated 'souq' area with traditional Moroccan crafts. Take a shopping
break to gawp at the two-storey-high aquarium, and fill up in the multinational food
court. On-site parking costs Dh5 per hour.

Anfa Place MALL
(Map p158; ☑ 0522 95 46 46; http://anfashopping.
com; Blvd de la Corniche, Ain Diab; ☉ 10am-9pm
Mon-Fri, to 10pm Sat & Sun; ☎) On the waterfront in Ain Diab, this new shopping mall
sports a supermarket, a food court and a
reasonable number of retail outlets. There's
paid parking and free wi-fi.

ℹ Orientation

The medina – the oldest part of town – is tiny and
sits in the north of the city close to the port. To
the south of the medina is Pl des Nations Unies, a
large traffic junction that marks the heart of the
city. The city's main streets branch out from here:
Ave des Forces Armées Royales (Ave des FAR),
Ave Moulay Hassan I, Blvd Mohammed V and Blvd
Houphouët Boigny.

Ave Hassan II leads to Pl Mohammed V, easily
recognised by its grand art deco administrative
buildings. Quartiers Gauthier and Maarif, west
and southwest of the Parc de la Ligue Arabe, are

home to upmarket housing, restaurants, cafes and retail outlets.

To the southeast is the Quartier Habous (also known as the Nouvelle Medina) and to the west is Ain Diab, the beachfront suburb whose Corniche is home to upmarket hotels, restaurants and nightclubs.

ℹ Information

EMERGENCY

Fire/Ambulance	150
Police	190
Service d'Aide Médicale Urgente (Private ambulance service)	0522 25 25 25

MEDICAL SERVICES

Dar Salam Clinic (Map p159; ☑ 0522 85 14 14; www.cliniquedarsalam.ma; 728 Blvd Modibo Keita, Tantonville; 🚇 Mekka) Near the Jardin Horticulture; 24-hour emergency department.

MONEY

There are banks – most with ATMs – on almost every street corner in the centre of Casablanca.

POST

Central Market Post Office (cnr Blvd Mohammed V & Rue Chaouia; ⊙8am-4pm Mon-Fri, 9am-noon Sat)

Main Post Office (Map p162; cnr Blvd de Paris & Ave Hassan II; ⊙8am-6pm Mon-Fri, to noon Sat)

Medina Post Office (Map p159; Pl Ahmed El Bidaoui; ⊙8.30am-4.30pm Mon-Fri)

TOURIST INFORMATION

Staff at your hotel will be the most reliable source of tourist information.

ℹ Getting There & Away

AIR

Casablanca's **Mohammed V International Airport** (Map p158; ☑ 0522 43 58 58; www.

onda.ma) is 30km southeast of the city on the Marrakesh road. Regular flights leave from here for most countries in Western Europe, as well as to West Africa, Algeria, Tunisia, Egypt, the Middle East and North America.

Internally, the vast majority of Royal Air Maroc's (RAM) flights go via Casablanca, so you can get to many destinations in Morocco directly from the city.

BUS

CTM bus station (Map p162; ☑ 0522 54 10 10; www.ctm.ma; 23 Rue Léon L'Africain; 🚇 Marché Central) Close to Ave des FAR. There are daily CTM bus departures to destinations across the country. Destinations include seven daily services (Dh110, 7¼ hours) and one premium service (Dh270, 6¾ hours) to Agadir; four services to Essaouira (Dh140, 7¼ hours); and seven daily services (Dh85, 7¼ hours) and one premium service (Dh120, four hours) to Marrakesh.

Gare Routière Ouled Ziane (Map p162) The main reason to trek out to this modern bus station 4km southeast of the centre is for services to destinations not covered by CTM – almost all non-CTM services depart from here. A taxi here will cost about Dh25; alternatively take **bus 10** from outside Cinema Rif on Ave des FAR.

SAT bus station Also on Rte Ouled Ziane, but more than 1km closer to town than Gare Routière Ouled Ziane. SAT runs national buses of a similar standard to CTM, though to fewer destinations. Fares are slightly cheaper.

CAR

Casablanca is well endowed with car-rental agencies, many with offices around Ave des FAR and Blvd Mohammed V, and at the airport.

Avis Airport (☑ 0522 53 90 72; Mohammed V International Airport; ⊙7am-11pm); **City** (☑ 0522 31 24 24; 19 Ave des FAR; ⊙8am-7pm Mon-Sat, to noon Sun; 🚇 Place Nations Unies)

Budget Airport (☑ 0522 53 91 57; Mohammed V International Airport; ⊙7am-10.30pm); **City** (☑ 0522 31 31 24; 5 Tours des Habous, Ave des

MAJOR TRAINS FROM CASA VOYAGEURS

TO	1ST-CLASS FARE (DH)	2ND-CLASS FARE (DH)	TIME (HR)	FREQUENCY (DAILY)
Azemmour	46	33	1	7
El Jadida	53	37	1½	8
Fez	174	116	3½-4½	16
Marrakesh	148	95	3¾	9
Meknès	143	95	3½	19
Nador	275	196	10½	1 direct
Oujda	322	216	10¾	2 direct
Tangier	195	132	5-6½	8

FAR; ⊕8.30am-noon & 2.30-7pm Mon-Sat,
9am-noon Sun; 🚇 Place Nations Unies)
President Car (☑ 0661 21 03 94, 0522 26
07 90; www.presidentcar.ma; 27 Rue el-Ghali
Ahmed; 🚇 Place Nations Unies)

TAXI

Most grands taxis arrive at and depart from Gare
Routière Ouled Ziane bus station.

Vendôme Transport Touristique (☑ 0522 27
76 19; vtt13@yahoo.com) This reliable company
has a fleet of cars and minivans with air-conditioning and functioning seatbelts (a rarity in
Moroccan taxis). It charges Dh300 for transfers
from Mohammed V International Airport to central Casablanca (one to three people), and can
also organise transfers to destinations across
the country. Other services include two-hour
city tours of Casablanca by car (Dh450 for one
or two people).

TRAIN

Casablanca has five train stations, but only two
are of interest to most travellers.

Casa Port (Map p162) train station is located a
few hundred metres northeast of Pl des Nations
Unies, in the port precinct. This is the station for
trains to/from Rabat (1st/2nd class Dh69/37, 70
minutes, every 30 minutes) and Kenitra (1st/2nd
class Dh95/51, 1¾ hrs, every 30 minutes to one
hour). The train to/from Mohammed V International Airport also starts/ends here.

Long-distance trains to all national destinations except Rabat and Kenitra arrive at and
depart from **Casa Voyageurs** train station. A
tramline connects the station with other parts of
the city including downtown and Ain Diab.

ℹ Getting Around

TO/FROM THE AIRPORT

Train Services run between the Mohammed V
International Airport and Casablanca's Casa
Port station at 4am and then on the hour from
6am to 10pm, with a final service at 11.45pm
(1st/2nd class Dh64/43, 45 minutes). Trains
stop at Oasis and Casa Voyageurs en route.
You'll need to change at Casa Port for Rabat
and Kenitra, and at Casa Voyagers for other
major destinations. Trains leave from below
the ground floor of Terminal 1. From Casa
Port train station, the first train to the airport
leaves at 3am and then every hour from 5am
to 10pm.

Grand Taxi The set price for a grand taxi between the airport and the city centre is Dh300,
though drivers work an unofficial cartel and
fares can ending up being much more at night
or at times of high demand – consider booking
an airport pick-up with **Vendôme Transport
Touristique** (p171) to be sure of getting the official price. Note that some taxi drivers receive

ℹ CASA STREET NAMES

Casablanca's French street names are
slowly being replaced with Moroccan
names. Our maps and directions use the
names that were on street signs at the
time of research, but these may change.
It is also worth noting that many locals,
including taxi drivers, have yet to make
the transition.

commissions if they bring clients to particular
hotels and can be unscrupulous in orchestrat-
ing this – don't believe any driver who tells you
your hotel of choice is closed.

BUS

Bus tickets cost Dh4 and there are at designated stops along each bus route; see http://
mdinabus.ma/docs/Lignesbus.pdf for details.
Travellers are likely to find the new tramway or
petits taxis much more useful.

CAR & MOTORCYCLE

Parking meters (Dh2 per hour, two hours maximum) operate from 8am to noon and 2pm to
7pm daily, except on Sunday and public holidays.
If you don't pay, you may be fined or have your
wheels clamped. On unmetered streets a guard
will often request a tip for watching your car; it is
common practice to pay Dh5.

TAXI

➤ Casa's red **petits taxis** will get you to your
destination faster than the tram or bus and are
hailed on the street.

➤ The fare for a short trip starts at Dh15, and
drivers will often stop to collect other passengers along the way. Drivers rarely if ever
use the meter, so be sure to negotiate the fare
before getting into the taxi. Prices rise by 50%
after 8pm.

➤ Have plenty of small coins to hand, and check
your change.

TRAM

➤ The excellent **Casa Tramway** (www.casa-
tramway.ma) makes getting across the city a
simple and comfortable exercise.

➤ The most useful section of line for travellers
is from Casa Voyageurs train station to Pl Mohammed V, via the Marché Central and Pl des
Nations Unies. Trams also go to Ain Diab (about
35 minutes from central Casablanca).

➤ Trams runs every 15 minutes, with the first
and last departures from the termini at 5.30am
and 10.30pm.

➤ Tickets are Dh7 for a single trip, bought
from easy-to-use machines on the platforms
(multiple-journey tickets are also available).

Rabat الرباط

POP 565,000

Morocco's political and administrative capital may be short on top-drawer tourist attractions, but it compensates with plenty of charm. The ville nouvelle's palm-lined boulevards are clean, well kept and relatively free of traffic – a blessed relief for those who have spent time in Casablanca. There's a clean central beach, an intact and evocative kasbah, and an attractive walled medina that is far less touristy than those in other large cities. All in all, the city is a good choice for a short sojourn.

History

The fertile plains inland from Rabat drew settlers to the area as far back as the 8th century BC. Both the Phoenicians and the Romans set up trading posts in the estuary of the Bou Regreg river in Sala, today's Chellah. The Roman settlement, Sala Colonia, lasted long after the empire's fall and eventually became the seat of an independent Berber kingdom. The Zenata Berbers built a *ribat*, a fortress-monastery from which the city takes its name, on the site of Rabat's present kasbah. As the new town of Salé (created in the 10th century) began to prosper on the north bank of the river, the city of Chellah fell into decline.

The arrival of the Almohads in the 12th century saw the *ribat* rebuilt as a kasbah, a strategic jumping-off point for campaigns in Spain, where the dynasty successfully brought Andalucia back under Muslim rule. Under Yacoub al-Mansour (the Victorious), Rabat enjoyed a brief heyday as an imperial capital, Ribat al-Fatah (Victory Fortress). Al-Mansour had extensive walls built, added the enormous Bab Oudaia to the kasbah and began work on the Hassan Mosque, intended to be the greatest mosque in all of the Islamic West, if not in all of the Islamic world.

Al-Mansour's death in 1199 brought an end to these grandiose schemes, leaving the great Hassan Mosque incomplete. The city soon lost all significance and it wasn't until the 17th century that Rabat's fortunes began to change.

As Muslim refugees arrived from Christian Spain, so did a band of Christian renegades, Moorish pirates, freebooters and multinational adventurers. Rabat and Salé became safe havens for corsairs – merciless pirates whom English chroniclers called the Sallee Rovers. At one point they even created their own pirate state, the Republic of Bou Regreg. These corsairs roved as far as the coast of North America seeking Spanish gold, and to Cornwall in southern England to capture Christian slave labour. The first Alawite sultans attempted to curtail their looting sprees, but no sultan ever really exercised control over them. Corsairs continued attacking European shipping until well into the 19th century.

Meanwhile, Sultan Mohammed ben Abdallah briefly made Rabat his capital at the end of the 18th century, but the city soon fell back into obscurity. In 1912 France strategically abandoned the hornet's nest of political intrigue and unrest in the traditional capitals of Fez and Marrakesh and instead shifted power to coastal Rabat, where supply and defence were more easily achieved. Since then, the city has remained the seat of government and official home of the king.

◉ Sights

◉ Central Rabat

Rabat Medina AREA
(Map p178; ⓜ Medina Rabat, Bab Chellah) When the French arrived in the early 20th century, this walled medina by the sea was the full extent of the city. Built on an orderly grid in the 17th century, it is small enough to be easily explored in half a day, but large enough to make getting lost inevitable. The main market street is Rue Souika, with local shopping on its western stretch and shops geared largely to tourists in the covered **Souq as-Sebbat** to its east.

The **Grande Mosquée de Rabat Medina** (off Rue Bab Chellah; ⓜ Bab Chellah), a 14th-century Merenid original that has been rebuilt in the intervening years, marks the start of the Souq as-Sebbat. If you continue past the Rue des Consuls (so called because diplomats lived here until 1912), you'll come to the *mellah* (Jewish quarter) just before Bab el-Bahr and the river. Turning north along Rue des Consuls, which is home to many jewellery shops, will take you to one of the more interesting areas of the medina, with *funduqs* (courtyard complexes) and some grand former diplomatic residencies. At its northern end the street terminates in an open area that was the setting for slave auctions in the days of the Sallee Rovers. From here you can make your way up the hill to the Kasbah Les Oudaias (p180).

RABAT IN...

One Day

Start your day by exploring Rabat's **medina** (p172), snacking on some traditional street food for lunch. Cross Blvd Tariq al-Marsa and enter the **Kasbah les Oudaias** (p180) through or near its spectacular main gate, Bab Oudaia. Climb to the top for magnificent views over the estuary and across to Salé, then stop for tea at atmospheric **Café Maure** (p182). In the evening, join the local promenade up and down Ave Mohammed V and enjoy a Moroccan dinner at **Le Petit Beur** (p180) or **Tajine Wa Tanjia** (p180).

Two Days

Take the tram to Salé (p184) and head into the medina to view the beautiful **medersa** (p185) of the **Grand Mosque** (p186). Then wander down to the river and be rowed across to Rabat, where you can spend the afternoon sunning yourself on the *plage* (beach) or take a taxi to the **Chellah** (p176) for some archaeological investigation. In the evening, enjoy French cuisine at **Cosmopolitan** (p181) or **Le Bistro du Pietri** (p180) in the ville nouvelle, or at **L'Entrecôte** (p181) in upmarket Agdal.

Most eateries are on the major pedestrian thoroughfare of Ave Mohammed V, which runs between the Medina Rabat tram stop and Ave Laalou, the medina's northern boundary. Popular fast-food joints with street seating include Bidawai (p182) and Inza (p182), and a parade of street vendors sell snacks such as *babouche* (small snails) served in a fragrant and spicy soup, freshly squeezed sugar-cane juice, *bisara* (a thick soup made from dried fava beans), syrup-drenched pastries, freshly baked bread and whatever fresh fruit is in season.

Museum of Modern & Contemporary Art   MUSEUM

(Musée Mohammed VI Art Moderne et Contemporain, MMVI; ☑ 0537 76 90 47; www.musee mohammed6.ma; cnr Aves Moulay Hassan & Allal ben Abdallah, Ville Nouvelle; permanent collection adult/child 12-18yr/child under 12yr Dh20/10/ free; ☺10am-6pm Wed-Mon; 🚋 Mohammed V/ Gare de Rabat) Looking more like a shopping mall than an art gallery, this institution was conceived and funded by the present king and opened in 2014. Billed as the first national museum of modern and contemporary art in the country, it hosts international travelling exhibitions of big-name artists and has a permanent exhibition of Moroccan works dating from the 1950s to the present day. Many of the works are decorative in nature, featuring rich colours and intricate detail.

Look out for paintings by Radia Bent El Houssein (1912–94), Abbés Saladi (1950–92), André Elbaz (b 1934), Mehdi Qotbi (b 1951) and Aziza Alaoui (b 1966). Also of note are photographs by Laila Essaydi (b 1965).

Archaeology Museum   MUSEUM

(Map p178; 23 Rue al-Brihi Parent; 🚋 Mohammed V/ Gare de Rabat) Closed for a major renovation at the time of research, this archaeological museum has traditionally been home to a particularly wonderful collection of ceramics, statuary and other artefacts from the Roman settlements at Volubilis, Lixus and Chellah. There has been some talk in the recent past of these collection highlights being relocated to other institutions around the country, so the unveiling of the renovated building and rejuvenated exhibits is being anticipated by locals with both excitement and trepidation.

Moroccan Museum of Money   MUSEUM

(Map p178; Musée de Bank Al-Maghrib; ☑ 0537 21 64 72; www.bkam.ma; cnr Ave Allal ben Abdellah & Rue Al-Qahira, Ville Nouvelle; adult/student Dh20/ free; ☺9am-5.30pm Tue-Fri, 9am-noon & 3-6pm Sat, 9am-1pm Sun; 🚋 Place al-Joulane) Numismatists will be in seventh heaven when visiting this well-curated and -presented museum. It offers an unexpectedly interesting tour of Moroccan history through currency, from the Roman period to today. There's also an exhibition of paintings from the Bank Al-Maghrib's collection of works by Moroccan artists and by foreign artists painting about Morocco. Entrance is free on Fridays.

St Pierre Cathedral   CHURCH

(Map p178; Cathédrale Saint-Pierre de Rabat; www. dioceserabat.org; Plal-Joulane, Ville Nouvelle; 🚋 Place al Joulane) Still operational, this cathedral dates from 1919, but its two art deco–style towers were added in the 1930s.

Rabat

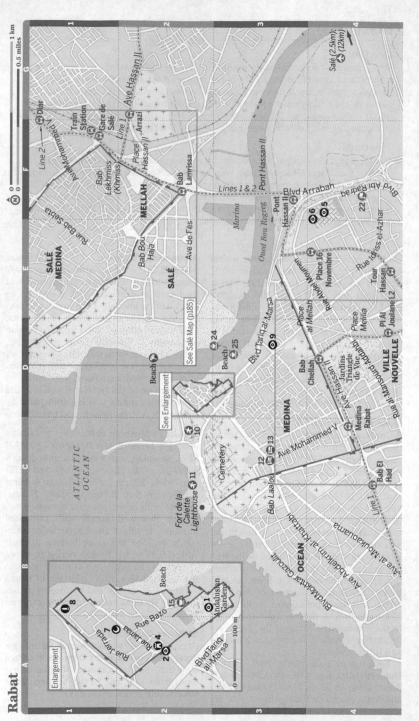

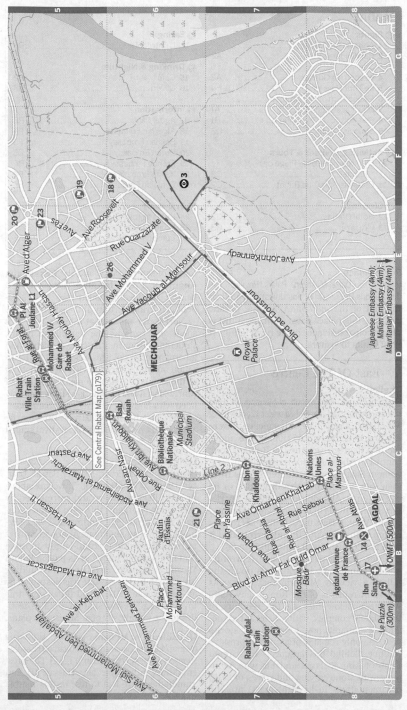

Rabat

◉ Sights
1 Andalusian Gardens	B2
2 Bab Oudaia	A2
3 Chellah	F6
4 Kasbah les Oudaias	A2
5 Le Tour Hassan	F4
6 Mausoleum of Mohammed V	F4
7 Mosque el-Atiqa	A1
8 Plateforme du Sémaphore	B1
9 Souq as-Sebbat	D3

◆ Activities, Courses & Tours
10 Club Nautique de la Plage de Rabat	C2
11 Oudayas Surf Club Rabat	C2

◉ Sleeping
12 Hôtel Darna	C3
13 L'Alcazar	C3

✖ Eating
14 L'Entrecôte	B8

◉ Drinking & Nightlife
15 Café Maure	B2
16 Oliveri	B8

ℹ Information
17 Agdal Clinic	B8
18 Algerian Embassy	F6
19 Belgian Embassy	F5
20 Dutch Embassy	E5
21 French Embassy	B6
22 Italian Embassy	F4
23 Tunisian Embassy	E5

ℹ Transport
24 Boats to Rabat	D3
25 Boats to Salé	D3
26 Europcar	E6

Royal Palace PALACE
(Map p175; Dâr-al-Makhzen, Palais Royale; Ave des Nations Unies; 🚇 Nations Unies) Located at the end of the *mechouar* (a large parade ground), this palace dates from 1864 and is the principal residence of the royal family. It is off-limits to visitors.

◉ East Of The Centre

Chellah HISTORIC SITE
(Map p175; cnr Ave Yacoub al-Mansour & Blvd Moussa ibn Nassair; adult/child under 12yr Dh10/3; ⊙ 8.30am-5.30pm) The Phoenicians were the first to settle on this sloping site above the Bou Regreg river, and the Romans took control in about AD 40, renaming the settlement Sala Colonia. Scattered stones from their city remain, but give little idea of its size or form. Abandoned in 1154, it lay deserted until the 14th century, when Merenid sultan Abou al-Hassan Ali built a necropolis on top of the Roman site and surrounded it with the defensive wall that stands today.

From the massive main gate (currently under restoration), a path heads down the hill to a viewing platform that overlooks the scant remains of the Roman city ('Site Antique'). Below this are the remains of the Islamic complex, with an elegant stone-and-tile minaret, now topped by a stork's nest, the only remains of a once-impressive mosque. Behind the mosque is the ruined tomb of Abu al-Hasan and his wife, complete with stone carving and traces of *zellij* ornamentation. To its right (east) are the tombs of several saints and the **Bassin aux Anguilles**, a pool that attracts women who believe that feeding boiled eggs to its resident eels brings fertility and easy childbirth.

Next to the minaret, at a lower level, is a small *medersa* with the remains of pillars, students' cells, a mihrab (prayer niche) and an ornamental pool. This was closed for restoration on our most recent visit. At the bottom of the site, on the slope beneath the tomb of Abu al-Hasan and his wife, is a shady walkway lined with flowers, palm trees and bamboo.

The Chellah is an evocative setting for the annual Jazz Au Chellah (p177) festival staged in September.

Le Tour Hassan HISTORIC SITE
(Map p174; Hassan Tower; Ave Tour Hassan, Quartier Hassan; 🚇 Pont Hassan II) Towering above the Bou Regreg estuary and surrounded by well-tended gardens, this 44m tower is Rabat's most prominent landmark. It was originally part of an ambitious Almohad project to build the world's second-largest mosque (after Samarra in Iraq), but its patron Sultan Yacoub al-Mansour died before the building was complete. The mosque was destroyed by an earthquake in 1755, and today only this tower and a forest of shattered pillars testifies to the grandiosity of al-Mansour's plans.

Mausoleum of Mohammed V MAUSOLEUM
(Map p174; Blvd Mohammed Lyazidi, Quartier Hassan; ⊙ sunrise-sunset; 🚇 Pont Hassan II) **FREE** The present king's father (the late Hassan II) and grandfather were laid to rest in this marble mausoleum, which is decorated with pat-

terned *zellij* and carved plaster. Its carved cedar ceiling is covered in gold leaf, and is quite magnificent. Visitors must be respectfully dressed, and can look down into the tomb from a gallery.

🏃 Activities

Oudayas Surf Club Rabat   WATER SPORTS
(Map p174; OSCR; ☑ 0537 26 06 83; www.surfmaroc.info/oscr; Plage des Oudaias; 90min surfboard/bodyboard lessons Dh150) One of Morocco's original surf clubs, OSCR offers lessons and board hire, and has a swish clubhouse-cafe facing the waves. King Mohammed VI was a founding member.

Club Nautique de la Plage de Rabat   WATER SPORTS
(Map p174; ☑ 0537 26 16 09; www.cnprabat.com; Plage des Oudaias) Located on Oudaias beach beneath the kasbah (p180), this club offers lessons and equipment hire for surfing, bodyboarding and sea kayaking at both the beach and the Bouregreg Marina.

🎓 Courses

Rabat has a number of language schools offering year-long courses or short-term classes.

Center for Cross-Cultural Learning   LANGUAGE
(Map p178; CCCL; ☑ 0537 20 23 65; www.cccl.ma; Ave Hassan II, Bab el-Had; ☒ Bab El Had) This private, US-affiliated school offers intensive short courses in Modern Standard Arabic and Darija.

🎉 Festivals & Events

Rabat hosts a number of festivals and events each year.

Festival Mawazine   MUSIC
(www.festivalmawazine.ma; ☺ May) This well established festival draws the biggest names from the international pop music scene, as well as some major Arabic music stars. Christina Aguilera's headline act in 2016 drew 250,000 people to the OLM Souissi, southeast of Agdal – claimed to be the biggest music concert in Moroccan history. Other venues include the Chellah (p176).

Jazz au Chellah   MUSIC
(☺ Sep) Partly funded by the EU, this long-running festival features collaborations between European and Moroccan jazz musicians and is staged in the atmospheric surrounds of the Chellah (p176). Check its Facebook feed for program details.

🛏 Sleeping

The medina has a host of low-budget options (many of them dives) as well as a few atmospheric riads (town houses set around an internal garden). There are more choices in the ville nouvelle, with a growing number of comfortable business hotels on offer.

🛏 Ville Nouvelle

Hôtel Central   HOTEL €
(☑ 0537 70 73 56; hotel.central.rabat@gmail.com; 2 Rue Al-Basra; s/d Dh170/250, without bathroom Dh120/180; 🖥; ☒ Mohammed V/Gare de Rabat) Its glory days are long gone, but this hotel just off Ave Mohammed V, is clean and cheap. Rooms have rock-hard beds and wifi is only available in the reception area. Rooms without shower have a sink; en suite rooms have a shower, but toilets are outside and shared. Hot showers for those who opt for a room without bathroom cost Dh10.

Hôtel Majestic   HOTEL €
(Map p178; ☑ 0537 72 29 97; www.hotelmajestic.ma; 121 Ave Hassan II; s/d Dh284/348; ☒ Medina Rabat) Sadly, this hotel, opposite the main entrance to the medina, is nowhere near as palatial as it sounds. Cramped rooms have wi-fi but that's all that can really be said in their praise. Despite the double glazing the rooms can be noisy, so it's best to forgo the medina view for a room at the back.

⭐ **Le Piétri Urban Hotel**   HOTEL €€
(Map p178; ☑ 0537 70 78 20; www.lepietri.com; 4 Rue Tobrouk; s incl breakfast Dh760-1020, d Dh860-1120, ste Dh1300; ☒@🖥; ☒ Mohammed V/Gare de Rabat) 🍃 If only all midrange hotels in Morocco

---

RABAT FOR CHILDREN

Other than the crowded *plage* (beach), which is child-friendly, there are few specific attractions in the city for younger visitors. Children may enjoy tram journeys and will almost certainly have fun crossing between Rabat and Salé on one of the commuter rowing boats. They will also enjoy exploring the **Kasbah les Oudaias** (p180), where they can pretend to be pirates or expend energy running around the Plateforme du Sémaphore and Andalusian Gardens.

Central Rabat

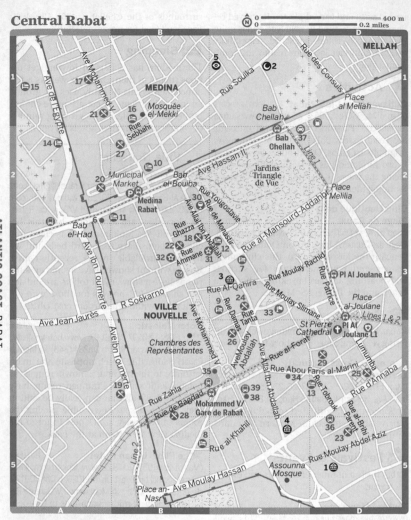

lived up to the standard set by this impressive business hotel! On offer are reasonable prices, a central location, helpful bilingual staff and 35 spacious and bright rooms with good beds, satellite TV, work desk and double-glazed windows. There's also an excellent restaurant, Le Bistro du Pietri (p180), where live jazz is performed on weekends.

Hôtel B&B Rabat Médina
HOTEL €€

(Map p178; ☑ 0537 70 30 74; www.hotelbb.ma; 2 Rue Ghandi; s/d/tr incl breakfast Dh1100/1200/1240; ℗❄☎; 📵 Pl al-Joulane) Geared towards business people, this friendly modern hotel located diagonally opposite the Moulina Mosque and

Jardin Nouzhat Hassan offers well-maintained and attractive rooms with double-glazed windows, good beds, reading lamps, work desk and satellite TV; some also have balconies overlooking the park. Breakfast is served in the hotel's bright and cheerful lobby cafe.

Hôtel Bélère
HOTEL €€

(Map p178; ☑ 0537 70 38 97; www.belere-hotels. com; 33 Ave Moulay Youssef; s incl breakfast Dh950-1080, d Dh1080-1180, ste Dh1240-1400; ❄❄☎; 📵 Mohammed V/Gare de Rabat) This reliable but characterless hotel offers small, comfortable rooms with tasteful (albeit dated) decor. It has a bar and restaurant and is handy to

Central Rabat

ATLANTIC COAST RABAT

the train station. Air-con units are in need of an overhaul and guests report that wi-fi can sometimes be patchy.

Hôtel Royal   HOTEL €€
(Map p178; ☏ 0537 72 11 71; 1 Rue Ammane; s/d Dh490/700; ☞; ⊟ Medina Rabat) In a very central location, the Royal has dowdy and musty rooms that are begging for refurbishment. Those on the 4th floor have the best views over the park and city; all are noisy. Breakfast (Dh55) is served in the downstairs restaurant.

⛵ Medina

★ Riad Meftaha   B&B €
(Map p178; ☏ 0537 72 14 06; www.riad-meftaha. com; 15 Rue Iran, Quartier Marassa Océan; d/tr/ ste incl breakfast Dh575/640/660; ❄ ☞; ⊟ Bab El Had, Medina Rabat) Owner Franck and his sidekick Khadija are friendly and helpful hosts, making this quiet riad just outside Bab Laalou an excellent choice. The building is modern and not particularly attractive, but rooms are pleasantly decorated. The pick of the bunch is undoubtedly the terrace suite. Note that double rooms lack air-conditioning; all have satellite TV. Breakfast is generous.

Hôtel Dorhmi   HOTEL €
(Map p178; ☏ 0537 72 38 98; 313 Ave Mohammed V, Medina; s/d/tr Dh100/140/210; ☞; ⊟ Medina Rabat) Immaculately kept, very friendly and dirt cheap, this family-run hotel (also known as the Doghmi) offers 10 ultrabasic rooms surrounding a central courtyard on the 1st floor above the Banque Populaire; some have no windows. Rooms have sinks (cold water) and a hot shower costs Dh10.

Hôtel Darna   HOTEL €
(Map p174; ☏ 0537 73 47 05; www.hoteldarna. ma; Ave Laalou, Medina; s/d/tr incl breakfast Dh350/550/650; ☞; ⊟ Medina Rabat) Just inside Bab Laalou on the edge of the medina, this safe but unexciting choice offers small rooms with double-glazed windows, comfortable beds and satellite TV. We liked the 3rd-floor restaurant with its medina view, but were disappointed by the dodgy plumbing and lack of hot water.

Rabat Youth Hostel   HOSTEL €
(Map p178; Auberge de Jeune Rabat; ☏ 0537725769; auberge.jeunes.rbt@hotmail.fr; 43 Rue Maressa Bab El Had, Quartier Bab El Had; dm Dh60; ☞; ⊟ Medina Rabat) A peaceful courtyard garden is the main reason to stay in this old-style hostel

occupying a riad next to Bab El Had bus station. There are two 16-bed male dorms and one 20-bed female dorm; none have air-con or fans. The shared bathrooms (four showers for men, three for women) are clean but lack hot water.

★ **L'Alcazar** BOUTIQUE HOTEL €€€
(Map p174; ☑ 0537 73 69 06; www.lalcazar.com; 4 Impasse Ben Abdellah, off Ave Laalou, Medina; r Dh1000-3500; P ❈ ☎; ☐ Medina Rabat) Rabat's most stylish hotel is entered through a royal-blue doorway at the end of an impasse (dead-end lane) near Bab Laalou. A chic French-style adaptation of a traditional riad, the hotel offers eight extremely comfortable rooms, a charming central dining area and a multitiered rooftop terrace with expansive medina views. Amenities are top-quality, breakfast is delicious and service is friendly.

Riad Oudaya RIAD €€€
(Map p178; ☑ 0537 70 23 92; www.riadrabat.com; 46 Rue Sidi Fateh, Medina; s/d incl breakfast Dh1100/1300, two-/ three-person ste Dh1650/1920; ☎; ☐ Medina Rabat) Tucked away down an impasse just north of Mosquée el-Mekki, this small French-owned riad is an oasis of style and tranquillity in the heart of the medina. There are two standard rooms on the rooftop and two suites sleeping two or three people downstairs. Dinner in the gorgeous open courtyard costs Dh250 but must be booked in advance.

Note that it is a great choice in autumn or spring but rooms are too hot in summer and the open courtyard means that the restaurant will be cold in winter. Credit cards are not accepted.

Eating

Considering its status as the nation's capital, Rabat's restaurant scene leaves a lot to be desired. The best of the local eateries are in the ville nouvelle, with one or two decent options in Agdal. Ave Mohammed V, just inside the medina gate, is a good place to find a cheap eat.

✗ Ville Nouvelle & Agdal

La Rive MOROCCAN €
(Map p178; ☑ 0537 73 00 01; www.restaurant-lariverabat.com; Pl Moulay Hassan, Ville Nouvelle; snacks from Dh 10; ☺ 7.30am-midnight ☐ Place al-Joulane) Modern and airy, this is one of three popular cafe-restaurants on this sunken plaza – it's a good spot away from the traffic and bustle. All three have terrace seating and offer set menus for less than Dh100.

La Comédie MOROCCAN €
(Map p178; 269 Ave Mohammed V; Ville Nouvelle; pastries from Dh10; ☺ 7am-10pm; ☐ Medina Rabat) Friendly and efficient staff serve excellent coffees and good pastries and gateaux at this popular cafe. Claim a table under the large trees and watch the passing parade on Ave Mohammed V.

EXPLORING RABAT'S HISTORIC NEIGHBOURHOOD

Rabat's historic citadel **Kasbah les Oudaïas** (Rue Jamaa; ☐ Bab Chellah) occupies the site of the original *ribat* (fortress-monastery) that gave the city its name. Predominately residential, its narrow streets are lined with whitewashed houses – most of which were built by Muslim refugees from Spain. There are scenic views over the river and ocean from the **Plateforme du Sémaphore** (Signal Platform; Kasbah les Oudaïas; ☐ Bab Chellah) at its highest point, and the attractive **Andalusian Gardens** (☺ sunrise-sunset; ☐ Bab Chellah) at its southern edge are a popular relaxation and meeting point for locals.

The most dramatic entry to the kasbah is through the enormous Almohad gate of **Bab Oudaïa**, built in 1195. Its location, facing the heart of the city and just outside the original palace, made it more ceremonial than defensive and the gateway is elaborately decorated with a series of carved arches. These days, it is only occasionally open so most visitors enter through a much smaller nearby gateway. Inside, the main street, Rue Jamaa, runs straight through the kasbah to the Plateforme du Sémaphore. About 200m ahead on the left is the oldest **mosque** (Rue Jamaa, Kasbah les Oudaïas) in Rabat, built in the 10th century and restored in the 18th with funds donated by an English pirate known as Ahmed el Inlisi, one of the feared Sallee Rovers (p187).

★ **Le Petit Beur**   MOROCCAN €€
(Map p178; ☑ 0537 73 13 22; 8 Rue Damas, Ville Nouvelle; salads Dh45, mains Dh80-120; ⊙ 11.30am-2pm & 7-11pm Mon-Sat; ◙ Mohammed V/Gare de Rabat) Known for its friendly waiters and fresh Moroccan food, this small restaurant offers an array of daily specials, tajines, brochettes, *briouates* and *pastillas*. The set menu of salad, brochettes and water for Dh90 is excellent value. Lunchtimes are quiet but it's wise to book for dinner, when an oud player serenades diners.

Ty Potes   FRENCH €€
(Map p178; ☑ 0537 70 79 65; http://typotes.com/; 11 Rue Ghafsa, Ville Nouvelle; salads Dh60-85, tartines Dh65-95; ⊙ noon-2.45pm Tue-Sat, 7-11pm Thu-Sat, 11am-3pm Sun; ◙ Place al-Joulane) Head to the leafy street behind the St Pierre Cathedral and Institut Française to find this popular expat haunt. The menu features sweet and savoury crêpes and galettes, salads and *tartines* (open-faced sandwiches), which are ideally enjoyed in the rear garden. The Sunday brunch (Dh120) is particularly popular. Both alcohol and charcuterie are served; service can be brusque.

Tajine Wa Tanjia   MOROCCAN €€
(Map p178; ☑ 0537 72 97 97; 9 Rue de Baghdad, Ville Nouvelle; tajines Dh65-86, tanjias Dh128-148, couscous Dh55-85; ⊙ noon-3pm & 7pm-midnight Mon-Sat; 🛜; ◙ Mohammed V/Gare de Rabat) Down-to-earth Moroccan dishes are the speciality at this friendly restaurant near the Rabat Ville train station. The menu is dominated by brochettes, *tajines* and *tanjias* (stews slow-cooked in a pottery vessel) prepared according to traditional recipes, with couscous served on Fridays only. The ambience is romantic at night, helped along by live loud music.

Le Bistro du Pietri   FRENCH €€
(Map p178; ☑ 0537 70 78 20; Le Piétri Urban Hotel, 4 Rue Tobrouk, Ville Nouvelle; mains Dh140-170; ⊙ noon-3pm Mon-Fri, 7-11pm daily; ❋🛜; ◙ Mohammed V/Gare de Rabat) We usually shy away from dining at restaurants in business hotels, but this eatery in the Le Piétri Urban Hotel (p177) is an exception to our self-imposed rule. The predominantly French food is well prepared and tasty. There's a good wine list, a kids menu and live jazz on Friday and Saturday between 9.30pm and midnight.

La Koutoubia   MOROCCAN €€
(Map p178; ☑ 0537 70 10 75; 10 Rue Pierre Parent, Ville Nouvelle; mains Dh80; ⊙ noon-3pm & 7-10.30pm; ◙ Mohammed V/Gare de Rabat) It opened way back in 1955, and this Moroccan restaurant, with attached bar, has managed to retain its clients and traditional decor over the decades. All the classic Moroccan dishes are available – tajines, brochettes, couscous and *pastillas* – and the helpful English-speaking owner is happy to translate the menu.

La Mamma   ITALIAN €€
(Map p178; ☑ 0537 70 73 29; 6 Rue Tanta, Ville Nouvelle; pastas Dh55-100, pizzas Dh55-90; ⊙ noon-3pm & 7.30pm-midnight; ◙ Place al-Joulane, Mohammed V/Gare de Rabat) This bistro serves some of the best Italian food in town, so the fact that the dining area is dark and slightly smelly is overlooked by regulars. Some of the pasta portions can be on the small side, but the wood-fired pizzas will leave you planning a return visit.

Cosmopolitan   MODERN FRENCH €€€
(Map p178; ☑ 0537 20 00 28; http://restaurant-cosmopolitan.eresto.net/; cnr Ave Ibn Toumert & Rue Abbou Abbas El Guerraoui; mains Dh160-250; ⊙ noon-2.30pm & 7.30-10.45pm; ◙ Mohammed V/Gare de Rabat) This swish place near Bab Ruach occupies a handsome art deco villa and is one of the only restaurants in town serving modern French cuisine. The menu changes daily according to what is fresh at the market, with seafood taking pride of place. Dine in the front courtyard in warm weather and upstairs during the cooler months. Excellent wine list.

L'Entrecôte   FRENCH €€€
(Map p178; ☑ 0661 15 59 59; http://lentrecote.ma/; 74 Blvd al-Amir Fal Ould Omar, Agdal; mains Dh80-180; ⊙ noon-11pm; ◙ Agdal/Ave de France) The menu at this old-fashioned eatery is classic French with occasional forays over the border into Spanish territory, and the result is popular with locals and tourists alike. Steak and seafood dishes dominate (vegetarians should steer clear), and there's a good value deal of a *plat et dessert du jour* for Dh120.

✖ Medina

Restaurant de la Libération   MOROCCAN €
(Map p178; 256 Ave Mohammed V; mains Dh60; ⊙ 11.30am-10pm Mon-Sat; ◙ Medina Rabat) Cheap, cheerful and marginally more classy than the string of other eateries along this road (it has plastic menus and tablecloths), this basic restaurant does a steady line in traditional favourites. Friday is couscous day, when giant platters of the stuff are delivered to the eager masses.

ATLANTIC COAST RABAT

SELF-CATERING

To stock up on picnic lunch supplies and your five-plus a day, head to the medina.

Fruit & Vegetable Market (Ave Hassan II; ⊙8am-7pm Mon-Sat; 🚇 Medina Rabat) has a good choice of fresh produce, dried fruits and nuts. You should be able to find everything else you need (including booze) at the surrounding stalls or along Rue Souika and near Bab el-Bouiba.

Inza
FAST FOOD €

(Map p178; Ave Mohammed V, Medina; pizza/panini/ shwarma Dh15/10/12; ⊙10am-11pm; 🚇 Medina Rabat) Popular fast-food joint on busy Ave Mohammed V, with street tables and a bustling atmosphere.

Bidawai
FAST FOOD €

(Map p178; Ave Mohammed V, Medina; pizza/shwarma/panini Dh15/12/10; ⊙10.30am-11pm Mon-Sat; 🚇 Medina Rabat) One of the most popular fast-food joints with seating on the street.

Boulangerie Pâtisserie Majestic
BAKERY €

(Map p178; ☑0537 20 71 86; cnr Rue Ammane & Ave Allal ben Abdallah, Ville Nouvelle; pastries from Dh10; ⊙7am-10pm; 🚇 Medina Rabat) The shaded terrace here is lovely and the pastries are excellent, but the service and coffee have been so terrible on our last few visits that our recommendation can only be half-hearted.

Drinking & Nightlife

Rabat's nightlife is a lot more limited – and subdued – than Casablanca's, but there are a few clubs and bars in the ville nouvelle and Agdal worth a visit. Expect to pay around Dh200 to enter clubs, and the same for drinks.

Café Maure
CAFE

(Map p174; Rue Bazo, Kasbah les Oudaias; ⊙9am-5pm; 🚇 Bab Chellah) Sit back, relax and gaze out over the estuary to Salé at this open-air cafe spread over several terraces above the Andalusian Gardens. Mint tea is the tipple of choice, accompanied by *cornes de gazelle* pastries (Dh8) ordered from the dedicated pastry seller.

Cafetéria du 7ème Art
CAFE

(Map p178; Ave Allal ben Abdallah; ⊙9am-9pm; 🛜; 🚇 Medina Rabat) Set in the shady grounds of a cinema, this popular outdoor cafe attracts a mixed clientele of students and

professionals. While most popular for a tea, coffee or ice cream, it also serves a set breakfast (Dh18) and snacks such as pizza (from Dh38) and sandwiches (Dh17).

Amnesia
CLUB

(Map p178; ☑0612 99 11 90; 18 Rue de Monastir, Ville Nouvelle; ⊙11.30pm-4am; 🚇 Medina Rabat) A Rabat institution (it opened in 1989), this huge, pricey and perennially popular club can accommodate over 1000 patrons and sees plenty of action on its dance floor. Resident DJs have a fondness for house and R&B.

Oliveri
CAFE

(Map p174; ☑0537 77 78 00; cnr Ave de France & Blvd Al-Amir Fal Ould Omar; ⊙7am-11pm; 🚇 Agdal/Ave de France) Agdal branch of a popular ice-cream cafe.

Le Puzzle
BAR

(Map p175; ☑0673 12 00 73; 79 Ave Ibn Sina, Agdal; ⊙5pm-2am; 🚇 Ibn Rochd) Predominantly a sports bar, with occasional live bands.

Entertainment

Cultural centres associated with Rabat's many foreign embassies often host music, dance, art and literary events. Most films are dubbed in French, unless marked as *version originale*.

When it opens, the new Grand Théatre de Rabat, designed by the late Zaha Hadid and currently under construction, will be the city's preeminent cultural and entertainment venue.

Cinéma Renaissance
CINEMA

(Map p178; ☑0537 72 21 68; www.renaissance.ma; 360 Ave Mohammed V; adult/student Dh50/30; 🚇 Medina Rabat) This large cinema complex on the main drag shows mainstream Hollywood flicks.

Cinéma du 7ème Art
CINEMA

(Map p178; ☑0537 73 38 87; Ave Allal ben Abdallah; 🚇 Medina Rabat) Art-house cinema screening Moroccan, Middle Eastern and European films.

Shopping

Rabat's great shopping secret is its laid-back merchants. There's little pressure to buy, so you can stroll the medina in relative peace, but there is also less room to bargain. There's a fair selection of good handicrafts on offer, particularly in and around the Rue des Consuls in the medina. Here you'll find everything from jewellery, silks, slippers and pottery to *zellij* and carved wooden furniture.

Information

EMERGENCY

Police Station (Map p178; Préfecture de Police; Ave Tripoli, Ville Nouvelle; 🚉 Place al-Joulane)

MEDICAL SERVICES

Town pharmacies open nights and weekends on a rotational basis; check the rota, posted in French and Arabic, in all pharmacy windows.

Agdal Clinic (Map p174; 📋 0537 77 77 77; www. clinique-agdal.com; 6 Pl Talhah, Ave Ibn Sina, Agdal; 🚉 Agdal/Avenue de France) Twenty-four hour emergency department.

SAMU (📋 0537 73 73 73; www.samu-rabat.org; ⊙24hr) Private ambulance service.

SOS Médecins (📋 0537 20 2020; ⊙24hr) Doctors on call.

MONEY

Numerous banks (with ATMs) are concentrated along Ave Mohammed V and the parallel Ave Allal ben Abdallah.

POST

Main Post Office (Map p178; cnr Rue Soékarno & Ave Mohammed V; ⊙8.30am-4.30pm Mon-Fri)

TOURIST INFORMATION

Office National Marocain du Tourisme (ONMT, 📋 0537 27 83 00; www.visitmorocco. com; cnr Rues Oued el-Makhazine & Zalaka, Agdal; ⊙8.30am-4.30pm Mon-Fri) Predominantly a marketing outfit, and offers little assistance to travellers.

Getting There & Away

AIR

Considering the notoriously long and chaotic immigration queues at Casablanca's Mohammed V International Airport, opting to fly in or out of Rabat-Salé Airport is a decent alternative option to consider.

➤ Rabat-Salé Airport, 10km northeast of town, is used by an ever-growing number of international airlines, including Ryanair, Air France, RAM, Lufthansa, KLM and Air Arabia.

➤ **Stareo** (Map p178; 📋 0530 27 87 00) buses travel between the airport and a stop on Ave Mohammed V, opposite Rabat Ville Train Station/ Mohammed V Tramway Station, between 6.30am and 8.45pm. These depart from the airport one hour after each arrival and from the city centre two hours before each flight (a schedule is posted on the bus stop). Tickets cost Dh20 and the journey takes approximately 30 minutes.

➤ A grand taxi to the airport should cost Dh150 daytime and Dh200 at night, although you will need to bargain to get these prices.

BUS

Intercity buses do service Rabat, but you are much better off using the train.

Rabat has two bus stations – the main **Gare Routière Kamra** (📋 0537 79 58 16; Blvd Hassan II/N1; 🚉 Ibn Rochd), from where most buses depart and arrive, and the less chaotic **CTM station**, 500m south. To get to the town centre from Kamra, take bus 30 (Dh4) or a petit taxi (Dh30). The closest tram stop, Ibn Rochd, is a 1.3km walk east along Ave Ibn Rochd.

Note that some intercity buses pass through central Rabat rather than stopping at Kamra.

Routes not covered by rail link include:

Agadir Dh240 to Dh280, 6¾ to 9½ hours, six daily

Er-Rachidia Dh165 to Dh175, 8¾ to 9½ hours, two daily

Laâyoune Dh490, 20¾ hours, two daily

Tetouan Dh120 to Dh155, 3½ to 6½ hours, five daily

CAR

Avis Ville Nouvelle (📋 0537 72 18 18; www. avis.com.au; 7 Rue Abou Faris al-Marini; ⊙8am-7pm Mon-Sat, to noon Sun; 🚉 Mohammed V/Gare de Rabat); **Airport** (📋 0537 83 11 98; www.avis.com.au; Rabat-Salé Airport; ⊙8am-midnight)

Budget Ville Nouvelle (📋 0530 20 05 20; http://locations.budget.com/ma; Rabat Ville train station, Ave Mohammed V; ⊙8.30am-noon & 2.30-7pm Mon-Sat, 9am-noon Sun; 🚉 Mohammed V/Gare de Rabat); **Airport** (📋 0660 17 41 11; http://locations.budget. com/ma; Rabat-Salé Airport; ⊙7am-10.30pm)

Europcar Ville Nouvelle (📋 0537 72 23 28; www.europcar.com.au; 25 Rue Patrice Lumumba, Ville Nouvelle; ⊙8.30am-noon daily, 2.30-7pm Mon-Sat); **Airport** (📋 0537 72 41 41; Rabat-Salé Airport; ⊙7am-11pm)

Hertz Ville Nouvelle (📋 0537 70 73 66; http:// en.hertz.ma; 467 Ave Mohammed V; ⊙8am-noon & 2-6.30pm Mon-Fri, 9am-noon & 3-6pm Sat, 9am-noon Sun; 🚉 Mohammed V/Gare de Rabat); **Airport** (📋 0537 82 97 00; http:// en.hertz.ma; Rabat-Salé Airport; ⊙7am-10pm)

TAXI

Grands taxis leave for Casablanca, Fez, Meknès and Salé from a lot opposite Bab Chellah, next to the petrol station.

TRAIN

Train is the most convenient way to arrive in Rabat, as the **Rabat Ville train station** (Map p175; not to be confused with Rabat Agdal train station, to the west of the city) is in the centre of the ville nouvelle and within easy walking distance of the medina. The station has a food court and wi-fi, as well as Budget car-rental and Supratours offices.

Trains run every 30 minutes from 6am to 10pm between Rabat Ville and Casa Port train stations (1st/2nd class Dh69/37, 70 minutes, every 30 minutes). You can connect with trains to Casablanca's Mohammed V International Airport at Casa Port.

On all long-distance routes there's always one late-night *ordinaire* train among the *rapide* services. Second-class *rapide* services include the following.

Fez 1st/2nd class Dh127/85, 2½ hours, hourly

Marrakesh 1st/2nd class Dh195/127, five hours, nine daily

Meknès 1st/2nd class Dh95/69, two hours, hourly

Oujda 1st/2nd class Dh285/190, 9½ hours, two daily

Tangier 1st/2nd class Dh153/101, four hours, eight daily

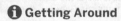 Getting Around

BOAT
Commuter rowing **boats** cross the estuary between Rabat and Salé between sunrise and sunset (Dh2.50).

BUS
Buses are horribly crowded and barely roadworthy; tickets can be purchased from conductors on board and cost Dh4.

CAR & MOTORCYCLE
➜ Blue lines around street car parks indicate that drivers must buy a ticket from a nearby machine (Dh2 per hour).

➜ City-centre parking restrictions apply from 8am to noon and 2pm to 7pm Monday to Saturday; metered parking costs Dh2 per hour.

➜ When there are no blue lines or machines, unofficial parking attendants will often help you park and expect a tip of Dh5 to Dh10.

TAXI
Rabat's blue petits taxis are plentiful, cheap and quick. A ride around the centre of town will cost between Dh15 and Dh30 – try to get the driver to use his meter. There's a petit-taxi rank near the entrance of the medina on Ave Hassan II and another at the train station. Note that petits taxis aren't allowed to drive between Rabat and Salé.

Larbi El Wardi (☑ 0661 71 20 17, 0603 48 43 23) is a friendly English-speaking taxi driver with a new car complete with air-con, wi-fi and functioning seatbelts. Can do short or long trips.

TRAM
The smart and efficient **Rabat-Salé tramway** (www.tram-way.ma) system is an excellent way to get around Rabat.

Line 1 runs along Ave Hassan II next to the medina, detouring past the Hassan Tower to Bab Lamrissa next to the Salé medina and then on to Hassan II.

Line 2 starts at Madinat Al Irfane, stopping at Agdal/Avenue de France, Mohammed V/Gare de Rabat in the ville nouvelle, Bab Lamrissa, Salé Ville trains station and Hay Karima.

Fares are Dh6, bought from ticket machines on the platforms (multiple journey tickets are also available).

Services run every 20 minutes, from 6am to 10pm.

Salé سلا
POP 980,000

The winds of change are blowing strongly through Salé, with a development boom and population explosion well and truly under way. Now considerably larger than its neighbour (Rabat) on the opposite bank of the Oued Bou Regreg, it is now functioning as an integrated part of the capital rather than the staid satellite town it once was. Assisted by an efficient modern tram link and the newly constructed marina just south of the medina, it is attracting industry, commerce and tourism, and looks set to prosper. That said, it has retained a traditional flavour and is noticeably more conservative than Rabat.

History

People began to settle in Salé in the 10th century and the town grew in importance as inhabitants of the older settlement at Sala Colonia began to move across the river to the new town. Warring among local tribes was still rampant at this stage and it was the Almohads who took control of the area in the 12th century, establishing neighbouring Rabat as a base for expeditions to Spain.

Spanish freebooters attacked in 1260; in response the Merenids fortified the town, building defensive walls and a canal to Bab Mrisa to allow safe access for shipping. The town began to flourish and established valuable trade links with Venice, Genoa, London and the Netherlands.

As trade thrived so too did piracy, and by the 16th century the twin towns prospered from the activities of the infamous Sallee Rovers pirates (p187).

Salé

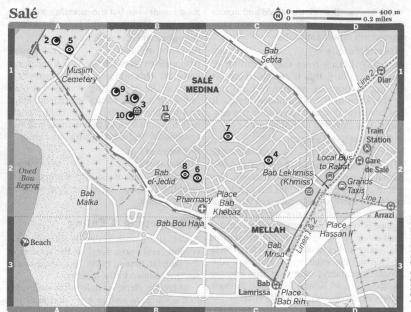

By the 19th century the pirates had been brought under control, Rabat had been made capital and Salé had sunk into an obscurity from which it is only now emerging.

⊙ Sights

The main entrance to the medina is Bab Bou Haja, near the Bab Lamrissa tram stop on the southwestern wall. From here walk left (north) to the souqs and the Great Mosque, 500m further northwest along Rue Ras ash-Shajara (also known as Rue de la Grande Mosquée). Alternatively, enter at Bab Lekhmiss (aka Khmiss), between the Bab Lamrissa and Gare de Salé tram stops, and walk straight ahead to find the souqs and mosque.

Salé Medina   AREA

(Map p185; 🚊 Bab Lamrissa) Retaining an almost medieval flavour, this 13th-century walled medina is visited on a regular basis by the city's pious, who come to worship in the Grand Mosque (p186) and three important shrines. Local housewives are also regulars, lured by its various souqs selling fresh produce and spices.

➡ **Medersa Abou al-Hassan**   HISTORIC BUILDING

(Map p185; Médersa des Mérinide; Dh10; ⊙8.30am-5pm) Attached to the magnificent Grand

Salé

⊙ Sights
1 Grand Mosque	B1
2 Koubba of Sidi Ben Ashir at-Taleb	A1
3 Medersa Abou al-Hassan	B1
4 Salé Medina	C2
5 Slave Prison	A1
6 Souq el-Ghezel	B2
7 Souq el-Kebir	C2
8 Souq el-Merzouk	B2
9 Zawiya of Sidi Abdallah Ben Hassoun	B1
10 Zawiya of Sidi Ahmed Tijani	B1

🛏 Sleeping
11 Repose	B1

Mosque (p186), this *medersa,* next to the mosque's monumental entrance gate, is a showcase of superb Merenid architecture and decorative arts. Both it and the mosque date from the first half of the 14th century and were commissioned by Almohad Sultan Abou al-Hassan. The *medersa* takes the form of a narrow courtyard surrounded by a gallery, and every available surface is encrusted in intricate *zellij,* carved stucco or elegant cedar woodwork.

Small student cells surround the gallery on the upper floor, from where you can climb through an aperture to the flat roof, which has excellent views of Salé and across to Rabat. The guardian who shows you around will expect a small tip.

➡ **Grand Mosque** MOSQUE

(Map p185) Dating from the beginning of the 11th century, this is the third-largest mosque in Morocco. An architectural mix of the Almoravid and Almohad styles, it has been rebuilt many times over the centuries. It is closed to non-Muslims.

➡ **Zawiya of Sidi Abdallah Ben Hassoun** ISLAMIC SHRINE

(Map p185; Rue Sidi Abdallah Ben Hassoun) Salé's patron saint, Sidi Abdallah ibn Hassoun, was a 16th-century Sufi cleric and teacher. He is revered by Moroccan Muslims as a patron of travellers in much the same way as St Christopher is revered among Catholics. An annual candlelit pilgrimage and procession in his honour makes its way through the streets of Salé on the evening of Mouloud (the Prophet's birthday), ending at this *zawiya* (religious shrine) behind the Grand Mosque (p186), which only Muslims may enter.

➡ **Slave Prison** NOTABLE BUILDING

(Map p185; Ave Sidi Ben Achir) Built by the dastardly Sallee Rovers pirates and recently restored, this slave prison next to the Muslim cemetery hadn't officially opened during our

most recent visit, but the caretaker was happy to show visitors around for a Dh20 tip.

➡ **Koubba of Sidi Ben Ashir at-Taleb** ISLAMIC SHRINE

(Map p185; cnr Aves Sidi Ben Achir & Abdelkader Al Harrati) This white *koubba* (shrine of a saint) at the edge of the medina was built to honour a 14th-century Spanish adherent and teacher of Sufism. The faithful come here to pray for cures to blindness and other ailments. Non-Muslims may not enter.

➡ **Zawiya of Sidi Ahmed Tijani** ISLAMIC SHRINE

(Map p185) Shrine of the 18th-century founder of the Tijaniyya Sufi order. Non-Muslims may not enter.

🛏 Sleeping & Eating

Now that the tram has made Salé more accessible, and encouraged by the success of the popular Repose (p186), guesthouses are starting to open in the medina.

There are plenty of hole-in-the-wall cafes in the souqs, as well as a popular juice bar and bakery just inside Bab Bou Haja.

Salé is an almost totally alcohol-free area; you'll need to go to one of the restaurants at the new marina or into Rabat if you want to drink alcohol.

★ **Repose** GUESTHOUSE €€

(Map p185; ☑ 0537 88 29 58; www.therepose.com; 17 Zankat Talaa, Ras Chejra, Salé Medina; ste incl breakfast Dh450-700; ❅ @ 🛜; 🚆 Bab Lamrissa) 🍃 Husband-and-wife team Jan and Rachid have restored this traditional medina house with great style, creating a delightful retreat. All four guest rooms have vibrant decor, sitting areas and excellent bathrooms. There's a sun-drenched roof terrace where breakfast is served, and three-course vegetarian or vegan dinners (Dh200) are also available. Other offerings include cooking classes (Dh400) and argan-oil massage (Dh200).

ℹ Information

There are banks with ATMs on Ave 2 Mars near Bab Bou Haja.

Pharmacy (Pl Bab Khebaz)

Post Office (Bab Khmiss; ⏱ 8am-4.15pm Mon-Fri, to 11.45am Sat)

ℹ Getting There & Away

Boat From the marina boats to Rabat leave when full and operate between sunrise and sunset (Dh2.50).

DON'T MISS

SALÉ SOUQ ACTION

Join in the bustle of local medina life in Salé's traditional souqs.

Souq el-Ghezel (Wool Market; Salé Medina) Shaded by trees and unchanged for centuries, the atmospheric Souq el-Ghezel makes an interesting stop on Tuesday and Thursday mornings, when men and women haggle over the price and quality of rough white wool as it hangs from ancient scales suspended from a large tripod.

Souq el-Merzouk (Salé Medina; 🚆 Bab Lamrissa) Textiles, basketwork and jewellery are crafted and sold in this souq. Also on sale are the woven grass mats used in mosques, for which Salé is famous.

Souq el-Kebir (Salé Medina; 🚆 Bab Lamrissa) The medina's main souq, selling household goods, leather and wood. The spice souq is nearby.

THE SALLEE ROVERS: SALÉ'S PIRATE GOVERNMENT

In 1619 a group of corsairs (pirates) declared the ancient port of Salé to be an independent republic and gave allegiance to their leader, Dutchman Jan Janszoon van Haarlem (c 1570–1641), rather than to the sultan. Known as the Sallee or Salé Rovers, they named their republic Bou Regreg and set up a government that consisted of 14 pirate leaders, with Janszoon, who was also known as Murat Reis the Younger, as both their president and the admiral of their 18-ship navy. After ordering an unsuccessful siege of the city, the sultan bowed to the inevitable and acknowledged the republic by declaring Janszoon governor in 1624.

Under the rule of the Sallee Rovers, Salé initially prospered. The Rovers patrolled the shipping routes between Atlantic colonial ports and Europe, seizing ships and their gold, and also selling the ships' crews into slavery. Fees from anchorage and other harbour dues also enriched the corsairs' coffers. Soon, though, the political climate worsened and Janszoon and most of his followers departed in 1627.

The exploits of the Rovers were recounted throughout Europe and the Americas, and even made it into fiction when, in 1719, Daniel Defoe's novel *Robinson Crusoe* was published. In it, Robinson Crusoe spends time being held captive by the Sallee Rovers and eventually sails off to liberty from the mouth of the Salé river.

Bus Salé's main bus station is 2km east of the medina, but buses from Rabat also stop outside Bab Lamrissa.

Tram The easiest way to travel between Rabat and Salé is by tram (Dh6).

Taxi Pick up a **grand taxi** in Rabat on Ave Hassan II opposite Bab Chellah; ask for the Bab Bou Haja or Bab Lamrissa. From Salé there are departures from Bab Lekhmiss and Bab Mrisa (D4 one way). Note that petits taxis are not permitted to travel between Rabat and Salé.

Train Trains run to/from Rabat, but the tram or grands taxis are probably the simplest options. Trains north to Kenitra run every 30 minutes (Dh16, 25 minutes).

Around Rabat & Salé

Jardins Exotiques   GARDENS
(☏0537 82 27 56; www.jardinsexotiques.com; Bouknadel; adult/child/family of 4 Dh20/15/50; ◷9am-6.30pm autumn & winter, to 7.30pm spring & summer) Created by French horticulturist Marcel François in 1951, these gardens were declared a Natural Heritage site in 2003. Though neither attractive nor particularly well maintained, they are a popular day trip for residents of Rabat and Salé. The gardens are 13km north of Rabat on the road to Kenitra. Take bus 9 from Bab Chellah in Rabat or from Bab Lekhmiss at the Salé medina.

Areas include the **Jardin Nature**, plantations that evoke the exotic vegetation the horticulturist encountered on his many travels; and the **Jardin Culture**, referring more to the philosophy of the garden in different cultures. There's also a vivarium for reptiles.

Musées Belghazi   MUSEUM
(☏0537 82 21 78; http://museebelghazi.maroc oriental.com; main collection Dh40, private rooms Dh100; ◷when staff available 9am-5pm; ⛟9 from Rabat & Salé) This forlorn ethnographic museum certainly isn't worth a dedicated visit from Rabat. It displays a dusty collection of traditional Andalucian, Jewish Moroccan and Islamic arts and crafts amassed by the Belghazi family, and the entry fee is overpriced for what is on offer. The museum is 17km from Salé on the road to Kenitra. Take bus 9 from Bab Chellah in Rabat or from Bab Lekhmiss at the Salé medina.

Displays include measuring instruments (one of the first Belghazis was an astrologist at the Qarawiyin court in Fez), carpets, leather saddles and slippers, jewellery, tools, pottery, embroidery and miniature copies of the Quran.

Plage des Nations   BEACH
The clean, sandy strip of beach at Plage des Nations, 17km north of Rabat, gets some serious wave action that's good for surfers, but the currents can be dangerous for swimming.

To get to the beach, drive north as far as the Musées Belghazis and turn left down a road known as Sidi Bouknadel. Bus 9 from Rabat or Salé will drop you at the turn-off, from where it's a 2km walk to the beach past huge developments of holiday apartments.

Lac de Sidi Boughaba   LAKE
This freshwater lake, part of the Lac Sidi Boughaba Parc National, is located in Mehdia, on the outskirts of industrial Kenitra. As a refuelling stop for thousands of birds

migrating between Europe and Sub-Saharan Africa, the lake provides some of the country's best birdwatching, especially between October and March. To get to the lake follow the signposts from the beach road to Mehdiya Plage, 300m past the Cafe Restaurant Belle Vue. If you're on foot, the lake is a 3.3km walk from the turn-off.

More than 200 species of birds have been spotted on the lake and many choose to winter or nest here – among them a number of rare or endangered species. This is one of the last places on earth where you can still see large numbers of marbled ducks, distinguished by the dark patch around their eyes. Other birds to look out for include the beautiful marsh owl (seen most often at dusk), crested coot, black-shouldered kite and greater flamingo.

The lake is also a popular place for gentle hiking, with well-appointed (but rubbish-strewn) walking trails in the forested hills around the lake.

Témara Plage   BEACH
Wild and sandy Témara Plage, 15km southwest of the city, is popular with surfers and sunbathers in summer; there are dangerous rips so swimmers should be cautious. The beach can be reached on bus 33 from Bab al-Had in Rabat.

Moulay Bousselham
مولاي بوسلهام
POP 26,545

Though inundated by holidaymakers in high summer, the small town of Moulay Bousselham is marvellously tranquil for the rest of the year. The sweeping beach, with its golden sand, is one of the most attractive on the North Atlantic coast, although its strong currents and crashing waves can be dangerous. The protected lagoon is one of the country's most important bird habitats, attracting twitchers from across the globe. If you have a car, it's a great place to chill for a few days.

The town is named after a 10th-century Egyptian saint who is commemorated in one of the *koubbas* that line the slope down to the sea, guarding the mouth of the river. All services – ATMs, shops, a pharmacy, cafes and taxi ranks – are on the main street.

◉ Sights

Merja Zerga National Park   NATIONAL PARK
One of the great pleasures of Morocco's Atlantic Coast is spending half a day on the calm Merja Zerga (Blue Lagoon) with an expert bird guide. The 73-sq-km Merja Zerga National Park (4 sq km of water and the rest marshland) attracts myriad migrant birds, including wildfowl, waders and flamingos in huge numbers, making it one of Morocco's prime birdwatching habitats. The best times to visit are September to October and March to April, but there are about 100 species all year-round.

You'll see herons, flamingos, ibises, the African marsh owl, spoonbills, plovers and egrets. Slender-billed and Audouin's gulls are regular visitors, as are shelducks, teals, terns, marsh harriers and peregrine falcons.

The lagoon is between 50cm and 4m deep depending on the tide. Ninety percent of the water comes from the sea, 10% is freshwater from the Oued Dredr, south of the lagoon.

There are six villages around the lake, four of which depend on agriculture, two on fishing. Many of the fishers take tourists around the lake as a sideline. Boat trips with the local boaters are easily arranged if you wander down to the small port where boats are moored. Expect to pay about Dh100 per hour for the boat. If possible, contact Khalil Fachkhir (p188) or Hassan Dalil (p188) in advance for a specialised birding tour; both have their own boats and speak English.

Hard-core birdwatchers may also want to explore Merja Khaloufa, an attractive lake about 8km east of Moulay Bousselham and part of the park, which offers good viewing of a variety of wintering wildfowl.

🏃 Activities

Hassan Dalil   BIRDWATCHING
(☑ 0668 43 41 10; per hr Dh100) A recommended bird guide.

Khalil Fachkhir   BIRDWATCHING
(☑ 0663 09 53 58; nidlettibou@yahoo.com; 90min guided tours per boat Dh250) Recommended English-speaking guide who knows the lagoon and its birds extremely well.

🛌 Sleeping

Most holidaymakers stay in private villas (many wealthy residents of Casablanca and Rabat have holiday villas here), but there are also two campgrounds and a few hotels and B&Bs. The prime location is on the Front de Mer (Beachfront).

Flamants-Loisirs   CAMPGROUND €
(☑ 0661 89 22 14; www.flamants-loisirs.fr; Rte secondaire BP 24; adult/child under 10 yr Dh20/10,

campsites Dh60, vehicles Dh50-80; P ➤) Moulay Bousselham is a camping-friendly destination, and this well-run and shady campsite is an ever-popular choice. The huge on-site pool costs Dh45/35 per adult/child per day, and there's also a cafe, a small shop and bungalows on-site (Dh450 to Dh650). You'll find it on the secondary (lower) road as you enter town, overlooking (but not on) the lagoon.

Villa Nora B&B €€
(☎ 0537 43 20 71; jeanoli@yahoo.uk; Front de Mer; s/d incl breakfast Dh300/400, with sea view Dh400/500; ➤) Its grandiose claim to be a 'residential cultural centre' may have applied long ago, but time hasn't been all that kind to this B&B. Its location overlooking the beach is wonderful, but furnishings (including beds) are worn and creature comforts such as hot water can't be taken for granted. Nevertheless, it's clean and the terrace is a perfect relaxation spot.

★ Villa Bea BOUTIQUE HOTEL €€€
(☎ 0537 43 20 87; www.vilabea.com; 41 Front de Mer; s incl breakfast Dh1200-1600, d Dh1300-1800; ⊙ closed Jan; P ❄ ➤ ➤) Once ensconced in this super-stylish beachside retreat, many guests refuse to step outside for the remainder of their stay. This is perfectly understandable – the large and luxurious rooms, spacious lounge and dining area and spectacular pool terrace are the stuff of which dreams are made. Three of the seven rooms have sea views (one has a private terrace); all have excellent beds.

Multilingual owner Béatrice and her staff are efficient and friendly, the villa has private access to the beach and three-course set dinners (Dh250) are available on request.

✗ Eating & Drinking

The pickings are slim when it comes to eating options, so most visitors self-cater. Note that alcohol isn't officially available in any of the town's restaurants, shops or hotels.

Restaurant Milano MOROCCAN €
(pastas Dh30-60, sandwiches Dh30-40, tajines Dh40-60; ⊙ 11am-4pm & 6-10pm) Located on the main street close to the mosque, this bustling place is popular with tourists but locals eat elsewhere. The menu holds few surprises, with sandwiches, salads, pastas, pizzas and tajines on offer. No alcohol.

Cafe Restaurant Izaguirra SEAFOOD €€
(☎ 0537 43 24 45; Rue du Port; tajines Dh55-60, fish mains Dh50-200; ⊙ 8am-10pm) Next to the fishing boats moored in the lagoon, this clean and cheerful restaurant specialises in the daily catch and is universally acknowledged to be the best eatery in town. Head up the stairs to find the blue-and-white terrace, where friendly waiters are rushed off their feet in the summer months. No alcohol.

Cafe Restaurant Nassim CAFE
(⊙ 8am-10pm) A good choice for coffee or a quick snack (paninis Dh25 to Dh30; omelettes Dh10 to Dh30), this bustling cafe near the grand taxi rank on the main street has an outdoor terrace that is a popular local meeting place.

ℹ Getting There & Away

Moulay Bousselham is about 40km due south of Larache. To travel between the two towns by public transport you'll need to detour to the little town of Souk el-Arba (grand taxi from Larache Dh40, 45 minutes), from where there are frequent grands taxis (Dh18, 45 minutes) to Moulay Bousselham. Grands taxis between Moulay Bousselham and Kenitra charge Dh50; the trip takes 1½ hours.

A private grand taxi from Larache to Moulay Bousselham will cost Dh250; it's Dh350 to the Kenitra Medina train station, from where you can make your way to Rabat, Casablanca, Meknès or Fez.

Larache العرائش
POP 124,800
Like the other towns on this stretch of coast, Larache is laid-back for most of the year but bursts into life in summer, when Moroccan tourists flock to nearby Ras R'mel beach. Occupied by the Spanish for most of the 17th century, the town developed a local industry building ships for the corsairs operating further south. It eventually became the main port of the Spanish protectorate in 1911. Though certainly as picturesque as its northern neighbour, Asilah, Larache gets far fewer visitors and is relatively hassle-free. Come here for local flavour rather than headline sights, and don't expect a lot in terms of accommodation and eating options.

◎ Sights

The ville nouvelle has some grand Hispano-Moorish architecture dating from the colonial era, particularly around lovely Pl de la Libération (the former Plaza de España), and the heavily populated blue-and-white medina is well worth a wander. On weekends

Larache

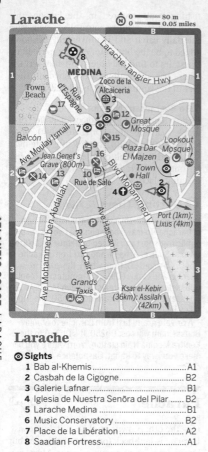

Larache

◎ Sights
1 Bab al-Khemis A1
2 Casbah de la Cigogne B2
3 Galerie Lafnar B1
4 Iglesia de Nuestra Señora del Pilar B2
5 Larache Medina B1
6 Music Conservatory B2
7 Place de la Libération A2
8 Saadian Fortress A1

⊜ Sleeping
9 Hôtel España A2
10 Hotel Hay Essalam A2
11 Hôtel Somarían A2
12 La Maison Haute B1
13 Pension Amal A2

⊗ Eating
14 Casa Ché A2
15 Restaurant Commercial B2
16 Restaurant Puerta Del Sol A2

☻ Drinking & Nightlife
17 Café Balcón Atlantico A1

---

and in the early evening, the pedestrianised *balcón* (elevated platform) overlooking the Atlantic is a popular spot for a promenade. North of the river Loukos, on the outer edge of town, sit the overgrown ruins of ancient Lixus, the legendary site of the Garden of the Hesperides.

Place de la Libération   SQUARE
(Map p190) Built by the Spanish, who named it Plaza de España, this circular plaza near Larache's old medina is the town's focal point and the place where most locals congregate to meet up with friends and relax over a coffee or tea. Surrounded by extremely handsome Hispano-Moorish buildings, most of which now house terrace cafes, it's decorated with palm trees and a fountain and is a perfect people-watching perch.

The medina can be entered through tiled **Bab al-Khemis** (p190) on its eastern side and the town's much-loved pedestrianised *balcón* (elevated platform) is one block north.

Larache Medina   AREA
(Map p190) Entered through Bab al-Khemis, a delightful Hispano-Moorish structure, Larache's blue-and-white medina has changed little over the past century. Mostly residential, it is arranged around the large colonnaded **Zoco de la Alcaiceria**, a *qissaria* (covered market) where fresh produce and household goods are sold. North of the *qissaria* is a labyrinthine arrangement of narrow lanes leading to the ruined, rubbish-filled Saadian Fortress (p190). South of the *qissaria,* up the hill, is the handsome Music Conservatory (p191) and a scenic lookout (p191).

➡ **Galerie Lafnar**   GALLERY
(Map p190; ☏ 0654 04 48 10; 58 Assadr Alaadam, Medina; ◷ 10am-1pm & 5-9pm) This art gallery stages occasional exhibitions of work by local and international artists. The building itself is an old wheat *fondouq* (rooming house) just off the Zoco de la Alcaiceria in the heart of the medina.

➡ **Saadian Fortress**   RUINS
(Map p190; Qebibat) Though this 16th-century European-style fortress is included on the Liste des Monuments et Sites Historiques Nationale du Maroc, it is disintegrating and filled with rubbish. Built on the ruins of an earlier fortress, it is perched on the edge of the medina. Nearby ramshackle tea stands overlook the port and estuary.

➡ **Music Conservatory**   NOTABLE BUILDING
(Map p190; Conservatoire de Musique de Larache) A wonderful example of Hispano-Moorish architecture, the town's crenellated music conservatory features ornately decorated

balconies and a minaret-style clock tower. It is closed to the public.

➡ **Casbah de la Cigogne** LANDMARK

(Map p190; Fortress of the Storks) Built by the Spaniards under Philip III, this now-crumbling 17th-century fortification on the path to the scenic lookout is closed to visitors.

➡ **Lookout** VIEWPOINT

(Plaza Dar El Majzen) Offering views over the port and estuary, this lookout is a popular local meeting and relaxation spot.

Iglesia de Nuestra Senõra del Pilar CHURCH

(Map p190; Blvd Mohammed V) This handsome 1920s church opposite the Hotel de Ville (Town Hall) was built by the Spanish and still hosts mass every Sunday morning.

Jean Genet's Grave LANDMARK

(Map p190) To the west of town, the old Spanish cemetery is the final resting place of French writer Jean Genet (1910–86). If the gate is locked, ring the bell for the caretaker. A small tip is expected for showing you to the grave.

Ras R'mel Beach BEACH

Larache has a small rubbish-strewn strip of sand below the town, but the best beach is across the Loukos Estuary, an 11km drive from the town centre. In summer, small boats ferry passengers across the estuary, from where the beach is a short walk across the dunes. You'll need to bargain with the boatman to get the best price and should pay around Dh10. At other times a petit taxi from the town centre will cost around Dh25.

Near the beach is a huge holiday resort, Port Lixus, with a golf course, several resort hotels, villas and a luxury marina.

🛏 Sleeping

Accommodation choices in Larache are predominantly in the budget category. Most hotels are clustered along the streets just south of Pl de la Libération.

Hotel Hay Essalam HOTEL €

(Map p190; ☑ 0539 91 68 22; 9 Ave Hassan II; s/d/tw with bathroom Dh116/133/166, without bathroom Dh90/116/140; ❄🛜) The best of Larache's budget accommodation options, this simple place run by a friendly lady offers a variety of room types; some have basic bathrooms and air-con, others are little more than unadorned cubes. Those at the front are light but noisy – light sleepers should opt for one at the rear. No English.

Hôtel España HOTEL €

(Map p190; ☑ 0539 91 31 95; www.hotelespanalarache.com; 6 Ave Hassan II; s/d/tw Dh260/300/320; 🅿❄@🛜) Housed in a handsome Hispano-Moorish building, this old-fashioned hotel is a safe and friendly accommodation choice. Rooms are clean, comfortable and well maintained, with satellite TV, a hard bed and double-glazed windows. The best are at the front, with balconies overlooking the action on Pl de la Libération.

Pension Amal HOTEL €

(Map p190; ☑ 0539 91 27 88; 10 Rue Abdallah ben Yassine; s/d without bathroom Dh50/100) Dirt cheap, this little pension off pedestrianised Ave Mohammed Ben Abdallah offers clean but spartan tiled rooms with shared facilities (hot showers are Dh12).

La Maison Haute PENSION €€

(Map p190; ☑ 0665 34 48 88; http://lamaisonhaute.free.fr; 6 Derb ben Thami, Medina; s/apt Dh350/600, d Dh450-500, tr Dh550-600, all incl breakfast) With bags of character but very little in the way of creature comforts, this Hispano-Moorish house overlooking Zoco de la Alcaiceria offers six rooms, an apartment sleeping four and a roof terrace with panoramic views over the medina and estuary. Rooms aren't as clean as one would like, and have extremely uncomfortable beds. Owner Hassan speaks English and French.

Hôtel Somarían HOTEL €€

(Map p190; ☑ 0539 91 01 16; hotelsomarian@live.fr; 68 Ave Mohammed Zerktouni; s/d/tr Dh400/500/600; @🛜) Housed in a spectacularly ugly modern hotel across the street from the covered central market, the Somarían offers gaudily decorated yet comfortable rooms, all of which have spotless bathrooms. It serves a predominantly business clientele.

🍴 Eating & Drinking

Eating out in Larache is cheap and cheerful with plenty of little places around Pl de la Libération. The Spanish influence lingers on in the paella and tortillas served in most restaurants.

Cafes with outdoor terraces surround Pl de la Libération and face the *balcón*. The town is almost entirely alcohol-free.

Casa Ché SEAFOOD €

(Map p190; ☑ 0677 83 02 00; 87 Ave Mohammed Zerktouni; mains Dh50; ⊙noon-3pm & 7-10pm Mon-Sat) This simple place near the covered central market is bedecked with portraits of

ATLANTIC COAST LARACHE

Che Guevara and serves Mediterranean, Moroccan and Basque dishes, with an emphasis on seafood.

Restaurant Commercial MOROCCAN €
(Map p190; Pl de la Libération; mains Dh40; ⊙ 11am-10pm) This basic and not particularly clean place on the main square does a roaring trade in simple soup, brochettes and fried fish. It's ultra cheap and its tables under the colonnade are great for people-watching.

Restaurant Puerta Del Sol MOROCCAN €
(Map p190; ☑ 0539 91 36 41; 5 Rue Ahmed Chaouki; sandwiches Dh20, mains Dh25-40; ⊙ noon-10pm Mon-Sat) Moroccan staples, including tajines and brochettes, join Spanish favourites such as paella and tortilla at this no-nonsense eatery close to Pl de la Libération.

Café Balcón Atlantico CAFE
(Map p190; cnr Rues de Casablanca & Tarik Ibnou Ziad; ⊙ 8am-11pm) Overlooking the *balcón*, and with Atlantic views, this bright, bustling cafe has plenty of outdoor seating and good coffee. It's the best spot in town for a relaxed breakfast or tea/coffee break.

ℹ Information

Banks with ATMs are found at the northern end of Blvd Mohammed V.

Post Office (Blvd Mohammed V; ⊙ 8am-4.15pm Mon-Fri, to 11.45am Sat)

ℹ Getting There & Away

The **bus station** (Gare Routière, Estación de Autobús; Rue Ibnou Khaldoun) is an easy walk south of Pl de la Libération, off Ave Mohammed ben Abdallah. Most major destinations are covered by CTM, including the following:
Agadir Dh310, 12½ hours, one daily
Casablanca Dh120, four hours, five daily
Fez Dh90, 4¼ hours, four daily
Marrakesh Dh200, 8¾ hours, one daily
Tangier Dh35, 1½ hours, four daily
Grands taxis (Map p190; Rue Ibnou Khaldoun) run from outside the bus station to Souk el-Arba (Dh40), Tangier (Dh35) and Kenitra (Dh50). Those heading to Asilah (Dh20) usually leave from outside the municipal produce market on Ave Malek Ben Marhal.
Petit taxis charge Dh20 to Lixus and Dh25 to Ras R'mel Beach.

Lixus ليكسوس

Set on a hill overlooking the Loukos Estuary, the Carthaginian and Roman ruins of Lixus

are evocative reminders that settlements on this coast are among the oldest in the country.

Few visitors make it here outside the summer months, and in winter your only companions will be the wind and the odd goat quietly grazing. A new visitor centre has been under construction near the site entrance for many years now, and locals have no confidence that it will open in the immediate future. In the meantime, there's no entrance fee. Tips to the site guardian are appreciated.

There is no food available on-site, so pack a picnic before heading off from Larache.

History

Megalithic stones found in the vicinity of Lixus suggest that the site was originally inhabited by a sun-worshipping people with knowledge of astronomy and mathematics. However, little more is known about the area's prehistory until the Phoenicians set up the colony Liks here in about 1000 BC. According to Pliny the Elder, it was here that Hercules picked the golden apples of the Garden of the Hesperides, thus completing the penultimate of his 12 labours. The golden apples may well have been Moroccan tangerines.

In the 6th century BC the Phoenician Atlantic colonies fell to the Carthaginians. Lixus remained a trading post, principally in gold, ivory and slaves and, by AD 42, had entered the Roman Empire. Its primary exports soon changed to salt, olives, wine and *garum* (an aromatic fish paste) and its merchants also grew rich from the export of wild animals for use in the empire's amphitheatres.

The colony at Lixus rapidly declined as the Romans withdrew from North Africa, and was abandoned completely in the 5th century, after the collapse of the Roman Empire. Later, the site became known to Muslims as Tuchummus.

◉ Sights

Lixus Ruins ARCHAEOLOGICAL SITE
(Larache-Tangier Hwy/N1) **FREE** The main gate to Lixus is just off the highway, off the road running in front of the estuary. Only about a quarter of the ancient city has been excavated, but the visible ruins, though badly damaged and overgrown, hint at how grand and important this city once was, and are worth a visit.

If there is more than one site guardian on duty, one is usually happy to lead visitors through the site for a small tip.

Immediately inside the gate is the lower town, with the remains of garum factories where fish was salted and the paste so beloved by the Romans was produced. A track leads up the hill to the acropolis, passing a steep amphitheatre built by the Romans along the way. Baths were originally built into the side of the amphitheatre, with some traces of mosaic flooring. Some mosaics from the site were removed and are now on display at the archaeology museum in Tetouan. Others are said to have been destroyed when the son of a former guardian of the site tried to dig them up so as to sell them on antiquities black market.

Continue up the path to the overgrown acropolis, which straddles the crest of the hill. From here there are lovely views down over the Loukos Estuary and salt fields below. The civic buildings (including temple sanctuaries) and original city ramparts are here, as are traces of pre-Roman structures.

ⓘ Getting There & Away

Lixus is approximately 5.5km north of Pl de la Libération in Larache, on the road to Tangier. A petit taxi costs Dh20 one way, but you may have trouble flagging down a bus or taxi on the highway for your return trip; it's best to organise for the taxi driver to pick you up at an agreed time.

Asilah أصيلة

POP 31,054

The tortilla, paella and rioja (Spanish wine) served in most of Asilah's restaurants are reminders that this compact town was Spanish territory for a long time. Today, it's an easy introduction to Morocco, offering a good selection of budget and midrange accommodation and an extremely pretty medina to explore. There are also plenty of clean swimming and surf beaches close by.

The town is sleepy for most of the year, but in the summer months its population triples and the streets and town beach are crammed with sun-seeking Moroccan and Spanish families, some of whom retain holiday houses here. The best time to visit is in spring or autumn when the weather is still pleasant but the holiday hordes have left.

History

This small but strategic port has had a turbulent history ever since it began life as the Carthaginian settlement of Zilis. During the Punic Wars the people backed Carthage, and when the region fell to the Romans, the locals were shipped to Spain and replaced with Iberians. From then on, Asilah was inexorably linked with the Spanish and with their numerous battles for territory.

As Christianity conquered the forces of Islam on the Iberian Peninsula in the 14th and 15th centuries, Asilah felt the knock-on effects. In 1471 the Portuguese sent 477 ships with 30,000 men, captured the port and built the walls that still surround the medina, a trading post on their famous gold route across Africa. In 1578 King Dom Sebastian of Portugal embarked on an ill-fated crusade from Asilah. He was killed, and Portugal (and its Moroccan possessions) passed into the hands of the Spanish, who remained for a very long time.

Asilah was recaptured by Moulay Ismail in 1691. In the 19th century, continuing piracy prompted Austria and then Spain to send their navies to bombard the town. Its most famous renegade was Er-Raissouli (p196), one of the most colourful bandits ever raised in the wild Rif Mountains. Early in the 20th century, Er-Raissouli used Asilah as his base, becoming the bane of the European powers. Spain made Asilah part of its protectorate from 1911 until 1956.

◎ Sights

Asilah has long had a reputation as a city of the arts. It all started in 1978 when several Moroccan artists were invited to hold workshops for local children and to paint some walls in the medina as part of the town's *moussem* (saint's day celebrations). Sadly, there's not much of artistic note happening here these days.

Asilah's main beach stretches north from town. It's a wide sweep of golden sand, but the ugly and noisy cafes along its length and the ever-present mounds of rubbish on the sand make it less than appealing. **Paradise Beach** at Rmilate, 7km south of town, is a much better choice for swimmers. **Sidi Mghayet**, approximately 13km further south, is a popular surf beach and nearby **Rada Beach** has a popular beach cafe.

Asilah Medina AREA
(Map p194) Asilah's largely residential medina is surrounded by sturdy stone fortifications built by the Portuguese in the 15th century. Within the walls are tranquil narrow streets lined by white houses with blue or green decorative touches; many of these have been purchased and painstakingly restored by foreigners. Although this restoration work has left the medina much sanitised, its winding

Asilah

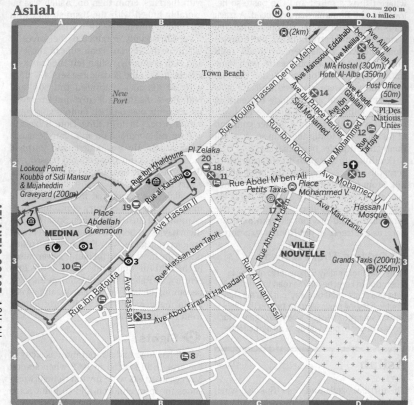

Town Beach

New Port

ATLANTIC COAST ASILAH

lanes, jalousies (wooden, trellis-like window shutters) and colourful murals – painted each year during the Asilah Festival (p195) – make it very photogenic.

Access to the ramparts is limited. The southwestern bastion is the best spot for views over the ocean and is a popular spot at sunset. It also offers a peek into the nearby **Koubba of Sidi Mansur** (which is otherwise closed to non-Muslims) and the **Mujaheddin Graveyard**.

The southern entrance to the medina, **Bab Homar** (Ave Hassan II), is topped by the much-eroded Portuguese royal coat of arms. The main entrance, **Bab al-Kasaba**, leads to the **Great Mosque** (Medina), which is closed to non-Muslims. The medina is busiest on Thursdays, Asilah's main market day.

Palais de Raissouli HISTORIC BUILDING
(Map p194; Palais de Culture; Medina) This palace was built in 1909 by Er-Raissouli the

pirate (p196) and stands as a testament to the sumptuous life he led at the height of his power. Beautifully restored, it is usually only open during the Asilah Festival (p195). The building includes a main reception room with a glass-fronted terrace overlooking the sea, from where Er-Raissouli forced convicted murderers to jump to their deaths onto the rocks 30m below.

**Centre de Hassan II
Rencontres Internationales** GALLERY
(Map p194; ☎ 0539 41 70 65; http://c-assilah.com; ☺8.30am-12.30pm & 2.30-5pm, to 8pm summer) **FREE** Located in a handsome house just inside the main entrance to the medina, this exhibition space hosts revolving exhibitions of international painting and sculpture in its gallery, and acts as the hub of the annual Asilah Festival (p195).

Asilah

◉ Sights

1	Asilah Medina	A3
2	Bab al-Kasaba	B2
3	Bab Homar	B3
4	Centre de Hassan II Rencontres Internationales	B2
5	Church of San Bartolome	D2
6	Great Mosque	A3
7	Palais de Raissouli	A3

⊜ Sleeping

8	Christina's House	B4
9	Dar Azaouia	A3
10	Dar Manara	A3
11	Hotel Patio de la Luna	C2
12	Hôtel Sahara	D2

✖ Eating

13	Ali Baba	B4
14	Casa García	D1
15	Central Market	D2
16	La Perle d'Asilah	D1
17	Restaurant Dar Al Maghrebia	C2
18	Restaurante Oceano Casa Pepe	C2

◉ Drinking & Nightlife

19	Al-Madina	B2
20	La Symphonie II des Douceurs	B2

Church of San Bartolome
CHURCH

(Map p194; cnr Aves du Prince Héritier & Mohammed V) Built in 1925 by Spanish Franciscans in a typical Hispano-Moorish style, this is one of the few churches in Morocco allowed to ring the bells for Sunday Mass.

✦ Festivals & Events

Asilah Festival
CULTURAL

(www.c-assilah.com; ⊘ Jul) The Centre de Hassan II Rencontres Internationales (p195) is the main focus for this annual festival, when artists, musicians, performers and spectators descend upon the town. Events include workshops, public art demonstrations, concerts and exhibitions.

🛏 Sleeping

During high season (Easter week and July to September) the town is flooded with visitors so it's advisable to book well in advance.

★ MIA Hostel
HOSTEL €

(☑ 0539 41 78 94; www.mia-hostels.com; 55 Lot Minza; dm Dh120-160, d/tw Dh580/640, all incl breakfast; @ 🛜) It takes its name from owners Mehdi, Ismael and Ali, and this excellent hostel does them all proud. Dorms and rooms have comfortable beds, there's plenty of hot water in the bathrooms, and facilities include a TV lounge, a book exchange, bike and surfboard rental, a communal kitchen and a rooftop terrace where summer BBQs are held (Dh50 to Dh100). Most rooms have air-con.

Hôtel Sahara
HOTEL €

(Map p194; ☑ 0539 41 71 85; 9 Rue Tarfaya; s/d without bathroom Dh90/150; 🛜) A good cheapie, this small hotel offers rooms set around an open courtyard. Patterned tiles and potted plants adorn the entrance, and the simple rooms are well maintained (though some have tiny

windows and are reminiscent of prison cells). The sparkling shared toilets and hot showers (Dh5) are well-kept. No English.

Christina's House
GUESTHOUSE €€

(Map p194; ☑ 0610 50 20 26; www.christinash ouseasilah.com; 26 Rue Ibn Khatib, off Blvd 16 Nov; s/d/tr incl breakfast Dh380/490/540; 🛜) A friendly guesthouse that feels more like a home than a hotel, this place is run by Spanish-born Sally and offers freshly painted rooms with tiled floors and simple bathrooms. There's a comfortable lounge, communal kitchen and huge rooftop terrace with plenty of seating. Meals are available on request.

Dar Manara
BOUTIQUE HOTEL €€

(Map p194; ☑ 0539 41 69 64; www.asilah-darmanara. com; 23 Rue M'Jimma, Medina; d & tw incl breakfast Dh700; ❄🛜) One of only a few accommodation options in the medina, this Spanish-owned riad has been elegantly restored and converted into an intimate hotel. Rooms are small but attractively presented, and common areas include an elegant salon with an open fireplace and an alluring roof terrace with traditional Moroccan seating. Our only caveat is that staff can be unfriendly.

Hotel Patio de la Luna
HOTEL €€

(Map p194; ☑ 0539 41 60 74; hotelpatiodelaluna@ gmail.com; 12 Pl Zellaka; s/tr Dh300/500, d Dh400-450; 🛜) Spanish-run, this small place near Bab al-Kasaba has seven rooms with minimalist decor, a shady rear courtyard and a windy roof terrace. The nicest rooms are on the 1st floor or the terrace at the front of the building, but these may be blighted by street noise in high summer. Cash only.

★ Dar Azaouia
BOUTIQUE HOTEL €€€

(Map p194; ☑ 0672 11 05 35; www.darazaouia-asilah.com; 16 Rue Moulay Driss N 6, near Bab

RASCALLY ER-RAISSOULI

Bandit, kidnapper and general troublemaker, Moulay Ahmed ben Mohammed er-Raissouli (or Raisuni) was one of Asilah's most legendary inhabitants. He started life as a petty crook in the Rif Mountains and saw no problem in bumping off unwilling victims, leading to him becoming renowned as a merciless murderer and feared right across the region.

Internationally, Er-Raissouli was best known for kidnapping Westerners. He and his band held various luminaries to ransom, including Greek-American billionaire Ion Perdicaris, who was ransomed in 1904 for US$70,000.

In an attempt to control the unruly outlaw, consecutive sultans appointed him to various political positions, including governor of Asilah and later Tangier. However, Er-Raissouli continued with his wicked ways, amassing great wealth in whatever way he could. He held considerable sway over the Rif tribes and the Spanish funded his arms in the hope of keeping order in the mountains, but Er-Raissouli often used them against his benefactors.

The Spaniards eventually forced Er-Raissouli to flee Asilah after WWI, but he continued to wreak havoc in the Rif hinterland until January 1925, when the Rif rebel Abd al-Krim arrested him and accused him of being too closely linked with the Spanish. Er-Raissouli died from natural causes two months later.

Homar; s/d/tr incl breakfast Dh800/850/950; (P)(⊙) Belgian owned and operated, this small, beautiful guesthouse comfortably blends Moroccan tradition with contemporary European style. Local textiles and objets d'art are scattered throughout the building and there are good beds, quality toiletries, a welcoming lounge and dining room and a small roof terrace. Dinner is available on request (Dh270) and alcohol is served. Prebooking is essential.

Hotel Al-Alba BOUTIQUE HOTEL €€€
(☏0613 42 91 90; www.hotelalalba.com; 35 Lot Nahil; s/d/ste incl breakfast Dh780/900/1020; (✳)(⊙)) Tucked behind Restaurant Annakhil on the edge of the town centre, this small and very comfortable hotel is decorated in blue and white as a homage to the medina. The young, multilingual staff go out of their way to be helpful (we love the complimentary mint tea) and the in-house hammam is a real draw (treatments Dh275 to Dh380, nonguests welcome).

There's an inhouse restaurant (three-course set menu Dh140), but the food is disappointing and no alcohol is available.

 Eating

The quality of restaurants here is generally low and prices high, so eating out isn't a highlight. There's a string of slightly grotty juice bars, cafes and fast food restaurants along the medina walls on Ave Hassan II. These fast-food joints serve carbon-copy menus of pizza (Dh30 to Dh55) and tajines (Dh40 to Dh50). All have street seating.

There are a few other cheap options around the central market (p197).

★**Restaurant Dar Al Maghrebia** MOROCCAN €
(Map p194; ☏0633 66 23 77; 7 Rue Al Banafsaje; mains Dh45-60; ⊙noon-3pm & 7-10pm) Deserving kudos for its bargain prices, tasty dishes and atmospheric surrounds, this small restaurant off Pl Mohammed V offers a selection of tajines, *pastillas*, brochettes, *briouats* and couscous dishes; all arrive in relatively small serves. Dine in the charming dining salon or at one of three streetside tables. No alcohol, but fruit cocktails are available (Dh30).

Ali Baba MOROCCAN €
(Map p194; ☏0633 58 00 50; www.restaurantalibaba.com; cnr Aves Abou Ferras El Hamadani & Hassan II; dishes Dh20-50; ⊙noon-1am) Extremely popular with local residents and workers, this impeccably clean place serves fresh and tasty *harira* (lentil soup), tajines, *shwarma* (meat sliced off a spit and stuffed in a pocket of pita-type bread), pizza and sandwiches. Eat in or take away.

Central Market MARKET €
(Map p194; Marché Central; Ave Mohamed VI; ⊙8am-8pm) Asilah's small central market is a good place to source fresh fruit, vegetables, meat, fish and spices. The restaurants in its front arcade serve excellent fresh fish at bargain prices.

Casa García SPANISH €€
(Map p194; ☑0539 41 74 65; 51 Rue Moulay Has-san ben el-Mehdi; mains Dh50-125; ⊙noon-3pm & 7-11pm) Spanish-style fish dishes are the speciality at this friendly restaurant a couple of streets back from the beach. The food is acceptable rather than inspired (the chef has an extremely heavy hand with garlic), but the breezy terrace is a pleasant spot on which to while away an evening with a bottle of wine.

Restaurante Oceano
Casa Pepe SEAFOOD €€
(Map p194; ☑0539 41 73 95; 8 Pl Zellaka; mains Dh60-350; ⊙noon-midnight) The surrounds are pleasant enough, but the food lacks flavour, freshness and finesse. Its location right in front of the main entrance to the medina is convenient, but if you choose to dine here we suggest that you stick to simple fried fish. Fortunately, it's licensed.

La Perle d'Asilah FRENCH €€€
(Map p194; ☑0618 55 69 80; cnr Rue Allal ben Ab-dallah & Ave Melilla; mains Dh120-250, 2-3-course menus Dh160/190; ⊙noon-3pm & 7-10.30pm) Generally accepted as Asilah's most impres-sive eating option, La Perle's menu leans heavily on the Gallic, with a handful of Spanish and Asian options thrown into the mix. Surrounds are classy, and the set two- and three-course menus are excellent value.

🍷 Drinking & Nightlife

Most drinking in town occurs in the Spanish restaurants, and there are no bars or clubs worthy of recommendation. Cafes are found on nearly every street corner in the blocks around Pl Mohammed V, but most have solely male clienteles.

La Symphonie II des Douceurs CAFE
(Map p194; 26 Pl Zellaka) A good place for a coffee or mint tea, with street-side tables overlooking Bab al-Kasaba. The waiters don't mind if you linger over your drinks, which is fortunate as there's plenty of people-watching potential.

Al-Madina CAFE
(Pl Abdellah Guennoun) The main attraction of this simple little cafe in the medina is its sunny seating area in the square in front of El-Khamra Tower. It's a great place to watch the world go by.

ℹ Information

There are plenty of banks with ATMs on Pl Mo-hammed V and along Ave 16 Novembre, south of Bab Homar.

Internet Alahram (Rue Al Banafsaje; per hr Dh5; ⊙10am-1am) Internet access, scanning and printing.

Police Station (Ave Mohammed V)

Post Office (Ave Khalid Ibn Al Ouaud/Tangier-Rabat Rd; ⊙8am-4.15pm Mon-Fri, to 11.45am Sat)

ℹ Getting There & Away

BUS

The **bus station** (Gare Routiere) is opposite the Shell petrol station on the Tangier–Rabat road, but few intercity buses stop here. The only useful and regular services are on local company Alsa to Tangier (Dh7) and on Supratour to Tetouan (DH35, 2¼ hours)

TAXI

Grands taxis to Tangier (Dh20) and Larache (Dh20) depart when full from a stand near the Shell petrol station on the Tangier–Rabat road. A taxi to Tangier's airport (only 26km from Asilah) costs Dh250.

TRAIN

The train station is 3km north of Asilah, (Dh10 in a petit taxi). Destinations include the following:

Fez 1st/2nd class Dh136/92, four hours, four daily

Marrakesh 1st/2nd class Dh196/301, 9½ hours. One overnight train goes direct to Marrakesh, but this train originates in Tangier, so buy your ticket in advance.

Rabat 1st/2nd class Dh130/88, three hours, eight daily

Tangier 1st/2nd class Dh27/16, 50 minutes, 12 daily

El Jadida الجديدة

POP 193.935

In July and August, this town transforms into a heaving holiday resort popular with Moroccan families. The only compelling rea-son for travellers to head here is to visit the Unesco-listed 16th-century Cité Portugaise, and this is something that can easily be done in an hour or two en route between Casa-blanca and towns further down the coast.

Just north of the town, on a gorgeous stretch of beach, is the recently opened tour-ist resort of **Mazagan**, which includes a golf course, casino, spa and large resort hotel.

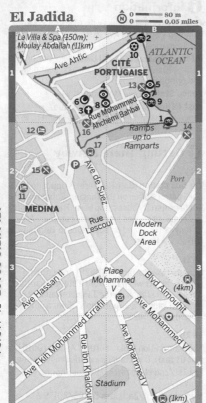

El Jadida

◎ **Sights**
1 Bastion de L'Ange B1
2 Bastion de St Sébastian B1
3 Church of the Assumption A1
4 Cité Portugaise A1
5 Communal Bakery B1
6 Grand Mosque A1
7 Porte de la Mer B1
8 Portuguese Cistern A1
9 Ramparts B1
10 Synagogue B1

◎ **Sleeping**
11 Hôtel Bordeaux A2
12 Riad Le Mazagao A2

◎ **Eating**
13 Café do Mar B1
14 Restaurant du Port B2
15 Restaurant Tchikito A2
16 Restaurante La Portugaise A2

◎ **Transport**
17 Local Bus 2 to Sidi Bouzid A2

History

The *cité* (fortress) was built by the Portuguese in 1506 to protect their ships heading down the West African coast. They baptised it Mazagan, and it soon developed into the country's most important trading post. Sultan Sidi Mohammed ben Abdallah seized Mazagan from the Portuguese following a siege in 1769, but the Portuguese blew up most of the fort before leaving. Most of the new settlers preferred to live in the new town and the citadel remained a ruin until the early 19th century when Sultan Abd er-Rahman resettled some of the Jews of Azemmour in old Mazagan and renamed the town El Jadida, 'the New One' in Arabic.

The large and influential Jewish community soon grew rich on trade with the interior. Unlike most other Moroccan cities, in El Jadida there was no *mellah*; the Jews mixed with the general populace and an attitude of easy

tolerance was established. During the French protectorate the town became an administrative centre and a beach resort, but its port gradually lost out to Safi and Casablanca.

◎ Sights

The beaches within and to the immediate north and south of town are packed in July and August, despite being quite filthy. **Sidi Bouzid**, 5km southwest of town, is a bit cleaner and as such is popular with both sunbathers and surfers. To get here, take local bus 2 (Dh5) from Pl Mohammed Ben Abdallah.

Cité Portugaise   HISTORIC SITE
(Map p198; Portuguese City) **FREE** Inscribed on Unesco's World Heritage list in 2004, the Cité Portugaise was one of the early settlements built by the Portuguese in West Africa. Dating from the early 16th century and originally called Mazagan, it is a fine example of Renaissance military design. Hefty, ochre-coloured ramparts in a loose star shape protect a compact maze of streets, the architecturally notable **Church of the Assumption** – now converted into a hotel – and an atmospheric cistern (p199).

The main entrance of the cité is just off Pl Mohammed ben Abdallah and leads into Rue Mohammed Ahchemi Bahbai. Immediately on the left is the former church and almost next door is the **Grand Mosque**

MONOLITHS OF M'SOURA

The mysterious Monoliths of M'Soura make an interesting half-day trip from Asilah. This prehistoric site consists of a large stone circle (actually an ellipse) of about 175 stones, thought to have originally surrounded a burial mound. Although many of the stones have fallen or been broken, the circle is still impressive, its strange presence heightened by the desolation of its location. The tallest stone reaches about 5.5m in height and is known as El-Uted (The Pointer).

The stone circle is about 25km (by road) southeast of Asilah. To get there you'll need a sturdy vehicle. Head for the village of Souq Tnine de Sidi el-Yamani, off highway R417, which branches east off the main Tangier–Rabat road. Veer left in the village and follow a poorly maintained, unsealed track 6km north to the site. It can be difficult to find so you may want to ask for directions or hire a guide in the village. Another interesting trip from Asilah is a visit to the lively Sunday market in the village of **Had Gharbia**, 16km north of town off the road to Tangier.

(Grande Mosquée; Cité Portugaise), with its unique pentagonal-shaped minaret.

Further down Rue Mohammed Ahchemi Bahbai is the **Porte de la Mer** (⏰10am-5pm), the original sea gate where ships unloaded their cargo and from where the Portuguese finally departed. To the left of the gate, through the archway, is a **communal bakery** where local women still bring their bread to be baked.

To the right of the sea gate, a ramp leads up to the **ramparts** (⏰9am-5pm) FREE and, in the southeast corner, the **Bastion de L'Ange** FREE, an excellent vantage point with views out to sea and over the new town and port. Walk along the ramparts to the left to reach the **Bastion de St Sebastian** FREE, in the northeast corner, from where you can look down on the ruined **synagogue**.

➡ **Portuguese Cistern** NOTABLE BUILDING
(Map p198; Citerne Portugaise; Rue Mohammed Ahchemi Bahbai; adult/child under 12yr Dh10/3; ⏰9am-1pm & 3-6pm) On the main street of the cité, amid the souvenir shops, is this atmospheric vaulted cistern lit by a single shaft of light. Built in the early 16th century, it is famous as the eerie location for the dramatic riot scene in Orson Welles' 1951 film *Othello*.

🎊 Festivals & Events

Festival International Jawhara CULTURAL
(☎0523 35 52 21; www.festivaljawhara.ma; ⏰Aug) Staged in the towns of El Jadida, Azemmour and Bir Jdid, this cultural festival includes sport, theatre and visual arts, but it concentrates on music, staging performances by big-name Moroccan and African artists.

🛌 Sleeping

Hôtel Bordeaux HOTEL €
(Map p198; ☎0523 37 39 21; 47 Rue Moulay Ahmed Tahiri; s/d Dh180/230, without bathroom Dh100/160,; ❄) The best of the cheapies, this basic hotel in a traditional (but characterless) house in the medina offers clean and well-maintained rooms with cramped bathrooms and wheezing air-conditioning units. No credit cards and no English spoken.

Riad Le Mazagao GUESTHOUSE €€
(Map p198; ☎0523 35 01 37; www.lemazagao. com; 6 Derb el-Hajjar; s/d with shared bathroom Dh330/440, d/f with private bathroom Dh440/765, all incl breakfast; ❄) This welcoming and highly atmospheric 19th-century guesthouse located above an arched entrance to the medina offers four large rooms decorated in a warm Moroccan style, with lots of textiles and original tiling. Two rooms have en suites and air-con; two share a bathroom and have no cooling. Breakfast is served on the lovely roof terrace and dinner can be arranged (Dh160).

⭐ **Dar Al Manar** B&B €€€
(☎0523 35 16 45; www.dar-al-manar.com; r incl breakfast Dh800-1000; ❄@) Five stylish and spacious rooms, decorated in a contemporary Moroccan style, await at this tranquil retreat near the Sidi M'sbah lighthouse 7km from El Jadida. Guests enjoy relaxing in the lovely garden or downstairs lounge, and can dine on the terrace (set meals Dh200 to Dh250). The English- and French-speaking owner is both charming and helpful.

La Villa & Spa HOTEL €€€
(☎0523 34 44 23; www.lavilladavid.com; 4 Ave Moulay Abdelhafid; r incl breakfast Dh860-1160,

BUS SERVICES FROM EL JADIDA

TO	COMPANY	FARE (DH)	TIME (HR)	FREQUENCY
Casablanca	CTM	45	2hr	4 daily
Essaouira	CTM	110	4½	1 daily
Marrakesh	STCR	55	4	hourly
Rabat	STCR	50	4	12 daily
Safi	CTM	60	2½	6 daily

ste Dh1380; ❋ 🛜 🌊) A French-owned hotel just north of the *cité*, La Villa has sleek modern rooms with good beds, excellent bathrooms and satellite TV. There is a rooftop bar and dining area (dinner Dh300), the top terrace has a hot tub (Dh80 per hour) and massages are available in a dedicated downstairs room (Dh350 per hour). Manager Oussama is a gem.

✗ Eating & Drinking

El Jadida lacks decent restaurants and cafes. For a relatively cheap eat, pull up a seat at one of the popular fried-fish restaurants on Ave de Suez, opposite the port. These all serve fried fish, salad and bread for around DH70

There are a number of sleazy bars around town, and these are resolutely off-limits to women. In summer, some of the licensed fish restaurants opposite the town beach and Sidi Bouzid morph into clubs after their dinner service and welcome a mixed crowd.

Café do Mar   CAFE €
(Map p198; Rue Mohammed Ahchemi Bahbai, Cité Portugaise; galettes Dh30-70, crêpes Dh20-35; ◷11am-7pm) Opposite the sea gate, this stylish cafe has indoor and roof-terrace seating with views over the ramparts, and is an excellent spot for a tea, coffee or light snack such as a *galette* (savoury pancake) or crêpe. There are also fresh juices, smoothies and ice cream on offer.

Restaurante La Portugaise   MOROCCAN €
(Map p198; Rue Mohammed Ahchemi Bahbai; mains Dh48; ◷noon-3pm & 7-11pm) Just inside the walls of the old city, this tourist-focused place with red-checked tablecloths offers a simple menu of Moroccan staples. No alcohol.

Restaurant Tchikito   SEAFOOD €
(Map p198; 4 Rue Mohammed Smiha; mixed fish platters Dh50; ◷11am-4pm Mon-Sat) This hole-in-the-wall is popular for its delicious and cheap fried fish served with a fiery chilli sauce.

Le Requin Blue   SEAFOOD €€
(☑0523 34 80 67; www.requinbleu.com; mains Dh85-135; ◷noon-3pm & 7-11pm) Overlooking the beach in Sidi Bouzid (5km southwest of El Jadida), Le Requin Blue serves excellent fish. In summer, it morphs into a nightclub after the dinner service.

Restaurant du Port   SEAFOOD €€
(Map p198; ☑0523 34 25 79; Port du Jadida; mains Dh90-130; ◷noon-3pm daily, 7-10pm Mon-Sat) Head into the port and up the stairs to find this restaurant, which very naturally focuses on fish and seafood. It's one of the few restaurants in town serving alcohol, and the small bar in the main dining space attracts some rather raddled types. Not great for solo women diners.

ℹ Information

There are numerous banks with ATMs located in the streets around Pl Mohammed V.

Main Post Office (Pl Mohammed V; ◷8.30am-4.30pm Mon-Fri)

Police Station (Ave Mohammed VI)

ℹ Getting There & Away

Bus The **bus station** (Ave Mohammed V) is a 10-minute walk from the medina and *cité*.

Taxi Grands taxis for Azemmour (Dh10, 15 minutes) and Casablanca (Dh35, one hour) leave from Ave Mohammed V, next to the bus station.

Train El Jadida train station is located 4km south of town. There are eight services a day to and from Casablanca's Casa Voyagers station (1st/2nd class Dh53/37, 80 minutes). A petit taxi to the centre will cost Dh15 to Dh20.

Local bus 2 for Sidi Bouzid (Dh4) leaves from Pl Mohammed Ben Abdallah, near the *cité*.

Azemmour   أزمور
POP 40,865

Azemmour has inspired many Moroccan artists over the decades, some of whom have chosen to live here. Although it is close to the cosmopolitan art market of Casablanca, in Azemmour life is still traditional and the surroundings provide plenty of artistic inspiration courtesy of a crumbling 16th-century medina squeezed between the Oud Er-Rbia (Mother of Spring River) and the ocean, with fields spread between.

The Portuguese built the town in 1513 as one of a string of trading posts along the coast. The town's most famous inhabitant was Estevanico the Black. Captured and made a slave, he later became one of the first four explorers to cross the entire mainland of North America from Florida to the Pacific.

◉ Sights

Azemmour Medina AREA
An ochre-walled warren of narrow winding streets, whitewashed houses and hole-in-the-wall shops, Azemmour's medina has yet to undergo the restoration that has enlivened (or should that be afflicted?) other Moroccan medinas. Built next to the banks of the Er-Rbia in the 16th century, it retains traces of its Portuguese heritage – especially ornate doorways. Residents have long been associated with arts and handicrafts – you'll see artisans weaving colourful textiles on old-fashioned looms and stroll past massive murals adorning crumbling walls.

A wander around the media offers an authentic glimpse of life in modern working-class Morocco. Enter through the large gate with its unusual semicircle-shaped arch; the ramparts can be accessed from here. Walk along the walls to see Dar el Baroud (the Powder House), a Portuguese gunpowder store of which only the tower remains. To the north of the medina is the *mellah* with a still-standing synagogue painted in blue and white. Further on, you'll get wonderful views over the river.

🛏 Sleeping & Eating

There are terrace cafes on the bank of the Oud Er-Rbia beneath the medina.

Dar Nadia B&B €
(📞 0661 31 62 42; 3 Rue Souika El Malah, Medina; r incl breakfast Dh370; 🛜) A traditional, lovingly restored *dar* (small house) in the centre of the medina, Nadia's house has a peaceful central courtyard and attractively decorated rooms with private bathrooms.

★ L'Oum Errebia BOUTIQUE HOTEL €€€
(📞 0523 34 70 71; www.azemmour-hotel.com; 25 Impasse Chtouka, Medina; s/d/f incl breakfast Dh600/800/1600, s/d with river view Dh900/1200; 🛜⚑) A showcase of local art, antiques and

artisanship, this French-owned B&B overlooking the river blends traditional Moroccan style with chic contemporary design. Each of the nine rooms feature lavishly tiled sunken showers and traditional *tadelakt* (plaster) floors and walls; two have river views. Relaxation areas include a lounge with an open fireplace, a rooftop terrace and a small swimming pool.

Communal meals (Dh250) are served at the big dining-room table. The in-house hammam offers *gommage* for Dh200 and massage for Dh250 per hour.

ⓘ Information

There are a couple of banks with ATMs on Ave Allal Ben Abdallah, the main street.

ⓘ Getting There & Away

The town is located between the Casablanca–El Jadida highway (N1) and the coastal road.

Trains now stop nine times daily at Azemmour Halte, 2km from the town centre. These link the town to El Jadida (1st/2nd class Dh27/16,17 minutes) and Casablanca (1st/2nd class Dh46/33, 80 minutes).

The town is also linked to El Jadida by grand taxi (Dh10) and bus (Dh4).

Oualidia الوالدية

The delightful resort town of Oualidia (Walidiya) spreads around a gorgeous crescent-shaped lagoon fringed with golden sands and protected from the wild surf by a rocky breakwater. With a good selection of accommodation and great fish restaurants (the town is particularly famous for its oysters), it's a popular weekend and summer retreat for Marrakshis and Casablancais, and a perfect destination for those needing a break after spending time fending off *faux guides* in the Marrakesh medina.

Out of season it is quiet, with little more to do than relax, surf and gorge on shellfish. In spring and autumn, birdwatchers arrive to observe migrating pink flamingos, avocets, stilts, godwits, storks, waders, terns, egrets and warblers on the lagoon and surrounding coastal wetlands.

Most hotels and restaurants are off the highway on the approach to town or down near the beach, 1km from the roundabout on Ave Hassan II in the upper town. You'll find a bank, a post office and grocery stores on Ave Hassan II.

BIRDWATCHING ON THE ATLANTIC COAST

The Atlantic Coast attracts hundreds of species of migrating birds and is known to aficionados the word over as prime birdwatching territory. The wild and blustery coastline is dotted with marshlands, salt pans and lagoons that offer birds shelter and abundant sustenance on their migrations between Europe and Africa in spring and autumn (fall).

Merja Zerga National Park (p188), near Moulay Bousselham, north of Rabat, is known for its birdlife, as are the lagoons in Oualidia (p201) and **Sidi Moussa**, south of Casablanca. Regularly spotted species include herons, flamingos, ibises, the African marsh owl, spoonbills, plovers, egrets, slender-billed and Audouin's gulls, shelducks, teals, terns, marsh harriers, avocets, stilts, godwits, storks and peregrine falcons. Shearwaters are often seen on the ocean reefs.

⊙ Sights & Activities

The town is named after the Saadian Sultan el-Oualid, who built the kasbah now atmospherically crumbling on the bluff overlooking the lagoon in 1634. The lagoon also attracted Morocco's royalty, and the grand villa on the water's edge was Mohammed V's summer palace. It is rarely if ever used these days.

The safe, calm waters of the lagoon are perfect for **swimming**, **sailing** and **fishing**, while the wide, sandy beach on either side of the breakwater is good for **windsurfing** and **surfing**.

On Saturdays, there's a traditional market when people from surrounding villages come to town to sell their wares.

Dream Surf Oualidia　　　WATER SPORTS
(☑0661 81 78 17; www.dreamsurfoualidia.com; Oualidia Plage; ⊙Apr–mid-Nov) Hire a surfboard (Dh200), bodyboard (Dh150), kiteboard (Dh700) or paddleboard (Dh300) for two hours. Also available are kayaks, quads and scooters.

🛌 Sleeping

There are plenty of accommodation options near the beach, and a few in the upper town. Properties with water frontage are under-

standably popular and should be booked well in advance, especially in high summer.

Hotel Restaurant Thalassa　　　HOTEL €
(r Dh150-200) Near the roundabout on the main street in the upper town, this no-frills place is cheap but doesn't have much else in its favour. Rooms are relatively clean; those at the front are noisy.

Dar Beldi　　　B&B €€
(☑0523 36 62 88; www.darbeldi.free.fr; Douar Moulay Abdessalam; s/d incl breakfast Dh650/750; ❋ ☎) The main-street entrance of this hidden B&B, surrounded by car mechanic workshops, is neither easy to find nor encouraging. Persistence pays off, though, because behind the high walls is a lush garden surrounded by five clean and thoughtfully decorated guest rooms. French owners Pierre-Yves and Guy are ebullient and helpful hosts, happy to arrange transport and activities.

Hôtel-Restaurant L'Initiale　　　B&B €€
(☑0523 36 62 46; initialhotel@gmail.com; Oualidia Plage; s/d/tr incl breakfast Dh450/500/600; ❋ ☎) Predominantly a tourist restaurant (pizzas Dh55 to Dh60, pastas Dh60 to Dh140), this modern hotel next to the *plage* has a warm orange interior and six comfortable rooms with tiny balconies. Restaurant noise can be a problem.

★ La Sultana　　　HOTEL €€€
(☑0524 38 80 08; www.lasultanahotels.com/oualidia; Parc à Huîtres No 3; r Dh4400-9100; ⊙closed Jan; P ♿ ❋ @ ☎ ≋ ❋) Each of the 11 spacious suites at this luxurious spa hotel has a private Jacuzzi and terrace overlooking the lagoon, but guests spend most of their waking hours lazing by the spectacular infinity pool, being pampered in the luxurious spa, feasting on seafood at the terrace restaurant (p203) or sipping sunset cocktails on the jetty. A lavish breakfast costs Dh180.

L'Hippocampe　　　HOTEL €€€
(☑0523 36 61 08; hotelhippocampe@hotmail.com; Rte du Palais; r Dh1200-1500, ste Dh2600, all incl breakfast; P ❋ ☎ ≋ ❋) Oddly enough, the spick-and-span standard and comfort rooms at this old-fashioned place are the best choices – suites are musty, with an ugly decor. The main draws are the flower-filled garden and utterly magnificent terrace overlooking the lagoon. There's a bar, an excellent restaurant (mains Dh80 to Dh210), a good-sized pool edged with lawn and access to a small private beach.

✗ Eating & Drinking

For cheap eats, head to Ave Hassan II in the upper town.

There is a pleasant lounge bar at L'Hippocampe (p202) hotel and an absolutely spectacular jetty bar at La Sultana (p202).

L'Araignée Gourmande SEAFOOD €€
(☎0523 36 64 47; www.araignee-gourmande. com; Oualidia Plage; 12 oysters Dh130, fried fish Dh100; ⊗noon-11pm) The town's best-known restaurant has lost its mojo in recent years – standards of service and food have dropped. That said, it's still a reasonable option if you order simply. No alcohol. The attached hotel isn't recommended.

La Sultana HOTEL €€€
(☎0524 38 80 08; www.lasultanahotels.com/ oualidia; Parc à Huîtres No 3; seafood platters Dh220-1000; ⊗8am-10pm; 🎧) Even if you can't stay in this luxury hotel (p202), you should consider enjoying a leisurely lunch at its terrace restaurant on the edge of the lagoon. It specialises in fresh shellfish, which is kept in high-tech tanks and served straight from tank to the table – the oysters, clams, sea urchins and spider crabs are delicious. Great wine list, too.

Ostréa II SEAFOOD €€€
(☎0523 36 64 51; www.ostrea.ma; Parc à Huîtres; 12 oysters Dh180-280; ⊗11am-10pm) Oualidia is famous for its oyster beds, which produce about 200 tonnes of oysters annually, and this restaurant attached to an oyster farm is a great place to slurp some bivalves. These come in three grades, with the difference being the size. Order them grilled, served with almonds or au naturel. Paella and fried fish are also available.

The well-signed access road to the restaurant is off the main highway, at the entrance to town. It's an easy 15-minute walk from the roundabout in the upper town.

❶ Getting There & Away

Grands taxis congregate on Ave Hassan II near **Hotel Restaurant Thalassa** (p202) and travel to/from Casablanca (Dh90, 2½ hours), El Jadida (Dh50, 40 minutes) and Safi (Dh50, 45 minutes). If you're heading to Marrakesh, a taxi *complet* (grand taxi functioning as a private taxi) will cost Dh800. From the main road, it's a 10-minute walk down to the lagoon and beach – grands taxis will ask for an extra tip to drop you down here.

Safi آسفي

POP 308,175

An industrial centre and thriving port, Safi is a lot less picturesque than neighbouring coastal towns but does offer an insight into the day-to-day life of a Moroccan city. Most tourists stop here en route to or from Essaouira to visit the giant pottery works that produce the typical brightly coloured Safi pottery.

The new town is pleasant enough, with tree-lined boulevards and whitewashed villas, but the alleys of the walled and fortified medina are more atmospheric to stroll through, and you often have the sites to yourself. The beaches are famous for their impressive surf.

History

Safi's natural harbour was known to the Phoenicians and the Romans, and in the 11th century it was a port for the trans-Saharan trade between Marrakesh and Guinea, where gold, slaves and ivory were sold. In the 14th century the town became an important religious and cultural centre when the Merenids built a *ribat* here. The Portuguese took the city for a brief spell from 1508 until 1541, when the Saadians took it back. They built the monumental Qasr al-Bahr fortress and generally expanded the town, but destroyed most monuments upon their departure.

In the 16th century Safi grew wealthy from the trade in copper and sugar, and European merchants and agents flocked to the city, but when the port at Essaouira was rebuilt in the 18th century Safi was largely forgotten.

Safi's real revival came in the 20th century when its fishing fleet expanded and huge industrial complexes were built to process the 30,000 tonnes of sardines caught annually. A major phosphate-processing complex was established south of the town and the city began to expand rapidly. Today, Safi is one of Morocco's largest ports.

◎ Sights

Medina MEDINA
(Map p204) Safi's walled medieval medina is sliced in two by the main street, Rue du Souq, which runs northeast from Bab Lamaasa to Bab Chaaba and is lined with shops. On the southern side of this street, down a twisting alley, are the remains of the 16th-century Cathédrale Portugaise. The Kechla, another structure built by the Portuguese, is located in the medina's southeastern corner. Shops

ATLANTIC COAST SAFI

Safi

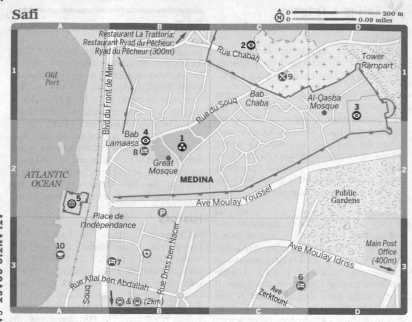

Safi

◉ Sights
1 Cathédrale Portugaise B2
2 Colline des Potiers C1
3 Kechla D1
4 Medina B2
5 Qasr al-Bahr A2

🛏 Sleeping
6 Golden Tulip Farah C3
7 Riad Asfi B3

8 Riad le Cheval Blanc B2

🍴 Eating
9 Café Restaurant Du Potier C1

🍷 Drinking & Nightlife
10 Espace Jalal Essafina A3

🛍 Shopping
Poterie Serghini .... (see 9)

and street stands selling Safi's famous ceramics are clustered around Bab Chaaba.

➡ **Cathédrale Portugaise** RUINS
(Map p204; Medina; adult/child under 12yr Dh10/3) Opposite the entrance to the Great Mosque and clearly signed from Rue du Souq, this ruined cathedral dates from 1519 and was built in the Manueline (Portuguese late Gothic) style. Its construction was never completed and most of the structure was demolished after the departure of the Portuguese. All that remains are parts of the choir and a side chapel.

Colline des Potiers LANDMARK
(Map p204; Potters' Hill; Bab Chaaba) The earthen kilns and chimneys of the Colline des Potiers are clearly seen from Bab Chaaba at the edge

of the medina. The skills used here are predominantly traditional and you can wander around the cooperatives and see the potters at work. If a potter invites you in to watch him at work, you'll be expected to give a small tip or buy an item or two from the shop.

Qasr al-Bahr HISTORIC BUILDING
(Map p204; Castle on the Sea; Dh10) The ruins of Safi's once-impressive castle are located next to the crashing waves of the Atlantic. Built to enforce Portuguese authority, house the town governor and protect the port, the **tower** once housed prisoners who were kept in the basement before being killed or shipped as slaves. In an appalling state of disrepair, the castle is closed to the public while it awaits a long-overdue restoration.

🛏 Sleeping

There are a handful of decent midrange hotels in Safi, but few of the budget options on offer are clean or comfortable.

Riad le Cheval Blanc
B&B €€

(Map p204; ☎0524 46 45 27; www.riad-cheval-blanc.com; 26 Derb El Kaouss, Bab Sidi Boudhab; s/d/tr Dh490/530/735; ❄🐾) A multistorey traditional *dar* hidden inside the medina near Bab Lamassa, this B&B is stronger on character than on comfort, but gets a warm recommendation from us for its reasonable prices, helpful management, panoramic roof terrace, handicraft-adorned interior and squeaky-clean bathrooms. Its major drawback is the lumpy and short beds.

Ryad du Pêcheur
HOTEL €€

(☎0524 61 02 91; www.ryaddupecheur.com; 1 Rue des Cretes; s Dh500, d Dh550-700, f Dh700-1100; 🅿❄🐾) The owner of this hotel is from a well-known family of local potters, so colourful tiles adorn every available surface. Double rooms and large family suites are set around the courtyard restaurant; all are clean but their decor won't suit everyone. Drawcards include the restaurant (p205), a hammam and a rooftop terrace with sweeping views over the port's ship-building yards.

Golden Tulip Farah
HOTEL €€

(Map p204; ☎0524 46 42 99; www.goldentulip farahsafi.com; Ave Zerktouni; s/d incl breakfast Dh690/980; 🅿❄🐾🏊) A good night's sleep is assured at this business hotel located in a quiet and leafy residential enclave high above the medina. Rooms are large and comfortable, with a nondescript decor in shades of beige. Facilities include a large outdoor pool, two restaurants (one Italian, one international), two bars, a gym and a spa with hammam (*gommage* DH90, massage DH250).

Riad Asfi
HOTEL €€

(Map p204; ☎0524 46 46 95; www.hotel riadasfi.com; 11 Pl de l'Indépendance; s Dh350, d Dh450-500, all incl breakfast; 🐾) The name is deceptive, as this place opposite the Qasr al-Bahr is an extremely ugly business hotel rather than a converted traditional house. Rooms are clean and reasonably comfortable, but we suggest avoiding those at the rear, which have no natural light – request a front one with balcony. Views from the 5th-floor restaurant are sensational.

🍴 Eating & Drinking

Sourcing a decent restaurant meal in Safi is a challenge, and we have listed the only eateries worthy of recommendation. Rather than opting for a sit-down meal, many visitors end up following the local lead and snacking on grilled sardines (a local speciality) at the ramshackle and less-than-hygienic eateries on the cliff face next to the Qasr al-Bahr.

To source an alcoholic drink, you'll need to dine at Restaurant La Trattoria (p205) or head to one of the bars or restaurants at the Golden Tulip Farah (p205).

Café Restaurant Du Potier
MOROCCAN €

(Map p204; 4 Rue des Forgeronts, Bab Chaaba; tajines Dh50-60, fresh juices Dh15-20; ⊙11am-10pm) You'll sit next to a tiled fountain under an orange tree and a fig tree if you choose to enjoy a simple Moroccan meal, glass of mint tea or fresh juice at this charming courtyard cafe near the Colline des Potiers. Owned by the Serghini family of potters, whose ceramics shop (p206) is attached, it's a lovely place in which to while away an hour.

Restaurant Ryad du Pêcheur
MOROCCAN €€

(☎0524 61 02 91; www.ryaddupecheur.com; 1 Rue des Cretes; pastas Dh50-80, mains Dh70-135; ⊙7-11.30am, noon-6pm & 7-11pm; 🐾) A lovely spot for a meal in the warmer months, this courtyard restaurant opposite the port serves simple pasta dishes, tajines and fried fish in a garden setting. No alcohol.

Restaurant La Trattoria
ITALIAN €€

(☎0699 04 40 63; www.restaurant-latrattoria.com; 2 Rue l'Aouinate; pizzas Dh50-70, pastas Dh60-70, mains Dh100-150; ⊙12.30-3pm & 7.30-10pm) Any Italian restaurant that substitutes grated supermarket-style mozzarella for Parmesan should be ashamed of itself; sadly, this is the case here. Avoid pastas and mains and instead order a mediocre pizza. It's licensed,

---

LOCAL KNOWLEDGE

BEACHSIDE SHELLFISH

From late afternoon on, head to the plaza next to the camping ground or to the beachfront to buy freshly gathered shellfish from crates on the backs of fishers' scooters. Oysters, clams, razor shells and sea urchins are shucked as fast as you can eat them and served with a squeeze of lemon for around Dh5 a shell. Divine.

ATLANTIC COAST SAFI

which is good, but attracts sleazy drunk businessmen, which is bad. You'll find it on Blvd du Front de Mer, 400m north of the medina.

Espace Jalal Essafina CAFE
(⊙10am-11pm) The location of this ice-cream cafe on Safi's clifftop promenade is superb, offering panoramic ocean views from a huge terrace. Staff make perfectly acceptable espresso coffee that locals tend to enjoy with a crêpe (Dh15 to Dh18) or ice-cream sundae (Dh10 to Dh30).

🛍 Shopping

It's all about Safi's signature pottery here. You can find some great items (as well as some awful tourist dross). Head to Colline des Potiers (p204) to scope out the full range of what's on offer.

★**Poterie Serghini** CERAMICS
(Map p204; ☐0661 34 69 10; www.poterie-serghini.com; 4 Rue des Forgeronts, Bab Chaaba; ⊙10am-7pm) Safi's famed ceramics are showcased in this huge shop and gallery near Bab Chaaba. English-speaking owner Mehdi Serghini is the seventh generation of a famous family of potters and is happy to show visitors his personal collection of ceramics. The ceramics for sale are well priced and of a high quality.

ℹ Information

There are plenty of banks and ATMs clustered around Pl de l'Indépendance and Pl Driss ben Nacer.
The official Safi website www.safi-ville.com includes some tourist information.
Main Post Office (Ave Sidi Mohammed Ben Abdallah; ⊙8.30am-4.30pm Mon-Fri)

ℹ Getting There & Away

Bus The **bus station** (Ave Président Kennedy) is quite a distance south from the centre of town. Most CTM buses stopping in Safi originate elsewhere, so consider booking in advance. Destinations include Agadir (Dh115, six hours, three daily), Casablanca (Dh100, 4¾ hours, eight daily), El Jadida (Dh60, 2¾, six daily) and Essaouira (Dh55, two hours, four daily).

Taxi There are grands taxis to Marrakesh (Dh100, 2½ hours) and Oualidia (Dh50, 45 minutes), among other destinations. These leave from the parking lot beside the bus station.

Train From Safi **train station** (Rue de R'bat) there are two services per day at 5.50am

and 3.50pm involving a change at Benguérir and calling at Casablanca (1st/2nd class Dh127/79, 4½ hours), Rabat (Dh203/116, 5¾ hours) and Fez (Dh308/195, 8¾ hours).

ℹ Getting Around

A metered petit taxi, from either the bus station or train station into the centre of town, costs around Dh10. Local buses operate from just north of Pl Driss ben Nacer.

Essaouira الصويرة
POP 77,426

It is the coastal wind – the beautifully named *alizee*, or *taros* in Berber – that has allowed Essaouira (*essa*-weera, or es-*sweera* in Arabic) to retain its traditional culture and character. For most of the year, the wind blows so hard here that relaxing on the beach is impossible, meaning that the town is bypassed by the hordes of beach tourists who descend on other Atlantic Coast destinations in summer. Known as the 'Wind City of Africa', it attracts plenty of windsurfers between April and November, but the majority of visitors come here in spring and autumn to wander through the spice-scented lanes and palm-lined avenues of the fortified medina, browse the many art galleries and boutiques, relax in some of the country's best hotels and watch fishing nets being mended and traditional boats being constructed in the hugely atmospheric port.

Essaouira lies on the crossroads between two tribes: the Arab Chiadma to the north and the Haha Berbers to the south. Add to that the Gnawa, who came originally from further south in Africa, and the Europeans, and you get a rich cultural mix.

Winter is the time to get closer to the real Essaouira, when the wind howls at its strongest and the waves smash against the city's defences. In summer the town is invaded by throngs of Moroccan tourists, the beach is crowded and it is hard to find accommodation.

History

Most of the old city and fortifications in Essaouira today date from the 18th century, but the town has a much older history that started with the Phoenicians. For centuries, foreigners had a firm grip over the town, and although Moroccans eventually reclaimed it, the foreign influence lingers on in the way the town looks and feels today.

In 1764 Sultan Sidi Mohammed ben Abdallah installed himself in Essaouira (then known as Mogador) so that his corsairs could launch attacks on the people of Agadir, who were rebelling against him. He hired a French architect, Théodore Cornut, to create a city in the middle of sand and wind, where nothing had previously existed. The combination of Moroccan and European styles pleased the sultan, who renamed the town Essaouira, meaning 'well designed'. The port soon became a vital link for trade between Timbuktu and Europe. It was a place where the trade in gold, salt, ivory and ostrich feathers was carefully monitored, taxed and controlled by a garrison of 2000 imperial soldiers.

By 1912 the French had established their protectorate, changed the town's name back to Mogador and diverted trade to Casablanca, Tangier and Agadir. It was only with independence in 1956 that the sleepy backwater again became Essaouira. Since Orson Welles filmed *Othello* here and hippies chose Essaouira as a hang-out, the town has seen a steady flow of visitors – everyone from artists, surfers and writers to European tourists escaping the crowds of Marrakesh.

◉ Sights

Although there aren't many formal sights in Essaouira, it's a wonderful place for rambling. The medina, souqs, ramparts, port and beach are perfect for leisurely discovery, interspersed with relaxed lunches and unhurried mint tea breaks.

★ Essaouira Medina   AREA
(Map p208; Essaouira's walled medina dates from the late 18th century and was added to Unesco's World Heritage list in 2001. It is an outstanding and well-preserved example of European military architecture in North Africa. For the visitor, the narrow streets, souqs, street vendors, leafy plazas and whitewashed houses with ornate wooden doors make it a wonderful place to stroll. Dramatic, wave-lashed ramparts surround the medina and were famously used in the opening scene of Orson Welles' 1951 film *Othello*.

➡ Skala de la Ville   FORT
(Map p208; Medina) Closed for restoration on our last visit, this bastion is part of the ramparts that protect the medina from the crashing Atlantic waves. The town's main woodworking souq is on the narrow street underneath.

ESSAOUIRA'S ART SCENE

The light and beauty have forever attracted artists to Essaouira, and the town has a flourishing art scene, with many artists living and working here, and a number of galleries selling their work. Many of these artists work in a naive style that employs broad brush strokes and rich colours, often incorporating Gnaoua imagery. You'll see their work for sale in galleries and souvenir shops and even on pavements throughout the medina.

More interesting are the local artists who specialise in calligraphy. These include Mohammed Zouzaf, who draws intricate black Berber signs and symbols on lambskin. Also of note is Mohammed Tifardine, an internationally acknowledged calligrapher who creates elegant coloured works featuring Arabic script. Both artists sell through the local gallery Espace Othello (p215).

➡ **Sidi Mohammed Ben Abdellah Museum**   MUSEUM
(Map p208; ☑ 0524 47 53 00; musee_amba_ess@gmail.com; Rue Laâlouj, Medina; adult/child under 12yr Dh10/3; ☺ 8am-5pm Wed-Mon) Housed in an old riad, this somewhat fusty museum has a small collection of jewellery, costumes, embroidery, woodcarving and weapons from the region. Its collection of ritual and musical instruments is particularly interesting.

Port   PORT
(Map p208) Essaouira's large working port is noisy, pungent and hugely atmospheric. Along with the flurry of boats arriving and departing, nets being repaired and the day's catch being landed, you can see traditional wooden boats being made. The boatbuilders supply fishing vessels for the entire Moroccan coast and even as far away as France, as the design is particularly seaworthy. It's also worth visiting the **fish auction**, which takes place in the market hall just outside the port gates.

Skala du Port   FORTRESS
(Map p208; adult/child under 12yr Dh10/3; ☺ 9am-5.30pm) Down by the harbour, this bastion offers picturesque views over the fishing port and the Île de Mogador. Looking back at the walled medina from here, through a curtain of swirling seagulls, you'll get the

Essaouira

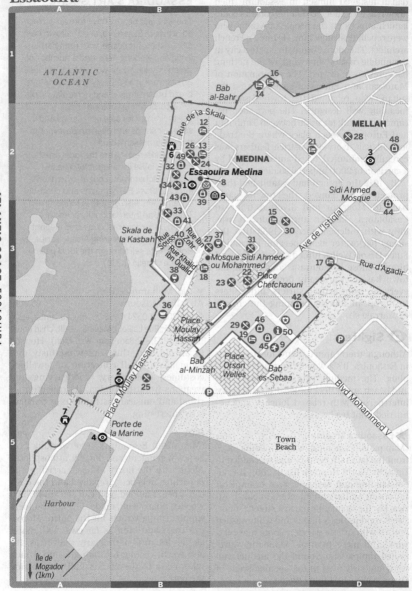

ATLANTIC
OCEAN

Bab
al-Bahr

Rue de la Skala

MELLAH

MEDINA

Essaouira Medina

Sidi Ahmed
Mosque

Skala de
la Kasbah

Rue Ibn Zohr

Rue Souss

Mosque Sidi Ahmed
ou Mohammed

Rue Khalid Ibn Oualid

Place
Chefchaouni

Ave de l'Istiqlal

Rue d'Agadir

Place
Moulay
Hassan

Place
Orson
Welles

Bab
al-Minzah

Bab
es-Sebaa

Blvd Mohammed V

Place Moulay Hassan

Porte de
la Marine

Town
Beach

Harbour

Île de
Mogador
(1km)

same evocative picture that is used on nearly all official literature.

Île de Mogador
ISLAND

Just off the coast to the southwest is Île de Mogador, which has some interesting structures. It's actually two islands and several tiny islets – also known as the famed Îles Purpuraires (Purple Isles) of antiquity. The uninhabited islands are a sanctuary for Eleonora's falcons, which can be easily seen through binoculars from Essaouira beach.

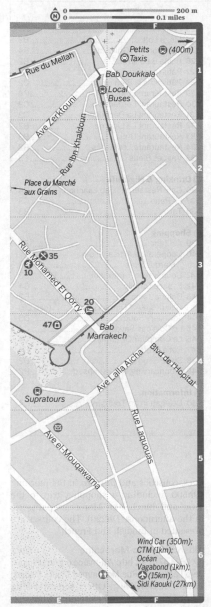

Town Beach
BEACH

Essaouira's wide, sandy beach is a great place for walking, but swimming and sunbathing can be difficult when the winds are strong. If you do swim, stick to the town stretch as the north beach (aka Plage de Safi) has dangerous currents.

Beach football is a popular activity on weekends and camel owners ply the sands on the southern stretch. Be firm if you don't want to take a ride (and bargain hard if you do).

If you're walking, head south across the Ksob River (impassable at high tide) to see the ruins of the Borj el-Berod, an old fortress and pavilion that's partially covered in sand. From here you can walk inland to the village of Diabat or continue along the sands to the sand dunes of Cap Sim.

Océan Vagabond
WATER SPORTS

(☑ 0524 78 39 34; www.oceanvagabond.com; Essaouira Beach; ⊘9am-6pm) This outfit gives two-hour group surfing (adult/child Dh440/220), windsurfing (Dh825/660) and kitesurfing (Dh825) lessons. It also rents out equipment for all three.

It has a cafe-restaurant on the beach with a laid-back terrace; this is open for lunch every day during the year, and stays open for drinks and dinner between mid-July and mid-September.

Hammam Villa de l'Ô
HAMMAM

(☑ 0524 47 63 75; www.villadelo.com; 3 Rue Mohamed Ben Messaoud, Medina; ⊘by appointment) The in-house spa at boutique hotel Villa de l'Ô (p213) has a lovely small hammam where you can enjoy a bath treatment (30-minute bath with *gommage* Dh400, one-hour bath with *gommage* and argan-oil massage Dh550). Also on offer are massages (one hour Dh400) and a variety of beauty treatments. Bookings essential.

Villa Maroc Oriental Spa
HAMMAM

(☑ 0524 47 61 47; www.villa-maroc.com; 10 Rue Abdullah Ben Yassine, Medina; bath Dh350, massages from Dh450) The in-house hammam at upmarket Villa Maroc (p213), just inside the medina walls near Bab al-Minzah, offers a range of bath, massage and beauty treatments. The 'Traditional Beauty' package (Dh600) includes *gommage, ghassoul* body wrap and 10-minute argan-oil massage, while beauty treatments include one-hour pedicures (Dh350) and facials (Dh350). Bookings essential.

🏃 Activities

Organised horse- and camel-riding is based a few kilometres south of Essaouira in Diabat (p216).

Essaouira

Spa Casa Lila　　　　　　　　　HAMMAM
(Map p209; ☑0524 47 55 45; www.riad-casalila.
com; 94 Rue Mohamed El Qorry, Medina; ☺by appointment) This small guesthouse hammam
and spa offers good-value massage and beauty treatments. A 90-minute session with a
30-minute *gommage* and one-hour massage
costs Dh440. Bookings are essential.

🗗 Courses

★**L'Atelier Madada**　　　　　　　COOKING
(☑0524 47 55 12; www.lateliermadada.com; 5
Rue Youssef el-Fassi, Medina; incl lunch Dh500;
☺10.30am-5pm Mon-Sat) Set in a stylishly
restored former almond warehouse and attached to Essaouira's best restaurant (p214),
this cookery school offers places for eight
people per session. Learn the secrets of ta-

jines, couscous and *pastilla* in the morning
(Dh500, including a shopping trip to the
souq and lunch), or Moroccan patisserie
in the afternoons (Dh220). The courses are
presented in English and French.

Alliance Franco-Marocaine　　　LANGUAGE
(☑0524 47 61 97; http://if-maroc.org/essaouira/;
Derb Lâalaouj, 9 Rue Mohammed Diouri, Medina;
☺Mon-Sat, closed Aug) Offers semester-long
French classes as well as regular films, ex-
hibitions and cultural events.

🗗 Tours

Ecotourisme et Randonnées　　　HIKING
(☑0615 76 21 31; www.essaouira-randonnees.
com; 8b Rue Houmman El Fatouaki, Medina) Offers
hiking tours in the countryside outside Es-

saouira (half-day tours Dh200, full-day tours Dh450), including to local argan groves, the Sidi M'Bark waterfall and the Ksob River. Strong on birdwatching. Its office is Restaurant La Découverte (p213).

✨ Festivals & Events

Gnaoua and World Music Festival
MUSIC

(www.festival-gnaoua.net; ⊘ late Jun) Essaouira overflows every year for the celebrated Gnaoua and World Music Festival, a four-day extravaganza with concerts staged at venues including the beach and Pl Moulay Hassan.

Festival des Andalousies Atlantiques
MUSIC

(www.facebook.com/FestivalDesAndalousiesAtlantiques; ⊘ late Oct) An eclectic mix of Andalucian music, art and dance featuring local and international performers.

🛌 Sleeping

Essaouira has a wonderful range of accommodation options catering for every taste and budget. Most of these are within the walls of the medina, so everything you need is within walking distance. In summer book ahead or at least arrive early in the day to find a room.

★ Hôtel Riad Nakhla
B&B €

(Map p208; ☑ tel/fax 0524 47 49 40; www.riadnakhla.com; 12 Rue d'Agadir, Medina; s/tr Dh250/490, d & tw Dh360, all incl breakfast; ☜) The dark and dingy entrance passageway is unprepossessing, but inside there's a lovely central courtyard surrounded by 16 clean and attractive rooms. All have good beds and satellite TV, some have seating alcoves and a few have sea views. Breakfast is served on the pleasant roof terrace, which has sea views. Ultrafriendly staff and bargain prices seal a great deal.

Riad Etoile d'Essaouira
B&B €

(Map p208; ☑ 0524 47 20 07; 2 Rue Kadissiya, off Ave Sidi Mohammed ben Abdallah; s/d/tr incl breakfast Dh195/270/435; ☜) Comfortably appointed and brightly decorated with local fabrics, this B&B in the *mellah* is an excellent budget option. English-speaking staff are friendly and guests enjoy breakfast on the terrace.

Hôtel les Matins Bleus
B&B €

(Map p208; ☑ 0524 78 53 63; www.les-matins-bleus.com; 22 Rue de Drâa, Medina; s/d incl breakfast Dh285/430; ☜) Hidden down a slightly scruffy dead-end street, this friendly B&B has neat and clean rooms surrounding a central courtyard. All but one have private bathrooms. There's no air-conditioning, so the rooms on the roof terrace can be hot in summer. A three-course set meal is available each evening (Dh95)

Dar Afram
B&B €

(Map p208; ☑ 0524 78 56 57; www.darafram.com; 10 Rue Sidi Magdoul, Medina; s Dh175, d Dh350-400, tr Dh525-575, all incl breakfast; ☜) This extremely friendly guesthouse has seven simple rooms with a funky vibe. The Aussie-Moroccan owners are musicians and an impromptu session often follows evening meals (Dh90) shared around a communal table. Guests love the summer BBQs held on the rooftop terrace with its sunloungers and sea view.

★ Jack's Apartments & Suites
APARTMENT €€

(Map p208; Jack's Bohemian Suites; ☑ 0524 47 55 38; www.jackapartments.com; 1 Pl Moulay Hassan, Medina; r Dh380-850, apt Dh740-1740; ☜) Swiss traveller Jack came to Essaouira to windsurf but ended up marrying a local and opening a business renting apartments and rooms, benefiting fellow travellers in the process. In various locations near Bab Skala, the apartments sleep between two and eight persons and are clean, stylish and extremely well-equipped;

JIMI HENDRIX: CASTLES OF SAND OR PIE IN THE SKY?

There are plenty of stories told about Jimi Hendrix in Essaouira. That the musician lived here on and off for a few years in the '60s. That he owned a riad in which you can now stay, or a restaurant in which you can eat. That he stayed in quite a few other riads, or a campervan, or perhaps a tent. That he tried to buy Île de Mogador and composed 'Castles Made of Sand' here. Even that he sired various children and shared a room with Timothy Leary.

Put simply, these stories are all bunkum. Hendrix visited Morocco once only, for about a week, in July 1969, and two or three days of this were spent in Essaouira. But he didn't even bring a guitar. This was 18 months after the album containing the song 'Castles Made of Sand' was released.

ARGAN OIL: MOROCCO'S FOODIE ESSENTIAL

Organic argan oil is 'the new olive oil', increasingly used in hip restaurants around the world to season salads with its nutty flavour. The wrinkled argan tree is unique to this part of the world and, as a result, the argan forests of the Souss Valley and the Haha Coast south of Essaouira have been designated by Unesco as a biosphere reserve.

The argan tree (*Argania spinosa*), is resistant to heat and survives temperatures up to 50°C, and so is an essential tool in the fight against desertification in southern Morocco. It has become vital to the local economy, providing firewood, fodder for the goats – you can see them actually climb into the branches – and oil for humans. Berber women harvest the fruits in spring. They then feed them to goats, whose digestive juices dissolve the tough elastic coating on the shell. The nuts are then recovered from the goats' dung, and the kernels are split, lightly toasted, pulped and pressed.

To produce just one litre of oil takes 30kg of nuts and 15 hours of manual labour, done solely by women. In a recent change to this tradition, some cooperatives have decided to cut the goats out of the process and are hand-picking fruits from the trees to produce a more subtle-tasting oil.

The Berbers have long used argan oil to heal, and modern research suggests that the oil may help reduce cholesterol and prevent arteriosclerosis. In the kitchen its rich and sweet nutty flavour works wonders as a salad dressing, or added to grilled vegetables or a tajine. Berbers mix it with ground almonds and honey to make *amlou*, a delicacy believed to have aphrodisiac properties.

Cold-pressed oil from untoasted nuts is increasingly recognised as a prized cosmetic, particularly for the hair. The oil has a high vitamin E content, which makes it a great addition to antiwrinkle creams, and is sometimes also used to treat skin conditions such as eczema.

If you have your own transport and are heading south, consider stopping en route at **Coopérative Al Amal** (☐0662 21 78 51; http://coopamal.com; Blvd Mohanned V, Tamanar; ⊙9am-7pm Mon-Fri, 10am-4pm Sat & Sun), 70km from Essaouira, which produces and sells quality argan-oil products, including foodstuffs and cosmetics.

---

some have private terraces and others can access a rooftop terrace with sea views.

The individually rented rooms are equally impressive, with a vibrant colour scheme and access to a communal kitchen and rooftop terrace.

The company office in Pl Moulay Hassan handles all bookings.

★ **Dar Al-Bahar**   B&B €€
(Map p208; ☐0524 47 68 31; www.daralbahar. com; 1 Rue Touahen; d & tw Dh550-825, tr Dh825, all incl breakfast; ☎) The nine immaculately kept rooms at this lovely guesthouse, under the ramparts near the Skala de la Ville, are simple and stylish, featuring good beds and small bathrooms with colourful tiles. Local art adorns the walls and the views from the roof terrace overlooking the ocean are magnificent.

Hotel Ríad Mémouna   HOTEL €€
(Map p208; ☐0524 78 57 53; www.riad-mimouna. com; 62 Rue d'Oujda, Medina; s Dh600-750, d Dh700-850, ste Dh1100-1800, all incl breakfast; ☎) On entry to this hotel overlooking the Atlantic, the signs are auspicious – an elegant Moorish-style foyer lounge and extremely friendly staff on the door and at reception. The 33 rooms are clean and comfortable, with those overlooking the water deserving their higher charge. The rooftop restaurant has panoramic ocean views, as does an adjoining sun terrace.

Dar Adul   B&B €€
(Map p208; ☐0524 47 39 10; www.daradul.ma; 63 Rue Touahen, Medina; s Dh450, d Dh500-1000, ste Dh1300, all incl breakfast; ☎) This lovingly restored house has five double rooms and two suites sleeping four; all have attractive decor, most have seating alcoves, and suites have satellite TV. Dinner is available in the licensed restaurant (mains Dh120 to Dh140) and there's a rooftop terrace with spectacular sea and rampart views.

Casa Lila & Spa   B&B €€
(Map p209; ☐0524 47 55 45; www.riad-casalila. com; 94 Rue Mohamed El Qorry; r Dh825-990, ste Dh1320, all incl breakfast; ❄☎) An excellent location near Bab Marrakech is one of a number of drawcards at this 10-room riad. Rooms are comfortable and pretty, featuring original *zellij* tiles, *tadelakt* walls and painted ceilings. The well-priced in-house

hammam (p210) is well regarded and there's also a small rooftop terrace with rooftop views. Three-course set dinners are available (Dh165).

★Palais Heure Bleue
HOTEL €€€

(Map p209; ☑0524 78 34 34; www.heure-bleue. com; Rue Ibn Batouta; d Dh1950-2460, ste Dh3340-5170, all incl breakfast; ✴🛜🏊) A decided hush falls as you walk through the doors of the Heure Bleue, Essaouira's top hotel. This swish riad has facilities galore – rooftop swimming pool, spa, bar, restaurant and private cinema. Chic European style and colonial charm meet in the foyer and gorgeous courtyard, and the rooms are lavishly appointed and extremely comfortable. Levels of service couldn't be better.

★Madada Mogador
BOUTIQUE HOTEL €€€

(Map p208; ☑0524 47 55 12; www.madada.com; 5 Rue Youssef el-Fassi, Medina; r Dh1250-1680, 4-person ste Dh1850, all incl breakfast; ✴🛜) If the definition of a boutique hotel is an establishment offering a chic interior, luxe rooms, quality toiletries and high levels of service, the Madada Mogador fits the bill. Seven rooms – some with sea views – are on offer, along with a stylish lounge and a spectacular roof terrace where drinks and tasty snacks are served.

Villa Maroc
HOTEL €€€

(Map p208; ☑0524 47 61 47; www.villa-maroc.com; 10 Rue Abdallah Ben Yassine; s/d incl breakfast Dh1050/1400, ste Dh1900-2100, all incl breakfast; 🛜) Housed in a large converted 18th-century town house, the Villa Maroc is a model of restrained chic, with airy whitewashed rooms offset by carefully chosen wood, wicker and fabric. The terrace offers great views, while the in-house spa (p209) is as well-regarded for pampering as the ground-floor restaurant is for intimate dining (set menu Dh450). Wi-fi is available in public areas only.

Villa de l'Ô
BOUTIQUE HOTEL €€€

(Map p208; ☑0524 47 63 75; www.villadelo.com; 3 Rue Mohamed Ben Messaoud; r Dh1650, ste Dh2300-2900, all incl breakfast; ✴🛜) Turning its back on the modernist minimalism embraced by most boutique hotels, this riad near Bab es-Sebaa offers comfortable, good-sized rooms with a vaguely bling-ish decor. There's an on-site restaurant, lovely spa (p209), lounge with open fire and huge roof terrace overlooking the beach.

✖ Eating

There are plenty of snack stands and hole-in-the-wall-type places along Rue Mohamed El Qorry, Ave Sidi Mohammed ben Abdallah and Ave Zerktouni.

Pasta Baladin
ITALIAN €

(Map p208; ☑0642 44 81 36; www.riadbaladin. com; Bab Skala, Medina; antipasti Dh40-50, pastas Dh50-70; ☺noon-4pm & 7-11pm Tue-Sun) Communal bar-style seating gets you chatting with your fellow diners at this cheery licensed restaurant. The menu is limited to pasta and choices are simple (10 sauces and five pasta types), but it's well cooked and quickly served. Tiramisu or panna cotta are the usual finales. Unsurprisingly popular.

Pâtisserie la Bienvenue
CAFE €

(Map p208; ☑0677 16 62 41; 7 Rue Abdel Aziz El Fachtall, Medina; corne de gazelle Dh5, gateaux Dh10; ☺10.30am-8pm) Head to this small salon du thé (teahouse) to sample some of the best Moroccan pastries and French gateaux in town, accompanied by a cup of coffee or tea. The *corne de gazelle* are absolutely delicious.

Vagues Bleus
ITALIAN €

(Map p209; 2 Rue Sidi Ben Abdellah; pastas Dh50, mains Dh45-50; ☺noon-3pm & 6.30-9pm Sat-Thu) This tiny hole-in-the-wall eatery painted in blue and white is cheap and cheerful, serving pasta dishes (the gnocchi is recommended) and veggie and meat mains. Everything is fresh and very tasty.

Restaurant La Découverte
MOROCCAN €

(Map p208; ☑0524 47 31 58; http://essaouira-ladecouverte.com; Rue Houmman El Fatouaki, Medina; mains from Dh50) A small, friendly French-run restaurant, offering a mix of Franco-Moroccan dishes. The *briouates* are particularly good, as are the creamy desserts.

Outdoor Fish Grill Stands
SEAFOOD €

(Map p208; port end of Pl Moulay Hassan; fish, bread & salad from Dh40; ☺11am-10pm) Eating here is one of the definitive Essaouira experiences, although the increasingly hard-sell-tactics of the stall owners is unfortunate. Choose what you want to eat from the colourful displays of freshly caught fish and shellfish at each grill, and wait for it to be cooked on the spot and served with a pile of bread and salad. Be sure to agree on the price before you order.

Café Restaurant L'Horloge
CAFE €

(Map p208; Pl Chefchaouni, Medina; omelettes Dh15-25, tajines Dh40-60; ☺noon-3pm & 7-10pm) Set on the attractive square beneath the clock tower, this popular cafe has an outdoor terrace and serves a basic Moroccan menu.

Pâtisserie Driss DESSERTS €
(Map p208; near Pl Moulay Hassan, Medina; set breakfasts Dh21-40, pastries from Dh4; ⊙ 8.30am-4.30pm) It opened way back in 1928, and this cafe with attached semihidden courtyard has many loyal regulars. Sadly, we have found its pastries almost inedible on our recent visits.

★**Loft** MEDITERRANEAN €€
(Map p208; ☑ 0524 78 44 62; 5 Rue Hajjali, Medina; mains Dh75-110; ⊙1-4pm & 6-11pm Wed-Mon; 🐾) The menu at this tiny eatery near Pl Moulay Hassan changes daily according to what's plentiful and good at the souqs, resulting in food that is fresh and full of flavour. Dishes have Mediterranean accents, but remain predominantly Moroccan – the tajines and couscous are delicious. Decor is retro-funky and the English-speaking waiters are friendly. Alcohol isn't available.

Restaurante Les Alizés MOROCCAN €€
(Map p208; ☑ 0524 47 68 19; 26 Rue de la Skala, Medina; set menus Dh129; ⊙ noon-2.30pm & 7-10pm) This popular place, run by a charming Moroccan couple in a 19th-century house, has delicious Moroccan dishes, particularly the couscous with fish and the tajine of *boulettes de sardines* (sardine balls). You'll get a very friendly welcome, and it's a good idea to book ahead. It's above Hôtel Smara.

Restaurant El-Minzah MOROCCAN €€
(Map p208; ☑ 0524 47 53 08; 3 Ave Oqba ben Nafii; mains Dh75-130; ⊙ noon-3pm & 7-11pm) Seating is on an outdoor terrace or inside a vaulted dining room at this long-standing restaurant facing the ramparts. The menu delivers Moroccan and French favourites, and there are good-value three-course (Dh110) and seafood four-course (Dh290) set menus. Live loud music at night.

Mega Loft INTERNATIONAL €€
(Map p208; ☑ 0613 98 19 87; 49 Rue Al Yeman, Medina; mains Dh70-120; ⊙ noon-11pm; 🍴) Retro furniture, delicious food, live music (often Gnaoua) and a funky vibe are the hallmarks at this popular restaurant-cafe near the Skala de la Ville. Unusually, it serves some vegetarian and vegan dishes. No alcohol, though.

Restaurant La Licorne MOROCCAN €€
(Mapp208;☑ 0524473626;www.restaurant-lalicorne-essaouira.com; 26 Rue de la Skala, Medina; mains Dh85-130; ⊙ 7-10pm Mon-Sat) This is a cosy place

with a most un-Essaouiran feel – wooden beams and heavy chairs give it the ambience of a European hunting lodge. A no-nonsense menu of Moroccan and French favourites is served up by friendly staff.

Restaurant Ferdaous MOROCCAN €€
(Map p208; ☑ 0524 47 36 55; 27 Rue Abdesslam Lebadi, Medina; mains Dh75, set menus Dh120; ⊙ noon-3pm & 7-10pm Tue-Sun) Long-standing favourite serving home-style traditional Moroccan food.

★**La Table by Madada** MEDITERRANEAN €€€
(Map p208; ☑ 0524 47 55 12; www.latablemadada.com; 7 Rue Youssef el-Fassi, Medina; mains Dh100-220; ⊙ 7-10.30pm Fri-Wed; ❄🐾) Style meets substance at Essaouira's best restaurant, which is housed in an old almond warehouse. The interior is an exhilarating and highly successful meld of traditional Moroccan and modern European, and the menu features contemporary rifts on Moroccan favourites such as tajines and *pastilla*. Fish and seafood dishes dominate. Service is friendly but could do with a polish.

Restaurant Umia MEDITERRANEAN €€€
(Map p208; ☑ 0524 78 33 95; umia.essaouira@gmail.com; 22 Rue de la Skala, Medina; ⊙ noon-3pm & 7-11pm Wed-Mon; 🐾) We were in two minds about whether to list this newcomer to Essaouira's restaurant scene. Its small interior is glamorous and staff are professional, but the dishes we've sampled were unsuccessful, with fussy presentation, clashing flavours and inept execution. This is a shame, as the restaurant's stated intention of making the most of market-fresh ingredients is laudable.

If you're one of those people who dislikes dining at communal tables, specify this when booking. Good wine list.

 Drinking & Nightlife

Essaouira's nightlife is lacklustre. Don't expect to party into the wee hours.

Taros BAR
(Map p208; ☑ 0524 47 64 07; www.tarosessaouira.com; Pl Moulay Hassan; ⊙ 9am-midnight) A great place for a sundowner, with a terrace looking over the square and port. There's often live music. It's also good for afternoon tea, or a drink at the bar.

Le Patio BAR
(Map p208; ☑ 0524 47 41 66; 28 Rue Moulay Rachid; ⊙ 7.30-11pm) For something sultry, this hip bar and restaurant is a candlelit den with blood-red furnishings and a black mirror ball. You'll

need to buy some tapas (Dh40) to just sit and drink. There's live music on Thursday, Friday and Saturday.

Café Restaurant
Bab Laachour CAFE
(Map p208; Pl Moulay Hassan; ☺noon-11pm) Somewhat sleazy, but its on one of the town's busiest squares serves alcohol and has a front terrace that's great for people-watching.

🔒 Shopping

Essaouira is famous for its woodworking, and particularly for products made from thuya wood, a dark-orange or reddish-brown wood with plenty of dark knots. Note that this is an endangered species – buying anything made from thuya threatens the last remaining stands of trees by increasing demand and therefore encouraging illegal logging.

★ Espace Othello ARTS & CRAFTS
(Map p208; So Art; ☑0524 47 69 60; 9 Rue Mohammed Layachi; ☺10am-1pm & 3-7pm Tue-Sun) Fantastic private gallery selling work by established and up-and-coming artists.

Az-Zahr HOMEWARES
(Map p208; ☑0524 78 43 52; az_zahr@yahoo.fr; 6 Rue Mohammed Diouri; ☺2-9pm) French-owned and *trés chic*, this hybrid homeware shop and salon du thé next to the Institut Français stocks textiles, ceramics and objets d'art.

Le Comptoir Oriental HOMEWARES
(Map p208; ☑0524 47 55 12; www.madada.com; 2nd fl, Rue Youssef el Fassi, Medina; ☺10am-7pm) Describing itself as an 'oriental vintage chic bazar', this homeware shop in an old apartment sells a heavily curated range of furniture, textiles, glassware, ceramics and handicrafts. Ring the bell for entrance and then head up the stairs.

Coopérative Tamounte ARTS & CRAFTS
(Map p208; ☑0524 78 56 11; www.tamounte-essaouira.com; 6 Rue Souss Essaouira; ☺10am-8pm) An excellent all-female cooperative selling argan-oil lotions and cosmetics (some medicinal), woodwork and ceramics. It's in a dingy passageway and can be a bit hard to find – look for the 'Commerce Équitable à la Coopérative Tamounte' sign.

Le Coin des Saveurs FOOD
(Map p208; ☑0524 78 51 93; Rue Mohammed Ben Messaoud, Medina) Concept store selling food products sourced from quality local suppliers and stocking a range of spices, jams and oils, as well as some artisan-made homeware.

> ## ESSAOUIRA MEDINA SOUQ SHOPPING
> ....
> **Jewellery Souq** (☺10am-8pm) A small area of jewellery shops with everything from heavy Berber beads to gaudy gold.
>
> **Spice Souq** (☺9am-8pm) This is the place to go for herbal Viagra, Berber lipstick, exotic spices and *ghassoul* (clay used in face masks). You can also buy argan-oil products here, as well as *amlou* (a mix of honey, almond and argan oil).
>
> **Fish Souq** (off Ave de l'Istiqlal; fish, bread & salad Dh30) Fresh fish is available here, but is better purchased down at the port.
>
> **Woodcarving Workshops** (☺10am-9pm) Essaouira is well known for its woodwork and plenty of wooden products are available at this string of shops beneath the Skala de la Ville.

Coopérative Artisanal
des Marqueteurs ARTS & CRAFTS
(Map p208; ☑0671 73 73 99; 6 Rue Khalid ibn Oualid; ☺10am-9pm) Come to this cooperative in an impasse (dead-end lane) off Pl Moulay Hassan for a wonderful range of wooden items.

Rafia Craft ARTS & CRAFTS
(Map p209; ☑0524 78 36 32; 82 Rue d'Agadir; ☺10am-8pm Mon-Sat) Designs and sells unusual shoes and sandals made from the fibres of the doum palm.

Galerie Jama ANTIQUES
(Map p208; ☑0670 01 64 29; galeriejama@gmail.com; 22 Rue Ibnou Rochd; ☺10am-7pm) Run by an affable chap who avoids hard-sell tactics, this small shop has an alluring range of antique rugs, clothing, textiles, ceramics and various objets d'art.

Galeries d'Art Damgaard ARTS & CRAFTS
(Map p208; www.galeriedamgaard.com; Ave Oqba ben Nafii; ☺9am-1pm & 3-7pm) This gallery is one of the oldest in town and features the work of local artists.

ⓘ Information

DANGERS & ANNOYANCES

Essaouira is still mostly a safe, relaxed tourist town but you should be on your guard in the backstreets of the *mellah* after dark – there are problems with drugs and drinking north of Ave

Zerktouni and east of Ave Sidi Mohammed ben Abdallah.

EMERGENCY

Police Station (☎ 024 78 48 80; Rue du Caire) Opposite the tourist office.

MONEY

There are banks with ATMs around Pl Moulay Hassan and along Ave de l'Istiqlal.

POST

Main Post Office (Map p209; Ave el-Mouqa-wama; ☺ 8.30am-4.15pm Mon-Fri, 8am-noon Sat)

Post Office (Rue Laâlouj; ☺ 8.30am-4pm Mon-Fri)

TOURIST INFORMATION

The **tourist office** (☎ 0524 78 35 32; www.essaouira.com; 10 Rue du Caire, Medina; ☺ 8.30am-4.30pm) can offer little assistance. Check www.essaouira.nu for practical and cultural information.

❶ Getting There & Away

AIR

Aéroport de Mogador (☎ 0524 47 67 04; www.onda.ma; Rte d'Agadir), 17km south of the medina, is used by Transavia, flying from Paris, and EasyJet, flying from London Luton.

BUS

The **bus station** (Map p209; Ave Ghazouat) is about 400m northeast of the medina, an easy walk to Bab Doukkala during the day but better in a petit taxi (Dh10) if you're arriving or leaving late at night. CTM buses leave from its dedicated **office,** (☎ 0522 54 10 10; Pl 11 Janvier, Lotissement Azlef) a Dh10 petit-taxi ride from the medina.

CTM destinations include Agadir (Dh75, 2¼ hours, three daily), Casablanca (Dh160, seven hours, four daily) via Safi (Dh55, two hours, four daily), El Jadida (Dh110, five hours, three daily) and Marrakesh (Dh80, 3½ hours, two daily).

Other companies run cheaper and more frequent buses to the same destinations as well as to Taroudannt (Dh90, six hours) and Tan Tan (Dh150, six hours).

Supratours (☎ 0524 47 53 17; Bin Lassour, off Ave Lalla Aicha), the ONCF subsidiary, runs coaches to Marrakesh train station (Dh70, three hours, five daily) to connect with trains to Casablanca from the station near Bab Marrakech. There's also a Dh100 'comfort plus' service once a day, and a daily departure to Agadir (Dh70, 3¾ hours). Book in advance for these services, particularly in summer.

Local bus 5 to Diabat (Dh5) and Sidi Kaouki (Dh6) leaves from Blvd Moulay Youssef outside

Bab Doukkala. There are about eight services a day.

TAXI

The grand-taxi rank lies immediately west of the bus station. Fares include Sidi Kaouki (Dh10, 15 minutes), Marrakesh (Dh90, 2½ hours) and Agadir (Dh80, two hours).

❶ Getting Around

To get to the airport, take bus 2, which passes the airport turning (Dh10, 15 minutes, every two hours), or a grand taxi (Dh150 to Dh200). The blue **petits taxis** are a good idea for getting to and from the bus station (Dh10), but they can't enter the medina. If you're happy to walk but don't want to carry your bags, there are plenty of enterprising men with luggage carts who will wheel your bags directly to your hotel for about Dh20.

Around Essaouira

Diabat الديابات

The sleepy Berber village of Diabat, 5km south of Essaouira, was once a dope-smoking colony popular with hippies. Today it is the site of a major new tourist development, Golf de Mogador, which comprises a luxury resort and two golf courses designed by Gary Player. Also in the village are two horse- and camel-riding ranches: Ranch de Diabet and Zouina Cheval.

♂ Activities

For something more serious than the horse and camel rides on the beach, several companies offer cross-country trekking and multiday rides in the countryside around Essaouira. Tailor-made horse trips can be arranged through Ranch de Diabat (p216) and Zouina Cheval. (p216)

Golf de Mogador (www.golf-mogador-essaouira.com) offers two six-tee courses suitable for players of all levels, as well as a golf academy and a clubhouse with restaurant.

Zouina Cheval   HORSE RIDING
(☎ 0682 65 27 42; www.zouina-cheval.com; Diabat; 1hr rides from Dh160, day rides incl picnic from Dh600) This outfit in Diabat is owned and run by Najib and Sophie, highly qualified and experienced instructors who cater for all levels, including children and beginners. Longer horse trekking and camping trips are also available.

Ranch de Diabat HORSE RIDING
(☎0524 47 63 82; www.ranchdediabat.com; Diabat; 30min horse/camel rides Dh150/250) This outfit, approximately 3km south of Essaouira, offers horse and camel riding, as well as quad excursions. Also on offer are hikes and four- to six-day trail rides in the desert or along the coast (Dh6065 to Dh8800).

Maison du Chameau CAMEL TREK
(☎0658 37 60 43; www.lamaisonduchameau.fr; Douar Al Arab; prices on application) This guesthouse is home to eight *meharis* (white Sudanese racing camels). It offers rides, weeklong camel-riding courses and shorter excursions. Accommodation is in simple but comfortable rooms (doubles including breakfast Dh1030), and there's a swimming pool for guest use. A set dinner costs Dh165. You'll find it approximately 20km from Essaouira, past Bouzama.

Sleeping

Auberge Tangaro BOUTIQUE HOTEL €€
(☎0524 78 47 84; www.aubergetangaro.com; Zone du Golf, Diabat; s/d Dh760/870, ste Dh975-1520, all incl breakfast; P 🛜 🏊) Set in flower-filled grounds, this 1915 house, close to the golf course in Diabat, offers 19 guest rooms decorated in a chic mod-Moroccan style. Facilities include a yoga studio (supposedly the only one in or near Essaouira), a hammam and a tranquil pool area. Meals are available.

Sofitel Essaouira Mogador Golf & Spa RESORT €€€
(☎0524 47 94 00; www.sofitel.com; Domaine Mogador; r Dh1800-2200, ste Dh2280-3800, villa Dh4370-5160; P ❄ @ 🛜 🏊 🐾) Part of the Golf de Mogador development, this luxury resort offers a range of rooms and suites as well as 28 villas with private swimming pool. Facilities include a luxury spa, two bars (one of which functions as a club in the high season), four restaurants and a large swimming pool. Breakfast costs Dh110.

Getting There & Away

To get to Diabat from Essaouira drive south on the coast road to Agadir and turn right just after the bridge about 5km out of town. Alternatively, local bus 5 leaves from outside Bab Marrakech (Dh5, every two hours).

Sidi Kaouki سيدي كاوكي

POP 4582

The constant blustery winds, wild beach and good budget accommodation at Sidi Kaouki have made it one of Morocco's top windsurfing and surfing spots. It's not for the faint-hearted (waves average 1m to 3m and the currents can be dangerous), but even if you don't take to the water, it's a chilled escape from Essaouira.

The large building on the rocks, washed by the sea, is the final resting place of Sufi saint Sidi Kaouki, who was known for his healing abilities. People still visit the shrine. For water sports, the quintessential surfers' hang-out on the beach is the Sidi Kaouki Surf Club, a brightly decorated cafe-clubhouse with a cool vibe. You can arrange lessons and hire surfing, windsurfing and kitesurfing gear here.

Activities

Sidi Kaouki Surf Club WATER SPORTS
(☎0672 04 40 16; www.sidi-kaouki.com) Offers surfboard hire (two hours Dh165, one day Dh270), windsurfer/windkite rental (three days Dh1570), and lessons. Can also book accommodation in a number of apartments and guesthouses in the village; check the website for information and rates.

MOGAsurf WATER SPORTS
(☎0618 91 04 31; www.mogasurf.com) This Essaouira-based company offers half-day kitesurf (Dh165), surfboard (Dh165) and paddleboard (Dh325) hire in Sidi Kaouki, as well as two-hour kitesurfing (Dh650), surfing and paddleboarding (Dh325) lessons.

Sleeping & Eating

A clutch of guesthouses are set back from the beachfront and can be booked through the surf club (p217) or the Al-Vent restaurant (p217).

Al-Vent INTERNATIONAL €€
(☎0623 83 66 15; http://sidikaoukihotel.com; Sidi Kaouki; paella Dh75-150, mains Dh50-125; ⏰10am-10pm; 🌿) This Spanish-owned place opposite the beach is popular with the ultrachilled surfer crowd, who can't get enough of the paella (fish, chicken or seafood), burgers and tajines. There are a number of options for vegetarians and vegans. The owners also offer backpacker-style accommodation in the village.

Getting There & Away

Sidi Kaouki is about 25km south of Essaouira. Bus 2 or 5 (Dh6) leaves from outside Bab Marrakech every two hours.

Mediterranean Coast & the Rif

شاطئ البحر المتوسط ومنطقة الريف

Best Places to Eat

➡ Auberge Dardara Restaurant (p257)

➡ Art et Gourmet (p229)

➡ Populaire Saveur de Poisson (p230)

➡ Blanco Riad (p247)

Best Places to Sleep

➡ Dar Nour (p226)

➡ Villa Josephine (p228)

➡ El Reducto (p246)

➡ Casa Hassan (p255)

Why Go?

Caught between the crashing waves of the Mediterranean and the rough crags of the Rif Mountains, northern Morocco is one of the most charming parts of the country. Tangier, the faded libertine of a port that links Africa and Europe, has shed its shady past to enjoy a rebirth as fashionable Moroccan riviera. To the east, the coast is dotted with high cliffs and sandy coves; the area booms as a Moroccan holiday destination.

The charming pastel blue medina of Chefchaouen deserves its reputation as a magnet for travellers, while Tetouan boasts the food and architecture of the Spanish protectorate era. Echoes of Spain continue with the medieval fortresses and modernist architectural treasures of the enclaves of Ceuta and Melilla.

Inland, you can get away from everything with treks in the Rif and walking in the little-visited remote Beni-Snassen 'national park'.

When to Go
Tangier

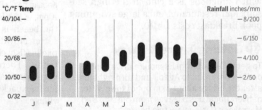

Apr Spring is perfect for trekking in the Rif or exploring national parks.

Jul Head to Chefchaouen for its annual arts festival.

Sep Mediterranean beaches await, without the crowds.

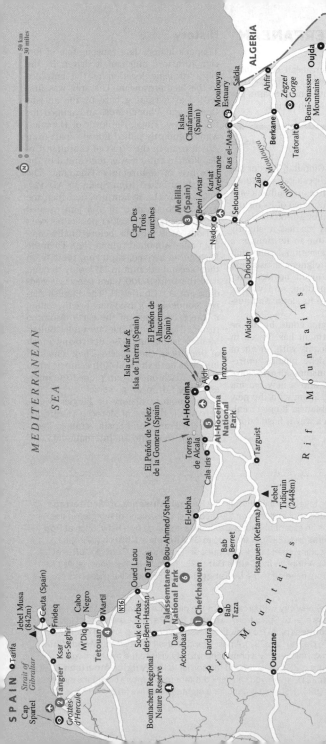

ALGERIA

MEDITERRANEAN SEA

SPAIN

50 km
30 miles

Mediterranean Coast & the Rif Highlights

1 **Chefchaouen** (p250) Getting happily lost in the blue-washed lanes and alleys of one of Morocco's most enchanting medinas.

2 **Tangier** (p220) Looking beyond this city's gleaming modern face to find traces of the artists, from Matisse to the Beat poets, who made it home.

3 **Melilla** (p268) Wandering around the modernist buildings and imposing medieval fortress, before indulging in tapas for lunch or dinner.

4 **Tetouan** (p243) Taking in the art and colonial history of this Riffian town's museums and its beautifully restored Spanish architecture.

5 **Al-Hoceima National Park** (p267) Exploring the remote hills and beaches while looking for birdlife in this overlooked national park.

6 **Talassemtane National Park** Looking for Barbary apes while trekking amid the forests and Berber villages of the Rif Mountains.

WEST MEDITERRANEAN COAST

Morocco's west Mediterranean coast takes in the area around the storied port city of Tangier, as well as Ceuta, one of Spain's few remaining enclaves in North Africa.

Tangier

طنجة

POP 950,000

Guarding the Strait of Gibraltar, Tangier has for centuries been Europes's gateway to Africa. Its blend of cultures and influences is unique in Morocco – for much of its history it wasn't even governed by Morocco.

Tangier has always carried a slightly seedy allure, in part due to its time as a semi-independent international zone that attracted eccentric foreigners, artists and spies. Officially sanctioned neglect later gave it a dismal reputation, and visitors were often quick to flee its sleaze and hustle.

Contemporary Tangier could hardly be more different. Investment has flowed in and the white city gleams with an air of confidence. The corniche bustles, entrepreneurs in the new business district have replaced the hustlers, and a new marina is under construction, along with the new TGV train line to Casablanca. Tangier's cultural life is buzzing in a way it hasn't done since the 1950s.

History

Tangier's history is a raucous tale of foreign invasion, much of it driven by the city's strategic location at the entrance to the Mediterranean. The area was first settled as a trading base by the ancient Greeks and Phoenicians, and named for the goddess Tinge, the lover of Hercules, who legendarily pulled Europe apart from Africa to form the Strait of Gibraltar. Under Roman rule, it was the capital of the province of Mauretania Tingitana. The Vandals attacked from Spain in AD 429, followed by the Byzantines, and then the Arabs, who invaded in 705 and quelled the Berber tribes. Tangier passed between various Arab factions before finally coming under Almohad rule in 1149. Then the Portuguese arrived, capturing the city on their second attempt in 1471, only to hand it to the British 200 years later as a wedding gift for Charles II. The English diarist Samuel Pepys lived here briefly, calling it 'the excrescence of the earth'. Morocco regained control of the city under Sultan Moulay Ismail in 1679, destroying much of the city in the process. They remained in power until the mid-19th century, when North Africa once again piqued the interest of the European powers.

The modern history of Tangier begins here. While the rest of Morocco was divided between France and Spain, strategic Tangier was turned into an 'International Zone'

TANGIER IN...

One Day

Starting in the kasbah, take a wander through the **Kasbah Museum of Mediterranean Cultures** (p223) and a meander down the medina streets. A cup of mint tea in the **Petit Socco** (p222) is an essential Tangier experience, followed by a fishy lunch at **Populaire Saveur de Poisson** (p230). Wander up to **St Andrew's Church** (p224) for a spot of gravestone reading, then take in the latest art exhibition at **Centre Culturel Ibn Khaldoun** (p224). A drink in the **Caid's Bar** (p232) is followed by dinner at **Art et Gourmet** (p229), before heading to the **Le Tangerine** (p233), just like a Beat poet.

Two Days

Discover the vibe of the new city with breakfast at the plush **La Giralda** (p230), where you can check the views over to Spain from **Terrasse des Paresseux** (p224). Head to **Librairie des Colonnes** (p234) to browse the historic bookshop and take coffee at the storied **Gran Café de Paris** (p232). A post-prandial stroll through the **Mendoubia Gardens** (p223) follows, followed by a photo-opportunity visit to the fresh produce market in **Grand Socco** (p223). Just around the corner is the **Tangier American Legation Museum** (p221), where you can seek out Morocco's *Mona Lisa*. Take dinner at **El Morocco Club** (p232), staying around for a nightcap and live jazz.

21ST CENTURY TANGIER

Times were that Tangier was exactly the Moroccan destination that you'd pass through – a rundown city full of hustlers trading on stories of a libertine past. Those days are long behind it, and Tangier has entered the 21st century with a fresh face and a confident spring in its step.

Tangier's renaissance began in 2007 when the main port was replaced by the Tanger Med facility, 40km along the coast, now one of the busiest ports not only in Africa but anywhere in the Mediterranean. The new port allowed investment to flow in, not least the flagship Renault-Nissan car plant. Tangier now makes over 200,000 vehicles a year, exporting to the European Union as well as selling on the domestic market – the majority of petits taxis are now locally made Dacias. The plant is entirely fuelled by biomass from Morocco's olive oil industry – a neat fusion of ancient and modern Moroccan know-how.

The next step has been the Tangier Metropolis program, remodelling the city's corniche, building a new marina (due to open in 2017) and redevelopment around the train station, and adding hotels, malls and the new TGV train station for the high-speed link to Casablanca. The medina has been cleaned up, and the plan is to put the city back at the forefront of Moroccan tourism. There's a strong focus on domestic, Gulf and package tourism, but Tangier still lags behind destinations such as Marrakesh when it comes to boutique offerings. In spite of this we'd suggest keeping your eyes on the kasbah area as the place for future developments. Still, with events like the hipper-than-thou Nuits Sonores electronic music festival, and the artsy digital start-up at Technopark, the city's forward motion is bringing an optimism that it hasn't known for decades.

of various sectors, similar to West Berlin in the Cold War. France, Spain, Britain, Portugal, Sweden, Holland, Belgium, Italy and the USA all had a piece of the pie, which was managed by the sultan, at least on paper. This situation lasted from 1912 until shortly after Moroccan independence, in 1956, when the city was returned to the rest of the country. During this famous Interzone period, expats flooded in, forming half the population, and a wild, anything-goes culture broke out, attracting all sorts of people, for reasons both high and low. Socialites, artists, currency speculators, drug addicts, spies, sexual deviants, exiles, eccentrics – the marginalia of humanity all arrived, giving the city a particularly sordid reputation.

When the Interzone period ended, Tangier entered a long period of decline. As the economic base moved on, so did the cultural scene. The city became a dreary port, while retaining its criminality. King Hassan II hated the city and starved it of funding. Street hustlers multiplied, turning off tourists. The number of expats dwindled, until there were only a few thousand left.

Since 1999, Tangier has been the site of major development, most notably its new port, Tanger Med, and the high speed TGV train line to Casablanca, currently under construction.

Sights

◉ Medina & Kasbah

★ Medina
AREA

(Map p225) The medina, the top attraction of Tangier, is a labyrinth of alleyways both commercial and residential. It's contained by the walls of a 15th-century Portuguese fortress, although most buildings are actually relatively young for a Moroccan medina. Clean and well lit as medinas go, the place is full of travellers' treasures, from glimpses of traditional living, to the more material rewards of the souqs.

➡ ★ Tangier American Legation Museum
MUSEUM

(Map p225; ☏ 0539 93 53 17; www.legation.org; 8 Rue D'Amerique; Dh20, guided tour Dh50; ⊙10am-5pm Mon-Fri, 10am-3pm Sat) **FREE** This museum, in an elegant five-storey mansion, is a must-see: Morocco was the first country to recognise the fledgling United States, in 1777, and this was the first piece of American real estate abroad, as well as the only US National Historic Landmark on foreign soil.

There are some unusual displays, including a Moroccan Stars and Stripes carpet, and an 1839 letter from a hapless US consul who had been given two lions as a diplomatic gift. The museum also holds an impressive

Tangier

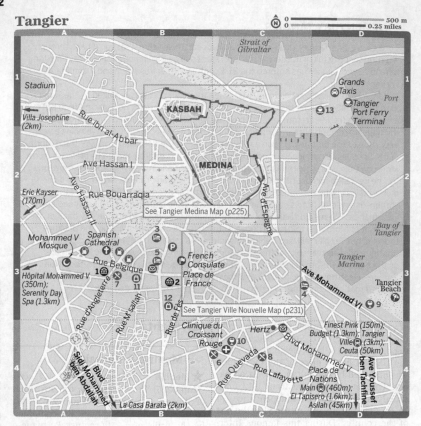

display of paintings that give a view of the Tangerine past through the eyes of its artists, most notably Scotsman James McBey, whose hypnotic painting of his servant girl, Zohra, has been called the Moroccan *Mona Lisa*. There is a small bookshop and a wing dedicated to Paul Bowles.

➡ Musée de la
Fondation Lorin   MUSEUM
(Map p225; ☎ 0539 93 03 06; fondationlorin@gmail.com; 44 Rue Touahine; donations appreciated; ⏲ 11am-1pm & 3.30-7.30pm Sun-Fri) **FREE** This eclectic museum is housed in a former synagogue. Here you will find an open two-storey room with an engaging collection of black-and-white photographs of 19th- and 20th-century Tangier on the walls. Meanwhile there will likely be a children's theatre production going on in the centre – as the museum doubles as a workshop for disadvantaged kids, bringing life to the static display.

➡ Old Spanish Church   CHURCH
(Map p225; 51 R as-Siaghin) Mother Teresa's Missionaries of Charity, a handful of Indian, French and Spanish nuns, work from the Old Spanish Church in the medina. They cope with heartbreaking situations: street children, abused children, marital violence, and drug and alcohol abuse.

➡ ★Petit Socco   SQUARE
(Map p225; Souq Dakhel) Officially named Pl Souq ad-Dakhil, this was once the most notorious crossroads of Tangier, the site of drug deals and all forms of prostitution. Today the facades are freshly painted, tourists abound and it's a wonderful square for people-watching over a mint tea.

➡ Grande Mosquée   MOSQUE
(Map p225) From the Petit Socco in the medina, Rue Jemaa el-Kebir leads east past this mosque, which at one time housed a Portuguese church.

Tangier

➜ **Tomb of Ibn Battuta**   TOMB
(Map p225) This modest tomb is purported to be the last resting place of Ibn Battuta, who was born in Tangier in 1304 and became the greatest traveller of the period – outpacing Marco Polo at an easy clip. A scholar and judge, Ibn Battuta travelled across North Africa through the Middle East then onto Russia, Central Asia and China, returning via Sri Lanka and East Africa.

After stopping at home, he then journeyed across the Sahara to West Africa, finally settling to write it all down in 1355. The tomb is frequently locked.

★**Kasbah Museum
of Mediterranean Cultures**   MUSEUM
(Map p225; ☑0539 93 20 97; Pl de la Kasbah; adult/child Dh20/10; ⊙10am-6pm Wed-Sun) This recently refurbished museum, recently refurbished, is housed in the former sultan's palace of Dar el-Makhzen. The focus is on the history of the area from prehistoric times to the 19th century. Exhibits are well-presented (information in French and Arabic only). Work your way anticlockwise around the first courtyard before heading inside to the rest of the displays, followed by a walk in the charming Andalucian garden.

Particular highlights are the mosaic of Venus from Volubilis and statuary, plus the giant replica maps. The first map tracks trade routes from the Phoenician trade in metals to the electronic goods of the 21st century; the second is a gorgeous map of the known world made in Tangier in 1154 (hint: it's upside down from the viewer's perspective) The museum is outside the medina – follow the perimeter all the way to the western end, to the highest part of the city, enter the Porte de la Kasbah, and follow the road to the museum.

⊙ Ville Nouvelle

With its Riviera architecture and colonial ambience, the stretch from Pl de France along Blvd Pasteur still hints at the glamour of the 1930s. It's a popular place for an early evening promenade, or a few hours sipping mint tea in one of the many streetside cafes – particularly the venerable landmark Gran Café de Paris, where you still might half-expect to bump into Truman Capote or Jean Genet.

★**Grand Socco**   LANDMARK
(Map p225) The Grand Socco (official name Pl du 9 Avril 1947) is the romantic entrance to the medina, a large, sloping, palm-ringed plaza with a central fountain that stands before the keyhole gate Bab Fass. Once a major market, its cobblestone circle is now the end of the line for taxis, the point at which the modern streets narrow into the past.

For the best ground-floor view, climb the steps at the highest point on the circle, across from the large tan building (the police station), to what locals simply call La Terrasse. This is what you came for, one of those dreamy moments when you think you've entered a movie set.

The Grand Socco is also the hub of several other sights, all visible from within it. First is the Cinema Rif (p233), which stands on the circle. The brightest light on Tangier's cultural scene, it is a combination art-house cinema, cafe and archive, and the focal point for anything to do with film. Young locals come to soak up the ambience and use the free wi-fi.

Mendoubia Gardens   PARK
(Map p225) This large park is full of strolling couples and children playing football. The Mendoubia Gardens are flanked by an elegant line of colonial buildings, perhaps

the most attractive of its kind in the city. At the top of the central hill is a monument flanked by cannons that contains the speech given by Mohammed V asking for independence.

St Andrew's Church
CHURCH

(Map p225; Rue d'Angleterre; donation requested; ⊙services 8.30am & 11am Sun) St Andrew's Church is one of the more charming oddities of Tangier. Completed in 1890, on land granted by Sultan Hassan, the interior of this Anglican church is decorated in high Fassi style, with the Lord's Prayer in Arabic over the altar. Behind the altar is a cleft that indicates the direction of Mecca, with carved quotes from the Quran.

The graveyard is worth lingering in. The journalist, Moroccan explorer and Tangerine socialite Walter Harris is buried here, along with Squadron Leader Thomas Kirby Green, one of the prisoners of war shot during the 'Great Escape'. There

---

EXPLORE TANGIER'S ART SCENE
....

Mohamed Drissi Gallery of Contemporary Art (52 Rue d'Angleterre; ⊙9am-1pm & 2-6pm Tue-Sun) Contemporary art gallery housed in the former British consulate.

Les Insolites (☑0534 59 29 83; http://lesinsolitestanger.com; 28 Rue Khalid Ibn Oualid; ⊙11am-8pm Mon-Sat) Photographic gallery with works by Moroccan artists, and a bookshop.

Galerie Conil (☑0534 37 20 54; conil.maroc@gmail.com; 7 Rue du Palmier, Petit Socco; ⊙11am-8pm Mon-Sat) This small gallery, just off the Petit Socco, shows local mixed-media artists and has a collection of books and clothing.

Galerie Delacroix (86 Rue de la Liberté; ⊙11am-1pm & 4-8pm Tue-Sun) The exhibition hall of the Institut Français; hosts temporary exhibitions.

Centre Culturel Ibn Khaldoun (Rue de la Liberté; ⊙10am-1pm & 4-8pm) Exhibition space specialising in contemporary art from Tangier and the surrounding region.

Instituto Cervantes Gallery (Rue Belgique; ⊙10am-1pm & 4-8pm Tue-Sun) Hosts exhibitions of contemporary artists from Tangier and beyond.

---

is also a sobering section of war graves of entire downed aircrews, their headstones attached shoulder to shoulder. Caretaker Yassine is always on-site and can offer you a tour.

Tangier Beach
BEACH

(Map p222) The wide town beach has been improved – it's actually cleanest in the bustling summer. It works well for a seaside stroll, and the corniche (beachfront road) from the new marina makes walking easy. There are plenty of attractive beaches down the nearby Atlantic Coast.

Terrasse des Paresseux
ARCHITECTURE

(Map p231; Idlers' Terrace) The aptly named Terrasse des Paresseux provides sweeping views of the port, Spain and, on a really clear day, Gibraltar. A set of ancient cannons faces the bay, symbolically warding off usurpers (apart from the children who love to climb them).

🏃 Activities

El-Minzah Wellness
SPA

(Map p231; ☑0539 93 58 85; www.elminzah.com; 85 Rue de la Liberté; fitness room Dh200) Pamper yourself at the luxury spa, where there's a fully equipped gym (with superb views to the sea), hammam, sauna and Jacuzzi, as well as a range of massage and other therapeutic treatments.

Serenity Day Spa
SPA

(Map p222; ☑0539 37 28 28; serenity@serenityspa.ma; Rue Adolfo Fessere, Quartier California; hammam & gommage Dh400) Here is a chance for women to escape the all-too-male world of Morocco, at least for a few hours, and indulge the body in luxurious surroundings. This female-only hammam gets high marks from local customers. It's west of Pl de Koweit, on the road to the golf course; take a cab.

Royal Club Equestre
HORSE RIDING

(☑0539 93 48 84; www.equestre.ma; Rte de Boubana; 30min Dh100, 1hr Dh150; ⊙8am-noon & 3-7pm Tue-Sun) Along the road to Cap Spartel, the stables are set in the midst of forested hills, a pleasant place to explore on horseback. All riders must be accompanied by a guide, included in the price of the horse hire.

👉 Tours

Hotels can provide recommended guides, usually at around Dh250 a day. Remember that any guide who takes you shopping receives a commission, although they'll often

Tangier Medina

Tangier Medina

find you things you wouldn't have found otherwise.

There is a series of colour-coded walks in the medina, with signs and maps throughout the medina in strategic spots:

Brown The kasbah

Green Rue Oued Aherdane from the kasbah to the Petit Socco

Purple Rue Dar ed-Baroud with its sea views down to the Hotel Continental

Yellow The south of the medina from the Petit Socco to the Tangier American Legation Museum

Blue Souk Dakhel: from the Petit Socco eastwards in a circle

Orange The ramparts around the medina, from the Grand Socco to the kasbah

Festivals & Events

There are two booklets listing events and local info: monthly *Urbain Tanger* and bi-monthly *Tanger Pocket*, both in French and available at most hotels and online at www.urbainmagazine.com and www.tanger pocket.com.

Salon International de Tanger des Livres et des Arts   LITERATURE
(www.if-maroc.org/tanger/spip.php?rubrique59; Institut Français, 41 Rue Hassan ibn Ouazzane; ☺May) Annual weeklong book festival with varying themes.

TANJAzz   MUSIC
(www.tanjazz.org; Tangier; ☺Sep) This ever-popular festival with a good reputation for attracting leading names, has been running for over 17 years and hosts concerts by local and international jazz musicians.

Nuits Sonores Tanger   MUSIC
(www.nuits-sonores.com/tanger; ☺Oct) This cutting-edge music festival is an offshoot of the original Nuits Sonores in Lyon, and leans heavily on contemporary electronic music and arts.

Festival du Court Métrage Méditerranéen   FILM
(International Mediterranean Short Film Festival; www.ccm.ma; ☺Nov) Weeklong festival of short films from around the Mediterranean.

Sleeping

Tangier's sleeping options cater to all budgets and styles, spanning the spectrum from the ultra-cheap *pensiónes* (guesthouses)

near the port to the chic hotels along the oceanfront. Ultra-budget accommodation options are clustered around the medina and close to the port gate. You can also find plenty of choice in the streets around Ave Mokhtar Ahardan and the Rue Magellan.

Medina

★**Melting Pot Hostel**   HOSTEL €
(Map p225; ☎0539 33 15 08; www.meltingpothostels.com/tanger; 3 Rue Tsouli; dm Dh130, d Dh330; ☎) This bright and cheerful hostel is a perfect backpacker's hub, with a big, clean kitchen and plenty of chill-out space including a roof terrace with terrific views. Shared facilities are clean and the staff very friendly and helpful. It's a short walk from Petit Socco or, if you're walking up from the port, the Hotel Continental.

Hotel Mamora   HOTEL €
(Map p225; ☎0539 93 41 05; 19 Ave Mokhtar Ahardan; s/d with shower Dh120/180, with bathroom Dh270/430) Readers enjoy this hotel in a good location near the Petit Socco, with its variety of rooms at different rates. There's a slight institutional air, like an old school, but it's clean, well run, and strong value for money. The rooms overlooking the green-tiled roof of the Grande Mosquée are the most picturesque, if you don't mind the muezzin's call.

★**Dar Nour**   GUESTHOUSE €€
(Map p225; ☎0662 11 27 24; www.darnour.com; 20 Rue Gourna, Kasbah; d/ste incl breakfast from Dh720/1300; ☎) This peppermint-walled guesthouse has no central courtyard, rooms here instead branch off two winding staircases, creating a maze of rooms and salons, each more romantic than the last. Rooms are stylishly decorated with objets d'art and packed with books, creating a relaxed and homely atmosphere, while bathrooms are *tadelakt* (polished plaster). Some rooms have a private terrace.

Once you get to the top of the house, there is an impressive view over the roofs of the medina. Breakfasts are huge and are usually served on the terrace.

La Tangerina   GUESTHOUSE €€
(Map p225; ☎0539 94 77 31 19; www.latangerina. com; Rue Sultan, Kasbah; d incl breakfast Dh750-1650; ☎) This is a perfectly renovated riad at the very top of the kasbah, with 10 rooms of different personalities. Bathed in light and lined with rope banisters, it feels like an elegant, Berber-carpeted steamship cresting

MATISSE IN TANGIER

Of the many artists who have passed through Tangier, Henri Matisse is one of the most famous. The French impressionist and leading light of the early-20th-century Fauvist movement called Tangier a painter's paradise. His two visits to the city, in the spring of 1912 and again the following winter, had a profound influence on his work.

Inspired by the luminous North African light and the colour and harmony found in traditional Moroccan art, Matisse completed some 20 canvases and dozens of sketches during his time in Tangier. In them he honed the qualities that define his mature work: bold abstract lines, two-dimensional shapes and vibrant, expressive – as opposed to natural – colours.

Matisse mainly looked to the daily life of the medina for his themes. He produced several striking portraits of Zohra, a local prostitute, and a wonderful painting of a strong-featured Riffian woman sitting legs akimbo against an azure sky.

However, it is Matisse's renditions of the city that really strike a chord. Two of the most evocative are *Vue sur la Baie de Tanger* (View of the Bay of Tangier) and *La Porte de la Casbah* (Entrance to the Kasbah). Both are relatively subdued in their use of colour, but in *Paysage Vu d'une Fenêtre* (Window at Tangier) the artist hits full stride. The painting shows the view from his window in the Grand Hôtel Villa de France (p229), looking out over St Andrew's Church, with its squat tower, to the kasbah beyond. The overriding colour is a pure, sizzling Mediterranean blue.

the medina. The roof terrace overlooks the ancient crenellated walls of the kasbah, while below, neighbourhood washing hangs from abandoned coastal cannons, proclaiming the passage of history.

Hotel Continental
HOTEL €€
(Map p225; ☑ 0539 93 10 24; hcontinental@menara.ma; 36 Rue Dar el-Baroud; s/d incl breakfast Dh795/850; ❖❋☎) Nothing appears to have been touched here for decades, making this piece of faded grandeur a fascinating bit of International Zone archaeology; parts of *The Sheltering Sky* were filmed here. The rooms are on the spartan side, though many have fine views overlooking the port and sea (as does the huge terrace). The hotel has a large craft shop.

Nord Pinus Tanger
GUESTHOUSE €€€
(Map p225; ☑ 0661 22 81 40; www.nord-pinus-tanger.com; Rue Riad Sultan, Kasbah; d €190, junior/deluxe ste €230/290, all incl breakfast €190/230/290; ❋☎) This is a very grand Kasbah house with somewhat Gothic stone columns and staircase. Rooms are a delight with eclectic decor and every comfort. Excellent meals are served on request (half-*pensión* €30) in the opulent dining room or on the roof terrace. The bar on the terrace overlooking the sea is a favourite for an aperitif.

Ville Nouvelle

Many of the unrated hotels and *pensiónes* along Rue Salah Eddine el-Ayoubi and Ave

d'Espagne are little better than the cheapies in the medina. This Salah/Espagne area can be dodgy at night, and questionable for women travelling alone. Nicer hotels line Ave Mohammed VI, offering views over the Bay of Tangier and close proximity to the attractions of the city, with a couple of options right in the centre.

Hotel El-Muniria
HOTEL €
(Map p231; ☑ 0539 93 53 37; www.hotelelmuniria.com; 1 Rue Magellan; s/d Dh200/250, on terrace Dh250/300; ☎) This is your best low-end option in the ville nouvelle, and is chock-full of Beat Generation history (William Burroughs famously lived here while writing *The Naked Lunch*). French windows and bright, flowery fabrics set it apart, revealing the careful touch of a hands-on family operation.

Room 4, a quiet corner double with lots of light, is a great hideaway, as is Room 8 on the terrace, a quiet double with a harbour view. Noise from Le Tangerine bar below can be an issue for some rooms.

Pension Hollanda
HOTEL €
(Map p222; ☑ 0539 93 78 38; 139 Rue de Hollande; s/d Dh250/350, loft r without bathroom per person Dh150) Tucked away in a quiet street a short walk from Pl de France, this former hospital has sparkling whitewashed rooms and high ceilings, with tiny bathrooms. All rooms have a TV and a sink; doubles come with a shower. Hot water is available on demand. For a budget steal, don't miss the loft rooms up the hidden spiral staircase.

DON'T MISS

SEEKING OUT TANGIER'S BEAT HERITAGE

The Beat Generation was a post-WWII American counterculture movement that combined visceral engagement in worldly experiences with a quest for deeper understanding. Tangier was a key location in its development. Writer Jack Kerouac and poet Allen Ginsberg both passed through here, visiting the father of the movement, William Burroughs, who had moved here in 1953. The Interzone of Burroughs' most famous work, *Naked Lunch*, was written in and directly inspired by Tangier. Burroughs' writing utilised the cut-up technique pioneered by the multitalented Brion Gysin, who also spent a significant part of his life here. Burroughs, along with Paul Bowles, inspired a coterie of local artists. The result was a mixed bag, from the heights of artistic creativity to the lows of moral depravity. Traces of Tangier's grimy literary history can still be found:

Hotel el-Muniria (p227) The hotel where William Burroughs wrote *Naked Lunch*, holed up with a supply of typewriter ribbons and methadone.

Le Tangerine (p233) A sleazy bar turned tourist and hipster hang-out, where Ginsberg, Kerouac and others drank: check the photos on the wall.

Café Central (p233) Burroughs' principal hang-out on the Petit Socco, where he sized up his louche opportunities.

Tangier American Legation Museum (p221) Houses a wing dedicated to Paul Bowles, as well as a small section on the Beats.

Hotel Continental (p227) Scenes from the movie version of Paul Bowles' *The Sheltering Sky* were filmed here.

Gran Café de Paris (p232) The main post-WWII literary salon during the Interzone, it also drew Tennessee Williams and Truman Capote.

For more on the Beats, and Tangier's other writers, read Josh Shoemakers essential *Tangier: A Literary Guide for Travellers*.

Hotel de Paris
HOTEL €
(Map p231; ☑0539 93 18 77; www.hoteldeparis-tanger.com; 42 Blvd Pasteur; s/d with bathroom & breakfast Dh450/580) This reliable choice in the heart of the ville nouvelle has a classy, old-world aura in its lobby. There is a variety of room types and prices depending on bathroom arrangements and balconies. All are clean and (for the most part) modern, but those overlooking Blvd Pasteur can get noisy. The multilingual front-desk staff are very helpful.

Hotel El Djenina
HOTEL €
(Map p222; ☑0539 92 22 44; eldjenina@menara.ma; 8 Rue al-Antaki; s/d incl breakfast Dh375/490; ❋🛜) This somewhat characterless hotel is close to the port; rooms are bright and modern. The cosy bar and restaurant with patio views to the sea are pleasant. Unexciting but reliable.

Hotel Rembrandt
HOTEL €€
(Map p231; ☑0539 33 33 14; www.hotelrembrandt.ma; Ave Mohammed V; s/d Dh700/900; ❋🛜🌊) Rooms here are pretty standard and are in marked contrast to the elegant downstairs lobby, with its classic elevator and curving staircase echoing its 1950s roots. However, the glassed-in restaurant is good, the green garden cafe is a tranquil spot to relax, and there's a reasonable bar for an evening drink. Rooms with a sea view cost around Dh100 extra.

★ Villa Josephine
HERITAGE HOTEL €€€
(Map p222; ☑0539 33 45 35; www.villajosephine-tanger.com; r Dh3600-7600; 🅿🛜🌊) A mansion or a palace? It's hard to decide at this restored 1920s residence, once a summer retreat for Moroccan royalty and partying European diplomats. Everything about the 10 rooms here is sumptuous, from the period decor to the up-to-the-minute amenities and service. All have balconies or terraces looking out to sea.

Relax in the delightful gardens or by the pool, or have pre-dinner drinks in the wood-panelled library. For a taste of the old Tangier of the monied classes, this is a real treat.

★ El-Minzah
HOTEL €€€
(Map p231; ☑0539 33 34 44; www.elminzahleroyal.com; 85 Rue de la Liberté; d/ste from Dh2000/3500; ❋🛜🌊) The classiest five-star

hotel in Tangier proper, and a local landmark, this beautifully maintained 1930s period piece offers three excellent restaurants, three equally good bars, a fitness centre, a spa, pleasant gardens and even a babysitting service. It's shaped like an enormous hollow square, with a tremendous Spanish-Moorish courtyard, and has history oozing from its walls.

Portside rooms offer beautiful views, but can be noisy when the wind is blowing.

★ Grand Hôtel
Villa de France   HISTORIC HOTEL €€€
(Map p222; Rue de la Liberté; s/d from Dh2000/2400, ste from Dh3000) Recently and gloriously refurbished, few hotel addresses are as venerable as Grand Hôtel Villa de France. French painter Eugène Delacroix stayed here in 1832, then his compatriot, Henri Matisse, followed just before WWI – you can enjoy the still-spectacular views he painted from his old room (35), decorated as it was in his day.

The period attention to detail in the salons and dining rooms is superb, and the service is attentive. There's a piano bar and suites around a pool at the rear, next to an old villa once occupied by the Napoleons.

✕ Eating

In the medina there's a host of cheap eating possibilities around the Petit Socco (Souq Dakhel) and the adjacent Ave Mokhtar Ahardan, with rotisserie chicken, sandwiches and brochettes all on offer. In the ville nouvelle, try the streets immediately south of Pl de France, which are flush with fast-food outlets, sandwich bars and fish counters.

For self-catering options, the covered markets near the Grand Socco are the best places for fresh produce, particularly on Thursday and Sunday, when Riffian women descend on the city wearing traditional straw hats with pompoms and candy-striped skirts to sell their agricultural products. **Casa Pepé** (☑ 5399 93 70 39; 39 Rue ibn Rochd; ☺ 9am-10.30pm) is one of several general stores in the area.

✕ Medina

El Morocco Café   MOROCCAN €€
(Map p225; breakfasts around Dh20, mains Dh65-85; ☺ 8am-9pm) Tucked into a tiny plaza in the kasbah, and shaded by trees and vines, El Morocco is an absolutely delightful place to while away an hour or so over a late breakfast, a juice or coffee or a light lunch.

It's the low-key street version of its posher sibling, El Morocco Club (p230).

Le Nabab   MOROCCAN €€
(Map p225; ☑ 0661 44 22 20; 2 Rue al Kadiria; mains Dh90, set menu Dh175; ☺ lunch & dinner Mon-Sat) This is a beautifully restored old *fondouq* (rooming house), all grey *tadelakt*, comfortable seating and swaths of airy fabrics. Dine around the huge fireplace or in a private alcove. The menu is Moroccan, the welcome friendly and it has an alcohol licence.

Café à l'Anglaise   MOROCCAN €€
(Map p225; 37 Rue de la Kasbah; mains Dh90-150; ☺ 10am-10pm) Decorated by way of an Anglo-Moroccan flea market, this blue-fronted shabby-chic cafe serves up some good fish and a variety of tajines and Moroccan salads. The downstairs is cosy but there's an upstairs terrace for when things get crowded. Tasty food, but the automatic 10% service charge on the bill is a little cheeky.

★ Art et Gourmet   MEDITERRANEAN €€€
(Map p225; ☑ 0539 37 12 51; 9 Pl du 9 Avril 1947; lunch menu Dh160, mains Dh180; ☺ noon-midnight; ☏) Overlooking the Grand Socco, the terrace of this restaurant has the best views in town. Inside, it's more formal. Menus are presented on the back of small paintings, and the *menu du jour* on a blackboard. There are lots of fish, organic vegetables and meat produced on the Boufalah farm in nearby Assilah, and fusion Moroccan dishes.

All is beautifully presented on a slate plate, and there's a good wine list. The service is excellent.

SPOT THE CELEB

Sashay past the doorman at **El-Minzah hotel** and glide down the stairs to the beautiful Andalucian courtyard where there are dozens of photographs of celebrity visitors around the walls. Most of the photos date from the 1950s and '60s. A suave Rock Hudson, Aristotle Onassis in a white car, Jackie O too, Winston Churchill with his cigar, and glitzy Rita Hayworth are just some that we spotted. Then head for Caid's Bar (p232) for a cocktail while you decide where they'll hang your photo.

★ **Populaire Saveur de Poisson** SEAFOOD €€€

(Map p231; ✍ 0539 33 63 26; 2 Escalier Waller; fixed-price menu Dh200; ⊙1–5pm & 8–11pm, closed Fri) This charming seafood restaurant offers an excellent, filling set menu in rustic surroundings. The owner serves a four-course meal of fish soup followed by inventive plates of fresh catch, olives and various fresh breads, all of it washed down with a homemade juice cocktail made from a dozen fruits. Dessert is honey and almonds. Not just a meal, a whole experience.

El Morocco Club MEDITERRANEAN, TAPAS €€€

(Map p225; contact@elmoroccoclub.ma; 1 Rue Kashla, Kasbah; mains Dh140-195, tapas Dh40-90; ⊙noon-10pm; P 🛜) A very smart renovation of this elegant building has resulted in a stylish restaurant upstairs and a more relaxed piano bar downstairs. It's all dramatic colours and the cosy bar has some fascinating photographs on the walls. During the day, there's a cafe (p229) outside under the trees.

✖ Ville Nouvelle

La Giralda CAFE €

(Map p231; ✍ 0539 37 04 07; 1st fl, 5 Blvd Pasteur; breakfast from Dh25; ⊙7am-midnight; ❄) The young and beautiful adore this grand cafe overlooking the Terrasse des Paresseux, with its sumptuous, Egyptian-influenced decor and intricately carved ceiling. Huge windows give great sea views. A light menu of crêpes and paninis make it a good lunch stop, too.

Champs Élysées CAFE €

(Map p231; 6 Ave Mohammed V; breakfast from Dh25; ⊙6am-10pm) This enormous cafe-in-the-round is high on opulence, with a huge central chandelier and red velour upholstery. Great sticky pastries.

Patisserie La Española PASTRIES €

(Map p231; 97 Rue de la Liberté; pastries from Dh8; ⊙7am-10.30pm winter, 7am-12.30am summer) A heavily mirrored tearoom, this cafe tempts people off the street with its pretty arrangements of cakes and pastries. Everyone seems to come here – locals and foreigners, businessmen and courting couples.

Fast Food Brahim FAST FOOD €

(Map p231; 16 Ave Mexique; sandwiches from Dh25; ⊙11am-midnight) Great made-to-order sandwiches. You can't go wrong here with half a baguette filled with *kefta* (spicy lamb meatballs) and salad to eat on the hoof. One of several fast-food places in this area.

Mix Max FAST FOOD €

(Map p231; 6 Ave Prince Héritier; meals Dh25-50; ⊙noon-2am) A trendy and popular fast-food joint, Mix Max serves up great paninis, *shwarma* (sliced meat, cooked on a spit, and stuffed in a flatbread) and other fast fare for meals on the hoof.

★ **Ana e Paolo** ITALIAN €€

(Map p222; ✍ 0539 94 46 17; 77 Rue Prince Héretier; mains from Dh85; ⊙12pm–3pm & 7.30–11pm, closed Sun) This is a genuine, family-run Italian bistro with Venetian owners; it feels like you've been invited for Sunday dinner. Expect a highly international crowd, lots of cross-table conversations about the events of the day, and wholesome food, including excellent charcuterie and pizzas, homemade pastas, meat and fish.

Eric Kayser PATISSERIE, FRENCH €€

(Map p222; cnr Rue des Amoureux & Rue Granada; mains from Dh140, dish of the day Dh120; ⊙7am-10.30pm) This renowned French *boulanger* has a bakery and restaurant that's trendy and stylish; it's very popular for its good French cuisine, though a little out of the way.

Number One MOROCCAN, FRENCH €€

(Map p231; ✍ 0539 94 16 74; 1 Ave Mohammed V; mains from Dh85; ⊙noon-11pm) The rose walls and white windows in this renovated apartment provide the feel of a holiday cottage, while the red lighting, background jazz and exotic mementoes lend it an intimate, sultry allure. The Moroccan-French cuisine gets high marks from locals, who have been coming here for almost 50 years. Alcohol is served.

Otori SUSHI €€

(Map p222; www.otorisushi.com; 41 Ave de la Résistance; 4 sushi pieces Dh25-50, mains Dh70-120; ⊙noon-11pm) Have a chilled beer or glass of wine in this dark-panelled sushi restaurant just off Ave Mohammed V. Sushi is carefully assembled, and tempura crisp fried. A pleasant escape from Tangerine excitements.

Le Pagode CHINESE €€

(Map p231; ✍ 0539 93 80 86; Rue al-Boussiri; mains from Dh80; ⊙noon-3pm & 7-11pm Tue-Sun) If you're tired of tajines and pasta, this realistic bit of Asia is a decent answer. An intimate and classy dining area, with lacquered furniture, white tablecloths and low lighting, is paired with a classic Chinese menu.

Tangier Ville Nouvelle

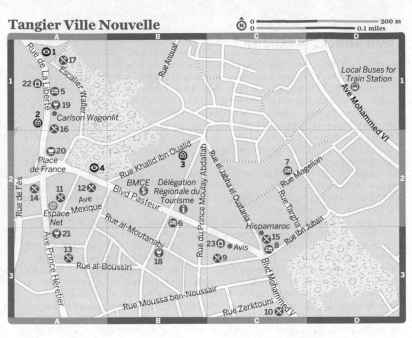

Tangier Ville Nouvelle

MEDITERRANEAN COAST & THE RIF TANGIER

La Fabrique   FRENCH €€€
(Map p222; ☑ 0539 37 40 57; Residence Salima, 7 Rue d'Angleterre; meals Dh250-350; ⊗ 7.30pm-11.30pm Mon-Sat) The minimalist decor and excellent French cuisine make this restaurant just the place to be seen. The *tournedos* (fillet steaks) is legendary, though there's not much choice for vegetarians. Service is attentive and there's a good winelist. Reserve ahead.

Restaurant el-Korsan   MOROCCAN €€€
(Map p231; ☑ 0539 93 58 85; El-Minzah Hotel, 85 Rue de la Liberté; mains around Dh160; ⊗ lunch & dinner) One of Tangier's top restaurants, this chic and classy place inside El-Minzah Hotel offers a smaller, more intimate version of the palace restaurant theme but without the bus tours. Well-presented Moroccan classics are served to soft live music, and

PAUL BOWLES IN TANGIER

Perhaps the best-known foreign writer in Tangier was the American author Paul Bowles, who died in 1999, aged 88. Bowles made a brief but life-changing trip to Tangier in 1910, on Gertrude Stein's advice, then devoted the next 15 years to music composition and criticism back home. In 1938 he married Jane Sydney Auer, but they were never a conventional couple – he was an ambivalent bisexual and she was an active lesbian. After WWII Bowles took her to Tangier, where he remained the rest of his life. Here he turned to writing amid a lively creative circle, including the likes of William Burroughs and Mohammed Choukri. Visiting writers, from Jean Genet to Truman Capote, all sought out Bowles.

During the 1950s Bowles began taping, transcribing and translating stories by Moroccan authors, in particular Driss ben Hamed Charhadi (also known by the pseudonym Larbi Layachi) and Mohammed Mrabet. He was also an important early recorder of Moroccan folk music.

Thanks partly to Bernardo Bertolucci's 1990 film, Bowles' best-known book is *The Sheltering Sky* (1949), a bleak and powerful story of an innocent American couple slowly dismantled by a trip through Morocco. His other works include *Let It Come Down* (1952), a thriller set in Tangier; *The Spider's House*, set in 1950s Fez; and two excellent collections of travel tales, *Their Heads Are Green* (1963) and *Points in Time* (1982). *A Distant Episode: the Selected Stories* is a good compilation of Bowles' short stories.

There is a dark and nihilistic undercurrent to Bowles' writing, as fellow writer Norman Mailer describes in *Advertisements for Myself* (1959): 'Paul Bowles opened the world of Hip. He let in the murder, the drugs, the death of the Square...the call of the orgy, the end of civilization'. The Tangier American Legation Museum (p221) has a wing dedicated to Bowles' life and work.

MEDITERRANEAN COAST & THE RIF TANGIER

often traditional dancing. Reservations are necessary, including one day's prior notice for lunch. Dress well.

🍷 Drinking & Nightlife

Given Tangiers hedonistic past, it's no surprise that the drinking scene here is firmly entrenched in Tangerine culture. It's equally unsurprising that bars are principally the domain of men, although there are a few more-Westernised places where women can have a drink. Many only get going after midnight.

Tangier's clubbing scene picks up in the summer, when Europeans arrive on the ferries. Discos cluster near Pl de France and line the beach, appealing to a wide range of clientele, from grey-haired couples to sex tourists. Cover charges vary and may be rolled into drink prices. If leaving late, have the doorman call a taxi.

★Gran Café de Paris   CAFE
(Map p231; Pl de France; ⊙ 6am-10.30pm) Gravity weighs upon the grand letters of the Gran Café de Paris, reminding us of its age at the crossroads of Tangier. Facing the Pl de France since 1927, this is the most famous

of the coffee establishments along Blvd Pasteur, most recently used as a setting in *The Bourne Ultimatum*. In the past it was a prime gathering spot for the Tangier literati.

Number One   BAR
(Map p231; ⊙11am-midnight) A perennially popular place with Tangerine expats, this small bar (there's a restaurant next door) does cold beer, decent wine and spirits, and a good stab at tapas. The decor is adorably funky, as is the bar's CD collection. Perfect for a low-key drink; women are welcome.

Caid's Bar   BAR
(Map p231; El-Minzah; 85 Rue de la Liberté; ⊙10am-midnight) Long the establishment's drinking hole of choice, this El-Minzah landmark is a classy relict of the grand days of international Tangier, and photos of the famous and infamous adorn the walls. Women are more than welcome and the adjacent wine bar (wine from Dh35) is equally good.

Piano Bar at El Morocco Club   BAR
(Map p225; Pl du Tabor, Kasbah; ⊙from 8pm Tue-Sun) An atmospheric medina bar on the edge of the kasbah, this is a good place for

a drink. There's usually live music at weekends, and a fresh breeze at any time.

Nord Pinus Tanger
BAR

(Map p225; Rue Riad Sultan, Kasbah; ☺11am-midnight) On the top floor of this kasbah guesthouse is a bar and terrace, with fabulous views across to Spain. Sip a cocktail in the retro-chic lounge full of quirky chairs, Moroccan cushions and contemporary photography. A great place for a chilled-out drink

Beach Club 555
CLUB

(Map p222; Ave Mohammed VI; ☺10am-3am; ☎) A beach club by day with pool, pizzeria and bar with a sports screen (admission Dh100), at night the Triple 5 morphs into one of the best discos in the city. Dance up a storm with the resident and visiting DJs.

Le Tangerine
BAR

(Map p231; 1 Rue Magellan, Hotel el-Muniria; ☺10.30pm-1am, to 3am Fri & Sat) A last holdout from the Beat days, the Tangerine (or 'Tangier Inn') was where William Burroughs took Kerouac and Ginsberg drinking. It's a little cleaner, with a hint of Moroccan hipster about it now, but still a decent place to grab a beer.

Café Central
CAFE

(Map p225; Petit Socco; ☺6am-11.30pm) The premier people-watching site in the medina, with tables on the pavement facing Petit Socco. See the local Mafiosi arrive in his new Benz, watch odd specimens of humanity drift past, hear the strange shouts echo down the alleys, and wonder what is going on upstairs. It's the perfect place to sip your coffee.

Americain's Pub
BAR

(Map p231; Rue al-Moutanabi; ☺noon-2am) Don't be fooled by the name: this pub is outfitted as an authentic part of the London underground, with white tiled walls, ubiquitous red trim and signage far more authentic than the Bobbies would appreciate. It's the perfect place to hide: there's no street number, and the phone is out of order.

Regine Club
CLUB

(Map p222; 8 Rue al-Mansour Dahabi; ☺10pm-3am Mon-Sat) Welcome to the 1980s. This disco has stayed the same so long it is a museum piece, replete with glass-reflecting ball and purple velour couches. It has a great atmosphere after midnight, especially on weekends.

Hole in the Wall Bar
BAR

(Map p231; Rue du Prince Heretier; ☺11am-midnight) For chuckles only, walk up Rue Prince Héretier from the Terrasse des Paresseux one-and-a-half blocks and you will see a pair of swinging black doors, Old West style. Welcome to the smallest bar in Tangier, if not the world. Beer (from Dh20) only.

☆ Entertainment

Cinema Rif
CINEMA

(Map p225; Cinematheque de Tanger; ☑0539 93 46 83; Grand Socco) In this fine, well-restored art-deco building you'll find both indie and mainstream films, mostly American, Moroccan, Spanish or French (with Spanish and American films typically dubbed into Arabic).

🛍 Shopping

🛍 Medina

Boutique Majid
ANTIQUES, JEWELLERY

(Map p225; ☑0539 93 88 92; Rue Les Almohades; ☺10am-7pm) You can get lost for hours in this exotic antique shop, but the real gem is Majid himself. Straight out of central casting (including his red fez), Majid will regale you with stories of the Rolling Stones and other luminaries while showing you his amazing collection of Moroccan doors, jewellery and artefacts, clothing, fabrics and carpets.

Laura Wefling
ARTS & CRAFTS, CLOTHING

(Map p225; Pl de la Kasbah; ☺11am-6pm) Next to the Kasbah Museum, this is a beautiful shop with some superb one-off pieces of clothing, bags, decor items and ceramics.

Bleu de Fès
ANTIQUES

(Map p225; ☑0539 33 60 67; www.bleudefes.com; 16 Rue Les Almohades, Petit Socco; ☺10am-7pm) Drool over stacks and stacks of Berber carpets from the Middle and High Atlas.

🛍 Ville Nouvelle

★DARNA, The Women's Association of Tangier
ARTS & CRAFTS

(Map p225; www.darnamaroc.com) The yellow building opposite La Terrasse is a small complex offering an inexpensive restaurant, a boutique shop with crafts and clothing, and a sunny courtyard, making it a popular stop for lunch or just a place to relax. Since 2002 DARNA has served as a community house to help local women in need, such as those suffering the after effects of divorce.

★ **Las Chicas** ARTS & CRAFTS, CLOTHING
(Map p225; ☎0539 37 45 10; 52 Kacem Guenoun, Porte de la Kasbah; ⊙10am-7pm Mon-Sat) Just outside the kasbah, this is an eclectic mixture of a shop, stocking art pieces, homeware, cosmetics and some exquisite designer clothes, alongside a cafe. Offering a fun twist on the usual Moroccan style, this place is an absolute treat.

Librairie des Colonnes BOOKS
(Map p231; ☎5399 93 69 55; 54 Blvd Pasteur; ⊙9.30am-1pm & 4-7pm Mon-Sat) A famous landmark boasting wonderful architecture, this is Tangier's best bookshop, with a decent English section. There are frequent book readings and events, including author appearances. It was once the haunt of Paul Bowles, Jean Genet, Samuel Becket and William Burroughs, and is an institution in Tangier.

Ensemble Artisanat ARTS & CRAFTS
(Map p222; cnr Rue Belgique & Rue M'sallah; ⊙9am-1pm & 3-7pm Sat-Thu) This government-backed arts-and-crafts centre is a good place to see the range of local crafts and watch the artisans at work. There's no haggling, as prices are fixed, and they are also much higher than in the souqs.

Bazar Tindouf ANTIQUES
(Map p231; 72 Rue de la Liberté; ⊙10am-7pm) This shop opposite El-Minzah Hotel is bursting to the seams with antiques, glassware, brassware, ceramics, lamps, jewellery, clothing and more. It's definitely worth a browse.

El Tapisero ARTS & CRAFTS
(Map p222; ☎0539 94 56 81; www.eltapisero.com; 61 Blvd Yacoub el Mansour, Charf; ⊙9.30am-1pm & 3-7pm Mon-Thu, 9.30am-noon Fri & Sat) Make like Madonna and order a handmade carpet at El Tapisero. The team at this carpet-weaving enterprise is very creative and works with some of the big European decorators. Expect to pay about €50 to €250 per square metre.

La Casa Barata MARKET
(Ave Abou Kacem Sebti; ⊙9am-8pm Thu & Sun) Literally 'the cheap house', this large flea market carries everything you can imagine, from vegetables to electronics to carpets. The best opportunity to find real treasure, and an experience unto itself.

Fès Market MARKET
(Map p222) This market, to the west of the city centre, is good for imported cheese and other treats.

❶ Information

ORIENTATION

Tangier is divided into the old walled city (medina) and the modern city (ville nouvelle). The medina contains a kasbah (the walled fortress of the sultan); the historic meeting place of Petit Socco (also known as Socco Chico) in the centre; and of course the souqs. The larger Grand Socco (now officially called Pl du 9 Avril 1947), a pleasant square with a central fountain, is the hinge between the two sides of town, and the postcard entrance to the medina.

DANGERS & ANNOYANCES

As in any big city, it's best to stick to the beaten path at all times, and to take cabs point to point at night. Solo women may be subject to being hassled after about 10pm, and should avoid the port area after dark. If you have a serious problem and need help from the authorities, contact the **Brigade Touristique** (Tourist Police; ☎177; Ave Mohammed VI, Tangier Port).

INTERNET

Espace Net (Map p231; 16 Ave Mexique; per hr Dh5; ⊙9.30am-1am)

MEDICAL SERVICES

Hopital Mohammed V (Map p222; ☎0539 93 08 56; Ave Moulay Rachid)
Clinique du Croissant Rouge (Map p222; Red Cross Clinic; ☎0539 94 69 76, 0539 94 69 76; 6 Rue al-Mansour Dahabi) On the road to the airport.
Pharmacy Anegay (Map p225; Rue as-Siaghin; ⊙8am-6pm Mon-Sat)

MONEY

Blvds Pasteur and Mohammed V are lined with numerous banks with ATMs and *bureau de*

TANGIER FOR CHILDREN

For kids, **M'Nar Park** (☎0539 34 38 29; www.facebook.com/pages/Mnar-Park-Piscine/485227728156690; Cap Malabata; aquapark adult/child Dh100/50; ⊙pool 15 Jun-15 Sep) is heaven. Located south of Cap Malabata, with great views across the Bay of Tangier, this cliffside resort offers a water park, an electronic game park, karting, a small train, a mini-football field, restaurants, a cafe and 38 residential bungalows for families.

In town and close to the Grand Socco, the Mendoubia Gardens (p223) is a park with grass for playing football and swings for letting off steam.

change counters. Outside of working hours, try the exchange bureaus in the big hotels.

BMCE (Map p231; Blvd Pasteur; ☺8am-4pm Mon-Fri) One of several in this area.

Société Générale Bank ATM and money exchange.

POST

Main Post Office (Map p222; cnr Rue Quevada & Ave Mohammed V; ☺8am-4pm Mon-Fri) Poste restante is at the counter furthest to the right; parcel post is on the south side of the building.

TOURIST INFORMATION

Délégation Régionale du Tourisme (Map p231; ☑0539 94 80 50; 29 Blvd Pasteur; ☺9am-1pm & 3-6pm Mon-Fri) The recent investment in tourism infrastructure hasn't made it here. Some verbal help, but no printed material. The Hotel de Paris across the road has lots of brochures and staff are willing to help.

TRAVEL AGENCIES

The following both sell ferry and air tickets.

Carlson Wagonlit (Map p231; ☑0539 33 10 24; 91 Rue de la Liberté; ☺9am-1pm & 3-6pm Mon-Fri)

Hispamaroc (Map p231; ☑0539 93 21 78; hispamaroc@mamnet.net.ma; 2 Rue el-Jabha el-Ouatania; ☺9am-1pm & 3-6pm Mon-Fri)

❶ Getting There & Away

With a ferry port, international airport, train station and buses, Tangier is possibly Morocco's best-connected city.

AIR

The **Ibn Batouta International Airport** (☑0539 39 37 20) is 15km southwest of the city centre. It attracts a number of budget airlines (including easyJet, RyanAir and Air Arabia) as well as Iberia and Royal Air Maroc. Check the internet for the latest service providers and schedules, as these are constantly changing.

BOAT

Tangier effectively has two ports: **Tangier Port** (Map p222; in the city) and the newer Tanger Med terminal, 48km east along the coast.

From Tangier Port, there are fast catamaran ferries run by **FRS** (www.frs.es) and **Inter Shipping** (www.intershipping.es) to Tarifa (Dh350, 40 minutes). There are more than a dozen sailings a day, with the ferry companies leaving on alternate hours. The service includes a free bus transfer to Algeciras (50 minutes) on presentation of your ferry ticket.

Tickets are available from the company **ticket booths** outside the ferry terminal building at Tangier Port, in the terminal itself, or from virtually any travel agency around town; be sure to pick up an exit form so you can avoid hassles later.

Services from Tanger Med are primarily to Algeciras. A shuttle bus (Dh25) leaves Tanger Med every hour on the hour for the Tangier bus station, taking 45 minutes.

Advance book during peak periods (particularly Easter, the last week in August and the last week in October), allow an hour before departure to get tickets and navigate passport control, and remember the time difference with Spain (Morocco is one hour behind, and two hours behind during Ramadan). If you're arriving in Morocco, remember to get your passport stamped on the ferry.

BUS

CTM buses depart from the **main bus station** (gare routière; ☑0539 94 69 28; Pl Jamaa el-Arabia), about 2km to the south of the city centre by the Syrian mosque – the distinctly un-Moroccan-looking minarets are a useful nearby landmark. Destinations include the following:

DESTINATION	COST (DH)	DURATION (HR)
Casablanca	150	5½
Chefchaouen	50	3
Fez	125	6
Marrakesh	250	10
Meknès	100	5
Rabat	115	4
Tetouan	25	1

Cheaper bus companies also operate from the main bus station. There are regular departures for all the destinations listed for CTM, plus services to Al-Hoceima (Dh105, 10 hours) and Fnideq (Dh25, 1½ hours) – a small town 3km from the Ceuta border. A metered petit taxi to/from the town centre is around Dh10.

The main bus station has a **left-luggage facility** (per item per 24hr Dh5-7; ☺5am-1am).

CAR

The major car-rental agencies are at the airport. The following have in-town locations:

Avis (Map p231; ☑0539 93 46 46; www.avis. com/car-rental/location/AFR/MA/Tanger; 54 Blvd Pasteur; ☺8am-7pm Mon-Sat, 8am-noon Sun)

Budget (Map p222; ☑0531 06 09 51; Tanger Ville station; ☺8.30am-noon & 2.30-7pm Mon-Fri, 9am-noon & 3-6pm Sat, 9am-noon Sun)

Hertz (Map p222; ☑0539 32 21 65; 36 Ave Mohammed V; ☺8am-noon & 2.30-6.30pm Mon-Fri, 9am-noon & 3-6pm Sat, 9am-noon Sun)

A reasonably secure and convenient **car park** (42 Rue Hollande; per hour/night/24hr Dh2/15/25) is next to the Dawliz complex.

There are a number of gas stations around town:

TAXI

The **grand-taxi** rank for places outside Tangier is across from the main bus station. The most common destinations are Tetouan (Dh35, one hour, change here for Chefchaouen), Asilah (Dh20, 30 minutes) and Larache (Dh35, 1½ hours). For Ceuta, travel to Fnideq (Dh30, one hour), 3km from the border. There are no direct taxis to the border (Bab Sebta). Grands taxis to Tetouan also frequently wait for arriving trains at Tanger Ville train station. For destinations on the outskirts of Tangier, such as the Caves of Hercules or Cap Malabata, use the **grand-taxi** rank on the Grand Socco.

TRAIN

Tanger Ville is a hassle-free train station, though under massive remodelling as a terminus for the planned TGV line to Casablanca. Trains depart throughout the day for Meknès (Dh90), Fez (Dh111), Rabat (Dh101), Casablanca (Dh132) and Marrakesh (Dh 216), including a night service with couchettes, the famed *Marrakesh Express*, which should be reserved in advance (single Dh660, double per person Dh470, Dh370 with couchette). A petit taxi to/from Tangier centre should cost around Dh10.

❶ Getting Around

TO/FROM THE AIRPORT OR TANGER MED

Ibn Batouta Airport From the port in the city to the airport, a grand taxi takes 25 minutes and costs Dh150 for the entire car. If you want to pick up a local bus from the airport, bus 17 and bus 70 run to the Grand Socco, but you'll need to walk 2km to the main road.

Tanger Med A shuttle bus (Dh25) runs every hour from Tanger Med to the main bus station (45 minutes). The driver will drop you off near the train station if you ask.

BUS

Buses aren't really necessary for getting around Tangier, but two potentially useful services are **bus 13**, which runs from the train station via Ave Mohammed VI to Tangier Port gate, and bus 17, which links the train station and the **main bus station**. (p235)

TAXI

Ultramarine with a yellow stripe down the side, petits taxis do standard journeys around town, charging 50% more at night. Tangier suffers a perennial shortage of taxis, especially during the busy holiday months, so it's good to remind yourself that you can (and should) flag down a taxi that has passengers but spare seats.

Cap Spartel   رأس سبارطيل

Just 14km west of Tangier lies Cap Spartel, the northwestern extremity of Africa's Atlantic Coast. It is a popular day trip with locals and tourists alike. A dramatic drive takes you through La Montagne, an exclusive suburb of royal palaces and villas, and over the pine-covered headland to the Cap Spartel Lighthouse (closed). The beaches to the south are clean and quiet outside the summer season, so you can find your own private cove.

◉ Sights

Grottes d'Hercule   CAVE
(Dh5; ⊙8am-dark) Below Cap Spartel, **Plage Robinson** stretches off to the south – a great place for a bracing beach walk. Five kilometres further you reach the Grottes d'Hercule, the mythical dwelling place of Hercules, next to Le Mirage hotel. Since the 1920s these caves have been quarried for millstones, worked by prostitutes, and used as a venue for private parties by rich celebrities from Tangier.

A much-photographed view of the Atlantic from within the cave resembles a map of Africa. Camel rides are available here, just before the entrance to the caves on the right. A beach ride is a special treat.

🛏 Sleeping & Eating

Camping Achakkar   CAMPGROUND €
(☑0612 24 97 27; camping per person Dh25, plus per tent/car/campervan Dh25/20/45, bungalows Dh250-550, hot showers Dh20; ❄) Inland from the grotto, this shady site has clean facilities and hot water (electricity Dh30). It has a shop that stocks essentials and a cafe serving breakfast (Dh35), paninis, *shwarma* and pasta.

Le Mirage   HOTEL €€€
(☑0539 33 33 32; www.lemirage.com; Cap Spartel; d from Dh2600; ❄☎❄) One of the finest hotels in the Tangier area, with a dramatic location perched on the cliff beside the grotto, Le Mirage offers a view of miles of broad Atlantic beach. The bungalows are exquisite, as the price suggests, and there's a spa and golf course.

Nonguests can get a taste of the opulence in the immaculate restaurant (meals around Dh500), or just stop by for a drink beneath the pergola. From the sunny terrace you can see the Roman ruins of Cotta, where fish oil was processed.

Cap Spartel Café & Restaurant
MOROCCAN €

(☑0539 93 37 22; Cap Spartel Rd; breakfast Dh22, paninis Dh30; ℗) This restaurant next to the lighthouse is popular on weekends. Set in a lovely garden overlooking the sea, it serves good juices, crêpes both savoury and sweet, paninis and pizza.

❶ Getting There & Away

Grands taxis from Tangier are the best way of getting to Cap Spartel. A round-trip charter should cost around Dh200, including waiting time. Taxis leave from the rank in front of St Andrew's Church in Tangier.

Road to Ceuta

The scenic road from Tangier to Ceuta is worth taking: green patchwork fields, alluring mountain roads, rolling hills, rocky headlands and good sandy beaches reveal a different side to Morocco.

The road begins at Cap Malabata, the headland opposite Tangier. There's a corniche with expensive apartments, a golf course and the large M'nar Park (p234), a great place for children and with a restaurant that has views back towards Tangier.

There's no more development until Ksar es-Seghir, 25km further around the coast. This small fishing port, dominated by the remains of a Portuguese fort, has a yacht basin and a beach that's popular in summer. Just beyond you'll spot Tanger Med, the massive container facility and ferry port, 48km from Tangier.

The great crag of Jebel Musa, one of the ancient Pillars of Hercule, rises up 10km or so further on, and views along the pretty mountain road are spectacular.

Grands taxis ply the route between Tangier and Fnideq, where you can catch links to Ceuta.

Ceuta (Sebta)
سبتة

POP 84,960

Ceuta is one of a handful of Spanish possessions on the coastline of Morocco. Located on a peninsula jutting out into the Mediterranean, it offers a compact dose of fantastic architecture, interesting museums, excellent food, a relaxing maritime park and bracing

---

SURVIVAL SPANISH

Hello/Goodbye ¡Hola!/¡Adios!

Yes/No Sí/No

Please/Thank you Por favor/Gracias

Where is...? ¿Dónde está...?

➡ **hotel** hotel

➡ **guesthouse** pensíon

➡ **camping** camping

Do you have any rooms available? ¿Tiene habita-ciones libres?

➡ **a single room** una habitación individual

➡ **a double room** una habitación doble

How much is it? ¿Cuánto cuesta?

What time does the next...leave? ¿A qué hora sale/llega el próximo...?

➡ **boat** barca

➡ **bus** autobús

I'd like a... Quisiera un...

➡ **one-way ticket** billete sencillo

➡ **return ticket** billete de ida y vuelta

➡ **beer** cerveza

➡ **sandwich** bocadillo

---

nature walks. The city is particularly beautiful at night, a skyline of artfully lit buildings and bursting palms.

If entering from Morocco, Ceuta is also an eye-opener. You cross a 400m no-man's-land of haphazardly placed barricades, part of the EU's efforts to prevent illegal immigration, and find yourself blinking in the light of Spanish culture, a relaxed world of well-kept plazas and tapas bars bubbling over until the wee hours. This cultural-island phenomenon is the essence of Ceuta. It explains the Spanish military presence, the immigrants, the duty-free shopping, the shady cross-border commerce and the tourism. It makes a perfect weekend getaway.

History

Ceuta served as one of the Roman Empire's coastal bases (its Arabic name, Sebta, stems from the Latin *septem*). After a brief stint under the control of the Byzantine Empire, the city was taken in AD 931 by the Arab rulers of Muslim Spain – the basis for Spain's claim of historical rights to the land. For the

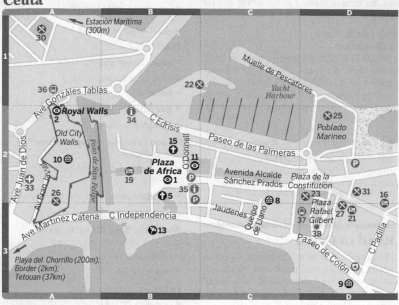

Ceuta

◉ Top Sights
1	Plaza de Africa	B2
2	Royal Walls	A2

◎ Sights
3	Baños Arabes	F2
4	Casa de Los Dragones	E3
5	Cathedral Santa Maria de la Asuncion	B2
6	Iglesia de San Francisco	E3
7	Museo de Ceuta	E3
8	Museo de la Basilica Tardorromana	C2
9	Museo de la Legión	D3
10	Museo de los Muralles Reales	A2
11	Palacio de Asamblea	B2
12	Parque Marítimo del Mediterráneo	E2
13	Playa de la Ribera	B3
14	Plaza de los Reyes	E3
15	Santuario de Nuestra Señora de Africa	B2

🛏 Sleeping
16	Hostal Central	D2
17	Hostal Plaza Ruiz	E3
18	Hotel Ulises	E3
19	Parador Hotel La Muralla	B2
20	Pensión Charito	F2
21	Pensión La Bohemia	D3

🍽 Eating
22	Cala Carlota	B1
23	Central Market	D2
24	Charlotte	E3
25	El Refectorio	D2
26	El Secreto de Yuste	A2
27	Gran Muralla	D3
28	Mesón el Bache	E3
29	Mesón el Cortijo	E3
30	Supersol Supermarket	A1
31	Vincentino Pastelería	D2

🍷 Drinking & Nightlife
32	Dublin	E2

ℹ Information
33	Instituto Gestión Sanitario	A2
34	Main Tourist Office	B2
35	Plaza de Africa Kiosk	B2

🚌 Transport
36	Buses to Border	A1
	Buses to Border	(see 37)
37	Local Bus Station	D3
38	Renfe Office	D3

next 500 years, however, this city at the tip of Africa was a prized possession, fought over and ruled successively by Spanish princes, Moroccan sultans and Portuguese kings. Things began to settle down when Portugal and Spain united under one crown in

tegic complexity, have been beautifully restored, with information boards in English.

➡ **Museo de los Muralles Reales** MUSEUM

(Map p239; Ave González Tablas; ⊙11am–2pm & 5–9pm Tue-Sat) **FREE** This gallery houses temporary art exhibitions. Squeezed out of the fort's unforgiving architecture, it's a beautifully designed space, worth visiting irrespective of what's on – although if you're lucky enough to catch local artist Diego Canca, don't miss his work.

Museo de la Basilica Tardorromana MUSEUM

(Map p238; ⊙10am-1.30pm & 5-7.30pm Mon-Sat, 10am-1.30pm Sun) **FREE** This superbly executed underground museum is integrated into the architectural remains of an ancient basilica discovered during street work in the 1980s, including a bridge over open tombs, skeletons included. The artefacts become a means of branching out into various elements of local history. In Spanish, but definitely worth a lap through. Enter via Calle Queipo de Llano.

Museo de la Legión MUSEUM

(Map p238; ☑0956 52 64 58; Paseo de Colón; donations appreciated; ⊙10am-1.30pm Mon-Sat) **FREE** This intriguing museum is dedicated to and run by the Spanish Legion, an army unit set up in 1920 that played a pivotal role in Franco's republican army. Loaded to the gills with memorabilia, weaponry and uniforms, not to mention glory, pomp and circumstance, it is a fascinating glimpse into the military culture that shaped the Spanish Morocco.

There's the imperious statue of fascist leader Franco, an explanation of how the legion's founder, Millan Astray, lost his right eye, and the history of the legion in cinema. There are guided tours in English.

Playa de la Ribera & Playa del Chorillo BEACH

(Map p238) Ceuta's two beaches are well kept and conveniently located, although the sand is a bland grey.

Casa de Los Dragones ARCHITECTURE

(Map p239; House of Dragons) The Casa de los Dragones on Plaza de los Reyes is a fantastic dream that has entered the real world. This former home is an extraordinary example of eclectic architecture, with Moorish arches, polished brick facades, mansard roofs, fabulous balconies, and the pièce de résistance,

1580, and Ceuta passed to Spain by default. When the two countries split in 1640, Ceuta remained Spanish, and has been ever since.

☉ Sights & Activities

★**Plaza de Africa** LANDMARK

(Map p238) This is the charming heart of Ceuta, with manicured tropical plantings, a square of cobblestone streets and some of the city's finest architecture.

Moving clockwise from the oblong **Commandancia General**, a military headquarters closed to visitors, you encounter the striking yellow **Santuario de Nuestra Señora de Africa** (⊙9am-1pm & 5-9pm Mon-Sat, 9am-1pm & 6.30-9pm Sun & holidays); the 19th-century **Palacio de Asamblea**; and finally the **Cathedral Santa Maria de la Asuncion** (☑0956 51 77 71; ⊙9am-1pm & 6-8pm Tue-Sun, museum 10am-1pm Tue-Sat) with its museum. The centre of the plaza contains a memorial to soldiers lost in the Spanish–Moroccan War of 1860, a conflict over the borders of Ceuta.

★**Royal Walls** ARCHITECTURE

(Map p238; ☑0956 51 17 70; Ave González Tablas; ⊙10am-2pm & 5-8pm) **FREE** The most impressive sight in Ceuta is the medieval Royal Walls, dating back to the 5th century. These extensive fortifications, of great stra-

SELF-CATERING

Stock up for ferry journey snacks and road trips here:

Central Market (⊙8am-3pm Mon-Sat) This cavernous market is the local spot for fresh meat and produce, and a vibrant experience as well.

Supersol Supermarket (Av Muelle Cañonero Dato; ⊙9am-9pm) This is the best place to stock up on essentials and treats alike; there's a smaller branch in the city centre on Dean Navarro Acuña.

four enormous dark dragons springing from the roof. If only it were open to the public!

Plaza de los Reyes   LANDMARK
(Map p239) With its green triumphal arch (inscribed 'a monument to coexistence') and fountain, this plaza borders the twin-towered yellow **Iglesia de San Francisco**.

Museo de Ceuta   MUSEUM
(Map p239; ☑0956 51 73 98; 30 Paseo del Revellín; ⊙11am-2pm & 6-9pm Mon-Sat Jun-Sep) FREE This ageing municipal museum has a small collection showing the peninsula's pre-Spanish history, with all labels in Spanish. The temporary exhibitions are of more interest.

**Parque Marítimo
del Mediterráneo**   PARK
(Map p238; adult/child €4.80/3.70; ⊙11am-8pm Jun-Aug) This creative maritime park is a real hit in the summer, and perfect for families. One of several parks developed by the artist and architect César Manrique, it borrows the city-walls theme to construct a huge pool deck on the sea, including a grand lagoon and two other saltwater pools, surrounded by 10 bars, pubs, restaurants, cafes and a disco.

A central island holds a fortress casino (open from 10pm). A pictorial display of Manrique's work lies just inside the entrance, 50m to the right.

Baños Arabes   HISTORIC BUILDING
(Map p239; Calle Arrabal 16; ⊙11.30am-1.30pm & 6.30-8.30pm) Accidentally discovered during street work, these ancient Arab baths sit on a main road, an incongruous sight. There are two of them, with barrel-vaulted roofs originally covered with marble – the high-tech spa of its time.

Monte Hacho   OUTDOORS
A walk around Monte Hacho is an option on a nice day; maps are available at the tourist office or you can wing it and follow the coast. Since it's an uphill slog from town, a good option is to start by taking a cab (€15) to the **Mirador de San Antonio** two-thirds of the way up, which offers magnificent views over Ceuta and north to Gibraltar.

The summit of the peninsula is crowned by the massive **Fortaleza de Hacho**, a fort first built by the Byzantines, and still an active military installation. No visitors are allowed. Back down at the main road, you keep going clockwise until you reach the **Castillo del Desnarigado** (☑0956 51 17 70; ⊙11am-2pm Sat & Sun) FREE.

García Aldave   OUTDOORS
If you've done everything else, the García Aldave can be crossed from coast to coast along the N354, either by car or on foot (a hiking map from the tourist office will help). The route contains a series of circular neo-medieval watchtowers, closed to visitors. Several of these are visible from the excellent **Mirador de Isabel II**, which offers great views across the isthmus to Monte Hacho.

On 1 November, the Day of the Dead, there is a mass pilgrimage here to remember the deceased.

The road ends at Benzú, a small town on the northern coast, which faces the grand sight of Jebel Musa rising across the border. The mountain is known here as the Dead or Sleeping Woman, because it resembles a woman, lying on her back. Contemplate mortality here over a cup of mint tea.

🛏 Sleeping

Ceuta isn't overrun with sleeping options, so if you'll be arriving late in the day, an advance reservation is a good idea. Most cheap places are *pensiónes,* some of which are identifiable by the large blue-and-white 'CH' plaque.

★**Pensión La Bohemia**   HOTEL €
(Map p238; ☑0956 51 06 15; 16 Paseo del Revellín; per person without bathroom €30) This well-run operation, one flight above a shopping arcade, offers a bright and spotless set of rooms arranged around a central courtyard. Bathrooms are shared, with plenty of hot water and communal showers. Rooms have small TVs and fans; some have internal windows only.

Pensión Charito
HOSTEL €

(Map p239; ☎0956 51 39 82; pcharito@terra.es; 1st fl, 5 Calle Arrabal; per person €25) A bold new CH sign that makes this place easy to find – look for the green-and-cream building next to the bar Bocatos José. Although it's a bit decrepit on the outside, the inside is clean and homey with hot showers and a small, well-equipped kitchen. If rooms are full, the staff may not be present.

Hotel Ulises
HOTEL €€

(Map p239; ☎0956 51 45 40; www.hotelulises. com; 5 Calle Camoens; s/d incl breakfast €76/82; ✳☏☀) This hotel offers a pretty decent deal: excellent location, parking nearby and great prices. The rooms aren't large, but come with TV and some have balconies. The cafe spills out onto the pavement and is perfect for people-watching over a drink and a few tapas.

Hostal Central
HOTEL €€

(Map p238; ☎0956 51 67 16; www.hostalceuta. com; Paseo del Revellín; s/d €45/52; ✳☏) This place is in a charming location and offers a warm welcome. Rooms are airy, with nice pine furniture; the best have wrought-iron balconies overlooking the cafes of the plaza. Bathrooms and fridges are standard.

Hostal Plaza Ruiz
HOTEL €€

(Map p239; ☎0956 51 67 33; www.hostalesceu- ta.com; 3 Plaza Ruiz; s/d €52/65; ✳☏) This good-value, two-star hotel in an excellent location has ultra-modern decor and is very welcoming. Rooms are tiny but spotless, and all come with bathroom and fridge. Low-season discounts are available.

Parador Hotel La Muralla
HOTEL €€€

(Map p238; ☎0956 51 49 40; www.parador.es/ en/paradores/parador-de-ceuta; 15 Plaza de Afri- ca; s/d from €115/135; ✳☏☀) This spacious four-star hotel is perfectly situated on the Plaza de Africa. Rooms are comfortable, but not luxurious, with simple wooden doors and plain ceramic tiles. Balconies overlook a pleasant garden overflowing with palm trees. A bar-cafe adds value.

✖ Eating & Drinking

There are numerous bars and fast-food res- taurants at Poblado Marinero, near Parque Marítimo del Mediterráneo.

★Mesón el Cortijo
TAPAS €

(Map p239; ☎0956 51 19 83; 14 Calle Cervantes; tapas from €2; ☺1pm-midnight) A classic neigh- bourhood gathering place that's heavy on tapas, *cerveza* (beer) and friendliness. Catch up on football, gossip and practise your Es- pañol.

Charlotte
CAFE €

(Map p239; Plaza de los Reyes; breakfast €4, tapas from €2; ☺9am-midnight) This is the perfect place for just about anything any time of day: it serves breakfast, a lunchtime sand- wich, beer, cocktail and tapas. Swift, efficient service and a prime people-watching spot on the square make it very popular.

Mesón el Bache
TAPAS €

(Map p239; ☎0956 51 66 42; Sargento Mena Alge- ciras; tapas €2.50, raciones from €10; ☺9am-3pm & 8.30pm-midnight Mon-Sat) Have your tapas in a rustic hunting lodge. The locals love it, especially for watching sport, and you get one free tapa with every drink. Just down- hill from Plaza de los Reyes, looking towards the port.

Vincentino Pastelería
CAFE €

(Map p238; Calle Alférez Bayton; sandwiches €2, bocadillos €2.50; ☺8am-11pm) This place buzz- es all day with people clamouring for its ice creams, sandwiches, delicious patisserie and excellent coffee. Sit inside or out.

El Secreto de Yuste
SPANISH €

(Map p238; ☎0659 67 18 14; 1 Muralles Reales; menu €6; ☺1.30pm-12.45am) Here's your chance to eat inside the Royal Walls. There's a small menu of local meats and seafood en- hanced by the unique atmosphere. You can sit outside by the moat.

Gran Muralla
CHINESE €

(Map p238; ☎0956 51 76 25; Plaza de la Constitu- tion; mains from €7; ☺12-4pm & 7-11pm Mon-Sat) If you've had enough local food, you'll find hearty portions of Chinese standards here. Window tables have views over the plaza and out to sea.

TAPAS BAR NEIGHBOURHOODS

The best places to look for tapas bars are in the streets behind the post office and around Calle Millán Astray to the north of Calle Camoens. In addition to tapas, they all serve more substantial *raciones* (a larger helping of tapas) and *bocadillos* (sandwiches).

MEDITERRANEAN COAST & THE RIF CEUTA (SEBTA)

Cala Carlota
SEAFOOD €€

(Map p238; ☎0956 52 50 61; Real Club Nautico, Calle Edrisis; mains from €8, set menu €15; ☺9am-3pm & 5pm-midnight Mon-Sat, 10am-3pm Sun) This simple restaurant has a prime location in the Club Nautico overlooking the yacht harbour, with outdoor seating in season. If you can see your way past the desultory service, the three-course *menú del diá* (daily set menu) is a good choice, and there are excellent fish main dishes.

To get there, the underpass beneath the busy highway starts at the main tourist office, and will save you a long walk.

★ El Refectorio
SPANISH €€€

(Map p238; ☎0956 51 38 84; www.elrefectorio. com; Poblado Marinero; menu around €40-55; ☺1pm-4.30pm Sun & Mon, 8.30pm-12.30am Tue-Sat) Considered by many to be Ceuta's best restaurant, El Refectorio has a good bar, and dining inside and out with magnificent sea views from the balcony. It excels at shellfish, fish and meats and has a good wine list.

Dublin
PUB

(Map p239; Calle Delgado Serrano; ☺4pm-3am Mon-Sat) It's like every other Irish pub you've ever been in, but if you need that Guinness fix, this is the place. If the volume gets to you, you can escape to the tables outside. Go down the steps where Calle Delgado Serrano takes a 90-degree bend.

ⓘ Information

To phone Ceuta from outside Spain, dial 0034. Remember that Ceuta is one hour ahead of Morocco (two during summer time), and that most businesses will be closed on Sunday.

MEDICAL SERVICES

Instituto Gestión Sanitario (Map p238; Ingesa; ☎0956 52 84 00; ☺24hr) Next to the Royal Walls.

MONEY

Euros are used for all transactions in Ceuta. ATMs are plentiful; outside banking hours you can change money at the more expensive hotels. There are informal moneychangers on both sides of the border, although it's technically illegal to take dirhams out of Morocco.

POST

Correos (Map p239; Post Office; 59 Calle Real; ☺8.30am-8.30pm Mon-Fri, 9.30am-2pm Sat)
Main Post Office (Plaza de España; ☺8.30am-8.30pm Mon-Fri, 9.30am-2pm Sat)

TOURIST INFORMATION

Ceuta's history is outlined by the *ruta monumenta*, a series of excellent information boards in English and Spanish outside key buildings and monuments.

Main Tourist Office (Map p238; ☎0956 20 05 60; Baluarte de los Mallorquines; ☺8.30am-8.30pm Mon-Fri, 9am-8pm Sat & Sun) Friendly and efficient, with good maps and brochures.

Plaza de Africa Kiosk (Map p238; ☎0956 52 81 46; ☺10am-1pm & 5-8pm 15 Sep-31 May, 10.30am-1.30pm & 6-9pm 1 Jun-14 Sep) A satellite of the main tourist office.

TRAVEL AGENCIES

Av Muelle Cañonero Dato and the approach to the *estación marítima* are lined with agencies selling ferry tickets to Algeciras.

ⓘ Getting There & Away

TO/FROM MOROCCO

Buses and grands taxis to Ceuta often terminate at Fnideq, rather than at the border (Bab Sebta). If so, the border is a further 1km walk, or Dh7 by taxi. Although the border is open 24 hours, public transport is sparse from 7pm to 5am.

On the Moroccan side, you'll either fill out a departure form at the passport window, if on foot, or at the vehicle registration window. Hustlers will sell you a form for a dirham or two. If you're driving a hire car, you will be required to show proof of authorisation to take the vehicle out of the country. The 100m crossing is surprisingly disorganised, with multiple people asking for your passport. Pedestrians must frequently walk in the car lanes.

Coming the other way, there is a large grand taxi lot next to Moroccan border control. Departures are plentiful to Tetouan (Dh20, 30 minutes), from where you can pick up onward transport. Taxis to Chefchaouen or Tangier are rare, and you'll most likely have to bargain hard to hire a vehicle for yourself (Chefchaouen, Dh300, 90 minutes; Tangier, Dh200, one hour). A good alternative is to take a grand taxi to Fnideq (Dh7, 10 minutes), just south of the border, from where transport to Tangier is more frequent (Dh35, one hour).

TO/FROM MAINLAND SPAIN

The unmissable **Estación Marítima** (Ferry Terminal; Calle Muelle Cañonero Dato) is west of the town centre. There are several daily high-speed ferries to Algeciras. **Ticket offices** (☎0956 50 62 75; ☺9am-9pm) are around the corner. **Baleària** (www.balearia.com), **Trasmediterranea** (www.trasmediterranea.es) and **FRS** (www.frs.es) also run ferries to Algeciras.

You can purchase train tickets to European destinations at the **Renfe office** (Map p238; ☎0956 51 13 17; 17 Plaza Rafael Gilbert;

9.30am-1pm & 4.30-8.30pm Mon-Fri,
9.30am-1pm Sat) or at a travel agency. Several
agencies in the ferry terminal also sell Enatcar
(the main Spanish coach company) bus tickets.

❶ Getting Around

Bus 7 runs up to the **border** *(frontera)* every
10 minutes or so from Plaza de la Constitution
(€1). If you arrive by ferry and want to head
straight for the border, there's a **bus stop** on
Ave González Tablaz opposite the entrance to
the ramparts. **Local buses** also stop on Ave
González Tablaz. There's also a taxi rank outside
the terminal building.

If you have your own vehicle, street parking is
restricted to a maximum of two hours (€1) during the day. If you are staying longer, use the **car
park** (Calle O'Donnell; per hr €0.50, per 12hr €4)
on Calle O'Donnell.

THE RIF MOUNTAINS

جبال الريف

(Map p267) The Rif is the most northerly of
Morocco's mountain chains. There are some
good hikes to be had in the region, from
the most popular town for tourists, Chefchaouen, with its pastel blue medina. An
alternative base in the Rif is Tetouan, which
has some fine Spanish colonial architecture.

Tetouan

تطوان

POP 330,000

Tetouan is a jewel of a town in a striking
location at the foot of the Rif Mountains,
and just a few kilometres from the sea. Despite seeing relatively few foreign visitors,
there's an air of authenticity here that adds
great value to a visit. The ancient medina,
a Unesco World Heritage site, looks like it
has not changed in several centuries. The
modern centre that abuts it gleams in white,
its Spanish facades given a recent facelift to
seductive affect.

That Spanish influence dates from 1912–
56, when Tetouan was the capital of the
Spanish protectorate, which encompassed
much of northern Morocco. The town's
long relationship with Andalucia has left it
with a Hispano-Moorish character that is
unique in Morocco, as physically reflected
in the white buildings and broad boulevards of the Spanish part of the city, known
as the Ensanche (extension).

History

From the 8th century onwards, the city
served as the main point of contact between Morocco and Andalucia. In the 14th
century the Merenids established the town
as a base from which to control rebellious
Rif tribes, and to attack Ceuta, but it was
destroyed by Henry III of Castille in 1399.
After the Reconquista (the reconquest of
Spain, completed in 1492), the town was rebuilt by Andalucian refugees. It prospered,
due in part to their skills, and to thriving
pirate activity.

Moulay Ismail built Tetouan's defensive
walls in the 17th century, and the town's trade
links with Spain developed. In 1860, the Spanish took the town under Leopoldo O'Donnell,
who extensively Europeanised it, but upon
recapture, two years later, the Moors removed
all signs of European influence.

At the turn of the 20th century, Spanish
forces occupied Tetouan for three years,
claiming it was protecting Ceuta from Rif
tribes. In 1913 the Spanish made Tetouan
the capital of their protectorate, which was
abandoned in 1956 when Morocco regained
independence. Lately the Andalucian government has provided a great cultural boost
to the city by financing various restoration
projects.

◎ Sights

◎ Medina

The whitewashed medina of Tetouan is
an authentic time machine, and very trav-
eller-friendly, with moped-free lanes, few
street hustlers, amiable residents and a general lack of congestion, particularly in the
large residential areas. In the commercial
spaces, the sights and sounds of traditional
life are everywhere: craftsmen pound brass,
silk merchants offer thousands of spools of
multicoloured thread and bakers tend the
public ovens. There are dedicated souqs for
carpentry, **leather** and **jewellery**. There
are some 35 mosques as well, of which the
Grande Mosquée and **Saïda Mosque**, both
northeast of Pl Hassan II, are the most impressive, although non-Muslims are not allowed to enter. If you get lost, a few dirhams
in local hands will get you to any doorstep.

The medina is bordered to the south by
the pretty **Lovers Park**, a pleasant escape.
The entrance to the medina is off the grand
Pl Hassan II, which faces the Royal Palace.

Tetouan

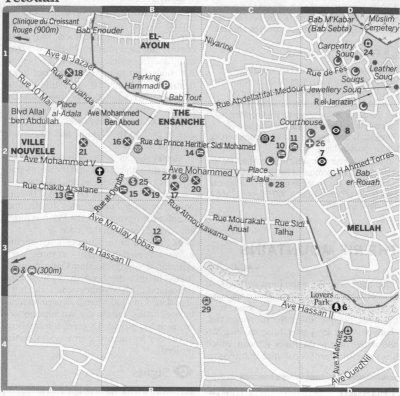

Tetouan

Place Hassan II LANDMARK

(Map p244) The broad and empty Pl Hassan II, which is mostly roped off for security reasons, links the medina to the Ensanche. It looks like it houses the Wizard of Oz, with guards standing in front of the long flat facade of the **Royal Palace**, and four somewhat bizarre columns towering all around.

These are not minarets, as one might suppose, but art-nouveau light towers designed by Enrique Nieto, a student of Gaudí, who lived in Melilla. The large decorations on the opposite wall are abstract Hands of Fatima, a common symbol used to ward off the evil eye. There are a few cafes that are good for a rest, particularly on the 2nd floor, which allows a grander view.

◉ The Ensanche

Take in the Ensanche by walking along Ave Mohammed V from **Place al-Jala** to **Place Moulayel-Mehdi**. The broad boulevard is lined with bright white Spanish colonial architecture, with a few art-deco elements, reminiscent of styles found elsewhere (eg in Casablanca and Larache) with restoration funded by the Andalucian government. You'll find hotels, banks and places to eat here.

Archaeology Museum MUSEUM

(Map p244; Ave al-Jazaer; Dh10; ◌10am-6pm Mon-Sat) A few blocks from Pl al-Jala there is an extensive museum with an excellent collection of artefacts from the Roman ruins at Lixus, displayed both inside and in the gardens. Labelling is in French, Spanish and Arabic.

Iglesia de Bacturia CHURCH

(Map p244; Pl Moulay el-Mehdi; ◌mass 7pm daily, 11am Sun) This Roman Catholic church was built in 1926 and is still active. We can't think of another place in Morocco where church bells sound the hour.

★Tetouan Museum of Modern Art MUSEUM

(Map p245; ☑0666 04 60 81; www.gotetouan. com/Museums.html; Ave Al Maki Al Naciri; ◌9am-7pm Mon-Sat) **FREE** Tetouan boasts one of only two schools of fine arts in Morocco (Casablanca has the other), so it's fitting that this museum should live here. The building itself is worth a visit: a magnificent Spanish-castle-like building that was once the railway station to Ceuta. It has been

Ethnographic Museum MUSEUM

(Bab el-Okla; Dh10; ◌9am-4pm Mon-Sat) Just inside the picture-perfect eastern gate, Bab el-Okla, is the Ethnographic Museum. It's worth a visit for the terrace views of the Rif (ask the caretaker to open it for you, if necessary), its pleasant garden with old cannons and the display of silk wedding gowns.

★Artisanal School NOTABLE BUILDING

(☑0539 97 27 21; Dh10; ◌8.30am-2.30pm Sat-Thu, to 11.30am Fri) Just outside Bab el-Okla is the best artisan centre in northern Morocco. This is a fascinating opportunity to see masters teaching apprentices traditional arts, including ornamental woodwork, silk costumes, carved plaster, intricate mosaics and decorative rifles. A fantastic central treasury holds the best of the best – don't miss the ceiling. Staff will open it upon request.

The building itself is of interest, set around a large courtyard, with fine doors upstairs.

carefully renovated to protect the artworks and to provide ample light inside.

The museum houses contemporary Moroccan art and has visiting exhibitions.

🛏 Sleeping

Tetouan has some reasonable sleeping options, both inside and out of the medina. If you want to be nearer the coast than the mountains, the port of Martil is only an inexpensive 15-minute cab ride away; M'Diq, the classier option, is twice that. The beachfronts are very quiet outside the holiday season of July to August.

Hotel Regina HOTEL €

(Map p244; ☑0539 96 21 13; 8 Rue Sidi Mandri; s/d Dh180/230; ☎) One of the larger budget choices, the Regina initially feels a bit stuck in the 1970s (be prepared to love the pebble-dashed walls), but the bright Riffian fabrics manage to wake you up. While the bathrooms are sometimes worn, everything is sparklingly clean, which makes it decent value for money. There's a cafe on the ground floor for breakfast.

Pension Iberia HOTEL €

(Map p244; ☑0539 96 36 79; 5 Pl Moulay el-Mehdi; s/d without bathroom Dh100/180) A good budget option, with shuttered balconies that open out onto Pl Moulay el-Mehdi. Views of the fountain below, and the city flowing over the hills add a dash of romance. Room 11 is a good choice. Poorly signed from the street, it's above the BMCE bank, on the 3rd floor of the building.

Hotel Paris HOTEL €

(Map p244; ☑0539 96 67 50; 31 Rue Chakib Arsalane; s/d Dh250/295) The simple, uninspiring rooms are clean, but the bathrooms are small. Institutional hallways accelerate you outdoors. Breakfast costs Dh40.

★ El Reducto GUESTHOUSE €€

(Map p244; ☑0539 96 81 20; www.riadtetouan. com; 38 Zanqat Zawiya; s/d incl breakfast from Dh400/550; ☀☎) The spotless, palatial rooms are truly fantastic: big bathrooms with lots of Spanish glazed tiles (one has a Jacuzzi for two), quality furniture and beautiful silk bedspreads. Climb the spiral staircase to the roof terrace for spectacular views. Some rooms are above the (excellent) restaurant while others are in the annexe on the opposite side of the lane.

The quixotic decision not to give guests building keys means that you'll need to find a waiter any time you want to get into the accommodation building.

Hotel Panorama Vista HOTEL €€

(Map p244; ☑0539 96 49 70; www.panorama-vista.com; Ave Moulay Abbas; s/d incl breakfast Dh295/395; ☀☎) Any place calling itself Panorama Vista has to be sure of its location,

---

THE CANNABIS INDUSTRY

Morocco is the largest producer of cannabis in the world, and most of it comes from the Rif. Almost 420 sq km of the region is under cultivation, with 700 tonnes of cannabis resin produced every year. European demand has soared to the point where profits have seen many regular farmers switch from traditional agriculture to cannabis (known in Morocco as kif). Put bluntly, kif production is the region's main economic activity. Alternative income projects, such as rural tourism, have been difficult to promote in the face of such economic dominance.

Cannabis cultivation started around Ketama in the 15th century. In 1912 the right to cultivate cannabis was granted to a few Rif tribes by Spain. In 1956, when Morocco gained independence, cannabis was prohibited, but Mohammed V later condoned cultivation in the Rif after the prohibition led to conflict there.

Most large shipments of Moroccan hashish (a concentrated form of marijuana) are smuggled into Europe by boat, including small speedboats that can make a round trip to Spain in an hour. The primary departure points are Martil, Oued Laou and Bou Ahmed, although the bigger ports of Nador, Tetouan, Tangier and Larache are also used. Traffickers also export hashish concealed in trucks and cars embarked on ferries leaving from the Spanish enclaves of Ceuta and Melilla or from Tangier. Not surprisingly, of all hashish seizures worldwide, half are made in Spain. There is much collaboration between traffickers and gangs smuggling Africans migrants to Europe.

Cannabis remains illegal in Morocco, although in 2016 several opposition parties called for its legalisation.

and, sure enough, rooms here offer dramatic views of the Rif Mountains. The rooms themselves are hotel-chain style without a lot of local ambience, but they're clean and everything works. The best value outside the medina. The cafe on the 1st floor offers a strong Moroccan-continental breakfast.

Blanco Riad GUESTHOUSE €€€

(Map p244; ☎ 0539 70 42 02; www.blancoriad.com; 25 Rue Zawiya Kadiria; d incl breakfast from Dh550, ste Dh1650; ❋❀) This beautiful medina house with its typical Tetouan architecture has been carefully restored and furnished with a blend of modern and antique pieces. It offers large, comfortable rooms and a Zen-like garden. One of the salons contains a good restaurant open to non-guests, and there's a boutique with a clothes designer doing clever things with traditional Riffian fabrics.

✖ Eating

Tetouan has not been known for its restaurants in the past, but things are looking up as tourism is encouraged. The best restaurants are those in medina guesthouses. Several places serve alcohol with meals.

Snack Taouss FAST FOOD €

(Map p244; ☎ 0533 23 11 58; 3 Rue 10 Mai; mains from Dh25; ☉11am-11pm) Known for its burgers and chips, this little snack bar has a Syrian influence and does good felafel and delicious *shwarma* as well as inexpensive pizzas, salads, *harira* (tomato and chickpea soup), tajines and more. There's a small seating area upstairs (handy if you're waiting for a pizza), or you can eat on the move.

Dallas PASTRIES €

(Map p244; ☎ 0533 96 60 69; 11 Rue Youssef ben Tachfine; pastries from Dh4; ☉6am-10pm; ☎) Yes, named after the TV show, but otherwise the name has no bearing on this place, a patisserie stacked to the rafters with plates of pastries. This is where local families come to load up on sweets. One block off Ave Mohammed V.

Birjiss FAST FOOD €

(Map p244; ☎ 0539 71 11 11; 8 Ave Mohammed Ben Aboud; panini from Dh20; ☉noon-11pm) Made-to-order sandwiches, burgers, pizzas and *shwarma* make this an excellent option. Choose from a smorgasbord of ingredients both typical and exotic.

LOCAL MARKETS

There's loads of fresh fruit and veg for sale in the medina on the road leading east to Bab el-Okla. The central market (closed Friday) around the corner from Lovers Park puts on a good display, with fish brought in from the coast.

Oahda CAFE €

(Map p244; ☎ 0533 96 67 94; 16 Rue al-Ouahda; pastries from Dh4; ☉7am-9pm, closed Fri afternoon) A female-friendly cafe popular with locals, where sticky cakes are a speciality. It's a bit claustrophobic on the upper floor.

Restaurant Albahr FAST FOOD €

(Map p244; ☎ 0533 68 96 75; 21 Rue Almoukawama; mains from Dh30; ☉10am-10pm) It's all shiny chrome and black decor here, with fried foods, burgers and good fish and chips on the menu. Salads are a plus, and there's couscous on Fridays (Dh50).

★ Blanco Riad MOROCCAN €€

(Map p244; ☎ 0539 70 42 02; 25 Rue Zawiya Kadiria; 3-course menu Dh150; ☉noon-10pm) The menu at this elegant riad is a cut above the usual, and features some innovative Moroccan dishes, heavy on local seasonal produce and a big change from the standard tajine menu. The garden is pleasant in summer, and the dining room has both Moroccan and Western seating. Reservations essential; no alcohol.

El Reducto MOROCCAN €€

(Map p244; ☎ 0539 96 81 20; 38 Zanqat Zawiya; mains from Dh80; ☉noon-10pm) Tuck into traditional Moroccan (and some Spanish) fare in the grand surroundings of this traditional house, which once belonged to Moroccan vizier and is decorated with antique glazed Seville tiles. Desserts are particularly good, and alcohol is served.

Restaurant Restinga MOROCCAN €€

(Map p244; 21 Ave Mohammed V; mains from Dh40, beer from Dh20; ☉9am-9pm) The open-air courtyard shaded by a huge ficus tree is this charming restaurant's primary attraction – along with the rare alcohol licence. A great place to duck out of the crowded boulevard for a rest and a beer, as well as some seafood from the coast.

Drinking

As is the Moroccan norm, Tetouan's drinking establishments are firmly in the male sphere. For a drop of the hard stuff, head for the dark and smoky bars along Rue 10 Mai, northwest of Pl Moulay el-Mehdi. If you just want a beer, Restaurant Restinga (p247) is the place, and is female-friendly.

Shopping

Wood and leatherwork are the local specialities; for the latter go straight to the source at the small tannery (p248) in the north of the medina.

Dar Lebadi ARTS & CRAFTS
(Map p245; ☎0533 97 38 56; Jenoui section; ☺10am-7pm) The shopping palace of the medina, this 200-year-old building, a former governor's house, has been meticulously restored. It is a clearing house for Berber artisans and Rabati carpets, and has friendly staff. Worth a stop just to see the building, but be careful: you may be there for hours.

Ensemble Artisanat ARTS & CRAFTS
(Map p244; Ave Hassan II; ☺8am-8pm Mon-Sat) This government-sponsored emporium is a hive of activity, with carpet weavers, leatherworkers, jewellers and woodworkers all plying their trades. Prices are fixed.

Tannery ARTS & CRAFTS
(Map p244; Bab M'Kabar; ☺closed Fri) Tetouan has traditionally been a leather-producing town, and there is a small tannery here. They're smaller than the tanneries at Fez, but still interesting, and there are leather shops in the vicinity.

Information

There are plenty of banks with ATMs along Ave Mohammed V.

BMCE (Map p244; Pl Moulay el-Mehdi; ☺8.45am-4pm Mon-Thu, 8.45-11am Fri, 8.45am-noon Sat)

Clinique du Croissant Rouge (Map p244; Red Cross Clinic; ☎0539 96 20 20; Pl al-Hammama, Quartier Scolaire)

Cyber Friends (Map p244; 19 Ave Mohammed V; per hr Dh5; ☺9am-11pm)

Pharmacie El-Feddan (Map p244; ☎0539 96 80 51; Pl Hassan II; ☺9am-1pm & 3.30-8pm) Useful pharmacy between the Ensanche and the medina.

Post Office (Map p244; Pl Moulay el-Mehdi; ☺8am-4pm)

Tetouan Hospital (Map p245; ☎0539 97 24 30; Ave Abdelkhalek Torres) About 2km out of town.

Voyages Hispamaroc (Map p244; fax 0539 71 33 38; 23 Ave Mohammed V; ☺8.30am-12.30pm & 3-7pm Mon-Fri, 9am-12.30pm Sat) Sells ferry tickets to Spain.

Voyages Travelmar (Map p244; ☎0539 71 42 37; 5 Ave Mohammed V; ☺9am-noon & 2.30-6.30pm Mon-Sat) Sells ferry tickets to Spain.

Getting There & Away

BUS

From Tetouan's modern **bus station** (Map p244; cnr Ave 9 Avril & Ave Meknes) you can get to any town in the north. There's a left-luggage office (medium/large bag Dh6/10). Local buses serve the following destinations:

Fnideq Dh12, 1¼ hours

Martil Dh6, 25 minutes

M'Diq Dh10, one hour

CTM (☎0539 96 16 88) has its own station; destinations include the following:

Fez Dh100, six hours

Marrakesh Dh240, 11½ hours

Rabat Dh120, four hours

TAXI

Grands taxis leave from the main bus station for Oued Laou (Dh20, 30 minutes), Al-Hoceima (Dh150, three hours), Chefchaouen (Dh35, one hour) and Tangier (Dh35, one hour).

Grands taxis leave from the CTM bus station for Fnideq (for Ceuta; Dh20, 30 minutes) and Martil (Dh7, 15 minutes).

Getting Around

Petits taxis are canary yellow; a ride around town should be around Dh10.

If you have your own vehicle, you can keep your car at the guarded **Parking Hammadi** (Map p244; Ave Al Jazaer; daytime per 4hr Dh10, per night Dh10).

Around Tetouan

While Tetouan sees few foreigners, in summer both local and Europe-based Moroccans flock to the golden beaches close to the town. The coast from Fnideq near Ceuta southwards to M'Diq, Cabo Negro and Martil sports two large golf resorts and swaths of holiday apartments along new corniches.

Cabo Negro & M'Diq
الراس الاسود والمضيق

Tucked into the lee of the north side of Cabo Negro is the surprising town of M'Diq. Once a small fishing village, it has rapidly grown into a classy resort, with a grand entrance, a fine beach, good hotels, the enormous Port de Plaisance shopping centre with lots of restaurants and the yacht club. There is really little to separate this place from Florida, but if you are suffering from medina fatigue, it's the perfect stop, and only 20 minutes from Tetouan.

🛏 Sleeping & Eating

M'Diq's sleeping options tend to cater to the summer tourist trade and ignore the lower end of the price bracket. Ask for discounts outside the summer months.

Golden Beach Hotel HOTEL €€
(☑ 0539 97 50 77; www.goldenbeachhotel.com; 84 Rte de Sebta; s/d incl breakfast Dh500/800, incl half-board Dh650/1050; 🛜🛏) This four-star, aptly named hotel, right on the beach, is worth the splurge – it's short on charm, but well run, well maintained and with good facilities, including a restaurant, a disco, a pool by the corniche and a piano bar with a most clever bar top: piano keys in marble.

Hotel Côte d'Or HOTEL €€
(Corniche; s/d incl breakfast Dh360/490) One of several new hotels along the corniche, this one is fairly bland with simple, modern rooms. Ask for a sea view. There are also apartments that sleep five (Dh1300). It is in a superb location opposite the beach, and there's a cafe and restaurant on the ground floor.

Café Olas SEAFOOD €
(☑ 0539 66 44 33; Corniche; mains from Dh65; ⊙ 9am-1pm) You can't miss this waterfront landmark dressed up as a lighthouse, with a hopping downstairs cafe and an upstairs seafood restaurant. The decor is snappy, the rooftop views superb, and they don't have to go far to get fresh catch. Located directly on the corniche car park.

La Table du Marché SEAFOOD €€€
(☑ 0661 47 85 56; Port de Plaisance; ⊙ 8pm-3am) Sitting at the end of a causeway in the sea, this Asian-inspired thatched-roof restaurant comes as quite a surprise. With branches in St Tropez and Marrakesh, perhaps this is the new face of Morocco. It offers seafood, sushi and Italian dishes in chic surroundings.

DRIVING THE COAST ROAD

The coast road, Rocade, now stretches from Fnideq all the way along the Mediterranean coast to Saïdia in the far east. From Fnideq to Martil there's a spanking new corniche along the beautiful beach. While there are few hotels, a huge number of holiday apartment blocks have been completed along this stretch, and more are being built. There are resorts at Plage Riffiyenne and the Marina Smir, and the enormous Ritz-Carlton resort under construction promises golf and another marina.

❶ Getting There & Away

Grands taxis and buses travelling between Tetouan and Fnideq (3km short of the border with Ceuta) pass through M'Diq. Grands taxis to Tetouan (Dh7, 15 minutes) depart from a stand near the Narjiss Hotel on Av Lalla Nezha. Those for the border (Dh15) gather opposite the Golden Beach Hotel.

Martil
مرتيل
POP 64355

Tetouan's port of Martil is a rapidly growing, modern beach town with a broad mountain view and a long corniche paralleled by streets full of apartment blocks, cafes, ice-cream shops and fast-food restaurants. The town also has a golf course and a pair of small shopping centres. It has year-round weekend visitors, and heaves in the summer, but is deserted the rest of the time. It's a viable base if you don't mind the 8km, 10-minute cab ride to Tetouan (p243).

🛏 Sleeping & Eating

Martil is chock-full of apartment rentals and resorts aimed squarely at local holiday makers. They're decent if a little bland. If you want something with more character, rest your head in nearby Tetouan.

The corniche is the place to go to eat, as there are a host of open-fronted restaurants facing the sea, as well as ice-cream parlours if you want a cone on your beach stroll. Cheap fast-food places are clustered in the streets near the bus station

Hotel Etoile de la HOTEL €
(☑ 0539 97 90 58; Ave Hassan II; s/d incl breakfast Dh320/374; 🛜) With its funky design – a cen-

tral, plant-filled atrium criss-crossed by stairways – and good location one block from the beach, this is Martil's best sleeping option. Riffian textiles and green paint brighten things up. The best rooms have balconies overlooking the sea, and the restaurant serves alcohol.

Camping al-Boustane CAMPGROUND €
(fax 0539 68 88 22; Corniche; camping per person Dh20, per tent/car/campervan Dh40/20/35, electricity Dh25; ☉ office 7.30am-noon & 7-11pm; 🛜 🐾) This secure campsite is one block from the beach, set in a pretty garden. Facilities are showing their age, but it does have a reasonable fish restaurant (mains from Dh75) and a pool in summer. There are serious drainage problems when it rains. Turn off the corniche at the fountain.

Le Guayana MOROCCAN €
(Corniche; salads Dh35, pizzas Dh45) One of a number of beach restaurants. Le Guayana serves juices, decent salads and ice cream as well as the usual burgers, pizzas and paninis.

❶ Getting There & Away

Local buses to Tetouan (Dh5, 15 minutes) leave from the bus station near the water tower at the southern end of the beach. You'll find grands taxis to Tetouan (Dh7, 10 minutes) near the big mosque.

Chefchaouen شفشاون

POP 42,800

Beautifully perched beneath the raw peaks of the Rif, Chefchaouen is one of the prettiest towns in Morocco, an artsy, blue-washed mountain village that feels like its own world. While tourism has definitely taken hold, the balance between ease and authenticity is just right. The old medina is a delight of Moroccan and Andalucian influence with red-tiled roofs, bright-blue buildings and narrow lanes converging on busy Plaza Uta el-Hammam and its restored kasbah. Long known to backpackers for the easy availability of kif (cannabis), the town has rapidly gentrified and offers a range of quality accommodation, good food, lots to do and no hassles to speak of, making it a strong alternative to a hectic multicity tour. This is a great place to relax, explore and take day trips to the cool green hills.

History

Chefchaouen was originally known as Chaouen, meaning 'peaks'. Under Spanish occupation the spelling changed to Xaouen, and in 1975 the town was renamed Chefchaouen (Look at the Peaks). These days the names are used interchangeably.

Moulay Ali ben Rachid founded Chaouen in 1471 as a base for Riffian Berber tribes to launch attacks on the Portuguese in Ceuta. The town expanded with the arrival of Muslim and Jewish refugees from Granada in 1494, who built the whitewashed houses, with tiny balconies, tiled roofs and patios (often with a citrus tree in the centre), that give the town its distinctive Spanish flavour. The pale-blue wash prevalent today was introduced in the 1930s – previ-

---

CLIMBING JEBEL EL-KELAÂ

Looming over Chefchaouen at 1616m, Jebel el-Kelaâ might initially appear a daunting peak, but with an early start, it can easily be climbed in a day if you're in reasonably good shape.

The hike starts from behind Camping Azilane, following the 4WD track that takes you to the hamlet of Aïn Tissimlane. Rocks painted with a yellow- and white- stripe indicate that you're on the right path. The initial hour is relatively steep as you climb above the trees to get your first views over Chefchaouen, before cutting into the mountains along the steady *piste* (track). You should reach Aïn Tissimlane within a couple of hours of setting out, after which the path climbs and zigzags steeply through great boulders for nearly an hour to a pass. Turn west along the track, which leads to the saddle of the mountain, from where you can make the final push to the summit. There's a rough path, although you'll need to scramble in places. The peak is attained relatively quickly, and your exertions are rewarded with the most sublime views over this part of the Rif.

It's straightforward and quick to descend by the same route. Alternatively, you can head north from the saddle on a path that takes you to a cluster of villages on the other side of the mountain. One of these villages, El-Kelaâ, has 16th-century grain stores and a mosque with a leaning minaret. From here, a number of simple tracks will take you back to Chefchaouen in a couple of hours.

ously windows and doors had been painted a traditional Muslim green.

The town remained isolated and xenophobic – Christians were forbidden to enter on pain of death – until occupied by Spanish troops in 1920. When the Spanish arrived they were surprised to hear the Jewish inhabitants still speaking a variant of medieval Castilian. The Spanish were briefly thrown out by Abd al-Krim during the Rif War in the 1920s, but they soon returned and remained until independence in 1956.

◉ Sights

Chefchaouen is split into an eastern half (the medina), and a western half (the *ciudad nueva*, or new city). The heart of the medina is Plaza Uta el-Hammam, with its unmistakable kasbah. The medina walls have recently been repaired, with Spanish funding. The principal route of the new city is Ave Hassan II, which stretches from Plaza Mohammed V, a leafy square designed by artist Joan Miró, past the western gate of Bab el-Ain, around the southern medina wall and into the medina itself. Here it dead-ends at Pl el-Majzen, the main drop-off point. The bus station is a steep 1.5km hike southwest of the town centre. The falls of Ras el-Maa lie just beyond the medina walls to the northeast.

◉ Medina   AREA

Chefchaouen's medina is one of the loveliest in Morocco. Small and uncrowded, it's easy to explore, with enough winding paths to keep you diverted, but compact enough that you'll never get too lost. Most of the buildings are painted a blinding blue-white, giving them a clean, fresh look, while terracotta tiles add an Andalucian flavour.

➡ **Kasbah**   LANDMARK
(Map p252; ☑ 0539 98 63 43; Plaza Uta el-Hammam; museum & gallery Dh10; ⊙ 9am-1pm & 3-6.30pm Wed, Thu & Sat-Mon, 9am-noon & 3-6.30pm Fri) The kasbah is a heavily restored walled fortress that now contains a lovely garden, a small **ethnographic museum** (museum & gallery Dh10; ⊙ 9am-1pm & 3-6.30pm Wed, Thu & Sat-Mon, 9am-noon & 3-6.30pm Fri), and an even smaller **art gallery**. The ethnographic museum contains some fascinating views of old Chefchaouen, including the plaza and the kasbah; the gallery promotes the work of local artists. The views from the kasbah tower over the medina are a delight.

THE SPANISH MOSQUE

Looking east, you'll easily spot the so-called **Spanish mosque** on a hilltop not far from the medina. It's a pleasant walk along clear paths and well worth the effort. Start at the waterfall Ras el-Maa (p251), just beyond the far northeastern gate of the medina. Continuing over the bridge, you can walk to the Spanish mosque following the hillside path. The mosque was built by the Spanish in the 1920s, but never used.

The mosque has been newly restored (by the Spanish, again) and there are plans for it to open as a cultural centre. From the hilltop minaret you'll have a grand view of the entire town sprawling over the green hills below.

➡ **Plaza Uta el-Hammam**   PLAZA
The heart of the medina is the shady, cobbled Plaza Uta el-Hammam, which is lined with cafes and restaurants, all serving similar fare. This is a peaceful place to relax and watch the world go by, particularly after a long day of exploration.

➡ **Grande Mosquée**   MOSQUE
(Plaza Uta el-Hammam) Noteworthy for its unusual octagonal tower, the Grande Mosquée was built in the 15th century by the son of the town's founder, Ali ben Rachid, and is closed to non-Muslims.

◉ Outside the Medina

Ras el-Maa   RIVER
The waterfall of Ras el-Maa is just beyond the far northeastern gate of Chefchaouen medina. It's here, where the water comes gushing out of the mountain, that local women come to do their washing. The sound of the water and the verdant hills just beyond the medina wall provide a sudden, strong dose of nature.

Talassemtane Eco-Museum   MUSEUM
(near Camping Azilane) This museum at the entrance to the Talassemtane National Park is well worth a visit. It has info on the park, maps of treks and an extensive display of the flora and fauna found in the park. Registration here is essential if you intend to camp during your trek.

Chefchaouen

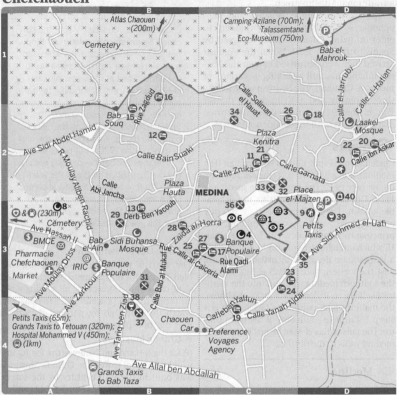

🏃 Activities

Hammams

Lina Ryad & Spa   SPA

(☎ 0645 06 99 03; www.linariad.com; Ave Hassan I; gommage Dh300, 1hr relaxation massage Dh300; ⏰ 10am-8pm) The spa at this riad has a hammam and various forms of massage, and a candlelit oriental bath for two. Finish with a facial to complete the picture.

Douches Barakat   HAMMAM

(Onsar; hammam Dh20; ⏰ men 8am-noon, women noon-8pm) The local hammam is the traditional way to get clean – and cheap with it.

Trekking

The **Talassemtane National Park** starts just outside Chefchaouen, and has numerous hiking options. If you're camping, you must register at the park entrance, where there's also an informative eco-museum (p251).

The **Bouhachem Regional Nature Reserve** lies between Tetouan, Chefchaouen and Larache, and has a number of treks of various lengths visiting local villages and exploring the mountains, forests and waterfalls. There are a several *gîtes* (trekkers' hostels) for overnight stays. The park is exceptionally beautiful and covers an enormous area of 80,000 sq km. Designated a Site of Biological and Ecological Interest, it is, along with the nearby Talassemtane National Park, one of the core areas of the Intercontinental Biosphere Reserve of the Mediterranean shared between Andalucia (southern Spain) and Morocco. The forest has various species of oak, maritime pine and cedar. The park is home to an important number of birds (99 species), mammals (32 species including the Barbary macaque) and reptiles (17 species).

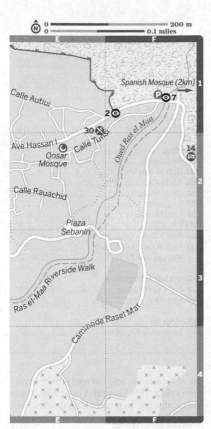

heating; if not, you will be sleeping beneath plenty of blankets during cold winter nights. Most other accommodation options are clustered along Ave Hassan II, which runs south of the medina alongside the old city walls.

🏨 Medina

★ Dar Baraka GUESTHOUSE €

(📱 0614 68 24 80; www.riad-baraka.com; 12 Derb Ben Yacoub; d with/without bathroom Dh275/Dh220, dm Dh100; 🛜) English-owned Dar Baraka is a bright and cheery place to rest your backpack. The rooms are comfortable and share spotless facilities, and there's a convivial terrace with good views for meeting fellow travellers. There are a handful of private rooms or dorms for four, with bunk beds. Map murals help orientate yourself in the medina.

Breakfast and laundry service are available on request.

Dar Terrae GUESTHOUSE €

(Map p252; 📱 0539 98 75 98; www.darterrae.com; Ave Hassan I; s/d Dh480/600, d/tr without bathroom Dh280/380, all incl breakfast; 🛜) This cute guesthouse has funky, cheerfully painted rooms, some with their own bathroom and fireplace, hidden up and down a tumble of stairs and odd corners. There's a good breakfast spread every day served on a small terrace, tea and coffee throughout the day and dinner on request. Also known locally as the 'Hotel Italiano'.

Hostal Gernika GUESTHOUSE €

(Map p252; 📱 0539 98 74 34; hostalgernika@hotmail.com; 49 Onssar; d/tr Dh250/350) This is a warm and charming place, with a very caring and attentive owner, near the Pl el-Majzen. Most rooms are large and bright, and face the mountains. There's a fire in winter and books to read. The terrace has spectacular views. Reservations are advisable in summer, Easter and December. Breakfast not included, plus a heating supplement in winter.

Hotel Koutoubia GUESTHOUSE €

(Map p252; 📱 0539 98 84 33; hotelkoutoubia@hotmail.fr; Calle Andalouse; r with medina/mountain views Dh250/350; 🛜) This hotel does quality budget accommodation well, with friendly and attentive management, a central location, traditional decor, spotless rooms and a closed-in roof terrace where you can have breakfast on those cold mornings.

Abdeslam Mouden TREKKING

(📱 0661 46 39 05; rifwalks@gmail.com; groups of up to 10 half-/full day Dh250/400, lunch per person in gîte Dh85) Abdeslam Mouden and his team of 13 trained guides lead treks lasting from half a day to several days in both parks, with optional visits to honey production, cheese-making and organic vegetable farming projects.

Chaouen Rural TREKKING

(📱 0539 98 72 67; www.chaouenrural.org; Pl el-Mazjen) Chaouen Rural offers treks in Talassemtane National Park, some with a focus on medicinal plants.

🛏 Sleeping

Chefchaouen has a large number of accommodation options. As the medina is what you'll come to Chefchaouen for, it's best to stay here, though there are some good options outside the walls. Some hotels have

Chefchaouen

Hotel Souika　　　　　　　HOSTEL €

(Map p252; ☑ 0539 98 68 62; www.hotelsouika. com; Derb Hadi Alami; dm Dh60) A hostel by any other name, Souika has a series of dorms with bunk beds, plus a couple of double rooms. The shared showers and toilets are adequate, and the decorator got so carried away with them he covered half the hostel with bathroom tiles. Hard to beat on value for the rock-bottom price.

Hotel Barcelona　　　　　　GUESTHOUSE €

(Map p252; ☑ 0539 98 85 06; hotelbarcelona2@ gmail.com; 12 Rue Targhi; d with/without bathroom Dh300/156; 🖥) A good budget option in bright Chefchaouen blue. The fixtures and fittings are pretty basic, but the hotel is well maintained, and the rooftop terrace is wonderful. The en-suite rooms have their own semi-private terrace area.

Pension Yasmina　　　　　　GUESTHOUSE €

(Map p252; ☑ 0539 88 31 18; yasmina@hotmail. fr; 12 Zaida al-Horra; r per person Dh100; 🖥) For the price bracket, this place sparkles. Rooms are bright and clean, though avoid the ones without windows. All bathrooms are shared. The location is a stone's throw from Plaza Uta el-Hammam, and the roof terrace is very welcoming. This bargain doesn't have many rooms, though, so it can fill up quickly.

Pension Mouritania　　　　　HOSTEL €

(Map p252; ☑ 0539 98 61 84; pension.mouritania@hotmail.com; Derb Hadi Alami; dm Dh70) Basic hostel with extremely simple dorms and a roof terrace that's been part of Chefchaouen's travel scene for as long as we can remember. Pleasant courtyard and helpful staff.

★ Casa Perleta　　　　　　GUESTHOUSE €€

(Map p252; ☑ 0539 98 89 79; www.casaperleta. com; Bab Souq; d incl breakfast Dh500-900; 🖥) This lovely house offers rooms sleeping two or three, and one suite for four. It's full of wonderful local fabrics and furniture and white walls that soothe after the blue medina. The cosy sitting room has a fireplace for chilly nights, and there's central heating in all rooms. Topping it off is a terrace with great views.

Dar Gabriel　　　　　　　　GUESTHOUSE €€

(Map p252; ☑ Spain 00 34 952 11 74 86; www.dargabriel.com; Bab Souq; s/d incl breakfast Dh350/500;

☎) The warmth of natural brick teamed with lots of local rugs and fabrics make this a comfortable option. The cosy lounge has a fireplace, there are three roof terraces and meals can be provided. Rooms are simple and individually decorated. Excursions into the mountains are on offer.

Dar Meziana GUESTHOUSE €€
(Map p252; ☎0539 98 78 06; www.darmeziana-hotel.com; Rue Zagdud; r incl breakfast & dinner Dh648-933; ❋☎) Beautifully decorated, this boutique hotel has a unique angular courtyard, lush plantings, lots of light, the highest quality furniture and extraordinary ceilings. On the edge of the medina and not well signposted, but lovely.

Dar Mounir GUESTHOUSE €€
Map p252; (☎0539 98 82 53; www.hotel-darmounier.com; Derb Hadi Alami; r Dh520-620; ☎) A cute guesthouse with helpful staff and a series of nicely presented rooms in tradtional style, piled on several floors leading up to a terrace with fine views. A few rooms are dark with internal windows only; others are much brighter and fresher. All come with a surfeit of horseshoe-shaped doorways and windows.

★**Casa Hassan** GUESTHOUSE €€€
(Map p252; Dar Baibou; ☎0539 98 61 53; www.casahassan.com; 22 Rue Targhi; s/d with half-board from Dh700/850; ❋) Don't be confused by the signs: Casa Hassan is now across the street from its sister restaurant of the same name. The move has much improved this long-established guesthouse – knocking together a couple of properties has provided airy, well-laid-out rooms, a couple of courtyards and a pleasant patio garden, as well as the obligatory roof terrace. A great choice.

Lina Ryad & Spa GUESTHOUSE €€€
(Map p252; ☎0645 06 99 03; www.linaryad.com; Ave Hassan I; s/d incl breakfast Dh1200/1400; ☎❋) The upmarket Lina Ryad is opulent and impeccably turned out – a brand-new building made to look traditional. It has large, comfortable rooms with TV (and free movies) and friendly staff. The roof terraces have fabulous views. An internal courtyard holds a delightful heated pool that's surprisingly private, and there's a restaurant serving mostly Moroccan cuisine (mains Dh100, no alcohol).

DON'T MISS

STROLLING THE RIVERSIDE

Exit the medina at **Bab el-Ansar** and head downhill a few metres until you cross the river. Turn right after the bridge and follow the path on the eastern side of the river, Oued Ras-el Maa. The route has been prettily landscaped, and meanders alongside the water. There are spectacular views of the medina, and it all makes a very pleasant downhill saunter of around half an hour. The path meets Ave Allal ben Abdallah, where you can hail a taxi to take you back to the medina.

Outside The Medina

Hotel Marrakesh HOTEL €
(Map p252; ☎0539 98 77 74; Hotel.Marrakech1@hotmail.com; 41 Ave Hassan II; s/d incl breakfast Dh150/220, d/tr with shower Dh250/300; ☎) Slightly outside the medina but with good access, the Marrakesh is a hotel with a bit of cheer. Bright pastel rooms invite the fresh air in, bathrooms have good showers, the common room attracts with its central fireplace, and the roof terrace offers fine views over the valley. All rooms share toilets; the more expensive rooms have a shower.

Hotel Salam HOTEL €
(Map p252; ☎0539 98 62 39; 39 Ave Hassan II; s/d Dh80/150) An out-of-medina experience on the main road up to the plaza, the Salam has bright courtyard rooms. Shared facilities are adequate, but sinks in all rooms are a bonus. Fairly priced for a simple experience.

Camping Azilane CAMPGROUND €
(☎0539 98 69 79; www.campingchefchaouen.com; Hay Ouatman; camping per adult Dh30, plus per tent/car/campervan Dh20/20/35, electricity Dh15; ☎❋) A shady setting with great views makes this site popular, although cleanliness is questionable. It is a stiff 20-minute walk from the medina. There's a small restaurant and a shop that sells some essentials, but otherwise facilities are pretty basic (hot showers Dh10). Fires and alcohol are not allowed.

★**Auberge Dardara** INN €€
(☎0539 70 70 07, 0661 15 05 03; www.dardara.ma; Rte Nationale 2; d/tr incl breakfast Dh600/750; ❋❋) This authentic French *auberge* in the Moroccan countryside offers large rustic suites with TVs and fireplaces and an

LOCAL KNOWLEDGE

FOODIE TREATS FROM THE MARKET

The market off Ave Hassan II is excellent for fresh fish, meat, fruit and vegetables, and gets particularly busy on Monday and Thursday, when people come from outside Chefchaouen to sell produce.

Several local specialities are worth checking out, particularly the fragrant mountain honey and soft ewe's cheese – both served up at breakfast. Add fresh *dial makla* (a type of bread) and you have your picnic.

excellent restaurant. The 10-hectare complex includes an active farm and gardens, a pool, a craft shop, a hammam, a fitness centre, fishing, biking, mule riding, trekking and treasure hunts. Guest programs include crafts, gardening and more. It's a 10-minute taxi ride (Dh5) to Bab Taza.

Dar Zman GUESTHOUSE €€
(Map p252; ☑ 0539 98 93 46; www.darzman.net; Bab el Hammar, Ave Hassan II; d incl breakfast from Dh350; ❋❀☞) A lovely, finely restored guesthouse with eight brightly painted rooms and a wonderful rooftop breakfast area, created by some ambitious young hoteliers. The faux artefacts revealed in the walls are a clever touch.

★ Dar Ech-Chaouen GUESTHOUSE €€€
(Map p252; ☑ 0539 98 78 24; www.darechchaouen. ma; 18 Ave Ras el-Maa; d incl breakfast from Dh610, ste d Dh850; ❋☞❀) Providing excellent accommodation, this guesthouse is close to Ras el-Maa, just outside the medina walls. It's well designed with even staircases, spacious, comfortable rooms and a shady garden terrace. There's a pool with great views, and a restaurant.

✗ Eating

Sip juice or mint tea while watching the world go by at the cafes on Plaza Uta el-Hammam. In the back rooms, local men play cards and smoke kif. Look out for the sticker in some restaurant windows announcing 'The Chefchaouen Network of Community-involved Restaurants'. These establishments support farmers by using local organic products.

La Lampe Magique MOROCCAN €
(Map p252; Rue Targhi; mains from Dh45, set menu Dh100; ❀11am-10pm) This magical

favourite overlooking Plaza Uta el-Hammam serves delicious Moroccan staples in a grand setting. Three bright-blue floors include a laid-back lounge, a more formal dining area and a rooftop terrace. The menu – featuring favourites such as lamb tajine with prunes and some great cooked salads – is much better than average, and the ambience relaxed.

Mandala ITALIAN €
(Map p252; ☑ 0539 88 28 08; mains from Dh40; ❀11am-10pm) Offering a welcome break from Chefchaouen's endless tajine parade, Mandala serves up some good pizzas and pastas, plus a serviceable steak. Surroundings are cosy and service is good. If you're feeling lazy, you can even get delivery to your guesthouse.

Lala Mesouda MOROCCAN €
(Map p252; Ave Hassan I; mains from Dh60; ❀lunch & dinner) This restaurant serves dishes not found elsewhere in the town. Both the steak with Roquefort sauce and the chicken with cream and mushrooms are recommended, and fish is also available. The interior is comfortable and intimate, if rather dark, and the welcome warm, but check ahead of time as opening hours can be erratic.

Assaada MOROCCAN €
(Map p252; ☑ 0666 31 73 16; Bab el-Ain; set menu Dh40; ❀9am-9pm) This reliable cheapie tries hard to please. Located on both sides of the alley just prior to Bab el-Ain, it offers the usual *menu complet* (complete menu), but also great fruit shakes and a funky graffiti rooftop terrace that exudes an urban charm. The staircase is not for the faint-hearted.

Plaza Café-Restaurants MOROCCAN €
(Map p252; Plaza Uta el-Hamman; breakfast from Dh25, mains from Dh40; ❀8am-11pm, closes earlier in winter) It's hard to make a choice between the dozen or so cafes on the main square. Menus are virtually identical – continental breakfasts, soups and salads, tajines and seafood – such that we wonder if they're all served by one giant kitchen, but the food is generally pretty good, the ambience lively and the location perfect for people-spotting.

Bab el-Ansar Café CAFE €
(Map p253; Bab el-Ansar; ❀8am-8pm) Set into the outside wall of the medina, this cafe has a great location overlooking the falls of Ras el-Maa, with three terraces tumbling down the hill. Views are particularly nice in the

late afternoon, with the sun catching the mountains opposite.

Chez Aziz
PASTRIES €

(Map p252; Ave Hassan II; pastries from Dh4; ☉8am-7pm) For a decent selection of pastries, make your way here. Pizzas and paninis are also on the menu. They squeeze a mean juice and make good coffee too, for a quick breakfast on the run.

★ Auberge Dardara Restaurant
MOROCCAN €€

(☑0661 15 05 03, 0539 70 70 07; www.dardara.ma; Rte Nationale 2; menu Dh120; ☉lunch & dinner) This is the best restaurant in the area, and worth the 10-minute drive from town (to Bab Taza, Dh5). The Tangerine owner uses only the freshest ingredients from the garden, bakes his own bread and makes his own olive oil and goat's cheese. Try the superb salads, and the venison cooked with dried figs or the succulent rabbit with quince.

Restaurant Tissemlal
MOROCCAN €€

(Map p252; Casa Hassan; 22 Rue Targhi; menu Dh90-120; ☉noon-9pm) Better known as Casa Hassan as it's part of the guesthouse (p255) of the same name, this restaurant serves the usual traditional dishes. It's particularly welcoming in winter when there's a roaring fire.

Restaurant Les Raisins
MOROCCAN €€

(Map p252; ☑0667 98 28 78; 7 Rue Sidi Sifri; tajines Dh25, set menu from Dh50; ☉7am-9pm) A bit out of the way, this family-run place is a perennial favourite with locals and tourists alike, and known for its couscous royal. Late, lazy lunches are the best, with the front terrace catching the afternoon sun.

Chez Hicham
MOROCCAN €€

(Map p252; Rue Targhi; mains around Dh80; ☉11am-10pm) Chez Hicham has a lovely warm interior, comfortable seating and views over the kasbah from the terrace. The usual suspects – tajines etc – are on the menu.

Drinking & Nightlife

While it's easy to find kif in Chefchaouen, it's hard to find a beer.

Atlas Chaouen
BAR, CLUB

(☉9am-11pm) The jazzy bar here is the smartest in Chefchaouen, but it's quite a hike. The hotel's disco (11pm to 3am) is the only nightclub in the area, but trim your expectations. Hotel guests are the clientele during the week, joined by locals on weekends.

Hotel Parador
BAR

(Map p252; ☑0539 98 61 36; Pl el-Majzen; ☉2-11pm) The bar here is OK for a beer, bottle of wine or spirits, but it's all rather soulless.

Bar Oum-Rabiá
BAR

(Map p252; Ave Hassan II; ☉10am-10pm) A very masculine option.

🛍 Shopping

Chefchaouen remains an artisan centre and, as such, an excellent place to shop – especially for Riffian woven rugs and blankets in bright primary colours. The largest concentration of tourist shops is around the Uta el-Hammam and Pl el-Majzen.

Ensemble Artisanat
ARTS & CRAFTS

(Map p252; Place el-Majzen; ☉10am-2pm & 4-6pm) Chefchaouen is an excellent place to shop for woven rugs and blankets. Most of the weaving nowadays is done with wool, one of the area's biggest products. It's worth stopping at the Ensemble Artisinat, if only for the sake of comparison.

ℹ Information

Banque Populaire (Map p252; Ave Hassan II, near Bab el-Ain; ☉8.45am-6pm Mon-Thu, 8.45am-noon Sat) Bank with ATM and money-changing facilities.

Banque Populaire (Map p252; Plaza Uta el-Hammam, Medina; ☉8.45am-6pm Mon-Thu, 8.45am-noon Sat) Bank with ATM.

BMCE (Map p252; Ave Hassan II; ☉8.45am-6pm Mon-Thu, 8.45am-noon Sat) Bank with ATM and money-changing facilities.

> **WORTH A TRIP**
>
> ### TAGHRAZOUTE
>
> Some 20km from Chefchaouen on the road to Oued Laou, **Le Caiat** (☑0666 28 87 15, 0671 85 49 97; www.caiat.com; RP 4105, Taghzoute; meals around Dh100, d with breakfast/half-board from Dh200/350) at Taghzoute is a wonderful mountain refuge. The Portuguese owner is a keen environmentalist and works with local Moroccans arranging treks between villages in the Talassemtane National Park. Trails of two hours to two days lead to cooling cascades and monkeys, rock pools and the rare black pine. There is a range of accommodation and a restaurant with breathtaking views across the valleys.

Hospital Mohammed V (Map p252; ☎ 0539 98 62 28; Ave al-Massira al-Khadra)

IRIC (Map p252; Institut Raouachid pour l'Information et le Commerce; Ave Hassan II; per hr Dh5; ☙ 8am-midnight) Internet cafe next to Librairie Al-Nahj.

Pharmacie Chefchaouen (Map p252; ☎ 0539 98 61 58; Ave Moulay Driss; ☙ 8am-6pm Mon-Sat) Useful pharmacy.

Post Office (Map p252; Ave Hassan II; ☙ 8am-4pm Mon-Fri, 8-11am Sat)

Preference Voyages Agency (Map p252; ☎ 0539 98 79 13; www.preferencevoyages.com; 39 Ave Hassan II; ☙ 9am-12.30pm & 3-6.30pm Mon-Fri, 9am-12.30pm Sat) This extremely helpful travel agency has tourist information and organises mountain treks with registered guides. English-speaking.

⑤ Getting There & Away

BUS

Bus services from Chefchaouen originate elsewhere, so are often full on arrival. Buy the ticket for your onward journey on arrival in Chefchaouen to secure a seat. The **bus station** (☎ 0539 98 76 69) is 1.5km southwest of the town centre at the far end of Ave Mohammed V (Dh10 in a petit taxi from Pl el-Majzen). CTM and all other buses use the same station.

CTM serves the following destinations.

DESTINATION	COST (DH)	DURATION (HR)
Casablanca	140	6
Fez	75	4
Nador	120	11½
Rabat	100	4½
Tangier	45	3

Other companies run a number of cheaper services to the same destinations, including a daily departure for Oued Laou (Dh32, 1½ hours).

TAXI

The fixed price for a grand taxi from Tangier airport to Chefchaouen is Dh650, and from Tanger Med Dh550. Unless you can find several people to split the fare with you, it is far cheaper to go to Tangier first, then hop to Chefchaouen via Tetouan. Even if you buy two places, you will save over Dh500 and add less than an hour.

Grands taxis north leave Chefchaouen from just below Plaza Mohammed V. Most just run to Tetouan (Dh35, one hour), where you must change for Tangier or Ceuta – direct taxis are rare.

Grands taxis headed south gather below the central market. Catch one to Ouezzane (Dh35, one hour), where you can pick up onward transport to Fez and Meknès. There is very little transport heading east to the coast. The best option is to take a grand taxi to Dardara junction (Dh8, 15 minutes) or Bab Taza (Dh15, 30 minutes) and hope for the best from there.

⑤ Getting Around

Some of Chefchaouen's blue **petits taxis** congregate on Pl el-Majzen; others can be found near the **market**. They're unmetered; most fares shouldn't top Dh10. The safe and convenient Hotel Parador **car park** (Pl el-Majzen; per night Dh10) can be used by nonguests.

Chaouen Car (☎ 0539 98 62 04; Ave Hassan II) rents cars and also organises 4WD trips and quad bikes.

TREKKING IN THE RIF MOUNTAINS: TALASSEMTANE NATIONAL PARK

There are numerous trekking opportunities of various durations in the vast 580-sq-km Talassemtane National Park, which begins just outside Chefchaouen. The name means 'cold spring' in Berber. Some popular destinations include the small villages of El-Kelaâ and Akchour, and God's Bridge, a natural formation that looks like a stone arch. The duration of these excursions depends on how much you wish to drive versus walk.

Chefchaouen to Bab Taza

This is the best introductory walk to the Rif Mountains. Within the Talassemtane National Park and starting from Chefchaouen, it takes in some spectacular scenery, including the geologically improbable God's Bridge, a natural stone arc spanning the Oued Farda. You are also likely to meet troupes of Barbary apes.

The full trek takes five days, but there are plenty of ways to shorten the distance or duration. One option would be to arrange transport from Akchour back to Chefchaouen at the end of day two. Transport isn't too hard to find in Akchour, or you can arrange for a grand taxi from Chefchaouen to pick you up at a specified time. Alternatively, you may be able to hike back along an alternate route.

The Talassemtane National Park is one of two parks in the Rif Mountains (the other being Bouhachem). It's a largely undiscovered area and yet these mountains make perfect trekking country, blessed with magnificent ranges, gorges and valleys, with forests of cedar, cork oak and fir. Being close to the Mediterranean, the Rif are also the greenest of Morocco's mountains, and springtime, with its riot of wildflowers, is one of the most delightful times to walk here.

One thing that does deter trekkers is the region's reputation as an area of drug production. But although cannabis takes up over three-quarters of cultivatable land east of Chefchaouen, trekkers have little reason to feel threatened, especially if travelling with a guide – villagers will be genuinely interested and welcoming. The trek detailed here, setting out from Chefchaouen, is well trodden and unproblematic in this respect. In a concerted effort to reduce reliance on the cannabis industry, local organisations, backed by the government, are setting up rural tourism facilities such as *gîtes* and homestays, managing routes and training guides.

The Rif Mountains rarely top more than 2500m in height, with most treks only occasionally venturing over 2000m, so altitude sickness isn't the worry it can be in other parts of Morocco.

Wildlife

The Rif's climate and proximity to Europe endows it with a Mediterranean vibe – the area closely resembles the sierras of southern Spain. Cedars make up the majority of tree species, including a rare endemic species *Abies maroccana,* a high-altitude variant of the Spanish cedar. In addition, cork oak, holm pine, wild olive, juniper and the rare carob are some that dot the limestone mountains. The stony land is hard to cultivate and thin in nutrients; deforestation is an issue here as in other parts of Morocco. Various herbs such as lavender and thyme thrive and are used by the local population as medicines.

Locals may say that there are wolves in the mountains, but it's a mistranslation – there are foxes. Wild boar are also native, but have a retiring nature that makes them hard to spot. The Rif's most famous mammals are the Barbary apes (known locally as *mgou*), whose range extends south into the Middle Atlas.

You'll have better luck with birdlife. Raptors easily spotted wheeling on thermals include black-shouldered kites, golden eagles and long-legged buzzards. Ravens can also be seen against the limestone cliffs.

TREK AT A GLANCE

Duration Four to five days

Distance 56km

Standard Medium

Start Chefchaouen

Finish Bab Taza

Highest Point Sfiha Telj Pass (approximately 1700m)

Accommodation *Gîtes* and camping

Public Transport Yes

Summary The walking here is relatively undemanding but the mountain scenery is spectacular, the tiny Riffian villages worth a detour, and the gorges and weird geology fascinating.

Scorpions present a small risk in the Rif, although less so than further south. Be wary of the red scorpion; stings are extremely painful. The venomous *fer à cheval* viper (named for the horseshoe-like mark on its head) is more likely to flee from you than vice versa.

Day 1: Chefchaouen to Afeska

DURATION 5½–6½ HOURS / DISTANCE 14.5KM / ASCENT 1200M / DESCENT 600M

An early-morning start is recommended for the first day, starting on the 4WD track behind Camping Azilane, with an initially steep ascent climbing through trees to give great views over Chefchaouen's medina. Skirting the southern slopes of **Jebel el-Kelaâ** (1616m), the track evens out to follow the stream passing through the hamlet of **Aïn Tissimlane**, before once again rising in an arc to a high pass by the jagged limestone crags of **Sfiha Telj**. The views here are astounding in both directions, and on a clear day you can see the Mediterranean in the distance. The climb is a killer with a full pack – the hardest of the trek – which explains the necessity for a cool early-morning start.

The track turns east before descending. Stopping regularly to enjoy the fine views, take the right (southern) fork where the track splits – this takes you down in an hour or so to the village of **Azilane**, where there's a homestay option and a *gîte*. If you don't want to stop here, continue for another hour along a mostly level path to **Afeska**, where there's another homestay and a *gîte*.

Day 2: Afeska to Akchour

DURATION 3½–4½ HOURS / DISTANCE 10KM / DESCENT 860M

From Afeska, the wide *piste* you've been following deteriorates to a smaller track. Heading north, you pass through more oak and pine woods to **Sidi Meftah**, where there's a *marabout* (mausoleum of a saint) and spring, before leaving the woods and descending the switchbacks to **Imizzar** on the **Oued Farda**. Once beside the river, turn left (away from the village, northwest), then cross the river below some impressive overhanging cliffs and continue heading northwest. You'll join a well-worn mule track that eventually leads down to **Pont Farda**, an ancient bridge over Oued Farda.

Cross to the west bank of the river and continue north, dwarfed by the surrounding scenery. After an hour, the trail bears left away from the river towards **Ouslaf**, which is overshadowed by a giant rock buttress, but keep on the same path while it bears right, descending to rejoin the river on the outskirts of **Akchour** (398m), which sits on the **Oued Kelaâ**.

Akchour is strung out along the river. As you approach it, you first come to a small cafe with very welcome river-cooled soft drinks, and a dam with a deep pool that seems made for swimming, although the water temperature means short dips only!

Akchour has a *gîte* that's very comfortable and provides excellent meals.

From Akchour, it's usually possible to get transport back to Chefchaouen – most likely one of the rugged vans or 4WDs that battle it out on the *piste*. If there's nothing going from Akchour, try **Talembote**, 2km further north, which has a market on Tuesdays with regular transport to Chefchaouen (Dh15). Most passing vehicles will stop to pick you up if they have space – a case of paid hitchhiking. They may drop you at Dar Ackoubaa, the junction town 10km north of Chefchaouen on the N2 highway.

SIDE TRIP: GOD'S BRIDGE

With an early start from Afeska, you can reach Akchour by lunchtime, allowing time for the short hike (1½ hours, 3km return) to **God's Bridge**, an unlikely geological structure that shouldn't be missed.

The path south from Akchour's dam up the Oued Farda is rough in places, but well worth any scrambling. You'll also have to cross the river twice but this is quite easy where it's not deep – if you don't mind the occasional splash. (However, if you're trek-

---

BEFORE YOU GO: CHEFCHAOUEN TO BAB TAZA CHECKLIST

Weather Trekking is possible year-round, though it can be bitterly cold with snow between November and March. There's frequent rain between late September and June. It's fiercely hot in summer, when some water sources dry up.

Guides Organise trekking guides through Abdeslam Mouden (p252) in Chefchaouen. Guides charge Dh400 per day.

Accommodation Many villages have simple *gîtes* that cost from Dh200 per person including dinner and breakfast. It's also possible to arrange *gîtes* in person during the trek, though there is a risk that the guardian may not be around and the *gîte* may be closed – not uncommon.

Camping is not encouraged as local people don't benefit. But in some areas there are no *gîtes*, so it's the only alternative. There's one official camping site at the village of Talassemtane. Permission to camp (free) must be obtained from the Eco-Museum in Chefchaouen in advance. Staying with families en route is an option in some villages and it is possible to stop for tea with locals and to visit weaving and cheese-making cooperatives.

Maps From the government 1:50,000 topographical series, survey sheets *Chaouen* and *Bab Taza* cover the Chefchaouen to Bab Taza trek.

The Eco-Museum at the entrance to the park has maps of the routes.

Equipment Where there are no *gîtes*, a tent is necessary. A decent sleeping bag is essential, as is a light waterproof jacket – rain showers are common. Food and fuel supplies can be bought in Chefchaouen.

Mules to carry your luggage cost from Dh250 per day including muleteer. From August to October, mules can be hard to organise as they're used for the kif harvest, and prices increase accordingly.

king in spring, check in Afeska that snow melt hasn't made the river impassable.) God's Bridge is about 45 minutes from Akchour. A huge red stone arch towers 25m above the river and it almost beggars belief that it was carved by nature and not by human hand. Over countless millennia, the river flowed as an underground watercourse, eroding the rock and carving a path deeper and deeper, leaving the bridge high and dry.

Day 3: Akchour to Pastures Above Abou Bnar

DURATION 4½–6 HOURS / DISTANCE 12KM / ASCENT 977M

An early-morning start (with full water bottles, since there are no springs on the route until you reach Izrafene) sees you leaving Akchour by heading to the north, crossing the bridge over the Oued Kelaâ and then cutting right (southeast) along the track to Izrafene. It's a particularly picturesque walk as you climb up and around **Jebel Azra** (1375m). Your eyes lift from the steep gorges you've trekked through and out over the sweep of open mountains. If you're up for some scrambling, add half an hour to attain the peak, from where you can drink in further gorgeous views.

Having cut around the mountain, the countryside becomes gentler – rolling even – as the trail heads south. The village of **Izrafene** marks the halfway point of the day's trek. Just before the village, a track bears east at a col, tempting the adventurous to abandon the Bab Taza hike and walk to Taourarte (where there's a homestay and a *gîte*) and on to **Bou-Ahmed** on the coast, a further two to three days' walk.

From Izrafene, the track turns into a 4WD *piste* – the first since Afeska. It follows a narrow valley, gradually turning east up onto a ridge with gentle views. Where it forks, turn left, and then, just 25m later, turn right onto a trail that heads southeast to **Abou Bnar** through a pretty stretch of oak wood. There's little to detain you here, so continue alongside the river (not the 4WD track) through the open, grassy country to the *marabout* of **Sidi Jil**. This is a pretty area for camping, but if you continue for another 30 minutes, you'll come to an even more beautiful spot, set in wide pasture near the El-Ma Souka spring – an idyllic place for a night's rest.

ALTERNATIVE ROUTE: RETURN TO CHEFCHAOUEN

It's possible to trek back to Chefchaouen from Akchour in a day by an alternate route. The route goes via the villages of **Ouslaf, Arhermane** and **El-Kelaâ**. El-Kelaâ is the site of the fascinating **Mosquée Srifi-yenne**, with its strange leaning tower. This route takes a quick six hours and avoids any major climbs or descents.

Day 4: Pastures Above Abou Bnar to Talassemtane Village

DURATION 2–2½ HOURS / DISTANCE 6KM / ASCENT 352M

From the camping site southwest of Abou Bnar, walk back to the 4WD track. Turn left and cross the river, and walk south into the pine woodland. You will quickly come to a T-junction, where you should keep on the right (the left goes downhill to Beni M'Hamed) where the path starts to ascend again.

Keep on the main track, ignoring further side tracks and junctions. As you rise and go through several mini-passes, the views return. To the west, the huge mass of **Jebel Lakraa** (2159m) dominates the countryside.

By late morning you'll reach **Talassemtane** village. A small sign indicates that you should turn left off the 4WD track to the house of the park's Eaux et Forêts guardian. There's an official camping site here.

SIDE TRIPS

The short walking day allows plenty of time to explore the area and watch wildlife, particularly Barbary apes.

Head north, back along the 4WD track above the *guardian's* house to a clearing and junction. Here you turn right and follow the track east into *mgou* country. Troupes are relatively common here, although they quickly retreat into the safety of the trees if you get too close. The track bends south, giving great views out across the valley to the long ridge of **Jebel Taloussisse** (2005m), before turning briefly east again. Here a trail on the right leads south over the spur of **Talassemtane** (1941m) to a football pitch – strange, but true! – on an area of flat land. From here it's possible to make a rocky traverse west, back to the campsite.

Climbing **Jebel Lakraa** is another alternative for gung-ho trekkers. The best approach is from the north of the mountain, trekking along the ridge to descend one of the stream gullies southeast of the summit. However, there's no fixed path and it's a scramble in places. Allow around 3½ hours return.

Day 5: Talassemtane Village to Bab Taza

DURATION 2½–3½ HOURS / DISTANCE 13.5KM / DESCENT 825M

The last day is a quick descent along the 4WD track to Bab Taza, where local kif cultivation is much in evidence. The trail swings through a wide pasture and on through the cork woodland of **Jebel Setsou** (1363m) before revealing the sprawl of **Bab Taza** (or so it seems after a few days in the mountains) below.

In Bab Taza, there are quite a few cafes and a couple of grotty-looking hotels strung along the main road. The main business seems to be in huge sacks of fertiliser used for growing kif. Grands taxis leave regularly throughout the day for Chefchaouen (Dh12, 30 minutes) from the western end of town.

Oued Laou   واد لاو

POP 8500

Don't let Oued Laou's dusty main street lined with slapdash construction fool you – if the tourist developments along this stretch of the coast continue apace, it will all look like Martil within a few years. For now, waterfront budget rooms and cheap beer and food along the new corniche back a very long, empty beach to make it a backpacker paradise, especially in summer. There's nothing to do aside from watching the fishermen haul their boats in the morning.

The road from Chefchaouen to Oued Laou has recently been upgraded and the journey is now reduced to a little over an hour.

Sleeping & Eating

Seafood is the order of the day here, with corniche restaurants serving fish fresh from the boat, along with the usual selection of tajines.

There are a few cheap bars serving cold beer and cheap wine, though they're not very female-friendly. It's nicer to linger over a coffee on the corniche.

Hotel Oued Laou   GUESTHOUSE €
(☑ 0650 18 43 38, 0655 21 37 89; Blvd Massira; s/d without bathroom Dh200/250) There are several new budget hotels to choose from, but this is the best. A new road splits it from its cafe-restaurant on the beach. Get a room with views to the sea.

Aramar   SEAFOOD €
(Corniche; mains from Dh60; ☉ noon-11pm, closes earlier out of season) The best of the fish restaurants along the corniche, the Aramar does a tasty platter of *poisson friture* (fried fish) for Dh80 while you watch the fishermen on the beach.

ⓘ Information

Cyber Costa (internet per hr Dh5; ☉ 9am-midnight) Opposite La Plage Restaurant but unlikely to be open out of season.

ⓘ Getting There & Away

If you're driving from Chefchaouen, turn off the main Tetouan road at Dar Ackoubaa, 11km north of Chefchaouen. It's a wonderful drive past the large hydroelectric dam and through rolling hills and the stunning Laou Gorge. Coming from Tetouan, the Rocade N16 hugs the dramatic coastline for 140km all the way to El-Jebha.

Three buses a day connect Tetouan and Oued Laou (Dh25, two hours). There's also one bus from Chefchaouen (Dh20, 90 minutes), which continues along the coast to El-Jebha (Dh35, five hours); the return service leaves El-Jebha early in the morning. However, at Oued Laou it dumps you out by the souq, which lmeans a 45-minute walk or Dh7 grand-taxi ride to town.

Grands taxis run from beside the mosque in Oued Laou to Tetouan (Dh30, one hour) via Dar Ackoubaa (Dh15, 20 minutes), where you can pick up a passing taxi for Chefchaouen.

Targa to El-Jebha   من تارجا الى الجبهة

This stretch of the coast is very dramatic, and still remote. Pine-clad hills are interspersed with valleys of cultivated fields that roll down to the sea and beaches of grey pebbles. However, the new coastal road (Rocade) linking Tetouan to El-Jebha promises massive development projects with golf courses, luxury hotels and apartments.

Seventeen kilometres southeast of Oued Laou, Targa is a little village with a history of piracy. High atop an outcrop of black rock, a stone fort, built during the Spanish protectorate, overlooks the village. The 13th-century mosque is associated with a local saint.

About 18km southeast of Targa, in the wide valley of Oued Bouchia, are the twin villages of Steha and Bou-Ahmed. Set back from the coast, the latter is the end point for a long-distance trek from Chefchaouen. There's an interesting souq every Tuesday, and a basic camping area in summer.

From here the road follows the coast on a splendid roller-coaster ride to the blue-and-white town of El-Jebha, 52km to the southeast. The rugged coastline forms a number of breathtaking and secluded bays – worth exploring if you have your own transport. Each Tuesday, the local souq draws Rif farmers from the surrounding villages. At El-Jebha you can turn south into the Rif to Issaguen, or continue on the Rocade to Al-Hoceima.

ℹ Getting There & Away

Grands taxis link Tetouan to Targa. From Targa, grands taxis run to El-Jebha, which has connections to Al-Hoceima.

Al-Hoceima الحسيمة

POP 57,000

Al-Hoceima is a great place to spend a few days. Quiet, safe, relaxing and hassle-free, this modern seaside resort is full of proud and genial Berbers with a surprisingly independent outlook that's far more Western than any other town in the north.

Founded by the Spanish as Villa Sanjuro, the town was built as a garrison after the Rif Wars in the early 20th century; rebel Abd al-Krim operated nearby. Independence brought the name change to Al-Hoceima, but Spanish influence remains strong in language, architecture and business.

In recent years a lot of money has been ploughed into the town, particularly into its booming tourism industry. The wide Pl Mohammed VI has fountains and a sweeping corniche following the coast and forms a natural centre to the town. The nearby Al-Hoceima National Park has been opened to rural tourism – an opportunity not to be missed.

⊙ Sights

In the summer, good options are the three beaches that begin 5km south of town. During the low season they tend to be strewn with rubbish. The best way to reach the beaches is by grand taxi. For the entire taxi, reckon on about Dh50 to **Cala Bonita** and Dh75 to **Plage Asfiha**. Local buses to Ajdir and Imzouren, which pass the turn-offs for the beaches (Dh5 to Dh7), leave from beside the Mobil petrol station at the south end of Blvd Mohammed V.

El Peñón de Alhucemas   FORT
One of the *plazas de soberanía* (places of sovereignty), this extraordinary white island fortress can be seen a few hundred metres off Playa Asfiha, along with the uninhabited Isla de Mar and Isla de Tierra, which fly the Spanish flag. Spanish rule dates back to 1559, when the Saadi dynasty gave it to Spain in exchange for military assistance.

In 1673, the Spanish military established a garrison there, and never left. Today, the fort hosts 60 soldiers, and cannot be visited. Spanish sovereignty has been contested by Morocco since independence in 1956.

Plage Quemado   BEACH
A pretty, steep-sided bay protects the yellow sand of the town beach. The place teems in the summer, providing a great view of Morocco at play. Pedalos are available to hire in season.

Plage Isly   BEACH
A grey-sand beach south of town, with a few eating shacks serving fish during the summer months.

The Port   PORT
The port is mainly used for a large commercial fishing operation. It is a great place to watch the catch being unloaded, and to find dinner: take your selected fish to the Club Nautique (p265) for cooking.

🛏 Sleeping

Accommodation is in high demand in the summer – book ahead. The streets between Pl du Rif and the souq are packed with ultra-cheap hotels. Some are pretty dingy, so look around before committing.

Hotel Villa Florido   HOTEL €
(📞0539 84 08 47; http://florido.alhoceima.com; Pl du Rif; s/d Dh301/393; 🛜) This curvaceous art-deco hotel dating from 1920, an island in the Pl du Rif, has some nice period charm. Rooms come in different sizes (the triples are huge) and have bathrooms and satellite TV, and most have a balcony. There's a smart cafe downstairs (breakfasts Dh40). All rooms face the streets, which can be noisy at night.

Hotel National   HOTEL €
(📞0539 98 21 41; 23 Rue Tetouan; s/d Dh288/322) A decent enough budget option, although some rooms are a little small, with windows facing into an internal courtyard and not getting a lot of light.

Hotel al-Hana   HOTEL €
(📞0666 90 32 00; 17 Calle Imzouren; s/d without bathroom Dh100/160) With rock-bottom prices, this simple hotel is tucked into the

Al-Hoceima

tiny streets east of Pl du Rif. All facilities are shared, including the clean squat toilets (hot showers are free). It's well kept, and the cafe on the ground floor is full of men throwing dice.

Hotel Rif
HOTEL €

(☎ 0539 98 22 68; 13 Calle Sultan Moulay Youssef; s/d without bathroom Dh100/150) If your budget is really maxed-out, you'll end up in this long hallway lined with simple rooms. Rooms are basic but reasonable for the price tag. You get a sink but bathrooms are shared (squat toilets).

La Perla
HOTEL €€

(☎ 0539 98 45 13; Ave Tariq ibn Zaid; s/d incl breakfast Dh700/850; ❄☀ 🕿) This modern mirrored-glass high-rise business hotel has comfortable rooms with satellite TV and large bathrooms. The location on a busy corner makes it quite noisy if you have rooms on the lower levels. There's a cafe on the ground floor with good breakfasts, and a restaurant upstairs. A little bland and modest for the price tag.

Hotel al-Khouzama
HOTEL €€

(fax 0539 98 56 69; Calle al-Andalous; s/d Dh288/376; 🕿) Just off Blvd Mohammed V, this two-star hotel is a long-time favourite of business travellers, and is suitably comfortable, with spacious rooms (though those facing away from the street are a bit dark). All come with bathrooms and satellite TV, and the guys at reception are friendly and helpful.

Mercure Quemado Resort
HOTEL €€€

(www.mercure.com; 1 Ave Ibn Tachfine; s/d Dh1515/1640; P🕿🕿🏊) Holiday-business hotel that has been plonked down on Plage Quemado like a cruise ship washed ashore. Rooms are spacious, comfy and well-maintained. There's a restaurant with buffet and à la carte options, and a bar where you can have a drink overlooking the beach.

Al-Hoceima

Suites Hotel Mohammed V HOTEL €€€
(☎0539 98 22 33; www.hotelsuitesmoham medv.com; Pl Mohammed VI; s/d Dh800/950; P❋✿❀) This hotel is modern but characterless. It occupies a prime position perched above Plage Quemado. Rooms are spacious and comfortable and have balconies giving truly grand views over the bay, but service is a little lackadaisical. There's a restaurant, a bar and a gym to complete the picture.

✕ Eating

Cheap restaurants cluster around Pl du Rif, serving up filling tajines, brochettes and a bit of seafood to the bus-station crowd from about Dh25 per head. There are also many snack shops around town.

Many small general food stores are dotted around town, including **Épicerie Hassouni** (Blvd Mohammed V) and **Supermarché el-Bouayadi** (Calle Abdelkrim Khattabi). For alcohol try **Bougamar** (near cnr of Rue Micra).

★ Club Nautique SEAFOOD €
(☎0539 98 14 61; Gate 2, Port d'Al-Hoceima; mains from Dh60; ⊙noon-11pm) This is the main restaurant at the port, and a good one. After 6pm you can buy your fish fresh off the boat and have them grill it for you (alternatively,

order straight from the menu). The 2nd floor overlooks the whole port and is a great place to relax and a have beer in the fresh air.

Café La Belle Vue CAFE €
(Map p264; 131 Blvd Mohammed V; breakfast Dh20; ⊙8am-10pm) This cafe-restaurant gets its name from the terrace at the back overlooking the bay – it really does offer a splendid vista. There are several similar cafes on this stretch of Mohammed V with great views.

Espace Miramar FAST FOOD €
(Map p264; ☎0531 98 42 42; Rue Moulay Ismail; mains from Dh35; ⊙9am-11pm) It's hard to go wrong at this 5000-sq-metre complex with a pizzeria, two cafes, a grill and restaurant as well as a children's playground, all of it perched on the cliffs overlooking the sea, and with occasional live music as well. It's a series of open-air terraces, so be careful not to get lost inside!

La Dolce Pizza FAST FOOD €
(Map p264; ☎0531 98 47 52; Pl du Rif; pizzas Dh37; ⊙11am-10pm) Also signed as DP, this cute Italian bistro, thrust out into the chaos of Pl du Rif, has just four tables inside and some on the pavement. Service is appallingly slow but the ambience makes it a pleasant place to people-watch and have some pizza, hamburgers or salads.

Boulangerie Patisserie Azir PASTRIES €
(Map p264; ☎0531 17 71 42; 14 Rue Yousef ben Tachfine; pastries from Dh4; ⊙5am-8.30pm) This patisserie is the town favourite, with great homebaked bread and tons of different sweets.

Basilic INTERNATIONAL €€
(Map p264; mains Dh40-130; ⊙8am-11pm) A classy glass-fronted restaurant on two levels and with quick service. Moroccan standards are all available here, plus plenty of seafood and some decent pasta, pizza and steaks.

⊒ Drinking & Nightlife

Perhaps its the seaside holiday air, but Al-Hoceima has more good options for having a drink than you might otherwise expect for a town of its size, including several places where you can sit outside.

Mercure Quemado Resort BAR
(Map p264; ⊙noon-11pm) The bar of the Mercure hotel is open to nonguests. It's not the cheapest place to have a drink in Al-Hoceima, but it may be the nicest – sitting out on the decking overlooking the beach.

SURVIVAL TARIFIT

Hello/Goodbye *msalkhir/baslama*

Yes/No *wah/alla*

Please *aafak*

Thank you *choukrane*

Where is...? *mani thadja (fem) or mani yadja (masc)*

➡ **hotel** *annoutir*

➡ **camping** *arihla*

Do you have any rooms available?
maghak cha akhamane akhwane?

➡ **a single room** *akham injnabnadam*

➡ **a double room** *akham ntnaine nyawdane*

How much is it? *mchhar tag tha?*

What time does the next...leave?
marmi ghayoya wanni dyouggane?

➡ **boat** *agharabo*

➡ **bus** *toubis*

I'd like a... *khsagh*

➡ **one-way ticket** *thawrikth ichtane waha*

➡ **return ticket** *thawrikth waakab*

➡ **beer** *berra*

➡ **sandwich** *bocadio*

Club Nautique BAR
(Gate 2, Port d'Al-Hoceima; ⊘noon-11pm) An atmospheric option, and the bar here usually attracts quite a crowd. It's a rarity in Morocco – a place where you can drink in the fresh air. Beers are Dh20.

Suites Hotel Mohammed V BAR
(Map p264; Pl Mohammed VI) The bar is a bit dingy, but the terrace has excellent views over Plage Quemado.

Shopping

There is a weekly market on Monday and Tuesday in the **souq** (⊘closed Fri).

❶ Information

Blvd Mohammed V has several banks with ATMs, including branches of BMCE, BMCI and Banque Populaire.

Travel agencies sell ferry tickets from AL-Hoceima to Motil in Spain during the summer, and Nador year-round.

Cyber Bades (Map p264; Calle al-Amir Moulay Abdallah; per hr Dh5; ⊘8am-9.30pm)

Délégation Provinciale de Tourisme (Map p264; Tourist Bureau; ☎0539 98 11 85; Zanqat Al Hamra, Cala Bonita; ⊘9am-1pm & 3-6pm Mon-Fri) Staff here are on the ball and have lots of information on the town and National Park.

Ketama Voyages (Map p264; ☎0539 98 51 20; www.ktmahu@menara.ma; 146 Blvd Mohammed V; ⊘9am-1pm & 3-6pm Mon-Fri, 9am-1pm Sat)

Pharmacie Nouvelle (Map p264; Calle Moulay Idriss Alkbar; ⊘8.30am-12.30pm & 3-7.30pm Mon-Thu, 8.30am-noon Fri, 8am-12.30pm Sat)

Post Office (Calle Moulay Idriss Alkbar; ⊘8am-4pm Mon-Fri)

❶ Getting There & Away

AIR

Royal Air Maroc flies from Amsterdam and in summer from Brussels to the small local airport located 12km (Dh175 by taxi) from town. Royal Air Maroc offers sporadic services from Paris and various parts of Spain, as well as Casablanca. Otherwise the best option is a flight to Nador, 150km east.

BOAT

Armas (www.navieraarmas.com) has summer ferries to Motil in Spain.

BUS

All the bus companies have offices around Pl du Rif, including **CTM**, but all depart from the **bus station** on the southern edge of town. CTM runs the following summer services:

Chefchaouen (Dh90, 5½ hours, three daily)

Nador direct (Dh55, three hours, two daily)

Year-round, CTM has the following departures:

Casablanca (Dh230, 10 hours, two daily) via Taza (Dh75, four hours)

Fez (Dh125, six hours)

Meknès (Dh145, seven hours)

Rabat (Dh175, eight hours)

Tetouan (Dh115, seven hours, three daily) via Chefchaouen (Dh90, 5½ hours)

Several small companies also serve the aforementioned destinations. There are at least three buses a day to Tetouan and Tangier (Dh90, 7½ hours), stopping in Chefchaouen. Heading east, there are also a couple of buses a day to Nador (Dh40, 2½ hours) and Oujda (Dh70, five hours).

TAXI

Grands taxis can be found at the bus station. The most popular destinations are Taza (Dh70, 2½ hours) and Nador (Dh60, 2 hours). For Melilla, change at Nador for the border at Beni Ansar.

The Rif Mountains

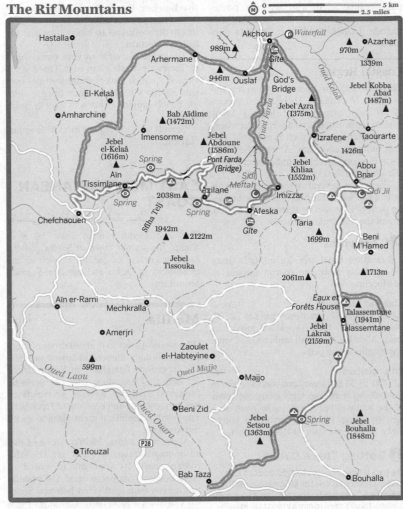

Al-Hoceima National Park
المنتزه الوطني للحسيمة

The undiscovered Al-Hoceima National Park is a hidden jewel of this region. The park extends to 485 sq km (including 190 sq km at sea). The area is dotted with Berber settlements and criss-crossed by dirt roads, making it ideal trekking and mountain-biking territory. Its isolation has helped preserve several at-risk species, from its thuya forests to an important colony of fish eagle. While a 4WD opens up your options, a 2WD will get you through the main tracks.

The park offers two regions: the central Rif bordered by the N16 in the south and west, and the coast.

Central Rif Region

Of the 15,000 people living in the park, most are Bokkoya Berbers and live in rural communities centred on fresh water supplies. The women have good knowledge of the medicinal use of local herbs such as the abundant lavender and thyme.

A number of rare trees can be found here, such as wild carob and the endangered thuya, highly prized for its wood.

Other plants include wild olive, ilex, pomegranate, ericas, bulbs and orchids. Animals include jackals, wild boar, rabbits and hares.

Coastal Region

This area of the park extends out to sea and is rich in biodiversity. There are 86 species of fish and three types of dolphin. Many species represented here are rare elsewhere in the Mediterranean, such as red coral, various molluscs and algae. Among the birds, there is a considerable population of osprey *(Pandion haliaetus)*.

There are several remote and scenic beaches, of which the highlight is the fantastic sight of El Peñón de Velez de la Gomera, one of the *plazas de soberanía*.

🏃 Activities

Information brochures including a map are available from the tourist bureau in Al-Hoceima.

Abdellah Massoudi   TREKKING
(☑ 0673 22 91 22; per person per day Dh200, minimum Dh500) French-speaking mountain guide Abdellah Massoudi leads treks of various lengths in the park.

Rif Croisiéres   BOATING
(☑ 0641 59 98 94; www.rifcroisieres.com; 90min tour Dh150) Offers boat trips along the coast of the national park, with some great seabird watching, including ospreys if you're lucky. Tours leave from Al-Hoceima port.

ℹ️ Getting There & Away

The park is best accessed by 4WD. You can also walk to El Peñón de Velez de la Gomera along the coast from Cala Iris in 1½ hours. Without your own transport, you'll need to hire a grand taxi. In summer there may be enough people to share one, otherwise expect to pay Dh150 one way.

Cala Iris & Torres de Alcala   كلا ايريس وطوريس القلعة

Cala Iris now lies inside the Al-Hoceima National Park. It has a small fishing port and a beautiful sandy beach that's empty out of season – for now. Construction of a resort was due to start in 2017. There's nowhere to stay here, but there is a rough-looking, nameless restaurant behind the Cooperative des Marins Pecheurs that serves typical Berber food. The port is flanked by attractive beaches: Yellich (to the east) faces an island that you can walk out to; Oued Sahfa lies to the west; and an hour's hike over the hill lies Mestaza.

There are a couple of very basic shops at Torres de Alcala, 5km east. Three semi-ruined Spanish towers stand sentinel over this scruffy village, set back from a shingle beach caught between two rocky headlands.

Grands taxis to Cala Iris from Al-Hoceima cost Dh25.

EAST MEDITERRANEAN COAST
الشاطئ الشرق للبحر المتوسط

The east Mediterranean coast takes in Nador, the seaside town of Saïdia and the Spanish enclave of Melilla as well as the inland city of Oujda and the Beni-Snassen Mountains

Melilla   مليلية
POP 84,500

Who would expect to find hundreds of modernist buildings, the second-largest such collection outside Barcelona, in North Africa? Yet here they are, along with one perfectly preserved medieval fortress, several fascinating museums and a wealth of tapas bars. The result is Melilla, a great place to spend the weekend.

Along with Ceuta, Melilla is one of two autonomous Spanish cities on the Moroccan coast. Its economy is rooted in cross-border commerce, and its population nearly equally divided between Spanish Christian and Berber Muslim, giving a strongly multicultural atmosphere. The enclave is tightly fenced and at the forefront of Spain's efforts to prevent Sub-Saharan African migrants and refugees from the Syrian and Libyan conflicts entering the European Union.

Melilla is very easy on the traveller, and tourist infrastructure is excellent. While ferry-loads of visitors pour in during summer, in the low season you'll have plenty of breathing room.

History

Melilla oozes with history, but it is neither as broad nor as deep as you might

THE LAST PIECES OF EMPIRE

Some of the most fascinating places in northern Morocco are not Moroccan at all, but Spanish. When Spain recognised Moroccan independence in 1956, it retained a collection of historical oddities that had predated the Spanish protectorate. Known by the euphemism *plazas de soberanía* (places of sovereignty), they have a population of 145,000, and are divided into two groups.

The *plazas mayores* (greater places), Ceuta and Melilla, contain virtually all the people. Politically these are 'autonomous cities', with governmental powers placing them somewhere between a city and a region of Spain.

The *plazas menores* (lesser places) are inhabited by a handful of Spanish legionnaires, if that. These include three islands in the Bay of Al-Hoceima: Isla de Mar, Isla de Tierra (both deserted, apart from Spanish flags) and El Peñón de Alhucemas, a striking white fortress that's home to some 60 soldiers. El Peñón de Velez de la Gomera, at the end of a long canyon in the Al-Hoceima National Park, is another ancient rock fortress, connected to the mainland by a narrow spit of sand – and a guardhouse, one of the oddest national borders you'll ever see. The Islas Chafarinas, 3km from Ras el-Mar, have three small islands: Isla del Congreso, Isla del Rey and Isla Isabel II, the last with a garrison of 190 troops. Spain also owns the tiny Isla Perejil, near Ceuta, which was the cause of one of the world's smallest conflicts, when Spanish troops evicted a handful of Moroccan soldiers in 2002; and the Isla de Alborán, about 75km north of Melilla, which has a small navy garrison.

While the two fortress *peñónes* (rocky outcrops) are must-sees, none of the *plazas menores* can be entered, as they are military sites. Morocco claims them all, making their defence necessary even though their strategic importance is limited.

Recent history has been focused on problems with Spain over immigration and political sovereignty. In 2006 youths set fire to several mosques in Ceuta after a number of local Muslims were arrested on the Spanish mainland in connection with the Madrid bombings. In 2007 the king of Spain visited the city for the first time in 80 years, sparking protests from the Moroccan government. So far none of this has closed a single tapas bar. In late 2010 Moroccan youths rioted in both Ceuta and Melilla over sovereignty of the cities, sparked by a lack of jobs. Tensions continue to simmer.

expect. While the area has been inhabited for more than 2000 years, the old city wasn't begun until after Spanish conquest in 1496, then built up in four stages. Up until the end of the 19th century, virtually all of Melilla was contained within a single impregnable fortress. Current borders were fixed by several treaties with Morocco between 1859 and 1894, the last following an unsuccessful siege by rebellious Rif Berbers. The method involved shooting a cannonball and seeing how far it went. More fighting with rebel Berbers broke out several times in the ensuing years, until the Spanish protectorate consolidated its grip in 1927. In 1936 Franco flew here from the Canary Islands to launch the Spanish Civil War. Local politics still tip to the right.

☉ Sights

Melilla is a semicircle of 12 sq km carved out of the Moroccan coastline. The old

town, Melilla la Vieja, is a highly complex, multilevel fortress that juts out into the sea. It contains numerous museums, as well as some small residential areas. The port and major beaches lie to the south, with the ferry terminal directly east.

The 'new town' is a broken grid of streets with an attractive commercial centre full of modernist buildings. The heart is the long triangular Parque Hernández, which ends at the circular Plaza de España. Most of the hotels, banks and restaurants are located to the north.

☉ Melilla la Vieja

★ **Melilla la Vieja** FORT
(Calle General Macías) Perched over the Mediterranean, Melilla la Vieja is a prime example of the fortress strongholds that the Spaniards built along the Moroccan littoral during the 16th and 17th centuries. Much

Melilla

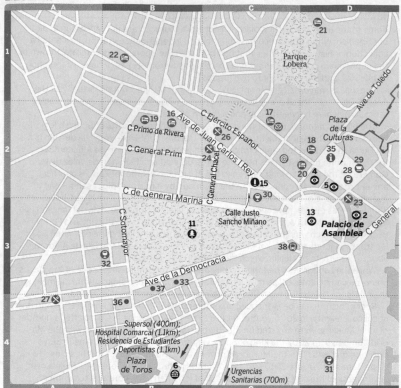

of it has been painstakingly restored in recent years. The main entrance is Puerta de la Marina, from where you ascend to the summit, passing several small museums.

Signage, in Spanish, French and English, is very good.

➡ **Puerta de la Marina**   GATE
(Calle General Macías) The main entrance to the Melilla la Vieja fortress is Puerta de la Marina, fronted by a statue of Franco – one of the few remaining on public display in Spain.

➡ **Museo Etnográfico de la**
Culturas Amazigh & Sefardí   MUSEUM
(Almacenes de la Peñuelas; ☑ 0952 97 62 16; Plaza Pedro de Estopiñán; ☉ 10am-2pm & 5-9pm Tue-Sat, 10am-2pm Sun summer, 10am-2pm & 4-8pm Tue-Sat, 10am-2pm Sun winter) **FREE** This charming newly opened museum charts the history of the Amazigh (Berber) and Sephardic (Jewish) cultures in Melilla, which

have contributed to the enclave's rich multicultural mix.

➡ **Aljibes de**
las Peñuelas   HISTORIC BUILDING
(☉ 10am-2pm & 5-9.30pm Tue-Sat, 10am-2pm Sun Apr-Sep) **FREE** The small door across the courtyard leads into the cave-like, other-worldly cistern that is still flowing.

➡ **Iglesia de la**
Purísima Concepción   CHURCH
(Parish of the Immaculate Conception; ☑ 0952 68 15 16; ☉ 10am-3pm & 4-9pm Tue-Sat, 10am-12.30pm Sun) This 17th-century church is worth a stop for its resplendent nave.

➡ **Las Cuevas del**
Conventico   HISTORIC BUILDING
(Caves of the Convent; ☑ 0952 68 09 29; €1.20; ☉ 10.30am-1.30pm & 4.30-8pm Tue-Sat, 10.30am-2pm Sun) These extensive and well-restored caves were used as a refuge during sieges, and pop out at a small beach below the cliffs.

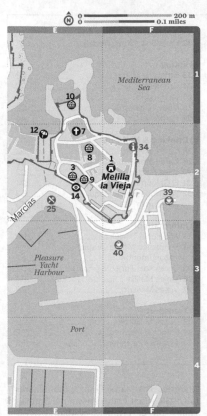

The Calle de la Concepción continues up to the baroque Iglesia de la Purísima Concepción and, just below it, the entrance to Las Cuevas del Conventico.

The Phoenicians first excavated the tunnels; later occupiers took turns enlarging them and they now extend over three levels. They are meticulously maintained and well lit, which sadly eliminates much of their mystery. A short film and guided tour (both in Spanish) detail the history of the caves and tunnels that lead to the cliff face.

➡ **Museo Militar**　　　　　MUSEUM
(Map p271; Melilla la Vieja; ☉10am-2pm Tue-Sun) **FREE** Near the Iglesia de la Concepción, the Museo Militar is perched high over the Mediterranean. Its two small rooms are stuffed full of exhibits from the Spanish military in Melilla: regimental flags, medals, some great old photos and a motley collection of weapons and the obligatory bust of Franco.

Playa de la Ensanada de los Galápagos　　　　　BEACH
(Map p271; The secluded beach of Playa de la Ensanada de los Galápagos is reached by taking a tunnel under Melilla's fortress. The beach is in a cove surrounded by cliffs and the fort walls, and is open May to September (with lifeguards on duty).

◉ New Town

Construction of the new part of town, west of the fortress, began at the end of the 19th century. Laid out by Gaudí-disciple Don Enrique Nieto, Melilla is considered by some to be Spain's 'second modernist city', after Barcelona. The highlight is Plaza de España, with the lovely facade of the Palacio de la Asamblea facing Parque Hernández.

At the turn of the 20th century, Melilla was the only centre of trade between Tetouan and the Algerian border. As the city grew, it expressed itself in the architectural style of Modernisme (not to be confused with the cultural movement of modernism), which was then in vogue. This trend continued locally even after it went out of fashion elsewhere. The result is a living museum of hundreds of modernist and art-deco buildings. Unlike Ceuta, many of these treasures have yet to be dusted off, but the overall architectural wealth is greater.

The best way to appreciate this heritage is to stroll through the area to the north of Parque Hernández; it's known as 'the golden triangle'.

★**Palacio de Asamblea**　　NOTABLE BUILDING
Map p270; Nieto's art-deco Palacio de Asamblea, whose floor plan depicts a ducal crown, is an operating town hall, although the staff at the entrance are willing to show tourists around upon request. Worth seeing are two rooms on the upper floor: Salon Dorado, which contains a large painting of the arrival of Spaniards in Melilla in 1497, and the Sala de Plenos, where the local congress meets.

Plaza de España　　　　　LANDMARK
Map p270; Several fine examples of the city's heritage are on the Plaza de España, including Nieto's **Casino Militar**, and the **Banco de España**.

With its central fountain, the Plaza is a pleasant place to sit. At the centre is an art-deco military monument to campaigns in Morocco.

Melilla

In the distance towards the sea you can spot Melilla's most striking contemporary building, the new courthouse, which looks like a flying saucer landed on the roof (closed to visitors).

Parque Hernández   PARK
(Map p270) FREE From the Plaza, take a pleasant stroll down the long, palm-lined Parque Hernández. At the end, turn left down Calle Sotomayor. **Plaza de Toros**, the only operating bull ring in Africa, lies straight ahead.

Gaselec Museum   MUSEUM
(Map p270; ☑ 0952 69 55 75; www.fundaciongaselec.es; Plaza Rafael Fernández de Castro y Pedrera; ⊗ 6-9pm Mon-Fri, 11.30am-1.30pm & 6-9pm Sat & Sun) FREE Just off Parque Hernandez is this intriguing oddity, the passion of the former president of the local gas and electric company. It houses a museum of Ancient Egypt composed entirely of reproductions, including King Tut's mask and sarcophagus.

Statue Grande Libre   MONUMENT
(Map p270; Avenida de Juan Carlos I Rey, New Town) Melilla's role in modern Spanish history isn't forgotten. The Statue Grande Libre marks 7 July 1936, when Franco began the campaign against the government in Madrid. With a soldier and lion backed by a Fascist eagle, it feels like a throwback to another, uncomfortable age.

🛏 Sleeping

There aren't many hotels in Melilla, so they tend to fill up even in the quieter months. Book ahead.

Hostal Cazaza   HOTEL €
(Map p270; ☑ 0956 68 46 48; 6 Calle Primo de Rivera; s/d €28/40) This old modernist building, with its high ceilings and small balconies, has ramshackle charm, and a central location in the golden triangle. Rooms are clean and management is friendly.

Hostal Residencia Rioja   HOSTEL €
(Map p270; ☑ 0956 68 27 09; 10 Calle Ejército Español; s/d €22/35) Don't be put off by the gloomy and uninspiring entrance. Rooms here at this rock-bottom pension are a little tired but wellkept. Rooms have basins; the bathrooms are shared.

Residencia de Estudiantes y Deportistas HOSTEL €
(Residence of Students & Athletes; ☑ 0952 67 00 08; Calle Alfonso X; per person incl breakfast €25, half-board €30, full-board €35; 🐾) A reasonable budget choice if you don't mind being away from the town centre, and like hanging out with students. There are 87 rooms, a cafeteria, a library and a TV lounge. Rooms above the 2nd floor have balconies.

Take local bus 3, which stops near Plaza España on Calle Marina every 10 minutes, though there are fewer services on weekends. The trip takes 10 to 15 minutes.

Pensíon La Rosa Blanca HOTEL €
(Map p270; ☑ 0952 68 27 38; 7 Calle Gran Capitán; s/d without bathroom €30/40) A very basic option; the rooms are clean but vary in quality, size and fittings, so make sure you look before you pay. Rooms have sinks but bathrooms are shared.

Hotel Rusadir HOTEL €€
(Map p270; ☑ 0956 68 12 40; www.hotelrusadir.com; 5 Calle Pablo Vallescá; s/d incl breakfast €68/80; 🖪🐾) This four-star hotel has been completely renovated to excellent effect, including an impressive lobby and design-conscious rooms with TVs, minibars and balconies. The restaurant puts out an impressive breakfast buffet. Good value.

Hotel Anfora HOTEL €€
(Map p270; ☑ 0956 68 33 40; www.hotelanfora.net; 8 Calle Pablo Vallescá; s/d incl breakfast €45/71; 🖪🐾) This three-star hotel is in an excellent location and offers good-sized, standard-fare rooms with TVs, fridges and balconies, as well as a gym. The rooftop restaurant serves a basic breakfast as you enjoy vistas of Melilla la Vieja and of the sea beyond. Popular and reliable, if unexciting.

Hotel Nacional HOTEL €€
(Map p270; ☑ 0956 68 45 40; 10 Calle Primo de Rivera; s/d €40/60; 🖪🐾) This hotel has mostly compact rooms, with minibars, quaint iron furniture and modern bathrooms. Those facing inside are a bit dark, so get one looking to the street. Management is friendly, and there's a restaurant.

Parador de Melilla HOTEL €€€
(Map p270; ☑ 0956 68 49 40; www.parador.es; Ave Cándido Lobera; r €150; 🖪🐾🎇) You'll need a vehicle to get to this classy choice with large, grand rooms, warm use of wood throughout, a high level of quality furnishings and bal-

conies with great views to sea. The circular dining room overlooking the city is an elegant touch. The adjacent Parque Lobera is great for kids.

🍴 Eating

Many of Melilla's restaurants are associated with hotels (like the Rusadir or the Parador), but there are plenty of others around Ave de Juan Carlos I Rey.

There are plenty of small grocery shops in the streets around Parque Hernández. **Supersol** (Calle General Polavieja; ⊙ 10am-10pm Mon-Sat) is on the road to the frontier.

Granier CAFE €
(Map p270; 7 Calle General Chacel; sandwiches from €2.50; ⊙ 7am-9pm; 🐾) This cafe and bakery with indoor and outdoor seating is good to grab a quick eat or while away an hour with a book and a coffee. The *bocadillos* (sandwiches) are a perfect lunchtime snack, and it does some delicious fruit smoothies.

Cafetéria Militar SPANISH €
(Map p270; Calle de Almovodar; mains €8; ⊙ 1-3.30pm Mon-Sat) A huge canteen-like affair on the side of the Palacio de Asamblea, with a few tables outside as well, this restaurant is hugely busy for its short lunchtime openings.

Parnaso BISTRO €
(Map p270; ☑ 0952 68 41 84; 30 Avenida Duquesa de la Victoria; sandwiches from €2.50; ⊙ 7am-1am Mon-Sat) This bistro with outdoor seating offers tasty sandwiches and tapas for an easy light meal with drinks. Popular during lunch and with the after-work crowd.

Nuevo California INTERNATIONAL €
(Map p270; ☑ 0952 68 22 64; Plaza Menéndez; ⊙ 7.30am-1.30pm & 4-9.30pm Mon-Fri) This modern cafeteria on a plaza terrace has a wide-ranging menu and friendly waiters eager to help your clumsy Spanish along. The sandwiches and pasta are particularly good, all washed down with a cold *cerveza* (beer).

★ La Pérgola SEAFOOD €€
(Map p271; ☑ 0952 68 56 28; Calle General Marcías; mains from €10; ⊙ noon-midnight) A waterfront terrace makes this classy spot beneath the fortress walls a very pleasant place for a meal, or just a late-afternoon drink. The speciality is barbecued seafood, and at €10 the prix-fixe menu cannot be beaten – as the crowds can attest. There's a lively atmosphere in the evenings.

🍷 Drinking & Nightlife

Tapas bars are a highlight of Melilla, especially if you've spent a lot of time in Morocco prior to arrival. Puerto Deportivo Noray is Melilla's bar zone, with a dozen different options grouped side by side on the waterfront. Enter through the car park next to the courthouse.

★ Casa Marta   TAPAS
(Map p270; Calle Justo Sancho Miñano; tapas from €2; ⊙1-3.30pm & 8pm-1am) This is a great tapas bar that brims with people of all ages both inside and out: outdoor seating is under a tent in the street. Free tapas is included with drinks; larger plates are available from the menu.

La Onubense de Moqui   TAPAS
(Map p270; 5 Calle Pareja; tapas from €2; ⊙noon-3pm & 7pm-midnight Mon-Sat) With its rough-hewn wood furniture and unpolished decor, this place looks like the quintessential tapas bar. The house speciality is spicy *bollito de Pringá* (meatball) and other classic tapas delicacies.

La Pérgola   CAFE
(Map p271; Calle General Marcías; ⊙3-11pm) This cafe-bar on the pleasure-yacht harbour is an exceedingly pleasant place for a drink in the late afternoon, particularly on its wide sunny terrace on the waterfront.

Café La Dolce Vita   TAPAS
(Map p270; Plaza de la Culturas; tapas from €1.50, raciones from €6; ⊙10am-11pm) This large, buzzy cafe and tapas bar has seating all around a corner of the plaza. Have a coffee, an ice cream or a drink with tapas while people-watching on the square.

El Galeón   BAR
(Map p270; ☎0952 69 55 25; Explanada de San Lorenzo, Hotel Melilla Puerto; ⊙5pm-midnight) With its long wooden bar and brass fixtures, the classy bar inside the Melilla Puerto follows the hotel's nautical theme. Don't dress too scruffily here, but apart from that it's a relaxed place to enjoy tapas and a few drinks.

Café Latoga   CAFE
(Map p270; Plaza de la Culturas; ⊙10am-1am) This small bar in the lee of a grand church has a local clientele happy to sip a beer or glass of wine and keep an eye on the plaza. Relaxed.

ℹ Information

To phone Melilla from outside Spain, dial 0034 and drop the first zero. Melilla is one hour ahead of Morocco, and two hours ahead during Ramadan. Most shops and businesses are closed on Sunday.

INTERNET ACCESS
There are a handful of internet cafes downtown, including **Locutoria Dosmil** (Map p270; 14-25 Calle Ejercito Español; per hr €2; ⊙9am-2pm & 4-9pm).

MEDICAL SERVICES
Hospital Comarcal (Map p270; ☎0956 67 00 00; Ave de la Juventud) South side of Río de Oro.

Urgencias Sanitarias (Map p270; ☎0956 67 44 00; 40 Alvaro de Bazan; ⊙5pm-9am Mon-Sat, 24hr Sun & public holidays) Night pharmacy.

MONEY
Euros are used for all transactions in Melilla. You'll find several banks (with ATMs) around Ave de Juan Carlos I Rey. Most will buy or sell dirham at an inferior rate to the Moroccan dealers hanging around the ferry port or the border.

On the Moroccan side of the border you can change cash at the Crédit du Maroc. There's also a Banque Populaire with an ATM 200m further into Morocco; walk straight ahead to the crossroads and it's on your left on the road to the port.

POST
Main Post Office (Map p270; Calle Pablo Vallescá; ⊙8.30am-8.30pm Mon-Fri, 9.30am-1pm Sat)

TOURIST INFORMATION
Fundación Melilla Ciudad Monumental (☎0952 97 62 01; www.melillamonumental. org; 13 Calle Miguel Acosta; ⊙10am-2pm & 4.30-8.30pm Mon-Sat, 10am-2pm Sun) In-depth information on local architecture.

Oficina del Turismo (main) (Map p270; ☎0952 97 61 89; www.melillaturismo.com; Plaza de la Culturas; ⊙10am-2pm & 4.30-8.30pm Mon-Sat, 10am-2pm Sun) Lots of maps and brochures and friendly, English-speaking staff. Offers special tours of religious sites. Website contains a comprehensive history and architectural tour.

TRAVEL AGENCIES
Andalucía Travel (☎0956 67 07 30; fax 0956 67 65 98; 11 Avenida de la Democracia) Will sell plane and ferry tickets.

Viajes Melilla (☎0952 67 93 52; 1 Ave Duquesa de la Victoria; ⊙9.30am-1pm, 3.30-

MODERNISME & MELILLA

Like many of the movements from which it drew its inspiration (eg the English Arts & Crafts movement), Modernisme was a broad reaction to the material values of an industrial age, which suffused culture with a machinelike spirit. Centred in Barcelona, it was the Catalan version of art nouveau. Modernisme architecture is characterised by the use of curves over straight lines, the frequent use of natural motifs (especially plants), lively decoration and rich detail, asymmetrical forms, a refined aesthetic and dynamism. Its chief proponent was Antoni Gaudí, the architect of Barcelona's famous Sagrada Família cathedral. But in Melilla, Modernisme is synonymous with Enrique Nieto.

A student of Gaudí, Nieto worked on his Casa Milà in Barcelona. Wanting to escape his master's shadow, however, he left for booming Melilla in 1909 and stayed the rest of his life, becoming city architect in 1931. His work included Melilla's main synagogue, the main mosque and several buildings for the Catholic Church, representing the diversity of the city's culture. Perhaps due to the distant location of his canvas, however, this great painter in concrete is not well-known outside of Melilla.

7pm Mon-Sat) Travel agent that can book ferries to Spain.

Viajes Melisur (☎ 0956 67 35 95, 0956 67 36 78; www.melisur.es; 13 Avenida de la Democracia) Travel agency selling plane and ferry tickets.

ⓘ Getting There & Away

AIR

Air Nostrum (www.airnostrum.com; Melilla Airport, Iberia Regional) offers four flights a day between Melilla and Málaga, nine daily flights to Madrid (two via Barcelona) as well as four a week to Almería and Madrid. **Air Europa** (www.aireuropa.com; Melilla airport) has two flights a day to Malaga. The airport is a 10-minute (€6) taxi ride from the town.

BOAT

Trasmediterránea (Map p271; ☎ 0952 45 46 45; trasmediterranea.es; Estación Marítima), part of Acciona, sails from Melilla daily to Málaga and Almería. Both voyages take six to eight hours depending on the schedule. Fares start at €35 for foot passengers.

Tickets for ferries to Spain are available at the **estación marítima** (Ferry Port; ☎ 0956 68 16 33) or **Melisur** (☎ 0956 68 66 13; www.melisur.es; 8 Calle de General Marina; ⊙ 9am-1pm & 5-7pm Mon-Fri, 9am-noon Sat).

BORDER CROSSING

To get to the border, you'll need to either take a taxi (€7) or catch local bus 2 (marked 'Aforos'), which runs between Plaza de España and the Beni Enzar border post (€0.85, every 30 minutes from 7.30am to 11pm). The bus drops you 50m from the Spanish border control. From here it's a 200m walk to the Moroccan border.

Before entering Morocco, fill in a white form and get your passport stamped at the booth.

Touts may try to sell you a form for €1, but they're free at the booths (get one before you start queueing). If you're driving into Morocco, remember to retain the green customs slip, which you must present when you (and your vehicle) leave the country. Large queues of vehicles entering Morocco are frequent and time-consuming; procedures for foot passengers are quick and easy.

On the Moroccan side of the border, grands taxis (Dh6, 15 minutes) to Nador are tucked away in a car park to the right of the crossroad – a 100m walk from the border.

When entering Melilla from Morocco, fill in a white form and get your passport stamped. Some nationalities require visas to enter Spain: if they don't stop you here, they will when you try to move on to the mainland. Bus 42 goes to Plaza de España (€0.85).

ⓘ Getting Around

The centre of Melilla is compact and easy to walk around. Buses ply the route between Plaza de España and the border. The local **taxi service** (☎ 0956 68 36 21) is also useful.

Nador الناظور

POP 159,000

The Rocade (coastal road) from Al-Hoceima to Nador (130km) is a delight to travel. It passes through red cliffs, verdant gorges and, midway, an enormous sculpture of deeply eroded hills.

Within 60km of Nador there are several ramshackle, clifftop cafes that are perfect for a mint tea as you gaze out over the sea. A few of the beaches tucked into coves have restaurants; others are dirty with litter.

Nador itself has few attractions. The corniche by the lagoon is pleasant to walk on, but everything feels on hold until the new development on the outskirts at Marchica is completed – currently an endless sprawl of concrete. There are few reasons to linger, although the city is a decent transport hub, with an airport, a ferry port and a train station that has a service to Fez.

🛏 Sleeping

There's no shortage of hotels of all classes in Nador, with the accommodation scene recently enlivened by the addition of the new Mercure Rif hotel (p276). The cheaper places are near the bus and grand-taxi stations.

Hotel Geranio   HOTEL €
(✆ 0536 60 28 28; 16 Rue No 20; s/d Dh160/190) Just away from the chaos of the bus station, streetside rooms here can be noisy, but the low prices make this the top budget option. Clean rooms come with tiny bathrooms. There's a ground-floor cafeteria as well.

Hotel Méditerranée   HOTEL €€
(✆ 0536 60 64 95; hotel.mediterranee@gmail. com; 2-4 Ave Youssef ibn Tachfine; s/d incl breakfast Dh515/700; ❄ 🖥) Views from this hotel have been annihilated by the now-abandoned hotel construction in front. But it's still only one block back from the corniche and lagoon. The corner rooms have plenty of light, and all have TVs. There's a dull restaurant on the ground floor serving breakfast, omelettes and fish.

Mercure Rif Nador   HOTEL €€€
(✆ 0536 32 85 00; www.mercure.com; 1 Ave Ibn Tacfine; s/d Dh1216/1343; ❄ 🖥 ⛱) The new belle of Nador's accommodation scene, the Mercure stands out on the corniche with its tinted blue glass facade, and neat attention to service. Rooms are large and with the comfort and amenities you'd expect from this international chain; some have views over the lagoon. The swimming pool on the roof terrace is a neat, pleasant surprise.

Hotel l'Aeroport   HOTEL €€€
(✆ 0536 381722; hotelnador@gmail.com; s/d Dh400/700) A little out of the way, this hotel will be closer to the centre of things when the surrounding developments are finished. In the meantime, it has good, clean and comfortable rooms, although they're a little tight. Ask for the swanky Café Select nearby when flagging a taxi (also a good option for meals).

Hotel Ryad   HOTEL €€€
(✆ 0536 60 77 17; hotel-ryad@menara.ma; Ave Mohammed V; s/d Dh750/980; ❄ 🖥) Once plush but now showing its age and somewhat overpriced, the Ryad is a large tired hotel with a noisy bar. The rooms have standard features and those on the top floor have views over the lagoon.

🍴 Eating & Drinking

There are numerous cheap eats around the CTM bus station, serving up quick brochettes, sandwiches and tajines. Ave Mohammed V is the place for a lazy coffee – street cafes line the road under shady orange trees.

Café Antalya   CAFE €
(Blvd Prince Héritier Sidi Mohammed; pizzas from Dh50; ⊙ 8am-10pm) All glass and chrome and spilling out onto the pavement, this smart cafe shows a new face of Nador. The pizzeria upstairs is popular with young trendies.

Romero   SEAFOOD €€
(mains from Dh55; ⊙ noon-10pm) Perennially popular restaurant, with a brightly painted pastel dining room and quite enormous plates of seafood served up very quickly.

Restaurant Marhaba   SEAFOOD €€
(✆ 0536 60 33 11; Calle ibn Rochd; mains from Dh70; ⊙ noon-11pm) One of the smartest restaurants in town, the Marhaba specialises in fish and does it very well. The main room is very large, but there's a cosier terrace at the back with fishing nets and plastic lobsters. There's no alcohol.

Café Club   CAFE
(Ave Mohammed Zerktouni; ⊙ 8.30am-10pm) Jutting into the lagoon at the far end of Mohammed V, this island cafe is a welcome bit of maritime focus in an otherwise concrete forest. It no longer serves food, but it's a nice place to sit over the sea.

ℹ Information

Credit Maroc (64 Ave Mohammed V; ⊙ 9am-4pm Mon-Thu, 9-11am Fri, 9am-noon Sat) One of several banks on Mohammed V with foreign-exchange services and ATM.

Pharmacy al-Farabi (✆ 0536 60 60 11; Ave Mohammed V; ⊙ 8am-6pm Mon-Sat)

Ketama Voyages (✆ 0536 60 61 91; ketamavoyage@hotmail.fr; 55 Ave Mohammed; ⊙ 9.30am-noon, 2.30-6.30pm Mon-Fri, 9.30am-noon Sat)

Royal Air Maroc (Ave Mohammed V; ☺8.30am-12.15pm & 2.30-7pm Mon-Fri, 9am-noon & 3-6pm Sat)

ℹ Getting There & Away

AIR

The airport is 23km south of Nador. Ryanair operates numerous flights to Brussels, Paris, Marseilles, Frankfurt and Barcelona. Eurowings flies to London, Cologne, Berlin, Prague and Zurich. Air Arabia flies to Barcelona, Cologne and Brussels. Royal Air Maroc flies to Casablanca, Amsterdam and Brussels.

BOAT

Trasmediterranea has 11 sailings a week to Almería (six hours). Naviera Armas sails twice a week to Motril (five hours), while Grandi Navi Veloci has a weekly ferry to Sete in France (29 hours). The port of Beni Enzar is 7km from the city but traffic makes it feel much further. The quickest way to get there is by grand taxi (Dh6, 15 minutes).

BUS

From the **CTM office** (☎ 0536 60 01 36; Rue Genéral Meziane) there are departures to all the usual suspects: Casablanca, Rabat, Meknès, Fez, Tangier, Larache, Sidi Kacem, Al-Hoceima, Chefchaouen and more. In the evening, several slightly cheaper Casablanca-bound coaches run by other companies leave from the same area. CTM also has a small office in the main bus station in addition to its main office.

The main bus station is southeast of the centre. There are frequent departures:

Al-Hoceima (Dh40, three hours)

Beni Enzar (Melilla border; Dh5, 25 minutes)

Fez (Dh60, 5½ hours)

Oujda (Dh30, 2½ hours) via Berkane (Dh20, 1½ hours)

Ras el-Maa (Dh20, one hour)

Tetouan (Dh120, nine hours), some via Dardara (for Chefchaouen, Dh100, six hours)

TAXI

The huge grand-taxi lot next to the main bus station serves plenty of destinations.

DESTINATION	COST (DH)	DURATION
Al-Hoceima	60	2 hr
Beni Enzar (the Melilla border)	6	15 min
Berkane	35	1 hr
Oujda	60	2 hr
Taza	70	3 hr

TRAIN

Nador Ville train station serves the following destinations:

Beni Enzar/Melilla border (Dh11, 18 minutes)

Fez (Dh104, six hours, four daily) Two of the Fez trains go via Taourirt, where you can change for Casablanca.

East of Nador

East of Nador, the coast is a mix of salt marsh and sand dunes, which attracts a wide variety of birdlife, including the greater flamingo. Two scruffy towns, Kariat Arekmane and Ras el-Maa, lie on the Rocade (N16) eastwards to Saïdia, which affords good views of the Islas Chafarinas, the last bit of Spain on the northern coast. Arekmane has a new corniche but no further development yet. The beach, with its fishing boats, is full of rubbish, and the wetlands inland of the corniche are in danger of disappearing.

Ras el-Maa, also known as Cap de l'Eau, is faring better. The pedestrianised corniche has a few small restaurants and a beautiful beach. The wetlands around the Moulouya rivermouth west of the small town are Ramsar-protected, making them a prime birdwatching area, especially for migrant fowl and waders from Europe.

From the eastern side of the Moulouya River estuary, the much-vaunted Station Balnéaire (seaside resort) runs for 5km to Saïdia along a truly magnificent beach. There are hundreds upon hundreds of blocks of apartments, mostly completed. They are largely only occupied during the high season (July and August), which gives the entire development a ghostly air. The development is mostly aimed at Moroccan holidaymakers (and Moroccans returning from abroad for their holidays).

The best area of beach along this 5km stretch is at Mediterreanéa Saïdia, known as Saïdia Med, where there are several golf courses, a large shopping centre and a marina with 740 berths. Here you can hire a jet ski (Dh800 per hour), a kayak (Dh40) or a motorboat (Dh1000).

🛏 Sleeping & Eating

Resort hotels dominate Saïdia Med, which is where you'll find the restaurants, unless you go into Saïdia proper for cheap, cheerful options.

Iberostar Hotel
HOTEL €€€

(☎ 0536 63 00 10; www.iberostar.com; Saïdia Med; s/d full board Dh1580/2680; P ❀ 🛜 🏊) The best option when it comes to resort hotels along Mediterreanéa Saïdia (Saïdia Med). It has extensive grounds and rooms, a spa, sporting facilities and several restaurants and bars. At the beach you can hire a jet ski, a kayak or a motorboat.

ℹ Getting There & Away

Grands taxis ply the routes between Saïdia, Saïdia Med and the Nador-Oujda corridor.

Saïdia
السعيدية

POP 3870

Saïdia has always been a sleepy little seaside town that springs into life in summer when it throngs with Moroccan holidaymakers, many staying in the apartment complexes reserved for government workers.

The large developments known as the Station Balnéaire and Saïdia Med, consisting of holdiay apartments and resorts under construction, lie to the west, but the town remains quite separate.

Saïdia has a superb beach with clean yellow sand. There are loungers and umbrellas to hire, jet skis and pedalos and, most unusually, girls in bikinis. The new corniche has fast-food restaurants and clubs along it, each pumping out its own brand of music. Most, though, are closed out of season. One block back from the beach, Blvd Hassan II has some pre-existing hotels, banks, cafes and internet facilities.

🛏 Sleeping & Eating

There are seafood restaurants along the corniche (Ave Mohammed V) and along Blvd Hassan II.

Hotel Atlal
HOTEL €€

(☎ 0536 62 50 21; atlalben@menara.ma; 44 Blvd Hassan II, Saïdia; d incl breakfast Dh510; ❀ 🛜) Large rooms are the order of the day at this hotel run by friendly staff. There's a bar and good restaurant, too. However, noise from the basement disco can be a problem.

Titanic Hotel
HOTEL €€

(☎ 0536 62 40 71; Ave Mohammed V; s/d Dh370/520; ❀ 🛜) A cheery blue-and-white hotel on the seafront with decent, breezy rooms and iceberg-free views of the water.

Restaurant Boughaz
FAST FOOD €

(Corniche, Saïdia; pizzas from Dh30; ⊙ 10am-10pm) One of many restaurants lining the corniche, the Boughaz serves the usual burgers, pizzas and fish. Inside it's cavernous, but there's a terrace overlooking the beach with wonderful sea views.

La Corniche
MOROCCAN €€

(Ave Mohammed V; mains Dh30-90; ⊙ 8am-10pm) Seafront restaurant with a terrace facing the water, with a mix of Moroccan staples, sandwiches, pasta and pizzas.

ℹ Getting There & Away

Politics keeps the nearby border with Algeria closed. There is little to no chance of it reopening soon.

AIR

Oujda-Angad Airport (☎ 0536 68 32 61) servs Saïdia. RAM has two (sometimes three) daily flights to Casablanca and direct flights to Paris Orly. Ryanair operates flights to Paris, Brussels, Marseille and Düsseldorf. EasyJet, Transavia, Jetairfly and Air Arabia all have flights to Paris.

BUS

CTM operates an early-morning bus from Nador (Dh35, two hours).

Other companies run several buses a day from Oujda to Saïdia (Dh17, one hour).

TAXI

Hiring a taxi from Oujda airport to Saïdia costs Dh150 and the journey takes an hour. A seat in a shared taxi from Oujda's bus station is Dh25.

Berkane

POP 80,000

Berkane is a dusty modern town about 80km southeast of Nador on the road to Oujda. It's famous for its oranges and everything in the town is indeed orange, from the taxis and buildings and the wonderful statue of an orange as you enter the town. It's most useful to travellers as a transit point, as well as a base for exploring the Beni-Snassen Mountains.

The town is easy to navigate as it's stretched along Blvd Mohammed V, which leads from the orange Grande Mosquée in the west to the large roundabout at the other end, dominated by a large orange municipal building. You'll find the post office and ATMs here, as well as a couple of hotels.

BENI-SNASSEN MOUNTAINS

جبال بني يزناسن

Inland from the eastern Mediterranean coast, the ruggedly beautiful Beni-Snassen Mountains are for all intents and purposes a national park. This is a verdant area of scenic gorges that few imagine when they think of Morocco, and even fewer visit.

Using the 'orange' town of **Berkane** as a base is the best way to explore the Beni-Snassen Mountains. If you don't have your own vehicle, the easiest way to access the park is to take a shared taxi from Berkane (Dh15). Alternatively, hire your own taxi; the minimum fare will be in the region of Dh250 for two hours, although not all drivers will be willing to take their vehicles along the poor roads near the hamlet of Zegzel. A cheaper alternative is to take a bus or grand taxi to Taforalt and walk down. Two buses each morning make the journey from Berkane (Dh12, 30 minutes), with return services in the afternoons. Grands taxis cost Dh15, and are most frequent on market days (Wednesday and Sunday).

From Berkane, take the national road to **Taforalt** (Tafoughalt), which passes through beautiful mountain scenery. Taforalt is a somewhat haphazard settlement that arose around a former French military installation, but the northern end, which you come upon first, contains a charming strip of cafes and restaurants; one of these is **Club Taforalt** (☉ Apr-Oct). You can stay at the nearby **Auberge Taforalt** (☑ 0662 04 51 19; www.taforalt-club.com; Taforalt; r incl breakfast Dh350, tent Dh250; ☂).

Soon after you enter Taforalt from Berkane, turn left at the post office, then immediately turn left again and follow signs to the Infokiosk, which has a small but informative display on the natural history of the park, and an observation platform with heavenly views of a distant mesa. If you're lucky you will catch sight of a big-horned Barbary sheep from the adjacent reserve. They generally arrive around 4pm, when it is cooler.

About 2km back down the national road is a right turn signposted for two *grottes* (caves). **Grottes des Pigeons** (1km) is the site of an active excavation by Oxford University and has revealed human remains from the Pleistocene era, including some early human jewellery (80,000 years old).

Another 5km brings you to **Grottes de Chameau**, a multistorey cave complex with three entrances that have been closed for years due to flooding damage. Three kilometres further brings you to the pretty **Zegzel Gorge** and a beautiful serpentine drive. Don't miss the chance to sample the cumquats, a local industry. Even the Romans remarked upon them.

The source of the **Charaâ River** provides a worthwhile detour. Follow signs to the tiny hamlet of Zegzel, 2km up a side road. At the end there's a popular picnic spot near where the river gushes out of the cliff. Not far from here, a spectacular ridge road cuts east to Oujda. You'll need a 4WD vehicle, a good map and an early start.

Halfway between is the main square, with the CTM station on the south side.

🛏 Sleeping & Eating

The main options for sleeping and eating are strung along or near Blvd Mohammed V.

Hotel Rosalina　　　　　HOTEL €
(☑ 0536 61 89 92; rosalina_hotel@hotmail.fr; 82 Blvd Mohammed V, Berkane; s/d incl breakfast Dh280/360) This modern hotel is pleasant, with lots of wood panelling and friendly staff. There's a cafe on the ground floor. Berkane's best sleeping option by some distance.

ⓘ Getting There & Away

Berkane's bus and taxi stands are scattered all over town.

CTM buses depart from a dedicated station near the main square. Most other long-distance buses gather in the streets behind the CMH petrol station. The buses to Nador (Dh22, one hour) stop immediately behind the petrol station, and run hourly until midafternoon.

Local buses for Taforalt (Dh8, 30 minutes) depart from Blvd Mohammed V twice a day, while grands taxis for Taforalt (Dh10, 25 minutes) and Nador (Dh30, one hour) use the car park on the opposite side of the road, between the Shell petrol station and the bridge.

Grands taxis for Oujda (Dh25, one hour) leave from near the bus station; for Saïdia (Dh10, 15 minutes) from the square in front of the municipal building at the end of Blvd Mohammed V; and for Nador from the car park opposite the Great Mosque.

Oujda

وجدة

POP 518,000

Oujda is the largest city in eastern Morocco, with a modern facade that belies its millennium-old age. Despite its heritage, it receives very few foreign travellers. The reason for this is found on the map: it was once the busiest border crossing with Algeria, making it popular with traders and tourists alike. When the border closed in 1995, Oujda's economy took a major hit. However, recent tourism development along the nearby Mediterranean coast, and the consequent rise in importance of the airport, are having a positive knock-on effect. In addition, Oujda's university remains a mainstay of the economy and the city's intellectual life.

Despite few attractions, it's hassle-free so you can catch your breath after heading down from the Rif Mountains or before travelling on to Figuig (p143) and the Sahara.

History

Oujda lies on the main axis connecting Morocco with the rest of North Africa (the Romans built a road through here). Like Taza, it occupied a key position in controlling the east and was often seen as a vital stepping stone for armies aiming to seize control of the heartland around it.

Founded by the Meghraoua tribe in the 10th century, Oujda remained independent until the Almohads overran it a century later. Under the Merenids, Algerian rulers based in Tlemcen took the town on several occasions, and in the 17th century it fell under the Ottomans in Algiers.

Moulay Ismail put an end to this in 1687, and Oujda remained in Moroccan hands until 1907, when French forces in Algeria crossed the frontier and occupied the town in one of a series of similar 'incidents'. The protectorate was still five years away, but the sultan was powerless to stop it.

The French soon expanded Oujda, which is still burgeoning as a provincial capital.

◉ Sights

Although full of new buildings, a few deco structures survive in the side streets of central Oujda. Walking south along Blvd Mohammed V, note the 1930s **clock tower**, and the impressive French neo-Moorish **Banque al-Maghrib** before arriving at the **Church of St Louis** (Pl 9 Juillet; ⊘ mass Sat 6.30pm, Sun 9am) with nesting storks on its towers. Ask at the presbytery for access to the church.

Medina   MEDINA

Oujda's medina isn't large but the walls and several surrounding squares have been rebuilt. Enter through the eastern gate, **Bab el-Ouahab**. It is chock-full of food stalls (Oujda olives are well regarded) and street cafes. Bustling without being overwhelming, it's a great slice of tradition and modernity.

➡ **Grande Mosquée**   MOSQUE

Also known as the Mosque of Omar ben Abdelaziz, this mosque was built in the early years of the French protectorate in a Mauresque style.

Parc Lalla Aicha   PARK

(Ave Yacoub Al-Mansour; ⊘ 7am-7pm) This beautiful park is worth a stroll. There's a swimming pool (summer only, Dh20), a cafe, tennis and horse riding.

✵✵ Festivals & Events

Oujda is renowned for its music: a cross-cultural mix of Algerian, Andalucian and Moroccan.

International Gharnati Festival (⊘ Jul) Gharnati is Algerian music from Andalucia (the name is derived from Granada) and is particularly renowned in nearby Tlemcen.

Oujda International Rai Festival (⊘ Aug) Rai music developed in Algeria in the 1930s as a form of protest folk music.

Sidi Yahia Moussem (⊘ Aug & Sep) Ben Younes, 6km south of Oujda. Patron saint of the city and venerated by Moroccans, Sidi Yahia is also thought to be John the Baptist or perhaps a Castilian rabbi. Thousands of pilgrims flock to the celebrations 6km south of Oujda. The trees around the shrine (closed to non-Muslims) are festooned with rags, tied to receive blessings – a throwback to pre-Islamic fertility beliefs. To get to Sidi Yahia, take bus 1 (Dh6) from outside Bab el-Ouahab in Oujda or a petit taxi (Dh30).

⊨ Sleeping

Hôtel Angad   HOTEL €

(Map p282; ☏ 0536 69 14 51; hotelangad@hotmail.fr; Rue Tafna; s/d Dh182/224, with air-con Dh223/274; ☏) The top pick of the budget hotels is this affordable two-star hotel. Rooms are basic, with a large bathroom and

TV; get a room at the back as streetside can be noisy. The downstairs cafe does breakfast and pizza.

Hôtel Tlemcen
HOTEL €

(Map p282; ☑ 0536 70 03 84; 26 Rue Ramdane el-Gadhi; s/d Dh90/180; ✳) This friendly little place offers excellent value, and has a grand-looking lobby. Quarters are small but bright, with bathroom and TV.

Hôtel Afrah
HOTEL €

(Map p282; ☑ 0536 68 65 33; 15 Rue Tafna; s/d Dh90/140) The tiles and plasterwork in the lobby lend some traditional Moroccan flavour here. Self-contained rooms are a bit boxy, but otherwise this is a good budget choice.

Hôtel Ibis Moussafir
HOTEL €€

(Map p282; ☑ 0536 68 82 02; www.ibishotel.com; Pl de la Gare; s/d Dh640/720; ✳ 🛜 ⧉) Bang in front of you on the left as you leave the train station, the Ibis has all the up-to-the-minute facilities and comfortable rooms you'd expect from this international hotel chain – you could be anywhere (or nowhere) in the world. Nonguests can use the pool for Dh100 per day.

Hotel Al Manar
HOTEL €€

(☑ 0536 68 88 55; hotelalmanara@menara.ma; 50 Blvd Zerktouni; s/d Dh360/420; ✳ 🛜) Centrally located, the Al Manar is suitably towering for its name, and has functional and practical decor. Rooms are fine value, although avoid the darker, small-windowed interior rooms.

Hotel Jeda
HOTEL €€

(☑ 0536 70 46 46; jeddahotel8@gmail.com; 13 Rue Ouartass; s/d Dh300/400; ✳ 🛜) Comfortably competent midrange option just away from the main action, with a pleasant ice-cream and pizza place out front.

Atlas Terminus & Spa
HOTEL €€€

(☑ 0536 71 10 10; www.hotelsatlas.com; Pl de la Gare; s/d incl breakfast Dh1380/1570; ✳ 🛜 ⧉) Sitting imperially next to the train station, the Atlas Terminus is very grand. Rooms and service are the best quality, with three restaurants, a bar and nightclub, a pool and a spa.

✗ Eating

There's a rash of new, modern cafes, and many serve good food. In the medina, the stalls inside Bab el-Ouahab offer more traditional fare, including *kefta*, bowls of *harira* and boiled snails.

★ Restaurant Nacional
MOROCCAN €

(☑ 0536 70 32 57; 107 Blvd Allal ben Abdallah; meals from Dh25; ⊘ noon-3pm & 7-10pm) This is a Oujda institution: people queue for tables at lunchtime (there's a big, packed salon upstairs). Salads are great, and waiters rush with plates of grilled meat, fried fish and tajines, and there's couscous on Fridays.

Trocadero
CAFE, ITALIAN €

(71 Blvd Allal Ben Abdellah Al Mahatta; mains Dh40-120; ⊘ 8am-10pm; 🛜) One of the new black, glass and chrome cafes, Trocadero has two floors and a pavement area. The food is excellent: try the chicken florentina or risotto.

L'Excellence
CAFE, ITALIAN €

(☑ 0536 71 28 18; 30 Blvd Mohammed V; pizza from Dh40; ⊘ 8am-10pm) A large, modern cafe over two floors with an excellent patisserie around the corner and a pizza restaurant upstairs.

Café Pâtisserie Colombe
CAFE €

(Blvd Mohammed V; croissants Dh2; ⊘ 8am-10pm) One of several popular and busy cafes along this stretch, this perennially busy place is particularly good for breakfast and people-watching.

Argana
CAFE €

(Pl Sidi Abdel Ouahab; tajines Dh25; ⊘ 9am-9pm) Join lots of Moroccan families and take the lift to this large, plant-filled cafe overlooking the square. There's (very loud) live music at night.

La Belle d'Orient
SEAFOOD €€

(☑ 0536 70 59 61; 65 Blvd Ahfir; mains from Dh75; ⊘ lunch) An excellent choice if you're in the mood for fish fresh from the coast. Sardines are grilled on the barbecue outside, there's a fish tagine (Dh100) or a platter of *poisson friture* (Dh75). Pizzas are also available.

Restaurant Le Comme Chez Soi
FRENCH €€

(☑ 0536 68 60 79; 8 Rue Sijilmassa; mains around Dh110; ⊘ noon-3pm & 7pm-midnight) This licensed restaurant has a French-influenced menu, with some good meat and fish dishes, plus a smattering of pastas and steaks.

Rihab
CAFE, ITALIAN €€

(☑ 0536 70 51 51; cnr Blvds Idriss Al-Akbar & Allal ben Abdallah; mains from Dh95; ⊘ 8am-11pm; 🛜) The ground and 1st floors are a swish, modern cafe, ice-cream parlour and excellent *boulangerie*, while on the 8th floor there's a good restaurant with a wide range of fish and Italian dishes.

Oujda

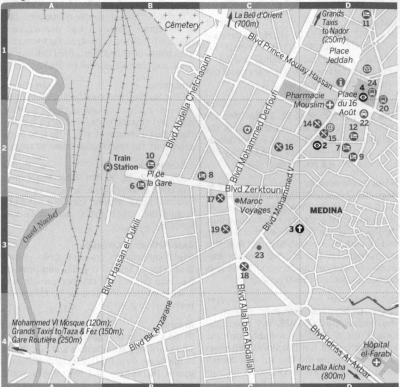

Map labels:
- Cemetery
- La Bell d'Orient (700m)
- Blvd Prince Moulay Hassan
- Grands Taxis to Nador (250m)
- Place Jeddah
- 11
- 4
- 24
- 20
- Blvd Abdella Chefchaouni
- Pharmacie Mouslim
- Place du 16 Août
- 14
- @
- 12
- 22
- 15
- 16
- 2
- 7
- 9
- Blvd Mohammed Derfoufi
- Train Station
- 10
- Pl de la Gare
- 6
- 8
- Blvd Zerktouni
- 17
- Maroc Voyages
- MEDINA
- Blvd Mohammed V
- 19
- 3
- 23
- Blvd Hassan el-Oukili
- 18
- Oued Nachef
- Mohammed VI Mosque (120m); Grands Taxis to Taza & Fez (150m); Gare Routière (250m)
- Blvd Bir Anzarane
- Blvd Allal ben Abdallah
- Blvd Idriss Al-Akbar
- Hôpital el-Farabi
- Parc Lalla Aicha (800m)

Sidebar (vertical): MEDITERRANEAN COAST & THE RIF OUJDA

ℹ Information

There are numerous banks with ATMs and *bureaux de change* located along Blvd Mohammed V.

Delegation Provinciale du Tourisme (Pl du 16 Aout; ⊗9am-4pm Mon-Thu, 9am-noon Fri) As usual, this is just an administrative office, but it does have a good map of the city.

Hôpital el-Farabi (☑ 0536 68 27 05; Ave Idriss el-Akbar)

Internet (Blvd Mohammed V; per hr Dh5; ⊗9am-10pm) Above the *téléboutique*.

Main Post Office (Blvd Mohammed V; ⊗8am-4pm)

Maroc Voyages (☑ 0536 68 39 93; 110 Blvd Allal ben Abdallah; ⊗9am-6pm Mon-Thu, 9am-noon Fri & Sat)

Pharmacie Mouslim (Blvd Mohammed V; ⊗8am-6pm)

Police Station (Blvd Mohammed Derfoufi)

ℹ Getting There & Away

AIR

Oujda-Angad Airport (p278) is 15km north of the town off the road to Saïdia. Grand-taxi fares are set at Dh150, but any bus to Nador, Berkane or Saïdia can drop you on the main road for a few dirham.

RAM (☑ 0536 68 39 09; 45 Blvd Mohammed V) has two (sometimes three) daily flights to Casablanca and direct flights to Paris Orly. Ryanair operates flights to Paris, Brussels, Marseille and Düsseldorf. EasyJet, Transavia, Jetairfly and Air Arabia all have flights to Paris.

BUS

The **main bus station** sits in the shadow of the huge Mohammed VI Mosque. **CTM** (☑ 0536 68 20 47; Rue Sidi Brahim) has an office just off Pl du 16 Août selling tickets to Casablanca (Dh210, nine hours overnight), Taza (Dh80, 3½ hours), Fez (Dh120, five hours), Meknès (Dh130, six

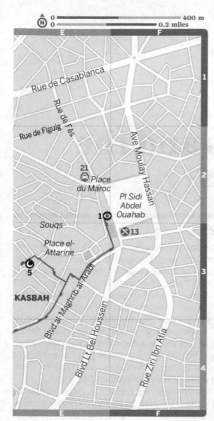

hours), Rabat (Dh180, 7½ hours); and Tangier (Dh200, 11 hours) also via Taza, Fez and Meknès. There is a service every other day to Figuig (Dh110, six hours).

Trans Ghazala runs several daily services to Casablanca via Taza, Fez, Meknès and Rabat. You also can buy tickets for these services at the **Trans Ghazala ticket office** (☑ 0536 68 53 87; Rue Sidi Brahim).

Numerous other companies with ticket offices in the bus station offer frequent departures for Taza, Fez and Meknès as well as Berkane (Dh18, 20 minutes) and Nador (Dh35, three hours). There are two daily buses to Figuig (Dh95, seven hours). There are also several buses a day to Saïdia (Dh15, one hour) and Al-Hoceima (Dh80, six hours). There are also two daily buses to Tangier via Tetouan

TAXI

Grands taxis leave regularly from the main bus station to Taza (Dh80, three hours). Change here for onward connections. Grands taxis heading north to Nador (Dh60, three hours), Saïdia (Dh25, one hour) and Berkane (Dh25, one hour) congregate north of town near the junction of Rue ibn Abdelmalek and Blvd Mohammed Derfoufi.

TRAIN

Oujda is the terminus of the northern branch of the Moroccan train line.

Oujda's train station is at the west end of Blvd Zerktouni. Four trains leave daily for Casablanca (Dh216, 10 hours) and four for Tangier (two via Sidi Kacem, Dh22, 10 hours). All stop at Taza (Dh78, 3½ hours), Fez (Dh1116, six hours) and Meknès (Dh137, 6½ hours).

ⓘ Getting Around

Red petits taxis are plentiful in Oujda. You're unlikely to pay more than Dh10 for any ride.

Fez, Meknès and the Middle Atlas

Why Go?

Humble villages and gentle mountain trails offer a charming counterpoint to imperial cities and ancient ruins in this area of Morocco. The fertile plains of the north have acted as Morocco's breadbasket for centuries. The Romans left remains at Volubilis, followed in turn by Muslim dynasties who created Morocco's grandest imperial city: Fez.

The narrow streets of the Fez medina are this region's major drawcard. Meknès, another old imperial capital, offers a more pocket-sized experience but some epic relics from Moulay Ismail's reign. Nearby, the picturesque pilgrimage town of Moulay Idriss – for centuries off-limits to non-Muslims – still quietly exerts a mystical force but remains little-visited.

The Middle Atlas, home to the Barbary macaque, rise to the south: the area is made for tranquil ambles and forest picnics. Across the mountains, Morocco's distinctive kasbahs begin to make an appearance – a sure sign that the southern desert isn't far away.

Best Places to Eat

➜ Ruined Garden (p307)

➜ Café Clock (p307)

➜ Dar El Mandar (p305)

➜ Dar Hatim (p308)

➜ Hôtel des Cèdres (p343)

Best Places to Sleep

➜ Ryad Mabrouka (p304)

➜ Funky Fes (p299)

➜ Ryad Bahia (p326)

➜ Dar Kamal Chaoui (p315)

➜ Dar El Mandar (p305)

When to Go
Fez

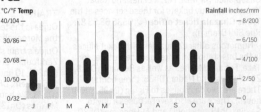

Apr Perfect spring weather and markets full of orange blossom scenting the air; the best time to visit Volubilis.

Jun Hit Fez for the Festival of World Sacred Music.

Sep Summer's heat has burned off making for perfect sightseeing conditions.

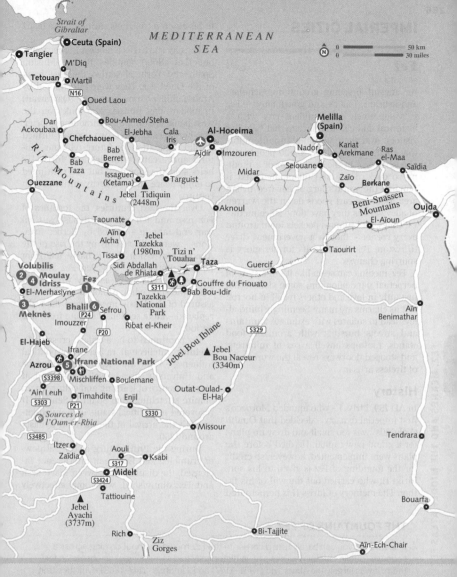

Fez, Meknès & Middle Atlas Highlights

① Fez (p286) Diving into the warren of this ancient city's medina looking for souqs and souvenirs, and enjoying the sound of the sublime at the Festival of World Sacred Music.

② Volubilis (p332) Time travelling through Morocco's finest Roman ruins, strewn with spectacular floor mosaics.

③ Meknès (p320) Exploring the outsized imperial architecture that characterised mighty Moulay Ismail's reign.

④ Moulay Idriss (p334) Spending a day and night on pilgrimage in this holy town.

⑤ Ifrane National Park (p338) Hiking in the rolling Middle Atlas mountains around Ifrane and Azrou, perhaps catching sight of a native monkey or two.

⑥ Bhalil (p315) Making like a troglodyte with a stay in this hilltop village famed for its cave dwellers.

IMPERIAL CITIES

Fez فاس

POP 1,150,131

An ancient breeding ground for scholars and artisans, imams and gourmands – Fez is a supremely self-confident city with a historical and cultural lineage that beguiles visitors. And there is something intangibly raw about a place where 70,000 people still choose to live in the maelstrom of a medina so dark, dense and dilapidated that it remains the world's largest car-free urban area. Donkeys cart goods down the warren of alleyways as they have done since medieval times, and ruinous pockets loom around every corner – though a government drive to restore Fès el-Bali to its former glory is spurring changes.

Fez' medina can seem like it's in a state of perpetual pandemonium; some visitors fall instantly in love and others recoil in horror. But its charms are many. Seemingly blind alleys lead to squares with exquisite fountains and streets bursting with aromatic food stands, rooftops unveil a sea of minarets, and stooped doorways reveal the workshops of tireless artisans.

History

In AD 789, Idriss I – who founded Morocco's first imperial dynasty – decided that Oualili (Volubilis) was too small and drew up plans for a grand new capital. He died before the plans were implemented, however, so credit for the founding of Fez is given to his son, Idriss II, who carried out the will of his father. The memory of Idriss II is perpetuated in his *zawiya* (religious shrine) in the heart of Fès el-Bali.

The city started as a modest Berber town, but then 8000 families fleeing Muslim Spain and Portugal settled the east bank of the Oued Fez. They were later joined by Arab families from Kairouan (Qayrawan) in modern-day Tunisia, who took over the west bank, creating the Kairaouine quarter. The heritages of these two peoples formed a solid foundation for future religious, cultural and architectural richness. Idriss II's heirs split the kingdom, but Fez continued to enjoy peace and prosperity until the 10th century.

Over the next centuries, the fortunes of Fez rose and fell with the dynasties. Civil war and famine – incited by Berber invasions – were relieved only by the rise of the Almoravids. When that dynasty fell from power around 1154, they fled Fez and destroyed the city walls as they went. Only when the succeeding Almohad dynasty was assured of the Fassis' loyalty were the walls replaced – large sections still date from this period.

Fez continued to be a crucial crossroads, wielding intellectual rather than political influence. With the Kairaouine Mosque and University already well established, it was the centre of learning and culture in an empire stretching from Spain to Senegal. It recovered its political status only much later, with the arrival of the Merenid dynasty around 1250.

During the 19th century, as central power crumbled and European interference increased, the distinction between Marrakesh and Fez diminished, with both effectively

THE FOUNTAINS OF FEZ

It seems like you can barely turn a corner in the Fez medina without coming across a *seqqâya* (public fountain) – Fassis have historically had something of an obsession for them. It was largely the Almoravid (1061–1147) and Almohad (1147–1248) dynasties that were the great water engineers. To supply their cities with water they diverted rivers, created lakes and constructed vast canal systems. While they did this across the country, fountain construction reached its zenith in imperial Fez.

There are well over 60 public fountains inside the medina. Along with the hammam, they are usually located near the neighbourhood mosque. Many were paid for by princes and wealthy merchants. Some of these fountains are simple basins against a wall. The majority are beautifully decorated structures of coloured tiles, often under a canopy of intricately carved wood. One of the finest is the Nejjarine fountain. Built in the 18th century, it features *zellij* (tilework) and stucco that form patterns as delicate as lacework.

Some fountains are still used for water collection and washing by their neighbourhoods; at some, the water supply has been cut as houses gain their own water supply.

serving as capitals of a fragmented country. Fez retained its status as the spiritual capital. It was here, on 30 March 1912, that the treaty introducing the French and Spanish protectorates over Morocco was signed. Less than three weeks later, rioting and virtual revolt against the new masters served as a reminder of the city's volatility.

The French may have moved the political capital to Rabat, but Fez remains a constituency to be reckoned with. The city's allegiance, or at least submission, has always been essential to whoever held Morocco's throne. Morocco's independence movement was born here, and when there are strikes or protests, they are often at their most vociferous in Fez.

As one of Morocco's most traditional cities, Fez is generally regarded with a certain amount of awe, perhaps tinged with jealousy, by the rest of the country. Indeed, a disproportionate share of Morocco's intellectual and economic elite hail from here and it's a widely held belief (especially among Fassis) that anyone born in the Fez medina is more religious, cultured, artistic and refined; the fact that the king's wife, Princess Lalla Salma is from Fez, and the royal family spend much time here is a source of great pride for the city.

◉ Sights

Travelling from the ville nouvelle to Fès el-Bali is like stepping back in time. The essential footprint of the medina hasn't changed in nearly a millennium, as the surrounding hills have constrained expansion – the last big growth of the traditional medina was in the 13th century with the construction of Fès el-Jdid. Today, around 156,000 Fassis still call this maze of twisting alleys, blind turns and hidden souqs home, while tourists call it one of the most mind-boggling places they'll visit in Morocco.

Bab Bou Jeloud in the west is the main entrance to the old city, with two main streets descending into the medina's heart. On your left as you enter is Talaa Kebira (Big Slope), with Talaa Seghira (Little Slope) on your right. Both converge near Pl an-Nejjarine, continuing to the Kairaouine Mosque and Zawiya Moulay Idriss II – the heart of the city. From here, it's uphill to reach the northern gates of Bab Guissa and Bab Jamaï, or head south towards Bab R'cif. The R'cif area has undergone a big facelift with a smart new gate and refurbished square and the

river is being upgraded. R'cif is likely to provide an alternate focus for the medina.

The major sights are really only a small part of the charm of the medina. It pays to do a little random exploration, and simply follow your nose or ears to discover the most unexpected charms of Fez' nature. Following your nose will lead you to women with bundles of freshly cut herbs, children carrying trays of loaves to be baked in the local bakery or a cafe selling glasses of spiced Berber coffee. Around the next corner you might find a beautifully tiled fountain, a workshop hammering pots, a camel's head announcing a specialist butcher, or just a gang of kids turning their alley into a football pitch. Everywhere, listen out for the call to prayer or the mule driver's cry 'balak!' ('look out!') to warn of the approach of a heavily laden pack animal.

Navigation can be confusing and getting lost at some stage is a certainty, but look at this as part of the adventure. A handy tip is to note the 'main' streets that eventually lead to a gate or landmark – just follow the general flow of people. Ask shopkeepers for directions, or you can fall back on the eager kids happy to rescue confused foreigners – though the remuneration they expect can be steep.

◉ The Medina (Fès el-Bali)

Bou Jeloud Square SQUARE
(Map p290; P) This square on the edge of the medina comes into its own at dusk, when locals emerge to stroll and chat. Concerts and a few storytellers sometimes pop up here, but it will never be Djemaa el-Fna.

★Medersa Bou Inania ISLAMIC SITE
(Map p290; Talaa Kebira; Dh20; ⊗9am-5pm, closed during prayers) A short walk down Talaa Kebira from Bab Bou Jeloud, the Medersa Bou Inania is the finest of Fez' theological colleges. It was built by the Merenid sultan Bou Inan between 1351 and 1357, and has been impressively restored with elaborate *zellij* (tiles) and carved plaster, beautiful cedar *mashrabiyyas* (lattice screens) and massive brass entrance doors. Whereas most *medersas* just have a simple prayer hall, the Bou Inania is unusual in that it hosts a complete mosque.

The mihrab (niche facing Mecca) has a particularly fine ceiling and onyx marble columns. It's thought that the *medersa* required a larger-scale mosque because there was none other nearby at the time; it includes a beautiful green-tiled minaret.

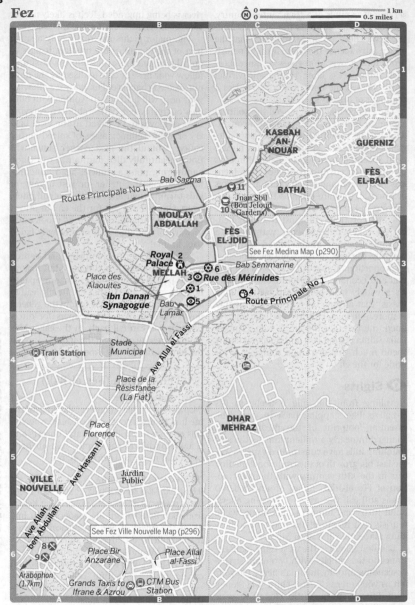

FEZ, MEKNÈS AND THE MIDDLE ATLAS FEZ

★**Nejjarine Museum of Wooden Arts & Crafts**   MUSEUM
(Map p290; ☎ 0535 74 05 80; Pl an-Nejjarine; Dh20; ☺10am-5pm) This museum is in a wonderfully restored *fondouq* (rooming house) – a caravanserai for travelling merchants who stored and sold their goods below and took lodgings on the floors above. Centred on a courtyard, the rooms are given over to displays of traditional artefacts of craftsmen's tools, chunky prayer beads and Berber locks, chests and musical instruments. Everything is beautifully presented, although the stun-

Fez

ning building gives the exhibits a run for their money. The rooftop cafe has great views over the medina. Photography is forbidden.

Henna Souq   MARKET

(Map p290; Rue Lfakharine) This souq, off Talaa Kebira, is one of the medina's oldest marketplaces. It's dominated by a huge graceful plane tree shading stalls selling ceramics and traditional cosmetics, including henna. This is a good place to come if you'd like to be talked through the fascinating array of natural products Moroccans routinely use – stall-holders are friendly and offer little hassle. The *mohtassib* (price-controller), now defunct, had his office here and you can still see his large scales.

Kairaouine Mosque & University   MOSQUE

(Map p291) One of Africa's largest mosques and possibly the oldest university in the world, this complex is the spiritual heart of Fez and Morocco itself. It's so large that it can be difficult to actually see: over the centuries the streets and houses of the Kairaouine quarter have encroached on the building so much they disguise its true shape. Non-Muslims cannot enter, but the university library has recently been impressively restored and opened to the public in 2016.

In the meantime, tourists will have to be content with glimpses of the mosque's courtyard from the main door on Derb Boutouil. Better still, take the view from any vantage point over the medina: the huge green pyramidal roof and minaret immediately an-

nounce their presence. The entrance to the library is at the other side of the complex, on Pl Seffarine.

The complex was established in 859 by Fatima el-Fihria, a female Tunisian refugee, and expanded by the Almoravids in the 12th century, and can accommodate up to 20,000 people at prayer.

★ Medersa el-Attarine   ISLAMIC SITE

(Map p291; Dh20; ⊙ 9am-5pm) Founded by Abu Said in 1325 in the heart of the medina, the Attarine was designed as an annexe to the nearby Kairaouine. The central courtyard displays the traditional patterns of Merenid artisanship, with magnificent *zellij*, carved plaster and cedar wood. Onyx columns flank the mihrab. Slightly smaller than the Medersa Bou Inania, it has been sensitively restored.

★ Chaouwara Tanneries   CRAFTS

(Map p291; Derb Chaouwara, Blida) The Chaouwara tanneries are one of the city's most iconic sights (and smells), offering a unique window into the pungent, natural process of producing world-class leather using methods that have changed little since medieval times. In 2015–16 they underwent a yearlong restoration to spruce up the crumbling environs surrounding the pits, including the viewing terraces, but fear not – the tanneries' atmosphere remains intact. Try to get here in the morning when the pits are awash with coloured dye.

Causing much frustration for visitors, the only way to see the tanneries in action is to dive into the lair of one of the many leather shops built into the walls surrounding the site. Displaying typical Fassi ingenuity, each shop has a terrace out back offering a different vantage point of the action – door No. 10 on Derb Chaouwara (keep an eye out for the number above the doorway) has one of the best views.

Salesmen will happily give an explanation of the processes involved and will expect a small tip in return or, even better, a sale. While this might feel a little commercialised, you probably won't find a better selection of leather in Morocco, and prices are as good as you'll get. The leather shops form a cooperative with the tannery workers and many of the salesmen are relatives of those doing the hard graft below.

Heading east or northeast from Pl as-Seffarine, you'll soon pick up the unmistakable waft of skin and dye that will guide you into the heart of the leather district. Beware the

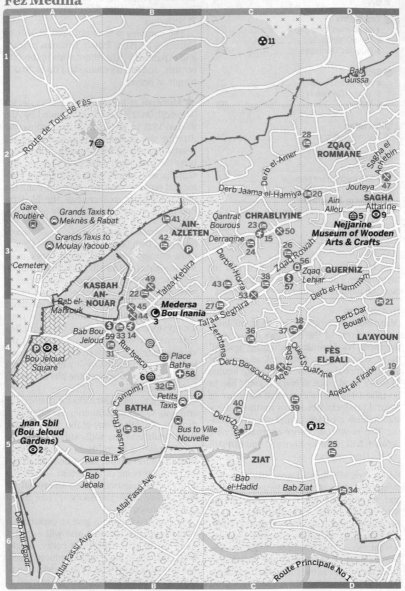

persistent touts, who will pounce on you as soon as you get within sniffing distance of the streets surrounding the tanneries: it is completely unnecessary to hire one and if you let a tout lead you into a shop, you'll pay more for anything you happen to buy there, to pay for his commission.

Batha Museum
MUSEUM

(Map p290; Musée du Batha; Rue de la Musée, Batha; Dh10; ⊙ 9am-5pm Wed-Mon) Housed in a

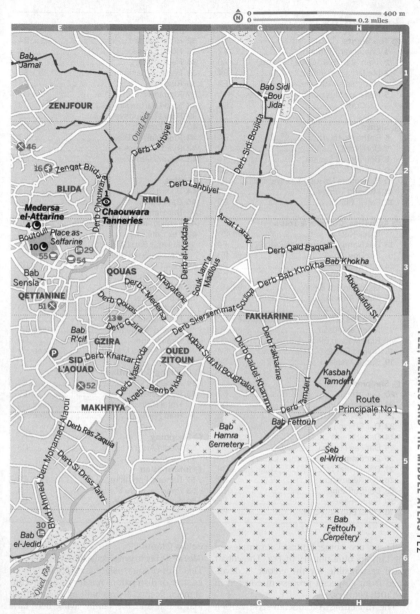

wonderful 19th-century summer palace and converted to a museum in 1915, the Batha Museum houses an excellent collection of traditional Moroccan arts and crafts. Historical and artistic artefacts include fine woodcarving, *zellij* and *tadelakt* (sculpted plaster), much of it from the city's ruined or decaying *medersas*. It also has some fine Fassi embroidery, colourful Berber carpets and antique instruments. The highlight of the museum is the superb ceramic collection dating from the 14th century to the present.

Fez Medina

These are some fantastic examples of the famous blue pottery of Fez. The cobalt glaze responsible for the colour is developed from a special process discovered in the 10th century.

The museum's Andalucian-style garden offers temporary respite from the bustle and noise of the medina, and the spreading holm oak provides a backdrop for the open-air concerts held here during the Sacred Music and Sufi Culture festivals.

Palais Glaoui PALACE
(Map p290; Douh Hamia, Batha; Dh30; ⊙9am-5pm)
This 18th-century palace is as fascinating for its state of disrepair as it is for its architectural magnificence. It was built by a pasha from Marrakesh and the family living here have been its guardians for 100 years. The main house is the height of Andalucian style and includes a well-preserved early-20th-century bathroom, still in use today. A hareem leads onto a large kitchen with gigantic cooking pots. The biggest surprise is the modern-art gallery in a salon at the back.

◉ Fès el-Jdid (New Fez)

Only in a city as old as Fez could you find a district dubbed 'New' because it's only 700 years old. The paranoid Merenid sultan Abu Yusuf Yacoub (1258–86) purpose-built the quarter, packing it with his Syrian mercenary guards and seeking to isolate himself from his subjects. Even today almost half of the area is given over to the grounds of the Royal Palace, still popular with Mohammed VI. Its other main legacy is the architectural evidence of its early Jewish inhabitants.

★ Jnan Sbil (Bou Jeloud Gardens)   GARDENS
(Map p290; Ave Moulay Hassan; ⊘ 8am-7pm) These lush gardens are a breath of fresh air after the intensity of Fez' medina. Although over a century old, extensive renovation and replanting have reinvigorated the gardens' splendour, and locals come in droves to promenade the leafy trails, cool off around the grand central fountains and lounge beside the bird-filled lake – especially at dusk. The main entrance is on Ave Moulay Hassan, but there's another at the opposite end of the park.

The gardens make a good halfway break between the *mellah* (Jewish quarter) and Bab Bou Jeloud.

★ Royal Palace   PALACE
(Map p288; Dar el-Makhzen; Pl des Alaouites) The entrance to Fez' Palais Royale is a stunning example of modern restoration, but the 80 hectares of palace grounds are not open to the public. Visitors must be satisfied with viewing its imposing brass doors, surrounded by fine *zellij* and carved cedar wood. Note the lemon trees to one side – tour guides are prone to plucking the fruit to demonstrate the juice's astringent cleaning properties on the palace gates. The entrance faces onto Pl des Alaouites.

Mellah   JEWISH SITE
(Map p288; In the 14th century Fès el-Jdid became a refuge for Jews, thus the creation of a *mellah*. The records suggest the move was orchestrated to offer the Jews greater protection, and they repaid the favour of the sultan with their loyalty during conflict. Around 250,000 Jews once lived here but now only 70 to 80 remain in Fez – all in the ville nouvelle. Their old houses remain, with their open balconies looking onto the streets a marked contrast to Muslim styles.

★ Rue des Mérinides   NOTABLE BUILDING
(Map p288) The most architecturally impressive street in the *mellah* is Rue des Mérinides, lined with houses that are distinguished by their wooden and wrought-iron balconies, as well as by their stucco work. Jewish ladies would have once sat at these upper balconies, watching the world go by and catching a cool breeze.

★ Ibn Danan Synagogue   SYNAGOGUE
(Map p288; off Derb Taquriri; donations welcome; ⊘ 9am-8pm) This pretty 17th-century synagogue was restored with the aid of Unesco in 1999. The doors are rarely flung wide, so you may need to find the guardian to invite you inside and point out the main features, including a *mikva* (ritual bath) in the basement. The original 17th-century torah scrolls, made of gazelle skin, are in a wooden cupboard on the far wall. The synagogue is well signposted.

Jewish Cemetery   CEMETERY
(Map p288; donations welcome; ⊘ 7am-7pm, to 5pm Fri) The southwest corner of the *mellah* is home to the sea of blindingly white tombs that stretch down the hill; those in dedicated enclosures are tombs of rabbis. One of the oldest, high up against the north wall, is that of Rabbi Vidal Hasserfaty, who died in 1600. The cemetery is still in use and has guardians. A warning: some dodgy characters hang around this area of the *mellah* – if you are offered entry to the cemetery after hours, respectfully decline.

On the slope below Vidal Hasserfaty's tomb, not far from the main entrance, the large tomb with green trimming is that of the martyr Solica. In 1834 this 14-year-old girl refused to convert to Islam or accept the advances of the governor of Tangier and subsequently had her throat slit. There's also a small synagogue on-site, but it's often locked so ask the guardians if you want to see inside.

Entry to the cemetery is via the southeastern street that runs parallel to Rue des Mérinides.

American Fondouk   ANIMAL SANCTUARY
(Map p288; www.americanfondouk.org; Rte de Taza; donations welcome; ⊘ 8am-noon Mon-Fri) **FREE** This nonprofit organisation's raison d'être is to help give the working equids of Fez medina a better life, and improve health and welfare education the often-poor families who depend on working donkeys, mules and horses for their livelihoods. The sanctuary

encourages visitors and veterinary volunteers (many from the University of Glasgow) happily give insightful, ad-hoc tours.

The American Fondouk has operated in Fez since 1927 but has gained new impetus under respected English director Dr Gigi Kay, who works tirelessly to ensure the veterinary care and conditions offered at the sanctuary are comparable to Western standards. There are 25 stables at the site and about 35 equids at any one time, many suffering from common complaints such as sores and hernias. What may surprise some visitors is that cases of outright cruelty are extremely rare; families depend on these pack animals and the equids are part of their lives. Sadly, it's often welfare education that's lacking.

Some owners have walked for miles from surrounding villages to bring their sick steeds here, and many owners visit frequently, sometimes daily, to spend time with their poorly animals while they are receiving medical treatment. Hearing their stories from the veterinary staff can be both heartbreaking and moving. Injuries can sometimes be graphically on view and upsetting to see; the sanctuary is not recommended for younger children.

◉ North Of The Medina

Viewed from the surrounding hills, Fez' jumbled buildings merge into a palette of white-flecked sandstone. Only here and there do the green-tiled roofs of the mosques and *medersas* provide a hint of colour.

Borj Nord   MUSEUM
(Map p290; ◔9am-noon & 2-5pm Tue-Sun) FREE
Like its counterpart on the southern hills (Borj Sud), Borj Nord was built by Sultan Ahmed al-Mansour in the late 16th century to monitor the potentially disloyal populace of Fez. Sitting on a level with the Merenid Tombs, it offers one of Fez' best lookouts, but in 2016 it also opened as a national armoury museum. Highlights include elaborately decorated sabres and muscats, traditional leather powder drums, and fascinating old photos. Signage is in French and Arabic; no photography permitted.

Merenid Tombs   RUINS
(Map p290) These tombs are dramatic in their advanced state of ruin, although little remains of their fine original decoration. The views over Fez are spectacular and well worth the climb. It's best at dusk as the lights

FEZ, MEKNÈS AND THE MIDDLE ATLAS FEZ

🚶 City Walk
Mazing Medina

START BAB BOU JELOUD
END R'CIF SQ
LENGTH 3KM; TWO TO THREE HOURS

This route takes you from Bab Bou Jeloud to the Kairaouine Mosque, then south to R'cif. It could take a couple of hours or all day, depending on the number of distractions.

Unlike much of the rest of the city walls and gates, the main entry, ❶ **Bab Bou Jeloud**, is a recent addition, built in 1913. Pass through it and you come upon a hive of activity. The pavement cafes here are excellent places for people-watching.

For the tour, take the first left and then right downhill along Talaa Kebira. This part of the street is a produce market – watch out for the camel butcher displaying the heads of his wares. Where the produce ends you're at the ❷ **Medersa Bou Inania** (p287), which represents the Merenid building style at its most perfect.

Opposite the entrance to the *medersa* (above eye-level) is the famous 14th-century ❸ **Magana hydraulic clock** designed by a clockmaker and part-time magician. Carved beams held brass bowls with water flowing between them to mark the hours, but the secret of its mechanism died with its creator.

Continuing downhill, notice the old *fondouq* (rooming house) on both sides of Talaa Kebira. These once hosted merchants and their caravans, and have rooms on several levels around a wide courtyard for both goods and pack animals. ❹ **Fondouq Kaat Smen** is particularly interesting, specialising in many varieties of honey and vats of *smen*, the rancid butter used in cooking.

About 400m from the Medersa Bou Inania, as you go around an unmistakable dogleg, you'll soon catch sight of the pretty, green-tiled minaret of the ❺ **Chrabliyine Mosque** (named for the slipper-makers who can still be found working in this area) straight ahead.

Still heading downhill, past the shoe sellers and leatherworkers, look out for a right turn onto Rue Lfkahrine and a sign indicating the entrance to a tiny tree-filled square (on your left) known as the

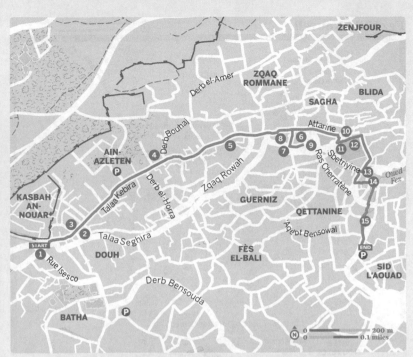

6 **henna souq** (p289) – if you start walking uphill, you've gone too far. Cosmetic shops sell oils and henna. Pottery and bric-a-brac stalls abound, too.

Exiting the henna souq the same way you entered, turn left (south). After 50m a right turn brings you into **7** **Place an-Nejjarine**. The lanes immediately north of the Nejjarine Museum of Wooden Arts & Crafts form part of the **8** **Souq an-Nejjarine** (Carpenters' Souq), where craftsmen create glittering wedding thrones.

From Pl an-Nejjarine, head back out the way you came in, turning left almost immediately and ducking under the bar that prevents the passage of mules and donkeys. The lane leads uphill between stalls piled high with candles and incense, to the entrance of the newly restored **9** **Zawiya Moulay Idriss II**. Non-Muslims cannot enter but can peer inside. To Fassis, this is the heart of their medina.

Afterwards, it's simplest to backtrack to Talaa Kebira along Rue Lfkahrine. Follow the lane east – over a slight hummock and past haberdashers' stalls – until it ends at a T-junction about 100m later, where you'll find the **10** **Medersa el-Attarine** (p289).

On emerging from the *medersa*, turn left (south) until the shops come to a sudden end at the walls of the great **11** **Kairaouine Mosque & University** (p289), right by Dar al Mouaqqit. The university is one of the world's oldest and this spot is where you'll find the main door. Again, non-Muslims cannot enter, but it's worth a peep in. Now backtrack and follow the university walls clockwise, passing **12** **Pâtisserie Kortouba**. Look out for the recently restored, 14th-century *fondouq* walls along the way.

Continue until the sound of metalworkers leads you into another small and attractive square, **13** **Place as-Seffarine** (Brass-makers' Sq). With the university walls (and the entrance to its library) at your back, there is the Medersa as-Seffarine on the square's east side. Built in 1280, it is the oldest *medersa* in Fez, and the only one still in use.

Pass the *medersa* and follow the lane, turning left at the mirror stalls. Ahead is the **14** **Dyers' Souq**. Walk through the souq into the **15** **R'cif market** (p307). Explore the market, or take any left into R'cif Sq where you can catch an onward petit taxi.

Fez Ville Nouvelle

come on and the muezzin's prayer calls echo around the valley, although you wouldn't want to hang about here after dark. A taxi from Bab Bou Jeloud should cost around Dh12; it's a 10-minute walk back downhill to the medina but the path's not great.

🏃 Activities

For a luxury experience, several guesthouses offer opulent hammam experiences. **Riad Laaroussa** (📞 0674 18 76 39; www.riad-laaroussa.com; 3 Derb Bechara; hammam Dh350; ⊙ 11am-9pm), **Riad Maison Bleue** (📞 0535 74 18 73; www.maisonbleue.com; 33 Derb el Mitter, Ain-Azleten; hammam from Dh300; ⊙ noon-8pm), Riad Fès (p304), **Palais Amani** (📞 0535 63 32 09; www.palaisamani.com; 12 Derb el Miter, Oued Zhoune; hammam from Dh395; ⊙ 8am-8pm) and Le Jardin des Biehn (p309) have excellent private spas, with hammam experiences starting from Dh350 and treatments Dh500.

Hammam Mernissi   HAMMAM
(Map p290; Derb Serrajine; public hammam Dh50; ⊙ women 11am-9pm, men 6-9am & 9pm-midnight) This renovated old hammam offers female tourists a special traditional hammam package for Dh200, comprising *savon beldi* (olive oil soap) and exfoliation with a *kis* (coarse glove). A massage will cost Dh100 extra.

Hammam Rihab   HAMMAM
(Map p290; 3 Chrabliyenne, Talaa Kebira; ⊙ women 8am-9pm, men 9pm-8am) A showstopping tiled doorway entices visitors into this ancient but refurbished hammam. Inside it's large, clean and used to tourists. Entrance is Dh20, but expect to pay around Dh100 for exfoliation and a massage.

Nausikaa   SPA
(📞 0535 61 00 06; www.nausikaaspa.com; Ave Bahnini, Rte Ain Smen; traditional hammam Dh100; ⊙ 10am-10.30pm) In the ville nouvelle, Nausi-

Fez Ville Nouvelle

kaa offers one of the most complete packages in Fez, blending hammam traditions with a modern spa experience. A variety of sumptuous massages and treatments are on offer, along with a gym and a pool.

◥ Courses

Clock Kitchen   COOKING
(☏ 0535 63 78 55; www.cafeclock.com; Derb el-Magana, Talaa Kebira; half-day course Dh600) Held in Café Clock, these classes are the place to perfect your tajine and couscous-making skills. After planning your menu, you shop for ingredients in the souq, spend the morning honing your technique and finish up enjoying the feast you've prepared. Other options include a two-hour bread-baking class and patisserie workshops.

Ruined Garden   COOKING
(☏ 0649 19 14 10; www.ruinedgarden.com; 13 Derb Idrissi; lunch course Dh550) One of Fez' best dining spots now offers cooking classes, giving aspiring chefs the run of the restaurant garden before opening time. To our knowledge, Ruined Garden is the only place in Fez to focus on vegetarian cuisine. Aided by in-house chef Najia, and Fatima for translation, you cook up a two-course feast including *maâkouda* (potato fritters), dips and a veggie tajine.

Or you can try your hand at baking bread, covering five different types of Moroccan breads and a trip to the local *ferran* (communal bread oven).

Dar Namir Gastronomic Retreats   COOKING
(tarastevens@gmail.com; 24 Derb Chikh el-Fouki; full-day class 2-4 people €350; live-in residencies incl breakfast from €450 per day) Established food writer Tara Stevens offers tailor-made luxury cooking experiences in her custom-built school. Tara's passion is modern Moroccan cuisine (she wrote the Café Clock cookbook). Courses also include Moroccan wine, and occasionally cheese, tastings. Tara has also launched an online Moroccan homewares business, www.anajamhome.com.

Fez Download   LANGUAGE
(☏ 0535 63 78 55; www.cafeclock.com; Derb el-Magana, Talaa Kebira; per person, minimum 2, incl refreshments Dh150) Spend 90 minutes with the affable Khalid learning basic phrases in Moroccan Arabic, etiquette and customs. At Café Clock.

Arabic Language Institute   LANGUAGE
(☏ 0535 62 48 50; www.alif-fes.com; 2 Rue Ahmed Hiba; 3-/6-week course Dh6300/10,900) Offers longer courses aimed at foreigners, and can assist in finding accommodation for students, in apartments or homestays. Lessons are held at the American Language Center where there's also a superb English-language bookshop stocking titles about Morocco.

Subul Assalam   LANGUAGE
(☏ 0535 63 79 36; www.sacal-fez.com; 19 Gzem Benameur; 3-week group course Dh6000, hourly lessons Dh250) This language school in R'cif touts its services in cross-cultural understanding. Subul Assalam ('Pathways to Peace') can arrange homestays for its longer courses, which are offered in Darija (Moroccan Arabic), modern standard and classical Arabic, as well as Tamazight Berber.

Arabophon   LANGUAGE
(☏ 0535 60 34 75; www.arabophon.com; 80 Rue Jaâfer ben Atiah, Aït Skato; half-/3-day course Dh500/Dh1500, 10-session online course Dh1100) Intensive Moroccan and Modern Standard Arabic courses, online courses and shorter courses aimed at travellers: the half-day Curious Explorer and three-day Serious Explorer. There are also classes in Tamazight Berber. Lessons are offered in English, French and Spanish, and the centre is south of the ville nouvelle.

FEZ, MEKNÈS AND THE MIDDLE ATLAS FEZ

☞ Tours

There are a series of well-signed self-guided walks through the old city; each highlights different aspects of traditional Fez:

Blue	Knowledge and learning
Brown	Monuments and souqs
Green	Palaces and Andalucian gardens
Orange	Walls and ramparts
Purple	Fès el-Jdid
Red	Artisanal crafts

The overhead signs are easy to follow, showing the direction of the next major landmark, and there are excellent English information boards at regular intervals. For an overview of the different trails, visit the main route map info board just off Talaa Kebira, where the Ain-Azleten parking is.

As well as pointing out incredible architecture and clandestine corners, guides can answer cultural questions, help overcome language barriers, and – perhaps most importantly – ward off other would-be guides. The standard rate for an official guide in Fez is Dh250 for a half-day tour, or Dh500 for a full day – always ask to see identification.

The quality of guides can vary considerably, so communication is very important to ensure that you get the best out of the experience. If you're not interested in shopping, say so firmly at the outset, although

WHAT'S ON IN THE VILLE NOUVELLE

Compared to the sensory overload provided by the medina, the ville nouvelle can seem boring: very modern, but with little actually going on. But for most Fassis, the ville nouvelle is where it's at and, far more interesting and progressive than crumbling Fès el-Bali. In the past few years, huge amounts of money have been poured into the area, the benefits of which can best be seen along the long boulevard of Ave Hassan II, with its manicured lawns, palm trees, flower beds and fountains. This is the 'real' Morocco as much as any donkey-packed lane in the old city. That said, Fez' ville nouvelle still lacks the panache of its equivalents in Marrakesh and Casablanca, and there's very little of interest here for visitors.

be aware that the guide who won't take a tourist to a single shop probably hasn't been born yet. It may be necessary to pay an extra Dh50 to Dh100 as a 'no shopping' supplement. If possible, arrange a guide through your hotel or guesthouse.

★ **Plan-it Morocco** TOURS
(☎ 0535 63 87 08; www.plan-it-morocco.com; Blvd Ahmed Mekouar, Batha; ⊗ 9am-6pm) Plan-it Morocco has carved out a niche organising unique cultural experiences in Fez and further afield, with excellent guides and unfaltering service. Excursions include streetside *tanjia* cooking, winery tours and architectural trails – the entertaining night-time street-food tasting trail is a highlight. Tours are private and exclusive and consequently not cheap, but they become more reasonable if there's two or more of you.

Artisanal Affairs CRAFTS
(☎ 0535 68 33 75; http://culturevulturesfez.org; 1-2 people Dh1500, 3 people Dh1800) This in-depth, highly interactive half-day tour explores the artisanal crafts of the Fez medina. It's a chance to meet and talk to coppersmiths, tanners, mosaic-tile-makers, cobblers, carpet makers and weavers. Note that it's not a traditional guided tour; the set-up is designed to enable tourists to ask questions and you'll get out of it what you put in.

There's no shopping involved, and groups are restricted to four. The organisers operate a similar tour in Sefrou (p314), too.

Photography Walking Tour TOURS
(☎ 0659 66 15 02; www.omarchennafi.com; 3hr tour Dh700) See the medina through the eyes of a local photographer on this laid-back three-hour walking tour, led by professional snapper Omar Chennafi. You'll learn plenty about local Fassi life while you're walking and Omar manages a good balance between technical advice and artistic insights. Tours can be tailored to your interests, focusing on geographical areas or subjects such as architecture or people.

Fes Rando WALKING
(☎ 0674 79 79 83; www.fesrando.com; per person from Dh300) A specialist walking-tour operator based out of Fez, offering day hikes on Mt Zalagh above Fez and further afield into the Middle Atlas. Longer treks to destinations such as Azrou's cedar forests and Tazekka National Park (p349) are also offered, and prices are reasonable.

✦ Festivals & Events

Fès Festival of World Sacred Music   MUSIC
(📞 0535 74 05 35; www.fesfestival.com; Fez;
☉ May/Jun) The Fès Festival of World Sacred
Music brings together music groups and
artists from all corners of the globe, and it
has become one of the most successful world
music festivals around. Based on the idea
that music can engender harmony between
different cultures, the festival has attracted
big international stars such as Ravi Shankar,
Bjork and Patti Smith.

Festival of Amazigh Culture   MUSIC
(☉ Jul) The festival, run in association with
the Institut Royal de la Culture Amazighe,
aims to promote and protect Amazigh (Berber) culture. Its program includes musical
performances, art workshops and handicraft exhibitions.

Moussem of Moulay Idriss II   RELIGIOUS
(☉ varies) Fez' biggest religious festival is also
one of the country's largest. The *moussem*
(festival in honour of a saint) of the city's
founder, Moulay Idriss, draws huge crowds.
Local artisans create special tributes and
there's a huge procession through the medina. Traditional music is played and followers dance and shower the musicians (and
onlookers) with orange-blossom water.

It's currently in September but the date
moves according to the Islamic calendar.

Festival of Sufi Culture   MUSIC
(☉ Oct) A series of events each year including talks and debates, and some spectacular
concerts held in the garden of the Batha Museum with Sufi musicians from across the
world. It used to be held in April but since
2016 the festival has been held in October.

🛏 Sleeping

Fez doesn't lack for variety in its accommodation options, but rates are higher than in
many other areas of Morocco.. Your main
choice is whether to stay in the colour and
chaos of the medina, or a petit-taxi ride
away in the ville nouvelle (where budgets
tend to go further). Booking in advance is
advised during high season, and especially
during the Festival of World Sacred Music.

🛏 Medina

Most of the cheapest options are within
touching distance of Bab Bou Jeloud, placing you right in the middle of the action.

ℹ RIAD BOOKING SERVICES

Fez Riads (📞 0672 51 33 57; www.
fez-riads.com) A percentage of profits is
donated to the High Atlas Foundation,
which supports grassroots development
projects in rural Moroccan communities.

Riads in the Fez medina are expensive
compared with elsewhere in the region. If
you're on a budget but want a private room,
look to the growing collection of backpacker
riads, which often have one or two private
rooms – some with en suites – at very reasonable prices.

★ Funky Fes   HOSTEL €
(Map p291; 📞 0535 63 31 96; www.funkyfes.com;
60 Arset Lamdelssi; dm Dh85-120, d Dh300; 🕸)
Fez' original, Spanish-owned hostel is still
the best, offering up good cheap backpacker beds close to Bab el-Jdid. It's a youthful
and social place, with more dorm beds than
you might imagine, and offers local tours,
activities, cooking classes and more. Cheap
in-house dinners cost Dh40 and the en-suite
double on the terrace is a great deal.

Dar Jannat   GUESTHOUSE €
(Map p290; 📞 0535 63 6000; www.riadjannat.com;
89 Derb Ahl Tadla, Talaa Seghira; dm €12, r from
€24; ❄🕸) This well-signposted cheapie is
a real bargain. The welcome is warm, the
atmosphere tranquil, and rooms are simple
yet charmingly furnished with traditional
textiles. A couple of rooms share bathrooms,
and there's a dorm as well as a larger family room sleeping up to four. Bathrooms are
very decent. Ask the owners if you need
transfers or tours.

Ziyarates Fes   HOMESTAY €
(📞 0620 30 37 92, 0535 63 46 67; www.ziyarates-
fes.com; s/d from Dh300/350) If you really
want to experience medina life up close,
this innovative homestay scheme can help.
Around 25 Fassi families rent rooms in their
homes to welcome foreign guests, while support from the regional tourism authorities
is meant to ensure the quality of the places
signed up. Organisation is excellent and you
can expect a warm welcome wherever you
stay, but cleanliness varies.

You might practise your Arabic, learn to
cook or just help the kids with their home-
work in this unique cultural exchange. Exact
prices vary, but all family homes are listed

THE MEDINA REVAMPED

Although visitors find medina life romantic, many residents have been happy to sell up to foreigners and swap their sometimes medieval living conditions for a modern apartment in the ville nouvelle. Certainly, years of neglect have taken their toll on Fès el-Bali (Old Fez) and restoration and modernisation efforts have been a long time coming.

The medina's riads were the first buildings to receive some tender loving care, mainly fuelled by money from expats, but now the city's *fondouqs* (rooming houses) and souqs are getting their slice of the action thanks to a government-backed drive to restore the medina to what it would have looked like in medieval times.

Souq by souq, metal doors are being ripped out of shops and replaced with the honey-coloured cedar wood that would have once been ubiquitous (a move that has caused the price of Morocco's most sought-after wood to skyrocket). Some workshops, little more than rough-hewn caves, are being rebuilt from scratch. The Chaouwara Tanneries have emerged from a year-long renovation to enhance the viewing platforms and workshops that surround it. Meanwhile, the river that bisects the city, for years virtually an open sewer hidden behind a high wall, is being cleaned up and revealed piece by piece. Riverside walkways designed to one day house artisan shops have been restored around PI R'Cif.

There is much to commend in this plan – for one thing, pollutants from the souqs (such as the newly restored Dyers' Souq) are now being diverted away from communities using the river to places where the water can be treated outside the city. Workers inside the medina are pleased to see Fès el-Bali finally receive some loving care and, for themselves, an improvement in working conditions. Yet there is also a fear that visitors will see the medina lose some of its charm for the sake of (mostly) cosmetic enhancements. Let's hope the authorities can strike the right balance between progress and preservation.

(with photos) on the organisation's website. Some rooms have shared bathrooms, while others might be en suite for the same price; it depends on the host.

Dar El Hana GUESTHOUSE €
(Map p290; ☑ 0535 63 58 54, 0665 81 98 36; www.darelhana.com; 22 Rue Ferrance Couicha, Chrabliyine; r incl breakfast Dh400-550; ☜) If there's a cosier and more intimate guesthouse in Fez than this *dar* (small house), we'd like to know about it. There are three rooms upstairs in the main house and another at ground level (though this last one feels ever so slightly cavelike), all charmingly presented. Guests are free to use the kitchen as they please; this is a real home away from home.

Dar Bouânania GUESTHOUSE €
(Map p290; ☑ 0535 63 72 82; darbouanania@gmail.com; 21 Derb Bensalem, Talaa Kebira; s/d Dh300/400, without bathroom Dh200/300, all incl breakfast; ✴☜) A popular choice with backpackers, this is a budget-style riad, though the array of intricate painted woodwork could make you think it's pricier than it is. The rooms are well sized and those that with en suite also have air-con; the rooms on the ground floor were being converted

into a restaurant during our visit. Shared bathrooms are clean, and there are a couple of roof terraces.

Hôtel Bab Boujloud HOTEL €
(Map p290; ☑ 0535 63 31 18; 49 Pl Isesco, Bab Bou Jeloud; s Dh170-200, d Dh300-350, all incl breakfast; ✴☜) Fantastically located, this hotel sits just outside Bab Bou Jeloud with all the medina action right on your doorstep. The rooms are as simple as the price tag suggests, but cosy enough and great value. There's also a good roof terrace.

Pension Campini GUESTHOUSE €
(Map p290; ☑ 0535 63 73 42; pensioncampini@gmail.com; Rue Campini, Batha; s/d Dh200/300; ☜) A short walk from the Batha Museum, this simple guesthouse is in a quiet location slightly outside the medina proper. Rooms have an en suite and are airy. There's a small terrace, with views just over the walls of Jnan Sbil (Bou Jeloud Gardens).

Hôtel Cascade HOTEL €
(Map p290; ☑ 0535 63 84 42; 26 Rue Serrajine, Bab Bou Jeloud; s/d Dh120/240) One of the grand-daddies of the Morocco shoestring hotels, the Cascade's Bab Bou Jeloud location is

hard to beat and it benefits from a pleasant rustic rooftop terrace restaurant with great views of the *bab* (gate). However, it's exceedingly basic so adjust your expectations accordingly: if you're impervious to the stench of urine, this place has merit.

Dar Roumana
GUESTHOUSE €€
(Map p290; ☑ 0535 74 16 37; www.darroumana. com; 30 Derb el-Amer, Zqaq Roumane; r incl breakfast €85-145; ✳ 🛜) Occupying a quiet corner within touching distance of the northern medina walls, Dar Roumana is a beautiful restoration job with hard-to-beat views from its roof terrace. Uncommonly, three of the rooms have wonderful baths (one a roll-top) and a couple of the rooms have external-facing windows. Push the boat out for the Yasmina suite, with its four-poster bed and leafy balcony.

A perennial favourite, it also has one of the medina's best restaurants (p308) to boot (reservations well in advance).

Dar Seffarine
GUESTHOUSE €€
(Map p291; ☑ 0671 11 35 28; www.darseffarine.com; 14 Derb Sbaalouyat, R'cif; r from €75, ste €110-130, all incl breakfast; ✳ 🛜) A short walk from Pl Seffarine, this classy *dar* stands on high ground, meaning it's filled with light and blessed with plenty of external-facing windows – the lovely roof terrace towers over much of the rest of the medina. Its owner is an Iraqi architect and graphic designer whose talents are reflected in the understated room interiors. Dinner (Dh200) and alcohol can be served in-house.

One of the suites is positively palatial, with a painted domed ceiling.

Ryad Salama
GUESTHOUSE €€
(Map p290; ☑ 0535 63 57 30; www.ryadsalama. com; 4 Derb el Tadla, Talaa Seghira; r incl breakfast €70-110; ✳ 🛜 🏊) Well located between Talaa Kebira and Talaa Seghira, this is a true riad with a lovely courtyard garden, inviting plunge pool and winter salon with an open fireplace. Upstairs rooms have delightful balconies to play Fassi Romeo and Juliet from. Rooms are finished to a very high standard, but the roof terrace is disappointingly small and basic. Alcohol is served.

Dar Fes Medina
GUESTHOUSE €€
(Map p290; ☑ 0673 31 41 07, 0535 63 83 92; www. darfesmedina.com; Derb Mokri, Ziat; s/d incl breakfast Dh550/660; ✳ 🛜) There's a clever trick being played here: walk through the 17th-century doors and you'll think you're in a restored

medina townhouse, but this *dar* is a recent build. You'll get the best of both worlds – slightly more spacious and modern rooms, but a pleasingly traditional veneer. The *Fassi owners have* expertly decorated the *dar* with antiques from their father's shop in Fez.

And its location near Bab Ziat provides another medina rarity: taxis can drop you right outside the front door. Nearby, the brothers who own this place have recently completed a more traditional restoration (Riad Mazar, from Dh770), but given it the same modern spin with orthopedic mattresses and high-tech temperature controls throughout.

Dar Bensouda
GUESTHOUSE €€
(Map p290; ☑ 0535 63 89 49; www.riaddarbensouda.com; 14 Zqaq Labghal, Qettanine; r incl breakfast from €85; ✳ 🛜) A converted palace, Dar Bensouda is one of the most impressive medina restoration projects in Fez. There's a large column-flanked traditional courtyard plus a more modern side annexe hosting a small but lovely pool with loungers. The scale here is grand without being overwhelming, and the service excellent. The only downside is its location: right at the heart of the labyrinthine medina.

That said, the staff are more than happy to collect you from, or guide you to, wherever you wish to go, and can even furnish you with a local phone.

Dar el Menia
GUESTHOUSE €€
(Map p290; ☑ 0535 63 31 64; www.darelmeniafez. com; 7 Derb el Menia, Talaa Kebira; standard/superior d incl breakfast €60/75; 🛜) Dar el Menia is a compact townhouse with four rooms tucked off the main drag. It's relatively restrained in its decor, giving an air of calm the moment you close the door. At the time of writing, the riad was under new management and upgrades such as luxury bedding and aircon were being installed. Cooking lessons and meals can be provided in-house.

Dar Finn
GUESTHOUSE €€
(Map p290; ☑ 0655 01 89 75, 0535 74 00 04; www. darfinn.com; 27 Zqaq Rowah; r Dh850-1300; ✳ 🛜) Fassi houses often surprise as they open up after passing through a dark medina doorway. Dar Finn manages the trick twice over, going from high Fassi style in the main house to an adjoining annexe with walled garden, plunge pool and a variety of patios. There's a lovely view from the multilevel roof and two rooms are suites with private terraces.

Of the five rooms, two lack air-con – no fun in Fez' sweltering summers.

1. Ceilings in Bahia Palace, Marrakesh 2. Tangier medina
3. Chefchaouen medina 4. Essaouira medina

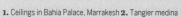

Winding Lanes

You could happily spend days in the best medinas of Morocco – getting lost, drinking tea, and getting lost again. The serendipity of chance discoveries are all part of the charm. Magical medinas are found in every part of the country, each with its own special flavour – here are some of the most atmospheric.

Marrakesh Medina

Inside 19km of ramparts, the theatrical Djemaa el-Fna (p50) is the beating, back-flipping heart of the Marrakesh medina. Follow crazy lanes – or thoroughfares if you forgot your compass – to sights such as Bahia Palace (p57).

Tangier Medina

Europe is just across the Strait of Gibraltar, but it feels a world away among the kasbah and souqs of the Tangier medina (p221). Spots like Petit Socco have been given a fresh coat of paint as part of the city's makeover.

Chefchaouen Medina

High in the Rif Mountains, Chefchaouen medina (p251) is painted a delightful Andalucian blue, fringed with terracotta tiles and green hills. You won't get too horribly lost in this compact mini-maze.

Essaouira Medina

In the salty embrace of Morocco's Atlantic sea, the fortified walls of Essaouira's laid-back medina (p207) trace the coastline and seagulls swarm overhead. It still has all the classic hallmarks: narrow twisty lanes, souqs and the aroma of spices – but here they combine with the damp sea air, smell of fish guts and crashing waves.

Fès el-Bali

Old Fez (p287) is Morocco's largest intact medina and embodies over 1200 years of history. Even old hands get lost in this maze of souqs and tanneries – you might chance upon a craft museum or a 14th-century *medersa* (theological college).

Riad Lune et Soleil
GUESTHOUSE €€

(Map p290; ☑ 0535 63 45 23; www.luneetsoleil. com; 3 Derb Skalia, Batha; r incl breakfast €65-90; ❄ 🛜) Each room at this French-owned riad is a cornucopia, filled with the evidence of a lifetime of collecting, from old postcards and embroidery to carvings and metalwork. It's not a museum, though; there's plenty of comfort too, and some rooms have their own Jacuzzi. There's also a good kitchen, a rooftop salon for colder weather and parking around the corner (Dh20 per night).

Hôtel Batha
HOTEL €€

(Map p290; ☑ 0535 74 10 77; hotelbatha@menara. ma; Pl Batha; s/d incl breakfast Dh350/500; ❄ 🏊) The great location, room capacity and pool keep the Batha permanently busy, and is popular with tour groups. It's a reasonably modern set-up, with fair rooms and a tranquil courtyard to retreat from the hustle of the medina. There's a convenient bar and nightclub next door for those looking for a drink in the medina.

Dar Attajali
GUESTHOUSE €€

(Map p290; ☑ 0535 63 77 28, 0677 08 11 92; www. attajalli.com; Derb Qettana, Zqaq Rommane; r incl breakfast Dh950-1300; ❄ 🛜) Dar Attajali is a magnificent testament to the art of patient and sympathetic restoration. Everything has been done to maintain the building's integrity, using a minimum of modern techniques, while producing a supremely comfortable guesthouse. Days kick off with organic, locally sourced breakfasts, and the guesthouse is known for its vegetarian and vegan food. Discounts of 20% are available July and August.

★ Ryad Mabrouka
GUESTHOUSE €€€

(Map p290; ☑ 0535 63 63 45; www.ryadmabrouka. com; 25 Derb el-Mitter, Ain-Azleten; d Dh1150-1450, ste Dh1300-2000, all incl breakfast; ❄ 🛜 🏊) 🍴 An old favourite, Mabrouka is a large, meticulously restored Arab-Andalucian townhouse whose owners go the extra mile for guests and strive to employ sustainable practices. There are eight rooms, all with little extras to make your stay more special: bathrobes and bathrooms equipped with traditional olive-pitt soap and scrubbing gloves are lovely touches. The courtyard opens onto a lush garden with medium-sized pool.

Enjoy a simple breakfast or an all-out Moroccan feast (set menu Dh130 to Dh240) on the view-tastic verandah overlooking the medina, or in bad weather there's a pretty 1st-floor, window-fronting tiled terrace –

wherever you desire. Massages can also be arranged and the owners will happily furnish you with a wealth of information on the city. Mabrouka's location is good for taxi drop-offs, too.

Riad Idrissy
GUESTHOUSE €€€

(Map p290; ☑ 0649 19 14 10; www.riadidrissy.com; 13 Derb Idrissi; d incl breakfast €85-140; ❄ 🛜) This magnificently restored townhouse wins extra points for its adjoining garden, a quirky green haven of huge papyrus and banana trees that has taken root in next door's crumbling foundations – now cleverly converted into one of Fez' best restaurants, the Ruined Garden (p307). Bedrooms are beautifully done, bathrooms have welcome modern flourishes and there's a lovely little Evita Balcony peeping over the garden.

Central African crafts and old Arabic vinyl records add an interesting decorative twist. The riad operates an informal room service and here's a nice touch: the friendly staff will put a basket of tea and coffee outside your door before 8am, so you can have drinks in bed before facing the world.

Riad Fès
GUESTHOUSE €€€

(Map p290; ☑ 0535 94 76 10; www.riadfes.com; 5 Derb ben Slimane, Zerbtana; d incl breakfast from Dh2100; ❄ 🛜 🏊) This labyrinthine riad has knocked together several houses to create a spacious hotel with stylish lounge areas, blending ancient and modern with impressive panache. The newer quarters wouldn't look out of place in a Parisian boutique hotel yet remain unmistakably Moroccan. Its location is also good: not too far from taxi drop-offs in Pl Batha, but also close to Talaa Seghira action.

The most recent renovations have gobbled up an adjoining house to create a unique hammam (☑ 0535 94 76 10; www.riadfes.com; Derb Zerbtana; hammam from Dh350; ⏰ noon-8pm) spectacularly sited around a riad courtyard, plus an enlarged pool area. If you can't afford to stay here, it's still worth coming for a drink (p309).

Riad Laaroussa
GUESTHOUSE €€€

(Map p290; ☑ 0674 18 76 39; www.riad-laaroussa. com; 3 Derb Bechara, Talaa Seghira; d incl breakfast Dh1200-2200, ste from Dh2700; ❄ 🏊) Entering through Laaroussa's cavernous dark entrance hall, it comes as a surprise to be greeted by such a large green space, with orange trees and a softly playing fountain. Indeed, there's loads of space here and the joy continues in the fine rooms, decorated with

SURVIVING THE FEZ MEDINA

If you're the type of person who likes a good lookout point, revels in bright sunshine and doesn't like confined airless spaces, spending too long in the bowels of the Fez medina might make the palms of your hands a little sweaty. Some tips for avoiding claustrophobia:

➡ Fez' medina is like a bowl that slopes down in the middle and rises around the edge: pick a riad that occupies a hilly spot. It'll be brighter and breezier inside as it's more likely to have external-facing windows. Dar Seffarine (p301) and Dar Roumana (p301) are good options.

➡ Ensure your hotel has a comfortable roof terrace, because if you've spent all day touring the medina you'll want to see Morocco's bright-blue sky in all its majesty at the end of the day. Alternatively, base yourself in the ville nouvelle.

➡ Dine high: some medina restaurants can be a bit cavelike, with no natural light, but several offer roof terrace dining. Café Clock (p307), Le 44 (p307), L'Amandier (p308) and Moi Anan (p308) are all good options.

➡ Head to Jnan Sbil (Bou Jeloud Gardens) (p293), just outside the medina, at dusk. With its lake, fountains and leafy trails it's a breath of fresh air after the medina and makes a gorgeous spot for strolling. Other good escape points are Borj Nord (p294) and the Merenid Tombs (p294), on the northern hills above the city.

➡ Factor time into your stay to escape the city completely. Consider a trip to a laid-back hill village such as Bhalil (p315), or spend a day eating, drinking and swimming in the countryside at Dar El Mandar (☑ 06 76 14 13 35; www.darelmandarfes.com; Douar Lahricha, Beni Mellala, Commune Rurale Kandar Sidi Khiar; d incl breakfast €40, lunch & pool day use €35; ℗).

modern art and eclectic furniture, and the outstanding (large!) dedicated pool annexe. One of Fez' best riad experiences.

There's also a hammam and restaurant (dinner Dh280) serving alcohol. Discounts available low season (July and August).

Riad Maison Bleue GUESTHOUSE €€€
(Map p290; ☑ 0535 74 18 73; www.maisonbleue.com; 33 Derb el-Mitter, Ain-Azleten; d/ste incl breakfast from Dh1900/2800; ℗ ❋ 🛜 🖂) You have to be careful not to get lost in this riad – it's four houses knocked together and even extended across the street. Start in the orange-tree-clad, Andalucian-style courtyard, then find your way to any of the 18 rooms, possibly stopping en route at the private spa, fashionably dark and plush Blue Lounge, or chic terrace restaurant-bar (nonguests welcome) with views to Borj Nord.

The latest addition to the stable is a well kitted-out, in-house cooking school – Maison Cordon Bleue – on the ground floor, offering a variety of culinary experiences (half-day class Dh850).

Palais Faraj HERITAGE HOTEL €€€
(Map p290; ☑ 0535 63 53 56; www.palaisfaraj.com; 16-18 Quartier Ziat, Derb Bensouda, Bab Ziat; d incl breakfast from €180; ℗ ❋ 🛜) It took four years to reinvent this 19th-century palace as the

bells-and-whistles heritage hotel that stands today. The Faraj retains some beautiful original features, but mixes them with edgy modern updates such as mirrored walls. There's an air of openness and calm, thanks to its location abutting a quiet wall of the medina, which also means it's a cinch to access by taxi.

The hotel is home to a recommended restaurant, L'Amandier (p308).

Riad Les Oudayas GUESTHOUSE €€€
(Map p290; ☑ 0669 10 94 90; www.lesoudayas.com; 5/6 Derb el-Hamiya, Ziat; r incl breakfast from Dh900; ❋ 🛜 🖂) The Moroccan owner is a Paris-based designer, something that certainly shows in this riad's careful blend of traditional styles and modern design aesthetic, in everything from the downstairs salons to the chic but comfortable bedrooms. There's a plunge pool in the courtyard garden and a private hammam leading off it. Alcohol is served in the ground-floor honesty bar.

Up top there's a large roof terrace, but if you crave privacy, two of the five rooms have private terraces.

Ville Nouvelle

In the ville nouvelle, room rates drop considerably compared with the more popular medina, so much of the time you can get midrange accommodation at budget prices. Although there are exceptions, note that hotels in this area of town can lack character and often allow smoking.

Hôtel Splendid
HOTEL €

(Map p296; ☑0535 62 21 48; splendidf@menara. ma; 9 Rue Abdelkarim el-Khattabi; s/d incl breakfast Dh353/432; ✻ ⊕ ⊠) Although in the budget category, this 69-room hotel makes a good claim for three stars and has bags more personality than many of its competitors. There's original art-deco character on the outside, while the rooms are modern and clean on the inside. The large courtyard pool is a bonus, though it's a little overlooked. There's also a restaurant (dinner Dh150).

Hôtel Central
HOTEL €

(Map p296; ☑0535 62 23 33; 50 Rue Brahim Roudani; s/d without shower Dh200/250, d with shower Dh300; ☏) A bright and airy budget option conveniently located just off busy Blvd Mohammed V. Most rooms have bathrooms, but even those without a shower have their own sinks. It's clean and good value, and many rooms come with petite wooden-shuttered balconies.

Hôtel Olympic
HOTEL €

(Map p296; ☑0535 93 26 82; www.hotelolympicfes. com; Rue Houman el Fatouaki, off Blvd Mohammed V; s/d Dh310/420; ✻ ☏) A handy choice near the central market, this hotel has nondescript but modern and comfortable rooms, equipped with bathrooms and TVs. Its central location means it's often heavily booked (it's popular with tour groups), so call in advance. Breakfast is Dh35.

Youth Hostel
HOSTEL €

(Map p296; ☑0535 62 40 85; www.hihostels.com; 18 Rue Abdeslam Serghini; dm incl breakfast Dh75, d without bathroom Dh170; ⊙ check-in 8am-9pm, gate open 24hr; ☏) One of the better youth hostels in Morocco, the Fez branch is a surprising leafy retreat where local Fassi pottery adds extra charm to a series of zellij-splashed patios. Tidy rooms and facilities (including Western-style toilets) are superbly clean, there's a communal kitchen and the staff can wrangle you discounts on official guides and tours. There's hot water mornings and evenings.

Across Hotel
HOTEL €€

(Map p296; ☑0535 94 06 12; www.acrosshotels.com; 76 Blvd Chefchaouni; s/d incl breakfast Dh1050/1350; �ⓟ ✻ ☏ ⊠) A sparkling modern hotel in a convenient location, the Across ticks all the boxes for its four stars. Rooms are as you'd expect, there's a gym, a hammam, a bar, a restaurant and a rooftop pool with amazing 360-degree views over the city and (wait for it!) a bar. Prices shown here are rack rates; you can bag a 40% discount if you book online.

Hôtel Mounia
HOTEL €€

(Map p296; ☑0535 62 48 38; www.hotelmouniafes. ma; 60 Blvd Zerktouni; s/d incl breakfast Dh551/702; ✻ ☏) A zellij lobby guides you into this modern hotel that's popular with tour groups. Rooms are bright and tidy, with satellite TV. There's a smoky bar as well as a nightclub (midnight to 3am). Rooms along corridors near the bar can be noisy. Staff are helpful, and good discounts are often available. There's a lift.

★ Hotel Sahrai
DESIGN HOTEL €€€

(Map p288; ☑0535 94 03 32; www.hotelsahrai. com; Dhar el-Mehraz; standard/deluxe ste incl breakfast from Dh2000/2500; ⓟ ✻ ☏ ⊠) This smart hotel venture from the owners of Riad Fès blends the comforts of a modern luxury stay with all the charm of Fez' Moroccan heritage. Oversized Fassi pottery and brass lanterns set the tone in the communal areas, while understated rooms feature sumptuous sunken baths and Acqua di Parma products. Deluxe rooms and junior suites have wonderful infinity-pool views.

High on the southern hills overlooking the medina, the Sahrai feels like it's in a world of its own – but there's still a convenient shuttle bus to ferry guests to the medina and back. That's if you can tear yourself away from the Givenchy spa, two restaurants and gorgeous rooftop cocktail bar.

Hotel Barceló Fès Medina
HOTEL €€€

(Map p296; ☑0535 94 88 00; www.barcelo.com; 53 Ave Hassan II; r Dh1760, ste from Dh1900; ✻ ☏ ⊠) One of Fez' chicest hotels, the 134-room Barceló sweeps elegantly around a corner opposite Pl de la Résistance, affording it excellent views of the medina. Despite its name, it is in the ville nouvelle. Rooms are well designed and spacious, with chic decor. There's a spa and a bar (serving alcohol – nonguests welcome), as well as a restaurant. Book online for discounts.

✗ Eating

Dining in Fez is something to be taken seriously. Fassi cuisine is famed across Morocco, and there are plenty of places in the medina to choose from. One of the most intimate experiences can be had dining at a riad, many of which are open to nonguests and offer excellent fare. A good range of cheaper places can be found around Bab Bou Jeloud. The ville nouvelle has more non-Moroccan options.

Medina

★ Café Clock   CAFE €

(Map p290; 0535 63 78 55; www.cafeclock. com; Derb el-Mergana, Talaa Kebira; mains Dh55-95; 9am-10pm;) This trendy place is a hive of activity laid out over a series of comfy rooms and terraces, and a hub for creative types involved in the cafe's culture program. Its refreshing menu mixes Moroccan and Western flavours: grilled sandwiches such as herbed chicken with preserved lemon mayo sit alongside interesting vegetarian options, a signature camel burger, and ras el hanout wedges.

The 'Clock Culture' program includes calligraphy and conversation classes, traditional storytelling, films and sunset concerts every Sunday (Dh20), attracting a good mix of locals, expats and tourists. The cafe is incredibly popular in the evenings: book ahead if you can.

Jawarat Bab Boujloud   MOROCCAN €

(Map p290; Bab Bou Jeloud; mains from Dh38; 8am-12.30am;) A friendly cheapie with an enviable spot snuggled up against the *bab*, this fresh place is the pick of Bou Jeloud's clamouring pavement cafes. Its *zellij* and a grand carved-wood open frontage make an impression, as do the good-value meals and petite roof terrace – practically close enough to touch the famed blue gate.

Le 44   CAFE €

(Map p290; 0634 70 75 13; 44 Derb Bensalem, Talaa Kebira; noon-10pm;) This friendly, relaxing place down a twisty street is a welcome change to most other medina cafes. Delicious healthy salads and juices, hot and cold soups and freshly made pasta dishes are the order of the day, served against a minimalist backdrop inside a medina *dar*. Work your way up to the roof and there's seating on a shaded terrace, too.

A big plus: the cafe is easy to find as it's well signposted off Talaa Kebira.

Famille Restaurant Berrada   MOROCCAN €

(Map p290; 0662 34 88 19; 57 Sagha el Achebine; mains around Dh50; noon-5pm Sat-Thu)

FEZ PRODUCE MARKETS

R'cif Market (inside Bab R'cif; 8am-8pm Sat-Thu;) Those who shop for fresh produce in the medina know that R'cif is the best place to go – its traders always have the freshest fruit, vegetables and meat.

Talaa Kebira Market (8am-8pm Sat-Thu) Tucked inside Bab Bou Jeloud, this market is easy to access and regularly enthralls tourists with its animal heads, live chickens, street-food stalls and local hagglers. It is home to Fez' two famed camel-meat vendors.

Central Market (Marché Municipal; Blvd Mohammed V; 8.30am-noon) If you're in the ville nouvelle and in need of fresh fruit and veggies, spices, nuts, olives or a parcel of delicious dates, you can't beat the new town's central market. It also has a couple of good cheese stalls.

'Famille restaurant' says it all here – a small medina place run with much hearty cheer. Everything is very traditional, but they're used to seeing tourists too, keeping dishes turned over quickly and inviting diners into the kitchen to taste the day's selections before ordering (there's no written menu). Dishes come with bread and salad.

B'sara Stalls   MOROCCAN €

(Map p290; Talaa Kebira; soup Dh6; 7am-2pm) Don't miss the Fassi speciality of *b'sara* (fava bean soup with garlic). Served from hole-in-the-wall places throughout the medina, our favourites are at the top of Talaa Kebira and in Achebine. Perfect fuel for exploring the city, the soup is ladled into rough pottery bowls and served with a hunk of bread, a dash of olive oil and a sprinkling of chilli.

Snail Stand   MOROCCAN €

(cnr Talaa Seghira & Derb el-Horra; snails small/large portions Dh6/10; noon-10pm) This permanent stand is a good place to fill up on a molluscan snack – the ultimate in pre-packaged fast food. Grab a pin to pluck the beasts out of their shells, then slurp down the aromatic broth. An acquired taste, but a Moroccan comfort food.

★ Ruined Garden   MOROCCAN €€

(Map p290; 0649 19 14 10; www.ruinedgarden. com; 13 Derb Idrissi; tapas selection Dh85, mains

SELF-CATERING IN FEZ

The first-ever shopping centre in Fez (with the first-ever escalator), large, modern **Borj Fes** (www.borjfez.com; Ave Allal el Fassi; ☺9am-9pm) has a large supermarket with a wider range of foodstuffs than you'll find in the medina, and an alcohol section. It also has a food hall with all the international fast-food outlets you could desire, if you're craving Western junk food.

Dh80-120; ☺1-9.30pm Thu-Tue; 🛜) An innovative approach to local street food is on the menu, served in this delightful garden or cosily around the fire in winter. Chef-gardener Robert Johnstone grows herbs and vegetables and smokes his own salmon. If you book ahead, they'll arrange a Sephardic feast or a traditional *mechoui:* (slow-roasted lamb). Guests can be escorted to and from the house on request.

If you like what you eat, you can participate in one of the restaurant's cooking classes.

Moi Anan   THAI €€
(Map p290; ☑0535 63 57 13; www.maisonmoianan. com; 30 Zkak Lma, Chrablyine; mains from Dh90; ☺7-11pm Mon-Thu & Sat; 🛜) A Thai restaurant in Fez? Sweep your reservations aside, because Moi Anan is worth a trip. Dishes are displayed on picture cards and while it's not all totally traditional Thai (alas there's no prawn crackers), all the food is incredibly fresh. The restaurant is set in a *dar*, with a warren of rooms washed in neutral grey and a quirky roof terrace.

Entry is through a chic designer boutique – the baby of Thai native Anan, the chef, who also happens to be a fashion designer.

Dar Hatim   MOROCCAN €€
(Map p291; ☑0666 52 53 23; 19 Derb Ezaouia Funduk Lihoudi; 3-course menus Dh130-250; ☺11am-late) A family-home-turned-restaurant with beautiful painted ceilings, this welcoming place pulls out all the stops in its food and service. Set menus include kebab and couscous options, as well as a special lamb tajine made to a family recipe. The owners Fouad and his wife Karima will happily arrange to collect you so you won't struggle to find it (because you *will* struggle).

Le Kasbah   MOROCCAN €€
(Map p290; Rue Serrajine; mains from DH70, set menu Dh100; ☺8am-midnight) On several floors opposite the cheap hotels at Bab Bou Jeloud, this restaurant occupies a prime spot. The top floor looks out over the medina. The menu itself isn't overly exciting – tajines, couscous and *pastillas* – and drinks are marked up if you're not eating.

★**Restaurant Dar Roumana**   MEDITERRANEAN €€€
Map p290; (☑0660 29 04 04, 0535 74 16 37; 30 Derb el-Amer, Zqaq Roumane; 2/3 courses Dh275/350; ☺7-9pm Tue-Sun; 🛜📶) Dining at Dar Roumana is a white-linen affair with fine service and fine food, and its gorgeous courtyard creates an atmospheric dining spot. French chef Vincent Bonnin's menu makes the best of local Moroccan produce while celebrating Mediterranean flavours. There are innovative salads and excellent fish and meat dishes, and vegetarians are well catered for (notify in advance). Alcohol is served.

Reserving well in advance is recommended; when booking, you can ask for an escort to and from the restaurant.

Restaurant Riad al Andalib   MOROCCAN €€€
(Map p291; ☑0535 76 45 65; www.riadandalib. ma; Ave Ahmed Ben Mohamed Alaoui, R'cif; mains Dh150; ☺noon-4pm & 6.30-10pm; 🛜) This large, light and airy place sits inside an upmarket R'cif heritage hotel, and makes an exceedingly pleasant retreat from the chaos of R'cif. The menu is traditional Moroccan fare, but there's a broad range including some lesser-seen dishes. Food is delicately spiced, thoughtfully presented and delicious. Service is attentive, and alcohol is served.

L'Amandier, Palais Faraj   MOROCCAN €€€
(Map p290; ☑0535 63 53 56; www.palaisfaraj. com; 16-18 Quartier Ziat, Derb Bensouda, Bab Ziat; mains from Dh150; ☺noon-11pm; ❋🛜) Excellent Moroccan cuisine is served in the restaurant or on the terrace of this exquisite heritage hotel, with spectacular views across the medina. All the classics are here, and they're served with attention to detail in the subtle spicing. Make the most of this elegant dinner choice by arriving early for a snoop around and a pre-dinner drink with a view in the adjoining bar.

Fez Café   FRENCH, MOROCCAN €€€
(Map p290; ☑0535 63 50 31; www.jardindesbiehn. com; 13 Akbat Sbaa, Douh; mains from Dh135; ☺noon-3pm & 7.30-10pm; 🛜📶) A charming restaurant set in a wonderful garden once owned by a pasha. The set-up is relaxed bistro-style, with a summery verandah and

unusual vintage-inspired interior: you won't find anything else like this in Fez. Chef Hicham presents dishes that are a delicious seasonal mix of French and Moroccan, chalked up afresh on a board each day. Alcohol, including cocktails, is served.

The restaurant entrance is low-key, but it's inside the **Jardin des Biehn** (☎0535 74 10 36; www.jardindesbiehn.com; Akbat Sbaa, Douh; hammam Dh330; ⏰9am-8pm); staff are usually happy to pick you up or drop you off if you can't find your way. Don't miss the gallery of African antiques near the door.

Ville Nouvelle

Chicken Mac MOROCCAN €

(Map p296; Ave Lalla Meriem; mains Dh25-40; ⏰9am-1am) Several eateries seem to run into each other along this strip in a continuously busy row of streetside tables and chairs. Chicken Mac is the last one away from Pl Florence, and quickly serves up generous plates of rotisserie chicken (Dh25), fried fish, couscous and other cheap, filling meals. If you're not in the mood to sit, takeaway sandwiches are available.

Restaurant Marrakech MOROCCAN €€

(Map p296; ☎0535 93 08 76; 11 Rue Omar el-Mokhtar; mains from Dh79; ⏰noon-3pm & 6pm-late; ❄) Hidden behind thick wooden doors, this restaurant exudes more charm than just about any other food stop in the ville nouvelle. Red *tadelakt* walls and dark furniture, with a cushion-strewn salon at the back, add ambience, while the menu offers some interesting variations on the usual Moroccan fare: specialities include couscous with spicy merguez sausage and a chicken *pastilla* (savoury pie) with almonds.

Kaï Taï ASIAN €€

(Map p288; ☎0535 65 17 00; 12 Rue Ahmed Chaouki; sushi Dh25-45, menus from Dh100; ⏰noon-3pm & 7-11pm; P❄📶) This is not going to be the best Asian food you've ever eaten, but Kaï Taï is one of the swankiest minimalist restaurants in the ville nouvelle and the Japanese and Thai dishes on offer add a chilli-zing to palates jaded by one tajine too many. It's opposite the new Marriott hotel.

MB Restaurant Lounge EUROPEAN €€€

(Map p288; ☎0535 62 27 27; 12 Rue Ahmed Chaouki; mains Dh130-220; ⏰noon-3pm & 7pm-midnight; ❄📶) Making a strong bid for Fez' classiest restaurant, MB is all about cool stylish minimalism with modern furniture and rough-hewn stone. Food has a strong French influence. Retire to the upstairs bar at the end of the evening or swing by in the middle of the day for the Dh200 lunch menu. It's opposite the new Marriott hotel.

Drinking & Nightlife

A stroll in the ville nouvelle is a favourite evening pastime. Stop for an ice cream or just sit on a bench and people-watch. Blvd Mohammed V and Ave Hassan II have the greatest concentration of cafes.

Many ville nouvelle hotels have their own bars serving alcohol; it's also possible to find a drinking spot in the medina, though the vast majority of licensed venues only serve alcohol with food.

★ **Abdullah's** CAFE

(Map p291; Rue Lmachatine; ⏰8am-8pm Sat-Thu) There's something a bit special about Abdullah's nook-in-the-wall tea shop, and it's not just the owner's beaming smile and *zellij*-decorated counter piled high with fresh herbs to pop in your brew. Abdullah swears by the water he uses to make his teas (featuring not just mint, but also herbs such as absinthe): it comes straight from the holy Kairaouine complex. A blessed infusion, indeed.

To find him, take the street off Pl Seffarine opposite Cremarie La Place until you're about halfway down, where a few of Abdullah's seats spill out onto the street.

★ **Riad Fès** BAR

(Map p290; www.riadfes.com; 5 Derb ben Slimane, Zerbtana; ⏰10am-midnight) You're spoilt for choice at Riad Fès, without doubt the classiest place for a drink in the whole city. Its courtyard Alcazar bar is a delight, with stucco columns that catch the light reflected off the central ornamental pool. The riad also now has a wine bar next to the new swimming pool, and an ultra-modern Sky Bar peeping over the medina rooftops.

Mezzanine BAR

(Map p288; 17 Kasbah Chams; ⏰noon-1am; 📶) Scoring highly on the fashion meter and for late opening, this bar is more Ibiza than Moulay Idriss, and popular with the hip young Fassi crowd. The covered roof terrace overlooking Jnan Sbil (Bou Jeloud Gardens) is a good place to chill with a beer or cocktail, and there are tapas and larger Mediterranean dishes if you're peckish.

Cremerie La Place CAFE

(Map p291; PI as-Seffarine; ⊕8am-6.30pm) Put a cafe in one of the most interesting spots in the medina, and you have a near-perfect combination. Over juice, tea, coffee and pastries, the parade passes before you, accompanied by the tapping of the square's coppersmiths.

MB BAR

(12 Rue Ahmed Chaouki; ⊕noon-3pm & 7pm-midnight) Dark leather, stylishly rough stone walls and a well-stocked bar make this place the perfect ville-nouvelle retreat for a classy drink or two, served with tapas. It's just a shame it's a little out of the way.

Hôtel Batha BAR

(Map p290; PI Batha; ⊕8am-10pm) There are a couple of options for drinks around this handily located medina hotel. The Churchill Bar is inside the hotel and in winter even features a log fire to warm yourself. At the back of the hotel (side entrance), the externally run Nightclub Batha (10.30pm to 2am) offers drinkers somewhere to wobble onto if the mood takes.

Café Restaurant La Noria CAFE

(Map p288; off Ave Moulay Hassan; ⊕7am-11.30pm) On the edge of the Jnan Sbil gardens and surrounded by crumbling city walls, this leafy cafe has seen better days but still makes a good refreshment break if you're strolling through the gardens en route to the *mellah*. It's named after an ancient *noria* (waterwheel) – still in situ but

no longer working. It's inaccessible from within the gardens; head around the back.

☆ Entertainment

Live-music buffs know the best time to visit Fez is during the well-respected Festival of World Sacred Music (p299). Café Clock (p307) has regular Sunday sunset concerts worth checking out.

Institut Français (Map p296; ☑0535 62 39 21; www.institutfrancaisfes.com; 33 Rue Loukili; ⊕8.30am-12.15pm & 2.30-6.30pm Mon-Fri) organises a packed program of films, concerts, exhibitions and plays.

🛍 Shopping

Fez is the artisanal capital of Morocco. The choice of crafts is wide, quality is high, and prices are competitive, so take your time to shop around. As usual, it's best to seek out the little shops off the main tourist routes (principally Talaa Kebira and Talaa Seghira in the medina).

For leather, the area around the tanneries, unsurprisingly, has the highest quality and best selection of goods – note that elsewhere in the medina there are some unscrupulous shops selling cheap imitation leather goods and trying to pass them off as the real deal.

In the medina, there are many well-restored riads and fondouqs that have been converted into carpet showrooms. While they certainly offer a great opportunity to sit with a mint tea in spectacular surroundings and look at some fabulous rugs, the hard sell

---

LIFE IN THE LEATHER DISTRICT

Tanneries provide perhaps the greatest illustration of how resolutely some parts of Morocco have clung to practices developed in medieval times. Moroccan leather, and more particularly the Fassi leather in Fez, which is mostly produced using natural methods, has for centuries been highly prized as among the finest in the world and is often exported to Europe. One type of leather, a soft goatskin used mainly in bookbinding, is simply known as 'morocco'.

It's claimed that tanning leather in Morocco goes back several millennia, and little has changed since medieval times. Donkeys still labour through the narrow streets carrying skins to dye pits, which are still constructed to traditional designs (with the addition of modern ceramic tiles). Tanners are organised according to ancient guild principles, with workers typically born into the job. Unfortunately, health and safety principles are similarly old-fashioned, and health problems among the workers, who are knee-deep in chemicals all day, are not uncommon.

Rank odours abound at the tanneries, and the delicate tourists who come to view the work will often be offered a sprig of mint to hold to their noses to take the edge off the pong (rain also dampens the smell). Major components in processing the skins are pigeon poo, salt and lime (the latter accounts for the whitish colour of the processing pits); more delicate ingredients such as indigo, saffron and poppy are added later for colour.

FASSI POTTERY

Ceramics are everywhere in Fez – from the distinctive blue pottery to the intricate mosaics decorating fountains and riads. **Art Naji** (📞 0535 66 91 66; www.artnaji.com; 20 Ain Nokbi; ⏱8am-6pm) is the place to go to see the real deal being made. The centre is a professional operation and free guides will take you through the entire production process, from pot-throwing to the painstaking hand painting and laying out of *zellij* (tilework) – it's a joy to behold. The potteries are about 500m east of Bab el-Ftouh, an easy trip in a petit taxi.

The clay to make the pottery comes from the hills around Fez and the region's fascinating traditional production methods are still very much *en vogue*. Pieces made here are of the highest quality and lead-free, and prices in the large showroom reflect that, running much higher than what you will see in the medina. Expect to pay from Dh100 for a tiny bowl – big plates start at about Dh500 (though there's no pressure to buy). You can even commission a mosaic and arrange for it to be shipped home.

---

is like no other place in Morocco. You can pick up some wonderful pieces, but also pay over the odds for factory-made rubbish.

Blue-and-white Fassi pottery is highly prized and everywhere in the medina. Head to Art Naji (p311) for the highest quality pieces and to see the fascinating production process from start to finish.

Médin Art　　　　　　　　　ARTS & CRAFTS
(Map p290; Talaa Seghira; ⏱10am-2pm & 4-7pm) Silky scarfs, beautiful leather bags, handmade books, boho clothes and oversized jewellery from French and Moroccan designers make this gallery-style shop a bit less bazaar and a bit more *oh là là* than Fez' usual shops. Note it's sometimes closed on Fridays.

ℹ️ Information

DANGERS & ANNOYANCES
➡ It's not really safe to walk on your own in the medina late at night, especially for women.

➡ Knife-point robberies are not unknown.

➡ Hotels and many restaurants are usually happy to provide an escort on request if you're out late.

➡ Fez has long been notorious for its *faux guides* (unofficial guides) and carpet-shop hustlers, all after their slice of the tourist dirham.

➡ *Faux guides* tend to congregate around Bab Bou Jeloud, the main western entrance to the medina, although crackdowns by the authorities have greatly reduced their numbers and hassle.

➡ Even many official guides will suggest visitors turn their tour into a shopping trip, and the pressure to buy can be immense. Fez' carpet sellers are masters of their game. If you really don't want to buy, it might be best not to enter the shop at all: once the parade of beautiful rugs begins, even the hardest-minded of tourists can be convinced to buy something they

didn't really want (honeyed words suggesting that you could always sell the carpet later on eBay at vast profit should be treated with extreme scepticism). It's also worth remembering that any time you enter a shop with a guide, the price of the goods immediately goes up to cover their commission. Shopping in Fez needn't be a battle – indeed it's best treated as a game – but it's worth being prepared.

➡ Beware the touts who board trains to Fez, often at Meknès. They can be very friendly, approaching you claiming to be students or teachers returning to Fez – they'll often have 'brothers' who have hotels, carpet shops or similar.

INTERNET ACCESS
Wi-fi is common across most midrange accommodation and above, as well as at most cafes and restaurants.

Cyber Batha (Rue Al Bard; per hr Dh10; ⏱10am-midnight) Has English as well as French keyboards.

Cyber Net (42 Blvd Mohammed V; per hr Dh6; ⏱9am-10pm)

Teleboutique Cyber Club (Map p296; Blvd Mohammed V; per hr Dh5; ⏱9am-11pm) Above *téléboutique* (telephone office) in the ville nouvelle.

MEDICAL SERVICES
Clinique al-Kawtar (📞 0535 61 19 00; Ave Mohamed el-Fassi, Route d'Immouzzer) Large modern hospital in the ville nouvelle, just off the main road to the airport.

Pharmacie Du Maroc (Map p290; Pl Batha; ⏱8.30am-12.30pm & 3-7.30pm Nov-Apr, 9am-1pm & 3.30-8pm May-Oct) An easily accessible modern pharmacy in the medina.

MONEY
There are plenty of banks (with ATMs) in the ville nouvelle along Blvd Mohammed V. In the medina there is an ATM at the Batha Post Office and at

banks around Place R'cif, as well as these useful spots:

Banque Populaire (Talaa Seghira; ⊕8.15am-3.45pm Mon-Fri)

Société Générale (Map p290; Bab Bou Jeloud; ⊕9.15am-5.15pm Mon-Thu, 8.15-11.45am Fri, 9.15-12.45pm Sat)

POST

Main Post Office (Map p296; cnr Ave Hassan II & Blvd Mohammed V; ⊕8am-4.30pm Mon-Fri & 8.30-noon Sat)

Post Office (Pl Batha; ⊕8am-4.15pm Mon-Fri) Located in the medina; also has an ATM.

TOURIST INFORMATION

There is no tourist office in the medina.

Délégation Régionale de Tourisme (Map p296; Tourist Information Office; ☑0535 94 24 92; Ave Mohammed es Slaoui; ⊕9am-1pm & 2-4pm Mon-Thu, 9am-1pm Sat & Sun) You can pick up a good-quality free map of Fez here and book official guides. Staff speak English.

TRAVEL AGENCIES

Carlson Wagonlit (Map p296; ☑0535 62 29 58; ⊕8.30am-12.30pm & 3-7pm Mon-Fri) Behind Central Market; useful for flights and ferries.

RAM (☑0535 94 85 51; 54 Ave Hassan II) There's a Royal Air Maroc office in the ville nouvelle for ticketing and flight enquiries.

USEFUL WEBSITES

Culture Vultures (www.culturevulturesfez.org) For arty Fez happenings including artisanal projects, tours, workshops, residencies, arts and culture.

View From Fez (www.theviewfromfez.com) News and views blog for keeping up to date with what's happening in Fez.

ⓘ Getting There & Away

AIR

Fes-Saïss Airport (☑0535 67 47 12) is 15km south of the city and has recently been expanded with a swanky new hall, though at the time of writing it had yet to open. **RAM** (p312) operates daily flights to Casablanca, as well as connections to Europe.

BUS

The main bus station for **CTM buses** (☑0800 09 00 30; www.ctm.ma) is in the southern ville nouvelle. Buy tickets for Chefchaouen in advance because the lack of other transport options means seats always get booked up quickly. Services can be reduced out of season.

CTM runs 16 buses a day to Casablanca (Dh90, 4½ hours) via Rabat (Dh75, three hours) between 1.30am and 7.15pm, plus one other premium bus to Rabat only at 9.30pm (Dh100). Buses to Meknès (Dh25, one hour) run 24 hours a day but departure times are irregular. There are seven buses a day to Marrakesh (Dh165 to Dh175, 9½ hours) between 6.30am and 8pm, plus a quicker premium bus departing at 9.30pm (Dh225).

Heading north and east, there are six buses for Tangier (Dh110, six to seven hours), three for Chefchaouen (Dh75, four hours), four for Tetouan (Dh100, five hours) and two for Al-Hoceima (Dh110, five hours), one of which is a night bus. Four go to Nador (Dh110 to Dh115, five hours), and six to Oujda (Dh115, 4½ to five hours).

International services to Spain with Eurolines (www.eurolines.com) also depart from the CTM bus station.

Non-CTM buses depart from the **Gare Routière** (☑0535 63 60 32) outside Bab el-Mahrouk on the edge of the medina, or from the streets immediately surrounding the bus station. Fares are slightly lower than CTM, and reservations can be made for popular routes. The Gare Routière has a left-luggage facility.

Long-distance buses run to Casablanca via Rabat (hourly), Midelt and Er-Rachidia, Rissani and Ouarzazate (six daily), Marrakesh (five daily), Taza (hourly), Oujda (10 daily), Tangier (13 daily), and Tetouan and Ouezzane (12 daily).

Locally, there are frequent departures to Azrou (Dh25, 1½ hours), Ifrane (Dh25, 1½ hours), Moulay Yacoub (Dh10, 30 minutes), Sefrou (Dh10, 45 minutes) and Meknès (frequently).

CAR

There are several guarded car parks around the medina: on Pl Bou Jeloud close to Bab Bou Jeloud, in Batha, north of Talaa Kebira at Ain Azleten and in the south at R'cif. In the ville nouvelle there's a guarded car park in front of the central market. **Chrifftans** (☑0615 45 01 28; www.chriftrans.com) is a reliable transport and vehicle-hire company, offering services from airport pick-ups to day trips from Fez and longer hires.

TAXI

There are several grand taxi ranks dotted around town. **Taxis for Moulay Yacoub** (Dh10, 20 minutes) and **taxis for Meknès** (Dh25, one hour) and Rabat (Dh80, 2½ hours) leave from in front of the main bus station (outside Bab el-Mahrouk). The **rank for Sefrou and Bhalil** (Dh12, 45 minutes) is located at Slaiki, southeast of Pl de la Résistance in the ville nouvelle. **Azrou** (Dh35, one hour) and Ifrane (Dh30, 45 minutes) taxis wait at a parking lot to the west of the CTM bus station in the south of the ville nouvelle.

Grands taxis outside the train station don't have specific destinations so cannot be shared.

TRAIN

Fez' shiny new **train station** is in the ville nouvelle, a 10-minute walk northwest of Pl Florence. There's no longer any left luggage at the station, but there's an ATM, some snack shops and decent cafes with wi-fi.

Trains depart almost hourly between 1.30am and 8.40pm to Casablanca (Dh116, four hours), via Rabat (Dh127, three hours) and Meknès (Dh30, 30 minutes). Eight trains go to Marrakesh (Dh206, eight hours) and four go direct to Tangier (Dh164, five hours) – two more go via Sidi Kacem. Some of the trains to Taza (Dh59, two hours, six daily) go on to Oujda (Dh169, 5½ hours, three daily).

ⓘ Getting Around

TO/FROM THE AIRPORT & TRANSPORT STATIONS

Fes-Saïss Airport Bus 6 service runs hourly between the airport and train station in the ville nouvelle. The set fare for a grand taxi from the airport to the medina is Dh120 (up to four people); transfers organised through your hotel vary in price, but expect to pay at least Dh100 per person. Heading back to the airport, you won't be able to hail a grand taxi from the medina; you'll have to get one from the train station or pay a higher rate by organising one through your hotel. Petits taxis don't run to the airport.

Train Station It's a 10-minute walk to Pl Florence, or a Dh12 petit-taxi ride to Bab Bou Jeloud in the medina.

CTM Station A taxi to Bab Bou Jeloud will cost around Dh12.

BUS

Fez' bus service can be unreliable, packed like sardine cans at certain times of day, and are notorious for pickpockets. The standard fare is Dh3.50. Some useful routes:

Bus 9 Bouramana and Pl Atlas via Blvd Chefchaouni (both in the ville nouvelle) to Pl Batha (Fès el-Bali); the bus returns via **Ave Hassan II** and Ave des FAR.

Bus 10 Train station via Bab Guissa (northern Fès el-Bali) to Bab Sidi Bou Jida (northeastern Fès el-Bali).

Bus 19 Train station via Ave Hassan II (in ville nouvelle) and Bab el-Jdid (southern Fès el-Bali) to Pl R'cif (central Fès el-Bali)

TAXI

Drivers of the red petits taxis generally use their meters without any fuss, but tourists are often hassled by touts at the train station. Insist on the meter, or walk further to hail a taxi. Expect to pay about Dh12 from the train or CTM station to Bab Bou Jeloud. There is a 50% surcharge after 8pm. You'll find taxi ranks outside all the gates of the medina, as well as at **Pl Batha**. Only grands taxis go out to the airport.

There is a convenient **petits taxis rank** near the giant Borj Fes shopping centre at Pl de la Résistance on the northern edge of the ville nouvelle.

Sefrou

POP 79,887

The small Berber town of Sefrou, just 30km southeast of Fez, is a picturesque place situated on the edge of the Middle Atlas. It has a small but interesting medina that was designated a Unesco World Heritage site in 2013. As such, the medina walls have been restored and some *funduqs* (hotels) are being rebuilt. Sefrou once hosted one of Morocco's largest Jewish communities (as many as 8000 people, according to some accounts), and it was here that Moulay Idriss II lived while overseeing the building of Fez.

It's an easy day trip from Fez. Time your visit with the Thursday souq, just south of the town centre, if you want to see a real local market without the tourist trappings.

⊙ Sights

Medina MEDINA
(Map p314; The Oued Aggaï flows through the centre of Sefrou's medina, opening the place up and giving it more of an airy feel than many old medinas. Although it's still a maze, there's not much to it so navigation is manageable; the best point of entry is the northerly Bab el-Maqam. From here the flow of people will take you downhill past pastel-hued souq shops and a lively local produce market.

Mellah AREA
(Map p314) Although Sefrou's Jewish population has gone, this district still retains a few distinctive wooden-galleried houses and lanes so narrow two people can only just pass. In its heyday, the *mellah* was so dark and crowded that street lamps had to be lit even in the middle of the day. Today it has an edgy feel and the area's dereliction has become a breeding ground for drugs and prostitution; sadly it's not considered safe to visit.

Jardin Al Kanatir Al Khairia PARK
Skirting the western walls of the medina, Sefrou's public gardens are wedged into a small depressed valley and feel a little like the lost world. Towering tangles of trees tripping down, down, down to the river create a cool retreat beloved by locals. There are peaceful paths and a couple of cafes. Enter off Ave Moulay Hassan or Blvd Mohammed V.

Jewish School JEWISH SITE
Just south of Bab Merba, this former Jewish school with its own synagogue is now closed, but you can still peak through the

Sefrou

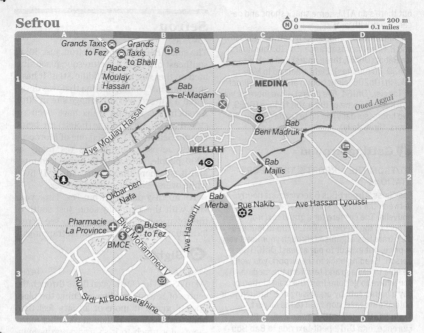

Sefrou

◉ Sights
1 Jardin Al Kanatir Al Khairia	A2
2 Jewish School	C2
3 Medina	C1
4 Mellah	B2

🛏 Sleeping
5 La Maison des Lallas	D2

✖ Eating
6 Restaurant Al Farah	C1

🍸 Drinking & Nightlife
7 Café Zahra el-Jebal	A2

🛍 Shopping
8 Ensemble Artisanal	B1

doors – it's pretty rundown. If you're interested to see more, try to find the guardians as they will usually let you in for a small donation of Dh10 to Dh20.

Cascades de Sefrou   WATERFALL
A 1.5km walk west of town are the Cascades, a modest waterfall. Follow the signs from Ave Moulay Hassan around Al-Qala' (a semifortified village) and along the river's lush valley.

👉 Tours

Sefrou Artisanal Tour   CRAFTS
(☎ 0535 68 33 75; www.culturevulturesfez.org; 1-2 people incl lunch Dh1200, 3 people Dh1400) Along the same lines as its sister tour in Fez (p298), this educational half-day excursion around Sefrou's medina provides a window into the lives of artisans working in Sefrou – giving you the chance to interact with, and visit the workshops of, local blanket weavers, iron-mongers, button makers and wood carvers. A particular focus is the town's disappearing Jewish heritage.

🎊 Festivals & Events

Cherry Festival   FOOD & DRINK
(Festival des Cerises; ☉ mid-Jun) This annual four-day festival celebrates the local cherry harvest. There's plenty of folk music, along with displays by local artists, parades, *fantasias* (musket-firing cavalry charges) and the crowning of the Cherry Queen. Sefrou lays claim to the longest-running town festival in Morocco – it will celebrate 100 years in 2020 and it was inscribed on the Unesco Intangible Cultural Heritage list in 2012.

🛏 Sleeping

La Maison des Lallas   GUESTHOUSE €
(☑ 0535 66 11 16; www.lamaisondeslallas.com; 304 Derb El Miter; d/ste incl breakfast from Dh396/400; ☎) This homely house in a quiet street has five bedrooms, each with a bathroom, centred on a lovely courtyard that's traditionally decorated. Welcoming Jamila can provide dinner (Dh132) and even a picnic basket (Dh44) if you're heading into the hills.

🍴 Eating & Drinking

Restaurant Al Farah   MOROCCAN €
(Pl Haddadine; meals about Dh25; ☺ 10am-9pm) The best of the bunch in Sefrou's medina is the Restaurant Al Farah. It's easy to find, opposite the knife-grinders and blacksmith with his fiery anvil (Haddadine means ironmongers), and with simple tables under a shady tree in this slim square. There's no menu: go for the spit-roast chicken with harissa for dipping, chips, bread and salad.

Café Zahra el-Jebal   CAFE
(Jardin Al Kanatir Al Khairia; ☺ 8am-7.30pm) Women will feel comfortable at this lovely cafe spread along the south side of the shady riverbank in Sefrou's popular park.

🔒 Shopping

Ensemble Artisanal   ARTS & CRAFTS
(Rte de Fès; ☺ 9.30am-1pm & 2.30-6.30pm Sat-Thu) Small shops selling a selection of mostly wood and jewellery, plus some rugs, at fixed prices.

ℹ Information

BMCE (Blvd Mohammed V; ☺ 8.15am-5.45pm Mon-Fri) Has an ATM.
Main Post Office (Blvd Mohammed V; ☺ 8am-4.30pm Mon-Fri, 8am-noon Sat)
Pharmacie La Province (Blvd Mohammed V; ☺ 8am-1pm & 3pm-9pm)

ℹ Getting There & Away

Regular **buses** (Dh8, 40 minutes) and **grands taxis** (Dh11, 30 minutes) run between Sefrou and Slaiki in Fez, just north of the CTM bus station in the ville nouvelle. If you'd prefer to get a private grand-taxi transfer from your hotel in Fez, expect to pay Dh250 to Dh300.

Grands taxis to Azrou (Dh28) go via Immouzzer (Dh14) and depart from the same walled grand-taxi lot just north of Pl Moulay Hassan. **Grands taxis to Bhalil** (Pl Moulay Hassan) (Dh3.50) depart from across the road, at the top of Pl Moulay Hassan.

Bhalil   البهاليل

POP 12,997

This curious village, 5km from Sefrou, is worth a trip for its troglodyte houses built into the picturesque mountainside and picked out in pastel hues of pink, yellow and blue. The cave dwellings date back to the 4th century and for hundreds of years have been inhabited by shepherds to protect against the elements. Some villagers go so far as to utilise caves for the primary room of the house. The result is a cool, spacious room, usually used as a salon, while bedrooms and private areas are built above.

The hassle often experienced in larger towns is entirely absent here: people are incredibly friendly and local women are often found sitting out on the streets making woven buttons for *jellabas* (Morocco's long traditional hooded capes) – one of the village's main industries. Bhalil has an excellent local guesthouse and can make a refreshing break from the big-city hustle of Fez.

🛏 Sleeping

★ Dar Kamal Chaoui   GUESTHOUSE €€
(☑ 06 43 03 24 44, 0678 83 83 10; www.kamal-chaoui.com; 6 Kaf Rhouni, Bhalil; d incl breakfast Dh605-715; ☎) Kamal Chaoui offers very comfortable accommodation in a traditional village house, and Naima cooks delicious dinners (Dh180). Decorated in local Berber style, it has a relaxing roof terrace with sweeping views. Kamal strives for a home-away-from-home atmosphere, and he and Naima join guests at mealtimes. In winter, the house is heated via an ingenious wood-fire system to keep things toasty.

Kamal, who speaks excellent English, French and German, is a pillar of the local community and a mine of information on the area. He can arrange mountain excursions – sometimes including lunch with Naima's Berber family – or a village tour with a visit to Bhalil's troglodyte caves for tea with the inhabitants (Dh275 per person). Naima also runs cooking classes (Dh330 per person). Money from the tours is funnelled back into the community, helping to clean up the streets and improve conditions for villagers.

ℹ Getting There & Away

To get here from Fez you'll need to head to Sefrou, from where a shared grand taxi to Bhalil costs Dh3.50.

Mountain Ranges

SIMON MONTGOMERY/ROBERTHARDING/GETTY IMAGES ©

Visible from both the Mediterranean and the Sahara, Morocco's mountains are as iconic as medinas and tajines – and they've been around much longer. They offer some of the best trekking landscapes in the world, from easy day walks to full-on expeditionary hikes.

Rif Mountains

Close to the Mediterranean coast, the Rif is Morocco's greenest range, and is covered in wildflowers in spring.

High Atlas

The High Atlas rolls from snow-covered peaks such as Jebel Toubkal to the Dadès and Todra Gorges. Those in good physical condition can climb Toubkal, but if grands taxis are your preferred mode of transport, the High Atlas is still memorable. Roads pass crumbling kasbahs and Berber villages, and wind up the Tizi n'Test and Tizi n'Tichka passes.

1. Chefchaouen (p250), Rif Mountains **2.** Tizi n'Tichka (p109), High Atlas **3.** The road from Imilchil (p138), Middle Atlas

Middle Atlas

You might think you're in the Alps when walking among the flowerbeds of Ifrane, or the fragrant cedar forests near Azrou.

Anti Atlas

Closer to the Sahara, the Anti Atlas is a land of jagged peaks such as quartzite Jebel L'Kest, with oasis villages in the valleys. The wild, arid Jebel Saghro is home to the seminomadic Aït Atta.

Top Mountain Treks

Rif Mountains From Chefchaouen through Talassemtane National Park.

M'Goun Traverse Prehistoric rock forms, ridges, escarpments and river gorges.

Jebel Toubkal The two-day ascent of North Africa's highest peak.

Jebel Saghro Palm and almond groves beneath twisted volcanic pinnacles.

Anti Atlas Unexplored trails among ochre cliffs and saffron fields.

3

Deserts & Oases

Morocco sits on the edge of the great Sahara, and its dunes and oases are a huge draw for travellers. Follow the paths of the old camel caravans that once trekked across the desert, carrying salt and gold from Timbuktu.

Erg Chebbi & Erg Chigaga

The dunes at Erg Chebbi (p148) and Erg Chigaga (p125), respectively rising to 160m and 300m, are Morocco's greatest desert sights. These are the places to disappear into the desert, accompanied by a camel and blue-robed guide, to see the sand sea by moonlight and sleep in a nomad camp.

Desert Valleys

Coming from Marrakesh, there are more accessible glimpses of the desert in the Drâa Valley, where a sign once advised desert caravans that Timbuktu was only 52 days away, and oases remain the region's lifeblood. In Ouarzazate the desert stretches to the foot of the Atlas, and palms can be spotted through slit windows in the Taourirt kasbah.

1. Dunes at Erg Chebbi (p148) 2. *Palmerie* outside N'Kob (p151) 3. The Anti Atlas mountains (p374)

The Deep South

Largely overlooked by travellers, the *hammada* (flat, stony desert) of the far south runs through the Western Sahara. It's a stark environment, mainly crossed by overlanders en route to Mauritania.

Top Oases

Figuig Seven traditional desert villages amid 200,000 date palms.

N'Kob Mudbrick castles overlook the *palmeraie* (palm grove).

Skoura The Unesco-protected 'Oasis of 1000 Palms'.

Afella-Ighir Rocky red gorges tower above the palms.

Ameln Valley Village *palmeraies* beneath Jebel L'Kest.

Tata Treetops are a welcome sight in this Saharan outpost.

Paradise Valley *Palmeraies,* oleanders and beehives line the gorge.

Meknès

مكناس

POP 835,695

Quieter and smaller than its grand neighbour Fez, Meknès feels rather overshadowed and receives fewer visitors than it should. It's more laid-back with less hassle, yet still has all the winding narrow medina streets and grand buildings that it warrants as an imperial city and one-time home of the Moroccan sultanate.

Sultan Moulay Ismail, the architect of Meknès' glory days, might be a little disgruntled at the city's current modesty, but visitors will find much to be enchanted by. Remnants of no less than three sets of fortifications, ingeniously incorporated into the city's road networks, make it clear how important this city once was. The king's tomb sits at the heart of what remains of the original imperial city, flanked by an almighty royal granary, the magnificent Bab el-Mansour – the likes of which even Fez can't compete with – and Pl el-Hedim, a local mini-me of Marrakesh's popular Djemaa el-Fna.

History

The Berber tribe of the Meknassis (hence the name Meknès) first settled here in the 10th century. Under the Almohads and Merenids, Meknès' medina was expanded and some of the city's oldest remaining monuments were built.

It wasn't until the 17th century that Meknès really came into its own. The founder of the Alawite dynasty, Moulay ar-Rashid, died in 1672. His successor and brother, Moulay Ismail, made Meknès his capital, from where he would reign for 55 years.

Ismail endowed the city with 25km of imposing walls with monumental gates and an enormous palace complex that was never completed. That he could devote the time and resources to construction was partly due to his uncommon success in subduing all opposition in Morocco and keeping foreign meddlers at bay, mainly because of his notorious Black Guard.

Ismail's death in 1727 also struck the death knell for Meknès. The town resumed its role as a backwater, as his grandson Mohammed III (1757–90) moved to Marrakesh. The 1755 earthquake that devastated Lisbon also dealt Meknès a heavy blow. As so often happened in Morocco, its monuments were subsequently stripped in order to be added to buildings elsewhere. It's only been in the past few decades, as tourist potential has become obvious, that any serious restoration attempts have taken place.

In 1912 the arrival of the protectorate revived Meknès as the French made it their military headquarters. The army was accompanied by French farmers who settled on the fertile land nearby. After independence most properties were recovered by the Moroccan government and leased to local farmers.

◉ Sights

The heart of the medina is around Pl el-Hedim and the monumental gateway of Bab el-Mansour. Behind the gate lies Moulay Ismail's imperial city. The narrow streets of the old *mellah* are in the west of the medina – look for the old balconied houses so distinctive of the Jewish quarter.

The easiest route into the medina's souqs is through the arch to the left of the Dar Jamaï Museum on the north side of Pl el-Hedim. Plunge in and head northwards, and you'll quickly find yourself amid souvenir stalls and carpet shops.

◉ Medina

★ **Place el-Hedim**　　　　　　　SQUARE

(Map p322) The heart of the Meknès medina is Pl el-Hedim, the large square facing Bab el-Mansour. Before Moulay Ismail swept through town a kasbah stood on this spot, but once the *bab* was erected the king ordered for it to be demolished in favour of a broad plaza from which the gate could be better admired. Originally used for royal announcements and public executions, it's a good place to sit and watch the world go by.

There's definitely parallels to be drawn between this square and its grand cousin, Marrakesh's Djemaa el-Fna. The Meknasi version, however, has a lot more of a local flavour. There's always something going on – kids playing football, musicians drawing crowds, and promenading families treating their toddlers to spins in electric toy cars. Sadly you'll also sometimes see shackled monkeys captured from the nearby Middle Atlas, providing local entertainment.

One edge is lined with cafes and restaurants; behind these is an excellent, covered produce market.

★ **Dar Jamaï Museum**　　　　　　MUSEUM

(📞 0555 53 08 63; Dh10; ⏰ 9am-noon & 3-6.30pm Wed-Mon) Overlooking Pl el-Hedim, Dar Jamaï,

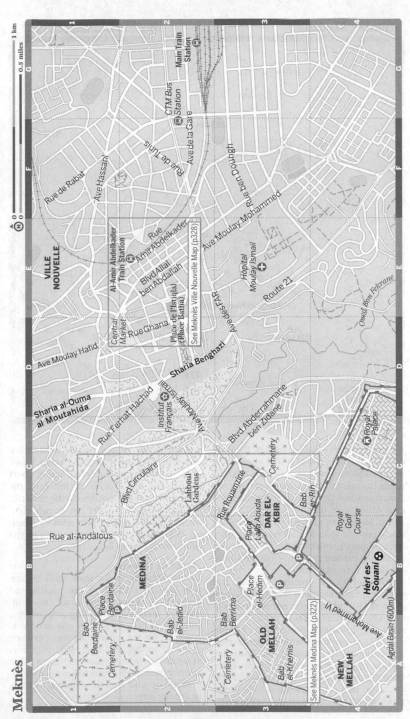

Meknès

VILLE NOUVELLE

Main Train Station

CTM Bus Station

Ave de la Gare

Rue de Tunis

Ave Hassani

Rue de Rabat

Rue ben Dough

Ave Moulay Mohammed

Al-Amir Abdelkader Train Station

Rue Amir Abdelkader

Blvd Allal ben Abdallah

Rue Ghana

Central Market

Place de l'Istiqlal (Place Batha)

See Meknès Ville Nouvelle Map (p328)

Hopital Moulay Ismail

Route 21

Oued Bou Fekrane

Ave Moulay Hafid

Ave des FAR

Sharia Benghazi

Sharia al-Ouma al Moutahida

Rue Ferhat Hachad

Institut Français

Ave Moulay Ismail

Blvd Abderrahmane ben Zidane

Cemetery

Royal Palace

Blvd Circulaire

Rue al-Andalous

Lahboul Gardens

Rue Rouamzine

MEDINA

Place Lalla Aouda

DAR EL KBIR

Bab er-Rih

Royal Golf Course

Bab Berdaine

Place Berdaine

Cemetery

Bab el-Jedid

Bab Berrima

Place el-Hedim

OLD MELLAH

Cemetery

Bab el-Khemis

NEW MELLAH

Heri es-Souani

Ave Mohammed VI

Agdal Basin (600m)

See Meknès Medina Map (p322)

0   1 km
0   0.5 miles

Meknès Medina

is a palace that was built in 1882 by the powerful Jamaï family, two of whom were viziers to Sultan Moulay al-Hassan I. Since 1920 the palace has housed a fine museum of traditional ceramics, jewellery, textiles and cedar-wood craft dating from the 14th century. The museum's Andalucian garden and courtyard are shady, peaceful spots amid overgrown orange trees, brimming with bird life – the crumbling palace and gardens are well worth the admission fee in their own right.

Look out for the brocaded saddles, and some exquisite examples of Meknasi needlework (including some extravagant gold and silver kaftans). The *koubba* (domed sanctuary) upstairs is furnished as a traditional salon complete with luxurious rugs and cushions. The museum also has some antique carpets, representing various styles from different regions of Morocco. The exhibits are well constructed if a little dusty; explanations are in French and Arabic only.

The history of the palace is tumultuous: when Sultan Moulay al-Hassan I died in 1894, the Jamaï family fell foul of court politics and lost everything, including the palace, which was passed on to the powerful Al-Glaoui family. In 1912 the French commandeered the palace for a military hospital, before it was taken over in 1920 by the Administration des Beaux Arts.

Musée de Meknès   MUSEUM
(Meknès Museum; Rte Dar Smen; Dh10; ⊘9am-6pm Tue-Sun) Housed in the peeling old Tribunal building, this small museum features metalwork, farming implements, clothing, jewellery, carpets and ceramics. Look out for the remarkable set of armour made of leather and encrusted with coral beads, turquoise studs and coins. This warrior was well protected with helmet, breastplate and gauntlets. Information is in French only.

Meknès Medina

⊙ **Top Sights**
1 Bab el-Mansour C4
2 Dar Jamaï Museum B3
3 Place el-Hedim B3

⊙ **Sights**
4 Koubbat as-Sufara' C4
5 Lahboul Gardens C2
6 Mausoleum of Moulay Ismail C4
7 Mausoleum of Sidi ben Aïssa A2
8 Medersa Bou Inania B3
9 Musée de Meknès C3
10 Place Lalla Aouda C3

🛏 **Sleeping**
11 Hôtel Maroc D3
12 Riad d'Or C3
13 Riad El Ma C3
14 Riad Felloussia C3
15 Riad Lahboul D3
16 Riad Meknès D4
17 Riad Yacout C3
18 Ryad Bahia B3

✗ **Eating**
19 Covered Market B3
20 Restaurant Mille et Une Nuits C3
21 Restaurant Oumnia D3
Restaurant Riad Meknès .... (see 16)
22 Restaurant Yahala C3
Ryad Bahia .... (see 18)
23 Sandwich Stands B3

⊙ **Drinking & Nightlife**
24 Cafe Restaurant Place
Lehdime B3
25 Pavillon des Idrissides C3

🛍 **Shopping**
26 Ensemble Artisanale B4
Pottery Stalls .... (see 19)

Medersa Bou Inania   ISLAMIC SITE
(Rue Najjarine; Dh10; ⊙10am-6pm) Opposite the Grande Mosquée, the Medersa Bou Inania is typical of the exquisite interior design that distinguishes Merenid monuments. It was completed in 1358 by Bou Inan, after whom a more lavish *medersa* in Fez is also named. This *medersa* is a good display of the classic Moroccan decorative styles – the *zellij* base, delicate stucco midriff and carved cedar-wood ceiling. You can climb onto the roof for views of the green-tiled roof and minaret of the Grande Mosquée nearby.

Students aged eight to 10 years once lived two to a cell on the ground floor, while older students and teachers lived on the 1st floor in the luxury of private rooms. On the right when you enter is the school room with a deep mihrab for natural amplification.

Lahboul Gardens   GARDENS
(Ave Moulay Al-Hassan ben Driss) **FREE** These gardens overlooking the medina have seen better days, but are still a tranquil place to stroll if you need to switch off from the souq biz of old Meknès. The gardens are split into two areas and the gate linking them isn't always open so sometimes you may have to backtrack to the main gate (at the southeastern edge) and re-enter further north. The northern section of the gardens is scattered with columns from Volubilis and an amphitheatre.

Mausoleum of Sidi ben Aïssa   MAUSOLEUM
Sidi ben Aïssa gave rise to one of the more unusual religious fraternities in Morocco, known for their self-mutilation and imperviousness to snake bites. His followers gather here at his mausoleum in spring (dates change with the lunar calendar) from all over Morocco and further afield. It's closed to non-Muslims.

⊙ Imperial City

★ **Bab el-Mansour**   GATE
(Map p322; The focus of Pl el-Hedim is the huge gate of Bab el-Mansour, the grandest of all imperial Moroccan gateways. The gate is well preserved with lavish (if faded) *zellij* and inscriptions across the top. It was completed by Moulay Ismail's son, Moulay Abdallah, in 1732. You can't walk through the *bab* itself (although it's sometimes open to host exhibitions), but instead have to make do with a side gate to the left.

The two white columns either side of the *bab* are Corinthian marble, plundered from a Marrakesh palace. They were acquired by Moulay Ismail during his lifetime but only added to the *bab* by Monlay Abdallah after his father's death. Along the top of the gate, the Arabic inscription extols Bab el-Mansour's virtues with a confidence befitting of the king. It reads: 'I am the most beautiful gate in Morocco. I'm like the moon in the sky. Property and wealth are written on my front.'

Place Lalla Aouda   SQUARE
(Map p322; Mechouar) South of Bab el-Mansour lies the *mechouar* (parade ground), now known as Pl Lalla Aouda, where Moulay Ismail inspected his famed Black Guard. After bringing 16,000 slaves from Sub-Saharan Africa, Moulay Ismail guaranteed the continued existence of his elite units by providing the

soldiers with women and raising their offspring for service in the guard. At the time of writing this area was being redeveloped into a garden with fountains and community space.

By the time of Moulay Ismail's death, the Black Guard had expanded tenfold. Its successes were many, ranging from quelling internal rebellions, to chasing European powers out of northern Morocco, to disposing of the Ottoman threat from Algeria.

Mausoleum of Moulay Ismail MAUSOLEUM
(Map p322; donations welcome; ☺8.30am-noon & 2-6pm Sat-Thu) A visit to the final resting place of the sultan who made Meknès his capital in the 17th century should be a rite of passage for those travelling through town. Moulay Ismail's stature as one of Morocco's greatest rulers means that non-Muslim visitors are usually welcomed into the sanctuary, but in 2016 the site closed for much-needed restoration work following pressure from Unesco. It was expected to reopen some time in 2018. The tomb hall is a lavish celebration of the best of Moroccan craftsmanship.

Entry is through a series of austere, peaceful courtyards meant to induce a quiet and humble attitude among visitors – an aim that's not always successful in the face of a busload of tourists. Photography is permitted, but non-Muslims may not approach the tomb itself. The mausoleum is diagonally opposite the Koubbat as-Sufara' in the Imperial City.

Koubbat as-Sufara' MONUMENT
(Map p322; Dh10; ☺10am-6pm Apr-Sep, to 5pm Oct-Mar) The Koubbat as-Sufara' was once the reception hall for foreign ambassadors and it's here that Unesco chose to place its World Heritage inscription when the city was designated in 1996. In front of the building is a broad clearing pockmarked with small subterranean windows providing light for a vast 40-hectare crypt of similar construction to the granary at Heri es-Souani. Take the stairs down to the right of the entrance to Koubbat as-Sufara'; the entrance fee covers both.

The dark and slightly spooky network of rooms below ground was a mystery when discovered. Historians now believe it was used for food storage, although tour guides will delight in recounting the (erroneous) story that it was used as a dungeon for the Christian slaves who provided labour for Moulay Ismail's building spree. Bring a torch.

★**Heri es-Souani** RUINS
(Map p322; Dh10; ☺9am-noon & 3-6.30pm) Nearly 2km southeast of Moulay Ismail's

---

THE ALMIGHTY MOULAY

Few men dominate the history of a country like the towering figure of Sultan Moulay Ismail (1672–1727). Originating from the sand-blown plains of the Tafilalt region, his family were sherifs (descendants of the Prophet Mohammed) – a pedigree that continues to underpin the current monarchy.

Ruthlessness as well as good breeding were essential characteristics for becoming sultan. On inheriting the throne from his brother Moulay ar-Rashid, Moulay Ismail set about diffusing the rival claims of his 83 brothers and half-brothers, celebrating his first day in power by murdering all those who refused to submit to his rule. His politics continued in this bloody vein with military campaigns in the south, the Rif Mountains and Algerian hinterland, bringing most of Morocco under his control. He even brought the Salé corsairs to heel, taxing their piracy handsomely to swell the imperial coffers.

The peace won, Moulay Ismail retired to his capital at Meknès and began building his grandiose imperial palace, plundering the country for the best materials, and building city walls, kasbahs and many new towns. This cultural flowering was Morocco's last great golden age.

Moulay Ismail also considered himself a lover. Although he sought (but failed to receive) the hand in marriage of Louis XIV of France's daughter, he still fathered literally hundreds of children. Rather foolishly, however, he did nothing to secure his succession. When he died the sultanate was rocked by a series of internecine power struggles, from which the Alawites never fully recovered.

Nevertheless, his legacy was to be the foundation of modern Morocco. He liberated Tangier from the British, subdued the Berber tribes and relieved the Spanish of much of their Moroccan territory. Moulay Ismail sowed the seeds of the current monarchy and beneath his strong-arm rule the coherent entity of modern Morocco was first glimpsed.

mausoleum, the king's immense granaries and stables, Heri es-Souani, were ingeniously designed. Tiny ceiling windows, massive walls and a system of underfloor water channels kept the temperatures cool and air circulating. Incredibly the building provided stabling and food for 12,000 horses, and Moulay Ismail regarded it as one of his finest architectural projects. The giant vaults are impressive and atmospheric – particularly in the darkest corners – with original cedar wood doors leaning against the walls.

Look for the *noria* room where horses would have once drawn up buckets of water from underground. Beyond the granary lies the stables, with row upon row cleverly set at angles to give the stable masters maximum visibility of their steeds across a huge area. Its flat roof caved in during an 18th-century earthquake and it is thought that before this event the stables were seven times longer than what can be seen today – quite a vision!

In summer it's a long hot walk here from Moulay Ismail's mausoleum, so you might want to catch a taxi or calèche (horse-drawn carriage). If you do decide to walk, follow the road from the mausoleum south between the high walls and past the main entrance of the Royal Palace (no visitors) to find the entrance straight ahead.

Agdal Basin   LAKE
(Map p321) Immediately north of the Heri es-Souani granaries and stables lies an enormous stone-lined lake, the Agdal Basin. Originally it was fed by a complex aqueduct system some 25km long and it served as both a reservoir for the sultan's gardens and a pleasure lake. Today the water is stagnant, but it's still a pleasant place to stroll, with a giant Giacometti-like statue of a traditional water-seller watching over it.

◉ Outside The Centre

Palais Al-Mansour   PALACE
[FREE] Little visited but rather glorious in its semi-state of repair, Palais Al-Mansour is an all-but-forgotten relic of Moulay Ismail's reign, in a quiet suburb of Meknès. The 17th-century palace was once the king's summer residence, built by the same architect who masterminded Bab el-Mansour. It is in the process of being resurrected from rubble but progress is slow. The round, domed reception room – architecturally magnificent with seven arches, but restrained in every other way, typical of Moulay Ismail's distinctive style – is a highlight.

Before you leave ask to be taken onto the roof, where the ruins of the residential palace rooms are open to the elements and the Imperial City can just about be spied from the balconies fronting the palace. In contrast to the stately ground floor, this rooftop residence would have once been highly decorated and you can still see pockets of original mosaic tiles in a couple of spots on the floor.

🧭 Tours

Compared with Fez and Marrakesh, the Meknès medina is fairly easy to navigate (but don't let that fool you into thinking you won't get lost). If you are short on time, or if you wish to gain some local insight, book an official guide through your hotel for Dh300/500 for a half-/full day.

Calèche rides of the imperial city with a guide are easy to pick up around Pl el-Hedim and behind Bab el-Mansour – a quick 30-minute 'grand tour' of the city's main attractions costs from Dh100 to Dh120.

🎊 Festivals & Events

Moussem of Sidi ben Aïssa   RELIGIOUS
One of the largest *moussems* in Morocco takes place on the eve of Moulid at Meknès' Mausoleum of Sidi ben Aïssa, outside the medina walls, in celebration of the Aïssawa Sufi brotherhood. It's a busy and popular festival with *fantasias*, fairs, singing and dancing. The dates change each year as they're fixed by the Islamic lunar calendar.

🛏 Sleeping

The riad scene has exploded in Meknès and there are now dozens of good options in the medina. Although your money will stretch further in the ville nouvelle, hotels lack atmosphere, often allow smoking and most are in need of a good refurb.

🛏 Medina

Most of Meknès' cheapies cluster along Rue Dar Smen and Rue Rouamzine on the edge of the old city. During festivals, they can fill up quickly. Riads are mostly clustered just north and east of Pl el-Hedim.

Hôtel Maroc   HOTEL €
(Map p322; ☑ 0535 53 00 75; 7 Rue Rouamzine; per person Dh100, roof terrace Dh50) A perennially popular shoestring option, the Maroc has the edge on location as it's just a five-minute

walk from the medina, Bab el-Mansour and Pl el-Hedim. Friendly and quiet, rooms (with sinks) are simple, and the shared bathrooms are clean. For a 50% discount you can sleep on a mattress on the roof terrace, surrounded by pot plants and washing.

★ Ryad Bahia GUESTHOUSE €€

(Map p322; ☎0661 81 52 37, 0535 55 45 41; www.ryad-bahia.com; Tiberbarine; s/d incl breakfast from Dh400/650; ❄📶) This charming riad, a converted family home, is just a stone's throw from Pl el-Hedim. The main entrance opens onto a cavernous courtyard, which also hosts a great restaurant (p328). Rooms are pretty and carefully restored, and the owners (keen travellers themselves) are eager to swap travel stories as well as guide guests in the medina; Bouchra is a licensed (female!) guide.

The riad also now opens its doors to nonguests for drinks and pastries each afternoon, so even if you don't stay, know that you are welcome to drop by.

Riad d'Or GUESTHOUSE €€

(Map p322; ☎0641 07 86 25; www.riaddor.com; 17 Derb el-Anboub; r/ste €50/80; ❄📶🏊) This labyrinthine riad is spread over two townhouses, with rooms tumbling around unexpected courtyards and staircases. The mix of traditional and modern-styled rooms caters to all tastes. Many can sleep four or more people and have sitting areas, and provide outstanding value for money. The biggest surprise is hidden on one of the roof terraces: a larger-than-average swimming pool.

Riad Lahboul GUESTHOUSE €€

(Map p322; ☎0675 71 69 17, 0535 55 98 78; www.riadlahboul.com; 6 Derb Ain Sefli, Rouamzine; s €40, d €60-70, f from €85, all incl breakfast; ❄📶) A musically minded Moroccan-English couple run this cosy riad, which has six rooms including a larger family room and a couple of others that can be combined to create petite two-bed apartments. Its *table d'hôte* (set menu Dh200) is a good option as the food gets rave reviews and local wine is served (nonguests welcome; book a day ahead).

If you're lucky, dinner might be accompanied by a performance from the owners. The leafy roof terrace is lovely – you almost feel part of the peaceful Lahboul Gardens, across the road.

Riad El Ma GUESTHOUSE €€

(Map p322; ☎0661 51 48 24; www.riad-el-ma.com; 4 Derb Sidi Besri; standard/red r Dh600/700, ste Dh900, all incl breakfast; ❄📶🏊) This pretty, traditional riad has a well-restored courtyard patio and a multilevel roof terrace with plunge pool and bird's-eye view of the Medersa Bou Inania. The spacious rooms are named after colours; note the standard rooms are better value than the larger ones as the size difference is minimal. El Ma is French-owned but run by two welcoming local ladies.

The managers offer an in-house dinner menu for Dh150.

Riad Yacout BOUTIQUE HOTEL €€

(Map p322; ☎0535 53 31 10; www.riad-yacout-meknes.com; 22 Pl Lalla Aoud; d incl breakfast Dh500-650, ste Dh750-850; ❄📶🏊) If you're after a combination of traditional touches and modern flair, you'll love Riad Yacout. Rooms are kitted out with hairdryers, flat-screen TVs and safety deposit boxes, bathrooms are a bit more shiny than those in most riads, and the staff work hard on service. There's a dip pool on the roof, where tables are set out for dinner and lunch.

The hotel is conveniently situated for parking and taxi drop-offs, as it's wedged into the walls of the Imperial City, right on Pl Lalla Aoud.

Riad Meknès BOUTIQUE HOTEL €€

(Map p322; ☎0535 53 05 42; www.riadmeknes.com; 79 Ksar Chaacha, Dar el-Kabir; s €35-40, d €45-50, all incl breakfast; ❄📶🏊) This large, airy riad is located amid the ruins of the Palais Ksar Chaacha, in a quiet area near Pl Lalla Aouda where few tourists venture. Rooms are tastefully decorated in a traditional-meets-modern style. It is noted for its restaurant (open to the public) and there's a chic plunge pool right in the colonnaded ruins. Signage is bad; arrange an escort.

Riad Felloussia GUESTHOUSE €€

(Map p322; ☎0676 98 77 17, 0535 53 08 40; www.riadfelloussia.com; 23 Derb Hammam Jdid; d €70-100; ❄📶) A well-located riad, easily accessible from Rue Dar Smen, Felloussia wins points for its roof terrace view over Pl el-Hedim, where hours could be spent just watching the nightly circus. There's a small, lush inner courtyard inhabited by tortoises, and traditional furnishings throughout. This riad can be booked online for half the advertised price, making it an excellent deal.

The largest ground-floor room has a mezzanine sleeping level that's like Marmite: guests either love it or hate it.

Ville Nouvelle

Its proximity to the CTM bus station and train stations can make the ville nouvelle a convenient place to bed down if you're arriving in town late at night – but bear in mind you'll spend your time travelling back and forth to the medina each day, as that's where all Meknès' attractions are.

Hôtel Majestic HOTEL €
(Map p328; ☑ 0535 52 20 35; 19 Ave Mohammed V; s/d incl breakfast Dh288/376; ☻) Open for business since 1937, the Majestic is one of the best deco buildings in Meknès. Rooms are comfortable, if a little small, and soundproofing isn't great, but there's plenty of character to compensate. A quiet courtyard, a roof terrace and friendly management, plus Majestic's location near the train station, make this a decent option.

Hôtel Palace HOTEL €
(Map p328; ☑ 0535 40 04 68; 11 Rue Ghana; s/d Dh180/230; ☐☎) The dour look of this hotel from the outside is matched by the dour staff inside, but the Palace is actually surprisingly good value: large airy rooms have attached bathrooms and many come with a teeny balcony. The trade-off for the price is ancient furnishings, and no restaurant, bar or breakfast.

Hôtel de Nice HOTEL €€
(Map p328; ☑ 0535 52 03 18; nice_hotel@menara.ma; cnr Rue Accra & Rue Antsirabé; s/d from Dh427/534; ☒) Friendly management helps elevate this hotel, but on the downside it still suffers from the same affliction as many other ville nouvelle options: the smell of lingering cigarette smoke. All rooms have a TV, a safety box and a hairdryer, and some have a balcony; decor is a little dated. The hotel has a pleasant bar in which nonguests are welcome.

Hôtel Akouas HOTEL €€
(Map p328; ☑ 0535 51 59 67; www.hotelakouas.com; 27 Rue Amir Abdelkader; s/d Dh360/446; ☒☒) This friendly, family-run hotel has a little more local colour than its rivals. Rooms, while not huge, are modern, serviceable and very fairly priced. The place also has a restaurant and nightclub (midnight til 3am), both serving alcohol. Breakfast costs an extra Dh40.

Hôtel Bab Mansour HOTEL €€
(Map p328; ☑ 0535 52 52 39; hotel_bab_mansour@menara.ma; 38 Rue Emir Abdelkader; s/d incl breakfast Dh399/525; ☒☎) It's a fine line between tasteful and characterless and, while comfortable enough, the Bab Mansour lacks personality. Rooms are a little old-fashioned and the hotel suffers from an all-pervasive smell of cigarette smoke. That said, it's well run, with everything you'd expect in a tourist-class hotel; there's a bar, a restaurant and a nightclub (midnight to 3am) on-site, all serving alcohol. Wi-fi in reception only.

Hôtel Rif HOTEL €€
(Map p328; ☑ 0535 52 25 91; hotel_rif@menara.ma; Rue Accra; s/d Dh618/736; ☒☎☒) The four-star Rif is a bit of a chocolate-concrete monstrosity from the outside, but inside it's got some charm, particularly in the traditional Moroccan salon oozing with pretty *zellij* tiling. The courtyard pool is good for dipping toes in, but as it's overlooked by the bar (nonguests welcome), female bathers will feel exposed. Breakfast costs Dh50 extra.

Le Jardin de Ryad Bahia GUESTHOUSE €€€
(☑ 0535 55 45 41; www.lesjardinsderyadbahia.com; Rte Agourai; r incl breakfast Dh700-1200; ☒☎☒) The owners of Ryad Bahia (p326) also run this airy, suburban house on the outskirts of Meknès. The lovely garden has a large pool, and there's a hammam (Dh350) and sauna that uses natural Moroccan beauty products. The modern house has nine bedrooms with balconies, and relaxing, traditionally styled living spaces. Cooking classes are a speciality (Dh400 per person).

Hôtel Malta HOTEL €€€
(Map p328; ☑ 0535 51 50 20; www.hotel-malta.ma; 3 Rue Charif Idrissi; s/d from Dh620/840; ☒☎) The Malta sets its aim a little higher than most other ville nouvelle hotels, which is reflected in the price. The spacious rooms are comfy and have satellite TV, though they may never win any design awards. A highlight has to be the entertaining bar with disco lighting, trussed up like a Moroccan palace with palm-tree columns. Breakfast is Dh50 extra.

Eating

There's not much variety in the Meknès restaurant scene – expect to find tajines, pastillas and couscous, and then more tajines, pastillas and couscous. Most of the best medina restaurants are to be found in riads, many of which open their doors to nonguests if you book ahead.

Meknès Ville Nouvelle

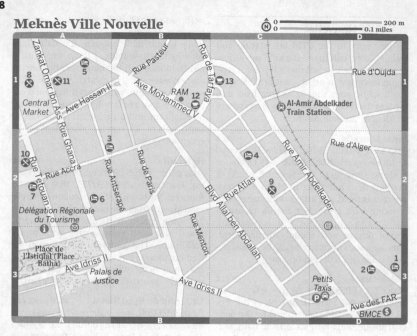

Meknès Ville Nouvelle

Sleeping

Eating

Drinking & Nightlife

Medina

Restaurant Oumnia
MOROCCAN €

(📞 0694 22 64 37; 8 Ain Fouki Rouamzine; set menu Dh95; ☺ noon-11pm) Thank goodness for this low-key restaurant, which is one of the only places in Meknès to eschew the standard Moroccan menu in favour of more unusual dishes, and will serve them alongside local beer or Meknès wine should you be hankering for it. The beef is particularly good,

such as *kamama* (beef with tomatoes and honey) and *kababe mardoure* (beef kebab with egg).

Sandwich Stands
FAST FOOD €

(Pl el-Hedim; sandwiches around Dh30; ☺ 7am-11pm) Take your pick of any one of the stands lining Pl el-Hedim (look for the ones grilling to order), and sit at the canopied tables to watch the scene as you eat. There are larger meals such as tajines, but sandwiches are the speciality. The friendly banter from the staff trying to pull you in to eat will keep you entertained, too.

Restaurant Riad Meknès
MOROCCAN €€

(📞 0535 53 05 42; 79 Ksar Chaacha; 3-course set menu Dh100-110; ☺ noon-3pm & 7-10pm; 📶) While all the riads in the Meknès medina have lovely restaurants, this is a great option for nonguests because its lush green courtyard with cacti garden and towering ruined walls is just so atmospheric. The menu of salads, tajines and couscous is simple, but it's all delicious and served with care and attention. No alcohol.

Ryad Bahia
MOROCCAN €€

(📞 0535 55 45 41; www.ryad-bahia.com; Tiberbarine; mains from Dh90, set menus Dh160-190; ☺ noon-3pm & 7-10pm; 📶) Nonresidents are welcome to eat at the restaurant of this riad (book well in advance), and it makes a pleasant evening dining spot with its candlelit tables around the courtyard. The menu is typically Moroccan, but everything is tasty and served and presented nicely.

Restaurant Yahala
MOROCCAN €€

(☑0649 98 88 16; restaurant.yahala@gmail.com; 10 Rue Sidi Amar Bouaouda; mains Dh60-95; ☜) There's a nice atmosphere at this petite restaurant, where chatter wafts down from the family kitchen in which the mother is cooking up a storm while her son bustles about eager to please diners downstairs. Everything in the white stuccoed dining salon is bright, clean and modern, though lacking in natural light, and the Moroccan dishes are cooked fresh to order.

Restaurant Mille et Une Nuits
MOROCCAN €€

(☑0535 55 90 02; off Pl el-Hedim; mains Dh75-95; ☉noon-10pm) Easily located off Pl el-Hedim, this friendly family restaurant feels like somebody's home that has received a glamorous makeover as a Moroccan palace – which is exactly what it is. It's a bit dark inside and ever so slightly shabby, but the traditional salon seating makes for a comfy lunch spot and the Moroccan fare on offer is very tasty.

✖ Ville Nouvelle

Marhaba Restaurant
MOROCCAN €

(Map p322; 23 Ave Mohammed V; mains from Dh25; ☉noon-10pm; ☜) This retro canteen-style place – the essence of cheap and cheerful – is hugely popular. At lunchtime, go for the freshly grilled meats. Later in the day do as everyone else does and fill up on a bowl of *harira* and a plate of *maâkouda* (potato fritters) with bread and hard-boiled eggs (served from 4pm) – and get change from Dh15.

Restaurant Gambrinus
MOROCCAN €

(Map p328; ☑0535 52 02 58; Zankat Omar ibn Ass; mains Dh50-70, set menu Dh77; ☉noon-6pm & 7-10pm) A good place for Moroccan food in a diner that doesn't look like it's changed much since the first Gambrinus rocked into town from Czechoslovakia in 1914 – the owner's immigrant past is something of a surprise considering the cuisine on offer. It's perennially popular with locals, who come for tajines such as rabbit and *kefta* (grilled minced beef or lamb with herbs and garlic), grilled lamb and steaks.

Palais Hassani du Poulet
FAST FOOD €

(Map p328; 4 Rue Tetouan; mains from Dh28; ☉noon-1am) Although tajines and couscous also feature on the menu, there's just one dish being served up at this popular fast-food joint: steaming piles of rotisserie chicken, chips, bread and salad. Choose between a streetside table on the covered terrace or a cool spot in the air-conditioned salon at the back. Order from the table, but pay at the counter by the door.

⚑ Drinking & Nightlife

It's a popular adage that Meknès has more bars than any other Moroccan city. However, it's still difficult to find a place to drink alcohol in the medina, where there are no bars. Restaurant Oumnia (p328) serves beers and local wines with meals.

Many ville nouvelle hotels have bars and a few even offer nightclubs (generally midnight to 3am).

Cafe Restaurant Place Lehdime
CAFE

(cnr Pl el-Hedim & Sidi Amar Bouaouda; ☉10am-10.30pm) Come dusk, this succession of roof terraces with front-row seats onto Pl el-Hedim is the place for young, trendy Meknès locals to come for a sundowner coffee. Courting couples vie with groups of friends for the best tables (at the very top) from which to watch the sun brush the Imperial City walls and Bab el-Mansour with gold. Service is slow at peak times.

Café Tulipe
CAFE

(Map p322; Rue de Tarfaya; ☉5.30am-11pm; ☜) The Tulipe is a much more modern affair than most Moroccan cafes, with a large shady terrace and very decent coffee. It's one of the most pleasant spots in which to kill an hour or two, and the patisserie on offer (sweet and savoury) is delicious. Pick from the sweets counter and then order drinks and pay at the till.

Café Opera
CAFE

(Map p328; 7 Ave Mohammed V; ☉6.30am-11pm) Airy and old-fashioned, this grand cafe is a classic, and among the most popular for Moroccan men to sip their mint tea. Sitting outside and people-watching is a great breakfast pastime. There's also a patisserie inside.

Pavillon des Idrissides
CAFE

(Map p322; 147 Dar Smen Lahdim; mains from Dh55; ☉9am-11pm; ☜) This rooftop cafe-restaurant has a coveted view overlooking Bab el-Mansour but it's not much of a dining

LOCAL KNOWLEDGE

SHOPPING IN THE SOUQS & QISSARIAT IN MEKNÈS

There are many *qissariat* (covered markets) in Meknès. A couple of these are devoted to textiles and carpets, which are noisily auctioned off on Sunday mornings. Okchen Market (auctions happen around 2pm) specialises in fine embroidery. On Rue Najjarine, leading away from the Medersa Bou Inania, you'll pass stalls of *babouches* (leather slippers) in multicoloured rows. Outside the western city wall, heading north from Bab Berrima, there's a colourful souq selling spices, herbs and nuts, and a lively *marché aux puces* (flea market).

spot: come for a quick coffee or fresh juice at sunset, like the locals do.

☆ Entertainment

Institut Français　　　PERFORMING ARTS
(Map p296; ☑ 05 35 51 65 00; inst.fr.mek@aim.net.ma; Rue Ferhat Hachad; ⊗ 9am-12.15pm & 2-6pm Mon-Sat) The centre of Meknès' cultural life, with films, plays, concerts and exhibitions. There's also a garden cafe.

🛍 Shopping

While the souqs of Meknès aren't as extensive as those of Fez or Marrakesh, the lack of hassle can make them a relaxed place to potter around looking for souvenirs. A particular speciality of Meknès is silver damascene, where metalwork is intricately inlaid with silver wire. There's a handful of good-value carpet shops opposite the Mausoleum of Moulay Ismail.

Ensemble Artisanale　　　ARTS & CRAFTS
(Map p322; Ave Mohamed VI; ⊗ 10am-1pm & 3-7pm Mon-Sat) This is the place to go if you want to get an idea of what to look for and how much to spend. Quality is high, but prices are fixed.

Pottery Stalls　　　ARTS & CRAFTS
(Map p322; Pl el-Hedim; ⊗ 9am-10pm) Set up on the western side of Pl el-Hedim, in front of the covered market.

ℹ Information

There are plenty of banks with ATMs both in the ville nouvelle (mainly on Ave Hassan II and Ave Mohammed V) and the medina (Rue Rouamzine).

BMCE (98 Ave des FAR; ⊗ 8.15am-5.45pm Mon-Fri) In the ville nouvelle, with a currency-exchange office that opens Saturdays.

BMCE (Rue Rouamzine; ⊗ 9am-5pm Mon-Fri) One of several banks along this street near Bab el-Mansour.

Délégation Régionale du Tourisme (☑ 0535 52 44 26, 0535 51 60 22; Pl de l'Istiqlal; ⊗ 8.30am-4.30pm Mon-Fri, 8-11.30am Sat) Meknes' main tourist office is in the ville nouvelle, but it doesn't keep to its advertised opening hours.

Hôpital Moulay Ismail (☑ 0535 52 28 05/06; off Ave des FAR)

Main Post Office (Pl de l'Istiqlal; ⊗ 8am-4.30pm Mon-Fri & 8am-noon Sat)

Pharmacy el-Fath (Map p322; Pl el-Hedim; ⊗ 9.30am-1pm & 3.30-8pm Mon-Fri, 9.30am-1pm Sat) Around the back of Pl el-Hedim.

Post Office (Map p322; Rue Dar Smen; ⊗ 8.30am-6pm)

Quick Net (28 Rue Amir Abdelkader; per hr Dh6; ⊗ 9am-9pm)

RAM (☑ 0535 52 09 63; 7 Ave Mohammed V; ⊗ 8.30am-12.15pm & 2.30-7pm Mon-Fri, 9am-4pm Sat) Handles tickets for Royal Air Maroc flights.

ℹ Getting There & Away

BUS

The **CTM bus station** (☑ 0522 43 82 82; Ave des FAR) is west of the ville nouvelle, a couple of blocks from the main train station.

CTM departures include Casablanca (Dh85, three to four hours, seven daily), some of which go via Rabat (Dh55, two hours, eight daily), as well as Fez (Dh25, one hour, 17 daily) and Marrakesh (Dh165, seven to eight hours, twice daily), Tangier (Dh90 to Dh100, five hours, four daily), Oujda (Dh130, 5½ to seven hours, three daily), Taza (Dh70 to Dh80, three hours, nine daily), Er-Rachidia (Dh110 to Dh120, six to seven hours, three daily) and Nador (Dh130, six hours, three daily).

Slightly cheaper than CTM, other buses depart from the **Gare Routière**, which is located just outside the medina's western Bab el-Khemis and has left-luggage and snack stands. However, these buses are not very reliable. Buses to Fez run hourly from 5am to 10pm and cost Dh15.

Tickets need to be purchased from the numbered windows:

Bus 1 Marrakesh (six daily, 5.30am to 6.30pm)

Bus 2 Midelt, Er-Rachidia, Ouarzazate and Rissani (one daily)

Bus 4 Rabat and Casablanca (hourly 5.30am to 4pm)

Bus 6 Tangier (seven daily), Tetouan via Chefchaouen (four daily)

Bus 7 Fez (hourly), Taza (one daily), Oujda (four daily) and Nador (six daily, indirect)

Note that the bus to Moulay Idriss is a red city bus (15), that departs from Bab el-Mansour (Dh7) rather than the bus station.

TAXI

The principal **grand-taxi rank** is a dirt lot next to the Gare Routière just outside the medina's Bab el-Khemis. There are regular departures to Fez (Dh25, one hour), Ifrane (Dh30, one hour), Azrou (Dh30, one hour) and Midelt (Dh45, three hours).

Grands taxis for Moulay Idriss (Dh10, 20 minutes) leave from opposite the Institut Français – this is also the place to organise round trips to Volubilis, for which there is an official rate (half-day trip Dh400, one to five people). Though note that it's very cheap to hire a taxi for the trip to Volubilis once you arrive at the taxi rank in Moulay Idriss.

Taxis run to Fes-Saïss Airport from Meknès for a fixed rate of Dh400/500 (day/night), or to Casablanca Airport for Dh1400.

TRAIN

Although Meknès has two train stations, head for the more convenient Al-Amir Abdelkader, east of the ville nouvelle. There are trains to Fez (Dh32, 45 minutes, hourly), Taza (Dh59, three to four hours, eight daily), some of which involve a change at Fez, and Oujda (Dh201, 6½ to seven hours, three daily). Trains also go to Casablanca (Dh143, three to 3½ hours, 19 daily) via Rabat (Dh95, two to three hours), and to Marrakesh (Dh280, seven hours, eight daily). For Tangier, there are four direct trains a day (Dh90, four to five hours) and two night trains that involve a change at Sidi Kacem.

ℹ️ Getting Around

BUS

City buses ply the route between the medina and ville nouvelle. The most useful are bus 2 (Bab el-Mansour to Blvd Allal ben Abdallah, returning to the medina along Ave Mohammed V) and bus 7 (Bab el-Mansour to the CTM bus station). Tickets are Dh2.50.

TAXI

Urban grands taxis (silver-coloured Mercedes Benz with black roofs) link the ville nouvelle and the medina, charging Dh2.50 per seat. Pale-blue **petits taxis** cost Dh7 to Dh10 for the same journey. Both can be caught from Pl el-Hedim. In the medina, petits taxis also congregate where Rue Dar Smen intersects with **Rue Rouamzine**. In the ville nouvelle, you'll find them in a parking lot close to where Ave des Far intersects with **Av Mohammed V**.

From Al-Amir Abdelkader train station to the Bab el-Mansour will cost Dh10 to Dh15 on the

meter, but watch out because the station is prime territory for opportunists. You may have to walk away from the station to find a driver willing to take you on the meter.

A more touristy way to get around the medina is by **calèche** (Pl el-Hedim), available for hire in front of Bab el-Mansour and just behind it, inside the Imperial City walls.

Volubilis (Oualili)   وليلي

The Roman ruins of Volubilis sit in the middle of a fertile plain about 33km north of Meknès, and can easily be combined with nearby Moulay Idriss to make a fantastic day trip from Meknès. The city is the best-preserved archaeological site in Morocco and was declared a Unesco World Heritage site in 1997. Its most amazing features are its many beautiful mosaics preserved in situ.

In the heat of a summer day, the sun can be incredibly fierce at Volubilis, so bring a hat and plenty of water. Spring is the ideal season, when wildflowers blossom amid the abandoned stones, and the surrounding fields are at their greenest. The best time to visit is either first thing in the morning or late afternoon; at dusk, when the last rays of the sun light the ancient columns, Volubilis is at its most magical.

History

Excavations indicate that the site was originally settled by Carthaginian traders in the 3rd century BC. One of the Roman Empire's most remote outposts, Volubilis was annexed in about AD 40. According to some

---

MEKNÈS MARKETS

Covered Market (Pl el-Hedim; ◷ 8.30am-10pm) This is the place in Meknès to get fresh produce, and is virtually a tourist attraction in itself, with its beautifully arranged pyramids of sugary sweet delicacies, dates and nuts, olives and preserved lemons in glistening piles. There's good-quality fruit and veg here, as well as meat – the faint-hearted may choose to avoid the automated chicken-plucking machines at the rear of the hall.

Central Market (Ave Hassan II; ◷ 7.30am-2.30pm) A good place to shop in the ville nouvelle, with a variety of fresh-food stalls and some imported foodstuffs.

historians, Rome imposed strict controls on what could and could not be produced in its North African possessions, according to the needs of the empire. One result was massive deforestation and the large-scale planting of wheat around Volubilis. At its peak, it is estimated that the city housed up to 20,000 people. The site's most impressive monuments were built in the 2nd and 3rd centuries, including the triumphal arch, capitol, baths and basilica.

As the neighbouring Berber tribes began to reassert themselves, so the Romans abandoned Volubilis around AD 280. Nevertheless, the city's population of Berbers, Greeks, Jews and Syrians continued to speak Latin right up until the arrival of Islam. Moulay Idriss found sanctuary here in the 8th century, before moving his capital to Fez. Volubilis continued to be inhabited until the 18th century, when its marble was plundered for Moulay Ismail's palaces in Meknès, and its buildings were finally felled by the Lisbon earthquake of 1755.

◉ Sights

Official guides hang about at the site and conduct good one-hour tours for Dh200. Between them, the guides speak virtually every language under the sun. To get the most out of your tour, insist on getting one that speaks your language fluently.

Visitor Centre & Museum　　　MUSEUM
(⊙8.30am-sunset; **P**) Volubilis' slick new Visitor Centre & Museum is just inside the main entrance gate to the site; however, at the time of visiting it wasn't yet open to the public. It will eventually display prized archaeological finds from Volubilis, with descriptions in French and Arabic. Some of the site's key artefacts are currently held by Rabat's archaeology museum and their return has been a point of dispute.

★Roman Ruins　　　RUINS
(admission adult/child Dh10/3; ⊙8.30am-sunset) Only about half of the 40-hectare site at Volubilis has been excavated. The better-known monuments are in the northern part of the site, furthest from the entrance in the south. Information boards are irregular, and other than that there's little in the way of signposting to indicate what you're actually seeing. It's well worth considering hiring a guide, especially if you're pressed for time. If you prefer to wander on your own, allow at least two hours to see the essentials. Although

parts of certain buildings are roped off, you are free to wander the site at will.

➡ Ancient Volubilis

Although the least remarkable part of the site, the **olive presses** here indicate the economic basis of ancient Volubilis, much as the plentiful olive groves in the surrounding area do today – look for the flat presses and stone storage vats dotted about the site. Wealthy homeowners had private olive presses.

➡ Buildings

Next to the House of Orpheus are the remains of **Galen's Thermal Baths**. Although largely broken, they clearly show the highly developed underfloor heating in this Roman hammam (look for the low arches). Opposite the steam room are the communal toilets – where citizens could go about their business and have a chat at the same time.

The **Capitol**, **Basilica** and 1300-sq-metre **Forum** are, typically, built on a high point. The Capitol, dedicated to the Triad of Jupiter, Juno and Minerva, dates back to AD 218; the Basilica and Forum lie immediately to its north. The reconstructed columns of the Basilica are usually topped with storks' nests – an iconic Volubilis image if the birds are nesting at the time of your visit. Around the Forum is a series of plinths carved with Latin inscriptions that would have supported statues of the great and good. Keep your eyes out for the carved stone drain-hole cover – an understated example of Roman civil engineering.

The marble **Triumphal Arch** was built in 217 in honour of Emperor Caracalla and his mother, Julia Domna. The arch, which was originally topped with a bronze chariot, was reconstructed in the 1930s, and the mistakes made then were rectified in the 1960s. The hillock to the east provides a splendid view over the entire site.

➡ Houses with Mosaics

The **House of Orpheus** is the finest and largest home, containing a mosaic of Orpheus charming animals by playing the lute, and a dolphin mosaic in the dining room. Note the private hammam has a caldarium (hot room) with visible steam pipes, a tepidarium (warm room) and a frigidarium (cold room), as well as a solarium.

On the left just before the triumphal arch are a couple more roped-off mosaics. One, in the **House of the Acrobat**, depicts an athlete being presented with a trophy for winning a desultory race, a competition in

Volubilis

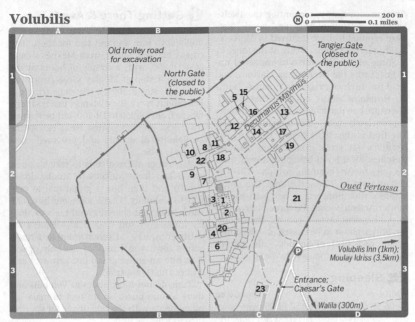

which the rider had to dismount and jump back on his horse as it raced along. To the west of here is the **House of the Dog**, famed not for its mosaics but a lonesome rock plinth with a giant phallus carved into the top of it – this establishment was once a brothel for weary warriors who would stop off here after making it back to the triumphal arch after battle.

From the arch, the ceremonial road, Decumanus Maximus, stretches up the slope to the northeast. The houses lining it on either side contain the best mosaics on the site. The first on the far side of the arch is known as the **House of the Ephebus** and contains a now-incomplete mosaic of Bacchus in a chariot drawn by panthers.

Next along, the **House of the Columns** is so named because of the columns arranged in a circle around the interior court – note their differing styles, which include spirals. Adjacent to this is the **House of the Knight**, also called House of the Cavalier/Rider with its incomplete mosaic of Bacchus and Ariadne. The naked Ariadne has suffered somewhat from the attentions of admirers.

The next four houses are named for their excellent mosaics: the **House of the Labours of Hercules**, the **House of Dionysus & the Four Seasons**, the **House of the**

Volubilis

Nymphs Bathing, though the nymph mosaics are heavily damaged, and the **House of the Wild Beasts**. The first is almost a circular comic strip, recounting the Twelve Labours. Several of Hercules' heroic feats were reputed to have occurred in Morocco, making him a popular figure at the time.

Some of the best mosaics are saved until last. Cross the Decumanus Maximus and head for the lone cypress tree, which marks the **House of Venus**, home of King Juba II. There are two particularly fine mosaics here, appropriately with semi-romantic themes. The first is the *Abduction of Hylas by the Nymphs*, an erotic composition showing Hercules' lover Hylas being lured away from his duty by two beautiful nymphs. The second mosaic is *Diana Bathing*. The virgin goddess was glimpsed in her bath by the hunter Acteon, whom she turned into a stag as punishment. Acteon can be seen sprouting horns, about to be chased and devoured by his own pack of hounds – the fate of mythical peeping toms everywhere.

🛏 Sleeping

Walila   GUESTHOUSE €€
(✆ 06 52 09 63 73, 06 62 52 81 05; www.walila. com; Oualili; d incl breakfast Dh550; ℗) Once the childhood home of a French minister, this 1920s farmstead is in a tranquil setting a five-minute walk from Volubilis. The original house offers three cosy (if a little basic) rooms mixing Berber textiles with French antiques and open fires, and the affable owner Azzeddine used to be a chef in Holland – guests rave about his organic modern Moroccan dinners (Dh150 to Dh200).

Azzeddine goes out of his way to make the place feel like a home away from home: you can get your hands dirty helping out, ride mules into the hills or simply lay back in the garden hammock and wait to be fed. At the time of writing an old stone barn was in the process of being converted into further accommodation, and you can book in for lunch here if you're in the area visiting Volubilis but don't fancy staying. This place is all about 'back to nature', which means no wi-fi.

Volubilis Inn   HOTEL €€€
(✆ 0535 54 44 05; hotelvolubilisinn@gmail.com; Rte de Meknès; s/d incl breakfast from Dh540/640; ℗ ❋ ☲) The best feature of this large four-star hotel on a rise above Volubilis is its expansive views over the Roman ruins and surrounding countryside. All rooms have a TV and a fridge, and benefit from the views – as do the terraces, pool and international restaurant (mains from Dh90). There's also a bar with an open fire. Overall, it lacks atmosphere.

ℹ Getting There & Away

The simplest and quickest way to get to Volubilis is to hire a grand taxi for the return trip. A half-day outing from Meknès should cost Dh350, with a couple of hours at the site and a stop at Moulay Idriss (worth an overnight stay in itself). The same trip from Fez (about twice the distance) can cost anywhere from Dh250 to Dh500, but be warned it's a less popular outing from Fez so the availability of drivers and proposed costs can be erratic.

A cheaper alternative is to take a shared grand taxi from Meknès to Moulay Idriss (Dh10) and then hire a grand taxi to take you to Volubilis (Dh30 complete hire, one way). Note that shared grand taxis to Moulay Idriss only run from near Meknès's Institut Français – at other grand-taxi ranks across town you'll be told the only option is to hire an entire grand taxi privately, at a cost of Dh90 (not true!).

Taxis do not hang about at Volubilis and there are no buses, so it's best to make arrangements with the taxi driver for your return journey as well.

If the weather isn't too hot, it's a lovely one-hour walk (one way) between Moulay Idriss and Volubilis.

Moulay Idriss   مولاي ادريس
POP 11,615

The whitewashed town of Moulay Idriss sits astride two green hills in a cradle of mountains slightly less than 5km from Volubilis, and is one of the country's most important pilgrimage sites. Given its picturesque setting, pretty historic core and national importance, it's a mystery why more tourists don't visit. The good news is that its lack of popularity means you can often have the place all to yourself.

Moulay Idriss' holy status kept it closed to non-Muslims until 1912 and it wasn't until 2005 that non-Muslims were allowed to stay overnight in the town. Its previous inaccessibility has helped protect the town's peaceful way of life and those who do stay are invariably charmed. Appealing local guesthouses cater to visitors and while it's no longer a safe haven from Morocco's dreaded tourist touts, it's still a relaxed place with a centre free of carpet shops.

The town is named for Moulay Idriss, a great-grandson of the Prophet Mohammed, the founder of the country's first real dynasty, Morocco's first Islamic leader, and its most revered saint. His tomb is at the heart of the town, and is the focus of the country's largest *moussem* every August.

Moulay Idriss fled Mecca in the late 8th century in the face of persecution at the hands of the recently installed Abbasid caliphate, which was based in Baghdad. Idriss settled at Volubilis, where he converted the locals to Islam, and made himself their leader, establishing the Idrissid dynasty.

◉ Sights

Mausoleum of Moulay Idriss   MAUSOLEUM
(Pl Mohammed VI) The Mausoleum of Moulay Idriss is Morocco's most important pilgrimage site and the town is swamped every August during the annual *moussem* to venerate it; it's said locally that five pilgrimages to Moulay Idriss during the *moussem* equals one haj to Mecca. The entrance is located at the top of the town's main square, via a three-arched gateway surrounded by shops selling religious trinkets – non-Muslims cannot enter beyond the inner barrier, but it's worth a peak inside the grand entrance.

Moulay Ismail created this pilgrimage site by building the mausoleum and moving the body of Moulay Idriss during the late 17th and early 18th century, in a successful attempt to rally the support of the faithful.

Grande & Petite Terrasses   VIEWPOINT
These lofty medina vantage points provide stunning views over Moulay Idriss and the green-roofed mausoleum. The Grande Terrasse is broader and better for capturing panoramic vistas of the hilltop town and surrounding landscape on camera. Both terraces are difficult to find on your own; keep heading uphill and you'll get near, but you may have to ask a local to help you get to the exact spots. Dar Zerhoune (p336) has a handy map.

Cylindrical Minaret   MOSQUE
(off Rue Ain Fakra) Moulay Idriss' green-tiled cylindrical minaret, built in 1939, is unique and worth a look. Although it's located inside the medina it's easy to find if you skirt around the western edge heading uphill (passing a communal olive press on your right) until you reach the Boulangerie Patisserie Moulay Idriss. Here, turn right into the medina, veer left as you climb uphill and you'll find it.

✺ Festivals & Events

Moussem of Moulay Idriss   RELIGIOUS
(☺ late Aug) Morocco's greatest annual *moussem* is held every August in the pilgrimage town of Moulay Idriss, which holds the tomb of Morocco's first Islamic ruler. The pilgrimage is accompanied by *fantasias*, markets and music; so important is the event that it sometimes attracts royalty. The town's guesthouses are crammed during the *moussem*, so book well ahead if you plan to attend.

⛺ Sleeping & Eating

Rooms are at a premium during the *moussem*, so book in advance.

The cheap food stands around the main square are all good for a quick snack. The grilled *kefta* with salad is something of a local speciality.

La Colombe Blanche   GUESTHOUSE €
(☏ 0535 54 45 96; www.maisonhote-zerhoune. ma; 21 Derb Zouak Tazgha; s/d incl breakfast Dh250/400; ▦ ⛊) A traditional home turned guesthouse – the family occupies a portion of this rambling house so they're always on hand to help. Rooms are decent, there are multiple terraces with lovely hill views, and Colombe Blanche also bills itself as a restaurant serving home-cooked meals (menus Dh60 to Dh120 – call ahead to book). At the mausoleum, turn right uphill and follow the signs.

Hotel Diyar Timnay   HOTEL €
(☏ 0535 54 44 00; amzday@menara.ma; 7 Aïn Rjal; s/d incl breakfast Dh160/240; ▦) Near the grands-taxis stands, this is Moulay Idriss's only hotel but it suffers from an air of neglect and the pong of cigarette smoke. The simple rooms mostly have en suites, although a few have separate (but still private) bathrooms. The enclosed 'terrace' restaurant (mains Dh70) has great hill views but feels a bit soulless. Timnay's saving grace is that it's cheap.

★ Dar Ines   GUESTHOUSE €€
(☏ 0535 54 49 07; www.dar-ines.com; 57 Hay Tazga, Derb Amjout; s/d incl breakfast from Dh350/440; ⛊) ⚐ This grand guesthouse with terrace views over the main square is actually two *dars* knocked together, offering seven traditional rooms with solar-heated showers, wrapped around two staircases. House manager Sahid is super helpful and his care and attention elevates this *dar* above the competition. In-house meals are excellent (guests/

Moulay Idriss Medina

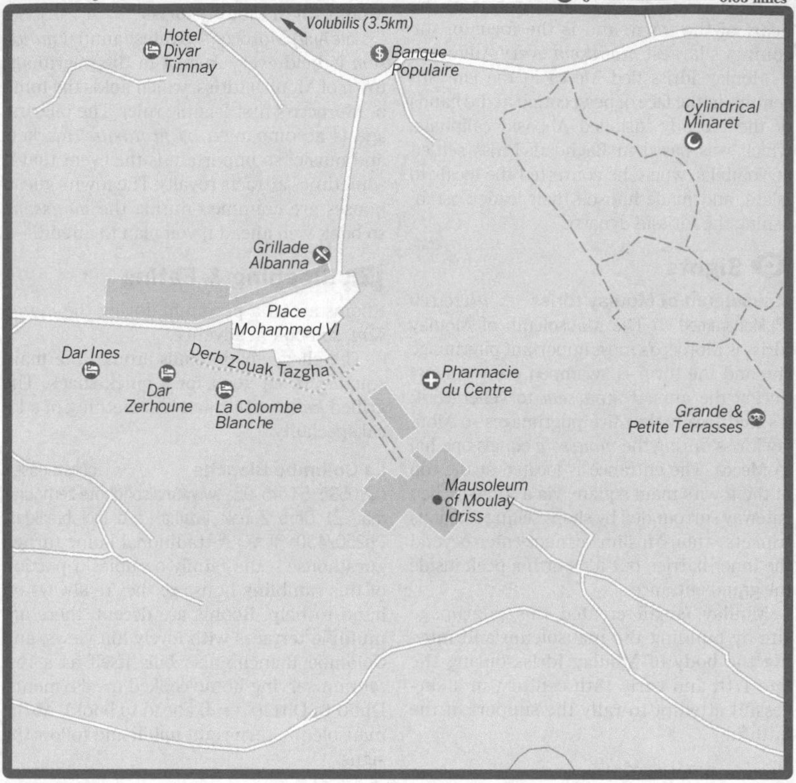
0 100 m
0 0.05 miles
Volubilis (3.5km)
Hotel Diyar Timnay
Banque Populaire
Cylindrical Minaret
Grillade Albanna
Place Mohammed VI
Dar Ines
Derb Zouak Tazgha
Dar Zerhoune
La Colombe Blanche
Pharmacie du Centre
Grande & Petite Terrasses
Mausoleum of Moulay Idriss

nonguests Dh120/140 – book ahead), and the owners offer craft courses and trekking excursions.

The only downside (if you're bothered by this sort of thing) is that wi-fi is restricted to one small downstairs salon.

Dar Zerhoune GUESTHOUSE **€€**
(☎06 42 24 77 93; www.darzerhoune.com; 42 Derb Zouak Tazgha; s/d incl breakfast Dh410/620;) To the right uphill from the mausoleum, this gem of a guesthouse has taken a left-field approach to *dar* decorating, with a refreshing white colour scheme in place of the dark wood, accented by pops of bright colour. The Kiwi owner offers tours, bike hire and cooking lessons, and you can book a meal on the panoramic terrace even if you're not staying there.

Grillade Albanna KEBAB **€**
(off Pl Mohammed VI; kefta Dh30; ⏲11am-9pm) Moulay Idriss is known for its *kefta* and this simple grillhouse just off the town's main square is a local favourite. Take a people-watching seat while you wait for your meat to be grilled to order; the kefta is fresh, packed with flavour and served simply with grilled tomatoes, fresh bread and ground chilli.

ℹ Information

There is a **Banque Populaire** (Rue Ain Fakra; ⏲8.15am-3.45pm Mon-Fri) uphill from the grand taxi rank, where the road forks just before the main square.

Pharmacie du Centre (Pl Mohammed VI; ⏲9am-2pm & 4-8.30pm Mon-Sat) is conveniently located on Moulay Idriss' main square, Pl Mohammed VI.

ℹ Getting There & Away

Grands taxis (Dh10, 20 minutes) to Moulay Idriss leave Meknès from outside the Institut Français. The red city bus, (15) runs from Bab el-Mansour in Meknès to Moulay Idriss (Dh7) throughout the day – you will not be able to catch a bus from the bus station.

Taxis leave Moulay Idriss from a stand at the bottom of town on the main road. If you want to get to Fez, you'll have to go via Meknès.

MIDDLE ATLAS

South of Fez and Meknès, the low-rise Middle Atlas mountains come into play. Oak and cedar forests create refreshing pockets of woodland and easy hiking terrain, connecting the dots between Berber hill towns and villages. Further south, towards Midelt, the forests give way to dramatic barren slopes as the desert calls.

Ifrane   فران

POP 14,659

As foreign tourists head to the medinas for a taste of the 'real' Morocco, Moroccan tourists find more favour with places such as Ifrane. Tidy, ordered and modern, it feels more like Switzerland relocated to the Middle Atlas than North Africa. Its clean air, scrubbed streets and leafy outlook make it popular with tour groups.

The French built Ifrane in the 1930s, deliberately trying to re-create an alpine-style resort. It has neat red-roofed houses, blooming flower beds and lake-studded parks. It is a popular summer day trip for picnickers; in the winter, the affluent flock here to ski, and the hoi polloi come for the pure fun of throwing snowballs.

The main road from Meknès is called Blvd Mohammed V and it runs through Ifrane from west to east. Most of the cafes and hotels are clustered in the centre along Rue de la Cascade and Ave de la Poste, close to the stone lion statue.

The nature around Ifrane is more alluring than the town itself. The woods of the national park virtually encroach on the urban area, and the region to the north is splashed with serene lakes.

◉ Sights & Activities

The lake- and wood-studded countryside around Ifrane, and particularly to the north, is good for horse riding, hiking and birdwatching. Le Gîte Dayet Aoua makes an excellent base from which to organise reasonably priced tours.

Stone Lion   MONUMENT

(Av Hassan II) Ifrane's cult landmark is the stone lion that sits on a patch of grass near the Hôtel Chamonix. It was carved by a German soldier during WWII, when Ifrane was used briefly as a prisoner-of-war camp, in exchange for the prisoner's freedom – or so the story goes – and commemorates the last wild Atlas lion, which was shot near here in the early 1920s. Having your picture taken with the lion is something of a ritual for Moroccan day trippers.

🛏 Sleeping

Hotel prices in Ifrane reflect the town's affluence, and its year-round popularity means demand for rooms runs high – particularly with tour groups. If you're on a budget, you'd be better off staying in Azrou.

Hotel les Tilleuls   HOTEL €€

(📞 0535 56 66 58, 06 61 16 11 86; hoteltilleuls@gmail.com; cnr Ave des Tilluels & Rue de la Cascade; s/d Dh300/400) 🏊 The cheapest hotel in Ifrane has been welcoming guests since 1935. These days it's a bit frayed around the edges and the owners know it: a series of renovations are underway but could take years to complete. In the meantime its selling points are large, en-suite rooms and its convenient location on the corner of Ifrane's main square.

Thursday to Saturday a nightclub takes up residence here, and the hotel has a bar.

Hôtel Chamonix   HOTEL €€

(📞 0535 56 60 28; lechamonix@yahoo.fr; Ave de la Mare Verte; s/d incl breakfast Dh489/557; ❄ 🛜) Right across the street from Ifrane's stone lion, this three-star place is well maintained and centrally located. Rooms are bright and spacious, if a little bland, with attached bathrooms and central heating. There's also a decent restaurant and bar. During the snow season, expect prices hikes of 15% to 20%.

Michlifen Ifrane   LUXURY HOTEL €€€

(📞 0535 86 40 00; www.michlifenifrane.com; off Ave Hassan II; low-/high-season r from Dh2500/4600; 🅿 ❄ 🛜 🏊) Overlooking Ifrane from the north, this oversized ski lodge is one of Morocco's most luxurious hotels. Local cedar is evident throughout the rather dark interior, with rooms echoing a luxury chalet. The view from the pool is sublime and you can even fish in the river that runs through the hotel grounds. There's also a sumptuous bar and a restaurant.

IFRANE NATIONAL PARK

This 500 sq km park encompasses Ifrane and Azrou as well as numerous Berber villages. It is known for its Atlas cedar trees and the Barbary macaque, an endangered species, and some 30 other mammals including wild pigs and wolves up on the high plateaus.

Bird life is exceptional and includes red kite, marbled teal, and common kestrel. Two Ramsar wetland sites and the lakes Dayet Ifrah and Dayet Aoua support ruddy shelduck and various coots. The lakes themselves, particularly those north of Ifrane, make for scenic touring and are popular with local day trippers from Meknès and Fez. Gentle hiking is the main pastime here.

Around Ifrane

Dayet Aoua North of Ifrane, Dayet Aoua is surrounded by woodlands in an area notably rich in bird life. The lake is a popular picnic destination for families on weekends, but during the week you'll get it largely to yourself. In summer the water all but dries up and locals trot around the lake bed on horseback. At other times you can rent pedalos here, and year round it makes a good bike circuit. From Ifrane, a one-way taxi to the lake costs about Dh250.

The lake attracts significant numbers of ducks and waders, including crested coot, woodpeckers, tree creepers and nuthatches, which flit among the trees around the south-eastern end of the lake. Also keep an eye out for raptors, including booted eagles, black and red kites and harriers.

Lake Circuit A pretty diversion north of Ifrane is the lake circuit around Dayet Aoua (p338). Signposted off the main Fez road 17km north of Ifrane, the route winds for 60km through the lake country between the P24 and P20. If you don't have your own vehicle, hiring a grand taxi in Ifrane for a day trip of this route should cost about Dh600.

Beyond Dayet Aoua, the road loops east and then south, skirting past small Dayet Hechlaf Ifrah and then Dayet Ifrah. Although this trip is billed as a scenic drive, the joy of the area is to get out and walk along the lake shore and enjoy the tranquillity of the scenery. This is an area made for hikers and mountain bikers. Note that the road is paved but a bit scarred in some parts, and liable to be snowbound in winter.

If you want to linger longer, there's a good sleeping option at Dayet Aoua: the delightfully rustic Le Gîte Dayet Aoua (p338).

Exploring the Azrou Area

Agdal Plateau & Kherzouza Cliffs This leisurely day hike starts from the forests at Moudmame just outside Azrou, climbing steadily through crops of oak trees that morph into fragrant cedar at about 1800m. You'll then strike out over the broad Agdal plateau, inhabited by Berber shepherds and honey farms, before dipping back into the forests and eventually emerging at the craggy Kherzouza cliffs, with spectacular views over Azrou.

Signposting for this walk is poor, and if you don't have a good map or GPS it's advisable to book a mountain guide. The walk is about 10km from Moudmame, though it can be done straight from Azrou if you fancy the 8km walk to get to Moudmame as well.

'Ain Leuh This pretty village, 25km southwest of Azrou, is within the Ifrane National Park, and crowned by a small 17th-century kasbah that would have been used to control the local Berber population during Moulay Ismail's time. It's a pleasant climb through the rough

Hôtel Perce-Neige HOTEL €€€
(☑ 0535 56 64 04; hperceneige@gmail.com; Rue des Asphodelles; s/d incl breakfast Dh650/810, ste Dh1000-1350; ❄ ☎) A pretty accommodation option down a leafy street about 200m southeast of the centre. The rooms could be a bit bigger and some are a little faded for the price, but they're very comfortable and come with satellite TV and bathrooms. Those at the front with balcony can be a bit noisy. The licensed restaurant is a good dining option (mains Dh80 to Dh150).

Out Of Town

★ **Le Gîte Dayet Aoua** LODGE €
(☑ 0535 61 05 75; www.gite-dayetaoua.com; Dayet Aoua; 8-person dm/d/ste incl breakfast Dh100/300/400; ℗ ☎) This delightfully rustic lodge offers comfortable rooms with

streets of flat-roofed houses to a waterfall at the town's northern edge (best in spring), surrounded by storks' nests and topped by a prettily situated cafe. Shared grand taxis from Azrou cost Dh15 and drop you on 'Ain Leuh's Blvd Hassan II.

From Blvd Hassan II, which is also where you'll find public parking, follow the road straight uphill and take the pastel-coloured steps up past a small tiered public garden – the cascade is at the top, just beyond the stone gate marking the edge of the village. At the bottom of the steps there's a **Women's Co-operative** (open 8am to 7pm Saturday to Tuesday and Thursday), where locals weave Berber carpets to sell and can explain the process to you.

The village also hosts a small weekly **souq** on Wednesday (the best day to get public transport – at other times you may have to visit on a private trip, costing about Dh500) that attracts market-goers from around the region, as well as a popular **Berber music festival** each August.

Sources de l'Oum-er-Rbia (parking Dh5, cave Dh5) Several dozen springs break out of the rocks to form a series of waterfalls at Oum-er-Rabia, but the attraction astonishment of visiting is not just seeing the cascades themselves (which virtually dry up during and after summer), but it's the makeshift cafes and restaurants that cling precariously to the rocks above the rushing water from where it tumbles down into the river. The road south from 'Ain Leuh deteriorates at some points but the scenery is stunning; expect the drive to take about an hour.

From Azrou it costs a hefty Dh1000 to hire a private grand taxi for this trip (including a stop in 'Ain Leuh), but the springs are also included in some Middle Atlas tours so ask about. From 'Ain Leuh, the road ascends through thick juniper, oak and cedar forests where troops of Barbary macaques are sometimes spotted, and skirts tiny Berber communities. Watch out for shepherds and their flocks, and working donkeys going about their daily tasks.

It's also possible to hike to the Sources de l'Oum-er-Rabia from one of the region's lakes: leave the road at Lac Ouiouane, about 20km south of 'Ain Leuh, and follow the path down past a number of farmhouses to a small valley, where a bridge crosses the Rbia river. From here, it's about a 15-minute walk to the gorge and its cascades. In total this trail will take you about three hours (approximately 10km).

Tours

Official Middle Atlas mountain guides work for set rates. It's Dh600/300 per whole/half-day, but this fee doesn't include lunch or transport. Including food and transport (depending on where you want to hike), expect to pay about Dh1000 per day for one to two people.

Multiday treks, including mule, accommodation, food and guiding cost Dh800 to Dh1200, depending on the number of hikers.

Boujmaa & Saleh Boudaoud (📱 0632 36 19 90; salehboudaoud@gmail.com) Official guides covering the Azrou/Ifrane area and sometimes further afield.

Abdellah Lahrizi (p343) Another official guide and owner of the rural guesthouse Les Jardins d'Azrou. He runs a useful website (in French) about trekking in the Middle Atlas: www.moyen-atlas-trekking.com.

bathroom, all decorated in local Berber style. There's a pool, an apple orchard, a Berber tent and a detached Moroccan salon with log fire, too. Have a few days of internet detox (there's no wi-fi here) and go cycling, horse riding or walking. Food is excellent Amazigh cuisine; enquire about half-board options and picnic lunches (Dh120).

If you're on a tight budget, the owner can organise mountain guides for Dh300 per day, which is half the price of an official Middle Atlas mountain guide.

🍴 Eating & Drinking

Virtually all the hotels in town have a bar that serves alcohol, and there's a nightclub (Thursday to Saturday) at Hotel les Tilleuls (p337).

FEZ, MEKNÈS AND THE MIDDLE ATLAS IFRANE

La Paix CAFE €

(Ave de la Mare Verte; ⊙ 9am-10pm; 🛜) Go ahead and rub your eyes, because you won't believe you're in Morocco once you've crossed the threshold of this upmarket cafe-patisserie. First there's the astroturfed outdoor patio with garden furniture; then there's the wide glass frontage and minimalist white interior to behold. La Paix is situated just up from the Hôtel Chamonix – come for a breakfast of croissant and coffee.

Forest Restaurant INTERNATIONAL €€

(cnr Ave del Porte & Rue de la Cascade; mains Dh55-150; ⊙ 7.30am-11pm Mon-Fri, to midnight Sat & Sun; 🛜) This chilled-out cafe attracts Ifrane's wealthy university students and it's a little on the pricey side, but if your Western palate is craving some decent international food, Forest is a treat. Start the day with eggs or croissants, or come later on for burgers, excellent pasta and pizzas; finish off with a warming dessert such as apple crumble.

ℹ️ Information

BMCE (Ave de la Mare Verte; ⊙ 8.30am-4pm) One of several banks with ATMs on this road.

Délégation Provinciale du Tourism (Tourism Office; ☎ 0535 56 68 21; Ave Prince Moulay Abdallah; ⊙ 8am-4pm Mon-Fri) If you're lucky, you might be able to pick up a map from Ifrane's tourist office, but set your expectations low.

Pharmacie Michliffen (Rue de la Cascade; ⊙ 9am-1pm & 3-10pm Mon-Fri, 9am-1pm Sat) Around the corner from Forest Restaurant.

Post Office (Ave de la Poste; ⊙ 8am-4.15pm Mon-Fri) Just uphill from La Paix cafe and Hôtel Chamonix. Has an ATM.

ℹ️ Getting There & Away

The new Gare Routière is south of town and services both CTM and local buses. The station has a cafe and left luggage.

Each morning and evening, CTM buses leave for Marrakesh (Dh155, eight hours) via Beni Mellal. There's a daily 9am departure for Casablanca (Dh120, five hours) via Meknès (Dh25, one hour) and Rabat (Dh90, 3½ hours).

There are frequent daily non-CTM bus departures to Fez, Azrou and Khenifra, as well as four daily to Marrakesh, five daily to Rabat and one daily to Casablanca, at 1pm.

Grands taxis also congregate at the bus station; they go to Fez or Meknès (Dh30) and Azrou (Dh9). Grands taxis to **Dayet Aoua** (p338) can be hired privately for Dh250, or it'll cost Dh600 for a full day trip of the **Lake Circuit** (p338).

Azrou أزرو

POP 54,350

Monkeys and fragrant cedar forest trails are what draw visitors to Azrou, but the town itself is a thoroughly unhurried, relaxing spot in which to wind down if you're feeling frazzled after too many big cities. It's an important Berber market centre deep in the Middle Atlas, with a shaggy mane of woods and high meadows that burst into flower every spring.

Azrou (Great Rock) takes its name from the isolated outcrop marking the town's western boundary. The big Ennour mosque, beautifully finished with local cedar, provides another handy landmark. Azrou's petite medina is most easily accessible from the south side of Pl Mohammed V, and is a refreshing place to wander without hassle.

◎ Sights

⭐ **Azrou Souq** SOUQ

(⊙ sunrise-sunset Tue) Azrou's weekly souq is one of the largest in the Middle Atlas and truly a sight to behold, but it's not a souvenir-fest: mountain people come from surrounding villages to trade and shop, and the real attraction is in observing a workaday Moroccan market bulging with local produce, livestock and clothes – come before 10am to see goats, sheep and cows being bartered.

The souq sprawls over an open plain 1.5km north of the town centre and is divided into three sections, with the livestock area the furthest from town. Start at this end and work your way back, stopping at the food tents (downhill from the livestock area) to see carcasses hanging ready for the grills and to grab a mint tea with the locals. Take care if it's been raining, as the souq area can easily turn into a quagmire.

Centre Culturel d'Azrou MUSEUM

(Pl Hassan II; ⊙ 8.30am-4.30pm Mon-Fri) **FREE** Azrou's new cultural centre houses a shiny museum with three rooms focusing on the ecology of the Middle Atlas, the cultural heritage of the local Amazigh people, and the region's broader history.

Moudmame FOREST

If you're desperate to see Azrou's furry famed locals, it's a piece of cake – just outside town, Moudmame is a popular picnic forest area where one of the region's Barbary macaque troops (p342) are guaranteed to

Azrou

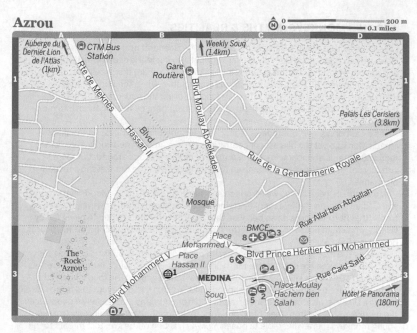

be found hanging out. But be prepared for the unpleasantness of seeing the macaques living in squalor: improper waste management has sadly turned the area into a dump and the monkeys have been conditioned to scavenge for food. Take Rte 13 from Azrou heading southeast, or it's a Dh100 grand-taxi round rip.

Opposite the picnic area, a broad space has been cleared and a museum about the region's cedar forests and industries built.

However, the opening has been delayed by drawn-out building concerns.

🏃 Activities

Monkey-spotting, horse riding (Dh200 per hour), mountain biking (Dh700 per day) and walking are popular pursuits in this area, but you may have to hire a mountain guide to facilitate these excursions.

Trails into the hills southeast of town can be reached on foot. From the centre of Azrou, ask for directions to the Sbab hammam, south of the medina. From here, take the road to the left of the hammam (alongside the men's entrance) and follow your nose uphill to the cemetery, which you should find on your left. The road will eventually peter out and be replaced by a pathway that follows the river and ascends into the mountains.

🛏 Sleeping

For its size, Azrou has a surprising number of sleeping options. Budget travellers are spoilt for choice, while it's more difficult to find decent midrange options. The most comfortable digs exist on the town's peripheries.

AZROU'S MONKEYS: MYTHS & REALITIES

Legend has it that Azrou's Barbary macaques are descended from an impish family who disrespected their hosts. One day the family went walking in the cedar forests, got lost and ran out of food. A charitable family invited them in to share their meal and, it being the day of prayers (Friday), it was couscous on the table. When the family had gorged themselves, they started to play with their food by rolling the couscous into balls to throw at each other. God was not happy and punished them by turning them into monkeys to run wild in the forests forever.

It's a cautionary tale, but today's reality is more sobering. Six thousand monkeys inhabit Morocco yet the biggest concentration is in this area of the Middle Atlas, where food and water is abundant. There are dozens of monkey troops around, but there's virtually nothing in the way of organised tourism to observe the monkeys in a responsible manner.

Most tourists head to two well-trodden spots just outside Azrou – Moudmame (p340) and Cedar Gouraud – where monkey sightings can be guaranteed. However, the two troops that hang out here do so because they have become habituated to being fed by visitors who claim not to know any better (though there are now educational info boards describing their plight).

Feeding the macaques causes them health problems, such as obesity, because the foods being offered are not suitable for their stomachs. Being around humans increases stress, and several are killed each year by cars due to begging on the road (though the authorities have recently reduced the speed limits in the park to prevent this from happening). Disease, also, can be transferred to and from humans – especially if people feed the monkeys straight from their hand or if they try to touch them. Feeding also makes young monkeys more vulnerable to poaching, which is one of the greatest threats to the species.

For more information on the macaques, visit the website of the Moroccan Primate Conservation Foundation (www.mpcfoundation.com).

Riad Azrou
GUESTHOUSE €

(☑ 06 61 06 42 42; www.riadazrou.com; Pl Moulay Hachem ben Saleh; s/d €30/35, without bathroom €25/30; ❄ ⏳) Azrou isn't awash with mid-range sleeping options but this budget riad offers a greater level of comfort and more amenities than its neighbours (reflected in the prices). En-suite rooms are large with decent bathrooms and traditional Berber furnishings; rooms with shared bathrooms are a little on the basic side for what you're paying. It's a family-run place with friendly staff.

Hôtel des Cèdres
HOTEL €

(☑ 0535 56 23 26; Pl Mohammed V; s/d Dh150/250; ⏳) Built in 1925, this hotel still has a hint of deco styling in its fixtures. In the past few years renovations have added en suite to every room, though they feel rather makeshift. Nevertheless, des Cèdres is good value. The downstairs square-fronting patio is a focal point for locals, and there's a good restaurant. Breakfast is Dh25 extra.

Hôtel le Panorama
HOTEL €

(☑ 0535 56 20 10; www.hotelpanorama.ma; Hay Ajelabe; s/d Dh283/348; ⏳) Built in a grand alpine-chalet style, this hotel most comfortable budget hotel. It's in a quiet wooded spot northeast of town (a very dark walk back at night!). Rooms are compact with balconies, but all are in need of a revamp. There are two bars in the hotel grounds, one of which is buzzing after dark. Breakfast is Dh36 extra.

Hôtel Salame
HOTEL €

(☑ 0535 56 25 62; salame_hotel@yahoo.fr; Pl Moulay Hachem ben Salah; s Dh80-120, d Dh160) Salame gets mixed reviews from travellers, but it's got charm and the staff are exceedingly helpful. Small, cute rooms are nicely presented with a smattering of traditional Berber decoration and shared bathrooms are kept constantly clean, with 24-hour hot showers. There's a functional roof terrace for washing clothes.

Hôtel Beau-Séjour
HOTEL €

(☑ 0535 56 06 92, 06 70 84 70 13; sadiki.tarik.40@gmail.com; 45 Pl Moulay Hachem ben Salah; s/d

Dh70/120, hot showers Dh10) Walls draped in Berber carpets (which are all for sale) welcome you into the 1st-floor reception of this decent budget option. Rooms are clean and simple, and a couple come with balconies overlooking the lively little square below. The roof terrace has good views across Azrou.

Auberge du Dernier Lion de l'Atlas
GUESTHOUSE €

(📞 0535 56 18 68; www.dernierlionatlas.ma; 16 Rte de Meknès; s/d Dh225/300; 🖥) A bit of a way from the centre of Azrou on the road to Meknès, this large orange villa has pleasant rooms and a smokey, *zellij*-covered Moroccan lounge area. If you're basing yourself in the Middle Atlas area, there's a good stash of tourist information at reception to help you find your feet.

🛏 Out Of Town

Camping Amazigh
CAMPGROUND €

(📞 0535 56 07 25, 0665 36 16 40; www.campinga-mazigh.com; Km 5, Rte d'Ifrane; camping per person D17, plus per tent/campervan Dh12/25, r in guesthouse Dh170) A delightfully rural campsite with very respectable bathrooms and hot-water showers. There's a small book exchange and communal area where you can hang out on chilly nights, and a slightly rundown kitchen with basic cooking facilities. There's also a simple lodge bedecked with Berber textiles. A log fire keeps things cosy in winter, but it can feel like an oven in summer. Campsite electricity costs Dh23 extra per night.

Les Jardins d'Azrou
GUESTHOUSE €€

(📞 0663 77 26 87; www.lesjardinsdazrou.com; Km 4 Afoud Douar Ait Ali, Rte d'Ifrane; s/d incl breakfast Dh450/550; 🅿) 🪴 The Swiss-Moroccan owners built this tranquil farm and guesthouse from scratch, installing solar panels and specialist equipment to harvest heat from the soil. What has been achieved is an exceedingly pleasant place to stay, with a peaceful patio fronting the farm and sublime views of Azrou's cedar forests from the bedrooms. Food, where possible, comes from the owners' farm or neighbouring gardens.

The farm is 1km down a dirt track just outside Azrou, but the owner is happy to ferry you to town and back should you need to go. Abdellah is also an official Middle Atlas mountain guide, making Jardins d'Azrou an ideal base for hikers.

Palais des Cerisiers
HOTEL €€€

(Rte du Cèdre Gorou btwn Azrou & Ifrane; s Dh765-965, d Dh930-1530, all incl breakfast; 🅿❄🖥❄) A smart upmarket choice, Cerisiers is surrounded by cherry blossoms in spring. Rooms are spacious with fridges and heating, plus there are free bikes, a spa, an elegant restaurant and a bar (nonguests welcome). The only downside is that it's 4km from Azrou and petite taxis from town won't come out here: this place is better suited to those with a car.

🍴 Eating & Drinking

The best cheap eats are found in three main areas – strung along Blvd Moulay Abdelkader south of the bus station, and clustered around Pl Hassan II and Pl Moulay Hachem ben Salah. You can find all the trusty favourites here – rotisserie chicken, brochettes and steaming bowls of *harira*.

If you're looking for an alcoholic drink in Azrou, Hotel le Panorama (p342) has two bars to choose from. Palais des Cerisiers (p343) offers a more upmarket setting for a drink, but it's a bit of drag to get to without a car.

Hôtel des Cèdres
MOROCCAN €

(📞 0535 56 23 26; Pl Mohammed V; mains from Dh50, menu of the day Dh100; ⏱11.30am-3pm; 7.30-10pm) Hôtel des Cèdres' restaurant is by far the best place to eat in Azrou. Inside there's a 1920s dining room and log fire; outside plaza-fronting terrace tables allow diners to sit cheek by jowl with the town's stalwart coffee-drinkers. The sustainable local trout is always good, plus there are some more unusual dishes such as rabbit tajine. Service is excellent.

Café Restaurant Bilal
CAFE €

(www.restaurant-bilal.com; Pl Mohammed V; sandwiches Dh15-25, mains Dh40-60; ⏱8am-10pm; 🖥) The streetside terrace at this cafe-restaurant is crammed with locals partaking in coffee and cake (the cafe doubles as a patisserie), but upstairs there's a quiet dining room that makes a good base for checking emails over a sandwich, tajine or pizza. Service is slow, but friendly.

🛍 Shopping

Ensemble Artisanal
ARTS & CRAFTS

(Blvd Mohammed V; ⏱10am-5pm Mon-Sat) This small artisan area has a few fixed-price shops and a number of craftsmen working on the premises, mostly carving the famous local cedar wood. You'll find it on the left as you enter through the grand cedar-wood door.

ℹ Information

Banks aren't hard to come by in Azrou and there are three ATMs around Pl Mohammed V.

BMCE (Pl Mohammed V; ⏱8.15am-4pm Mon-Fri) Includes a *Bureau de change.*

Pharmacie Sakhra (Pl Mohammed V; ⏱9.30am-1.30pm & 4-9pm Mon-Fri, 9.30am-1.30pm Sat)

Post Office (Blvd Prince Héritier Sidi Mohammed; ⏱8am-4.15pm Mon-Fri)

ℹ Getting There & Away

Azrou sits at a crossroads, with one axis heading northwest to southeast from Meknès to Er-Rachidia, and the other northeast to Fez and southwest to Marrakesh. Its location makes it a transport hub for the region and buses heading all over Morocco pass through here. There's no train station.

BUS

CTM (Blvd Hassan II) offers daily departures from its bus station on Blvd Hassan II to Casablanca (Dh130, six hours), Fez (Dh35, one hour), Marrakesh (Dh150, eight hours) and Meknès (Dh30, two hours).

Other cheaper companies leave from the **Gare Routière** (Blvd Moulay Abdelkader.) on Blvd Moulay Abdelkader. There are frequent daily departures to Fez (Dh20), Meknès (Dh20), Ifrane (Dh10), Marrakesh (Dh120), Midelt (Dh40 to Dh50) and Er-Rachidia (Dh80). Three buses a day run to Casablanca (Dh70 to Dh80).

TAXI

The grand-taxi lot is down a stepped path below the Gare Routière. Taxis go to Fez (Dh35, one hour), Meknès (Dh30, one hour), Khenifra (Dh35, one hour) and Ifrane (Dh9, 10 minutes), and less frequently to Midelt (Dh55, two hours). Those for 'Ain Leuh (Dh14, 30 minutes) wait beside the Shell petrol station on the main road out to the southwest (by the police station).

If you want a private taxi out of town, head to the grand-taxi rank behind the mosque, on Blvd Moulay Abdelkader.

Midelt   ميدلت

POP 55,304

Midelt sits in apple country between the Middle and the High Atlas and makes a handy break between Fez and the desert. Coming from the north, in particular, the landscape offers some breathtaking views, especially of the eastern High Atlas, which seem to rise out of nowhere.

Midelt consists of little more than one main street (Ave Mohammed V in the north, which becomes Ave Hassan II to the south), a modest souq and a number of oversized hotel-restaurants, which cater to the tourist buses whistling through on their way south. The town itself is of little interest to tourists, but it makes a good base for some off-*piste* exploring of the Jebel Ayachi region.

⊙ Sights

Kasbah Myriem   ARTS CENTRE

(Atelier de Tissages et Broderie; ☎06 64 44 73 75; ⏱8am-noon & 2-6pm Mon-Thu & Sat, 9-11am & 3-5pm Fri) If you're in the mood for carpets, this Kasbah-styled workshop, about 1.5km west of town, is worth a look. It helps Berber women develop their embroidery and weaving. The workshop provides looms and materials, as well as a simple place to work. Local girls – aged 15 or so – come here in order to learn these skills from more experienced women. Literacy lessons are also offered. Follow the signs from the main road, then enter behind the clinic.

Kasbah Myriem Monastery   MONASTERY

(⏱services 7.15am daily & 11am Sun) This monastery is home to a few Franciscan monks and the grounds are an interesting place to wander. Ring the bell at the big wooden doorway next to the Kasbah Myriem carpet centre to gain entry.

Apple Statue   LANDMARK

The lands around Midelt are apple-growing country, hence this oversized statue of an apple perched atop Midelt's main roundabout in the centre of town. It makes a good orientation point.

🛏 Sleeping & Eating

Central Midelt lacks decent hotels, and many of the more comfortable options are slightly further out – not that this is a problem for most visitors, who simply use Midelt as a stopover to break up the long journey south to the desert.

Most of the bigger hotels in and around Midelt have licensed restaurants.

Hôtel Atlas   HOTEL **€**

(☎0535 58 29 38; 3 Rue Mohammed el-Amraoui; s/d Dh60/120) It's a bit cramped and rough around the edges, but this pension's friendly family owners make up for its shortcomings. *Zellij* decoration adds character and there's a small home-run restaurant on-site (mains from Dh35). Rooms are predictably simple and some are without windows, but they're clean, as are the shared bathrooms with squat toilets (hot showers cost Dh10).

Hôtel Kasbah Asmaa
HOTEL €€

(☑ 0535 58 04 08; Rte Er-Rachidia; s/d/apt incl breakfast Dh400/550/950; P ❋ ☎ ☒) About 3km from central Midelt, this large kasbah-style hotel announces that you're on the road south. It has comfortable rooms and apartments, an inviting pool at the centre of the property and opulent common areas. Its lunchtime buffet is a favourite with tour groups, but there's also a licensed restaurant (ask for half-board discounts).

Riad Villa Midelt
GUESTHOUSE €€

(☑ 0535 36 08 51; www.hotel-riad-villa-midelt. com; 1 Pl Verte; s/d incl breakfast Dh450/600; P ❋ ☎ ☒) In a garden setting, this large 10-room suburban house offers spacious rooms, some with balconies. The biggest surprise is the lovely pool in a walled adjunct to the house. The friendly staff can whip up dinner for Dh150. The villa is well signposted from central Midelt and a petit taxi to/from the bus station costs Dh10.

Restaurant Adnane
FAST FOOD €

(Ave Hassan II; mains from Dh20; ⊙ 8am-12.30am; ☎) The leafy corner terrace at Adnane is a perfect spot for watching the world go by while you wait for a delicious plateful of rotisserie chicken. Here it's served with bread and olives, lentils, fragrant rice, herby tomato salad and tasty chicken gravy: possibly the best spread you'll find in any similar joint across Morocco. Staff are friendly, too.

Complexe Touristique Le Pin
MOROCCAN €€

(☑ 0535 58 35 50; Ave Hassan II; menu Dh70; ⊙ 8am-9pm; ☎ ♨) There's a faint air of neglect hanging about this large cafe-restaurant site but it still manages to draw in coach groups with its decent food, friendly service and pleasant garden. The restaurant is at the back to the left of the entrance and serves a *menu du jour* (Dh70) featuring a couple of tajines. It is open for breakfast, lunch and dinner.

ℹ️ Information

BMCI (Ave Hassan II; ⊙ 8.15am-4pm Mon-Fri) One of several banks with ATMs on this street.
Cyber Cafe (Ave Hassan II; per hr Dh5; ⊙ 10am-11pm)
Post Office (off Ave Hassan II; ⊙ 8am-4.15pm Mon-Fri, 8.30am-12.30pm)

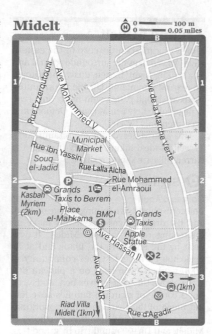

Midelt

🛏 **Sleeping**

🍴 **Eating**

ℹ️ Getting There & Away

The Gare Routière is 2km east of central Midelt and CTM buses run from here, too (mostly at night). There's an evening departure to Casablanca (Dh175, seven hours) via Rabat (Dh145, five hours), and to Rissani (Dh95, four hours) via Er-Rachidia (Dh50, two hours) and Erfoud (Dh80, 3½ hours). There are also night-time services for Azrou (Dh55, two hours), Meknès (Dh80, three hours) and Fez (Dh90, five hours).

Other buses cover the same routes at more sociable hours – Fez (Dh60, five hours) is serviced by four departures through the day.
Grands taxis to Azrou (Dh70, two hours), Er-Rachidia (Dh50, two hours), Meknès (Dh80, three hours) and Fez (Dh110, three hours) depart from a lot near the central Apple Statue off Ave Hassan II; **grands taxis to Berrem** (Dh6) depart from a different square off Ave Hassan II.

Around Midelt

Midelt's location on the cusp of the eastern High Atlas makes the surrounding rural areas a striking sight: barren, dusty and framed by rearing mountains. Off the main routes, roads are rough *pistes*, with many only really negotiable between May and October and even then only by 4WD.

This area is heaven for mountain bikers, as well as ideal hiking country (though the barren hills are short on shade).

⊙ Sights

Gorges d'Aouli   RUINS
The eerie ghost-town mining village of Aouli and the dramatic crevasse it fills make an interesting road trip from Midelt. It was built by the French in the 1930s and at its peak housed an industrious community of 6000 workers, who lived on a plateau 660 steps above the gorge's river bed. Today, all but a couple of guardian families have left, but much of the abandoned mine workings remain. It's a scenic 25km drive northeast of Midelt, and Dh400 round trip by grand taxi.

Before you reach the village of Aouli itself, stop off at *le galleries* – one of the locations where workers would have burrowed into the hills extensively for lead, copper and silver. The domed caverns, carved into hillocks, are just the type of place where you might expect to hear goblin drums rising out of the depths. They're difficult to find; look for a dirt track on your left, seemingly to nowhere, just after the start of the only village along the S317 coming from Midelt.

After *le galleries*, the road starts to deteriorate in places as you get deeper into the hills. Keep following the track and it'll be clear when you reach Aouli itself – note the open shafts, some halfway up the cliffside, the railway line that disappears 20km into the mountainside, and the furnaces. Continue along the road through the village and the road will eventually start to ascend, doubling back on itself to reach an abandoned mosque and hundreds of rows of crumbling workers' houses overlooking the gorge.

In total, it'll take at least two hours to get here and back from Midelt.

🏃 Activities

Cirque Jaffar   SCENIC DRIVE
The Cirque Jaffar winds through the foothills of Jebel Ayachi, 25km southwest of Midelt. It's a rough *piste*, and regular cars will grumble on the route in all seasons, but the dramatic crests of the Atlas are otherworldly driving companions. The highlight of this drive is a dramatic walk-through gorge. Ksar Timnay Inter-Cultures (p346) offers this circuit as a day tour.

Gorges des Berrem   HIKING
(Kasbah des Noyers) The village of Berrem, 6km west of Midelt and a Dh50/6 private/shared grand-taxi ride, is also known as the Kasbah des Noyers for its ancient walnut trees and makes a good starting point for a day hike to a scenic overlook of the Gorges des Berrem. Head to the village's colourful mosque and cross the bridge to join the thin trail. There's no shade.

🛏 Sleeping

Auberge Jaafar   HOTEL €
(☎0535 36 02 02; http://aubergejaafar.free.fr; Rte du Cirque de Jaafar & d'Imilchil, Berrem; s/d incl breakfast Dh300/350; ▣ ⌘) This petite, ramshackle kasbah-style complex is about 6km west of Midelt through peaceful apple orchards, just past the village of Berrem. Basic rooms of all shapes and sizes are set up around terraces and a blooming courtyard, and there's a raised pool (though it's seen better days). Note that it's not feasible to stay here unless you have your own car.

Ksar Timnay Inter-Cultures   RESORT €€
(☎0535 58 34 34; www.ksar-timnay.com; btwn Zaida & Midelt; s/d incl breakfast Dh320/450, Riad Mimouna Dh450/550; ▣ ✳ ⌂ ⌘) On the dusty highway 20km north of Midelt, this kasbah hotel-motel sits in large leafy grounds and offers a wide range of accommodation from rooms to family apartments, as well as camping and caravanning. Rooms are large and comfortable enough; those in fancier Riad Mimouna aren't a whole lot nicer than the standard rooms. The restaurant is poor.

The owners are passionate about the region and offer excursions at Dh300 per person per day, as well as trekking to Jebel Masker (3265m) and Jebel Ayachi (3737m). The snag is that all of its trips are a minimum of four people – and the hotel rarely gets busy enough to put together a group of that size.

ⓘ Getting There & Away

Public transport only runs between populated areas so, for example, you'll be able to catch a shared grand taxi to Berrem from Midelt, but not to Gorges d'Aouli.

Once you're off the main highway the roads around Midelt are bad. This means seemingly short trips can take longer than you'd think, which can also push up the costs if you need to hire a grand taxi. Expect to pay about Dh500 for half-day hire.

Ksar Timnay Inter-Cultures (p346), north of Midelt, will rent you a 4WD (with driver) for around Dh1200 – good value if there's a group of you.

Taza

POP 148,456

Taza fulfils all the criteria of a sleepy provincial centre and if it weren't for the deep caves and empty trails on its doorstep, it probably wouldn't be worth stopping by. In town, climb the impressive restored fortifications up to Taza Haute, the walled medina, for panoramic views of the Rif to the north and the Middle Atlas to the south. Then head out to explore the eastern Middle Atlas, including Gouffre du Friouato (one of the most incredible open caverns in the world) and Tazekka National Park.

Taza is divided neatly in two: the ville nouvelle (also called Taza Bas, or Lower Taza), centred on Pl de l'Indépendance, and the walled medina (Taza Haute), occupying the hill 2km to the south. The unremarkable ville nouvelle is of little interest to visitors but this is where most of the accommodation is, along with the bus and train stations.

History

The fortified citadel of Taza is built on the edge of an escarpment overlooking the only feasible pass between the Rif Mountains and the Middle Atlas. It has been important throughout Morocco's history as a garrison town from which to exert control over the country's eastern extremities.

The Tizi n'Touahar, as the pass is known, was the traditional invasion route for armies moving west from Tunisia and Algeria. This is, in fact, where the Romans and the Arabs entered Morocco. The town itself was the base from which the Almohads, Merenids and Alawites swept to conquer lowland Morocco and establish their dynasties.

All Moroccan sultans had a hand in fortifying Taza. Nevertheless, their control over the area was always tenuous because the fiercely independent and rebellious local tribes continually exploited any weakness

in the central power in order to overrun the city. Never was this more so than in the first years of the 20th century, when 'El-Rogui' (Pretender to the Sultan's Throne) Bou Hamra held sway over most of northeastern Morocco.

The French occupied Taza in 1914 and made it the main base from which they fought the prolonged rebellion by the tribes of the Rif Mountains and Middle Atlas.

◉ Sights

Medina Walls HISTORIC SITE

The impressive restored medina walls, around 3km in circumference, are a legacy from when Taza served briefly as the Almohad capital in the 12th century. The two most interesting sections are the crumbling bastion, and the Bab er-Rih. The outer road that leads to Bab er-Rih is also interesting for its richly decorated doorways and windows high up in the walls, guarded by old, carved cedar screens.

➡ **Bab er-Rih** VIEWPOINT

(Gate of the Wind) The most interesting section of Taza Haute's fortified wall is around Bab er-Rih, from where there are superb views over the surrounding countryside. Look southwest to the wooded slopes of Jebel Tazzeka in the Middle Atlas, and then to the Rif in the north, and it's easy to see the strategic significance of Taza's location. Two tranquil cafes with mountain views sit opposite this section of the wall.

➡ **Bastion** VIEWPOINT

Taza Haute's bastion, where the medina walls jut out to the east, was added in the 12th-century fortifications 400 years later by the Saadians, but it's not been restored so you'd be forgiven for thinking it the oldest part. Duck under the archway just before Pl de la Resistance to see how it is being used today: as a grain store.

Grande Mosquée MOSQUE

Not far from Bab er-Rih, and visible over the top of the houses, is the Grande Mosquée, which the Almohads began building in 1135; the Merenids added to it in the 13th century. Non-Muslims are not allowed to enter, and it's difficult to get much of an impression from the outside of the building. From here the main thoroughfare wriggles its way southeast to the far end of the medina.

Taza Haute

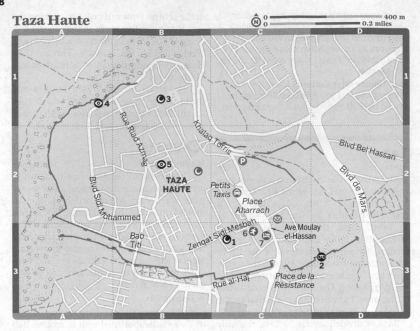

Taza Haute

⊙ Sights

1 Andalous Mosque C3
  Bab er-Rih ....(see 4)
2 Bastion D3
3 Grande Mosquée B1
4 Medina Walls A1
5 Souqs B2

⊕ Activities, Courses & Tours

6 Hammam C3

⬛ Sleeping

7 Hôtel de l'Étoile C3

Andalous Mosque   MOSQUE

The main street into the medina off Pl Aharrach stretches past hole-in-the-wall bakeries before reaching this mosque, constructed in the 12th century. There is no sign and from within the medina it's difficult to tell it's a mosque; look for the two green mosaic doors, where men and women enter separately. Non-Muslims cannot enter.

Souqs   MARKET

The souqs and *qissaria* (covered market) are at the heart of Taza's medina, offering food stuffs and domestic goods. The *qissaria* glitters with jewellery, and also sells clothes.

🏃 Activities

Hammam   HAMMAM

(off Zenqat Sidi Mesbah; Dh12.50; ☺men 5am-noon & 7pm-midnight, women noon-7pm) Just off Pl Aharrach, around the back of the Hotel de l'Etoile, this local hammam is a good place to scrub away the cares of the road.

🏃 Around Taza

★ Gouffre du Friouato   CAVE

(☎ 06 68 57 61 94, 06 66 01 47 90; Dh5, guide Dh200, protective clothing & headlamp Dh50; ☺8am-6pm) At over 20m wide and 230m deep, the Gouffre du Friouato is said to be the deepest cavern in North Africa, and the cave system is possibly the most extensive. In 2016 a section of the roof collapsed, killing some schoolchildren, and at the time of writing the caves were still closed – ask in Taza before heading out here. A return grand taxi from Taza Haute costs Dh200 upwards – depending on how much time you want in the caves.

Gouffre du Friouato is well signposted, up a very steep road 25km from Taza. It was first investigated in 1935 and access is via 520 precipitous steps (with handrails) that lead you to the floor of the cavern. It's a strenuous climb back up. At the bottom, you can squeeze through a hole to start exploring the fascinating chambers that are found 200 more steps below. It's dark and eerily beautiful: wear clothes you don't mind dirtying.

The most spectacular chambers, full of extraordinary formations, are the Salle de Lixus and the Salle de Draperies. They do indeed resemble thin sheets of curtains, frozen and calcified. Allow at least three hours there and back. Speleologists have explored to a depth of 300m, but they believe there are more caves another 500m below.

The admission fee allows you to enter the cavern mouth at a depth of 160m. Beyond that, a guide is needed to go further underground to the grandest chambers. Bank on the occasional scramble, and squeezes through narrow sections; not recommended for claustrophobes. Overalls, nonslip overshoes and a helmet with lamp must be rented.

Tazekka National Park   HIKING

Stands of cork oak and gently rising hills make the terrain of Tazekka National Park a joy to hike through, yet it flies under the radar of most visitors to Morocco. The small park was designated in 1950 and unfurls for 137 sq km southwest of Taza, bordering the Gouffre du Friouato. Its competent Tourist Information Office (p350), at Bab Bou-Idir, promotes numerous hikes through information boards and maps; walks range from a 1.4km stroll to a serious 17km day trek.

North African Barbary deer were introduced to the park 20 years ago with great success, and other fauna such as wild pigs, Barbary squirrels and bats proliferate here, as well as dozens of bird species.

Shared grands taxis to Bab Bou-Idir (Dh13) are frequent in July and August (when its summer chalets and camping are open), but at other times of year you'll most likely have to hire a grand taxi privately to get out here (Dh78).

Jebel Tazekka Circuit   SCENIC DRIVE

This scenic driving route loops around Tazekka National Park along twisty mountain roads, but it's quite an expensive day trip if you don't have your own car: expect to pay Dh600 for a grand taxi. The route passes the Cascades de Ras el-Oued (though they virtually dry up in summer), the Gouffre du Friouato, Bab Bou-Idir and the gorges of Oued Zireg.

🛌 Sleeping

Taza has only a handful of hotels, mostly in the ville nouvelle, and the amount of business they do can be gauged by the general readiness to offer discounts if you stay more than a night.

Grand Hôtel du Dauphiné   HOTEL €

(☎ 0535 67 35 67; Pl de l'Indépendance; s/d Dh185/290) Ideally located on the ville nouvelle's main square, the Dauphiné is good value in the budget category but suffers from noisy plumbing and a noisy downstairs bar. Rooms are decent if unexciting, and all benefit from small balconies. On the ground floor there's also a restaurant (p350). A fair option if you decide to stay in the ville nouvelle.

Hôtel de l'Étoile   HOTEL €

(☎ 0535 27 01 79; 39 Ave Moulay el-Hassan; s/d without bathroom Dh60/100) This cheapie on the cusp of Pl Aharrach is easy to miss (the sign is hidden under the arcaded front), but inside the strawberry-pink paint job is hard to escape. Friendly enough, it's as basic as the tariff suggests, with shared showers (Dh10 extra) and a mix of Western and drop toilets. Rooms open onto a pleasant courtyard and all have sinks.

Hôtel La Tour Eiffel   HOTEL €€

(☎ 0535 67 15 62; tourazhar@hotmail.com; Blvd Bir Anzarane; s/d Dh330/417; ❄ 🛜) Stuck on the road out of town heading towards Oujda, the Tour Eiffel is named for its high aspirations. Past the cramped lobby, a lift swishes you up to well-sized and fairly comfy rooms with TVs and fridges, many with great views out towards the mountains. Breakfast is an extra Dh42, and there's an in-house restaurant.

🍴 Eating & Drinking

Taza Haute has the usual selection of kebab-touting snack stalls and coffee-touting cafes around the main square, Pl Aharrach. In the ville nouvelle, the streets fanning out from Pl de l'Indépendance (particularly Ave Mohammed V and Ave Moulay Youssef) are lined with restaurants and patisseries.

There's a hopping bar attached to the Grand Hôtel du Dauphiné (p349) in the ville nouvelle (look for the terrace cafe with mirrored windows).

Taza Ville Nouvelle

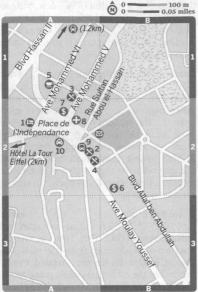

La Casa
MOROCCAN €

(Ave Mohammed V; sandwiches from Dh10; ⊘5am-10pm; 📶) One of a rash of modern places that look quite out of place in sleepy Taza; there's a cafe at the front with pavement seating and a dimly lit restaurant at the back. It does the usual paninis and *shwarma,* as well as unexpectedly delicious pizzas. Breakfast and ice cream are also served (though not at the same time!).

Mou Mou
FAST FOOD €

(Ave Moulay Youssef; mains from Dh30; ⊘11.30am-midnight) Come night-time, happy customers – including lots of families and women – spill out the door of this packed-out corner joint with Moroccan music joyously blaring out. Tasty fast food is the order of the day here: kebabs, paninis and pizzas, including one topped with *merguez* (spicy North African lamb sausage). Juices are also good.

Café Amsterdam
BAKERY €

(Ave Moulay Youssef; pastries from Dh2; ⊘6am-10pm; 📶) Follow your nose to the piles of freshly baked savoury and sweet pastries, croissants and breads at Café Amsterdam, where a steady stream of locals file in and out to collect daily packages. This is a great breakfast stop, with a welcoming interior and a smattering of pavement seating.

Grand Hôtel du Dauphiné
MOROCCAN €€

(📋0535 67 35 67; Pl de l'Indépendance; meals Dh80; ⊘7-10pm) On the ground floor of the hotel, the Dauphiné serves up the usual range of Moroccan standards, plus a handful of Continental dishes. The dining room is utterly lifeless; alcohol is served.

Café la Joconda
CAFE

(Ave Mohammed VI; ⊘6.30am-10pm) A modern cafe with plenty of pavement seating, and one that's not threatened by the concept of female customers – though don't expect to see any here.

ℹ Information

Attijariwafa Bank (Ave Moulay Youseff; ⊘8.15am-3.45pm Mon-Fri) Has an ATM.

BMCI (Pl de l'Indépendance; ⊘8.15am-4pm Mon-Fri) Has an ATM.

Cyber Friwato (Ave Mohammed VI; per hr Dh4; ⊘8am-midnight)

Main Post Office (Pl de l'Indépendance; ⊘8am-4.15pm Mon-Fri & 8.30-12pm Sat)

Pharmacy Centrale (Pl de l'Indépendance; ⊘9am-1pm & 3-7.30pm Mon-Fri, 9am-1pm Sat) On the main square in the ville nouvelle.

Post Office (Ave Moulay el-Hassan; ⊘8am-4.15pm Mon-Fri) In the medina.

Tazekka National Park Information Office (📋0535 28 00 96, 06 61 04 72 92; www.tazekka.com; Bab Bou-Idir; ⊘8am-6pm Sat & Sun) is located at Bab Bou-Idir, a summer holiday camp 30km southwest of Taza. It's not open during the week but if you desperately want to speak to somebody, call the office and they may come down and meet you. The most useful information boards with maps are outside the office, so are still accessible when it's closed.

Getting There & Away

BUS

Few buses actually originate in Taza, but plenty pass through on their way between Oujda and points west of Taza such as Fez, Tangier and Casablanca, as well as to the coast.

The **CTM office** (☎ 0535 28 20 07; Pl de l'Indépendance; ⏲ 24hr), which doubles as the bus stop, is located in the ville nouvelle. Buses run to Casablanca (Dh155, seven hours), Fez (Dh45 to Dh50, two to 2½ hours), Meknès (Dh70 to Dh80, 2½ to 3½ hours), Rabat (Dh125, five hours), Oujda (Dh75, three hours) and Nador (Dh70, 2½ to three hours).

The Gare Routière is on Blvd Bir Anzarane – the same road the train station is just off – but frequent CTM and train services to/from Taza mean you're unlikely to need it.

TAXI

Grands taxis to the attractions around Taza depart from a dusty lot just north of the medina in an area called Kocha. A return trip to the Gouffre du Friouato costs Dh200, including wait time (more if you want to spend the whole day exploring the site).

TRAIN

Taza's location on the train line makes rail the best transport option. Six trains a day run to Fez (Dh59, two hours), Rabat (Dh117, 5½ hours) and Casablanca (Dh215, 6½ hours), and there are seven daily trains to Meknès (Dh87, three hours). There is one direct train to Tangier (Dh148, seven hours), and three changing at Sidi Kacem or Fez. Several of the other trains noted here also involve a change in Fez (check online for details; www.oncf-voyages.ma). In the opposite direction, three trains go to Oujda (Dh117, 3½ hours).

Note there is no snack bar or shop to buy water from at the train station.

Getting Around

Sky-blue petits taxis (Dh5 to Dh7) run regularly between the **ville nouvelle** (Pl de l'Indépendance) and **Taza Haute** (Pl Aharrach).

Southern Morocco & Western Sahara
جنوب المغرب والصحراء الغربية

Best Places to Eat

→ Nomad (p393)

→ Pure Passion (p359)

→ Cafe Mouja (p365)

→ À l'Ombre du Figuier (p386)

→ Casa Lola (p405)

Best Places to Sleep

→ Amouage (p365)

→ Logis La Marine (p391)

→ Ryad Tafilag (p369)

→ El Malara (p377)

→ Lunar Surf House (p363)

Why Go?

The Souss Valley, where goats climb argan trees beneath the sun-baked Anti Atlas, draws a line across Morocco. South of this fertile valley, the pace of life in mountain villages and Saharan gateways is seductively slow.

A sense of somewhere really fresh and undiscovered gusts through the region like the spring winds – and you'll want to savour it. On elegantly wrecked seafronts, sip a mint tea and gaze at the wild Atlantic Coast. When trekking, mountain biking or driving through wrinkled Anti Atlas foothills, stop before the next oasis village and appreciate the silence.

The locals, from Chleuh Berbers in the Souss to Western Sahara's Saharawi people, seem determined to complement the landscapes. Their light robes flutter under desert skies, and their dark herds dot rocky hillsides.

Continue even further south to Dakhla for some of the world's best kitesurfing, and an emerging scene for outdoor activities and desert exploration.

When to Go

Agadir

Feb Trek the Anti Atlas and hit the Atlantic Coast for winter sun and surf.

Mar See almond trees blossom, celebrated by Tafraoute's harvest festival.

Nov Catch Taliouine's saffron festival and Immouzzer des Ida Outanane's olive harvest.

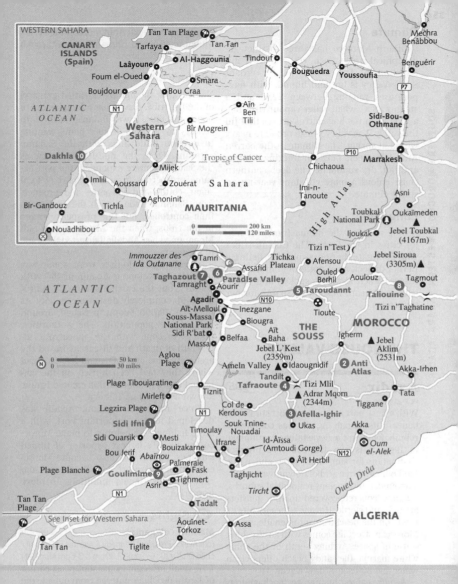

Southern Morocco & Western Sahara Highlights

1 Stroll past art-deco relics in seaside **Sidi Ifni** (p390)

2 Trek, drive or cycle through the **Anti Atlas** (p374)

3 Explore green *palmeraies* at **Afella-Ighir** (p377)

4 Visit traditional Berber houses and cycle around **Tafraoute** (p374)

5 Hit the medina souq in the bustling trading centre of **Taroudannt** (p366)

6 Meander up the accessible part of the western High Atlas at **Paradise Valley** (p365)

7 Hang loose in Morocco's premier surf spot, **Taghazout** (p364)

8 Taste saffron and argan oil in **Taliouine** (p372)

9 Put your feet up on the Sahara's fringes in the *palmeraie* accommodation around **Goulimime** (p395)

10 Sail, windsurf or kiteboard on the expansive lagoon at **Dakhla** (p402)

Climate

Southern Morocco has three distinct geographical areas, each with its own micro-climate. The semitropical, verdant Souss Valley is hot and humid, with temperatures ranging between 22°C and a steamy 38°C, when water vapour rises like a mist from the huge citrus groves that fill the valley. The valley is also prone to heavy winds in spring. The climate of the barren Anti Atlas veers between freezing winters and hot, dry summers. The deep southern coast enjoys a more constant year-round sunny climate.

Language

Arabic remains the lingua franca of major cities in the south. The Chleuh tribes who dominate the Souss speak Tashelhit, a Berber dialect, most noticeable in the Anti Atlas. French is widely spoken and Spanish is still heard in some of Spain's former territories.

THE SOUSS VALLEY

Agadir   اكادير

POP 679,000

With a busy port and beach resort sprawling beneath its kasbah, Agadir was completely rebuilt following a devastating earthquake in 1960. It is now the country's premier destination for sun, sand, pubs and pizza. Laid out as a large grid of downtown streets, surrounded by spacious residential suburbs, Agadir's concrete-covered inland quarters are ugly and sterile. However, the city hits its stride on the beachfront promenade, where Moroccan street life comes with a refreshing sense of space. Arching south of the shiny white marina, the sandy beach offers clean water and 300 sunny days a year.

Agadir caters mainly to package-tour holidaymakers, and will appeal less to independent travellers. Families will also enjoy relaxing on the beach and wandering around the handful of sights. If you do not have children in tow, however, we recommend heading elsewhere to make the most of a visit to Morocco.

The city spreads over a large area, both along the coast and inland from the huge swath of beach. From the northern end of the beach, near the marina and port, three parallel streets – 20 Août, nearest the ocean, Mohammed V and Hassan II – run through the main tourist area.

History

Named after the *agadir* (fortified granary) of the Irir tribe, Agadir has a long history of boom and bust. It was founded in the 15th century by Portuguese merchants wanting to develop trade links with the Saharan caravans. From the mid-16th century, as the Saadian empire expanded, the port became prosperous from the export of local sugar, cotton and saltpetre, and products from Saharan trade, which the Moroccans then controlled. But this prosperity ended in the 1760s, when the Alawite Sultan Sidi Mohammed ben Abdallah diverted the trade to Essaouira.

The French colonists went some way towards redeveloping Agadir in the 20th century, but the earthquake on 29 February 1960 completely destroyed the city. As many as 18,000 people perished, around half of the population. The authorities, unable to cope with the apocalyptic aftermath of death and disease, sprayed the area with lime and DDT, and left the dead where they had been buried, in the collapsed city. The mound this created is now known as Ancienne Talborjt.

Since its reconstruction, Agadir has developed into an important port, with a large fishing fleet helping to make Morocco the world's largest exporter of tinned sardines. Agadir has also become Morocco's top beach resort, and the luxury marina complex signals ambitions to move upmarket.

◉ Sights

Mémoire d'Agadir   MUSEUM
(cnr Ave du Président Kennedy & Ave des FAR; adult/child Dh20/10; ⊙9am-12.30pm & 3-6pm Mon-Sat)
This small museum in the southwest corner of Jardin de Olhão, entered from outside the park, is dedicated to the 1960 earthquake. Displays include interesting photos of Agadir since the 1920s, while others show the effects of the quake.

Jardin de Olhão   PARK
(Ave du Président Kennedy; ⊙2-6pm Tue-Sun)
FREE A cool, relaxing garden created in 1992 to mark the twinning of Agadir with the Portuguese town of Olhão.

Agadir

Map scale: 0 — 400 m / 0 — 0.2 miles

Labels on map:
- Ancienne Talborjt (290m)
- Blvd Hassan II
- Carrefour (60m)
- CTM
- Musée de l'Argan (350m)
- Jardin de Olhão
- NOUVEAU TALBORJT
- Ave des FAR
- Ave du Président Kennedy
- Place Lahcen Tamri
- Pharmacie du Talborjt
- Supratours
- Rue des Oranges
- Car Hire Agencies
- Ave du Général Kettani
- Car Hire Agencies
- ONMT (350m)
- Rue Chinguit
- Ave du Prince Moulay Abdallah
- Ave du 29 Février
- Clinique al-Massira
- Rue al-Jazouli
- Jardin ibn Zaidoun
- Rue de Marrakesh
- Rue de la Foire
- Rue 18 Novembre
- Car Hire Agencies
- Riad Les Chtis D'Agadir (110m)
- Tourist Police (200m);
- Jour et Nuit (280m);
- Pistachios (350m);
- Club Royal de Jet-Ski (580m);
- Havana (900m);
- Les Blancs (900m)
- Passage Aït Souss
- Stadium
- Blvd Hassan II
- Rue de Fès
- Rue Oued Souss
- Ave Mohammed V
- ATLANTIC OCEAN
- Blvd du 20 Août
- Le Sò (450m)
- Gare Routière (2km); Inezgane (13km); Al-Massira (28km)

Agadir

◉ Sights
1 Jardin de Olhão	C1
2 Mémoire d'Agadir	C1
3 Musée du Patrimoine Amazigh	C3
4 Vallée des Oiseaux	B2

◈ Activities, Courses & Tours
5 Palm Beach	A4
6 Petit Train d'Agadir	A3
7 Sunset Beach	A3

⊟ Sleeping
8 Hotel Atlantic	C2
9 Hotel Clichy	C1
10 Hôtel Kamal	B2
11 Hôtel Petite Suède	A1
12 Hotel Sindibad	D1
13 Hôtel Tiznine	C1
14 Kenzi Europa	A3
15 Royal Atlas	A3
16 Studiotel Afoud	C3

⊗ Eating
17 Côte Court	C3
18 Daffy	B1
Dolce & Caffe	(see 10)
19 K Moon	B1
20 La Scala	B4
21 La Siciliana	B2
22 Le P'tit Dôme	B4
Marché Central	(see 33)
23 Mezzo Mezzo	C3
24 Snack Stands	D1
25 Tafarnout	C3

⊙ Drinking & Nightlife
26 Cafe III	C3
27 English Pub	B3
28 La Verandah	C2
29 Orange Café	B1
30 Papa Gayo	B4

⊞ Shopping
31 Al Mouggar Bookshop	C2
32 Ensemble Artisanal	D1
33 Marché Central	B1
34 Tafoukt Souq	A3

Musée du Patrimoine Amazigh
MUSEUM

(☑ 0528 82 16 32; Passage Aït Souss; adult/child Dh10/5; ⊙ 9.30am-12.30pm & 2-5.30pm Mon-Sat) With an excellent display of Berber artefacts, especially jewellery, the museum is a great place to learn about the traditional life and culture of the region's Berber people.

Vallée des Oiseaux
PARK

(Valley of the Birds; ⊙ 11am-6pm) FREE A leafy city-centre retreat in the dry riverbed running down from Blvd Hassan II to Blvd du 20 Août, with a shaded children's playground, an aviary and a small zoo. It's also a handy – and more scenic – way to walk to the beach area from the centre of town.

Kasbah
HISTORIC SITE

(off Ave al-Moun) Offering superb views and 7km northwest of the centre, the hilltop kasbah is a rare survivor of the 1960 earthquake. Built in 1541 and restored in the 1740s, the area once housed 300 people. All that remains is the outer wall, though traces of the dwellings can still be made out. The inscription over the entry arch in Dutch and Arabic ('Believe in God and respect the King') is a reminder of the beginning of trade with the Low Countries.

The walk up to the kasbah is long, hot and uncomfortable: get a taxi (about Dh30) and walk back down.

Ancienne Talborjt
HISTORIC SITE

(off Ave al-Moun) The grassy area below the kasbah covers the remains of old Agadir town and constitutes a mass grave for all those who died in the 1960 earthquake.

Marina
AREA

(☑ 0661 21 57 46; www.portmarinaagadir.com; off Ave Mohammed V) The city's most modern attraction is a billion-dirham pleasure port between the beach and commercial port. As well as mooring for your floating gin palace, the complex of faux white kasbahs has holiday apartments, shops (mostly international brands), cafes, restaurants and boat trips for groups.

🏄 Beaches

Agadir's glory is its crescent beach, which usually remains unruffled when the Atlantic winds are blustering elsewhere. It's clean and well maintained, spotlit at night and patrolled by lifeguards and police during peak periods (mid-June to mid-September). There is a strong undertow.

The beach is mostly hassle-free, but single females or families will have a more relaxed time at one of the private beaches near the marina, or in front of the big hotels around **Sunset Beach** and **Palm Beach** (deckchair & umbrella DH30). Facilities include showers, toilets and children's' play areas; deckchairs and umbrellas can be hired.

The shops on the promenade just south of the marina sell bodyboards for about Dh130. Many larger beach hotels and surf clubs rent out windsurfing equipment, jet skis, bodyboards and surfboards.

At sunset and into the evening, Agadir's activity of choice is strolling along the promenade that runs runs south from the marina.

🏃 Activities

Club Royal de Jet-Ski
WATER SPORTS

(☑ 0665 95 24 35; www.agadiradventure.com) Offers jet-skiing and flyboarding on the beach near the marina. Quad bike and ATV trips on nearby beaches can also be booked.

Musée de l'Argan
HAMMAM

(☑ 0528 84 87 82; www.lemuseedelargan.com; Ave Moulay Youssef; hammam & scrub Dh150; ⊙ 10am-9pm) Geared towards tourists, this unisex hammam offers massages and argan-based treatments.

👉 Tours

Local tour operators can arrange day trips to destinations including Taroudant, Paradise Valley and Essaouira.

Petit Train d'Agadir
TOUR

(Blvd du 20 Août; adult/child Dh18/12; ⊙ every 40min from 9.15am) This chain of buggies snakes around the city centre and along the beach for 35 minutes.

✨ Festivals & Events

Festival Timitar
MUSIC

(www.festivaltimitar.ma; ⊙ Jul) Festival Timitar attracts Moroccan and international musicians and DJs to Agadir every July. Expect an eclectic world-music focus and visiting acts from other parts of Africa.

Concert for Tolerance
MUSIC

(⊙ Oct) Agadir's annual Concert for Tolerance takes place on the northern end of the beach in October. The concert's diverse program of DJs, dance music and local rap is wildly popular with Agadir's younger residents.

🛏 Sleeping

Agadir targets midrange and top-end visitors but away from the beach are more affordable options. Booking ahead is recommended for Easter, summer and Christmas/New Year.

Luxury beachfront hotels and resorts runs south of the centre on Rue Oued Souss and Chemin des Dunes, and riads and kasbahs are found inland of Agadir or to the south en route to Inezgane.

🛏 Centre & Seafront

Riad Les Chtis D'Agadir GUESTHOUSE €
(☑0528 82 19 96; www.maisondhoteschtis agadir.com; 27 Rue Houmane El Fetouaki; s/d incl breakfast from Dh330/429; 🖃) Located in a quiet residential neighbourhood, this family-owned guesthouse has colourful if compact rooms opening onto a pleasant central courtyard. Not much English is spoken by the French-expat owners, but they're friendly and eager to please. Breakfast is taken at a shared table with other guests, and this homely spot is a refreshing alternative to Agadir's lookalike hotels.

Hôtel Petite Suède HOTEL €
(☑0528 84 07 79; www.petitesuede.com; cnr Blvd Hassan II & Ave du Général Kettani; s/d incl breakfast Dh190/325; 🖃) Readers recommend this simple but perfectly located hotel, five minutes' walk from the beach, with good service and a roof terrace for breakfast and ocean views. It's one of Agadir's more Moroccan-styled hotels, with an attractive, rug-scattered interior.

Kenzi Europa HOTEL €€
(☑0528 82 12 12; www.kenzi-hotels.com; Blvd du 20 Août; r from Dh600; 🕸🖃🏊) This Kenzi hotel is about the most stylish and restrained thing in tacky Agadir. Curvy lampshades and flat surfaces abound in the calm, minimal rooms; facilities include a spa, a restaurant and a bar; and a band tinkles away in the lobby. Only the plastic octopus and dolphins in the children's pool detract from the overall smoothness. Specials are offered online.

Hotel Atlantic HOTEL €€
(☑0528 84 36 61; www.atlantichotelagadir.com; off Blvd Hassan II; s/d incl breakfast Dh550/700; 🕸🖃🏊) The three-star Atlantic is one of the best deals in Agadir, offering comfortable rooms and, in the cool and breezy reception, professional service. It has a spa, a lovely little pool, and tours on offer.

Studiotel Afoud APARTMENT €€
(☑0528 84 39 99; www.studiotel-afoud.com; Rue de la Foire; apt from Dh800; 🕸🖃🏊) If you would like to self-cater, these studios are simple but pleasant, each featuring a kitchen with hob and fridge, and a balcony overlooking the peeling neighbouring buildings. On the ground floor there's a restaurant, a grocery booth and a bookcase of paperback novels.

Hôtel Kamal HOTEL €€
(☑0528 84 28 17; www.hotel-kamal.com; Blvd Hassan II; s/d Dh404/465; 🖃🏊) A popular and well-run downtown hotel in a white block overlooking Pl de L'Esperance, the Kamal manages to appeal to a range of clients, from package-tourists to travelling Moroccans. Rooms are tired, but the staff are helpful, the pool is large enough to swim laps in, and there is a bar.

Royal Atlas HOTEL €€€
(☑0528 29 40 40; www.hotelsatlas.com; Blvd du 20 Août; s/d incl breakfast Dh1428/1657; 🕸@🖃🏊) This beachfront colossus ticks all the five-star boxes with a Moroccan flourish. Carpets and antiques dot the tiled floors leading to the palm-fringed bar and pool area, and the 350 rooms and suites. Facilities include a nightclub, a gym, Daniel Jouvance spa, a private beach, Italian and Moroccan restaurants, and all the extras you would expect.

🛏 Nouveau Talborjt

The best area for budget options is away from the ocean in Nouveau Talborjt, where there are three budget hotels on Pl Lahcen Tamri. The all-night bus activity ensures that most hotel receptions here are open 24 hours; the area is a little seedy.

Hotel Clichy HOTEL €
(☑0528 84 42 00; contact@hotelclichy.ma; 48 Ave du President Kennedy; s/d Dh230/270) The rooms certainly aren't as flash as the over-the-top tiled reception, but a recent makeover has definitely resurrected this midrange hotel on the edge of the Nouveau Talborjt neighbourhood. Bathrooms are especially spick and span, and the modern and shiny downstairs terrace cafe is popular with Agadir locals. Ask for a rear room to minimise occasional traffic noise.

Hotel Sindibad   HOTEL €
(☎0528 82 34 77; sinhot@menara.ma; Pl Lachen Tamri; s/d Dh300/350; ❋🛜🌊) This blue-and-white building has compact en-suite rooms, and the star attraction is the hotel's pint-sized rooftop pool. New downstairs rooms facing an expansive square are good value.

Hôtel Tiznine   HOTEL €
(☎0528 84 39 25; 3 Rue Drarga; s/d without bathroom Dh100/150, with shower Dh120/150; 🛜) A dozen good-sized rooms surround a green-and-white tiled flowering courtyard. Some rooms have bathrooms but most share facilities.

🏠 Out Of Town

⭐ **Atlas Kasbah**   BOUTIQUE HOTEL €€
(☎0661 48 85 04; www.atlaskasbah.com; Rte d'Azrarag, Tighanimine El Baz; r/ste incl breakfast from Dh880/1650; 🛜❋🌊) Located on a spectacular hilltop 15km inland from Agadir, the 11 rooms and suites in this Berber-style fortress are the ideal overnight haven after partaking in Atlas Kasbah's busy menu of ecofriendly and cultural activities. Guests can indulge in hammam and massage treatments, learn about Moroccan cuisine and crafts, or go hiking or donkey riding to nearby Berber villages.

The team behind Atlas Kasbah is strongly focused on sustainable practices and has won awards for its responsible approach to tourism.

⭐ **Paradis Nomade**   BOUTIQUE HOTEL €€
(☎0671 12 15 35; www.paradis-nomade.com; Douar Azarag; s/d incl breakfast from Dh405/590, tents per person Dh155; @🛜🌊) Located in pleasant rural surroundings around 15km from Agadir, Paradis Nomade combines

---

SELF-CATERING
··
For beach lunches and road journeys stock up here:

Carrefour (Rue Yacoub El Mansour; ⊙9am-10pm) The biggest and best supermarket in central Agadir. Handy for picnic fixings if you're heading to the surf beaches north of Agadir or inland to Paradise Valley.

Marché Central (off Blvd Hassan II; ⊙8am-4pm Mon-Sat) Has a fresh food market on the ground floor.

---

very impressive suites, smaller but still comfortable rooms, and the option of staying in Berber-style tents. A Berber ambience is also carried through to the best of the rooms, and the garden surroundings are enlivened with a compact swimming pool and a spacious restaurant and bar area.

🍴 Eating

There's a great choice of cafes and patisseries, where you can start the day with coffee and pastries or recover from the rigours of the beach. Some restaurants in Agadir are licensed, and the city's beachfront promenade is packed with touristy restaurants serving everything from burgers to Indian and Spanish cuisine.

🍴 Centre & Nouveau Talborjt

K Moon   MOROCCAN €
(☎0528 82 47 61; 58 Rue des Oranges; mains Dh25-42; ⊙noon-11pm) Colourful parasols and a sunny outdoor terrace combine at this local spot serving well-priced grills – the merguez plate for lunch will set you up for an afternoon's exploring of Agadir – and hearty tagines packed with vegetables. If you're hungry and travelling in a small group, push the boat out with the 1kg mixed grill.

Pistachios   CAFE, ICE CREAM €
(Rue La Plage; ice cream from Dh8; ⊙10am-10pm) Colourful outdoor tables and energetic English-speaking staff are standouts at this modern cafe with some of the best ice cream in town. Cool down with the lemon, melon or orange flavours, or linger over coffee and cheesecake as you take in the views of Agadir's beachfront promenade.

Tafarnout   PASTRIES €
(Blvd Hassan II; snacks Dh30; ⊙7am-11pm) Agadir's smartest patisserie, with indoor and outdoor seating and a wide range of gâteaux, tarts, croissants, crêpes and biscuits. Good luck in choosing from the mouthwatering selection.

Daffy   MOROCCAN €
(Rue des Oranges; mains Dh70; ⊙11am-11pm) This popular unlicensed tourist restaurant offers tastes of Moroccan cuisine, including couscous (on Friday) and tajines, as well as seafood and salads.

Dolce & Caffe   CAFE, ICE CREAM €
(Blvd Hassan II; snacks Dh30; ⊙8am-10pm; 🛜) One of Agadir's coolest cafes, serving

delectable gâteaux, tarts, ice cream, crêpes, light meals and breakfasts with an R&B soundtrack.

La Siciliana
PIZZA €

(Blvd Hassan II; mains Dh70-110, pizza Dh40-80; ☺noon-11.45pm) In a line of Italian eateries, this unlicensed restaurant is the most atmospheric of the lot. Between noon and 5pm weekdays, its pizza and pasta deals are popular.

Côte Court
SEAFOOD €€

(☏0528 82 65 33; off Blvd Hassan II; mains Dh70-160; ☺noon-3pm & 7-11pm) This restaurant at the Royal Tennis Club occupies a lovely outdoor area, which is equal parts chichi garden and nomad camp, with up-lit trees, basket lamps and the pizza oven flickering away. The service is attentive and the menu incorporates a range of Asian, Mediterranean and Spanish influences. Good-value two- or three-course lunch specials start at Dh70.

Mezzo Mezzo
ITALIAN €€

(☏0528 84 88 19; www.facebook.com/MezzoMezzoAgadir; Blvd Hassan II; mains Dh90-130; ☺7pm-1am; 🖥) A shining beacon among Agadir's many stodgy pizzerias, Mezzo Mezzo offers a good range of pizzas, daily specials and wine by the glass. The kitchen also produces pasta and fish dishes, and there's a smooth European sophistication to the decor and service. Secure an outdoor table, order a cold Casablanca lager, and watch the world go by.

Le P'tit Dôme
MOROCCAN, INTERNATIONAL €€

(☏0528 84 08 05; www.facebook.com/Ptitdome; Blvd du 20 Août; mains Dh80-125; ☺10am-late) In a line of tourist restaurants, Le P'tit Dôme offers good service, black-and-white decor and a touch more class than its neighbours. The usual pizza, meat, seafood and Moroccan dishes are served, and the three-course set menu (Dh120) is good value. Outdoor terrace seating provides a pleasant dining environment.

La Scala
SEAFOOD €€€

(☏0528 84 67 73; Rue Oued Souss; meals Dh150-250) One of Agadir's best fish restaurants, with two pages of the menu devoted to seafood. Pasta and meat dishes are also available, and the food is generally elegant, fresh and beautifully presented.

✖ Marina

The upmarket marina at the northern end of the seafront promenade has a concentra-

---

TOP EATING SPOTS IN AGADIR

Passage Aït Souss Opposite the museum on this pedestrianised walkway, cafes serve everything from Moroccan dishes to pizza.

Souq al-Had (p360) At lunchtime, tajines bubble away outside the many cheap cafes.

Nouveau Talborjt In the morning, **snack stands** (Ave du 29 Février; snacks from Dh20) are popular for Moroccan pancakes and mint tea; for lunch or dinner, budget cafes and restaurants have seats on Pl Lahcen Tamri.

Port At the entrance to the port, off Ave Mohammed V, you can pick up an ultra-fresh, no-nonsense fish meal from around Dh70. Check costs before ordering; the various catches differ greatly in price (seafood such as crab is about Dh300 per 1kg). The **stalls** (meals around Dh50; ☺11.30am-10pm) close in the early evening during the winter.

---

tion of midrange and top-end restaurants and cafes, where you can dine in style on international food.

Les Blancs
SEAFOOD €€

(☏0528 82 83 68; www.facebook.com/lesblanc; mains Dh130-190; ☺11am-midnight) Occupying a series of elegant white blocks by the beach at the entrance to the marina, Les Blancs serves seafood and meat dishes including paella, the house speciality (two people minimum). In season, book ahead to score an outside table. For a sunset snack, pizza (Dh90) is served in the terrace bar.

★ Pure Passion
INTERNATIONAL €€€

(☏0528 84 01 20; www.purepassion.ma; Agadir Marina; mains Dh150-240; ☺noon-11pm) Vintage clocks and elegant lighting reinforce a stylish ambience at this restaurant adjudged one of Agadir's best. Try and score a front table for Marina views, and sample scallops topped with argan oil, fresh Dakhla oysters and good vegetarian options. The wine, beer and cocktail list runs across multiple pages, and Pure Passion's three-course lunch menu (Dh160) is excellent value.

33 Yacht Adress
SEAFOOD, MOROCCAN €€€

(☏0529 90 09 00; mains Dh150-170; ☺noon-3pm & 6-11pm) This upmarket restaurant

WORTH A TRIP

SOUQ AL-HAD

Leave the seafront to shop with the locals at the **Souq al-Had** (Blvd Abderrahim Bouabid; ⊙7am-11pm Tue-Sat), which slaps a big, messy dollop of Moroccan atmosphere onto concrete Agadir. Stalls sell everything from jellabas (a popular flowing garment) to fish, and include some good handicrafts, leatherwork and lanterns. Among the lines of fresh fruit and veg from the Souss Valley, look out for Berber apothecaries selling herbal incense, lipstick and potions that have all sorts of effects on the bowels.

is an excellent spot for sundowners, with superb views down the beach. The menu, prepared by three French chefs, is a good mix of seafood (sole, lobster, bouillabaisse) and meat dishes, such as chicken *pastilla* (savoury pie) and shoulder of lamb.

La Madrague MEDITERRANEAN, SEAFOOD €€€
(☑0528 84 24 24; mains Dh130-240; ⊙11am-11pm) This stylish restaurant occupies a quiet corner of the marina, with a view of the kasbah above the boats. It specialises in dishes such as pasta, risotto, crab and prawns, and offers a three-course weekday lunch special (Dh180).

🍷 Drinking & Nightlife

Blvd du 20 Août and Rue Oued Souss are good for bars and nightclubs. At the marina and along the promenade there are also plenty of cafes and bars. Beers are typically Dh5 to Dh10 more expensive at night, but many bars extend their daytime prices during early-evening happy hours. Many also offer the dubious pleasure of karaoke or crooning entertainers.

Havana BAR
(☑0528 84 65 41; www.facebook.com/havanarestaurant; Agadir Marina; ⊙noon-11pm) Once you've spotted Havana's bright yellow American vintage car parked outside, you'll have found this fun bar that has live music most nights. The food – Moroccan flavours and international snack food – is only OK, but the real attraction is Havana's menu of cocktails and cold beer.

Orange Café CAFE
(Rue des Oranges; ⊙10am-8pm; 🛜) This cool little courtyard cafe, with chilled Arabic

electronica on the stereo and a fountain gurgling away, serves coffee and light meals (Dh25 to Dh35).

English Pub PUB
(Blvd du 20 Août; mains from Dh75; ⊙noon-late) Come to this Union Jack–festooned bar for Stella Artois, all-day breakfasts and karaoke. A bevy of TV screens and resourceful bar staff usually means you can watch pretty well any live football game from across Europe.

Le So CLUB
(Sofitel Royal Bay, Chemin des Dunes; ⊙6pm-late) The hippest club in Agadir and one of the most expensive, laid out on several levels with features including champagne and vodka bars, a live-music stage and a restaurant. Local players save this one for the climax of the evening's entertainment.

Cafe III SHEESHA
(off Rue de la Foire; ⊙noon-1am) Hip young locals of both sexes come here to smoke sheesha beneath flat-screen TVs.

La Verandah CAFE
(Immeuble Oumlil, Blvd Hassan II; ⊙9am-8pm) This meeting point offers strong coffee and light meals on its glassed-in verandah. Snacks cost around Dh20 to Dh45.

Jour et Nuit CAFE
(Rue de la Plage; ⊙24hr) A popular spot for a seafront sundowner. The newer of the two neighbouring branches has a panoramic terrace with brilliant views of the beach.

Papa Gayo CLUB
(Chemin des Dunes; ⊙6pm-late) One of Agadir's most popular nightclubs, attracting international DJs. Dance the night away and chill on the beach.

Shopping

Souvenirs are often trucked into Agadir from other parts of Morocco and tend to be of low quality, although Marrakshi vendors have started to outsource production here. The options in the centre are unatmospheric but low-pressure environments offering easy shopping.

Ensemble Artisanal ARTS & CRAFTS
(☑0528 82 38 72; Ave du 29 Février; ⊙10am-12.30pm & 2.30-5pm Mon-Sat) Some of the best craftwork found in Agadir can be found in this store.

Tafoukt Souq GIFTS & SOUVENIRS
(Blvd du 20 Août; ⊙ 9.30am-12.30pm & 2-6pm) A touristy bazaar with everything from Berber jewellery to football tops. There's also a handy mini-supermarket selling snacks, souvenirs, and beer and liquor.

Marché Central ARTS & CRAFTS
(off Blvd Hassan II; ⊙ 8am-4pm Mon-Sat) Pick up presents ranging from chessboards to leatherwork in and around this concrete building.

Al Mouggar Bookshop BOOKS
(cnr Ave du Prince Moulay Abdallah & Ave du 29 Février; ⊙ 9am-3pm) Has a wide selection of French books, and some English paperback novels.

ⓘ Information

There are banks all over the centre, most with ATMs and exchange facilities, and exchange booths and ATMs at the airport. Large hotels can also usually exchange cash, albeit at an inferior rate.

There are internet cafes around Nouveau Talborjt:

Adrar Net (Ave du Prince Moulay Abdallah; per hr Dh5; ⊙ 9am-10pm)

Teleboutique le Musée (Passage Aït Souss; per hr Dh5; ⊙ 10.30am-11pm)

Most of the larger hotels are able to recommend reliable, English-speaking doctors. Pharmacy windows display a list of that week's *pharmacies de garde*, which open 24 hours on a rotating basis.

Clinique al-Massira (🕿 0528 38 08 42; Ave du 29 Février; ⊙ 24hr) Medical clinic.

Pharmacie du Talborjt (off Pl Lahcen Tamri; ⊙ 9am-12.30pm & 2.30-5pm Mon-Sat)

Main Post Office (Ave Sidi Mohammed; ⊙ 8.30am-4.15pm Mon-Fri, 9am-3pm Sat)

Police (🕿 19; Rue du 18 Novembre)
There's also a Nouveau Talborjt office on **Pl Lahcen Tamri**, and a **Tourist Police** post on the promenade.

Post Office (Ave du 29 Février; ⊙ 8.30am-4.15pm Mon-Fri, 9am-3pm Sat)

TOURIST INFORMATION

Information Booth (🕿 0528 83 91 02; www.visitagadir.com; Al-Massira Airport) Open 24 hours at the airport and has useful maps and brochures.

ONMT (Délégation Régionale du Tourisme; 🕿 0528 84 63 77; www.visitagadir.com; Immeuble Ignouan, Ave Mohammed V; ⊙ 8.30am-4.30pm Mon-Fri) In the blue building next to DHL; not particularly helpful.

TRAVEL AGENCIES

There are many travel agencies around the junction of Blvd Hassan II and Ave des FAR, variously representing major airlines and offering tours and day trips.

ⓘ Getting There & Away

AIR

Al-Massira Airport (🕿 0528 83 91 02; www.onda.ma; N10), mainly served by Royal Air Maroc and European charter flights and budget airlines, is 28km southeast of Agadir en route to Taroudannt. Facilities include a post office, bag-wrap service, cafes, souvenir shops and wi-fi hotspots.

BUS

Although a good number of buses serve Agadir, it is quite possible you'll end up in Inezgane, 13km south, the regional transport hub. Check before you buy your ticket. Plenty of grands taxis (Dh7) and local buses (Dh10) shuttle between there and Agadir.

All the major bus companies, and plenty of smaller companies, serve the massive circular **gare routière** (Bus Station; Blvd Abderrahim Bouabid), past Souq al-Had. If you want to travel on a specific bus, it is worth booking ahead.

CTM (🕿 0528 82 53 41; www.ctm.ma), which has a Nouveau Talborjt ticket office off Pl Lahcen Tamri, has several daily departures to destinations including Casablanca (Dh270, eight hours), Dakhla (Dh395, 20 hours), Essaouira (Dh75, 3½ hours), Laâyoune (Dh240, 11½ hours), Marrakesh (Dh110, 3½ hours), Rabat (Dh230, nine hours), Tangier (Dh340, 13½ hours), Taroudannt (Dh35, two hours) and Tiznit (Dh40, 1¾ hours).

Supratours (🕿 0528 84 12 07; www.supratours.ma), which has a city-centre ticket office on Rue des Oranges, offers similar services.

CAR & MOTORCYCLE

The distances involved in touring southern Morocco make it worthwhile considering car rental. It is cheapest to book a vehicle online in advance; www.economycarrentals.com offers good deals in Agadir and at Al-Massira Airport.

Local agencies charge from about Dh300 for a small car for one day, though there's usually room for haggling. Note that you'll need to stump up an additional cost to reduce your insurance excess.

Local agencies are clustered in the **arcade** (Ave du Prince Moulay Abdallah) across Ave du Prince Moulay Abdallah from the bottom of Ave du 29 Février; around the **junction** of Ave des FAR and Blvd Hassan II, and the **corner** of Ave Mohammed V and Ave du Général Kettani. Avis, Budget, Europcar and Hertz have offices both in the latter location and at the airport, where

ℹ AIRPORT TAXIS

You can catch a taxi straight from Al-Massira Airport to numerous destinations. Tariffs for private hire are displayed at the airport information booth, and include the following destinations: Agadir or Inezgane (Dh200), Essaouira or Goulimime (Dh1000), Mirleft (Dh700), Tafraoute (Dh900), Taghazout (Dh300), Taroudannt or Tiznit (Dh450).

Thrifty and Sixt also have desks. Most accommodation options can also arrange car hire, Scooters and motorbikes are also available, but check the state of the machines carefully.

There is a centrally located **petrol station** at the southern end of Rue Palais Municipal.

TAXI

The main grand-taxi rank is located at the south end of Rue de Fès. Destinations include Essaouira (Dh100), Inezgane (Dh10) and Taroudannt (Dh40).

ℹ Getting Around

TO/FROM THE AIRPORT & BUS STATION

Al-Massira Airport Taxis from the airport to Agadir or Inezgane cost Dh200. Bus 37 runs from outside the airport (about 500m straight out on the road) to Inezgane (Dh10, 6.45am to 10.15pm), from where you can continue to Agadir and destinations throughout southern Morocco.

Agadir Bus Station From Agadir's *gare routière*, a taxi to central hotels and resorts is around Dh15. Some intercity buses for Agadir may terminate in the suburb of Inezgane, from where shared taxis and buses continue to central Agadir.

BUS

Journeys within Agadir cost Dh5 and you can buy tickets on the bus. Buses run along Ave Mohammed V between the port and Inezgane. Catch bus 32 for Tamraght and Taghazout.

TAXI

Orange petits taxis run around Agadir. Prices are worked out by meter; ask for it to be switched on. It should cost about Dh15 to cross town.

Souss-Massa National Park

One of Morocco's most significant national parks and bird reserves, Souss-Massa (www.visitnationalparksoussmassa.jimdo.com)

stretches down the coast from Inezgane, a block of over 330 sq km of protected land between the main north–south highway and the beach. It is a spectacular and wild place of cliffs, sand dunes, farmland, coastal steppes and forests.

The park was created in 1991 in recognition of its importance as a feeding ground for birds. The Souss estuary, at the northern end of the park, and in particular the Massa coastal lagoon, near the southern end, are popular with birdwatchers.

The best times for birdwatching are from March to April and October to November. Birds found here include ospreys, marbled ducks, cormorants, greater flamingos, flocks of sandgrouse and warblers. But the biggest attraction is the northern bald ibis. These birds, revered in ancient Egypt and once widespread in central Europe, North Africa and the Middle East, are an endangered species, with the world's only sizeable population found on this stretch of coast. Tourism development is an ongoing threat to the four local breeding grounds, which remain off-limits, but you can spot ibises around Oued Massa or at the mouth of the Tamri River.

The park is a great place for walking. Animals such as jackals, red foxes, wild cats, genets and Eurasian wild boars are found here, while a large fenced area in the north of the park contains species that have disappeared from the south, including Dorcas and dama gazelles, addaxes, red-necked ostriches and scimitar-horned oryxes.

Guides can be arranged in the village of Massa, some 60km south of Agadir (signposted from the N1). From there, a track leads along the river to the estuary mouth (5km) and a tarred road leads to Sidi R'bat (8km). This tiny village has two claims to fame. Supposedly it is where the biblical Jonah was vomited up by a whale, and also where Uqba bin Nafi, the 7th-century Arab conqueror of Morocco, rode his horse triumphantly into the sea and called on God to witness that he could find no land left to conquer.

🛏 Sleeping & Eating

There are restaurants at both accommodation options, and the simple cafe at La Dune is open to nonguests. Try the Berber omelette.

La Dune   GUESTHOUSE €€
(📞0666 80 78 24; www.ladune.de; Sidi R'bat; s/d incl breakfast Dh400-650, tent per person incl breakfast from Dh100; ❄) La Dune has basic two- and four-person Berber tents, a pleas-

antly cool tented restaurant (dinner Dh70) and African-themed, occasionally garish rooms with balconies. It's an easy walk downhill through the dunes to the beach.

Ksar Massa   HOTEL €€€
(☏0661 28 03 19; www.ksarmassa.com; Sidi R'bat; s/d incl breakfast Dh1500/2000, tent s/d Dh750/1200; ❄️🛜🏊) Spectacularly located on Sidi R'bat beach, Ksar Massa is a fantastical destination in itself. The terracotta-and-blue contemporary kasbah is a wonderful place to unwind, with hazy ocean views from its perch above the pale sands. Luxuriously spacious rooms and suites are painted in bright colours and meals (lunch/dinner Dh170/300) are sumptuous affairs with multiple dishes. Management can arrange guided trips into the park.

To get there, follow the signs from Massa or 3km south of Belfaa.

ⓘ Getting There & Away

From Agadir and Inezgane, Tiznit-bound local buses and grands taxis will drop you in Belfaa or Massa (about Dh30). From either, a grand taxi to Sidi R'bat costs about Dh220. Accommodation options in Sidi R'bat also offer transfers to/from Agadir airport (about Dh450). From Massa, it is about an hour's walk to Oued Massa river mouth; 4WDs also head into the park, but both Oued Massa and Oued Souss are usually accessible by 2WD (or grand taxi).

Travel agencies in Agadir also offer convenient day trips to the area.

North of Agadir

Despite the villas, fun parks, golf courses and development projects colonising the coast around Agadir, if you're looking for surf and less crowded beaches, head north. There are sandy coves every few kilometres, and welcoming accommodation and eateries make it a good place to relax for a few days even if you don't surf.

ⓘ Getting There & Away

Grands taxis travel between Agadir and Taghazout (Dh10) via Aourir and Tamraght. Another option is bus 32 (Dh5) running along Ave Mohammed V in Agadir.

Tamraght & Aourir

Aourir and Tamraght are known collectively as Banana Village because of the banana groves alongside Oued Tamraght, which separates the villages. Respectively some 12km and 14km north of Agadir, they share Banana Beach, which can be good for beginner surfers at its southern end. Aourir has facilities such as a petrol station, a post office and banks.

At Rocher du Diable, round the headland to the north of Banana Beach, Surf Maroc offers surfboard rental and lessons. As in Taghazout, various companies offer accommodation and surf packages.

Accommodation owners in Tamraght are keen to expand the area's reputation beyond surfing, and can arrange market visits, cooking classes, hammam and yoga sessions, and workshops learning traditional Berber and Moroccan crafts.

🏃 Activities

Lunar Surf House   ART, COOKING
(☏0679 53 50 49; www.thelunarsurfhouse.com; Tamraght; per person from Dh270) Various activities including pottery, carpet weaving, *tadelakt* (lime plaster), traditional fabric dyeing, Berber embroidery and wood carving are available through Lunar Surf House's program of Creative Expression workshops. Excursions to Banana Beach's Wednesday souq followed by a Moroccan cookery class (Dh220) are also on offer.

Surf Maroc   SURFING
(www.surfmaroc.com; surfboard/bodyboard/paddleboard rental from Dh/70/35/100, surf lessons from Dh150) From its oceanside base on Imourane Beach, Surf Maroc offers lessons and surfboard, bodyboard, paddleboard and wetsuit rental.

🛏️ Sleeping

⭐Lunar Surf House   GUESTHOUSE €
(☏0679 53 50 49; www.thelunarsurfhouse.com; dm/d incl breakfast from Dh140/325; 🛜) Run by a young switched-on Australian –Moroccan couple, Lunar Surf House is – despite its name – also an excellent place to stay, even if you're not into surfing. Adil and Irene can certainly arrange surfboard hire and lessons, but the colourfully decorated and spotless rooms and dorms are also the perfect base for trips to Paradise Valley, yoga sessions or creative workshops.

Breakfast on the funky rooftop terrace and other meals get rave reviews from guests.

Hotel Littoral   HOTEL €
(☏0528 31 47 26; www.hotellittoral.com; Rte d'Essaouira, Aourir; s/d/apt Dh251/310/650;

(🛜 ❄) The kitschy Hotel Littoral is basic but comfortable, with a bar-restaurant and well-equipped en-suite rooms. It's handily located for transport options north to Essaouira or south to Agadir. Breakfast is an additional Dh30.

Riad Dar Haven

B&B €€

(☏ 0528 31 54 34; www.riad-dar-haven; Hay Ait Soual, Tamraght; r/ste incl breakfast from Dh880/960; 🛜 ❄) Concealed behind a simple door in a nondescript Tamraght street, this lovely riad run by a Moroccan–Australian couple features nine rooms and suites arrayed around a swimming pool and shaded courtyard. A hammam and spa services are also available, and an adherence to sustainable practices has seen the property afforded Green Key status. Excellent lunches and dinners are also available.

Outside guests are welcome for these meal occasions (Dh190 per person), but priority is given to in-house guests so phone ahead to check availability and make bookings.

Villa Mandala

GUESTHOUSE €€

(☏ 0528 31 47 73; www.surfmaroc.com; Aourir; r per week incl all meals Dh9000; 🛜 ❄) This beachfront villa at the southern end of Banana Beach is run by Surf Maroc and can be booked for yoga-focused stays of one or two weeks. The decor mixes traditional and contemporary with a curvy pool and a white rug-scattered interior. Prices include all meals enjoyed at a communal shared table, and surfing is also available.

✖ Eating

Babakoul

CAFE €

(☏ 0611 14 76 25; Tamraght; mains Dh20-50; ⊙8am-11pm) With a breezy outdoor patio and a crazy paving mosaic floor, this cool little cafe is a relaxing spot to hang out in after a day's swimming or surfing. The versatile menu stretches from crêpes to grills and pizza, and fresh fruit juices and smoothies are also good.

Chez Brahim

SEAFOOD €€

(Rocher du Diable; mains Dh70; ⊙noon-10pm) The smartest of the restaurants near Banana Beach and Rocher du Diable, Chez Brahim serves hearty fish or meat platters (from Dh150) on its seafront terrace.

Banana Beach

SEAFOOD €€

(mains Dh70; ⊙8am-4pm) At the northern end of the beach, Banana Beach is the perfect spot to while away a few hours, offering sunloungers on the sands and seafood, omelettes, sandwiches and cold beer.

Taghazout

تغازوت

POP 5400

Six kilometres from Tamraght, the laid-back fishing village of Taghazout, once famous for calamari and hippies, is now considered Morocco's premier surfing destination for both pros and learners.

The scruffy roadside village is a mixed-up place – a largely dry tourist town where surf culture dominates. The main beach is great for swimming, but during and after the Moroccan summer holiday, the influx of domestic tourists can overwhelm the village's infrastructure.

Between Taghazout and Tamraght to the south, there is ongoing development of new accommodation and residential areas. Some of these projects have been put on hold, creating a forlorn landscape of cranes and building sites, but the easygoing village ambience of Taghazout itself is still largely intact.

🏃 Activities

Surf breaks such as Hash Point, Panorama, Anchor Point, La Source, Killer Point and Mysteries surround the village, and the surf is most reliable from October to April.

The leading operator for lessons, board hire and accommodation packages is British-owned Surf Maroc (p364), but numerous locals have followed in its wake, offering accommodation and surf packages, and board and wetsuit hire is available from many places in town.

★ Surf Maroc

SURFING

(☏ 0528 20 02 30; www.surfmaroc.com) Run by a group of passionate British surfers, Surf Maroc offers surfing lessons, board hire and yoga, and also operates three excellent cafes and interesting accommodation options around Taghazout and near Tamraght. All-inclusive surfing packages, including lessons, board hire, meals and accommodation, begin at Dh600 per night, and accommodation only is also available on a per-night basis.

Check the Surf Maroc website for more information on its diverse range of accommodation and activities.

🛏 Sleeping

Taghazout has a good range of accommodation from, simple auberges through to a very comfortable luxury designer guesthouse.

Locals also rent out apartments and rooms, which may be your only option in summer if you have not booked ahead.

Taghazout Surf Hostel
HOSTEL €

(☑ 0676 06 94 95; www.taghazoutsurfhostel.com; behind West Coast restaurant; r incl breakfast from Dh330; ⊛) Run by the friendly Yassine, this accommodation has basic double, twin, quadruple and six-bed rooms with shared bathrooms. Surfing lessons and gear hire is also available.

Taghazout Villa
GUESTHOUSE €

(☑ 0528 20 02 30; www.surfmaroc.com; r per person incl breakfast Dh210-460; ⊛) Undergoing careful refurbishment when we dropped by, Taghazout Villa is Surf Maroc's good-value option for guests keen for a longer stay to learn how to surf. Nine rooms have a beachy ambience and the village location is excellent. Self-contained apartments nearby are also available for independent surfers keen to explore the breaks around Taghazout.

L'Auberge
GUESTHOUSE €

(☑ 0528 20 02 72; www.surfmaroc.com; r per person from Dh210; ⊛) This beachfront white-washed building was actually Taghazout's first guesthouse, and it's still a great place to stay with simple but stylish rooms giving front row access to the village's compact town beach and a few good cafes.

★ Amouage
BOUTIQUE HOTEL €€

(☑ 0528 20 02 30; www.surfmaroc.com; dm/r incl breakfast per person from Dh400/450; ⊛☒) Effortlessly raising the bar in Taghazout, Surf Maroc's newest opening is this super-stylish 'designer guesthouse'. Brilliant local art and photography fill the airy public spaces, an infinity pool with day beds segues to the Atlantic's horizon, and a hammam and massage centre is ideal after days spent surfing or exploring. There's also a restaurant and bar open to nonguests for lunch and dinner.

Nonguests can also buy a pass to use Amouage's pool and facilities – dependent on how full the hotel is – for a day (Dh120) or a week (Dh720).

✗ Eating & Drinking

The cafes near the main beach are good for coffee and juices, while Cafe Mouja has occasional music and cinema nights. There is a licensed bar at Amouage, which nonguests can enjoy over dinner.

Dar Jospehine
INTERNATIONAL, MOROCCAN €

(mains Dh50-70; ⊙ 9am-10pm) The best of the cafes along Taghazout's main street, Dar Josephine features shaded tables under a grape arbour, and a band of friendly local cats. The three-course menu (Dh97) is good value and options for mains include roast chicken with garlic-and-thyme potatoes and a robust *kefta* (spiced lamb or beef meatballs) tagine. International influences creep in with zingy tzatziki and a hearty lasagne.

Cafe Aftas
CAFE €

(Taghazout Beach; breakfast Dh15-25; ⊙ 8am-10pm) Juices, smoothies and great espresso with absolute beachfront views make this hole-in-the-wall a perfect spot to kick off another day in Taghazout.

Cafe Mouja
CAFE €€

(www.surfmaroc.com; snacks & mains Dh40-90; ⊙ 7am-11pm) Expansive windows with brilliant Atlantic Ocean views and chunky wooden furniture both feature at this coolly hip cafe behind Surf Maroc's shop. The menu straddles Moroccan favourites and Western comfort food – think chicken baguettes or beetroot-and-lentil salad – and good smoothies, juices and vegetarian offerings are all healthy options. Music and movie nights are regular events.

L'Auberge Resto
INTERNATIONAL €€

(mains Dh60-80; ⊙ 8am-11pm) The cafe at L'Auberge is a funky hangout serving Moroccan and international food. Comfort food options include nachos, a shared antipasto plate, and excellent salads and curries. Named after a nearby surf break, the Killers burger combines cheese, avocado and caramelised onions. Moroccan options include tagines and a great Moroccan chicken stew, and the patio setting is quite romantic.

ⓘ Information

Taghazout has internet cafes and a pharmacy, but most facilities – including an ATM– are in Aourir.

Immouzzer des Ida Outanane
ايموزار ادا وتنان

The village of Immouzzer des Ida Outanane is in the High Atlas foothills, around 60km (two hours' drive) northeast of Agadir). Nearby is the aptly named **Paradise Valley**, an oleander- and palm-lined gorge, and a popular picnic and swimming spot. Local producers have formed a **route du miel** (honey route), and stalls sell the sweet stuff as well as argan oil. Signs by the road point to walking trails.

The area turns white in February and March when the almond trees blossom. There is a honey harvest and festival in July and August, and around late November you may be lucky enough to witness the olive harvest. Locals climb into the trees to shake olives from the branches and oil is pressed in the village. Thursday is souq day.

◉ Sights

The famous cascades of Immouzzer are one of North Africa's most beautiful waterfalls. The calcium-rich water flows most strongly between February and August, although recent droughts have frequently reduced it to a trickle. Given the stream of tourist stalls and *faux guides* (unofficial guides) leading to the falls, you may prefer Paradise Valley.

When it's flowing, water falls off the edge of the plateau in several chutes, running down one cliff face known as the Bride's Veil. The path to the foot of the falls finishes at an iridescent blue plunge pool with overhanging rocks and foliage. If you can cross the river here, you can climb to a plateau and see the top plunge pool, and caves once inhabited by hippies. The steep, 4km road from Immouzzer village down to the falls is one of many walks in the region.

⊨ Sleeping & Eating

There are cafes at the bottom of the path to the falls, and on the way up. Accommodation options around Paradise Valley all have good cafes with excellent views. Try the local honey.

Auberge le Panoramic HOTEL €€
(☑ 0528 21 67 09; www.auberge-le-panoramic.com; Paradise Valley; s/d incl half-board Dh280/500; ❄ ⊛) The newer block at this friendly stop on the *route du miel* (honey route) is the pick of Paradise Valley's accommodation, with almost vertigo-inducing views from the balcony of en-suite rooms. The restaurant serves tajines, omelettes, brochettes and a breakfast featuring three honeys, produced by the beehives on the slopes below.

Auberge Bab Immouzer HOTEL €
(☑ 0670 13 10 06; www.aubergebabimouzer.com; Paradise Valley; r Dh250-300; ❄⊛) Well kept but low on atmosphere, Bab Immouzer has six en-suite rooms and a series of terraces overlooking the neighbouring *palmeraie*

(palm grove) and valley. Poolside rooms have balconies with a view.

Hotel Tifrit HOTEL €
(☑ 0528 21 67 08; www.hotel-tifrit.net; Paradise Valley; s/d incl half-board Dh300/450; ❄⊛) Right by the river in the *palmeraie*, near the waterfall of the same name, Tifrit has six en-suite rooms with big windows overlooking the palms.

Hôtel des Cascades HOTEL €€
(☑ 0528 82 60 23; www.cascades-hotel.net; s/d Dh460/572; ⊛⊛) In a wonderful location on the edge of Immouzzer village, perched high above the valley, this hotel is set in a riotous garden with tennis courts. Flower baskets and artwork decorate the terrace and corridors; the 27 rooms have small balconies, and there's a licensed restaurant (mains Dh80 to Dh120). Paths descend 4km from the garden to the cascades.

Tour groups arrive at the restaurant around 12.30pm so try and time a lunch visit before or after then. The hotel also has a self-catering house 20km away, en route to Essaouira.

ⓘ Getting There & Away

Buses and grands taxis run between Aourir and Immouzzer (Dh30) until about 4pm. From Agadir, it is hard to visit the falls in a day by public transport; you can visit on a tour or hire a grand taxi. Thursday, when Immouzzer's weekly market takes place, is a good day to pick up a lift, but a bad time to drive as the narrow road is busy. Between October and May, the river sometimes destroys the road.

Taroudannt تارودانت

POP 80,149

Taroudannt (also spelled Taroudant) is sometimes called 'Little Marrakesh', but that description doesn't do the Souss Valley trading centre justice. Hidden by magnificent red-mud walls, and with the snowcapped peaks of the High Atlas beckoning beyond, Taroudannt's souqs and squares have a healthy sprinkling of Maghrebi mystique. Yet it is also a practical place, a market town where Berbers trade the produce of the rich and fertile Oued Souss plain.

There aren't any must-see sights. Instead, the medina is a place to stroll and linger. The two souqs are well worth a browse, more laid-back than Marrakesh, but with an atmosphere of activity that is missing in Agadir. With the little-explored western High Atlas, the Anti Atlas and the coast all nearby, the town makes a good base for trekking and activities. Just 65km inland from Al-Massira Airport, it is a more atmospheric staging post to/from the airport than Agadir.

History

Taroudannt was one of the early bases of the Almoravids, who established themselves here in 1056 AD, at the beginning of their conquest of Morocco. In the 16th century, the emerging Saadians made it their capital for about 20 years. By the time they moved on to Marrakesh, they had turned the Souss Valley, in which the city stands, into the country's most important producer of sugar cane, cotton, rice and indigo; all valuable trade items on the trans-Saharan trade routes the dynasty was keen to control. The Saadians constructed the old part of town and the kasbah, though most of it was destroyed and the inhabitants massacred in 1687 by Moulay Ismail, as punishment for opposing him. Only the ramparts survived. Most of what stands inside them dates from the 18th century.

Taroudannt continued to be a centre of intrigue and sedition against the central government well into the 20th century, and indeed played host to El-Hiba, a southern chief who opposed the Treaty of Fès, the 1912 agreement that created the French Protectorate.

Sights

Ramparts   HISTORIC SITE
The 7.5km of ramparts surrounding Taroudannt are among the best-preserved pisé walls in Morocco. Their colour changes from golden brown to deepest red depending on the time of day. They can easily be explored on foot (two hours), preferably in the late afternoon; or take a bike or calèche and see the walls by moonlight.

Bab el-Kasbah   NOTABLE BUILDING
Built in the 16th and 17th centuries, a string of mighty defensive towers create the gates of the city. Considered the main gate, the triple-arched Bab el-Kasbah (also known as Bab Essalsla) is approached via an avenue of orange trees. Steps lead to the top of the tower, where you can walk along the ramparts.

Kasbah   AREA
The old kasbah quarter, originally a fortress built by Moulay Ismail, is today a poor but

---

TIOUTE KASBAH

Southwest of Taroudannt, this kasbah is so picture-perfect that it was used as a location in the 1954 French production of *Ali Baba and the Forty Thieves*. The stone kasbah overlooks a *palmeraie* and a couple of restaurants, with the High and Anti Atlas in the distance. Visit early to ensure you find a grand taxi (Dh15, 30 minutes) there and back, and to beat the tour groups.

---

safe residential area, where winding lanes and low archways lead to tiny squares and dead ends. The governor's palace, on the eastern side of the kasbah, now forms part of Hôtel Palais Salam.

Place al-Alaouyine   SQUARE
(Pl Assarag) During Moroccan holidays, Pl al-Alaouyine is like Marrakesh's Djemaa el-Fna in miniature, with storytellers, snake charmers, escapologists and performers working the crowds.

Activities

Taroudannt is a great base for trekking in the western High Atlas region, including the secluded **Tichka Plateau**, a delightful area of highland meadows and hidden gorges (two days minimum). The **Afensou** and **Tizi n'Test** areas are ideal for day walks. Agencies in town offer treks; insist on travelling with a qualified guide. Charges start at about Dh350 per person per day, including transport and picnic.

★**La Maison Anglaise**   CULTURAL
(☑0661 23 66 27; www.cecu.co.uk/contact; 422 Derb Afferdou) Excellent guides and activities including trekking, Berber village visits, wildlife trips, cookery lessons, and visits to the soap-making and beekeeping cooperatives they support. Day trips to the valley at Afensou in the High Atlas involve walking through olive groves to a swimming hole.

Calèche   TOURS
You can tour the ramparts in a calèche. The horse-drawn carriages gather just inside **Bab el-Kasbah**, on **Pl al-Alaouyine** and at other prominent spots. A one-way trip across town should cost roughly the same as by petit taxi, although the driver may disagree; don't pay more than Dh25. For a one-hour tour, including the medina, a circuit of

Taroudannt

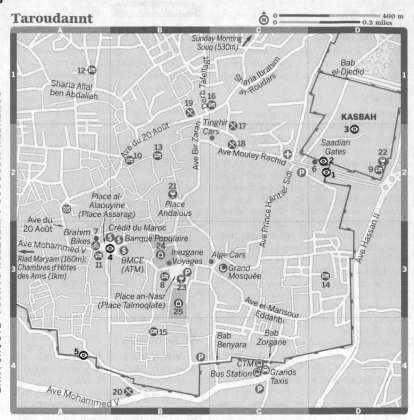

the ramparts and a small tannery, don't pay more than Dh120.

Abdellatif Abassi HIKING
(📱 0670 59 13 88; abdelroudana@gmail.com) In addition to the trekking guides available through accommodation, Abdellatif Abassi is uncertified but recommended by readers, and can organise mules and village homestays.

🛏 Sleeping

Hotel Saadiens HOTEL €
(📱 0528 85 25 89; hotelsaad@menara.ma; Ave du 20 Août; s/d Dh220/280; 🛜🕱) Signposted from all over town, Saadiens has aged but spacious rooms with reasonable en suites, stripy bedspreads and Berber designs on the doors. Despite the gloomy, echoing corridors, it is a central retreat from the medina, with a 1st-floor lounge and mountain views from the roof terrace. Ave du 20 Août is a

thoroughfare, so ask for a room at the rear. Half-board is available.

**Chambres d'Hôtes
des Amis** GUESTHOUSE €
(📱 0667 60 16 86; www.chambresdesamis.com; Sidi Belkas; s/d incl breakfast Dh80/160; 🛜) This good-value guesthouse has aged but sizeable rooms, basic bathrooms with intermittent hot water, a couple of salons, and a roof terrace for breakfast. It's 800m west of Bab Taghount (on the west side of the ramparts) at the beginning of the open countryside, although street noise and the nearby mosque overwhelm any suburban tranquility.

The proprietor, Said Dayfollah, offers bike hire, trekking and activities, pick-ups from Al-Massira Airport (Dh350) and meals on request (Dh70).

Hôtel Taroudannt HOTEL €
(📱 0528 85 24 16; Pl al-Alaouyine; s/d from Dh70/120; 🕱) In this central option, tiled

Taroudannt

corridors lead past a restaurant and jungly courtyard to rooms with simple bathrooms. A drawback is noise from Pl al-Alaouyine. The hotel used to offer a male-dominated bar proffering cheap beer but that has now closed.

Hôtel el-Warda HOTEL €
(☏ 0528 85 27 63; Pl an-Nasr; s/d Dh80/100) This ultra-cheapie has a *zellij* (tilework) terrace overlooking Pl an-Nasr and basic 2nd-floor rooms with shared toilets and showers. Solo female travellers might find the alley entrance and male-dominated 1st-floor cafe difficult.

★ **Ryad Tafilag** BOUTIQUE HOTEL €€
(☏ 0528 85 06 07; www.riad-tafilag.com; Derb Tafellagt; s/d incl breakfast from Dh550/605; ❀@☎☀) Consisting of adjoining medina houses, this creative hotel is a warren of

staircases, terraces, lounges and a hammam. The nine rooms and suites, three of which have private terraces, place guests' needs above the dictates of design, managing to be unfussily artistic throughout. Free bikes are offered to guests, and evening meals are served in an elegant dining room.

There is a compact plunge pool concealed amid the Moroccan design wizardry.

La Maison Anglaise GUESTHOUSE €€
(☏ 0661 23 66 27; www.cecu.co.uk/contact; 422 Derb Afferdou; s/d incl breakfast Dh400/600; ❀@☎) On a quiet street north of Taroudant's central hubbub, this Green Key-certified medina house makes a welcoming base run by a brilliant team of locals. As well as nine en-suite rooms, there is a kitchen for self-catering, a roof terrace with views of the High and Anti Atlas, and a small library. Meals get raves reviews from guests.

What really makes this British-owned option special is the staff, who help you get to grips with local culture, whether on their tours or by just pointing you in the right direction. As the name suggests, English is spoken. If you're keen to stay here, phone ahead to check there is room available as La Maison Anglaise is popular with groups. Evening meals are also available for nonguests (Dh110 to Dh130), but bookings need to be made by email (cecuecotours@gmail.com) at least one day prior.

Riad Ain Khadra GUESTHOUSE €€
(☏ 0528 85 41 42; www.riad-ain-khadra.com; r/ste incl breakfast from Dh550/770; ❀☎☀) Recommended by some of Southern Morocco's best trekking guides, Riad Ain Khadra is located 10km south of Taroudannt in a rural setting. The quiet location is further enhanced by a garden pool, a hammam, a Jacuzzi and massage services. One of the area's more luxurious but still low-key options, Riad Ain Khadra is a soothing in contrast to the energy of the medina.

Riad Taroudant GUESTHOUSE €€
(☏ 0528 85 25 72; www.riadtaroudant.com; 243 Ave Al Quds, Derb J'Did; s/d incl breakfast Dh300/400; ❀☎☀) In a residential neighbourhood near the medina's southern entrance, the highlight of Riad Taroudant is the rooftop terrace. Breakfast is served with medina views and the attention of a playful duo of cats, and downstairs a compact pool provides a haven from the Moroccan heat. Rooms are simply furnished but comfortable, and evening

meals and 4WD desert excursions can be booked.

Air-con is available but is subject to a small additional charge.

Riad Maia B&B €€
(📞 0641 03 79 89; 12 Tassoikt Ighezifen; s/d incl breakfast from Dh380/490) Possibly one of Tardoudannt's most concealed riads – don't worry, there is plenty of signage – Riad Maia is a great example of how to maximise a small space. Stairways lead to rooftop terraces and Maia's four elegant en-suite rooms, allowing glimpses of a well-ordered courtyard garden. Because of the stairs, Riad Maia is not suitable for children under six.

Palais Oumensour BOUTIQUE HOTEL €€
(📞 0528 55 02 15; www.palaisoumensour.com; Al Mansour Borj Oumensour Tadjount; r/ste incl breakfast Dh600/800; ❄️ 🛜 🏊) Tasteful and tranquil, Palais Oumensour hides away on a medina lane by the Catholic church garden. Above the central courtyard with its jade pool, the four doubles and six suites combine modern comforts and traditional materials, with Georges Braque prints and *tadelakt* walls. Elegant public spaces include a hammam, a massage room, a roof terrace with High Atlas views and a bar.

Hôtel Palais Salam HERITAGE HOTEL €€
(📞 0528 85 25 01; Kasbah; s/d/ste incl breakfast from Dh582/674/1424; 🛜 🏊) This former pasha's residence, entered through the east wall of the kasbah, lives up to its palatial name, with gardens, pools, courtyards and fountains (one inhabited by turtles) on various levels. With their traditional decor, the older, ground-floor rooms have an authentic feel, but the newer rooms, behind pink walls and blue shutters, are more spacious.

Rooms and bathrooms are disappointing compared with newer options, as is the service, but it remains a wonderful environment, with a bar and Moroccan and international restaurants.

✕ Eating

The hotel cafes and touristy eateries on Pl al-Alaouyine are good for breakfast on the square, and serve tajines and simple grills later in the day. The best place to look for cheap eats is around Pl an-Nasr and north along Ave Bir Zaran, where you will find the usual tajines, *harira* (lentil soup) and salads.

Chez Nada MOROCCAN €
(📞 0528 85 17 26; Ave Moulay Rachid; mains Dh55-95, set menu Dh80; ⊙ noon-3pm & 6-10pm; ❄️) This 60-year-old restaurant specialises in tajines, including one with pigeon (or chicken), prunes and grilled almonds. Above the male-dominated ground-floor cafe and elegant white 1st-floor dining room, the roof terrace has views over public gardens. *Pastilla* and royal couscous (Dh75 to Dh95) should be ordered two hours ahead.

Big Restaurant MOROCCAN, FAST FOOD €
(mains Dh20-35; ⊙ 11am-11pm) The American-diner ambience is a tad incongruous for Taroudannt's storied medina, but look behind the burger menu to decent pizzas and well-priced Moroccan-style grills of merguez sausages, chicken and lamb. Salads are fresh and zingy, and in a town where evening dining options are limited, Big Restaurant is a handy option.

Jnane Soussia MOROCCAN €€
(📞 0528 85 49 80; Ave Mohammed V; mains Dh70-100; ⊙ 10am-11pm; ❄️) This recommended garden restaurant has tented seating areas set around a large swimming pool adjacent to the ramparts. The house specialities, which include *mechoui* (whole roast lamb) and pigeon *pastilla,* have to be ordered in advance, but the chicken tajine with lemon and olives is good for a light lunch, and everything is decent.

Riad Maryam MOROCCAN €€
(📞 0666 12 72 85; www.riadmaryam.com; Ave Mohhamed V; menu Dh200; ⊙ 7-10pm) The first Taroudannt riad to open as accommodation, Riad Maryam has been overtaken by other flasher options, but it is still a wonderful location for an evening meal. Multicourse menus, including soup, salad and dessert, are served in the verdant inner courtyard. Prior booking is essential, so follow the signs and visit in the morning to book for the evening.

The family owners speak French but little English.

🍷 Drinking & Nightlife

Hotel Palais Salam BAR
(⊙ 2-11pm) Tucked away poolside in the lush gardens of the Hotel Palais Salam, this is a pleasant place to relax over a cold beer away from the hubbub of the medina.

WORTH A TRIP

ARGAN COUNTRY

As you travel along the N10 east of Taroudannt you will see frizzy argan trees, beloved of local goats and international chefs, growing near the road.

Approaching the mountains, the Tizi n'Test road leads through a lush state-run argan preserve – a dream destination for mountain goats accustomed to slim pickings in the High Atlas. Stop here to picnic in the shade among frolicking kids, or stake out the herds for the ultimate Anti Atlas postcard shot: a goat casually balanced on a treetop, munching on sun-ripe argan nuts.

Sleeping

The best accommodation is in Ouled Berhil at the historic Hôtel Palais Riad Hida.

Hôtel Palais Riad Hida (☑ 0528 53 10 44; www.riadhida.com; s/d incl half-board from Dh616/1023; ❄ ❐ ﹡) In a restored 19th-century mansion on the edge of the Berber village of Ouled Berhil, some 45km northeast of Taroudannt, is Hôtel Palais Riad Hida. The village's best accommodation is in nondescript bungalows, but it's a special environment from the moment you cross the tiled threshold and clap eyes on the central courtyard, with its towering palms and long pools.

Getting There & Away

Exploring this area – and especially reaching where the argan tree goats can be seen – it's best to have your own transport. Some 10km further on from Ouled Berhil, a signpost indicates the Tizi n'Test road, one of the most spectacular and perilous passes in the country, leading northeast over the High Atlas to Marrakesh.

Cafe Andalous　　　　　　　JUICE BAR
(Pl Andalous; smoothies & juices Dh10-15; ⊙10am-10pm) Beneath a dentist's sign on a small square adjoining Ave Bir Zaran, this cheerful place is good for a mixed-fruit smoothie.

Orange-Juice Stands　　　　　JUICE BAR
Freshly squeezed OJ is just Dh5 at these simple stalls.

🔒 Shopping

Taroudannt is the central Chleuh city of the Souss, so it is a good place to look for the quality silver jewellery for which this tribe is renowned. The jewellery is influenced both by Saharan tribes and by Jewish silversmiths, who formed a significant part of the community until the late 1960s.

Souq Arabe　　　　　　　ARTS & CRAFTS
(⊙10am-11pm) The main souq, also known as the *grand souq,* has antique and souvenir shops hidden in the quiet streets. The area southwest of the mosque is good for present shopping, with a small square of jewellery shops just off Ave Bir Zaran.

Souq Berbère　　　　　　ARTS & CRAFTS
(⊙10am-11pm) Also known as the *marché municipal,* this souq, on the south side of Pl an-Nasr, sells carpets, jewellery, argan oil,

musical instruments, lamps, leatherwork and ceramics – past the trainers and mobile phones on the central thoroughfare.

Sunday Morning Souq　　　FOOD & DRINKS
(⊙7am-1pm) This large market, held outside Bab el-Khemis north of the kasbah, brings in people from the whole region.

ℹ Information

Taroudannt has no 'European' quarter or ville nouvelle (new town). Most facilities are found on and around the two central squares, Pl al-Alaouyine (formerly Pl Assarag) and Pl an-Nasr (formerly Pl Talmoqlate).

Internet cafes are found along Aves Bir Zaran and Mohammed V.

Banks on Pl al-Alaouyine have ATMs, money-changing facilities and visa services.

Banque Populaire (Pl al-Alaouyine; ⊙8.30am-6.30pm Mon-Fri)

BMCE ATM (Pl al-Alaouyine)

Crédit du Maroc (Pl al-Alaouyine; ⊙8.30am-6.30pm Mon-Fri)

Hospital (Ave Moulay Rachid)

Inezgane Voyages (☑ 0528 55 06 46; Pl an-Nasr; ⊙9am-12.30pm & 2.30-5pm Mon-Sat) Represents airlines including RAM.

Post Office (Ave du 20 Août; ⊙8.15am-4pm Mon-Fri & 9am-3pm Sat)

TRAVEL AGENCIES

ⓘ Getting There & Away

Accommodation providers can organise pickups from Agadir Al-Massira Airport.

BUS

Buses depart from the **station** outside Bab Zorgane. **CTM** (☑ 0528 85 38 58; www.ctm.ma; Bab Zorgane) has the most reliable buses, with at least one daily service to each of the following destinations: Agadir (Dh35, three hours), Casablanca (Dh190, eight hours), Marrakesh (Dh105, four hours) and Ouarzazate (Dh115, five hours)

Other companies serve Agadir and Inezgane (Dh30, 1½ hours, hourly), Taliouine (Dh80, 1½ hours, daily) and Tata (Dh90, five hours, daily).

CAR

The best option is to hire a car from one of the major companies operating at Agadir Al-Massira Airport. There are local agencies in Taroudannt, including **Alge Cars** (☑ 0615 09 04 13; alge-cars@yahoo.fr; Ave Prince Héretier Sidi Mohammed, opposite mosque; per day around Dh500) and **Tinghir Cars** (☑ 0661 19 02 89; Ave Moulay Rachid; per day around Dh500).

TAXI

Grands taxis gather just outside Bab Zorgane. Destinations include the following: Agadir (Dh40), Inezgane (Dh34), where you can change for more frequent, services to Agadir, and Marrakesh (Dh150). To travel via the mountainous and spectacular Tizi n'Test, you will need to hire the entire taxi (around Dh1100).

ⓘ Getting Around

Taroudannt is a good place to cycle; bikes can be rented at **Brahim Bikes** (☑ 0662 74 10 91; Pl al-Alaouyine; per hr/day Dh10/60) on the main square. Petits taxis charge Dh8 per trip (Dh12 after 8pm).

Taliouine تالوين

POP 6000

The straggling village of Taliouine, halfway between Taroudannt and Ouarzazate, is dominated by hills and the impressive Glaoui kasbah.

Taliouine is the African centre of *l'or rouge* (red gold) – saffron, the world's most expensive spice. Numerous shops and boutiques sell it here for about Dh35 to Dh40 per gram. The purple *crocus sativus* flower, from which the spice comes, grows only above 1200m. It flowers between mid-October and mid-November, when you can see locals picking the flowers around villages 12km east of Taliouine. A saffron festival takes place – around the first weekend of November – which usually incorporates nightly concerts from some of Berber music's biggest names, and massed *ahouach* (celebratory) dancing to the beat of *bendirs* (traditional hand drums).

Beware 'counterfeit saffron'; the genuine article should stain your fingers yellow (rather than red), taste bitter (rather than sweet) and carry a spicy price tag.

◎ Sights

★ **Calligraphie Tifinaghe** ARTS CENTRE
(☑ 0601 35 31 51; www.molidaz.blogspot.com; ◎ 8.30am-12.30pm & 2-6.30pm) Amazigh poet and calligrapher Mouild Nidouissadan paints Berber proverbs and colourful compositions. Free to every visitor is a rendition of their name in Berber – crafted via a theatrical combination of saffron 'ink' and a blowtorch. Other interesting and well-priced souvenirs include T-shirts and tote bags. Mouild speaks a smidgen of English but is more comfortable speaking French.

Dar Azaafaran MUSEUM
(☑ 0528 53 44 13; ◎ 8am-7pm) **FREE** This modern information centre is devoted to *l'or rouge*, with a small museum, saffron for sale by local cooperatives and a display of the current going rate. Most displays are in French but there is some information in English. Opening hours are not strictly adhered to.

Coopérative Souktana du Safran MUSEUM
(☑ 0528 53 44 52; ◎ 8.30am-6.30pm) ☑ **FREE** Founded in 1979, the largest and oldest of Taliouine's saffron cooperatives has 160 members (four are women). The centre is well worth visiting for the museum, calligrapher and informative employees. They can explain saffron production, give you a tasting and sell you the spice, plus related products including chocolates, cosmetics and calligraphy ink.

Kasbah HISTORIC SITE
Gazing at the brown hills, the kasbah is mostly disintegrating, but it makes a pleasant sunset stroll.

Souq SOUQ
(◎ 7am-1pm) The village comes to life during the Monday souq, near Auberge le Safran.

⚡ Activities

Taliouine is a popular trekking centre for nearby Jebel Sirous, which offers some of the finest walking in the Anti Atlas. Trekking guides can be arranged through accommodation or local operators.

Maroc Inedit   HIKING
(☏0673 56 90 82; www.maroc-inedit.com) Organises trekking around the Jebel Siroua region as well as trips exploring other parts of Morocco. Taliouine-based guides speak English, French and Spanish. Owner Annie Lauvaux is active in community development work around the Taliouine area. See www.ecotourisme-solidaire-taliouine.com.

Zafrani   HIKING, CULTURAL TOUR
(☏0613 88 05 26; www.zafrani.ch; Taliouine) This Swiss-Moroccan company specialises in trekking, but also organises cultural tours and activities including stargazing, skiing and meditation, catering to individuals and families of all ages. Recent additions to its program include trekking trips incorporating the region's saffron and argan heritage, and cooking courses. Accommodation can also be arranged, as well as treks in other parts of Morocco.

Siroua Discovery   HIKING
(☏0617 03 07 03; www.siroua-discovery.com) Headed by respected Taliouine trekker Nourdine Alhyane.

🛏 Sleeping & Eating

The best of Taliouine's accommodation is slightly out of town in more rural surroundings, often with views of the atmospheric kasbah.

For dinner, ask for half-board at your accommodation or try Auberge le Safran or Souktana. At the west end of the main drag near the *gare routière*, grills smoke away, and you can get a tajine (around Dh50), made with saffron, at Auberge Siroua. There are also cheap hotels on the main street.

Auberge le Safran   HOTEL €
(☏0668 39 42 23; www.auberge-safran.com; d/ ste from Dh170/300; ❄ 🛜 ⊠) Le Safran has basic, colourful en-suite rooms, with two budget doubles on the roof terrace and a spacious four-person suite. The salon looks across the fields at the kasbah, and downstairs is a Berber tent on the patio. The hotel harvests its own saffron, which it sells in the on-site shop-museum and uses in the delicious meals.

Friendly owner Mahfoud offers activities including trekking, hammam visits, saffron-based cookery courses, and a saffron and argan producers tour. Ask for a room at the back to minimise road noise.

Auberge Souktana   HOTEL €
(☏0528 53 40 75; souktana@menara.ma; s/d Dh180/220, bungalow s/d Dh100/160, tents 1/2 people Dh50/80; 🛜) At this trekking-orientated auberge, guests consult maps in the relaxing communal area, and owner Ahmed can offer advice and arrange guides. Half-board is available (Dh220 per person) and the colourful rooms are pleasantly decorated in traditional style. It's east of the village, across the N10 from the kasbah with great views of the crumbling fort.

Chez Souad   GUESTHOUSE €
(☏0671 05 68 46; moradchoukri@yahoo.fr; r per person from Dh60) Overlooking a dusty soccer pitch, this sprawling family home has a rooftop terrace with views of the kasbah and town. There are eight rooms accommodating up to four people each, three with private bathroom. Half-board is available (Dh160 per person), and Souad's brother, Morad Choukri, is a trekking guide.

Escale Rando   GUESTHOUSE €€
(☏0662 54 78 28; www.escalerando.fr; s/d Dh330/440, without bathroom Dh242/330; 🛜) Abutting the kasbah, Escale Rando is a romantic little guesthouse centred on a courtyard with gardens, lights, fountains and tortoises. There are four high-ceilinged rooms, a fully equipped kitchen and, for hot nights, a terrace where guests can sleep alongside the kasbah battlements. Half-board is an extra Dh55 per person and activities can be arranged. Excellent English is spoken here.

Auberge Tobkal   CAMPGROUND, APARTMENT €€
(☏0528 53 43 43; aubergetoubkal@yahoo.fr; camping Dh60, bungalows per person incl half-board Dh220, apt Dh800-1200; 🛜 ⊠) This tidy campground, on the main road 500m east of the turn-off for the kasbah, also has bungalows with en suite and four new apartments.

ℹ Information

On the main road near near Dar Azaafaran are banks and an internet cafe.

ⓘ Getting There & Away

BUS

Taliouine has a small *gare routière*. There are not always seats available on the buses passing through town, so grands taxis, also found at the bus station, are a better option.

TAXI

Grands taxis run from Taliouine to Ouarzazate, but direct taxis are rare and you will normally have to change at Tazenakht (Dh35). For Taroudannt there are relatively frequent direct taxis, but it is often quicker to change at Ouled Berhil (Dh32).

THE ANTI ATLAS

الأطلس الصغير

The Anti Atlas remains one of the least-visited parts of Morocco's mountainscape, which is surprising, as it is beautiful and close to Agadir. The mountains are the stronghold of the Chleuh tribes, who live in a loose confederation of villages strung across the barren mountains, some of them still far beyond the reach of any central authority. Living in areas moulded by the demanding landscape of granite boulders and red-lava flows, the Chleuh have always been devoted to their farms in the lush oasis valleys, now some of the country's most beautiful *palmeraies*.

Tafraoute

تافراوت

POP 5000

Nestled in the gorgeous Ameln Valley, the village of Tafraoute is surrounded on all sides by red-granite mountains. Despite its unassuming appearance, the area is quite prosperous due to the hard-earned cash sent home by relatives working in the big cities or abroad. It is a pleasant and relaxed base for exploring the region.

🏃 Activities

The best way to see the beautiful surrounding countryside is by walking or cycling, and several companies and guides offer mountain-biking and trekking trips. Operators have booths west of Hôtel Salama.

Cycling

The palm-filled Aït Mansour Gorges, leading towards the bald expanses of the southern Anti Atlas, and the Pierres Bleues are great destinations. Several places rent out bikes of varying quality; expect to pay about Dh60/120 per day for a road/mountain bike with helmet, pump and puncture-repair kit.

Maison de Vacances   CYCLING
(☑0528 80 01 97; www.tafraout.info; bike rental per day Dh60-120; ⊗8.30am-10pm) Has good mountain bikes.

Tafraoute VTT   CYCLING
(☑0670 40 93 84; www.tafraout-vtt.cla.fr; rack rental per day Dh70-100) Has bike racks for cars – useful for a drive-and-cyle trip to Aït Mansour.

Hammams

Tafraoute is a good place for an authentic hammam experience as some houses here still lack water. There are three in town; massages are available at the **new hammam** (Dh12; ⊗men 7am-10pm, women to 7pm) behind Auberge Les Amis, although the male-only **old hammam** (Dh12; ⊗men 7am-10pm), just behind the market, is more authentic.

Trekking & Climbing

Tafraoute and the Anti Atlas offer numerous climbing routes and trekking possibilities, though most of the walks are strenuous.

Au Coin des Nomades   CLIMBING, HIKING
(☑0661 62 79 21; tafraoutdesert@gmail.com) Houssine Laroussi, a respected climber, is a good source of trekking and climbing information, guides, books and topographical maps. He can also organise village homestays and advise on buses to get to lesser-visited areas such as Afella-Ighir and Aït Mansour.

Tawada   HIKING, CLIMBING
(☑0661 82 26 77; www.guide-tafraout.com) Accredited English-speaking guide Brahim Bahou offers information and guided treks lasting for one day or more, and can organise mules.

🎊 Festivals & Events

Almond Blossom Festival   CULTURAL
(⊗Mar) The Tafraoute area celebrates its almond harvest at the Almond Blossom Festival.

🛌 Sleeping

Accommodation in town is good value; staying in the nearby Ameln Valley is also an option. There are two campgrounds 1km west of town on the Tiznit road (R104).

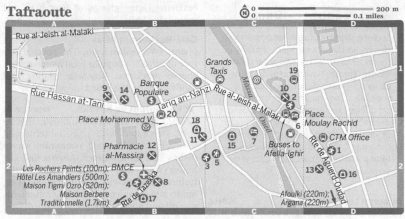

Tafraoute

Maison Tigmi Ozro GUESTHOUSE€

(☑0699 91 69 79; bouchra2.hani@gmail.com; Blvd Mokhtar Soussi; s/d incl breakfast Dh187/220; ❋❅) Courtesy of living and working in London, owner Bouchra Hani speaks perfect English and her cosy and colourful guesthouse, a short walk from central Tafraoute, is a relaxing place to stay. The three rooms all have private bathrooms, and a quiet courtyard is dotted with almond and pomegranate trees. Breakfast is enjoyed on a roof terrace with excellent mountain views.

Hôtel Salama HOTEL€

(☑0528 80 00 26; R104, riverside in central Tafraoute; s/d Dh200/300; ❋❅) Readers recommend this hotel mixing local materials and modern standards, with Berber artefacts decorating the corridors, and helpful staff who speak some English. The roof terrace has mountain views and some rooms have balconies overlooking the market square, which the cafe-restaurant (breakfast/menu Dh23/65) opens onto. Recent renovations make the Salama the best hotel in central Tafraoute.

Les Rochers Peints HOTEL€

(☑0528 80 00 32; hotelrocherpeints@gmail.com; s/d Dh200/300; ❅) The former Riad Tafraout offers colourful artworks, furniture, rugs and textiles and Berber decor and vintage French posters. Located on the edge of town, it has a wraparound terrace with good mountain views and an airy cafe in reception. The only let-down is the 10 en-suite rooms, which are small and stuffy. Breakfast is an additional Dh25.

Tafraoute

Argana HOSTEL€

(☑0528 80 14 96; www.argana-tafraout.com; s/d incl breakfast from Dh120/200; ❋❅) Recommended by readers, Argana has comfortable backpacker-style rooms of various sizes with shared bathrooms. Also on offer are a laundry service, good breakfasts, a lounge, terraces, and advice from the helpful owner Mustapha, an English-speaking trekking aficionado.

ℹ️ TAFRAOUTE CLIMBING

Oxford Alpine Club (www.oxfordalpine-club.co.uk) There is excellent climbing in the mountains and valleys around Tafraoute. The UK-based **Oxford Alpine Club** have been pioneers in mapping the area across recent years and have produced excellent pocket guidebooks detailing around 2000 different climbs of varying difficulty across the Anti Atlas mountains. Order the hard-copy books from its website or access digital versions online.

Auberge Les Amis　　　　　　HOTEL €
(☑ 0528 80 19 21; auberge.lesamis@yahoo.fr; Pl Moulay Rachid; s/d Dh130/200, r without bathroom Dh170, all incl breakfast; ❄ 🤶) Overlooking Pl Moulay Rachid, Les Amis has nine basic rooms across three floors and a welcoming team at reception. A new rooftop tent (Dh60 per person) was on order when we dropped by, promising to offer a more breezy alternative to the simple rooms with a subtle Berber ambience.

Afoulki　　　　　　　　　GUESTHOUSE €
(☑ 0528 80 14 92; www.maisondhotes-afoulki.com; s/d Dh100/200; 🤶) Above its cafe-restaurant (breakfast/menu Dh25/80), Afoulki's white rooms are bland but large and clean, with shared bathrooms and a roof terrace.

Hôtel Les Amandiers　　　　HOTEL €€
(☑ 0528 80 00 88; www.hotel-lesamandiers.com; s/d Dh385/496; ❄🤶🏊) This kasbah-like hilltop pile has 60 reasonably attractive rooms with small balconies taking in incredible views of the rock formations ringing Tafraoute. The pool and restaurant share the views, but the bar is tucked away inside without any vistas. The hotel is feeling a little tired and needs a renovation, but you may have the place to yourself.

🍴 Eating & Drinking

L'Étoile d'Agadir　　　　　　CAFE €
(breakfast Dh30; ⏰ 8am-6pm) Recommended by readers, this is Tafraoute's favourite cafe for a continental breakfast in the morning sun. After serving breakfast, L'Etoile remains open for drinks throughout the day.

Cafe-Restaurant Panorama　　　CAFE €
(mains Dh70; ⏰ 11am-10pm; 🤶) Recommended locally, this terrace eatery dishes up tajines, omelettes, large glasses of fruit juice and mountain views.

Café-Restaurant Atlas　　　　CAFE €
(mains Dh40; ⏰ 8am-10pm) The covered terrace at Atlas is a popular local hangout, with cheese omelettes, brochette, tajines and sandwiches on the broad menu.

⭐**Restaurant La Kasbah**　　MOROCCAN €€
(☑ 0672 30 39 09; set menu Dh100; ⏰ noon-9pm) Decorated with rugs, lanterns and jewellery, this licensed restaurant serves dishes including tajines, *harira* and the house speciality, nomad tortilla: *kalia* (minced mutton with tomato, peppers, egg, onion and 44 spices served in a tajine). Argan oil and spices abound in all the dishes.

Restaurant L'Étoile du Sud　　MOROCCAN €€
(☑ 0528 80 00 38; set menu Dh90; ⏰ moon-3pm & 6pm-late) L'Étoile du Sud serves a good set menu in a rather kitsch Bedouin-style tent. You may have to share the place with tour groups, particularly at lunchtime, but the service is professional and on warm nights it's one of the best places to eat.

Hôtel Les Amandiers　　　　　　BAR
(beer Dh20-30; ⏰ 4-11pm) Order a Flag Special or Heineken from the inside bar and then retire to the outside deck for great views. Just the ticket if you've been mountain biking or hiking amid Tafraoute's quirky landscapes. Note it's an uphill walk of around 1km from the centre of town.

🛍️ Shopping

Several slipper shops around the market area sell the traditional leather slippers (yellow for men, red for women). Look out, too, for people selling local argan and olive oil. Numerous shops around the post-office square sell Berber jewellery, argan products and souvenirs, and shopping here is less pressurised than in the cities.

Maison du Troc　　　　　　ARTS & CRAFTS
(⏰ 9am-9pm) A good range of Berber and Tuareg products, including pottery, jewellery, cactus-silk blankets and camel-wool kilims (carpets). Products are sourced from across the Anti Atlas region, not just locally.

Au Coin des Nomades　　GIFTS & SOUVENIRS
Berber handiwork and local souvenirs at reasonable prices. Hours are sporadic but

adjacent shopkeepers usually phone owner Houssine Laroussi if he is not around.

Maison Tuareg ARTS & CRAFTS
(⊙9am-12.30pm & 2.30-6pm Mon-Sat & by appointment) Stocks Berber and Tuareg carpets, jewellery and souvenirs from the Atlas, Rif and Sahara. Also has a booth opposite Hôtel Salama.

Souq ARTS & CRAFTS
(⊙Tue & Wed) A lively weekly souq takes place near Hôtel Salama. Small dealers sometimes sell Berber carpets here.

❶ Information

For tourist information and local events, visit www.tafraout.info.

There are numerous banks with ATMs and exchange facilities in the centre.

Banque Populaire (Pl Mohammed V; ⊙8.15am-3.45pm Mon-Fri)

BMCE (behind L'Étoile d'Agadir; ⊙8.30am-6.30pm Mon-Fri)

Internet Amelen (off Rue al-Jeish al-Malaki; per hr Dh5; ⊙8.30am-10pm)

Pharmacie al-Massira (☑0528 80 01 60; Pl al-Massira; ⊙8am-8.30pm)

Post Office (Pl Mohammed V; ⊙8am-4.15pm Mon-Fri) Has a *bureau de change.*

❶ Getting There & Away

BUS
Buses for regional destinations depart from outside the various company offices, mostly on

Rue al-Jeish al-Malaki. **CTM** (☑0528 80 17 89; www.ctm.ma; Rte Aguerd-Oudad) has departures to Tiznit (Dh35), Agadir (Dh70) and Sidi Ifni (Dh30).

Local **buses** to the Ameln Valley (Dh5) leave from outside Cafe Paris every half-hour, stopping on request at different villages. Lux bus 20 to Tiznit (Dh40) leaves from a **stop** near Pl Mohammed V.

Four buses from 11am Monday to Saturday travel to **Afella-Ighir** and Aït Mansour (Dh26) from outside the Auberge Les Amis. This service can be infrequent so check with Houssine Laroussi at Au Coin des Nomades to make sure it is still running.

TAXI
Station wagons and Land Rovers do the rounds of various villages in the area, mostly on market days. They hang around the post-office square, and on Rue al-Jeish al-Malaki by the Afriquia petrol station at the bottom of Tariq an-Nahzi. **Grands taxis** leave for Tiznit (Dh50) in the morning from the latter location.

Around Tafraoute

Tafraoute makes a good base for exploring some interesting landmarks and geological features around the area.

Tazekka & Tirnmatmat

The closest of the easily accessible examples of prehistoric rock engravings found in the Tafraoute area, the **Carved Gazelle** is 2km

---

WORTH A TRIP

RURAL RETREATS

Tizourgane Kasbah (☑0661 94 13 50; www.tizourgane-kasbah.com; Rte d'Agadir, Idaougnidif; r per person incl half-board Dh330; ☗) Overlooking the main road roughly 65km from Tafraoute and 100km from Agadir, is this stunning renovated 13th-century kasbah. Rooms are simply decorated, with carpets, stripy bedspreads, fans and shared bathrooms, but derive extra romance from the setting. There's a hammam, and a terrace restaurant surveys the wrinkled hillsides, scattered villages and Jebel L'Kest.

The kasbah was essentially a fortified town, enclosing 25 houses, a mosque, a granary and a prison, and thick stone walls tower above the passages around the ancient structure. If you're just passing, you can tour the kasbah for Dh10. Buses on the Aït Baha route to Agadir can drop you here.

El Malara (☑0658 18 18 36; www.elmalara.com; per person half-board Dh410; ❇☗⊠) Located above a mountain valley, expat French owners Bernardette and Jean have crafted a beautiful Moroccan guesthouse with six stylish rooms. Shared public spaces including a salon, a lounge and a bar, and a fine attention to detail flows through to traditional decor throughout the property. El Malara is located around 15km from Tafraoute down a piste road via the Painted Rocks.

El Malara is best visited with your own transport.

away in the village of Tazekka. It's a simple carving on the top face of a fallen block. The easiest way to find it is to walk along Rte de Tazekka, then make enquiries when you reach the village. It's not far from Camping Tazka on the Tiznit road (R104), so you could, alternatively, ask for directions there.

It's a pleasant mountain-bike ride or walk of around 2km from central Tafraoute.

◎ Sights

**Maison Berbere
Traditionnelle** NOTABLE BUILDING
(☑0673 82 90 54; Maisonberbere30@yahoo.fr; adult Dh15; ☺8am-6pm) Maison Traditionnelle stands in the largely uninhabited old hilltop village, where bulging boulders have been incorporated into the pisé walls of the centuries-old houses. You can visit the Carved Gazelle as part of a tour of the four-floor dwelling, where the knowledgeable proprietor Mahfoud's family once lived. It's possible to stay the night here (Dh150/230 per person including breakfast/half-board).

Mahfoud, a trekking guide, offers Berber music soirées and tea ceremonies.

Tirnmatmat ARCHAEOLOGICAL SITE
To find the rock engravings at Tirnmatmat, take the Tiznit road (R104), then after 14km turn north at Tahala towards Aït Omar. Just before the village, an unmarked piste (track) leads to Tirnmatmat, where you will find the gravures (engravings) along the riverbed (the local kids will lead you there, or you can engage a guide from Tafraoute). The village sits in a lovely spot and there are excellent walks in all directions.

Le Chapeau de Napoléon & the Pierres Bleues

The village of Aguerd-Oudad, 3km south of Tafraoute, makes for a nice stroll or bike ride. From the roundabout by the Afriquia petrol station in Tafraoute, take the road to Tiznit via Izerbi. On the way you will see the unmistakable rock formation known as Le Châpeau de Napoléon (Napoleon's Hat).

Some 7km south of Tafraoute, 500m past the foot of the road to the Afella-Ighir oasis, a *touristique piste* leads uphill to the right – to the Pierres Bleues (Painted Rocks), the work of Belgian artist Jean Verame.

Verame spray-painted the smooth, rounded boulders in shades of blue, red, purple and black in 1984 and, although the rocks have a faded air, they remain strange and impressive against the landscape. Local lore has it that the villagers give these incongruous tourist attractions a fresh coat of paint every year.

The packed-earth track is passable in a normal car, but this is prime mountain-biking territory. You can see the rocks a couple of kilometres from Tafraoute, then ride or drive right up to them some 5km away. The track leads 9km to the village of Afella Ouaday, 5km from Tafraoute on the Tiznit road (R104).

Ameln Valley & Jebel L'Kest

وادي اميلن وجبل لكست

Tafraoute lies in a basin, largely surrounded by craggy brown cliffs and rocks. To the northwest lies one such ridge, on the other side of which runs the Ameln Valley. North of the valley is Jebel L'Kest (2359m). From Tafraoute you can make out a rock formation in this range that resembles a lion's face. Villagers will jokingly tell you that he is there to guard the women while their husbands are away working.

From Tafraoute, the Agadir road (R104) takes you to the valley, dotted with picturesque Berber villages. Four kilometres out of Tafraoute, the road forks with the right branch turning east up the valley towards Agadir.

◎ Sights

Maison Traditionnelle MUSEUM
(☑0666 91 81 45; www.maisontraditionnelle. ma; Oumesnate; Dh10; ☺8am-sunset) At Oumesnate, 6km from Tafraoute, follow the signs through the village and then the footpath to this mountainside museum house. The three-storey granite, palm and argan house, some 400 years old, was inhabited by 20 family members – three generations – until 1982. The owners will take you on a fascinating tour, telling tales of traditional life.

🛏 Sleeping

The villages have numerous basic *gîtes* (trekkers' hostels), *maisons d'hôtes* (small hotels) and homestays; Au Coin des Nomades (p374) can organise a stay.

L'Arganier d'Ammelne HOTEL, CAMPGROUND €
(☑0528 80 00 69; www.arganierammelne. com; Rte d'Agadir, Tandilt; s/d incl half-board

Dh250/360; ❄📶🏊) L'Arganier d'Ammelne's pink, yellow and pisé rooms open onto a flowery garden. The terrace restaurant (meals/menu Dh40/80) serves dishes including local specialities and the recommended beef tajine with apricots, almonds and prunes. Five new rooms and a new swimming pool are evidence the friendly owners are keen to make sure their accommodation remains one of the best in the region.

Oumesnate Maison d'Hôte GUESTHOUSE €
(☎0661 51 37 93; www.maisontraditionnelle.ma; Oumesnate; s/d incl half-board Dh250/400; ❄📶) Staying in the guesthouse next to Oumesnate's Maison Traditionnelle – run by the same family – is a wonderful way to get an insight into Berber village life. If you have a car, spending a night here would be more interesting than Tafraoute. Rooms have en suites, and meals (Dh70) are available with notice. Trekking, 4WD and bike tours can be arranged.

Yamina GUESTHOUSE €
(☎0528 21 66 21, 0670 52 38 83; www.yamina-tafraout.com; Tandilt; r per person incl half-board Dh220; ❄📶) At the top of the village, Yamina is run by a Berber woman and her French husband, who have created a unique cross between a comfortable guesthouse and a *maison traditionnelle* (traditional house). Reached along terraces, courtyards and earthen walkways with low ceilings, the simple rooms are beautifully decorated with cheery paintwork on the walls and beams.

Chez Amaliya HOTEL €€
(☎0528 80 00 65; www.chezamaliya.com; Tazoulte; s/d incl breakfast from Dh330/500; ⌚closed Jun; ❄📶🏊) A few hundred metres past the turning for Tandilt, Oumesnate and Agadir, this Dutch-owned hotel is one of the valley's grandest options. A Berber tent and Jebel L'Kest's lion face rise above the pool, and paintings and local maps decorate the lobby. Rooms are comfortable, and there are three more spacious rooftop apartments (Dh1000) perfect for groups and families.

Chez Amaliya has the most well-stocked bar for many a mountain valley, and the smart restaurant (menu Dh100) is open from noon to 9pm and accepts nonguests. The chicken pastilla is recommended, but you'll need to give the kitchen at least two hours' notice.

ℹ Getting There & Away

Grands taxis (Dh8) head along the main road between the villages and Tafraoute has regular bus services (Dh5). Note these buses also double as the school bus and only run during the day.

Tata طاطا

POP 42,000

Situated on the Saharan plain at the foot of Jebel Bani, Tata was an oasis settlement along the trade route from West Africa. Its name, which roughly means 'take a break' in Tashelhit, recalls those days of Saharan caravans, as do the turban-wrapped men sipping tea in the shade. Close to the Algerian border, the small town has a garrison feel, with four types of police and military stationed here, and you may be questioned on your way into town. With good infrastructure and less hassle than other Saharan spots, Tata is poised to become more of a destination for travellers.

The town's *palmeraie* is well worth exploring. You can drive a 7km circuit of it, or catch a local bus (Dh5). Above the village at the far end of the *palmeraie* is a white hilltop *marabout* (saint's tomb), which you can see from Tata.

Activities

Tata is best as a base for off-the-beaten-track excursions, such as desert camping; Akka oasis, kasbah and *agadir*; and the rock engravings at Tiggane, Oum el-Alek and Tircht, among the finest in Morocco.

Maison du Patrimoine OUTDOORS
(☎0613 24 13 12; issam3599@hotmail.com; Ave Mohammed V; ⌚10am-4pm) Helpful multilingual Berber guide Isam, based at souvenir shop Maison du Patrimoine, charges about Dh350 per day for one or two people (Dh900 including 4WD). Opening hours are very flexible and it is best to contact him by email or phone prior to arriving in Tata.

Sleeping

Oasis Dar Ouanou GUESTHOUSE, CAMPGROUND €
(☎0660 23 25 38; www.dar-wanou.e-monsite.com/; Akka Izankad; per tent incl shower from Dh75, s/d incl breakfast Dh350/450; ❄📶) By the N12 3km southwest of Tata, this ramshackle but clean building has cool rooms, a courtyard with fountains and palms, and oasis and mountain views from the roof terrace.

Highly recommended if you have your own transport.

Hotel Les Relais des Sables   HOTEL €
(📞0528 80 23 01; Ave des FAR; s/d from Dh220/280; ❋ 🛜 🏊) Popular with tour groups and overlanders, the pool, bar, restaurant and gardens are more impressive than the small en-suite rooms in stuffy bungalows. Even if you're not staying here it's worth popping in for a frosty Flag Special – it's the only place you'll get a cold beer for many a kilometre.

Municipal Campsite   CAMPGROUND €
(Ave Mohammed V; per tent incl shower from Dh30) Next to the dry river, with a reasonable ablutions block that has flush toilets.

Hôtel La Renaissance   HOTEL €
(📞0528 80 22 25; larenaissance1982@gmail.com; Ave des FAR; s/d Dh150/200; 🛜) This central stalwart with *palmeraie* views has small but comfortable rooms and a pleasant lounge and breakfast area. The only downsides are the cramped bathrooms and the somewhat gloomy downstairs bar.

Dar Infiane   GUESTHOUSE €€€
(📞0528 80 21 04, 0661 61 01 70; www.darinfiane. com; Indfiane; r incl breakfast Dh884-1860, meals Dh200; ❋) Tata's old kasbah, perched above the *palmeraie,* has been turned into a Green Key guesthouse. Off a carpet-strewn central courtyard lie 10 rooms, in which the French owners have kept the original eccentricities such as low beams intact. The *dar* (house) has both loyal fans and detractors, with some guests raving about magical evenings on the rooftop terrace in the still of the Sahara night, while others criticising the service.

✗ Eating & Drinking
A few simple cafes dot Ave Mohammed V, Tata's main street, and most accommodation places also provide the option of half-board.

Oasis de Rêve   MOROCCAN €
(Ave Mohammed V; mains Dh30-40; ⏱8am-11pm) Located on the edge of the souq at the southern end of Tata's main drag, Oasis de Rêve has a friendly owner with a smidgen of English and the ability to rustle up something good most times of the day. How does chicken brochettes, chips and salad for around Dh40 sound? Don't forget to add a refreshing glass of homemade lemonade.

Hotel Les Relais des Sables   BAR
(Ave des FAR; ⏱4-11pm) The ambience inside this hotel bar is a tad smokey and blokey, but it's far more enjoyable having a Moroccan dust-dousing beer outside, sitting around the pool. Order the slightly more expensive Flag Special beer as the Stork brand is watery, soapy, and just maybe the world's worst beer.

ℹ Information
On Ave Mohammed V there's a post office, an internet cafe, banks with ATMs and money-changing facilities, and the seldom-open **Délégation de Tourisme** (📞0528 80 20 76; www.crt-guelmim.com/prevince-tata-en.html; ⏱10am-12.30pm & 2-5pm Mon-Fri).

ℹ Getting There & Away

BUS
Tata's new **Gare Routière** is located just south of the centre of town. CTM and Supratours do not serve Tata, but **Satas** (📞0672 31 18 43; Gare Routière; ⏱8.30am-12.30pm & 2-6pm Mon-Sat) has daily departures to the following destinations: Agadir (Dh100, eight hours), Goulimime (Dh102, five hours), Marrakesh (Dh170, 10 hours), Taroudannt (Dh60, five hours), Tiznit (Dh80, 6½ hours) and Zagora (Dh92, eight hours).

TAXI
Grands taxis leave from Pl de la Marche Verte to the following destinations: Akka-Irhen for Taliouine (Dh30), Agadir (Dh100), Bouizakarne for Tiznit (Dh100), Goulimime (Dh80), Igherm for Tafraoute (Dh50), Ouarzazate (Dh140) and Taroudannt (Dh80).

TREKKING IN THE ANTI ATLAS

The arid, pink- and ochre-coloured Anti Atlas are the last significant mountains before the Sahara, are little visited by trekkers, and yet they offer some wonderful trekking opportunities. Taliouine is well set up for trekking, and Tafraoute is the centre of the region. The quartzite massif of Jebel L'Kest (2359m), the 'amethyst mountain', lies about 10km north of Tafraoute, and the twin peaks of Adrar Mqorn (2344m) are 10km southeast. Beneath the jagged mass of these peaks lie lush irrigated valleys and a string of oases.

At the eastern end of the Anti Atlas near Taliouine, almost due south of Jebel Toubkal,

Jebel Siroua (3305m) rises starkly above the landscape. This dramatic volcano makes an excellent centrepiece of varied long-distance treks.

For further advice, and to arrange guides, mules and gear, contact operators in Tafraoute, Taliouine and Taroudannt.

Around Tafraoute

Morocco has such a wealth of trekking options that perhaps it is not surprising that an area with the potential of Tafraoute has not yet been fully exploited. The adventurous trekker will find here, as elsewhere in the Moroccan south, many challenging and rewarding treks. Because of local depopulation caused by movement to the cities, and the decline in the use of mules for agriculture, many paths are partially abandoned and nature is particularly wild here. Trekkers might spot Cuvier's gazelles, wild boars, Barbary sheep and rich endemic vegetation.

This is a tougher area than the M'Goun Massif or Tichka Plateau and trekkers will need to cope with a lack of facilities and the harsh climate. This close to the Sahara, summer (June until mid-September) is blisteringly hot, and winter sees the occasional snowfall on the high passes and peaks, so the region is best walked at the end of winter. Late February is ideal. Daytime temperatures may be 20°C, but at night it can drop below freezing.

Other than the odd small store, you won't find many supplies in the area, so the great challenge is carrying enough food and water to keep you going. As with other remote Moroccan areas, it is often possible to stay in village houses, but you must still be prepared to camp and to carry food and water.

The best way of doing this is by hiring a guide and mules; there are trekking guides – and *faux guides* – in Tafraoute. As ever, insist on seeing a guide's ID card before you start discussing possibilities. As a rule, trained mountain guides do not tout for business in the street. Mules are rarely found around Tafraoute, but you may be able to arrange this through your guide.

Jebel L'Kest and the approaches from Tafraoute are covered by the 1:50,000 map sheets *Had Tahala* and *Tanalt,* while the whole area is covered by 1:100,000 sheets *Annzi, Tafrawt, Foum al-Hisn* and *Taghjijt.* You should be able to find these maps in Au Coin des Nomades (p374), in specialist bookshops, or in good big-city bookshops in Morocco.

This part of the Atlas is not well developed for tourism, and transport is an issue throughout. *Camionettes* (pick-up trucks) and minibuses provide a reliable though infrequent service to some villages and grands taxis run on souq days, but at other times you may need to hire one to get to trailheads.

Jebel L'Kest

The area's star attraction is this massive quartzite ridge that stretches away northwest of Tafraoute. Despite the harshness of the landscape, the Berbers who live in local villages manage to grow the mountain staples of wheat, barley, olives, figs and almonds. The village of Tagdichte is the launching point for a day ascent of Jebel L'Kest (2359m). Tagdichte can be accessed by minibus or taxi, and homestay accommodation can be arranged there.

Ameln Valley

There are some 26 villages neatly spaced out through the Ameln Valley, which runs along the south side of Jebel L'Kest, and they make for a great walk. You'd need weeks to do a full circuit, but a stunningly beautiful and suitably stretching five-day walk would start in Oumesnate, take in several villages, and head up to Tagdichte for an ascent of Jebel L'Kest. Alternatively, the ascent could be tackled as part of a gentle trek east through the valley from, say, Tirnmatmat to Oumesnate, both just off the road. You could also base yourself at Oumesnate Maison d'Hôte (p379) and go on treks from there.

Adrar Mqorn & Around

Southeast of Tafraoute the possibilities are also exciting. The scramble up Adrar Mqorn (2344m) is hard but worthwhile. Due south of its twin peaks are the palm-filled gorges of Aït Mansour and Timguilcht, which make up Afella-Ighir oasis.

Jebel Aklim

Jebel Aklim (2531m) sits in an even remoter area than Jebel L'Kest, yet is surrounded by Berber villages in valleys guarded by old kasbahs. From the top, there are great views over to the High Atlas and Jebel Siroua. It makes a great focal point for a four- or five-

AFELLA-IGHIR

Southeast of Tafraoute is the pretty oasis of Afella-Ighir. Leave Tafraoute on the Aguerd-Oudad road, turning left a few kilometres south of the village, and travel roughly 25km over a mountain pass through Tlata Tasrirte to the start of the dramatic Aït Mansour Gorges. You can see the Pierres Bleues from the road up to the pass, which is often foggy and sometimes snowed over in winter.

You can drive through the gorges in a normal car if it hasn't rained, but walking or mountain biking is the best way to appreciate this atmospheric area, where red cliff faces tower above the palms.

Follow the road through a string of villages perched above the oasis, until you reach the T-junction in Gdourt after about 8km. Turn right here for Tiznit or to loop back to Tafraoute. Turning left, the next village is Souq el-Had Issi, a rather depressing settlement that accommodates workers from the nearby gold mine. From Souq el-Had Issi, the road leads south to Aït Herbil. After about 12km, there are some impressive rock carvings in Ukas, although you need a guide to find them.

A turn-off 1km beyond Souq el-Had Issi leads 5km northeast to the village of Tiwadou. In a 4WD, you can continue from Tiwadou through the Timguilcht Gorges to Tlata Tasrite (about 20km). At the time of writing, it was not possible to drive this circuit in a 2WD vehicle, as the road disintegrates after Tanrarte; the tarred road was being extended, so it should be possible in the future.

Contact Houssine Laroussi at Au Coin des Nomades (p374) in Tafraoute to book accommodation in these areas and also confirm bus details from Tafraoute.

Sleeping

Auberge Aït Mansour (☎ 0676 73 51 98; r per person Dh80, with half-board Dh170) In the village of Aït Mansour at the beginning of the gorges and oasis, Auberge Aït Mansour offers mattresses on the floor and new flush toilets. Owner Abdou can guide you to the old village nearby for oasis views and cooks a mean Berber omelette.

Auberge Sahnoun (☎ 0528 21 83 65, 0667 09 53 76; maisonsahnoun@gmail.com; r per person incl half-board Dh150) A turn-off 1km beyond Souq el-Had Issi leads 5km northeast to the village of Tiwadou, where the family-run Auberge Sahnoun is on the edge of a *palmeraie* (palm grove). It has three basic rooms, with mattresses on the floor and a shared bathroom with hot water, and a roof terrace. The auberge's late owner, Mohamed Sahnoun, was involved in village development projects.

day walk out of Igherm, which is roughly equidistant from Tafraoute (to the southwest), Taroudannt, Taliouine and Tata.

Jebel Siroua

Some way south of the High Atlas, at the eastern edge of the Anti Atlas, the isolated volcanic peak of Jebel Siroua offers unique trekking opportunities. Remote villages, tremendous gorges, a tricky final ascent and some dramatic scenery all make this an excellent place for trekkers in search of solitude, stark beauty and a serious walk.

The Jebel Siroua ascent is the most obvious walk, but, as ever in Morocco, lasting memories will be found elsewhere: in the beauty of lush valleys, in the hospitality shown in Berber homes, in the play of light on rock and in the proximity of the Sahara. So if you don't fancy the climb to the summit, the mountain circuit still makes a wonderful trek, with diverse scenery, traditional activities in the villages and beautiful, well-maintained agricultural terraces.

Mules can also be hired at short notice (often the next day) at villages around the mountain.

The 1:100,000 *Taliwine* and 1:50,000 *Sirwa* maps cover the route. In winter it can be fiercely cold here, so the best times to trek are autumn, when the saffron harvest takes place, and spring. You should be able to find these maps in Au Coin des Nomades (p374), in specialist bookshops, or in good big-city bookshops in Morocco.

If you need supplies, there are small stores in Taliouine and Tazenart, and weekly markets take place in Taliouine, Aoulouz, Askaoun, Tazenakht and Igli.

Routes

There's a challenging, week-long trek that allows you to walk out of Taliouine along a gentle dirt trail, which heads eastward up the **Zagmouzen Valley** to **Tagmout**. The route then heads northeast through **Atougha**, from where the summit of Jebel Siroua is best reached in two days, with a night at **Tegragra**. Walking at a regular pace, you'll ascend the summit on the morning of the fourth day.

After descending into the gorges, you'll reach the extraordinary cliff village of **Tizgui**, where you can spend the night, before continuing to **Tagouyamt** on the fifth day. The village has limited supplies and, in case you can't find a room, a good place to camp in the amazing **Tislit Gorge**. From Tislit, the valley continues to Ihoukarn, from where you can head south to the Taliouine–Ouarzazate road at Tizi n'Taghatine (organise beforehand in Taliouine to be picked up here); or complete the circuit by walking west back to Taliouine (two days from Tislit via Tagmout and the Zagmouzen Valley).

An alternative circuit that is even less trekked starts at the village of Tamlakout, where there is a classified *gîte,* and takes in Aït Tigga, the Assif Mdist and the foot of Jebel Siroua. It then ascends the mountain, continues to Aziouane and exits via the Amassines. Some of the trek is strenuous but should not involve more than six hours' walking in any day.

Taliouine and Anezale (for Tamlakout) are both on the main Taroudannt–Ouarzazate road, regularly served by grands taxis and buses.

SOUTHERN ATLANTIC COAST

Tiznit تزنيت

POP 53,600

South of the Souss Valley and at the western end of the Anti Atlas, Tiznit is an old walled medina town surrounded by modern development. It was originally the site of a cluster of forts that were encircled in the 19th century by some 5km of pisé wall. It quickly became a trade centre and remains a provincial capital and centre for Berber jewellery, with a souq devoted to the silver stuff. This slow-paced and authentic spot, with its dusty medina lanes and conservative but friendly inhabitants, is a convenient stop-off between the Anti Atlas and Atlantic Coast.

History

In 1881 Sultan Moulay al-Hassan (1873–94) founded Tiznit as a base from which to assert his authority over the rebellious Berber tribes of the south. To do this, he built the town's perimeter walls. Jewish silversmiths were moved into the town and gave it a reputation for silver workmanship.

However, Tiznit remained embroiled in local sedition, and was a centre of dissent against the 1912 treaty that turned Morocco into a French and Spanish protectorate. This resistance movement was led by El-Hiba, the so-called 'Blue Sultan' from the Western Sahara, who earned his nickname for always wearing his Saharawi veil.

Following Sultan Moulay Hafid's capitulation to the French at the Treaty of Fès, El-Hiba proclaimed himself sultan here in 1912. The southern tribes rose to support him and El-Hiba marched north at the head of an army of men from the Tuareg and Anti Atlas tribes. They were welcomed as liberators in Marrakesh, but much of the army was slaughtered by the French as it moved towards Fez. El-Hiba retreated to Taroudannt, then Tiznit, then up into the Anti Atlas, where he pursued a campaign of resistance against the French until his death in 1919.

◉ Sights

Tiznit medina is a sleepy place where it is fun to wander around spots such as the jewellery souq and Rue Imzilne, a street of leather-sandal shops. The Berber traders here are tough salesmen, but it is still worth trying to strike a bargain. Things liven up considerably on Thursday, which is market day.

City Walls HISTORIC SITE
It's possible to climb onto sections of the 5km-long city walls, which have some 30 towers and nine gates. On the northern side of the medina, **Bab Targua** overlooks a *palmeraie* with a natural spring, used as a laundry by local women.

Grande Mosquée MOSQUE
The minaret of the Grande Mosquée (closed to non-Muslims) is studded with jutting wooden sticks. Local legend suggests this is where the souls of the dead congregate. More likely, these were left in place by the

Tiznit

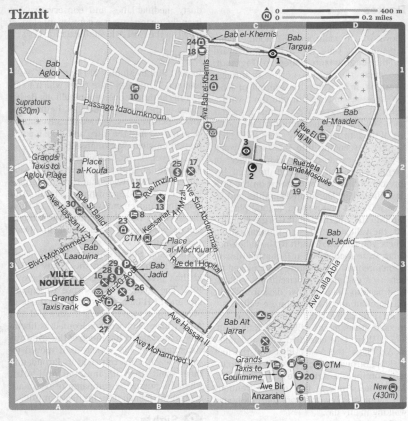

Tiznit

◉ Sights
1 City Walls...C1
2 Grande Mosquée......................................C2
3 Source Bleue...C2

🛏 Sleeping
4 Bab el Maader..D2
5 Camping Municipal....................................C4
6 Hôtel Al Amal..C4
7 Hôtel de Paris...C4
8 Hôtel des Touristes...................................B2
9 Hotel Tiznit...C4
10 Maison Du Soleil......................................B1
11 Riad Janoub...D2
12 Riad Le Lieu...B2

🍴 Eating
13 À l'ombre du figuier..................................B2
14 Food Market...B3
15 Idou Tiznit Supermarket...........................C4
16 La Ville Nouvelle.......................................A3
   Restaurant Al Amal.........................(see 6)
   Riad Le Lieu...................................(see 12)

17 Snack Stands...B2

🍷 Drinking & Nightlife
18 Cafe Panoramique....................................B1
19 Espace Asrir...C2
20 Hotel Mauritania......................................C4

🛍 Shopping
21 Bijouterie Ban Alkhmis............................C1
22 Ensemble Artisanal..................................B3
23 Jewellery Souq...B3
24 Trésor du Sud...B1

ℹ Information
25 Bank...B2
26 Banque Populaire......................................B3
27 BMCE...A4
28 BMCI..B3
29 Tiznit Voyages..B3

ℹ Transport
30 Bus Stop for Sidi Ifni, Mirleft and
   Tiznit..A2

masons who built the minaret to help them climb up and replaster. A similar arrangement is used on minarets in Mali and Niger.

Recently added signage – in French, Arabic and Berber – explains the history of the mosque.

Source Bleue
HISTORIC SITE

The original town spring is now a shallow, stagnant pool, and green rather than blue. Legend claims a woman of ill repute, Lalla Zninia, stopped to rest here at what was then plain desert. She spent the next three days repenting her wicked ways, and God was so impressed that he showed forgiveness by having a spring gush beneath her feet.

Her name was thus given to the village that preceded Sultan Moulay al-Hassan's 19th-century fortress town. The adjacent citadel is undergoing careful restoration and is also worthy of a quick stroll. Nearby are more jewellery and Berber crafts shops.

🛏 Sleeping

Hotels are gathered around the large roundabout to the southeast of Bab Oulad Jarrar, with a few options in the medina.

Maison Du Soleil
GUESTHOUSE €

(☑ 0672 311 353; www.facebook.com/maisondus oleiltiznit; 470 Rue Tafoukt; r incl breakfast Dh350; 🗦) In a residential area in the northwestern medina, the 'House of the Sun' fulfills its name on the rooftop terrace and the two spacious en-suite rooms adjoining it. The rooms with shared bathrooms downstairs are more prosaic, but host Sliman is friendly and super-organised. The bright interior decor is a colourful surprise just metres from the medina's neutral walls.

Bab el Maader
GUESTHOUSE €

(☑ 0673 90 73 14; www.bab-el-maader.com; 132 Rue El Haj Ali; r Dh330; ⊘ Sep-Jun) This traditional house in the medina is one of Tiznit's best addresses, a five-room guesthouse with a courtyard, plenty of great decorative touches and good use of Moroccan fabrics and materials. The French-Moroccan team can give pointers and arrange trips in the region.

Riad Le Lieu
GUESTHOUSE €

(☑ 0528 600 019; riadlelieu@hotmail.fr; 273 Impasse Issaoui; r/ste/apt Dh220/290/320; 🗦) Five double rooms and suites and a four–person apartment share this former courthouse with the restaurant of the same name. One suite has a private shower, but otherwise the rooms and suites share bathrooms. Rooms

are poky, but the warm welcome and copious breakfast (Dh30) make this a relaxing haven in the medina.

Hotel Tiznit
HOTEL €

(☑ 0528 86 24 11; tiznit-hotel@menara.ma; Ave Bir Anzarane; s/d Dh260/350; 🗦☀) Set in leafy grounds with a large pool, Tiznit is unexciting and a little rundown but comfortable and welcoming. The pink rooms are reasonably spacious with TV and small bathroom.

Hôtel de Paris
HOTEL €

(☑ 0528 86 28 65; www.hoteldeparis.ma; Ave Hassan II; s/d Dh120/160; ❊🗦) The rooms with en suites are clean but simple, and a friendly welcome and a handy cafe-restaurant downstairs makes Hôtel de Paris a good choice if you're just overnighting between buses.

Hôtel des Touristes
HOTEL €

(☑ 0528 86 20 18; Pl al-Méchouar; s/d from Dh50/90; 🗦) This welcoming 1st-floor hotel is a dependable, central budget option. Rooms are entered from a quiet, cheerful communal area with a book exchange; those overlooking Pl al-Méchouar have small balconies, but all lack fans. The room next to the flush toilet is particularly hot and noisy.

Camping Municipal
CAMPGROUND €

(☑ 0528 60 13 54; Bab Oulad Jarrar; per person Dh36) The municipal campground is next to the old walls.

★ Riad Janoub
GUESTHOUSE €€

(☑ 0679 00 55 10; www.riadjanoub.com; 193 Rue de la Grande Mosquée; r incl breakfast from Dh750; ❊🗦☀) French couple Gilbert and Claudine are attentive hosts in this modern riad, which has Moroccan and European salons, a massage room, a hammam and a roof terrace, all overlooking the pool and garden of palms and cacti. The six comfortable rooms, including a wheelchair-accessible option, have soft colour schemes, rugs and traditional trimmings.

Hôtel Al Amal
HOTEL €€

(☑ 0528 862 462; 465 Ave Bir Anzarane; s/d incl breakfast Dh400/450; 🗦) Tiznit's newest hotel features spotless, if slightly compact, rooms, a good cafe downstairs and a rooftop pizza restaurant. Decor combines calming neutral tones and the colourful accent of Moroccan art. The Al Amal had only opened for six months when we visited; get in before the telltale odour of secondhand cigarette smoke takes hold.

SELF-CATERING IN TIZNIT

Stock up before hitting the long road south:

Idou Tiznit Supermarket (Bab Oulad Jarrar; ⊙9am-12.30pm & 2.30-8pm Mon-Sat) Behind the hotel of the same name, selling a range of local and imported food.

Food Market (Ave du 20 Août; ⊙9am-4pm Mon-Sat) Good option for picnic supplies.

Eating

Restaurant Al Amal MOROCCAN, PIZZA €
(☑0528 862 462; 465 Ave Bir Anzarane; mains Dh30-50; ⊙8am-11pm; ⊛) Tiznit's newest hotel also hosts a couple of good eating options pitched at a higher level than most of the city's other cafes and restaurants. Seafood, tagines and good pasta are the standouts, the downstairs cafe is known for good breakfasts, and the Al Amal's rooftop terrace has pizza-enhanced views of Tiznit's busy main intersection.

La Ville Nouvelle CAFE €
(17 Ave du 20 Août; mains Dh30-66; ⊙7am-9pm; ⊛) At this popular multistorey cafe, brisk waiters serve the classic salads, brochettes, tajines and *kefta* (spiced lamb or beef meatballs). It's also a top spot for a coffee, some of Tiznit's best French-style baked goods, and there's even a special nonsmoking floor.

Snack Stands FAST FOOD €
(snacks from Dh5; ⊙11am-10pm) Along Ave Sidi Abderhman, the main road through the medina.

★ **À l'Ombre du Figuier** MOROCCAN, INTERNATIONAL €€
(☑0528 861 204; www.facebook.com/ombredu figuier; 22 Passage Akchouch, Quartier Idzakri; mains Dh60-75; ⊙11.30am-3pm & 6-10pm) Follow the signs through alleyways and under low doorways to one of southern Morocco's best restaurants. Colourful tables are arrayed under the dappled shade of a sprawling fig tree, and the concise menu offers just five meat or seafood dishes. Chicken, beef, shrimps and calamari all feature, and side dishes include a delicious cucumber and melon soup or Moroccan salad.

Definitely leave room for dessert of chocolate mousse or chilled pineapple gazpacho.

Riad Le Lieu MOROCCAN €€
(☑0528 60 00 19; riadlelieu@hotmail.fr; 273 Impasse Issaoui; mains Dh35-95; ⊙8am-10pm; ⊛) The charming Aïcha attracts locals and tourists alike with her daily specials, which typically include tomato and goat's-cheese salad, *pastilla* and camel, beef or sardine tajine. The intimate setting is a yellow courtyard with foliage and lanterns overhead. There are just four tables, so it pays to drop by and book ahead.

 Drinking & Nightlife

Espace Asrir CAFE
(☑0662 767 904; 133 Rue Id Ali Oubihi; ⊙10am-11pm; ⊛) Housed in a heritage courtyard house, Asrir is a surprising find amid the winding laneways of Tiznit's medina. Excellent juices and coffee are served to a soundtrack of delicate birdsong, and old radios and a piano fill nooks and crannies perfect for escaping the Moroccan sun. Tiznit's hipper younger residents come to chat over sheesha, mint tea and light snacks.

Hotel Mauritania BAR
(Ave Bir Anzarane; ⊙10am-10pm) Quite probably the only place in town to get a cold beer, the back bar at the Hotel Mauritania dispenses icy Heineken and Flag Special, making it a favourite watering hole of visiting motorcycle riders and 4WD desert-bashing enthusiasts.

Cafe Panoramique CAFE
(Ave Sidi Abderhman; ⊙8.30am-6pm) Panoramique has views of the city walls and surrounding countryside from its roof terrace.

Shopping

Bijouterie Ban Alkhmis JEWELLERY
(☑0644 977 387; bablhkmiss@gmail.com; Ave Sidi Abderhman; ⊙9am-6pm) A good location for traditional silver and Berber handcrafts but you'll need to bargain hard over multiple cups of mint tea.

Jewellery Souq JEWELLERY
(⊙8.30am-8pm Mon-Sat) With its long history of silversmiths, the jewellery souq has some of southern Morocco's best work. It's a pleasant place to wander, with blue-doored shops and windows full of silverware. Some of the jewellery is made in Tiznit, and some bought from Saharan tribes to the south. You'll need time to look around and bargain to get the best prices.

Trésor du Sud JEWELLERY
(www.tresordusud.com; Bab el-Khemis, Ave Sidi Abderhman; ☺9am-5pm Mon-Sat & by appointment) Jewellery shops are found along Ave Sidi Abderhman, the main road through the medina. At the top, Trésor du Sud is not the cheapest, but the work is good and it deals in hallmarked solid silver.

Ensemble Artisanal JEWELLERY
(Ave du 20 Août; ☺9am-12.30pm & 2.30-8pm Mon-Sat) Craftsmen ply their wares in a hassle-free environment.

ⓘ Information

EMERGENCY
Police Post (Ave Sidi Abderhman)

INTERNET ACCESS
There are internet cafes around Pl al-Méchouar.

MONEY
Most banks with ATMs and exchange facilities are in the **ville nouvelle** (Ave Sidi Abderhman; ☺8.30am-6.30pm Mon-Fri), but there are banks in the medina.

Local branches include **BMCE** (Ave Mohammed V; ☺8.30am-6.30pm Mon-Fri), **BMCI** (Ave du 20 Août; ☺8.30am-6.30pm Mon-Fri) and **Banque Populaire** (Ave du 20 Août; ☺8.30am-6.30pm Mon-Fri).

POST
Main Post Office (Ave du 20 Août; ☺8.30am-4.30pm Mon-Fri) In the ville nouvelle.

Post Office (Ave Sidi Abderhman; ☺8.30am-4.30pm Mon-Fri) In the medina.

TOURIST INFORMATION
Tiznit Voyages (☑0528 86 21 17; Ave Hassan II; ☺9am-12.30pm & 2-5pm Mon-Sat) This RAM agent also organises excursions and has local maps.

ⓘ Getting There & Away

BUS
Inter-city will eventually leave from the **new bus station** just off the Tafraoute road, but at the time of writing this new departure point was still not open. CTM has an **office** closer to the centre on the same road, and also one on **Pl al-Méchouar** in the medina. CTM serves the following destinations: Agadir (Dh40, two hours), Dakhla (Dh370, 20 hours), Goulimime (Dh45, 2½ hours), Laâyoune (Dh210, nine hours), Tafraoute (Dh40, 2½ hours) and Tan Tan (Dh95, 4½ hours).

BEYOND THE GLITTER

Berber jewellery serves a much wider purpose than simple adornment. A woman's jewellery identifies her as a member of a clan or tribe, it is a sign of her wealth, it reflects cultural traditions, and it has power beyond the visual – to protect her from the evil eye.

A woman will receive jewellery from her mother until she marries. For her marriage, her future husband will commission his mother or sister to provide jewellery. These pieces will be kept by her as a dowry and added to throughout her life; they will always be made of silver, as gold is considered evil.

Necklaces are important; the traditional assemblage in the southern oasis valleys sometimes features talismans of silver, pink coral, amazonite, amber, Czech glass and West African ebony beads. Women will also own bracelets, *fibulas* (elaborate brooches, often triangular, used for fastening garments), anklets, earrings and headdresses. Some jewellery will be worn every day, while the finest pieces will be saved for occasions such as festivals, pilgrimages and funerals.

Jewellery's protective, medicinal and magical properties are extremely important. The necklaces contain charms bought from magicians or holy men, offering protection against the evil eye, disease, accidents and difficulties in childbirth. Silver is believed to cure rheumatism; coral symbolises fertility and is thought to have curative powers; amber is worn as a symbol of wealth and to protect against sorcery (it's also considered an aphrodisiac and a cure for colds); amazonite and carnelian stones are used in divining fortunes; and shells traded from East Africa symbolise fertility.

Talismans feature stylised motifs of animals, the sun, moon and stars, which are all believed to have supernatural powers. A common symbol to ward off the evil eye is the hand of Fatima, daughter of the Prophet Mohammed. Any depiction of the hand (which represents human creative power and dominance), or of the number five, is believed to have the same effect as metaphorically poking your fingers into the evil eye with the words *khamsa fi ainek* (five in your eye).

Supratours (www.supratours.ma) offers similar services from its office northwest of the medina.

Cheaper bus-company offices are clustered on Ave Lalla Abla, just northeast of the roundabout near Bab Oulad Jarrar.

Green Lux buses leave from a stand near Bab Laaouina on the western edge of the medina. Bus 18 travels to Sidi Ifni (Dh20) via Mirleft (Dh10) and bus 20 (Dh40) to Tiznit.

TAXI

Taxis leave from the main grand-taxi rank, opposite the main post office in the western part of town, serving the following destinations: Agadir (Dh35), Inezgane (Dh30), Mirleft (Dh20), Sidi Ifni (Dh30) and Tafraoute (Dh40).

Taxis for Aglou Plage (Dh5) leave from a stand on Ave Hassan II, and for Goulimime (Dh42) from a stand just south of the roundabout near Bab Oulad Jarrar, (across Rte de Goulimime from the Total garage).

ⓘ Getting Around

Red petits taxis charge Dh7 for a journey (Dh10 after 7.30pm).

Aglou Plage   شاطئ اكلو

Aglou Plage, 14km northwest of Tiznit, is a long beach with good surf, although the strong undertow makes it dangerous for swimming most of the time. When the Atlantic winds start blustering, it's a wild and woolly sort of place. Development is taking its toll, but the settlement has some charm, with a raised walkway for promenading between the seafront cafes.

If you're driving from Tiznit to Mirleft, the route via Aglou Plage takes you along a beautiful stretch of coastline.

🛏 Sleeping & Eating

Besides Le Chant du Chameau, accommodation includes campgrounds and cheap hotels.

Aglou Plage has many cafes serving good seafood with a side order of ocean views.

Le Chant du Chameau   GUESTHOUSE €
(☑0667 90 49 91; www.chantduchameau.com; per person incl breakfast/half-board Dh275/385) Le Chant du Chameau is a delightful French-Moroccan-run guesthouse at the south end of Aglou beach. Apart from a rust-red house, some fantasy tents, and a dramatic view of the beach and sea, it also offers excursions in the area and a weeklong course in *tadelakt,* the local plasterwork.

ⓘ Getting There & Away

Lux bus 1 (Dh5) runs from Tiznit to Aglou Plage. Bus 18 links Tiznit to Sidi Ifni via Mirleft and some departures also stop at Aglou Plage en route. Grand taxis (Dh5) run from Tiznit to Aglou Plage.

Mirleft   ميرلفت

POP 6500

One of the region's most beautiful roads runs south of Aglou Plage, offering wonderful views of the ocean, rugged hills and the occasional empty cove. Then comes Mirleft, with a burgeoning surf scene and beckoning cafes under the arches on its main street. Historically popular with artists, musicians and overlanders recovering from Saharan crossings, this cosmopolitan little spot is developing as fans of water and wind sports discover the area. Mirleft also has a healthy share of the best coastal accommodation south of Essaouira. The climate is gentle, the air clear, the views magnificent – and the fledgling tourism development has largely been the work of individuals, rather than corporations or chains.

⊙ Sights & Activities

Stroll down the arcaded main street, which resembles the set of a cowboy film. Under the pink-and-blue arches you will find arts and crafts, argan products, souvenirs, carpets, surfboards, beach-tennis sets and two small vegetable markets.

If at first the scruffy village seems uninspiring, the gentle bustle soon becomes contagious. A social morning coffee is followed by a trip to the beach – choose from the village's largest beach, Imin Tourga (also known as *la grande plage*), Fish Beach, Camping Beach, Coquillage Beach, Aftas Beach, Plage Sauvage and Marabout's Beach. The last is the most dramatic, with its marabout's tomb and savage-looking rocks.

There are plenty of activities to keep you busy, with several surf schools, mostly located on the road to Imin Tourga. The beach is good for surf casting (fishing), and hotels and guides can organise trips from trekking to desert excursions.

Le Jardin d'Orient   HAMMAM, MASSAGE
(☑0652 241 020; 1hr treatment Dh100; ⊙by appointment) Look for the blue door behind the fish market to discover this stylish

combination of massage and hammam. Beauty therapies are also available.

Spot-M
SURFING

(☑0661 44 19 33; www.surfingholidaysmorocco. com) British-owned surf specialist with a fully equipped surf shop in the middle of town and accommodation in a beach house in Imin Tourga. Beginner and intermediate surfers are welcomed and one- to five-night trips exploring remote Saharan waves are also offered.

Surf en Marruecos
SURFING

(☑0615 99 04 70; www.surfenmarruecos.com) This Spanish-owned surf school has spearheaded Mirleft's development as a surf destination, organising an international longboard competition here every August.

Le Nid d'Aigle
PARAGLIDING

(☑0658 45 82 23; www.nidaigle.com) Tandem paragliding flights begin at €50 and accommodation, including half-board, is €45 per night.

Paraglide Morocco
PARAGLIDING

(☑0676 31 86 55; www.paraglidemorocco.com) The British-owned outfit is geared towards seasoned paragliders, but tandem flights (Dh550) are available.

🛏 Sleeping

As well as decent hotels and bed and breakfasts, there are plenty of short-let apartments in Mirleft, costing from about Dh220 per night; ask at the entrance to the village.

Hôtel Abertih
HOTEL €

(☑0528 71 93 04; www.abertih.com; s/d incl breakfast Dh200/300, without bathroom Dh180/240; ☎) Looking like it popped out of a Cubist painting, blue-and-yellow Abertih is equally colourful inside, where open courtyards lead to 11 rooms above the licensed ground-floor restaurant. The French-owned hotel offers half-board and hire-car packages, making it popular with paragliding groups.

Hotel du Sud
HOTEL €

(☑0528 71 94 07; www.hotel-mirleft.fr; s/d Dh120/170; ☎) The Sud's basic upstairs rooms are simply but tastefully decorated, with colourful bedspreads and vintage postcards. The rudimentary shared bathrooms have showers in stalls, but the turquoise patio and roof terrace are cool refuges on hot days.

Hotel Atlas
HOTEL €

(☑0528 71 93 09; atlasmirleft@gmail.com; s/d Dh200/300, s/d without shower Dh120/240, meals from Dh20, all incl breakfast; ☎) French-owned Atlas' palatial roof terrace is a popular fixture on the southern surf circuit. The blue-shuttered rooms, entered from a corridor open to the elements, are pleasantly rustic and the hotel has a 1st-floor balcony and ground-floor restaurant (meals from Dh20).

Aftas Beach House
HOSTEL €

(☑0675 164 271; www.aftasmirleft.com; Aftas Beach; s/d from Dh170/220; ☎) This whitewashed house overlooking the rocky cove of Aftas Beach has simple but clean rooms, all with shared bathroom facilities. Nearby are three beachfront cafes and endless Atlantic waves, and surf lessons can be arranged. There's normally a two-night minimum stay.

Sally's Bed & Breakfast
B&B €€

(☑0528 71 94 02; www.sallymirleft.com; Les Amicales; r incl breakfast Dh600-1300; ☎) Created by a horse-loving Englishwoman, Sally, this gorgeous cliff-top villa above Imin Tourga, one of Mirleft's largest and cleanest beaches, has breathtaking views up the coast. With six en-suite rooms and antiques decorating the lounge, it's a stylish and comfortable hideaway.

Aftas Trip
GUESTHOUSE €€

(☑0666 02 65 37; www.aftas-trip.com; tents Dh330, r Dh550; ☎) Superb Atlantic views and a versatile range of accommodation combines at this hilltop destination around 5km north of Mirleft town. Rooms range from family-friendly mini-apartments through to more prosaic Berber-style tents, and the English-speaking Aftas Trip team can arrange surfing, paddleboarding, fishing and desert explorations by trekking or 4WD. Meals are served in a large Berber tent in the pretty garden.

★ Les 3 Chameaux
GUESTHOUSE €€€

(☑0528 71 91 87; www.3chameaux.com; s/d/ste incl half-board Dh1200/1490/1790; ❈🛜🏊) High on the hill, in a renovated 1930s military fort, is Mirleft's best address, a lovely guesthouse with fabulous views over the village to the sea beyond. It's worth paying extra for one of the suites, which have balconies and bathroom windows surveying the sea or the valley behind the property. Rooms are less impressive, without TV or air-conditioning.

Facilities include the pool (heated during the winter), hammam, licensed restaurant and boutique. The only sound is the roar of the surf far below, and you'll feel yourself unwinding as soon as you arrive.

Dar Najmat
BOUTIQUE HOTEL €€€

(☏ 0528 71 90 56; www.darnajmat.com; s/d incl half-board Dh1290/1640, apt Dh1900; ❄ ⎙ ⛱) With its infinity pool seemingly melting into Marabout's Beach, Dar Najmat's view is one of the best on the Moroccan coast. You'll want to start taking photos as soon as you pull off the road, 2km south of Mirleft. The decor in the seven rooms and two-bedroom apartment is perfectly judged, with Moroccan materials achieving a contemporary and harmonious ambience.

✖ Eating & Drinking

The highly convivial bar at the Hôtel Abertih serves decent wine and exceptionally cold San Miguel lager.

La Bonne Franquette
MOROCCAN €

(Hotel du Sud; mains Dh40-70; ⊙ noon-3pm & 6-10pm) Mirleft's best daytime dining option is La Bonne Franquette, the downstairs restaurant at the Hotel du Sud. Standout dishes include seafood – try the shrimp tagine or calamari – and a few more surprising plates on offer are rabbit with mustard or camel brochettes.

Cafe Aftas
CAFE €

(☏ 0670 72 95 83; www.cafeaftas.com; Aftas Beach; snacks Dh20-30; ⊙ 8am-10pm; ⛱) Mint tea, coffee and omelettes combine with up close and personal views of Aftas Beach at this fun spot with a funky beach-shack ambience. Colourful murals and the easygoing vibe of owner Najib create one of Morocco's most laid-back cafes. He can also hook you up with surfing lessons through his Chasseurs de Vagues surf school.

Tifawin Cafe
CAFE €

(☏ 0611 908 323; www.facebook.com/Tifawin-Cafe; snacks & mains Dh20-30; ⊙ 7.30am-10pm; ⛱) Tifawin's laid-back cosmopolitan style includes excellent juices and smoothies – especially anything incorporating creamy avocado – and Moroccan pancakes with honey or *amlou* (a winning combination of honey and almonds). Comfort food for hungry surfers includes muesli, omelettes and toasted sandwiches, and Tifawin's bright blue-and-yellow decor adds a colourful touch to Mirfelt's arcaded main drag.

Restaurant Ayour
BERBER €

(☏ 0528 71 91 71; meals Dh70; ⊙ noon-10pm) Cosy Ayour is one of Mirleft's better standalone restaurants. It's slightly overpriced but tajines, spaghetti and fish dishes are all on the menu.

★ Hôtel Abertih
MOROCCAN €€

(☏ 0528 71 93 04; Hôtel Abertih; mains Dh60-120; ⊙ 7pm-late) The restaurant and bar at the Hôtel Abertih puts a cosmopolitan after-dark spin on Mirleft. Round tables host diners for an ever-changing menu of seafood and meat dishes, and after grilled sole or couscous with chicken, leave room for dessert with one of coastal Morocco's better crème caramels. There's also a compact wine list and a lots of cold beer.

Book ahead if you can, but Damien the friendly French owner usually finds room for additional diners on the 1st floor.

ⓘ Getting There & Away

Lux bus 18 links Mirleft to Tiznit (Dh10) and Sidi Ifni (Dh10). Grand taxis also run to Sidi Ifni (Dh13) and Tiznit (Dh15) from Mirleft.

Sidi Ifni
سيدي إفني

POP 21,618

Only returned to Morocco by the Spanish in 1969, Sidi Ifni retains an atmospheric Iberian flair, and the faded art-deco buildings are a haunting reminder of colonial ambitions. At the heart of what was the Spanish Sahara, Ifni was once a base for slave-trading operations and later a large exporter of fish to the Spanish mainland. When the sun sets on the ocean esplanade and dilapidated *calles* (streets), and the Atlantic rolls in, Ifni seems an eerie outpost.

The locals have painted the town blue and white, and continue the colour scheme in their turbans and robes. They support Spanish football teams, take siestas and are more likely to greet travellers with *hola* than *bonjour*. You might hear Spanish beats blaring from a cafe, and the expats and local cafe crowd are laid-back even by Moroccan standards. Equally easygoing are visiting surfers, seeking out excellent Atlantic waves on nearby beaches.

History

Spain acquired the enclave of Sidi Ifni after defeating the Moroccan forces in the war of 1859. They christened their new possession

Santa Cruz del Mar Pequeña, but seem to have been uncertain as to what to do with it as they did not take full possession until 1934. Most of Ifni dates from the 1930s and features an eclectic mix of art deco and traditional Moroccan styles.

On Moroccan independence in the late 1950s, Spain refused to withdraw, citing the fact that some 60% of the town's population was Spanish. The protracted dispute over territorial rights included the Ifni War, in which the town was besieged. It eventually ended in 1969, when the UN brokered an agreement for Spain to cede the enclave back to Morocco. Santa Cruz was renamed Sidi Ifni, after a holy man buried in the town in the early 1900s. Ifni still celebrates 'Independence Day' (30 June) with a festival on the abandoned airfield.

Ifni is mostly a contented place, but clashes occasionally erupt between the police and townsfolk, sparked by high unemployment and the marginalisation of the independently spirited town.

◉ Sights

Sidi Ifni has a unique atmosphere, which has lured many a passing foreigner to settle. The small old Spanish part of town is one of the main attractions. At its heart is Pl Hassan II (often still called Plaza de España), the colonial centrepiece. The large square with a small park in the middle is surrounded by the main administrative buildings: **law courts (former church), royal palace, former Spanish consulate** and **town hall**, mostly in grand art-deco style.

Other interesting remnants of the colonial era include the Hôtel Bellevue (p391), also on Pl Hassan II, a nearby **lighthouse** and the clifftop **ship house**, which served as the Spanish Naval Secretariat. There's also some art-deco architecture in the streets east of Pl Hassan II, including the derelict nightclub **Twist Club** (off Ave Hassan II) and cinema **Cine Avenida** (Ave Hassan II). The post office still has a **letterbox** (Ave Mohammed V) outside marked 'Correos – Avion/Ordinario' (Post – Air Mail/Ordinary).

Beach BEACH
The beach is big and rarely busy, though not always clean. At the south end is the port: Ifni's economy is based on small-scale fishing, with most of the catch sold in Agadir. The odd construction just offshore is the remains of an old land-sea conveyor, which was used to take cargo from ships to the old Spanish port.

🏄 Activities

There's some excellent surfing around Ifni and paddlboarding is also becoming popular.

Ifni Surf SURFING
(📞 0662 53 37 17; www.ifnisurf.com; Ave Moulay Youssef; board & wetsuit rental per day Dh150, 2hr lesson incl equipment Dh200, kayak & wetsuit rental per hr Dh60) The most well-established of Ifni's surf companies also offers kayaking at Legzira Plage, quad bike and 4WD desert excursions, and market visits and cooking classes. Check the website for accommodation and surfing packages at its bases at Sidi Ifni and Legzira.

🛏 Sleeping

Hôtel Bellevue HOTEL €
(📞 0528 87 52 72; Pl Hassan II; s/d Dh170/200, without bathroom Dh105/130) The art-deco charms of the Bellevue's exterior do not continue inside, where you'll find just a few lampshades and stained-glass windows. Nonetheless, it is a reasonable budget option on the main square, with coastal views from the bar-restaurant and room balconies. Request an en-suite room upstairs; those downstairs are darker and the shared shower is a frugal rooftop affair.

Hôtel Ère Nouvelle HOTEL €
(📞 0528 87 52 98; Ave Sidi Mohammed ben Abdallah; s/d Dh35/70) Above a local restaurant, this central cheapie has spartan rooms with narrow beds. The shared bathrooms sport that classic shower and squat toilet combination. However, it's welcoming and secure, and the breakfast of bread, honey and snow-white butter is delicious.

Camping Sidi Ifni CAMPGROUND €
(📞 0658 019 813; off Ave Al Hourria; tent/caravan/r Dh35/75/120) Next to the outdoor swimming pool at the north end of the beach. Popular with visiting Europeans in campervans.

★Logis La Marine B&B €€
(📞 0641 76 60 96; www.logislamarine.com; 1 Ave My Abdellah; s/d/f incl breakfast from Dh600/660/880; 📶) Formerly the headquarters of the Spanish navy, this art-deco clifftop mansion has superb views of the Atlantic. Charming Belgian owners Benoit and Dominique have adorned many rooms with heritage art-deco furniture and local art,

Sidi Ifni

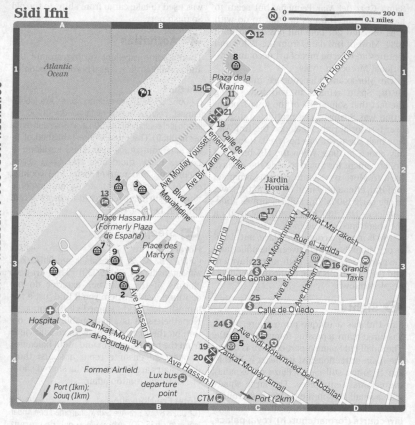

Sidi Ifni

◉ Sights

1	Beach	B1
2	Cine Avenida	B3
3	Former Spanish Consulate	B2
4	Law Courts (Former Church)	B2
5	Letterbox	C4
6	Lighthouse	A3
7	Royal Palace	A3
8	Ship House	C1
9	Town Hall	B3
10	Twist Club	B3

⊕ Activities, Courses & Tours

11	Ifni Surf	C1

🛏 Sleeping

12	Camping Sidi Ifni	C1
13	Hôtel Bellevue	A2
14	Hôtel Ère Nouvelle	C4

15	Logis La Marine	B1
16	Maison d'hôtes Tiwaline	D3
17	Xanadu	C2

✖ Eating

	Cafe Ere Nouvelle	(see 14)
18	Chez Sofia	C1
19	Gran Canaria	C4
20	Municipal Market	C4
21	Nomad	C1

🍷 Drinking & Nightlife

22	Eddib	B3
	Hôtel Bellevue	(see 13)

ⓘ Information

23	Attijariwafa Bank	C3
24	Banque Populaire	C4
25	BMCE	C3

and shared breakfasts and dinners (Dh165) are enjoyed in a shaded garden populated by a posse of shy tortoises. Bathrooms are relatively compact.

Ask Dominique about looking through the photo albums crammed with poignant images of Sidi Ifni's relatively recent Spanish heritage.

Maison d'hôtes Tiwaline
GUESTHOUSE €€

(📞0528 875 660; www.maison-tiwaline-ifni.com; 21 Rue Casablanca; s/d Dh330/450; 🔊) French expat Michel has created this cool and calming guesthouse a short walk downhill from Sidi Ifni's main street. Crisp blue-and-white decor combines with stylish design touches – we especially like all the retro travel posters dotted throughout the building – and social breakfasts complete with fresh baguettes and homemade jams are shared around a big downstairs table.

Xanadu
GUESTHOUSE €€

(📞0528 876 718; www.maisonxanadu.com; 5 Rue el Jadida; s/d incl breakfast Dh360/550; @🔊) Tucked away on a lane off Ave Mohammed V, this restored house offers a contemporary take on the Ifni aesthetic, with soothing colours pervading the five rooms. Breakfast on the roof is a pleasure and the book-filled lounge is ideal for whiling away an evening. The charming French host, Patrick, speaks some English, and offers guided hikes and 4WD excursions.

🍴 Eating

For fresh produce head to the **fruit and vegetable market** (⊙7am-3pm), off Zankat Marrakesh or stock up at the weekly souq (p377), held on Sundays, 1km out of town on the road to the port.

Cafe Ere Nouvelle
MOROCCAN €

(📞0528 87 52 98; Ave Sidi Mohammed ben Abdallah; mains Dh20-40; ⊙8am-8pm) This simple eatery under a budget hotel is recommended by multiple locals as one of the best places in town for a cheap and authentic meal. Tagines are the highlight, but a few Spanish flavours also creep in with good tortilla and other dishes. If you don't get breakfast at your accommodation this is where to come.

Chez Sofia
SEAFOOD, MOROCCAN €

(Mar Pequeña; Calle de Teniente Carlier; mains Dh60-80; ⊙noon-3pm & 6-10pm) The well-established family business fills a compact corner location with a few tables and the aromas of daily specials including seafood couscous,

chicken pastilla or decent-value three-course menus of the day (Dh100 to Dh120). There are usually a few vegetarian options available including mushroom frittata or zucchini and cheese.

Municipal Market
SEAFOOD, MARKET €

(cnr Ave Mohammed V & Ave Hassan II; mains Dh15-40; ⊙10am-10pm) In addition to the fish market, fruit and vegetable market and surrounding cafes, look out for the courtyard of smoking grills. In this atmospheric outdoor spot, where cooks fan the coals and call out to punters, you can get grilled seafood – including sardines, fish and prawns – served with salad and bread.

★ Nomad
MOROCCAN, SEAFOOD €€

(📞0662 173 308; abdellahnomad@gmail.com; 5 Ave Moulay Youssef; mains Dh70-100; ⊙noon-3pm Tue-Thu, Sat & Sun, 6-11pm nightly) The best restaurant in Sidi Ifni serves excellent grills and seafood, often to a soundtrack of Western music – English-speaking owner Abdellah is a big fan of the blues – amid an elegant Moorish-style interior. Beer and wine are both served, and especially good is the plate-covering Pariada of the Sea (Dh180), a mixed grill of fish, calamari and octopus.

Caution: you must like loads of garlic and the occasional air guitar flourish from the chatty owner.

Gran Canaria
INTERNATIONAL, SEAFOOD €€

(Ave Mohammed V; mains Dh35-100; ⊙noon-11pm) Sidi Ifni's best pizzas and expertly cooked seafood – try the octopus tagine – all feature at this popular spot with a terraced view of Ave Mohammed V. Downstairs is an espresso-fuelled cafe, but upstairs Gran Canaria's chef adds a few idiosyncratic touches such as spectacularly presented brochettes and a basil-laden caprese salad that comes piled high on the plate.

🍸 Drinking & Nightlife

Eddib
CAFE

(Ave Hassan II; coffee Dh8; ⊙8am-late) Our favourite of the laid-back cafes lining Ave Hassan II. Order up a robust *cafe noir*, tune in to the bouncy 1960s Spanish pop music, and take in views across the street of the cool art-deco profile of the Cine Avenida. The friendly owner speaks good English.

Hôtel Bellevue
BAR

(Pl Hassan II; ⊙11am-11pm) On a terrace above the beach, the bar at Hôtel Bellevue is a pleasant spot for a beer. Avoid the cheaper

Stork brew and order a Casablanca lager instead. Atlantic views come with a side order of complimentary olives.

ℹ️ Information

See www.ifniville.com for images, music and information pertaining to Sidi Ifni.

Local bank branches offering ATMs and exchange facilities include **Attijariwafa Bank** (Ave Mohammed V; ⊘ 8.30am-6.30pm Mon-Fri), **BMCE** (Ave Mohammed V; ⊘ 8.30am-6.30pm Mon-Fri) and **Banque Populaire.** (Ave Mohammed V; ⊘ 8.30am-6.30pm Mon-Fri).

Hassan Cyber (Ave Hassan I; per hr Dh4; ⊘ 10am-2pm & 5pm-midnight Sat-Thu, 5pm-midnight Fri)

Hospital Sidi Ifni's main medical centre.

Pharmacies can be found along Ave Mohammed V.

Police Station Just off Ave Mohammed V.

Post Office (Ave Mohammed V; ⊘ 8.15am-4pm Mon-Fri)

ℹ️ Getting There & Away

BUS

CTM (✆ 0528 78 00 50; www.ctm.ma; Ave Hassan II) has daily departures to destinations including Casablanca (Dh270, 12 hours), Marrakesh (Dh170, 7½ hours), Agadir (Dh70, four hours) and Laâyoune (Dh180, eight hours). **Lux bus** 18 travels via Mirleft (Dh10) to Tiznit (Dh20).

TAXI

The **grand-taxi station** is on the east side of town. Taxis serve Goulimime (Dh25), Legzira Plage (Dh13), Mirleft (Dh13), Tiznit (Dh27) and Agadir (Dh60).

Around Sidi Ifni

The most popular location around Sidi Ifni is the beach and spectacular natural archway at Legzira Plage.

Legzira Plage

El Gzira, usually called Legzira Plage, is a superb secluded bay 10km north of Ifni, with excellent sand and a dramatic natural stone arch reaching over the sea. Until September 2016, there were actually two arches, but the smaller one further south towards Sidi Ifni collapsed in the dark of night. The arch that remains standing is the more spectacular of the two, and the beach is still definitely worth visiting.

It's accessible from Rte 104 but better reached by walking along the beaches and cliffs. This is only possible at low tide, so check tide times before you start walking. Tourism development is slowly spreading down the access road from Rte 104, but the beach itself remains pristine and largely undeveloped.

🛏️ Sleeping & Eating

Beachfront cafes charge around Dh50 for mains and the seafood is always good.

Beach Club   PENSION €

(✆ 0670 52 28 00; www.legzirabeachclub.com; s/d from Dh175/275) Beach Club has the best rooms along Legzira Plage, some with shared sea-facing balconies. You'll find the accommodation at the quieter northern end of the beach.

Sables d'Or   PENSION €

(✆ 0661 30 24 95; eddibmohamed2@yahoo.se; r Dh150-300) Sables d'Or has small but comfortable rooms, opening onto terraces with sea views. Public areas have recently been renovated, and the restaurant is adorned with colourful Berber carpets and wall hangings.

ℹ️ Getting There & Away

Grands taxis stop on Rte 104 between Sidi Ifni (Dh10) and Mirleft (Dh15). Buses also run from Sidi Ifni (Dh10) and Mirleft (Dh15).

Mesti

This Berber village is 25km southeast of Sidi Ifni on the road through the prickly-pear-covered hills to Goulimime. At the turnoff for Mesti and the back road to Tiznit, you can do a tasting at the shop of honey cooperative Miel Afoulki.

Mesti has no accommodation and is best visited from Sidi Ifni.

🛍️ Shopping

Miel Afoulki   FOOD

(✆ 0661 47 24 33; www.cooperativeafoulki.net) The shop of Miel Afoulki, a honey cooperative, sells some extraordinary local flavours, including orange and euphorbia. Hours are flexible but someone usually shows up to let visitors in.

Tafyoucht Cooperative   FOOD, BEAUTY

(✆ 0528 21 84 16) The Tafyoucht Cooperative, at the Berber village of Mesti, 25km south of Ifni on the Goulimime road, is a women's cooperative that produces oil and cosmetic products from the versatile argan tree. Opening hours are flexible but visitors are welcome.

ⓘ Getting There & Away

Public transport to Mesti is very sporadic and is best visited with your own transport or in a petit taxi from Sidi Ifni.

Goulimime كلميم

POP 118.300

Once the 'Gateway of the Sahara', dusty Goulimime (or Guelmim) sprang up as a border town where farmers from the fertile Souss traded with nomads from the south. If you have come from the north, you will still recognise Goulimime as a border town: for the first time, you will see Saharawi in the majority.

The main reason to stop here is the Saturday-morning souq, which includes a camel market and takes place a few kilometres from town on the Tan Tan road. A week-long *moussem* (festival) and camel fair is held here around the end of July.

There are plans for an international airport to be built at Goulimime, and subsequent hope this could increase visitor numbers to this relatively remote area of southern Morocco.

🛏 Sleeping & Eating

Many Goulimime hotels are basic and some may not appeal to women. If you have transport, there is better accommodation outside town. An exception to this is the newly opened Oasis Palm Hotel.

Around the bus station and north of the post office are good areas for cafes and restaurants.

Hôtel Ijdiguen HOTEL €
(☑ 0528 77 14 53; Blvd Ibnou Battouta; s/d Dh80/160) Across the road from the grand-taxi station, Ijdiguen ('Ichdigen') is clean and welcoming, with tiled corridors, reasonable rooms and shared showers.

Oasis Palm Hotel HOTEL €€
(☑ 0528 77 93 00; www.oasispalmhotel.com; Rte d'Agadir RN1; s/d incl breakfast from Dh660/825; ✹ 🐕 ⌸) Located 10km northeast of the city near the airport, Goulimime's newest and most comfortable hotel has more than 100 rooms arrayed around pleasant palm-fringed patios and an expansive swimming pool. Facilities include three restaurants and two bars, as well as two hammams and gyms. As a haven from Goulimime's busy and dusty streets, this new opening really is an oasis.

Hôtel Hamza HOTEL €€
(☑ 0528 87 39 75; off Rte d'Agadir; s/d Dh360/460; ✹ @ 🐕) In this quiet and welcoming caravanserai near the tourist office, expansive corridors lead to cool and spacious rooms with bathrooms of varying quality.

Hôtel Adil Moussafir HOTEL €€
(☑ 0528 77 29 30; Ave Mohammed V, off Rte d'Agadir; s/d Dh480/550; 🐕) One of Goulimime's grander options, the Adil Moussafir has a restaurant (mains Dh70) and spacious, comfortable rooms with slightly tired bathrooms.

La Plage Blanche MOROCCAN €
(Ziz garage, Rte d'Agadir; meals Dh50-80; ⊘ 8am-10pm) Near Pl Bir Anzarane, this Western-ised snack bar serves dishes ranging from pizzas, burgers and spaghetti to tajines and *pil-pil* prawns. On Friday, join the locals and treat yourself to the couscous, while the masses pray outside the mosque across the road.

ⓘ Information

Pl Bir Anazarane is the centre of town, and near here you'll find banks, internet cafes and the post office.

Tourist Office (☑ 0528 87 29 11; www.crt-guelmim.com; 3 Résidence Sahara, Rte d'Aga-dir; ⊘ 8.30am-4.30pm Mon-Fri) Around 400m northeast of Pl Bir Anazarane on the main road to Agadir.

ⓘ Getting There & Away

AIR

RAM (www.royalairmaroc.com) links Goulimime Airport to Casablanca.

BUS

The **bus station** (Gare Routiére) is a 10-minute walk north of Pl Bir Anazarane.

CTM (www.ctm.ma; Blvd Ibnou Battouta) and **Supratours** (www.supratours.ma) have regular departures to the following places: Agadir (Dh85, five hours), Casablanca (Dh295, 12 hours), Dakhla (Dh330, 16 hours), Laâyoune (Dh170, 7½ hours), Marrakesh (Dh195, 7½ hours), Rabat (Dh325, 13½ hours), Tan Tan (Dh50, two hours) and Tiznit (Dh40, 2¾ hours). Daily **Satas** (☑ 0528 87 22 13; Gare Routière)

SOUTHERN MOROCCO & WESTERN SAHARA TAN TAN & TAN TAN PLAGE

AROUND GOULIMIME

Tighmert oasis makes a scenic drive from Goulimime, with views of the distant Anti Atlas. You can drive a circuit of this *palmeraie* (palm grove) in an hour or two on Rte d'Asrir, returning to town along the Goulimime–Assa road.

There are a few basic guesthouses in the oasis, mostly located some 20km southeast of Goulimime off Rte d'Asrir. **Maison d'Hôtes Nomades** (☑0667 90 96 42; d/tr from Dh200/250, breakfast/dinner/picnic Dh30/80/50) is a family-run guesthouse deep in the oasis (there are some tight corners on the drive there), with rugs and farming implements decorating the pisé walls and simple rooms with shared or private bathroom. Accommodation is also available in a Berber tent (Dh60 per person) and dinner features dishes such as dromedary tajine. Camel rides and other activities are offered, but you may prefer to just lounge on the roof terrace taking in the views.

Accessed from the N12 between Goulimime and Tata (or along back roads from the Anti Atlas), the oasis village of **Id-Aïssa**, also known as Amtoudi, after the gorge it occupies, has walking trails to two agadirs, a waterfall and cave paintings. One of the *agadirs* is particularly impressive, towering above the village on a spindly outcrop. In the second half of September, a festival and *fantasia* (musket-firing cavalry charge) takes place in the nearby village of **Aït Herbil**, also known for its rock engravings.

Id-Aïssa is 30km from the N12, signposted from near the village of Taghjicht. To get there by grand taxi from Goulimime, you will likely have to change in Bouizakarne and Souk Tnine-Nouadai. A shared/private taxi from Bouizakarne costs about Dh35/210. From Tata, pick up a ride to Goulimime or Bouizakarne and alight in Taghjicht, from where a private taxi costs Dh120.

On the other side of Goulimime, French resort **Fort Bou-Jerif** (☑0528 87 30 39; www.fortboujerif.com; campsites from Dh70, s incl half-board Dh490-600, d incl half-board Dh800-1000, khaïma per person incl half-board Dh320; ☒) offers a taste of the desert, 40km northwest of town via the Sidi Ifni and Plage Blanche roads (it's well signposted).

Getting There & Away

Tighmert can be reached by a grand-taxi from Goulimime, but private transport – preferably 4WD – is needed to reach Fort Bou-Jerif.

---

buses are a slightly cheaper option to most of these destinations.

TAXI

You can catch grands taxis from behind the bus station to Inezgane (Dh80), Laâyoune (Dh220), Sidi Ifni (Dh25), Tan Tan (Dh50) and Tiznit (Dh40).

Tan Tan & Tan Tan Plage
طانطان وشاطئ طانطان

POP 50,000

South of Goulimime, across the dry Oued Drâa, you enter the Sahara proper. The 130km of desert highway to Tan Tan is impressive for its bleak emptiness and harsh *hammada* (flat, stony desert).

If you weren't stopped by security on the way in, you could probably drive along the N1 (known as Ave Hassan II within Tan Tan's boundaries) without realising you were in the town, which spreads mostly south of the highway. The majority of the inhabitants are nomads who settled here, and blue robes are a big feature. The army and police presence is also noticeable, due to the proximity of the disputed Western Sahara.

Tan Tan Plage, also known as Al-Ouatia, 25km west of Tan Tan, is a dilapidated seaside resort overlooking a long, windswept beach. The town only briefly comes to life during the Moroccan summer holiday, but staying here is nonetheless preferable to Tan Tan.

Tan Tan was founded in the 1940s during the Spanish Protectorate, but had its moment in 1975, when the area was the departure point for the Green March. It's a run-down place with tough but not unfriendly inhabitants. The Sunday souq is held 1.5km south of town.

✿✿ Festivals & Events

Tan Tan Moussem   CARNIVAL
(www.moussemdetantan.org/en) A Unesco-protected *moussem* takes place in September, featuring camel racing and music.

🛏 Sleeping & Eating

In Tan Tan, there are cheap eateries on Ave Hassan II, Ave Mohammed V and around the *gare routière*, although many close at lunchtime or take a while to rustle up food. Hôtel Sable d'Or is a popular choice. Fresh seafood is a standout in the cafes of Tan Tan Plage. The town's interesting main square has everything from bakeries to grill restaurants specialising in meaty cuts of camel and lamb from adjacent butcheries.

Hôtel Belle Vue   HOTEL €
(☑ 0528 87 91 33; Ave Mohammed V, Tan Tan Plage; s/d from Dh150/300; 🛜) This appropriately named family-run seafront hotel has basic en-suite rooms, reached along white corridors hung with cheery paintings. The cafe-restaurant (breakfast and meals Dh25 to Dh90) is one of Tan Tan Plage's best, serving tajines, omelettes, sardines and calamari.

Hôtel Sable d'Or   HOTEL €
(☑ 0528 87 80 69; Ave Hassan II, Tan Tan; s/d Dh150/200; 🛜) Next to the banks on the main road, this friendly family-run hotel has comfortable en-suite rooms with flat-screen TV. Ask for a room at the rear, away from the main road. There's a cafe-restaurant with a pool table.

Hôtel Bir Anzarane   HOTEL €
(☑ 0528 87 78 34; hotelbiranzarane@hotmail.fr; Ave Hassan II, Tan Tan; s/d Dh80/100; 🛜) A worn but clean place, next to the royal palace (soldiers patronise the cafe here) on the west side of the river. Above the breezy cafe, the small but neat rooms share bathrooms with squat and flush toilets.

Riad Essadia   GUESTHOUSE €€
(☑ 0528 87 92 14; riad.essadia@gmail.com; Ave Mohammed V, Tan Tan Plage; s/d from Dh400/500; 🛜) The best place to stay in either Tan Tan or Tan Tan Plage, Riad Essadia has eight rooms opening onto a spacious central courtyard which flows out onto the beach. The charmingly decorated rooms lack external windows so natural light is limited, but the lovely shared public spaces easily offset this. Breakfast and other meals are enjoyed with Atlantic views.

Kasba Hotel   HOTEL €€
(☑ 0528 87 98 98; www.hotelkasbatantan.com; 9 Ave Mohammed V, Tan Tan Plage; r incl breakfast Dh600-810; 🛜) A tad overpriced maybe, but the rooms at the Kasba are the best in Tan Tan Plage, especially the ones at the front enjoying Atlantic views. The team at reception usually speaks good English and bring an open mind to negotiation. Get a good deal and secure an ocean vista and you'll be sorted. The downstairs restaurant is also good.

La Scala   SEAFOOD, MOROCCAN €
(Chez Abdellah; ☑ 0528 87 93 24; mains Dh45-70; ⊙ noon-3pm & 6-10pm) A short walk from Tan Tan Plage's main square, La Scala is one of the town's best seafood restaurants. The friendly owner Abdellah is eager to please visitors who've made the big trek south, and plates of octopus salad, grilled calamari and sole are very generous servings. Italian and Spanish influences also feature, with paella and pizza on the menu.

ℹ Information

Banks with ATMs and exchange facilities are clustered around the junction of Aves Hassan II and Mohammed V in Tan Tan.

Club Internet (off Ave Hassan II; per hr Dh3; ⊙ 9am-midnight) Next to the Samir Oil petrol station in Tan Tan.

Post Office (Pl de la Mare Verte, Tan Tan; ⊙ 8.15am-4pm Mon-Fri) Centrally located in Tan Tan.

Tan Tan Plage has a post office and two banks with ATMs and exchange facilities.

ℹ Getting There & Away

AIR
RAM (www.royalairmaroc.com) flies between Tan Tan Airport and Casablanca.

BUS
In Tan Tan **CTM** (☑ 0528 76 58 86; www.ctm.ma; Ave Hassan II, Tan Tan) has daily departures to: Agadir (Dh130, six hours), Dakhla (Dh300, 14 hours), Goulimime (Dh50, 1½ hours), Laâyoune (Dh130, five hours) and Tiznit (Dh95, 3½ hours). **Supratours** (☑ Tan Tan Plage 0528 87 96 65, 0528 87 77 95; www.supratours.ma; Ave Hassan II, Tan Tan), which stops in Tan Tan and also at its office in Tan Tan Plage, opposite the Dubai Hotel, operates similar services at slightly higher prices. Other, cheaper companies, all serving the same destinations, use Tan Tan **gare routière** (Pl de la Marche Verte, Tan Tan), off Ave Mohammed V, about 1km south of Ave Hassan II.

TAXI
From Tan Tan *gare routière*, grands taxis head to Agadir (Dh110), Goulimime (Dh50), Inezgane (Dh110), Laâyoune (Dh160), Tan Tan Plage (Dh15), Tarfaya (D160) and Tiznit (Dh80).

Grands taxis to Tan Tan Plage also leave from the top of Blvd el-Amir Moulay Abdallah, a few hundred metres south of Ave Hassan II.

Tarfaya طرفايه

POP 6000

The fishing port of Tarfaya was the centre of the Spanish Protectorate of Cap Juby, now known as the Tarfaya Strip. A Scottish trader, Donald Mackenzie, created the original settlement in the late 19th century, building a small trading post on a rock just offshore, which he called Port Victoria. When the Spanish took over, they appropriated the building, now known as Casa Mar. The area gained independence from Spain in 1958.

The Moroccan government upgraded Tarfaya's municipal status to provincial centre in 2009, and the town is on the cusp of big developments. A new port is being constructed, with hopes for the relaunch of the ferry connection to the Canary Islands and greater tourist numbers. A new beachfront promenade is also a relaxing spot. For now, however, Tarfaya's charm remains; it's a friendly outpost with a seductively remote feel to the sand blowing between its crumbling colonial relics.

◎ Sights & Activities

There are some good fishing, surfing and kitesurfing spots around Tarfaya. Ask your accommodation or Les Amis de Tarfaya about organising an expedition.

Musée Saint-Exupéry   MUSEUM
(☑ 0661 07 94 88; Dh10; ⊙ 8.30am-4.30pm Mon-Fri, by appointment Sat & Sun) Tarfaya will forever be associated with the French pilot and writer Antoine de Saint-Exupéry. In 1926 he began flying in the airmail service between France and Senegal, and Cap Juby was one of the stops. This museum tells the stories (in French) of Saint-Exupéry, the airmail service's founder, Pierre-Georges Latécoère, and the incredible service itself, which eventually became part of Air France.

In 1927 Saint-Exupéry was appointed station manager for Cap Juby and he spent a couple of years here, writing his first novel *Courrier Sud* (Southern Mail) in which an airmail pilot dies south of Boujdour in the desert of Rio de Oro. He also picked up inspiration for his most famous story, *Le Petit Prince* (The Little Prince), which features a pilot lost in the desert.

★ Historic Sites   HISTORIC SITE

Numerous dilapidated buildings recall the days when Saint-Exupéry touched down here. The **Casa Mar** is abandoned but still standing, and can be easily reached at low tide. At the north end of the beach, a **monument** honours Saint-Exupéry's memory: a dinky green Bréguet 14 biplane, the sort he used to fly. Nearby, the **Spanish fort** now houses military barracks, and behind the museum is the 1930s **cinema**; in the same area, swashbucklers swapped anecdotes between flights at **Bar des Pilotes**.

The **wrecked Armas ferry**, *Assalama*, 2km south of town, put paid to the short-lived connection between Tarfaya and Fuerteventura when it went down in 2008.

✤ Festivals & Events

Rallye Toulouse Saint-Louis   FESTIVAL
(www.rallyetoulousesaintlouis.com; ⊙ late Sep/early Oct) The airmail service is remembered when light aircraft fly from France to Senegal and back, landing in Tarfaya en route.

⛏ Sleeping & Eating

For a small centre, Tarfaya has surprisingly comfortable accommodation options. There are numerous self-catering apartments in Tarfaya. Les Amis de Tarfaya can help you find an apartment.

Residence Armas   APARTMENT €
(☑ 0673 54 66 47; ste from Dh350; ☎) Self-contained suites and apartments that can be booked through Les Amis de Tarfaya.

Residence Hôtelière Canalina APARTMENT €€
(☑ 0641 78 55 21; www.tarfayahotelcanalina.com; Ave Mohamed V; s/d Dh330/440) Spacious mini-apartments, all with compact kitchens, are a good accommodation solution for groups and families. Downstairs there's a good Spanish restaurant that unfortunately keeps very irregular hours, If you're in town, it's worth dropping by to see if it's open. The Residence Hôtelière Canalina is around 400m along the road from the Musée Saint-Exupéry (away from the waterfront).

Hotel Tarfaya   HOTEL €€
(Aoudate; ☑ 0528 89 58 68; r per person incl breakfast from Dh300; ☎) Available with or without balcony and private bathroom, the Tarfaya's 35 rooms have attractive checkered bedding and satellite TV, with sea views from the upper floors. The ground-floor cafe is a favourite of locals watching Spanish football,

and when we last visited, the energetic English-speaking team on reception were planning on launching desert tours around the Tarfaya hinterland.

Casa Mar CAFE, SEAFOOD €

(☎ 0528 89 53 26; casamarhotel@gmail.com; breakfast/mains Dh30/70; 🛜) Just outside the port entrance, Casa Mar's cafe-restaurant serves a good selection of seafood dishes, ranging from mixed grilled fish to calamari tajine. The cafe, a popular meeting point, is a good place to check your emails and watch local characters stroll in. Accommodation is available: rooms in the hotel's old section are mediocre (singles/doubles without bathroom from Dh100/120), but newer en-suite rooms have port views (singles/doubles Dh180/250).

ⓘ Information

Tarfaya has a medical centre, pharmacies, internet cafe, laundrette and banks with ATMs and exchange facilities.

Les Amis de Tarfaya (☎ 0661 07 94 88; sadat@yours.com) Information is available from the English-speaking Sadat at this local tourism association, based at Musée Saint-Exupéry.

ⓘ Transport

Bus companies, including CTM, stop in Tarfaya, but **Supratours** (☎ 0528 89 52 84; www.supratours.ma; Rte du Port) has the only reliable office. It has the best buses and so is the best option anyway, given the brutal journey times in the Sahara. Daily Supratours departures head for: Agadir (Dh190, eight hours), Dakhla (Dh210, 10 hours), Goulimime (Dh130, six hours), Laâyoune (Dh50, two hours), Marrakesh (Dh265, 13 hours), Tan Tan (Dh80, three hours) and Tiznit (Dh150, seven hours).

Grands taxis go to Laâyoune (Dh45) and Tan Tan (Dh90). Tarfaya has petrol stations, car-washing services and mechanics.

WESTERN SAHARA

After crossing the rocky and forlorn expanses of the *hammada* south from Tarfaya, the Western Saharan city of Dakhla is an appealingly relaxed destination. A constant feature is the cobalt intensity of the Atlantic Ocean, softened here by palm trees, a pleasant oceanfront esplanade and a shallow island-studded lagoon.

The region's recent Spanish past echoes languidly in cafes and restaurants, while one of the world's best kiteboarding scenes attracts international visitors seeking a more energetic Western Saharan experience.

Occasional roadblocks on the fringes of the desert reinforce this is a disputed region, despite what is indicated by the Moroccan flags shifting in tropical breezes.

Against this subdued background of international contention, a small group of pioneering expats are developing eco-aware and low-impact tours exploring the lagoon and surrounding desert.

History

Despite its windswept desolation, the Western Sahara has a long and violent history. Islamic missionaries started to spread Islam among the Zenata and Sanhaja Berber tribes here in the 7th century. A second wave of Arab settlers, the Maqil from Yemen, migrated to the desert in the 13th century, and the whole region became predominantly Arabic.

In the 19th century, the Spanish grabbed the Western Sahara and renamed it Rio de Oro. In reality, Sheikh Ma El-Ainin and his son El-Hiba controlled the desert and the nomadic tribes well into the 20th century. From the 1930s, an uneasy colonial peace prevailed until Moroccan independence in

---

DISPUTED TERRITORY

Ask most Moroccans about the status of the Western Sahara and they will insist it belongs to their country, yet the UN maintains it is under dispute. Local maps may show this region as a continuation of the *hammada* around Tarfaya, but many outside Morocco disagree.

It's one of the world's most sparsely populated territories, and despite the 1991 ceasefire in the war between Morocco and the separatist Polisario Front, the Moroccan military sometimes seems to outnumber civilians.

Largely comprising the former colonies of Spanish Sahara and part of the Tarfaya Strip, this seemingly barren environment has phosphate, oil and fishing potential – all significant factors in the dispute.

SAFE TRAVEL IN THE WESTERN SAHARA

Despite ongoing tensions in the Western Sahara, travel in much of the west of this region is still considered safe by most government travel advisories. Flying in and out of Dakhla from Casabanca or Agadir is straightforward and safe.

Spain has been most critical of Morocco's presence in the Western Sahara, so Spanish travellers are most likely to field questions from Moroccan officials. Occupations likely to ring alarm bells at police posts are journalist or aid worker. If police confirm that you work in an occupation of that nature, you could be followed, detained, sent back to Morocco proper or even deported. Authorities tend to be more wary of travellers visiting Laâyoune than Dakhla or Tarfaya.

That said, Spanish and other nationalities visiting for legitimate purposes of tourism are likely to have no problems at all.

Travelling overland, and approaching the Western Sahara through towns such as Tarfaya, Tan Tan, Goulimime and Tata, you should also be prepared for the regular occurrence of police checkpoints. Foreigners are invariably asked about their occupation, reason for visiting, and next destination, and passports are requested so details can be recorded.

For most people exchanges between police and travellers at checkpoints usually dissolve quickly into the relative merits of the Barcelona and Real Madrid football teams. However, everyone should treat the checkpoint stops seriously, tedious though they are, as there is a small risk of travellers being mistaken for a journalist or Polisario sympathiser.

In the Western Sahara, your passport and visa details will be noted down, along with your vehicle details if you are driving. If you're on a bus, you can usually stay in your seat while the police take your ID and write down your particulars. To streamline these encounters, it's a good strategy is to have multiple photocopies of the identification pages from your passport, to hand over, rather than the actual document.

Once in both Laâyoune (especially) and Dakhla, you will be aware of the military and police, both of whom are sensitive to photography around military installations. Similarly, they will not take too kindly to you photographing or trying to visit the refugee camps around both cities, where many Saharawi still live.

the late 1950s, when new nationalist fervour saw the genesis of the Polisario Front and a guerrilla war against the Spanish.

When it was abandoned by Spain in 1975, Morocco and Mauritania both raised claims to the desert region, but Mauritania soon bailed out. In November 1975 King Hassan II orchestrated the Green March – 350,000 Moroccans marched south to stake Morocco's historical claim to the Western Sahara.

Over the following years, Rabat poured in 100,000 troops to stamp out resistance, and gained the upper hand. The UN brokered a ceasefire in 1991, but the promised referendum, in which the indigenous Saharawi could choose between independence and integration with Morocco, has yet to materialise.

Ever since, Morocco has strengthened its hold on the territory, pouring money into infrastructure projects, particularly offshore oil exploration, and attracting Mo-

roccans from the north to live here tax-free. Until late 2010, the troubled area seemed to be lying dormant, with the dispute largely forgotten by the world beyond this remote region. However, on 8 November 2010, Moroccan security forces stormed the Gadaym Izik camp near Laâyoune, in an attempt to break up the 15,000-strong protest camp. Both sides incurred fatalities in the ensuing clashes, which turned into riots and engulfed the city, with 700-plus Saharawi injuries, and scenes of fire and destruction in the international media. The region has seen several clashes and riots since then, most recently in 2014 in Laâyoune, and Africa's longest-running territorial dispute continues.

Since 2014, the Moroccan government has further advanced activities to solidify its hold on the region, including ongoing migration of Moroccans to the cities and the establishment of smaller communities along the coast, and in November 2015 the Moroccan King Mohammed VI visited to announce multi-million-dollar investments aimed at promoting economic development in the region. In December 2013, a four-year deal signed between Morocco and the European Union to allow European vessels to fish off the Moroccan coast also included the disputed waters off Western Sahara.

Dakhla locals report of a cautious rapprochement between the Moroccan and Saharawi communities – including marriages between the two groups – but the referendum promised back in 1991 still shows no sign of being scheduled. If and when it does take place, the ongoing economic and social expansion of Morocco in the area means probably only restricted autonomy and not full independence for the Saharawis will be on the table.

For the most up-to-date information on the Western Sahara, or the Saharawi Arab Democratic Republic (as the separatist government calls the occupied territory), check these resources:

➡ ARSO (www.arso.org)

➡ BBC (www.bbc.co.uk/news/world-africa-14115273)

➡ CIA World Factbook (www.cia.gov/library/publications/the-world-factbook/geos/wi.html)

➡ Global Voices (globalvoicesonline.org)

➡ UN (www.un.org)

Laâyoune (Al-'Uyun) العيون

POP 248,000

The Spanish created Laâyoune as an outpost from which to administer the nearby Bou Craa phosphate mines. The Moroccans had bigger ambitions and spent more than US$1 billion turning it into the Western Sahara's principal city. Now neither Saharawi nor Spanish, Laâyoune's population is mostly Moroccans, lured from the north by the promise of healthy wages and tax-free goods.

A government centre and military garrison with UN Land Cruisers drifting along its drab avenues, Laâyoune is not worth a visit for its own sake. Indeed, given the occasional tensions between Moroccans and Saharawi – protests were experienced across the territory in 2014 – we recommend it's only worth passing through if you're travelling overland to Mauritania.

Whether you're heading north or south, distances are so great that you may have to stop here, but try to plan your trip so you pause in Tarfaya or Dakhla instead.

🛌 Sleeping & Eating

The UN maintains a significant presence in Laâyoune and tends to fill the better hotels, so you would be wise to book well ahead. Unsurprisingly, good accommodation in this desert outpost is expensive by Moroccan standards.

There are simple restaurants around Pl Dchira, where around Dh35 should get you a filling meal. More lively food stalls can be found at the Souq Djemal. Otherwise, wander down Blvd de Mekka or head to a hotel restaurant.

Hôtel Jodesa HOTEL €
(📞 0528 992064; 223 Blvd de Mekka; s/d Dh120/190, with shower Dh170/220; 🛜) Behind its dilapidated two-tone facade, this central cheapie has basic but reasonably spacious rooms.

Hôtel Nagjir HOTEL €€
(📞 0528 89 41 68; Pl de la Résistance; s/d incl breakfast from Dh545/670; ❄🛜) Beyond its grand reception, the four-star Nagjir has a restaurant and small but comfortable rooms with tiled floors. It has another, equally '70s hotel, Nagjir Plage, by the sandy beach at Foum el-Oued, 22km from town.

Sahara Line Hotel HOTEL €€
(📞 0528 99 54 54; Blvd el-Kairaouane; s/d Dh450/560; ❄🛜) A UN favourite, the three-star Sahara Line has swish, carpeted rooms with fridge, bathroom and TV. There's a restaurant on the top floor, but no bar.

Hôtel Parador HOTEL €€€
(📞 0528 892814; Ave de l'Islam; s/d Dh1100/1400; ❄❄) This survivor from Spanish days, built in hacienda style around gardens, has a faintly colonial bar and a good restaurant. The rooms are equipped with all the creature comforts you'd expect and each has a small terrace.

Le Poissonier SEAFOOD €
(183 Blvd de Mekka; mains from Dh50; ⏰ 11am-midnight) One of the city's best restaurants, serving catches from the Atlantic. There are worse ways to spend your time in Laâyoune than over a fish soup or lobster here.

Pizzeria la Madone ITALIAN €
(☎0528 99 32 52; 141 Ave Chahid Bouchraya; pizzas Dh50; ◷11am-midnight) A cosy place to eat, although it also does a brisk takeaway trade, la Madone specialises in pasta dishes and thin-crust pizzas.

❶ Information

The city's showpiece is the vast Pl du Méchouar, but there is no obvious centre. The post office, banks and most hotels are along Ave Hassan II and Blvd de Mekka, and internet cafes are on Blvd de Mekka. Bored youths hang about at Pl du Méchouar at night.

Délégation Régionale du Tourisme (☎0528 89 16 94; Ave de l'Islam; ◷9am-noon & 2.30-4.30pm Mon-Fri) Opposite Hôtel Parador.

El Sahariano (☎0528 98 12 12; www.facebook.com/elsaharianotravel; Blvd de Mekka) Well-established travel agency booking flights and other transport.

❶ Getting There & Away

AIR

Hassan I Airport (☎0528 89 37 91; www.onda.ma) Located 1.5km southwest of Laâyoune. Flights from Agadir to Dakhla sometimes transit here.

Binter Canarias (www.bintercanarias.com) Flights to/from various destinations in the Canary Islands.

Royal Air Maroc (RAM; ☎0528 89 40 77; www.royalairmaroc.com; Immeuble Nagjir, Pl de la Résistance) Fights to/from Casablanca, Agadir and Dakhla.

BOAT

At the time of writing there were no ferries linking Laâyoune with the Canary Islands, but there were plans to restart a service linking Tarfaya to Fuerteventura.

BUS

Buses mostly leave from the offices towards the southern end of Blvd de Mekka; however, a new bus station located to the west of central Laâyoune was awaiting completion at the time of research. Book ahead for daily **CTM** (www.ctm.ma; Blvd de Mekka) departures to: Agadir (Dh240, 11 hours), Dakhla (Dh175, eight hours), Goulimime (Dh170, seven hours), Marrakesh (Dh350, 14 hours), Tan Tan (Dh130, five hours) and Tiznit (Dh210, nine hours). **Supratours** (www.supratours.ma; Pl Oum Saad) services cost slightly more than CTM's; **SATAS** (Blvd de Mekka) services cost the same or marginally less.

TAXI

Red-and-white petits taxis charge about Dh5 to take you across town, including to the main grand-taxi station, located about 2km east of the centre along Blvds Prince Moulay Abdallah and Abou Bakr Seddik. Grand-taxi services include Tarfaya (Dh45), Tan Tan (Dh150), Goulimime (Dh200), Inezgane (for Agadir; Dh220) and Dakhla (Dh200).

Dakhla (Ad-Dakhla) الداخلة

POP 106.277

Established by the Spanish in 1844 and formerly called Villa Cisneros, Dakhla lies just north of the Tropic of Cancer on a sandy peninsula stretching 40km from the main coastline. It's a very lonely 500km drive from Laâyoune (more than 1000km from Agadir) through endless *hammada*, and Dakhla is actually closer to Nouâdhibou (Mauritania) than any Moroccan city.

And yet Dakhla feels less remote than many southern towns and certainly more prosperous, with good hotels, restaurants and an emerging tourism scene driven by kitesurfing.

Although Western Saharan tensions do still linger under the carefree, sea-breeze surface, Dakhla's inhabitants appear relatively modern and progressive. Investment by the Moroccan government and developers continues, and the population continues to grow with new arrivals from the north. New apartment blocks stretch the town boundaries, the presence of the Moroccan navy and army is tangible, and Dakhla's port is home to Morocco's largest fishing fleet.

🏃 Activities

Kitesurfing is the biggest game in town, with dynamic breezes and the calm waters of the lagoon providing year-round access to some of the best conditions on the planet. When the Moroccan royal family holidayed and kitesurfed here in 2016, the profile of Dakhla for Moroccan visitors from the northern cities surged overnight.

Windsurfing and paddleboarding are also popular if the wind is not quite right, and the resorts offer desert trips and surfing to their guests.

Sailing on the lagoon and exploring Dakhla's desert hinterland is also possible, and fishing excursions can be booked through the better hotels.

Dakhla

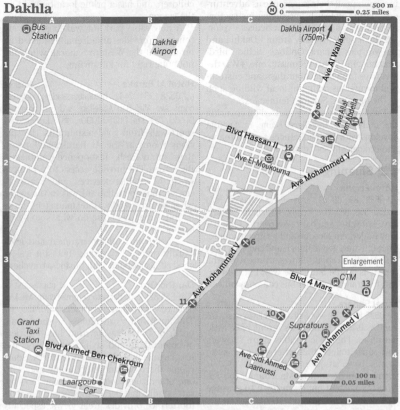

The team at Hotel Al Baraka can book 4WD excursions incorporating visits to remote beaches, hot springs and an ostrich farm. Ask about incorporating lunch at the Dakhla oyster farm. Excursions for up to six people cost from Dh88,000 to Dh154,000 per vehicle.

★**Sahara Sailing**   BOATING
(☑0619 250 454; www.saharasailing.com; 1hr Dh350, half-/full-day Dh650/1200) British expats Neil and Jackie Hutchinson are joined by local sailors as they negotiate their catamaran around the lagoon. Excursions incorporate lunch – including terrific carrot cake – and guests are encouraged to be as active or relaxed as they wish in sailing the boat. Helping the crew hoist sails is a good way to earn another slice of cake.

★**Dakhla Rovers**   OUTDOORS
(☑0636 808 514, 0636 808 515; www.dakhla-rovers.com) Italian couple Nico and Martina

Dakhla

🛏 Sleeping
1 Dar Rio Oro	D2
2 Hôtel Aigue	C4
3 Hotel Al Baraka	D2
4 Hôtel Erraha	B4
5 Hôtel Sahara	C4

🍽 Eating
6 Café Restaurant Samarkand	C3
7 Café-Restaurant Bahia	D4
8 Casa Lola	D2
9 Casa Luis	D4
10 Gladys	C4
11 La Maison du Thé	B3

🍷 Drinking & Nightlife
12 Hassan Fruits	C2

🛍 Shopping
13 Complexe d'artisanat de Dakhla	D3
14 Ensemble Artisinal	D4

incorporate all their experience as adventurers, marine biologists and diving instructors in providing a range of experiences exploring the natural diversity around Dakhla and the Western Sahara. Options include birdwatching in Dakhla's Ramsar zone, 4WD desert trips from two to four days, and customised excursions taking in local wildlife such as the big-eared Saharan fennec fox.

Dakhla Rovers is very focused on ensuring the embryonic travellers' scene in Dakhla develops with good adherence to sustainable and ecologically sound practices.

🛏 Sleeping

Hôtel Erraha
HOTEL €

(☎0528 89 88 11; Ave Banchekroune; s/d Dh250/350; 🖥) The Erraha's spacious rooms have hot water and balconies overlooking the new Edderhem Mosque and its green square. The staff are a genial bunch and there's a cafe. The location, about 1km southwest of the centre, is a little out of the way, but convenient for grands taxis and bus company offices.

Hôtel Sahara
HOTEL €

(☎0528 89 77 73; Ave Sidi Ahmed Laaroussi; s/d from Dh60/80) The Sahara's rooms have little balconies. The basic options share showers and squat toilets; the better-value en-suite rooms have sit-down toilets and TVs. If you're headed south to Mauritania, the Sahara is your best option in town to arrange a place in a car or grand taxi. Just ask at the downstairs cafe or at reception upstairs.

Hôtel Aigue
HOTEL €

(☎0528 89 73 95; Ave Sidi Ahmed Laaroussi; s/d Dh80/120) In a tall, narrow building, the Aigue is one of the central budget hotels overlooking the pedestrianised shopping lanes just southwest of the waterfront promenade. It has basic, pokey rooms with shared showers and squat toilets, but it's clean, secure, and centrally located near transport and eating opportunities.

Dakhla Attitude
RESORT €€

(☎0661 835 010; www.dakhla-attitude.ma; Km 30, Dakhla Lagoon; s/d incl full board from Dh1045/1540; 🖥) The first of Dakhla's kitesurfing camps has now evolved into an expansive and very comfortable resort with breezy hillside bungalows, an excellent restaurant, and a sandy beachfront bar attended by quite possibly the most laid-back dogs in all Morocco. It's a true destination resort with yoga, massage and activities for children, and has a prime location right on the lagoon.

A new cable park for wakeboarding enthusiasts provides an adrenaline-fuelled alternative if the Western Saharan winds are not quite right for kitesurfing.

Hotel Al Baraka
HOTEL €€

(☎0528 934 744; hotelalbarakadakhla@gmail.com; Ave Allal Ben Abdellah; s/d incl breakfast Dh550/759, ste Dh850-1000; 🖥) Located a short walk from good restaurants, the spacious rooms at the Al Baraka still retain that minty-fresh just-opened ambience. Big-screen TVs provide access to a planet's worth of satellite services, and a new licensed rooftop restaurant was in the works when we dropped by. Hotel manager Charlie definitely has his pulse on what's going on around town.

A few points off for cramped and awkwardly shaped bathrooms, but still a very good choice popular with business travellers.

Dar Rio Oro
GUESTHOUSE €€

(☎0655 821 260; dar.rio.oro@gmail.com; Ave Mohammed V; s/d incl breakfast from Dh400/450; 🖥) This multistorey townhouse a short walk north of Dakha's waterfront has a variety of comfortable and stylish rooms and mini-apartments with kitchen facilities. Some rooms share bathrooms, but only ever with one other guest room. The decor incorporates traditional Berber motifs and the rooftop terrace provides great views, especially at sunset. Excursions and rental cars can be arranged.

Ocean Vagabond
RESORT €€€

(☎0613 037 861; www.oceanvagabond.com; Km 28, Lagoon; s/d incl full board from Dh1125/1700; 🖥) Popular with French travellers, Ocean Vagabond combines brilliant ocean views with a beach bar, yoga and massage pavilions and a pleasing New Age vibe courtesy of massive day beds and lagoon-side fire pits. Villas and bungalows are stylish, and the focus on providing a brilliant kitesurfing experience is maximised with a well-stocked gear shop and lessons from world champion kitesurfers.

Ocean Vagabond has also been awarded Green Key status for sustainable tourism practices, including solar electricity and a massive tree-planting program.

Zenith Dakhla
RESORT €€€

(www.zenith-dakhla.com; Km 27, Lagoon; s/d incl full board from Dh950/1350; 🖥🏊) Located across the road from the lagoon, this new

German-owned kitesurfing resort compensates for its slightly inferior location with stellar design features, including a stunning swimming pool, and a restaurant with soaring ceilings and furniture crafted from recycled timber. The chic design continues to the rooms and villas with rainforest outdoor showers, cooling tones and romantic and classy bathrooms.

✕ Eating & Drinking

Central Dakhla has a couple of surprisingly stylish eateries and a good cafe, while the restaurants at the kitesurfing resorts are also well regarded. Unfortunately, only grands taxis are authorised to visit this area from town, making a journey just for a meal an expensive exercise.

Options for a drink include La Maison du Thé and Casa Lola. The team at Casa Lola will probably serve your beer with an empty non-alcohol beer bottle beside the glass. Don't worry, the Casablanca lager is still the real deal. Things are more open at the funky beachside bars in the kitesurfing resorts.

Gladys MOROCCAN €
(mains Dh20-30; ☺6pm-10pm) Located on a busy shopping street lined with tailors and mobile phone shops, Gladys serves up well-priced tagines to a loyal band of locals including savvy Dakhla expats and thrifty businessmen. The kitchen is helmed by female members of a single family, and no, we don't know why it is called Gladys.

Café Restaurant
Samarkand SEAFOOD, MOROCCAN €
(✐0528 89 83 16; Ave Mohammed V; mains Dh50-70; ☺8am-11pm) This waterfront cafe has views of the white cliffs of Africa from its Silk Road–inspired pergolas. The menu features fish and other dishes; order in advance for couscous or fish *pastilla*. An upstairs pavilion is a great escape from Dakhla's dusty streets, and Samarkand is one of the town's only cafes where the clientele regularly includes both men and women.

★Casa Lola SPANISH, SEAFOOD €€
(✐0528 930 692; casalola.dakhla@gmail.com; Ave Al Wallae; tapas Dh45-85, mains Dh85-120; ☺1-3.30pm Mon-Fri plus 8.30pm-midnight daily) This stylish eatery celebrates the region's recent Spanish heritage with hot and cold tapas – the shrimp croquettes and the calamari are both very good – while local

octopus and grilled *merlan* (whiting) are popular menu items. The erstwhile Lola keeps regular business visitors from the Canary Islands very happy, dispensing both good humour and complimentary *aperitivo* shots.

Beer and wine are also served.

Casa Luis SEAFOOD, SPANISH €€
(✐0528 898 193; Ave Mohammed V; mains Dh70-120; ☺8.30am-11pm) Spanish flavours and Atlantic seafood come together at this long-established local favourite. The inner dining room is a bit formal, so try and secure a table on the outside patio for lobster, paella and well-priced grilled fish including meaty *corvina* (sea bass). Chicken and grilled beef also feature, and beer and wine is served.

Café-Restaurant Bahia SEAFOOD €€
(✐0528 93 00 62; 16 Ave Mohammed V; mains Dh50-70; ☺noon-10pm) A good, unlicensed fish restaurant serving catches including calamari and octopus. It's pretty smokey and blokey, but staff will serve you a furtive cold beer (concealed in a tea cup) if you ask them in your best French.

La Maison du Thé MOROCCAN €€€
(✐0673 224 110; 100 Ave Mohammed V; mains Dh130-180; ☺7-11pm) Trimmed with Asian design cues, this elegant lounge and bar would be more at home in cosmopolitan Casablanca. Blackboard menus highlight fragrant tagines and an excellent seafood *pastilla*, and the wine list with French, Spanish and Moroccan varietals is the best in town. The dining room segues to exterior terraces with ocean views, a great spot to share a shisha.

At the time of writing, the owners were putting the finishing touches on an adjacent boutique hotel.

Hassan Fruits JUICE BAR
(Ave al-Walae; juices & smoothies from Dh15; ☺6pm-late) Across the pedestrian crossing from the Dakhla peninsula monument, this is popular for a slice of gâteau and a mixed fruit cocktail. Look for the fluorescent plastic chairs out front.

🛍 Shopping

A pedestrianised shopping lane runs north from Ave Sidi Ahmed Laaroussi between Hôtel Sahara and Hôtel Aigue. Vendors here sell goods ranging from argan oil to bright *melhaf* (fine, colourful Saharan fabrics).

The striking new Complexe d'artisanat de Dakhla is also worth a look.

Complexe d'artisanat de Dakhla   ARTS & CRAFTS

(cnr Ave Mohammed V & Blvd 4 Mars; ⊙6-10pm) This brand new building is one of most striking structures in town and hosts a variety of local artisans working with silver, textiles and other traditional crafts. There will eventually be around 20 stalls across three levels. Hours were limited to evenings at the time of writing, but will probably increase when it becomes more busy.

Ensemble Artisinal   JEWELLERY, SOUVENIRS

(Ave el-Moukouama; ⊙noon-10pm) Marrakesh medina it ain't, but you can find last-minute gifts here, particularly Saharan jewellery.

❶ Information

Your best bet for local information and the current ins and outs of travel to Mauritania is Charlie, an affable Frenchman managing the Hotel Al Baraka. Look for the guy wearing the stylish hat.

Banks with ATMs and exchange facilities are clustered around the waterfront along Ave Mohammed V.

Post Office (Ave el-Moukouama; ⊙8am-4pm Mon-Fri, 9am-noon Sat)

❶ Getting There & Away

As the distances in Western Sahara are so great, flying direct from Agadir or Casablanca is recommended.

AIR

Dakhla Airport (☏0528 93 06 30; www.onda. ma) Located a short 2.5km drive north of the waterfront. A shared taxi from the airport to central hotels costs Dh15.

Royal Air Maroc (RAM; ☏0528 89 70 49; www.royalairmaroc.com) Regular flights to/from Casablanca and Agadir, and to Las Palmas on Gran Canaria (Tuesday only).

BUS

CTM (☏0528 89 81 66; Blvd 4 Mars) and **Supratours** (Ave Mohammed V) both have offices in the centre.

Bus companies also have offices on and around Ave Banchekroune, between the grands-taxis station and the Edderhem Mosque.

Dakhla also has a new bus station (Gare Routière) west of the waterfront in the new town, and some buses from the north terminate here.

Book ahead for popular daily services to: Agadir (Dh395, 20 hours), Laâyoune (Dh175, 8½ hours), Marrakesh (Dh490, 23 hours) and Tan Tan (Dh300, 13½ hours). These fares and durations are for CTM buses.

For onward travel south to Mauritania, Supratours runs daily services leaving Dakhla at 8.30am and 7.30pm (Dh160) south to Gargarate, around 5km north of the border. At the border, Mauritanian taxi drivers will want around Dh200 per person to drive you through the border and a further 25km into Mauritania for onward transport. At the time of writing, Mauritanian visas (a whopping €120) were not available at the border so arrange one at the Mauritanian embassy in Rabat prior to travelling. Note that the border is open from 9am to 6pm, and while the Supratours 8.30am departure from Dakhla is scheduled to arrive at 2pm in Gargarate, it sometimes runs late and arrives after the border is closed. There is one very basic guesthouse near the border on the Moroccan side and more comfortable accommodation 80km north of the border at Motel Barbas.

CAR

There are plenty of mechanics, mostly in the newer part of town to the southwest, who can service vehicles before a trek south. **Laargoub Car** (☏0528 93 04 47; www.laargoubcar.com; Ave Ahmed Bahnini) has one-way car rental available within Morocco.

TAXI

The grand-taxi station is in al-Messira, southwest of the centre. Destinations include Inezgane (for Agadir; Dh440) and Laâyoune (Dh200).

Shared grands taxis run from Dakhla all the way through to Nouadibhou (around Dh450 per person) or Nouakchott (around Dh700 per person) in Mauritania. Ask around at the Hôtel Sahara or see Charlie at Hotel Al Baraka to find out when one is leaving. The potential advantage for a taxi over travelling south on the bus is that there is less risk of arriving after the border closes at 6pm.

❶ Getting Around

White-and-turquoise petits taxis whiz around town (average trip day/night Dh5/6).

Understand Morocco

Morocco Today

Morocco in the early 21st century is a confident country, increasingly sure of its role as a stable link between Europe, Africa and the Arab world, and a place that welcomes tourists and investors alike. It sailed through the Arab Spring unscathed, and while the perennial question of Western Sahara shows no sign of resolution, the nation is taking big steps to cement its role as a regional player, and a leader in renewable energy and responses to climate change.

Best on Film

Casanegra (Nour-Eddine Lakhmari; 2008) A film about two friends growing up as hustlers on the gritty side of Casablanca.

La Grande Villa (Latif Lahlou; 2009) Tale of a Franco-Moroccan couple moving from Paris to Casablanca.

A Thousand Months (Faouzi Bensaidi; 2003) A family epic and winner of the 2003 Premier Regard at Cannes.

Marock (Laila Marrakchi; 2005) A Muslim girl and a Jewish boy are star-crossed lovers in Casablanca.

Behind Closed Doors (Mohammed Ahed Bensouda; 2013) Call to arms against sexual harassment of women.

Best in Print

The Sacred Night (Tahar ben Jelloun; 1987) This tale of a Marrakesh girl raised as a boy won France's prestigious Prix Goncourt.

Dreams of Trespass: Tales of a Harem Girlhood (Fatima Mernissi; 1994) The author's memoirs of 1940s Fez blend with other women's stories.

The Polymath (Bensalem Himmich; 2004) A fictionalised retelling of the life of 14th-century scholar Ibn Khuldun.

For Bread Alone (Mohamed Choukri; 1973) A gritty autobiographical novel of growing up in extreme poverty, translated by Paul Bowles.

The Tourist Dirham

Tourism remains a key plank of Morocco's vision of the future. Tourism – through both direct and indirect jobs – is responsible for almost 18% of GDP and 16% of the nation's jobs. Around eight million tourists visit Morocco every year, a number that's doubled in the last decade, and would undoubtedly be higher were it not for the global economic downturn.

Newly refurbished airports continue to attract low-cost European and Gulf airlines, while the 'Plan Azur' has seen the number of coastal resorts, aimed at servicing the increasing popularity of Morocco as a destination for Arab as well as European travellers, greatly increase – a sign of traditional Moroccan flexibility in adapting to changing global travel patterns.

Regional Ambitions

On the geopolitical front, the unresolved conflict in Western Sahara has continued to make headlines. Morocco briefly threatened to expel the UN peacekeeping mission there after the UN secretary general used the word 'occupation' in relation to Morocco's presence in the disputed territory. Tensions flared further in 2016 when Morocco deployed new troops to the border with Mauritania, ostensibly to crack down on smuggling but raising protests from Saharawis.

Despite this, Western Sahara may no longer be the stumbling block to Morocco's regional ambitions that it once was. In July 2016 Morocco asked to rejoin the African Union, the regional body it had left in protest in 1984 when the Western Saharan government-in-exile was admitted. This move reflected Morocco's desire to flex its economic muscles in the region, and build on its growing economic influence in West Africa.

Part of Morocco's economic plan is to become Africa's flagship for green energy. The government has invested heavily in renewable energy, and Morocco has both the continent's largest wind farm and solar power plant, powered by Atlantic breezes and Saharan sun respectively. These credentials were at the forefront when Marrakesh hosted the UN climate change conference in November 2016.

Speeding Ahead?

The construction of the high-speed TGV train line between Tangier and Casablanca has been Morocco's flagship infrastructure project, with the first trains due to start rolling out in 2017. It's part of the building boom that has occurred over the last 10 years, and seen major towns and cities receive much-needed facelifts, but while the train reflects an aspirational vision of the future, some Moroccans have criticised it as an extravagance when a sizeable proportion of the population scrape along near the poverty line with poor access to education and healthcare.

Unemployment hovers around 45% for youth, while the regular blocking of internet communications apps such as Skype and WhatsApp by telecommunications companies speaks to a disconnect between the authorities and the populace (as well as the easy skirting of such regulations by an innovative populace). Although there have been modest improvements on free speech issues, social, Islamist and human-rights organisations have faced continued hurdles to operate without restriction, and direct political criticism of the palace remains a deep taboo.

As Morocco's economy has slowed, an important issue in the most recent parliamentary elections – the statistic that around 40% of young Moroccans would emigrate if they were given the chance – continues to sting. As Morocco attempts to redefine itself for the 21st century, the challenges – and opportunities – are myriad.

Do

Conserve water Water is a scarce and valuable resource in this Sub-Saharan country.

Cover your knees and shoulders Regardless of whether you're a man or woman; it shows your respect for your Moroccan hosts.

Learn basic greetings Learn a few words in Darija or Berber to delight your hosts, who will also make an effort to speak your language.

Don't

Give money, sweets or pens to children It encourages begging and shames families.

Eat in public during Ramadan Or drink alcohol within view of a mosque.

Skip pleasantries Say hello before asking for help or prices.

POPULATION: **33,655,800**

AREA: **446,550 SQ KM**

GDP PER CAPITA: **US$8200**

LIFE EXPECTANCY: **76.9 YEARS**

ADULT LITERACY: **68.5%**

if Morocco were 100 people

67 would be 16-64 years old
26 would be 0-15 years old
7 would be 65 years and older

belief systems
(% of population)

99 Muslim
1 Other

population per sq km

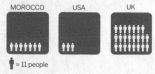

MOROCCO USA UK

= 11 people

History

Morocco is an old nation. The current king, Mohammed VI, is part of the Alawite dynasty that has ruled the country since the 17th century. Before that, empires and invaders left their mark, from the Romans to the Arabs who brought Islam and made Morocco what it is today. Its ties across the Mediterranean to Europe and across the Sahara to the rest of Africa have given rise to a unique nation with a singular history.

The Berbers meet the Romans

Morocco's earliest inhabitants were ancestors of Morocco's Amazigh (plural Imazighen, loosely translated as 'free people'), who may have been distant cousins of the ancient Egyptians. They were joined by Mediterranean anglers and Saharan horse-breeders around 2500 BC, with Phoenicians showing up fashionably late around 800 BC and East Africans around 500 BC. When the Romans arrived in the 4th century, they didn't know quite what to make of this multicultural milieu. The Romans called the expanse of Morocco and Western Algeria 'Mauretania' and the indigenous people 'Berbers', meaning 'barbarians'. The term has recently been reclaimed and redeemed by the Berber Pride movement, but at the time it was taken as quite a slur.

The symbol on the Berber flag is the Tifinagh letter 'yaz', and symbolises a free person *(amazigh)*, the Berbers' name for themselves.

The ensuing centuries were one long lesson for the Romans in minding their manners. First the Berbers backed Hannibal and the Carthaginians against Rome in a protracted spat over Sicily known as the Punic Wars (264–202 BC). Fed up with the persistently unruly Berbers, the new Roman Emperor Caligula finally declared the end of Berber autonomy in the Maghreb (northwest Africa) in AD 40.

Defying Orders under Roman Noses

True to his ruthless reputation, Caligula divided relatively egalitarian Berber clans into subservient classes of slaves, peasants, soldiers and Romanised aristocrats. This strategy worked with Vandals and Byzantines, but Berbers in the Rif and the Atlas drove out the Romans with a campaign of harassment and flagrant disregard for Roman rules. Many Berbers refused to worship Roman gods, and some practised the new renegade religion of

TIMELINE	Origin	248,000–73,000 BC	5000–2500 BC
	According to Amazigh folklore, the earth's first couple birthed 100 babies and left them to finish the job of populating the planet.	Precocious 'pebble people' begin fashioning stone tools far ahead of the European Stone Age technology curve.	Once the Ice Age melts away, the Maghreb becomes a melting pot of Saharan, Mediterranean and indigenous people. They meet, mingle and merge into a diverse people: the Amazigh.

Christianity in open defiance of Roman rule. Christianity took root across North Africa; St Augustine himself was a Berber convert.

Ultimately Rome was only able to gain a foothold in the region by crowning local favourite Juba II king of Mauretania. The enterprising young king married the daughter of Mark Antony and Cleopatra, supported scientific research and performing arts, and helped foster Moroccan industries still vital today: olive-oil production from the region of Volubilis (near Meknès), fishing along the coasts, and vineyards on the Atlantic plains.

The Roman foothold in Mauretania slipped in the centuries after Juba II died, due to increasingly organised Berber rebellions inland and attacks on the Atlantic and Mediterranean coasts by the Vandals, Byzantines and Visigoths. But this new crop of marauding Europeans couldn't manage Mauretania, and neither could Byzantine Emperor Justinian. Justinian's attempt to extend his Holy Roman Empire turned out to be an unholy mess of treaties with various Berber kingdoms, who played their imperial Byzantine connections like face cards in high-stakes games. The history of Morocco would be defined by such strategic gamesmanship among the Berbers, whose savvy, competing alliances helped make foreign dominion over Morocco a near-impossible enterprise for more than a millennium.

Islam Arrives in Morocco

By the early 7th century, the Berbers of Morocco were mostly worshipping their own indigenous deities, alongside Jewish Berbers and a smattering of local Christian converts. History might have continued thus, but for a middle-aged man thousands of miles away who'd had the good fortune to marry a wealthy widow, and yet found himself increasingly at odds with the elites of his Arabian Peninsula town of Mecca. Mohammed bin Abu Talib was his given name, but he would soon be recognised as the Prophet Mohammed for his revelation that there was only one God, and that believers shared a common duty to submit to God's will. The polytheist ruling class of Mecca did not take kindly to this new religion, which assigned them shared responsibilities and took away their minor-deity status, and kicked the Prophet out of town on 16 July AD 622.

This Hejira (exile) only served to spread the Prophet Mohammed's message more widely. By the Prophet's death in 632, Arab caliphs – religious leaders inspired and emboldened by his teachings – were carrying Islam east to Central Asia and west to North Africa. But infighting limited their reach in North Africa, and it took Umayyad Arab leader Uqba bin Nafi until 682 to reach the Atlantic shores of Morocco. According to legend, Uqba announced he would charge into the ocean, if God would only give him the signal. But the legendary Algerian Berber warrior Queen Al-Kahina would have none of Uqba's grandstanding, and with her warriors soon forced Uqba to retreat back to Tunisia.

Pre-Islamic Sites

Carved Gazelle, Tafraoute

Roman Diana mosaics at Volubilis

Phoenician/Roman ruins at Lixus

Prehistoric petroglyphs, Oukaïmeden

Roman Sala Colonia, Chellah

1600 BC	950 BC	800–500 BC	4th–1st century BC
Bronze Age petroglyphs in the High Atlas depict fishing, hunting and horseback riding – a versatile combination of skills and cultures that would define the adaptable, resilient Amazigh.	Amazigh rebuff Rome and its calendar year, and start tracking Berber history on their own calendar on 13 January; it's maintained for centuries after the Muslim Hejira calendar is introduced.	The Maghreb gets even more multiculti as Phoenicians and East Africans join the Berbers, making the composition of the local population as complex as a *ras al hanout* spice blend.	Romans arrive to annex Mauretania, and 250 years later they're still trying, with limited success and some Punic Wars to show for their troubles.

Although an armed force failed to win the Berbers over to Islam, force of conviction gradually began to succeed. The egalitarian premise of Islam and its emphasis on duty, courage and the greater good were compatible with many Berber beliefs, including clan loyalty broadly defined to include almost anyone descended from the Berber equivalent of Adam and Eve. Many Berbers willingly converted to Islam – and not incidentally, reaped the benefits of Umayyad overland trading routes that brought business their way. So although Uqba was killed by his Berber foes before he was able to establish a solid base in Morocco, by the 8th century his successors were able to pull off this feat largely through diplomatic means.

Islam Stays, but Umayyads Must Go

The admiration between the Berbers and the Arab Umayyads was not always mutual, however. While the Umayyads respected Jews and Christians as fellow believers in the word of a singular God, they had no compunction about compelling polytheist Berbers to pay special taxes and serve as infantry (read: cannon fodder). The Umayyads greatly admired Berber women for their beauty, but this wasn't necessarily advantageous; many were conscripted into Umayyad harems.

Even the Berbers who converted to Islam were forced to pay tribute to their Arab overlords. A dissident school of Islamic thought called Kharijism critiqued the abuses of power of the Umayyads as a corruption of the faith, and called for a new moral leadership. In the mid-8th century, insurrections erupted across North Africa. Armed only with slings, a special force of Berbers defeated the elite Umayyad guard. The Umayyads were soon cut off from Spain and Morocco, and local leaders took over an increasingly lucrative trade in silver from the Western Sahara, gold from Ghana and slaves from West Africa.

A Death-Defying Dynasty: The Idrissids

Looking back on early Berber kingdoms, the 14th-century historian Ibn Khuldun noted a pattern that would repeat throughout Moroccan dynastic history. A new leadership would arise determined to do right, make contributions to society as a whole and fill the royal coffers, too. When the pursuit of power and royal comforts began to eclipse loftier aspirations, the powers that be would forfeit their claim to moral authority. A new leadership would arise determined to do right, and the cycle would begin all over again.

So it was with the Idrissids, Morocco's first great dynasty. A descendant of the Prophet Mohammed's daughter Fatima, Idriss I fled Arabia for Morocco in AD 786 after discovering ambitious Caliph Haroun ar-Rashid's plan to murder his entire family. But Idriss didn't exactly keep a low profile. After being proclaimed an imam (religious leader) by the local Berbers, he unified much of northern Morocco in the name of Islam. Just a few

49 BC	25 BC–AD 23	200–429	533
North African King Juba I supports Pompey's ill-fated power play against Julius Caesar. Rome is outraged – but senators pick up where Pompey left off, and assassinate Caesar.	Rome gets a toehold in Mauretania with farms, cities and art, thanks to Juba II. He expands Volubilis into a metropolis of 20,000 residents, including a sizeable Jewish Berber community.	Vandals and Visigoths take turns forcing one another out of Spain and onto the shores of Morocco, until local Rif warriors convince them to bother the Algerians instead.	Justinian ousts the last Vandals from Morocco, but his grand plans to extend the Holy Roman Empire are soon reduced to a modest presence in Essaouira, Tangier and Salé.

days after he'd finally settled into his new capitol at Fez in 792, Haroun ar-Rashid's minions finally tracked down and poisoned Idriss I. Yet death only increased Idriss I's influence; his body was discovered to be miraculously intact five centuries later, and his tomb in the hillside town of Moulay Idriss remains one of the holiest pilgrimage sites in Morocco.

His son Idriss II escaped Haroun's assassins and extended Idrissid control across northern Morocco and well into Europe. In perhaps the first (but certainly not the last) approximation of democracy in Morocco, Idriss II's 13 sons shared power after their father's death. Together they expanded Idrissid principates into Spain and built the glorious mosques of Fez: the Kairaouine and the Andalous.

Warriors Unveiled: The Almoravids

With religious leaders and scholars to help regulate trade, northern Morocco began to take shape as an economic entity under the Idrissids. But the south was another story. A dissident prophet emerged near Salé brandishing a Berber version of the Quran, and established an apocryphal Islam called Barghawata that continued to be practised in the region for centuries. The military strongmen who were left in control of trading outposts in the Atlas Mountains and the Sahara demanded what they called 'alms' – bogus religious nomenclature that didn't fool anyone, and stirred up resentments among the faithful.

From this desert discontent arose the Sanhaja, the pious Saharan Berber tribe that founded the Almoravid dynasty. While the Idrissid princes were distracted by disputes over Spain and Mediterranean Morocco, the Sanhaja swept into the south of Morocco from what is today Senegal and Mauritania. Tough doesn't do justice to the Sanhaja; they lived on camels' meat and milk instead of bread, wore wool in the scorching desert and abstained from wine, music and multiple wives. Their manly habit of wearing dark veils is still practised today by the few remaining Tuareg, the legendary 'Blue Men' of the desert (and the many tourists who imitate them in camel-riding photo-ops). When these intimidating shrouded men rode into Shiite and Barghawata outposts under the command of Yahya ibn Umar and his brother Abu Bakr, they demolished brothels and musical instruments as well as their opponents.

From Marrakesh to Barcelona; the Ultimate Power Couple

After Yahya was killed and Abu Bakr was recalled to the Sahara to settle Sanhaja disputes in 1061, their cousin Youssef ben Tachfine was left to run military operations from a campsite that would become Marrakesh the magnificent. To spare his wife the hardships of life in the Sahara, Abu Bakr divorced brilliant Berber heiress Zeinab en-Nafzawiyyat and arranged

Key Islamic Sites Open to Non-Muslims

Tin Mal Mosque, High Atlas

Medersa Bou Inania, Fez

Zawiya Nassiriyya, Tamegroute

Hassan II Mosque, Casablanca

Ali ben Youssef Medersa, Marrakesh

662–682	711	788–829	8th century
Arabs invade the Maghreb under Umayyad Uqba bin Nafi, introducing Islam to the area. Berber warriors eventually boot out the Umayyads, but decide to keep the Quran.	Northern Morocco and most of Spain come under Umayyad control, and Berbers are strategically settled throughout Andalucia.	Islam takes root in Morocco under Idriss I and Idriss II, who make Fez the epitome of Islamic art, architecture and scholarship and the capital of their Idrissid empire.	Through shared convictions and prudent alliances, Arab caliphates control an area that extends across the Mediterranean and well into Europe, just 320km shy of Paris.

her remarriage to his cousin. Though an odd romantic gesture by today's standards, it was an inspired match. It would be Zeinab's third marriage: before marrying Abu Bakr, she was the widow of one of the leading citizens of Aghmat, and had considerable fortune and political experience at her command. Between Ben Tachfine's initiative and Zeinab's financing and strategic counsel, the Almoravids were unstoppable.

The Almoravids took a while to warm up to their new capital of Marrakesh – too many mountains and rival Berbers around, and too few palm trees. To make themselves more at home, the Almoravids built a mud wall around the city, 8m high and 19km long, and set up the ingenious *khettara* (underground irrigation) system that still supports the *palmeraie* – a vast palm grove outside Marrakesh now dotted with luxury villas. The Jewish and Andalucian communities in Fez thrived under Ben Tachfine, a soft-spoken diplomat and, like his wife, a brilliant military strategist. His Spanish Muslim allies urged him to intercede against Christian and Muslim princes in Spain, complaining bitterly of extortion, attacks and debauchery. At the age of almost 80, Ben Tachfine launched successful campaigns securing Almoravid control of Andalusia right up to the Barcelona city limits.

Sticks & Stones: The Almohads

Youssef ben Tachfine was a tough act to follow. Ali was his son by a Christian woman, and he shared his father's commitments to prayer and urban planning. But while the young idealist Ali was diligently working wonders with architecture and irrigation in Marrakesh, a new force beyond the city walls was gathering the strength of an Atlas thunderstorm: the Almohads.

Almohad historians would later fault Ali for two supposedly dangerous acts: leaving the women in charge and allowing Christians near drink. While the former was hardly a shortcoming – after all, his stepmother's counsel had proved instrumental to the Almoravids – there may be some merit in the latter. While Ali was in seclusion praying and fasting, court and military officials were left to carry on, and carry on they did. Apparently, Almoravid Christian troops were all too conveniently stationed near the wine merchants of Marrakesh.

Queen Al-Kahina had one distinct advantage over the Umayyads: second sight. The downside? She foretold her own death at the hands of her enemy.

The Hard Knocks of Ibn Tumart

None of this sat well with Mohammed ibn Tumart, the Almohad spiritual leader from the Atlas who'd earnt a reputation in Meknès and Salé as a religious vigilante, using his walking stick to shatter wine jars, smash musical instruments and smack men and women with the audacity to walk down the street together. Ibn Tumart finally got himself banished from Marrakesh in the 1120s for knocking Ali's royal sister off her horse with his stick.

But though Ibn Tumart died soon after, there was no keeping out the Almohads. They took over Fez after a nine-month siege in 1145, but reserved

1062	1069	1082	1121–30
With the savvy Zeinab as his wife and chief counsel, Berber leader Youssef ben Tachfine founds Marrakesh as a launching pad for Almoravid conquests of North Africa and Europe.	The Almoravids take Fez by force and promptly begin remodelling the place, installing mills and lush gardens and cleaning up the city's act with running water and hammams.	Almoravid control stretches south to Ghana and Timbuktu, east to Algiers, and north from Lisbon to Spain's Ebro River, near Barcelona.	Almohad spiritual leader Mohammed ibn Tumart loudly condemns Almoravid indulgence in music and wine, but also champions scientific reasoning and political organisation based on a written constitution.

their righteous fury for Marrakesh two years later, razing the place to the ground and killing what was left of Ali's court (Ali died as he lived, quietly, in 1144). Their first projects included rebuilding the Koutoubia Mosque – which Almoravid architects, not up on their algebra, had misaligned with Mecca – and adding the soaring, sublime stone minaret that became the template for Andalucian Islamic architecture. The Tin Mal Mosque was constructed in the High Atlas to honour Ibn Tumart in 1156, and it remains a wonder of austere graces and unshakable foundations.

Almohad Demolition & Construction Crews

A bloody power struggle ensued between the sons of Ibn Tumart and the sons of his generals that wouldn't be settled definitively until 1185, when Abu Yusuf Yacoub, the young son of the Muslim governor of Seville and Valencia, rode south into Morocco and drove his foes into the desert. But he also kept and expanded his power base in Spain, winning so many victories against the princes of Spain that he earned the moniker Al-Mansour, 'the Victorious'. He modelled Seville's famous La Giralda after Marrakesh's Koutoubia minaret, and reinvented Marrakesh as an Almohad capital and learning centre to rival Fez.

Yacoub el-Mansour's urban-planning prowess also made Fez arguably the most squeaky-clean city of medieval times, with 93 hammams, 47 soap factories and 785 mosques complete with ablutions facilities. Yacoub el-Mansour was also a patron of great thinkers, including Aristotle scholar Ibn Rashid – whose commentary would help spark a Renaissance among Italian philosophers – and Sufi master Sidi Bel-Abbes. However, Yacoub's enlightenment and admiration of architecture was apparently not all-encompassing; several synagogues were demolished under his rule.

Defeated by Bulls & Betrayal

Similar thinking (or lack thereof) prevailed in 12th-century Europe, where a hunt for heretics turned to officially sanctioned torture under papal bulls of the egregiously misnamed Pope Innocent IV. Bishop Bernard of Toledo, Spain, seized Toledo's mosque, and rallied Spain's Castilian Christian kings in a crusade against their Muslim rulers. The Almohads were in no condition to fight back. When Yacoub's 16-year-old son was named caliph, he wasn't up to the religious responsibilities that came with the title. Instead, he was obsessed with bullfighting, and was soon gored to death.

Yacoub el-Mansour must have done pirouettes in his grave around 1230, when his next son tapped as caliph, Al-Mamun, allied with his Christian persecutors and turned on his fellow Almohads in a desperate attempt to hang onto his father's empire. This short-lived caliph added the ultimate insult to Almohad injury when he climbed the Koutoubia *minbar* (pulpit) and announced that Ibn Tumart wasn't a true Mahdi (leader) of the faithful. That title, he claimed, rightfully belonged to Jesus.

Key Moroccan Dynasties

Idrissid
(8th–10th century)

Almoravid (11th–12th century)

Almohad (12th–13th century)

Merenid (13th–15th century)

Saadian (16th–17th century)

Alawite (17th century–present)

In Morocco's lower parliament, 60 seats out of 395 are reserved for women (30 are reserved for men aged under 40).

1147	1199	1276	1324–52
The Almohads finally defeat the Almoravids and destroy Marrakesh after a two-year siege, paving the way for Yacoub el-Mansour and his architects to outdo the Almoravids with an all-new Marrakesh.	A vast swath of prime Mediterranean commercial real estate from Tripoli to Spain is consolidated under Almohad control.	Winds of change blow in from the Atlas with the Zenata Berbers, who oust the Almohads and establish the Merenid dynasty with strategic military manoeuvres and even more strategic marriages.	Tangier-born adventurer Ibn Battuta picks up where Marco Polo left off, travelling from Mali to Sumatra and Mongolia and publishing *Rihla* – an inspired though not entirely reliable travel guide.

By Marriage or Murder: The Merenids

When Zenata Berbers from the Anti Atlas invaded the Almohad capital of Marrakesh in 1269, the Almohad defeat was complete. The Zenata had already ousted the Almohads in Meknès, Salé and Fez and along most of the Atlantic Coast. To win over the devout, they promised moral leadership under their new Merenid dynasty. Making good on the promise, the Merenids undertook construction of a *medersa* (school of religious learning) in every major city they conquered, levying special taxes on Christian and Jewish communities for the purpose. In exchange, they allowed these communities

BERBER PRIDE & PREJUDICE

Despite a rich tradition of poetry, petroglyphs, music and art dating as far back as 5000 BC, the Amazigh were often misconstrued as uneducated by outsiders, because no standard written system had been consistently applied to their many distinct languages. The Romans tried for 250 years to take over Amazigh territory and institute Roman customs – and when that failed they bad-mouthed their adversaries, calling them 'Berbers', or Barbarians. The name stuck, and so did anti-Amazigh prejudice.

The protectorate established French as the official language of Morocco to make it easier to conduct (and hence control) business transactions and affairs of state. Complex Amazigh artistic symbolism and traditional medicine were dismissed as charming but irrelevant superstition by those not privy to the oral traditions accompanying them, and the educated classes were encouraged to distance themselves from their Berber roots. But Amazigh languages and traditions have persisted in Morocco, and the Berber Pride movement has recently reclaimed 'Berber' as a unifying term.

After independence (1955–56), Arabic was adopted as the official language, though French continues to be widely spoken among the elite, and Darija is the commonly understood Moroccan Arabic dialect. As recently as the 1980s, the use of Berber script was subject to censure in Morocco. But with the backing of King Mohammed VI – who is part Berber himself – the ancient written Tifinagh alphabet that first emerged around the time of Egyptian hieroglyphics was revived in 2003, and a modernised version is now being taught in many state schools as a standardised written language. In 2011 Berber became an official state language.

More than 60% of Moroccans now call themselves Amazigh or Berber, and Berber languages are currently spoken by some 8.5 to 10 million Moroccans. Berber Pride is now mainstream in Morocco, with the introduction of the official Moroccan broadcaster Chaîne Amazigh, offering TV and radio programs in three Amazigh languages. Yet Human Rights Watch reported that in 2010, parents who gave their children Amazigh names were told the names were rejected by state bureaucrats as 'not recognizably Moroccan'. After a public outcry, the policy was reversed, so babies too can show Berber Pride in Morocco.

1348	1377	1415	1480–92
Bubonic plague strikes Mediterranean North Africa; Merenid alliances and kingdoms crumble. Rule of law is left to survivors and opportunists to enforce, with disastrous consequences.	At Kairaouine University in Fez, Ibn Khaldun examines Middle Eastern history in his groundbreaking *Muqaddimah*, explaining how religious propaganda, taxation and revisionist history make and break states.	In search of gold and the fabled kingdom of Prester John (location of the Fountain of Youth) Portuguese Prince Henry the Navigator begins his conquests of Moroccan seaports.	Ferdinand and Isabella conquer Spain, and the persecution of Muslims and Jews escalates.

to practise key trades, and hired Christian mercenaries and Jewish policy advisors to help conduct the business of the Merenid state.

But this time the new rulers faced a tough crowd not easily convinced by promises of piety. Fez revolted, and the Castilian Christians held sway in Salé. To shore up their Spanish interests, the Merenids allied with the Castilian princes against the Muslim rulers of Granada. Once again, this proved a losing strategy. By the 14th century, Muslim Spain was lost to the Christians, and the Strait of Gibraltar was forfeited. The Merenids also didn't expect the Spanish Inquisition, when over one million Muslims and Jews would be terrorised and forcibly expelled from Spain.

Without military might or religious right to back their imperial claims, the Merenids chose another time-tested method: marriage. In the 14th century, Merenid leaders cleverly co-opted their foes by marrying princesses from Granada and Tunis, and claimed Algiers, Tripoli and the strategic Mediterranean port of Ceuta.

Death by Plague & Office Politics

But the bonds of royal marriage were not rat-proof, and the Merenid empire was devastated by plague. Abu Inan, son of the Merenid leader Abu Hassan, glimpsed opportunity in the Black Death, and proclaimed himself the new ruler despite one minor glitch: his father was still alive. Abu Hassan hurried back from Tripoli to wrest control from his treacherous son in Fez, but to no avail. Abu Inan buried his father in the royal Merenid necropolis outside Rabat in 1351, but he too was laid to rest nearby after he was strangled by one of his own advisors in 1358.

The Merenids had an unfortunate knack for hiring homicidal bureaucrats. To cover his tracks, Abu Inan's killer went on a royal killing spree, until Merenid Abu Salim Ibrahim returned from Spain and terminated this rampaging employee. Abu Salim's advisor sucked up to his boss by offering his sister in marriage, only to lop off Abu Salim's head after the wedding. He replaced Abu Salim with a Merenid patsy before thinking better of it and strangling the new sultan, too. This slippery advisor was assassinated by another Merenid, who was deposed a scant few years later by yet another Merenid – and so it continued for 40 years, with new Merenid rulers and advisors offing the incumbents every few years. While the Merenids were preoccupied with murderous office politics in Meknès and Fez, the Portuguese seized control of coastal Morocco.

Victory is Sweet: The Saadians

Much of Portugal (including Lisbon) had been under Muslim rule during the 12th century, and now the Portuguese were ready for payback – literally. The tiny, rugged kingdom needed steady supplies of food for its people and gold to fortify its growing empire, but Morocco stood in the way. No nation

Berber Languages in Morocco

....

Tashelhit, Central Morocco

....

Tamazight, Middle Atlas

....

Tarifit, Rif

....

Tuareg (Tamashek), Sahara

1497–1505	1498	1525	1578
Moroccan ports are occupied by English, Portuguese and Spanish forces and sundry pirates, from Mediterranean Melilla to Agadir on the Atlantic coast.	Church Inquisitors present European Muslims and Jews with a choice: conversion and persecution; or torture and death. Many choose neither of these, and escape to Morocco.	Like a blast of scorching desert wind, the Beni Saad Berbers blow back European and Ottoman encroachment in Morocco, and establish a new Saadian dynasty in Marrakesh.	The Saadians fight both alongside and against Portugal at the Battle of Three Kings, ending with 8000 dead, a scant 100 survivors and the decimation of Portugal's ruling class.

could wrest overland Saharan trade routes from the savvy Berber warriors who'd controlled key oases and mountain passes for centuries. Instead, the Portuguese went with tactics where they had clear technical advantages: naval warfare and advanced firearms. By systematically capturing Moroccan ports along the Mediterranean and Atlantic coasts, Portuguese gunships bypassed Berber middlemen inland, and headed directly to West Africa for gold and slaves.

Sugar Caravans

Once trade in the Sahara began to dry up, something had to be done. Entire inland communities were decimated, and formerly flush Marrakesh was wracked with famine. The Beni Saad Berbers – now known to history as the Saadians – from the Drâa Valley took up the fight against the Portuguese. With successive wins against European, Berber and Ottoman rivals, the Saadians were able to reinstate inland trade. Soon the Saadians were in control of such sought-after commodities as gold, slaves, ivory, ostrich feathers and the must-have luxury for trendy European royals: sugar.

The Saadians satisfied European sugar cravings at prices that make today's oil and cocaine cartels look like rank amateurs. With threats of full-scale invasion, the Saadians had no problem scaring up customers and suppliers. The most dangerous sugar-dealer of all was Saadian Sultan Ahmed al-Mansour ed-Dahbi, who earned his names Al-Mansour (the Victorious) for defeating foes from Portugal to the Sudan, and Ed-Dahbi (the Golden) for his success in bilking them. This Marrakshi Midas used the proceeds to line his Badi Palace in Marrakesh from floor to ceiling with gold and gems. But after the sultan died, his short-lived successor stripped the palace down to its mudbrick foundations, as it remains today. The Saadian legacy is most visible in the Saadian Tombs, decked out for a decadent afterlife with painted Carrara marble and gold leaf. The Saadians died as they lived: dazzling beyond belief and a touch too rich for most tastes.

The Rise of Mellahs

Under the Saadians, Jewish communities also took up crucial roles as dealers of the hottest Moroccan commodities of the time: salt and sugar. When European Jewish communities faced the Inquisition, forced conversions and summary executions, the comparatively tolerant Saadian dynasty provided Jewish communities with some security, setting aside a section of Marrakesh next to the royal kasbah as a Jewish quarter, or *mellah* – a name derived from the Arabic word for salt. This protection was repaid many times over in taxes levied on Jewish and Christian businesses, and the royally flush Saadians clearly got the sweet end of the deal. Yet several Jewish Moroccans rose to

An incisive look at religious life on opposite ends of the Muslim world, anthropologist Clifford Geertz's groundbreaking *Islam Observed: Religious Development in Morocco and Indonesia* reveals complex variations within the vast mosaic of Islam.

A Travellers History of North Africa, by Barnaby Rogerson, is a handy and accessible guide that puts Morocco amid the wider currents of regional history.

1591	1610–14	1659–66	1662
With 4000 European mercenaries, Ahmed al-Mansour ed-Dahbi crosses the Sahara and defeats a 40,000-strong army for control of the fabled desert caravan destination of Timbuktu.	Oxford graduate and erstwhile lawyer Henry Mainwaring founds the Masmouda Pirates Republic near Rabat, pillaging Canadian cod, French salt-fish and Portuguese wine. He is later elected to Britain's parliament.	The Alawites end years of civil war, and even strike an uneasy peace with the Barbary pirates controlling Rabati ports.	Portugal gives Tangier to the British as a wedding present for Charles II. After a lengthy siege, it is eventually returned to Moroccan control in 1684.

2000 YEARS OF MOROCCAN JEWISH HISTORY

By the 1st century AD, Jewish Berber communities that were already well established in Morocco included farmers, metalworkers, dyers, glassblowers and bookbinders. The Merenids established the first official Jewish quarter in Fez, where Jewish entrepreneurs excluded from trades and guilds in medieval Europe were able to conduct business. Jewish Moroccans were taxed when business boomed for the ruling dynasty and sometimes blamed when it didn't, yet they managed to flourish under the Merenids and Saadians, while European Jews faced the Inquisition and persecution.

Under Alawite rule in the 17th to 19th centuries, the official policy toward Jewish Moroccans was one of give and take: on the one hand they had opportunities as tradespeople, business leaders and ambassadors to England, Holland and Denmark in the 19th century; on the other hand they were subjected to taxes, surveillance and periodic scapegoating. But in good times and bad, Jewish Moroccans remained a continuous presence.

By 1948, some 300,000 Jewish Moroccans lived in Morocco. Many left after the founding of the states of Morocco and Israel, and today only an estimated 3000 to 8000 remain, mostly in Casablanca. A Jewish community centre in Casablanca was a bombing target in 2003, and though no one was harmed at the community centre, trade-centre blasts killed 33 and wounded 100. Yet the Casablanca community remains intact, and Casablanca is home to the recently expanded Moroccan Jewish Museum.

Under the current king, Jewish schools now receive state funding, and a few Jewish expatriates have responded to a royal invitation to return, contributing to the revival of Essaouira's *mellah*. Yet the everyday champions of Jewish heritage in Morocco remain ordinary Moroccans, the one million people worldwide of Moroccan Jewish heritage, and culturally engaged travellers, who together ensure Moroccan Jewish customs, festivals, and landmarks get the attention they deserve.

prominence as royal advisors, and in the Saadian Tombs of Marrakesh, trusted Jewish confidantes are buried closer to kings than royal wives.

By day, Jewish merchants traded alongside Christian and Muslim merchants, and were entrusted with precious salt, sugar and gold brought across the Sahara; by night they were under official guard in their quarters. Once the *mellahs* of Fez and Marrakesh became overcrowded with European arrivals, other notable *mellahs* were founded in Essaouira, Safi, Rabat and Meknès, and the traditions of skilled handicrafts that flourished there continue to this day. The influence of the *mellahs* spread throughout Morocco, especially in tangy dishes with the signature salted, pickled ingredients of Moroccan Jewish cuisine.

1672	18th century	1757–90	1767–1836
The Alawite Moulay Ismail takes the throne. One of the greatest Moroccan sultans, he rules for 55 years and the Alawite succession lasts to the present day.	The Alawites rebuild the ancient desert trading outpost of Sijilmassa, only to lose control of it to Aït Atta Berber warriors, who raze the town. Only two not-so-triumphal arches remain.	Sidi Mohammed III makes a strategic move to the coast, to rebuild Essaouira and regain control over Atlantic ports. Inland imperial cities of Fez and Meknès slip into decline.	Cash-strapped Morocco makes extraordinary concessions to trading partners, granting Denmark trade monopolies in Agadir and Safi, and France and the US license to trade in Morocco for a nominal fee.

Pirates & Politics: The Early Alawites

The Saadian empire dissolved in the 17th century like a sugar cube in Moroccan mint tea, and civil war prevailed until the Alawites came along. With illustrious ancestors from the Prophet Mohammed's family and descendants extending to the current King Mohammed VI, the Alawites were quite a change from the free-wheeling Saadians and their anarchic legacy. But many Moroccans might have preferred anarchy to the second Alawite ruler, the dreaded Moulay Ismail (1672–1727).

A despot whose idea of a good time included public disembowelments and amateur dentistry on courtiers who peeved him, Moulay Ismail was also a scholar, dad to hundreds of children and Mr Popularity among his royal European peers. European nobles gushed about lavish dinner parties at Moulay Ismail's palace in Meknès, built by conscripted Christian labourers. Rumour has it that when these decidedly non-union construction workers finished the job, some were walled in alive. The European royal party tab wasn't cheap, either, but Moulay Ismail wasn't worried: piracy would cover it.

In Her Majesty's Not-So-Secret Service: Barbary Pirates

Queen Elizabeth I kicked off the Atlantic pirate trade, allying against her arch-nemesis King Phillip II of Spain with the Saadians and specially licensed pirates known as privateers. The most notoriously effective hires were the Barbary pirates, Moriscos (Spanish Muslims) who'd been forcibly converted and persecuted in Spain and hence had an added motivation to shake down Spaniards. James I outlawed English privateering in 1603, but didn't seem to mind when his buddy Moulay Ismail aided and abetted the many British and Barbary pirates who harboured in the royal ports at Rabat and Salé – for a price.

But pirate loyalties being notoriously fickle, Barbary pirates attacked Ireland, Wales, Iceland and even Newfoundland in the 17th century. Barbary pirates also took prisoners, who were usually held for ransom and freed after a period of servitude – including one-time English allies. Captives were generally better off with Barbary pirates than French profiteers, who typically forced prisoners to ply the oars of slave galleys until death. Nevertheless, after pressure from England secured their release in 1684, a number of English captives were quite put out about the whole experience, and burned the port of Tangier behind them. But other English saw upsides to piracy and kidnapping: when the Portuguese were forced out of Essaouira in the 17th century, a freed British prisoner who'd converted to Islam joined a French profiteer to rebuild the city for the sultan, using free labour provided by European captives.

Global Voices Morocco provides a roundup of Moroccan news and opinion online, including English translations of bloggers' responses to Moroccan news at www.globalvoicesonline.org/-/world/middle-east-north-africa/morocco.

Whatever happened to Barbary pirates? How did Islam mesh with Berber beliefs? And why was Morocco the exception to Ottoman rule? Jamil Abun-Nasr unravels these and other Moroccan mysteries in *A History of the Maghreb in the Islamic Period*.

1777	1830	1860	1880
A century after the English leave Tangier a royal wreck, Morocco gets revenge and becomes the first country to recognise the breakaway British colony calling itself the United States of America.	France seizes the Algerian coast, increasing pressure on the Moroccan sultan to cede power in exchange for mafia-style protection, along Morocco's coasts, from the advancing Ottomans.	If at first you don't succeed, try for seven centuries: Spain takes control of a swath of northern Morocco reaching into the Rif.	France, Britain, Spain and the US meet in Madrid and agree that Morocco can retain nominal control over its territory – after granting themselves tax-free business licenses and duty-free shopping.

Troubled Waters for Alawites

After Moulay Ismail's death, his elite force of 50,000 to 70,000 Abid, or 'Black Guard', ran amok, and not one of his many children was able to succeed him. The Alawite dynasty would struggle on into the 20th century, but the country often lapsed into lawlessness when rulers overstepped their bounds. Piracy and politics became key ways to get ahead in the 18th and 19th centuries – and the two were by no means mutually exclusive. By controlling key Moroccan seaports and playing European powers against one another, officials and outlaws alike found they could demand a cut of whatever goods were shipped through the Strait of Gibraltar and along the Atlantic Coast.

In the late 18th century, when Sidi Mohammed ben Abdullah ended the officially condoned piracy of his predecessors and nixed shady side deals with foreign powers, the financial results were disastrous. With added troubles of plague and drought, Morocco's straits were truly dire.

With Friends Like These: European Encroachment

For all their successful European politicking, the early Alawites had apparently forgotten a cardinal rule of Moroccan diplomacy: never neglect Berber alliances. Sultan Moulay Hassan tried to rally support among the Berbers of the High Atlas in the late 19th century, but by then it was too late. France began to take an active interest in Morocco around 1830, and allied with Berbers across North Africa to fend off the Ottomans. After centuries of practise fighting Moroccans, Spain took control of areas of northern Morocco in 1860 – and generated lasting resentment for desecrating graveyards, mosques and other sacred sites in Melilla and Tetouan. While wily Queen Victoria entertained Moroccan dignitaries and pressed for Moroccan legal reforms, her emissaries were busy brokering deals with France and Spain.

Footloose & Duty-Free in Tangier

Order became increasingly difficult to maintain in Moroccan cities and in Berber mountain strongholds, and Moulay Hassan employed powerful Berber leaders to regain control – but accurately predicting Moulay Hassan's demise, some Berbers cut deals of their own with the Europeans. By the time Moulay Hassan's teenage successor Sultan Moulay Abdelaziz pushed through historic antidiscrimination laws to impress Morocco's erstwhile allies, the Europeans had reached an understanding: while reforms were nice, what they really wanted were cheap goods. By 1880, Europeans and Americans had set up their own duty-free shop in Tangier; an 'international zone' where they were above the law and beyond tax collectors' reaches.

HISTORY WITH FRIENDS LIKE THESE: EUROPEAN ENCROACHMENT

Historic Moroccan Mellahs

Tamnougalt

Demnate

Fez

Zagora and Amezrou

Essaouira

Marrakesh

Moulay Ismail was pen pals with England's James II and Louis XIV of France, and tried to convert the Sun King to Islam by mail.

1906	1912	1921–26	1942
The controversial Act of Algeciras divvies up North Africa among European powers like a *Pastilla* (pigeon pie), but Germany isn't invited – a slight that exacerbates tensions among European powers.	The Treaty of Fez hands Morocco to the French protectorate, which mostly protects French business interests at Moroccan taxpayer expense with the ruthless assistance of Berber warlord Pasha el-Glaoui.	Under the command of Abd el-Krim, Berber leaders rebel against Spanish rule of the Rif, and Spain loses its foothold in the mountains.	In defiance of Vichy France, Casablanca hosts American forces staging the Allied North African campaign. This move yields US support for Moroccan independence and the classic Humphrey Bogart film *Casablanca*.

Impress Moroccans with your knowledge of the latest developments in Moroccan society, Amazigh culture and North African politics, all covered in English at www.moroccoworldnews.com

But the lure of prime North African real estate proved irresistible. By 1906, Britain had snapped up strategic waterfront property in Egypt and the Suez; France took the prize for sheer acreage from Algeria to West Africa; Italy landed Libya; Spain drew the short stick with the unruly Rif and a whole lot of desert. Germany was incensed at being left out of this arrangement and announced support for Morocco's independence, further inflaming tensions between Germany and other European powers in the years leading up to WWI.

France Opens a Branch Office: The Protectorate

Whatever illusions of control Morocco's sultanate might've been clutching slipped away at the 1906 Conference of Algeciras, when control of Morocco's banks, customs and police force was handed over to France for 'protection'. The 1912 Treaty of Fez establishing Morocco as a French protectorate made colonisation official, and the French hand-picked a new sultan with all the backbone of a sock puppet. More than 100,000 French administrators, outcasts and opportunists arrived in cities across Morocco to take up residence in French villes nouvelles (new towns).

Résident-Général Louis Lyautey saw to it that these new French suburbs were kitted out with all the mod cons: electricity, trains, roads and running water. Villes nouvelles were designed to be worlds apart from adjacent Moroccan medinas (historic city centres), with French schools, churches, villas and grand boulevards named after French generals. No expense or effort was spared to make the new arrivals feel right at home – which made their presence all the more galling for Moroccans footing the bill through taxes, shouldering most of the labour and still living in crowded, poorly serviced medinas. Lyautey had already set up French colonial enterprises in Vietnam, Madagascar and Algeria, so he arrived in Morocco with the confidence of a CEO and a clear plan of action: break up the Berbers, ally with the Spanish when needed and keep business running by any means.

Nationalist Resistance

Once French-backed Sultan Yusuf died and his French-educated 18-year-old son Mohammed V became sultan, Lyautey expected that French business in Morocco would carry on as usual. He hadn't counted on a fiery young nationalist as sultan, or the staunch independence of ordinary Moroccans. Mining strikes and union organising interfered with France's most profitable colonial businesses, and military attention was diverted to force Moroccans back into the mines. Berbers had never accepted foreign dominion without a fight, and they were not about to start. By 1921 the Rif was up in arms against the Spanish and French under the leadership of Ibn Abd al-Krim al-Khattabi. It took five years, 300,000 Spanish and French forces and

Read first-hand accounts of Morocco's independence movement from Moroccan women who rebelled against colonial control, rallied and fought alongside men in Alison Baker's Voice of Resistance: Oral Histories of Moroccan Women.

1943–45	1944–53	1955–56	1961
When the Allies struggle in Italy, US General Patton calls in the Goums, Morocco's elite force of mountain warriors. With daggers and night-time attacks, they advance the Allies in Tuscany.	Moroccan nationalists demand independence from France with increasing impatience. Sultan Mohammed V is inclined to agree, and is exiled to Madagascar by the protectorate for the crime of independent thought.	Morocco successfully negotiates its independence from France, Spain cedes control over most of its colonial claims within Morocco, and exiled nationalist Mohammed V returns as king of independent Morocco.	When Mohammed V dies suddenly, Hassan II becomes king. He transforms Morocco into a constitutional monarchy in 1962, but the 'Years of Lead' deal heavy punishments for dissent.

WESTERN SAHARA

Talk of 'Greater Morocco' began in the 1950s, but in the 1970s it became the official explanation for Morocco's annexation of phosphate-rich Spanish Sahara. There was a snag: the Popular Front for the Liberation of the Sagui al Hamra and the Rio di Oro (Polisario – Saharawi pro-independence militia) declared the region independent. Putting his French legal training to work, Hassan II took the matter up with the International Court of Justice (ICJ) in The Hague in 1975, expecting the court would provide a resounding third-party endorsement for Morocco's claims. Instead the ICJ considered a counter-claim for independence from the Polisario, and dispatched a fact-finding mission to Spanish Sahara.

The ICJ concluded that ties to Morocco weren't strong enough to support Moroccan sovereignty over the region, and Western Sahara was entitled to self-determination. In a highly creative interpretation of this court judgment, Hassan II declared that Morocco had won its case and ordered a celebratory 'peace march' of more than 350,000 Moroccans from Marrakesh into Western Sahara in 1975. This unarmed 'Green March' was soon fortified by military personnel and land mines, and was vehemently resisted by armed Polisario fighters. The Green March is no longer the symbol of national pride it once was; Green March murals that once defined desert-cafe decor have been painted over with apolitical dune-scapes, and images of the march have been removed from the new Dh100 note.

In 1991 a truce was brokered between Morocco and Polisario and continues to be monitored by UN peacekeepers. As part of the deal a referendum on independence was promised, but Morocco has never allowed it to be held. At best, Rabat maintains that it will grant Western Sahara autonomous status. Today, the status of Western Sahara remains unresolved in international law, a rallying cry for many Saharawi, a political taboo in the national conversation and an awkward conversation nonstarter for many deeply ambivalent Moroccan taxpayers.

two budding Fascists (Francisco Franco and Marshal Pétain) to capture Ibn Abd al-Krim and force him into exile.

The French won a powerful ally when they named Berber warlord Thami el-Glaoui pasha of Marrakesh, but they also made a lot of enemies. The title gave the pasha implicit license to do as he pleased, which included mafia-style executions and extortion schemes, kidnapping women and children who struck his fancy, and friendly games of golf at his Royal Golf Club with Ike Eisenhower and Winston Churchill. The pasha forbade talk of independence under penalty of death, and conspired to exile Mohammed V from Morocco in 1953 – but Pasha Glaoui would end his days powerless, wracked with illness and grovelling for King Mohammed V's forgiveness.

Although the French protectorate of Morocco was nominally an ally of Vichy France and Germany in WWII, independent-minded Casablanca provided crucial ground support for the Allied North African

1975	1981	1984	1994
The UN concludes that the Western Sahara is independent, but Hassan II concludes otherwise, ordering the Green March to enforce Morocco's claims to the region and its phosphate reserves.	After the Casablanca Uprising, the military rounds up dissenters and unionists nationwide. But demands for political reforms increase, and many political prisoners are later exonerated.	Morocco leaves the Organisation of African States (now the African Union) in protest against the admission of Saharawi representatives. It finally asks to rejoin in 2016.	Years of poor relations between Morocco and Algeria, primarily over the Western Sahara issue, lead to the permanent closure of the border between the two countries.

campaign. When Morocco's Istiqlal (Independence) party demanded freedom from French rule in 1944, the US and Britain were finally inclined to agree. Under increasing pressure from Moroccans and the Allies, France allowed Mohammed V to return from exile in 1955. Morocco successfully negotiated its independence from France and Spain between 1956 and 1958.

A Rough Start: After Independence

When Mohammed V died of heart failure in 1961, King Hassan II became the leader of the new nation. Faced with a shaky power base, an unstable economy and elections that revealed divides even among nationalists, Hassan II consolidated power by cracking down on dissent and suspending parliament for a decade. With heavy borrowing to finance dam-building, urban development and an ever-expanding bureaucracy, Morocco was deep in debt by the 1970s. Attempts to assassinate the king underscored the need to do something, quickly, to turn things around – and then in 1973, the phosphate industry in the Spanish-controlled Western Sahara started to boom. Morocco staked its claim to the area and its lucrative phosphate reserves with the Green March, settling the area with Moroccans while greatly unsettling indigenous Saharawi people agitating for self-determination.

Years of Lead

According to the 2014 Human Development Index, the annual gross national income (GNI) in Morocco is US$6850 per capita, but 13.3% of its population live on US$2 a day.

Along with the growing gap between the rich and the poor and a mounting tax bill to cover Morocco's military spending in Western Sahara, King Hassan II's suppression of dissent fuelled further resentment among his subjects. By the 1980s, the critics of the king included journalists, trade unionists, women's-rights activists, Marxists, Islamists, Berbers advocating recognition of their culture and language, and the working poor – in other words, a broad cross-section of Moroccan society.

The last straw for many came in 1981, when official Moroccan newspapers casually announced that the government had conceded to the International Monetary Fund to hike prices for staple foods. For the many Moroccans subsisting on the minimum wage, these increases meant that two-thirds of their income would be spent on a meagre diet of sardines, bread and tea. When trade unions organised protests against the measure, government reprisals were swift and brutal. Tanks rolled down the streets of Casablanca and hundreds were killed, at least 1000 wounded, and an estimated 5000 protesters arrested in a nationwide *laraf*, or roundup.

1999	2002–07	2004–05	2004
Soon after initiating a commission to investigate abuses of power under his own rule, Hassan II dies. All hail Mohammed VI, and hope for a constitutional monarchy.	Historic reforms initiated under Mohammed VI include regular parliamentary and municipal elections across Morocco, plus the Mudawanna legal code offering unprecedented protection for women.	Equity and Reconciliation Commission televises testimonies of the victims of Moroccan human-rights abuses during the 'Years of Lead'; it becomes the most watched in Moroccan TV history.	Morocco signs free-trade agreements with the EU and the US, and gains status as a non-NATO ally.

Far from dissuading dissent, the Casablanca Uprising galvanised support for government reform. Sustained pressure from human-rights activists throughout the 1980s achieved unprecedented results in1991, when Hassan II founded the Equity and Reconciliation Commission to investigate human-rights abuses that occurred during his own reign – a first for a king. In his first public statement as king upon his father's death in 1999, Mohammed VI vowed to right the wrongs of the era known to Moroccans as the Years of Lead. The commission has since helped cement human-rights advances, awarding reparations to 9280 victims of the Years of Lead by 2006.

New Regime, New Hopes

As Moroccans will surely tell you, there's still room for improvement in today's Morocco. The parliament elected in 2002 set aside 30 seats for women members of parliament, and implemented some promising reforms: Morocco's first-ever municipal elections, employment non-discrimination laws, the introduction of Berber languages in state schools, and the Mudawanna, a legal code protecting women's rights to divorce and custody. But tactics from the Years of Lead were revived after the 2003 Casablanca trade-centre bombings and a 2010 military raid of a Western Sahara protest camp, when suspects were rounded up – in 2010 Human Rights Watch reported that many of them had been subjected to abuse and detention without counsel. Civil society is outpacing state reforms, as Moroccans take the initiative to address poverty and illiteracy through enterprising village associations and non-governmental organisations.

The most comprehensive Berber history in English is *The Berbers*, by Michael Brett and Elizabeth Fentress. The authors leave no stone carving unturned, providing archaeological evidence to back up their historical insights.

Morocco's Arab Spring

In early 2011 Morocco was rocked by the Arab Spring protests that were sweeping across the Middle East and North Africa. Protestors demanded more devolution of power and political accountability. Mohammed VI reacted with a deftness that eluded many other leaders, and announced a series of constitutional reforms, which included giving more power to parliament and making Berber an official state language. The reforms were quickly passed in a national referendum. Although some demonstrators have continued to call for deeper reforms, Morocco's stability continues be a valued prize for most of its citizens.

2006	2011	2016
Morocco proposes 'special autonomy' for the Western Sahara, and holds the first direct talks with Polisario in seven years – which end in a stalemate.	Pro-democracy revolutions in Tunisia and Egypt inspire Morocco's February 20 Movement; in response the king announces limited constitutional reform, passed by national referendum.	Elections in October see the ruling moderate Islamist Justice and Development Party (PJD) increase their representation in parliament as well as providing Morocco's prime minister.

A Day in the Life of Morocco

For travellers Morocco can be about haggling for carpets, romantic dreams of sunsets over the Sahara, dodging snake charmers in Marrakesh and chasing urban legends about decadent Tangier. It certainly makes for an exciting picture, but what is it like for Moroccans? Taking some time to explore the major themes in Moroccan society and daily life will enrich anyone's visit to this culturally fruitful country.

Language & Identity

Morocco's original inhabitants were Berber, but the arrival of Arabs with the introduction of Islam has, over the centuries, mixed and remixed the two populations to a point where the line between Arab and Berber is frequently rather blurred. However, culturally there has frequently been a clear demarcation between speakers of Arabic (in its Moroccan form known as Darija) and Berber languages (known as Amazigh).

Arab speakers, personified in the Alawite dynasty that has ruled Morocco since the 17th century, have traditionally held the upper hand, despite speakers of Berber languages often holding a demographic majority. This position was institutionalised by the French in the 1930s when they passed laws to discriminate against Berbers. For much of the 20th century it was illegal to even register many traditional Berber names at birth, and Berber education was banned.

In 21st-century Morocco, Berber culture is having something of a renaissance. In 2011 the constitution was revised to make Amazigh an official national language. The effects of this are most immediately visible by the new Amazigh signage that adorns government buildings (and, increasingly, road signs) along with Arabic and French. Berber education, now formally encouraged, still lags behind in quality due to poor training and facilities, although it's still early days in a renaissance in national identity for a culture whose roots are so deep in Moroccan culture.

The rise of Berber is reflected in the relative fall from grace of French, the language of Morocco's colonial past. French is no longer listed as an official state language, though it remains a language of much business and the ability to speak it is frequently perceived as a marker of social status. In higher education today, however, many lessons are taught in English; some argue that French should ultimately be done away with altogether, and English tuition encouraged to increase Morocco's competitiveness in a global economy.

Social Norms

Family Values

Family life remains at the heart of much of Moroccan life, and while individuals may have ambitions and ideas of their own, their aspirations are often tied in some way to family – a much-admired trait in Morocco. Success for the individual is seen as success for the family as a whole. Even major status symbols such as cars or satellite TVs may be valued less as prized possessions than as commodities benefiting the entire family. This is beginning to change, as the emerging middle class represents moves out of large family homes and into smaller apartments in the suburbs, where common property is not such a given. But family connections remain paramount. Even as Morocco's economy has grown, remittances from Moroccans living in Spain and France to family back home represent as much as 7% of GDP.

Since family is a focal point for Moroccans, expect related questions to come up in the course of conversation: Where is your family (the idea of holidaying without your family can be anathema)? Are you married, and do you have children? If not, why not? These lines of enquiry can seem a little forward, but are a roundabout way of finding out who you are and what interests you. Questions about where you work or what you do in your spare time are odd ice-breakers, since what you do for a living or a hobby says less about you than what you do for your family.

Education & Economy

One of the most important indicators of social status in Morocco is education. As a whole, the country has an adult literacy rate of 67%, with slightly more men than women being literate. The disparity is heightened in poorer rural areas. Here, three-quarters of women cannot read or write and less than 50% of first-graders complete primary school. Schooling to age 14 is now officially mandated, and local initiatives are slowly improving opportunities for education in the Moroccan countryside.

For vulnerable rural families, just getting the children fed can be difficult, let alone getting them to school. Around a quarter of Moroccans are judged to live in near or absolute poverty, and suffer from food insecurity (living in fear of hunger). Under-employment often means that a steady income is a rarity, and 35% of the average Moroccan income covers basic foodstuffs. Only 10% of Moroccans can afford imported foods at the supermarket, let alone eating at restaurants. Although the Moroccan economy has grown well in the 21st century, and Morocco has a burgeoning middle class, its benefits have not always been spread equally: improvements are needed in education to match the growth of Morocco's service industry, which in recent years has even overtaken agriculture for its contribution to GDP.

For a millennia-old civilisation, Morocco looks young. Half the population is under 25, almost a third is under 15, and just 4% is over 65.

THE FOREIGNERS NEXT DOOR

With an attractive climate and exchange rate, Morocco has 100,000 foreign residents – and counting. Many Moroccan emigrants from Europe and the US are returning to Morocco to live, retire or start businesses, creating a new upper-middle class. The carefree spending of returnees is a source of revenue and a certain amount of resentment for Moroccans, who grumble openly about returnees driving up costs and importing a culture of conspicuous consumption that's unattainable and shallow.

An international vogue for riads has seen many Europeans buying and restoring historic structures – and sometimes pricing Moroccans out of the housing market and leaving medina neighbourhoods strangely empty and lifeless off-season. It's a double-edged sword: maintenance and restoration of centuries-old medina houses is often beyond the reach of the families who live in them, and who grab with both hands the chance to upgrade to homes with modern amenities in the villes nouvelles. At the same time, others grumble that the European influx brings to mind colonial-era enclaves.

Travellers can make the exchange more equitable by venturing beyond riad walls to explore Moroccan culture, meet Moroccans on their own turf and ensure Moroccans benefit from tourism.

Frustratingly for many Moroccans, getting ahead can still be a case of who you know as much as what you know. Morocco rates low on Transparency International's corruption perception index, and most Moroccan families at some time will have butted up against the concept of *wasta*, the need to have a well-connected middleman to get a job or access a service. This is particularly frustrating for an increasingly educated youth suffering high levels of unemployment, who demand a more meritocratic society.

Shifting Gender Roles

Morocco is a male-dominated society, particularly in the public sphere. Take one look at the people nursing a coffee all afternoon in a pavement cafe and you might even ask, where are all the women? However, significant progress is being made on women's rights, and the push for change has been led from the ground up, with women's groups creating a singular brand of Islamic feminism to affect change.

Two decades ago most of the people you'd see out and about, going to school, socialising and conducting business in Morocco would have been men. Women were occupied with less high-profile work, particularly in rural areas, such as animal husbandry, farming, childcare, and fetching water and firewood. Initiatives to eliminate female illiteracy have given girls a better start in life, and positive social pressure has greatly reduced the once-common practice of hiring girls under 14 years of age as domestic workers. Women now represent nearly a third of Morocco's formal workforce, forming their own industrial unions, agricultural cooperatives and artisans' collectives. Over 40% of university graduates today are women.

A major societal change came in 2004, with the overhaul of Morocco's Mudawanna legal code. Revising these laws guaranteed women crucial rights with regard to custody, divorce, property ownership and child support, among other protections. The direction of travel hasn't been universally smooth, however. In 2012, Moroccan society was shocked by the case of a 16-year-old girl who committed suicide after being forced to marry her rapist, drawing attention to a clause in the law that allowed a man to be 'forgiven' his crime by marrying his victim. The law was amended after a public outcry, but although the legal age of marriage remains 18 years, child marriages may still be allowed if a special dispensation is given by an Islamic judge.

The modern Moroccan woman's outlook extends far beyond her front door, and female visitors will meet Moroccan women eager to chat, compare life experiences and share perspectives on world events.

The Majlis, Morocco's lower parliament, has 60 seats (of 395) reserved for women. On regional councils (which are directly elected), one-third of seats are reserved for women.

Best-selling Moroccan feminist writer Fatima Mernissi exposes telling differences and uncanny similarities in the ideals of women in Europe and the Middle East in *Scheherazade Goes West: Different Cultures, Different Harems*.

DRESSING TO IMPRESS IN MOROCCO

A common question is 'how best to dress as a visitor in Morocco?'

Women aren't expected to cover their head in Morocco. Some Moroccan women do and some don't wear the *hijab* (headscarf). Some wear it for religious, cultural, practical or personal reasons, or alternate, wearing a head covering in the streets but taking it off at home and work. A full face-covering veil is unusual in cities, and even rarer among rural women working in the fields. Context is important. Likewise, that chic knee-length skirt you see a Moroccan woman wearing in a Marrakesh restaurant is likely to be swapped for more conservative jellaba while visiting the medina.

That said, your choice of attire may be perceived as a sign of respect for yourself and Moroccans alike. For both men and women, this means not wearing shorts, sleeveless tops or clingy clothing. If you do, some people will be embarrassed for you and the family that raised you, and avoid eye contact. So if you don't want to miss out on some excellent company – especially among older Moroccans – dress modestly.

MOROCCAN SOCIAL GRACES

Many visitors are surprised at how quickly friendships can be formed in Morocco, and are often a little suspicious. True, carpet-sellers aren't after your friendship when they offer you tea, but notice how Moroccans behave with one another, and you'll see that friendly overtures are more than a mere contrivance. People you meet in passing are likely to remember you and greet you warmly the next day, and it's considered polite to stop and ask how they're doing. Greetings among friends can last 10 minutes, as each person enquires after the other's happiness, well-being and family.

Moroccans are generous with their time, and extend courtesies that might seem to you like impositions, from walking you to your next destination to inviting you home for lunch. To show your appreciation, stop by the next day to say hello, and be sure to compliment the cook.

Male-female interactions are still sometimes stilted by social convention (though you'll surely notice couples meeting in parks, at cafes and via webcam), but conversations about hijab that obsess the media in some parts of the world seem less relevant here, where you'll see a devout young woman covering her hair walking with a friend with free-flowing hair and another wrapped up in a headscarf worn purely as a fashion statement. These are young Moroccan women on the move, commuting to work on motor scooters, taking over sidewalks on arm-in-arm evening strolls, and running for key government positions.

To avoid conflict, French Resident-Général Lyautey banned non-Muslims from mosques in Morocco. Moroccans appreciated the privacy so much that they ousted the French from Morocco, and kept the ban.

Social Behaviour

At times it can feel as if there is one rule for behaviour in public and another for private. The key word is discretion. A decade ago, Morocco's gay community was beginning to seek tentative public approbation, but a conservative shift has seen a number of high-profile prosecutions (some including foreigners) and a shutting of the closet door. Morocco's relationship with alcohol can feel similarly complicated: despite the popularity of bars and a booming brewing industry aimed almost entirely at a domestic market, a traveller who accidentally clinks his bottles together while getting in a petit taxi to go to a medina is liable to be asked to get out, as medinas are seen as more socially and religiously conservative. Yet with proper discretion, there is plenty of latitude when it comes to socially acceptable behaviour.

Religion

Morocco is 99% Muslim. Christian and Jewish communities have existed here for centuries, although in recent years their numbers have dwindled.

Although the Moroccan constitution guarantees freedom of religion, it is illegal to proselytise for Christianity or own a Bible translated into Arabic.

The Five Pillars of Islam

Soaring minarets, shimmering mosaics, intricate calligraphy, the muezzin's call to prayer: much of what thrills visitors in Morocco today is inspired by a deep faith in Islam. Islam is built on five pillars: *shahada*, the affirmation of faith in God and God's word entrusted to the Prophet Mohammed; *salat* (prayer), ideally performed five times daily; *zakat* (charity), a moral obligation to give to those in need; *sawm*, the daytime fasting practised during the month of Ramadan; and *haj*, the pilgrimage to Mecca that is the culmination of lifelong faith for Muslims.

Moroccan Islam

While all Muslims agree on these basic tenets received by the Prophet Mohammed, doctrinal disagreements ensued after his death. The

Umayyads challenged his son-in-law Ali's claim to the title of caliph, or leader of the faithful. Some Muslims continued to recognise only successors of Ali; today they are known as Shiites. But in numerical terms, the Umayyad caliphate's Sunni Muslim practice is more common today.

It was the Umayyads who brought Islam to Morocco at the end of the 7th century, and hence Morocco today is almost entirely Sunni. Morocco's ruling Alawite dynasty claims descent from the Prophet Mohammed, and King Mohammed VI holds the unusual position of *Amir al-Mumineen*, (Commander of the Faithful), making him the spiritual leader of the country as well as head of state.

Morocco follows the Maliki school of Sunni thought. Historically this school has been less strict, with Maliki *qaids* (judges) applying the sharia (religious code) according to local custom instead of absolutist rule of law. This applies mainly in the case of family law *(mudawanna)* such as marriage and inheritance.

Farida ben Lyzaid's film *A Door to the Sky* tells the story of an émigré's return to Morocco, and her delicate balancing act between activism and tradition.

Marabouts & Zawiyas

An important Moroccan tradition is the custom of venerating *marabouts* (saints). *Marabouts* are devout Muslims whose acts of devotion and professions of faith are so profound, their very presence is considered to confer *baraka,* or grace, even after their death. Moroccans go out of their way to visit *marabout* mausoleums and *zawiyas* (shrines).

This practice of honouring *marabout*s is more in line with ancient Berber beliefs and Sufi mysticism than orthodox Islam, which generally discourages anything resembling idol worship. Visits to *zawiyas* are side trips for the many devout Moroccans who spend a lifetime preparing and planning for the haj.

Sufism in Morocco

It's often commented that Morocco follows one of the most moderate forms of Islam. One reason for this is the strong roots that Sufism has in the country. Sufism is the mystical strand of Islam, where adherents seek perfection of worship in their quest to encounter the divine. This often involves the use of music and repetitive prayer *(dhikr)* to help gain spiritual enlightenment.

Morocco, 1980–2010

Life expectancy increased by 14 years.

Expected years of schooling increased by five years.

GNI per capita increased by 86% (UNDP).

Sufism revolves around orders or brotherhoods known as *tariqas*, founded by a spiritual leader. The most famous worldwide are the Mevlevis, followers of the Sufi poet Rumi, also known as the 'whirling dervishes' of Turkey. In Morocco, two of the most important *tariqas* are the Tijaniyya and the Boutchichiyya. The Tijanniyya was founded in the late 18th century by al-Tijani, who died and is buried in Fes. The Boutchichiyya was founded around the same time, and today many in the order hold high-ranking positions in the Moroccan government.

Many observers cite the continued influence of Sufism in Morocco as an important bulwark against the rise of more religiously conservative and politically radical forms of Islam such as Salafism.

Moroccan Cuisine

Moroccan cuisine is a lot more than just couscous and tajines. From cooked vegetable salads and slow-cooked meats to fresh fruits and flaky pastries with orange-flower water, the flavours on offer are mouth-watering. _B'saha_ – here's to your health.

Food

The food you find in Morocco is likely to be fresh, locally grown and homemade, rather than shipped in, microwaved and served semi-thawed. Most Moroccan ingredients are cultivated in small quantities the old-fashioned way, without GMOs (genetically modified organisms), chemical fertilisers, pesticides or even mechanisation. These technologies are far too costly an investment for the average small-scale Moroccan farmer, as is organic certification and labelling – so though you may not see a label on it to this effect, much of the Moroccan produce you'll find in food markets is chemical- and GMO-free.

Produce

The splendid appearance, fragrance and flavour of Moroccan market produce will leave you with a permanent grudge against those wan, shrivelled items trying to pass themselves off as food at the supermarket. There's a reason for this: Moroccan produce is usually harvested by hand when ripe, and bought directly from farmers in the souqs. Follow the crowds of Moroccan grandmothers and restaurant sous-chefs to the carts and stalls offering the freshest produce. Just be sure to peel, cook or thoroughly wash produce before you eat it, since your stomach may not yet be accustomed to local microbes.

Meats

Carnivores and sustainability-minded eaters can finally put aside their differences and enjoy dinner together in Morocco. As you may guess from watching sheep and goats scamper over mountains and valleys in Morocco, herds live a charmed existence here – at least until dinnertime. Most of the meat you'll enjoy in Morocco is free-range, antibiotic-free, and raised on a steady diet of grass and wild herbs. If you wonder why lamb and mutton is so much more flavourful in Morocco than the stuff back home, you'll find your answer scampering around the High Atlas foothills.

Seasonal Variations

If there is one food you adore or a dish you detest, you might want to plan the timing of your visit to Morocco accordingly. Morocco offers an incredible bounty of produce, meats and fish, but these vary seasonally. The country's relative lack of infrastructure and hard currency can be advantageous to visitors – hence the picturesque mountain villages that seem untouched by time, and the jackpot of dirhams you get for your euros – but this also makes importing produce tricky. This means

---

What's in Season in Morocco?

....

Autumn: Figs, pomegranates, grapes

....

Spring: Apricots, cherries, strawberries, peaches

....

Summer: Watermelon, wild artichokes, tomatoes

....

Winter: Oranges, mandarins, onions, beets, carrots, potatoes and other root vegetables

---

For anyone wanting to learn about Moroccan food (and food culture) the bible is Madame Guinaudeau's lyric _Traditional Moroccan Cooking – Recipes from Fez._ It evens contains a recipe for camel tajine for 20 diners!

Moroccan Sauces

Mhammar: paprika, cumin and butter

Mqalli: saffron, oil and ginger

Msharmal: saffron, ginger and a dash of pepper

Qadra: Smen (seasoned butter with vegetable stock, chickpeas and/or almonds)

that if you're visiting in autumn, you may have to enjoy fresh figs instead of kiwi fruit (not exactly a hardship).

When you consider your menu options, you'll also want to consider geography. Oualidia oysters may not be so fresh by the time they cross mountain passes to Ouarzazate, and Sefrou cherries can be hard to come by in Tiznit. So if your vacation plans revolve around lavish seafood dinners, head for the coasts; vegetarians visiting desert regions in autumn should have a high tolerance for dates.

Quitting While You're Ahead

One final and important Moroccan dining tip: pace yourself. Moroccan meals can be lengthy and generous, and might seem a bit excessive to an unyielding waistband. Take your time and drink plenty of water throughout your meal, especially with wine and in dry climates. There are better ways to end a meal than with dehydration and bloating – namely, a dessert *bastilla* (multilayered pastry) with toasted almonds, cinnamon and cream. Your Moroccan hosts may urge you on like a cheerleading squad in a pie-eating contest, but obey your instincts and quit when you're full with a heartfelt *alhamdulallah!* (Thanks to God!).

Al-ftour (Breakfast)

Even if your days back home begin with just coffee, it would be a culinary crime to skip breakfast in Morocco. Whether you grab yours on the go in the souq or sit down to a leisurely repast, you are in for a treat. Breakfasts are rarely served before 9am in guesthouses and hotels, so early risers in immediate need of coffee will probably have to head to a cafe or hit the souqs.

Breakfast of Champions

As a guest in a Moroccan home, you'd be treated to the best of everything, and the best guesthouses scrupulously uphold this Moroccan tradition each morning. You'll carb-load like a Moroccan marathoner, with some combination of the following to jumpstart your day:

➡ **Ahwa** (Coffee) *Ahwa* is one option, but also *café au lait, thé b'na na* (tea with mint) or *thé wa hleb* (tea with milk), *wa* (with) or *bla* (without) *sukur* (sugar).

➡ **Aseer limoon** Orange juice.

➡ **Bayd** (Eggs) Cooked in omelettes, with a dash of *kamun* (freshly ground cumin) or *zataar* (cumin with toasted sesame seeds).

Food Facts - Morocco's Farmers

40% of Morocco's population lives in rural areas

39% of the country is involved in food production, mostly small-scale

18% of Morocco's land is arable

➡ **Beghrir** Moroccan pancakes with an airy, spongy texture like crumpets, with honey or jam.

➡ **French pastries** Croissants, *pain au chocolat* and others.

➡ **Khoobz** Moroccan bread, usually served with butter and jam or olive oil and *zataar*.

➡ **Rghaif** Flat, buttery Moroccan pastries.

➡ **Sfenj** Moroccan doughnuts (sometimes with an egg deep-fried in the hole).

Street Eats

Sidewalk cafes and kiosks put a local twist on the Continental breakfast, with Moroccan pancakes and doughnuts, French pastries, coffee and mint tea. Follow your nose and rumbling stomach into the souqs, where you'll find tangy olives and local *jiben* (fresh goat's or cow's milk cheese) to be devoured with fresh *khoobz* (Moroccan-style pita bread baked in a wood-fire oven until it's crusty on the outside, yet fluffy and light on the inside). *Khoobz* can be found wrapped in paper at any *hanout* (cupboard-sized corner shops found in every neighbourhood).

In the souqs, you can't miss vendors with their carts piled high with fresh fruit. You'll never know how high oranges can be stacked or how delicious freshly squeezed *aseer limoon* (orange juice) can be until you pay a visit to a Moroccan juice-vendor's cart.

One savoury southern breakfast just right for chilly mornings is *bessara* (a steaming-hot fava-bean and garlic soup with cumin, olive oil and a dash of paprika), best when mopped up with *khoobz* still warm from the communal oven right down the street. For a twist on the usual French breakfast pastries, try *rghaif* (flaky, dense Moroccan pastries like flattened croissants), typically served with warm honey, apricot jam or, if you're lucky, nutty *tahalout* (date syrup). The truly adventurous can start their day with a rich stew of lamb's head or calves' feet, generously ladled into an enamel bowl from a huge vat precariously balanced on a makeshift gas burner.

Vitamin-rich Moroccan argan oil is popular as a cosmetic, but also as a gourmet treat: the toasted-hazelnut flavour makes an intriguing dipping oil and exotic salad dressing.

El-Ghda (Lunch)

Lunch is traditionally the biggest meal of the day in Morocco, followed by a nice nap through the heat of the day. The lunch hour here is really a three- to four-hour stretch from noon to 3pm or 4pm, when most shops and facilities are closed, apart from a few stores catering to tourists.

For speed eaters this may seem inconvenient, but especially in summer it's best to do as the locals do, and treat lunchtime as precious downtime. Tuck into a tajine, served à la carte with crusty bread, or upgrade to a *prix fixe*, three-course restaurant lunch. Afterwards, you'll have a whole new appreciation for mint tea and afternoon naps.

Moroccan Snacks

roasted corn fresh off the brazier

sandwiches of brochettes or merguez with cumin, salt and harissa

escargot (snails) in broth

ice cream

Moroccan and French pastries

Snak Attack

If you're still digesting your lavish guesthouse breakfast come lunchtime, try one of the many *snak*s (kiosks) and small restaurants offering lighter fare – just look for people clustered around sidewalk kiosks, or a sign or awning with the word *snak*. Many hard-working locals do not take afternoon siestas, and instead eat sandwiches on the go. At the risk of stating the obvious, always join the queue at the one thronged with locals: Moroccans are picky about their *snak*s, preferring the cleanest establishments that use the freshest ingredients.

EATING DURING RAMADAN

During Ramadan, most Moroccans observe the fast during the day, eating only before sunrise and after sunset. Dinner is eaten later than usual and many wake up early for a filling breakfast before dawn. Another popular strategy is to stay up most of the night, sleep as late as possible, and stretch the afternoon nap into early evening. Adapt to the local schedule, and you may thoroughly enjoy the leisurely pace, late-night festivities and manic feasts of Ramadan.

Although you will not be expected to observe the fast, eating in public view is still frowned upon. Hence many restaurants are closed during the day until *lftour*, the evening meal when the fast is broken – though if you call ahead to restaurants in tourist areas, you may have luck. With a little planning, there are plenty of other workarounds: load up on snacks in the market to eat indoors, make arrangements for breakfast or lunch in the privacy of your guesthouse, and ask locals about a good place to enjoy *lftour*.

Lftour comes with all the traditional Ramadan fixings: *harira* (a hearty soup), dates, milk, *shebbakia* (a sweet, coiled pastry that's guaranteed to shift your glucose levels into high gear) and *harsha* (buttery bread made of semolina and fried for maximum density). You may find that *harira* is offered free; even Moroccan McDonald's offers it as part of their special Ramadan Happy Meal.

Here's what you'll find on offer at a *snak*:

➡ **Brochettes** Kebabs rubbed with salt and spices, grilled on a skewer and served with *khoobz* and *harissa* (capsicum-pepper sauce), cumin and salt. Among the most popular varieties are lamb, chicken, *kefta* (spiced meatballs of ground lamb and/or beef) and the aggressively flavourful 'mixed meat' (usually lamb or beef plus heart, kidney and liver).

➡ **Merguez** Hot, spicy, delicious homemade lamb sausage, not to be confused with *teyhan* (stuffed spleen; like liver, only less bitter and more tender) – *merguez* is usually reddish in colour, while *teyhan* is pale.

➡ **Pizza** Now found at upscale *snaks* catering to the worldly Moroccan middle class. Look for *snaks* boasting wood-fired ovens, and try tasty local versions with olives, onions, tomatoes, Atlantic anchovies and wild thyme.

➡ **Shwarma** Spiced lamb or chicken roasted on a spit and served with *tahina* (sesame sauce) or yoghurt, with optional onions, salad, *harissa* and a dash of *sumac* (a tart, pickle-flavoured purple spice; highly recommended).

➡ **Tajines** The famous Moroccan stews cooked in conical earthenware pots that keep the meat unusually moist and tender. The basic tajines served at a roadside *snak* are usually made with just a few ingredients, pulled right off a camping stove or *kanun* (earthenware brazier), and plonked down on a ramshackle folding table. Often you can pick your tajine; point to one that's been bubbling for an hour or two, with nicely caramelised onions and well-reduced sauce. Don't let appearances fool you: this could be one of the best tajines you'll eat in Morocco. Pull up a stool and dig in, using your *khoobz* as your utensil.

Before dinner, your host may appear with a pitcher and a deep tray. Hold out your hands, and your host will pour water over them.

The Moroccan Power Lunch

Some upscale Moroccan restaurants that serve an evening *diffa* (feast) to tourist hordes serve a scaled-down menu at lunch, when waitstaff are more relaxed and the meal is sometimes a fraction of the price you'd pay for dinner. You might miss the live music and inevitable belly dancing that would accompany a fancy supper – but then again, you might not. Three courses may seem a bit much for lunch, but don't be daunted: what this usually means is a delightful array of diminutive vegetable dishes, followed by a fluffy couscous and/or a small meat or chicken tajine, capped with the obligatory mint tea and biscuits or fruit.

➡ **Mezze** (Salad course) This could be a meal in itself. Fresh bread and three to five small, usually cooked vegetable dishes that might include lemony beet salad with chives, herbed potatoes, cumin-spiked chickpeas, a relish of roasted tomatoes and caramelised onions, pumpkin purée with cinnamon and honey, and roasted, spiced eggplant dip so rich it's often called 'aubergine caviar'.

➡ **Main** The main course is usually a tajine and/or couscous – a quasi-religious experience in Morocco not to be missed, especially on Fridays. The most common tajine choices are *dujaj mqalli bil hamd markd wa zeetoun* (chicken with preserved lemon and olives, zesty in flavour and velvety in texture); *kefta bil matisha wa bayd* (meatballs in a rich tomato sauce with a hint of heat from spices and topped with a sizzling egg); and *lehem bil berquq wa luz* (lamb with prunes and almonds served sliding off the bone into a saffron-onion sauce). If you're in Morocco for a while, you may tire of these classic tajine options – until you come across one regional variation that makes all your sampling of chicken tajine with lemon and olives worthwhile. That's when you cross over from casual diner to true tajine connoisseur, and fully appreciate the passionate debates among Moroccans about such minutiae as the appropriate thickness of the lemon rind and brininess of the olives. Variations on the classics are expected, but no self-respecting Moroccan restaurant should ever serve you a tajine that's stringy, tasteless, watery or overcooked.

➡ **Dessert** At lunchtime, dessert is usually sweet mint tea served with almond cookies. You may not think you have room, but one bite of a dreamy *kaab el-ghazal* (crescent-shaped 'gazelle's horns' cookie stuffed with almond paste and laced with orange-flower water) will surely convince you otherwise. A light, refreshing option is the tart-sweet *orange á canelle* (orange slices with cinnamon and orange-flower water).

Cooking at guesthouses is usually done by *dadas*, who are champions of Morocco's culinary traditions, cooking feasts with whatever's freshest in the market, usually without a recipe or a measuring cup. If a *dada's* delights impress you, ask to thank her personally – it's good form, and good *baraka* (auspicious omen) besides.

VEGETARIANS: YOUR MOROCCAN MENU

➡ **Breakfast** Load up on Moroccan pastries, pancakes, fresh fruit and fresh-squeezed juice. Fresh goat's cheese and olives from the souq are solid savoury choices with fresh-baked *khoobz* (bread). *Bessara* is a delicious bean soup that's typically meat-free, but steer clear of bubbling roadside vats if you're squeamish – they may contain snails or sheep's-head soup.

➡ **Lunch** Try the *mezze* of salads, which come with fresh bread and may range from delicate cucumbers in orange-blossom water to substantial herbed beets laced with kaffir lime. Vegetarians can sometimes, but not always, order a Berber vegetable tajine or Casablanca-style couscous with seven vegetables. Ingredients are bought fresh daily in small quantities and the chef may not have factored vegetarians into the restaurant's purchases – so call ahead if you can. Pizza is another widely available and inexpensive menu option, best when spiked with local herbs and olives.

➡ **Snacks** Market stalls feature cascades of dried figs, dates and apricots alongside towering cones of roasted nuts with salt, honey, cinnamon, cane sugar or hot pepper. Chickpeas and other pulses are roasted, served hot in a paper cone with cumin and salt, and are not to be missed. Tea-time menus at swanky restaurants may feature *briouats,* cigar-shaped pastries stuffed with goat's cheese or egg and herbs, plus finger sandwiches, pastries and cakes. If that's not enough, there's always ice cream, and mint tea with cookies or nuts are hardly ever more than a carpet shop away.

➡ **Dinner** For a hearty change of pace from salads and couscous, try a vegetarian pasta (anything with eggplant is especially tasty) or omelette (usually served with thick-cut fries). If you're staying in a Moroccan guesthouse, before you leave in the morning you can usually request a vegetarian tajine made to order with market-fresh produce.

L'Asha (Dinner)

Dinner in Morocco doesn't usually start until around 8pm or 9pm, after work and possibly a sunset stroll. Most Moroccans eat dinner at home, but you may notice young professionals, students and bachelors making a beeline for the local *snak* or pizzeria. In winter you'll see vendors crack open steaming vats of *harira* – a hearty soup with a base of tomatoes, onions, saffron and coriander, often with lentils, chickpeas and/or lamb. Dinner at home may often be *harira* and lunch leftovers, with the notable exception of Ramadan and other celebrations.

Hold the hot sauce: dousing your tajine with *harissa* (capsicum-pepper sauce) is generally done in Tunisia, Morocco's chief rival in the kitchen and on the football field.

Diffa

With enough hard currency and room in your stomach, you might prefer restaurants to *snak* fare for dinner. Most upscale Moroccan restaurants cater to tourists, serving an elaborate *prix fixe* Moroccan *diffa* (feast) in a palatial setting. This is not a dine-and-dash meal, but an evening's entertainment that often includes live music or belly dancing and wine or beer.

Fair warning about palace restaurants: your meal may come with a side order of kitsch. Many palace restaurants appear to have been decorated by a genie, complete with winking brass lamps, mirrors, swagged tent fabric and tasselled cushions as far as the eye can see. Often it's the ambience you're paying for rather than the food, which can vary from exquisitely prepared regional specialities to mass-produced glop. Here's a rule of thumb: if the place is so cavernous that your voice echoes and there's a stage set up for a laser show, don't expect personalised service or authentic Moroccan fare.

Ras el hanout (head of the shop) is Morocco's ubiquitous spice mix. Each spice shop makes up its own particular blend, but cumin, coriander, cinnamon, cloves and ginger all feature.

Whether you're in for a *diffa* at a Moroccan home (lucky you) or a restaurant, your lavish dinner will include some combination of the following:

➡ **Mezze** Up to five different small salads (though the most extravagant palace restaurants in Marrakesh and Fez boast seven to nine).

➡ **Briouat** Buttery cigar-shaped or triangular pastry stuffed with herbs and goat's cheese, savoury meats or egg, then fried or baked.

➡ **Pastilla** The justly famed savoury-sweet pie made of *warqa* (sheets of pastry even thinner than filo), painstakingly layered with pigeon or chicken cooked with caramelised onions, lemon, eggs and toasted sugared almonds, then dusted with cinnamon and powdered sugar.

HEAVENLY COUSCOUS

Berbers call it *seksu*, *New York Times* food critic Craig Claiborne called it one of the dozen best dishes in the world, and when you're in Morocco, you can call couscous lunch. You know that yellowish stuff that comes in a box, with directions on the side instructing you to add boiling water and let stand for three minutes? That doesn't count. What Moroccans call couscous is a fine, pale, grain-sized, hand-rolled pasta lightly steamed with aromatic broth until toothsome and fluffy, served with a selection of vegetables and/or meat or fish in a delicately flavoured reduction of stock and spices.

Since preparing and digesting a proper couscous takes a while, Moroccans usually enjoy it on Fridays, when many have the day or the afternoon off after Friday prayers. Couscous isn't a simple side dish but rather the main event of a Moroccan Friday lunch, whether tricked out Casablanca-style with seven vegetables, heaped with lamb and vegetables in Fez, or served with tomatoes, fish and fresh herbs in Essaouira. Many delicious couscous dishes come without meat, including the pumpkin couscous of Marrakesh and a simple yet savoury High Atlas version with stewed onions. But scrupulous vegetarians will want to enquire in advance as to whether that hearty stock is indeed vegetarian. Sometimes a couscous dish can be ordered à la carte, but usually it's the centrepiece of a multicourse lunch or celebratory *diffa* – and when you get a mouthful of the stuff done properly, you'll see why.

> ### TASTY BEAST: MECHOUI
> ....
> Special occasions call for Morocco's very best beast dish: *mechoui*, an entire slow-roasted lamb. The whole beast is basted with butter, garlic, cumin and paprika, and slow-roasted in a special covered pit until it's ready to melt into the fire or your mouth, whichever comes first. Local variations may include substituting a calf instead, or stuffing the lamb with some combination of almonds (or other nuts), prunes (or other dried fruit) or couscous. Sometimes *mechoui* is accompanied by kebabs or *kwa* (grilled liver kebabs with cumin, salt and paprika). Other than Moroccan weddings, the best place to have *mechoui* is right off Marrakesh's Djemaa el-Fna around lunchtime, served with olives and bread in Mechoui Alley. Do not attempt to operate heavy machinery or begin a whirlwind museum tour post-*mechoui;* no amount of post-prandial mint tea will make such exertions feasible without a nap.

➡ **Couscous** Made according to local custom; couscous variations may be made of barley, wheat or corn.

➡ **Tajine** Often your choice of one of a couple of varieties.

➡ **Mechoui** Or some regional speciality.

➡ **Dessert** This may be *orange á canelle,* a dessert *bastilla* (with fresh cream and toasted nuts), *briouat bil luz* (*briouat* filled with almond paste), *sfaa* (sweet cinnamon couscous with dried fruit and nuts, served with cream) or *kaab el-ghazal.*

Drinks

To wash your *diffa* down and stay hydrated, you'll need a good amount of liquid. Day and night, don't forget to drink plenty of bottled or purified water. Vying to quench your thirst are orange-juice vendors loudly singing their own praises, and water vendors in fringed tajine-shaped hats clanging brass bowls together.

Moroccan tap water is often potable, though not always – so stick with treated water or local mineral water. Sidi Ali and Aïn Saiss are the biggest brands, along with sparkling Oulmes.

If you're offered Moroccan mint tea, don't expect to bolt it and be on your way. Mint tea is the hallmark of Moroccan hospitality, and a sit-down affair that takes around half an hour. If you have the honour of pouring the tea, pour the first cup back into the teapot to help cool it and dissolve the sugar. Then starting from your right, pour each cup of tea from as high above the glass as you can without splashing. Your hosts will be most impressed.

Moroccan mint tea ('Berber whiskey') may be ubiquitous after meals, but you can find a mean cup of coffee in Morocco, too. Most of it is French-pressed, and delivers a caffeine wallop to propel you through the souqs and into the stratosphere. Moroccans tend to take their coffee thick and black; ask for *nus-nus* ('half and half') to have it mixed with steamed milk.

> Foodies who equate Middle Eastern food with Lebanese cuisine stand corrected by Claudia Roden's *Arabesque: A Taste of Morocco, Turkey and Lebanon,* which showcases Moroccan cuisine and won the 2007 James Beard Award (the culinary Oscar).

Moroccan Beer, Wine & Spirits

Yes, you can drink alcohol in Morocco without offending local sensibilities, as long as you do it discreetly. Serving alcohol within Moroccan medinas may be frowned upon, and liquor licences an expensive bureaucratic nightmare – but many Moroccan guesthouses and restaurants get around these hurdles by offering booze in a low voice, and serving it out of sight indoors or on a terrace. So if you're in the mood for a beer and don't find it on the menu, you might want to ask the waiter in a low voice, speakeasy-style.

One note of caution: quality assurance is tricky in a Muslim country where mixologists, micro-brewers and licensed sommeliers are in understandably short supply, and your server may not be able to make any personal recommendations from the wine menu. Since wines are subject to unpredictable heat exposure in transit and storage, be sure to taste your wine before the server leaves the table – red wines are especially subject to spoilage. Don't hesitate to send back a drink if something about it seems off; your server will likely take your word for it.

Beer

➡ **Casa** A fine local pilsner beer

➡ **Flag Special** Affordable and the most popular beverage in Morocco (25 million units consumed annually)

Wine

➡ **White** Moroccan white wines are a solid bet, including the crisp, food-friendly Larroque; well-balanced, juicy Terre Blanche, a Chardonnay/Viognier/Sauvignon Blanc blend; citrusy, off-dry Cuvée du Président Sémillant; and Siroua S, a cool coastal Chardonnay.

➡ **Gris & Rosé** These are refreshing alternatives, especially not-too-fruity Medaillon Rosé de Syrah; peachy-keen Eclipse Grenache/Cinsault blend; fresh, fragrant Domaine Rimal Vin Gris; the juicy, aptly named Rosé d'un Nuit d'Eté (Summer's Night Rosé) of Grenache/Syrah; and the crisply top-range Volubilia.

➡ **Red** Reliable reds include the quaffable Burgundian-style Terre Rouge from Rabati coastal vineyards; well-rounded Volubilia from Morocco's ancient Roman wine-growing region; and spicier Merlot-Syrah-Cabernet Sauvignon Coteaux de L'Atlas Premier Cru. Guerrouane Rouge is a heavy red at the cheaper end of the scale, while Morocco's Jewish community has bequeathed the country an interesting selection of kosher wines.

Spirits

Mahia, a Moroccan spirit distilled from figs, is around 80% proof, with a flavour somewhere between Italian grappa and Kentucky moonshine. You won't find it on most menus, because it's usually made in home distilleries for private consumption. If you're staying at a guesthouse, your hosts may know where you can get some, but they may try to warn you off the stuff – *mahia* hangovers are legendary.

> For recipes and writing on Moroccan food, check out the mouth-watering website of food blogger Maroc Mama (www.marocmama.com).

BEEN THERE, EATEN THAT

Eat your way across Morocco, north to south, with these outstanding regional dishes:

Casablanca *Seksu bedawi* (couscous with seven vegetables)

Chefchaouen *Djaj bil berquq* (chicken with prunes)

Demnate *Seksu Demnati* (couscous made with corn or barley instead of semolina)

Essaouira *Hut mqalli* (fish tajine with saffron, ginger and preserved lemons); *djej kadra toumiya* (chicken with almonds, onions and chickpeas in buttery saffron sauce)

Fez *Kennaria* (stew with wild thistle or artichoke, with or without meat); *hut bu'etob* (baked shad filled with almond-stuffed dates)

High Atlas *Mechoui* (slow-roasted stuffed lamb or beef)

Marrakesh *Bessara* (fava beans with cumin, paprika, olive oil and salt); *tanjia* (crock-pot stew of seasoned lamb cooked for eight to 12 hours in the fire of a hammam)

Meknès *Kamama* (lamb stewed with ginger, *smen,* saffron, cinnamon and sweet onions)

Southern Coast *Amlou* (argan-nut paste with honey and argan oil)

Tangier Local variations on tapas and paella

Music

Any trip to Morocco comes with its own syncopated soundtrack: the early-evening *adhan* (call to prayer), and the ubiquitous donkey-cart-drivers' chants of *Balek!* – fair warning that since donkeys don't yield, you'd better, and quick. Adding to the musical mayhem are beats booming out of taxis, ham radios and roadside stalls, and live-music performances at restaurants and weddings, on street corners, and headlining at festivals year-round. There are plenty of Maghrebi beats to tune into.

Classical Arab-Andalucian Music

Leaving aside the thorny question of where exactly it originated (you don't want to be the cause of the next centuries-long Spain–Morocco conflict, do you?), this music combines the flamenco-style strumming and heartstring-plucking drama of Spanish folk music with the finely calibrated stringed instruments, complex percussion and haunting half-tones of classical Arab music. Add poetic lyrics and the right singer at dinner performances, and you may find that lump in your throat makes it hard to swallow your *pastilla* (pigeon pie).

You'll hear two major styles of Arab-Andalucian music in Morocco: Al-Aala (primarily in Fez, Tetouan and Salé) and Gharnati (mostly Oujda). The area of musical overlap is Rabat, where you can hear both styles. Keep an eye out for concerts, musical evenings at fine restaurants, classical-music festivals in Casablanca and Fez, and look especially for performances by Gharnati vocalist Amina Alaoui, Fatiha El Hadri Badraï and her traditional all-female orchestras from Tetouan, and Festival of World Sacred Music headliner Mohamed Amin el-Akrami and his orchestra.

Gnaoua

Joyously bluesy with a rhythm you can't refuse, this music may send you into a trance – and that's just what it's meant to do. The brotherhood of Gnaoua began among freed slaves in Marrakesh and Essaouira as a ritual of deliverance from slavery and into God's graces. A true Gnaoua *lila* (spiritual jam session), may last all night, with musicians erupting into leaps of joy as they enter trance-like states of ecstasy that can send fez-tassels spinning and set spirits free.

Join the crowds watching in Marrakesh's Djemaa el-Fna or at the annual Gnaoua & World Music Festival in Essaouira, and hear Gnaoua on Peter Gabriel's Real World music label. Gnawa *mâalems* (master musicians) include perennial festival favourites Abdeslam Alikkane and his Tyour Gnaoua, crossover fusion superstar Hassan Hakmoun, Saïd Boulhimas and his deeply funky Band of Gnawas, Indian-inflected Nass Marrakech and reggae-inspired Omar Hayat. Since Gnaoua are historically a brotherhood, most renowned Gnaoua musicians have been men – but the all-women Sufi group Haddarates plays Gnaoua trances traditionally reserved for women, and family acts include Brahim Elbelkani and La Famille Backbou.

No, that's not a musical rugby scrum: the *haidous* is a complex circle dance with musicians in the middle, often performed in celebration of the harvest.

MOROCCAN MUSIC FESTIVALS

March Rencontres Musicales de Marrakesh (classical); Tremplin (urban music)

April Festival of Sufi Culture (www.par-chemins.org); Jazzablanca (http://jazzablanca.com)

May Jazz aux Oudayas, in Rabat; L'Boulevard (www.boulevard.ma); Mawazine Festival of World Music (www.festivalmawazine.ma)

June Festival of World Sacred Music (www.fesfestival.com); Gnaoua & World Music Festival (www.festival-gnaoua.net)

July Marrakesh Popular Arts Festival (www.marrakechfestival.com); Voix des Femmes (Women's Voices), in Tetouan; Festival Timitar (Amazigh Music), in Agadir; Festival du Desert (www.festivaldudesert.ma)

September TANJAzz (www.tanjazz.org)

October Nuits Sonores Tangier (www.nuits-sonores.com/tanger)

Berber Folk Music

There's plenty of other indigenous Moroccan music besides Gnaoua, thanks to the ancient Berber tradition of passing along songs and poetry from one generation to the next. You can't miss Berber music at village *moussem*s (festivals in honour of a local saint), Agadir's Timtar Festival of Amazigh music, the Marrakesh Festival of Popular Arts and Imilchil's Marriage Festival, as well as weddings and other family celebrations.

The most renowned Berber folk group is the Master Musicians of Joujouka, who famously inspired the Rolling Stones, Led Zeppelin and William S Burroughs, and collaborated with the Stones' Brian Jones on experimental music with lots of clanging and crashing involved. Lately the big names are women's, including the all-woman group B'net Marrakech and the bold Najat Aatabou, who sings protest songs in Berber against restrictive traditional roles.

> To explore Amazigh music in a variety of styles, languages and regions, check out samples, musician bios and CDs from basic bluesy Tartit to '70s-funky Tinariwen at www.azawan.com.

From Marock to Hibhub

Like the rest of the Arab world, Moroccans listen to a lot of Egyptian music, but Moroccopop is gaining ground. A generation of local DJs with cheeky names such as Ramadan Special and DJ Al Intifada have mastered the art of the unlikely mashup. And so have some of the more intriguing talents to emerge in recent years: Hoba Hoba Spirit, whose controversy-causing, pop-punk 'Blad Skizo' (Schizophrenic Country) addresses the contradictions of modern Morocco head-on; Moroccan singer-songwriter Hindi Zahra, Morocco's answer to Tori Amos, with bluesy acoustic-guitar backing; Darga, a group that blends ska, Darija rap and a horn section into Moroccan surf anthems; and the bluntly named Ganga Fusion and Kif Samba, who both pound out a danceable mix of funk, Berber folk music, reggae and jazz. Algerian influences are heard in Morocco's raï scene, most notably Cheb Khader, Cheb Mimoun and Cheb Jellal.

> **Marock on Film**
>
> *This Is Maroc (2010)* Hat Trick Brothers' road trip
>
> *I Love HipHop in Morocco (2007)* H-Kayne, DJ Key, Bigg and other hip-hop groups struggle to get gigs

But ask any guy on the street with baggy cargo shorts and a T-shirt with the slogan MJM (*Maroc Jusqu'al Mort* – Morocco 'til Death) about Moroccan pop, and you'll get a crash course in *hibhub* (Darija for hip hop). Meknès' H-Kayne raps gangsta-style, while Tangier's MC Muslim raps with a death-metal growl, and Fez City Clan features a talented rapper and an Arabic string section. The acts that consistently get festival crowds bouncing are Agadir's DJ Key, who remixes hip-hop standards with manic scratching and beat-boxing, and Marrakesh's Fnaire, mixing traditional Moroccan sounds with staccato vocal stylings. Rivalling 'Blad Skizo' for youth anthem of the decade is Fnaire's 'Ma Tkich Bladi' (Don't Touch My Country), an irresistibly catchy anthem against neocolonialism with a viral YouTube video.

International musicians find themselves increasingly attracted to Morocco. The Festival of World Sacred Music held in Fez attracts an ever-more diverse range of headline acts, from Björk to Patti Smith, while Rabat's Mawazine Festival of World Music brings in the pop mainstream from Beyoncé to Elton John. The latter highlighted the sometimes delicate nature of the position of music in Morocco – while the government defended Elton John's homosexuality against Islamist criticism, Moroccan musicians have to tread a finer line, especially if commenting on social issues. In 2012, and following the the Arab Spring, rapper El Haked was imprisoned for a year for 'undermining the honour' of public servants when the video for his song 'Klab ed-Dawla' (Dogs of the State) pictured corrupt police wearing the heads of donkeys. El Haked had previously been jailed for criticising the monarchy.

Literature & Cinema

Morocco's rich oral tradition has kept shared stories and histories alive. Watch the storytellers and singers in Marrakesh's Djemaa el-Fna in action and you'll understand how the country's literary tradition has remained so vital and irrepressible, despite press censorship. More recently, novelists such as Tahar ben Jelloun have brought their rich prose to bear on the national experience. Moroccan cinema is younger still, but the country is actively moving beyond being a glitzy film location to being a producer in its own right.

Literature

A Different Beat

Grab a copy of Josh Shoemake's *Tangier: A Literary Guide for Travellers* for an essential tour of this most storied of Moroccan cities, with appearances by everyone from William Burroughs to Mohamed Choukri.

The international spotlight first turned on Morocco's literary scene in the 1950s and '60s, when Beat Generation authors Paul and Jane Bowles took up residence in Tangier and began recording the stories of Moroccans they knew. *The Sheltering Sky* is Paul Bowles' most celebrated Morocco-based novel, while the nonfiction *Their Heads Are Green and Their Hands are Blue* is a valuable travelogue. Following exposure from the Beats, local writers broke onto the writing scene. Check out Larbi Layachi's *A Life Full of Holes* (written under the pseudonym Driss ben Hamed Charhadi), Mohammed Mrabet's *Love With a Few Hairs* and Mohamed Choukri's *For Bread Alone*. Like a lot of Beat literature, these books are packed with sex, drugs and unexpected poetry – but if anything, they're more streetwise, humorous and heartbreaking.

Coming up for Air

In *Moroccan Folk Tales*, Jilali El Koudia presents 31 classic legends ranging from a Berber version of *Snow White* to the tale of a woman who cross-dresses as a Muslim scholar.

Encouraged by the outspoken Tanjaoui authors, Moroccan poet Abdellatif Laâbi founded the free-form, free-thinking poetry magazine *Anfas/Souffles* (Breath) in 1966, not in the anything-goes international zone of Tangier, but in the royal capital of Rabat. What began as a journal became a movement of writers, painters and filmmakers all heeding Laâbi's editorial outcry against government censorship. *Anfas/Souffles* published another 21 daring issues, until the censors shut it down in 1972 and sent Laâbi to prison for eight years for 'crimes of opinion'.

The literary expression Laâbi equated to breathing has continued unabated. In 1975 *Anfas/Souffles* cofounder and self-proclaimed 'linguistic guerrilla' Mohammed Khaïr-Eddine published his confrontational *Ce Maroc!*, an anthology of revolutionary writings. A Souss Berber himself, Khaïr-Eddine called for the recognition of Berber identity and culture in his 1984 *Legend and Life of Agoun'chich,* which served as a rallying cry for today's Berber Pride movement.

Living to Tell

Still more daring and distinctive Moroccan voices have found their way into print over the past two decades, both at home and abroad. Among the most famous works to be published by a Moroccan author are *Dreams of Trespass: Tales of a Harem Girlhood* and *The Veil and the Male Elite:*

A *Feminist Interpretation of Women's Rights in Islam*, both by Fatima Mernissi, an outspoken feminist and professor at the University of Rabat. In Rabati author Leila Abouzeid's *Year of the Elephant* and *The Director and Other Stories from Morocco*, tales of Moroccan women trying to reinvent their lives on their own terms become parables for Morocco's search for independence after colonialism.

The past several years have brought increased acclaim for Moroccan writers, who have continued to address highly charged topics despite repeated press crackdowns. Inspired by *Anfas/Souffles*, Fez-born expatriate author Tahar ben Jelloun combined poetic devices and his training as a psychotherapist in his celebrated novel *The Sand Child*, the story of a girl raised as a boy by her father in Marrakesh, and its sequel *The Sacred Night*, which won France's Prix Goncourt. In *The Polymath*, 2009 Naguib Mahfouz Prize–winner Bensalem Himmich reads between the lines of 14th-century scholar and political exile Ibn Khaldun, as he tries to stop wars and prevent his own isolation. Several recent Moroccan novels have explored the promise and trauma of emigration, notably Mahi Binebine's harrowing *Welcome to Paradise*, Tahar ben Jelloun's *Leaving Tangier*, and Laila Lalami's celebrated *Hope and Other Dangerous Pursuits*. In 2016 Leila Slimani won the Prix Goncourt, France's top literary prize, for her novel *Chanson Douce*.

In *Stolen Lives: Twenty Years in a Desert Jail*, Malika Oufkir describes her demotion from courtier to prisoner after her father's plot to assassinate Hassan II. Unsurprisingly, it was initially banned in Morocco on its publication.

Cinema

On Location in Morocco

Until recently Morocco had been seen mostly as a stunning movie backdrop, easily stealing scenes in such dubious cinematic achievements as *Sex and the City 2*, *Prince of Persia*, *Alexander* and *Sahara*. But while there's much to cringe about in Morocco's IMDb filmography, the country had golden moments on the silver screen in Hitchcock's *The Man Who Knew Too Much*, Orson Welles' *Othello* and David Lean's *Lawrence of Arabia*.

Morocco has certainly proved its versatility: it stunt-doubled for Somalia in Ridley Scott's *Black Hawk Down*, Tibet in Martin Scorsese's *Kundun*, Lebanon in Stephen Gaghan's *Syriana*, and Iraq in Clint Eastwood's *American Sniper*. Morocco also stole the show right out from under John Malkovich by playing itself in Bernardo Bertolucci's *The Sheltering Sky*, and untrained local actors Mohamed Akhzam and Boubker Ait El Caid held their own with Cate Blanchett and Brad Pitt in the 2006 Oscar-nominated *Babel*.

Cafe Clock in Marrakesh has weekly storytelling sessions, inviting the Djemma el Fna's last traditional storyteller to weave his magic, while teaching a new generation this dying oral art form.

Morocco's Directorial Breakthrough

Historically, Morocco has imported its blockbusters from Bollywood, Hollywood and Egypt, but today, Moroccans are getting greater opportunities to see films shot in Morocco that are actually by Moroccans and about Morocco. In 2015 half of the top 10 box office hits in Morocco were locally made.

Moroccan filmmakers are putting decades of Ouallywood filmmaking craft and centuries of local storytelling tradition to work telling epic modern tales, often with a *cinéma vérité* edge. Morocco's 2010 Best Foreign Film Oscar contender was Nour-Eddine Lakhmari's *Casanegra*, about Casablanca youth thinking fast and growing up faster as they confront the darker aspects of life in the White City. Other hits include Latif Lahlou's *La Grande Villa* (2010), tracking one couple's cultural and personal adjustments after relocating from Paris to Casablanca.

Euro-Moroccan films have already become mainstays of the international festival circuit, notably Faouzi Bensaïdi's family-history epic

None of the 1942 classic *Casablanca* was actually shot in Casablanca. It was filmed on a Hollywood back lot, and the Rick's Café Américain set was reputedly based on the historic El-Minzah hotel in Tangier.

MOROCCO'S LANDMARK CINEMA REVIVAL

Despite Morocco's creative boom, cinephiles have begun to fear for Morocco's movie palaces, since ticket prices can't compete with cheap pirated DVDs. In 2007 only 5% of Morocco's population went to the movies, while more than 400,000 pirated DVDs were symbolically seized from souq stalls in Rabat and Casablanca. Thirty years ago there were 250 cinemas in Morocco; in 2010 only 30 were left.

Moroccan cinema buffs have rallied to preserve and promote Morocco's historic movie palaces as architectural wonders and key modern landmarks in Morocco's ancient storytelling tradition. Tangier's 1930s Cinema Rif reopened in 2006 as Cinematheque de Tanger, a nonprofit cinema featuring international independent films and documentaries. Cinéma Camera in Meknès – possibly Morocco's most glorious art-deco movie theatre – continues to thrive on mainstream Egyptian, Hollywood and Bollywood fare. Check out its fabulous 'Golden Era Hollywood' mural as its stairs sweep up to the auditorium.

Morocco doesn't just provide filming locations for movies. Smash-hit TV series *Game of Thrones* has used the ramparts of Essaouira and Aït Benhaddou as backdrops for its wandering dragon queen Daenerys Targaryen.

A Thousand Months, winner of the 2003 Cannes Film Festival Le Premier Regard, and Laïla Marrakchi's *Marock,* about a Muslim girl and Jewish boy who fall in love, which screened at Cannes in 2005. With their stylish handling of colliding personal crises in *Heaven's Doors* (2006), Spanish-Moroccan directors Swel and Imad Noury hit the festival circuit with *The Man Who Sold the World,* a Dostoyevsky-existentialist fable set in Casablanca.

Thanks to critical acclaim and government support, new voices and new formats are emerging in Moroccan cinema. Young directors are finding their voices through a new film school in Marrakesh and short-film showcases, including back-to-back short-film festivals in Rabat and Tangier in October. Women directors have stepped into the spotlight, from Farida Benlyazid's 2005 hit *The Dog's Life of Juanita Narboni,* a Spanish expat's chronicle of Tangier from the 1930s to the 1960s, to star Mahassine El Hachadi, who won the short-film prize at the 2010 Marrakesh International Film Festival while still in film school.

How big is Bollywood in Morocco? Around a third of all films shown in Morocco originate in Bollywood, and stars from Shah Rukh Khan to Amitabh Bachchan make regular appearances at Marrakesh's international film festival.

Leila Kilani's *Les Yeux Secs* (2003) broke further ground by not only being filmed in Amazigh rather than Arabic, but tackling hard subjects such as female trafficking and prostitution. The use of social critique hasn't been without criticism, but filmmakers have been unafraid to push back in the name of artistic freedom. Star director Nabil Ayouch's *Much, Loved* (2014) was banned for discussing prostitution, but *Behind Closed Doors*, directed the same year by Mohammed Ahed Bensouda, focused on workplace sexual harassment of women and led to a national discussion on changing Moroccan laws.

Arts & Crafts

The usual arts and crafts hierarchy is reversed in Morocco, where the craft tradition is ancient and revered, while visual art is a more recent development. Ornament is meant to be spiritually uplifting, while nonfunctional objects and representational images have traditionally been viewed as pointless – or worse, vanity verging on idolatry. While Morocco's contemporary visual-arts scene remains small, its many beautiful crafts – from carpets and leather to pottery and metalwork – make the quintessential souvenir of any trip.

Visual Arts

Perhaps because it has been relegated to a marginal position, Moroccan contemporary art has particular poignancy and a sense of urgency, expressing aspirations and frustrations that can be understood instinctively – while eluding media censorship.

The new artworks emerging from Morocco are not kitschy paintings of eyelash-batting veiled women and scowling turbaned warriors, though you'll still find these in tourist showrooms. These form a 19th-century French Orientalist tradition made largely for export, and contemporary Moroccan artists such as Hassan Hajjaj are cleverly tweaking it. Hajjaj's provocative full-colour photographs of veiled women are not what you'd expect: one tough lady flashing the peace sign wears a rapper-style Nike-logo veil, emblazoned with the slogan 'Just Do It' across her mouth, while his 'Kesh Angels' series showed women bikers on the streets of Marrakesh.

Morocco's visual-art scene put down roots in the 1950s and '60s, when folk artists in Essaouira and Tangier made painting and sculpture their own by incorporating Berber symbols and locally scavenged materials. Landscape painting became a popular way to express pride of place in Essaouira and Asilah, and abstract painting became an important means of poetic expression in Rabat and Casablanca.

Marrakesh's art scene combines elemental forms with organic, traditional materials, helping to ground abstract art in Morocco as an indigenous art form. The scene has taken off in the past decade, with the Marrakech Biennale (p67) launched in 2005 and Morocco's first International Art Fair in 2009.

Mahi Binebine creates ethereal figures in beeswax, colliding, pulling apart, not seeing one another; Hassan Echair designs objects hanging in tenuous balance: white fence-posts, charcoal, twigs wrapped in string; Larbi Cherkaoui's work contains gestural and seemingly urgent calligraphic flourishes on goatskin.

Calligraphy

Calligraphy remains Morocco's most esteemed visual art form, practised and perfected in Moroccan *medersas* (theological schools) over the last 1000 years. In Morocco, calligraphy isn't just in the Quran: it's on tiled walls, inside stucco arches, and literally coming out of the woodwork. Look carefully, and you'll notice that the same text can have an incredibly different effect in another calligraphic style. One calligrapher might take up a whole page with a single word, while another might turn it into a flower, or fold and twist the letters origami-style into graphic patterns.

The style most commonly used for Qurans is Naskh, a slanting cursive script introduced by the Umayyads. Cursive letters interlaced ingeniously

You can try your hand at traditional Arabic calligraphy, and learn some of its history, with lessons at Cafe Clock in Fez and Marrakesh.

BUYING SUSTAINABLE SOUVENIRS

Used tyres don't biodegrade, and burning them produces toxic fumes – but when cleverly repurposed by Moroccan artisans, they make fabulous home furnishings. Tyre-tread mirrors make any entryway look dashingly well-travelled and inner-tube tea trays are ideal for entertaining motorcycle gangs. For the best selection, visit the tyre-craft *mâalems* (master artisans) lining the south end of Rue Riad Zitoun el-Kedim in Marrakesh.

to form a shape or dense design are hallmarks of the Thuluth style, while high-impact graphic lettering is the Kufic style from Iraq. You'll see three main kinds of Kufic calligraphy in Morocco: angular, geometric letters are square Kufic; those bursting into bloom are foliate Kufic; and letters that look like they've been tied by sailors are knotted Kufic.

Lately, contemporary artists have reinvented calligraphy as a purely expressive art form, combining the elegant gestures of ancient scripts with the urgency of urban graffiti. Farid Belkahia's enigmatic symbols in henna and Larbi Cherkaoui's high-impact graphic swoops show that even freed of literal meanings, calligraphy can retain its poetry.

To find out more about where those splendid traditional designs originated and learn to trace a few yourself, check out *The Splendour of Islamic Calligraphy* by Abdelkebir Khatibi and Mohammed Sijelmassi.

Crafts

For instant relief from sterile modernity, head to your nearest Moroccan souq to admire the inspired handiwork of local *mâalems* (master artisans). Most of Morocco's design wonders are created without computer models or even an electrical outlet, relying instead on imagination, an eye for colour and form, and steady hands you'd trust to take out a tonsil.

All this takes experience. In Fez, the minimum training for a ceramic *mâalem* is 10 years, and it takes a *zellij* mosaic-maker three to four months to master a single shape – and with 360 shapes to learn, mastery is a lifelong commitment. When you watch a *mâalem* at work, it's the confidence of the hand movements, not the speed, that indicates a masterwork is in the making. Techniques and tools are handed down from one generation to the next, and friendly competition among neighbours propels innovation.

Khadija Kabbaj makes basketry tables, mummified Barbies and other subversively applied traditions; Hicham Benohoud produces self-portraits with faces obliterated by shredded paper, sticky notes, corks; Hassan Hajjaj creates mock fashion photos of women in Louis Vuitton veils and Moroccan-flag jellabas.

Instead of sprawling factory showrooms, *mâalems* work wonders in cubby holes lining souqs, each specialising in a traditional trade. But artisans in rural areas are not to be outdone: many Moroccan villages are known for a style of embroidery or a signature rug design. Most of the artisans you'll see in the souqs are men, but you're likely to glimpse women *mâalems* working behind the scenes knotting carpets in Anti Atlas and Middle Atlas villages, weaving textiles along the Southern coast and painting ceramics in Fez, Salé and Safi.

Carpets

If you manage to return from Morocco without a carpet, you may well congratulate yourself on being one of few travellers to have outsmarted the wiliest salespeople on the planet.

Moroccan carpets hook travellers almost every time because there's a right carpet for almost everyone – and if that sounds like something your mother once said to you about soul mates, it's not entirely a coincidence. Women in rural Morocco traditionally created carpets as part of their dowries, expressing their own personalities in exuberant colours and patterns, and weaving in symbols of their hopes for health and married life. Now carpets are mostly made as a way to supplement household income, but in the hands of a true *mâalem,* a hand-woven carpet brings so much personality and *baraka* (blessings) underfoot, it could never be mistaken for a mere doormat.

Carpets you see in the souqs may already have been bought and sold three or four times, with the final price representing a hefty mark-up over what the weaver was paid for her work. Consider buying directly from a village association instead: the producer is more likely to get her fair share of the proceeds, you'll get a better deal without extensive bargaining, and you may meet the artisan who created your new rug.

Textiles

Anything not nailed down in Morocco is likely to be woven, sewn or embroidered – and even then, it might be upholstered. Moroccan women are the under-recognised *mâalems* of Moroccan textiles, and the tradition they've established has recently helped attract emerging fashion enterprises and global brands to Morocco. One-third of Moroccan women are employed in Morocco's industrial garment industry, but for meticulous handiwork with individual flair, check out traditional textile handicrafts.

Embroidery

Moroccan stitchery ranges from simple Berber designs to minutely detailed *terz Fezzi,* the elaborate nature-inspired patterns that are stitched in blue upon white linen and that women in Fez traditionally spend years mastering for their dowries. Rabati embroidery is a riot of colour, with bold, graphic flowers in one or two colours of silk thread that almost completely obscures the plain-cotton backing. But the ladies of Salé also deserve their due for their striking embroidery in one or two bold colours along the borders of crisp white linen.

Passementerie

What's that guy doing with a blow-dryer and silk thread down a medina side alley? That would be a *passementerie* (trims) *mâalem* at work, using a repurposed blow-dryer to spin thread from a nail stuck in the wall, until it's the perfect width and length to make into knotted buttons, silken tassels and snappy jellaba trim. In a cupboard-sized Moroccan

The most reliable resource in English on Moroccan carpets is the (aptly named) *Moroccan Carpets*, by Brooke Pickering, W Russell Pickering and Ralph S Yohe. It's packed with photos to help pinpoint the origins and style of any carpet that mysteriously followed you home.

Top Moroccan Modern Textiles

Cooperative Tigmi, Aït Oudinar

Al Nour, Marrakesh

Cooperative Artisanale des Femmes de Marrakesh

Sidi Ghanem, Marrakesh

WHEN PURPLE WAS PURE GOLD

The port that is today called Essaouira was hot property in ancient times, because it had one thing everyone wanted: the colour purple. Imperial purple couldn't be fabricated, and was the one colour strictly reserved for Roman royalty. This helps explain the exorbitant asking price, which according to Aristotle was 10 to 20 times its weight in gold. The natural dye came from the spiky murex marine snails that clung to the remote Purpuraire (Purple) Islands – as though that could save them from the clutches of Roman fashionistas.

Technically the Phoenicians were there first and discovered the stuff, but everyone wanted purple power. Savvy King Juba II established a coastal dye works in the 1st century BC to perform the tricky task of extracting murex dye from the vein of the mollusc, and kept his methods a closely guarded secret. The hue became wildly popular among royal celebrities of the day; Cleopatra loved the stuff so much that she dyed the sails of her royal barge purple before she went to meet Mark Antony.

But violet soon turned to violence. Legend has it that Juba's son Ptolemy was murdered by Emperor Caligula for having the audacity to sport a purple robe, making trendy Ptolemy possibly the world's first fashion victim. The bright, nonfading dye was never successfully produced commercially, and the secret extraction methods were assumed lost in the siege of Constantinople in 1453. But in Essaouira the stuff is mysteriously still available, for a price. The mysteries of the colour purple are still passed down from one generation of murex collectors to the next, and are jealously guarded.

ARTS & CRAFTS CRAFTS

Answers to your every 'how'd they do that?' are on display at state-run Ensemble Artisanales, where you can watch *mâalems* at work and purchase their handiwork at fixed (if somewhat stiff) prices.

passementerie shop, you'll find enough gold braid to decorate an army of generals and more tassels than a burlesque troupe could spin in a lifetime – but you'll also find a jackpot of small, portable gifts. Moroccan *mâalems* have made a stand-alone art of trimming, wrapping wire and washers with silk thread to create mod statement necklaces, napkin-ring holders, knotted keychains and curtain-pulls.

Felt

Handmade felt hats, slippers, coats, pillows, bags or floor coverings really put wool through the wringer: it's dyed, boiled and literally beaten to a pulp. Instead of being woven or sewn, felt is usually pounded with *savon noir* (natural palm soap), formed into the intended shape on a mould and allowed to dry gradually to hold its shape. Felt makers are usually found in the wool souq in major cities.

Weaving

Beyond the sea of imported harem pants and splashy synthetic jellabas in the souqs, hand-woven Moroccan fabrics with exceptional sheen and texture may catch your eye: nubby organic cotton from the Rif, shiny 'cactus silk' *(soie végétale)* woven with cotton and rayon from the south, sleek Marrakesh table linens and whisper-soft High Atlas woollen blankets. Some lesser-quality knock-offs are industrially produced, but connoisseurs seek out the plusher nap, tighter weave and elegant drape of hand-woven Moroccan fabrics.

The Art of the Islamic Tile, by Gerard Degeorge and Yves Porter, celebrates the splendours of ceramics across the Middle East, from Istanbul to Fez.

In souqs, village cooperatives and Ensemble Artisanal showrooms, you might glimpse two to four women at a time on a loom, working on a single piece. Men work larger looms for jellaba fabric, pushing the shuttle with arms as they pound pedals with their feet – producing one yard of fabric this way is a workout equivalent to running several miles while dribbling a basketball. You can buy linens and clothing ready-made or get hand-woven fabric by the bolt or metre, and have Moroccan decor and couture custom-made to your specifications. Tailors can be found in every major city, but be sure to leave enough time for the initial consultation plus two fittings for clothing.

CARPET CATEGORIES

Rabati carpets Plush pile carpets in deep jewel tones, featuring an ornate central motif balanced by fine detail along the borders. Many of the patterns may remind you of a formal garden, but you may see newer animal motifs and splashy modern abstract designs. Rabati carpets are highly prized, and could cost you Dh2000 per sq metre.

Chichaoua rugs Simple and striking, with spare zigzags, asterisks, and enigmatic symbols on a variegated red or purple background (about Dh700 to Dh1000 per sq metre).

Hanbels or kilims These flat-woven rugs with no pile make up for a lack of cushiness with character. Some *hanbels* include Berber letters and auspicious symbols such as the evil eye, Southern Cross and Berber *fibule* (brooch) in their weave. Ask the seller to explain them for you – whether it's folklore or fib, the carpet-seller's interpretation adds to the experience (from Dh400 to Dh900 per sq metre).

Zanafi or glaoua Kilims and shag carpeting, together at last. Opposites attract in these rugs, where sections of fluffy pile alternate with flat-woven stripes or borders. These are usually Dh1000 to Dh1800 per sq metre.

Shedwi Flat-woven rugs with bold patterns in black wool on off-white, so au naturel you can still feel the lanolin between your fingers when you rub it. For as little as Dh400 for a smaller rug, they're impressive yet inexpensive gifts.

Leatherwork

Now that there's not much call for camel saddles anymore, Moroccan leather artisans keep busy fashioning embossed leather book-covers and next season's must-have handbags with what look like medieval dentistry tools. Down medieval *derbs* (alleys), you'll discover freshly tanned and dyed lime-green leather sculpted into fashion-forward square pouffes (ottomans), yellow pompoms carefully stitched onto stylish fuchsia kid-skin gloves, or shocking silver leather stretched and sewn into flouncy bedroom slippers. Along these leather souqs, you might spot artisans dabbing henna onto stretched goatskin to make 'tattooed' leather candle-holders, lampshades or stand-alone artworks. If you're in town for a couple of days, you might even commission an artisan to make you a custom-made bag, lambskin leather jacket or jodhpurs.

If it's an authenticity trip you're after, for men you'll prefer the traditional yellow *babouche*s (slippers) or 'Berber Adidas', slippers with soles made from recycled rubber tyres. Women's *babouche*s come in a broader range of colours and designs, and you may see vats of vibrant dye used for them in tanneries in Fez. But as colourful as they may look from afar, the tanneries give off a putrid stench – many medina residents would prefer to see them outside the city limits.

Never let it be said that Moroccan leatherwork can't keep up with modern trends: look out for the traditional *babouche* (pointed slippers) branded with English and Spanish football club logos – and Raja Casablanca and MAS Fes for the domestic tourism market.

Ceramics

Moroccan ceramics are a delight, and excellent value – a decorative tajine may cost you Dh150 to Dh400, depending on size and decoration. Different regions have their own colour schemes: Meknès ceramics tend to be green and black, Fassi pottery is blue, Safi offers black-and-white Berber patterns, and Tamegroute makes a distinctive green glaze from oxidised copper. Salé is strong on yellow and turquoise, geometric patterns and intricate dot-patterned dishes. Marrakesh specialises in monochrome ceramics in red, graphite or orange instead of elaborate decoration. Many rural areas specialise in terracotta crockery, with plain, striking shapes and Berber good-luck symbols painted in henna.

Plain terracotta cooking tajines are oven safe, fine for stovetop cooking and cost less than Dh80. Wrap them well to guard against breakages on the trip home.

Zellij

To make a Moroccan fountain, grab your hammer and chisel, and carefully chip a glazed tile into a geometrically correct shape. Good job – now only 6000 more to go to finish your water feature. Then again, you might leave it to the Moroccan mosaic masters to spiff up your foyer with glittering *zellij* end tables, entryway mirrors and fountains of all sizes. Fez has a reputation for the most intricate, high-lustre *zellij*, and the historic fountains around town dating from the Middle Ages are convincing advertisements for Fassi masterworks.

Lots of the 'amber' you'll see in souqs is plastic. Genuine amber will have a faint incense smell when you light a match near it, and a slightly waxy feel.

Brass, Copper & Silver

Tea is a performance art in Morocco, requiring just the right props. As if tea poured from over your head wasn't dramatic enough, gleaming brass teapots and copper tea trays are hammered by hand to catch the light and engraved with calligraphy to convey *baraka* on all who partake. Pierced brass lamps and recycled tin lanterns add instant atmosphere – and if all else fails to impress, serve your guests a sliver of cake with an inlaid knife from Morocco's dagger capitol, Kelaâ M'Gouna.

Most 'silver' tea services are actually nickel silver, and should cost accordingly – about Dh50 to Dh250 for the teapot, and usually more for the tray (depending on size and design).

TOP CARPET-BUYING TIPS

→ Know your limits, namely how much blank wall and floor space you actually have, your airline's luggage weight limit, the cost of shipping and duty, and purchase price.

→ Tread cautiously with antique rugs. Precious few genuine antique rugs are left in Morocco. New rugs are aged by being taken out back and stomped on, bleached by the sun or otherwise treated.

→ Inspect the knots. You'll be asked to pay more for carpets with a higher number of knots per sq cm, which you'll begin to discern by examining the back of carpets to look for gaps between knots. Some carpets are washed in hot water to bind the wool together more tightly, but you can often distinguish these shrunken rugs by their misshapen, irregular borders.

→ Get plenty of vegetables. Prices are often higher for carpets whose wool is coloured using vegetable dyes (which tend to fade faster) instead of synthetics; you can usually tell these by their muted tones, and the carpet seller may be able to tell you what plant was used to make the dye.

→ There's no set price, so enjoy the transaction. Banter before you bargain, keep your sense of humour, come back tomorrow, and drink mint tea so sweet you'll want to brush your teeth twice. Besides fond memories, at the end of it all you should have a carpet that suits you.

Fair-Trade Carpets

Jemaite Tifawin Carpet Cooperative, Anzal

Cooperative Feminin de Tissage Aït Bououli, Aït Bououli

Kasbah Myriem, Midelt

Coopérative de Tissage, Ouarzazate

Ensemble Artisanales in cities nationwide

Jewellery

Not all that glitters is gold in Morocco, since many Berbers traditionally believe gold to be a source of evil. You may see some jewellers with magnifying glasses working a tricky bit of gold filigree, but most gold you see in the souqs is imported from India and Bali. Sterling will be marked with 925, and is often sold by weight rather than design. Morocco's mining operations are more concerned with phosphates and fossils than with precious gems, but you will see folkloric dowry jewellery and headdresses with semiprecious stones, including coral, agate, cornelian and amber.

But Moroccan *mâalems* don't need precious materials to create a thing of beauty. Ancient ammonite and trilobite fossils from Rissani make fascinating prehistoric amulets, and striking Berber *fibules* (brooches) in silver are Tiznit's speciality. Layered wood, nickel silver and brightly coloured enamel make groovy cocktail rings in Marrakesh, and desert Tuareg talismans in leather and silver are fitting gifts for a man of the world.

Woodwork

The most pleasingly scented part of the souq is the woodworkers' area, aromatic from the curls of wood carpeting the floors of master-carvers' workshops. These are the *mâalems* responsible for the ancient carved, brass-studded cedar doors and those carved cedar *muqarnas* (honeycomb-carved) domes that cause wonderment in Moroccan palaces. Tetouan, Meknès and Fez have the best reputations for carved wood ornaments, but you'll see impressive woodwork in most Moroccan medinas.

For the gourmets on your gift list, hand-carved orangewood *harira* (lentil soup) spoons are small ladles with long handles that make ideal tasting spoons. Cedar is used for ornate jewellery boxes and hefty chip-carved chests are sure to keep the moths at bay. The most prized wood is thuya wood, knotty burl from the roots of trees indigenous to the Essaouira region. Buy from artisans' associations that practise responsible tree management and harvesting.

Architecture

Stubbed toes come with the territory in Morocco: with so much intriguing architecture to gawp at, you can't always watch where you're going. Some buildings are more memorable than others – as in any developing country there's makeshift housing and cheap concrete – but it's the striking variation in architecture that keeps you wondering what's behind that wall or over the next mountain pass. Here are some Moroccan landmarks likely to leave your jaw on tiled floors, and your toes in jeopardy.

Deco Villas

When Morocco came under colonial control, villes nouvelles (new towns) were built outside the walls of the medina, with street grids and modern architecture imposing strict order. Neoclassical facades, mansard roofs and high-rises must have come as quite a shock when they were introduced by the French and Spanish.

But one style that seemed to bridge local Islamic geometry and streamlined European modernism was art deco. Painter Jacques Majorelle brought a Moroccan colour sensibility to deco in 1924, adding bursts of blue, green and acid yellow to his deco villa and Jardin Majorelle.

In its 1930s heyday, Casablanca cleverly grafted Moroccan geometric detail onto whitewashed European edifices, adding a signature Casablanca Mauresque deco look to villas, movie palaces and hotels, notably Marius Boyer's Cinéma Rialto (1930) and the Hôtel Transatlantique (1922). Tangier rivalled Casablanca for Mauresque deco decadence, with its 1940s Cinematheque and 1930s El-Minzah Hotel – the architectural model for Rick's Cafe Americain in the 1942 classic *Casablanca*. Mauresque elements can be seen in cities all over Morocco.

Top Deco

Villa des Arts, Casablanca

Jardin Majorelle, Marrakesh

Cinéma Rif, Tangier

Plaza de España, Melilla

El-Minzah Hotel, Tangier

Foundouqs

Since medieval times, these creative courtyard complexes featured ground-floor stabling or artisans' workshops and rented rooms upstairs – from the nonstop *foundouq* flux of artisans and traders emerged cosmopolitan ideas and new inventions. *Foundouqs* once dotted caravan routes, but as trading communities became more stable and affluent, most *foundouqs* were gradually replaced with private homes and storehouses. Around 140 *foundouqs* remain in Marrakesh alone, including historic *foundouqs* near Pl Bab Fteuh, several lining Rue Dar el-Bacha and one on Rue el-Mouassine featured in the film *Hideous Kinky*. In Fez, an exemplary *foundouq* dating from 1711 underwent a six-year renovation to become the spiffy Nejjarine Museum of Wooden Arts & Crafts.

Eight of the world's leading Islamic architectural scholars give you their best explanations in *Architecture of the Islamic World: Its History and Social Meaning*, by Oleg Grabar et al.

Hammams

These domed buildings have been part of the Moroccan urban landscape since the Almohads, and every village aspires to a hammam of its own – often the only local source of hot water. Traditionally they are built of mudbrick, lined with *tadelakt* (satiny hand-polished limestone plaster that traps moisture) and capped with a dome that has star-shaped vents to let steam escape. The domed main room is the coolest area, with side rooms offering increasing levels of heat to serve everyone from the vaguely arthritic to the woefully hung-over.

The boldly elemental forms of traditional hammams may strike you as incredibly modern, but actually it's the other way around. The hammam is a recurring feature of landscapes by modernist masters Henri Matisse and Paul Klee, and Le Corbusier's International Style modernism was inspired by the interior volumes and filtered light of these iconic domed North African structures. *Tadelakt* has become a sought-after surface treatment for pools and walls in high-style homes, and pierced domes incorporated into the 'Moroccan Modern' style feature in umpteen coffee-table books. To see these architectural features in their original context, pay a visit to your friendly neighbourhood hammam – there's probably one near the local mosque, since hammams traditionally share a water source with ablutions fountains.

Historic Hammams

Hammam Dar el-Bacha, Marrakesh

Douches Barakat, Chefchaouen

Hammam Bab Doukkala, Marrakesh

Archaeological excavations, Aghmat

Kasbahs

Wherever there were once commercial interests worth protecting in Morocco – salt, sugar, gold, slaves – you'll find a kasbah. These fortified quarters housed the ruling family, its royal guard, and all the necessities for living in case of a siege. The *mellah* (Jewish quarter) was often positioned within reach of the kasbah guard and the ruling power's watchful eye. One of the largest remaining kasbahs is Marrakesh's 11th-century kasbah, which still houses a royal palace and acres of gardens, and flanks Marrakesh's *mellah*. Among the most photogenic northern kasbahs are the red kasbah overlooking all-blue Chefchaouen, and Rabat's whitewashed seaside kasbah with its elegantly carved gate, Bab Oudaïa.

Unesco World Heritage designations saved Taourirt kasbah in Ouarzazate and the rose-coloured mudbrick Aït Benhaddou, both restored and frequently used as film backdrops. To see living, still-inhabited kasbahs, head to Anmiter and Kasbah Amridil in Skoura Oasis.

In 2009, Dh230 million was set aside to restore *ksour* and kasbahs, with top priorities in Er-Rachidia, Erfoud and Rissani.

Ksour

The location of *ksour* (fortified strongholds, plural of *ksar*) in southern Morocco are spectacularly formidable: atop a rocky crag, against a rocky cliff, or rising above a palm oasis. Towers made of metres-thick, straw-reinforced mudbrick are elegantly tapered at the top to distribute the weight, and capped by zigzag *merlon* (crenellation). Like a desert mirage, a *ksar* will play tricks with your sense of scale and distance with its odd combination of grandeur and earthy intimacy. From these watchtowers, Timbuktu seems much closer than 52 days away by camel – and in fact, the elegant mudbrick architecture of Mali and Senegal is a near relative of Morocco's *ksour*.

To get the full effect of this architecture in splendid oasis settings, visit the *ksour*-packed Drâa and Dadès Valleys, especially the fascinating

ENDANGERED MONUMENTS: GLAOUI KASBAHS

The once-spectacular Glaoui kasbahs at Taliouine, Tamdaght, Agdz, and especially Telouet have been largely abandoned to the elements – go and see them now, before they're gone. These are deeply ambivalent monuments: they represent the finest Moroccan artistry (no one dared displease the Glaoui despots) but also the betrayal of the Alawites by the Pasha Glaoui, who collaborated with French colonists to suppress his fellow Moroccans. But locals argue Glaoui kasbahs should be preserved, as visible reminders that even the grandest fortifications were no match for independent-minded Moroccans.

ancient Jewish *ksar* at Tamnougalt and the pink,gold, and white *ksar* of Aït Arbi, teetering on the edge of the Dadès Gorge. Between the Drâa Valley and Dadès Valley, you can stay overnight in an ancient *ksar* in the castle-filled oases of Skoura and N'Kob, or pause for lunch at Ksar el-Khorbat and snoop around 1000-year-old Ksar Asir in Tinejdad.

Caravan stops are packed with well-fortified *ksour,* where merchants brought fortunes in gold, sugar and spices for safekeeping after 52-day trans-Saharan journeys. In Rissani, a half-hour circuit will lead you past half a dozen splendid ancient *ksour,* some of which are slated for restoration. Along caravan routes heading north through the High Atlas toward Fez, you'll spot spectacular *ksour* rising between snowcapped mountain peaks, including a fine hilltop tower that once housed the entire 300-person community of Zaouiat Ahansal.

Medersas

More than schools of rote religious instruction, Moroccan *medersas* have been vibrant centres of learning for law, philosophy and astronomy since the Merenid dynasty. For enough splendour to lift the soul and distract all but the most devoted students, visit the *zellij*-bedecked 14th-century Medersa el-Attarine in Fez and its rival for top students, the intricately carved and stuccoed Ali ben Youssef Medersa in Marrakesh. Now open as museums, these *medersas* give some idea of the austere lives students led in sublime surroundings, with long hours of study, several roommates, dinner on a hotplate, sleeping mats for comfort and one communal bathroom for up to 900 students. While other functioning *medersas* are closed to non-Muslims, Muslim visitors can stay overnight in some Moroccan *medersas,* though arrangements should be made in advance and a modest donation is customary.

Mosques

Even small villages may have more than one mosque, built on prime real estate in town centres with one wall facing Mecca. Mosques provide moments of sublime serenity in chaotic cities and busy village market days, and even non-Muslims can sense their calming influence. Towering minarets not only aid the acoustics of the call to prayer, but provide a visible reminder of God and community that puts everything else – minor spats, dirty dishes, office politics – back in perspective.

Mosques in Morocco are closed to non-Muslims, with two exceptions that couldn't be more different: Casablanca's sprawling Hassan II Mosque and austere Tin Mal Mosque nestled in the High Atlas. The Hassan II Mosque was completed in 1993 by French architect Michel Pinseau with great fanfare and considerable controversy: with room for 25,000 worshippers under a retractable roof and a 210m-high laser-equipped minaret, the total cost has been estimated at €585 million, not including maintenance or restitution to low-income former residents moved to accommodate the structure. At the other end of the aesthetic spectrum is the elegant simplicity of Tin Mal Mosque, built in 1156 to honour the Almohads' strict spiritual leader, Mohammed ibn Tumart, with cedar ceilings and soaring arches that lift the eye and the spirits ever upward.

Muslims assert that no Moroccan architecture surpasses buildings built for the glory of God, especially mosques in the ancient Islamic spiritual centre of Fez. With walls and ablutions fountains covered in lustrous green and white Fassi *zellij* (ceramic-tile mosaic), and mihrabs (niches indicating the direction of Mecca) swathed in stucco and marble, Fez mosques are purpose-built for spiritual glory. When vast portals are open between prayers, visitors can glimpse (no photos allowed) Fez' crowning glory: Kairaouine Mosque and Medersa,

Pick up a copy of Tahir Shah's *The Caliph's House* for a rollicking account of his project to restore an old Casablanca mansion, starting with exorcising the resident djinns before the builders would start work.

The only fully active mosque non-Muslims are allowed to visit in Morocco is Casablanca's Hassan II Mosque. It can hold 25,000 worshippers inside (and another 80,000 outside), so you won't be cramping anyone's style.

LOST IN THE MEDINA MAZE? FOLLOW SOUQ LOGIC

In labyrinthine Moroccan medinas, winding souqs hardly seem linear, but they do adhere to a certain logic. Centuries ago, market streets were organised by trade so that medieval shoppers would know where to head for pickles or camel saddles. More than other medinas, Fez souqs maintain their original medieval organisation: kiosks selling silver-braided trim are right off the kaftan souq, just down the street from stalls selling hand-woven white cotton for men's jellabas. What about wool? That's in a different souq, near stalls selling hand-carved horn combs for carding wool. The smelliest, messiest trades were pushed to the peripheries, so you'll know you're near the edge of the medina when you arrive at tanneries, or livestock markets. In Marrakesh, the saddle-making souq is at the northeast end of the souq, not far from the tanneries.

In addition to ancient fortress walls, 3m- to 6m-high border barriers wrap the Mediterranean towns of Ceuta and Melilla. Spain and Morocco dispute their sovereignty, and local architecture does nothing to resolve the conflict: the Spanish point out Andalucian elements, which Moroccans as will certainly remind you, developed under Almohad rule.

founded in the 8th century by a Fassi heiress. Non-Muslims can also see Morocco's most historic *minbar* (pulpit): the 12th-century Koutoubia *minbar,* inlaid with silver, ivory and marquetry by Cordoba's finest artisans, and housed in Marrakesh's Badi Palace.

Ramparts

Dramatic form follows defensive function in many of Morocco's trading posts and ports. The Almoravids took no chances with their trading capital, and wrapped Marrakesh in 16km of pink pisé (mudbrick reinforced with clay and chalk), 2m thick. Old Fez is similarly surrounded. Coastal towns like Essaouira and Asilah have witnessed centuries of piracy and fierce Portuguese–Moroccan trading rivalries – hence the heavy stone walls dotted with cannons, and crenellated ramparts that look like medieval European castle walls.

Riads

Near palaces in Morocco's major cities are grand riads, courtyard mansions where families of royal relatives, advisors and rich merchants whiled away idle hours gossiping in *bhous* (seating nooks) around arcaded courtyards paved with *zellij* and filled with songbirds twittering in fruit trees. Not a bad set-up, really, and one you can enjoy today in one of the many converted riad guesthouses in Marrakesh and Fez.

So many riads have become B&Bs over the past decade that 'riad' has become a synonym for 'guesthouse' – but technically, an authentic riad has a courtyard garden divided in four parts, with a fountain in the centre. A riad is also not to be confused with a *dar*, which is a simpler, smaller house constructed around a central light well – a more practical structure for hot desert locales and chilly coastal areas. With several hundred riads, including extant examples from the 15th century, Marrakesh is the riad capital of North Africa.

From outside those austere, metre-thick walls, you'd never guess what splendours await beyond brass-studded riad doors: painted cedar ceilings, ironwork balconies and archways dripping with stucco. Upkeep isn't easy, and modernising ancient structures with plumbing and electricity without destabilising the foundations is especially tricky. Built in clay or mudbrick with a thick lime plaster covering, their walls insulate against street sound, keep cool in summer and warm in winter, and wick away humidity instead of trapping it like mouldy old concrete – building materials of the future, as well as the past.

Souqs

In Morocco, souqs – the market streets of a medina – are often covered with wooden grilles for shade and shelter, and criss-crossed with smaller streets lined with food stalls, storerooms and cubby-hole-sized artisans' studios carved into thick mudbrick walls. Unlike souqs, these smaller streets often do not have names, and are together known as a *qissaria*. Most *qissariat* are through streets, so when (not if) you get lost in them, keep heading onward until you intersect with the next souq or buy a carpet, whichever happens first.

Zawiyas

Don't be fooled by modest appearances or remote locations in Morocco: even a tiny village teetering off the edge of a cliff may be a major draw across Morocco because of its *zawiya* (shrine to a *marabout*, or saint). Just being in the vicinity of a *marabout* is said to confer *baraka* (a state of grace). Zawiya Nassiriyya in Tamegroute is reputed to cure the ill and eliminate stress, and the *zawiya* of Sidi Moussa in the Aït Bougomez Valley is said to increase the fertility of female visitors.

To boost your *baraka* you can visit the Tamegroute and Aït Bougomez *zawiyas* as well as the *zawiya* of Moulay Ali ash-Sharif in Rissani, which is now open to non-Muslims. Most *zawiyas* are closed to non-Muslims – including the famous Zawiya Moulay Idriss II in Fez, and all seven of Marrakesh's *zawiyas* – but you can often recognise a *zawiya* by its ceramic green-tiled roof and air of calm even outside its walls. In rural areas, a *marabout's* shrine (often confusingly referred to as a *marabout* rather than *zawiya*) is typically a simple mudbrick base topped with a whitewashed dome – though in the Ourika Valley village of Tafza you can see a rare red-stone example.

Top Souqs

Okchen Market, Meknès

Souq Sebbaghine (Dyers' Souq), Marrakesh

Souq an-Nejjarine (Carpenters' Souq), Fez

Souq el-Ghezel (Wool Souq), Salé

Marché Central, Casablanca

ARCHITECTURE SOUQS

Medinas: Morocco's Hidden Cities explores the shadows of ancient Moroccan walled cities, with painterly images by French photographer Jean-Marc Tingaud and illuminating commentary by Tahar Ben Jelloun.

Natural Wonders

A day's journey in Morocco can take you from Atlantic beaches through rich farmland, and over high mountain passes to the Sahara itself. The human landscape is no less fascinating – half of all Moroccans still live in rural areas, and everywhere you'll spot people working this extraordinary land, harvesting barley on tiny stone-walled terraces hewn from cliffsides, tending to olive and argan groves, or leading their flocks of sheep to mountain pastures.

Coastline

If you're going for a dip, be aware that the Atlantic rollers can hide some fearsome riptides, and once you're in the waters there's nothing between you and the Americas (or at best, the Canary Islands).

When the Umayyads arrived in Morocco, they rode their horses onto Atlantic beaches and dubbed the country *Al-Maghreb* (where the sun sets), knowing that the sea marked the westernmost limit of their conquests. The coast has played a central role in Moroccan history, from the Barbary pirates to the Allied landings of WWII; today the country is developing stretches of both its Atlantic and Mediterranean coastlines into shiny new tourist hubs complete with villas, resorts and golf courses. Luckily for nature lovers, there's still pristine coastline in between, with rare shorebirds and cliff's-edge vistas.

Fishing and international trade have defined the Atlantic coastal economy ever since the Phoenicians and Romans established their port at Lixus. But the Atlantic also has its wild side, with raw, rocky beaches around whitewashed Asilah, and wetland habitats, such as the lagoon of Merja Zerga National Park, attracting flamingos and rare African wildfowl. South of Casablanca are the ports of Oualidia and Essaouira, former pirates' coves where rare wildlife still flourishes and Morocco's best seafood is served port-side. South of the commercialised boardwalks of Agadir, resort beaches empty into great sandy expanses stretching through Western Sahara to Mauritania.

By 2019, 600 mosques in Morocco will have been converted into showcases for green living, with LED lighting, solar thermal water heaters and photovoltaic electrical systems.

By contrast, the craggy Mediterranean coast has remained relatively undeveloped until recently, despite a spectacular coastline of sheltered coves and plunging cliffs. Tangier and the port towns of Ceuta and Melilla make the best of their advantageous positions, with scenic overlooks and splendid coastal villas. The major barrier to the east is the Rif Mountains, rugged terrain inhabited by staunchly independent Berbers, but the new highways that skirt along the Rif to Saïdia and Ouda have made this stretch of coast accessiable as never before.

Mountains

Three mountain ranges ripple diagonally across a topographical map of Morocco: the Rif in the north, the Middle Atlas (south of Fez) and the High Atlas (south and northeast of Marrakesh), with the southern subchain of the Anti Atlas slumping into the desert. The monumental force of plate tectonics brought these ranges into existence. Around 60 million years ago, a dramatic collision of Africa and Eurasia plates lifted up the High Atlas, while closing the Strait of Gibraltar and raising the Alps and Pyrenees. More recently, the mountains have provided shelter for self-sufficient Berbers, a safe haven for those fleeing invaders and a strategic retreat for organising resistance against would-be colonisers.

In the north, the low Rif Mountains form a green, fertile arc that serves as a natural coastal barrier. Even the Vandals and Visigoths were no match for independent-minded Riffian Berbers, who for millennia successfully used their marginal position to resist incursions from Europe and Africa alike. The Rif has remained politically marginalised, which has had one highly debatable advantage until now: kif (cannabis) is widely grown in the region east of Tetouan. It's taken huge government investment to improve access to the region via new infrastructure. Well-graded roads make exploring the Rif more possible than ever before.

The Middle Atlas is the Moroccan heartland, a patchwork of farmland that runs from Volubilis to Fez and gradually rises to mountain peaks covered with fragrant forests of juniper, thuya and cedar. This sublime trekking country is also home to the Barbary ape, Morocco's only (nonhuman) primate. Running northeast to southwest from the Rif, the range soars to 3340m at its highest point.

But the real drama begins east of Agadir, where foothills suddenly rise from their crouched position to form the gloriously precipitous High Atlas Mountains. South of Marrakesh, the High Atlas reach dizzy heights at Jebel Toubkal, North Africa's highest summit (4167m). On the lower flanks, the mountains are ingeniously terraced with orchards of walnuts, cherries, almonds and apples, which erupt into bloom in spring. The High Atlas hunkers down on to the southeast into the Anti Atlas range, which protects the Souss Valley from the hot winds of the rising Sahara Desert.

When hiking in the Rif, try not to step on the kif. Morocco is the one of the world's largest producers of cannabis, most of it destined for markets in Western Europe.

Desert

No landscape is more iconic in Morocco than the desert, with rolling dunes and mudbrick *ksour* (fortified strongholds) rising majestically from hidden palm oases. But most of the desert is neither oasis nor dune, and it's virtually uninhabitable. Vast tracts of barren, sunbleached *hammada* (stony desert) are interrupted by rocky gorges, baked over millions of years by the desert's ovenlike heat until the blackened surface turns glassy. The desert forms still-disputed borders east and south to Algeria and Mauritania. South of the Anti Atlas, the barren slopes trail off into the stony, almost trackless desert of Western Sahara.

Even today, the sight of an oasis on this desolate desert horizon brings a rush of elation and wonder – but when ancient caravans emerged after a gruelling 52-day trans-Saharan journey with final

---

DUST-UP IN THE DESERT

To see the desert the way nature intended, take a dromedary instead of an all-terrain vehicle. The 4WDs break up the surface of the desert, which is then scattered into the air by strong winds. By one estimate, the annual generation of dust has increased by 1000% in North Africa in the last 50 years – a major contributor to drought, as dust clouds shield the earth's surface from sunlight and hinder cloud formation. What happens in the desert has far-reaching consequences: dust from the Sahara has reached as far away as Greenland. If you travel by dromedary instead, desert wildlife won't be scared off by the vibrations, and you're much more likely to spot small, sensitive and rather adorably big-eared desert creatures like the fennec fox, jerboa and desert hedgehog.

stretches of dunes at Erg Chigaga and Tinfou, the glimpse of green on the horizon at Zagora was nothing short of life-saving. From Zagora, caravans heading to Middle Atlas laden with gold proceeded warily through the Drâa Valley from one well-fortified *ksar* to the next, finally unloading the camels and packing up mules at Skoura Oasis.

Some caravans passed through the ancient desert gates of Sijilmassa (near Rissani), though there was no easy route: one approach was via the rose-gold dunes of Erg Chebbi at Merzouga, while the other led past formidable Jebel Sarhro, inhabited by equally formidable seminomadic Aït Atta warriors. Today the mood in oases is considerably more relaxed, with a slow pace in the daytime heat and sociable evenings as visitors and locals gather around a warming fire.

Sahara: A Natural History, by Marq de Villiers and Sheila Hirtle, is a highly readable account of the Sahara's wildlife, its people and geographical history.

Wildlife

Even after millennia of being inhabited, farmed and grazed, Morocco still teems with wildlife – a testament to sustainable traditional practices and careful resource management handed down through generations. Today Morocco's 40 different ecosystems provide a habitat for many endemic species, including flora and fauna that are rare elsewhere. Industrialisation has put considerable pressure on Morocco's delicately balanced natural environments, and while steps are being taken to create wildlife reserves for Morocco's endangered species, visitors can do their part to preserve natural habitats by staying on marked *pistes* (tracks) and taking out waste.

Coastal Species

You might occasionally see live hedgehogs for sale in Moroccan souqs. While they can be eaten for food, they're also used as remedies against witchcraft and the evil eye.

Away from the urban sprawl of port cities and resort complexes are long stretches of rugged Moroccan coastline, where people are far outnumbered by abundant bird populations and marine mammals such as dolphins and porpoises. Along beaches, you'll spot white-eyed gulls, Moroccan cormorants and sandwich terns. Seabirds and freshwater birds thrive in preserves such as Souss-Massa National Park, where you might spy endangered bald ibis along with the ducks and waders who migrate here from Europe for the winter.

Desert Habitats

The Sahara may seem like a harsh place, but it's home to numerous creatures, including several furry, cuddly ones: several varieties of fluffy gerbils; long-eared, spindly-legged, cartoonish jerboas; and the desert hedgehog, the world's tiniest hedgehog and tipping the scales at between 300g and 500g. The delightful fennec fox has fur-soled feet and huge batlike ears to dissipate The Saharan heat; pups look like Chihuahuas, only fuzzier. This desert fox is stealthy and nocturnal, but

SOLAR SAHARA

One thing the desert has in copious amounts (apart from sand) is sunshine, and in November 2009 Morocco revealed a US$9 billion investment plan to generate 20% of its energy from solar energy by the year 2020. Much of it will be produced in the Moroccan Orient, the region running along the Algerian border from the Mediterranean to Figuig. The upgrading of infrastructure on the highway south of Oujda (proclaimed from dozens of roadside billboards) point to the money pouring into the region. In addition, a great deal of investment is earmarked for the Ouarzazate region.

The programs are being financed by private investors as well as the World Bank, the European Investment Bank, and Spain, France, Germany and Saudi Arabia.

THE BARBARY LION – BACK FROM THE DEAD?

When Morocco's national football team – the Atlas Lions – takes to the pitch, it's honouring one of the country's most iconic animals, albeit one that has long been on the extinct species list.

The Barbary Lion was North Africa's top predator. It was the largest and heaviest of all lion subspecies, with the males famed for their thick black manes. They were hunted by the Romans to provide sport for the gladiatorial combats of the Colosseum, while Moroccan sultans later gave them as diplomatic gifts. Slowly exterminated across the region through hunting and habitat loss, the lions persisted in heavily forested parts of Morocco's Atlas and Rif Mountains well into the 20th century. The last wild lion is thought to have been shot in 1942, although recent research suggests that populations survived into the 1960s – no doubt aided by their naturally solitary behaviour, rather than living in prides as lions do in the rest of Africa.

Remnant lion populations of mixed heritage survived in zoos across the world, including the personal zoo of the current king of Morocco. In recent years a captive breeding program, coupled with the latest genetic fingerprinting techniques, has been attempting to re-create a genetically pure and viable population of the big cats. The ultimate aim of the International Barbary Lion Project is to create a protected reserve in the Atlas Mountains large enough to allow a limited reintroduction program. While this is a long way off – and the willingness of locals to share land with a top predator remains unknown – perhaps the last roar of this magnificent animal is yet to be heard.

if you're travelling by dromedary and staying overnight in the desert, you might catch a brief glimpse.

While desert heat makes most humans sluggish, many desert creatures are elegant and swift. Dorcas gazelles are common, and you might also catch a glimpse of a rare, reddish Cuvier's gazelle. Lizards you might see darting through the desert include skinks and spiny-tailed lizards, and you might catch sight of the devilish-looking (though not especially poisonous) horned viper. Golden jackals are the most common predator in the Sahara, though in the more remote parts of the Western Sahara a few desert-adapted cheetahs may yet survive.

Mountain Wildlife

Forested mountain slopes are Morocco's richest wildlife habitats, where it's easy to spot sociable Barbary macaques (also known as Barbary apes) in the Rif and Middle Atlas, especially around Azrou. Less easy to track are mountain gazelles, lynx and the endangered mouflon (Barbary sheep). The mouflon are now protected in a High Atlas preserve near the Tizi n'Test, where its only predator is the critically endangered Barbary leopard – the last population of leopards in North Africa.

Golden eagles soar in Atlas mountain updrafts, and High Atlas hikes might introduce you to red crossbills, horned larks, acrobatic booted eagles, Egyptian vultures, and both black and red kites. In springtime, butterflies abound in the mountains, including the scarlet cardinal and bright-yellow Cleopatra.

National Parks

With cities encroaching on natural habitats, the Moroccan government is setting aside protected areas to prevent the further disappearance of rare plant and animal species. Toubkal National Park in the High Atlas Mountains was the first national park to be created in 1942. After the

One less-than-charming fact about snake charming: to prevent them from biting handlers, snakes' mouths are sometimes stitched closed. This often causes fatal mouth infections and leaves snakes unable to feed. To discourage this practice, don't pose with or tip snake charmers handling snakes whose mouths are stitched shut.

vast Souss-Massa National Park was founded in 1991 outside Agadir, Morocco created four new national parks in 2004: Talassemtane (589 sq km) in the Rif; Al-Hoceima (485 sq km) in the Mediterranean, with outstanding coastal and marine habitats along the Mediterranean that include one of the last outposts of osprey; Ifrane National Park (518 sq km) in the Middle Atlas, with dense cedar forests and Barbary macaques; and the Eastern High Atlas National Park (553 sq km).

Today Morocco's 14 national parks and 35 nature reserves, forest sanctuaries and other protected areas overseen by Morocco's Direction des Eaux et Forêts are conserving species and advancing natural sciences. The park staff are tracking the region's biodiversity through botanical inventories, bird censuses, primate studies and sediment analyses. These studies are critical to understanding the broader causes of habitat loss, in Morocco and beyond; the Spanish and American Park Services have studied Morocco's parklands to better understand biodiversity concerns.

Parks have proven a boon to local wildlife, but a mixed blessing for human residents. While national parks protect local ecosystems and attract tourist revenue, access for local communities to water, grazing land and wild plants harvested for food and medicine has been limited or cut off entirely. But by conserving parkland, the Ministries of Tourism and Agriculture aim to help local ecosystems flourish, gradually restore arable land, and ultimately benefit local communities with ecotourism that provides a profitable alternative to kif cultivation. In the near future, fees for park admission may be instituted to support the parks' conservation, scientific and community missions. Meanwhile, the best sights in Morocco are still free and visitors can show their appreciation to local communities by supporting local NGOs along their route.

The endangered Houbara bustard is making a comeback with the release of 5000 captive-bred birds into a 40,000-sq-km protected zone in Morocco's eastern desert – among the largest reintroduction of any endangered species in the world. Bustards are notoriously difficult to breed in captivity due to their intricate mating behaviour and nervous disposition.

Creative Conservation

The only thing more natural than the wonders of Morocco is the impulse to preserve them. Morocco is in a fortunate position: to envision a more sustainable future, it can look to its recent past. Ancient *khettara* (irrigation systems), still in use, transport water from natural springs to fields and gardens in underground channels, without losing precious water to evaporation. Although certification is still a novel concept, most small-scale Moroccan farming practices are organic by default, since chemical fertilisers are costly and donkey dung pretty much comes with the territory. Community hammams use power and water for steamy saunas more efficiently than individual showers or baths. Locally made, detergent-free *savon noir* ('black soap' made from natural palm and olive oils) is gentle enough for a shave and effective as laundry soap, without polluting run-off – and leftover 'grey water' can be used for gardens and courtyard fountains. With Morocco's traditional mudbrick architecture, metre-thick walls provide natural insulation against heat in summer and chill in winter, eliminating most street noise and the need for air-con and central heating.

Morocco is also thinking fast on its feet, becoming an early adopter of resource-saving new technologies. The pioneering nation already has Africa's biggest wind farm at Tarfaya, while Ouazazarte is home to what will ultimately be the world's largest solar power plant. By 2020 almost half of Morocco's energy will be provided by renewables.

The Sahara Conservation Fund (www.saharaconservation.org) is dedicated to preserving the wild creatures of the Sahara, and provides a preview of wildlife you might spot in this vibrant desert ecosystem.

NOTABLE NATIONAL PARKS

NATIONAL PARK	LOCATION	FEATURES	ACTIVITIES	BEST TIME TO VISIT
Al-Hoceima National Park	Al-Hoceima	thuya forest, limestone escarpments, fish eagles	hiking, birdwatching	May-Oct
Bouarfa Wildlife Sanctuary	Bouarfa	red rock steppe	hiking, climbing	Apr-Oct
Lac de Sidi Bourhaba	Mehdiya	lake & wetlands; 200 migratory bird species, including marbled duck, African marsh owl & flamingo	swimming, birdwatching, hiking	Oct-Mar
Merja Zerga National Park	Moulay Bousselham	lagoon habitats; 190 species of waterfowl, including African marsh owl, Andouin's gull, flamingo & crested coot	wildlife-watching	Dec-Jan
Souss-Massa National Park	south of Agadir	coastal estuaries and forests; 275 species of birds, including endangered bald ibis, mammals & enclosed endangered species	hiking, wildlife-watching, birdwatching	Mar-Oct
Talassemtane National Park	Chefchaouen	cedar & fir forests; Barbary macaque, fox, jackal & bats in the cedar forest	wildlife-watching, hiking	May-Sep
Tazzeka National Park	near Taza	oak forests & waterfalls	hiking	Jun-Sep
Toubkal National Park	near Marrakesh	highest peak in North Africa	hiking, climbing	May-Jun

To tackle challenges still ahead, Morocco will need all the resourcefulness it can muster. Due to the demands of city dwellers and tourist complexes, 37% of villages around Marrakesh now lack a reliable source of potable water. Damming to create reservoirs frequently strips downstream water of valuable silts needed to sustain farms and coastal wetlands. Forests are also under threat, with around 250 sq km of forest lost each year, including Moroccan pine, thuya and Atlas cedar. Pollution is a weighty concern, literally: Morocco's cities alone produce an annual harvest of 2.4 million tonnes of solid waste.

Everywhere you travel in the country, you'll notice minor modifications that collectively make major savings in scarce resources – and you're invited to participate. Plastic bags were banned in 2016.

Solar water heaters provide instant hot water for showers in the afternoon and evening, so taking showers at those times saves water that might otherwise be wasted by running the tap while gas heaters warm up. Reforestation programs are helping prevent erosion, and you can help by staying on marked mountain paths and supporting local NGO reforestation initiatives. Organic gardens provide fresh ingredients for meals, reducing the dependence on food transported over long distances – and ordering local, seasonal specialities provides positive reinforcement for local food sourcing. Morocco's Green Key program also certifies hotels and guesthouses that institute a range of resource-conserving measures, from low-flow toilets to environmentally friendly cleaning products, although it has received criticism from some quarters for granting certificates to hotels with distinctly high-impact facilities such as swimming pools.

Add these traditional, national and local resource-saving practices together, and Morocco is poised not only to make the switch to sustainable tourism, but to show Europe how it's done.

Many of the Barbary apes around Azrou have been habituated to people, who stop in their cars to feed them cookies and other high-sugar items. Such behaviour is frowned on, but by trekking further into the Middle Atlas you can still encounter wild troupes.

Survival Guide

Directory A–Z

Accommodation

A wide range of accommodation options is available in Morocco. In our listings, the official, government-assigned rates (including taxes) are quoted, although these are intended as a guide only.

Hotels Range from the most basic to the glitziest.

Riads The country has become famous for its traditional medina houses converted into boutique guesthouses.

Camping Mostly restricted to trekkers, who can also access mountain refuges in some areas.

Camping

➡ You can camp anywhere in Morocco if you have permission from the site's owner.

➡ There are many official campsites.

➡ Most official sites have water and electricity; some have a small restaurant, a grocery store and even a swimming pool.

➡ Most of the bigger cities have campsites, although they're often some way from the centre.

➡ Such sites are sometimes worth the extra effort to get to, but often they consist of a barren and stony area offering little shade and basic facilities.

➡ Particularly in southern Morocco, campsites are often brimming with the enormous campervans so beloved of middle-aged French tourists.

COSTS

➡ At official sites you'll pay around Dh10 to Dh20 per person, plus Dh10 to Dh20 to pitch a tent and about Dh10 to Dh15 for small vehicles.

➡ Parking a campervan or caravan typically costs around Dh20 to Dh30, although this can rise as high as Dh45.

➡ Electricity generally costs another Dh10 to Dh15.

➡ A hot shower is about Dh5 to Dh10.

➡ Many campsites have basic rooms or self-catering apartments.

Gîtes d'Étape, Homestays & Refuges

➡ *Gîtes d'étape* are homes or hostels, often belonging to mountain guides, which offer basic accommodation (often just a mattress on the floor) around popular trekking routes in the Atlas and Rif Mountains.

➡ *Gîtes* have rudimentary bathrooms and sometimes hot showers.

➡ Larger than *gîtes*, mountain *refuges* offer Swiss-chalet-style accommodation.

➡ Accommodation at *refuges* is usually in dormitories with communal showers, and often includes a lively communal dining-living room.

➡ **Club Alpin Français** (CAF; Map p158; ☑0522 27 00 90; www.ffcam.fr; 50 Blvd Moulay Abderrahman, Quartier Beauséjour, Casablanca) runs *refuges* in the High Atlas.

➡ If you are trekking in the High Atlas or travelling off the beaten track elsewhere, you may be offered accommodation in village homes.

➡ Many homestays won't have running water or electricity, but you'll find them big on warmth and hospitality. You should be prepared to pay what you would in *gîtes d'étape* or mountain *refuges*.

BOOK YOUR STAY ONLINE

For more accommodation reviews by Lonely Planet authors, check out http://lonelyplanet.com/hotels. You'll find independent reviews, as well as recommendations on the best places to stay. Best of all, you can book online.

Hostels

Part of Hostelling International, **Fédération Royale Marocaine des Auberges de Jeunes** (☎0522 47 09 52; www.auberges-de-jeunesse. com/en/maroc) has reliable youth hostels in Casablanca, Fez, Marrakesh, Meknès, Ouarzazate and Rabat.

➡ If you're travelling alone, hostels are among the cheapest places to stay (from Dh60 a night), but many are inconveniently located.

➡ Some offer kitchens, family rooms and breakfast.

➡ If looking for a budget hostel, beware of individuals' houses converted in the dead of night without the appropriate licences.

Hotels

➡ You'll need your passport number (and entry-stamp number) when filling in a hotel register.

➡ Some hotels in more isolated regions offer half-board (*demi-pension*), which means breakfast and dinner are included, or full-board (*pension*), also including lunch. This can be a good deal.

BUDGET

➡ You'll find cheap, unclassified (without a star rating) or one-star hotels clustered in the medinas of the bigger cities. Some are bright and spotless; others haven't seen a mop for years.

➡ Cheaper prices usually mean shared washing facilities and squat toilets.

➡ Many budget hotels don't supply soap in the bathrooms, so bring your own.

➡ Occasionally there is a gas-heated shower, for which you'll pay an extra Dh5 to Dh10.

➡ Where there is no hot water at all, head for the local hammam.

➡ Many cheap hotels in the deep south offer a mattress

on the roof terrace (Dh25 to Dh30); others also have traditional Moroccan salons, lined with banks of seats and cushions, where you can sleep for a similar price.

MIDRANGE

➡ Midrange hotels in Morocco are generally of a high standard.

➡ Options range from hotels offering imitation Western-style rooms, which are modern if a little soulless, to riads and *maisons d'hôtes* (small hotels), which capture the essence of Moroccan style with both comfort and character.

➡ In this price range you should expect a room with an en suite (shower) and breakfast.

➡ In cheaper areas such as the south, you may find midrange standards at budget prices.

TOP END

➡ Hotels in this bracket are similar to midrange places but with more luxurious levels of comfort and design.

➡ In resorts such as Agadir, many top-end hotels are self-contained holiday complexes, offering features such as golf courses, nightclubs and multiple restaurants.

Rental Accommodation

➡ If travelling in a small group or as a family, consider self-catering options, particularly in low season, when prices can drop substantially.

➡ Agadir, nearby Taghazout, Essaouira, Asilah and the bigger tourist centres on both coastlines have a fair number of self-catering apartments and houses, sometimes in tourist complexes.

Riads, Dars & Kasbahs

For many guests, the chance to stay in a converted traditional house is a major drawcard of a trip to Morocco. These midrange and top-end options are the type of accommodation that the term 'boutique hotel' could have been invented for, and no two are alike. Service tends to be personal, with many places noted for their food as much as their lodgings.

Locations Marrakesh is the most famous destination for riads (there are several hundred); Fez, Meknès, Essaouira and Rabat are also noteworthy. With their popularity seemingly unassailable, you can increasingly find riads in the most unexpected corners of the country.

Riads and dars Although the term riad is often used generically, a riad proper is a house built around a garden with trees. You'll come across plenty of *dars* (traditional townhouses with internal courtyards) labelling themselves as riads.

Kasbahs Often functioning as hotels, kasbahs (old citadels) are found in tourist centres in central and southern Morocco. Rooms in kasbahs are small and dark, due to the nature of the building, but are lovely and cool in summer.

Booking Most riads require booking, and it's worth planning ahead, as most only have a handful of rooms and can fill quickly. Booking well in advance often means that someone from the riad will be sent to meet you outside the medina when you arrive: labyrinthine streets conspire against finding the front door on your first attempt.

Rates Room rates are generally comparable to four- or five-star hotels. Many riads list their online rates in euros, rather than dirham, at exchange rates favourable to themselves, so always double-check the prices when booking.

Customs Regulations

Importing or exporting dirham is forbidden, although checks are rare so don't worry about the loose change you may have at the end of a drink. Forbidden items include 'any immoral items liable to cause a breach of the peace', such as 'books, printed matter, audio and video cassettes'.

Duty-free allowances:

➡ up to 200 cigarettes, or 25 cigars, or 250g of tobacco

➡ 1L of alcoholic drink

➡ 150ml of perfume

➡ presents or souvenirs worth up to Dh2000.

Electricity

Electricity is reliable, but bring a torch for off-the-beaten-track destinations in the mountains.

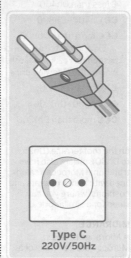

**Type C
220V/50Hz**

Embassies & Consulates

The Moroccan Ministry of Foreign Affairs and Cooperation (www.diplomatie.ma/en) has a list of embassies and consulates in Morocco. Most embassies and diplomatic representation are in Rabat, and open from about 9am until noon, Monday to Friday. Rabat embassies include the following:

Algerian Embassy (Map p174; ☑0537 66 15 74; algerabat@iam.net.ma; 46-48 Ave Tariq ibn Zayid, Quartier Hassan; 🚇Tour Hassan) Also has a consulate-general in Casablanca and consulate in Oujda.

Canadian Embassy (☑0537 54 49 49; www.canadainternational.gc.ca/morocco-maroc; 66 Mehdi Ben Barka Ave, Souissi; ⊙8am-4.30pm Mon-Thu, to 1.30pm Fri) Also provides consular assistance to Australians.

Dutch Embassy (Map p174; ☑0537 21 96 00; http://marokko.nlambassade.org; 40 Rue de Tunis, Quartier Hassan; 🚇Tour Hassan) Also has a consulate-general in Casablanca.

French Embassy (Map p174; ☑0537 67 87 00; www.consulfrance-ma.org; 1 Rue Aguelmane Sidi Ali, Agdal; ⊙8.30am-1.45pm Mon-Fri; 🚇Bibliotèque Nationale) Also has consulates in Agadir, Casablanca, Fez, Marrakesh, Rabat and Tangier.

German Embassy (☑0537 21 86 00; www.rabat.diplo.de; 7 Rue Madnine, Ville Nouvelle; ⊙9am-noon Mon-Fri; 🚇Place al-Joulane) Also has a consulate in Rabat and honorary consulates in Agadir and Casablanca.

Mauritanian Embassy (off Map p174; ☑0537 65 66 78; 6 Rue Thami Lamdaouar, Soussi)

Spanish Embassy (☑0537 63 39 00; www.exteriores.gob.es/embajadas/rabat; Rue Ain Khalouiya, Souissi; ⊙8.30am-4.30pm Mon-Fri) Also has consulates-general in Agadir, Casablanca, Larache, Nador, Rabat, Tangier and Tetouan.

UK Embassy (☑0537 63 33 33; www.gov.uk; 28 Ave S.A.R. Sidi Mohammed, Souissi; ⊙8am-4.15pm Mon-Thu, to 1pm Fri) Also has honorary consulates in Agadir, Marrakesh and Tangier.

US Embassy (☑0522 64 20 99; http://rabat.usembassy.gov; Km 5.7, Ave Mohamed VI, Souissi; ⊙8am-5pm Mon-Fri) Also has a consulate-general in Casablanca.

Australia, New Zealand and Ireland do not have embassies in Morocco.

Gay & Lesbian Travellers

➡ Homosexual acts (including kissing) are illegal in Morocco, and carry a potential jail term of up to three years and/or a fine. Moroccan authorities have recently shown an increased tendency to prosecute.

➡ In practice, although not openly admitted or shown, sex between men is not uncommon, even if few people actively self-identify as gay.

➡ Platonic affection is freely shown among Moroccans, more so between men than women.

➡ For travellers, discretion is the key in most places. Avoid public displays of affection.

➡ Be extremely circumspect about using using social media apps to make contact with local gay men. There have been several instances of robbery and assault in recent years.

➡ Some towns are more gay-friendly than others, with Marrakesh winning the prize, followed by Tangier. However, there are no dedicated gay destinations; nightlife in the bigger cities has become increasingly discreet in recent years.

➡ The pressures of poverty mean many young men will consider having sex for money or gifts. Exploitative relationships form an unpleasant but real dimension of the Moroccan gay scene.

➡ Lesbians shouldn't encounter any problems, though it's commonly believed by Moroccans that there are no lesbians in their country.

Insurance

A travel-insurance policy to cover theft, loss and, in particular, medical problems is strongly recommended for all visitors to Morocco.

Activities Some policies specifically exclude 'dangerous activities', which can include scuba diving, motorcycling, skiing and even trekking, so ensure your policy covers these if needed.

Driving Make sure you have adequate travel medical insurance and any relevant car insurance if you're driving.

Extensions If you need to extend your cover on the road, do so before it expires or a more expensive premium may apply.

Flights Paying for your airline ticket with a credit card often provides some travel-accident insurance, but take note of exclusions. You may be able to reclaim the payment if the operator doesn't deliver.

Purchase Buy travel insurance as early as possible. Buying just before you leave home may mean you're not covered for delays to your flight caused by strike action that began, or was threatened, before you took out the insurance.

Online insurance Worldwide travel insurance is available at www.lonelyplanet.com/insurance. You can buy, extend and claim online any time – even if you're already on the road.

Internet Access

➡ Moroccan internet cafes are common, efficient and cheap (Dh5 to Dh10 per hour), usually with reasonable connection speeds.

➡ Two irritants for many travellers are the widespread French and Arabic (nonqwerty) keyboards, and Moroccan men's common use of internet cafes to view pornographic websites and similar.

➡ Wi-fi is widely available in midrange and top-end accommodation and in many of the better budget options. It is slowly becoming more widespread in destinations that host lots of foreigners.

➡ If you're bringing a laptop, check the power-supply voltage and bring a universal adapter. USB modems are widely available from mobile-phone shops, and cost around Dh100 for one month's internet access. Buy them at a phone shop from Maroc Telecom, Meditel or Inwi (ID is required – take your passport).

TAXES & REFUNDS

Value-added tax (VAT) is a 20% sales tax levied on most goods and services. Some purchases may be eligible for tax refunds when presented with a receipt; this service is available at Casablanca and Marrakesh airports only.

Language Courses

There are courses in Arabic – both modern standard and Moroccan (Darija) – in most major towns in Morocco, with a high concentration in Fez, Rabat and Casablanca, where long- and short-term programs are offered.

Arabophon (☎0535 60 34 75; www.arabophon.com; 80 Rue Jaâfer ben Atiah, Aït Skato; half-/3-day course Dh500/Dh1500, 10-session online course Dh1100) has intensive Moroccan and Modern Standard Arabic courses. Shorter courses are aimed at travellers: the half-day Curious Explorer and three-day Serious Explorer. There are also courses in Tamazight Berber. Lessons are offered in English, French and Spanish.

Jeunesse des Chantiers Marocains (http://perso.menara.ma/youthcamps) offers language and cultural-immersion programs in Marrakesh.

Legal Matters

Drugs Moroccan law prohibits the possession, offer, sale, purchase, distribution and transportation of cannabis (known locally as kif). The penalties for possessing even small amounts of drugs are severe, and include up to 10 years' imprisonment, with no remission for good behaviour, heavy fines and confiscation of your vehicle or vessel. Acquittals in drugs cases are rare.

PRACTICALITIES

➡ **Weights & Measures** The metric system is used in Morocco.

For a list of Moroccan newspapers online, visit www.onlinenewspapers.com/morocco.htm.

➡ A good English-language news website is Morocco World News (www.moroccoworldnews.com).

➡ French-language dailies include the semi-official *Le Matin* (www.lematin.ma), and the opposition *Libération* (www.libe.ma), *L'Opinion* (www.lopinion.ma) and *Al-Bayane*. The weekly *Telquel* (www.telquel.ma) magazine is an excellent news source.

➡ Major European, British and American papers (or their foreign editions) and magazines are available in most of the main cities.

Most Moroccan radio stations broadcast in Arabic or French on AM or FM.

➡ Broadcasting across North Africa and Europe from Tangier, Maghrebi affairs and music station Médi 1 is available via radio (105.3MHz in Marrakesh and 95.3 or 101 in Tangier) and www.medi1.com.

➡ State-run SNRT (www.snrt.ma) has regional and national stations, including the urban Chaine Inter, available via radio (98.8MHz in Marrakesh and 90MHz in Casablanca) and www.chaineinter.ma.

➡ Satellite dishes are everywhere, and pick up foreign stations.

➡ The major TV station, 2M, is partly state-owned and broadcasts in languages including Arabic and French via satellite, analogue and www.2m.ma.

➡ Médi 1's news and current-affairs broadcasts are available via satellite and www.medi1tv.com.

➡ Moroccan DVDs share region 5 with much of Africa and Asia (North America is region 1, Europe is mostly region 2 and Australia is region 4).

Help & advice If you get into trouble, your first call should be to your embassy or consulate; remember that it's not unknown for local police to be in on scams. The London-based Fair Trials International (www.fairtrials.net) provides legal assistance and advocacy to individuals facing criminal charges in a foreign country.

Police If you get arrested by the Moroccan police, you won't have much of a legal leg to stand on. It's unlikely that any interpreter on hand will be of sufficient standard to translate an accurate statement that will, nonetheless, play a vital part in subsequent judicial proceedings. According to some human-rights groups, physical abuse while in custody is not unknown.

Maps

Few decent maps of Morocco are available in the country itself, so get one before leaving home.

Michelin's No 742 (formerly No 959) map of Morocco is arguably the best. It has the following features:

➡ The 1:4,000,000 scale map of the whole country includes the disputed Western Sahara.

➡ Features a 1:1,000,000 enlargement of Morocco.

➡ Features 1:600,000 enlargements of Marrakesh and the High Atlas, Middle Atlas and Fez areas.

➡ Shows sites of weekly markets, kasbahs and *marabouts* (holy mausoleums of local saints).

➡ Notes particularly scenic roads.

➡ Available in major Moroccan cities.
The GeoCenter World Map *Morocco* is preferred by many and has similar, often clearer, detail. Features:

➡ Shows Morocco at a handy 1:800,000 scale

(and the Western Sahara at 1:2,500,000).

➡ Occasionally available in Morocco.
Additionally, several maps include Morocco as part of northwestern Africa. An overlanding classic, Michelin's No 741 (formerly Nos 953 and 153) map covers all of west Africa and most of the Sahara. It has a scale of 1:4,000,000.

Soviet survey maps of Morocco, with scales ranging from 1:100,000 to 1:1,000,000, are available online and at good map shops worldwide. They often have to be ordered and can take up to six weeks to arrive.

Money

The Moroccan currency is the dirham (Dh), which is divided into 100 centimes. You might also occasionally hear older people give prices in rials – an old unofficial usage, whereby one dirham equals 20 rials.

You will find notes in denominations of Dh20, Dh50, Dh100 and Dh200. Coins come in denominations of Dh1, Dh2, Dh5 and Dh10, as well as, less frequently, 10, 20 and 50 centimes. Break big notes whenever possible. Moroccans guard their small change jealously (taxi drivers never seem to have any), and so should you. The Dh20 note is the most useful note in your wallet.

The dirham is a restricted currency, meaning that it cannot be taken out of the country and is not available abroad. The dirham is fairly stable, with no major fluctuations in exchange rates. Euros, US dollars and British pounds are the most easily exchanged currencies.

ATMs

➡ ATMs (guichets automatiques) are the easiest way to access your money in Morocco.

➡ A common sight even in the smallest towns, virtually all accept Visa, MasterCard, Electron, Cirrus, Maestro and InterBank cards. Most banks charge you for withdrawing money from foreign cash machines; check before travelling.

➡ BMCE (Banque Marocaine du Commerce Extérieur), Banque Populaire, BMCI (Banque Marocaine pour le Commerce et l'Industrie), Société Générale and Attijariwafa Bank all offer reliable service.

➡ The amount of money you can withdraw from an ATM generally depends on the conditions attached to your card; machines will dispense no more than Dh2000 at a time.

Black Market

The easy convertibility of the dirham leaves little room for a black market, but you'll find people in the streets asking if you want to exchange money, especially in Tangier, Casa-

blanca and on the borders of (and just inside) the enclaves of Ceuta and Melilla. Avoid these characters; there's no monetary benefit to be had from such transactions and scams are common.

Cash

You'll need to carry some cash with you. Many riads accept payment in euros, but often at less preferential rates than you can get at the bank.

➡ Keep a handful of small denomination notes in your wallet, or just in a pocket (but never a back pocket), for day-to-day transactions.

➡ Put the rest in a money belt or another safe place.

➡ If you're travelling in out-of-the-way places, make sure you have enough cash to last until you get to a decent-sized town.

➡ Keep a small stash of euros in case of emergency.

➡ The endless supply of small coins may be annoying, but they're handy for taxis, tips, guides and beggars.

Credit Cards

➡ Major credit cards are widely accepted in the main tourist centres.

➡ They often attract a surcharge of up to 5% from Moroccan businesses.

➡ The main credit cards are MasterCard and Visa; if you plan to rely on plastic cards, the best bet is to take one of each.

➡ Many large bank branches will give you cash advances on Visa and MasterCard. Take your passport with you.

Money Changers

➡ Any amount of foreign currency may be brought into the country.

➡ It is illegal to import and export dirham.

➡ Banks and exchange bureaus change most currencies, but Australian, Canadian and New Zealand dollars are often not accepted. You'll occasionally be asked for ID when changing money.

➡ Moroccan banking services are reasonably quick and efficient.

➡ Rates vary little from bank to bank, although it doesn't hurt to look around.

➡ Hang on to all exchange receipts. They show you changed money legally, and you'll need them to convert leftover dirham at most Moroccan banks and bureaux de change.

CEUTA & MELILLA

➡ In the Spanish enclaves of Ceuta and Melilla the currency is the euro.

➡ The Moroccan banks on the enclaves' borders exchange cash only.

➡ Banks in Ceuta and Melilla deal in dirham, but at rates inferior to those in Morocco.

Tipping

➡ Tipping is an integral part of Moroccan life; almost any

TIPPING IN MOROCCO

SERVICE	TIP
Baggage handlers	Dh5
Cafe	Dh2
Car-park attendants	Dh3-5; Dh10 for overnight parking
Porters	Dh10-20
Public-toilet attendants	Dh1-2
Restaurant	10%

BARGAINING

Bargaining or haggling is part and parcel of the Moroccan experience, especially for tourist goods and services. If you want to avoid this, many tourist shops have fixed prices.

service can warrant a tip. *Baksheesh*, frequently taken to mean a bribe, generally means money paid for a service rendered, and can include tipping.

➡ Don't be railroaded, but the judicious distribution of a few dirham for a service willingly rendered can make your life a lot easier.

➡ Bear in mind that unskilled workers in Morocco earn less than Dh100 per day.

Travellers Cheques

➡ Travellers cheques are not recommended in Morocco – even large city banks often do not accept them.

➡ If you want to carry some anyway, as a fallback in the event of theft, American Express (Amex), Visa and Thomas Cook cheques are the most useful, and have efficient replacement policies.

➡ Keeping a record of the cheque numbers and those you have used is vital when it comes to replacing lost travellers cheques.

➡ Make sure you keep this record separate from the cheques.

➡ Almost all banks charge commission on travellers cheques. Normally the commission is around Dh10 to Dh20 per cheque; check before changing.

Opening Hours

Although it's a Muslim country, for business purposes, Morocco follows the Monday to Friday working week. Friday is the main prayer day, however, so many businesses take an extended lunch break on Friday afternoon. During Ramadan the rhythm of the country changes, and office hours shift to around 10am to 3pm or 4pm.

Hours often vary between medinas and villes nouvelles (new towns): most businesses close on Sundays in villes nouvelles, whereas those in medinas usually open continuously from about 9am to 7pm except on Fridays.

Medina souqs and produce markets in the villes nouvelles of the bigger cities tend to wind down on Thursday afternoon and are usually empty on Friday. Business hours are highly variable for cafes and snack stands, which can be both seasonal and subject to to the owner's mood.

Souqs in small villages start early and generally wind down before the onset of the afternoon heat.

In cities, pharmacies open all night on a rotating basis. All pharmacies should have a list in their window of that week's night pharmacies.

In the main tourist cities, *bureaux de change* (foreign-exchange bureaus) are often open until 8pm and over the weekend.

*Téléboutique*s (private telephone offices) and internet cafes often stay open late into the night, especially in cities.

Banks 8.30am to 6.30pm Monday to Friday

Bars 4pm till late

Government offices 8.30am to 6.30pm Monday to Friday

Post offices 8.30am to 4.30pm Monday to Friday

Restaurants noon to 3pm and 7pm to 10pm (cafes generally open earlier and close later)

Shops 9am to 12.30pm and 2.30pm to 8pm Monday to Saturday (often closed longer at noon for prayer)

Photography

➡ Morocco is a photographer's dream, but never point your camera at anything that's vaguely military or could be construed as 'strategic'. This includes airports, bridges, government buildings and members of the police or armed forces.

➡ Hide your camera when going through checkpoints in and near the Western Sahara.

➡ It is common courtesy to ask permission before taking photographs of people. Urban Moroccans are generally easygoing about it. Women, older people and rural folk often don't want to be photographed. Respect their right to privacy and don't take photos.

➡ Memory cards and batteries for digital cameras are quite easy to find in photography shops in major cities (especially Marrakesh and Casablanca).

➡ A USB memory stick is useful for backing up photos, but most internet cafes can burn you a CD if needed.

➡ Camera film is increasingly hard to find. If you buy film in Morocco, check expiry dates.

➡ Professional photo labs offer the most professional processing services.

➡ Lonely Planet's *Travel Photography* provides comprehensive advice on taking terrific photos when you're on the road.

Post

➡ Offices of Poste Maroc (www.poste.ma) are distinguished by a yellow 'PTT' sign or the 'La Poste' logo.

➡ *Tabacs*, the small tobacco and newspaper kiosks scattered about city centres, often sell stamps, and have shorter queues.

➡ The postal system is fairly reliable, if not terribly fast.

➡ It takes at least a week for letters to reach European destinations, and two weeks to get to Australia and North America.

➡ Sending post from a city normally gives mail a head start.

➡ Worldwide postcards cost around Dh25 to send.

Sending Parcels

➡ The parcel office, indicated by the sign 'colis postaux', is generally in a separate part of the post-office building.

➡ A 1kg package costs around Dh150 to send via airmail to the UK, Dh180 to the USA and Dh240 to Australia.

➡ Parcels should not be wider, longer or higher than 2m; weight limit varies according to the destination, but it's typically 30kg. To ship goods home, buy a box and a shipping form at the post office and take them to the shop where you purchased your wares.

➡ The shopkeeper knows the product and can wrap and pack the pieces well with newspaper and cardboard.

➡ If you've purchased carpets, the vendor should have rolled and bound them in plastic sacks; if not, return and ask them to do so.

➡ Label the outside of the package in several places with a waterproof pen.

➡ Be very clear about the destination country; marking it in French as well as English helps.

➡ Indicate the value of the contents if you like, but you may be charged taxes at the receiving end.

➡ Don't seal the box! Customs officers at the post office need to view the contents.

➡ Your packages will be weighed and you will be charged Par Avion (air) freight rates unless you specify that you prefer the items to be shipped by land.

➡ The overland service is considerably less expensive but can take three months.

➡ Valuable speciality items such as large furniture may involve customs clearance.

➡ Shopkeepers should be able to arrange clearance and shipping for you, but make sure you keep copies of all documentation in case the goods never arrive.

Express Mail & Couriers

➡ There is usually an Express Mail Service (EMS), also known as Poste Rapide, in the same office as parcel post.

➡ A 500g package costs from Dh350 to send to the UK or Europe, and Dh380 to North America or Australia.

➡ Private courier companies, with offices in the major cities, are faster and more expensive. International couriers with offices throughout Morocco include DHL (www.dhl-ma.com) and TNT (www.tnt.com).

Receiving Mail

➡ Having mail addressed to 'Poste Restante, La Poste Principale' of any big town should not be a problem.

➡ Some offices only hang on to parcels for a couple of weeks before returning them.

➡ You'll need your passport to claim mail and you'll be charged around Dh5 for collection.

Public Holidays

Banks, post offices and most shops shut on the main public holidays, although transport still runs.

New Year's Day 1 January

Independence Manifesto 11 January – commemorates the publication in Fez of the Moroccan nationalist manifesto for independence

Labour Day 1 May

Feast of the Throne 30 July – commemorates King Mohammed VI's accession to the throne

Allegiance of Oued Eddahab 14 August – celebrates the 'return to the fatherland' of the Oued Eddahab region in the far south, a territory once claimed by Mauritania

Anniversary of the King's and People's Revolution 20 August – commemorates the exile of Mohammed V by the French in 1953

Young People's Day 21 August – celebrates the king's birthday

Anniversary of the Green March 6 November – commemorates the Green March

---

ETIQUETTE

Morocco is a famously tolerant country, but following a few rules of etiquette will make your travels smoother and avoid embarrassment.

➡ Greetings are formal. Handshakes are followed by lightly touching your heart with your right hand. Men should wait for Moroccan women to offer handshakes.

➡ Both sexes should dress to cover their shoulders. Outside the cities, where people are more conservative, above-the-knees shorts may be seen as inappropriate.

➡ The left hand is considered unclean as it's used for toilet duties. Don't handle food with your left hand, particularly if eating from a communal dish such as a tajine.

MAJOR ISLAMIC HOLIDAYS

The rhythms of Islamic practice are tied to the lunar calendar, which is slightly shorter than its Gregorian equivalent, so the Muslim calendar begins around 11 days earlier each year.

The following principal religious holidays are celebrated countrywide, with interruptions and changes of time to many local bus services and increased pressure on transport in general. Apart from on the first day of Ramadan, offices and businesses close.

Moulid (or Mouloud) an-Nabi celebrates the birth of the Prophet Mohammed. Children are often given presents.

Eid al-Fitr (Feast of the Breaking of the Fast), also known as Eid as-Sagheer (the Small Feast), is the end of Ramadan. The four-day celebration begins with a meal of *harira* (lentil soup), dates and honey cakes, and the country grinds to a halt during this family-focused period.

Eid al-Adha (Feast of the Sacrifice) sees sheep traded for the ritual sacrifices that take place throughout the Muslim world during this three-day celebration. Also known as the Eid al-Kabeer (Grand Feast), it commemorates Ibrahim's sacrifice. The sheep sacrifice is often a very public event – be prepared for the possibility of seeing blood running in the gutters and sheep heads being flamed over fires in the street.

Because the precise date of an Islamic holiday is in doubt until a few days before the start of that month, the following dates are only approximate.

HOLIDAY	2017	2018	2019	2020
Moulid an-Nabi	1 Dec	20 Nov	9 Nov	29 Oct
Ramadan begins	27 May	16 May	6 May	24 Apr
Eid al-Fitr	25 Jun	16 Jun	4 Jun	24 May
Eid al-Adha	1 Sep	21 Aug	11 Aug	31 Jul
New Year begins (year)	21 Sep (1439)	11 Sep (1440)	31 Aug (1441)	20 Aug (1442)

'reclaiming' the Western Sahara on November 1975

Independence Day 18 November – commemorates independence from France

Safe Travel

Morocco is a pretty safe country that can be navigated with a bit of common sense, but there are a few things to be aware of:

➜ getting lost in winding medina streets

➜ getting hassled by unofficial guides (known as 'faux guides')

➜ the widespread use of marijuana (kif), which is grown in Morocco.

Drugs

➜ Morocco's era as a hippie paradise, riding the Marrakesh Express and all

that, has been consigned to history.

➜ Marijuana (known as kif) is widely grown in the Rif Mountains. It's illegal to buy, sell or consume marijuana or hashish in Morocco. If you're going to smoke kif, don't do it in public and be extremely circumspect about who you buy it from.

➜ If caught with marijuana, you may be looking at a fine and, in the worst case, a prison sentence.

➜ Although some locals smoke marijuana as a recreational pastime, as a tourist you're more vulnerable.

SCAMS & HASSLE

Many Moroccan stories of extortion and rip-offs are drug-related. Recent legislation and a hard government line may have forced deal-

ers to give up their more aggressive tactics, but the hassle has not disappeared.

A traditional ploy is to get you stoned, force you to buy a piece of hash the size of a brick and then turn you over to the police (or at least threaten to). Once you've purchased hash, or even just smoked some, you're unlikely to call the cops, and the hustlers know it.

HOT SPOTS

➜ New arrivals should ignore late-night offers of hashish. These dealers have a sixth sense for greenness, and won't miss an opportunity to squeeze ridiculous amounts of money out of frightened people.

➜ Issaguen (Ketama) and the Rif Mountains are Morocco's kif-growing heartland. Issaguen in particular can be a bag-load of trouble, and is best avoided unless you're accompanied by a reliable guide.

MAJOUN

➜ You may occasionally be offered *majoun*, a traditional sticky fudge made of butter, dried fruits, seeds, spices – and cannabis resin.

➜ A small ball of *majoun* can send you reeling (see Paul Bowles' *Their Heads Are Green* or *Let It Come Down* for descriptions).

➜ Anyone with a slight tendency to paranoia when smoking dope should be aware that this is a common reaction among first-time *majoun* munchers.

SPAIN

Although the Spanish police have a relaxed attitude towards small amounts of cannabis for private use, Spanish customs will come down hard on people entering the country from Morocco in possession of the drug, and you could be done for trafficking.

➜ If you're taking a car across, the chances that it will be searched are high.

➜ Never carry parcels or drive vehicles across borders for other people.

Getting Lost

➜ A minor irritation is the ever-changing street names in Moroccan cities.

➜ For years, there's been a slow process of replacing old French, Spanish and Berber names with Arabic ones.

➜ The result so far is that, depending on whom you talk to, what map you use or which part of the street you are on, you're likely to see up to three different names.

➜ The general Arabic word for street is *sharia*, or *derb* in medinas (*zankat* for smaller ones).

➜ The French avenue, boulevard and *rue* are still common. In the north and far south you'll still find the Spanish *calle* and *avenida*.

➜ In some cases the Arabic seems to have gained the upper hand. This is reflected in our listings; streets appear as *sharia* or *zankat* if local usage justifies it.

MEDINAS

➜ Street names won't help much in the labyrinthine medinas, although in theory a compass might.

➜ If you feel you're getting lost, stick to the main paths (which generally have a fair flow of people going either way) and you'll soon reach a landmark or exit.

➜ Kids will sometimes offer to direct you for a few dirhams; corner shops are better places to ask for directions. Carry a businesscard from your hotel to show.

Theft

On the whole, theft is not a huge problem in Morocco. Travellers can minimise risk by being vigilant (but not paranoid) in the major cities and taking some basic precautions. As the saying goes, 'Trust in God, but tie your camel'.

➜ When wandering around the streets, keep the valuables you carry to a minimum.

TRAVEL DURING RAMADAN

Ramadan Mubarak! (Happy Ramadan!) Ramadan is a lunar month dedicated to *sawm* (fasting) – from sun-up to sundown, the faithful abstain from food, drink, tobacco and sex to concentrate on spiritual renewal – and *zakat* (charity).

Many businesses operate with limited hours and staff, so try to book accommodation, transport and tours in advance. Call offices to ensure someone will be there. Most restaurants close by day; pack lunches or reserve at tourist restaurants. Stores often close in the afternoon; bargaining is better before thirst is felt in the midday heat. For the next few years from 2017, Ramadan falls in the summer, so be prepared for long, hot days.

Sunset streets fill with Ramadan finery, light displays, music, tantalising aromas and offers of sweets. After an *iftar* (fast-breaking meal) of dates, soup or savoury snacks, people gobble sweets until the late-night feast. More visits and sweets follow, then sleep, and an early rise for the *sahur* (meal before the sunrise).

Tourists are exempt from fasting; it's hard enough at home under controlled conditions. To show support, avoid eating, drinking or smoking in public, and grant people privacy at prayer times. Taxi drivers don't appreciate being flagged down minutes before the evening call to prayer announcing *iftar*.

When a new friend offers you sweets or invites you to a feast, you honour by accepting; refusal is crushing. You're not obliged to return the favour or eat the sweets; reciprocate the *zakat* by giving to a local charity perhaps.

GOVERNMENT TRAVEL ADVICE

For the latest travel information refer to the following websites:

➡ **Australian Department of Foreign Affaris** (www.smartraveller.gov.au)

➡ **Canadian Consular Services Bureau** (www.voyage.gc.ca)

➡ **Japanese Ministry of Foreign Affairs** (www.mofa.go.jp)

➡ **New Zealand Ministry of Foreign Affairs and Trade** (www.safetravel.govt.nz)

➡ **UK Foreign & Commonwealth Office** (www.fco.gov.uk/travel)

➡ **US State Department** (www.travel.state.gov)

➡

➡ Keep what you must carry around with you well hidden.

➡ Be vigilant when withdrawing money from ATMs.

➡ External money pouches attract attention. Neck pouches or moneybelts worn under your clothes attract less attention. They are better places to keep your money, passport and other important documents, but keep a small amount of everyday cash easily accessible to avoid having to flash your stash.

➡ If you prefer to keep things in your room (preferably locked inside your suitcase), nine times out of 10 you'll have no trouble.

➡ Rooms in top-end hotels often have safes.

➡ Other hotels sometimes have a safe at reception, where you could stow valuables such as a camera.

➡ Leaving anything in a car, even out of sight, is asking for trouble.

➡ In the large cities, notably Casablanca, there are some desperate people, and physical attacks on foreigners occasionally occur.

➡ Treat the medinas with particular caution at night.

➡ The medinas in Marrakesh, Casablanca and Tangier have a particular reputation for petty theft. A common tactic is for one person to distract you while another cleans out your pockets. Late-night knife crime isn't uncommon.

Touts, Guides & Hustlers

Morocco's notorious hustlers and *faux guides* (unofficial guides) remain an unavoidable part of the Moroccan experience.

➡ *Brigades touristiques* (tourist police) were set up in the principal tourist centres, and anyone suspected of trying to operate as an unofficial guide could face jail and/or a huge fine. This has greatly reduced, if not eliminated, the problem.

➡ You'll generally find *faux guides* hanging around the entrances to the big cities' medinas, and outside bus, train and ferry stations.

➡ Having a siege mentality would be an overreaction. Indeed, when arriving in a place for the first time, you might benefit from the services of a guide, official or otherwise.

➡ Although high unemployment rates drive the numbers of *faux guides*, not all are complete imposters. Many are very experienced and speak half a dozen languages.

➡ Sometimes their main interest is the commission gained from certain hotels or on articles sold to you in the souqs.

DEALING WITH GUIDES

➡ Agree on a price before setting off on a tour.

➡ Set some parameters on what you expect to see and the number of shops you're taken to. If you don't want a shopping expedition included in your tour, make this clear beforehand.

➡ Unofficial guides charge around Dh50 to Dh100 per day. Rates should always be per guide, not per person.

➡ A few dirham will suffice if you want to be guided to a specific location (like a medina exit).

➡ Whatever you give, you'll often get the 'you can't possibly be serious' look. The best reply is the 'I've just paid you well over the odds' look.

➡ Maintain your good humour and, after a couple of days in a place, the hassle tends to lessen considerably.

➡ Official guides can be engaged through tourist offices and some hotels at the fixed price of around Dh250/300 per day (plus tip) for a local/national guide.

➡ It's well worth taking a guide when exploring Fez and Marrakesh medinas. The guide can help you find interesting sights and shops in the melee, stop you from getting lost and save you from being hassled by other would-be guides.

DRIVING & TRANSPORT

➡ Drivers should note that motorised hustlers operate on the approach roads to Fez and Marrakesh. These motorcycle nuisances are keen to find you accommodation and so on, and can be just as persistent as their counterparts on foot.

➡ Travellers disembarking from (and embarking on) the ferry in Tangier may receive some hassle from touts and hustlers.

➡ Arriving by train in cities like Fez and Marrakesh, you may run into 'students' or similar, with the uncanny knowledge that your preferred hotel is closed or full, but they just happen to know this great little place...

Smoking

➡ Smoking is a national pastime in Morocco and nonsmoking restaurants and hotels are rare.

➡ Most popular eateries and cafes have outdoor seating, so the problem is reduced.

➡ Only the very top-end hotels and some riads have a nonsmoking policy.

Women

➡ In Muslim countries, it is often considered unacceptable for women to smoke. This is a cultural rather than religious dictate.

➡ Particularly outside the big cities, you'll seldom see women smokers.

➡ Although most religious leaders condemn smoking, like drinking, as *haram* (forbidden), only during daylight hours of the holy month of Ramadan is the habit seriously eschewed.

➡ This shouldn't affect foreigners too much, although women may wish to refrain from smoking within local homes and be discreet elsewhere.

Telephone

➡ Within Morocco, always dial the local four-digit area code even if you are dialling from the same town or code area.

➡ You can make calls from *téléboutiques* (private telephone offices) and public payphones.

➡ Attendants at *téléboutiques* will usually change small notes into coins.

➡ Most payphones are card-operated.

➡ You can buy *télécartes* (phonecards) at *tabacs* and *téléboutiques*.

➡ Payphones have easy-to-follow instructions.

➡ Calling from a hotel normally doubles the cost of your call.

➡ Moroccan landline numbers start with 05, mobile numbers with 06.

Mobile Phones

GSM phones work on roaming. For unlocked phones, local mobile SIM cards are a cheaper option.

➡ Morocco has three GSM mobile-phone networks: Méditel (www.meditelecom.ma), Maroc Telecom (www.iam.ma) and Inwi (www.inwi.ma).

➡ Coverage is generally excellent, apart from in the mountains and deserts. 4G is available in most cities and many towns.

➡ If your mobile phone is unlocked, buying a prepaid mobile SIM card will likely be cheaper than using your phone on roaming. Offers change frequently, but at the time of research, Dh100 got you around 200 minutes of calls plus up to 10Gb of

data. Not all packages offer international SMS services.

➡ Domestic calls cost from Dh1 per minute, international calls from Dh2.50 per minute.

➡ Calls are cheaper between 8am and 8pm.

➡ You need to show a passport or other form of identification when buying a SIM card.

➡ *Téléboutiques*, newsstands and grocery stores sell scratch cards for topping up your credit. Look out for special deals offering double recharge credit.

Internet Phone Apps

➡ Moroccan telecommunications companies tend to block internet phone call applications (VOIP) like Skype and Whatsapp, for fear of lost revenues.

➡ Messaging services on these services are not blocked. If you want to make calls, however, install a VPN (Virtual Private Network) app on your laptop or smartphone before arriving in Morocco.

Time

Standard Moroccan time is on GMT/UTC.

Daylight saving Daylight saving runs from the end of March to the end of October. The exception is during Ramadan, when Morocco reverts to GMT, but it goes back again to daylight saving afterwards.

EMERGENCY PHONE NUMBERS

Always dial the local four-digit area code even if you are dialling from the same town or code area.

Ambulance	☎15
Fire	☎15
Police (city)	☎19
Gendarmerie (police outside cities)	☎177

USEFUL NUMBERS
. . . .

Morocco country code	☎212
International access code from Morocco	☎00
Directory enquiries	☎160
Spain country code (including Melilla and Ceuta)	☎34

Daylight saving almost always causes confusion in Morocco; watch out for 'city time' and 'medina time' – many people in medinas never bother to change their clocks either way.

Spain If you're travelling to/from Spain (including Ceuta and Melilla), note that Spanish clocks run on GMT+1 (+2 in summer), so double-check your times if catching a ferry.

Local attitudes Time is something that most Moroccans seem to have plenty of; they're not in nearly as much of a hurry to get things done as most Westerners. Rather than getting frustrated by this, learn to go with the flow a little.

Toilets

➡ Flush toilets are a luxury in a country struggling with water shortages. Outside midrange and top-end hotels and restaurants, toilets are mostly of the squat variety.

➡ Squat toilets feature a tap, hose or container of water for sluicing – the idea being to wash yourself (with your left hand) after performing.

➡ There's often no toilet paper (papier hygiénique) so keep a supply with you.

➡ Don't throw the paper into the toilet as the plumbing is often dodgy; instead discard it in the bin provided.

➡ Women will need to take along a plastic bag for disposing of tampons and pads.

➡ Public toilets are rare outside the major cities.

➡ If you find a public toilet, you'll need to bring a tip for the attendant, stout-soled shoes, and very often a nose clip.

Tourist Information

Some cities and larger towns have tourist offices, which are normally repositories of brochures run by uninformed staff and, as such, usually best avoided. Often the receptionist in your hotel or another local will be more helpful than such bureaus. The best tourist offices are found in smaller destinations that are trying to promote themselves.

The Moroccan National Tourist Office (www.visitmorocco.com) runs most tourist offices.

Travellers with Disabilities

Morocco has few facilities for the disabled, but the country is not necessarily out of bounds for travellers with a physical disability and a sense of adventure. Some factors to be aware of:

➡ The awkward nature of narrow medina streets and rutted pavements can make mobility challenging at times even for the able-bodied.

➡ Not all hotels (almost none of the cheaper ones) have lifts, so booking ground-floor hotel rooms ahead of time is essential. Riads invariably have steep, narrow and twisting stairs.

➡ Only a handful of the very top-end hotels have rooms designed for the disabled.

➡ Travelling by car is probably the best transport, though you'll be able to get assistance in bus and train stations (a tip will be required).

➡ Many tour operators can tailor trips to suit your requirements.

➡ Vision- or hearing-impaired travellers are poorly catered for. Hearing loops, Braille signs and talking pedestrian crossings are nonexistent. Download Lonely Planet's free Accessible Travel guide from http://lptravel.to/AccessibleTravel.

Resources

Organisations that disseminate information, advice and assistance on world travel for the mobility impaired include the following:

Access-able Travel Source (www.access-able.com) An information provider for travellers with mobility problems.

Apparleyzed (www.apparleyzed.com) For paraplegic and quadriplegic people and others with spinal-cord injuries, featuring travel information.

Disabled Travelers Guide (www.disabledtravelersguide.com) A general guide for travellers with disabilities.

Mobility International USA (www.miusa.org) Promoting the inclusion of people with disabilities in international programs, with a page of air-travel tips.

Society for Accessible Travel & Hospitality (www.sath.org) Has news, tips and members' articles and blogs.

Visas

➡ Holders of UK, EU, US, Canadian, Australian and New Zealand passports may remain in the country for 90 days on entry.

➡ In all cases, your passport must be valid for at least six months beyond your date of entry.

➡ Nationals of Israel and many Sub-Saharan African countries (including South Africa) must apply in advance for a three-month visa (single/double entry about US$30/50).

➤ Applications are normally processed in 48 hours.

➤ You need three passport photos.

➤ In Morocco's neighbouring countries, there is a Moroccan embassy in Madrid (Spain) and consulates-general in locations including Algeciras; an embassy in Nouakchott (Mauritania) and a consulate-general in Nouâdhibou; and diplomatic missions in Algeria including an embassy in Algiers.

➤ Further information, including a list of Morocco's diplomatic missions, is available from the Moroccan Ministry of Foreign Affairs and Cooperation (www. diplomatie.ma/en).

➤ As visa requirements change, it's a good idea to

VISAS FOR NEIGHBOURING COUNTRIES

Embassies for the following countries are in Rabat.

Algeria

➤ Diplomatic disputes have kept the Morocco–Algeria border closed since 1994. The main border crossing was between Oujda and Tlemcen in Algeria. Don't hold your breath for positive developments on this front.

➤ Visas are required by everyone except nationals of Arab League countries.

➤ Algeria prefers applicants to apply in their country of residence.

Mauritania

➤ Everyone, except nationals of Arab League countries, needs a visa to enter Mauritania.

➤ At the time of writing, Mauritanian visas were being issued at the border for €120, but this frequently changes so check before travelling.

➤ The Mauritanian embassy in Rabat issues 30-day visas (€120). Multiple-entry visas are sometimes available, but purely at the discretion of the consular officer on the day.

➤ Visa applications are received Monday to Thursday 9am to 11am. Arrive well before the embassy opens and be prepared for queues. In the crowd of applicants, there's often someone organised enough to operate a list of those queuing – if so make sure your name is added, to keep your place in the queue.

➤ You need two passport photos and a photocopy of your passport. Local fixers may approach you offering forms and help filling them in (and pointers to the nearest copy shop), for a small fee.

➤ Visa costs and requirements can change regularly – for updates see Sahara Overland (https://sahara-overland.com/) or the North Africa forum at Horizons Unlimited (www. horizonsunlimited.com).

Spain

➤ Spain is in the European Union and the Schengen Area.

➤ The Schengen Area covers 30 European countries, including Spain and all other EU-member countries apart from the UK and the Republic of Ireland.

➤ Ceuta and Melilla, the two Spanish enclaves in Morocco, have the same visa requirements as mainland Spain.

➤ Nationals of EU-member countries do not need a visa to enter Spain.

➤ Nationals of countries including Australia, Canada, Israel, Japan, New Zealand and the USA do not need a Schengen visa to cross a Schengen border.

➤ Your passport will be stamped upon arrival in the zone, and you can then stay for up to 90 days (straight or cumulative) within 180 days. This means, for example, that when you leave the zone at the end of a three-month stay, you are not permitted to re-enter for three months.

➤ For more information, see Spain's Ministry of Foreign Affairs and Cooperation (www.exteriores.gob.es).

check with the Moroccan mission in your country or a reputable travel agency before travelling.

Visa Extensions

➜ Travellers requiring a visa extension find it easiest to head to mainland Spain, or one of the Spanish enclaves in Morocco, and re-enter after a few days.

➜ Although doing a visa run generally presents few problems other than travel costs, it leaves you at the mercy of individual immigration officers on re-entry. Travellers have occasionally come unstuck this way.

➜ An alternative is to apply for a visa extension, issued by the Directorate General of National Security. In practice, these are unobtainable.

➜ Residence (Carte de Sejour) is also available, but it is difficult to get and requires proof of employment.

➜ Go to the nearest police headquarters (Préfecture de Police) to check what documents they require. If possible, take a Moroccan friend to help you deal with the bureaucracy.

International Health Certificate

An international certificate of vaccination (or yellow-fever certificate) is no longer required for entry into Morocco, even if coming from a country where yellow fever is endemic.

We recommend, however, that travellers carry a certificate if they have been in an infected country during the previous month to avoid any possible difficulties with immigration.

There is always the possibility that a traveller without an up-to-date certificate will be vaccinated and detained in isolation at the port of arrival for up to 10 days, or possibly repatriated.

Volunteering

There are many international and local organisations that arrange voluntary work on regional development projects in Morocco.

They generally pay nothing, sometimes not even providing lodging, and are aimed at young people looking for something different to do for a few weeks over the summer.

Some of these organisations are really just summer camps and international exchange programs. Always ask of the organisation 'who benefits?' Good volunteering projects should be aimed at providing outcomes for beneficiaries not the volunteer.

A good starting point is Lonely Planet's The Big Trip, a guide to gap years and overseas adventures that includes a chapter on volunteering and working overseas, as well as a directory of resources.

Organisations

International or local organisations that sometimes have Morocco placements or camps:

Chantiers Sociaux Marocains (CSM; ☎0537 26 24 00; www.csmorocco.org) Rabat-based NGO engaged in nationwide health, education and development projects, with international volunteers aged 18 to 35.

Morocco Exchange (www.moroccoexchange.org) Offers short-term student exchange and travel programs with a focus on cross-cultural education through visiting cities and rural villages. Previous custom-made programs have explored Morocco's medical system, the use of the French language, and women's rights.

Peace Corps (www.peacecorps.gov) Long-established US volunteer scheme with deep roots in Morocco; volunteer programs lasting two years.

Idealist.org Has volunteering and job opportunities in Morocco.

Go Abroad (www.goabroad.com) A good place to start looking for volunteer places, as it provides links to organisations with Moroccan programs.

International Cultural Youth Exchange (www.icye.org) Allows you to search for upcoming Moroccan volunteer opportunities.

Women Travellers

➜ Prior to marriage, many Moroccan men have little opportunity to meet and get to know women outside their family – a major reason why Western women receive so much attention.

THANKS BUT NO THANKS

Faux guides abound in tourist hot-spots, hustling to 'help' you and earn some commission from souvenir shops. The following are useful tactics for dealing with unwanted attention:

➜ Politely decline all offers of help you don't want, and exchange a few good-humoured remarks (preferably in Arabic), but don't shake hands or get involved in any lengthy conversation.

➜ Give the impression that you know exactly where you're going, or explain that you employed a guide on your first day and now you'd like to explore on your own.

➜ Wear dark sunglasses and retreat to a cafe, restaurant or taxi if you're beginning to lose your cool.

➜ In extreme situations, use the word 'police' (shurta or ibulees) and look like you mean it.

→ Frequent unwanted looks and comments can come as something of shock to first-time visitors and the constant attention can be extremely wearing.

→ Some women choose to develop a thick skin and ignore the hassle and it's worth keeping in mind that low-level harassment rarely goes any further.

→ A benefit is that unlike male travellers, you'll have opportunities to meet local women.

→ Tampons can be hard to buy in Morocco. Carrefour is the only dependable supermarket to stock them, and even then offers limited choice.

Dress

→ Dress modestly. It's expected you will cover your shoulders and knees, and avoid low-cut tops altogether.

→ Bikinis are OK on private beaches. Play things by ear in hotel pools – some are fine, at others it will attract unwanted attention.

→ Sunbathing topless on the beach is never appropriate in Morocco.

Havens & Pitfalls

→ If the hassle gets too much, look for the ever-increasing number of places accustomed to having the business of single Moroccan women.

→ The upper floor of a *salon de thé* (teahouse), a restaurant or a hotel terrace are also good bets.

→ Hammams are good male-free zones for a relaxing reprieve.

→ Hotel and public swimming pools usually attract groups of men, whether they be swimming or drinking at a poolside bar.

→ Be aware that some budget hotels double as brothels; any cheap hotel above a popular locals' bar is a likely contender.

ANNOYANCES: MOROCCAN PLUMBING

→ Patience is required when it comes to Moroccan plumbing.

→ In cheap, unclassified hotels without star ratings, trickling cold water and squat toilets are common.

→ Sometimes hot water is enthusiastically promised, but it may be tepid at best and only available at certain times of the day.

→ In rural areas, water is sometimes heated by a wood fire, but this comes at an environmental cost. Wood is expensive, water is often in short supply and deforestation is a major problem in Morocco.

→ In small towns and rural areas the hammam may be a better bet.

→ Take tissues with you when using toilets at roadside restaurants on bus trips, plus a dirham or two to tip the attendant.

→ If you want an alcoholic drink, head to a large hotel rather than braving a bar, as these are generally male-dominated establishments. Local women who frequent watering holes (even the posher ones) are generally prostitutes.

Male Travelling Companions

→ Women travelling with male companions are less likely to experience much of the hassle that solo women inevitably encounter.

→ It may be better to claim to be a married couple rather than just friends (the latter concept is usually greeted with disbelief).

→ If you are a Moroccan woman (or Moroccan in appearance) travelling with your non-Moroccan spouse, it is advisable to carry a copy of your marriage certificate. Premarital sex for Muslims is forbidden and Morocco has a stern attitude to prostitution.

→ For the same reason, if your partner is thought to be Muslim, you may meet with some uncomfortable situations at hotel reception desks. This is less of an issue in larger cities.

Transport

→ Try to sit next to a woman on public transport, especially in grands taxis where you're squeezed in closely, and on trains, where you could potentially be trapped inside a compartment.

→ Many women travel in grands taxis without problems, regardless of where they sit, but you could pay for two seats to get a ride by yourself in the front. It would be considerably more comfortable.

→ Hitchhiking isn't recommended – female travellers looking for free rides may be assumed by male drivers as being prepared to offer sexual favours in return.

Safety Precautions

Women travellers should take a few sensible precautions:

→ Avoid wandering about alone at night, as there's an attitude that all 'good women' should be at home after dark; take a taxi.

→ Avoid walking alone in remote areas such as isolated beaches, forests and sand dunes.

DIFFERENCES FROM STANDARD MOROCCAN TIME

COUNTRY	CAPITAL CITY	DIFFERENCE FROM MOROCCO
Australia	Canberra	+11hr
Canada	Ottawa	-5hr
France	Paris	+1hr
Germany	Berlin	+1hr
Japan	Tokyo	+9hr
Netherlands	Amsterdam	+1hr
New Zealand	Wellington	+13hr
Spain	Madrid	+1hr
UK	London	0hr
USA	Washington DC	-5hr

➡ Wearing dark glasses is good for avoiding eye contact, but don't spend your entire Moroccan journey hiding behind them.

➡ A simple *non merci* or *la shukran* ('no thank you') is much more effective than reacting with aggression (which could be returned in kind).

➡ The key concept is 'respect', something that most Moroccans hold dear. *Hashouma!* ('shame!') can also be used to embarass would-be harassers.

➡ A wedding ring may help you avoid unwanted attention – along with a photo of your 'husband' and 'child'. The fact that you're travelling without them will arouse suspicion, but you could counter this by saying you'll be meeting them at your next destination.

➡ Take extra care at music festivals (and other large gatherings) as complaints have been made of physical harassment

Work

➡ With huge unemployment and a largely out-of-work youthful population, Morocco isn't fertile ground for job opportunities.

➡ A good command of French is a prerequisite and some Arabic would help.

➡ If you secure a position, your employer will have to help you get a work permit and arrange residency, which can be a long process.

➡ There are more volunteering opportunities.

Teaching English

There are a few possibilities for teaching English as a foreign language in Morocco, although they are not terribly well paid. Rabat is one of the best places to start looking.

The best times to try are around September and October (the beginning of the academic year) and, to a lesser extent, early January. Having a TEFL (Teaching English as a Foreign Language) qualification will be useful.

American Language Centers (www.aca.org.ma) Ten schools around the country.

TEFL.com Has a database of vacancies.

Transport

GETTING THERE & AWAY

Entering Morocco

Transport reform has encouraged the explosion of visitor numbers to Morocco. The government's 'open skies' policy has allowed the European budget airlines into the country.

Alternatively, there are numerous ferry services from Europe, a more romantic and lower carbon option than flying, crossing to Africa and connecting Morocco to the European rail network.

Flights, tours and rail tickets can be booked online at www.lonelyplanet.com/bookings.

Air

Direct flights are available from cities across Europe,
the Middle East, West Africa and North America.

Airports & Airlines

Royal Air Maroc (RAM; ☑0890 00 08 00; www.royalairmaroc. com) is Morocco's national carrier. For information about Moroccan airports, visit the website of Office National des Aéroports (www.onda.ma). Casablanca's Mohammed V International Airport is the country's main gateway, followed by Menara airport (Marrakesh). Other important airports include Fes–Saïss (Fez), Ibn Batouta International (Tangier), as well as Ouazazarte, Agadir, Essaouira, Oujda and Nador.

Departure tax is included in the price of a ticket.

Land

Border Crossings

Algeria This border remains closed. Algeria is reluctant to reopen it until the status of the
Western Sahara is resolved – don't hold your breath.

Mauritania The only crossing is in the Western Sahara between Dakhla (Morocco) and Nouâdhibou (Mauritania).

Spain You can cross to mainland Spain via the Spanish enclaves of Ceuta and Melilla in northern Morocco.

Continental Europe

BUS

Buses mostly enter Morocco on the ferries from Spain, with connections from across Europe. Routes are busiest during major Spanish or French holidays, as buses fill up with Moroccans working abroad.

CTM (☑in Casablanca 0800 0900 30; www.ctm.ma) Compagnie de Transports au Maroc, Morocco's national line, operates buses from Casablanca and other Moroccan cities to Spain, France, Belgium, Germany and Italy.

CLIMATE CHANGE & TRAVEL

Every form of transport that relies on carbon-based fuel generates CO_2, the main cause of human-induced climate change. Modern travel is dependent on aeroplanes, which might use less fuel per kilometre per person than most cars but travel much greater distances. The altitude at which aircraft emit gases (including CO_2) and particles also contributes to their climate change impact. Many websites offer 'carbon calculators' that allow people to estimate the carbon emissions generated by their journey and, for those who wish to do so, to offset the impact of the greenhouse gases emitted with contributions to portfolios of climate-friendly initiatives throughout the world. Lonely Planet offsets the carbon footprint of all staff and author travel.

Eurolines (www.eurolines.com) A consortium of European coach companies operating across Europe and into Morocco (partnering with CTM).

Supratours (www.oncf.ma) Run by train company ONCF, has weekly departures from the major northern Moroccan cities to destinations across Spain, France and Italy.

CAR & MOTORCYCLE

European hire companies do not usually permit their vehicles to be driven to Morocco.

If you intend to take a Moroccan hire car to the Spanish enclaves of Ceuta or Melilla, you must have a letter from the hire company authorising you to take the car out of Morocco.

Some hire companies will not allow you to take their car out of the country.

TRAIN

You can travel from London to Tangier via Paris and Madrid in less than 48 hours, with a night in Algeciras (Spain).

Morocco is no longer part of the InterRail/Eurail systems, so you will have to buy tickets locally to add the country onto a European trip.

In Algeciras, the train station is about 10 minutes' walk from the ferry terminals for Morocco. If you arrive during the day you should be able to quickly transfer to the ferries.

A useful resource is the website Man in Seat 61 (www.seat61.com), which has comprehensive, regularly updated information on getting to Morocco by train.

Mauritania

The trans-Saharan route via Mauritania is the main route from North Africa into Sub-Saharan Africa.

From Dakhla follow the N1 south along the coast for 328km to the border, past Nouâdhibou and south to the Mauritanian capital, Nouakchott.

While this route is generally regarded as safe, check both Western Sahara and Mauritania safety advice before travelling. Take plenty of water and food, and set off early in the morning.

This route is entirely paved (apart from a 5km stretch in the no-man's land between the two border posts). Moroccan border formalities are processed at Guergarat. The border is mined, so stay on the road. From the border, it's a 41km drive along the peninsula to Nouâdhibou.

Mauritanian currency (ouguiya, UM) is available at the border, and on the black market in no-man's land.

Vehicle searches and requests for a *petit cadeau* (little present) are not unknown in Mauritania, particularly if officials find alcohol on you (illegal in Mauritania).

Prepare a *fiche* (form) or *ordre de mission* (itinerary) for Mauritanian checkpoints. List all your passport and visa details, occupation, destination and your vehicle's make, colour and registration number. Make plenty of photocopies.

Useful resources include the Moroccan/North African forums at overland motorbiking website Horizons Unlimited (www.horizonsunlimited.com) and Sahara Overland (https://sahara-overland.com).

CAR & MOTORCYCLE

Some stations south of Dakhla may be out of fuel, in particular the last station 50km before the border.

As well as getting stamped in by the police, you need to buy a 30-day temporary-vehicle-import form (€10).

MINIBUS & JEEP

There are ad hoc transport links from Dakhla to the Mauritanian border and beyond. Minibuses and 4WDs leave from the military checkpoint on the road out of Dakhla.

Grands taxis occasionally run to the border from the main station (Dh220). You'll then need to hitch to get to the Mauritanian checkpoint, as walking across the border is forbidden. A lift all the way to Nouâdhibou is preferable, or you will likely have to pay extortionate fees to travel on from the border.

In Dakhla, hotels Erraha and Sahara and the Sahara Regency are good places to pick up information and arrange transport, with locals or overlanders.

From Nouâdhibou, bush taxis to the border/Dakhla cost around UM2000/11,500, leaving in the early morning.

Sea

There are extensive ferry links between northern Morocco and southern Europe, the most popular of which is Algeciras (Spain) to Tangier. Ferries to Tangier now dock at Tanger Med terminal, except for those from Tarifa, 40km from Tangier.

➡ From southern Spain and northern Morocco, you can just turn up at the dock and buy a ticket for the next ferry, but book in advance online during high season (mid-June to mid-September, Christmas, New Year and Easter).

➡ In Tangier and Algeciras, avoid touts who try to guide you towards travel agencies for commission.

➡ Discounts for students and young people with an ISIC card or similar, and InterRail or Eurail passholders are common. Children aged between two and 12 years often travel for half the fare, those aged under two travel free, and over-60s can often get reductions.

➡ Vehicles can be taken on most ferries for an extra fee; bicycles are normally free.

Ferry Routes

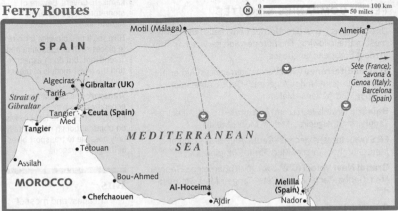

→ Cabins are available on longer crossings.

France

→ The journey from Sète (two hours by train from Marseilles) to Tangier takes 36 hours, to Nador takes 28 hours.

→ There are three sailings weekly to Tangier, and one to Nador.

Gibraltar

→ There's one ferry a week from Tangier Med.

→ The trip takes a similar length of time to sailings to/from Algeciras (90 minutes), and tickets cost the same.

→ Algeciras is a better option as it's a busier port with more choice.

Spain

→ Ferries from Spain to Morocco are plentiful. Tickets start at about €30, depending on season.

→ Hydrofoils and catamarans (also referred to as fast ferries) are used extensively.

→ Spanish passport control is uncomplicated, but non-EU citizens and Schengen visa-holders should make sure they get an exit stamp before boarding the ferry.

→ You need to fill in an embarkation form on board, and get your

passport stamped before disembarking.

ALGECIRAS TO TANGIER MED

→ The busiest crossing between Europe and Morocco. Ferries run at least every 90 minutes, and hourly in the summer. The crossing usually takes an hour.

→ Services typically run from 7am (or 6am in summer) until 10pm, but during peak demand in August 24-hour services aren't unknown.

ALGECIRAS TO CEUTA

→ Several daily high-speed ferries (30 minutes to one hour) leave in both directions.

ALMERÍA TO MELILLA

→ Two sailings most days of the week. Crossings take up to eight hours.

ALMERÍA TO NADOR

→ Daily departures in either direction, taking six/eight hours to Almería/Nador.

BARCELONA TO TANGIER

→ Two companies offer this route to Tangier, one stopping in Barcelona en route from Genoa (Italy).

→ The three weekly sailings; takes about 36 hours.

MÁLAGA TO MELILLA

→ The daily (apart from Sunday) service is normally an afternoon/night ferry between Motil (Málaga) and Melilla.

→ It takes up to eight hours.

TARIFA TO TANGIER

→ Catamarans leave every hour or so and cross the strait in 40 minutes, making this the fastest and most practical route.

→ The fare includes a free bus transfer to Algeciras on presentation of your ferry ticket.

→ The transfer takes 50 minutes, making the trip via Tarifa a faster way to get to Algeciras than the slower direct ferries.

MOTIL TO AL-HOCEIMA

→ Naviera Armas has summer services between Motil and Al-Hoceima.

→ Sailings are every Saturday.

Italy

→ Two companies sail the Mediterranean from Italy to Tangier, from Genoa (via Barcelona) and Savona.

→ The twice-weekly Genoa service takes 48 hours.

→ The weekly Savona service takes 48 hours.

FERRY COMPANIES & ROUTES

Direct Ferries (www.directferries.com) sells tickets for most of the following. The Europe-wide service has sites in most European languages.

Trasmediterranea (www.trasmediterranea.es) Almería–Melilla, Almería–Nador, Algeciras–Ceuta, Algeciras–Tangier Med, Málaga–Melilla.

Baleària (www.balearia.com) Algeciras–Ceuta, Algeciras–Tangier Med, Algeciras-Melilla, Motril-Melilla.

FRS (www.frs.es) Algeciras–Ceuta, Algeciras–Tangier Med, Gibraltar–Tangier Med, Tarifa–Tangier.

Grandi Navi Veloci (GNV; www.gnv.it) Barcelona–Tangier Med, Genoa–Tangier Med, Sète–Tangier Med, Sète–Nador.

Grimaldi Lines (www.grimaldi-lines.com) Savona–Tangier Med, Barcelona–Tangier Med.

GETTING AROUND

Getting around Morocco is pretty straightforward – transport networks between towns are good, and even off the beaten track there's often something going your way. Royal Air Maroc offers internal flights, the rail network is excellent in linking the major cities (with a high-speedTGV line between Tangier and Casablanca currently under construction), and large bus companies such as CTM are comfortable and efficient. Local networks are cheaper and more cheerful and do the job.

Car hire is relatively expensive but gives you the most freedom, although navigating the big cities can be stressful. Good sealed roads are generally the order of the day, with much investment being poured into areas like the Rif to improve their connectivity. Roads in remote mountain and desert areas are often just a *piste* (unsealed track or road).

Air

➡ National carrier **Royal Air Maroc** (RAM; ☐0890 00 08 00; www.royalairmaroc.com) is the main domestic airline. All flights are via its hub at Mohammed V International Airport, Casablanca.

➡ RAM serves Tangier, Nador, Oujda, Fez, Er-Rachidia, Marrakesh, Essaouira, Agadir, Laâyoune and Dakhla.

➡ Flying is relatively expensive but may be worth it if you are pushed for time. The 2¼-hour flight from Casablanca to Dakhla costs from Dh980, compared with Dh600 for a 1st-class seat on the 32-hour CTM bus journey.

➡ You can buy tickets online and at RAM offices and travel agencies.

➡ English is spoken at RAM's call centre.

Bicycle

Mountain biking can be a great way of travelling in Morocco. There are plenty of opportunities for getting off the beaten track, with thousands of kilometres of remote *pistes* to be explored.

Hazards Surfaced roads are generally well-maintained once completed, but they tend to be narrow and in less-frequented areas may have jagged edges, which can be hairy given the kamikaze drivers. Beware of stone-throwing children in remote areas.

Hire You'll find bicycles for hire in places such as Essaouira and Taroudannt, but don't expect to find the latest models of mountain bike.

Transport Bus companies will generally carry bicycles as luggage for an extra fee. Likewise on trains, although it's generally only possible to transport bikes in the goods wagon.

Bus

The cheapest and most efficient way to travel around the country, buses are generally safe, although drivers sometimes leave a little to be desired.

Bus stations Some Moroccan bus stations are like madhouses, with touts running around calling any number of destinations of buses about to depart. Most cities and towns have a single central bus station (*gare routière*), but Supratours and CTM often maintain separate terminals, and often have offices outside the station. Occasionally, there are secondary stations for a limited number of local destinations.

Touts Touts will happily guide you to a ticket booth (and take a small commission from the company). Always double-check that their recommended service really is the most comfortable, direct and convenient option.

Luggage Bus stations in the main cities have left-luggage depots (*consigne*), sometimes open 24 hours. Padlock your bags. More often than not you'll be charged for baggage handling – Dh5 is common.

Costs Bus travel is cheap considering the distances covered. CTM fares from Casablanca to Marrakesh, Fez and Tangier are Dh90, Dh100 and Dh145 respectively.

Reservations Where possible, and especially if services are infrequent or do not originate in the place you want to leave, book ahead for CTM and Supratours buses. Particularly busy routes are Marrakesh–Essaouira and Casablanca–Marrakesh, where you may need to reserve seats two days in advance in high season.

Daytime journeys Many buses have rather meagre curtains, so to avoid melting in the sun, pay attention to where you sit. Heading from north to south, sit on the right in the morning and the left in the afternoon; east to west, sit on the right, or on the left if travelling from west to east. You will often be assigned a seat when you purchase your ticket, but you can ask to choose a place.

Night-time journeys Operating on many intercity routes, night buses can be both quicker and cooler, although risks from other road users are considerably heightened.

Stops Bus trips longer than three hours incorporate a scheduled stop to stretch your legs and grab a snack. Buses are sometimes delayed at police checkpoints for about 10 minutes – longer than grands taxis, whose local drivers usually know the police.

Bus Operators
CTM
With the most comprehensive nationwide network, **CTM** (☑ in Casablanca 0800 0900 30; www.ctm.ma) serves most destinations of interest to travellers. Established in 1919, it's Morocco's oldest bus company.

➧ On CTM buses, children aged four years and over pay full fares, which tend to be 15% to 30% more expensive than most other lines – comparable to 2nd-class fares on normal trains.

➧ Tickets can normally be purchased in advance; check departures with the online timetable.

➧ CTM coaches are modern and comfortable, with air-conditioning and heating (they sometimes overdo both).

➧ Some routes between major cities offer a premium service, with comfier seats, more legroom and free wi-fi. Fares are around 40% higher than the regular service.

➧ There is an official Dh5-per-pack baggage charge on CTM buses.

➧ Once you have bought your ticket, you get a baggage tag, which you hand over when you've reached your destination.

SUPRATOURS
The ONCF train company runs **Supratours** (www.oncf.ma) to complement its rail network. For example, train passengers continuing south from Marrakesh link up at the station with coaches to destinations including Agadir and Ouarzazate. Supratours also runs the busy Marrakesh–Essaouira coach service.

➧ It's possible, at train ticket offices, to buy a ticket covering a complete trip with both rail and bus components.

➧ On trains, travellers with tickets for connecting buses have priority.

➧ Supratours is similar to CTM in terms of both its fares and the comfort of its buses. Check departures with the online timetable.

OTHER COMPANIES
In the south of the country, Satas and SAT are good second-tier choices, as is Trans Ghazala in the north.

At the bottom end of the price range, and on shorter routes, there are a fair number of two-bit operations with one or two well-worn buses. These services depart when sufficiently full, and frequently stop to recruit more passengers.

Car & Motorcycle
Morocco is a country made for touring, and offers freedom to explore the more unusual routes in your own time.

Daylight driving is generally no problem and not too stressful, though Moroccan drivers often need to be treated with caution and safe distances.

The roads connecting Morocco's main centres are generally good, and there's an expanding motorway network (which attract small tolls). The main routes:

➧ From Tangier down the Atlantic Coast to Safi (via Casablanca and Rabat)

➧ From Rabat inland to Oujda via Meknès and Fez

TRAVELLER ETIQUETTE
When travelling on public transport, it's considered both selfish and bad manners to eat while those around you go without. Always buy a little extra to offer to your neighbours.

Next comes the ritual. If you offer food, etiquette dictates that your fellow passengers should decline it. It should be offered a second time, a little more persuasively, but again it will be turned down. On a third, more insistent offer, your neighbours are free to accept the gift if they wish to.

If you are offered food, but you don't want it, it's good manners to accept a small piece anyway, and to pat your stomach contentedly to indicate that you are full. In return for participating in this ritual, you should be accorded great respect, offered protection and cared for like a friend.

➜ From Casablanca south to Agadir via Marrakesh

➜ From Tangier to Oujda via Tetouan and Nador

Bringing Your Own Vehicle

➜ Every vehicle should display the nationality plate of its country of registration, and you must always carry proof of ownership of a private vehicle. Moroccan law requires a Green Card (carte verte, or International Motor Insurance Card), as proof of insurance. A warning triangle (to be used in case of breakdown) is compulsory.

➜ Obtain insurance and a Green Card before leaving home. Otherwise local insurance (assurance frontière), costing about Dh650 for 10 days, must be purchased at the ferry port or a nearby broker (bureau d'assurance).

➜ Ask for the optional constat amiable form, which both parties fill out in the event of a minor road accident. They can also be purchased at tabacs in cities.

➜ At the port, or on the ferry on longer crossings, you must also fill in the TVIP form (temporary vehicle importation declaration – declaration d'admission temporaire de moyens de transport), valid for six months. Present this form when you (and your vehicle) leave the country. You can also download the form from the website of Morocco Customs (www.douane.gov. ma), where it's referred to as D16TER.

➜ There is no need for a carnet de passage en douane for temporarily importing your vehicle to Morocco.

Driving Licences

➜ International driving permits are recommended for Morocco by most automobile bodies, but many foreign, including EU, licences are accepted

provided they bear your photograph.

➜ You must carry your licence or permit as well as your passport when driving.

Fuel & Spare Parts

Availability The country is well served with petrol stations, although they're fewer and further between in Western Sahara. If you're travelling off the beaten track, refuel at every opportunity. Keep a close eye on the gauge in the southern desert and fill up wherever you get a chance, as stations don't always have supplies of fuel.

Costs Leaded and less-common unleaded (sans plomb) petrol cost around Dh10 per litre and diesel (gasoil) is around Dh11. In the Western Sahara, tax-free petrol is about 30% cheaper. Fuel in the Spanish enclaves of Ceuta and Melilla is comparably priced to Morocco.

Parts Moroccan mechanics are generally good and decent-sized towns should have at least one garage. If you can fit replacement parts yourself, ask a Moroccan friend to help you buy the parts, as this may help to keep the price closer to local levels.

Hire

Costs Renting a car costs about Dh300 per day for a week or so with unlimited mileage. For longer rentals, lower daily rates are sometimes available. Pre-booking gives the cheapest deals. Most companies demand a (returnable) cash deposit (Dh3000 to Dh5000) or take an impression of your credit card.

Operators With international firms such as Hertz, Budget, Europcar, National and Avis, you can pre-book online. There are also numerous local agencies.

Potential pitfalls Make sure you understand what is included in the price and what your liabilities are. Always check the car's condition before signing up, and make sure it comes with a spare tyre, tool kit and full documentation – including insurance cover. Keep the car's documents and your licence with you, rather than in the car, as you'll

need them if the car is stolen or damaged. Keep receipts for oil changes or mechanical repairs; these costs should be reimbursed.

Insurance and tax Insurance must, by law, be sold along with all rental agreements. Make sure that prices include collision damage, insurance and tax (20%). You should also take out Collision Damage Waiver insurance, typically about Dh35 to Dh60 a day (often with an excess of up to Dh5000). Super Collision Damage Waiver, which eliminates or minimises the excess, may be available for an extra Dh60 or so a day.

Piste Unless you hire a 4WD, your rental agreement will probably not allow off-road (piste) driving, making you liable for potential damages.

Motorcycle

➜ Motorcycle touring is popular, but many bikes are unfamiliar in Morocco, particularly those with larger capacity engines, so repairs can be tricky.

➜ Carry a good tool kit and all necessary spares, including cables and levers, inner tubes, puncture repair kit, tyre levers, pump, fuses, chain, washable air filter and cable ties.

➜ Some insurance policies do not allow foreign motorcycle licences to be used in Morocco.

➜ See Horizons Unlimited (www.horizonsunlimited. com) for detailed advice on biking in the region.

Parking

➜ Parking zones are often watched by gardiens de voitures (car-park attendants). Payment of a few dirhams gives a trouble-free parking experience.

➜ In the big city centres, parking tickets are issued from kerbside machines (Dh2 to Dh3 per hour for a maximum stay of two hours). Parking is free on Sundays.

➡ Parking is not allowed at kerbsides painted in red-and-white stripes. Stopping is not allowed on green-and-white stripes.

➡ Fines for illegally parked cars can reach Dh1500.

Roadblocks

➡ Police control points are common on main roads in and out of most sizeable towns.

➡ Foreigners are unlikely to be stopped, but it's still a good idea to slow down and put on your best smile.

➡ Roadblocks are also common in sensitive areas like the Western Sahara, the Rif Mountains around the cannabis-producing region of Ketama, and the road to Figuig near the Algerian border.

➡ Police are more vigilant in these areas, but at most, you'll be asked to show your passport, driving licence and the vehicle's papers, and asked the purpose of your visit and destination.

Road Hazards

Road accidents are as common in Morocco as offers of mint tea from carpet sellers. Treat all vehicles as ready to veer out and cut you off at inopportune moments.

Cyclists and pedestrians often have poor traffic awareness. Roads are often busy with people (including groups of schoolchildren), bicycles, horse and carts, donkeys and so on.

Desert In the *hammada* (stony desert), tar roads sometimes disappear without warning, replaced by stretches of sand, gravel and potholes. If a strong *chergui* (dry, easterly desert wind) is blowing and carrying a lot of dust, you'll have to wait until it eases off if you don't want to do your car considerable damage.

Mountains High and Middle Atlas passes are often closed due to snow in winter. Seek local advice before travelling, or check the road signs along the routes.

Medinas Entering cities and towns, park outside the medina or find out if the route to your accommodation is easily drive-able – narrow medina streets weren't designed for cars.

Night Driving at night is particularly hazardous: it's legal (and very common) for vehicles travelling under 20km/h to drive without lights.

Road Rules

➡ Drive on the right-hand side of the road.

➡ Give way to traffic entering a roundabout from the right when you're already on one.

➡ The fine for missing a red stop sign is Dh700.

➡ The speed limit in built-up areas is 40km/h, and 100km/h outside the towns (120km/h on motorways). Police with radar guns are common, so watch your speed.

➡ It's the law to wear a seatbelt.

➡ Tolls apply on the motorways – for example, Rabat–Tangier is about Dh60 and Rabat–Casablanca is Dh20. You take a ticket upon entering the motorway and pay at the end.

➡ In the event of an accident, especially involving injuries, drivers are officially required to remain at the scene. Vehicles cannot be moved until the police have arrived – this may take hours.

➡ Pick up a *constat amiable* form in case you have an accident; they can be purchased at *tabacs* in cities.

Local Transport

Bus

➡ The bigger cities have public bus services.

➡ Tickets are typically Dh5.

➡ Buses can be ludicrously overcrowded and routes often hard to discern.

➡ Petits taxis are often an easier and faster option.

Grand Taxi

The Mercedes saloons you'll see on Moroccan roads and gathered near bus stations are shared taxis (grands taxis in French or *taxiat kebira* in Arabic). On many routes the older cars are being replaced with newer people carriers.

The Ziz and Drâa Valleys, the Tizi n'Test and the Rif Mountains, all scenic areas not well-served by buses, are good to visit in a taxi.

Routes Grands taxis link towns to their neighbours, often in a relay system that may necessitate changing a few times on longer journeys. Taxis sometimes ply longer routes but these services are rarer and usually leave first thing in the morning.

Seats Grands taxis take six cramped passengers (two in the front, four in the back) and leave when full. It can often be advantageous to pay for two seats to get the taxi going earlier, and give yourself more space. This is particularly useful for lone women, as you should get the front seat to yourself.

Fares The fixed-rate fares are a little higher than bus fares, but still very reasonable. Make it clear you want to pay for *une place* (one spot) in a *taxi collectif* (shared taxi). Another expression that helps explain that you don't want the taxi to yourself is *ma'a an-nas* (with other people). If you've got particularly heavy/bulky luggage, there might be a surcharge.

Private hire Hiring an entire taxi is sometimes a good option – especially if you're travelling with a small group, or you want to travel along an unpopular route without waiting hours for other passengers. The fare should be six times the cost for one place. If you'll be travelling through a scenic area, make sure plans for stopping en route are clear.

Hazards Grand-taxi drivers often have a boy-racer mentality. Overtaking on blind corners can be a badge of honour, and speed limits are only adhered to when there's a police roadblock in sight. Night-time journeys are best avoided. Seatbelts are a rarity – and questioning this may be taken as a slur on your driver's skills.

Petit Taxi

➔ Cities and bigger towns have local petits taxis and are a different colour in every city.

➔ Petits taxis are licensed to carry up to three passengers, but are not permitted to go beyond the city limits.

➔ Petits taxis are metered in cities, less commonly so in smaller towns. To ask in French for the meter to be switched on, say 'tourne le conteur, si'l vous plaît'. Where taxis are not metered, agree on a price beforehand.

➔ If the driver refuses to use the meter and won't give you a price, ask to stop and get out. Most petit-taxi drivers are perfectly honest, but those in Marrakesh and Casablanca are notoriously greedy with tourists.

➔ Multiple hire is common. The price should be the same whether you hail an empty taxi and pick up other passengers en route, or there are already others in a taxi you wave down, or you travel alone.

➔ From 8pm (often 9pm in summer) there is normally a 50% surcharge.

Pick-up Truck & 4WD

➔ In more remote areas, especially the Atlas Mountains, locals travel between villages in Berber camionettes (pick-up trucks), old vans or the back of trucks.

➔ When travelling between remote towns and villages, the best time to find a lift is early on market days (generally once or twice a week). Waits for departures can be considerable.

➔ On remote pistes that would destroy normal taxis, 4WD taxis operate.

Tram

Casablanca and Rabat both have new and modern tram networks, which are an excellent and cheap way to explore those cities. A third tram network is reportedly planned for Marrakesh.

Tours

Atlas Sahara Trek (www.atlas-sahara-trek.com) Winter camel-treks to Erg Chigaga and summer hikes into the M'Goun valley.

Authentic Morocco (www.authentic-morocco.com) This reliable company supports local communities and practises low-impact tourism, offering itineraries from camel treks to tours of Roman ruins.

Desert Majesty (www.desert-majesty.com) A highly recommended local agency offering trips to the High Atlas and the desert. Airport pick-ups, multilingual guides originating in Erfoud, Merzouga, M'Hamid and Taouz and reassuringly safe drivers are offered at competitive prices. Booking queries are handled by Felicity who is fluent in English, German, French and Darija.

Equatorial Travel (www.equatorialtravel.co.uk) Tailor-made trips and set itineraries, focused on areas including music, photography and walking, run by a small agency based on the fair-trade concept.

Journeys Elite (www.journeyselite.com) Offers tailor-made trips such as Anti Atlas by 4WD, and High Atlas gorges to Erg Chebbi.

Nature Trekking Maroc (www.maroctrekking.com) Off-the-beaten-track trekking, horse riding, mountain biking, skiing and 4WD trips.

Wildcat Adventures (www.wildcat-bike-tours.co.uk) Offers road- and mountain-bike tours in the High Atlas and Anti Atlas, plus a bike-trek-camel itinerary.

Wilderness Travel (www.wildernesstravel.com) Much-applauded culture, wildlife and hiking specialist, with itineraries from High Atlas treks to cruising the coastline.

Yallah (www.yallahmorocco.com) The decade-old company offers tailor-made tours plus two itineraries covering the imperial cities and southern Morocco, both ending in luxury in Marrakesh.

Train

Morocco's excellent train network is one of Africa's best, linking most of the main centres. Trains are reasonably priced, and preferable to buses where available. Trains are comfortable, fast and generally run to their timetables. The ONCF (Office National des Chemins de Fer; www.oncf.ma) runs the network.

➔ There are two main lines: Tangier down to Marrakesh via Rabat and Casablanca; and Oujda or Nador in the northeast down to Marrakesh, passing Fez and Meknès before joining the line from Tangier at Sidi Kacem.

➔ A high-speed (TGV) line to link Tangier, Rabat and Casablanca is under construction and due to open in July 2018. When finished, the travel time between Tangier and Casablanca will be reduced from five hours to just over two hours, with trains travelling at 320km/h. For more information see www.tgvmaroc.ma.

➔ Also operated by ONCF, Supratours buses link many destinations to the train network.

➔ Trains are particularly convenient around Casablanca and Rabat, with services leaving every 30 minutes between the two cities.

➔ The overnight Tangier–Marrakesh and Oujda–Casablanca trains have sleeping cars.

Supratours & Train Network

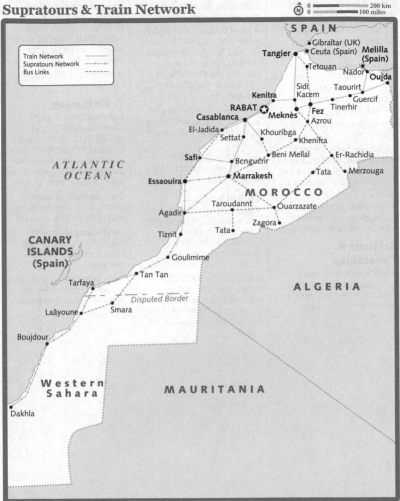

Classes & Costs

There are two types of train, and the main difference between the two is comfort, rather than speed:

➡ *Rapide* (Train Rapide Climatisé, TCR) – standard for intercity services.

➡ *Ordinaire* (Train Navette Rapide, TNR) – less comfortable, without air-conditioning, apart from the double-decker TNR Rabat–Casablanca shuttle.

Mostly late-night and local services.

Additional information:

➡ Prices given here are for *rapide* trains (*ordinaire* trains are around 30% cheaper).

➡ First- and 2nd-class fares are available, with six seats in 1st-class compartments and eight in 2nd class.

➡ First-class tickets include a reserved seat, while in 2nd class you just sit in an empty seat.

➡ Second class is more than adequate on short journeys. For longer trips, the extra for 1st class is worth paying.

➡ Shuttle services operate regularly between Kenitra, Rabat, Casablanca and Mohammed V International Airport, and they supplement the *rapide* services on this line.

Sample 2nd-class fares:

➡ Casablanca to Marrakesh (Dh95, three hours)

→ Rabat to Fez (Dh85, 2 ½ hours)

→ Tangier to Marrakesh (Dh216, 9½ hours) Additional information:

→ All journeys in sleeping cars cost Dh370 in a four-bed couchette, and Dh480/690 for a single/double compartment.

→ Children aged under four travel free.

→ Children between four and 12 years get a discount (normally 50%, less in a few cases including sleeping cars).

→ At weekends travellers get a 25% discount on return trips, on major-line trains.

Stations & Timetables

→ Stations aren't usually well signposted and announcements (in both French and Arabic) are frequently inaudible, so keep an eye out for your stop.

→ Most stations are located in the ville nouvelle. In cities such as Tangier, Marrakesh, Fez and Rabat, the main stations are sleek affairs with free wi-fi and decent restaurants.

→ Stations usually have left-luggage depots, which only accept luggage that can be locked.

→ Check on the ONCF website (www.oncf.ma) for times and prices.

Tickets

→ Buy tickets at the station, as a supplement is charged for buying tickets on the train. Automatic ticket machines are becoming more widespread at stations.

→ Buy your ticket the day before you want to travel if possible, particularly if you want to travel 1st class. Second-class seats cannot be reserved. First-class tickets can be bought up to a month before travel – advisable if travelling during major holidays, and for sleeper services.

→ Inspectors check tickets on the trains.

Train Passes

Rail Pass This is available for seven/15/30 days (Dh600/1170/2100 to travel in 2nd class, Dh900/1600/3150 for 1st class). Pass prices drop for travellers aged under 26, and again for those under 12 years.

Carte Chahab (six months, Dh265) If you're under 26, this offers 25% to 50% discounts.

Carte Hikma (six months, Dh105) For those aged over 60, this offers 25% to 50% discounts.

Carte Ousraty (one year, Dh50 per person) For families, this offers 10% to 25% on group tickets.

Health

Prevention is the key to staying healthy in Morocco, and a little planning before departure will save you trouble later. With luck, your worst complaint on your trip will be a bad stomach; infections are usually associated with poor living conditions and poverty, and can be avoided with a few precautions. Car accidents are a common reason for travellers to need medical help. Medical facilities can be excellent in large cities, but in more remote areas may be basic.

BEFORE YOU GO

Insurance

➡ Adequate health insurance is vital when travelling to Morocco. The national health service isn't always great and the few good private hospitals are expensive.

➡ You may prefer a policy that pays the medical facility directly rather than you having to pay on the spot and claim later, although in practice most Moroccan doctors and hospitals insist on payment up front.

➡ If you have to claim later, make sure you keep all documentation.

➡ Carry proof of your insurance with you; this can be vital for avoiding any delays to treatment in emergency situations.

➡ Some policies ask you to call (reverse charge) a centre in your home country, which makes an immediate assessment of your problem; keep your insurer's emergency telephone number on you.

➡ Find out which private medical service your insurer uses in Morocco so that you can call them direct in the event of an emergency.

➡ Your policy should ideally cover emergency air evacuation home, or transport by plane or ambulance to a hospital in a major city, which may be essential for serious problems.

➡ Some policies offer lower and higher medical-expense options; the higher ones are chiefly for countries such as the USA, which have extremely high medical costs.

RECOMMENDED VACCINATIONS

Although no specific vaccinations are required for Morocco, America's Centers for Disease Control and Prevention (CDC) suggests the following as routine:

➡ diphtheria

➡ tetanus

➡ measles

➡ mumps

➡ rubella

➡ polio

The CDC also suggests the following for Morocco:

➡ hepatitis A and B

➡ typhoid

➡ rabies

Don't leave health matters until the last minute: some vaccines don't ensure immunity for two weeks, so visit a doctor four to eight weeks before departure.

Before leaving home, ensure that all your routine vaccination cover is complete. Ask your doctor for an international certificate of vaccination, listing all the vaccinations you've received.

Medical Checklist

Consider packing the following items in your medical kit:

➡ antibiotics (if travelling off the beaten track)

➡ antibacterial hand gel

➡ antidiarrhoeal drugs (eg loperamide)

➡ paracetamol or aspirin

➡ anti-inflammatory drugs (eg ibuprofen)

➡ antihistamines (for hay fever and allergic reactions)

➡ antibacterial ointment (eg Bactroban) for cuts and abrasions

➡ steroid cream or cortisone (for allergic rashes)

➡ bandages, gauze and gauze rolls

➡ adhesive or paper tape

➡ scissors, safety pins and tweezers

➡ thermometer

➡ pocket knife

➡ DEET-containing insect repellent

➡ insect spray for clothing, tents and bed nets

➡ sun block

➡ oral rehydration salts (eg Dioralyte)

➡ iodine or other water-purification tablets

➡ syringes and sterile needles (if travelling to remote areas)

Bring medications in their original, clearly labelled containers. A signed and dated letter from your physician describing your medical conditions and medications, including generic names, is also helpful. If carrying syringes or needles, ensure you have a physician's letter documenting their medical necessity. See your dentist before a long trip; carry a spare pair of contact lenses and glasses (and take your optical prescription with you).

Other Preparations

Those heading to very remote areas may like to do a first-aid course, such as those offered by the American Red Cross and St John's Ambulance. Particularly if you're going trekking, you could take a wilderness medical training course, such as that offered by the Royal Geographical Society (www.rgs.org).

Websites

Useful to consult prior to departure:

CDC (www.cdc.gov/travel) US government website.

Health Canada (http://www.hc-sc.gc.ca/hl-vs/travel-voyage/index-eng.php) Canadian government website.

International Association for Medical Advice to Travellers (www.iamat.org) Gives access to its online database of doctors with recognised training.

NHS (www.fitfortravel.nhs.uk) UK government website.

Smarttraveller (www.smarttraveller.gov.au) Australian government website.

WHO (www.who.int/ith)

IN MOROCCO

Availability & Cost of Health Care

Primary medical care is not always readily available outside major cities and towns. Your hotel may be able to recommend the nearest source of medical help, and embassy websites sometimes list doctors and clinics. In an emergency, contact your embassy or consulate.

Pharmacies These are generally well stocked, and pharmacists can provide advice (usually in French) covering common travellers' complaints. They can sell over-the-counter medication, often including drugs only available on prescription at home, and advise when more specialised help is needed. Double-check any unfamiliar purchases; readers have reported receiving incorrect and potentially dangerous medication for their conditions.

Doctors and clinics If you are being treated by a doctor or at a clinic, particularly outside the major cities, you will often be expected to purchase medical supplies on the spot – even including sterile dressings or intravenous fluids.

Dental care Standards are variable – Marrakshi street dentists around the Djemaa el-Fna aren't recommended! Travel insurance doesn't usually cover dental work other than emergency treatment.

Infectious Diseases

Hepatitis A

Spreads Through contaminated food (particularly shellfish) and water.

Symptoms and effects Jaundice, dark urine, a yellow colour to the whites of the eyes, fever and abdominal pain. Although rarely fatal, it can cause prolonged lethargy and delayed recovery.

Prevention Vaccine (Avaxim, VAQTA, Havrix) is given as an injection, with a booster extending the protection offered. Hepatitis A and typhoid vaccines can also be given as a combined single-dose vaccine (hepatyrix or viatim).

Hepatitis B

Spreads Through infected blood, contaminated needles and sexual intercourse.

Symptoms and effects Jaundice and liver problems (occasionally failure).

Prevention Travellers should make this a routine vaccination, although Morocco gives hepatitis B vaccination as part of routine childhood vaccination. It is given singly, or at the same time as hepatitis A.

HIV & AIDS

Morocco has an HIV infection rate of 0.15%, primarily among men who have sex with men, sex workers and intravenous drug users.

Spreads Through infected blood and blood products; sexual intercourse with an infected partner; 'blood to blood' contacts, such as through contaminated instruments during medical, dental, acupuncture and other body-piercing procedures, or sharing used intravenous needles.

Leishmaniasis

Spreads Through the bite of an infected sandfly or dog. It may be found in rural areas in the Atlas Mountains, where sandflies are more prevalent between June and October.

Symptoms and effects Slowly growing skin lump or sores. It may develop into a serious, life-threatening fever, usually accompanied by anaemia and weight loss.

Prevention and treatment Avoid sandfly bites. There is no vaccine, but treatment with an antimonial drug such as Glucantime or Pentostam is straightforward, usually involving an injection.

Rabies

Spreads Through bites or licks on broken skin from an infected animal. Rabies is endemic to Morocco.

Symptoms and effects Initial symptoms are pain or tingling at the site of the bite with fever, loss of appetite and headache. If untreated, both 'furious' and less-common 'dumb' rabies are fatal.

Prevention and treatment People travelling to remote areas, where a reliable source of post-bite vaccine is not available within 24 hours, should be vaccinated.

Any bite, scratch or lick from a warm-blooded, furry animal should immediately be thoroughly cleaned. If you have not been vaccinated and you get bitten, you will need a course of injections starting as soon as possible after the injury. Vaccination does not provide immunity, it merely buys you more time to seek medical help.

Tuberculosis

Spreads Through close respiratory contact and, occasionally, infected milk or milk products.

Symptoms and effects Can be asymptomatic, although symptoms can include a cough, weight loss or fever months or even years after exposure. An X-ray is the best way to confirm if you have tuberculosis.

Prevention BCG vaccine is recommended for those mixing closely with the local population, whether visiting family, planning a long stay, or working as a teacher or health-care worker. As it's a live vaccine it should not be given to pregnant women or immuno-compromised individuals.

Typhoid

Spreads Through food or water that has been contaminated by infected human faeces.

Symptoms and effects Initially, usually fever or a pink rash on the abdomen. Septicaemia (blood poisoning) may also occur.

Prevention Typhim Vi or typherix vaccine. In some countries, the oral vaccine Vivotif is also available.

Yellow Fever

A yellow fever certificate (proof of vaccination) is not required for entry to Morocco

Traveller's Diarrhoea

Causes Strains of travel – unfamiliar food, heat, long days and erratic sleeping patterns – can all make your body more susceptible to an upset stomach.

Prevention Water is generally safe to drink in cities, but elsewhere you should only drink treated water. Eat fresh fruits or vegetables only if they are cooked or if you have washed or peeled them yourself. Buffet meals, which may have been kept sitting warm for some time, can be risky; food should be piping hot. Meals freshly cooked in front of you (like much street food) or served in a busy restaurant are more likely to be safe. Be sensible, but not paranoid: food is one of the treats of visiting Morocco, so don't miss out.

Hygiene Pay close attention to personal hygiene. Many Moroccan meals are eaten with the hand, so always wash before eating and after using the toilet. Even the smallest restaurant will have a sink, but soap is less common, especially at cheap hotels. Antibacterial hand gel, which cleans without needing water, is useful.

Treatment Drink plenty of fluids, and preferably an oral rehydration solution; pharmacies stock these inexpensive *sels de réhydration orale*. Avoid fatty food and dairy products. A few loose stools don't require treatment, but if you start having more than four or five a day, take an antibiotic (usually a quinolone drug) and an antidiarrhoeal agent (such as loperamide). If diarrhoea is bloody, persists for more than 72 hours, and is accompanied by fever, shaking chills or severe abdominal pain, seek medical attention.

Environmental Hazard

Altitude Sickness

Causes Lack of oxygen at high altitudes (over 2500m) affects most people to some extent. The effect may be mild or severe, and occurs because less oxygen reaches the muscles and the brain at high altitudes, requiring the heart and lungs to compensate by working harder. There is no hard-and-fast rule as to what is too high: Acute Mountain Sickness (AMS) has been fatal at 3000m, although 3500m to 4500m is the usual range.

Symptoms and effects Symptoms of AMS usually (but not always) develop during the first 24

hours at altitude. Mild symptoms include headache, lethargy, dizziness, difficulty sleeping and loss of appetite. Potentially fatal, AMS may become more severe without warning. Severe symptoms include breathlessness, a dry, irritative cough (which may progress to the production of pink, frothy sputum), severe headache, lack of coordination, confusion, irrational behaviour, vomiting, drowsiness and unconsciousness.

Prevention If trekking, build time into your schedule to acclimatise, and ensure your guide knows how to recognise and deal with altitude sickness. Morocco's most popular trek, to Jebel Toubkal, reaches the 4167m summit relatively quickly, so many people may suffer even mildly. The longer treks in the M'Goun Massif also reach heights of around 4000m. Treks in the Rif Mountains and Jebel Sarhro are considerably lower, so don't carry the same risks.

Treatment Treat mild symptoms by resting at the same altitude until recovery, or preferably descend – even 500m can help. Take paracetamol or aspirin for headaches. If symptoms persist or become worse, immediate descent is necessary. Drug treatments should never be used to avoid descent or to enable further ascent. Diamox (acetazolamide) reduces the headache of AMS and helps the body acclimatise to the lack of oxygen. It is only available on prescription, and those who are allergic to sulfonamide antibiotics may also be allergic to Diamox.

Heat Illness

Causes Occurs following heavy sweating and excessive fluid loss

with inadequate replacement of fluids and salt. This is particularly common in hot climates when taking unaccustomed exercise before full acclimatisation.

Symptoms and effects Headache, dizziness and tiredness.

Prevention Dehydration is already happening by the time you feel thirsty – drink sufficient water to produce pale, diluted urine. Morocco's sun can be fierce, so bring a hat.

Treatment Consists of fluid replacement with water, fruit juice, or both, and cooling by cold water and fans. Treating salt loss consists of consuming salty fluids such as soup or broth, and adding a little more table salt to foods than usual.

Heatstroke

Causes Extreme heat, high humidity, physical exertion or use of drugs or alcohol in the sun and dehydration. Occurs when the body's heat-regulating mechanism breaks down.

Symptoms and effects An excessive rise in body temperature leads to the cessation of sweating, irrational and hyperactive behaviour, and eventually loss of consciousness, and death.

Treatment Rapid cooling by spraying the body with water and fanning is ideal. Emergency fluid and electrolyte replacement by intravenous drip is usually also required.

Insect Bites & Stings

Causes Mosquitoes, sandflies (found around the Mediterranean beaches), scorpions (common in southern Morocco), bees and wasps, bedbugs and scabies

(both found in cheaper accommodation).

Symptoms and effects More likely to be an irritant than a health risk. Sandflies have a nasty, itchy bite, and can carry the rare skin disorder leishmaniasis. Scorpions have a painful sting that is rarely life-threatening. Bedbugs lead to very itchy, lumpy bites. Tiny scabies mites live in the skin, particularly between the fingers, and cause an intensely itchy rash.

Prevention and treatment DEET-based insect repellents. Spraying a mattress with an appropriate insect killer will do a good job of getting rid of bedbugs. Scabies is easily treated with lotion available from pharmacies; people you come into contact with also need treatment to avoid spreading scabies between asymptomatic carriers.

Snake Bites

The chances of seeing a snake in Morocco, let alone being bitten by one, are slim. Nevertheless, there are a few venomous species, such as the horned viper, found in the southern desert areas. Snakes like to bask on rocks and sand, retreating during the heat of the day.

Prevention Do not walk barefoot or stick your hand into holes or cracks.

Treatment If bitten, do not panic. Half of those bitten by venomous snakes are not actually injected with poison (envenomed). Immobilise the bitten limb with a splint (eg a stick) and apply a bandage over the site, with firm pressure, similar to applying a bandage over a sprain. Do not apply a tourniquet, or cut or suck the bite. Get the victim to medical help as soon as possible so that antivenin can be given if necessary.

Women's Health

➡ Tampons can be hard to buy in Morocco. Carrefour is the only dependable supermarket to stock them, and even then offers limited choice.

WATER

Tap water is chlorinated in Morocco's cities and generally safe to drink – certainly safe to clean your teeth with. Elsewhere, stick to treated water – filter or purify it.

Bottled water is available everywhere, although there is an environmental cost through the mountains of discarded (and unrecycled) plastic bottles.

Off the beaten track, water drawn from wells or pumped from boreholes should be safe, but never drink water from rivers or lakes, as this may contain bacteria or viruses that can cause diarrhoea or vomiting.

Language

The official language in Morocco is Arabic, which is used throughout the country. Berber is spoken in the Rif and Atlas Mountains. Most Berbers also speak at least some Arabic. French is still regularly used in the cities, but much less so among rural Berbers.

MOROCCAN ARABIC

Moroccan Arabic (Darija) is a variety of Modern Standard Arabic (MSA), but is so different from it in many respects as to be virtually like another language. This is the everyday spoken language you'll hear when in Morocco.

All publications and signs, however, are written in Modern Standard Arabic (MSA), which is the common written form in all Arabic-speaking countries. Note though that in Morocco, standard Western numeric symbols are used rather than those normally used in Arabic.

In this language guide we've represented the Arabic phrases with the Roman alphabet using a simplified pronunciation system. The vowels are:

a	as in 'had'
aa	like the 'a' in 'father'
ai	as in 'aisle'
ay	as in 'day'
e	as in 'bet'
ee	as in 'beer', only softer
i	as in 'hit'
o	as in 'note'

WANT MORE?

For in-depth language information and handy phrases, check out Lonely Planet's *Moroccan Arabic Phrasebook*. You'll find it at **shop.lonelyplanet.com**, or you can buy Lonely Planet's iPhone phrasebooks at the Apple App Store.

oo	as in 'food'
ow	as in 'how'
u	as in 'put'

Note that when double consonants occur in the pronunciation guides, each consonant is pronounced. For example, hammam (bath) is pronounced 'ham-mam'. The apostrophe (') represents the glottal stop (like the closing of the throat before saying 'Oh-oh!'). Other consonant sounds to keep in mind are:

dh	like the 'th' in 'this'
gh	a throaty sound like the French 'r'
h	a strongly whispered 'h'
kh	as the 'ch' in the Scottish loch
q	a strong, throaty 'k' sound

Basics

When addressing a man, the polite term more or less equivalent to 'Mr' is aseedee (shortened to see before a name); for women it's lalla, followed by the first name. To attract the attention of someone in the street or a waiter in a cafe, the word shreef is used.

The abbreviations 'm/f/pl' (male/female/plural) are used where applicable.

Hi.	la bes (informal)
	bekheer (response)
Hello.	es salaam alaykum (polite)
	wa alaykum salaam (response)
Goodbye.	bessalama/m'a ssalama
Please.	'afak/'afik/'afakum (said to m/f/pl)
Thank you.	shukran
You're welcome.	la shukran 'la wejb
Excuse me.	smeh leeya
Yes./No.	eeyeh/la
How are you?	keef halek?
Fine, thank you.	bekheer, lhamdoo llaah

What's your name?	asmeetek?
My name is ...	esmee ...
Do you speak English?	wash kat'ref negleezeeya?
I don't understand.	mafhemtsh

Accommodation

Where is a ...?	feen kayn ...?
campsite	shee mukheyyem
hotel	shee ootayl
youth hostel	daar shshabab

Is there a room available?
wash kayn shee beet khaweeya?

Can I see the room?
wash yemkenlee nshoof lbeet?

How much is a room for one day?
bash hal kayn gbayt l wahed nhar?

I'd like a room ...	bgheet shee beet ...
for one person	dyal wahed
for two people	dyal jooj
with a bathroom	belhammam

air-conditioning	kleemateezaseeyun
bed	namooseeya
blanket	bttaaneeya
hot water	lma skhoon
key	saroot
sheet	eezar
shower	doosh
toilet	beet lma

Directions

Where is the ...?
feen kayn ...?

What is the address?
ashnoo hoowa l'unwan?

Please write down the address.
kteb l'unwan 'afek

Please show me on the map.
werri liya men l kharita 'afak

How far?
bshhal b'ayd?

Go straight ahead.
seer neeshan

Turn ...	dor ...
at the corner	felqent
at the traffic lights	fedo elhmer
left/right	'al leeser/leemen

Question Words – Arabic

How?	keefash?
What?	ash?
When?	eemta?
Where?	feen?
Which?	ashmen?
Who?	shkoon?
Why?	'lash?

behind	men luy
here	hna
next to	hedda
opposite	'eks
there	hunak

north	shamel
south	janoob
east	sherq
west	gherb

Eating & Drinking

A table for..., please.
tabla dyal ... 'afak

Can I see the menu, please?
nazar na'raf lmaakla lli 'andkum?

What do you recommend?
shnoo tansaani nakul?

I'll try what she/he is having.
gha nzharrab shnoo kaatakul hiyya/huwwa

I'm a vegetarian.
makanakoolsh llehem

I'd like something to drink.
bgheet shi haazha nashrubha

Please bring me ...	llaa ykhalleek zheeb li ...
a beer	birra
a glass/bottle of red/white/ rose wine	kaas/qar'a dyal hmar/byad/ roozi shshrab
a napkin	mandeel
some bread	shwiyya dyaal lkhoobz
some pepper	shwiyya dyaal lebzaar
some salt	shwiyya dyaal lmelha
some water	shwiyya dyaal lmaa

I didn't order this.	tlabtsh had shshi
Without ..., please.	bla ... 'afak
This is excellent!	had shshi ldeed bezzef!
Cheers!	bsaha!
The bill, please.	lahsaab, 'afak

Meat & Fish

anchovies	shton
beef	baqree
camel	lehem jemil
chicken	farooj/dujaj
cod	lamoori
fish	hut
kidneys	kelawwi
lamb	lehem ghenmee
liver	kebda
lobster	laangos
meat	lehem
sardines	serdeen
shrimp	qaimroon
sole	sol
tuna	ton
whiting	merla

Fruit & Vegetables

apple	teffah
apricot	meshmash
artichoke	qooq
aubergine	lbdanzhaal
banana	banan/moz
cucumber	khiyaar
dates	tmer
figs	kermoos
fruit	fakiya
garlic	tooma
grapes	'eineb
green beans	loobeeya
lentils	'aads
lettuce	khess
mushroom	fegg'a
olives	zeetoun
onion	besla
orange	limoon
peas	zelbana bisila
pomegranate	reman
potatoes	batatas
tomato	mataisha tamatim
vegetables	khoodar
watermelon	dellah
white beans	fasooliya

Other

bread	khoobz
butter	zebda

cheese	fromaj/jiben
chips	ships
eggs	bayd
oil	zit
pepper	filfil/lebzaar
salt	melha
soup	shorba
sugar	sukur
yoghurt	zabadee/laban/danoon

LANGUAGE MOROCCAN ARABIC

Emergencies

Help!	'teqnee!
Help me, please!	'awennee 'afak!
Go away!	seer fhalek!
I'm lost.	tweddert
Thief!	sheffar!
I've been robbed.	tsreqt
Call the police!	'ayyet 'la lbùlees!
Call a doctor!	'ayyet 'la shee tbeeb!
There's been an accident!	uq'at kseeda!
Where's the toilet?	feen kayn lbeet lma?

Numbers – Arabic	
1	wahed
2	jooj
3	tlata
4	reb'a
5	khamsa
6	setta
7	seb'a
8	tmenya
9	tes'ood
10	'ashra
20	'ashreen
30	tlateen
40	reb'een
50	khamseen
60	setteen
70	seb'een
80	tmaneen
90	tes'een
100	mya
200	myatayn
1000	alf
2000	alfayn

I'm sick.	ana mreed
It hurts here.	kaydernee henna
I'm allergic to (penicillin).	'andee lhsaseeya m'a (lbeenseleen)

Shopping & Services

Where is the ...?	feen kayn ...?
bank	shee baanka
barber	shee hellaq
chemist/pharmacy	farmasyan
... embassy	ssifaara dyal ...
market	souk
police station	lkoomeesareeya
post office	lboostaa
restaurant	ristura/mat'am
souvenir shop	baazaar
travel agency	wekaalet el aasfaar

I want to change ...	bgheet nserref ...
some money	shee floos
travellers cheques	shek seeyahee

I'd like to buy ...	bgheet nshree ...
I'm only looking.	gheer kanshoof
Can I look at it?	wakhkha nshoofha?
I don't like it.	ma'jebatneesh
How much is it?	bshhal?
That's very expensive.	ghalee bezzaf
Can I pay by credit card?	wash nkder nkhelles bel kart kredee?

big	kabeer
small	sagheer
open	mehlool
closed	masdood

Time & Dates

What time is it?	shal fessa'a?

yesterday	lbareh
today	lyoom
tomorrow	ghedda

morning	fessbah
afternoon	fel'sheeya
evening	'sheeya

day	nhar
week	l'usbu'
month	shshhar
year	l'am

early/late	bekree/m'ettel
quickly/slowly	dgheeya/beshweeya

Monday	nhar letneen
Tuesday	nhar ttlat
Wednesday	nhar larb'
Thursday	nhar lekhmees
Friday	nhar jjem'a
Saturday	nhar ssebt
Sunday	nhar lhedd

January	yanaayir
February	fibraayir
March	maaris
April	abreel
May	maayu
June	yunyu
July	yulyu
August	aghustus/ghusht
September	sibtimbir/shebtenber
October	uktoobir
November	nufimbir/nu'enbir
December	disimbir/dijenbir

Transport
Public Transport

When does the ... leave/arrive?	wufuqash kaykhrej/ kaywsul ...?
boat	lbaboor
city/intercity bus	ttubees/lkar
train	tran
plane	ttayyyaara

I'd like a ... ticket.	'afak bgheet wahed lwarka l ddar lbayda ...
return	bash nemshee oo njee
1st/2nd class	ddaraja lloola/ttaneeya

Where is the ...?	feen kayn ...?
airport	mataar
bus station	mhetta dyal ttobeesat
bus stop	blasa dyal ttobeesat
ticket office	maktab lwerqa
train station	lagaar

What's the fare?
shhal taman lwarka?

Please tell me when we get to ...
'afak eela wselna l ... goolhaleeya

I want to pay for one place only.
bgheet nkhelles blaasaawaheda

Stop here, please.
wqef henna 'afak

Please wait for me.
tsennanee 'afak

Driving & Cycling

Where can I hire a ...?	feen yimkin li nkri ...?
bicycle	bshklit
camel	jmel
car	tumubeel
donkey	hmar
horse	'awd

Can I park here?
wash nqder nwakef hna?

How long can I park here?
sh-hal men waket neqder nstatiun hna?

How do I get to ...?
keefesh ghaadee nuwsul l ...?

Where's the next petrol station?
fin kayna shi bumba dyal lisans griba?

I'd like ... litres.
bgheet ... itru 'afak

Please check the oil/water.
'afak shuf zzit/lma

We need a mechanic.
khesna wahed lmikanisyan

The car has broken down at ...
tumubeel khasra f ...

I have a flat tyre.
'ndi pyasa fruida

BERBER

There are three main dialects among Berber speakers, which in a certain sense also serve as loose lines of ethnic demarcation.

In the north, in the area centred on the Rif, the locals speak a dialect that has been called Riffian and is spoken as far south as Figuig on the Algerian border. The dialect that predominates in the Middle and High Atlas and the valleys leading into the Sahara goes by various names, including Braber or Amazigh.

More settled tribes of the High Atlas, Anti Atlas, Souss Valley and southwestern oases generally speak Tashelhit or Chleuh. The following phrases are a selection from the Tashelhit dialect, the one visitors are likely to find most useful.

Basics

Hello.	la bes darik/darim (m/f)
Hello. (response)	la bes
Goodbye.	akayaoon arbee
See you later.	akranwes daghr
Please.	barakalaufik
Thank you.	barakalaufik
Yes.	yah
No.	oho
Excuse me.	samhiy
How are you?	meneek antgeet?
Fine, thank you.	la bes, lhamdulah
Good.	eefulkee/eeshwa
Bad.	(khaib) eeghshne

Practicalities

food	teeremt
mule	aserdon
somewhere to sleep	kra lblast mahengane
water	arman
Is there ...?	ees eela ...?
Do you have ...?	ees daroon ...?
How much is it?	minshk aysker?
Give me ...	fky ...
I want ...	reegh ...
a little/lot	eemeek/bzef
no good	oor eefulkee
too expensive	eeghla
I want to go to ...	addowghs ...
Where is (the) ...?	mani gheela ...?
Is it near/far?	ees eeqareb/yagoog?
straight	neeshan
to the left	fozelmad
to the right	fofasee
mountain	adrar
river	aseef
the pass	tizee
village	doorwar
yesterday	eedgam
today	(zig sbah) rass
tomorrow	(ghasad) aska

GLOSSARY

This glossary is a list of Arabic (A), Berber (B), French (F) and Spanish (S) terms that are used throughout this guide. For a list of trekking terms, see p38.

agadir (B) – fortified communal granary

'ain (A) – water source, spring

aït (B) – family (of), often precedes tribal and town names

Alawite – hereditary dynasty that has ruled Morocco since the late 17th century

Allah (A) – God

Almohads – puritanical Muslim group (1147–1269), originally Berber, that arose in response to the corrupt Almoravid dynasty

Almoravids – Muslim group (1054–1147) that ruled Spain and the Maghreb

bab (A) – gate

babouches (F) – traditional leather slippers

banu (A) – see beni

baraka (A) – divine blessing or favour

Barbary – European term used to describe the North African coast from the 16th to the 19th centuries

ben (A) – (or ibn) son of

beni (A) – 'sons of', often precedes tribal name (also banu)

Berbers – indigenous inhabitants of North Africa

borj (A) – fort (literally 'tower')

brigade touristique (F) – tourist police

bureau des guides (F) – guides' office

caid/caliph – town official

calèche – horse-drawn carriage

calle (S) – street

camionette (F) – minivan or pick-up truck

capitol – main temple of Roman town, usually situated in the forum

caravanserai – large merchants' inn enclosing a courtyard, providing accommodation and a marketplace (see also funduq)

chergui (A) – dry, easterly desert wind

Compagnie de Transports Marocaine – CTM; national bus company

corniche (F) – coastal road

corsair – 18th-century pirate based at Salé

dar (A) – traditional town house with internal courtyard

Délégation Régionale du Tourisme – tourist office; see also ONMT

derb (A) – lane or narrow street

djemaa (A) – Friday mosque (also jami', jemaa and jamaa)

douar (A) – generally used for 'village' in the High Atlas

Eaux et Forêts – government ministry responsible for national parks

eid (A) – religious festival

Ensemble Artisanal – government handicraft shop

erg (A) – sand dunes

fantasia (S) – military exercise featuring a cavalry charge

faux guides (F) – unofficial or informal guides

foum (A) – usually the mouth of a river or valley (from Arabic for 'mouth')

funduq (A) – caravanserai (often used to mean 'hotel')

gardiens de voitures (F) – car-park attendants

gare routière (F) – bus station

gîte, gîte d'étape (F) – trekkers' hostel, sometimes a homestay

Gnaoua – bluesy Moroccan musical form that began with freed slaves in Marrakesh and Essaouira

grand taxi (F) – (long-distance) shared taxi

haj (A) – pilgrimage to Mecca, hence haji or hajia, a male or female who has made the pilgrimage

halqa (A) – street theatre

hammada (A) – stony desert

hammam (A) – Turkish-style bathhouse with sauna and massage

hanbel (A) – see kilim

haram (A) – literally 'forbidden', the word is sometimes used to denote a sacred or forbidden area, such as the prayer room of a mosque

Hejira – flight of the Prophet from Mecca to Medina in AD 622; the first year of the Islamic calendar

ibn (A) – son of (see also ben)

Idrissids – Moroccan dynasty that established a stable state in northern Morocco in the 9th century

iftar (A) – breaking of the fast at sundown during Ramadan; breakfast (also ftur)

imam (A) – Muslim cleric

Interzone – name coined by author William Burroughs for the period 1923–56, when Tangier was controlled by nine countries

jebel (A) – hill, mountain (sometimes djebel in former French possessions)

jedid (A) – new (sometimes spelled jdid)

jellaba (A) – popular flowing garment; men's jellabas are usually made from cotton or wool, while women's come in light synthetic fabrics

kasbah (A) – fort, citadel; often also the administrative centre (also qasba)

kif (A) – marijuana

kilim (A) – flat-woven blankets or floor coverings (also hanbel)

koubba (A) – sanctuary or shrine (see also marabout)

ksar (A) – fort or fortified stronghold (plural ksour)

mâalem – master artisan

Maghreb (A) – (literally 'west') area covered by Morocco, Algeria, Tunisia and Libya

maison d'hôte (F) – guesthouse, often a restored traditional Moroccan house

majoun (A) – sticky paste made of crushed seeds of the marijuana plant

marabout – holy man or saint; also often used to describe the mausoleums of these men

mechouar (A) – royal assembly place

medersa (A) – college for teaching theology, law, Arabic literature and grammar (also called *madrassa*)

medina (A) – old city; used to describe the old Arab parts of modern towns and cities

mellah (A) – Jewish quarter of the medina

Merenids (A) – Moroccan dynasty (1269–1465), responsible for the construction of many of Morocco's *medersas*

mihrab (A) – prayer niche in the wall of a mosque indicating the direction of Mecca (the *qibla*)

minbar (A) – pulpit in mosque; the *imam* delivers the sermon from one of the lower steps because the Prophet preached from the top step

moulay (A) – ruler

Mouloud – Islamic festival celebrating the birth of the Prophet

moussem (A) – pilgrimage to *marabout* tomb; festival in honour of a *marabout*

muezzin (A) – mosque official who sings the call to prayer from the minaret

muqarna (A) – decorative plasterwork

musée (F) – museum

ONMT – Office National Marocain du Tourisme, national tourist body, sometimes called Délégation Régionale du Tourisme

ordinaire (F) – less comfortable train, slightly slower than a *rapide*

oued (A) – river or stream, including dry riverbeds (sometimes *wad* or *wadi*)

oulad (A) – sons (of), often precedes tribal or town name

palmeraie (F) – palm grove

pastilla – a rich, savoury-sweet chicken or pigeon pie made with fine pastry; a dish of layered pastry with cinnamon and almonds served as dessert at banquets

pasha – high official in Ottoman Empire (also *pacha*)

pensióne (S) – guesthouse

petit taxi (F) – local taxi

pisé (F) – building material made of sundried clay or mud

piste (F) – unsealed tracks, often requiring 4WD vehicles

place (F) – square, plaza

plage (F) – beach

plazas de soberanía (S) – 'Places of sovereignty', the name given to the Spanish possessions in North Africa

Prophet (Mohammed), the – founder of Islam, who lived between AD 570 and AD 632

qissaria (A) – covered market sometimes forming the commercial centre of a medina

Quran – sacred book of Islam

Ramadan (A) – ninth month of the Muslim year, a period of fasting

rapide (F) – type of train more comfortable and slightly faster than an *ordinaire*

refuge (F) – mountain hut, basic hikers' shelter

riad (A) – traditional town house set around an internal garden

ribat (A) – combined monastery and fort

Saadians – Moroccan dynasty that ruled in the 16th century

sharia (A) – street

sherif (A) – descendant of the Prophet

Shiites – one of two main Islamic sects, formed by those who believed the true *imams* were descended from the Prophet's son-in-law Ali (see also *Sunnis*)

sidi (A) – honorific (equivalent to 'Mr'; also *si*)

souq (A) – market

Sufism – mystical strand of Islam that emphasises communion with Allah through inner attitude

Sunnis – one of two main Islamic sects, derived from followers of the Umayyad-caliphate (see also *Shiites*)

Syndicat d'Initiative (F) – government-run tourist office

tabac (F) – tobacconist and newsagency

tadelakt (A) – waterproof lime plaster mixed with pigments and polished with a stone to give it a smooth, lustrous finish, originally used for the walls of *hammams* but now a favourite of interior designers

tariq (A) – road, avenue

téléboutique (F) – privately operated telephone service

tizi (B) – mountain pass

Tuareg – nomadic Berbers of the Sahara, also known as the Blue Men because of their indigo-dyed robes

ville nouvelle (F) – new city; town built by the French alongside existing towns

vizier – another term for a provincial governor in the Ottoman Empire, or adviser to the sultan in Morocco

zawiya (A) – religious fraternity based around a *marabout*; location of the fraternity (also *zaouia*)

zellij (A) – ceramic

Behind the Scenes

SEND US YOUR FEEDBACK

We love to hear from travellers – your comments keep us on our toes and help make our books better. Our well-travelled team reads every word on what you loved or loathed about this book. Although we cannot reply individually to your submissions, we always guarantee that your feedback goes straight to the appropriate authors, in time for the next edition. Each person who sends us information is thanked in the next edition – the most useful submissions are rewarded with a selection of digital PDF chapters.

Visit **lonelyplanet.com/contact** to submit your updates and suggestions or to ask for help. Our award-winning website also features inspirational travel stories, news and discussions.

Note: We may edit, reproduce and incorporate your comments in Lonely Planet products such as guidebooks, websites and digital products, so let us know if you don't want your comments reproduced or your name acknowledged. For a copy of our privacy policy visit lonelyplanet.com/privacy.

OUR READERS

Many thanks to the travellers who used the last edition and wrote to us with helpful hints, useful advice and interesting anecdotes:

Akis Vasileiadis, Alejandro Leano, Angela Parlane, Anne Hlinka, Asmus Dall Gregersen, Barbara Freeman, Beth Fertig, Carlos de Bustos, Claire Knight, Claire Patrick, Cornelis Faling, Daniel Schechter, Daniel Klement, Denise Chiarioni, Florian Rieger, Floris van Halm, Gail Doherty, Geeske Saad-Beukema, Harald Luckerbauer, Ilene Aveling, Jean-Claude Latombe, Julie Bartlett-Hejira, Katleen Matthieu, Keith Johnson, Krzysztof Świątly, Leonard Naymark, Leonie Hutch, Martin Briggs, Michelle Leicester, Mirjam Brusius, Mirka Costanzi, Nick Cross, Nick McWilliam, Peter & Emma Greenhalgh, Ray Stokes, Rebecca Lebow, Rebekka van Roemburg, Rein Boumans, Renata Haffaf, Rob Buzacott, Rob Keereweer, Rose Button, Ruben Lelivelt, Sally Kondziolka, Sally Norris, Sam Firth, Sam Pulfer, Sander Steel, Sara Rei, Simon Carlile, Sophie Bull, Steven & Roberta Haas, Tessa Hatlelid, Tina Woodhouse , Zenon Lewycky

WRITER THANKS

Jessica Lee

A huge shukran to all the Marrakshis who always make coming to Marrakesh such a pleasure. Big thanks to Youssef, Fatima, Hasan, and Amine; to Mark for a lowdown on the local scene over beers; Cyril for tips and advice; and in particular to Mohammed Nour for

taking time out of his schedule to help out. Also thanks to Virginia and Peter for restaurant-checking fun.

Brett Atkinson

A big *shukran* to the following: Ben and Ollie in Taghazout, Irene in Tamraght, Jane in Taroudannt, Sissi and Mafhoud in Taliouine, Sadat in Tarfaya, Houssine and Liesbeth in Tafraoute, and Sally in Mirleft. Special thanks to Neil, Jackie and the kids in Dakhla. At LP, thanks to Helen Elfer for the opportunity to explore North Africa, my fellow authors and the hardworking editors and cartos, and final thanks to Carol for holding the fort back home in New Zealand.

Paul Clammer

This was my first Morocco update job where I could commute from home, our house in the Fes medina. So, thanks and above all to Robyn for her amazing restoration job, and to Monkey the accidentally adopted mosque roof cat, for not smashing ALL the glassware when I was in Tangier. On the roof, my continued *salaams* to petit taxi drivers everywhere who put the meter on without asking.

Virginia Maxwell

Greatest thanks go to my travelling companion, Peter Handsaker. Thanks also to Tine Riera, Marie-Christine Martinet, Mustapha Bouamara, Helen Ranger and Jess Lee.

Lorna Parkes

Thanks to Helen Elfer, who gave me the best excuse to travel back to one of my favourite cities. To Said at Dar Bensouda, without whom I would have got lost in the Fez medina many more times than I did. Thanks also to Jess Stephens and Liz Campbell for their trusted insights, and to Robert Johnstone for his offerings of food. Biggest thanks of all goes to Rob, for looking after our son, Austin, and to Austin himself, for joining me on part of the adventure.

Regis St Louis

Countless people across Morocco showed me such enormous and humbling hospitality. In particular, I'm grateful to Abdel Haydar, Lahcen Igdem, Almodhik Aissa, Mohamed El Qasemy and Carolyn, Tahrbilte Rachid, Abdel Jalil, Omar and Ibrahim of Dar Sofian, Rashid and Doreen (and Jack the donkey), Ziad and Amqrane Tair (and family), Vanessa and Xavier, Toufiq Mousaoui, and Abdel Benalila and his family. Biggest thanks to Cassandra and our daughters, Magdalena and Genevieve, for their enduring support.

ACKNOWLEDGEMENTS

Climate map data adapted from Peel MC, Finlayson BL & McMahon TA (2007) 'Updated World Map of the Köppen-Geiger Climate Classification', Hydrology and Earth System Sciences, 11, 163344.

Cover photograph: Chefchaouen, Jan Wlodarczyk/4Corners ©

THIS BOOK

This 12th edition of Lonely Planet's *Morocco* guidebook was researched and written by Jessica Lee, Brett Atkinson, Paul Clammer, Virginia Maxwell, Lorna Parkes and Regis St Louis. This guidebook was produced by the following:

Destination Editor Helen Elfer

Product Editors Genna Patterson, Anne Mason

Senior Cartographer David Kemp

Book Designer Gwen Cotter

Assisting Editors Imogen Bannister, Andrea Dobbin, Victoria Harrison, Gabby Innes, Ilana Myers, Susan Paterson, Christopher Pitts

Assisting Cartographer Rachel Imeson

Cover Researcher Naomi Parker

Thanks to Ronan Abayawickrema, Heather Champion, Kate Chapman, Grace Dobell, Sandie Kestell, Ilana Myers Claire Naylor, Karyn Noble, Lauren O'Connell, Kirsten Rawlings, Kat Rowan, Jessica Ryan, Ellie Simpson, Angela Tinson, Tony Wheeler

Index

Map Legend

Sights

- Beach
- Bird Sanctuary
- Buddhist
- Castle/Palace
- Christian
- Confucian
- Hindu
- Islamic
- Jain
- Jewish
- Monument
- Museum/Gallery/Historic Building
- Ruin
- Shinto
- Sikh
- Taoist
- Winery/Vineyard
- Zoo/Wildlife Sanctuary
- Other Sight

Activities, Courses & Tours

- Bodysurfing
- Diving
- Canoeing/Kayaking
- Course/Tour
- Sento Hot Baths/Onsen
- Skiing
- Snorkelling
- Surfing
- Swimming/Pool
- Walking
- Windsurfing
- Other Activity

Sleeping

- Sleeping
- Camping

Eating

- Eating

Drinking & Nightlife

- Drinking & Nightlife
- Cafe

Entertainment

- Entertainment

Shopping

- Shopping

Information

- Bank
- Embassy/Consulate
- Hospital/Medical
- Internet
- Police
- Post Office
- Telephone
- Toilet
- Tourist Information
- Other Information

Geographic

- Beach
- Gate
- Hut/Shelter
- Lighthouse
- Lookout
- Mountain/Volcano
- Oasis
- Park
- Pass
- Picnic Area
- Waterfall

Population

- Capital (National)
- Capital (State/Province)
- City/Large Town
- Town/Village

Transport

- Airport
- Border crossing
- Bus
- Cable car/Funicular
- Cycling
- Ferry
- Metro station
- Monorail
- Parking
- Petrol station
- Subway station
- Taxi
- Train station/Railway
- Tram
- Underground station
- Other Transport

Note: Not all symbols displayed above appear on the maps in this book

Routes

- Tollway
- Freeway
- Primary
- Secondary
- Tertiary
- Lane
- Unsealed road
- Road under construction
- Plaza/Mall
- Steps
- Tunnel
- Pedestrian overpass
- Walking Tour
- Walking Tour detour
- Path/Walking Trail

Boundaries

- International
- State/Province
- Disputed
- Regional/Suburb
- Marine Park
- Cliff
- Wall

Hydrography

- River, Creek
- Intermittent River
- Canal
- Water
- Dry/Salt/Intermittent Lake
- Reef

Areas

- Airport/Runway
- Beach/Desert
- Cemetery (Christian)
- Cemetery (Other)
- Glacier
- Mudflat
- Park/Forest
- Sight (Building)
- Sportsground
- Swamp/Mangrove

Lorna Parkes

Fez Meknes and the Middle Atlas Londoner by birth, Melburnian by palate and ex-Lonely Planet staffer in both cities, Lorna has spent more than 10 years exploring the globe in search of the perfect meal, the friendliest B&B, the best-value travel experience, and the most spectacular lookout point – both for her own pleasure and other people's. She's discovered she writes best on planes, and has contributed to numerous Lonely Planet books and magazines. Wineries and the tropics (not at the same time!) are her go-to happy places. Follow her @Lorna_Explorer.

Regis St Louis

Central Morocco Regis grew up in a small town in the American Midwest—the kind of place that fuels big dreams of travel—and he developed an early fascination with foreign dialects and world cultures. He spent his formative years learning Russian and a handful of Romance languages, which served him well on journeys across much of the globe. Regis has contributed to more than 50 Lonely Planet titles, covering destinations across six continents. His travels have taken him from the mountains of Kamchatka to remote island villages in Melanesia, and to many grand urban landscapes. When not on the road, he lives in New Orleans.

OUR STORY

A beat-up old car, a few dollars in the pocket and a sense of adventure. In 1972 that's all Tony and Maureen Wheeler needed for the trip of a lifetime – across Europe and Asia overland to Australia. It took several months, and at the end – broke but inspired – they sat at their kitchen table writing and stapling together their first travel guide, *Across Asia on the Cheap*. Within a week they'd sold 1500 copies. Lonely Planet was born.

Today, Lonely Planet has offices in Franklin, London, Melbourne, Oakland, Dublin, Beijing and Delhi, with more than 600 staff and writers. We share Tony's belief that 'a great guidebook should do three things: inform, educate and amuse'.

OUR WRITERS

Jessica Lee

Marrakesh Jess high-tailed it for the road at the age of 18 and hasn't looked back since. In 2011 she swapped a career as an adventure-tour leader for travel writing and since then her travels for Lonely Planet have taken her across Africa, the Middle East and Asia. She has lived in the Middle East since 2007 and tweets @ jessofarabia. Jess has contributed to Lonely Planet's *Egypt*, *Turkey*, Cyprus, *Marrakesh*, Middle East, Europe, *Africa*, *Cambodia*, and *Vietnam* guidebooks and her travel writing has appeared in Wanderlust magazine, the Daily Telegraph, the Independent, BBC Travel and Lonelyplanet.com.

Brett Atkinson

Southern Morocco and Western Sahara For this new edition of *Morocco*, Brett travelled from his New Zealand home to explore the fascinating medinas of Taroudannt and Tiznit, the spectacular Atlantic coastline, and the compellingly wild desert vistas of the Sahara. An absolute highlight was the poignant and elegant Spanish Art Deco architecture of Sidi Ifni. Brett's contributed to Lonely Planet guidebooks spanning Europe, Africa, Asia and the Pacific, and covered over 60 countries as a food and travel writer. See www.brett-atkinson.net for his latest adventures.

Paul Clammer

Mediterranean Coast and the Rif Paul Clammer has worked as a molecular biologist, tour leader and travel writer. Since 2003 he has worked as a guidebook author for Lonely Planet, contributing to over 25 LP titles, covering destinations including swathes of South and Central Asia, West and North Africa and the Caribbean. In recent years he's lived in Morocco, Jordan, Haiti and Fiji, as well as his native England. Find him online at paulclammer.com or on Twitter as @ paulclammer.

Virginia Maxwell

Atlantic Coast Although based in Australia, Virginia spends at least half of her year updating Lonely Planet destination coverage in Europe and the Middle East. The Mediterranean is her favourite place to travel, and she has covered Spain, Italy, Turkey, Syria, Lebanon, Israel, Egypt and Morocco for LP guidebooks – there are only eight more countries to go! Virginia also writes about Armenia, Iran and Australia. Follow her @maxwellvirginia on Instagram and Twitter.

OVER MORE
PAGE WRITERS

Published by Lonely Planet Global Limited
CRN 554153
12th edition – August 2017
ISBN 978 1 786 570 321
© Lonely Planet 2017   Photographs © as indicated 2017
10 9 8 7 6 5 4 3
Printed in Singapore